P9-CNG-417

# THE
# VICTORIAN KITCHEN
## Book of
# PASTRIES & PUDDINGS

# THE
# VICTORIAN KITCHEN
## Book of
# PASTRIES & PUDDINGS

**JG PRESS**

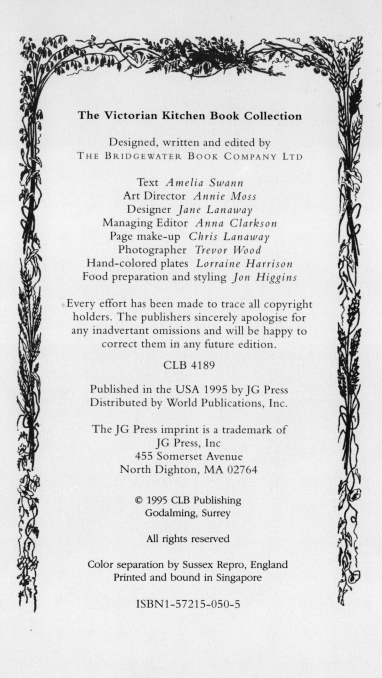

**The Victorian Kitchen Book Collection**

Designed, written and edited by
THE BRIDGEWATER BOOK COMPANY LTD

Text *Amelia Swann*
Art Director *Annie Moss*
Designer *Jane Lanaway*
Managing Editor *Anna Clarkson*
Page make-up *Chris Lanaway*
Photographer *Trevor Wood*
Hand-colored plates *Lorraine Harrison*
Food preparation and styling *Jon Higgins*

Every effort has been made to trace all copyright
holders. The publishers sincerely apologise for
any inadvertant omissions and will be happy to
correct them in any future edition.

CLB 4189

Published in the USA 1995 by JG Press
Distributed by World Publications, Inc.

The JG Press imprint is a trademark of
JG Press, Inc
455 Somerset Avenue
North Dighton, MA 02764

© 1995 CLB Publishing
Godalming, Surrey

All rights reserved

Color separation by Sussex Repro, England
Printed and bound in Singapore

ISBN 1-57215-050-5

# CONTENTS

# INTRODUCTION

> *I think I could eat one of Bellamy's veal pies.*
>
> **Alleged last words of WILLIAM PITT THE YOUNGER (1759–1806)**

BEFORE THE DAYS of cars and central heating, before labor-saving devices and mechanization released most people from a daily grind of hard physical work, well-filled pastries and good, substantial puddings that really lined the stomach were a vital source of heat and energy. These days, it may not be advisable to consume such calorie-laden goodies on a daily basis, but they are unbeatable as an occasional treat or for a special celebration.

The recipes in this book represent only a fraction of the huge range of baked, steamed, and boiled puddings and pies, tarts, and pastries made by Victorian cooks. All the recipes are based on authentic recipes of the period, but have been carefully adapted to suit smaller families and the less heroic appetites of today.

## MRS. BEETON'S PASTRY HINTS

*Here are Mrs. Beeton's main commandments, rendered into modern English.*

*1* **Touch the pastry as little as possible.**
*2* **Work with cool hands on a cool surface, such as a marble slab.**
*3* **Add liquids gradually and work them in with a flat blade.**
*4* **Work as fast as possible to keep the pastry light.**

### BOILED PUDDING HINTS

*1* **Simmer custard-based puddings rather than boiling them fiercely, or they will be honeycombed with air holes.**
*2* **Always fill the pudding mold up completely.**
*3* **Keep enough water in the boiling saucepan.**
*4* **Stand the pudding to rest for five minutes when it is cooked to let out the steam.**

> *Variety in the ingredients, we think, is held only of secondary consideration with the great body of people, provided that the whole is agreeable and of sufficient abundance.*
>
> **MRS. BEETON ON PUDDINGS**

## PREPARING THE MOLDS

Make sure all molds, basins, or dishes are clean and dry. For substantial puddings, be generous when you butter the molds. For lighter puddings, brush the molds with clarified butter.

## CRUSTS AND PASTES

*The Victorian cook* enjoyed an impressive repertoire of pastry (which was called crust or paste), apart from shortcrust in its varying degrees of richness or sweetness. Suet and butter crust were used for puddings; cream crust, French crust (today called *pâté brisée*), and puff paste were used for sweet and savory pies and tarts.

## Suet for Pastry

Suet is obtained from hard animal fat. The fat from beef and veal is preferable, and the best comes from the fatty cushion that protects the animal's kidneys. It must be carefully chopped to remove all trace of meat fiber, then minced very finely before use.

Pastry is one of the most important branches of culinary science. It increasingly occupies itself with ministering pleasure to the sight as well as the taste.

MRS. BEETON

A PANTRY FULL OF AUTHENTIC VICTORIAN
PASTRIES AND PUDDINGS

BAKEWELL PUDDING, A TRULY DELICIOUS CLASSIC DISH

## Lady Shaftesbury's Pudding

EMILY SHAFTESBURY (1810–1872), wife of the philanthropic Lord Shaftesbury, kept a recipe book. Among other dishes and household hints, there was a recipe for Bakewell Pudding with a meringue topping.

*This pudding is famous not only in Derbyshire, but in several of our northern counties, where it is usually served on all holiday occasions.*

ELIZA ACTON

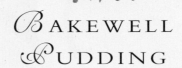

# BAKEWELL PUDDING

This is a truly delicious classic dish, based on Mrs. Beeton's recipe; she describes it as "very rich." It should always be called a pudding, not a tart. Eliza Acton's recipe incorporated candied peel in the jam, but she herself regarded this as "unrefined."

### INGREDIENTS

¼lb. Puff Pastry

Jam

5 Fresh Eggs

1 cup Sugar

½ cup Melted Butter

⅓ cup Ground Almonds

### METHOD

❦ Roll the puff pastry out thinly and line a 9-inch flan ring. Over the base, spread a good, thick layer of jam, preferably homemade and strawberry.

❦ Into a mixing bowl place the yolks of four eggs and the yolk and white of the fifth, and beat thoroughly. Add the sugar, melted butter, and almonds and mix until well incorporated. Pour the mixture over the jam and spread out evenly.

❦ Bake at 350°F for about 30 minutes, or until the crust has turned a beautiful golden brown.

## Windsor Castle Staff Carrot Pudding

In Queen Victoria's day, the army of staff that ran her palaces needed a lot of feeding. One of their favorite dishes was carrot pudding. It was essentially the same as Mrs. Beeton's recipe, but made with industrial amounts of carrots, flour, suet, and dried fruit; three cupfuls of orange peel were added as well as some baking powder to lift the load. It took five hours to boil.

CARROT PUDDING, A FAVORITE WITH CHILDREN

## A Sweet Vegetable

Carrots contain a lot of sugar and 19th-century cooks in France, Italy, and England used them for all manner of delicious sweet tarts, cakes, and puddings. There was even a carrot jam, made in southwest France; it was imaginatively named *Cheveux d'Ange*, or Angel's Hair.

# CARROT PUDDING

*This is based on a Mrs. Beeton recipe; the natural sweetness of carrots makes a filling, wholesome dessert suitable for hungry children. Serve it with custard sauce.*

### INGREDIENTS

³/₄lb. Fresh Carrots
3 Eggs
4 cups Fresh Breadcrumbs
1 cup Suet
³/₄ cup Raisins
³/₄ cup Currants
¹/₂ cup Sugar
Milk
Confectioner's Sugar

### METHOD

❦ Peel the carrots and place in a pan of fresh water to boil until soft. Remove from the heat and drain. Put the carrots in a large mixing bowl and mash to a purée.

❦ Stir in the eggs and the remaining dry ingredients along with sufficient milk to make a thick, batter-like mix. Pour into a well-greased pie dish.

❦ Cook for one hour at 350°F, until it is well risen and the crust has browned nicely. Sift thickly with confectioner's sugar just before serving.

# PLUM PUDDING OF FRESH FRUIT

*Mrs. Beeton considered raw plums, although refreshing, to lack nourishment. Her reservations did not extend to cooked fruit, "which even the invalid may eat in moderation." This is one of the most delicious ways to eat cooked plums.*

### INGREDIENTS

*³/₄lb. Suet Crust Pastry*
*1³/₄lb. Fresh Plums*
*²/₃ cup Moist Brown Sugar*

### METHOD

❦ Roll the suet pastry out to roughly ¹/₂-inch thickness and line a pudding bowl, reserving some pastry for the lid. Wash the plums thoroughly and cut in half, removing all the stones. Fill the lined basin with the fruit, sprinkling the sugar in between layers.

❦ Roll out the reserved pastry and make a lid for the bowl, pinching the edges together tightly to prevent any juices from leaking. Dust a pudding cloth with a little flour, tie tightly over the top of the bowl, and place the pudding in a saucepan of boiling water to cook for 2 hours.

❦ When ready, lift the pudding from the water and remove the covering. Serve with a custard sauce.

### Eliza Acton's Vegetarian Plum Pudding

This economical recipe used mashed potatoes, carrots, flour, currants, sugar, suet, nutmeg, and salt. She points out that the "cost of the ingredients does not exceed half a crown (12½ pence) and the pudding is of sufficient size for a party of 16 persons."

*Life's a pudding full of plums.*
W. S. GILBERT

### COOK'S TIP

When the pudding has been taken out of the water, allow it to stand for a few minutes to cool slightly and "shrink away" from the sides of the basin. This will allow you to turn it out onto a serving dish more easily.

*I'm not so think as
you drunk I am.*

SIR JOHN SQUIRE,
BALLADE OF SOPORIFIC ABSORPTION

TIPSY PUDDINGS, JUST THE THING
FOR A FRIVOLOUS LUNCHTIME INTERLUDE

# TIPSY PUDDINGS

*These gorgeous rum-soaked puddings are based on a Mrs. Beeton recipe. They are quick and easy to make, just right for an impromptu celebration. Try them with champagne.*

## INGREDIENTS

2 Eggs

$^1/_2$ cup Sugar

$^3/_4$ cup Flour

3–4 T. Dark Rum

Shredded Coconut to Decorate

## METHOD

❧ Break the eggs into a bowl and beat together with the sugar until the mixture is smooth. Lightly fold in the flour until it is all incorporated, taking care to keep the mixture light.

❧ Grease six small molds suitable for the oven with a little butter and sprinkle lots of sugar into them. Fill them three-quarters full with the mixture and bake at 350°F until they are well risen and firm to the touch (about 20 minutes).

❧ Remove from the oven and soak each pudding with some of the dark rum. Sprinkle with a little coconut before serving.

### A Large Tipsy Pudding

You can also make a single, large tipsy pudding for an after-dinner dessert. According to one traditional Victorian recipe, you make the pudding in one mold, turn it out and then pour over "as much warm Madeira as it will imbibe." Mask the (by now) tipsy pudding with apricot jam and decorate with slivers of blanched almonds.

### CHAMPAGNE CHARLIE

*Champagne Charlie is my name*
*Champagne drinking is my game*
*There's no drink so good as*
*fizz, fizz, fizz*
*I drink every drop there is, is, is.*
*All around town they know*
*my name*
*By pop! pop! pop! I rose to fame*
*I'm the idol of the barmaids*
*And Champagne Charlie is*
*my name.*

GEORGE LEYBOURNE
AND ALFRED LEE

# CHRISTMAS PUDDING

*E*very *Victorian cook had her own closely-guarded recipe for Christmas Pudding. This is just one of Mrs. Beeton's selection: she called it "very good." She also offered a Rich Christmas Pudding, an inexpensive one, and a Fruitarian Pudding, which omits the suet.*

CHRISTMAS PUDDING, THE UNDISPUTED STAR
OF THE LAVISH VICTORIAN CHRISTMAS

### INGREDIENTS

3 cups Flour

4 cups Fresh Breadcrumbs

4 cups Shredded Suet

3 cups Raisins

2 cups Currants

3/4 cup Chopped Mixed Peel

1/2 cup Soft Brown Sugar

1/2 cup Chopped Blanched Almonds

1/4 cup Ground Mixed Spice

Good Pinch of Salt

6 Eggs

1 cup Milk

1/4 cup Brandy

*Heap on more wood! The wind is chill;
But let it whistle as it will
We'll keep a merry Christmas still.*

SIR WALTER SCOTT

### METHOD

❦ In a large bowl, mix together all the dry ingredients; to ensure that everything is thoroughly incorporated, it is best to use your hands for this.

❦ Lightly beat the eggs and stir into the mixture, then add the milk and brandy, and stir until the pudding has a soft consistency. Pack the mixture into a buttered basin, pressing down well, and tie a layer of waxed paper over the top. Finish off with a pudding cloth tied tightly over the waxed paper.

❦ Place in a saucepan of boiling water that comes about two-thirds of the way up the side of the basin, and boil for about six hours. When cooked, remove the cloth and waxed paper, and turn out onto a serving dish.

*Buckingham Palace
Plum Pudding*

Each Christmas, 150 small plum puddings were made for the Royal Household. The recipe called for 60 lb. of flour, 30 lb. of sugar, 40 lb. each of raisins and currants, 30 lb. of candied peel, 50 lb. of beef suet, 150 eggs, 4 gallons of strong ale, 1 lb. of mixed spice, and a bottle apiece of rum and brandy.

**COOK'S TIP**

For an even richer pudding, you can substitute cream for the milk, add an extra egg, and sprinkle candied peel in among the sultanas.

# BREAD AND BUTTER PUDDING

Bread and Butter Pudding, the mainstay of the Victorian schoolroom and Gentlemen's Clubs, can be as plain or as rich as you like. This recipe is based on Mrs. Beeton's Baked Bread and Butter Pudding.

INGREDIENTS

8 Slices of Stale, Buttered White Bread
½ cup Sultanas
3 Eggs
¼ cup Sugar
2½ cups Fresh Milk
⅔ cup Heavy Cream
Zest of 1 Lemon

METHOD

❦ Cut the bread into triangles and layer it in a lightly-greased pie dish, with a sprinkling of sultanas and a little lemon zest between each layer.

❦ Lightly beat the eggs and sugar in a mixing bowl and add the milk and cream, stirring to combine all the ingredients. Strain the mixture over the bread and allow to stand for one hour so that the milk can soak into the bread.

❦ Bake at 350°F until the egg custard is firm to the touch and the top layer of bread is golden brown.

BREAD AND BUTTER PUDDING, EATEN IN NURSERIES AND GENTLEMEN'S CLUBS WITH EQUAL RELISH

BAKED APRICOT PUDDING, WARM AND GOLDEN, AND
DELICIOUS WITH CREAM

## METHOD

❦ Cut the apricots in half and remove the stones. Place the fruit in a saucepan with a little water and boil until the flesh has become soft. Pass the apricot pulp through a sieve to remove the skins, and put the purée to one side.

❦ Bring the milk to the boil and pour over the breadcrumbs, mix well and allow to cool a little. Lightly whisk the egg yolks and add to the milk mixture along with the sugar, sherry, and prepared fruit.

❦ Roll out the pastry, line an ovenproof dish, and fill with the mixture. Bake in a moderate oven (350°F/), until firm to the touch.

### COOK'S TIPS

For a more intense flavor, crush some of the apricot kernels and add them to the fruit purée.

If apricots are not in season, use well-drained tinned or preserved fruit. Add a tablespoon of flaked almonds to make up for the missing apricot kernels.

# BAKED APRICOT PUDDING

This delectable pudding is based on a recipe from Mrs. Beeton. For a dressier dessert, take the dish out of the oven as soon as the pudding has set, and add a layer of meringue spangled with slivers of crystallized apricot.

INGREDIENTS

12 Apricots
2½ cups Milk
3 cups Fresh Breadcrumbs
½ cup Sugar
4 Egg Yolks
5 T. Sherry
4oz Pastry

# ROLY POLY PUDDING

The delight of English schoolboys of all ages, this rib-sticking pudding is traditionally served with custard. Any cook worth her salt would have a recipe; this is based on Mrs Beeton's.

INGREDIENTS

12 oz. Suet Pastry
1 cup Your Favorite Homemade Jam

METHOD

❦ Roll out the pastry into a large rectangle about ½ inch thick. Spread the jam evenly over the pastry to within 1 inch of the edge all around. Carefully roll the pudding up and seal the end with a little water.

❦ Place on a greased baking sheet and cook in a fairly hot oven (400°F) for about 30 minutes or until nicely brown on top.

*As for the Roly-Poly,
it was too good.*

WILLIAM THACKERAY,
THE BOOK OF SNOBS

**COOK'S TIP**

You can make an
excellent pudding
using marmalade or
mincemeat instead
of jam.

# BACHELOR'S PUDDING

This simple yet tasty pudding is based on Mrs. Beeton's recipe for A Bachelor's Pudding. It has an austere, masculine air about it, but tastes very good with sweet butter sauce.

### INGREDIENTS

1 Apple, Peeled and Cored
2 cups Fresh Breadcrumbs
¾ cup Currants
¼ cup Soft Brown Sugar
3 Eggs, Whisked
Rind of 1 Lemon
Freshly Grated Nutmeg

### METHOD

❧ Chop the apple finely and mix together thoroughly with the rest of the ingredients. Allow to stand for 30 minutes.

❧ Pack into a well-greased pudding basin. Add a drop of milk if the mixture appears a little stiff.

❧ Cover tightly with foil and place in a saucepan that is two-thirds full of water; boil for about 3 hours.

❧ When cooked, gently turn the pudding out onto a dish and serve immediately.

Two old bachelors
were living in
one house,
One caught a Muffin,
the other caught
a Mouse.

EDWARD
LEAR

BACHELOR'S PUDDING, ORIGINALLY MADE AS HOME
COMFORTS FOR HARD-WORKING SCHOLARS

# FIG PUDDING

$A$*very dignified pudding based on a recipe of Mrs. Beeton's. Figs, like rhubarb, appealed to the valetudinarian leanings of the Victorians, although there is no medicinal taste about this sticky, delicious pudding.*

## INGREDIENTS

$2^{3}/_{4}$ *cups Dried Figs*
2 *cups Chopped Suet*
$1^{1}/_{3}$ *cups Flour*
4 *cups Fresh Breadcrumbs*
1 *Egg, Beaten*
*Milk*

## METHOD

❦ Chop the figs into small pieces and place in a large bowl along with the suet, flour, and breadcrumbs. Mix together well with the egg and sufficient milk to form a stiff mixture, and pack firmly into a well-greased pudding basin.

❦ Cover tightly with a piece of foil and a pudding cloth and place in a saucepan two-thirds full of water to boil for three hours. When cooked, carefully turn the pudding out of the mold and serve with Wine Sauce.

*Train up a fig tree in the way it should go and when you are old sit under the shade of it.*

CAPTAIN CUTTLE IN *Dombey and Son,*
CHARLES DICKENS

RIPE FIGS FOR A MOUTH-WATERING FIGGY PUDDING

CABINET PUDDING FREQUENTLY GRACED THE
HIGH TABLES OF THE VICTORIAN ESTABLISHMENT

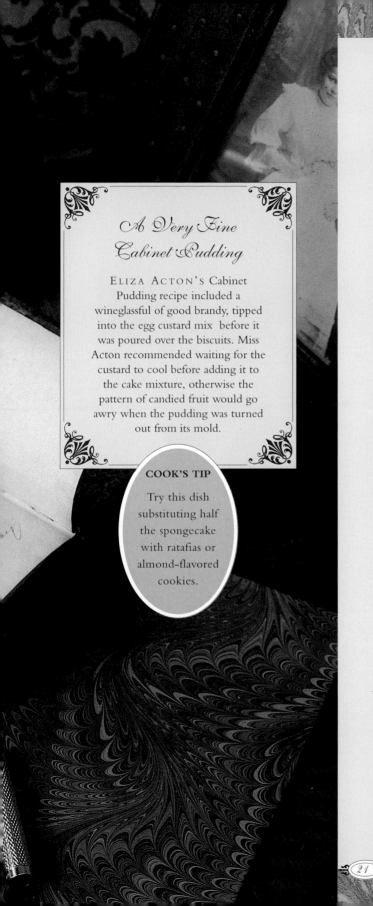

## A Very Fine Cabinet Pudding

ELIZA ACTON'S Cabinet Pudding recipe included a wineglassful of good brandy, tipped into the egg custard mix before it was poured over the biscuits. Miss Acton recommended waiting for the custard to cool before adding it to the cake mixture, otherwise the pattern of candied fruit would go awry when the pudding was turned out from its mold.

### COOK'S TIP

Try this dish substituting half the spongecake with ratafias or almond-flavored cookies.

# CABINET PUDDING

This solid, manly pudding is based on Mrs. Beeton's recipe; she also calls it Chancellor's Pudding. It should be served with a sweet sauce or, according to Eliza Acton, a "well-made wine sauce."

### INGREDIENTS

$^1/_3$ cup Chopped Candied Peel
$^2/_3$ cup Currants
$^2/_3$ cup Sultanas
Spongecake, Sliced
Melted Butter
4 Eggs
$^1/_4$ cup Sugar
Rind of 1 Lemon
$2^1/_2$ cups Milk

### METHOD

❦ Thoroughly grease a pudding basin with a little butter and place the chopped peel and a few currants and sultanas in the bottom of the basin. Cover the fruit with a layer of sliced spongecake and brush with the melted butter.

❦ Continue building up layers with the fruit and spongecake until the basin is nearly full. Break the eggs into a bowl and beat well. Add the sugar, lemon rind, and milk and beating again until all the ingredients are thoroughly mixed.

❦ Strain the mixture over the prepared pudding and allow to stand for one hour to soak into the spongecake. Bake at 350°F until the egg custard is firm. This takes about 30 minutes.

APPLES FROM THE WINTER STORE
FOR WHOLESOME FAMILY FARE

## Suet Crust Pastry

"This crust is so much lighter, and more wholesome, than that which is made with butter, we cannot refrain from recommending it in preference to our readers." Thus Eliza Acton eulogized suet crust pastry, giving several recipes for it. Mrs. Beeton also considered it suitable for children and recommended that it be made by mixing 1½ cups finely chopped beef suet to every 2¼ cups flour and making it into a paste with 1¼ cups water.

*Coleridge holds that a man cannot have a pure mind who refuses apple-dumplings.*

CHARLES LAMB

# BAKED APPLE DUMPLING

*These dumplings, simple yet delicious, are based on Mrs. Beeton's recipe. She calls them "a plain family dish."*

INGREDIENTS

*6 Medium Apples*
*Sugar*
*12 oz. Suet Crust Pastry*
*Confectioner's Sugar to Decorate*

**COOK'S TIP**
Use puff pastry instead of suet crust for richer dumplings.

METHOD

❦ Carefully peel and core the apples, taking care not to damage the fruit, and liberally sprinkle each one with sugar.

❦ Roll out the pastry and wrap each apple individually, taking care to join the pastry edges neatly so that round balls are formed.

❦ Place the dumplings on a baking sheet and cook at 350°F for 30 minutes. When cooked, remove from the oven and sift thickly with confectioner's sugar.

FASHIONABLE
DUMPLINGS

*Eliza Acton gives a fascinating recipe entitled "Fashionable Apple Dumplings;" the dumplings are boiled in little knitted snoods to give a "pretty effect."*

# PUBLISHER'S PUDDING

This is an adaptation of Eliza Acton's recipe. She observed rather drily that "this pudding can scarcely be made too rich." Presumably, she devised it for the delectation of her publisher's tastebuds. Her Modern Cookery for Private Families was published in 1845. The pudding is light, though rich; she recommends that it is served with German Sauce, a thick, creamy custard flavored with vanilla and cinnamon.

### INGREDIENTS

1 cup Ground Almonds
1 cup Fresh Breadcrumbs
1¼ cups Heavy Cream
1 cup Crushed Macaroons
2 cups Beef Suet
1 cup Flour
1 cup Sugar
1 cup Glacé Cherries
1¼ cups Raisins
1 cup Candied Peel
6 Egg Yolks
Grated Rind Of 1 Lemon
3 to 4 T. Brandy
Good Pinch of Salt

PUBLISHER'S PUDDING, EXCELLENT
WITH A GOOD BOOK

### METHOD

❧ Put the ground almonds and breadcrumbs into a large mixing bowl and pour over the cream, which has been brought to the boil. Put to one side and allow to cool.

❧ Add the rest of the ingredients one by one, mixing thoroughly until all are fully incorporated. Pour the mixture into a well-greased pudding basin, filling it to the top.

❧ Cover tightly with foil and a pudding cloth and place in a saucepan of water to boil for four hours. When cooked, allow the pudding to stand for several minutes before turning out onto a serving dish.

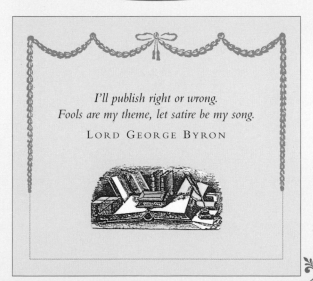

I'll publish right or wrong.
Fools are my theme, let satire be my song.

LORD GEORGE BYRON

# PARADISE PUDDING

*This heavenly mixture of brandied apple and light pudding is based on a recipe from Mrs. Beeton. Presumably, its name refers to the apples in it.*

### INGREDIENTS

1 lb. Apples
2 cups Fresh Breadcrumbs
$^1/_2$ cup Sugar
$^1/_2$ cup Raisins
Rind of 1 Lemon
3 Eggs
3 or 4 T. Brandy

### METHOD

❧ Peel and core the apples and chop them into small pieces. Place them in a mixing bowl with the remaining dry ingredients and combine thoroughly.

❧ Beat the eggs and add them to the bowl along with the brandy, and stir until well mixed. Pour the mixture into a well-buttered basin and cover with a pudding cloth. Place in a saucepan of water and boil for $1^1/_2$ hours. Serve with a sweet sauce.

*All Paradise opens! Let me die eating ortolans to the sound of soft music.*

BENJAMIN DISRAELI

# CANARY PUDDING

*This is based on a recipe from Mrs. Beeton. The light, lemony, delicious pudding turns out a beautiful yellow color, hence the name.*

### INGREDIENTS

¾ cup Butter

1 cup Sugar

Rind of 1 Lemon

¾ cup Flour

3 Eggs

### METHOD

❦ Melt the butter in a saucepan and stir in the sugar and lemon rind. Slowly sieve in the flour, continually stirring until it is fully incorporated.

❦ Whisk the eggs and add to the mixture; beat thoroughly. Pour the pudding into a buttered basin, cover with foil, and tie over a pudding cloth.

❦ Place in a saucepan of water and boil for two hours. Serve with a sweet sauce.

### COOK'S TIP

Mrs. Beeton suggests that you add two tablespoons of raspberry jam to the ingredients to convert it into Washington Pudding.

CANARY PUDDING,
PERFECT FOR A LADIES' LUNCH

# BREAD PUDDING

⚭

This is based on Mrs. Beeton's recipe for Queen of Bread Pudding and would grace any formal dinner table. Her more everyday versions were frugal exercises involving stale bread crumbs, dried fruit, and chopped suet.

INGREDIENTS

2 ½ cups Milk

5 cups Breadcrumbs

⅛ cup Butter

¼ cup Sugar

Rind of 1 Lemon, Grated

2 Eggs

Homemade Jam of Your Choice

METHOD

❦ Bring the milk to the boil and pour over the breadcrumbs, butter, sugar, and lemon rind in a mixing bowl. Put to one side and allow to cool.

❦ Separate the eggs. Beat the yolks and add to the cooling mixture, stirring thoroughly. Grease an 8-inch pie dish and pile the mixture into it. Bake at 400°F until the pudding sets.

❦ Remove from the oven and spread a good, thick layer of jam over the pudding. Top off with the egg whites that have been beaten until very stiff. Sift over lots of sugar and return to the oven for the meringue to cook and take on a little color.

THE HUMBLE BREAD PUDDING MAKES A FORMAL APPEARANCE AT THE TABLE, TOPPED WITH A LAYER OF MERINGUE

## A PLAIN RECEIPT

Eliza Acton's recipe,
which omits the meringue
topping, is very similar,
but Mrs. Acton
considered it "quite a
plain receipt." She
advocated the addition of
a small glass of brandy, a
handful of candied peel,
and some currants; then
"a very excellent pudding
will be obtained."

*They lived at the bottom of a well.*
*They lived on treacle.*
*It was a treacle well.*

LEWIS CARROLL,
ALICE IN WONDERLAND

MOLASSES PUDDING, A WINTER WARMER FOR
THE COLDEST OF DAYS

# MOLASSES PUDDING

This melting, multi-layered pudding is based on a recipe from Mrs. Beeton. It's very filling and even more delicious served with a custard sauce.

INGREDIENTS

1½ cups Flour
1 cup Chopped Suet
½ cup Breadcrumbs
Molasses
Grated rind of 1 Lemon
⅛ cup Baking Powder
Pinch of Salt
A Little Cold Water

METHOD

❦ In a bowl, mix together the flour, suet, baking powder, and salt, and add enough cold water to make a firm pastry. Split the pastry into two halves and use one half to line a pudding basin. Spread a thin layer of molasses over the bottom of the lined basin and sprinkle over plenty of breadcrumbs and a little lemon rind.

❦ Roll out the remaining half of the pastry thinly and cut a circle to completely cover the first layer of molasses. Dampen the edges lightly and press into place, ensuring it seals to the pastry lining. Repeat the process of layering the molasses and pastry until the basin is full.

❦ Cover with a layer of foil and steam in a double boiler for approximately 2½ hours. This is a very filling pudding that is even more delicious served with a custard sauce.

Georgie Porgie, Pudding and Pie
Kissed the girls and made them cry
When the boys came out to play
Georgie Porgie ran away.

TRADITIONAL NURSERY RHYME

# CHOCOLATE TARTLETS

*A chocoholic's dream, these tartlets are based on a recipe of Mrs. Beeton's. They are delicious with morning coffee.*

INGREDIENTS

*2 Eggs*

*½ cup Sugar*

*2 oz. Grated Plain Chocolate*

*2 cups Cake Crumbs*

*⅛ cup Cornstarch*

*¼ cup Melted Butter*

*½ lb. Shortcrust Pastry*

*Chocolate Icing For Decoration*

METHOD

❦ Separate the eggs and cream the yolks and sugar together. Stir in the grated chocolate, cake crumbs, cornstarch, and melted butter, and ensure it is all mixed together well.

❦ In a clean bowl, whisk the egg whites until they form stiff peaks and gently fold into the filling mixture. Roll out the pastry thinly and line some shallow muffin tins.

❦ Spoon in the chocolate filling and cook at 350°F for 20 minutes. When cool, spread with chocolate icing.

> *Doubtless God could have made a better berry (than the strawberry) but doubtless God never did.*
> WILLIAM BUTLER

# STRAWBERRY TARTLETS

*These delicious pink summer tartlets are based on an Eliza Acton recipe. She pronounced them "good," which hardly does them justice.*

INGREDIENTS

*2 cups Fresh Strawberries*

*½ cup Confectioner's Sugar*

*4 Eggs, Whisked*

*½ lb. Shortcrust Pastry*

METHOD

❦ Thoroughly wash the strawberries and remove any remaining stalks, then mash the fruit down to a fine pulp. Stir in the sugar until well mixed and slowly add the eggs a little at a time until all are incorporated.

❦ Roll out the shortcrust pastry thinly and, using pastry cutters, cut out discs to line some shallow muffin tins. Fill each pastry about two-thirds full with the strawberry mixture and bake at 400°F for ten minutes.

> *The Queen of Hearts*
> *She made some tarts*
> *All on a Summer's day;*
> *The Knave of Hearts*
> *He stole the tarts*
> *And took them clean away.*
> NURSERY RHYME

*And spectral dance, before the dawn*
*A hundred vicars down the lawn;*
*Curates, long dust, will come and go*
*On lissom, clerical, printless toe;*
*And oft betweeen the boughs unseen*
*The sly shade of a Rural Dean.*

RUPERT BROOKE,
THE OLD VICARAGE, GRANTCHESTER.

# CURATE'S PUDDING

*A frugal, filling pudding constructed from simple kitchen ingredients and one of the less exciting fruits from the kitchen garden; just the thing to satisfy a curate without tempting him to indulge, unless you serve it with cream. This is based on a recipe from Eliza Acton.*

INGREDIENTS

2 lb. Fresh Rhubarb
1 cup Sugar
8 Thin Slices of Bread
1½ cups Fresh Breadcrumbs
½ cup Butter

METHOD

❦ Wash the rhubarb and cut into 1-inch lengths. Spread a layer of the fruit over the bottom of a deep pie dish and sprinkle with a third of the sugar.

❦ Remove the crusts from the sliced bread and use half of them to cover the fruit over completely. Continue building up the pudding with alternating layers of rhubarb, sugar, and bread. Top the final layer of rhubarb with the remaining sugar and breadcrumbs mixed together.

❦ Melt the butter and pass it through a clean muslin cloth to clarify. Pour over the pudding and cook at 400°F for about 30 minutes.

**COOK'S TIP**

According to Eliza Acton, apples or blackcurrants, sweetened and flavored with nutmeg and lemon, rind also "make an excellent pudding of this kind;" if you use apples, butter the slices of bread.

# RHUBARB PIE

*This recipe is based on one of Mrs. Beeton's, who considered rhubarb to be "one of the most useful of all garden productions that are put into pies or puddings."*

INGREDIENTS

½ lb. Puff Pastry
2 lb. Fresh Rhubarb
½ cup Sugar

METHOD

❦ Roll out the puff pastry thinly and line a deep pie dish. Wash and dry the rhubarb and cut into small pieces roughly 1 inch in length. Pile the prepared fruit into the lined dish and sprinkle over the sugar; do not worry if the fruit is higher than the top of the dish, as it will reduce during cooking.

❦ Roll out some more pastry and cover the pie with a lid. Brush the top with a little beaten egg and sprinkle generously with sugar.

❦ Cook at 400°F for 30–45 minutes or until the pastry has risen and turned a golden brown.

# BEEFSTEAK PUDDING

*This savory batter pudding is based on Mrs. Beeton's recipe for Baked Beefsteak Pudding. It makes a refreshing change from the more familiar steamed suet variety.*

### INGREDIENTS

*1 cup Flour*

*2 Eggs*

*2 cups Fresh Milk*

*1lb. 8oz. Rump Steak, Cubed*

*8 oz. Kidney, Cubed*

*Salt and Pepper*

### METHOD

❦ Sieve the flour and a pinch of salt into a large mixing bowl and make a well in the center. Break the eggs into the well and add a little of the milk. Stirring with a wooden spoon, gradually incorporate the flour into the egg mixture and slowly pour in the rest of the milk until you have a smooth, thick batter.

❦ Pour a little of the batter into the bottom of a pie dish and add the cubed steak and kidney. Season well with pepper and salt and pour over the remaining batter.

❦ Place in hot oven and cook at 425°F for one hour or until the batter has risen and turned a deep brown.

*Dr. Johnson's morality was as English an article as a beefsteak.*

NATHANIEL HAWTHORNE

## Ruth Pinch's Celebrated Pudding

In Charles Dickens' *Martin Chuzzlewit*, Ruth, the pretty sister of the saintly Tom Pinch, makes a beefsteak pudding for her brother to celebrate their setting up home together. Eliza Acton quotes the recipe in her *Modern Cookery for Private Families*, published in 1845, just a year after Dickens' novel. Ruth used a very rich butter crust, moistened with egg yolks. Her pudding was also called Beefsteak Pudding a la Dickens.

Beefsteak Pudding for a hearty lunch to satisfy the most Dickensian of appetites

**COOK'S TIP**

Boil the pudding in a
long loaf shape; slice it just
before dinner is served and
brown the slices in the meat
juices of the roasting pan.

∽

Take care to top up the
saucepan with extra
boiling water if needed.

PEASE PUDDING, A TRADITIONAL
SAVORY PUDDING TO ACCOMPANY BOILED BÁCON

# PEASE PUDDING

Recipes for pease pudding are among the oldest in England, as pease pudding with bacon is one of the oldest dishes. Serve this pease pudding, based on a recipe of Mrs. Beeton's, with boiled bacon and onion sauce. It's so filling that you will not need potatoes.

INGREDIENTS

3 ½ cups Dried Split Peas
½ cup Butter
2 Eggs
Salt and Pepper
Handful Fresh Mint, Finely Chopped

METHOD

❦ Put the peas in a bowl, cover with water and allow to soak overnight. The following day, drain off the soaking water, put the peas into a saucepan, and cover with fresh, cold water. Bring to the boil, then reduce to a simmer and cook for 1 ½ hours until the peas are soft.
❦ When cooked, drain them well and press them through a sieve. Add the remaining ingredients and mix together until all are thoroughly incorporated. Spoon the prepared pudding into a well-greased pudding basin and cover tightly with a piece of foil.
❦ Place it in a saucepan half full of water and boil for 45 to 60 minutes, until the pudding is firm.

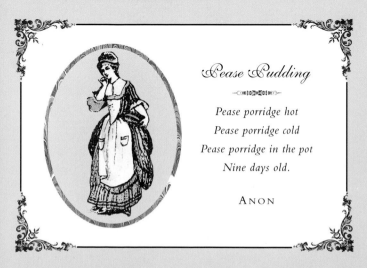

## Pease Pudding

Pease porridge hot
Pease porridge cold
Pease porridge in the pot
Nine days old.

ANON

## An Economical Plan

This is Mrs. Beeton's artful suggestion for frugal living. "Where there is a large family of children, and the means of keeping them are limited, it is a most economical plan to serve up the pudding before the meat as, in this case, consumption of the latter article will be much smaller than it otherwise would be."

### KENTISH SUET PUDDING

Eliza Acton's recipe, which she called Kentish Suet Pudding, adds an egg to the basic recipe. Miss Acton maintains that it is "very good sliced and broiled or browned in a Dutch oven, after having become quite cold."

# SUET PUDDING TO EAT WITH BEEF

This traditional and very tasty accompaniment to the Sunday roast is based on Mrs. Beeton's recipe for "Suet Pudding to Eat with Roast Meat."

INGREDIENTS

3 cups Flour
1 ½ cups Chopped Beef Suet
1 ¼ cups Fresh Milk
Good Pinch of Salt and Pepper

METHOD

❦ Place the flour and suet in a mixing bowl along with the seasoning and mix well. Slowly stir in the milk until a smooth paste is formed.
❦ Pour the prepared pudding into a buttered basin, cover with foil, and stand in a saucepan half full of water to boil for 2 ½ hours.

# GAME PIE

*This is based on Mrs. Beeton's recipe for Raised Game Pie, an elaborate and complicated affair involving a raised pie crust and marrow-bone jelly. Game pies should be eaten cold and so are excellent for picnics; in Victorian times they would have been sent out for shooting party luncheons.*

### INGREDIENTS

1 Large Fowl or 2 Pheasants
4 cups Brown Breadcrumbs
³/₄ cup Shredded Beef Suet
1 cup Fresh Chopped Parsley
1 Egg
1 lb. Shortcrust Pastry
¹/₂ lb. Good Sliced Ham
Salt and Pepper
Cornstarch
Egg for Glazing

### METHOD

❦ Prepare and clean the birds and cut into portions; put them in a pan with just enough water to cover them, and bring to the boil. Reduce to a simmer and cook until the flesh comes away from the bone. Remove the meat from the pan and cut into chunks, reserving the cooking liquor.

❦ Prepare the forcemeat by mixing together the breadcrumbs, suet, and parsley and adding the beaten egg to bind it all together. Roll out the pastry and line a deep pie dish, reserving enough to make a lid. Build the pie up in alternating layers of cooked game, forcemeat, and sliced ham, with a little seasoning between each.

❦ Once the pie dish is full, reduce the reserved stock and thicken with a little cornstarch dissolved in water. Pour the sauce over the prepared pie. Roll out a lid using the reserved pastry; brush the edges with cold water to ensure it seals well. Brush the top of the pie with a beaten egg and cook at 400°F for 30 minutes, until the crust is golden.

# LITTLE RAISED PORK PIES

❧

These delicious little pies, just right for a picnic or a lunch box, are based on a traditional Victorian recipe. Mrs. Beeton also gives a recipe, but for so large a number that she must have been catering for a house party.

### INGREDIENTS

$^1\!/_2$ cup Butter

3 cups Flour

1 cup Shredded Beef Suet

2 lb. Lean Pork, Minced

Salt and Pepper

1 Egg, Beaten

**MAKES ABOUT 10 LITTLE PIES**

❧

### METHOD

❦ Place the butter in a saucepan and gently melt over a low heat; add the flour, suet, and a good pinch of salt and mix into a stiff paste. Taking small pieces of the warm paste, form into little pots, remembering to leave enough pastry for the lids.

❦ Fill the pots with the minced pork and add a pinch of seasoning before covering with the lids. Brush thoroughly with beaten egg. Cook at 350°F until the pastry has turned a deep brown color.

RAISED PORK PIES AND GAMES PIES, TRADITIONAL FARE FOR PICNICS AND SHOOTING PARTIES

**COOK'S TIP**

Mrs. Beeton suggested that you "Clean three of the pigeon feet and place them in a hole made in the crust at the top; this shows the kind of pie it is."

*Promises and pie crusts are made to be broken.*

JONATHAN SWIFT

# Pigeon Pie

This is based on a Beeton recipe called "Epsom Grandstand recipe." Before she married, Mrs. Beeton actually lived in the Grandstand at Epsom where her stepfather, Henry Dorling, was Clerk of the Course. Isabella helped to run the extended household; Pigeon Pie must have been a regular on the menu.

INGREDIENTS

2 Pigeons, Prepared
$1/4$ cup Butter
1 lb. Fresh Rump Steak
$1\frac{1}{4}$ cup Chicken Stock
Salt and Pepper
$1/2$ lb. Puff Pastry
1 Egg Yolk

METHOD

❦ With a sharp knife, cut the pigeons in half lengthways. Season well with salt and pepper. Heat the butter in a pan and quickly brown the birds on all sides. Remove from the heat and put to one side.

❦ Line the bottom of a pie dish with the rump steak cut into cubes, and lay the pieces of pigeon on top. Bring the stock to the boil, adjust the seasoning, and pour into the pie dish. Roll out the pastry to make the lid, but line the rim of the dish with a strip of paste first. This will ensure the lid stays firmly in place during cooking.

❦ Brush the top of the pie with beaten egg yolk and cook at 350°F for about an hour until the pastry has risen and turned golden brown.

# GROUSE PIE

A hearty pie based on Mrs. Beeton's recipe. Grouse is in season in England between August and the end of December, so this is a treat to be savored.

INGREDIENTS

1 lb. Fresh Rump Steak
A Brace of Grouse, Plucked and Drawn
Cayenne Pepper
Salt and Pepper
$1\frac{1}{4}$ cups Chicken Stock
$1/2$ lb. Puff Pastry
1 Egg Yolk

METHOD

❦ Cut the rump steak into cubes and line the bottom of a pie dish. Joint the grouse, season well with cayenne, salt, and black pepper, and lay in the dish on top of the meat. Pour over the stock.

❦ Roll out the puff pastry evenly and line the rim of the dish first before covering the pie with its pastry lid.

❦ Beat the egg yolk and brush the pie over before cooking at 350°F for 45 minutes.

*GROUSE PIE with hare in the middle is fare Which duly concocted with science and care Doctor Kitchener says is beyond all compare And tenderer leveret Robin had never ate.*

INGOLDSBY LEGENDS

PIGEON AND GROUSE PIE, RELISHED IN GRAND DINING
ROOMS AND POACHERS' COTTAGES ALIKE

# RICH RABBIT PIE

*Rabbit pie is an ancient country dish relished by poachers and gamekeepers alike. Many recipes for it abound, but this is based on Mrs. Beeton's version.*

### INGREDIENTS

1 Rabbit, Skinned and Jointed
½ cup Fresh Cold Water
4oz Bacon
4 Hard Boiled Eggs, Quartered
4 cups White Breadcrumbs
¾ cup Shredded Suet
1 cup Fresh Chopped Parsley
1 Egg, Beaten
Salt and Pepper
½ lb. Puff Pastry
Egg Yolk for Glaze

### COOK'S TIP

You can leave the pie to cool so that the stock turns to jelly. Then the pie can be eaten cold for picnics or summer luncheon parties.

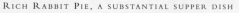

RICH RABBIT PIE, A SUBSTANTIAL SUPPER DISH

### METHOD

❧ Bone the rabbit pieces and cut the flesh into slices. Place the bones in a saucepan and cover with water. Bring to the boil, then simmer gently until well reduced. Strain off and reserve the stock. Place the rabbit meat in a pie dish along with the bacon cut into strips and the hard boiled eggs.

❧ Mix the breadcrumbs, suet, and chopped parsley in a bowl and bind together with the beaten egg. Form this forcemeat into little balls and add to the pie dish. Season the pie well with salt and pepper, pour in the cold water, and cover with a puff pastry lid. Make a hole in the center of the lid with a knife and brush the top thoroughly with the beaten egg yolk.

❧ Cook at 400°F for about an hour. Reduce the reserved stock made from the bones and pour it through the hole in the lid.

*Bye Baby Bunting*
*Daddy's gone a hunting*
*Gone to get a rabbit skin*
*To wrap the Baby Bunting in*
*Bye Baby Bunting.*

NURSERY RHYME

### COOK'S TIP

If the pastry begins to brown too much, cover with a sheet of waxed paper for the remainder of the cooking time.

# INDEX

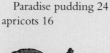

P9-EF

...se studies of the historical process of ec... ...ange in nineteenth- and twentieth-century United States, Canada, and the British West Indies represent a major step in ongoing efforts to understand the sources of economic growth. Developed from a National Bureau of Economic Research Conference on Income and Wealth, the papers are collected into four main sections:

*national product, in the tradition of national accounts study, including new Canadian national product series and estimates of United States transactions costs over the past century;
*capital stock and the distribution of wealth, including new United States nineteenth-century capital stock estimates;
*analyses of fertility, health, and mortality, and the free and slave labor supply, using such important sources as the manuscript census, the Moser sample on the sexual lives of middle-class women at the turn of the century, the Mormon genealogical collection in Salt Lake City, and slave registration from the British West Indies;
*sectoral studies on the United States and Canada that include agriculture, manufacturing, transportation, and government, with pathbreaking work in each area, including a new analysis of United States manufacturing growth before the Civil War and a framework for estimating revenues and expenditures at the state and local level.

Some papers rely on a national accounts orientation, while others draw on rich sources of primary micro data only recently made available to researchers, allowing the exploration of new topics in various areas. These well-written studies offer original research results and basic data not available elsewhere. Scholars interested in American economic history and the growth and development

P9-EFG-907

These studies of the historical process of ec........
change in nineteenth- and twentieth-century
United States, Canada, and the British West Indies
represent a major step in ongoing efforts to understand the sources of economic growth. Developed
from a National Bureau of Economic Research
Conference on Income and Wealth, the papers are
collected into four main sections:

*national product, in the tradition of national
accounts study, including new Canadian
national product series and estimates of United
States transactions costs over the past century;
*capital stock and the distribution of wealth,
including new United States nineteenth-century
capital stock estimates;
*analyses of fertility, health, and mortality, and
the free and slave labor supply, using such important sources as the manuscript census, the
Moser sample on the sexual lives of middle-class
women at the turn of the century, the Mormon
genealogical collection in Salt Lake City, and
slave registration from the British West Indies;
*sectoral studies on the United States and
Canada that include agriculture, manufacturing, transportation, and government, with path-
breaking work in each area, including a new
analysis of United States manufacturing growth
before the Civil War and a framework for estimating revenues and expenditures at the state
and local level.

Some papers rely on a national accounts orientation, while others draw on rich sources of primary
micro data only recently made available to researchers, allowing the exploration of new topics in
various areas. These well-written studies offer
original research results and basic data not available elsewhere. Scholars interested in American
economic history and the growth and development

of the North American economy as well as questions of economic growth in general will find this
volume a valuable resource. A major contribution
to the literature, *Long-Term Factors in American
Economic Growth* lays the groundwork for future
research in the field.

# Long-Term Factors in American Economic Growth

Studies in Income and Wealth
Volume 51

National Bureau of Economic Research
Conference on Research in Income and Wealth

# Long-Term Factors in American Economic Growth

Edited by  Stanley L. Engerman and
Robert E. Gallman

The University of Chicago Press

*Chicago and London*

Stanley L. Engerman is John H. Munro Professor of Economics
and professor of history at the University of Rochester. Robert E.
Gallman is Kenan Professor of Economics and History at the
University of North Carolina, Chapel Hill. Both editors are
research associates of the National Bureau of Economic
Research.

The University of Chicago Press, Chicago 60637
The University of Chicago Press, Ltd., London

© 1986 by the National Bureau of Economic Research
All rights reserved. Published 1986
Printed in the United States of America
95 94 93 92 91 90 89 88 87 86    5 4 3 2 1

**Library of Congress Cataloging in Publication Data**

Long-term factors in American economic growth.
    (Studies in income and wealth; v. 51)
    Includes indexes.
    1. North America—Economic conditions.   2. United
States—Economic conditions.   I. Engerman, Stanley L.
II. Gallman, Robert E.   III. Series.
HC106.3.C714      vol. 51     330 s [330.973]     86-11408
[HC95]
ISBN 0-226-20928-8

## National Bureau of Economic Research

Franklin A. Lindsay, *chairman*
Richard Rosett, *vice-chairman*
Martin Feldstein, *president*

Geoffrey Carliner, *executive director*
Charles A. Walworth, *treasurer*
Sam Parker, *director of finance and administration*

### Directors at Large

Moses Abramovitz
Andrew Brimmer
George T. Conklin, Jr.
Jean A. Crockett
Morton Ehrlich
Martin Feldstein
Edward L. Ginzton
David L. Grove
George Hatsopoulos

Walter W. Heller
Saul B. Klaman
Franklin A. Lindsay
Roy E. Moor
Geoffrey H. Moore
Michael H. Moskow
James J. O'Leary
Robert Parry

Peter G. Peterson
Robert V. Roosa
Richard N. Rosett
Bert Seidman
Eli Shapiro
Stephen Stamas
Donald S. Wasserman
Marina v.N. Whitman

### Directors by University Appointment

Marcus Alexis, *Northwestern*
Charles H. Berry, *Princeton*
James Duesenberry, *Harvard*
Ann F. Friedlaender, *Massachusetts Institute of Technology*
J. C. LaForce, *California, Los Angeles*
Paul McCracken, *Michigan*
James L. Pierce, *California, Berkeley*

Nathan Rosenberg, *Stanford*
James Simler, *Minnesota*
James Tobin, *Yale*
John Vernon, *Duke*
William S. Vickrey, *Columbia*
Burton A. Weisbrod, *Wisconsin*
Arnold Zellner, *Chicago*

### Directors by Appointment of Other Organizations

Carl F. Christ, *American Economic Association*
Robert S. Hamada, *American Finance Association*
Edgar Fiedler, *National Association of Business Economists*
Robert C. Holland, *Committee for Economic Development*
Douglas Purvis, *Canadian Economics Association*
Douglass C. North, *Economic History Association*

Rudolph A. Oswald, *American Federation of Labor and Congress of Industrial Organizations*
James Houck, *American Agricultural Economics Association*
Albert Sommers, *The Conference Board*
Dudley Wallace, *American Statistical Association*
Charles A. Walworth, *American Institute of Certified Public Accountants*

### Directors Emeriti

Arthur Burns
Emilio G. Collado
Solomon Fabricant

Frank Fetter
Thomas D. Flynn
Gottfried Haberler

George B. Roberts
Willard L. Thorp

Since this volume is a record of conference proceedings, it has been exempted from the rules governing critical review of manuscripts by the Board of Directors of the National Bureau (resolution adopted 8 June 1948, as revised 21 November 1949 and 20 April 1968).

30.973
85e

To Raymond Goldsmith
and to the memory of Simon Kuznets,
pioneers of quantitative economic history

# Contents

# Prefatory Note

This volume contains the papers and discussion presented at the conference on Long-Term Factors in American Economic Growth held in Williamsburg, Virginia, on March 22–24, 1984. Funds for the Conference on Research in Income and Wealth are provided to the National Bureau of Economic Research by the National Science Foundation; we are indebted for its support. We also thank Stanley L. Engerman and Robert E. Gallman, who served as co-chairmen of the conference and editors of this volume.

## Executive Committee, March 1984

F. Thomas Juster, chairman
Orley Ashenfelter
Christopher Clague
Martin David
W. Erwin Diewert
Robert T. Michael

John R. Norsworthy
Eugene Smolensky
Helen Stone Tice
Robert J. Gordon, NBER
   representative
Zvi Griliches, NBER
   representative

## Volume Editors' Acknowledgments

Kathi Smith handled local arrangements for the meetings on which this volume is based, Mark Fitz-Patrick prepared the papers for the press, and Annie Spillane skillfully advised the editors. Lance E. Davis, Peter H. Lindert, and Gavin Wright served as referees and offered exceptionally insightful comments and suggestions, while the discussants were unusually responsible and helpful. The editors give their thanks to these contributors to the volume and to the principal contributors, the authors of the papers.

# 1  Introduction

Stanley L. Engerman and Robert E. Gallman

The present volume differs from its recent Income and Wealth predecessors in two respects. The first is the breadth of its topic, *Long-Term Factors in American Economic Growth*. Narrowly defined analytical subjects (e.g., *The Measurement of Economic and Social Performance*, Vol. 38, *New Developments in Productivity Measurement and Analysis*, Vol. 44, and *The Measurement of Labor Costs*, Vol. 48) have been the norm. The second is that its papers are concerned with the historical process of economic change. Although historical papers have appeared previously (see, e.g., Vol. 46) and for a time seemed to be becoming a common feature (see Vol. 33 and 34), most Conference volumes have not had a historical dimension. This is surprising in view both of the concern of the Conference's founders—particularly Raymond Goldsmith and Simon Kuznets—with the measurement and analysis of long-period change and of the contributions economic history can make to analyzing problems that have long engaged the Conference.

Two preceding volumes—owing in considerable measure to the encouragement of Goldsmith and Kuznets—are exceptions: *Trends in the American Economy in the Nineteenth Century* (Vol. 24) and *Output, Employment, and Productivity in the United States after 1800* (Vol. 30). Both address broad subjects in the field of economic growth; both resulted from collaborative meetings of the Economic History Association and the Conference, in which economic historians played prominent roles. The Planning Committee for the first, held in Williamstown

Stanley L. Engerman is the John H. Munro Professor of Economics and professor of history at the University of Rochester, and a research associate of the National Bureau of Economic Research. Robert E. Gallman is Kenan Professor of Economics and History at the University of North Carolina at Chapel Hill and a research associate of the National Bureau of Economic Research.

in 1957, consisted of Harold F. Williamson (chairman), Stanley Lebergott, and John E. Sawyer; the resulting volume was edited by William N. Parker. The Planning Committee for the second, held in Chapel Hill in 1963, comprised Parker (chairman), Richard A. Easterlin, and Raymond W. Goldsmith; Dorothy S. Brady edited the published papers.

Most students of the subject find the origins of the new economic history—cliometrics—in these two meetings. Cliometrics has two branches, one with a strong national accounts orientation, the other stressing, more generally, the use of economic theory and econometrics in the study of historical problems. Both branches were represented at Williamstown and Chapel Hill, but true to the leading interests of the Conference at that time, only the first is represented in Volumes 24 and 30. The remaining papers were published elsewhere, notably in the proceedings issue of the *Journal of Economic History,* but also in other *JEH* issues, in the *Journal of Political Economy,* and in other places.[1] Among these papers were two hortatory and influential pieces by Alfred H. Conrad and John R. Meyer on how economic history should be practiced, one ("Economic Theory, Statistical Inference, and Economic History," published in the December 1957 *Journal of Economic History*) arguing in the abstract, the other ("The Economics of Slavery in the Ante-bellum South," *Journal of Political Economy,* April 1958) by way of a case study. The latter, with Robert W. Fogel's "A Quantitative Approach to the Study of Railroads in American Economic Growth" (*Journal of Economic History,* June 1962), launched a heated discussion over methods in the study of economic history.

The present volume is a lineal descendant of Volumes 24 and 30, the kinship showing clearly in its principal features. These consist of an abundant display of primary evidence (or the results of the manipulation of primary evidence) organized for long reaches of time, and frequently presented within the framework of the national accounts. (See, e.g., the papers by Urquhart, Green, McInnis, Weiss, Sylla, and Gallman, for examples of the last characteristic; examples of the first two are to be found in virtually all of the papers in this volume.) But kin are never identical and frequently far from it; Volume 51 has features that distinguish it from its predecessors.

The papers that are organized within the general framework of the national accounts either fill gaps left by Volumes 24 and 30 (see the papers by Sylla and Green), offer replacements for series appearing in the previous volumes (Urquhart, McInnis), or set afoot plans to extend existing series into new temporal periods (Gallman) or geographic regions (Weiss).

The paper by Richard Sylla employs archival materials and devises methods of assembling the evidence drawn from them into a coherent description of the fiscal activities of state and local governments, and, in addition, contributes to the fiscal history of North Carolina. It proposes ways of handling nineteenth-century state and local evidence—evidence that has rarely been treated systematically—and urges a general assault on state archival materials, thereby accepting the challenge laid down almost twenty years ago by Lance Davis and John Legler ("The Government in the American Economy, 1815–1902: A Quantitative Study," *Journal of Economic History,* December 1966). If the Sylla study is replicated for other states, one of the major gaps in the quantitative record of United States economic change will be filled. A set of such records for a wide variety of states would also permit potentially fruitful comparative analyses.

The Green and McInnis papers are drawn from a major study of Canadian economic growth in the latter part of the nineteenth century and the early part of the twentieth. The papers consider changes in output and productivity in railroads and agriculture. In addition to their significance to the reinterpretation of Canadian economic history, they open opportunities for comparative analysis (which they, in some measure, exploit) with the papers by Fishlow, in Volume 30, and by Towne and Rasmussen and Gallman in Volume 24. Urquhart's paper, deriving from the same project as Green's and McInnis's, a project under the general direction of Urquhart, offers a new, detailed, carefully assembled set of estimates of Canadian national product. These estimates are linked with the official series, which begins in 1926, and are intended to replace the series from the path-breaking Firestone study of a quarter of a century ago (see Firestone's paper in Vol. 24). Urquhart and his discussant, John Dales, suggest ways in which the new work may influence the interpretation of Canadian economic growth, but their exchange is only the beginning of what promises to be an animated discussion.

The Green, McInnis, and Urquhart papers report on a project drawing to a close; Weiss's paper describes the first steps in a new project intended to supply estimates of the labor force at the state level and at decadal intervals in the nineteenth century. Weiss plans to use Stanley Lebergott's procedures (perhaps in modified form) in his estimations, and he describes the tests he conducted on them and on the Lebergott estimates. As Weiss had expected, these tests demonstrated the sturdiness of Lebergott's original work. However, they also gave Weiss reason to revise Lebergott's sectoral distribution of his aggregate series, revisions that have implications for our understanding of early nineteenth-century economic growth.

Gallman's paper contains new estimates of the aggregate capital stock and its components, 1840–1900, at decade intervals, including comprehensive estimates of the value of agricultural land improvements. The series eventually will be extended to the early nineteenth century. They are readily linked with Goldsmith's twentieth-century series.

The papers of Volume 51 that follow a national accounts form of organization thus combine with the papers of Volumes 24 and 30 to form a quantitative description of the scale and structure of the United States and Canadian economies in the nineteenth century.[2] Although the story is still incomplete (for example, these volumes contain very little on finance), it is nonetheless remarkably full. Most of these papers provide series that link with twentieth-century series, permitting analysis of economic change over very long periods. One may hope that future meetings of the Conference will continue to fill out systematically the quantitative record of these two national economies.

Not all of the Volume 51 papers are organized on a national accounts basis, however. The two streams of cliometrics, separated in the publication of the proceedings of the Williamstown and Chapel Hill meetings, are rejoined here. Many of the Williamsburg papers have both the micro focus and the highly analytical character of papers (such as the Conrad and Meyer piece on slavery) presented at the Williamstown and Chapel Hill meetings but omitted from Volumes 24 and 30. In addition, many depend on samples drawn from large rich sources of primary micro data, a change that reflects the computational revolution that has taken place since the meeting that led to Volume 30. The first important step in this direction had, in fact, been taken in the period between the Williamstown and Chapel Hill meetings. The University of North Carolina Library, at the behest of William Parker, assembled microfilms of the manuscript census of population, agriculture, and industry for the American South in the mid–nineteenth century. Parker's goal was to draw a matched sample (matching entries from the agricultural, slave population, and free population schedules) to enable him to study the Southern cotton economy. At that time the University of North Carolina's computer facilities consisted of a Univac 1105, a vacuum tube instrument with computational power modestly inferior to a 1984 IBM personal computer. Under the circumstances, Parker's plan must be regarded as bold—indeed, audacious—as well as innovative. The projects from which at least seven of the papers in Volume 51 are drawn (those by Newell, Kearl and Pope, Fogel, Sokoloff, Wahl, Weiss, and Gallman) make some use of the manuscript census, and large samples figure in most of them. The manuscript census had been known and used before Parker came on the scene, of course, but large samples could not be handled effectively without modern computing facilities.

Other samples of micro data also contribute to the Volume 51 papers. The enormous genealogical collection at Salt Lake City plays a central role in the Kearl and Pope, Fogel, and Wahl papers. Newell and Kearl and Pope use tax and probate records (in the latter case following in the footsteps of Alice Hanson Jones in *American Colonial Wealth,* 2d ed., 3 vols. [New York: Arno Press, 1977]); Sokoloff, the McLane Report on manufacturing in 1832; Fogel, military, school, and shipping records; Goldin, city directories; David and Sanderson, the Mosher sample dealing with the sexual behavior of middle-class women; Higman, plantation records, slave registrations, and records of slave compensation claims.

These new forms of evidence have opened new topics, untreated in Volumes 24 and 30 and having to do chiefly with population and human development. The Fogel paper is concerned with the timing, pace, and determinants of the modern decline of mortality. As David and Sanderson point out, most research on the United States fertility transition has been concerned with demand-side phenomena. Their paper treats the supply side: the modes of behavior and the devices that led to lower levels of fertility. Wahl and Newell are both interested in the influence of one generation on the next: Newell in the intergenerational transmission of wealth, Wahl in the intergenerational transmission of fertility patterns. Kearl and Pope, who have elsewhere explored intergenerational mobility, here focus their attention on intragenerational mobility. Sokoloff uses micro data from the manuscript census and the McLane Report to describe and explain patterns of widespread productivity change in manufacturing in the early decades of United States modernization, change more dramatic than previous scholarship had suspected.

Finally, Volume 51 addresses a number of important conceptual topics. Claudia Goldin considers the impact on United States economic growth of the shift of female work activities from the home to the market. In doing so, she enters a domain that William Parker, in his introduction to Volume 24, argued was a difficult one in which to conduct quantitative work. Goldin pushes forward with imagination and skill. While Robert Fogel is chiefly concerned with mortality, his work has led him to proffer an alternative, sensitive index of human welfare, one that, he tells us, is able to capture changes in well-being missed by standard indices such as per capita income or the real wage rate. Moreover, this index is also available for periods of time for which systematic wage and income data are unavailable. John Wallis and Douglass North take up a topic that has long engaged the attention of students of growth (see, e.g., Simon Kuznets, *Economic Change* [New York: Norton, 1953], Ch. 6; William D. Nordhaus and James Tobin, "Is Growth Obsolete?", *Studies in Income and Wealth,* Vol. 38): the extent to which the rise of transaction costs has offset the benefits of economic growth. Their contribution to the subject—the first part of a larger project—is to define transaction costs, to measure the principal United States costs of this type, and to show how far the deduction of such costs affects the United States national product and the long-term rate of growth.

Volume 51, then, is a descendant of Volumes 24 and 30, but with characteristics peculiar to itself. These three volumes, together with the historical papers from Volumes 33, 34, and 46, constitute a very substantial quantitative historical record. Gaps, however, remain. There is little on the financial sector. While four of the papers treat Canada and the British West Indies, neither the Dominion nor the Caribbean receives all the attention it deserves, and there are no papers on any other part of the world. In the United States colonial America is virtually unrepresented, although a substantial volume of quantitative work has been completed and more is under way. Opportunities for further useful historical volumes are emerging. One may hope that the time span between the Williamsburg meetings and the next set of meetings with a historical orientation will be shorter than the interval between Chapel Hill and Williamsburg.

## Notes

1. One of them, Moses Abramovitz's "The Welfare Interpretation of Secular Trends in National Income and Product," was clearly concerned with a subject of interest to the Conference, but Abramovitz chose to place it in Bernard Haley's festschrift: *The Allocation of Economic Resources: Essays in Honor of Bernard Francis Haley.*

2. The Gallman and Weiss paper prepared for Volume 34 should also be added to the list. Read with the Volume 24 paper by Gallman, it describes the sectoral distribution of economic activity in the nineteenth century.

# I    The National Product

# 2 New Estimates of Gross National Product, Canada, 1870–1926: Some Implications for Canadian Development

M. C. Urquhart

This paper has its genesis in a project devoted to the preparation of national income estimates for Canada for the years 1870–1926: the delimitation of the period is explained by the twin facts that the first Canadian census after confederation was taken in 1871 and that the official estimates of the national income of Canada begin in 1926. The estimates are now complete—just barely. In this paper, I examine some of the consequences of the availability of the new data for the interpretation of Canadian economic development in the period covered by the estimates. In my discussion I barely scratch the surface, largely because the preparation of the estimates themselves absorbed nearly all of my time until very recently.

Before getting on with the main task I should say just a word about the new estimates. I shall be brief at this juncture, even though it is perhaps fair to say that they are the main contribution of this paper.

The estimates comprise: annual estimates of gross domestic product, at factor cost by industrial sector, and of gross national product at market prices, all in current prices; annual estimates of gross national product at market prices in constant dollars; annual estimates of government expenditure on goods and services, by level of government; annual estimates of the main components of the balance of international payments, a large part of which has been newly estimated; annual estimates of capital formation in residential construction throughout the period and of producers' durables from 1870 to 1895, which, together with new capital formation estimates for nonresidential investment prepared by Statistics Canada, provide a new series for gross

M. C. Urquhart is the Sir John A. Macdonald Professor of Political and Economic Science in the Economics Department of Queen's University, Ontario, Canada.

domestic capital formation for the entire period. They are the product of a collaborative work by seven of us in academia, assisted by at least a score of research assistants, over a decade, mostly on a spare-time basis. I had hoped myself to be pretty much chairman of the board, but it did not work out that way, with the result that I must take responsibility for large parts of the new estimates as well as for the delays in their production. The division of responsibility for the various parts of the estimates is given in appendix 1.

As for the quality of the new estimates, I have considerable confidence in them, comparatively speaking, which is not to say that they do not have limitations. But then, which country's estimates do not? The estimates have been prepared from a mass of data. The basic source information, frequently hitherto untapped, proved to be substantially better than we had expected it to be. And we have put a good deal of effort into developing processes that make the greatest feasible use of that information. Having said this much, I hasten to add, as I am sure everyone knows, that the basic information was considerably less in quantity and quality than that on which the official estimates for Canada, beginning in 1926, are based. Ultimate judgment of the quality of the estimates must come, of course, from others than those of us who were engaged in the project. A general statement of the sources of the data is given in appendix 2; a detailed statement would be of such volume as to be unmanageable on this occasion.

I do not intend to proceed with a detailed discussion of the basis of the estimates but rather to see what inferences, if any, can be easily made from them about the nature of Canadian economic development. However, given that the estimates are the most important part of the paper, I present them immediately. They are given on an annual basis because the annual data contain much information, useful to my later musings, that would be submerged in annual averages.

Table 2.1 presents gross domestic product (GDP) at factor cost, by industry, and gross national product (GNP) at market prices. For all industries but two the data are given on an annual basis; the industry groups, "wholesale and retail trade" and "community, business and personal services," have been given only for census dates and for 1926, the first year of the official accounts, these being the years for which primary data are available and there being no satisfactory specific annual interpolaters. The aggregate GDP at factor cost was interpolated between census years and to 1926 on the basis of the sum of those series for which annual estimates are available—the latter make up by far the larger part of GDP.

Table 2.2 presents data on gross capital formation broken down by a number of categories. As has been stated already, our project's contribution to this material is limited to the estimates for residential con-

**Table 2.1  Gross National Product, Canada (Thousands of Dollars)**

| | 1870 | 1871 | 1872 | 1873 | 1874 | 1875 | 1876 | 1877 | 1878 | 1879 | 1880 | 1881 |
|---|---|---|---|---|---|---|---|---|---|---|---|---|
| Agriculture | 143797 | 145281 | 147381 | 144490 | 154516 | 146516 | 139172 | 144466 | 134193 | 158421 | 159339 | 197021 |
| Forestry (excluding agriculture) | 5790 | 6960 | 7669 | 9175 | 9257 | 8184 | 7101 | 7244 | 6565 | 5911 | 5908 | 7923 |
| Hunting, trapping | 211 | 306 | 516 | 867 | 998 | 1047 | 1047 | 894 | 850 | 752 | 1019 | 1101 |
| Fisheries | 2921 | 3362 | 4249 | 4775 | 5186 | 4596 | 4936 | 5330 | 5868 | 6007 | 6540 | 6978 |
| Mining | 4431 | 5354 | 5507 | 5436 | 4762 | 6109 | 5906 | 5237 | 4736 | 5385 | 5289 | 5404 |
| Manufacturing | 76983 | 89406 | 98954 | 123997 | 107930 | 97479 | 84232 | 93173 | 83725 | 86996 | 103615 | 122923 |
| Manufactured gas | 399 | 505 | 641 | 744 | 778 | 813 | 848 | 562 | 534 | 825 | 719 | 847 |
| Construction | 20000 | 21000 | 26300 | 28700 | 32000 | 29000 | 22700 | 19500 | 17300 | 17400 | 20400 | 22400 |
| Transportation | 20000 | 22609 | 22014 | 23372 | 23777 | 19690 | 19849 | 19323 | 21454 | 21249 | 25001 | 27929 |
| Electric light & power | | | | | | | | | | | | |
| Communications | | | | | | | | | | | | |
| Banking & finance | 7000 | 8000 | 10000 | 10000 | 10000 | 8000 | 9000 | 9000 | 8000 | 9000 | 10000 | 12000 |
| Residential rents | 20756 | 21959 | 26609 | 28209 | 28769 | 27725 | 27123 | 26779 | 26515 | 26290 | 27275 | 28654 |
| Federal government | 4595 | 5268 | 6086 | 7989 | 7914 | 8689 | 8782 | 8474 | 8385 | 7723 | 7980 | 8404 |
| Provincial government | 1589 | 1756 | 2230 | 2548 | 3076 | 3058 | 2933 | 2890 | 2604 | 2607 | 2541 | 2704 |
| Municipal services | 3441 | 3587 | 3908 | 4202 | 4476 | 4748 | 4986 | 5340 | 5395 | 5482 | 5586 | 5711 |
| Education, public | 3480 | 3438 | 3978 | 4428 | 4800 | 5120 | 5355 | 5935 | 5900 | 6105 | 6198 | 6221 |
| Universities | 200 | 203 | 223 | 243 | 263 | 283 | 303 | 323 | 343 | 363 | 383 | 420 |
| Wholesale & retail trade | 21176 | | | | | | | | | | | |
| Community, business, and personal service | 26454 | | | | | | | | | | | |
| GDP (old official basis) | 363223 | 391060 | 423498 | 462612 | 462896 | 432007 | 401742 | 414588 | 389621 | 423581 | 456664 | 539010 |
| Public revenues from resource royalties | 1027 | 1120 | 1718 | 1451 | 1230 | 864 | 1040 | 999 | 807 | 862 | 1340 | 1871 |
| GDP (new basis) | 364250 | 392180 | 425216 | 464063 | 464126 | 432871 | 402782 | 415587 | 390428 | 424443 | 458004 | 540881 |
| Less: net interest & dividends paid abroad | 5412 | 4034 | 4991 | 5409 | 7039 | 8192 | 9079 | 9804 | 10047 | 11993 | 14286 | 14727 |
| GNP at factor cost | 358838 | 388146 | 420225 | 458654 | 457087 | 424629 | 393703 | 405783 | 380381 | 412450 | 443718 | 526154 |
| Indirect taxes less subsidies | 23715 | 24550 | 27029 | 29114 | 28456 | 27773 | 27967 | 28913 | 29268 | 32677 | 38236 | 42535 |
| GNP at market prices | 382553 | 412696 | 447254 | 487768 | 485543 | 452452 | 421670 | 434696 | 409649 | 445127 | 481954 | 568689 |

(continued)

Table 2.1 (continued)

| | 1882 | 1883 | 1884 | 1885 | 1886 | 1887 | 1888 | 1889 | 1890 | 1891 | 1892 | 1893 |
|---|---|---|---|---|---|---|---|---|---|---|---|---|
| Agriculture | 204892 | 185086 | 173396 | 165035 | 158063 | 175819 | 170638 | 177122 | 184656 | 189108 | 189499 | 181588 |
| Forestry (excluding agriculture) | 8940 | 9297 | 8685 | 8136 | 9343 | 9458 | 10170 | 10697 | 10933 | 11105 | 11422 | 11575 |
| Hunting, trapping | 798 | 745 | 924 | 1101 | 1130 | 1246 | 1280 | 1134 | 992 | 985 | 1013 | 1084 |
| Fisheries | 7459 | 7640 | 8044 | 8090 | 8385 | 8347 | 8143 | 8031 | 8279 | 8682 | 8668 | 9623 |
| Mining | 5740 | 5498 | 6065 | 6250 | 7500 | 8083 | 9155 | 10348 | 12350 | 14729 | 12285 | 14505 |
| Manufacturing | 142493 | 148958 | 132910 | 127817 | 133241 | 141622 | 148915 | 156984 | 171691 | 172454 | 165317 | 158575 |
| Manufactured gas | 769 | 906 | 950 | 1166 | 1281 | 1467 | 1361 | 1506 | 1705 | 1642 | 1715 | 1715 |
| Construction | 30000 | 34000 | 38000 | 25700 | 25500 | 30200 | 31600 | 34200 | 30100 | 31200 | 28600 | 26200 |
| Transportation | 29051 | 31301 | 31015 | 28672 | 32168 | 33604 | 36177 | 36320 | 40460 | 39840 | 42429 | 42234 |
| Electric light & power | | | | | | 526 | 548 | 636 | 936 | 1012 | 1089 | 1166 |
| Communications | | | | | | | | | 745 | 855 | 921 | 1162 |
| Banking & finance | 13000 | 14000 | 14000 | 14000 | 15000 | 17000 | 18000 | 19000 | 18000 | 20000 | 22000 | 21000 |
| Residential rents | 31080 | 30687 | 30112 | 29689 | 28986 | 33892 | 35496 | 36580 | 37493 | 38724 | 41267 | 42442 |
| Federal government | 9240 | 10259 | 11091 | 12436 | 11249 | 11297 | 11250 | 11117 | 11416 | 11565 | 11818 | 12275 |
| Provincial government | 2882 | 3014 | 2984 | 3013 | 3186 | 3423 | 3451 | 3957 | 3904 | 4388 | 4119 | 4091 |
| Municipal services | 5904 | 6067 | 6205 | 6554 | 6788 | 6954 | 7766 | 8447 | 8635 | 9505 | 9202 | 9437 |
| Education, public | 6339 | 6580 | 6733 | 7045 | 7268 | 7152 | 7501 | 7663 | 7987 | 8285 | 8552 | 8479 |
| Universities | 456 | 493 | 530 | 566 | 603 | 640 | 676 | 713 | 749 | 786 | 804 | 821 |
| Wholesale & retail trade | | | | | | | | | 53052 | | | |
| Community, business, and personal service | | | | | | | | | 60143 | | | |
| GDP (old official basis) | 590448 | 586489 | 560657 | 530544 | 537061 | 587438 | 602482 | 630731 | 664226 | 681001 | 676116 | 660909 |
| Public revenues from resource royalties | 1982 | 1663 | 1379 | 1483 | 1675 | 2021 | 2739 | 2388 | 2080 | 2564 | 3649 | 3193 |
| GDP (new basis) | 592430 | 588152 | 562036 | 532027 | 538766 | 589459 | 605221 | 633119 | 666306 | 683565 | 679765 | 664102 |
| Less: net interest & dividends paid abroad | 15745 | 16846 | 17291 | 17961 | 22199 | 24817 | 24687 | 26920 | 29904 | 30313 | 31156 | 31951 |
| GNP at factor cost | 576685 | 571306 | 544745 | 514066 | 516537 | 564642 | 580534 | 606199 | 636402 | 653252 | 648609 | 632151 |
| Indirect taxes less subsidies | 42200 | 40221 | 40432 | 40463 | 44196 | 46434 | 49770 | 49561 | 49017 | 50253 | 51676 | 50257 |
| GNP at market prices | 618885 | 611527 | 585177 | 554529 | 560733 | 611076 | 630304 | 655760 | 685419 | 703505 | 700285 | 682408 |

| | 1894 | 1895 | 1896 | 1897 | 1898 | 1899 | 1900 | 1901 | 1902 | 1903 | 1904 | 1905 |
|---|---|---|---|---|---|---|---|---|---|---|---|---|
| Agriculture | 172555 | 167159 | 157150 | 186915 | 188867 | 200280 | 207828 | 243414 | 280116 | 267048 | 278782 | 303838 |
| Forestry (excluding agriculture) | 10732 | 10973 | 12162 | 12697 | 12318 | 13020 | 13137 | 14439 | 14749 | 15109 | 15594 | 17263 |
| Hunting, trapping | 1113 | 1119 | 1132 | 1046 | 1008 | 1084 | 1127 | 1143 | 1399 | 1508 | 1504 | 1611 |
| Fisheries | 9790 | 9517 | 9809 | 10656 | 9625 | 10504 | 10649 | 12155 | 10640 | 11291 | 11454 | 14089 |
| Mining | 14296 | 15010 | 16500 | 21126 | 28607 | 36481 | 47713 | 47922 | 44548 | 42291 | 40682 | 44686 |
| Manufacturing | 145114 | 137998 | 138751 | 156082 | 169539 | 179188 | 200146 | 203941 | 243475 | 259771 | 254645 | 308439 |
| Manufactured gas | 1728 | 1532 | 1366 | 1285 | 1255 | 1195 | 1309 | 1219 | 1238 | 1469 | 1755 | 1899 |
| Construction | 21300 | 21100 | 20000 | 23300 | 30000 | 30400 | 32500 | 40900 | 46800 | 59100 | 67500 | 78500 |
| Transportation | 42044 | 38658 | 43488 | 45107 | 52077 | 55589 | 62083 | 63794 | 73574 | 84534 | 86345 | 92760 |
| Electric light & power | 1241 | 1320 | 1395 | 1471 | 1546 | 1625 | 1700 | 2124 | 2652 | 3234 | 4985 | 6023 |
| Communications | 1162 | 1162 | 1162 | 1162 | 1512 | 1600 | 1818 | 2192 | 2548 | 2981 | 3429 | 4164 |
| Banking & finance | 22000 | 22000 | 24000 | 25000 | 28000 | 32000 | 39000 | 41000 | 48000 | 57000 | 45000 | 56000 |
| Residential rents | 44012 | 44544 | 46537 | 46138 | 49252 | 53288 | 60453 | 65529 | 68857 | 72380 | 77769 | 87312 |
| Federal government | 12085 | 11397 | 11987 | 12631 | 14166 | 14107 | 15672 | 17259 | 17575 | 19456 | 23380 | 23934 |
| Provincial government | 4334 | 4142 | 4523 | 4573 | 4687 | 4726 | 5240 | 5462 | 5872 | 6012 | 6146 | 6565 |
| Municipal services | 9572 | 9443 | 9763 | 10295 | 10540 | 10725 | 11330 | 12419 | 13508 | 14825 | 16504 | 17458 |
| Education, public | 9234 | 9280 | 9694 | 9737 | 9741 | 9939 | 10158 | 10687 | 11043 | 11662 | 12715 | 13435 |
| Universities | 839 | 857 | 874 | 892 | 910 | 928 | 945 | 963 | 1126 | 1289 | 1452 | 1615 |
| Wholesale & retail trade | | | | | | | 65553 | | | | | |
| Community, business, and personal service | | | | | | | 84469 | | | | | |
| GDP (old official basis) | 631077 | 611950 | 615771 | 688069 | 740798 | 792874 | 872830 | 950875 | 1074408 | 1127842 | 1151915 | 1310935 |
| Public revenues from resource royalties | 2353 | 2481 | 2341 | 3833 | 3849 | 4150 | 4740 | 4634 | 4878 | 5886 | 6300 | 5702 |
| GDP (new basis) | 633430 | 614431 | 618112 | 691902 | 744647 | 797024 | 877570 | 955509 | 1079286 | 1133728 | 1158215 | 1316637 |
| Less: net interest & dividends paid abroad | 31380 | 29998 | 30499 | 31195 | 34450 | 35673 | 37120 | 39540 | 41493 | 42485 | 45765 | 49639 |
| GNP at factor cost | 602050 | 584433 | 587613 | 660707 | 710197 | 761351 | 840450 | 915969 | 1037793 | 1091243 | 1112450 | 1266998 |
| Indirect taxes less subsidies | 49361 | 48985 | 53204 | 56315 | 59175 | 64631 | 66907 | 74694 | 81806 | 86907 | 93366 | 94545 |
| GNP at market prices | 651411 | 633418 | 640817 | 717022 | 769372 | 825982 | 907357 | 990663 | 1119599 | 1178150 | 1205816 | 1361543 |

(continued)

Table 2.1  (continued)

| | 1906 | 1907 | 1908 | 1909 | 1910 | 1911 | 1912 | 1913 | 1914 | 1915 | 1916 | 1917 |
|---|---|---|---|---|---|---|---|---|---|---|---|---|
| Agriculture | 318796 | 354676 | 335689 | 402554 | 402327 | 469654 | 477958 | 517812 | 490900 | 686638 | 771679 | 935133 |
| Forestry (excluding agriculture) | 19466 | 19795 | 18049 | 21187 | 22995 | 25066 | 25329 | 24341 | 24048 | 23453 | 26208 | 37850 |
| Hunting, trapping | 1947 | 1812 | 1652 | 2276 | 2774 | 2641 | 3249 | 3683 | 2318 | 2823 | 3666 | 5021 |
| Fisheries | 12961 | 12651 | 12356 | 14177 | 14359 | 16119 | 16059 | 16039 | 15409 | 17252 | 19269 | 25593 |
| Mining | 49306 | 53077 | 52388 | 52979 | 61975 | 57026 | 75072 | 81903 | 74860 | 81724 | 107252 | 117201 |
| Manufacturing | 363617 | 401828 | 349336 | 406284 | 452122 | 469566 | 516339 | 517791 | 447723 | 475178 | 664054 | 960072 |
| Manufactured gas | 1679 | 2146 | 2141 | 1921 | 2078 | 2203 | 3181 | 3535 | 3042 | 1953 | 3067 | 3653 |
| Construction | 91000 | 113100 | 113800 | 124100 | 158500 | 178200 | 215600 | 219600 | 172800 | 126500 | 116300 | 122000 |
| Transportation | 108661 | 132799 | 131485 | 132869 | 153591 | 174855 | 207943 | 246670 | 222008 | 190025 | 229617 | 260507 |
| Electric light & power | 6790 | 7660 | 8553 | 9512 | 9503 | 13786 | 16103 | 17995 | 20611 | 22080 | 23861 | 27551 |
| Communications | 4860 | 8223 | 8807 | 9306 | 10401 | 11387 | 13467 | 15795 | 17507 | 17549 | 20127 | 22503 |
| Banking & finance | 71000 | 77000 | 76000 | 75000 | 73000 | 92000 | 104000 | 125000 | 114000 | 93000 | 104000 | 131000 |
| Residential rents | 96564 | 105533 | 115264 | 120417 | 132764 | 142948 | 162753 | 181142 | 182980 | 181795 | 186371 | 203125 |
| Federal government | 18265 | 27448 | 30782 | 27759 | 32556 | 37194 | 42137 | 50515 | 79830 | 151371 | 239223 | 264918 |
| Provincial government | 8288 | 10165 | 11628 | 13450 | 15465 | 17792 | 20904 | 22849 | 21050 | 20588 | 19589 | 23135 |
| Municipal services | 19439 | 21078 | 23030 | 24722 | 27888 | 29838 | 34715 | 36692 | 40525 | 46275 | 48725 | 50274 |
| Education, public | 14333 | 15387 | 17399 | 18976 | 20776 | 22229 | 25235 | 27274 | 30464 | 34428 | 34491 | 36595 |
| Universities | 1779 | 1942 | 2105 | 2268 | 2431 | 2594 | 3088 | 3582 | 4075 | 4569 | 5062 | 5556 |
| Wholesale & retail trade | | | | | 204444 | | | | | | | |
| Community, business, and personal service | | | | | 148359 | | | | | | | |
| GDP (old official basis) | 1469022 | 1662569 | 1596733 | 1780389 | 1948308 | 2149376 | 2383463 | 2557526 | 2366984 | 2601585 | 3110974 | 3826914 |
| Public revenues from resource royalties | 5677 | 7082 | 7267 | 6816 | 8653 | 9218 | 9202 | 9877 | 9874 | 7776 | 7415 | 8048 |
| GDP (new basis) | 1474699 | 1669651 | 1604000 | 1787205 | 1956961 | 2158594 | 2392665 | 2567403 | 2376558 | 2609361 | 3118389 | 3834962 |
| Less: net interest & dividends paid abroad | 56030 | 60586 | 68628 | 77439 | 86239 | 105303 | 118759 | 141168 | 153271 | 173251 | 172294 | 173505 |
| GNP at factor cost | 1418669 | 1609065 | 1535372 | 1709766 | 1870722 | 2053291 | 2273906 | 2426235 | 2223587 | 2436110 | 2946095 | 3661457 |
| Indirect taxes less subsidies | 107216 | 119341 | 118421 | 128577 | 152088 | 179874 | 219970 | 225237 | 224992 | 252469 | 296627 | 330415 |
| GNP at market prices | 1525885 | 1728406 | 1653793 | 1838343 | 2022810 | 2233165 | 2493876 | 2651472 | 2448579 | 2688579 | 3242722 | 3991872 |

| | 1918 | 1919 | 1920 | 1921 | 1922 | 1923 | 1924 | 1925 | 1926 |
|---|---|---|---|---|---|---|---|---|---|
| Agriculture | 906176 | 943779 | 1042279 | 677845 | 720736 | 778527 | 783897 | 991144 | 927356 |
| Forestry (excluding agriculture) | 42285 | 49270 | 63740 | 37689 | 48229 | 46876 | 58588 | 66000 | 66000 |
| Hunting, trapping | 8188 | 12716 | 11536 | 9876 | 12376 | 11507 | 11159 | 10855 | 11807 |
| Fisheries | 29239 | 28042 | 25134 | 19118 | 21489 | 21480 | 22198 | 23919 | 27547 |
| Mining | 139388 | 113996 | 147166 | 115178 | 127971 | 136465 | 137769 | 132514 | 154000 |
| Manufacturing | 1084026 | 1042248 | 1271069 | 873027 | 865311 | 954824 | 899777 | 953898 | 1067402 |
| Manufactured gas | 3129 | 4660 | 6202 | 7558 | 8640 | 8811 | 6793 | 8759 | 9174 |
| Construction | 109700 | 148500 | 184600 | 175400 | 182400 | 215900 | 193900 | 198200 | 203200 |
| Transportation | 256400 | 334555 | 381516 | 347987 | 355327 | 363993 | 345071 | 368982 | 405179 |
| Electric light & power | 30858 | 32963 | 37353 | 39495 | 43718 | 46733 | 51635 | 59354 | 69877 |
| Communications | 25344 | 32031 | 31035 | 34156 | 34380 | 35418 | 37216 | 39815 | 46688 |
| Banking & finance | 132000 | 163000 | 221000 | 193000 | 169000 | 157000 | 168000 | 183000 | 209000 |
| Residential rents | 218207 | 242426 | 283216 | 314351 | 331245 | 344563 | 352049 | 357484 | 359551 |
| Federal government | 324396 | 172761 | 103221 | 98038 | 89769 | 87800 | 87632 | 91128 | 91954 |
| Provincial government | 25409 | 31316 | 39681 | 43758 | 49251 | 50666 | 49026 | 51564 | 50964 |
| Municipal services | 54540 | 58518 | 66621 | 76081 | 75599 | 75631 | 75941 | 75134 | 78671 |
| Education, public | 41168 | 47073 | 57043 | 68458 | 74549 | 77606 | 77443 | 79032 | 81111 |
| Universities | 6050 | 6543 | 7037 | 7335 | 7632 | 7930 | 8228 | 8526 | 8825 |
| Wholesale & retail trade | | | 439432 | | | | | | 534000 |
| Community, business, and personal service | | | 303245 | | | | | | 506000 |
| GDP (old official basis) | 4053209 | 4106737 | 4722126 | 3767062 | 3906309 | 4200995 | 4179100 | 4643179 | 4908306 |
| Public revenues from resource royalties | 8969 | 11612 | 14081 | 14978 | 13790 | 13175 | 15829 | 16974 | 18009 |
| GDP (new basis) | 4062178 | 4118349 | 4736207 | 3782040 | 3920099 | 4214170 | 4194929 | 4660153 | 4926315 |
| Less: net interest & dividends paid abroad | 176060 | 178467 | 186029 | 210928 | 225335 | 231279 | 241200 | 243394 | 208000 |
| GNP at factor cost | 3886118 | 3939882 | 4550178 | 3571112 | 3694764 | 3982891 | 3953729 | 4416759 | 4718315 |
| Indirect taxes less subsidies | 375364 | 427499 | 510708 | 502713 | 539181 | 572375 | 547796 | 578989 | 627000 |
| GNP at market prices | 4261482 | 4367381 | 5060886 | 4073825 | 4233945 | 4555266 | 4501525 | 4995748 | 5345315 |

**Table 2.2**    **Gross Fixed Capital Formation, Current Dollars (Millions of Dollars)**

| Year | Total Manufacturing | Railway & Telegraph | Other Business | Housing Construction | Total Private Business | Public Schools | Government Total | Grand Total |
|---|---|---|---|---|---|---|---|---|
| 1870 | | | | 23.2 | | | | 60.0 |
| 1871 | 5.4 | 12.4 | 11.7 | 31.2 | 60.7 | 0.7 | 1.5 | 62.9 |
| 1872 | 6.1 | 27.0 | 13.2 | 27.5 | 73.8 | 1.3 | 2.8 | 77.9 |
| 1873 | 6.6 | 29.3 | 14.2 | 29.6 | 79.7 | 1.7 | 2.9 | 84.3 |
| 1874 | 6.6 | 25.3 | 15.2 | 35.3 | 82.4 | 2.1 | 8.0 | 92.5 |
| 1875 | 6.6 | 24.1 | 14.6 | 30.5 | 75.8 | 2.1 | 7.3 | 85.2 |
| 1876 | 6.1 | 15.3 | 14.2 | 23.8 | 59.4 | 1.7 | 9.0 | 70.1 |
| 1877 | 5.9 | 8.7 | 14.3 | 19.6 | 48.5 | 1.4 | 11.6 | 61.5 |
| 1878 | 5.6 | 6.4 | 14.2 | 17.4 | 43.6 | 1.3 | 10.4 | 55.3 |
| 1879 | 5.9 | 8.7 | 14.1 | 17.4 | 46.1 | 0.9 | 9.0 | 56.0 |
| 1880 | 8.9 | 14.1 | 14.7 | 20.6 | 58.3 | 0.9 | 6.9 | 66.1 |
| 1881 | 14.6 | 18.3 | 18.2 | 18.2 | 69.3 | 0.8 | 7.1 | 77.2 |
| 1882 | 19.7 | 44.0 | 22.1 | 14.3 | 100.1 | 1.0 | 5.7 | 106.8 |
| 1883 | 18.9 | 57.5 | 24.3 | 12.0 | 112.7 | 0.9 | 7.4 | 121.0 |
| 1884 | 14.1 | 72.5 | 20.0 | 14.4 | 121.0 | 0.9 | 8.0 | 129.9 |
| 1885 | 12.3 | 33.8 | 16.9 | 16.6 | 79.6 | 0.9 | 6.4 | 86.9 |
| 1886 | 12.5 | 23.7 | 18.1 | 22.7 | 77.0 | 1.0 | 7.5 | 85.5 |
| 1887 | 13.5 | 23.4 | 20.9 | 31.7 | 89.5 | 1.3 | 8.6 | 99.4 |
| 1888 | 14.1 | 20.7 | 25.8 | 38.2 | 98.8 | 1.5 | 5.6 | 105.9 |
| 1889 | 14.3 | 22.1 | 24.0 | 41.8 | 102.2 | 2.1 | 7.5 | 111.8 |
| 1890 | 13.8 | 15.3 | 21.8 | 39.7 | 90.6 | 1.8 | 6.2 | 98.6 |
| 1891 | 12.0 | 14.2 | 28.4 | 42.2 | 96.8 | 1.7 | 6.8 | 105.3 |
| 1892 | 11.8 | 12.0 | 26.8 | 39.2 | 89.8 | 1.5 | 6.1 | 97.4 |
| 1893 | 11.2 | 12.9 | 29.0 | 30.4 | 83.5 | 1.4 | 7.5 | 92.4 |
| 1894 | 10.5 | 8.8 | 21.8 | 22.2 | 63.3 | 1.4 | 10.2 | 74.9 |
| 1895 | 10.5 | 6.6 | 27.0 | 19.4 | 63.5 | 1.3 | 13.2 | 78.0 |
| 1896 | 12.6 | 7.4 | 25.3 | 20.2 | 65.5 | 1.1 | 7.2 | 73.8 |
| 1897 | 14.4 | 10.7 | 33.0 | 23.5 | 81.6 | 1.0 | 7.5 | 90.1 |
| 1898 | 19.1 | 18.6 | 42.4 | 26.9 | 107.0 | 1.4 | 10.1 | 118.5 |
| 1899 | 24.9 | 15.8 | 42.7 | 28.0 | 113.3 | 1.2 | 11.9 | 126.4 |
| 1900 | 30.2 | 18.7 | 51.4 | 25.6 | 125.9 | 1.3 | 13.0 | 140.2 |
| 1901 | 37.2 | 21.7 | 76.8 | 28.3 | 164.0 | 1.6 | 14.6 | 180.2 |
| 1902 | 42.8 | 24.3 | 90.1 | 32.8 | 191.0 | 1.6 | 16.0 | 208.6 |
| 1903 | 54.9 | 33.2 | 104.1 | 42.9 | 235.1 | 1.7 | 18.4 | 255.2 |
| 1904 | 55.5 | 37.6 | 105.6 | 54.5 | 253.2 | 2.3 | 21.6 | 277.1 |
| 1905 | 57.3 | 48.3 | 107.8 | 71.0 | 284.4 | 3.6 | 24.0 | 312.0 |
| 1906 | 61.4 | 63.4 | 128.3 | 83.9 | 337.0 | 4.1 | 18.6 | 359.7 |
| 1907 | 72.1 | 103.9 | 146.3 | 83.2 | 408.5 | 6.2 | 33.0 | 447.7 |
| 1908 | 70.0 | 103.0 | 137.7 | 78.2 | 388.9 | 7.1 | 42.0 | 438.0 |
| 1909 | 74.2 | 92.9 | 165.4 | 101.2 | 433.7 | 7.5 | 35.8 | 477.0 |
| 1910 | 97.9 | 109.5 | 204.1 | 131.0 | 542.5 | 9.1 | 45.3 | 596.9 |
| 1911 | 123.2 | 125.2 | 230.7 | 148.2 | 627.3 | 11.0 | 55.0 | 694.2 |
| 1912 | 155.8 | 157.0 | 282.1 | 171.0 | 765.9 | 14.8 | 69.4 | 850.1 |
| 1913 | 157.6 | 175.4 | 268.6 | 155.7 | 757.3 | 16.7 | 96.5 | 870.5 |
| 1914 | 108.7 | 126.6 | 197.0 | 108.6 | 540.9 | 18.9 | 100.5 | 660.3 |
| 1915 | 85.9 | 97.7 | 130.4 | 61.4 | 375.4 | 16.8 | 78.5 | 470.7 |

**Table 2.2**    (continued)

| Year | Total Manufac-turing | Railway & Telegraph | Other Business | Housing Construc-tion | Total Private Business | Public Schools | Govern-ment Total | Grand Total |
|------|------|------|------|------|------|------|------|------|
| 1916 | 135.0 | 49.0 | 190.6 | 60.2 | 434.8 | 11.6 | 54.5 | 500.9 |
| 1917 | 143.4 | 76.0 | 263.1 | 58.1 | 540.6 | 11.6 | 39.6 | 591.8 |
| 1918 | 100.4 | 86.5 | 247.8 | 59.1 | 493.8 | 10.7 | 44.9 | 549.4 |
| 1919 | 96.2 | 95.1 | 286.9 | 96.6 | 574.8 | 14.9 | 70.8 | 660.5 |
| 1920 | 152.1 | 115.5 | 335.9 | 127.3 | 730.8 | 20.7 | 87.7 | 839.2 |
| 1921 | 99.7 | 100.0 | 273.1 | 136.2 | 609.0 | 26.2 | 93.8 | 729.0 |
| 1922 | 92.1 | 50.5 | 227.7 | 180.9 | 551.2 | 27.6 | 90.7 | 669.5 |
| 1923 | 141.5 | 102.9 | 300.3 | 176.0 | 720.6 | 31.3 | 109.5 | 861.5 |
| 1924 | 136.7 | 83.1 | 252.6 | 164.0 | 636.4 | 22.1 | 102.9 | 761.4 |
| 1925 | 119.1 | 52.2 | 298.5 | 168.2 | 638.0 | 21.7 | 107.4 | 767.1 |
| 1926 | 129.8 | 84.3 | 304.0 | 184.2 | 702.3 | 19.7 | 84.4 | 806.4 |

struction and the estimates of investment in machinery and equipment before 1896 which are necessary to obtain estimates of total fixed capital formation, 1870–95. The other estimates are those of Statistics Canada. They have been prepared as a part of Statcan's program to obtain capital stock estimates for 1926 and later years by the perpetual inventory method (Statcan 1981).

Table 2.3 presents estimates of government expenditure on goods and services by federal, provincial, and municipal government and by public schools. The last is included because, in Canada, public education has been, in the main, organized under local school boards and, in our period, financed mainly by property taxes.

Table 2.4 presents data on the main components of the balance of international payments, both current and capital account. A great deal of work has been done on these data for this project. Some parts of earlier estimates have been used, but much is new. And everything has been rechecked and reexamined.

Now to return to the main task, my scheme, in broad terms, is to address conflicting interpretations of Canadian development from 1870 to the mid-1920s that have been a subject of controversy. One interpretation of Canadian development, the traditionalist view, is that, at least until the Second World War, the pace of Canadian economic growth was determined by the presence or absence of export staples. The best-known expositer of this view is perhaps H. A. Innis in his works on the fur trade and the codfisheries. And Arthur Lower has emphasized the exploitation of the forest. It was W. A. Mackintosh, however, who dealt most specifically and in greatest detail with the

**Table 2.3**        **Government Expenditure on Goods and Services (Millions of Dollars)**

| Year | Federal | Provincial | Municipal | Public Education | Total |
|------|---------|-----------|-----------|------------------|-------|
| 1870 | 7.0 | 1.8 | 4.7 | 5.0 | 18.5 |
| 1871 | 8.9 | 2.9 | 4.9 | 5.0 | 21.7 |
| 1872 | 9.6 | 3.6 | 5.8 | 6.2 | 25.2 |
| 1873 | 12.5 | 4.0 | 6.2 | 7.1 | 29.8 |
| 1874 | 14.9 | 4.9 | 8.5 | 7.9 | 36.2 |
| 1875 | 14.6 | 4.9 | 8.6 | 8.3 | 36.4 |
| 1876 | 15.6 | 4.7 | 9.6 | 8.3 | 38.2 |
| 1877 | 13.9 | 4.7 | 10.9 | 8.7 | 38.2 |
| 1878 | 13.8 | 4.3 | 10.6 | 8.6 | 37.3 |
| 1879 | 13.2 | 4.3 | 10.0 | 8.5 | 36.0 |
| 1880 | 13.3 | 4.1 | 9.5 | 8.6 | 35.5 |
| 1881 | 14.3 | 4.2 | 9.6 | 8.5 | 36.6 |
| 1882 | 15.6 | 4.6 | 9.3 | 8.9 | 38.4 |
| 1883 | 20.8 | 5.0 | 10.2 | 9.0 | 45.0 |
| 1884 | 19.4 | 5.1 | 10.6 | 9.2 | 44.3 |
| 1885 | 32.4 | 5.1 | 10.5 | 9.6 | 57.6 |
| 1886 | 18.8 | 5.5 | 11.1 | 10.0 | 45.4 |
| 1887 | 21.7 | 6.1 | 11.8 | 10.0 | 49.6 |
| 1888 | 20.1 | 5.9 | 11.6 | 10.6 | 48.2 |
| 1889 | 17.9 | 7.1 | 13.0 | 11.3 | 49.3 |
| 1890 | 18.5 | 7.2 | 12.9 | 11.5 | 50.1 |
| 1891 | 20.7 | 7.6 | 14.0 | 11.8 | 54.1 |
| 1892 | 19.6 | 7.0 | 13.4 | 11.9 | 51.9 |
| 1893 | 20.8 | 7.0 | 14.2 | 11.7 | 53.7 |
| 1894 | 20.5 | 7.2 | 15.3 | 12.6 | 55.6 |
| 1895 | 19.8 | 6.8 | 16.2 | 12.6 | 55.4 |
| 1896 | 21.5 | 7.4 | 14.6 | 13.1 | 56.6 |
| 1897 | 22.3 | 7.4 | 15.4 | 13.0 | 58.1 |
| 1898 | 24.7 | 7.4 | 16.8 | 13.4 | 62.3 |
| 1899 | 25.7 | 7.4 | 17.7 | 13.5 | 64.3 |
| 1900 | 27.5 | 8.2 | 18.9 | 13.9 | 68.5 |
| 1901 | 32.1 | 8.5 | 20.9 | 14.8 | 76.3 |
| 1902 | 31.5 | 9.1 | 22.7 | 15.3 | 78.6 |
| 1903 | 41.8 | 9.3 | 25.2 | 16.1 | 92.4 |
| 1904 | 43.8 | 9.5 | 28.6 | 18.0 | 99.9 |
| 1905 | 46.3 | 10.2 | 30.6 | 20.2 | 107.3 |
| 1906 | 46.8 | 12.9 | 31.1 | 21.8 | 112.6 |
| 1907 | 53.0 | 16.3 | 38.9 | 25.2 | 133.4 |
| 1908 | 61.3 | 19.5 | 45.0 | 28.6 | 154.4 |
| 1909 | 56.6 | 22.3 | 44.6 | 31.0 | 154.5 |
| 1910 | 61.6 | 25.8 | 52.4 | 34.8 | 174.6 |
| 1911 | 74.8 | 30.5 | 58.2 | 39.4 | 202.9 |
| 1912 | 78.5 | 35.9 | 69.9 | 46.0 | 230.3 |
| 1913 | 101.2 | 40.1 | 82.9 | 50.4 | 274.6 |
| 1914 | 173.7 | 36.8 | 89.2 | 56.6 | 356.3 |
| 1915 | 257.5 | 33.2 | 89.1 | 59.4 | 439.2 |

**Table 2.3**    (continued)

| Year | Federal | Provincial | Municipal | Public Education | Total |
|------|---------|-----------|-----------|-----------------|-------|
| 1916 | 361.4 | 31.6 | 82.2 | 54.3 | 529.5 |
| 1917 | 361.1 | 36.6 | 79.2 | 53.9 | 530.8 |
| 1918 | 457.9 | 40.1 | 88.8 | 61.6 | 648.4 |
| 1919 | 515.9 | 51.7 | 104.8 | 173.1 | 745.5 |
| 1920 | 325.1 | 70.3 | 108.0 | 91.2 | 594.6 |
| 1921 | 281.1 | 76.0 | 118.6 | 110.9 | 586.6 |
| 1922 | 247.8 | 85.4 | 119.9 | 119.8 | 572.9 |
| 1923 | 188.0 | 85.6 | 127.0 | 127.3 | 527.9 |
| 1924 | 168.8 | 81.7 | 125.0 | 117.9 | 493.4 |
| 1925 | 174.0 | 85.1 | 128.9 | 119.4 | 507.4 |
| 1926 | 169.5 | 82.8 | 119.4 | 120.0 | 491.7 |

period from Confederation (1867) to the 1930s, and many others elaborated on his work.

The traditionalist view was that the period from 1870 to 1900 was a period of laggard growth because Canada had lost external markets for wheat and forest products with the evolution of free trade in Britain and the end of reciprocity with the United States (in 1866) and with the substantial replacement of activities based on wood, wind, and water, such as wooden ship building and other construction, by those based on steam and iron (or steel). The loss of markets for forest products stemmed directly from the decline in use of lumber and timber; the loss of the grain market stemmed indirectly from the competition with grain from the Middle West of the United States made more than competitive by the presence of the new railways. Then, from the mid- or late 1890s onward, when some cost and price changes occurred into which we need not go, the development of new export staples and most especially of wheat as the country's great export staple, supplemented later by the development of base and precious metals and by pulp and paper, led to a period of unprecedented growth. In fact, so the argument goes, the emergence of Canada as a developed economy stems from the emergence of wheat and to a lesser degree pulp and paper and base and precious metals: the agricultural expansion provided a market for industrial products for the two big central provinces, Ontario and Quebec, and this led to the economic integration of the various polities that had joined together at Confederation and afterwards.[1]

Following the Second World War a twofold questioning of this view took place. On the one hand, it was argued that there was a considerable growth in manufacturing output and in productivity in manufacturing even from 1870 to 1900 and that the process of growth in manufacturing from 1900 onward was merely a continuation of what went before. On

**Table 2.4  Canada's Balance of International Payments (Thousands of Dollars)**

| | 1870 | 1871 | 1872 | 1873 | 1874 | 1875 | 1876 | 1877 | 1878 | 1879 | 1880 |
|---|---|---|---|---|---|---|---|---|---|---|---|
| **Credits** | | | | | | | | | | | |
| Exports (adjusted) | 66385 | 72981 | 81777 | 85609 | 80789 | 76781 | 76137 | 76080 | 74020 | 77470 | 90841 |
| Exports of gold coin & bullion | 700 | 1600 | 3000 | 1200 | 1900 | 3100 | 2100 | 1600 | 2100 | 600 | 1800 |
| Freight | 1328 | 1459 | 1636 | 1712 | 1616 | 1536 | 1523 | 1522 | 1480 | 1549 | 1817 |
| Tourist receipts | 2100 | 2400 | 2600 | 3300 | 3300 | 3300 | 3300 | 3300 | 3300 | 4100 | 4100 |
| Migrants' capital (net) | 804 | 1195 | 1466 | 2409 | 1303 | 688 | 419 | 711 | 790 | 2109 | 1723 |
| Noncommercial remittance | | | | | | | | 4328 | | | |
| Insurance | | | | | | | | | | | |
| Interest & dividends | 850 | 1151 | 710 | 856 | 838 | 1173 | 975 | 973 | 858 | 1010 | 1116 |
| Total current | 72167 | 80787 | 91189 | 95086 | 89746 | 86578 | 84453 | 88513 | 82548 | 86838 | 101397 |
| Capital (long term) | 3394 | 13290 | 8019 | 22742 | 38509 | 14709 | 16303 | 10900 | 11414 | 14262 | 12358 |
| Capital (short term) | | 7350 | | 289 | | 3303 | 36 | 1913 | | | |
| Net errors & omissions | 25470 | 13519 | 35699 | 22443 | 17454 | 18267 | 10341 | 12200 | 14401 | 3719 | 6546 |
| Total current & capital | 101031 | 114944 | 134907 | 140559 | 145709 | 122858 | 111133 | 113526 | 108363 | 104819 | 120300 |
| **Debits** | | | | | | | | | | | |
| Imports (adjusted) | 81220 | 100267 | 115557 | 123169 | 121044 | 104679 | 93064 | 93785 | 85484 | 81698 | 93565 |
| Imports of gold coin & bullion | | | | | | | | | | | |
| Freight | 5463 | 5957 | 7498 | 6985 | 7399 | 5579 | 4660 | 6141 | 5492 | 4772 | 4607 |
| Tourist payments | 2400 | 2500 | 2600 | 2500 | 2400 | 2200 | 2200 | 2200 | 2400 | 2500 | 2700 |
| Migrants' capital | | | | | | | | | | | |
| Noncommercial remittance | 553 | 658 | 785 | 835 | 755 | 696 | 666 | 624 | 583 | 541 | 550 |
| Insurance | 129 | 378 | 335 | 805 | 655 | 339 | 489 | 967 | 543 | 543 | 1067 |
| Interest & dividends | 6262 | 5185 | 5701 | 6265 | 7877 | 9364 | 10054 | 10777 | 10905 | 13003 | 15402 |
| Total current | 96026 | 114944 | 132476 | 140559 | 140129 | 122858 | 111133 | 113527 | 105831 | 103057 | 117891 |
| Capital (short term) | 5005 | | 2431 | | 5580 | | | | 2532 | 1762 | 2409 |
| Total current & capital | 101031 | 114944 | 134907 | 140559 | 145709 | 122858 | 111133 | 113527 | 108363 | 104819 | 120300 |

| | 1881 | 1882 | 1883 | 1884 | 1885 | 1886 | 1887 | 1888 | 1889 | 1890 | 1891 |
|---|---|---|---|---|---|---|---|---|---|---|---|
| **Credits** | | | | | | | | | | | |
| Exports (adjusted) | 98782 | 98807 | 92548 | 87402 | 85252 | 86376 | 89085 | 88164 | 89868 | 94477 | 103388 |
| Exports of gold coin & bullion | 1600 | 1500 | 1000 | 1200 | 400 | 2000 | 800 | | 4800 | | 1400 |
| Freight | 1976 | 1976 | 1851 | 1748 | 1705 | 1728 | 1782 | 1763 | 1797 | 1890 | 2068 |
| Tourist receipts | 4100 | 4100 | 4100 | 4700 | 4700 | 4700 | 4700 | 4700 | 4900 | 4900 | 4900 |
| Migrants' capital (net) | 612 | 3935 | 4425 | 2130 | 494 | 1046 | 2219 | 1704 | 1270 | 336 | 2907 |
| Noncommercial remittance | | | | | | | | | | | |
| Insurance | | | | | | | | | | | |
| Interest & dividends | 1050 | 1146 | 1175 | 1463 | 1211 | 1237 | 1358 | 1845 | 2440 | 2412 | 2023 |
| Total current | 108119 | 111464 | 105099 | 98643 | 93762 | 97086 | 99944 | 98177 | 105076 | 104014 | 116686 |
| Capital (long term) | 25775 | 10310 | 18704 | 23927 | 46870 | 35200 | 15632 | 66519 | 21334 | 22478 | 15048 |
| Capital (short term) | | | | 5052 | | | | | 569 | | |
| Net errors & omissions | 3210 | 29450 | 32409 | 10754 | | 10654 | 41087 | | 32407 | 39975 | 41938 |
| Total current & capital | 137104 | 151224 | 156212 | 138375 | 140632 | 142940 | 156663 | 164695 | 159386 | 166461 | 173671 |
| **Debits** | | | | | | | | | | | |
| Imports (adjusted) | 109819 | 122777 | 120823 | 108387 | 101871 | 105090 | 108786 | 109684 | 115652 | 117435 | 119736 |
| Imports of gold coin & bullion | | | | | | | | 1900 | | 800 | |
| Freight | 5699 | 5676 | 6198 | 5130 | 4549 | 5693 | 5412 | 5561 | 6145 | 5701 | 5865 |
| Tourist payments | 2900 | 3300 | 3200 | 3200 | 3200 | 3800 | 3800 | 3800 | 4100 | 4100 | 4100 |
| Migrants' capital | | | | | | | | | | | |
| Noncommercial remittance | 688 | 1179 | 1444 | 1946 | 1946 | 1869 | 1861 | 1987 | 2105 | 2028 | 1899 |
| Insurance | 303 | 817 | 763 | 958 | 1184 | 643 | 884 | 1451 | 2024 | 1735 | 984 |
| Interest & dividends | 15777 | 16891 | 18021 | 18754 | 19172 | 23436 | 26175 | 26532 | 29360 | 32316 | 32336 |
| Total current | 135186 | 150640 | 150449 | 138375 | 131922 | 140531 | 146918 | 150915 | 159386 | 164116 | 164918 |
| Capital (short term) | 1918 | 584 | 5763 | | 533 | 2409 | 9745 | 11900 | | 2345 | 8753 |
| Errors & ommissions | | | | | 8177 | | | 1880 | | | |
| Total current & capital | 137104 | 151224 | 156212 | 138375 | 140632 | 142940 | 156663 | 164695 | 159386 | 166461 | 173671 |

(continued)

**Table 2.4**  (continued)

| | 1892 | 1893 | 1894 | 1895 | 1896 | 1897 | 1898 | 1899 | 1900 | 1901 | 1902 |
|---|---|---|---|---|---|---|---|---|---|---|---|
| **Credits** | | | | | | | | | | | |
| Exports (adjusted) | 111896 | 113806 | 111220 | 111004 | 122498 | 142958 | 152908 | 153399 | 168695 | 179216 | 198499 |
| Exports of gold coin & bullion | 2238 | 2276 | 2224 | 2220 | 2450 | 2900 | 12900 | 22100 | 24800 | 21500 | 13700 |
| Freight | | | | | | 2859 | 3058 | 3068 | 3374 | 3584 | 3970 |
| Tourist receipts | 4900 | 4900 | 4700 | 4700 | 4700 | 4700 | 4500 | 9600 | 7000 | 8000 | 11000 |
| Migrants' capital (net) | 859 | 777 | 11 | | | 39 | 2037 | 2385 | 5537 | 6915 | 13412 |
| Noncommercial remittance | | | | | | | | | | | |
| Insurance | | | | | | | | | 1196 | 214 | |
| Interest & dividends | 2373 | 2771 | 3156 | 3351 | 3576 | 4024 | 4294 | 4506 | 4945 | 4831 | 5979 |
| Total current | 122266 | 124530 | 121311 | 121275 | 133224 | 157480 | 179697 | 195058 | 215547 | 224260 | 246560 |
| Capital (long term) | 28625 | 15921 | 31101 | 6568 | 10559 | 28036 | 16722 | | 25350 | 33161 | 20367 |
| Capital (short term) | | | | | | | | | 2860 | | |
| Net errors & omissions | 30207 | 35853 | 10071 | 31627 | 29446 | | 9388 | 42144 | | 27737 | 22800 |
| Total current & capital | 181098 | 176304 | 162483 | 159470 | 173229 | 185516 | 205808 | 237202 | 243757 | 285158 | 289727 |
| **Debits** | | | | | | | | | | | |
| Imports (adjusted) | 121689 | 117975 | 109672 | 106921 | 111248 | 122538 | 144055 | 166632 | 180572 | 192136 | 213450 |
| Imports of gold coin & bullion | 3300 | 1600 | 600 | 300 | 2900 | | | | | | |
| Freight | 6072 | 6024 | 6095 | 6397 | 6361 | 7649 | 10148 | 10983 | 11142 | 11068 | 11981 |
| Tourist payments | 4100 | 4300 | 4400 | 4500 | 5000 | 5300 | 5500 | 5300 | 4900 | 5400 | 6100 |
| Migrants' capital | | | | 187 | 174 | | | | | | |
| Noncommercial remittance | 1662 | 1695 | 1768 | 1514 | 1311 | 1352 | 1484 | 1800 | 2487 | 3484 | 4335 |
| Insurance | 793 | 363 | 556 | 666 | 952 | 404 | 565 | 46 | | | 3123 |
| Interest & dividends | 33529 | 34722 | 34536 | 33349 | 34075 | 35219 | 38744 | 40179 | 42065 | 44371 | 47472 |
| Total current | 171145 | 166680 | 157628 | 153834 | 162021 | 172462 | 200496 | 224940 | 241166 | 256459 | 286461 |
| Capital (long term) | | | | | | | | 1285 | | | |
| Capital (short term) | 9953 | 9624 | 4855 | 5636 | 11208 | 6741 | 5312 | 10977 | 2592 | 28699 | 3266 |
| Errors & omissions | | | | | | 6313 | | | | | |
| Total current & capital | | | | | | | | | | | |

| | 1903 | 1904 | 1905 | 1906 | 1907 | 1908 | 1909 | 1910 | 1911 | 1912 | 1913 |
|---|---|---|---|---|---|---|---|---|---|---|---|
| **Credits** | | | | | | | | | | | |
| Exports (adjusted) | 199704 | 188580 | 209015 | 239512 | 250527 | 251756 | 281116 | 285361 | 295366 | 348265 | 421392 |
| Exports of gold coin & bullion | 6800 | 6500 | 12500 | 3900 | 1400 | | 2700 | | | 11300 | |
| Freight | 3994 | 3772 | 4180 | 4790 | 5011 | 5035 | 5622 | 5708 | 5907 | 6965 | 8428 |
| Tourist receipts | 10500 | 12800 | 13300 | 16800 | 16200 | 19200 | 19600 | 24700 | 26200 | 29400 | 30500 |
| Migrants' capital (net) | 15264 | 12326 | 17191 | 18292 | 18258 | 9397 | 19825 | 26639 | 28023 | 24092 | 21366 |
| Noncommercial remittance | | 4799 | | | | | | | | | |
| Insurance | | | | | | | | | | | |
| Interest & dividends | 6110 | 5441 | 6287 | 6918 | 6418 | 5545 | 9243 | 10587 | 9552 | 9690 | 9682 |
| Total current | 242372 | 234217 | 262474 | 290212 | 297814 | 290933 | 338106 | 352994 | 365049 | 429712 | 491368 |
| Capital (long term) | 30290 | 79091 | 108438 | 81306 | 69847 | 177045 | 185176 | 222072 | 172535 | 277868 | 326413 |
| Capital (short term) | 16723 | | | 12514 | 21824 | | | | | 182 | |
| Net errors & omissions | 19914 | 32422 | 21 | 25215 | 71842 | 71577 | 5288 | 25886 | 189348 | 164151 | 113384 |
| Total current & capital | 309299 | 345730 | 370933 | 409246 | 461327 | 539555 | 528570 | 600952 | 726932 | 871913 | 931165 |
| **Debits** | | | | | | | | | | | |
| Imports (adjusted) | 235037 | 246848 | 263513 | 303919 | 346256 | 307148 | 354317 | 429411 | 500023 | 631720 | 632593 |
| Imports of gold coin & bullion | | | | | | 19100 | | 4100 | 21800 | | 7400 |
| Freight | 12410 | 12347 | 14521 | 15194 | 16080 | 13992 | 16131 | 18783 | 23882 | 32550 | 30160 |
| Tourist payments | 6000 | 6900 | 9400 | 12900 | 13400 | 15100 | 16600 | 21600 | 25200 | 29000 | 33200 |
| Migrants' capital | | | | | | | | | | | |
| Noncommercial remittance | 5640 | 7280 | 9054 | 11624 | 17690 | 17029 | 19829 | 27014 | 36056 | 47483 | 55797 |
| Insurance | 1616 | | 2734 | 2661 | 897 | 555 | 1409 | 874 | 1666 | 2711 | 2403 |
| Interest & dividends | 48595 | 51206 | 55926 | 62948 | 67004 | 74173 | 86682 | 96827 | 114855 | 128449 | 150850 |
| Total current | 309299 | 324580 | 355148 | 409246 | 461327 | 447096 | 494968 | 598609 | 723482 | 871913 | 912403 |
| Capital (short term) | | 21150 | 15785 | | | 92459 | 33602 | | | | 18762 |
| Errors & omissions | | | | | | | | 2344 | 3450 | | |
| Total current & capital | 309299 | 345730 | 370933 | 409246 | 461327 | 539555 | 528570 | 600952 | 726932 | 871913 | 931165 |

(continued)

**Table 2.4** (continued)

| | 1914 | 1915 | 1916 | 1917 | 1918 | 1919 | 1920 |
|---|---|---|---|---|---|---|---|
| **Credits** | | | | | | | |
| Exports (adjusted) | 442587 | 678205 | 1039296 | 1462570 | 1336938 | 1300372 | 1265965 |
| Exports of gold coin & bullion | 22600 | | 14000 | | 16300 | 15700 | 34200 |
| Freight | 41100 | 70700 | 91700 | 84100 | 83800 | 86900 | 114400 |
| Tourist receipts | 29600 | 36600 | 53200 | 64400 | 66100 | 73000 | 64200 |
| Migrants' capital / Noncommercial remittance | 28200 | 18300 | 19200 | 20000 | 21600 | 32200 | 40700 |
| Insurance | 3900 | 2000 | 3600 | 6600 | 3200 | 2900 | 4800 |
| Interest & dividends | 10400 | 9600 | 14100 | 19300 | 18900 | 20000 | 20900 |
| Total current | 578387 | 815405 | 1235096 | 1656970 | 1546839 | 1531072 | 1545165 |
| Capital (long term) | 381836 | 28633 | 95823 | 55720 | 53570 | 57811 | 132745 |
| Capital (short term) | 21200 | | | 10800 | | | 42400 |
| War finance, external | 24300 | 60400 | | | | | 31000 |
| Net errors & omissions | | 90583 | 113097 | | 69624 | 4450 | |
| Total current & capital | 1005723 | 995021 | 1444015 | 1723489 | 1670031 | 1593332 | 1751310 |
| **Debits** | | | | | | | |
| Imports (adjusted) | 521572 | 516370 | 783825 | 958428 | 953372 | 1053065 | 1225783 |
| Imports of gold coin & bullion | | 9400 | | 1700 | | | |
| Freight | 80200 | 101000 | 145500 | 139000 | 144100 | 125600 | 170100 |
| Tourist payments | 35000 | 25000 | 29000 | 27000 | 30000 | 47000 | 48400 |
| Migrants' capital / Noncommercial remittance | 20100 | 11300 | 12300 | 18000 | 21200 | 12100 | 10000 |
| Canadian expend frce | 5000 | 30000 | 100000 | 175000 | 170000 | 95000 | 20000 |
| Insurance | 6100 | 5700 | 5000 | 8300 | 8600 | 14800 | 19400 |
| Interest & dividends | 163671 | 182851 | 186394 | 192805 | 194960 | 198467 | 206929 |
| Total current | 831643 | 881621 | 1262015 | 1520233 | 1522231 | 1546032 | 1700611 |
| War finance, external | | | 52600 | 113100 | 119300 | 25600 | |
| Capital (short term) | | 113400 | 129400 | | 28500 | 21700 | |
| Net errors & omissions | 174080 | | | 90156 | | | 50699 |
| Total current & capital | 1005723 | 995021 | 1444015 | 1723489 | 1670031 | 1593332 | 1751310 |

| | 1921 | 1922 | 1923 | 1924 | 1925 | 1926 |
|---|---|---|---|---|---|---|
| **Credits** | | | | | | |
| Exports (adjusted) | 894290 | 918272 | 1042507 | 1075538 | 1270589 | 1272000 |
| Exports of gold coin & bullion | 42200 | | 82200 | 4600 | 15100 | 30000 |
| Freight | 84300 | 78500 | 89200 | 83000 | 86700 | 96000 |
| Tourist receipts | 68300 | 78900 | 103300 | 117000 | 128500 | 152000 |
| Migrants' capital | 36300 | 31900 | 38000 | 37800 | 37800 } | 83000 } |
| Noncommercial remittance | | | | | 15700 | |
| Insurance | 4100 | 6500 | 8100 | 10500 | | |
| Interest & dividends | 19200 | 13400 | 12300 | 12800 | 13500 | 32000 |
| Total current | 1148690 | 1127472 | 1375607 | 1341238 | 1567889 | 1665000 |
| Capital (long term) | 50516 | 131453 | 117150 | 152563 | 55438 | 52300 |
| Capital (short term) | 144400 | 27000 | | | | |
| War finance, external | | | | | | |
| Net errors & omissions | 27900 | 46800 | 63800 | 20700 | 1900 | 2300 |
| Total current & capital | 1371507 | 1332725 | 1556557 | 1514501 | 1625227 | 1719600 |
| **Debits** | | | | | | |
| Imports (adjusted) | 890409 | 807417 | 891996 | 840267 | 915483 | 973000 |
| Imports of gold coin & bullion | | 45300 | | | | |
| Freight | 116500 | 94300 | 121400 | 99100 | 106400 | 105000 |
| Tourist payments | 43300 | 40900 | 43900 | 49100 | 55900 | 99000 |
| Migrants' capital | 23100 | 16900 | 8400 | 9400 | 20800 } | 121000 } |
| Noncommercial remittance | | | | | 18600 | |
| Canadian expend frce | | | | | | |
| Insurance | 10600 | 9900 | 9900 | 14100 | | |
| Interest & dividends | 230128 | 238736 | 243579 | 254000 | 256894 | 240000 |
| Total current | 1314037 | 1253453 | 1319175 | 1265967 | 1374077 | 1538000 |
| War finance, external | | | | | | |
| Capital (short term) | 57470 | 79273 | 224682 | 232834 | 158350 | 129800 |
| Net errors & omissions | | | 12700 | 15700 | 92800 | 51800 |
| Total current & capital | 1371507 | 1332725 | 1556557 | 1514500 | 1625227 | 1719600 |

the other hand, there was an attempt to show that the rents from wheat production produced by the populating of the prairies by 1910 were so small that settlement of the latter could have had little effect in the growth of per capita income that took place from 1900 to 1910. Both approaches downplayed the role of the staple.[2]

It is not the aim of this paper to try to reconcile the contending views of Canadian growth or to try to pick a winner, if indeed there is one. But our data do provide a considerable amount of new information that has a bearing on the contending interpretations, and it is to these that we turn.

I present the remaining material of this paper in three parts. First, some background facts, not new to this paper but of relevance to our material, are presented. Second, the relationships among the aggregates are examined. Third, the nature of changes in the structure of GNP are examined.

## 2.1  Background Facts

A most important set of facts relates to the underlying population base and its growth. On one hand, Canada failed to retain the natural increase in its population in each decade from 1870 to 1900, despite having a substantial number of immigrants; on the other hand, it gained large numbers from net immigration in 1900–1921 (and to 1926). The relevant data are shown in table 2.5: it relates to the population 10 years of age and over, since only for them could estimates of survival from the last census be made—the natural increase, the immigration and emigration all apply to the 10 and over age groups.

The loss from net out-migration in the 10-year and older age group in each decade from 1871 to 1901 averages 4.9% of the beginning population. Other data show that Quebec's net loss by migration of pop-

Table 2.5     **Population and Changes in Population 10 Years of Age and Over, by Decades, 1861–1931 (Thousands of Persons)**

| Decade | Population at End of Decade | Natural Increase | Immigration | Emigration | Net Migration |
|--------|--------|--------|--------|--------|--------|
| 1861–71 | 2630 | 563 | 186 | 376 | −191 |
| 1871–81 | 3164 | 619 | 353 | 438 | −85 |
| 1881–91 | 3628 | 669 | 903 | 1108 | −205 |
| 1891–1901 | 4101 | 654 | 326 | 507 | −181 |
| 1901–11 | 5528 | 711 | 1782 | 1066 | +715 |
| 1911–21 | 6677 | 916 | 1592 | 1360 | +233 |
| 1921–31 | 8169 | 1389 | | | +103 |

*Source: Historical Statistics of Canada, 1st ed., p. 22.*

ulation was very high in both 1881–1891 and 1891–1901 and that insofar as they were nativeborn most of the migrants left the country; Ontario also lost large numbers, especially in 1891–1901, but a quite large part of the loss comprised migration of the nativeborn to Western Canada.

By contrast, in 1901–11 the countrywide net inflow of migrants aged 10 years and over was of the same order as the natural increase in the same age group, and the net inflow remained substantial although smaller in the succeeding two decades. Supplementary data show that Quebec and the Maritime Provinces continued to lose population by migration—in this regard Quebec's relatively high rate of natural increase should be kept in mind—that the Prairie Provinces were big gainers in 1901–11 and 1911–21, that British Columbia was a big gainer in all three decades, and that Ontario also gained substantial numbers from net in-migration in all three decades, a point of which we shall see the relevance later. The figures for total population in Canada and the significant provincial groupings are given in table 2.6.

While there are differing estimates of the labor force and its industrial distribution before 1901, the general lines of the division between agricultural and other pursuits are sufficiently accurate to be useful. The so-called gainfully occupied and the numbers engaged in agriculture are given in table 2.7. It should be noted at once that in 1900 the numbers in agriculture and total gainfully occupied are too low owing to the omission of a considerable number of unpaid farmers' sons from the count.

A next "fact" concerns the railways in Canada. Of 1870, it can be said, with only slight exaggeration of fact, that the Canadian railways system was limited to a main line from north of Quebec City, through Montreal and Toronto to Sarnia (near Detroit) with a connection from Montreal to Portland, Maine, lines from the Niagara Peninsula and from Hamilton to Detroit, and a few short spurs from these lines; the Maritime Provinces had only 379 miles in 1867 at Confederation. Rail-

**Table 2.6    Population of Canada and Five Provincial Groups, Census Dates 1871–1931 (Thousands of Persons)**

| Year | Canada | Maritime Provinces | Quebec | Ontario | Prairie Provinces | British Columbia |
|------|--------|--------------------|--------|---------|--------------------|------------------|
| 1871 | 3689 | 768 | 1192 | 1621 | 73 | 36 |
| 1881 | 4325 | 871 | 1359 | 1927 | 89 | 49 |
| 1891 | 4833 | 881 | 1488 | 2114 | 252 | 98 |
| 1901 | 5371 | 894 | 1649 | 2183 | 469 | 179 |
| 1911 | 7207 | 938 | 2006 | 2527 | 1343 | 393 |
| 1921 | 8768 | 1000 | 2361 | 2934 | 1968 | 525 |
| 1931 | 10377 | 1009 | 2875 | 3432 | 2367 | 694 |

*Source: Historical Statistics of Canada, 1st ed., p. 14.*

Table 2.7    Total Gainfully Occupied and the Numbers Engaged in
             Agriculture, Census Dates, 1871–1921 (Thousands of Persons)

| Year | Total Gainfully Occupied | Total Engaged in Agriculture | Proportion Engaged in Agriculture |
|------|--------------------------|------------------------------|-----------------------------------|
| 1871 | 1130 | 579  | 0.5124 |
| 1881 | 1378 | 667  | 0.4803 |
| 1891 | 1606 | 744  | 0.4633 |
| 1901 | 1783 | 717  | 0.4021 |
| 1911 | 2724 | 958  | 0.3517 |
| 1921 | 3164 | 1041 | 0.3290 |
| 1931 | 3922 | 1128 | 0.2875 |

*Source: Historical Statistics of Canada,* 1st ed., p. 59; and R. M. McInnis, "Output and Productivity in Canadian Agriculture," in this volume; Firestone 1958, p. 184, for gainfully occupied in 1871.

Table 2.8    Railway Track and Equipment, Selected Years, 1870–1925

| Year | Miles of First Main Track in Operation | Number of Locomotives | Number of Passenger Cars | Number of Freight Cars |
|------|----------------------------------------|-----------------------|--------------------------|------------------------|
| 1870 | 2617  |      |      |        |
| 1875 | 4331  | 980  | 1000 | 20297  |
| 1880 | 6858  | 1157 | 1170 | 24079  |
| 1885 | 10273 | 1524 | 1655 | 38318  |
| 1890 | 13151 | 1771 | 2018 | 49356  |
| 1895 | 15977 | 2023 | 2658 | 56963  |
| 1900 | 17657 | 2282 | 2828 | 64979  |
| 1905 | 20487 | 2906 | 3006 | 86196  |
| 1910 | 24730 | 4079 | 4320 | 119713 |
| 1915 | 34882 | 5486 | 6326 | 201690 |
| 1920 | 38805 | 6030 | 6557 | 224489 |
| 1925 | 40350 | 5752 | 6839 | 224227 |

*Source: Historical Statistics of Canada,* 1st ed., pp. 528, 532, 533.

way building played a major role in Canadian development from 1870 to the First World War both in the direct impact of the railway building on the economy and through its contribution to freight and passenger movement once it was built. Some measure of its impact is given by the miles of line in operation and the equipment in use which is given in table 2.8. We will return to the railways later.

Finally, there is a question about the course of prices through this period and how movements in real GNP differ from those measured in current prices. Estimates of GNP measured in 1900 dollars along with an implicit price index and real GNP per capita are given in table 2.9. The deflation of GNP in current prices was essentially done by two components. Gross domestic fixed capital formation in current prices broken into residential and nonresidential items was deflated by indexes of costs of capital goods appropriate to each of the items. All of the remaining part of the GNP was deflated by an index of consumer prices, part of which was constructed within this project.[5]

The deflation procedure can probably be improved, but I have sufficient confidence in our findings that I do not expect further refinements in the deflation process to result in changes that would lead to any significant reinterpretation of the meaning of the data.

In order to aid the interpretation of the data in table 2.9, certain growth ratios calculable from it are given in table 2.10 and for comparative purposes comparable growth rates are given for the United States. The entries are usually for decadal periods; however, the first entry in each panel is for 9 years and the final entry in panel C, real GNP per capita, is for 19 years. For both countries, the rates of growth of population are between the single years at the beginning and end of each period; for both countries, the rates of growth of real GNP are those between the averages of 3 years centered on the beginning and on the ending year of each period. I am most indebted to Robert Gallman for providing me with the estimates of the growth of real GNP and real GNP per capita in the United States from 1871 to 1900.

We should note at once that there is a considerable arbitrariness in the growth rates that are obtained for each period determined by the choice of beginning and ending years of the period. Thus, if the first decade were made to end in 1882 and the second in 1892, the calculated growth rate for income in Canada for the first period would be raised and that for the second period lowered; or if we divide the decade from 1890 to 1900 into two parts, we can see from table 2.9 that all of the growth in per capita income took place between 1896 and 1900. It is important that we keep these properties of the data of table 2.10 in mind when we come to draw inferences from them.

The main series of relationships among aggregates which utilize our new data and that appear to be relevant to the issues about the nature of Canadian development are given in table 2.11. The figures are given on an annual basis because the year-to-year movements themselves contain valuable information. The ratios are between values in current dollars.

A few comments about the data of table 2.11 are in order. First, all of the absolute values from which the ratios are calculated appear in other tables and hence are not given here. Second, the gross fixed capital formation ratio includes public as well as private capital formation; the public component—budgetary capital formation—is ordi-

**Table 2.9    Gross National Product in Current and Constant Dollars and Real Gross National Product per Capita, 1870–1926**

| Year | GNP in Current Market Prices ($mm) | GNP in Constant (1900) Prices ($mm) | Implicit Price Index 1900 = 100 | Population in Thousands of Persons | Real GNP per Capita in 1900 Dollars |
|------|------|------|------|------|------|
| 1870 | 382.6 | 369.5 | 104 | 3625 | 102 |
| 1871 | 412.7 | 385.9 | 107 | 3689 | 105 |
| 1872 | 447.3 | 382.8 | 117 | 3754 | 102 |
| 1873 | 487.8 | 419.3 | 116 | 3826 | 110 |
| 1874 | 485.5 | 427.8 | 113 | 3895 | 110 |
| 1875 | 452.5 | 417.1 | 108 | 3954 | 105 |
| 1876 | 421.7 | 391.1 | 108 | 4009 | 98 |
| 1877 | 434.7 | 416.5 | 104 | 4064 | 102 |
| 1878 | 409.6 | 402.6 | 102 | 4120 | 98 |
| 1879 | 445.1 | 441.8 | 101 | 4185 | 106 |
| 1880 | 482.0 | 462.1 | 104 | 4255 | 109 |
| 1881 | 568.7 | 527.0 | 108 | 4325 | 122 |
| 1882 | 618.9 | 547.2 | 113 | 4375 | 125 |
| 1883 | 611.5 | 545.7 | 112 | 4430 | 123 |
| 1884 | 585.2 | 592.0 | 99 | 4487 | 132 |
| 1885 | 554.5 | 556.3 | 100 | 4537 | 123 |
| 1886 | 560.7 | 559.4 | 100 | 4580 | 122 |
| 1887 | 611.1 | 579.0 | 106 | 4626 | 125 |
| 1888 | 630.3 | 616.1 | 102 | 4678 | 132 |
| 1889 | 655.8 | 620.9 | 106 | 4729 | 131 |
| 1890 | 685.4 | 657.4 | 104 | 4779 | 138 |
| 1891 | 703.5 | 679.9 | 104 | 4833 | 141 |
| 1892 | 700.3 | 676.2 | 104 | 4883 | 138 |
| 1893 | 682.4 | 666.9 | 102 | 4931 | 135 |
| 1894 | 651.4 | 700.6 | 93 | 4979 | 141 |
| 1895 | 633.4 | 698.9 | 91 | 5026 | 139 |
| 1896 | 640.8 | 680.7 | 94 | 5074 | 134 |
| 1897 | 717.0 | 757.2 | 95 | 5122 | 148 |
| 1898 | 769.4 | 786.5 | 98 | 5175 | 152 |
| 1899 | 826.0 | 857.8 | 96 | 5235 | 164 |
| 1900 | 907.4 | 907.8 | 100 | 5301 | 171 |
| 1901 | 990.7 | 984.1 | 101 | 5371 | 183 |
| 1902 | 1119.6 | 1073.6 | 104 | 5494 | 195 |
| 1903 | 1178.2 | 1115.1 | 106 | 5651 | 197 |
| 1904 | 1205.8 | 1131.4 | 107 | 5827 | 194 |
| 1905 | 1361.5 | 1248.2 | 109 | 6002 | 208 |
| 1906 | 1525.9 | 1380.6 | 111 | 6097 | 226 |
| 1907 | 1728.4 | 1456.0 | 119 | 6411 | 227 |
| 1908 | 1653.8 | 1383.3 | 120 | 6625 | 209 |
| 1909 | 1838.3 | 1520.4 | 121 | 6800 | 224 |
| 1910 | 2022.8 | 1655.4 | 122 | 6988 | 237 |

**Table 2.9**    (continued)

| Year | GNP in Current Market Prices ($mm) | GNP in Constant (1900) Prices ($mm) | Implicit Price Index 1900 = 100 | Population in Thousands of Persons | Real GNP per Capita in 1900 Dollars |
|------|------|------|------|------|------|
| 1911 | 2233.2 | 1770.7 | 126 | 7207 | 246 |
| 1912 | 2493.9 | 1905.4 | 128 | 7389 | 258 |
| 1913 | 2651.5 | 1979.8 | 134 | 7632 | 259 |
| 1914 | 2448.6 | 1835.6 | 133 | 7869 | 233 |
| 1915 | 2688.6 | 1964.4 | 137 | 7981 | 246 |
| 1916 | 3242.7 | 2182.5 | 149 | 8001 | 273 |
| 1917 | 3991.9 | 2273.2 | 176 | 8060 | 282 |
| 1918 | 4261.5 | 2141.4 | 199 | 8148 | 263 |
| 1919 | 4367.4 | 1994.9 | 219 | 8311 | 240 |
| 1920 | 5060.9 | 1992.0 | 254 | 8556 | 233 |
| 1921 | 4073.8 | 1800.3 | 226 | 8788 | 205 |
| 1922 | 4233.9 | 2060.9 | 205 | 8919 | 231 |
| 1923 | 4555.3 | 2194.0 | 208 | 9010 | 244 |
| 1924 | 4501.5 | 2210.1 | 204 | 9143 | 242 |
| 1925 | 4995.7 | 2450.3 | 204 | 9294 | 264 |
| 1926 | 5345.3 | 2611.8 | 205 | 9451 | 276 |

narily less than 10% of the total, as may be seen from table 2.2. Third, the net capital inflow has been measured, for all years, by the current account balance on international account. Fourth, the implied domestic saving is simply the difference between the gross fixed capital formation ratio and the capital inflow ratio. Fifth, the export ratio and the government expenditure ratio are, respectively, for merchandise exports and for government expenditures on goods and services. Finally, the ratio of export prices to import prices, the terms of trade, are given to show the qualitative nature of the impact of international prices on real income in Canada.

We are now in a position to examine the bearing of the data that we have considered on the matter at issue. I shall not go into the details of the way in which the traditionalists saw the staples as contributing to growth nor the arguments of the critics about the inadequacies of the traditionalists' explanations: such would take too much space. A well-rounded analytical statement and evaluation of the issues and contentions is given in Richard E. Caves's "Export-Led Growth and the New Economic History" in the Kindleberger festschrift (Caves 1971). Rather, I shall just examine the extent to which our data at least seem consistent with what the traditonalists or their critics would expect us to observe. Suffice it to say that in a period of expansion the traditionalists saw a growth of the export sector of the economy (the

**Table 2.10**  **Comparative Growth Rates of Canada and the United States (All Growth Rates in Compound Rates Percent per Annum)**

| Years | Canada | United States |
|---|---|---|
| *A. Population* | | |
| 1871–80 | 1.6 | 2.3 |
| 1880–90 | 1.2 | 2.3 |
| 1890–1900 | 1.0 | 1.9 |
| 1900–1910 | 2.8 | 2.0 |
| 1910–20 | 2.0 | 1.4 |
| 1920–25 | 1.7 | 1.7 |
| *B. Total Real GNP* | | |
| 1871–80 | 2.6 | 5.7 |
| 1880–90 | 3.2 | 3.5 |
| 1890–1900 | 3.5 | 3.6 |
| 1900–1910 | 6.0 | 3.8 |
| 1910–20 | 1.6 | 2.5 |
| 1920–25 | 4.7 | 4.7 |
| *C. Real GNP per Capita* | | |
| 1871–80 | 1.0 | 3.3 |
| 1880–90 | 2.0 | 1.2 |
| 1890–1900 | 2.4 | 1.7 |
| 1900–1910 | 3.2 | 1.8 |
| 1910–20 | −0.4 | 1.1 |
| 1920–25 | 2.9 | 2.9 |
| 1871–90 | 1.5 | 2.2 |

*Source:* For Canada, calculated from the data of table 2.9. For the United States, for 1871–1900, real GNP and per capita growth rates provided by Robert Gallman from data underlying his paper in vol. 30 of the Conference series; for 1900–1925, Kendrick 1961, pp. 298–99, and *Historical Statistics of U.S., Colonial Times to 1970*, p. 8.

high-productivity sector) lead to a more general expansion that permeated from the export sector to most other parts of the economy. For example, for the period 1895–1920, W. A. Mackintosh, in describing the main measured dimensions of growth—in which, incidentally, the high population growth was mentioned first—wrote:

> The most fundamental single characteristic of the period was a high rate of investment induced by improved expectations of profit from the exploitation of natural resources, which had been newly discovered, newly tapped by the extending railways, subjected to new productive techniques, or converted into profit possibilities by favourable shifts in costs and prices. Overwhelmingly most important were the wheat lands of the Prairie Provinces. Prospective profitableness in the exploiting industries created markets for other industries and for a time investment fed on itself. (Mackintosh 1939, p. 41)

There remains one matter of contention that requires comment. The traditionalists did not elaborate on whether economic growth meant

**Table 2.11**    **Ratios of Selected Aggregate Expenditure Items to GNP and Terms of Trade**

| Year | Capital Formation/ GNP[a] | Capital Inflow/ GNP[b] | Implied Savings Ratio[c] | Exports/ GNP[d] | Government Spending/ GNP[e] | Export/ Import Prices[f] |
|------|------|------|------|------|------|------|
| 1870 | 0.157 | 0.062 | 0.095 | 0.174 | 0.048 | 0.68 |
| 1871 | 0.152 | 0.083 | 0.069 | 0.177 | 0.053 | 0.66 |
| 1872 | 0.174 | 0.092 | 0.082 | 0.183 | 0.056 | 0.72 |
| 1873 | 0.173 | 0.093 | 0.080 | 0.176 | 0.061 | 0.76 |
| 1874 | 0.191 | 0.104 | 0.087 | 0.166 | 0.075 | 0.78 |
| 1875 | 0.188 | 0.080 | 0.108 | 0.170 | 0.080 | 0.82 |
| 1876 | 0.166 | 0.063 | 0.103 | 0.181 | 0.091 | 0.82 |
| 1877 | 0.141 | 0.058 | 0.083 | 0.175 | 0.088 | 0.89 |
| 1878 | 0.135 | 0.057 | 0.078 | 0.181 | 0.091 | 0.88 |
| 1879 | 0.126 | 0.036 | 0.090 | 0.174 | 0.081 | 0.86 |
| 1880 | 0.137 | 0.034 | 0.103 | 0.188 | 0.074 | 0.86 |
| 1881 | 0.136 | 0.048 | 0.088 | 0.174 | 0.064 | 0.91 |
| 1882 | 0.173 | 0.063 | 0.110 | 0.160 | 0.062 | 0.93 |
| 1883 | 0.198 | 0.074 | 0.124 | 0.151 | 0.074 | 0.92 |
| 1884 | 0.222 | 0.068 | 0.154 | 0.149 | 0.076 | 0.93 |
| 1885 | 0.157 | 0.069 | 0.088 | 0.154 | 0.104 | 0.95 |
| 1886 | 0.152 | 0.077 | 0.075 | 0.154 | 0.081 | 0.99 |
| 1887 | 0.163 | 0.077 | 0.086 | 0.146 | 0.081 | 1.06 |
| 1888 | 0.168 | 0.084 | 0.084 | 0.140 | 0.076 | 0.99 |
| 1889 | 0.170 | 0.083 | 0.087 | 0.137 | 0.075 | 1.01 |
| 1890 | 0.144 | 0.088 | 0.056 | 0.138 | 0.073 | 2.00 |
| 1891 | 0.150 | 0.069 | 0.081 | 0.147 | 0.077 | 1.05 |
| 1892 | 0.139 | 0.070 | 0.069 | 0.160 | 0.074 | 1.05 |
| 1893 | 0.135 | 0.062 | 0.073 | 0.167 | 0.079 | 1.08 |
| 1894 | 0.115 | 0.056 | 0.059 | 0.171 | 0.085 | 1.13 |
| 1895 | 0.123 | 0.051 | 0.072 | 0.175 | 0.087 | 2.06 |
| 1896 | 0.115 | 0.045 | 0.070 | 0.191 | 0.088 | 1.09 |
| 1897 | 0.126 | 0.021 | 0.105 | 0.199 | 0.081 | 1.09 |
| 1898 | 0.154 | 0.027 | 0.127 | 0.199 | 0.081 | 1.07 |
| 1899 | 0.153 | 0.036 | 0.117 | 0.186 | 0.078 | 1.00 |
| 1900 | 0.155 | 0.028 | 0.127 | 0.186 | 0.075 | 1.02 |
| 1901 | 0.182 | 0.033 | 0.149 | 0.181 | 0.077 | 1.06 |
| 1902 | 0.186 | 0.036 | 0.150 | 0.177 | 0.070 | 1.07 |
| 1903 | 0.217 | 0.057 | 0.160 | 0.169 | 0.078 | 1.05 |
| 1904 | 0.230 | 0.075 | 0.155 | 0.156 | 0.083 | 1.03 |
| 1905 | 0.229 | 0.068 | 0.161 | 0.154 | 0.079 | 1.05 |
| 1906 | 0.236 | 0.078 | 0.158 | 0.157 | 0.074 | 1.04 |
| 1907 | 0.259 | 0.095 | 0.164 | 0.145 | 0.077 | 1.06 |
| 1908 | 0.265 | 0.094 | 0.171 | 0.152 | 0.093 | 1.14 |
| 1909 | 0.259 | 0.085 | 0.174 | 0.153 | 0.084 | 1.14 |
| 1910 | 0.295 | 0.121 | 0.174 | 0.141 | 0.086 | 1.12 |
| 1911 | 0.311 | 0.160 | 0.151 | 0.132 | 0.091 | 1.13 |
| 1912 | 0.341 | 0.177 | 0.166 | 0.140 | 0.092 | 1.11 |
| 1913 | 0.328 | 0.159 | 0.169 | 0.159 | 0.104 | 1.04 |
| 1914 | 0.270 | 0.114 | 0.156 | 0.199 | 0.146 | 1.15 |
| 1915 | 0.175 | 0.025 | 0.150 | 0.252 | 0.163 | 1.24 |

*(continued)*

Table 2.11    (continued)

| Year | Capital Formation/ GNP[a] | Capital Inflow/ GNP[b] | Implied Savings Ratio[c] | Exports/ GNP[d] | Government Spending/ GNP[e] | Export/ Import Prices[f] |
|------|------|--------|--------|--------|--------|--------|
| 1916 | 0.154 | 0.008 | 0.162 | 0.321 | 0.163 | 1.13 |
| 1917 | 0.148 | −0.034 | 0.182 | 0.366 | 0.133 | 1.29 |
| 1918 | 0.129 | 0.006 | 0.123 | 0.314 | 0.152 | 1.22 |
| 1919 | 0.151 | 0.003 | 0.148 | 0.298 | 0.171 | 1.18 |
| 1920 | 0.166 | 0.031 | 0.135 | 0.250 | 0.117 | 1.08 |
| 1921 | 0.179 | 0.041 | 0.138 | 0.220 | 0.144 | 1.06 |
| 1922 | 0.158 | 0.030 | 0.128 | 0.217 | 0.135 | 1.05 |
| 1923 | 0.189 | −0.012 | 0.201 | 0.229 | 0.115 | 0.96 |
| 1924 | 0.169 | −0.017 | 0.186 | 0.239 | 0.108 | 1.02 |
| 1925 | 0.154 | −0.039 | 0.193 | 0.254 | 0.100 | 1.13 |
| 1926 | 0.151 | −0.040 | 0.191 | 0.242 | 0.091 | 1.16 |

[a]Ratio, gross fixed capital formation to current GNP (both in current prices).
[b]Ratio, inflow of capital to GNP (current account balance to GNP).
[c]Implied domestic savings ratio.
[d]Ratio, exports of goods to GNP.
[e]Ratio of government expenditure on goods and services to GNP.
[f]Ratio of export prices to import prices 1899 = 1.

rapid extensive growth (growth in population) or intensive growth (growth in income per capita) or some combination of the two. They usually argued that the emergence of staples led to periods of rapid population growth which would, of course, cause growth of aggregate output. In fact, Mackintosh judged the relative growth in the Province of Canada in the 1850s and 1860s by the relative rates of population growth in the two decades and, indeed, noted that a central objective of national policy after confederation was the settlement of the west, and that objective, on a grand scale, presumably meant substantial aggregate population growth. It was perhaps implied that a rise in per capita income was necessary to acquire the additional people, but that point was not made explicit.

The revisionists have tended to base their arguments on the growth of income per capita, which has been described as intensive growth. They have argued that growth of per capita output was not greatly affected by the presence or absence of exports in the period to which our data apply. Such per capita growth as there is comes from other sources. They presumably would not deny that sufficiently high growth in per capita productivity might lead to immigration and hence extensive as well as intensive growth; but they do not ordinarily go into that.

The ratios of table 2.11 are not as enlightening as one would like since the process of drawing inferences from them is complicated by the interactions between the development of exports, population growth, and capital formation. In accordance with the staple hypothesis, one might expect to take the ratio of exports to GNP as an indicator of the role of the export sector, the high productivity sector, in driving the economy. Yet the way in which growth in the export sector works in causing economic growth in the early phases of expansion may be only in small part in its direct effect on GNP but more largely through its effect on population growth and capital formation, both of which in turn affect directly the size of GNP. If an initial growth of exports stimulates both rapid population growth and capital formation in anticipation of further export growth, the consequent rise in GNP may cause the ratio actually to decline. The process of growth is a dynamic one with leads and lags, and the growth of the export sector to maturity may take many years. I propose then to leave examination of the export sector ratios until we have looked at the way in which related variables and particularly investment have moved.

As for fixed capital formation, and especially its relationship to GNP as shown in table 2.11, there are three periods when it was especially important. It was relatively robust, for its time, in the first half of the 1870s, again through the mid- to late 1880s, and, above all, in the period from 1900 to 1914. Capital formation in the railways was important in all three of these periods. It involved the building of the intercolonial railway (a government undertaking) in the early 1870s. And it was especially the major factor in the 1880s with the building of the Canadian Pacific Railway line to the west coast, 1881–85, a private undertaking that was greatly aided by very generous treatment from the federal government and that was supplemented by a building boom in the late 1880s in Montreal, a boom most likely consequent on the building of the railway. Had it not been for this building of the CPR in the 1880s, the period from the late 1870s to the mid-1890s would have been one of continuously low investment and bleak prospects. As it was, the railway building of the 1880s ameliorated the sad export performance of the decade. However, its main impact as a going concern only came 10 years later when the volume of freight began to increase rapidly. Railway building was important also in 1900–1914, but the investment was also very broadly based in that period, as may be seen in table 2.2.

The period from 1900 to 1914 epitomizes a classic investment boom, a major part of it related directly or indirectly to the settlement of the west. In the latter regard, much of the railway building was directed toward the west—two new transcontinental lines and many branch lines in the prairies were built. And as can be seen from tables 2.5, 2.6, and 2.10, there was an extraordinarily high rate of population growth of which a most disproportionate part took place on the prairies. That the settlement of the west was based on the expectation, in the minds of the settlers, of there being a viable market for wheat is beyond doubt. But the great engine of growth of the period was the enormous investment expenditure associated with that settlement.

During the 1914–18 war, investment expenditure languished and, although recovering somewhat from wartime levels in the 1920s, it did not retain anything like the relative eminence of the lusty levels of 1900–1914.

We shall return to the roles and interrelationships of investment and exports, but first we should look at some other relevant items.

Caves (1971) has made the point that export-led growth might affect the levels of saving, hence presumably the level of domestically financed capital formation, and hence growth rates. Our measure of the level of saving (table 2.11) leaves much to be desired since it is calculated as the residual of fixed capital formation less capital inflow and there are considerable errors of measurement in the latter. However, it seems most improbable that such revision as might be made would alter the general tenor of the inference we draw about saving. This inference is that the level of saving was of a quite different order after 1900 than it had been before. As a ratio of GNP, overall gross savings averaged 8.8% in 1870–79, 10.0% in 1880–89, and 8.3% in 1890–99. In contrast, it averaged 15.7% for 1900–1909, 16.3% for 1910–14, and 16.9% for 1921–26—the wartime years have been omitted. That there was a substantial increase in the saving rate appears to be quite clear.

Next there are the growth rates of production and of productivity which have been matters of issue and for which there are the data in table 2.10. It is clear that growth rates of population and of total real GNP in Canada were much higher after 1900 than before. The contrast would have been considerably stronger had the dividing point been taken at 1896, the date generally taken as the turning point in Canada's fortunes: in that event, the annual rate of increase of real GNP from 1871 to 1895 (3 years centered in each case) is 2.5% and from 1895 to 1913 (3 years centered) is 5.8%. The per capita real income growth rates are interesting. They do support the view that there was considerable growth in output per capita before 1900 with some increase in this growth of real output per capita in peacetime years after 1900. Again if one takes 3-year averages at the beginning and ending of the two periods from 1871 to 1895 and 1895 to 1913, the respective annual compound rates of growth of per capita real income are 1.2% and 3.4%. (If one wishes to take alternate periods of comparison, that can be done by use of the data of table 2.9.)

Account should be taken of the fact that the proportion of the population of working age that belongs to the gainfully occupied category changed from decade to decade. Unfortunately, until 1921, figures for the gainfully occupied are available only for census years (see table

2.7). Further, it is generally accepted that there was an undercount of the agricultural labor force in 1901 and hence that the figure for the gainfully occupied persons for 1901 is too low. In light of the 1901 undercount and the fact that the expansion of exports began in the 1890s and was especially significant from 1896 onward (table 2.11), we compare growth of the output per worker for three periods.[6] The average annual rate of growth was 1.1% from 1871 to 1891, 2.3% from 1891 to 1911, and 4.3% from 1921 to 1926 (end years centered on 3-year averages in each case). The high rate of growth from 1921 to 1926 may in part be a matter of recovery from a small decline in productivity per worker in the decade covering the wartime years.

Comparison with the United States shows the following. Population growth rates were clearly higher in the United States from 1871 to 1900 and in Canada from 1900 to 1920. Growth rates of aggregate real GNP in the United States were substantially higher than those in Canada in the 1870s and substantially lower than those in Canada in the decade 1900–1910; for other periods (the wartime decade excluded) the real GNP growth rates were about equal. Growth rates of real income per capita, which may be somewhat arbitrarily allocated among periods by choice of beginning and ending years, give a mixed picture. If the 1870s and the 1880s are taken together, United States per capita growth rates clearly exceeded those of Canada in 1871–90 but fall short of the Canadian rates in 1890–99. Following 1900, Canadian per capita growth rates substantially exceeded those of the United States in the decade 1900–1910 but lost such ground in the wartime years that over the whole period from 1900 to 1926 the per capita growth rates were about equal.

Now what inferences can be drawn from the export ratios of table 2.11? In order to try to abstract from influences on the data of lags between the initial and final impact of export (staple) growth on the performance of the economy, I compare first the export ratios of 1870–1900, which preceded the period of the wheat economy, with those after 1920 when the wheat economy was in full flourish. The relatively large increase in the export ratio was much more than accounted for by the increase in the value of wheat exports, which were supplemented in an important way from 1918 onward by those other resource-based (though more highly processed) exports of newsprint and wood pulp and of nonferrous metals: it was a product of the increase in exports of staple-based products. In order to give some indication of the significance of these ratios, I just mention for comparative purposes that the similar United States export rates were for the 3 years centered on 1890 just over .07 and for the 3 years centered on 1925 just under .07.

An examination of the export ratios within the period 1870–1900 should be supplemented by a look at the movement of total exports and of wheat exports given in table 2.12. Export ratios held up moderately well in the 1870s, but that was only because neither exports in total nor income grew through that decade; the complete absence of wheat exports and a decline in forest product export values were masked by a modest growth in some agricultural products exports—most notably barley to the United States, an item that disappeared in the early 1890s. Exports languished badly in the 1880s in the sense that they did not grow with the overall growth of the economy. They appear to have been an increasingly expansionary force in the 1890s, lead by a recovery in the export of wheat (from the pre-Confederation period), by growing exports of cheese and meats, and by some growth of exports of base and precious metals. The potentialities for wheat production on the prairies were clearly evident by 1900, when wheat production in the prairie region had reached 23 million bushels in a year (decennial census data) when yields were considerably below average. As a probably

**Table 2.12**    **Total Exports, Declared Values and at 1900 Prices and Net Exports of Wheat in Bushels, 1870–1915 (Values in Millions of Dollars, Wheat in Millons of Bushels)**

| Year | Declared Value | Value 1900 Prices | Wheat Exports (Net) | | Declared Value | Value 1900 Prices | Wheat Exports (Net) |
|---|---|---|---|---|---|---|---|
| 1870 | 66 | 74 | −1 | 1893 | 114 | 114 | 11 |
| 1871 | 67 | 72 | −3 | 1894 | 116 | 115 | 11 |
| 1872 | 79 | 82 | −1 | 1895 | 109 | 113 | 9 |
| 1873 | 86 | 87 | −1 | 1896 | 116 | 124 | 10 |
| 1874 | 87 | 86 | −1 | 1897 | 134 | 148 | 10 |
| 1875 | 77 | 73 | −2 | 1898 | 159 | 165 | 24 |
| 1876 | 80 | 73 | — | 1899 | 155 | 162 | 14 |
| 1877 | 75 | 77 | −4 | 1900 | 183 | 183 | 20 |
| 1878 | 79 | 78 | −1 | 1901 | 195 | 190 | 15 |
| 1879 | 71 | 77 | 4 | 1902 | 210 | 201 | 31 |
| 1880 | 86 | 92 | 7 | 1903 | 225 | 209 | 39 |
| 1881 | 97 | 100 | 4 | 1904 | 211 | 194 | 24 |
| 1882 | 102 | 95 | 5 | 1905 | 201 | 191 | 20 |
| 1883 | 97 | 89 | 7 | 1906 | 247 | 218 | 47 |
| 1884 | 89 | 85 | −1 | 1907 | 245 | 207 | 47 |
| 1885 | 87 | 88 | — | 1908 | 263 | 212 | 47 |
| 1886 | 85 | 89 | 4 | 1909 | 260 | 210 | 57 |
| 1887 | 90 | 93 | 7 | 1910 | 299 | 239 | 68 |
| 1888 | 90 | 89 | 3 | 1911 | 290 | 235 | 62 |
| 1889 | 87 | 86 | — | 1912 | 307 | 255 | 97 |
| 1890 | 94 | 91 | — | 1913 | 377 | 308 | 115 |
| 1891 | 98 | 94 | 3 | 1914 | 455 | 389 | 135 |
| 1892 | 113 | 109 | 10 | 1915 | 461 | 377 | 85 |

*Source: Historical Statistics of Canada, 1st ed., pp. 175, 363–64.*

fairly minor point we should note that the building of the intercolonial railway, especially in 1874–75, and the building of the Canadian Pacific Railway in 1881–84 were isolated exogenous events, undertaken respectively by government and by a private corporation with very heavy government subsidization, that undoubtedly tended to increase GNP in those years in cyclical fashion: they increased the denominator of the export ratio accordingly.

We come now to the 1900–1914 period. As can be seen from table 2.12, the value of exports increased two and one-half–fold between the year ending June 30, 1900 and that ending March 31, 1915 (fourfold from 1896 to 1915) and the great expansion of wheat exports was yet to come. Yet from 1900 to 1913 the ratio of exports to GNP in this great period of growth was at about the levels of the 1870s and 1880s. The explanation of the apparent conundrum has been given already. The settlement and growing cultivation of new lands based initially on expectations of future production and sale of wheat led to an enormous increase in capital formation that, along with a very rapid expansion of the population and labor force (see tables 2.5, 2.6, 2.7, and 2.9), led to a great increase in GNP even before the major increase in production of the wheat staple. The matter cannot be better put than in the words of Mackintosh that have been already quoted. At this stage of development the great source of expansion was the prospective production of great quantities of wheat even though the actual production in large quantity did not come until later.

One other matter deserves attention. As already noted, in 1900 the high-productivity export sector was relatively no larger than in the pre-1896 period. Yet it was a period of very high growth of aggregate GNP as well as GNP per capita. Clearly the capital formation sector, which is the major direct stimulus to growth, must have been a sector of reasonably high productivity. The expectations of purchasers of capital goods were sufficiently sanguine that they were prepared to pay good prices for structures and equipment.

The two remaining ratios of table 2.11 may be dealt with summarily. First, the ratio of government expenditure on goods and services to GNP shows that aside from the years of war and its immediate aftermath government purchases of goods and services for the ordinary functions of government were relatively small. The smallness of these figures may not reflect the government role well since governments did guarantee railway bonds in large quantity as well as build some line in the 1900–15 period in addition to the earlier participation which we have noted already. Governments also ran some market-oriented operations, including the Canadian National Railway after the bankruptcy of its constituent lines during the war. But it remains true that the government role was much less in 1900–1915 than in many other countries in their periods of rapid growth. Second, the terms of trade moved in Canada's favor in two significant periods. The improvement from the early 1870s to the mid-1890s was quite substantial and would play some part in contributing to the favorable conjunctures of the late 1890s. The other period of improvement from 1900 to 1915 would play some role in the expansion of that time, especially in its effects on the expectations that underlay the capital formation performance.

One final point about the aggregates must be made. In general, such stimulus to the economy as there has been from the export trade has not come because exports of goods and services exceeded imports of goods and services. In general, until the First World War, not only did current account receipts, on international account, fall quite substantially below current account expenditures, but in most years merchandise exports fell short of merchandise imports; only the years 1894–98 showed merchandise trade surpluses (usually very small). In most of these years net capital inflows were large. With the First World War and in the 1920s the international current account came roughly into balance and net capital inflows more or less disappeared. This last change was a significant development in the Canadian economy, but it nevertheless still remained true that Canada's international transactions did not directly increase the aggregate demand for Canadian goods and services.

I turn briefly now to the inferences one may draw from these data about the differences between the traditionalists and the revisionists. At the outset I wish to make it clear that I am not working with a model specified in a way that makes possible the shaping and application of specific tests. Rather, I just try to see in more general fashion whether the developments of the economy appear to be consistent with what the traditionalists specify or imply would occur according to their hypothesis or whether they fit better with the view of the revisionists or both. This procedure is not rigorous, but it is all that can be done now. I make just three points.

First, I would find it very difficult, in the light of our data, not to conclude that the staple, wheat, played the role assigned to it by the traditionalists in the extensive growth (aggregate growth) of the Canadian economy from the late 1890s onward. It is true that in the years 1870–1895 the relatively low growth of population and aggregate real GNP took place in a world setting that was not buoyant, and 1895 or there abouts is regarded as a low point of world growth. Nevertheless, in these years the United States maintained population growth rates much above those of Canada, and growth rates of aggregate real GNP considerably higher than Canada's (see table 2.11). This was the time when Canada's wheat exports, the major export of the 1850s, had disappeared and exports of forest products were faltering. In the period from the opening and growth of the wheat economy from the 1890s onward, Canadian population growth rates exceeded those of the United States from 1900 to 1920 and matched the United States rate from 1920 to 1926; and extensive growth of GNP in Canada exceeded that in the United States from 1900 to 1910 and again from 1920 to 1926. That a major part of the growth was associated with the settlement of the prairies, and definitely based on the objectives of growing wheat, is clear. The stimulus came first through the enormous induced investment of the 1900–1915 years and then in the 1920s with the export flow of wheat and the concomitant realization of the gains of international specialization. (I omit mention of the development of newsprint and woodpulp production and export rather late in our period, and of base metal production and export somewhat earlier, which were important but played subordinate roles to wheat.) Even given the upturn in world economic activity from 1895 onward, I find it very difficult to see how balanced aggregate growth in the Canadian economy could have been induced at close to the rate of the unbalanced expansion of the post-1900 period, especially when the role of the induced investment is considered.

Second, with regard to the growth of per capita product, the revisionists have a point. There was considerable growth in GNP per capita from 1870 to 1900 even with the relatively slow aggregate growth. As to whether or not the rate of growth of product per capita increased with the expansion of the wheat boom, the picture is not entirely clear. That the intrusion of the war had adverse effects on productivity is clear, but what effect it had on cumulative productivity from 1900 to 1926 is not evident. The fact that there seems to be an acceleration in per capita product from 1896 onward (table 2.9) after a flat performance from 1890 to 1896 leads one to believe that part of the 1896–1900 per capita growth may be cyclical recovery and part true long-term growth. That there were indeed the beginnings of the influence of western growth at this time will be seen from the fact that there were already about 420,000 persons in the three prairie provinces at the 1901 census. In these circumstances it may be best to compare per capita growth from 1890 to 1910 with that from 1871 to 1890. Such a comparison (table 2.10) shows clearly that the per capita growth rate by the 1890–1910 period substantially exceeds that for 1871–90. The same comparison for productivity per worker also shows a much higher per worker productivity growth rate in the 1891–1911 period (2.3%) than in the 1871–91 period (1.1%). This increase in the rate of growth of productivity in the staple period cannot necessarily be attributed to the development of the wheat staple, but, at the same time, it does not contradict the view that such could be the case—in other words, that the wheat staple led to intensive as well as extensive growth.

Third, the higher saving rates after 1900 than before should make possible higher rates of growth of GNP. Our data are not adequate to explain why savings rates increased, but whatever the cause it must be associated with developments after 1900.

## 2.2   Changes in the Structure of GDP

I turn now to see what easy inferences, if any, emerge from the nature of changes in the relative contributions of various industrial groups during the country's development. The industrial distribution of GDP at factor cost in percentage form is given in table 2.13. But before examining its implications I should mention one or two of the idiosyncrasies of the industrial distribution.

Among these idiosyncrasies, the most important one relates to the manufacturing and the trade sectors. In the early part of the period covered here, many of the trading functions were carried out in the

Table 2.13     **Percentage Distribution of Gross Domestic Product at Factor Cost, Average of 3 Years Centered on Census Years and of 1925, 1926**

|  | 1870 | 1880 | 1890 | 1900 | 1910 | 1920 | 1926 |
|---|---|---|---|---|---|---|---|
| Agriculture | 37.1 | 36.2 | 27.8 | 24.8 | 21.6 | 20.9 | 20.0 |
| Forestry, hunting, trapping & fishing | 2.7 | 3.0 | 3.1 | 3.0 | 2.1 | 2.0 | 1.6 |
| Mining | 1.3 | 1.1 | 1.9 | 5.0 | 2.9 | 3.0 | 3.0 |
| Manufacturing | 22.4 | 21.9 | 25.3 | 22.2 | 22.5 | 25.1 | 21.1 |
| Manufactured gas | 0.1 | 0.2 | 0.3 | 0.1 | 0.1 | 0.2 | 0.2 |
| Construction | 5.7 | 4.2 | 4.8 | 3.9 | 7.8 | 4.0 | 4.2 |
| Transportation | 5.5 | 5.2 | 5.9 | 6.9 | 7.8 | 8.5 | 8.1 |
| Electric light & power |  |  | 0.1 | 0.2 | 0.6 | 0.9 | 1.3 |
| Communications |  |  | 0.1 | 0.2 | 0.5 | 0.8 | 0.9 |
| Banking & finance | 2.1 | 2.2 | 2.9 | 4.3 | 4.1 | 4.6 | 4.1 |
| Residential rents | 5.9 | 5.8 | 5.7 | 6.8 | 6.7 | 6.7 | 7.5 |
| Federal government services | 1.3 | 1.7 | 1.8 | 1.8 | 1.6 | 3.0 | 1.9 |
| Provincial government services | 0.5 | 0.6 | 0.6 | 0.6 | 0.8 | 0.9 | 1.1 |
| Municipal services | 0.9 | 1.2 | 1.3 | 1.3 | 1.4 | 1.6 | 1.6 |
| Education | 1.0 | 1.4 | 1.2 | 1.2 | 1.1 | 1.6 | 1.9 |
| Wholesale & retail trade | 5.9 | 7.0 | 7.5 | 7.5 | 10.4 | 9.3 | 10.8 |
| Community, business and personal service | 7.4 | 8.1 | 9.6 | 9.6 | 7.6 | 6.4 | 10.3 |
| Public resource royalties | 0.3 | 0.3 | 0.5 | 0.5 | 0.4 | 0.3 | 0.4 |

*Source:* Calculated from the data in table 2.1.

*Note:* The percentages for wholesale and retail trade and for community, business, and personal service are taken from data for the single years given in the heading, and consequently the sums of the percentages vary slightly from 100.

so-called manufacturing establishments. Tailors, dressmakers, hatters, shoemakers, blacksmiths, and gristmillers, to mention only a few cases, dealt directly with the consumers and hence performed, in part, a function that was later performed by specialized merchants. Hence, in a sense, the income produced in the manufacturing function tends to be overstated and income generated in trade function tends to be understated in the early period. There was the added feature that some activities, such as blacksmithing, which had a large genuine manufacturing component in the earlier period, changed to producing mainly a service function. An attempt was made to retain the manufacturing component of these types of activity in the manufacturing sector.

Given these limitations—and of course, there are many others—what does the change in the industrial distribution show? The most dramatic point, in my view, is the fact that, in a time that is regarded as a great period of industrialization in Canada, from 1900 to the 1920s, agriculture's share in GDP fell so little; and such a fall as there was appears to have taken place largely between 1900 and 1910. There can be no doubt about where the growth in agricultural income occurred. Table 2.14 presents the components of agricultural gross revenue in this period. It was the emergence of wheat that explains the maintenance of agriculture as a principal income earner: the share of wheat in gross farm revenue (table 2.14) rose from less than 13% in the 3-year average centered on 1900 to more than 33% in the 3 years centered on 1925. To complete the agricultural income information, table 2.15 gives agricultural expenses and table 2.16 gives income of farmers.

The fact that the share of manufacturing did not increase more than it did is hard to interpret. In fact, the rise was much greater than apparent because much of the trading function did become separate, the evidence of the separation appearing in the growth of the share of income generated in trade. Further, just the maintenance of a constant share of income produced would represent a high rate of growth. But Canada did remain a substantial net importer of manufactured products, which explains, in part, why manufacturing's share of output did not grow more.

Tables 2.17 and 2.18, showing the distribution of manufacturing domestic product among groups, reflect some of the changes that took place in the structure of manufacturing. Unfortunately at the level of detail in tables 2.17 and 2.18 the more significant changes that took place in manufacturing do not always show up. Some things are evident, however: the declines of the leather products industry and the wood products industry (lumber, furniture, etc.) are very clear; similarly, the growth of the paper products industry (newsprint and woodpulp), the nonferrous metals products industry, the chemical industry, and the printing and publishing industry is equally evident. However, the changes

**Table 2.14    Farm Revenue from Off-Farm Sales and Farm Consumption (Thousands of Dollars)**

| | 1870 | 1871 | 1872 | 1873 | 1874 | 1875 | 1876 | 1877 | 1878 | 1879 | 1880 |
|---|---|---|---|---|---|---|---|---|---|---|---|
| Wheat | 22160 | 23979 | 25601 | 25088 | 20283 | 23564 | 25696 | 24361 | 25533 | 37181 | 32244 |
| Oats | 3275 | 3215 | 3316 | 3521 | 4505 | 3680 | 3694 | 3638 | 2997 | 4993 | 4120 |
| Barley | 3688 | 3981 | 3546 | 5089 | 6608 | 9414 | 5234 | 4824 | 5219 | 5057 | 7946 |
| Rye | 174 | 185 | 201 | 209 | 257 | 171 | 97 | 269 | 380 | 714 | 806 |
| Hay | 3125 | 3918 | 3463 | 3059 | 2859 | 2897 | 2649 | 2868 | 2774 | 2771 | 5178 |
| Vegetables | 8558 | 11047 | 9597 | 8185 | 10705 | 7648 | 8553 | 10685 | 10566 | 11466 | 6586 |
| Potatoes | 7463 | 10009 | 6704 | 5885 | 8507 | 5956 | 6717 | 8363 | 11652 | 10720 | 4684 |
| Hops | 149 | 539 | 348 | 246 | 365 | 245 | 354 | 224 | 206 | 576 | 239 |
| Flax seed | 161 | 209 | 253 | 47 | 129 | 101 | 85 | 125 | 58 | 60 | 75 |
| Tobacco | 63 | 72 | 81 | 69 | 88 | 86 | 77 | 71 | 74 | 82 | 91 |
| Flax fiber | 112 | 115 | 86 | 113 | 164 | 165 | 182 | 98 | 46 | 95 | 67 |
| Eggs | 4579 | 4835 | 5414 | 5560 | 5168 | 5475 | 5347 | 5307 | 4241 | 5327 | 5386 |
| Maple sugar & syrup | 1649 | 1709 | 1302 | 1673 | 1718 | 2324 | 1853 | 2101 | 2000 | 1345 | 1743 |
| Honey | 351 | 355 | 264 | 336 | 336 | 445 | 348 | 385 | 358 | 233 | 292 |
| Apples | 2480 | 2988 | 3607 | 3058 | 3452 | 2566 | 3073 | 3615 | 2301 | 3265 | 2883 |
| Small fruit | 1730 | 2064 | 2538 | 2131 | 2468 | 1881 | 2229 | 2583 | 1630 | 2334 | 1860 |
| Grapes | 102 | 109 | 131 | 168 | 239 | 236 | 209 | 208 | 233 | 311 | 362 |
| Orchard fruit | 241 | 317 | 426 | 397 | 481 | 378 | 505 | 615 | 423 | 589 | 776 |
| Cattle & calves | 32561 | 28751 | 29935 | 30233 | 24586 | 21866 | 21084 | 23332 | 22478 | 22324 | 23983 |
| Hogs | 16153 | 11429 | 11542 | 11211 | 13614 | 15120 | 13752 | 11245 | 8531 | 9912 | 11027 |
| Sheep & lambs | 4202 | 4642 | 4728 | 4177 | 3853 | 4821 | 3903 | 4078 | 4475 | 5439 | 5676 |
| Poultry | 1383 | 1540 | 1686 | 1787 | 1501 | 1700 | 1716 | 1622 | 1289 | 1682 | 1805 |
| Cheese | 2271 | 2663 | 3126 | 4638 | 4610 | 4304 | 4261 | 4514 | 3932 | 4278 | 6008 |
| Butter | 12853 | 14325 | 13117 | 15275 | 20899 | 17439 | 18500 | 18922 | 14208 | 16574 | 21578 |
| Fluid milk | 8700 | 8912 | 7988 | 9366 | 13196 | 11031 | 10006 | 10208 | 7811 | 9315 | 10892 |
| Horses | 2586 | 2567 | 2371 | 2194 | 2087 | 2024 | 2115 | 2375 | 2336 | 2810 | 3094 |
| Seed, grass & clover | 351 | −15 | −193 | −216 | −119 | 177 | 88 | −56 | −29 | 563 | 79 |
| Wool | 2272 | 3098 | 2814 | 2220 | 1985 | 2197 | 2214 | 2027 | 1919 | 2424 | 2248 |
| Forest products | 16402 | 17621 | 20492 | 21896 | 20122 | 16773 | 15583 | 15873 | 15559 | 15941 | 17749 |
| Grand total | 159808 | 165192 | 164498 | 167615 | 174676 | 164695 | 160138 | 164492 | 153214 | 178394 | 179489 |

| | 1881 | 1882 | 1883 | 1884 | 1885 | 1886 | 1887 | 1888 | 1889 | 1890 | 1891 |
|---|---|---|---|---|---|---|---|---|---|---|---|
| Wheat | 38437 | 33381 | 26223 | 21291 | 24088 | 26430 | 23340 | 26429 | 25484 | 26658 | 33720 |
| Oats | 5874 | 4586 | 4279 | 4034 | 4911 | 4188 | 4203 | 4529 | 3895 | 5053 | 6316 |
| Barley | 11379 | 7183 | 5819 | 5629 | 5659 | 5558 | 6562 | 7158 | 5089 | 3373 | 3272 |
| Rye | 1314 | 772 | 680 | 292 | 216 | 203 | 79 | 113 | 346 | 313 | 275 |
| Hay | 4143 | 4035 | 3715 | 4469 | 4481 | 4169 | 4922 | 6472 | 4707 | 3667 | 5157 |
| Vegetables | 13413 | 13252 | 14682 | 9619 | 10532 | 10085 | 13116 | 8614 | 12825 | 13094 | 9749 |
| Potatoes | 13981 | 11261 | 11715 | 6848 | 9900 | 8845 | 14014 | 6783 | 11021 | 10703 | 7669 |
| Hops | 347 | 890 | 313 | 262 | 195 | 56 | 171 | 270 | 64 | 374 | 186 |
| Flax seed | 103 | 100 | 109 | 195 | 105 | 96 | 145 | 91 | 130 | 115 | 92 |
| Tobacco | 113 | 132 | 149 | 164 | 159 | 164 | 172 | 212 | 192 | 231 | 232 |
| Flax fiber | 85 | 108 | 73 | 59 | 49 | 78 | 80 | 121 | 175 | 181 | 112 |
| Eggs | 6906 | 7927 | 9347 | 9231 | 8653 | 7496 | 8022 | 8490 | 8278 | 8501 | 8090 |
| Maple sugar & syrup | 1581 | 1557 | 1409 | 1918 | 1629 | 1691 | 2184 | 1599 | 1744 | 1798 | 1678 |
| Honey | 290 | 312 | 302 | 447 | 403 | 441 | 601 | 459 | 527 | 565 | 409 |
| Apples | 3742 | 4320 | 4311 | 3803 | 3230 | 3529 | 3485 | 3805 | 4283 | 5129 | 4114 |
| Small fruit | 2235 | 1907 | 1921 | 1766 | 1791 | 2180 | 1804 | 1018 | 1251 | 1878 | 1901 |
| Grapes | 506 | 573 | 486 | 651 | 791 | 721 | 760 | 825 | 1027 | 453 | 511 |
| Orchard fruit | 1325 | 1676 | 1578 | 1862 | 2380 | 1495 | 1903 | 1232 | 1806 | 3053 | 1343 |
| Cattle & calves | 20998 | 38135 | 34953 | 34307 | 28400 | 22828 | 25207 | 25595 | 24593 | 30443 | 31243 |
| Hogs | 15449 | 15579 | 12854 | 12026 | 11235 | 11748 | 13667 | 14427 | 14328 | 12779 | 8929 |
| Sheep & lambs | 8308 | 6312 | 7718 | 4617 | 4052 | 4146 | 4846 | 5313 | 6407 | 5423 | 5463 |
| Poultry | 2169 | 2784 | 2980 | 2836 | 2955 | 1850 | 2066 | 2526 | 2748 | 2472 | 2038 |
| Cheese | 5925 | 6822 | 7382 | 8279 | 6506 | 7154 | 8916 | 8814 | 9099 | 9032 | 11142 |
| Butter | 21722 | 22139 | 21274 | 19778 | 17393 | 18410 | 20291 | 20109 | 18462 | 22257 | 26530 |
| Fluid milk | 11141 | 12757 | 11553 | 11773 | 10480 | 10643 | 12360 | 12574 | 12787 | 14623 | 16528 |
| Horses | 4742 | 5437 | -2010 | 6209 | 4572 | 4162 | 6528 | 6592 | 9154 | 5634 | 5064 |
| Seed, grass & clover | 693 | 7 | -182 | -133 | -219 | -251 | -219 | -510 | -237 | 56 | 95 |
| Wool | 2137 | 2681 | 2361 | 2007 | 1563 | 1366 | 1374 | 1282 | 1631 | 1785 | 1709 |
| Forest products | 19840 | 21439 | 21553 | 20534 | 19627 | 19937 | 18621 | 19715 | 20583 | 21046 | 21275 |
| Grand total | 218911 | 228077 | 207548 | 194786 | 185749 | 179431 | 199230 | 194670 | 202411 | 210702 | 214854 |

(continued)

Table 2.14 (continued)

| | 1892 | 1893 | 1894 | 1895 | 1896 | 1897 | 1898 | 1899 | 1900 | 1901 | 1902 |
|---|---|---|---|---|---|---|---|---|---|---|---|
| Wheat | 26427 | 20725 | 18746 | 29715 | 22876 | 35754 | 26269 | 30505 | 28160 | 37127 | 45252 |
| Oats | 6450 | 5087 | 4076 | 3771 | 4170 | 5516 | 6168 | 5717 | 5912 | 7534 | 7213 |
| Barley | 1498 | 806 | 1218 | 884 | 1000 | 496 | 754 | 1544 | 1650 | 1206 | 1227 |
| Rye | 142 | 87 | 108 | 106 | 129 | 498 | 223 | 321 | 402 | 298 | 346 |
| Hay | 4771 | 5639 | 4617 | 6922 | 4941 | 3740 | 3122 | 4788 | 5820 | 7929 | 7552 |
| Vegetables | 10948 | 12962 | 10868 | 8360 | 7559 | 13058 | 12275 | 12089 | 8428 | 13834 | 15519 |
| Potatoes | 8845 | 9656 | 9270 | 4095 | 6044 | 9562 | 9982 | 8748 | 5051 | 9879 | 13284 |
| Hops | 365 | 358 | 143 | 165 | 145 | 211 | 181 | 112 | 180 | 157 | 288 |
| Flax seed | 95 | 83 | 390 | 784 | 229 | 220 | 340 | 345 | 197 | 238 | 530 |
| Tobacco | 270 | 288 | 281 | 362 | 382 | 606 | 542 | 719 | 754 | 809 | 852 |
| Flax fiber | 124 | 268 | 151 | 128 | 304 | 38 | 75 | 196 | 235 | 143 | 175 |
| Eggs | 7199 | 8294 | 7291 | 7408 | 7465 | 6912 | 8218 | 9819 | 9848 | 9337 | 10550 |
| Maple sugar & syrup | 1692 | 1604 | 1497 | 1350 | 1511 | 1014 | 1352 | 2433 | 1427 | 1747 | 1761 |
| Honey | 398 | 371 | 369 | 362 | 390 | 303 | 301 | 364 | 356 | 411 | 401 |
| Apples | 5678 | 5183 | 4886 | 4868 | 4379 | 5854 | 6578 | 6606 | 5058 | 6271 | 7505 |
| Small fruit | 2114 | 1533 | 1542 | 1776 | 1357 | 1578 | 1367 | 1376 | 1408 | 1837 | 1627 |
| Grapes | 395 | 634 | 546 | 731 | 720 | 827 | 569 | 600 | 1166 | 1182 | 1249 |
| Orchard fruit | 2148 | 1267 | 1320 | 697 | 925 | 1181 | 1005 | 1050 | 1805 | 1102 | 1034 |
| Cattle & calves | 30504 | 30486 | 24976 | 24047 | 23279 | 28718 | 32192 | 34578 | 36732 | 42722 | 51781 |
| Hogs | 14582 | 10285 | 19457 | 13577 | 13754 | 15949 | 19685 | 17835 | 17993 | 26944 | 32380 |
| Sheep & lambs | 8095 | 6468 | 6376 | 7516 | 4434 | 3559 | 4980 | 5331 | 5718 | 6037 | 5852 |
| Poultry | 1897 | 2438 | 2184 | 2357 | 2697 | 2354 | 2399 | 3103 | 3379 | 3622 | 3615 |
| Cheese | 12621 | 14444 | 13346 | 12576 | 13268 | 15699 | 14976 | 18528 | 19250 | 17994 | 22812 |
| Butter | 27177 | 27778 | 25562 | 23327 | 23511 | 23613 | 26187 | 23379 | 29586 | 31209 | 33531 |
| Fluid milk | 16797 | 17061 | 17326 | 15831 | 14288 | 14505 | 16580 | 16867 | 19083 | 17450 | 17899 |
| Horses | 2746 | 316 | -1035 | 30 | 1249 | 985 | 1552 | 4460 | 6563 | 6464 | 10041 |
| Seed, grass & clover | -233 | 145 | 325 | -254 | -237 | -87 | 304 | -232 | 14 | 785 | 359 |
| Wool | 1690 | 1719 | 1655 | 1375 | 1445 | 1490 | 1432 | 2057 | 1609 | 1382 | 1534 |
| Forest products | 20978 | 21012 | 20147 | 20350 | 21065 | 21164 | 20700 | 20952 | 21604 | 22686 | 24128 |
| Grand total | 216425 | 207007 | 197652 | 193229 | 183291 | 215330 | 220320 | 234201 | 239375 | 278350 | 320310 |

| | 1903 | 1904 | 1905 | 1906 | 1907 | 1908 | 1909 | 1910 | 1911 | 1912 | 1913 |
|---|---|---|---|---|---|---|---|---|---|---|---|
| Wheat | 39026 | 49105 | 56401 | 53547 | 70128 | 76691 | 119799 | 84584 | 124116 | 120913 | 137734 |
| Oats | 6428 | 6268 | 6811 | 7925 | 13131 | 8604 | 7626 | 8942 | 10272 | 9643 | 16716 |
| Barley | 1297 | 1423 | 1363 | 1420 | 2475 | 2523 | 2025 | 1939 | 3282 | 5564 | 6417 |
| Rye | 195 | 211 | 188 | 103 | 207 | 291 | 247 | 195 | 139 | 117 | 216 |
| Hay | 5958 | 5506 | 5754 | 6388 | 9276 | 7434 | 9709 | 8974 | 17573 | 12712 | 11273 |
| Vegetables | 19796 | 15743 | 18312 | 17134 | 20931 | 16707 | 15191 | 19918 | 21107 | 17512 | 21538 |
| Potatoes | 19882 | 14077 | 14467 | 15138 | 19278 | 16796 | 13411 | 18041 | 22108 | 16883 | 20152 |
| Hops | 271 | 304 | 157 | 227 | 132 | 112 | 311 | 290 | 519 | 374 | 348 |
| Flax seed | 400 | 462 | 599 | 968 | 1867 | 1415 | 2941 | 8472 | 25788 | 24846 | 15708 |
| Tobacco | 975 | 953 | 1054 | 1221 | 1352 | 1406 | 1597 | 1569 | 1242 | 669 | 1450 |
| Flax fiber | 271 | 410 | 244 | 73 | 163 | 120 | 84 | 125 | 72 | 24 | 46 |
| Eggs | 10275 | 13753 | 12720 | 15690 | 18132 | 17807 | 21702 | 22310 | 27128 | 26984 | 32387 |
| Maple sugar & syrup | 1922 | 1807 | 1864 | 2926 | 2374 | 2232 | 2211 | 2514 | 2594 | 2598 | 2471 |
| Honey | 370 | 361 | 383 | 567 | 652 | 699 | 769 | 713 | 729 | 790 | 760 |
| Apples | 9057 | 7003 | 9599 | 7281 | 10053 | 7677 | 9734 | 7840 | 10291 | 9515 | 11200 |
| Small fruit | 1703 | 1498 | 2027 | 2179 | 2634 | 2196 | 1975 | 2467 | 2840 | 1809 | 2108 |
| Grapes | 1182 | 887 | 1344 | 1384 | 1212 | 1215 | 1153 | 1217 | 823 | 857 | 1056 |
| Orchard fruit | 1418 | 1350 | 1248 | 1674 | 2739 | 1355 | 1984 | 1824 | 1786 | 709 | 1125 |
| Cattle & calves | 46816 | 47304 | 48633 | 41582 | 41686 | 36809 | 44997 | 55761 | 63530 | 68968 | 74552 |
| Hogs | 30739 | 30744 | 30439 | 37426 | 30109 | 30643 | 38803 | 47606 | 46275 | 48438 | 59899 |
| Sheep & lambs | 4971 | 3593 | 4623 | 4129 | 5686 | 5102 | 4953 | 5218 | 6122 | 7412 | 6524 |
| Poultry | 3465 | 3621 | 3921 | 6979 | 4670 | 5633 | 6757 | 9016 | 9437 | 10978 | 11189 |
| Cheese | 22056 | 18399 | 22880 | 26525 | 22085 | 20078 | 20860 | 19997 | 20809 | 20755 | 19240 |
| Butter | 33063 | 33274 | 40906 | 40195 | 42766 | 48186 | 46825 | 50725 | 40670 | 50565 | 46763 |
| Fluid milk | 18461 | 19089 | 21907 | 22315 | 25881 | 29256 | 27601 | 25855 | 24005 | 30073 | 28238 |
| Horses | -1894 | 14878 | 10353 | 17954 | 20070 | 12570 | 23560 | 21107 | 15391 | 22764 | 29316 |
| Seed, grass & clover | 971 | 51 | 1011 | -129 | -208 | -674 | -203 | 564 | -14 | -714 | -392 |
| Wool | 1636 | 1730 | 1961 | 1727 | 1748 | 1413 | 1506 | 1615 | 1472 | 1548 | 1945 |
| Forest products | 25014 | 24848 | 25612 | 30275 | 34076 | 30792 | 31765 | 33437 | 37969 | 38051 | 37549 |
| Grand total | 305738 | 318666 | 346796 | 364836 | 405315 | 385101 | 459897 | 462846 | 538087 | 551367 | 597540 |

(continued)

**Table 2.14** (continued)

| | 1914 | 1915 | 1916 | 1917 | 1918 | 1919 | 1920 |
|---|---|---|---|---|---|---|---|
| Wheat | 127468 | 298784 | 280766 | 376802 | 275169 | 291538 | 383267 |
| Oats | 16149 | 25515 | 48549 | 38384 | 22295 | 31325 | 23152 |
| Barley | 3635 | 5581 | 8195 | 9022 | 9993 | 15861 | 10976 |
| Rye | 364 | 597 | 1491 | 1690 | 402 | 3360 | 4476 |
| Hay | 13406 | 15144 | 11470 | 12617 | 20465 | 19709 | 22493 |
| Vegetables | 18463 | 26474 | 32053 | 37444 | 41046 | 39899 | 46290 |
| Potatoes | 19648 | 24458 | 34254 | 44187 | 42556 | 46110 | 46676 |
| Hops | 214 | 170 | 216 | 80 | 81 | 206 | 455 |
| Flax seed | 6552 | 8472 | 17940 | 15261 | 16478 | 20175 | 14059 |
| Tobacco | 1020 | 801 | 677 | 1265 | 2476 | 7564 | 12599 |
| Flax fiber | 34 | 86 | 277 | 370 | 827 | 1439 | 1298 |
| Eggs | 32346 | 31285 | 46955 | 53764 | 61108 | 69557 | 72514 |
| Maple sugar & syrup | 2678 | 3062 | 3263 | 4608 | 7261 | 8828 | 9376 |
| Honey | 657 | 788 | 831 | 984 | 1535 | 1492 | 1633 |
| Apples | 7709 | 8328 | 9073 | 8883 | 13476 | 15858 | 15016 |
| Small fruit | 2255 | 2126 | 2010 | 2521 | 3782 | 6105 | 6957 |
| Grapes | 958 | 959 | 1059 | 1359 | 1029 | 1761 | 2328 |
| Orchard fruit | 1045 | 701 | 1368 | 1461 | 2477 | 1890 | 4130 |
| Cattle & calves | 86110 | 93108 | 106691 | 124018 | 134806 | 106956 | 124546 |
| Hogs | 56676 | 52962 | 65234 | 73320 | 103446 | 111234 | 83357 |
| Sheep & lambs | 7230 | 7455 | 9960 | 15655 | 17739 | 16613 | 8957 |
| Poultry | 10879 | 10794 | 11552 | 14415 | 21309 | 19043 | 20389 |
| Cheese | 20010 | 26296 | 36278 | 39176 | 37774 | 45267 | 39240 |
| Butter | 45154 | 51320 | 57336 | 71057 | 82494 | 98805 | 108841 |
| Fluid milk | 29152 | 32482 | 38484 | 38768 | 54265 | 61501 | 72811 |
| Horses | 22823 | 13799 | 11932 | 22410 | 16859 | −3155 | 20003 |
| Seed, grass & clover | −1898 | −2121 | −500 | −422 | 1649 | 740 | −447 |
| Wool | 2136 | 2967 | 3363 | 4435 | 5316 | 6755 | 6213 |
| Forest products | 41147 | 40888 | 38739 | 49884 | 63452 | 61666 | 67047 |
| Grand total | 574030 | 783293 | 879529 | 1063431 | 1061579 | 1108113 | 1228662 |

| | 1921 | 1922 | 1923 | 1924 | 1925 | 1926 |
|---|---|---|---|---|---|---|
| Wheat | 227439 | 307491 | 307525 | 291319 | 413771 | 386002 |
| Oats | 15746 | 16547 | 18653 | 26143 | 20062 | 11532 |
| Barley | 6323 | 7163 | 7312 | 21507 | 19085 | 21182 |
| Rye | 2445 | 5994 | 3467 | 7812 | 4326 | 5318 |
| Hay | 16783 | 9622 | 10942 | 9676 | 10526 | 11428 |
| Vegetables | 37283 | 29474 | 32067 | 36249 | 51206 | 41708 |
| Potatoes | 36803 | 25648 | 29578 | 25190 | 66623 | 49421 |
| Hops | 311 | 142 | 329 | 235 | 279 | 318 |
| Flax seed | 4506 | 8461 | 12174 | 19817 | 10542 | 8845 |
| Tobacco | 2252 | 4177 | 3833 | 3255 | 4924 | 4265 |
| Flax fiber | 167 | 331 | 185 | 400 | 109 | 28 |
| Eggs | 61342 | 56727 | 58052 | 57566 | 50484 | 67757 |
| Maple sugar & syrup | 4397 | 4188 | 5957 | 5991 | 5287 | 4896 |
| Honey | 1345 | 1068 | 1174 | 1510 | 1756 | 2164 |
| Apples | 35821 | 24692 | 24489 | 19747 | 20057 | 9688 |
| Small fruit | 3235 | 3114 | 3051 | 2566 | 2385 | 2581 |
| Grapes | 2812 | 3515 | 2742 | 1470 | 1750 | 720 |
| Orchard fruit | 3394 | 2577 | 2886 | 1718 | 1463 | 2234 |
| Cattle & calves | 45920 | 52198 | 61843 | 58488 | 75247 | 80375 |
| Hogs | 63057 | 82013 | 75916 | 73068 | 109471 | 113929 |
| Sheep & lambs | 8596 | 6276 | 8059 | 11315 | 9895 | 8592 |
| Poultry | 23964 | 23131 | 26312 | 28848 | 31013 | 32695 |
| Cheese | 28186 | 22682 | 28202 | 26199 | 37553 | 28851 |
| Butter | 91342 | 79029 | 89690 | 91446 | 93368 | 98144 |
| Fluid milk | 57158 | 47961 | 54343 | 52020 | 54921 | 59116 |
| Horses | 4879 | -3297 | 3738 | -1868 | 1623 | -4369 |
| Seed, grass & clover | -311 | -223 | 772 | 1009 | 1862 | 2084 |
| Wool | 2853 | 3017 | 3304 | 4274 | 4042 | 3648 |
| Forest products | 51408 | 50965 | 57421 | 60385 | 57698 | 54882 |
| Grand total | 839462 | 874694 | 934029 | 937367 | 1161345 | 1108046 |

**Table 2.15    Farm Expenses of Production (Thousands of Dollars)**

| | 1870 | 1871 | 1872 | 1873 | 1874 | 1875 | 1876 | 1877 | 1878 | 1879 | 1880 | 1881 |
|---|---|---|---|---|---|---|---|---|---|---|---|---|
| Repairs to farm buildings | 2965 | 3054 | 3047 | 3084 | 3258 | 3115 | 3006 | 3108 | 2880 | 3428 | 3401 | 3526 |
| Repairs to machinery & equipment | 1402 | 1444 | 1441 | 1458 | 1540 | 1473 | 1422 | 1470 | 1362 | 1621 | 1608 | 1993 |
| Tractor expenses | | | | | | | | | | | | |
| Fertilizer expense | | | | 22 | 14 | 22 | 29 | 24 | 24 | 3 | 2 | 4 |
| Truck & auto expense | | | | | | | | | | | | |
| Mill feeds | 1720 | 5176 | 2264 | 7984 | 4302 | 2652 | 5651 | 4234 | 3856 | 2844 | 2971 | 2640 |
| Binder twine | | | | | | | | | | | | |
| Blacksmithing | 4313 | 4454 | 4596 | 4738 | 4879 | 5021 | 5163 | 5305 | 5446 | 5588 | 5730 | 5749 |
| Miscellaneous | 5609 | 5779 | 5767 | 5835 | 6163 | 5892 | 5691 | 5882 | 5451 | 6487 | 6435 | 7974 |
| Total operating expense | 16011 | 19911 | 17117 | 23125 | 20160 | 18179 | 20966 | 20026 | 19021 | 19973 | 20151 | 21890 |

| | 1882 | 1883 | 1884 | 1885 | 1886 | 1887 | 1888 | 1889 | 1890 | 1891 | 1892 | 1893 |
|---|---|---|---|---|---|---|---|---|---|---|---|---|
| Repairs to farm buildings | 3651 | 3862 | 4057 | 4153 | 4247 | 4372 | 4505 | 4598 | 4651 | 4731 | 4813 | 4886 |
| Repairs to machinery & equipment | 2076 | 1859 | 1734 | 1656 | 1600 | 1805 | 1750 | 1821 | 1901 | 1952 | 1959 | 1855 |
| Tractor expenses | | | | | | | | | | | | |
| Fertilizer expense | 5 | 4 | 6 | 5 | 8 | 14 | 16 | 13 | 37 | 43 | 61 | 38 |
| Truck & auto expense | | | | | | | | | | | | |
| Mill feeds | 3331 | 3589 | 2599 | 1978 | 2598 | 3141 | 3544 | 3853 | 3813 | 2875 | 3137 | 2897 |
| Binder twine | | 242 | 484 | 727 | 969 | 1212 | 1454 | 1697 | 1939 | 1779 | 2217 | 1195 |
| Blacksmithing | 5815 | 5466 | 5571 | 5565 | 5540 | 5646 | 5759 | 6019 | 6098 | 6550 | 6899 | 7122 |
| Miscellaneous | 8305 | 7437 | 6936 | 6626 | 6402 | 7221 | 7000 | 7286 | 7604 | 7811 | 7837 | 7421 |
| Total operating expense | 23185 | 22462 | 21390 | 20714 | 21368 | 23411 | 24032 | 25289 | 26046 | 25745 | 26926 | 25419 |

| | 1894 | 1895 | 1896 | 1897 | 1898 | 1899 | 1900 | 1901 | 1902 | 1903 | 1904 |
|---|---|---|---|---|---|---|---|---|---|---|---|
| Repairs to farm buildings | 4912 | 4951 | 4986 | 5061 | 5128 | 5229 | 5343 | 5962 | 6570 | 7190 | 7693 |
| Repairs to machinery & equipment | 1788 | 1729 | 1639 | 1916 | 1970 | 2121 | 2187 | 2576 | 2939 | 2773 | 2900 |
| Tractor expenses | | | | | | | | | | | |
| Fertilizer expense | 80 | 94 | 124 | 126 | 140 | 175 | 244 | 302 | 318 | 355 | 334 |
| Truck & auto expense | | | | | | | | | | | 17 |
| Mill feeds | 2622 | 3840 | 3010 | 4351 | 5580 | 5213 | 3453 | 2743 | 4597 | 4626 | 4494 |
| Binder twine | 1335 | 1213 | 2252 | 1413 | 2585 | 3971 | 2171 | 3486 | 4017 | 2856 | 2559 |
| Blacksmithing | 7201 | 7320 | 7567 | 7842 | 8176 | 8720 | 9394 | 9560 | 9994 | 9792 | 10280 |
| Miscellaneous | 7155 | 6919 | 6559 | 7666 | 7881 | 8487 | 8751 | 10304 | 11756 | 11093 | 11603 |
| Total operating expense | 25097 | 26070 | 26141 | 28379 | 31453 | 33921 | 31547 | 34936 | 40194 | 38690 | 39884 |

| | 1905 | 1906 | 1907 | 1908 | 1909 | 1910 | 1911 | 1912 | 1913 | 1914 | 1915 |
|---|---|---|---|---|---|---|---|---|---|---|---|
| Repairs to farm buildings | 8266 | 8917 | 9314 | 9907 | 10471 | 11123 | 11952 | 12531 | 12813 | 13209 | 13583 |
| Repairs to machinery & equipment | 3151 | 3248 | 3651 | 3530 | 4224 | 4218 | 4918 | 5059 | 5593 | 5322 | 7393 |
| Tractor expenses | | | | | | | | | | | |
| Fertilizer expense | 398 | 485 | 96 | 266 | 435 | 678 | 1452 | 3147 | 3704 | 3462 | 3922 |
| Truck & auto expense | 20 | 48 | 621 | 705 | 766 | 773 | 1023 | 1112 | 1092 | 2336 | 2197 |
| Mill feeds | 5297 | 6208 | 40 | 76 | 102 | 204 | 586 | 1224 | 1504 | 1785 | 2499 |
| Binder twine | 2655 | 2979 | 8880 | 7302 | 8764 | 9884 | 11442 | 11415 | 8780 | 12653 | 10741 |
| Blacksmithing | 10574 | 11166 | 1662 | 1487 | 3047 | 3660 | 3206 | 3233 | 6940 | 4896 | 7725 |
| Miscellaneous | 12604 | 12993 | 11763 | 12015 | 12630 | 13103 | 14175 | 15445 | 16922 | 18173 | 19016 |
| Total operating expense | 42968 | 46040 | 14607 | 14120 | 16899 | 16873 | 19674 | 20239 | 22373 | 21289 | 29574 |

*(continued)*

Table 2.15  (continued)

| | 1916 | 1917 | 1918 | 1919 | 1920 | 1921 | 1922 | 1923 | 1924 | 1925 | 1926 |
|---|---|---|---|---|---|---|---|---|---|---|---|
| Repairs to farm buildings | 14131 | 14551 | 16361 | 17959 | 18655 | 18302 | 18172 | 18171 | 18206 | 18093 | 18100 |
| Repairs to machinery & equipment | 8347 | 9982 | 9825 | 10301 | 11484 | 7760 | 8200 | 8738 | 8731 | 10866 | 10404 |
| Tractor expenses | 4140 | 5956 | 8838 | 14650 | 21309 | 20510 | 20534 | 17580 | 18742 | 19154 | 24215 |
| Fertilizer expense | 4990 | 5574 | 6316 | 2084 | 7120 | 6113 | 5710 | 5855 | 5945 | 5963 | 6182 |
| Truck & auto expense | 3418 | 6938 | 10407 | 13085 | 18901 | 18391 | 18340 | 16860 | 19028 | 19896 | 25508 |
| Mill feeds | 9155 | 9364 | 27349 | 37400 | 26816 | 20648 | 19242 | 21940 | 18152 | 20638 | 24671 |
| Binder twine | 10508 | 14899 | 14729 | 5236 | 12334 | 16380 | 9892 | 11113 | 10707 | 14095 | 13353 |
| Blacksmithing | 19769 | 21101 | 22270 | 22408 | 23822 | 22465 | 21062 | 20289 | 19030 | 18028 | 16634 |
| Miscellaneous | 33389 | 39930 | 39303 | 41206 | 45938 | 31043 | 32802 | 34952 | 34924 | 43464 | 41619 |
| Total operating expense | 107850 | 128298 | 155403 | 164334 | 186383 | 161617 | 153958 | 155502 | 153470 | 170201 | 180690 |

**Table 2.16**    **Gross Farm Income and Farm Gross Domestic Product (Thousands of Dollars)**

| Year | Gross Income | Operating Costs | Farm GDP |
|------|-------------|-----------------|----------|
| 1870 | 159808 | 16011 | 143797 |
| 1871 | 165192 | 19911 | 145281 |
| 1872 | 164498 | 17117 | 147381 |
| 1873 | 167615 | 23125 | 144490 |
| 1874 | 174676 | 20160 | 154516 |
| 1875 | 164695 | 18179 | 146516 |
| 1876 | 160138 | 20966 | 139172 |
| 1877 | 164492 | 20020 | 144466 |
| 1878 | 153214 | 19021 | 134193 |
| 1879 | 178394 | 19973 | 158421 |
| 1880 | 179489 | 20151 | 159339 |
| 1881 | 218911 | 21890 | 197021 |
| 1882 | 228077 | 23185 | 204892 |
| 1883 | 207548 | 22462 | 185086 |
| 1884 | 194786 | 21390 | 173396 |
| 1885 | 185749 | 20714 | 165035 |
| 1886 | 179431 | 21368 | 158063 |
| 1887 | 199230 | 23411 | 175819 |
| 1888 | 194670 | 24032 | 170638 |
| 1889 | 202411 | 25289 | 177122 |
| 1890 | 210702 | 26046 | 184656 |
| 1891 | 214854 | 25745 | 189108 |
| 1892 | 216425 | 26926 | 189499 |
| 1893 | 207007 | 25419 | 181588 |
| 1894 | 197652 | 25097 | 172555 |
| 1895 | 193229 | 26070 | 167159 |
| 1896 | 183291 | 26141 | 157150 |
| 1897 | 215330 | 28379 | 186915 |
| 1898 | 220320 | 31453 | 188867 |
| 1899 | 234201 | 33921 | 200280 |
| 1900 | 239375 | 31547 | 207828 |
| 1901 | 278350 | 34936 | 243414 |
| 1902 | 320310 | 40194 | 280116 |
| 1903 | 305738 | 38690 | 267048 |
| 1904 | 318666 | 39884 | 278782 |
| 1905 | 346796 | 42968 | 303828 |
| 1906 | 364836 | 46040 | 318796 |
| 1907 | 405315 | 50639 | 354676 |
| 1908 | 385101 | 49412 | 335689 |
| 1909 | 459897 | 57343 | 402554 |
| 1910 | 462846 | 60519 | 402327 |
| 1911 | 538087 | 68433 | 469654 |
| 1912 | 551367 | 73409 | 477958 |
| 1913 | 597540 | 79728 | 517812 |
| 1914 | 574030 | 83130 | 490900 |
| 1915 | 783293 | 96655 | 686638 |
| 1916 | 879529 | 107850 | 771679 |
| 1917 | 1063431 | 128298 | 935133 |

(*continued*)

Table 2.16    (continued)

| Year | Gross Income | Operating Costs | Farm GDP |
|------|--------------|-----------------|----------|
| 1918 | 1061579 | 155403 | 906176 |
| 1919 | 1108113 | 164334 | 943779 |
| 1920 | 1228662 | 186383 | 1042279 |
| 1921 | 839462 | 161617 | 677845 |
| 1922 | 874694 | 153958 | 720736 |
| 1923 | 934029 | 155502 | 778527 |
| 1924 | 937367 | 153470 | 783897 |
| 1925 | 1161345 | 170201 | 991144 |
| 1926 | 1108046 | 180690 | 927356 |

that took place in the iron and steel products industry and the transportation equipment industry are not nearly as apparent. For the former industry the relative decline of blacksmithing and other such small industry and the growth of the modern iron and steel industry with blast furnaces and steel mills is masked. For the latter industry, the relative decline in production of horse-drawn vehicles and, to some extent, the production of railway equipment, on the one hand, and the growth of the automotive industry, on the other hand, are also submerged.

Another feature is the growth of the mining industry proper. The income produced in 1900 is exaggerated by the production and sale of gold from the Klondike. But the emergence of base metal mining in the late nineteenth century and its growth in the twentieth, together with a continuation of coal and gold mining from the earlier period, established the mining industry as a substantial one. We have noted already the concomitant growth of the nonferrous metals industry in manufacturing.

I mention forestry (wood operations) just briefly. It was the principal component of the category "Forestry, . . . fishing," in table 2.13. After 1900, and especially from the 1914 war onward, the relative decline in logging for lumber was progressively offset by the great growth of pulpwood production. It is of interest, first, that during its period of development the pulp and paper manufacturing industry was much more export oriented than had been the saw and planing mill industry which it was to some extent replacing and, second, that the paper and pulpwood exports had a much larger manufacturing component than primary industry component in contrast to the agricultural exports.

Finally, the banking and finance industry (table 2.13) provides a good indication of growth of an increasingly specialized economy. By 1890 there was a fairly good banking system, but the remainder of the financial system was ill developed. A great growth of this sector after

**Table 2.17    Gross Domestic Product in Manufacturing at Factor Cost, by Industry, 1870–1926 (Thousands of Current Dollars)**

| | 1870 | 1871 | 1872 | 1873 | 1874 | 1875 | 1876 | 1877 | 1878 | 1879 | 1880 | 1881 |
|---|---|---|---|---|---|---|---|---|---|---|---|---|
| 1. Food & beverage | 11263 | 12522 | 13697 | 14787 | 13179 | 12162 | 12022 | 14783 | 11967 | 12677 | 14413 | 16355 |
| 2. Tobacco & products | 1014 | 1077 | 1150 | 1403 | 1693 | 1699 | 1665 | 1374 | 1021 | 982 | 1207 | 1421 |
| 3. Rubber products | 112 | 141 | 168 | 199 | 222 | 146 | 123 | 171 | 141 | 153 | 243 | 390 |
| 4. Leather products | 11717 | 13811 | 12632 | 10721 | 11137 | 8814 | 7314 | 9105 | 8428 | 9420 | 12825 | 14450 |
| 5. Textiles (excl. clothing) | 2691 | 3751 | 3547 | 2710 | 2761 | 3047 | 2999 | 3248 | 3228 | 4314 | 5116 | 6021 |
| 6. Clothing | 5386 | 7230 | 7664 | 7027 | 7052 | 6707 | 6270 | 6925 | 7120 | 8519 | 9373 | 10712 |
| 7. Wood products | 16173 | 16743 | 16944 | 25499 | 24051 | 19937 | 15802 | 18960 | 15601 | 16776 | 22227 | 28488 |
| 8. Paper products | 670 | 791 | 777 | 925 | 984 | 1044 | 1007 | 992 | 987 | 953 | 1035 | 1166 |
| 9. Printing and publishing | 2270 | 2739 | 2930 | 3525 | 3880 | 4000 | 3816 | 3865 | 3906 | 3743 | 3579 | 4793 |
| 10. Iron and steel products | 12803 | 16834 | 23698 | 34585 | 21633 | 21382 | 13459 | 14586 | 11813 | 10940 | 15485 | 18102 |
| 11. Transportation equipment | 5943 | 5952 | 7104 | 13134 | 12883 | 9648 | 9978 | 9394 | 9844 | 7940 | 7105 | 9626 |
| 12. Nonferrous metal products | 770 | 882 | 992 | 1103 | 1212 | 1322 | 1429 | 1534 | 1640 | 1745 | 1849 | 1852 |
| 13. Electric apparatus & supplies | | | | | | | | | | | | |
| 14. Nonmetallic minerals | 2398 | 2521 | 2642 | 2761 | 2876 | 2991 | 3102 | 3212 | 3320 | 3425 | 3528 | 3383 |
| 15. Petroleum and coal | 1119 | 1352 | 1642 | 1822 | 601 | 1074 | 1822 | 1156 | 1055 | 1563 | 1308 | 1334 |
| 16. Chemical products | 1560 | 1759 | 1908 | 1993 | 2128 | 1974 | 2024 | 2234 | 2166 | 2224 | 2332 | 2509 |
| 17. Miscellaneous industries | 1094 | 1301 | 1459 | 1803 | 1638 | 1532 | 1400 | 1634 | 1488 | 1622 | 1990 | 2321 |
| Total GDP | 76983 | 89406 | 98954 | 123997 | 107930 | 97479 | 84232 | 93173 | 83725 | 86996 | 103615 | 122923 |

(continued)

Table 2.17    (continued)

| | 1882 | 1883 | 1884 | 1885 | 1886 | 1887 | 1888 | 1889 | 1890 | 1891 | 1892 | 1893 |
|---|---|---|---|---|---|---|---|---|---|---|---|---|
| 1. Food & beverage | 17739 | 17681 | 18077 | 16785 | 17028 | 18754 | 22768 | 24207 | 26232 | 27785 | 26170 | 23685 |
| 2. Tobacco & products | 1556 | 1738 | 2118 | 1938 | 1586 | 1886 | 2102 | 2255 | 2713 | 2914 | 2881 | 2908 |
| 3. Rubber products | 394 | 328 | 352 | 342 | 346 | 435 | 545 | 508 | 505 | 556 | 580 | 635 |
| 4. Leather products | 14357 | 13347 | 13374 | 15502 | 16486 | 14468 | 12730 | 12102 | 14810 | 15073 | 14504 | 13378 |
| 5. Textiles (excl. clothing) | 7836 | 7180 | 6293 | 6672 | 7150 | 7458 | 8159 | 9246 | 9380 | 9524 | 9840 | 9134 |
| 6. Clothing | 13456 | 12583 | 11653 | 12520 | 13925 | 14099 | 15099 | 18288 | 19251 | 18739 | 19028 | 17811 |
| 7. Wood products | 35098 | 39031 | 33868 | 30067 | 30925 | 31438 | 32256 | 32679 | 35035 | 35257 | 29452 | 29658 |
| 8. Paper products | 1366 | 1625 | 1718 | 1768 | 1762 | 1936 | 2086 | 2236 | 2393 | 2581 | 2794 | 3017 |
| 9. Printing and publishing | 5610 | 5244 | 4439 | 4496 | 4393 | 5309 | 6601 | 6391 | 5809 | 6199 | 7961 | 8222 |
| 10. Iron and steel products | 22277 | 28292 | 21204 | 18669 | 19319 | 23810 | 23679 | 24652 | 27070 | 24780 | 24141 | 21615 |
| 11. Transportation equipment | 11015 | 10215 | 9079 | 8276 | 8885 | 9844 | 10140 | 10305 | 11806 | 12178 | 12413 | 11868 |
| 12. Nonferrous metal products | 1942 | 1621 | 1164 | 1339 | 1943 | 1998 | 2458 | 3026 | 3337 | 4480 | 3394 | 3533 |
| 13. Electric apparatus & supplies | | | | | | | | | 416 | 435 | 461 | 520 |
| 14. Nonmetallic minerals | 3236 | 3085 | 2928 | 2769 | 2605 | 3032 | 3211 | 3798 | 5209 | 4209 | 4062 | 5285 |
| 15. Petroleum and coal | 1064 | 1108 | 1036 | 1138 | 1127 | 1167 | 982 | 989 | 1020 | 1011 | 1090 | 1122 |
| 16. Chemical products | 2902 | 3160 | 3140 | 3177 | 3323 | 3417 | 3366 | 3433 | 3596 | 3577 | 3532 | 3318 |
| 17. Miscellaneous industries | 2645 | 2720 | 2467 | 2359 | 2438 | 2571 | 2733 | 2869 | 3109 | 3156 | 3014 | 2866 |
| Total GDP | 142493 | 148958 | 132910 | 127817 | 133241 | 141622 | 148915 | 156984 | 171691 | 172454 | 165317 | 158575 |

| | 1894 | 1895 | 1896 | 1897 | 1898 | 1899 | 1900 | 1901 | 1902 | 1903 | 1904 |
|---|---|---|---|---|---|---|---|---|---|---|---|
| 1. Food & beverage | 22891 | 24050 | 24262 | 30203 | 30991 | 29327 | 33172 | 34653 | 37761 | 40929 | 43355 |
| 2. Tobacco & products | 2884 | 2857 | 3185 | 4070 | 3937 | 3535 | 4012 | 4055 | 4343 | 4905 | 5332 |
| 3. Rubber products | 588 | 663 | 818 | 1036 | 1269 | 1471 | 1516 | 1385 | 1421 | 1899 | 2450 |
| 4. Leather products | 9859 | 12122 | 11361 | 17243 | 18719 | 17175 | 15863 | 17217 | 20889 | 20836 | 17535 |
| 5. Textiles (excl. clothing) | 8014 | 7690 | 7360 | 9167 | 11036 | 12286 | 12825 | 13020 | 13599 | 13300 | 12454 |
| 6. Clothing | 16451 | 16405 | 15816 | 16998 | 18751 | 20760 | 21669 | 23103 | 26223 | 28129 | 29024 |
| 7. Wood products | 27959 | 23781 | 26109 | 27106 | 26126 | 29950 | 34024 | 33477 | 39258 | 44346 | 43470 |
| 8. Paper products | 3287 | 3242 | 3254 | 3550 | 3831 | 4203 | 4752 | 4596 | 5471 | 5893 | 6299 |
| 9. Printing and publishing | 6559 | 6574 | 7074 | 7298 | 7510 | 8035 | 8952 | 8955 | 9015 | 9521 | 10509 |
| 10. Iron and steel products | 18994 | 14716 | 17801 | 14902 | 18684 | 20072 | 29077 | 23682 | 39683 | 39436 | 31718 |
| 11. Transportation equipment | 11741 | 8855 | 6730 | 7732 | 9214 | 11045 | 10765 | 11833 | 15062 | 17303 | 16335 |
| 12. Nonferrous metal products | 3138 | 3162 | 3105 | 4113 | 5169 | 5682 | 6257 | 8316 | 8496 | 9489 | 11060 |
| 13. Electric apparatus & supplies | 587 | 634 | 714 | 792 | 1076 | 1269 | 1628 | 2190 | 2438 | 2607 | 3028 |
| 14. Nonmetallic minerals | 5319 | 6533 | 4454 | 4608 | 5271 | 5981 | 6329 | 7233 | 8064 | 8343 | 8229 |
| 15. Petroleum and coal | 1168 | 1067 | 983 | 954 | 964 | 949 | 1075 | 1059 | 1135 | 1420 | 1791 |
| 16. Chemical products | 3029 | 3090 | 3144 | 3338 | 3794 | 4123 | 4523 | 5404 | 6238 | 6769 | 7488 |
| 17. Miscellaneous industries | 2646 | 2557 | 2581 | 2972 | 3197 | 3325 | 3707 | 3763 | 4379 | 4646 | 4568 |
| Total GDP | 145114 | 137998 | 138751 | 156082 | 169539 | 179188 | 200146 | 203941 | 243475 | 259771 | 254645 |

(*continued*)

**Table 2.17** (continued)

| | 1905 | 1906 | 1907 | 1908 | 1909 | 1910 | 1911 | 1912 | 1913 | 1914 | 1915 |
|---|---|---|---|---|---|---|---|---|---|---|---|
| 1. Food & beverage | 48452 | 46528 | 50453 | 55998 | 61065 | 64767 | 64267 | 69030 | 66643 | 70857 | 82568 |
| 2. Tobacco & products | 5703 | 5533 | 5910 | 7720 | 8430 | 8585 | 9430 | 9767 | 9735 | 10261 | 10327 |
| 3. Rubber products | 2735 | 2983 | 3247 | 2629 | 3878 | 4497 | 5369 | 6749 | 5850 | 5964 | 8355 |
| 4. Leather products | 21408 | 27282 | 19818 | 14197 | 25789 | 26746 | 30113 | 39097 | 27271 | 31448 | 26747 |
| 5. Textiles (excl. clothing) | 13018 | 14323 | 13531 | 12156 | 14688 | 17894 | 14846 | 14984 | 15565 | 13678 | 17668 |
| 6. Clothing | 32547 | 37089 | 38632 | 33675 | 43239 | 50605 | 45579 | 49244 | 50958 | 43019 | 47377 |
| 7. Wood products | 49604 | 61148 | 67417 | 59614 | 66468 | 72168 | 78640 | 67843 | 62903 | 56641 | 56984 |
| 8. Paper products | 7178 | 8449 | 9787 | 9985 | 11387 | 12388 | 11295 | 11240 | 12701 | 16320 | 18722 |
| 9. Printing and publishing | 11086 | 11944 | 12266 | 13958 | 15667 | 15765 | 17282 | 18795 | 20559 | 20997 | 21006 |
| 10. Iron and steel products | 50976 | 69246 | 87249 | 57338 | 68102 | 75808 | 78188 | 95780 | 103973 | 60352 | 72491 |
| 11. Transportation equipment | 18565 | 23677 | 32452 | 27221 | 29415 | 31302 | 38919 | 44854 | 53299 | 43301 | 33281 |
| 12. Nonferrous metal products | 17401 | 20941 | 22341 | 18324 | 20240 | 24169 | 22760 | 28287 | 26281 | 20128 | 28364 |
| 13. Electric apparatus & supplies | 3782 | 4949 | 5789 | 6384 | 6778 | 7280 | 8471 | 7806 | 7633 | 7635 | 7181 |
| 14. Nonmetallic minerals | 9706 | 11699 | 12686 | 11199 | 11058 | 17076 | 19261 | 22384 | 23458 | 18831 | 14245 |
| 15. Petroleum and coal | 2047 | 1827 | 2358 | 2379 | 2155 | 2355 | 2779 | 4494 | 5640 | 5531 | 4089 |
| 16. Chemical products | 8828 | 9801 | 11097 | 10460 | 10852 | 12890 | 14670 | 17918 | 17637 | 16160 | 18926 |
| 17. Miscellaneous industries | 5403 | 6198 | 6795 | 6099 | 7073 | 7827 | 7697 | 8067 | 7685 | 6600 | 6847 |
| Total GDP | 308439 | 363617 | 401828 | 349336 | 406284 | 452122 | 469566 | 516339 | 517791 | 447723 | 475178 |

| | 1916 | 1917 | 1918 | 1919 | 1920 | 1921 | 1922 | 1923 | 1924 | 1925 | 1926 |
|---|---|---|---|---|---|---|---|---|---|---|---|
| 1. Food & beverage | 103300 | 144219 | 156916 | 169843 | 187062 | 152471 | 141002 | 143715 | 150220 | 156065 | 169158 |
| 2. Tobacco & products | 11884 | 15997 | 20060 | 13957 | 19557 | 16646 | 18358 | 16960 | 16879 | 9779 | 12918 |
| 3. Rubber products | 12744 | 17935 | 19665 | 22929 | 30558 | 18097 | 22236 | 24430 | 27188 | 32405 | 28366 |
| 4. Leather products | 42026 | 39180 | 36692 | 43937 | 45462 | 36716 | 40818 | 38661 | 37228 | 35700 | 38795 |
| 5. Textiles (excl. clothing) | 22932 | 36734 | 47618 | 54141 | 58872 | 46725 | 54141 | 54099 | 41450 | 41083 | 50047 |
| 6. Clothing | 68874 | 80108 | 91133 | 107804 | 109493 | 83249 | 87978 | 89630 | 83364 | 84810 | 93436 |
| 7. Wood products | 56703 | 85863 | 93048 | 107388 | 137470 | 87188 | 84079 | 101393 | 88223 | 87215 | 93509 |
| 8. Paper products | 31507 | 47850 | 60691 | 74242 | 134378 | 71203 | 78066 | 92893 | 86010 | 94258 | 105444 |
| 9. Printing and publishing | 26477 | 33403 | 32504 | 42105 | 54323 | 52162 | 52235 | 53007 | 53327 | 54537 | 58047 |
| 10. Iron and steel products | 124805 | 185523 | 198134 | 158876 | 207531 | 125452 | 98746 | 132855 | 114033 | 124093 | 147981 |
| 11. Transportation equipment | 37544 | 76866 | 106980 | 110800 | 111534 | 61432 | 58043 | 68923 | 61191 | 79775 | 95991 |
| 12. Nonferrous metal products | 41393 | 45321 | 35666 | 33352 | 36970 | 17595 | 21204 | 26784 | 26380 | 33445 | 34170 |
| 13. Electric apparatus & supplies | 10178 | 15909 | 12108 | 14707 | 22213 | 20141 | 18603 | 19744 | 26292 | 28506 | 32401 |
| 14. Nonmetallic minerals | 14918 | 17950 | 17792 | 19664 | 33494 | 25481 | 28856 | 29060 | 27932 | 28207 | 29365 |
| 15. Petroleum and coal | 7621 | 10531 | 13169 | 14730 | 17208 | 10942 | 11553 | 4711 | 8254 | 8325 | 15129 |
| 16. Chemical products | 41941 | 93829 | 124797 | 34433 | 39688 | 28061 | 29704 | 37941 | 35911 | 38497 | 43259 |
| 17. Miscellaneous industries | 9207 | 12854 | 17053 | 19340 | 25256 | 19416 | 19689 | 20018 | 15895 | 17198 | 19387 |
| Total GDP | 664054 | 960072 | 1084026 | 1042248 | 1271069 | 872977 | 865311 | 954824 | 899777 | 953898 | 1067403 |

Table 2.18          Percentage Distribution of Gross Domestic Product,
                    Manufacturing, Census Years, 1870–1920 and 1926

|  | 1870 | 1880 | 1890 | 1900 | 1910 | 1920 | 1926 |
|---|---|---|---|---|---|---|---|
| Food & beverage | 14.6 | 13.9 | 15.3 | 16.6 | 14.3 | 14.7 | 15.9 |
| Tobacco & products | 1.3 | 1.2 | 1.6 | 2.0 | 1.9 | 1.5 | 1.2 |
| Rubber products | 0.2 | 0.2 | 0.3 | 0.8 | 1.0 | 2.4 | 2.7 |
| Leather products | 15.2 | 12.4 | 8.6 | 7.9 | 5.9 | 3.6 | 3.6 |
| Textiles (excl. clothing) | 3.5 | 4.9 | 5.5 | 6.4 | 4.0 | 4.6 | 4.7 |
| Clothing | 7.0 | 9.1 | 11.2 | 10.8 | 11.2 | 8.6 | 8.8 |
| Wood products | 21.0 | 21.4 | 20.4 | 17.0 | 16.0 | 10.8 | 8.8 |
| Paper products | 0.9 | 1.0 | 1.4 | 2.4 | 2.7 | 10.6 | 9.9 |
| Printing & publishing | 3.0 | 3.5 | 3.4 | 4.5 | 3.5 | 4.3 | 5.4 |
| Iron & steel products | 16.6 | 14.9 | 15.8 | 14.5 | 16.8 | 16.3 | 13.9 |
| Transport equipment | 7.7 | 6.9 | 6.9 | 5.4 | 6.9 | 8.8 | 9.0 |
| Nonferrous metal products | 1.0 | 1.8 | 1.9 | 3.1 | 5.4 | 2.9 | 3.2 |
| Electric apparatus and supplies | — | — | 0.2 | 0.8 | 1.6 | 1.8 | 3.0 |
| Nonmetallic minerals | 3.1 | 3.4 | 3.0 | 3.2 | 3.8 | 2.6 | 2.8 |
| Petroleum and coal products | 1.5 | 1.3 | 0.6 | 0.5 | 0.5 | 1.4 | 1.4 |
| Chemical products | 2.0 | 2.3 | 2.1 | 2.3 | 2.9 | 3.1 | 4.1 |
| Miscellaneous industries | 1.4 | 1.9 | 1.8 | 1.9 | 1.7 | 2.0 | 1.8 |

1890 is evident from the data, a growth in which several Canadian institutions, especially the banks, became big players in the world scene.

## 2.3 Conclusion

What does this add up to? In the interests of brevity and to focus our attention, I make just two points.

First, the Canadian economy developed in a fundamentally different way after 1900 than it had before. The best evidence in support of this statement from our data is provided by the performance of capital formation. Levels of sustained capital formation relative to GNP were of a distinctly higher order after 1900 than before; equivalently, levels of domestic saving appear to have been clearly of a much higher order after 1900 than before. Of particular significance, the level of investment in manufacturing became permanently much higher than it had been (table 2.2): Canadian manufacturing underwent a fundamental change between 1890 and 1910. Accompanying the change in manufacturing, the specialized trade sector and the financial sector went a long way toward assuming their modern form. And the electric power and communications system underwent like development (table 2.1).

Second, the evidence of our data supports most strongly the presumption that the growth and many of the changes in the Canadian economy were a consequence of the settlement of the prairies. The continued high level of the contribution of agriculture to GDP was a direct result of this settlement. And one should add that the foundation of western settlement was the production or prospect of production of wheat. The effects of western settlement and of the incomes consequent on it were felt strongly in Central Canada, where the manufacturing financial, and commercial functions were performed predominantly. Ontario gained population by net in-migration from 1900 onward.

I have put the matter rather starkly. Of course, other factors entered the picture. I have mentioned already the growth of the mining industry, itself highly dependent on external markets. I have not mentioned the effects of the war, which led to large growth of some sectors of the manufacturing industry. But these events were of the second order of magnitude.

I leave the matter there. I do not attempt to resolve the dispute between the traditionalists and the revisionists. I would just say that I do not see that their views are entirely antithetical. Of more importance, I hope that the new data provided herein stimulate further research. There are many things still to be explained.

# Appendix 1
## *The Background of the Project*

This project began, on my initiative, about nine years ago as a collaborative undertaking among seven of us in academia. The final project is attributed as follows with special reference to the industrial categories of table 2.1.

Alan Green was responsible for the estimates in transportation, communications, and electric light and power. This included estimates for the steam railways, the electric railways, the telegraph, the telephone, and the electric utilities.

Duncan McDougall prepared estimates of wage and salary payments and of outlays on goods and services of federal and provincial governments, in great detail for 1910 and in somewhat lesser detail for 1900, 1890, 1880, and 1870. I was responsible for estimates for provinces for 1920 and also for the interpolation of the yearly data between census years and between 1920 and 1926 when the official estimates begin. Duncan McDougall was also responsible for the preparation of the major part of the fisheries estimates; I did some work in reconciling the estimates at a point of junction of two series where the nature of the underlying data changed.

Marvin McInnis and I developed the methodology of estimation of income for the agricultural sector in preparing an estimate for 1910. Marvin McInnis then wrote up the estimates for that year. I did the detailed direction of the preparation of the estimates for the full period and must bear the responsibility for their quality. Marvin McInnis is doing the detailed writeup of the preparation of the estimates.

Thomas Rymes, of Carleton University, prepared the estimates for the finance, insurance, and real estate sector.

Alasdair Sinclair, of Dalhousie University, prepared the balance of payments estimates.

Marion Steele, of the University of Guelph, prepared the estimates of residential rent and also the estimates of capital formation through residential construction.

I am responsible for the preparation of the remainder of the estimates.

We were assisted in our work at various times by a score or so of research assistants.

The project was supported by a grant from Killan Fund of the Canada Council.

# Appendix 2
## *Notes on Methods and Sources*

This note contains two parts. First, the method of estimation of GDP for the period 1870–1926 and the rationale for the use of this method are presented. Second, the major sources of data and their strengths and weaknesses are described.

### The Method of Estimation of GDP

There are three possible methods of estimating GDP or the closely related GNP which are not necessarily alternatives but which, in fact, often are just that, at least for the preparation of historical estimates. It is about the method appropriate for historical estimates that I shall speak, although I shall also make reference, at times, to current practice.

### *The Expenditure Method*

One such method comprises the estimation of expenditure (actual and imputed) on final goods and services, on consumer commodities, on capital goods, on goods and services purchased by government, and on net purchases of goods and services by residents of foreign countries, to obtain GNP. It is then adjusted for net international income flows to obtain GDP. Practically all countries make estimates of such expenditure in their current preparation of their national accounts and, more important, make such estimates from data that are, for the most part, independent of those used to estimate GNP or GDP by alternative methods as well. However, most countries do not have the luxury of being able to make good historical estimates, from independent data, by both the expenditure method and either one or a combination of the two other methods that can be followed and consequently rely primarily on one method or another.

Many countries do not depend primarily on expenditure estimates for historical periods. However, the United States is one country that does. The historical GNP estimates for early years for the United States (before 1919) are based primarily on Kuznets's work; he obtained his estimates by use of the expenditure method. This method was reasonably appropriate for the United States since its census of manufactures obtained a large amount of commodity data from as early as 1869. These data made it possible to separate finished products from intermediate products and, in turn, along with such items as trade data, data on production of agricultural products, information on freight costs and on trade margins, and reports of government bodies, made possible the derivation of reasonably decent estimates for large components of gross national expenditure.

This method was much less appropriate for Canada because her census of manufactures did not report commodity data until 1917: only the value of output was reported. Hence it is much more difficult to separate production of intermediate products from final products and to divide the latter among consumer goods, capital goods, and goods sold to governments in Canada than in the United States. And we decided at an early stage not to use this method.

*The Income Method*

A second method of estimating GDP is to add together factor costs of production to obtain national income at factor cost, to further add on capital consumption allowances to obtain GDP at factor cost, and then, finally, if desired, to add indirect taxes less subsidies to obtain GDP at market prices. One can then, if one wishes, obtain GNP at market prices by subtracting factor incomes paid abroad and adding factor incomes received from abroad.

This factor income method is widely used currently to obtain most of the items of the factor income and GNP statements of the national accounts. Its use depends on the direct availability of data on, first, labor income and, second, property income. Such data are now available in Canada and many other countries from personal and corporate income tax returns and from many surveys done by statistical agencies. However, in the historical period in which we are interested, before the widespread use of income taxes to obtain revenue, data on property income are not directly available, and while reports of wage data are somewhat better, even they may be incomplete. Hence many countries find the use of this method unsatisfactory for estimation of historical GNP. The United Kingdom is an exception: its continuous use of the income tax dates from 1842/43. There are few data for Canada to yield direct estimates of property income before the First World War—reports for the banks, insurance companies, railways, and governments are exceptions—and so this method has for Canada only limited use for historical estimates.

### The Value-Added Method

The third method involves obtaining estimates of GDP at factor cost by the value-added method and then deriving from them estimates of GNP by adding factor incomes received from abroad and subtracting factor incomes paid abroad. Basically, the value-added method of estimation involves subtracting nonfactor costs of production from gross value of production or gross sales on an industry basis in order to obtain gross value added by industry (that is, the sum of factor costs and depreciation). This is the method used even yet in the official estimates of agriculture income in Canada: a synthetic account is set up in which estimated nonfactor costs of farming items such as cost of feed, fertilizer, machinery operating costs, and farm taxes are subtracted from farm sales plus an imputation of income in kind for farm products consumed as final products on the farms on which they were produced.

This method is often the one most suited, at least for a first approach, to making historical estimates of GDP at factor cost for both the farm sector and the manufacturing sector, which are, by any measure and by a substantial margin, the two largest sectors in Canada throughout the period 1870–1926 and which are really dominant in the earlier part of this period. Other goods-producing industries such as mining, forestry, construction, and even the fisheries may be approached by the factor income method.

### The Method Adopted

The method adopted in our project may best be given by a brief description of the procedure followed for selected industries, tedious as that procedure may be. Accordingly, I give now such an industry description.

*Agriculture.* Estimates for agriculture were made by the value-added method: the method is described more fully in the section of this paper that gives the estimates of income generated in agriculture. Here I just note that the main innovation is the direct estimation, in the first instance, of off-farm sales and farm consumption of farm products without its being necessary to deal with the presence of intermediate farm products that are used in further production in the farm sector itself. The only expenses that are relevant then are the costs of purchases from outside the farm sector.

*Manufacturing.* The value-added method is used: a general outline of the method is given in the section of this paper that deals with the manufacturing data. Basically, the method involves subtracting cost of materials, cost of fuel and electricity, and "miscellaneous" expenses (items like repair and maintenance expenditures, insurance, and office supplies) from gross value of production to obtain GDP at factor cost. The labor income component of GDP can be estimated directly from data collected in censuses of manufactures, and the property income emerges as a residual.

*Mining.* The value-added method is used for 1921–26 by use of Dominion Bureau of Statistics census of industry data. For 1870–1920 the estimates were made separately for each of five groups into which total mining was divided, namely, metallic mines; coal (further divided by province); asbestos; other nonmetallic minerals and fuels; and sand, gravel, and stone. For each of these, it was possible to get long annual series of gross value of production (GVP) running right back to 1886 for all minerals but coal and gold and for coal and gold themselves back to 1870. For the first four groups noted above we also had wage and salary costs for 1900, 1910, 1921–26, and for coal alone for 1917–18. The ratio of these wage and salary costs to GVP was constant for all of these aforementioned years. Estimates of annual wages and salaries were obtained by assuming that the ratios of wages and salaries to GVP, by groups, were the same before 1900 as in 1900 and that these ratios could be interpolated linearly between 1900 and 1910 and between 1910 and 1920 (with the exception of coal for which there were additional ratios for 1917 and 1918). Multiplication of gross values of products by these ratios then yielded estimates of wages and salaries.

In the absence of data before 1921, to permit a direct estimate of property income an improvisation was necessary. Ratios of property income to labor income were available by groups for 1921–26, and for 1966 onward (Corporation Financial Statistics). Overall ratios for mining were also available from the *National Accounts* for 1926 onward. There was sufficient stability in these ratios through time to suggest that we might assume that such stable ratios existed prior to 1921 at the level of industry subdivision that we used.

A variation of the method was used for the sand, gravel, and stone subdivision, but it is not worth detaining us for the details at this point, particularly since this item was very small in early years.

After the above calculations were made, a small percentage was added to the whole series to take account of income of the self-employed. This percentage was based on data for the national accounts from 1926 onward.

*Transportation: The railways.* For as far back as 1907 both wage and salary payments and property income are calculated from annual reports, submitted to the government, which are published. Prior to 1907 other methods were necessary, since the necessary data were not available in published reports. However, wage and salary data were available for a quite large sample of companies, in material housed in the national archives, for many years in the earlier period. By relating them to operating data one could obtain ratios that formed a basis for estimation of wages and salaries for all companies, since operating data were reported for all companies from 1875 onward. Property income was calculated from bond interest expenses—bonded indebtedness was fully known—and from reports of dividends paid in Poor's, an allowance being made for undistributed profits.

These estimates can be taken as being quite reliable.

*Finance, insurance, and real estate, excluding house rents.* The estimates for finance and insurance were prepared predominantly by the income method. Insurance companies of all kinds have long had to report to the Federal Superintendent of Insurance for federally incorporated companies or to provincial counterparts for provincially incorporated companies. These reports contained the material from which estimates of both labor and property income could be made. Labor income included a large component of "commissions." It required summing of information for each company to obtain the aggregates.

The estimates for banks were also derived basically by the income method but with an added wrinkle. First, annual estimates of both wages and salaries and property income were obtained from records of two of the major banks made available by the banks themselves: for one of the banks both wage and salary income and property income were obtained directly from the bank statements; for the other bank wages and salaries were obtained directly but property income was obtained from the statements by the value-added method. GDP for the whole banking industry was obtained by multiplying the GDP for the two banks by the ratio of assets of all banks to the assets of the two banks.

Labor income of loan and mortgage companies and the real estate and brokerage sections of the "Finance, etc." industry was obtained by extrapolating estimates prepared by Statistics Canada (previously the Dominion Bureau of Statistics) for the 1920s backward, on the basis of assets of building societies and mortgage loan companies and of trust companies. The real estate and brokerage section extrapolation was tied into estimates of wage and salary income of real estate dealers and brokers for 1911 derived from wage and salary data obtained in the population census of 1911. The labor income of all of the financial operations described in this paragraph are a relatively small part of such income for the whole finance, insurance, and real estate industry.

*Government: Federal, provincial, municipal, public education.* The main income item for all of the government components is salary and wage expense. Estimates of labor income for all of the government components are from annual reports that are reasonably complete for the federal and provincial governments and for education, and sufficiently good to permit passable estimates of municipal wages and salaries.

*Miscellaneous service industries.* These industries include wholesale and retail trade, business service, health and welfare, religion, recreation, other community services, and personal and domestic service. Labor income makes up a very large part of GDP in all of these industries. The estimation of labor income in all of these groups depends very heavily on the use of data collected in the population census on occupations of the gainfully occupied persons in all censuses from 1871 onward and on wages and salaries of every employed person in the censuses of 1901, 1911, 1921, and 1931. Labor income for the self-employed is imputed at rates that are derived from wages and salaries paid to hired workers. For census years before 1901, one obtains estimates of labor income by projecting wages and salary rates in 1900 by such items as average earnings in manufactures, reports of wages and salaries in Royal Commission reports and records of hearings (e.g., Royal Commission on the Relations of Labour and Capital in Canada; *Report,* 1889), reports of wage and salary rates in both agriculture and industry by the Ontario Bureau of Industries in the 1880s (and later for agriculture only), reported wage and salary rates for public servants and schoolteachers, and a considerable amount of other such information.

*Residential rents.* The new estimates of residential rents are much more firmly based than those available hitherto. The preparation of the estimates are best summarized in the words of Marion Steele, the author.

Estimates of residential rent in Canada 1871–1925 currently do not exist, except for those of Firestone (1958) for decade-ending years. In this note we present and describe new annual estimates for 1871–1930. The fundamentals of our estimation procedure are simple. First we estimate mean paid and imputed rent in 1931, using the Census data of that year. Next we estimate an index of mean rents back to 1870; this index is a patchwork of separate indexes which we estimate from sources as diverse as surveys carried out by Ontario Bureau of Industry in the 1880s and James Mavor's Toronto survey in the 1900s. Third, we estimate the stock of dwelling units by urbanization level—urban, rural nonfarm, farm—and so derive gross rents by urbanization level. Finally we estimate deductions from gross rents: expenditure on repairs and maintenance and on fire insurance premiums.

## Major Sources of Data

It would take far too much space to even list all sources of data. Hence only the most important ones will be covered. The sources of data are grouped into three classes: benchmark data sources, annual data sources, and occasional data sources.

### Benchmark Data Sources

The data for some years are sometimes much more complete than those for adjacent years. These are the benchmark years. The main benchmark years for 1870–1926 are the decennial census years. The decennial census was taken in the first half of the first year of each decade. The production data collected in the census were for the preceding year. For example, the production data collected in the census of 1901 are for the year 1900. In the census years the following relevant special census data were obtained.

a) Census of manufactures for 1870, 1880, 1890, 1900, and 1910. (The annual census of manufactures began in 1917, and hence this census was separated from the decennial census.) Later I elaborate on these data.

b) Census of agriculture for each decennial census year from 1870 to 1980. Special data continued to be collected for decennial census years, even after the annual censuses of production in agriculture began. Quantities of products only were obtained in the censuses of 1870, 1880, and 1890. Quantities and values of products were collected in 1900 and later censuses. There was not much collected in the way of cost data until the census of 1920, and even then the information obtained was quite limited. Further information on these data is contained in the discussion of the agricultural data that are presented later.

c) A usable census of mineral products was taken with each of the decennial censuses of 1900 and 1910. Quantities and values of minerals produced were obtained. The numbers of persons employed and their wages or salaries were also obtained. There were no other cost data, but there was a description of plant and equipment.

d) A census of forest production was taken from 1870 onward to 1910, but it was of limited use until 1900, in which year it appears to have been quite complete. It covered only production on farms in 1910. There were no cost data.

e) The decennial census of population contained two valuable sources of data. First, from 1870 onward, in every census, the occupations of the gainfully occupied were obtained: the occupational data of the 1910 census were particularly valuable because they were classified on an industrial basis very much like the 1948 standard industrial classification. In addition to obtaining occupational data, the population censuses from 1901 to 1931 (and beyond) obtained records of remuneration in the form of wage or salary from every hired person in the population. Information on the number of weeks worked as well as age and sex characteristics were also obtained (on the same census form, of course). These data were tabulated according to occupational classifications that corresponded with those used for the gainfully occupied population.

Special mention must be made of the wage and occupational data for 1910. The tabulations by the census office for this year were much more elaborate than those for either 1900 or 1920. There was the additional fact that since the classification was like that of the 1948 standard industrial classification, it was possible to compare wages and salaries reported in the population census with those reported in the census of manufactures, in the census of mines, in reports of government bodies on the wage bill of the public service, in reports of teachers' wage bills in departmental reports, in reports of the railways on wages and salaries, and in other such reports. In general the correspondence was quite good. Such satisfactory correspondence gives one confidence in the reliability of the labor income data for other workers for whom there is ordinarily little information. Thus, it seemed appropriate to use these wage and salary data for such industries as trade (wholesale and retail), business service, recreation, domestic service, and other such groups for 1910. The year 1910 became in effect a benchmark year par excellence.

*Annual Data Sources*

The number of sources of relevant annual data is very large; only a small selection is mentioned here.

a) External trade data provide continuous annual series from Confederation onward. They are most important for the balance of payments. They have many other uses, of which I shall give only two examples. First, exports of wheat (quantity and value) help in the earlier years in the estimation of wheat production. Second, imports of raw cotton (and cotton thread) can be used as an interpolater between census years of value of production of the cotton textile industry.

b) Mineral production statistics, collected or assembled by the Geological Survey of Canada and successor bodies, are available on an annual basis for all minerals from 1886 onward; output of coal and gold is available annually back to 1870 from both provincial and federal government sources.

c) Agricultural field crop production data are available annually for Ontario from 1882 onward (Ontario Bureau of Industries); stocks of animals are available also for Ontario from 1882 onward and sales and slaughter are available from 1892; cheese production is available from 1882. Similar data are available from provincial sources for Manitoba from 1883, for New Brunswick from 1898, and for the Northwest Territories (Alberta and Saskatchewan) from 1898. From 1908 onward the federal Census and Statistics Office collected crop production data and data on numbers of animals annually for all but British Columbia, which was added in 1911; with the establishment of the Dominion Bureau of Statistics in 1918, annual production data on meat, dairy, and poultry products were added.

d) Government annual reports provide information on wages and salaries in the public service at all levels of government; they also provide expenditures on educational salaries for all provinces.

e) Government reports of excise and bounty data and on inspection services provide annual data on items such as pig iron production, tobacco products made, production of beer and spirits, production of petroleum products, and other items.

f) Forestry branches of the federal government collected annual output of sawmill products from 1908 onward.

g) Government bodies collected railway statistics annually from 1875 onward and banking and insurance company data from Confederation onward.

h) Price data are available from many sources right from 1867. Chief among these are the work of H. Michell in *Statistical Contributions to Economic History, Volume 2,* of R. H. Coats in *Wholesale Prices 1890–1909* and subsequent annual volumes, and of DBS once it was established. The basis of much of this work was newspaper price quotations.

i) And then there are all the Dominion Bureau of Statistics data from 1917 onward in the census of industry, the census of agriculture, and so forth.

*Occasional Data Sources*
There were several occasional data sources:
a) Ontario Bureau of Industry Reports in the 1880s give a wide range of wage data for many occupations and also price data.

b) Some data came from commissions or committees of inquiry. Perhaps chief of these was the Report of the Inquiry into the Cost of Living (1915) of the Federal Department of Labour which was mainly Coats's work and which contains an enormous amount of data of many kinds.

c) Some data were collected on a nonrepetitive basis by government statistical agencies, for example, municipal financial data in the Statistical Yearbook of 1894, the predecessor of the Canada Year Book published by the Census and Statistics Office.

# Appendix 3
## *Notes on the Estimates of Income Produced in Agriculture, Canada, 1870–1926*

### Concept of National Income Produced in Agriculture

The ultimate objective is to make an estimate of gross and net income originating in Canadian agriculture regardless of who receives this income. Thus it includes rent paid to nonresident owners of farms, interest paid to nonfarm holders of farm mortgages, and wages paid to hired farm labor, as well as all income from farm operations accruing from farm operations in Canada to the farmers themselves. Conversely, it does not include income accruing to Canadian farmers from sources outside of the farm sector of Canada, such as property income from nonfarm property or labor income received by farmers for work they have done outside of the farm sector. Gross income produced in Canadian agriculture is gross of capital consumed in agricultural production. Net income produced is obtained by deducting capital consumption allowances from gross income produced.

### Coverage

The income estimates provide only a total for all Canada. Geographically, they cover the provinces of New Brunswick, Nova Scotia, Ontario, Quebec, and Prince Edward Island for all years from 1870 to 1879, even though the latter province did not enter confederation until 1873; they cover all of present-day Canada, excluding Newfoundland, from 1880 to 1926.

The income estimates cover all activity that results in an output of agricultural products wherever it takes place. Thus, they include the feeding of animals on commercial feedlots as well as on farms. They cover production of all crops and especially fruits and vegetables on small lots. They cover the very considerable production of dairy and poultry products in villages, towns, and cities by nonfarmers, and they cover output of farm products consumed by farmers or owners of small lots themselves. Only the products of urban kitchen gardens are excluded.

The income is measured for each year from 1870 to 1926. The estimates for census years are particularly important since they are based on more complete data than those for other years. But, except for the 1870s, there are many production data for intercensal years.

Methodology

Two alternative methods, basically, are available for estimating agricultural income produced. The first method involves adding the value of consumption of farm-produced products by farm families (income in kind) to the value of off-farm sales of farm products for the whole agricultural sector and then subtracting the expenses of those nonfactor inputs that are purchased from off the farms to arrive at income produced on the farms themselves. The second method involves making estimates of the values of all products that are produced on farms, regardless of whether they are consumed by farm families themselves, used as intermediate commodities for use in further farm production (mainly feed crops), or sold off farms, and then subtracting the values of the intermediate products used for further farm production and also the expenses of off-farm purchases of nonfactor inputs, in order to arrive at income produced on the farms.

If marketing data (or information that serves the same purpose) can be obtained for the sale of farm products, the advantages lie with the first method. Its use eliminates the necessity to estimate the value of the intermediate farm products that are used for further farm production. The first method has been used by Statistics Canada for many years and is the basis on which the offical statistics have been prepared for as far back as 1926.

The advantage of the second method, if market data are not available, is that agricultural statistics, once they are collected, have typically provided gross production data—that is, data on the total quantities of crops and other commodities produced regardless of whether they are sold off the farm or used on the farm for further production. If, then, some information can be obtained about the parts of gross farm production that are used as intermediate inputs, the second method may be better than the first. In the pre–World War II period the Dominion Bureau of Statistics had some such information, obtained from farmers, and used this second method.

A variant of the first method was used for two reasons. First, there is scarcely any information on the amounts of feed crops and other farm products that are used on the farms themselves for further farm production in the period before World War I. It would be very risky to assume that the ratio of intermediate products to the total gross output of all products was the same in the pre–World War I period as in the post–World War I period. The bulk of the intermediate products is made up of field crops, and the proportion of field crops that are used on the farms varies greatly between types of farms, especially between grain farms and livestock farms. Grain farms output grew much more rapidly than livestock farms output after 1900. Second, we have been able to find data that we believe permit us to make reasonably good estimates of the part of crops that is for off-farm disposal or for farm family consumption without getting involved in estimating the production of intermediate products in any major way.

## The Estimation of Net Farm Output of Final Products

We give now the general method of arriving at off-farm disposal and farm family consumption of crops and other vegetable products, on the one hand, and livestock and dairy products on the other. The general practice, in almost every case, was to estimate the volume of such movements, first, and then to obtain a unit money value which permitted a valuation of total farm product, net of intermediate products.

The disposal of farm crop and vegetable products, net of intermediate products, is composed of human consumption (of both farm and nonfarm families), plus nonhuman off-farm uses in Canada, plus net exports (exports minus imports), plus increases (or minus decreases) of inventories. If we can estimate each of these for each product, we would have one way of estimating the volume of farm products produced, net of intermediate products. Let us deal with these in turn.

First, total human consumption of each product was calculated from estimates of per capita consumption and the numbers in the Canadian population. The numbers in the Canadian population are readily available on an annual basis throughout the whole period. Estimates of per capita consumption were arrived at in various ways, depending on the product. The way in which the per capita consumption estimates were obtained was specific to each product. It is sufficient at this point to note that it has been possible to obtain estimates in which one may have a considerable degree of confidence.

Second, nonhuman off-farm uses of field crops were calculated by a variety of methods, the chosen method being suited to the crop. The amounts of hay and oats sold to feed nonfarm horses were calculated by making estimates of consumption of each product per horse and of the number of off-farm horses. Barley used for malting could be obtained from excise figures; the consumption of grains for distillation was obtained in like manner. In some years the supply of flax fiber could be obtained from statements of raw materials used in scutching mills, and so forth. Fortunately, our decision to include commercial feedlots and nonfarm production of milk and poultry products in the agriculture sector eliminated the need to estimate the feeds that went from farms to these particular nonfarm uses.

Third, external trade data, both exports and imports, were obtainable from the published trade returns for every fiscal year from 1870 onward. Usually the information was given in sufficient detail to provide information for individual commodities. However, in some cases, in the earlier years of our period, data were grouped in the source, and it was necessary to estimate individual commodities from the grouped data. The export figures used were those for Canadian products only, and the import figures were "imports for consumption."

Fourth, except for wheat, there are practically no data on inventories throughout the period. The lack of availability of inventories may affect the assignment of income to particular years. However, at this stage in Canadian development, carryovers at the end of crop years from one year to the next were probably rather small but, of course, insofar as minimum inventories, on the average, did increase, our estimates omit that part of the disposition of products that was directed toward the building up of inventories.

Of course, we also made use of whatever production data of field crops and fruits and vegetables were available. These production data, along with the trade data, for decennial census years often provided the basis of the estimates of human consumption in Canada, for census years, of those grains, fruits, or vegetables that were not intermediate products. Of course, a reconciliation of production and use data, where such is possible, provides the best ultimate check on reliability.

In some cases the production data alone provided the basis of the estimates. At the same time, the production data were of little help for those products for which a large part of the output is intermediate.

There was such diversity in the way that the farm prices, for valuing the farm products, were obtained that a general description of our method in short compass is not possible. The way in which individual prices were obtained was specific to each product.

Estimates of the net value of products of livestock and poultry were obtained in a fashion similar to that for crops, with one difference. For all but the earliest decades of our period we had annual direct estimates of the production of crops and fruits and vegetables, for Ontario from

1882 onward, for Manitoba from 1885 onward, for Alberta and Saskatchewan from 1898 onward, for New Brunswick from 1898 onward, for all provinces except British Columbia from 1908 onward, and for British Columbia from 1911 onward. In the case of the provincial data on livestock we had estimates of the stocks of animals on farms for those periods described in the preceding sentence but, with one exception, not for off-farm disposition and farm family consumption. The exception was Ontario, for which many livestock sales and slaughter data were available from 1892 onward. Of course, the decennial census from 1870 provided production data as well as stocks for most livestock products. The nature of the data available meant that, for provinces other than Ontario and even for some of Ontario's products, in making our estimates for intercensal years, we had to infer production of livestock products from data on stocks of livestock and poultry. The availability of data on stocks of animals meant that we could take account of changes in inventories from year to year, a procedure that we could not follow in the case of crops.

## The Estimation of Expenses of Off-Farm Purchases of Inputs

The expenses of off-farm purchases of inputs must be subtracted from the net value of products to obtain farm income produced. These purchases cover the acquisition of such items as tractor oil and grease, binder twine, blacksmithing, commercial fertilizers, fencing materials, harness and saddlery, and many other such items. Fortunately, many items that are expenses for an individual farm are only intermediate products for the agricultural sector as a whole, and our method of estimation is such that we do not have to estimate the quantities and values of these intermediate products. In addition, since we are interested in income originating in agriculture, we do not have to estimate the cost of hired labor, the interest paid on farm indebtedness, and the rents of farmland.

These circumstances still leave a formidable list of expenses to be calculated. The data for their estimation are best at the end of our period and become increasingly less satisfactory as we go back in time. Luckily, expenses for off-farm purchases become relatively less important the further back we go. For example, there were no purchases of oil for farm tractors when there were no farm tractors or only steam tractors; these expenses increased more than in proportion to output as the use of farm tractors became increasingly widespread. Similarly, as the use of increasingly elaborate machinery grew with the passing of time, outlays on machinery parts and machine service grew. The introduction and spread of the use of binder twine, from about 1890 onward, added an element to off-farm costs that grew through the years. And one can add to the list readily. There were some elements of substitution, of course. For example, the interchangeable part probably replaced one element of the blacksmith's services. But these appear not to have been of great importance.

The quality of the estimates of farm expenses is best for the late years and less good the further back in time we go. They are sufficiently small in the earliest part of the period that even if the margin of error of their estimation is quite large it does not have an important effect on the estimates of income produced in agriculture.

Sources of Data

The details of the sources of data are too voluminous to be given here; it is possible to give only the general sources of information. These include: the decennial census reports for the Dominion together with the quinquennial reports for the Prairie Provinces; the reports of first the Census and Statistics Office (based in the Federal Department of Agriculture) and later the Dominion Bureau of Statistics (DBS) on an annual basis from 1908 onward; provincial reports on agricultural production; the external trade reports; and finally, certain publications that give us prices.

From the agricultural censuses for 1870 onward, the data collected in the decennial census included the quantity of output of the main field crops and the larger types of livestock. In addition the numbers on farms, at a specific date, of the main types of livestock were obtained. No valuations of products were obtained until the census of 1900; from 1900 onward values as well as quantities produced and numbers and values of the inventory of livestock were obtained. The collection of data for some minor products was added in 1900.

The Census and Statistics Office collected annual data from 1908 onward on production and values of field crops, vegetables and fruit, and of numbers and values of the inventory of livestock (but not annual slaughter). For 1920 onward DBS made estimates of off-farm disappearance. Many of these data appear in a series, *Handbook of Agricultural Statistics,* in a number of volumes prepared by DBS after World War II.

Several provinces collected provincial data on an annual basis before the Dominion reporting system was set up in 1908. The Province of Ontario began the annual collection of data on the production of most field crops, of the numbers of livestock on farms, of capital invested in farms, and of prices of farm products in 1882; data collection on the sale or slaughter of farm animals was begun in 1892. The Province of Manitoba began the collection of considerable amounts of agricultural data in 1883, Alberta and Saskatchewan (initially the Western Territories) in 1898, and New Brunswick in 1898.

External trade data, both quantities and values, are available for every year from 1870 (and before) onward. Unit values of exports and imports may be calculated from these data.

In addition to the price or unit value data available from these just enumerated sources, there are two other general sources that give considerable agricultural price data. They are H. Michell in Taylor and Michell, *Statistical Contributions to Canadian Economic History,* volume 2, and Department of Labour, *Wholesale Prices, Canada 1890–1909,* along with its successor annual publication, *Wholesale Prices,* which begins with 1911.

There were, in addition to these general sources of data, many other sources that apply to more limited periods or to specific agricultural products.

# Appendix 4
## *Notes on the Estimates of Income Produced in Manufacturing, Canada, 1870–1926*

The estimates for the manufacturing industry, like those of most other sectors, were prepared by the income-produced method.

The source data for manufactures estimates were of three main sorts. First, the most basic data were obtained from censuses of manufactures, which themselves were of three types: a census of manufactures was taken with each decennial census, from 1871 to 1911, the data applying to the calendar year preceding the census date—these censuses of manufactures were taken by enumerators; two postal censuses were taken for the years 1905 and 1915, both of which suffered from incomplete coverage; an annual census of manufactures was taken from 1917 onward. Second, a large quantity of data of many kinds and from many miscellaneous sources, nearly all of them official documents, were used to obtain estimates for the intercensal years. Third, quite extensive use was made of data on occupations and wages collected in the censuses of population. The 1911 census was the most valuable for this purpose. In that year the equivalent of an industrial classification of the labor force, very similar to the standard industrial classification of 1948, was used to classify the labor force. The part of the labor force classified to manufacturing matched very closely that of the numbers recorded in the census of manufactures. In addition, in 1911 the wages and salaries of every employed person collected in the census were useful for comparative purposes as well as for filling gaps for those industries employing fewer than five persons that were omitted from the 1911 census. Similar data from the 1901 and the 1921 censuses were likewise useful, though in a more limited fashion since there was not as satisfactory an industrial classification of the labor force for these years.

The information obtained in the censuses before 1917 was limited. The basic data obtained were gross value of products, costs of materials, payments of wages and salaries, cost of fuels beginning in 1900, and in one year, 1900, outlays on other miscellaneous expenses. In all of these early censuses there was a quite fine breakdown of industries, the number of individual industries varying from slightly less than 200 upward to 250, but there was no commodity detail.

For the years from 1917 onward the censuses contained considerably more information than hitherto. The largest change was the addition of the collection of commodity data. In addition, for the years 1917–23 data on "miscellaneous" expenses were obtained.

Three features of the set of data should be noted immediately. First, from 1870 to 1915 the census included what has variously been called custom and repair work or the hand trades, and, indeed, data were collected for these trades, although tabulated separately, in the annual census from 1917 to 1921. It was not feasible to separate the data for custom and repair from manufacturing proper before 1917, and consequently the estimates for 1870–1916 include these trades. In order to maintain comparability from 1917 onward, custom and repair, though tabulated separately, were also included with the various manufacturing industries to which they were related. This procedure is in contrast to the official estimates, which begin in 1926 and do not include custom and repair with manufactures.

Second, the censuses of 1900, 1905, 1910, and 1915 all fell somewhat short of complete coverage of the manufacturing industry. The census of 1900 did not cover businesses employing fewer than five persons, except in the cases of cheese factories and of brick and tile yards, which were covered completely. The census of 1910, in general, also did not include businesses employing fewer than five persons, but the exceptions for which full coverage was taken were extended to cover such industries as sawmills and flour and grist mills, with the result that the undercoverage was much less than in 1900. The censuses of 1905 and 1915, the first postal censuses, also had their shortcomings: the number of establishments covered in the census of 1905 appears small in comparison with the numbers in 1900 and 1910, and in any event, information on cost of materials was not obtained; the census of 1915 omitted collection of data from businesses producing products valued at less than $2,500, irrespective of the number of persons employed, except for flour and grist mills, butter and cheese factories, fish-preserving factories, sawmills, brick and tile yards, lime kilns, and electric light plants, which were covered whatever their size. The greatest shortfall in coverage in 1915 would be bakeries, tailoring, and blacksmithing; sawmills were also considerably underreported. The shortfalls in the coverage of 1900 and 1910 required the construction of special estimates to fill in the gaps of the census data for those years.

Third, for the first volume of *Historical Statistics of Canada,* the manufacturing data for all censuses from 1870 to 1959 were classified, on as nearly a uniform basis as possible, into 17 industry groups in accordance with the Canadian standard industrial classification of 1948; this work was done in the DBS. This classification was most useful since the entire industrial distribution of GDP by industry in the official accounts for the years 1926–46 is based on the Standard Industrial Classification of 1948.

## The Basic Estimates

The most basic estimates are those for the decennial census years of 1870, 1880, 1890, 1900, 1910, for 1915, and for each year from 1917 to 1926, all years in which a census of manufactures was taken. As has been noted, some supplemental estimation for the omitted establishments employing fewer than five persons in 1900, 1910, 1915, and 1917 was necesssary, but a description of the method of calculating income generated in manufacturing in the decennial census benchmark years and in the later annual census of manufactures years is given.

The method is very simple. In the census of manufactures all business establishments reported the gross value of their products, the costs of materials, and wage and salary and piecework costs. In addition, in the 1900 census an estimate (provided by the establishments themselves) of the numbers engaged and of the value of labor services of owners and firm members was obtained. Also, in 1900 and in 1917–23 the costs of miscellaneous expenses, which included such items as rent of works and offices, insurance, travel, taxes, repairs, advertising, interest, royalties, and ostensibly all other expenses, were collected. If these expenses were complete, GDP at factor cost in manufacturing should be derivable by a process of subtracting the cost of materials, of fuel and power, and of such part of the miscellaneous expenses as contains items that are true costs and not themselves a part of factor returns from gross value of production. In fact, the method followed was actually to subtract relevant costs from gross value of production, the estimation process being done at the level of each of the 17 industry groups of the 1948 standard industrial classification.

The question then becomes one of trying to obtain estimates of gross value of product, of cost of materials, of cost of fuel and power, and of miscellaneous expenses that are as correct as possible. These items are dealt with in order.

Gross Value of Product

As for estimates of gross value of product (GVP), the amounts reported in the census returns themselves were accepted without amendment for the part of manufacturing that was covered in the censuses. It was accepted that the coverage was complete in 1870, 1880, 1890, and virtually complete in 1917–26; in 1900 and 1910, it was necessary to add estimates of output of those businesses employing fewer than five persons that were omitted in these censuses; in 1915 it was necessary to add estimates for those businesses producing less than $2,500 output; and for 1917–26 it was necessary to estimate custom and repair work. A rather extensive examination of some individual establishment returns for 1870, the only year for which individual establishment data are available, suggests that sometimes minor products and their values were not reported in that year. Hence the reported total of product values for that year is probably understated by an unknown amount. But there is no basis for making any revision of the reported figures. Further, it seems probable that in 1870 the cost of raw materials was also understated— the inspection noted above suggested that minor raw materials might have been omitted. If both GVP and costs of raw materials were understated, the biases would be offsetting for calculating GDP.

A scrutiny of the questionnaires used in the censuses shows the following. For 1870, 1890, and 1900, the questionnaires under the heading "Products" (1870 and 1890) or "Goods Manufactured" (1900) simply asked for "kind" or "classes" of products, "quantities," and "values" (1870 and 1890) or "value or price at work" (1900), with a single line being left for each of these stubs; in 1880 the request was limited to "aggregate value in $ of products"; in 1910 the headings were like those for 1890 but there were several blank lines to allow the listing of products. A request "Received for custom work and repairing" was added in 1900. It was not until 1915 that the instruction on the questionnaire specifically requested the inclusion of by-products and the value of containers sold with goods, and that a request for the item "all other products (value only)" was specifically printed on the questionnaire. The censuses from 1917 onward specified the commodity detail desired on forms that were specific to each industry and probably elicited full reporting.

Three other points are relevant. First, there is little or no information on instructions given to the enumerators about the taking of the censuses of manufactures. Second, there is no indication of whether or not construction work (of a capital account nature) done by establishments for their own use was included in value of product—it most likely was not. (Some information on establishments' construction with their own workforce was sought in 1919, but there is no evidence that the resulting information was used.) Third, it is probably safe to say that goods were valued at the works from 1900 onward although the specific instruction to so value them was not contained in the 1910 schedule; the instructions for 1870, 1880, and 1890 do not specify the place of valuation.

Cost of Materials

The figures reported in the censuses for cost of materials were also accepted as reported (except for such adjustment as was necessary owing to the undercoverage of small businesses in 1900, 1910, and 1915 and custom work, 1919–26).

There are some uncertainties about the reliability of the recorded raw material costs on which some light is cast by the questions in the questionnaires. The exact wording of the relevant parts of the census questionnaire for censuses from 1870 to 1915 follows.

WORDING ON CENSUS OF MANUFACTURES
re information on raw materials and entire exact wording on form
1870    Raw material
        12. Kind
        13. Quantities
        14. Aggregate value, in dollars
1880    17. Aggregate value in $ of raw material
1890    Materials used
        18. Kind
        19. Quantities
        20.  Cost at the factory using them including freight charges
1900    Materials used
            In crude state
        42. Kinds
        43. Cost delivered, $
            In partly manufactured state
        44. Kinds
        45. Cost delivered, $
1905    No information on raw materials
1910    39. Kind or class of raw or partly finished materials used at
            the works in year.

        ———
        ——— (several lines left)

        ———
        40. Cost value of raw or partly finished materials used at
            works in year.

        ———
        ——— (several lines left)

        ———

1915    4. Materials used:

Give cost values including freight, duty, etc., of all materials actually used in the manufacture of goods, whether raw or partly manufactured or whether entering into the product, used as containers (boxes, barrels, cans, etc.), or consumed in the process or manufacturing. Do not consider stock used as identical with stock purchased. Materials produced by the establishment itself and used by it for further manufacture are not to be included.

Total cost value of all materials used—$_____.

Itemize principal materials used in the following schedule:

|          | Articles | Quantities | Cost Values |
|----------|----------|------------|-------------|
| 1.       |          |            |             |
| 2.       |          |            |             |
| 3.       |          |            |             |
| 4.       |          |            |             |
| 5.       |          |            |             |
| 6.       |          |            |             |
| 7.       |          |            |             |

8. Fuel for power purposes
9. All other (value only)

1917    (onward)

From 1917 onward itemized forms for material costs specialized to industries were used. I have several of these. It would appear that in some industries in 1917 the listing of material inputs was not complete, since there was no heading for "all other materials" and containers were not included; in other industries the specifications were fairly complete even in 1917. In all industries the specifications were quite complete by 1920–22. From then on containers, etc., and other package materials were always included with costs where relevant. The consequence is that for some industries the 1917–19 figures for materials used are too low.

Cost of Fuel and Power

The data reported for cost of fuel and light and rent of power and heat are less well covered than those for GVP and for cost of material. Such data were not collected at all before 1900, although some part (probably small) of fuel costs may have been included in the cost of materials. In 1900, the money cost of "rent of power and heat" and expenses of "fuel and light" were collected explicitly; in 1910, the weight of coal used and the value of all fuels consumed were collected but not the cost of purchased power which, although requested on the form, was not tabulated; in 1915, although cost of fuel used for power purposes was collected, it was not tabulated separately and is most likely included in cost of materials for that year—fuel-for-power costs were collected in the same section as material costs; from 1917 onward, costs of fuel of all kinds and of rent of power were collected. It became necessary, then, to make estimates for the census years not covered. Only the simplest methods could be used. Purchased power for 1910 was estimated by first interpolating linearly the percentage of costs of purchased power to GVP for each of the 17 industry groups, between 1900 and 1917, and then applying the relevant percentage figure for each group in 1910 to the GVP in 1910. The purchased power costs were then added to fuel costs, which were collected in the census of 1910, to obtain fuel and power costs. Fuel and power costs for each industry in 1915 were estimated by linear interpolation between 1910 and 1917 of the ratio of such costs to GVP and then applying the 1915 ratios to GVP in 1915. For 1870, 1880, and 1890, the ratios of fuel and power costs to GVP for each of the 17 industries were taken as being the same as in 1900, and the estimates were made on that basis. The changes between 1900 and 1917 were sufficiently moderate that one has a reasonably comfortable feeling in following this procedure.

Miscellaneous Expenses

The most difficult problem to deal with was the estimation of "miscellaneous expenses." The purpose of obtaining these miscellaneous expenses presumably was to collect all expenses of manufacture other than material and fuel costs and salary and wage cost, excepting only capital consumption allowances.

The history of the collection of these costs is of some interest. "Miscellaneous expenses" under the headings given here were first requested on the questionnaire in the census of manufactures for 1900.

Headings of Miscellaneous Expenditure, 1900

Rent of works (if any), $                Rent of offices, interest, in-
Rent of power and heat (if any), $        surance, internal revenue
Fuel and light, $                            tax, etc. $
Municipal taxes, $                        Amount paid for contract
Provincial taxes, $                          work (if any), $

The largest item reported is the second from the last in the list ("rent of offices," etc.): it was obviously a catchall item—it frequently amounted to one-half or more of the total—but just what was included is not clear. For example, it is not clear whether or not it includes costs of repairs and maintenance, office supplies, postage, travel, local transportation costs, and other such items.

It was not until 1917 that the same kind of information was collected again. From 1917 to 1921 "miscellaneous expenses" were collected under headings like those for 1919 enumerated here, which are typical of other years.

Miscellaneous Expenses during the Year 1919

Rent of offices, works, and machinery
Cost of purchased power
Insurance (premium for year only)
          Excise
Taxes §    Excess Profits Tax
          Provincial and Municipal
Royalties, use of patents, etc.
Advertising expenses
Travelling expenses
Repairs to buildings and Machinery
All other sundry expenses (do not include fuel costs, materials used, salaries and wages).
                                   Total:

In 1922 and 1923 only the totals for all miscellaneous expenses (without any details) were collected; thereafter, this information was no longer obtained in the census of manufactures. In the enumerated data for 1917–21 the item "all other sundry expenses" was the largest one, often amounting to one-half or more of the total.

There was one other important body of data on miscellaneous expenses. At the time of preparation of the national income estimates for the Royal Commission on Dominion-Provincial Relations, in the late 1930s, a questionnaire requesting a great deal of information on value of products, cost of materials, wage and salary costs, depreciation, and a very wide range of miscellaneous expenses for the years 1929, 1933, and 1936 was sent to a very large number of manufacturing establishments, and a large response was obtained. The listing of expense items was quite exhaustive. By means of its use it was possible to ascertain that the "miscellaneous expenses" obtained by 1921 in the census of manufactures were quite complete, except for depreciation.

There are some items in the "miscellaneous expenses," as recorded in the census of manufactures data, that should not be treated as an expense for the purposes of estimating GDP. Thus, excess profits tax, royalties, use of patents, etc., and interest paid should not be deducted as expenses. A basis for calculating the interest payments (included in sundry expenses) was obtained from the royal Commission data alluded to above. These items were removed from the miscellaneous expense series used as a cost item in the calculation of GDP.

Basic data on miscellaneous expenses, then, were available by industrial groups for the years 1900 and 1917–23. Estimates for the

years 1924–26 were made by interpolation of the ratios of miscellaneous expenses to GVP between 1923 and 1929, the data for the
later year being the Royal Commission material. The data for 1900
yielded estimates that appeared to be much too low in comparison
both with years 1917–26 in Canada and especially with estimates for
the United States for 1889, 1899, 1904, and 1910. A considerable
amount of supplementary material along with the material of the
census was used to obtain individual industry benchmarks in 1900.
Estimates for each year from 1901 to 1916 were made, for each of 17
industry groups, by linear interpolation of the ratio of miscellaneous
expenses to GVP between 1900 and 1917. The expense ratios for the
years 1870–99 were assumed to be the same as in 1900.

I have some reservations about these estimates of miscellaneous
expenses for the earlier years. I believe that the supplementation of
the data for 1900 with other information was justified: the figures
that were used reflected my best judgment of reality. Yet it remains
true that an element of estimation not based on complete information was involved. It is possible also that even if the 1900 figures are
reasonably accurate, the ratios might have been somewhat lower in
the 1870s and 1880s; but the absence of data precludes taking a different course than that followed.

Such then were the procedures used to obtain estimates of GDP in
manufacturing.

# Appendix 5
## *The Cost of Living Index*

The cost of living index that was used to deflate the component of GNP
(expenditure) that excluded gross fixed capital formation was prepared
from three temporally distinct segments that were linked together at
overlapping years.

The first segment, covering the years 1913–26, was a full-blown
estimate prepared by the Dominion Bureau of Statistics. It appears as
series Kl in *Historical Statistics of Canada,* 2d edition.

The second segment, covering the years 1900–1913, was based on
an index prepared by Gordon W. Bertram and Michael B. Percy which
appeared in "Real Wage Trends in Canada, 1900–26: Some Provisional
Estimates," *Canadian Journal of Economics* (May 1979). Bertram and
Percy revised the federal Department of Labour's "Index Numbers of
a Family Budget," which covered the years 1900, 1905, and 1909–26
(Urquhart and Buckley, p. 303) in two ways. First, they used an im-

proved weighting system for aggregating the basic data, which were fully available. Second, they added a clothing component, prepared from mail-order catalogs of the T. Eaton Company for the years 1900–13, to the existing Department of Labour components of food, fuel and light, and rent.

The Bertram-Percy index was used as given for the years which they covered from 1900 to 1913. It remained to fill in figures for the years 1901–4 and 1906–8, which they, following the Department of Labour, had not covered. The latter years were interpolated between 1900 and 1905 and 1905 and 1909, respectively, by use of the wholesale price index, excluding gold (Urquhart and Buckley, ser. J 34).

The third segment, covering the years 1870–1900, was based on a cost of living index for Kingston, Ontario, prepared by R. F. J. Barnett and appearing in his M. A. thesis at Queen's University, "A Study of Price Movements and the Cost of Living in Kingston, Ontario, for the Years 1865 to 1900" (1963). Barnett prepared his index by using newspaper material on prices supplemented by information obtained from good records of a food store that was in business throughout his period, similar types of records for a fuel company, and records of expenditures by the House of Industry (the poor house), which records were in the archives of the City of Kingston.

Barnett's weighting system used all available Canadian and United States data relevant to the period and, in addition, information on consumer expenditure patterns collected by the Ontario Bureau of Industry for the 1880s. It was quite good for what it covered. However, Barnett was able to cover only food and fuel and light, which made up a large part of the consumer budget of the time but omitted clothing and rent (as well as items like household furnishing, etc.).

Although it was not possible, at this time, to do anything about the omission of clothing, it was possible to make an improvisation for rent. In her work on estimating expenditure on residential housing, Marion Steele had prepared a construction cost index for housing. This index was used as a surrogate for an index of rents. Such a procedure is, of course, a makeshift measure. However, a check with United States rent data (the Rees-Long-Hoover data noted below) and United States construction cost indexes (United States Historical Statistics, Colonial Times to 1970, Series N138 and N139) showed a not unreasonable correspondence in the period from 1870 to 1900. And so a rental index component was added to Barnett's index, the weight given to rent being based on data for Kingston in the 1880s from the Ontario Bureau of Industry surveys of the time. (The actual weight was 0.2.)

I believe that the resulting index for Kingston, although admittedly based on narrow regional data, reflects living cost movements considerably better than does a wholesale price index. It lacks a clothing component, which perhaps biases the index downward in the 1870s. However, at the same time the use of a construction cost index as a surrogate for rental rates may constitute a slight upward bias in the 1870s.

For readers to make their own judgments, I give table 2.A.1 (see p. 88) for comparing movements in our cost of living with a comparable one for the United States and with the DBS wholesale price index (Urquhart and Buckley, ser. J34). The United States index is derived by linking together Rees's index for 1890–1900 (Albert Rees, *Real Wages in Manufacturing 1890–1914*, p. 74) with Clarence Long's index for 1880–90 and Ethyl Hoover's index for 1860–80 (Clarence Long, *Wages and Earnings in the United States 1860–1890*, pp. 156, 157). The United States index for 1870–78 is adjusted downward by the amount of the premium on gold in United States currency for that time. Concerning the DBS wholesale price index, I just note that an alternative index by H. Michell (Urquhart and Buckley, ser. J1) shows considerably lower relative prices in the 1870s than does the DBS index.

# Notes

1. In response to suggestions made at the Williamsburg Conference, I have made two small additions to the paper as it was originally presented. First, estimates of indirect taxes less subsidies have been prepared, making possible the presentation of GNP at market prices. Second, an improved estimate of real GNP replaces the notional estimates of the original paper, and real growth rates are presented.

2. The actual procedure used was to calculate the ratio of gross product at factor cost in "trade" and in "community . . . services" to gross product in all other industries in census years and in 1926, to interpolate this ratio linearly between census years and to 1926, and then, in effect, to get annual intercensal data for these two industries by multiplying, year by year, the interpolated ratios by the sum of gross product at factor cost in all other industries. The actual figures for intercensal years for these two industries are not reproduced in the table just because for these years they have not been estimated from basic data in the style of all other industries.

3. The best single reference to what I have called the traditionalist view is in the Royal Commission on Dominion-Provincial Relations *Final Report* (1940).

4. I give two references for the revisionists: Bertram 1963, and Chambers and Gordon 1966.

5. See appendix 5 for a description of the construction of the consumer price index.

6. Even if a reasonable correction is made to the numbers of gainfully occupied persons reported in 1901 census, the actual output per gainfully occupied person increased at a somewhat more rapid compound annual rate for the decade 1891–1901 (3 years centered in each case) than for the decade 1901–11 (3 years centered in each case). All of this increase in productivity in the 1891–1901 decade occurred after 1896. Part of the growth of output per gainfully occupied person from 1896 onward to 1901 must have reflected cyclical upswing, but some considerable part must have reflected long-term growth. Unless the growth of these years 1896–1901 is an artifact of the statistics, and I do not believe that it is, an investigation of the rapid productivity increase in these years should be well worth while.

**Table 2.A.1**     Comparison of Barnett and Rees-Long-Hoover Cost of Living Indexes and Canadian Wholesale Price Index, 1871–1900 (Base of Index 1900 = 100)

| Year | Barnett (Canadian) | Rees-Long-Hoover (U.S.) | DBS Wholesale Price Index | Year | Barnett (Canadian) | Rees-Long-Hoover (U.S.) | DBS Wholesale Price Index |
|---|---|---|---|---|---|---|---|
| 1870 | 107 | 135 | 128 | 1886 | 103 | 111 | 100 |
| 1871 | 108 | 134 | 130 | 1887 | 109 | 112 | 102 |
| 1872 | 116 | 133 | 145 | 1888 | 105 | 112 | 106 |
| 1873 | 115 | 129 | 146 | 1889 | 107 | 109 | 106 |
| 1874 | 112 | 128 | 138 | 1890 | 105 | 108 | 108 |
| 1875 | 108 | 118 | 133 | 1891 | 105 | 108 | 108 |
| 1876 | 109 | 117 | 124 | 1892 | 105 | 108 | 100 |
| 1877 | 106 | 125 | 118 | 1893 | 104 | 107 | 101 |
| 1878 | 104 | 121 | 109 | 1894 | 95 | 102 | 95 |
| 1879 | 103 | 120 | 105 | 1895 | 91 | 100 | 93 |
| 1880 | 106 | 121 | 115 | 1896 | 95 | 100 | 90 |
| 1881 | 111 | 121 | 116 | 1897 | 96 | 99 | 91 |
| 1882 | 118 | 121 | 116 | 1898 | 100 | 99 | 95 |
| 1883 | 119 | 119 | 113 | 1899 | 97 | 99 | 97 |
| 1884 | 104 | 117 | 107 | 1900 | 100 | 100 | 100 |
| 1885 | 104 | 114 | 101 | | | | |

# Comment    J. H. Dales

For the better part of a decade Professor Urquhart and a small band of colleagues have doggedly pushed forward with the preparation of a completely new set of historical National Accounts for Canada. This paper, along with those of McInnis and Green, gives us our first substantial view of a project that has increased the volume of numbers available to students of the Canadian economy by many orders of magnitude. The project was initiated by Urquhart, and has been animated and directed by him; and in the end he also became directly responsible for a large portion of the new figures.

The quantitative output of the project is, quite simply, stupefying. The core of the work is the set of detailed, annual estimates of GNP at factor cost for the whole period from 1870 (the first Canadian census) to 1926 (when official National Accounts figures became available). In addition, A. Sinclair of Dalhousie University has completed "annual estimates of the main components of the balance of international payments, a large part of which has been newly estimated"; and there are new data on investment—an annual series on residential capital formation prepared by Marion Steel of the University of Guelph, and a series on investment in producer's durables from 1870 to 1985 prepared by Urquhart. Despite all this new work there is still one obvious soft spot in our national accounts history. As Urquhart notes, the GNP figures have not yet been deflated,* implicit prices appear in the agricultural, but not in the manufacturing or total GNP estimates. It would indeed be a pity to deflate these high-quality estimates by the coarse price indexes that are currently available, and the new estimates have given a new urgency to historical work on prices in Canada.

The new estimates constitute the second attempt to provide a comprehensive set of historical National Accounts for Canada; the first such estimates were prepared by O. J. Firestone some 30 years ago and published in his 1958 volume, *Canada's Economic Development, 1867–1953*. Since the two sets of numbers are bound to be compared, I hope Urquhart will prepare a short account of the major differences between them and possible explanations for the differences. (McInnis provides a good commentary on the agricultural figures, perhaps the main source of these major differences.) The point would only be to satisfy our gross curiosity; the estimates differ in concept, construction, and especially in the amount of raw data that underlies them, and it would be pointless to attempt to reconcile them in any detailed way.

J. H. Dales is professor emeritus in the Department of Economics at the University of Toronto.
*These remarks by Dales relate to the draft of Urquhart's paper delivered at Williamsburg. Urquhart subsequently computed deflators. (EDS.)

Here I comment on the estimates from the point of view of their probable effect on research in Canadian economic history. In retrospect I find it rather surprising that Firestone's estimates have stimulated so little research. Two reasons may be suggested. First, the Firestone figures were simply too skeletal, consisting essentially of estimates at census dates, with only a few annual series for large aggregates that represented interpolations made on a more or less mechanical basis between census years. Second, the worksheets of the people involved in the Firestone project were apparently never brought together in a safe repository, and over time they became lost. The result was that the scholarly community was faced with numbers that could be used to calculate decadal growth rates for a few major aggregates, but not for much else. More important, there was not much chance of fleshing out the skeleton by building on the raw data and attempting to improve the estimates, which is why improved estimates necessitated a whole new start.

If the Firestone estimates had a low research multiplier, I feel sure that the Urquhart estimates will greatly enrich the study of Canadian economic history. The main reason is their richness in detail. The GNP totals, for example, are built up from estimates for twenty sectors: agriculture, manufacturing, and six lesser commodity sectors; construction; transportation; residential rents; three government sectors; public education; three minor service sectors, and two large ones—trade, and personal and business services. Of these only the last two, constituting about 15% of the total, have had to be interpolated on a mechanical basis between census years; enough ancillary data have been found to develop annual series that can be used as interpolators for the other 18 sectors. Moreover, the sectors are themselves constructed from subsectors: some 28 separate commodity series for agriculture, and 17 separate series for manufacturing. There is more than enough here to enrich scores of doctoral dissertations, and it is hard to think of any research in the field that will not benefit from this new material. Constant use, in turn, will act as a continuous testing of the data, and, when anomalies appear, will lead to attempts to improve individual series. Our new numbers can confidently be expected to increase our research metabolism. (To make sure I was saying what I wanted to say, I checked "metabolism" in *The Concise Oxford Dictionary,* and was delighted to find that it is the process by which "nutritive material is built up into living matter.")

I now turn away from the numbers themselves, as Urquhart has done, in order to speculate about how they may affect current interpretations of Canadian development between Confederation and 1930. I begin with a telling quotation from an article on "The Political Economy of National Statistics" by William Alonso and Paul Starr in the Social Science Research Council's *Items* of September 1982:

Statistics are lenses through which we form images of our society. Frederick Jackson Turner announced his famous views on the significance of the closing of the frontier on the basis of data from the 1890 Census. Our [the American] self-image today is confirmed or challenged by numbers which tell of drastic changes in the family, the reversal of rural-to-urban migration . . . and many others. Whether the meanings read into the data are reasonable or fanciful, these numbers provide a common reference in popular and professional discussion. Even when they misrepresent reality, they often standardize our perception of it.

The process is thus recursive. Winston Churchill observed that first we shape our buildings and then they shape us. The same may be said of our statistics. (P. 30)

Of course there are lenses other than statistics. The time-honored view of Canadian economic history is that the economy suffered from something like secular stagnation from 1870 to 1900. This view was based primarily, it seems, on the fact that no new major staple export industry appeared in Canada between Confederation in 1867 and the wheat boom that got under way in western Canada at the turn of the century; but it may also have reflected the two most readily accessible statistics for the period, those that demonstrated falling prices and net emigration throughout at least the first 25 years of these 3 decades.

In the past quarter century a somewhat different interpretation has become quite common. It may very well have developed from Firestone's numbers, and especially from the emphasis he put on the growth of manufacturing in Canada in the nineteenth century. The new interpretation rather diffidently suggests that the 30 years after Confederation may not have been such a washout after all, and rather more stridently blames the "staple theory" for putting far too much emphasis on the western wheat boom and giving far too little attention to central Canadian manufacturing *and* agriculture, both before and after 1900.

Neither view is very carefully specified, and their proponents quite often talk past one another rather than disagreeing with one another. No one would dispute the view that the Canadian *economy,* or national GNP, grew much more slowly from 1870 to 1900 than it did in either of the 3 decades before and after this period, and very much more slowly than the United States economy during the same 30-year period. On the question of growth in the well-being of Canadians, or national GNP per person, there is less discussion. In traditional accounts, the great contrast drawn between the years before and after 1900 no doubt left the impression that per capita trends moved with the total trends, but Canadian historians have displayed a remarkable lack of interest in discussing trends in the Canadian standard of living. On the general question of emphasis, I offer two comments that weigh in on the revisionist side of the debate, which in truth might more accurately be described as a duel in the dark.

First, net emigration from Canada over the period can be viewed positively, that is to say as a necessary means of supporting the standard of living during these years, rather than negatively as clear evidence of a national catastrophe. If the various parts of Canada are viewed as regions in North America, the emigrations may appear less shocking, and indeed as a process that has on occasion occurred in different parts of the United States. It remains true that after 1870 all sections of Canada had bad luck at the same time, and that the growth of Canadian manufacturing, though not insignificant, could not begin to compensate for the decline in the Maritimes' shipping and shipbuilding industries and for the rapid growth of population in Quebec where agricultural land was already fully occupied. Even in Ontario, where the economy was much more buoyant, the good land had all been taken up and farmers' sons made the sensible decision to head for the American West, despite the lamentations of journalists, notably of George Brown, one of the fathers of Confederation.

Second, nearly all students would agree that the positive effect of western development on the Canadian standard of living after 1900 was flawed, to an unknown extent, by government support for a ridiculous amount of overinvestment in railways. The efficiency of the economy must also have been reduced, but again to a completely unknown extent, by government policies promoting uneconomically rapid settlement of the West (the Canadian homestead program was on a much larger scale, proportionally, than the American program), and perhaps also by the effect of western development in expanding tariff-protected manufacturing in central Canada.

Urquhart makes no claim that his new estimates settle this debate. He thinks the new figures may give marginal support to the traditionalists, mainly on the ground that agriculture is shown to have grown much more slowly before 1900, and considerably more rapidly after 1900, than Firestone's figures implied. The same pattern is repeated in the total GNP figures in current dollar terms. Indeed, the new estimates of GNP are some 15%–20% below Firestone's estimates for the years before 1900, and only a favorable deflator can save our forebears from the prospect of an even lower standard of living than we had imagined they had attained. The Urquhart numbers for manufacturing are also lower than Firestone's, but the revisionists will be able to take a little bit of comfort from the fact that the ratio of manufacturing to agricultural output is marginally higher in the new series, and that manufacturing's growth rate is slightly higher both before and after 1900 than in Firestone's figures. But deflators can be dynamite, and we are all of us, both traditionalists and revisionists, hoping for the best, but fearing the worst, about what constant dollar figures will show. In the meantime we *do* have a more accurate picture of the western boom than we have had in the past. Urquhart shows that it was at first primarily an investment boom, and that wheat exports did not explode until after 1910.

Allow me, in closing, to make a strong plea for someone to provide us users of statistics with sectoral workforce statistics of a quality to match our new output statistics, so that reliable sectoral productivity estimates may be calculated. My reason is that I have become sated with growth rates and am anxious to trade off a good deal of additional knowledge about economic *performance* for a better understanding of economic *process*. I have always delighted in the way that Gallman's sectoral productivity figures meshed so neatly with Salter's theoretical analysis of how differential sectoral productivities worked their way through the price system to produce easily observable features of the growth process. One of the great virtues of Urquhart's new estimates is that they bring us within a relatively short distance of several additional breakthroughs in our understanding of Canada's economic past.

# Reference

Bertram, G. W., 1963. Economic growth in Canadian industry: The staple model and the take-off hypothesis. *Canadian Journal of Economics and Political Science*.

Chambers, E. J., and Gordon, D. F. 1966. Primary products and economic growth: An empirical measurement. *Journal of Political Economy*.

―――.1967. Rejoinder. *Journal of Political Economy*.

Caves, R. E. 1971. Export-led growth and the new economic history. In *Trade, balance of payments and growth*, ed. J. N. Bhagwati et al. Amsterdam and Oxford: New York: American Elsevier.

Dales, J. H., et al. 1967. Primary products of economic growth: A comment. *Journal of Political Economy*.

Firestone, O. J. 1958. *Canada's economic development, 1867–1953*. International Association for Research in Income and Wealth, vol. 7. London: Bowes & Bowes.

Friedman, Milton, and Schwartz, Anna Jacobsen. 1963. *A monetary history of the United States, 1867–1960*. Princeton: Princeton University Press (for NBER).

Innis, H. A. 1956. *The fur trade in Canada*. Reprint. Toronto: University of Toronto Press. (Originally published, Yale University Press, 1930.)

————.1933. *Problems of staple production in Canada*. Toronto: Ryerson Press.

Kendrick, John W., ed. 1961. *Productivity trends in the United States*. Princeton: Princeton University Press (for NBER).

Kuznets, Simon, ed. assisted by Jenks, Elizabeth. 1961. *Capital in the American economy: Its formation and financing*. Princeton: Princeton University Press (for NBER).

Mackintosh, W. A. 1964. *The economic background to Dominion–provincial relations*. Appendix III of Report of the Royal Commission on Dominion–Provincial relations. Carleton Library no. 13. Reprint, Toronto: McClelland & Stewart. (Originally published King's Printer, 1939.)

Royal Commission on Dominion–Provincial Relations. 1940 *Final report*. Ottawa: King's Printer.

Statistics Canada. 1981. *Fixed capital flows and stocks, 1926–1978*. Catalogue no. 13568. Ottawa: Statistics Canada.

Urquhart, M. C., and Buckley, K. A. H., eds. 1965. *Historical statistics of Canada*. Cambridge: Cambridge University Press; Toronto: Macmillan of Canada.

# 3 Measuring the Transaction Sector in the American Economy, 1870–1970

John Joseph Wallis and Douglass C. North

Economists since Adam Smith have extolled the benefits to humanity of specialization and the division of labor. If economists have a philosopher's stone it is the principle of comparative advantage. Output can be increased without increasing the number of producers simply by reallocating production to those producers with the lowest opportunity costs. Likewise reallocating goods and services between consumers with different preferences can increase the welfare of society without actually increasing the number of goods and services.

In recent decades economists have come to realize that the gains from specialization and the division of labor are not a free lunch. Beginning with Coase's article on "The Nature of the Firm" the role of "transaction costs"—that is, the costs of making exchanges—has become more important in explaining the structure of market and nonmarket forms of economic organization (Coase 1937, 1960). This voluminous literature offers the promise of new insights into the way economic systems evolve, but to this point it has not resulted in an empirical definition or measure of transaction costs. This paper is a preliminary attempt to identify and measure those costs in the American economy between 1870 and 1970.

Given the size of the transaction costs literature it is surprising that there has not been an attempt to measure them. Perhaps this stems

John Joseph Wallis is assistant professor of economics at the University of Maryland. Douglass C. North is the Luce Professor of Law and Liberty at Washington University in Saint Louis, Missouri.

We thank Andy Rutten, Tom Weiss, Robert Gallman, Barry Weingast, Edward Denison, Yoram Barzel, David Galeson, Stanley Engerman, Mark Plummer, Randy Rucker, and workshops at Washington University, the University of Maryland, and the University of Chicago for helpful comments; Matthew Wallis for computational assistance; and particularly Lance Davis, whose comments substantially affected the final draft of this paper.

from a general lack of consensus over what the most important elements of transaction costs are. Williamson's work focuses on the costs of cheating or opportunistic behavior, the work initiated by Stigler concentrates on the costs of obtaining information (even when no one is lying), Alchian and Demsetz take up the problem of coordinating diverse inputs in the production process, Jensen and Meckling address the principal-agent problem, and Barzel has brought to light the problems of measurement.[1] We try to encompass these various concepts of transaction costs into a single unified definition.

Another reason for the lack of empirical measures of transaction costs stems from the comparative-static nature of much of the theoretical work. For the most part the approach is to identify, theoretically, the effects of increasing or decreasing transaction costs. In that context the central distinction is between situations in which transaction costs (of whatever form) are high and situations in which they are low.[2] This is understandable, since the industrial organization literature is primarily concerned with explaining alternative forms of organization and one potential explanation is high (or low) transaction costs. Distinguishing between high and low transaction costs, however, gives us no guidelines when the problem of measuring the *level* of transaction costs is addressed, and that is the problem we face.

In a fundamental sense we have no quantitative measure of transaction costs because we do not have a clear, general theoretical concept of the costs of exchange. As Kuznets has pointed out, "no economic measure is neutral, that is unaffected by economic theories of production, value, and welfare, and the broader social philosophy encompassing them."[3] We spend the first section developing a theoretical definition of transaction costs and the transaction sector. We have three purposes. The first is to integrate these estimates into the existing transaction cost literature. Second, we hope eventually to incorporate the notion of the transaction sector into the structure of the national income and product accounts, the current standard measure of the performance of economies over time. Finally, and most apparent, we hope to provide the framework of the empirical estimates that follow in sections 3.2 and 3.3. The potential implications of integration of the transaction sector into the accounts is the subject of section 3.4.

## 3.1  Defining the Transaction Sector

Constructing a definition of transaction costs is no easy matter. General definitions abound. "The costs of exchanging property rights," "the costs of making and enforcing contracts," and the one that we began our investigation with, "the costs of capturing the gains from specialization and division of labor," are all too broad to be of operational use. In what follows we adopt a slightly less general notion of what transaction costs are and then translate our notion into explicit categories of economic activity consistent with the historical income accounts and labor force series.

While as economists we wish to separate transaction costs from other costs, individual economic actors have no such motivation. People maximize net benefits, the difference between total benefits and total costs, where total costs include both transaction and other costs.[4] Every economic activity involves elements of transaction and other costs. Ideally our measure of transaction costs would delve into each exchange and separate these costs. Unfortunately, data are not available for such a measure. Instead our basic approach is to segregate economic activities and actors into those that are primarily associated with making exchanges and those that are not. The sum of the resources used by those associated with transacting make up our estimate of the transaction sector.

To make clear the rationale underlying our segregation of economic activity into different categories, we employ the terms "transaction function" and "transformation function." Transaction costs are the costs associated with making exchanges, the costs of performing the transaction function. Transformation costs are the costs associated with transforming inputs into outputs, the costs of performing the transformation function. From the viewpoint of the individual both of these functions are "productive"; that is, transaction and transformation costs are incurred only if the expected benefits from doing so exceed the costs of doing so. The behavioral similarity of transaction costs and transformation costs is critical, since it implies that we do not need a new "transaction costs theory" of human behavior to deal with transaction costs; simple price theory will suffice.

Within a general economic theory of behavior, which need not draw a distinction between transaction and transformation costs, it is nevertheless possible to distinguish the two functions in a meaningful way, one that gives rise to reasonable guidelines for dividing the two functions empirically. We define inputs in the standard economic way: the land, labor, capital, and entrepreneurial skill used in the process of economic activity. To perform either the transaction or transformation function requires the use of inputs. When we speak of transaction costs we mean the economic value of the inputs used in performing the transaction function. The empirical categories of transaction costs and, for example, labor costs are not and cannot be mutually exclusive. Transaction costs include the value of the labor, land, capital, and entrepreneurial skill used in making exchanges. We measure the size of the transaction sector by determining which labor, land, and capital costs should be included in the transaction sector.

We develop the definition of transaction costs and its empirical counterpart by first examining the simple relationship between a buyer and a seller. We then examine, in turn, the transaction costs that occur within firms and through intermediaries of various types. Finally we look into the special problem of protecting property rights. For purposes of illustration, consider the production and exchange of a house.

To the consumer seeking to purchase a good (or service), we define transaction costs as all costs borne by the consumer that are not transferred to the seller of the good. In the case of the house this would encompass all of the resources expended in purchasing the house that are not transferred to the seller, including the time spent looking at houses, obtaining information on prices and alternative housing, legal fees, the costs of establishing credibility as a buyer, and so on. Note that all of these actions are part of transaction costs, although some of them result in a second transaction, for example, hiring a lawyer. In that case hiring the lawyer is part of the transaction costs of buying the house. The key element is that transaction costs are that part of the cost of purchasing the house that the producer does not receive.

On the producer's side, the transaction costs of selling (producing) the house are those costs which the producer would not incur were he selling the house to himself. While such a transaction may seem to strain our credulity, remember that the cost of owning a house is the opportunity to sell it, an opportunity forgone every day that the house is owned. In effect every owner "sells" himself his possessions on a regular basis by choosing not to sell them to someone else. The seller's transaction costs include the realtor, advertising, time spent waiting while people tramp through the house, title insurance, the cost of establishing credibility as a seller, and so on. Again, some of these transaction costs themselves are a second transaction, for example, hiring a realtor.[5]

Not all of the transaction costs, for either the buyer or seller, occur at the point of exchange. Some costs occur before the exchange. These include gathering information about prices and alternatives, ascertaining the quality of the goods and the buyer's or seller's credibility, and so on. Other costs occur at the point of exchange. These include waiting in lines, paying notaries, purchasing title insurance, etc. Finally, some transaction costs occur after the exchange. These include the cost of ensuring that the contract is enforced, monitoring performance, inspecting quality, obtaining payment, and so on. The terms "coordinating," "enacting," and "monitoring" costs refer to the time dimension of transaction costs, whether the costs occur pre, during, or post exchange.

The simple example of a single seller/producer and single buyer/consumer illustrates two aspects of transaction costs that we wish to stress. First, a transaction cost is a cost like any other cost to both the buyer and the seller. The buyer will, for example, decide whether to acquire more information about alternative house prices, thereby incurring a transaction cost, only if he feels it will result in a commensurate reduction in the purchase cost of the house he ultimately buys (see Stigler 1961). The seller will, for example, weigh the alternative costs of expending more on advertising or lowering the asking price on the house as possible ways to attract a buyer.[6] The transaction costs and transformation costs of buying (or selling) the house are, at the appropriate margins, substitutes for one another and therefore can be treated the same theoretically.

Second, although all of the transaction costs in the exchange are borne by the buyer or the seller, some of those costs are occasioned by market activity (hiring lawyers and realtors) while others are not (time spent looking for houses or waiting for buyers to come by). While there is no conceptual difference between these two types of transaction costs, empirically they are a world apart. We can observe and measure the transaction costs embodied in the marketed services of the lawyers and realtors; we cannot observe the transaction costs of searching for houses or waiting for buyers. In our nomenclature those transaction costs which result in the exchange of a marketed good or service are the purchase of "transaction services." Transaction services are the observable element of transaction costs. In the example of the house, lawyers and realtors provide transaction *services*. We attempt to measure the level of transaction *services* provided in the economy, not the level of total transaction *costs*.

Our notion of transaction services and transaction costs is perfectly analogous to the notion of market income and total income in the national income accounts. GNP does not claim to measure the total income of individuals in a society, but the income that individuals generate through the market process (aside from imputed nonmarket items, such as owner-occupied housing and nonmarketed farm output). In the same way transaction services capture only that part of transaction costs that flows through the market.

The situation is somewhat more complicated when the seller (or buyer) is not an individual but a group of individuals: a firm. Going beyond individual buyers and sellers to the level of the firm is particularly important, since most of the available data are collected at the firm level. For illustration, consider an automobile manufacturer like Henry Ford.

Part of the transaction costs incurred by the firm are identical to those of the simple example. When Ford sells cars the transaction costs of doing so are those costs that Ford would not incur were he selling the cars to himself. Selling costs such as those associated with marketing, advertising, sales agents, the legal staff, and the shipping department are all part of transaction costs. Similarly, when Ford purchases inputs from his suppliers, we apply the rule that transaction costs are those costs borne by Ford that are not transferred to the supplier. Items such as purchasing departments, receiving clerks, legal staff, personnel departments (hiring), and the like are transaction costs.

The most difficult conceptual problem is created by those transaction costs that arise within the firm. Following Coase and the industrial organization literature, we regard the firm as a bundle of contracts.[7] One way to think of the bundle is as a sequential series of contracts between owners and managers, managers and supervisors, and supervisors and workers. At the top of the sequence Henry Ford (or he and the stockholders) buys cars from his managers. Ford incurs transaction costs in that payments to accountants, lawyers, and secretarial staff are necessary for him to coordinate, enact, and monitor his exchanges with the managers. The managers in turn bear costs in producing cars for Henry Ford that would not be borne if Ford produced cars for himself; again the costs of accountants, lawyers, and secretarial staffs. A hierarchy of such exchanges would exist, down through owners, managers, supervisors, and workers.

At the top of the sequence the bulk of the transaction costs involve the processing and conveying of information, a task carried on primarily by clerical workers. As we move down the sequence toward the workers the transaction costs involve both conveying information (foremen) and monitoring the labor contract (foremen and inspectors).

In the simplest scheme, Ford purchases the firm's output and the producers (sellers) are the people actually making the cars. All of the intermediate occupations (foremen, inspectors, supervisors, clerks, and managers) generate costs that Ford bears which are not transferred to the producers. That is, Ford purchases the transaction services of the intermediate occupations in order to coordinate, enact, and monitor the exchange he makes with those who provide transformation services.

Whether we wish to think of the firm using the complicated or simple set of contracts, making detailed decisions on who does and who does not perform transaction functions in a given firm or industry is impossible short of an intimate and exhausting study of the process of transforming inputs into outputs in each industry. We have chosen a compromise method to get at transaction services within firms. We divide occupations into those that provide primarily transaction services to the firm and, by elimination, those that provide primarily transformation services. (Detailed descriptions of the occupational breakdowns are provided in sec. 3.2.) The wages of employees in these "transaction occupations" constitute our measure of the transaction sector within firms.

Let us summarize our approach to estimating the transaction sector within firms. First, we identify occupations that are primarily concerned with transaction functions. These include occupations concerned with the purchase of inputs, the distribution of outputs, and the coordination and monitoring of the transformation function within the firm. Second, we estimate the wage payments going to employees in transaction occupations. Those wage payments constitute our measure of the size of the transaction sector within firms. Therefore, our measure includes only labor costs.

A specific type of firm, intermediaries, poses a special problem and therefore receives a different treatment. Intermediaries could be regarded in the same way as other firms, but they are primarily providers of transaction services. Go back to the house example for a moment. When the seller pays the real estate agent, everything the seller pays is part of the transaction costs of selling the house. *All* of the real estate fee should be included in the transaction sector. This is true even though the realtor in turn hires the transformation services of inputs (like buildings and janitors) that are used to produce the transaction service sold by the realtor to the seller of the house.

We want to treat all of the resources—that is, the total value of the inputs used by intermediaries—as a part of the transaction sector. The problem, of course, is to determine which firms (industries) are properly classified as intermediaries, or what we call "transaction industries." Three cases that seem clear are real estate and finance, whose role is primarily to facilitate the transfer of ownership; banking and insurance, whose role is to intermediate in the exchange of contingent claims; and the legal profession, whose primary role is to facilitate the coordination, enactment, and monitoring of contracts.

Wholesale trade, retail trade, and transportation present a more complicated case. Merchants often do more than transfer ownership of goods between parties, since they take ownership of the goods and transform the product in different ways. Perhaps the most important transformation is transporting the good from the producer to the consumer. The question is whether or not we wish to consider transportation costs as part of the transaction services provided by merchants. Our treatment of the transportation industry will also depend on the answer to this question.

To think about the problem, consider a living room couch purchased from a store that can be delivered to your home or picked up at the store. Should the freight charges of home delivery be considered part of transaction services or not? The answer is no. To show this it is necessary to make very clear the definition of the good in question. Specifically, are we talking about the exchange of a couch in the store or about the exchange of a couch in the living room?

In the case of the couch in the store the producer incurs no delivery charges, but are the resources used by the buyer to get the couch home a transaction cost? No. Resources expended by the buyer to get the couch home are not transferred to the producer, but what is the producer selling? He is selling a couch in the store, and that is what is being purchased. The transportation is, in this case, "home-produced" transformation services.[8]

Now consider the couch delivered by the producer to the living room. Are the costs of delivering the couch transaction costs? No. The producer is now selling a "couch in the living room." He would have had to transport the couch to the living room even had he sold the couch to himself (if it was his own living room). The transportation costs are not transaction costs but transformation costs: the act of moving the couch "transforms" it. When the couch is bought in the store and carted home by the customer the transportation services are home produced; when the couch is delivered the transportation services are market produced. In neither case, however, should the transportation costs be included in the transaction sector.

The implications are that the transportation industry should not be considered as a transaction industry. The wholesale and retail trade industries engage chiefly in transaction activities but also undertake some transformation activities. In the section that follows we include in the transaction sector the resources used in Finance, Insurance, and Real Estate (hereafter FIRE), Wholesale Trade, and Retail Trade; these are transaction industries.[9]

Before going to the empirical sections there are two problems that our definition of transaction cost leaves dangling: the protection of property rights and the "newly painted" house problem. That the protection of property rights is a problem may seem strange, since we often think of transaction costs as the costs of exchanging and *enforcing* property rights. If I enter into a contract with you, and you subsequently fail to fulfill the contract, I can get a lawyer and have you prosecuted. All of those costs that would be part of monitoring the contract and legitimate are transaction costs.

But consider the following problem. You are stranded on a deserted island and build a house. There is a door to the house which keeps the local animals out. An intelligent monkey figures out how to open the door and, in retaliation, you put a lock on the door. Is the cost of the lock a transaction cost? You are enforcing your property rights in your house, but there has not been any exchange, no transaction. Now move the house into the middle of Manhattan. Is the door lock a transaction cost? Does it matter whether it is a man or a monkey breaking into your house?

Frankly we do not know the answer, but feel uncomfortable putting what we might call "protective services" into the nontransaction sector. As a result we have included police, guards, sheriffs, and the like in the transaction sector, but will at the appropriate time indicate what the magnitude of their contribution is.

The second problem is the "newly painted house." We stated that the cost of painting the house should not be included in transaction costs, since what is being exchanged is now a newly painted house (see note 6). But the example does serve to illustrate a source of transaction costs, one emphasized by both Williamson (cheating) and Barzel (measurement). The owner may paint the house in order to make it more difficult for the prospective buyer to ascertain the quality of the house. Obviously, the owner believes that the obfuscation will result in an increase in the selling price of the house, but now the buyer incurs higher transaction costs, since it is more costly to measure the true condition of the building. Note that those individuals are acting rationally, but the result is to increase transaction costs and thereby reduce net social welfare.

To summarize, we are concerned with measuring the costs of making exchanges, of transaction costs, in the economy. Given the limitations placed on our ability to observe the elements of transaction costs as delineated by our definition, we are only able to measure "transaction services." Transaction services are that part of transaction costs that result in a market exchange. In order to measure the level of transaction services we focus on two basic types of measures, to be explained in detail in the next section. First, we include all of the resources used in providing transaction services in the open market. To do this we have classified certain types of economic activity as "transaction industries." These encompass the normal NIPA categories of Finance, Insurance, and Real Estate; Wholesale Trade; and Retail Trade. Transportation is not considered as a transaction industry (government is considered separately in the third section of the paper). Our second measure of transaction services includes transaction costs that occur within firms in nontransaction industries. To do this we divide occupations into those that provide primarily transaction services and those that provide primarily transformation services. We estimate the wages of employees in transaction occupations and use that as our measure of the transaction services provided by those workers and as an estimate of the size of the transaction sector in the nontransaction industries.

Because we focus on transaction services rather than transaction costs, our measure should not be interpreted as an estimate of the level of transaction costs within the economy, any more than GNP numbers should be taken as a direct measure of well-being. We wish to highlight how the attempt to capture the benefits of specialization and division of labor has changed the organization of economic activity in the United States over the last century. Remember that none of our transaction services are unproductive. They all represent the resource costs of making exchanges which, on net, made the parties to those exchanges better off (even when transaction costs are included). As such, our estimates form a starting point for a deeper investigation of the nature of economic organization, economic growth, and economic change.

## 3.2   The Private Transaction Sector

Our fundamental objective in this essay is to measure the changing size of the transaction sector in the American economy. This section measures the transaction sector in the private economy, following the general definition of transaction costs laid out in the previous section. The section has two parts. The first examines the nontransaction industries and the second the transaction industries.

### 3.2.1   The Nontransaction Industries

The *nontransaction* industries are those that produce primarily nontransaction goods and services.[10] Firms in these industries do engage in exchange, however. Purchasing inputs, coordinating and monitoring factors of production, and selling outputs all involve transaction costs. Disentangling *all* of the resources devoted to transacting from those devoted to transformation is, at this point, beyond our abilities. We focus only on the labor costs associated with the transaction sector.

The first step is to divide occupations into transaction and nontransaction occupations following the guidelines laid down in section 3.1. The share of transaction workers in all workers is determined for each industry. That share is used to divide the total wage bill in each industry between transaction workers and other workers. Compensation of the transaction occupations is then summed across all nontransaction industries. This sum is the measure used to estimate the size of the transaction sector in the nontransaction industries.

Our ability to separate transaction from nontransaction occupations is constrained by the available structure of occupational classifications. The census definitions were not designed to illuminate the distinction between transaction and transformation workers. In most cases, though, the classification of occupations is straightforward. Those are occupations primarily concerned with purchasing inputs or distributing output, that is, the purchasing and sales parts of the firm. Two other groups were easy to classify: the professional workers concerned with processing information and making exchanges, such as accountants, lawyers, judges, and notaries, and the protective service workers concerned with protecting property rights, such as police, guards, watchmen, and others. Two other groups are more difficult. Both involve the transactions that occur within the firm. One group consists of those employees who coordinate and monitor the complex of long-term contracts (relational contracts in Williamson's terms) that make up a firm: the owners, managers, proprietors, supervisors, foremen, and inspectors. It is, of course, the activity of these employees (and self-employed) who distinguish the firm from the market. As Coase observed:

> Outside the firm, price movements direct production, which is co-ordinated through a series of exchange transactions on the market, . . . Within a firm, these market transactions are eliminated and in place of the complicated market structure with exchange transactions is substituted the entrepreneur co-ordinator, who directs production. It is clear that these are alternative means of coordinating production. (1937, p. 388)

Within the firm that coordination is accomplished by a variety of "managers," from the owner himself down to the inspector or foreman.

The work of the managers and foremen requires a well-developed support network, whose primary purpose is to supply information to the managers. This group of occupations encompasses the clerical occupations. A detailed list of the census occupations that make up the transaction occupations is given in the Appendix.

A general picture of the importance of these occupations in this century is presented in table 3.1. For expositional convenience we call the transaction occupations "type I" occupations. As the table indicates, these workers have grown considerably in importance since the turn of the century, expanding from 15% to 38% of the labor force. Although all the occupations have grown, numerically the most important is the clerical group, followed closely by managers and salesworkers.

Our method of calculating the size of the transaction sector in the nontransaction industries is first to find the share of type I workers in total employment for each industry. Using that share, we then divide wage payments in each industry between type I and other workers. The summation of type I employee compensation across industries constitutes our measure of the transaction sector in the nontransaction industries. Type I employment in each industry is available after 1910 in existing census data. Before 1910, however, employment by industry must be inferred from the occupational data similar to those underlying table 3.1.

Table 3.2 presents information on type I occupations as a percentage of employment, by industry, for 1910–70. As is to be expected, the share of type I employment in total employment grows steadily from 1910 to 1970, just as it does in table 3.1 (differences between tables 3.2 and 3.1 are owing to the detailed occupational breakdowns used in table 3.2). Type I employment roughly doubles its share of total em-

**Table 3.1  Employees in Transaction-related Occupations "Type I Workers," 1900–1970 (Thousands of Employees)**

| Occupation | 1970 | 1960 | 1950 | 1940 | 1930 | 1920 | 1910 | 1900 |
|---|---|---|---|---|---|---|---|---|
| Accountants | 712 | 477 | 390 | 238 | 192 | 118 | 39 | 23 |
| Lawyers & judges | 273 | 213 | 184 | 182 | 161 | 123 | 115 | 108 |
| Personnel & labor relations[a] | 296 | 99 | 53 | | | | | |
| Farm managers[b] | 94 | 50 | 53 | 55 | 68 | 93 | 50 | 17 |
| Managers | 6,463 | 5,489 | 5,155 | 3,770 | 3,614 | 2,803 | 2,462 | 1,697 |
| Clerical | 14,208 | 9,617 | 7,232 | 4,982 | 4,336 | 3,385 | 1,987 | 877 |
| Salesworkers | 5,625 | 4,801 | 4,133 | 3,450 | 3,059 | 2,058 | 1,755 | 1,307 |
| Foremen | 1,617 | 1,199 | 867 | 585 | 551 | 485 | 318 | 162 |
| Inspectors[c] | 201 | 169 | 144 | 116 | 100 | 93 | 68 | 30 |
| Guards & police[d] | 747 | 543 | 478 | 397 | 317 | 228 | 162 | 121 |
| Total | 30,236 | 22,657 | 18,689 | 13,775 | 12,398 | 9,386 | 6,956 | 4,342 |
| Total as % of all workers | 38% | 33% | 32% | 27% | 25% | 22% | 19% | 15% |

Source: United States Department of Commerce 1975, pp. 140–145.

[a]Personnel and labor relations workers were not counted separately prior to 1950.

[b]Includes farm foremen.

[c]Includes surveyors and timber inspectors.

[d]Includes government police, private police, marshalls, and sheriffs.

**Table 3.2**    **Employment in Transaction-related Occupations as a Percentage of Total Employment, by Industry, 1910–70**

| Occupation | 1970 | 1960 | 1950 | 1940 | 1930 | 1910 |
|---|---|---|---|---|---|---|
| All employment | | | | | | |
| With military[a] | 37.29% | 32.45% | 30.98% | 28.13% | 26.02% | 17.45% |
| Without military | 38.78 | 33.72 | 31.77 | 28.27 | 26.35 | 17.49 |
| *Nontransaction Industries* | | | | | | |
| Agriculture, forestry, & fisheries | 3.75 | 1.92 | 5.05 | 0.65 | 2.05 | 0.51 |
| Mining | 25.40 | 21.03 | 10.81 | 11.80 | 8.79 | 5.95 |
| Construction | 20.32 | 17.72 | 15.72 | 11.48 | 9.45 | 1.41 |
| Manufacturing | 30.22 | 27.88 | 24.30 | 22.22 | 19.27 | 12.53 |
| Transportation, communications, & utilities | 37.62 | 37.43 | 33.63 | 36.44 | 32.46 | 28.29 |
| Services | 28.09 | 23.09 | 19.78 | 12.46 | 12.70 | 5.40 |
| Government | | | | | | |
| With military[b] | 28.53 | 26.17 | 30.11 | 42.90 | 36.69 | 37.92 |
| Without military | 38.53 | 37.46 | 42.88 | 46.40 | 38.71 | 40.38 |
| NEC[c] | — | 2.62 | 14.14 | 29.56 | 24.00 | — |
| *Transaction Industries* | | | | | | |
| Retail trade | 57.54 | 59.85 | 64.12 | 65.21 | 85.74 | 86.41 |
| Wholesale trade | 63.59 | 67.06 | | | | |
| FIRE | 92.02 | 88.51 | 84.34 | 83.04 | 93.69 | 98.94 |

*Source:* Census reports on occupations are from 1910, 1930, 1940, 1950, 1960, and 1970. See Appendix for details.

[a]The first row includes personnel on active military duty in the labor force; the second row uses civilian labor force.

[b]The first row includes personnel on active duty, and the second row excludes them from government employment.

[c]Not elsewhere classified.

ployment, but as the table indicates, the growth in type I employment varies widely across industries. The transaction industries, Trade and FIRE, have high levels of type I employment declining slightly over time. Type I employment in the nontransaction industries grows significantly. Over 60% of the increase in type I workers in the whole economy between 1910 and 1970 (from 17% to 39%) is accounted for by increases in type I workers in nontransaction industries, particularly increases in manufacturing and services.[11] The primary source of growth in transaction occupations was the nontransaction industries.

It is more difficult to determine occupational employment by industry before 1910. The census did not collect information on employment by industry, only on employment by occupation. Based on the work of Edwards (1943), the occupational distribution of employment by industry in 1910 and 1930 has been used to estimate employment by industry for earlier census years from available information on employment by occupation. Since employment by industry before 1910 is derived from employment-by-occupation data, estimates of employment by industry required to calculate type I employment shares before 1910 are essentially transformations of the employment-by-occupation data. Therefore the employment by industry and occupation by industry are not independent estimates. Fortunately, with the exception of clerical workers, type I employees can be allocated among industries with some confidence before 1910.

The problem, here as in other studies, is determining the level of total employment by industry.[12] Table 3.3 uses Carson's employment by industry to calculate the share of type I employment by industry for the period 1870–1910 (Carson 1949). Carson's estimates of employment in trade are notoriously low, as is shown in the table, where over 100% of the employees in trade have type I occupations.[13] Differences in the type I shares for 1910 in tables 3.2 and 3.3 result from the use of Edwards's occupation-by-industry classifications in 3.3 and our use of the complete detailed census classifications in 3.2 (see the appendix). Those caveats aside, the two tables tell a fairly consistent tale: type I employment is high and stable in trade and government;

| Table 3.3 | Employment in Transaction-Related Occupations as a Percentage of Total Employment, by Industry, 1870–1910 | | | | |
|---|---|---|---|---|---|
| Occupation | 1910 | 1900 | 1890 | 1880 | 1870 |
| All Employment | 18.93% | 16.43% | 13.70% | 11.09% | 9.63% |
| | *Nontransaction Industries* | | | | |
| Agriculture, forestries, & fisheries | 0.56 | 0.53 | 0.52 | 0.45 | 0.43 |
| Mining, | 5.78 | 5.08 | 5.36 | 3.14 | 2.81 |
| manufacturing & construction | 9.79 | 6.46 | 4.89 | 3.70 | 3.54 |
| Transportation, communications, & utilities | 27.93 | 21.87 | 19.36 | 16.81 | 13.31 |
| Services | 10.04 | 8.81 | 8.00 | 7.54 | 6.62 |
| Government, NEC | 31.26 | 33.01 | 27.28 | 24.19 | 21.32 |
| | *Transaction Industries* | | | | |
| Trade & FIRE | 106.86 | 114.08 | 106.99 | 110.90 | 104.95 |
| | (78.00)[a] | (79.37) | (71.86) | (69.99) | (66.34) |

*Source:* Edwards (1943) and Carson (1949). See Appendix for details.

[a]Figures in parentheses use Lebergott's estimates of trade employment to calculate the type I employment share. Lebergott's figures are not as detailed as Carson's, and using Lebergott's estimates for manufacturing, agriculture, and mining does not significantly alter our estimates. Lebergott (1964), p. 510.

low and stable in agriculture; and low and rising in mining, construction, manufacturing, and transportation.

The next step is to convert these employment shares into actual dollar values of resources used as inputs in each industry. Because of the break in employment series and the availability of appropriate national income data, the calculation is done first for the years after 1930, then for years 1900–1940, and finally for the years 1870–1900. The method of estimating the compensation of these employees in each of the periods follows the same procedure, described in detail in the appendix. Briefly, an estimate of employee compensation by industry (for all employees) was taken directly or derived from existing series on compensation, wages, employment, and other data.[14] The employee compensation series was then multiplied by the share of type I employment in total employment, from tables 3.3 or 3.4, to yield an estimate of type I employee compensation by industry. The type I compensation figures were summed over all nontransaction industries; that total was divided by GNP. The results of these calculations are found in table 3.4.

Both the data and the methods used to generate the estimates can be improved upon. However, it is not likely that such improvements would change the basic message of the table: compensation of transactions employees in nontransaction industries rose continuously from the mid-nineteenth century up until the present time. The share of national income/GNP going to type I employees in nontransaction industries rose from 1.4% in 1870 to 10% in 1970. If we were to treat government as a nontransaction industry (a subject that will be dealt with in more detail in the following section), the income share of type I employees in nontransaction industries would reach 14% in 1970, from 1.5% in 1870.

Limitations of the data and our method of estimating the share of resources going to these workers create several potential biases in our estimates. First, the number of workers in type I occupations may have been undercounted in the early census years. This seems to be the case with clerical workers, particularly in the 1870 census. This gives an upward bias to the trend in the share of type I workers. A similar bias could result from the classification of multiple-occupation employees. For example, a firm with 10 employees may employ one person half-time as a foreman and half-time as, say, a carpenter, yet he may report his principal occupation as carpenter. When employment grows to 20 workers, he becomes a foreman full time, and the apparent share of type I employees goes from zero to 5%, while the true share has remained constant.

These two biases are partially offset by other biases. First, we have included number of owners, managers, and proprietors in our type I employees (although not their earnings). These workers are like the

Table 3.4    Percentage of National Income/GNP Going to Type I Employees in Nontransaction Industries, 1870–1970

| Year | (1) | (2) | (3) | (4) | (5) | (6) | (7) | (8) | (9) | (10) |
|---|---|---|---|---|---|---|---|---|---|---|
| 1870 | 2.16 | (2.37) | | | | | | | | |
| 1880 | 2.50 | (2.74) | | | | | | | | |
| 1890 | 4.18 | (4.66) | | | | | | | | |
| 1900 | 4.70 | (4.98) | 3.32 | (4.62) | | | | | | |
| 1910 | | | 4.30 | (5.49) | 4.32 | (5.87) | | | | |
| 1920 | | | | | 7.25 | (8.85) | | | | |
| 1930 | | | | | 6.84 | (9.20) | 6.03 | (8.12) | 6.21 | (8.35) |
| 1940 | | | | | 6.50 | (9.23) | 6.23 | (8.85) | 6.67 | (10.43) |
| 1950 | | | | | | | | | 7.98 | (10.45) |
| 1960 | | | | | | | | | 9.52 | (12.25) |
| 1970 | | | | | | | | | 10.40 | (14.11) |

*Source*: See Appendix. Nontransaction industries are agriculture, forestry and fishing, mining, construction, manufacturing, transportation, communications and utilities, services, and (government). For a description of calculations, see Appendix, section 2. Figures in parentheses, columns (2), (4), (6), (8), and (10) include government as a nontransaction industry. Columns (1), (3), (5), (7), and (9) exclude government. In brief:

*Column 1*: Calculated from Gallman (1966) value-added series, using Edwards (1943) 1870–1910 type I employment shares, and Gallman GNP.

*Column 2*: Column 1 + type I employee compensation in government.

*Column 3*: Calculated from Lebergott (1964) wage payment series, using Edwards (1943) type I employment shares, and Kuznets's (1961) GNP.

*Column 4*: Column 3 + type I employee compensation in government.

*Column 5*: Calculated using Lebergott (1964) wage payment series, 1910–1970 Census Type I employment shares, and Kuznets's (1961) GNP.

*Column 6*: Column 3 + type I employee compensation in government.

*Columns 7 & 8*: Same as column 5 and column 6 using NIPA (United States Department of Commerce 1981), GNP.

*Column 9*: Calculated using NIPA employment compensation series, 1910–1970 census type I employment shares, and NIPA GNP.

*Column 10*: Column 7 + type 1 employee compensation in government. For details on all calculations, see Appendix.

foreman in the example, only their bias runs the other way. A larger share of the labor force was self-employed in earlier years, and over time these workers have probably increased the share of their labor time spent on managing and decreased time in actual production. Second, in calculating the type I shares for the years before 1910, we built an upward bias into the estimates for the early years. For several categories of type I employment, separate numbers were not reported before 1910. To estimate them we used the 1910 share of specific type I occupations in an industry to approximate that occupation's share of industry employment back to 1870. Since the overall share of type I workers falls as we go back in time, we overmeasure the share of type I workers in those industries where we inferred their employment share in this manner.[15] Finally, the problem with multiple-occupation employees, while potentially important, is also a symmetric bias. That is, the number of multiple-occupation employees who initially report their occupations as type I rather than their other occupation may be as large as the number of multiple-occupation employees who initially report the non–type I occupation (in the example, the man could have reported himself as a foreman initially). There is, of course, no way to know, even roughly, how large these biases are or the extent to which they cancel each other out.

Our other major concern is with the method of generating the estimates. First, we have ignored the capital resources associated with these workers. It is possible that type I workers worked with larger (smaller) amounts of capital goods in early years than they did in later years, in which case our trend in resources used by type I workers is biased upward (downward). Second, our measures operate on a highly aggregated level. They could be improved by using wage, hour, and employment data for specific occupations within industries. Finally, our margins of error in calculating the amount of resources used by type I workers in nontransaction industries must be multiplied by the margins of error inherent in the estimates of GNP used to calculate the share of resources used by these workers. The confidence intervals on the estimates in table 3.4 are therefore quite large. On the other hand, there is no compelling reason to believe that biases or errors in the estimates are systematic enough to obliterate the strong upward trend in the resource share going to type I workers.

### 3.1.2  The Transaction Industries

We turn now to the second set of estimates, the resources used by the transaction industries: trade and FIRE. We want to estimate *all* of the resources used in the transaction industries. We assume, for the moment, that all inputs into trade and FIRE go to transaction services.[16] Such a measure does not correspond to the measures of industry output, value added, or income originating that we usually use to characterize the contributions of an industry to GNP. We are concerned only with the value of resources that transaction industries use. We do not attempt to impute anything about the value of the services they provide to the economy, and we do not face the standard problem of double counting that necessitates careful attention to net and gross distinctions in the standard income accounts.

Table 3.5 reports our estimates of total resources used by trade for the period 1869–1970. Before 1948 we utilized Barger's estimates of gross distribution markups to estimate the total resources used in trade. We took measures of final commodity output from Gallman and Kuznets, multiplied by Barger's estimates of the total share of commodity output going through retail distribution channels, and multiplied again by Barger's estimates of gross distributive markup. After 1950 we took estimates of resources used in trade directly from the input/output tables used by the Commerce Department to estimate GNP.[17]

As the table indicates, resources used in trade grew from 16% of GNP in 1869 to 22% in 1948, falling to 18% in 1972. While this estimate could be improved by combining a more detailed breakdown of commodity output with Barger's detailed estimates of distributive markup by type of store, there is no reason to suppose that the table would be greatly affected by that adjustment.

Estimating the amount of resources used in the other transaction industry, FIRE, is more difficult. Earlier attempts to estimate GNP

**Table 3.5**    **Resources Used in Trade, in Billions of $ and as Percentage of GNP, 1865–1972**

| Year | | Billions of $ (1) | Percentage of GNP (2) |
|------|------|------|------|
| 1870 | (1869)[a] | 1.27 | 16.14 |
| 1880 | (1879) | 1.72 | 18.02 |
| 1890 | (1889) | 2.22 | 18.07 |
| 1900 | (1899) | 3.10 | 19.15 |
| 1910 | (1909) | 5.64 | 19.07 |
| 1920 | (1919) | 13.74 | 19.57 |
| 1930 | (1929) | 16.45 | 18.74 |
| 1940 | (1939) | 18.09 | 20.54 |
| 1950 | (1948) | 52.25 | 21.87 |
| 1960 | (1958) | 92.3 | 21.18 |
| 1970 | (1972) | 216.4 | 18.25 |

*Sources:*
Column 1:   1870–1950: table 3.A.5, col. 4.
              1960–70: table 3.A.4, col. 3.
Column 2: table 3.A.4, col. 6.
[a]The years in parentheses are the years for which calculations were actually made.

have finessed the financial sector by imputing some value to its output or calculated it as a residual category.[18] Our method, therefore, is quite simple. From 1958 to 1972 we base our estimate of gross resources used in FIRE on the Commerce Department input/output tables.[19] The estimates were extended back to 1920 using NIPA and Kuznets's data on national income in FIRE as an index. From 1870 to 1900 we used Gallman and Weiss's estimate of value of total output in banking and insurance.[20] The results of the estimates are presented in table 3.6.

Taken together, tables 3.4, 3.5, and 3.6 make up our estimate of the transaction sector in the private portion of the economy. The private transaction sector rises from roughly 18% of GNP in 1870 to 41% of GNP in 1970. The 1870 figures are probably too high; the share of resources going to FIRE and the share of type I employee compensation in nontransaction industries are overstated. The 1930–70 figures are based on solid data and can be taken with some confidence. The strong upward trend in the transaction sector share of GNP is, if anything, biased downward. The reasons underlying this trend will be discussed in section 3.4, but first we turn our attention to the public sphere.

### 3.3 The Public Transaction Sector

In this section we examine the provision of transaction services by governments. In a fundamental sense our broad conception of trans-action services would include all of government in the transaction sec-

Table 3.6            Resources Used in Finance, Insurance, and Real Estate, in Billions of Dollars and as a Percentage of GNP, 1870–1970

| Year | | Billions of $ (1) | Percentage of GNP (2) |
|---|---|---|---|
| 1870 | (1869)[a] | .310 | 4.19 |
| 1880 | (1879) | .453 | 4.75 |
| 1890 | (1889) | .845 | 6.87 |
| 1900 | (1899) | 1.29 | 7.96 |
| 1910 | | — | 8.12 |
| 1920 | | 5.5 | 8.28 |
| 1930 | | 9.5 | 12.61 |
| 1940 | | 9.6 | 9.88 |
| 1950 | | 23.1 | 10.45 |
| 1960 | (1958) | 55.7 | 10.61 |
| 1970 | (1972) | 120.8 | 12.15 |

*Sources:*
Column 1: table 3.A.8, col. 1 + 2.
Column 2: table 3.A.8, col. 5.
Note that 1930 values are the average of the two 1930 values in table 3.A.8.
[a]Years in parentheses are years for which calculation was actually made.

tor. A function of "governing" is to provide the sociopolitical assets that underlie all economic activity; that is, government incurs the social overhead costs that enable specialization and division of labor to occur. In our more limited definition of transaction costs, however, only a range of government services is properly considered transaction services. Particularly important are the costs of enforcing contracts (the court and police systems) and the costs of protecting property rights on a larger scale (national defense).

A second group of government activities is more difficult to classify. It includes education, transportation facilities, and basic public services such as fire protection, hospitals, health services, public sanitation, and housing. These activities all have an element of social overhead capital; they are part of the cost of maintaining our existing social order. Maintaining that order is, of course, a prerequisite for specialization and division of labor.

Finally, a third group of government activities has little to do with transaction services, particularly income redistribution. These activities are not, however, completely unimportant to the size of the transaction sector. Just as the nontransaction industries in the private economy utilize transaction services, so too the government requires the use of transaction services in order to carry out its nontransaction activities. In this section we discuss each of these three types of government activity and develop a method to estimate the transaction sector in each that follows closely the method used to estimate the size of the transaction sector in the private economy.

Table 3.7 breaks down government expenditures for activities that correspond to the three categories. Table 3.8 presents expenditures for each category as a share of GNP for selected years in this century. As the table indicates, each expenditure category has tended to grow consistently over this century.

The first category of expenditures includes basic expenditures to secure property rights and facilitate trade. By far the largest single item in this category is defense.[21] A breakdown of transaction service expenditures into components is shown in table 3.9. Including police and general government in the transaction sector seems straightforward. There are, however, legitimate reasons to question whether all of the defense budget should be included in transaction service expenditures. The rise of the "military-industrial complex" may give rise to some defense expenditures, like cost overruns, that should fall under transfer payments. Increases in defense spending since World War II are associated with a larger United States role in international affairs, and can be considered as political/diplomatic expenditures rather than as defense. Finally, defense expenditures fluctuate from year to year and administration to administration, and there is no way to measure the

**Table 3.7**      **Classification of Expenditures by Type**

*Transaction services*

National defense, military + foreign relations + veterans
Postal service
Police
Air transportation
Water transportation
Financial administration + general control

*Social overhead*

Education
Highways
Hospitals
Health
Fire
Sanitation
Natural resources
Housing and urban renewal

*Other*

Public welfare
Farm price supports
Social insurance administration
Insurance trust expenditures
    OASDI
      Unemployment compensation
      Employee retirement
Space research
Local parks
Interest on general debt
Utility and liquor stores
Other and unallocable

effect of those expenditures on our level of security, nor is opinion by any means unanimous that higher defense expenditures are related positively to higher levels of national security.

These questions arise because it is unclear exactly what the government buys when it spends money for defense. Beyond doubt, however, these expenditures are the expenses of maintaining national security, given our current political and social arrangements. Rather than attempting to divide defense spending into defense and nondefense activities, we treat it all uniformly and present two alternate measures below. One gives less weight to defense expenditures in the transaction sector.

The second category of expenditures poses a more difficult problem of classification. Expenditures by major component of expenditure are given in table 3.10. Individual components were included in this category for the following reasons. Education involves an element of transaction services to the extent that education (1) informs individuals

**Table 3.8**    **Government Expenditures by Type as a Percentage of GNP, 1902-70**

| Year | Transaction Services (1) | Social Overhead (2) | Other (3) | Total (4) |
|------|------|------|------|------|
| 1902 | 2.8 | 2.8 | 1.6 | 6.9 |
| 1913 | 2.8 | 3.3 | 2.0 | 8.0 |
| 1922 | 3.9 | 5.2 | 3.7 | 12.6 |
| 1927 | 3.1 | 5.4 | 3.3 | 11.7 |
| 1932 | 6.2 | 9.4 | 6.4 | 21.4 |
| 1938 | 4.5 | 9.2 | 9.3 | 20.9 |
| 1942 | 19.1 | 4.9 | 5.9 | 28.9 |
| 1948 | 9.5 | 6.1 | 6.5 | 21.5 |
| 1952 | 16.7 | 6.5 | 6.4 | 28.9 |
| 1957 | 13.5 | 7.5 | 8.0 | 28.4 |
| 1962 | 12.8 | 8.7 | 11.3 | 31.5 |
| 1967 | 12.4 | 9.7 | 11.4 | 32.7 |
| 1970 | 11.3 | 10.3 | 12.1 | 33.5 |

*Sources:* GNP figures are from Department of Commerce, *Historical Statistics of Government, Finance and Employment* (Washington, D.C.: Government Printing Office, 1969), p. i.

1902–1967, United States Department of Commerce (1969), table 3.

1970, United States Department of Commerce (1984), p. 274; GNP data from p. 420.

**Table 3.9**    **Government Expenditures on Transaction Services, by Component, as a Percentage of GNP, 1902-70**

| Year | Military (1) | Police (2) | General Governing (3) |
|------|------|------|------|
| 1902 | 1.26 | 0.21 | 1.33 |
| 1913 | 1.06 | 0.23 | 1.53 |
| 1922 | 1.86 | 0.28 | 1.75 |
| 1927 | 1.24 | 0.30 | 1.55 |
| 1932 | 2.84 | 0.60 | 2.75 |
| 1938 | 1.93 | 0.45 | 2.09 |
| 1942 | 17.12 | 0.28 | 1.64 |
| 1948 | 7.79 | 0.28 | 1.40 |
| 1952 | 14.69 | 0.42 | 1.59 |
| 1957 | 11.50 | 0.49 | 1.54 |
| 1962 | 10.60 | 0.57 | 1.74 |
| 1967 | 10.01 | 0.57 | 1.77 |
| 1970 | 9.05 | 0.49 | 1.81 |

*Source:* See table 3.8.

Column 1: Military = (military + foreign + veterans)

Column 2: Police = (police + corrections)

Column 3: General governing = (general government + financial control + postal)

**Table 3.10**     **Government Social Overhead Expenditures, by Component, as a Percentage of GNP, 1902–70**

| Year | Education (1) | Highways (2) | Urban Services (3) |
|------|------|------|------|
| 1902 | 1.07 | 0.72 | 0.64 |
| 1913 | 1.44 | 1.04 | 0.71 |
| 1922 | 2.31 | 1.75 | 0.95 |
| 1927 | 2.33 | 1.89 | 0.98 |
| 1932 | 4.01 | 3.04 | 1.75 |
| 1938 | 3.13 | 2.54 | 1.47 |
| 1942 | 1.71 | 1.12 | 1.14 |
| 1948 | 3.01 | 1.20 | 1.27 |
| 1952 | 2.78 | 1.36 | 1.64 |
| 1957 | 3.42 | 1.80 | 1.59 |
| 1962 | 4.07 | 1.88 | 1.95 |
| 1967 | 5.09 | 1.78 | 2.01 |
| 1970 | 5.62 | 1.68 | 2.24 |

*Source:* See notes to table 3.8.

Column 3: Urban services = fire + water + sanitation + hospitals + housing + urban renewal (see table 3.7).

about the existing legal and social arrangements regarding exchange; (2) reinforces the socialization process regarding the legitimization of contracts, which lowers the costs of enforcing contracts to the extent that people do not engage in "strategic behavior" or arrangements regarding exchange; and (3) directly reduces the costs of dealing with different social, ethnic, and cultural groups within society by providing all individuals with a common language, history, and cultural values.

The transportation services provided by government (highways, air, and water terminals) fall between transaction and transformation services. As discussed in the first part of the paper, we do not wish to treat transportation costs as a part of the transaction sector. Accordingly, publicly provided transportation services should not be included there. However, the part these services play in determining the level of transportation costs within the economy is crucial in determining the degree of specialization and division of labor, and therefore the level of transaction costs in the economy. It is for this reason that we include them here, even though we do not include government expenditures on transportation facilities in the transaction sector in what follows.

The third group of government-provided social overhead services can be lumped together under the title "urban services." Urban services indirectly lower transaction costs by making urban living less costly. A major advantage of living in an urban area is the reduction in transaction costs associated with having a large number of buyers and sellers in close proximity. Public provision of urban services directly reduces the cost of living in urban areas, increasing the number of individuals who can profitably move to cities and capture the gains from specialization and division of labor at lower transaction costs than they could in rural areas.

Even those who completely agree with our characterization of these functions will admit, as we do, that any partition of expenditures on education, transportation facilities, and urban services into transaction and nontransaction components is arbitrary. Therefore we have chosen not to go any farther than table 3.10. We do not include expenditures on these functions in our measure of public transaction services, but note that some portion of these expenditures would be included if we had a better understanding of the nature of government activity and its relationship to the economy.

Despite our exclusion of social overhead and other expenditures from the transaction sector, it is necessary to include the transaction services involved in administering those programs in our measure of the public transaction sector. Just as there are transaction services involved in the production and distribution of goods in the nontransaction industries, so there are transaction services involved in the production and distribution of government-provided goods and services.

**Table 3.11**    **Government Expenditures for Transaction Services and Compensation of Employees in Transaction-Related Occupations in Social Overhead and Transfer Programs, as a Percentage of GNP, 1902–70**

| | | Government Expenditures on Transaction Services (1) | Compensation of Employees in Transaction-Related Occupations in Other Government Programs (2) | Total (3) |
|---|---|---|---|---|
| 1900 | (1902)[a] | 2.8 | .87 | 3.67 |
| 1910 | (1913) | 2.8 | .86 | 3.66 |
| 1920 | (1922) | 3.9 | .97 | 4.87 |
| 1930 | (1932) | 6.2 | 1.97 | 8.17 |
| 1940 | | 4.04 | 2.56 | 6.60 |
| 1950 | | 9.24 | 1.71 | 10.95 |
| 1960 | | 12.18 | 1.86 | 14.04 |
| 1970 | | 11.3 | 2.60 | 13.90 |

*Sources:* Column 1: Table 3.8, col. 1.
Column 2: Table 3.A.9, col. 4.
[a]Years in parentheses refer to year for which calculation was actually made.

We employ the same technique to estimate this part of the public transaction sector as was used earlier to estimate the transaction sector in nontransaction industries. We multiply the share of employment in transaction occupations (type I employees) in all government employment by employee compensation in nontransaction government functions to obtain our estimate of the transaction sector in the nontransaction part of government. To that we then add the value of all resources, labor and capital, used in producing transaction services by the government. Our estimates using this method appear in table 3.11, where transaction expenditures as a share of GNP are reported separately from type I employee compensation in nontransaction expenditures. As the table indicates, the measure rises from 3.67% of GNP in 1902 to 13.90% of GNP in 1970. The importance of transaction services fluctuates somewhat, because of the influence of war expenditures. Employee compensation of transaction occupations in other government functions as a percentage of GNP grows fairly steadily throughout the period.

A second method is less complete in its coverage, but it avoids the problem of classifying defense expenditures and provides a minimum estimate of the transaction sector in government. The method simply treats all government as a nontransaction industry. Table 3.12 presents the results of the alternative estimates. Type I employee compensation as a percentage of GNP was derived by combining type I employment in government, table 3.2, with compensation of civilian government employees. To that is added compensation of military employees, em-

| Table 3.12 | Compensation of Transaction-Related Employees in Government, as Percentage of GNP, 1900–1970 | | |
|---|---|---|---|
| Year | Percent GNP Type I Employees (1) | Percent GNP Military Employees (2) | Total (3) |
| 1900 (1902)[a] | 1.30 | 0.41 | 1.71 |
| 1910 (1913) | 1.55 | 0.38 | 1.93 |
| 1920 (1922) | 1.60 | 0.47 | 2.07 |
| 1930 (1932) | 2.14 | 0.48 | 2.62 |
| 1940 | 3.76 | 1.07 | 4.83 |
| 1950 | 2.47 | 1.86 | 4.33 |
| 1960 | 2.73 | 1.32 | 4.05 |
| 1970 | 3.71 | 2.15 | 5.86 |

*Sources:* Column 1: Table 3.4.
Column 2: Table 3.A.10, col. 4.
Column 3: (1) + (2)
[a]Years in parentheses are years for which calculations were actually made.

ployees excluded from transaction-related employees in our treatment of the census occupation data. The table follows the same trend as table 3.11, although, as expected, the share of GNP is lower. Taken as a minimum estimate of the transaction sector in government, it rises from 1.71% of GNP in 1900 to 5.86% of GNP in 1970.

Extending the estimates back into the nineteenth century is difficult. There are no solid data on state and local expenditures before 1880, and even the census material for 1880 and 1890 are not complete. The work of Davis and Legler (1966) on government activity in the nineteenth century does not suggest that government, as a share of GNP, changed markedly between 1870 and 1900. Given their findings and the lack of detailed data, we have chosen to assume that the public transaction sector from 1870–1900 was identical to its actual size in 1900.

To summarize, we treat the public part of the economy in much the same way as the private part. Government activity is broken into transaction and nontransaction services. All resources used in activities that provide transaction services and employee compensation of transaction occupations in other government activities are included in the transaction sector. As a more conservative alternative we also treat the entire public sector as a nontransaction industry and proceed as we did in section 3.2.

## 3.4  Interpreting the Data

Before we get too deeply enmeshed in a discussion of why the transaction sector has grown, let us review briefly the magnitude of that growth. Table 3.13 assembles our various estimates of the private and public transaction sector shares of GNP. Keeping in mind that the 1870–90 estimates are probably high, the transaction sector grows from roughly one-quarter of GNP in 1870 to over one-half of GNP in 1970. Even with the qualifications on data and methods discussed in the text and appendix, the amount used in the transaction sector is high and rising.

Economists and economic historians have described fundamental structural changes in the American economy in the past century. These have included the shift from rural to urban living, the shift in the composition of output away from agricultural and extractive industries toward manufacturing, and then, more recently, the growth of services and the growth of government, the changing size of firms from the late nineteenth century on, and the growing sophistication of economic organization. Our interpretation of the role of transaction costs is consistent with these structural shifts, but leads to a different interpretation of the American economy than has been traditionally associated with this evidence.

Economics and theories of economic growth revolve around the gains from trade arising from specialization and division of labor. Productiv-

Table 3.13          The Transaction Sector as a Percentage of GNP

|  | | Public | | Total | |
|---|---|---|---|---|---|
| Year | Private (1) | I (2) | II (3) | I (4) | II (5) |
| 1870 | 22.49 | 3.6[a] | 1.7[a] | 26.09 | 24.19 |
| 1880 | 25.27 | 3.6[a] | 1.7[a] | 28.87 | 26.97 |
| 1890 | 29.12 | 3.6[a] | 1.7[a] | 32.72 | 30.82 |
| 1900 | 30.43 | 3.67 | 1.71 | 34.10 | 32.14 |
| 1910 | 31.51 | 3.66 | 1.93 | 35.17 | 33.44 |
| 1920 | 35.10 | 4.87 | 2.07 | 39.98 | 37.17 |
| 1930 | 38.19 | 8.17 | 2.62 | 46.35 | 40.81 |
| 1940 | 37.09 | 6.60 | 4.83 | 43.69 | 41.92 |
| 1950 | 40.30 | 10.95 | 4.33 | 51.25 | 44.63 |
| 1960 | 41.30 | 14.04 | 4.05 | 55.35 | 45.36 |
| 1970 | 40.80 | 13.90 | 5.86 | 54.71 | 46.66 |

*Sources:* Column 1 is taken from tables 3.4, 3.5, and 3.6. See appendix table 3.A.12.
Column 2: table 3.11.
Column 3: table 3.12.
Column 4 = columns 1 + 2.
Column 5 = columns 1 + 3.
[a]Assumes that the public transportation sector in 1870–90 is approximately the same as 1900.

ity increase comes from increasing the efficiency of the inputs in the transformation process. But such gains are only realized through exchange, and traditionally economic theory has assumed that exchange is costless. Our essential point is that transaction costs are a significant part of the cost of economic activity. One implication of this is that, throughout history, the costs of transacting may have been as much a limiting factor on economic growth as transformation costs. This perspective turns the traditional analysis of economic growth on its head. Until economic organizations developed to lower the costs of exchange we could not reap the advantage of ever greater specialization. Economic history is then the story of the reduction of transaction costs that permit the realization of gains from greater specialization. The development of specialized banking, finance, trade, and other transaction functions are the necessary requirements for enhancing productivity, and so is the role of government in specifying and enforcing a system of property rights. Our argument stresses two points.

First, while competition in the private sector ensures that more efficient organizational forms will replace less efficient ones, no such constraint operates on government (see North 1981). Governments may impede or promote economic growth, but it would be ignoring one of the most important aspects of economic history not to recognize that in all high-income countries government has played an increasingly important role in the economy, a role that must be sufficiently positive to enable society to realize the enormous production potential of the revolution of science and technology of the past century and a half. That the resources devoted to transacting by governments are (with the ambiguous exception of military expenditure) a relatively small part of the total costs of transacting may mislead us into believing that government has played no significant role. To the contrary, the public resources devoted to the specification and enforcement of property rights has been so efficient that it has made possible the enormous burgeoning of the contracting forms that undergird our modern economy and is the key to explaining the contrast between the high-income countries and Third World countries.

Our second point is that the growth of the transaction sector is a necessary part of realizing the gains from trade. Part of transaction sector growth is simply a shift from nonmarket (and therefore non-observed) transaction costs to the market (and therefore counted in our transaction sector). But part of the growth constitutes real investment of resources. These resources have to be devoted to the maintenance of the economy's institutional fabric in order to realize the enormous production potential of the revolution in science and technology, which necessarily requires an increase in specialization and therefore a growth in exchange.

In our view, there are three major reasons why transaction costs have risen over the last century. First, the costs of specifying and enforcing contracts became more important with the expansion of the market and growing urbanization in the second half of the nineteenth century. As the economy becomes more specialized and urbanized, more and more exchanges are carried out between individuals who have no long-standing relations, that is, impersonal exchange. In contrast to personal exchange, where repeated dealing and intimate knowledge of the other party reduced the cost of contracting, impersonal exchange required detailed specification of the attributes of what was being exchanged or of the performance of agents, as well as elaborate enforcement mechanisms. This in itself would suggest a radical change in the cost of transacting. The growth of markets and urbanization was dramatically quickened by falling transportation costs after 1850. Consumers were able to purchase goods from wider distances and a greater number of suppliers. An effect of this greater variety is a reduction in the personal contact between buyers and sellers. Rational consumers substitute more search and information-gathering activity (including purchasing information through middlemen, i.e., transaction services) as they come to know less and less about the persons from whom they buy their products. The same holds for sellers who come to service a wider range of buyers.

The second part of our story is the effect of technological change in production and transportation on transaction services. The new capital-intensive production techniques were often more profitable to operate (i.e., lower costs) at high output levels. The high output levels required a steady flow of inputs and a well-developed system of disposing of the product. The complex organizations within firms that arose to purchase inputs and distribute outputs were providing transaction services within the firm. Reduction in costs and increases in the speed of transportation made possible larger business organizations and placed a premium on the coordination of inputs and outputs and monitoring the numerous contracts involved in production and distribution. As in production, new technical advances in transportation placed a premium on transaction services, which led to more of those services being provided within firms and through the market.

The third part of our story is the declining costs of using the political system to restructure property rights. The consequence of this change, the breakdown of the Madisonian system, has been documented already (North 1978). It consisted of changing the cost of using the political system via the development of commissions, which replaced the decision-making unit of entire legislatures and the development of rule-making ability by executive departments of the government. This type of government growth imposed transaction costs on the rest of the economy.

In our view, then, the transaction sector has grown for three major reasons: increasing specialization and division of labor; technological change in production and transportation accompanied by increasing firm size; and the augmented role of government in relationship to the private sector. Of course, this paper presents no conclusive proof that any or all of these three elements is the correct explanation of the growing importance of transaction services within the economy. Satisfactory explanations will await more detailed investigations into the transaction sector itself, and its behavior in different industries and in different periods of time. In lieu of those investigations, however, allow us to suggest some implications of our results for two important and interrelated areas of economic history: the study of economic growth and the measurement of economic activity.

Explaining economic growth is perhaps economic history's central task. Growth is a function of productive technology, the quality of inputs, and the institutional structure of the economy. The study of each of these potential sources of growth has dominated inquiry in different periods of time, but the study of institutional structures and economic growth has not enjoyed the melding of statistical inquiry, theoretical formulation, and historical analysis that technology and human capital have received. For the most part institutions are treated theoretically as a kind of disembodied economic factor: the rules of the game rather than the actual players.

Institutions, however, are not just rules, they require labor, capital, and other real resources in order to operate. The approach of this paper provides important information on the actual costs of implementing institutional structures. Even if one doubts the trend growth of the transaction sector, it is difficult to ignore the sheer volume of resources that go into supporting the most fundamental economic institution: the market. Systematic identification of certain kinds of activities (like secretaries, clerks, foremen, etc.) with what we believe to be important parts of the institutional structure can provide an empirical wedge into understanding the process of institutional change.

For whatever reason, and the three given at the beginning of this section are prime candidates, most firms found it necessary to devote more resources to coordinating, enacting, and monitoring exchange over the last century. The growing importance of these transaction workers raises a series of questions. Were they essential for competitive success in the marketplace? Did firms that moved early into providing transaction services internally prove to be more successful than those that did not? What would a standard partitioning of factors that explain productivity changes indicate in these industries if the labor input were divided into transaction and transformation workers?

Chandler's *Visible Hand* portrays vividly how managers, clerks, and secretaries become essential elements in the growth of the new large industrial enterprises (Chandler 1977). Their importance was both external and internal to the firm. Controlling the flow of inputs into the production process and distributing outputs was as critical as coordinating the production process within the firm. What we wish to stress about Chandler's observations is that all these managerial activities are essentially transaction services.

This study also raises issues with regard to another central area of economic history: the measurement of economic growth through national income accounting. At the outset we cited Kuznets's observation that no structure of economic accounts is "unaffected by economic theories." The size of the transaction sector documented here suggests that a theoretical structure in which transaction costs are assumed to be zero may be inadequate for measuring changes in economically valuable outputs in a world of pervasive transaction costs. Particularly important is the distinction between final and intermediate goods when the "output" of the transaction industries is being considered, a subject beyond the scope of this study but one of considerable importance when we wish to evaluate the performance of the American economy over time.[22]

A more pedestrian, but equally important, issue is the internal organization of the accounts. With the exception of calculating the employment shares of transaction-related workers, none of the data used in our study are original. All of it comes directly from the classical works on national income accounting. We have simply repackaged the accounts utilizing a new set of internal divisions, using the transaction and transformation functions as our guide for segregating economic activity rather than the typical industrial divisions.

Recasting the accounts will not change the trend of per capita income over time, but it can change our interpretation of how changes in income come about. The existing internal structure of the accounts was designed to illuminate business cycle movements. The accounts can yield more information about economic growth and the composition of economic activity, but only if we are willing to pose new questions and exploit the rich variety of information built into the accounts by those who first constructed estimates of national income.

This essay has sought to establish one historical series: a measure of the transaction sector in the American economy from 1870 to 1970. Despite reservations one may have about the accuracy of the data or the appropriateness of the estimation methods, the magnitude of the increase in the resources used by the transaction sector over the last century is a phenomenon that must be dealt with. The growth of the transaction sector is the growth of a function necessary to the coordination of the tremendous amount of resources that have been committed to the market over the last hundred years. Transaction *costs* in the aggregate may or may not have risen in the last century, but certainly we can conclude that transaction *services*—the number of people, and the resources they command, who coordinate the flows of inputs into production, monitor the production process itself, and coordinate the flow of goods from producers to consumers—have risen continuously since 1870. The growth of the transaction sector is a structural change of the first order.

The growing size of the transaction sector poses a major explanatory challenge to economists and economic historians. What is the relationship of those inputs to their outputs? How have transaction and transformation costs interacted in the transformation of the economy? What are the implications of the growing sector for a variety of social and institutional changes? These are only a few important questions that should be explored in the context of structural change implied by this study.

# Appendix

This appendix describes the construction of the various data series presented in the text. The first section describes the transaction-related (type I) employment series, taken from various census sources; the second, the estimates of type I employment compensation in nontransaction industries; the third, the trade estimates; the fourth, the finance, insurance, and real estate (FIRE) estimates; the fifth, the public sector estimates; the sixth, GNP estimates; and the last, the combination of the estimates in table 3.13.

## 1.  Type I Employment

The series on type I employment by industry is broken into two parts. The first covers census years from 1910 to 1970, years with available data on occupational employment by industry. The second covers census years from 1870 to 1910.

### 1910 to 1970

The general classification of type I workers remained consistent over the census years. A listing of type I occupations is followed by detailed notes for each of the census years.

Type I includes:

Managers, owners, and proprietors: including other managers, administrators, dealers (in trade), bankers (in FIRE);

Foremen: including foremen, inspectors, gaugers, weighers, postmasters, and conductors;

Sales workers: including a variety of agents, shipping agents, purchasing agents, insurance and real estate agents; sales clerks, sales workers, newsboys, sales agents, and other sales workers;

Clerical workers: bookkeepers, cashiers, secretaries, stenographers, office machine operators, telephone operators, typists, shipping clerks, receiving clerks, clerks, and other clerical workers;

**Table 3.A.1    Division of Clerical Employment by Industry, 1910**

| Industry | Number of Employees | Employment as Percentage of All Clerical Employment |
|---|---|---|
| Agriculture, forestry, and fishing | 2,801 | 0.16 |
| Mining | 12,373 | 0.72 |
| Construction | 14,260 | 0.83 |
| Manufacturing | 305,129 | 17.76 |
| Transportation, communications, and utilities | 459,120 | 27.72 |
| Trade | 540,120 | 31.43 |
| Finance, insurance, and real estate | 180,167 | 10.48 |
| Services | 67,214 | 3.91 |
| Government | 137,272 | 7.99 |

Source: "Population," *1910 Census of Population*, table 4, pp. 302–433.

Professional workers: accountants, lawyers, judges, notaries, and personnel and labor relations workers;

Protective workers: police, guards, watchmen, marshalls, sheriffs, detectives, and constables.

In all years we exclude farm owners, military personnel, and teachers. In table 3.2 all type I employment shares are calculated using industry employment figures reported in or calculated from the occupational census figures. Although the categories explicitly considered in the census were refined in later census years, the categories are quite comparable from year to year. The major worries are over the number of "other" workers and "not elsewhere classified" workers. The extent to which these workers are type I workers is unknown.

*Notes for Specific Years*

*1970:*[23] Includes all workers in the major categories of managers and administrators (excluding farm owners); sales workers; and clerical workers. Also included are lawyers and judges; accountants; foremen; checkers, examiners, and inspectors; guards and watchmen; graders and sorters; and personnel and other labor relations workers.[24]

*1960:*[25] Includes all workers in the major categories of managers, officials, and proprietors (excluding farm owners); clerical and kindred workers; and sales workers. Also included are accountants and auditors; lawyers and judges; public relations workers;[26] foremen; guards, watchmen, and doorkeepers; checkers, examiners, and inspectors; and graders and sorters.

*1950:*[27] Includes all workers in major categories: managers, officials, and proprietors (excluding farm owners); clerical and kindred workers; and sales workers. All foremen, inspectors, and police that could be allocated to an industry were. Some occupations could not be allocated to specific industries, including accountants and auditors, lawyers and judges, personnel and labor relations, guards, watchmen and doorkeepers, guards and bridgetenders, and private police and detectives. These constituted 1.86% of the labor force, and were divided among all industries on the basis of each industry's share in total employment.[28]

*1940:*[29] Includes all workers in major categories: proprietors, managers, and officials (excluding farm owners); clerical, sales, and kindred workers; and protective service workers (excluding soldiers, sailors, marines, and coast guard). Also includes all foremen and inspectors that could be placed in industries. Those foremen, inspectors, lawyers, and judges who could not be placed in an industry were evenly distributed over all industries (they constitute 0.39% of the labor force). Accountants are included, although they are now listed as clerical, rather than professional workers. Personnel and labor relations disappear as a category altogether.

*1930 and 1910:* The information in the 1910 and 1930 census volumes is in a different form from that for later years. Employment by occupation is reported for individual industries, and totals are not presented for the major industry groups. Therefore the estimates are built up from individual calculations made for each industry. As a result the occupational classifications are considerably more detailed. We report the major divisions, and will supply a complete listing on request.

*1930:*[30] A variety of occupations is listed. Occupations reported by the census fall into five major groups.

—Proprietary, official, and supervisory pursuits: We include owners, operators, proprietors, managers, building contractors, foremen and overseers, conductors, postmasters, bankers, brokers, dealers in wholesale and retail trade, and like occupations.

—Professional pursuits: We include only lawyers.

—Clerical and kindred pursuits: We include accountants and auditors, bookkeepers and cashiers, clerks (including sales), shipping clerks, stenographers and typists, agents (purchasing and others), messenger, errand, and office boys and girls, weighers, other clerical pursuits, and like occupations.

—Skilled trades: No type I workers.

—Other pursuits: We include inspectors, scalers, and surveyors, guards and watchmen, and police.

*1910:*[31] A wide variety of occupations are listed. Basic groups and their constituent elements include:

—Proprietary, officials, and owners: We include owners and proprietors, managers and officials, bosses and foremen, overseers, builders and building contractors, contractors, bankers and bank officials, a variety of dealers in wholesale and retail trade, conductors, and postmasters.

—Clerical and kindred workers: We include agents, clerks, collectors, messengers, errand and office boys, purchasing agents, stenographers and typists, weighers, bookkeepers, cashiers, accountants, collectors, credit men, canvassers, commercial travelers, office appliance operators, telephone operators, advertising agents, and like occupations.

—Other occupations: We include inspectors, guards and watchmen, police, and like occupations.

The 1910 census reports judges, justices, and magistrates; lawyers; and abstractors, notaries, and justices of the peace in professional service rather than in industry categories. We divided lawyers and the like between "Services" and "Public Service" on the basis of their division in 1930.[32]

*Government Employees*

The estimates of type I employees in government required additional manipulation of the census numbers. First, the census classified some government workers in industries other than public administration or public service. From 1950 to 1970 public education is listed as a minor industry in the service category, and it was a minor matter to shift those workers back into public administration. In 1940, however, education is listed as a single category in the service industry (public and private education are not distinguished), and in 1910 and 1930 education is not identified as a minor industry at all. In 1940 we took 74% of all education employees (the average ratio of public employees to all employees in education in 1950–70) and moved them into public administration (making a corresponding reduction in services). We also assumed that the share of type I employees in education equals the share in the service sector, an assumption roughly accurate for 1950–70.

To break out education in 1910 and 1930 we obtained an estimate of employment in education for those years,[33] assumed that 74% of those people were in public education, and assumed again that the type I share of employment in education equaled the type I share in total services. Our estimated public education workers were added to public government and deleted from the service industry. A similar adjustment was made for postal workers, who were also included in the service industry. Tables 3.2 and 3.A.2 reflect these adjustments.

The second problem regards the classification of government employment in the census. What we have called "government" in table 3.2 when calculating the type I employment shares includes what the census labels "public administration, NEC" (not elsewhere classified). Although we have reclassified the two most important groups of public employees, postal and education workers, there are still some unclassified government workers in other industries. Potentially important are welfare workers in the service industry. We have been unable to establish the number of these "elsewhere classified" workers. Although they are probably few, their reclassification into public administration could potentially affect our estimates of type I employment shares in government used to estimate the size of the public transaction sector.

*1870–1910:*

The estimates of type I employment that appear in table 3.3 are derived from Edwards's *Comparative Occupation Statistics for the United States, 1870 to 1940*. Edwards has been discussed at length elsewhere, and we will not delve deeply into his methods here.[34]

The figures in table 3.3 are taken from Edwards, with one modification. Edwards reported employment by occupation for each industry.

Table 3.A.2    Employment by Industry, as Percentage of Total Employment, 1910–70

| Industry | 1970 | 1960 | 1950 | 1940 | 1930 | 1910 |
|---|---|---|---|---|---|---|
| Agriculture, forestry, and fisheries | 3.73 | 6.73 | 12.44 | 18.86 | 22.21 | 33.26 |
| Mining | .83 | 1.01 | 1.65 | 2.03 | 2.40 | 2.78 |
| Construction | 6.03 | 5.90 | 6.12 | 4.57 | 5.32 | 8.96[a] |
| Manufacturing | 25.86 | 27.09 | 25.91 | 23.52 | 24.35 | 19.60[a] |
| Transportation | 6.78 | 5.51 | 7.71 | 6.93 | 8.58 | 7.95 |
| Retail trade | 15.97 | 14.82 | 18.76 | 16.77 | 12.26 | 10.01 |
| Wholesale trade | 4.04 | 3.42 | | | | |
| Finance, insurance, and real estate | 5.02 | 4.17 | 3.41 | 3.27 | 3.29 | 1.36 |
| Services | 20.35 | 17.04 | 15.27 | 16.53 | 13.82 | 12.71 |
| Government | 11.39 | 8.88 | 7.16 | 5.99 | 5.28 | 3.37 |
| Other, NEC | — | 5.42 | 1.50 | 1.53 | 2.76 | — |
| Totals | 100.0 | 100.0 | 100.0 | 100.0 | 100.0 | 100.0 |

Sources: Occupational Reports of the various censuses between 1910 and 1970. See appendix notes for references.

[a]In 1910, hand trades included in construction; all other years, hand trades included in manufacturing.

We allocated managers, owners, proprietors, and foremen and like occupations to the type I category in each industry. But Edwards did not distribute clerical workers, protective service workers, professional service workers, and distributive occupations (agents, collectors, and the like) between industrial categories, a task we were obliged to carry out.

Examination of the distributive occupations that Edwards assigned to "trade" (an industry encompassing FIRE as well as wholesale and retail trade and enclosed in quotation marks to distinguish it from wholesale and retail trade), revealed that his numbers correspond closely to the numbers in trade and FIRE reported in the census for 1910. Therefore we left all Edwards's "trade" workers in the trade industry. Our figure on type I employment in trade takes all employment reported in Edwards, excluding only delivery men, undertakers, and laborers.

The protective service workers in the private economy (primarily guards and watchmen, with a small number of private police), were classified by Edwards as "public service." We could have distributed these workers back over the other industries, but their number was so small (0.2% of total employment in 1910) that we simply left them in "public service."

In professional service we had to contend with lawyers, judges, and justices, abstractors, notaries, and justices of peace. As mentioned above, for 1910 in table 3.2 we divided workers in these categories between the "service" and "government" categories. Table 3.3, follows the same convention.

Finally, we had to distribute the clerical workers among industries. Clerical workers were a significant share of the labor force in 1910 (4.6%) and between 1870 and 1910 they were also the fastest growing of the type I occupations.[35] We used the following method of distributing the clerical workers. First we calculated the share of all clerical workers working in each industry in 1910, using the published census data that underlie table 3.2. We then assumed that the distribution of clerical workers between industries was the same between 1870 and 1910. The total number of clerical workers in each year, reported by Edwards, was then distributed amongst the various industries on the basis of this distribution. The fraction of clerical workers distributed to each industry between 1870 and 1910 is reported in table 3.A.1.

As tables 3.2 and 3.3 show, the distributions of type I workers among industries in 1910 estimated by the two methods are close but not identical. The differences arise from two sources. First, our distribution of workers in trade, professional service, and protective service (Edwards's categories) between industries is a close, but not exact, duplicate of the 1910 census distribution of those occupations between industries. We were not able to identify all of the 1910 census categories in Edwards (e.g., weighers). Those occupations ended up in Edwards's "other" category and therefore could not be distributed.

Second, in table 3.2 we used the estimates of total employment by industry that were built into the census data. Employment by industry as a share of total employment is shown in table 3.A.2 for 1910 through 1970. Table 3.3 does not use the same information since the census has no data on employment by industry before 1900. Edwards generated an industrial distribution of workers by classifying occupations into industries. That, of course, was precisely what we wanted to avoid, preferring instead to see all occupations represented in each industry.

We compromised by using Carson's original estimates of employment by industry. There are problems with Carson's numbers, and they have been pointed out elsewhere.[35] The biggest appears to lie with the estimates for "trade" (as defined above). Since we do not use type I employment in trade in our examination of nontransaction industries, this was not a serious problem from our point of view, except to the extent that it means other industries were mismeasured.

There are no other complete series on employment by industry by decade for the entire period and all industries.[36] Therefore we used Carson's estimates combined with type I employees by industry taken from Edwards to calculate the share of type I workers by industry. Carson's employment shares by industry are shown in table 3.A.3. As

Table 3.A.3      Employment by Industry, as a Percentage of Total Employment, 1870–1910

| Industry | 1910 | 1900 | 1890 | 1880 | 1870 |
|---|---|---|---|---|---|
| Agriculture, forestry, and fishing | 31.42 | 37.54 | 42.85 | 50.03 | 50.21 |
| Mining | 2.86 | 2.61 | 2.00 | 1.81 | 1.53 |
| Construction | 6.23 | 5.72 | 6.09 | 4.77 | 5.82 |
| Manufacturing | 22.32 | 21.81 | 20.00 | 18.23 | 17.38 |
| Transportation | 8.19 | 7.00 | 6.22 | 4.69 | 4.77 |
| Trade | 9.13 | 8.46 | 7.69 | 6.64 | 6.07 |
| Finance, insurance, and real estate | 1.40 | 1.04 | .69 | .36 | .33 |
| Services | 12.88 | 11.81 | 11.25 | 10.06 | 10.74 |
| Government | 3.54 | 2.76 | 2.51 | 2.28 | 1.94 |
| Other | 2.03 | 1.25 | .71 | 1.14 | 1.19 |
| Totals | 100.0 | 100.0 | 100.0 | 100.0 | 100.0 |

*Source:* Daniel Carson 1949, table 1, p. 47.

Note that services include professional services and amusements and domestic and personal service.

comparison with table 3.A.2 shows, the 1910 census data are not exactly the same as Carson's.

## 2.  Combining Type I Employment with Employee Compensation

After constructing the type I employment share estimates reported in tables 3.2 and 3.3, it was necessary to combine them with a measure of employee compensation in each industry to determine the amount of resources going to those workers reported in table 3.4. The calculation was carried out separately for three periods: 1930–70, 1900–1940, and 1870–1900. Where possible we overlapped dates to provide a basis for comparison of the different methods.

### 1930–70

The calculation for this period—columns 9 and 10 of table 3.4—is straightforward. We multiplied the type I employment shares from table 3.2 by employee compensation by industry for all nontransaction industries. Summing over the industries gave a total type I employee wage bill, which was then divided by GNP. Both employee compensation and GNP were taken from the *National Income and Product Accounts* (NIPA).[37]

### 1900–1940

This calculation—columns 5 and 6—was slightly more complicated. Type I employment shares by industry for 1920 were estimated by taking the average of the type I shares in 1910 and 1930. Wage compensation by industry was calculated from Lebergott's data on employment by industry and average annual wages by industry.[38] The total wage bill for each industry—the product of employment and annual wages—was then multiplied by the type I employment shares to derive type I employee compensation by industry. The totals were then summed over all nontransaction industries. To determine the percentage of GNP going to type I employees, the total was divided by Kuznets's Variant I estimate of GNP.[39] Columns 7 and 8 are divided by GNP reported in NIPA for 1930 and 1940.

Columns 3 and 4 are similar calculations for 1900 and 1910 using the type I employment shares derived from the Edwards data instead of the census data. The difference for 1910 in columns 3 and 5 and in columns 4 and 6 are not substantial.

### 1870–1900

For the early period we utilized data from Gallman on value added by industry and Gallman and Weiss on the service industries in the nineteenth century.[40] Following the approach of Gallman and Weiss, we first calculated the income originating in agriculture, mining, manufacturing, and construction by multiplying Gallman's value added by industry by the extrapolating ratios contained in Gallman and Weiss (.6525 for agriculture and .6556 for other industries).[41] Then income originating in each industry was converted into the wage bill by multiplying by Budd's (1960, table 2, p. 373) factor shares. Then these estimated wage bills were multiplied by industry share of type I employment from table 3.3 to obtain the type I wage bill by industry.

For transportation we took the Gallman and Weiss estimates of value added and applied the Budd factor share directly to value added to estimate the wage bill. For services and government, value added was equal to total wages. The type I wage bill for each industry was calculated by multiplying the industry share of type I employment times the wage bill. These were summed across all industries. The estimate of the total type I wage bill was then divided by Gallman's estimates of GNP to derive the estimates in columns 1 and 2 in table 3.4. As the table indicates, the estimates for 1900 derived by the value-added method (cols. 1 and 2) are reasonably close to the estimates derived by the wage bill method (cols. 3 and 4).

### 3.   Trade

We tried two ways of estimating the value of resources used in wholesale and retail trade. The first measure was derived directly from the commodity flow of GNP estimates. The commodity flow estimates begin with the value of commodity output in producer prices, then (adding transportation costs at appropriate stages) inflate the value of commodities from producer to consumer prices by applying an estimate of the distributive markup involved in getting a product from the producer to the consumer.[42] The direct approach is to extricate from the income accounts the implicit gross distributive margin. The gross distributive margin can be used as a measure of the amount of resources used in trade, after an adjustment is made to include resources used to distribute intermediate goods, which are not included in the commodity flow estimates.

This would be sufficient if available estimates of the gross distributive margins implicit in the income accounts were readily available for the entire period, but they are not. An alternative method (the reverse commodity flow method) is to work back from the commodity flow estimates of GNP in consumer prices to generate an independent estimate of resources used in trade. This method has the virtue of continuity, but it is an additional step removed from the actual data. We have used the second method in the text, and present the results of the direct measures for comparison.

There is a conceptual difficulty in using the commodity flow estimates to generate a measure of the resources used in trade. Some goods sold to wholesalers are resold to producers rather than to retailers. The commodity flow estimates of GNP do not include the costs of distributing these intermediate goods in the gross distributive margin, since including them would inflate distributive markups and lead to an overestimate of commodity flows in consumer prices. For our purposes, however, we want to include all the resource costs of distributing all goods, final and intermediate.

For later years this is not a problem. In four years after 1958 the total resources used by wholesale and retail trade are available from the input/output tables prepared by the Commerce Department. For 1919 and 1929 Kuznets provides what appears to be a measure of the total resources used in trade, although one that is built up from the commodity flow estimates (discussed below). Before 1919, however, it is necessary to approximate the total resources used in trade from the existing data on commodity flows. This involves a combination of the work of Barger and Gallman. Table 3.A.4 presents the resources used in trade as reported by Gallman, Kuznets, and the Commerce Department, expressed as a percentage of GNP for years where figures were available.

Gallman, column 1, calculated value added in trade from the distributive trade margins in Barger and commodity flow data from Shaw. The Gallman series measures the implicit gross distributive margins that underlie Gallman's GNP estimates.[43]

The Kuznets data, column 2, were taken from *Commodity Flow and Capital Formation,* for 1919 and 1929. Kuznets reports the value of

Table 3.A.4     **Measures of Total Resources Used in Trade, as Percentage of GNP**

| Year | Gallman (1) | Kuznets (2) | Commerce (3) | Adjusted Gallman (4) |
|---|---|---|---|---|
| 1870 (1869) | 13.11 | — | — | 14.23 |
| 1880 (1879) | 13.56 | — | — | 15.40 |
| 1890 (1889) | 15.80 | — | — | 17.69 |
| 1900 (1899) | 16.38 | — | — | 17.92 |
| 1910 (1909) | — | — | — | — |
| 1920 (1919) | — | 19.28 | — | — |
| 1930 (1929) | — | 18.97 | — | — |
| 1940 (1939) | — | — | — | — |
| 1950 (1948) | — | — | — | — |
| 1960 (1958) | — | — | 21.18 | — |
| (1963) | — | — | 20.21 | — |
| 1970 (1967) | — | — | 20.43 | — |
| (1972) | — | — | 18.25 | — |

| Year | Combined Series (5) | Estimated Series (6) |
|---|---|---|
| 1870 (1869) | 14.23 | 16.14 |
| 1880 (1979) | 15.40 | 18.02 |
| 1890 (1889) | 17.69 | 18.07 |
| 1900 (1899) | 17.92 | 19.15 |
| 1910 (1909) | — | 19.07 |
| 1920 (1919) | 19.28 | 19.57 |
| 1930 (1929) | 18.97 | 18.74 |
| 1940 (1939) | — | 20.54 |
| 1950 (1948) | — | 21.87 |
| 1960 (1958) | 21.18 | 21.18 |
| 1970 (1967) | 20.43 | 20.43 |

*Sources:*

Column 1: Value added in Trade, Gallman and Weiss 1969, p. 306; as percentage of Gallman GNP, table 3.A.11, col. 1.

Column 2: Kuznets 1938. Calculated from table V–6, p. 309, by taking sales at retail prices (or wholesale prices for goods sold to consumers directly by wholesalers) and subtracting sales at producers prices, including transportation, for each of the commodity groups. As percentage of Kuznets GNP, table 3.A.11, col. 1.

Column 3: United States Department of Commerce, *Survey of Current Business,* for various years: 1958 from September 1965, pp. 38–39; 1963 from November 1969, pp. 34–35; 1967 from February 1974, pp. 42–43; and 1972 from April 1979, pp. 66–67. As percentage of NIPA GNP, table 3.A.11, col. 2.

Column 4: Column 1 times an adjustment factor taken from Barger. The adjustment factors for each year were: 1869, 1.09; 1879, 1.14; 1889, 1.12; 1899, 1.09. See text for references.

Column 5: Combination of cols. 2, 3, and 4.

Column 6: See table 3.A.5, col. 5, except for 1960 and 1970 when we took the Commerce Department estimate for the appropriate year from col. 3.

*Note:* The first year listed refers to the year we list in the text. The year in parenthesis refers to the year for which calculation was actually made.

goods in producer prices plus transportation costs and the value of the goods in consumer prices for the major types of goods. The difference in the two series is the gross distributive margin that underlies Kuznets's GNP estimates.[44] Kuznets included an estimate of the costs of distributing intermediate goods as well, so column 2 represents the total costs of resources used in wholesale and retail trade.

The Commerce estimates (col. 3) were taken directly from the input/output tables for 1958, 1963, 1967, and 1972. Column 3 measures the total resources used by wholesale and retail trade, including the costs of distributing intermediate goods between producers and all final goods to consumers.

The pre-1900 figures, column 1, are too low, as they exclude resources used in distributing intermediate goods to producers. To adjust the nineteenth-century numbers, we utilized Barger. He reports a "value added" in trade figure which appears to include all resources in trade, not merely those costs associated with distributing final goods (Barger 1960, table 5, p. 332). Barger also presents estimates of gross distributive margins for final goods only (Barger 1955, table 20, p. 70, table 23, p. 77). The difference between Barger's value-added series and his gross distributive margin series indicates that the costs of distributing intermediate goods were roughly 10% of all resource costs in trade. Since Barger and Gallman were working within the same basic framework and with the same sources, the 10% difference should be applicable to the Gallman estimates by the ratio of Barger's value-added series to his gross margin series for each year.[45] The adjusted Gallman figures are reported in column 4 of the table.

The series is put together in column 5 of the table. It has two obvious problems. First, there are gaps in 1910, 1940, and 1950. Second, the long gap falls between the Kuznets and Commerce figures, and we are concerned about the comparability of the two series (the Gallman numbers were designed to be compatible with Kuznets). Given the long gap there was no way to insure that conceptual differences in the two series would be minor. Our solution was to construct a series that could be linked up with the Commerce series for total resources in trade and benchmarked to the Kuznets numbers for 1919 and 1929. The method involved working backward from commodity flows valued in consumer prices. Table 3.A.5 provides details of the calculation. We began with the flow of goods to consumers for perishables, semidurables, and durables, producers' durables, and construction materials from Gallman, Kuznets, and Shaw for years between 1869 and 1949, column 3. Then we took Barger's estimate of the share of all commodities that go through distributive channels, column 1, and his estimate of the average distributive markup as a percentage of retail prices, column 2. We multiplied the commodity flows by those two figures and then

**Table 3.A.5**          **Estimating the Gross Resources Used in Trade by Reversing the Commodity Flow Method**

| Year | | Percentage of Finished Goods Going through Trade (1) | Distributive Markups as Percentage of Retail Price (2) | Commodity GNP in Trade (Billions) (3) | Resources Used in Trade (Billions) (4) | Percentage of GNP in Trade (5) |
|---|---|---|---|---|---|---|
| 1870 | (1869) | 65 | 32.7 | 5.63 | 1.27 | 16.14 |
| 1880 | (1879) | 71 | 33.7 | 6.77 | 1.72 | 18.02 |
| 1890 | (1889) | 71 | 34.7 | 8.50 | 2.22 | 18.07 |
| 1900 | (1899) | 75 | 35.4 | 11.01 | 3.10 | 19.15 |
| 1910 | (1909) | 75 | 36.5 | 19.43 | 5.64 | 19.07 |
| 1920 | (1919) | 75 | 36.5 | 47.29 | 13.74 | 19.57 |
| 1930 | (1929) | 77 | 37.0 | 54.42 | 16.45 | 18.74 |
| 1940 | (1939) | 80 | 37.3 | 57.14 | 18.09 | 20.54 |
| 1950 | (1948) | 80 | 37.4 | 164.57 | 52.25 | 21.87 |

*Sources:*
Column 1: Barger 1955, table 10, p. 22.
Column 2: Barger 1955, table 26, p. 92.
Column 3: 1869–99: Commodity flows were taken from Gallman (1966), and from Shaw (1947). Commodity flows include flows to consumers of perishables, semidurables, and durables (Gallman, table A–2, p. 27); manufactured durables (Gallman, table A–3, p. 34); and construction materials (Shaw, table I 1, p. 65).
1909–48: commodity flows were taken from Kuznets (1961), and Shaw (1947). Flow of goods to consumers includes perishables, semiperishables, and durables (Kuznets, table R–27, pp. 565–66); gross producers' durables (Kuznets, table R–33, pp. 596–97); and construction materials from Shaw. For 1909 and 1919 construction materials were taken directly from Shaw (table I 1, pp. 64–65). For 1929–48 we estimated the volume of construction materials by extrapolating construction materials on the basis of the volume of gross construction, reported in Kuznets, p. 524. The extrapolation ratio was .4831, the average ratio of construction materials to gross construction reported by Kuznets and Shaw for the period 1869–1919.
Note that the Gallman data are decade averages, the Kuznets data are 5-year averages, and the Shaw data are single-year estimates.
Column 4: (1) * (2) * (3) * 1.0612. The adjustment factor, 1.0612, was used to benchmark the series to the estimates of gross distributive margins in Kuznets (1938), as reported in col. 2 of table 3.A.4.
Column 5: Column 4 as percentage of Gallman/Kuznets GNP, table 3.A.11, col. 1.
*Note:* The estimating method is described in the text. The year listed first is reported in the text; the year in parenthesis is the year for which the calculation was actually made.

benchmarked the estimates to Kuznets's gross distributive margins in 1919 and 1929, column 4. The total resources were then converted to a percentage of GNP, column 5. They are also reported in column 6 of table 3.A.4.

This method has several advantages. First, it gives us a continuous and conceptually consistent measure for the entire period from 1869 to 1948. Second, the estimates of resources used in trade are consistent with Gallman's and Kuznets's GNP series. Third, the estimates link up chronologically with the Commerce estimates, although they do not overlap. As a comparison of columns 5 and 6 indicates, the two methods of estimating resources used in trade generate similar results, the major difference being a lower level of resources used in trade in the early part of the period in the Gallman series. Table 3.5 in the text uses the figures in column 6 of table 3.A.4.

As discussed in section 3.1, we do not want to include transportation costs in trade as part of the transaction sector. Investigation indicated that the total resources used for transportation in wholesale and retail trade were fairly small, around 5% of total resources in trade. From the input/output tables it was possible to determine the volume of intermediate inputs purchased by the trade industries that were used for transportation. These included purchases from the petroleum refining and related industries; motor vehicles and equipment; aircraft and parts; and transportation and warehousing. For the years 1958, 1963, 1967, and 1972 these categories averaged 1.855% of total resources used in trade, surely an overestimate of expenditures on transportation, given the volume of petroleum products used for heating. The occupational data from the census of 1970 enabled us to construct an estimate of transportation-related employment in trade by using the following categories: transport equipment operatives; automobile mechanics and repairmen; and freight, stock, and materials handlers. Again, the latter category includes a significant number of nontransportation workers. Total employment in these categories was 7.88% of total employment, and 7.88% of employee compensation in trade would account for 3.35% of total resources used in trade. Similar calculations for earlier years could not be made because of a lack of detail for female employees, but male employment in the transportation occupations was similar for earlier years. Given that transportation accounts for a small part of the resources used in trade, and lacking an effective way of extending that estimate into the earlier years, we chose not to net transportation out of the resources used in trade.

## 4.   Finance, Insurance, and Real Estate

The estimates of resources used in FIRE (table 3.6) presented several problems: finding comparable data series, dealing with the imputed services of owner-occupied housing and rental income, and working out a method to extend the series back to 1870. Our starting point was the input/output tables for 1972, 1967, 1963, and 1958. Finance and insurance were considered separately from real estate.

Table 3.A.6 provides the series used to construct the finance and insurance estimates. After 1958 the input/output tables provide a direct measure of the total resources used in finance and insurance, column

**Table 3.A.6**    **Estimates of Resources Used in Finance and Insurance, from Input/Output, NIPA, and Kuznets 1920–72 (Billions of Dollars)**

| Year | National Income Finance & Insurance (1) | Actual Resources (2) | Estimated Resources (3) | Ratio Actual/ Estimated (4) | Estimated Resources Finance & Insurance (5) |
|------|------|------|------|------|------|
| 1958 | 14.16 | 26.4 | 25.3 | 1.042 | — |
| 1963 | 17.89 | 33.7 | 32.0 | 1.054 | — |
| 1967 | 26.33 | 47.8 | 47.1 | 1.015 | — |
| 1972 | 40.39 | 77.9 | 72.2 | 1.079 | — |
| Mean |      |      |      | 1.047 |   |
| 1920* | 1.69 | — | — | — | 3.2 |
| 1930* | 2.47 | — | — | — | 4.6 |
| 1930 | 2.90 | — | — | — | 5.4 |
| 1940 | 2.63 | — | — | — | 4.9 |
| 1950 | 7.00 | — | — | — | 13.1 |
| 1960 | 16.34 | — | — | — | 30.6 |
| 1970 | 34.06 | — | — | — | 63.8 |

*Sources:*
Column 1: 1930–72: National income in finance and insurance from United States Department of Commerce 1981, table 6.3, pp. 229–33.
1920*–1930*: Kuznets 1941, table F–1, p. 731.

Column 2: United States Department of Commerce, *Survey of Current Business,* for various years: 1958 from September 1965, pp. 38–39; 1963 from November 1969, pp. 34–35; 1967 from February 1974, pp. 42–43; and 1972 from April 1979, pp. 66–67. Includes the sum of materials used and value added in finance and insurance.

Column 3: To account for the use of materials in finance and insurance, the income-originating figure was multiplied by 1.7882. Materials averaged .7882 of value added for the 4 years covered by the input/output tables.

Column 4: (2)/(3).

Column 5: National income in finance and insurance times 1.8597. National income in finance and insurance from col. 1. The 1.8597 figure is the product of the adjustment factor for materials (1.7882) and the adjustment factor to benchmark the estimates to the input/output estimates (1.047).

2. To extend the series back to 1920 we utilized information on national income in finance and insurance from NIPA and Kuznets, column 1. First we estimated the intermediate goods used in finance and insurance by taking the average ratio of value added to intermediate goods in finance and insurance from the input/output tables. We then adjusted national income in finance and insurance to reflect intermediate purchases, column 3. We found, however, that in the years for which we had both the input/output estimates and national income data (1958, 1963, 1969, 1972) this method underestimated total resources used by about 5% (col. 4). In making the estimates for the earlier years (1920–70) we accounted for this by transforming national income in finance

and insurance by a constant factor, which accounted for intermediate purchases and the underestimate, column 5.

Table 3.A.7 provides the series used to construct the estimates of total resources used in real estate. There were two problems with extending these estimates back to earlier years: netting out rental income, and accounting for the purchase of intermediate goods. We began by taking national income from housing, column 1, and then subtracted rental income in housing (both actual and inputed), column 2. Had we been able to establish a relationship between the volume of intermediate good purchases and national income from housing we could then have modified column 3 as we did for finance and insurance. It was not possible to do so, however, since evidence from the input/output tables did not indicate a stable relationship between value added and inter-

**Table 3.A.7**  **Estimates of Resources Used in Real Estate, from Input/Output, NIPA, and Kuznets, 1920–72 (Billions of Dollars)**

| Year | National Income Real Estate (1) | Rental Income Real Estate (2) | Nonrental Income Real Estate (3) | Estimated Resources Real Estate (4) | Actual Resources Real Estate (5) |
|------|------|------|------|------|------|
| 1958 | 29.97 | 17.6 | 12.26 | 23.38 | 21.33 |
| 1963 | 39.93 | 26.8 | 13.13 | 25.03 | 27.69 |
| 1967 | 51.10 | 34.7 | 16.40 | 31.26 | 41.75 |
| 1972 | 74.21 | 48.0 | 26.21 | 49.97 | 66.18 |
| 1920* | 5.79 | 4.29 | 1.50 | 2.86 | — |
| 1930* | 7.30 | 4.27 | 3.03 | 5.78 | — |
| 1930 | 8.17 | 5.20 | 2.97 | 5.65 | — |
| 1940 | 6.20 | 3.60 | 2.60 | 4.96 | — |
| 1950 | 16.24 | 7.40 | 8.84 | 16.85 | — |
| 1960 | 33.66 | 21.30 | 12.36 | 23.55 | — |
| 1970 | 61.24 | 40.40 | 20.84 | 39.74 | — |

*Sources:* Column 1: 1930–72: National income in real estate, United States Department of Commerce 1981, table 6.3, pp. 229–33. 1920*–1930*: Net income originating in real estate from Simon Kuznets 1941, table F–1, p. 731.

Column 2: 1930–72: Rental income, United States Department of Commerce, 1981, table 1.20, pp. 69–70.
1920*–1930*: Net rent to individuals, Kuznets 1941, table F–2, p. 732.

Column 3: (1) − (2)

Column 4: (3)/0.5245. The average ratio of col. (3)/(4) for 1963 and 1958 is 0.5245.

Column 5: The difference between total resources used in real estate and gross housing output. Resources used in real estate is the sum of intermediate goods used and value added from United States Department of Commerce, *Survey of Current Business*: 1958 from September 1965, pp. 38–39; 1963 from November 1969, pp. 34–35; 1967 from February 1974, pp. 42–43; and 1972 from April 1979, pp. 66–67; includes the sum of materials used and value added in real estate. Gross housing output from NIPA, table 1.20, pp. 69–70.

mediate purchases in the nonrental part of real estate. So we went directly from national income in nonrental real estate, column 3, to an estimate of resources in real estate, column 4. We calculated the ratio of national income in nonrental real estate, column 3, to total resources in nonrental real estate from the available series on national income in nonrental real estate (we used the ratio from 1958 and 1963, as the ratios for 1967 and 1972 were considerably different). The estimated resources used in real estate appear in column 4 of table 3.A.7.

A major problem—both for finance and insurance and for real estate—is extending the series back before 1920. We used Gallman and Weiss's work on the service industries in the nineteenth century. They estimate value added in banking and insurance at decade intervals between 1839 and 1899. Table 3.A.8, column 1, presents those estimates. There is no series available for real estate. The average ratio of resources used in real estate to resources used in finance and insurance between 1920 and 1972 was used to extrapolate the volume of resources used in real estate. We applied that ratio to value added in banking and insurance for earlier years. The estimates appear in column 2 of the table.

Columns 3 and 4 of the table give the resources (as a share of GNP) for finance and insurance and for real estate for all years between 1870 and 1970. Column 5 combines the estimates for both industry groups. We bridged the 1910 break in the series by interpolating the 1900 and 1920 values. These are the figures that appear in table 3.6 in the text.

5. Government Expenditures on Transaction Services

The estimates of the transaction sector in government are detailed in tables 3.A.9 and 3.A.10. We used two methods. In the first, table 3.11, we included all government expenditures on transaction services from table 3.12, as well as transaction-related (type I) employee compensation in other types of government expenditure. The calculation of type I employee compensation in nontransaction government functions is shown in table 3.A.9. The total (col. 4) was calculated by taking government expenditures on nontransaction services (net of interest payments) (col. 3), multiplying by the percentage of government expenditures going to employee compensation (col. 2), and multiplying again by the percentage of all government employees working in transaction-related occupations (col. 1).

The second method utilized estimates from table 3.4. We simply treated government as a nontransaction industry and took the compensation of transaction-related workers directly from table 3.4. It is necessary to add to this the compensation of military personnel, excluded from table 3.4. Table 3.A.10 details the calculation of military pay. We begin with the number of active personnel, column 1, and

**Table 3.A.8    Combination of the Estimates of Resources Used in Finance, Insurance, and Real Estate, 1870–1970**

| Year | Resources Used in Finance and Insurance (Billions) (1) | Resources Used in Real Estate (Billions) (2) | Finance as Percentage of GNP (3) | Real Estate as Percentage of GNP (4) | Total (5) |
|---|---|---|---|---|---|
| 1870 | .158 | .152 | 2.14% | 2.05% | 4.19% |
| 1880 | .231 | .222 | 2.42 | 2.33 | 4.75 |
| 1890 | .431 | .414 | 3.51 | 3.37 | 6.87 |
| 1900 | .658 | .632 | 4.06 | 3.90 | 7.96 |
| 1910 | — | — | — | — | 8.12[a] |
| 1920* | 3.2 | 2.86 | 4.34 | 3.94 | 8.28 |
| 1930* | 4.6 | 5.78 | 5.78 | 7.22 | 13.00 |
| 1930 | 5.4 | 5.65 | 5.99 | 6.23 | 12.22 |
| 1940 | 4.9 | 4.96 | 4.92 | 4.96 | 9.88 |
| 1950 | 13.1 | 16.85 | 4.57 | 5.88 | 10.45 |
| 1960 (1958)[b] | 26.4 | 21.33 | 5.87 | 4.74 | 10.61 |
| 1970 (1972) | 77.9 | 66.18 | 6.57 | 5.58 | 12.15 |

*Sources:*
Column 1: 1870–1900: Value of output in finance and insurance, Gallman and Weiss 1969, tables A–5 and A–6, pp. 319–320. 1920–1970: table 3.A.6, (of this paper) col. 5; except for 1960 and 1970, from col. 2 of table 3.A.6.

Column 2: 1870–1900: (1) * 0.9607. The ratio of resources in finance and insurance to resources in real estate from 1910 to 1920 was 0.9607, and we used that ratio to estimate the earlier years.
1920–70: table 3.A.7, col. 4; except for 1960 and 1970, col. 5, table 3.A.7.

Column 3: Column 1 as percentage of GNP, using Gallman-Kuznets GNP for 1870–1930* (table 3.A.11, col. 1); and NIPA GNP for 1930–70 (table 3.A.11, col. 2).

Column 4: Column 2 as percentage of GNP, using same GNP as col. 3.

Column 5: Cols. (3) + (4). NIPA GNP for 1930–70 (table 3.A.11, col. 2).

[a]Value for 1910 interpolated between 1900 and 1920.

[b]Years in parentheses represent year for which calculation was made.

multiply by basic pay plus allowances, column 2, to get military payrolls for the years between 1900 and 1940, column 3. After 1950 we took compensation of military employees, column 3, directly from NIPA.

## 6.  A Note on GNP

We used GNP series constructed by Gallman, Kuznets, and the Commerce Department (NIPA). The relevant figures are shown in table 3.A.11. Several words of caution are in order.

First, the Gallman figures were designed to be compatible with Kuznets, and we use Gallman/Kuznets as a continuous series. The Gallman estimates are, however, decade averages, while the Kuznets estimates

Table 3.A.9    **Compensation of Government Employees in Transaction-Related Occupations in Nontransaction Service Programs 1900–1970**

| Year | Percentage of All Employees in Transaction-Related Occupations (1) | Employee Compensation as Percentage of All Government Expenditures (2) | Government Expenditures in Nontransaction Services, as Percentage of GNP (3) | Total as Percentage of GNP (4) |
|------|------|------|------|------|
| 1900 (1902)[a] | 40.38 | 58.43 | 3.70 | 0.87 |
| 1910 (1913) | 40.38 | 44.39 | 4.80 | 0.86 |
| 1920 (1922) | 39.55 | 35.28 | 6.99 | 0.97 |
| 1930 (1932) | 38.71 | 38.02 | 13.35 | 1.97 |
| 1940 | 46.40 | 37.46 | 14.75 | 2.56 |
| 1950 | 42.88 | 29.19 | 13.70 | 1.71 |
| 1960 | 37.46 | 26.17 | 15.93 | 1.86 |
| 1970 | 38.53 | 33.18 | 20.38 | 2.61 |

*Sources:*
Column 1: Table 3.2, type 1 employees as a percentage of all government employees.
Column 2: United States Department of Commerce 1975. Figures are expenditures for personal services (ser. Y-530, pp. 1119–20) as a percentage of total expenditures (ser. Y-522, pp. 1119–20).
Column 3: Table 3.8, col. (2) + (3).
Column 4: Columns (1) * (2) * (3).
[a]Year in parentheses is year for which calculation was actually made.

are 5-year averages. We take comparable data on other variables (e.g., trade, employee compensation, etc.) from the year on which the GNP estimate is centered. When the other variables are taken from Gallman or Kuznets they are usually 10- or 5-year averages, but when they are taken from other sources (e.g., Barger) they are often single-year numbers. We have not attempted to correct for any errors that might result from this procedure.

Second, the NIPA figures are for single years and, as is well known, the conceptual framework of the NIPA figures differs from Kuznets. Particularly important is the treatment of government. We have not addressed either of these potential difficulties directly. We have simply tried to be as clear as possible about which GNP series we are using.

Third, different series were available for different dates. Tables in the text are dated at decade intervals, but often the actual calculation was done for a nearby year (these dates are noted in the relevant tables). This often results in an estimate of the size of the transaction sector built up from different years. For example, the data for 1950 include trade data from Barger and Kuznets for 1948, and employee compensation data from NIPA for 1950. In each case the relevant magnitudes

Table 3.A.10    Compensation of Military Personnel, as a Percentage of GNP, 1900–1970

| Year | Active Military Personnel (Thousands) (1) | Basic Pay Allowance (Dollars) (2) | Total Payroll (Millions of Dollars) (3) | Total as Percentage of GNP (4) |
|---|---|---|---|---|
| 1900 | 126 | 528 | 66.53 | 0.41 |
| 1910 | 139 | 968 | 134.55 | 0.38 |
| 1920 | 343 | 1,248 | 428.41 | 0.47 |
| 1930 | 283 | 1,530 | 432.99 | 0.48 |
| 1940 | 592 | 1,811 | 1,072.11 | 1.07 |
| 1950 | 1,813 | 2,942 | 5,333.85 | 1.86 |
| 1960 | 1,690 | 3,949 | 6,673.81 | 1.32 |
| 1970 | 3,273 | 6,534 | 21,385.78 | 2.15 |

*Sources:*
Column 1: 1900–1920: United States Department of Commerce 1975 ser. Y-904, p. 1141. 1930–70: United States Department of Commerce 1981, table 6.11.

Column 2: 1900–1940: United States Department of Commerce 1975, ser. D-924, pp. 175–76. The years are somewhat different than given in the table: 1900 = 1898, 1913 = 1918, and 1940 = 1945; 1920 and 1930 were interpolated linearly between the 1918 and 1945 figures.
1950–70: We had compensation of military personnel from United States Department of Commerce 1981 (see notes to col. 3. For these years the basic pay plus allowances was computed as cols. 3/1.

Column 3: 1900–1940: cols. (1) * (2).
1950–70: Employee compensation of military employees from United States Department of Commerce 1981, table 6.5, pp. 238–42.

Column 4: Column 3 as a percentage of NIPA GNP, table 3.A.11, col. 2, except for 1900 taken from col. 1.

are converted into a percentage of GNP for the appropriate year. That is, in 1950, the trade data are a percentage of GNP in 1948 and the employee compensation data are a percentage of GNP in 1950.

7.   Combining the Estimates

Table 3.13 presents the final results of our estimates. Column 1 of the table combines the estimates for the nontransactions industries, trade and FIRE. Table 3.A.12 details the combination of those elements. For 1930, where there were two estimates, we took the average of the Kuznets figure and the NIPA figure.

**Table 3.A.11**    **GNP Estimates, 1869–1972 Gallman, Kuznets, and Commerce Department Current Prices (Billions of Dollars)**

| Year | | Gallman-Kuznets (1) | Commerce NIPA (2) | Commerce (3) |
|------|------|------|------|------|
| 1870 | (1869) | 7.4 | — | — |
| 1880 | (1879) | 9.54 | — | — |
| 1890 | (1889) | 12.30 | — | — |
| 1900 | (1899) | 16.20 | — | — |
| 1902 | | — | — | 24.2 |
| | (1909) | 29.60 | 33.4 | — |
| 1910 | (1910) | 30.90 | 35.4 | — |
| 1913 | | — | — | 40.3 |
| | (1919) | 70.20 | 84.2 | — |
| 1920 | (1920) | 72.60 | 91.5 | — |
| 1922 | | — | — | 74.0 |
| | (1929) | 87.80 | 103.4 | — |
| 1930 | (1930) | 80.00 | 90.7 | — |
| 1932 | | — | — | 58.0 |
| | (1939) | 88.10 | 85.2 | — |
| 1940 | (1940) | 95.90 | 100.0 | — |
| | (1948) | 219.40 | 259.5 | — |
| 1950 | (1950) | 254.70 | 286.5 | — |
| | (1958) | — | 449.7 | — |
| 1960 | (1960) | — | 506.5 | — |
| 1963 | | — | 596.7 | — |
| 1968 | | — | 873.4 | — |
| 1970 | (1970) | — | 992.7 | — |
| | (1972) | — | 1,185.9 | — |

*Sources:*
Column 1: 1869–99: Gallman 1966, table A-1, p. 26. Note that the figure reported for 1869 is a single-year number, which was graciously provided by Gallman from his worksheets. Otherwise the data represent decade averages (e.g., 1880 equals 1874–1883).
1909–50: Kuznets 1961, table R-25, pp. 561–62, Variant I. The data are 5-year moving averages centered on the parenthetical year.
Column 2: United States Department of Commerce, 1981.
1909–20: Table 1.22, p. 72.
1929–72: Table 1.1, pp. 1–2.
Column 3: United States Department of Commerce 1969, p. i.

Table 3.A.12    The Size of the Transaction Sector in the Private Sector of the Economy as a Percentage of GNP, 1870–1970

| Year | Compensation of Employees in Transaction-Related Occupations (1) | Trade (2) | Finance, Insurance, and Real Estate (3) | Total (4) |
|---|---|---|---|---|
| 1870 | 2.16% | 16.14 | 4.19 | 22.49 |
| 1880 | 2.50 | 18.02 | 4.75 | 25.27 |
| 1890 | 4.18 | 18.07 | 6.87 | 29.12 |
| 1900 | 3.32 | 19.15 | 7.96 | 30.43 |
| 1910 | 4.32 | 19.07 | 8.12 | 31.51 |
| 1920 | 7.25 | 19.57 | 8.28 | 35.10 |
| 1930 | 6.84 | 18.74 | 12.61 | 38.19 |
| 1940 | 6.67 | 20.54 | 9.88 | 37.09 |
| 1950 | 7.98 | 21.87 | 10.45 | 40.30 |
| 1960 | 9.52 | 21.18 | 10.61 | 41.31 |
| 1970 | 10.40 | 18.25 | 12.15 | 40.80 |

Sources:
Column 1: Table 3.4. For years 1870–1890, col. 1
                                      1900, col. 3
                              1910–30, col. 5
                              1940–70, col. 9
Column 2: Table 3.5, col. 2.
Column 3: Table 3.6, col. 2.

# Notes

1. For Williamson's work, see Williamson (1975, 1979, 1981). Also see Stigler (1961), Alchian and Demsetz (1972), Jensen and Meckling (1976), and Barzel (1982).
2. For example, see Williamson's detailed classification system for different types of transactions in Williamson (1979), pp. 246–48.
3. Simon Kuznets, "Quantitative Economic Research: Trends and Problems," 50th Anniversary Colloquium, NBER, pp. 18–19.
4. Williamson (1979, p. 245) explicitly recognizes this when he says, "The object is to economize on the *sum* of production and transaction costs."
5. Note that things like "establishing credibility as a seller" can include a variety of activities: establishing brand names, investing in unsalvageable assets, making "ideological" efforts to convince the buyer that the seller is honest, etc.
6. Note that transaction costs do not include costs incurred to change the good. In this example, the seller may choose to paint the house rather than lower the asking price. The cost of painting is not a transaction cost, since what will now be exchanged is a "newly painted" house, and the seller would have had to incur the costs of painting the house if he were selling a "newly painted" house to himself. This is discussed in more detail later in the section.
7. For example, Williamson (1981, p. 1537) takes as his central theme that "the modern corporation is mainly to be understood as the product of a series of organizational innovations that have had the purpose and effect of economizing on transaction costs."
8. Some reflection on this emphasizes the importance of the definition of the good being exchanged. You can buy cut flowers from a florist or seeds from a gardening store. Are the costs of planting, weeding, and watering the transaction costs of buying the

seeds? Clearly not. The good being exchanged in the first instance is flowers, in the second instance it is seeds. Making seeds into flowers requires home production. Planting, weeding, and watering are transformation, not transaction, costs.

9. The actual amount of nontransaction services provided by wholesale trade and retail trade turns out to be small, as we show in the appendix. As a result we treat all of the resources used in Wholesale and Retail Trade as part of the transaction sector.

10. The nontransaction industries are agriculture, manufacturing, construction, transportation, services, mining, communications, and utilities. We include government in this sector but keep it separate from the other nontransaction industries.

11. The figure was derived by taking the 1970 share of total employment in each industry and weighting them by the type I employment shares from 1910 for each industry. The share of type I employment rose from 17.45% in 1900 to 38.78% in 1970. Of the 21.33% increase, 12.2% is attributable to increasing shares of type I employment in nontransaction industries, excluding government.

12. See the discussion and references in Lebergott (1966), pp. 132–33, and detailed notes following.

13. See Lebergott (1966), table 1, p. 118, and the discussion, pp. 188–90, and Ann Miller and Carol Brainerd (1957). Since we do not use the type I share of employment in trade in constructing our estimates, we have not attempted to reconcile the different estimates.

14. After 1930, employees' compensation was taken directly from the United States Department of Commerce (1981), table 6.5, pp. 238–47. Between 1900 and 1940 total wage bills by industry were calculated from Lebergott (1964), tables A-5, p. 514, and A-18, pp. 525–57. Between 1870 and 1900 income by industry was approximated by using Gallman's series on value added for major sectors, adjusted to reflect wage payments by using Budd's labor factor shares (see appendix).

15. Our method assumes, for example, that the percentage of foremen in manufacturing was the same in 1870 as in 1910. The occupations estimated in this manner account for 23% of all type I employment in nontransaction industries in 1910.

16. We have included some elements of trade and FIRE which may not be transaction services; for example, transportation costs in trade, and safe deposit boxes, perhaps, in FIRE.

17. See tables 3.A.4 and 3.A.5 for details.

18. See Kuznets (1961, app. B; 1946, pt. 3), Kendrick (1961, app. J); and Gallman (1966, pp. 57–60).

19. United States Department of Commerce, "Input-Output Structure of the U.S. Economy," *Survey of Current Business,* for various years: April 1979, February 1974, November 1969, and September 1965.

20. See tables 3.A.6, 3.A.7, and 3.A.8 for details.

21. We include in defense expenditures costs of international relations and veterans' benefits. The former are clearly transaction services, as they are necessary for foreign trade and for national defense. The latter are deferred compensation of military employees.

22. As Kuznets wrote, "The flow of services to individuals from the economy is a flow of economic goods produced and secured under conditions of internal peace, external safety, and legal protection of specific rights, and cannot include these very conditions as services. To include the latter implies feasibility of national income and of a flow of services to individuals outside the basic social fabric within which economic activity takes place. There is little sense in talking of protection of life and limb as an economic service to individuals—it is a pre-condition of such services, not a service in itself. . . . It is difficult to understand why the net product of the economy should include not only the flow of goods to ultimate consumers but also the increased cost of government activities necessary to maintain activities necessary to the social fabric within which the flow is realized" (Simon Kuznets, quoted in Studenski 1958, p. 198).

23. United States Department of Commerce (1972), table 1, pp. 1–16.

24. We have stayed with standard industrial classifications of activities. The transportation, communication, and utilities industry includes all type I workers reported in: railroads and railway express service; trucking service and warehousing; other transportation; communications; and utilities and sanitary services. The retail trade industry includes all workers in food and dairy products stores, and milk retailing; general merchandise and limited price variety stores; eating and drinking places; and other retail

trade. Services includes all workers in business services; hotel and lodging places; other personal services, including private household; entertainment and recreation; medical and other health services; private education; organizations; and other professional and related services.

25. United States Department of Commerce (1964), table 209, pp. 557–61.

26. 1960 is the only year in which public relations men and publicity writers appear. They number 23,350, or .054% of the labor force.

27. United States Department of Commerce (1954), table 124, pp. 261–66, and table 134, pp. 290–91.

28. That is, we assumed that 1.86% of the labor force in each industry was represented by these groups.

29. United States Department of Commerce (1943), table 58, pp. 75–80, and table 32, pp. 233–34.

30. United States Department of Commerce (1933), table 2, pp. 412–587.

31. United States Department of Commerce (1913), table VI, pp. 302–433.

32. In 1930 less than 5% of lawyers and judges worked outside of the public service or service industries. Following the 1930 distribution of lawyers between industries we allocated 90% of the lawyers to the private service industry and 10% to government.

33. United States Department of Commerce (1975), ser. Y272, p. 1100.

34. See Carson (1949); Lebergott (1966); and Miller and Brainerd (1957).

35. Employment in the clerical occupation, as classified by Edwards, table 8, pp. 104–12, increases from 0.63% of the labor force in 1910, to 8.24% in 1930. Brainerd and Miller identify clerical workers as a problem group (p. 398), and they adopt methods to distribute them among industries in 1880 and 1900 (pp. 480–88). We wanted a simpler method that could be applied to all years between 1870 and 1910. Our estimates for 1880 and 1900 do not differ significantly from theirs.

36. For example, Lebergott (1966, table 1, p. 118) covers the time period but does not give a complete industrial specification of employment. Brainerd and Miller (1957, table 2.8, p. 399) cover the industries but omit 1870 and 1890.

37. Employee compensation by industry was taken from United States Department of Commerce (1981), table 6-5, pp. 238–42. GNP was taken from table 1-1, pp. 1–2.

38. Stanley Lebergott (1964). Employment was taken from table A-5 and annual earnings from table A-18.

39. See table 3.A.11 for GNP data and sources.

40. Gallman (1960), table A-1, p. 43; and Gallman and Weiss (1969), table A-1, p. 306.

41. See Gallman and Weiss (1969), source notes, table 1, pp. 288–89.

42. Of course, this process is quite complicated, involving different markups for different kinds of wholesale and retail outlets, different amounts of product distributed direct, through wholesalers, and through wholesalers and retailers. See the extended discussion in Kuznets (1938, vol. 1, pts. III, IV, and V) and Barger (1955).

43. The series is taken from Robert Gallman and Thomas Weiss (1969, pp. 305–7). As Gallman and Weiss indicate, their series on value added in trade is the same series that Gallman used in constructing his nineteenth-century GNP estimates, Gallman (1966). We have called it the Gallman estimate in the text.

44. The figures are reported for different types of goods and for different methods of distribution, i.e., direct from wholesaler, direct from retailer, and through wholesaler and retailer. See Kuznets (1938).

45. Gallman's figures are based on Barger's figures. The difference is that Gallman uses Barger's numbers as a basis for extrapolation back from Kuznets's 1909 figures on gross distributive margins rather than using Barger's numbers directly. See Gallman (1966, pp. 36–37).

# Comment     Lance E. Davis

Wallis and North have set out to measure the level of "transaction costs" in the American economy and to examine changes in the levels of those costs over the past hundred-odd years. Such a task is indeed a bold undertaking; however, like any sea captains undertaking a voyage into uncharted waters, they should be aware of dangerous lee shores marked by uncharted and threatening reefs—and in this instance, none seem more threatening than those raised by language and logic. On the one hand, the concept of transaction costs, although living an apparently robust life in the modern economic literature, has never been well defined. On the other, measurement by its nature demands a taxonomy, but the scheme, if it is to be useful, must be tailored to the questions to be answered. In this instance it is not at all clear that the taxonomy chosen will lead to a useful analysis of the questions North and Wallis would like to see answered or indeed how it necessarily relates to the existing literature. Consider for a moment the words in a famous dialogue (Carroll 1981, p. 169):

> "When I use a word . . . it means just what I choose it to mean—neither more nor less."
> "The question is . . . whether you can make words mean many different things."
> "The question is . . . which is to be master—that's all."

Professors Wallis and North have cast themselves in the role of Humpty Dumpty; and at times it appears that Alice's concerns may be warranted.

It has been alleged that transaction costs have provided the refuge for those economists who take the Coase "theorem" as an act of faith, and who find that the world does not appear to behave in a way that conforms to the predictions of that "theory." Thus transaction costs have been defined by one, perhaps not unprejudiced, theorist as "anything necessary to make the Coase 'theorem' go through." Or, according to a second—and perhaps less critical—economist, "transactions costs are a useful notion whose usefulness declines proportionately with the preciseness of the definition."[1] The term is used to cover a variety of phenomena not normally included in economists' models; and as economic fashion has changed, so has the definition. Originally there were marketing costs, and for economists whose interests were not in trade or location, transport costs as well. To those time has added information, monitoring, and negotiation costs; but, as interest

---

Lance E. Davis is Mary Stillman Harkness Professor of Social Science at the California Institute of Technology in Pasadena.

1. Many theorists blanch at the use of the term "theorem" in reference to the Coase conjecture. The economists cited are James Quirk and Charles Plott.

in the spatial allocation of economic activity expanded, transport costs have often come to be considered independently; and, more recently, it appears that retail and wholesale trade may have been excluded as well.

While agreement is far from complete, a list that encompassed the costs associated with "greasing" markets and including, but not limited to, (1) obtaining information, (2) monitoring behavior, (3) recompensing middlemen, and (4) enforcing contract, might well encompass most of the transaction costs to which economists refer. They are the factors that drive a wedge between actual markets and the competitive ideal; and they are factors that have traditionally been excluded from the economists' models. To Wallis and North transaction costs are "the resource costs of maintaining and operating the institutional framework associated with capturing the gains from trade." They admit, however, that it is difficult to operationalize this broad definition and therefore attempt to ease the problem by distinguishing transaction costs and transaction services (that fraction of transaction cost that actually passes through the marketplace). It is the latter they attempt to estimate. But like Letty Palmer's dog who thought he knew what a cat was until he met a leopard, neither definition provides a formula for converting the "useful notion" into a set of estimates (Huxley 1959).

On a second, closely related point, Wallis and North may, perhaps, legitimately cry foul. They have established a taxonomy that might permit Chang to distinguish Nubian from jungle cats; but unlike Chang, it is not yet clear just why they care. Since the purpose of the categorization is only partially revealed, it may well be unfair to criticize them for producing a taxonomy that may not provide the distinctions that they desire.

The literature raises a number of questions that might be answered by an analysis somewhat similar to that of Wallis and North. Almost 40 years ago Simon Kuznets drew attention to the distortions in international income comparisons that arise from the inclusion in the calculation of the service income of developed countries certain charges that represent costs rather than income:

> First such activities as beyond any doubt represent payments by consumers for services that are nothing but occupational facilities should be excluded from the estimates for both types of country. Clear examples are commutation to and from work, and payments to unions and employment agencies; but one might add almost the entire gamut of what the Department of Commerce classifies as business services. . . . Second, where in industrial societies the costs of consumer services are inflated by the difficulties of urban life, some revaluation of these services by comparison with their costs in rural communities is in order. . . . Finally, it seems indispensable to include

in national income only such governmental activities as can be classified as direct services to ultimate consumers. (Kuznets 1947, 5:219)

A second class of problems was raised by Seymour Melman (1956) almost 30 years ago, as he attempted to explain the growth of industrial productivity in Britain and America between 1900 and 1950. Melman found that the ratio of administrative personnel to production workers had increased in both countries; and he concluded that this growth acted as a brake on total productivity increase since productivity growth in the administrative areas has been slow. Henry Ford, it might be noted, had the same feeling, and it is alleged that he attempted to solve the problem by periodically firing alternate rows of accountants (Sorenson 1957; Hughes 1966).

From the tone of this work, it is questions like those of Kuznets and Melman that will be the subject of the next canto of the Wallis and North epic. If that assumption is correct, then the operational taxonomy they have selected may well make analysis difficult, if not impossible. Kuznets recognized the problems involved in constructing such a taxonomy, but concluded, "This most important and inescapable step is urged here in full cognizance of the statistical difficulties, which are great."

Obviously both transformation and transaction costs are important, and equally obviously economists have tended to ignore some transaction costs. Costs are costs, however, and while all should be recognized in most economic analysis, it makes little difference into which category they fall. Consider the following example. A firm produces widgets with an average cost function of the form $C = L$. Mother nature is tough, and for the firm to maintain a required inventory level it is necessary that they produce two widgets for every one they sell. Then the total cost involved in the production of a widget is $2L$. In the Wallis and North taxonomy all of their costs are transformation costs. Assume that an intermediary capable of capturing certain economies of scale inherent in inventory centralization opens with average transaction cost of the form $C = 1/2 L$.

It is not important that average transaction costs have risen from zero to $1/2 L$ or that transformation costs have fallen from $2L$ to $L$. All that is relevant is that total costs have declined from $2L$ to $3/2 L$. Wallis and North are correct in arguing that all costs should be recognized. They are incorrect in their assertion that it makes any difference whether the costs are transaction or transformation.

Wallis and North classify all costs into their "production" and "transaction" components. While that goal may be unexceptionable, the location of the intercost boundary becomes critical, if the purpose is to answer questions similar to those articulated by Kuznets and

Melman. Wallis and North argue that "the transaction sector involves all the resources necessary to coordinate, execute, monitor, and enforce exchanges of property rights to goods and services." While that definition may be intellectually adequate, it is not operationally so, and it can serve as no more than a rough guide for an attempt to actually disaggregate and recombine a myriad of statistics collected with a variety of other purposes in mind. The problem is enormous, but the authors attack it with verve and with at least a dull ax if not a razor-sharp scalpel. As a first step, they divide the economy into public and private sectors, and they begin their analyses with the former. In that sector, they argue, for certain industries all costs are transaction costs. For the remainder (industries with a production cost component) there are some activities that should be classified in the transaction sector. The problem, however, still remains the same—where do you draw the line both between and within industries?

It is difficult to define precisely the line the authors have chosen to draw, but loosely it appears that they have placed activities associated with a physical transformation of the final product into production costs while all other activities have been consigned to the transaction sector.[2] On the basis of this or perhaps some other criterion, they place whole-sale and retail trade and finance, insurance, and real estate completely within the transaction sector. For the remainder of the private business sector, five classes of activities (owners, managers, and proprietors; clerical workers; sales workers; foremen and inspectors; and police and guards) are also assigned to the transaction sector. (Accountants and lawyers and judges are somehow included in these categories.) Thus equipped, the authors examine the trends in the private sector's transaction costs.

Their estimates indicate that over the period from 1870 to 1970 the share of the transaction sector rose from something less than 25% to almost 40% of the labor force (tables C3.1 and C3.2). This conclusion, however, depends on the line they have drawn between production and transaction costs, and it is not robust to relatively minor respecifications. If farmers (they were, after all, sole proprietors with substantial managerial responsibilities) are included and clerical workers excluded (one can certainly argue that some of their activity is product enhancing) from the transaction sector, the proportion, instead of rising by one-half, falls by one-third.[3] Similarly, a redefinition of the finance, insurance, and real estate industry to exclude commercial banking would reduce that industry's contribution to total transaction costs by about 15%.

---

2. To the extent that this inference is correct, one might ask why transport is not part of the transaction sector.

3. See table 3.C.2. Under the recalculation the proportion falls from 32% to 22%.

**Table C3.1**    **Type I Workers**

| Occupation | 1900 | 1910 | 1920 | 1930 | 1940 | 1950 | 1960 | 1970 |
|---|---|---|---|---|---|---|---|---|
| Accountants | 23 | 39 | 118 | 192 | 238 | 390 | 477 | 712 |
| Lawyers & judges | 108 | 115 | 123 | 161 | 182 | 184 | 213 | 273 |
| Personnel & labor relations | | | | | | 53 | 99 | 296 |
| Farm managers | 17 | 50 | 93 | 68 | 55 | 53 | 50 | 94 |
| Managers | 1697 | 2462 | 2803 | 3614 | 3770 | 5155 | 5489 | 6463 |
| Clerical | 877 | 198 | 3385 | 4336 | 4982 | 7232 | 9617 | 14208 |
| Sales workers | 1307 | 1755 | 2058 | 3059 | 3450 | 4133 | 4801 | 5625 |
| Foremen | 162 | 318 | 485 | 551 | 585 | 867 | 1199 | 1617 |
| Inspectors | 30 | 68 | 93 | 100 | 116 | 144 | 169 | 201 |
| Police & guards | 121 | 162 | 228 | 317 | 397 | 478 | 543 | 747 |
| Total | 4342 | 6956 | 9386 | 12398 | 13775 | 18689 | 22657 | 30236 |
| Total labor force | 28947 | 36611 | 42664 | 49592 | 51019 | 58403 | 68658 | 79568 |
| Total as % of all | 15% | 19% | 22% | 25% | 27% | 32% | 33% | 38% |

**Table C3.2**  Type I Workers (Alternative Definition)

| Occupation | 1970 | 1960 | 1950 | 1940 | 1930 | 1920 | 1910 | 1900 |
|---|---|---|---|---|---|---|---|---|
| Accountants | 712 | 477 | 390 | 238 | 192 | 118 | 39 | 23 |
| Lawyers & judges | 273 | 213 | 184 | 182 | 161 | 123 | 115 | 108 |
| Personnel & labor relations | 296 | 99 | 53 | | | | | |
| Farm managers | 94 | 50 | 53 | 55 | 68 | 93 | 50 | 17 |
| Farmers | 1428 | 2501 | 4290 | 5324 | 5992 | 6384 | 6132 | 5752 |
| Managers | 6463 | 5489 | 5155 | 3770 | 3614 | 2803 | 2462 | 1697 |
| Sales workers | 5625 | 4801 | 4133 | 3450 | 3059 | 2058 | 1755 | 1307 |
| Foremen | 1617 | 1199 | 867 | 585 | 551 | 485 | 318 | 162 |
| Inspectors | 201 | 169 | 144 | 116 | 100 | 93 | 68 | 30 |
| Police & guards | 747 | 543 | 478 | 397 | 317 | 228 | 162 | 121 |
| Total | 17456 | 15541 | 15747 | 14117 | 14054 | 12385 | 11101 | 9217 |
| Total labor force | 79568 | 68658 | 58403 | 51019 | 49592 | 42664 | 36611 | 28947 |
| Total as % of all | 22% | 23% | 27% | 28% | 28% | 29% | 30% | 32% |

The problem is twofold. On the one hand, an operational definition is necessary to distinguish between production and transaction activities. On the other hand, even that definition may be insufficient to disentangle the activities given the way the data are reported. The standard taxonomy is based on a "one man/one job" philosophy; and it is not necessary that an individual's activities always fall completely into either the production or transaction sectors. The farmer who is part manager and part field hand is a case in point.

The latter problem becomes particularly troubling when an attempt is made to compare structures at widely separated points in time. Two caveats, both involving comparative advantage, must be kept in mind. First, as the size of an enterprise increases, it may be possible to divide tasks between individuals and thus capture the gains from specialization and trade. These gains rest on an indivisibility and are the basis for Adam Smith's oft-quoted dictum, "the division of labor is limited by the extent of the market."[4] The census does not report that a farmer is one-third a manager and two-thirds a field hand, but it may well report that a somewhat larger farm is operated by one manager and two field hands. Second, even in the absence of scale economies technological progress may have changed the relative prices of generalized and specialized activities and therefore altered comparative advantage. An adjustment to capture these potential gains could result in an increase in the reported size of the transaction sector even if the result had been a net reduction in the costs of transaction services.

If the theoretical problems of measurement in the private sector were difficult, they pale in comparison to those raised by the public. Wallis and North are not blind to the magnitude of their task. They argue: "In a fundamental sense our broad conception of transaction services would include all of government in the transaction sector." The theoretical gain from that decision is somewhat opaque, but it certainly would have eased the measurement problems—problems that arise not from a shortage of data but from difficulties in classification.

Wallis and North begin (like Caesar) by dividing all Gaul into three parts: (1) expenditures for the defense and enforcement of property rights and investments in large social overhead public works, that are designed to facilitate trade, (2) expenditures in support of basic services, and (3) transfer payments. The first they classify as purely transaction costs (in a manner similar to their treatment of W&RT and FIRE in the private sector); the latter two as "output producing" but with some transaction components. Both present problems.

---

4. Some economists have argued that a transaction cost is any cost beyond those that would have been incurred in a Robinson Crusoe economy. It has, however, been noted that even Crusoe had to devote some resources to keeping the mice out of his bread, and thus all of his labors should not have been assigned to the production sector. For that reason John Wallis has termed the indivisibility problem the "mouse problem."

As to the first, included in expenditures of type I are defense, the postal service, certain public works, and general administrative costs. The authors explicitly recognize some, but not all, of the problems inherent in this classification. They note that a portion of the military expenditures may really be transfer costs reflecting nothing but realized American economic philosophy: socialism for the rich and capitalism for the poor. While the "military-industrial" complex may receive a substantial subsidy, it is not clear that there are not other transfers lurking in the expenditure totals. How much, for example, of veterans' programs should be viewed as payments for services received and how much as subsidies? In a similar vein, one might wonder what fraction of jobs in the postal service or the governmental administrative bureaucracy have a substantial transfer component. An interest-free loan of $15,000 appears to have produced an annual family income of nearly $100,000 in a recent example.[5]

The authors also do not appear to recognize a second and perhaps even more troublesome source of problems. Even in these "clean" transaction categories, a fraction of the expenditures may, in Kuznetsian terms, provide direct services to ultimate consumers. There is certainly a consumption component in both the post office and in the expenditures on airports and air control. One has only to contrast the 40 and 8 character of a coach section of a transcontinental flight with the uncrowded luxury of the adjacent first-class compartment to get a feel for the transaction/consumption ratio of the air transport industry or watch a mailman drive his route through suburban Belair under the watchful surveillance of a dozen security guards to understand that there are many besides businesses who use the mails. Those examples are clear-cut, but one might also wonder, although perhaps partly in jest, if there is not a consumption component in defense expenditures as well. It has long been argued that the British empire in the late nineteenth-century provided consumption for the middle and working classes, and certainly the same specter has been raised by the Far Left about more recent American adventures. While the latter obviously political charges clearly do not deserve a response, one might still wonder what behavior the next generation of historians will adduce to explain the recent fiasco in Grenada.

Finally, and more troubling, is the authors' response to their own question of the theoretical implications of the transfer component of the defense budget: "but beyond a doubt, these expenditures are the expenses of maintaining national security, given our current political

---

5. If the indivisibility can be called the mouse problem, this problem might be dubbed the "meese problem."

and social arrangements." There is no evidence at all that this conclusion is correct, and even if it were, it seems totally misdirected. The authors' research agenda appears to be directed at the design of institutions capable of minimizing transaction costs. Next year the taste for "star wars" weapons systems may decline and the transfers reappear in new disguises (perhaps like the Chrysler bailouts, perhaps somewhere in the Commerce Department budget). It may be economically efficient to maintain a strong defense posture (and those costs can be viewed as transaction costs), and it may be a political necessity that we subsidize the arms merchants, but to lump the two together and argue that they are the same animal casts substantial doubt on the ultimate usefulness of the taxonomy, if its purpose is institutional design or redesign.

The authors next explore governmental expenditures on basic services and transfers. For those classes they admit a production component and include only the "transaction workers" in their calculations. Again, however, the transfer problem raises its head; some fraction of those workers' activities can best be viewed as transfers rather than as costs (production or transaction). The Indiana personal property tax that raised just enough income to pay the assessors (who were also the party workers) and Mayor Washington's decision to keep all city workers (including the 8,000 precinct captains) on their jobs on primary day, which created political chaos in Chicago, are two cases in point.

From their analyses of these "productive" governmental sectors, Wallis and North conclude that "these [transaction] costs are higher in the public than private sector"; but this "conclusion" may well be tautological given their definition. There are, after all, few factory workers, barbers, or fieldhands working for the government.

Even if one accepts the Wallis and North taxonomy, these figures indicate that a large fraction of the observed trends in governmental transaction costs are rooted in the defense sector alone. Even if we assume that there is neither a transfer nor a consumption component in these activities, one may still wonder whether the "growth of the transaction sector" reflects much besides perceived change in the foreign climate. An extension of table 3.12 to 1980, for example, causes the percentage of pure governmental transaction expenditures in GNP to fall from 11.3 to 8.5. A further extension to 1984 would undoubtedly show a second reversal. In both instances it is difficult to see what has changed, except the party in power.

With their public and private estimates in hand, the authors merge the two to provide a single measure of the trends in "transaction costs"; and, in their conclusion, they provide some interpretation of those results.

The same questions raised about the public and private sector estimate cloud the merged series; and further questions are raised by interpretations, as cautious as they are, presented by Wallis and North. First, they have a tendency to assert conclusions that cannot be inferred from their logical structure. For example, they have presented evidence that transaction costs are important and perhaps too frequently overlooked by economists. That assumption is insufficient to support their conclusion that throughout economic history transaction costs have been as much a limiting factor in the growth of specialization as transformation costs and that economic history is the story of the reduction of transaction costs that permit the realization of gains from specialization. These are strong statements and cannot be inferred merely from a recognition of the fact that transaction costs can be important.

Second, some of Wallis and North's conclusions are presented with neither logical nor empirical support. For example, they argue: "First, while competition in the private sector ensures that more efficient organizational forms will replace less efficient ones, no such constraints operate on government. . . . Our second point is that the *growth* of the transaction sector is a necessary part of realizing the gains from trade." They adduce no evidence in support of either assertion; in fact, they suggest the governmental institutions have been very efficient in specifying and enforcing property rights.

Third, Wallis and North argue that the explanation for the growth of the transaction sector is rooted in three historical developments (costs of enforcing contracts rise with the growth of markets and urbanization; transaction costs rise more than proportionately as firm size increases; and the costs of political manipulation have decreased over time). All three raise either empirical or theoretical questions. Since, however, the authors themselves admit that "this paper presents no conclusive proof that any or all of these three elements is the correct explanation of the growing importance of the transaction services within the economy," it may not be productive to raise them.

Finally, the authors conclude that their restructuring of the national accounts can produce new insights into the forces effecting growth and changes in the structure of economic activity. Such a result would be very important, but unfortunately Wallis and North do not make it at all clear exactly which new questions should be posed nor how the accounts should be manipulated to obtain the desired results.

Wallis and North have set out a major research agenda; it is an agenda that focuses on the set of institutional arrangements that shape the direction and speed of growth and change in the economy; and it is an agenda that, if completed, would provide the glue to meld market and nonmarket analysis together in a true theory of political economy. The project is indeed immense, and that the authors have not totally succeeded is hardly surprising. Wallis and North end by concluding "that the growth of the transaction sector is a structural change of the first order"; however, in the next phase of their research they must more explicitly relate their theory to their estimates and they must begin to explicate the implications of those transaction costs (however defined) for economic change. Otherwise there will be a strong tendency to look back to Kuznets and say, "So what else is new?"

# References

Alchian, Armen, and Demsetz, Harold. 1972. Production, information costs, and economic organization. *American Economic Review* 62 (December): 777–95.

Barger, Harold. 1960. Income originating in trade, 1869–1929. In *Trends in the American economy in the nineteenth century,* ed. William Parker. Princeton: Princeton University Press (for NBER).

———. 1955. *Distribution's place in the American economy.* Princeton: Princeton University Press (for NBER).

Barzel, Yoram. 1982. Measurement costs and the organization of markets. *Journal of Law and Economics* (April): 27–48.

Budd, Edward. 1960. Factor shares, 1850–1910. In *Trends in the American economy in the nineteenth century,* ed. William Parker. Princeton: Princeton University Press (for NBER).

Carroll, Lewis. 1981. *Alice's adventures underground; and, Through the looking-glass.* New York: Bantam.

Carson, Daniel. 1944. Changes in the industrial composition of manpower since the Civil War. In *Studies in income and wealth,* Vol. 11. New York: NBER.

Chandler, Alfred D. 1977. *The visible hand.* Boston: Belknap.

Coase, Ronald H. 1937. The nature of the firm. *Economica* 4 (November): 386–405.

———. 1960. The problem of social cost. *Journal of Law and Economics* 3 (October): 1–44.

Davis, Lance, and Legler, John. 1966. The government in the American economy, 1815–1902. *Journal of Economic History* (December): 514–22.

Edwards, Alba M. 1943. *Comparative occupation statistics for the United States, 1870 to 1940.* In *Sixteenth census of the United States: 1940.* Washington: Government Printing Office.

Gallman, Robert E. 1966. Gross national product in the United States. In *Output, employment, and productivity in the U.S. after 1800*, ed. Dorothy Brady. New York: Columbia University Press (for NBER).

————. 1960. Commodity output, 1839–1899. In *Trends in the American economy in the nineteenth century*, ed. William Parker. Princeton: Princeton University Press (for NBER).

Gallman, Robert E. and Weiss, Thomas J. 1969. The service industries in the nineteenth century. In *Production and productivity in the service industries*, ed. Victor Fuchs. New York: NBER.

Hughes, J. R. T. 1966. *The vital few*. Boston: Houghton Mifflin.

Huxley, Elspeth. 1959. *The flame trees of Thika*. New York: Morrow.

Jensen, Michael C., and Meckling, William H. 1976. Theory of the firm: Managerial behavior, agency costs and ownership structure. *Journal of Financial Economics* (October): 305–60.

Kendrick, John. 1961. *Productivity trends in the United States*. Princeton: Princeton University Press (for NBER).

Kuznets, Simon. Quantitative economic research: Trends and problems. *50th Anniversary Colloquium*. New York: NBER, pp. 18–19.

————. 1938. *Commodity flow and capital formation*. New York: NBER.

————. 1941. *National income and its composition, 1919–1939*. New York: NBER.

————. 1946. *National product since 1869*. New York: NBER.

————. 1947. National income and industrial structure. *Proceedings of the International Statistical Conference*. 5:219.

————. 1961. *Capital in the American economy*. Princeton: Princeton University Press (for NBER).

Lebergott, Stanley. 1966. Labor force and employment, 1800–1960. In *Output, employment, and productivity in the United States after 1800*, ed. Dorothy Brady. New York: Columbia University Press (for NBER).

————. 1964. *Manpower in economic growth*. New York: McGraw-Hill.

Melman, Seymour. 1956. *Dynamic factors in industrial productivity*. New York: Wiley.

Miller, Ann, and Brainerd, Carol. 1957. In *Population, redistribution, and economic growth, 1870–1950*, ed. Everett Lee et al. Philadelphia: American Philosophical Society.

North, Douglass C. 1981. *Structure and change in economic history*. New York: Norton.

————. 1978. Structure and performance: The task of economic history. *Journal of Economic Literature* (September): 963–78.

Shaw, William. 1947. *Value of commodity output since 1869*. New York: NBER.

Sorenson, Charles E. 1957. *Forty years with Ford*. London: Cape.

Stigler, George J. 1961. The economics of information. *Journal of Political Economy* (June): 213–25.

Studenski, Paul. 1958. *The income of nations: Theory, measurements, and analysis: past and present*. New York: New York University Press.

United States, Department of Commerce. 1981. *National income and product accounts, 1929–1976*. Washington: Government Printing Office.

———. 1984. *Statistical abstract of the U.S., 1982–1983*. Washington: Government Printing Office.

———. 1979. Input-output structure of the U.S. economy. *Survey of Current Business*. Various years: April 1979, February 1974, November 1969, and September 1965.

———. 1975. *Historical statistics of the United States: Colonial times to 1970*. Washington: Government Printing Office.

———. 1969. *Historical statistics of government finance and employment*. Washington: Government Printing Office.

———. 1972. Occupation by industry. *1970 Census of Population, final report PC(2) - 7C*. Washington: Government Printing Office.

———. 1964. *Eighteenth census of population: 1960, Vol. I, Part 1*. Washington: Government Printing Office.

———. 1954. *Seventeenth census of population: 1950, Vol. II, Part 1*. Washington: Government Printing Office.

———. 1943. *Sixteenth census of population: 1940, Vol. III, Part 1*. Washington: Government Printing Office.

———. 1933. *Fifteenth census of population: 1930, Vol. V*. Washington: Government Printing Office.

———. 1913. *Thirteenth census of population: 1910, Vol. 1*. Washington: Government Printing Office.

Williamson, Oliver E. 1979. Transaction-cost economics: The governance of contractual relations. *Journal of Law and Economics* 22 (October): 233–60.

———. 1981. The modern corporation: Origins, evolution, attributes. *Journal of Economic Literature* 19 (December): 1537–68.

———. 1975. *Markets and hierarchies*. New York: Free Press.

# II    Capital and Wealth

# 4    The United States Capital Stock in the Nineteenth Century

Robert E. Gallman

## 4.1  Introduction

This paper describes the results of work begun many years ago by Edward S. Howle and me and carried forward intermittently since then by me. Howle and I estimated the value of the United States fixed capital stock (current and 1860 prices) at decade intervals, 1840–1900, and circulated in mimeographed form a manuscript describing our estimating procedures (Gallman and Howle, n.d.). This manuscript was never published, although it served as the basis for a number of descriptive and analytical papers by us and by others (Gallman and Howle 1971; Davis and Gallman 1973, 1978; Davis et al. 1973, chap. 2; Gallman 1965, 1972). While Howle and I thought the estimates were fundamentally sound, we regarded the project as incomplete and chose to delay publication until we were more fully satisfied with it. We wanted to run additional tests; in particular, Howle thought that appropriate samples from the manuscript census (Soltow's [1975] work ultimately met our requirements) would give us the means for strong tests of a set of important estimating decisions. A number of minor sectoral estimates had been hastily made, and we believed that they could be improved with more research and a little ingenuity. We also wanted to extend the series to earlier years, add figures for elements of the capital stock ignored in our original manuscript, and work out regional distributions of the totals.

Robert E. Gallman is Kenan Professor of Economics and History at the University of North Carolina at Chapel Hill and a research associate of the National Bureau of Economic Research.

I thank Edward S. Howle and Colleen Callahan, the first for collaborating with me at the beginning of this work, the second for recent assistance. The research reported in this paper has been supported by the NBER and by a grant from the National Science Foundation.

Our decision to delay was a mistake. Both of us were drawn off into other work, I temporarily, Howle permanently. The manuscript entered the underground of research; it was occasionally cited and our data were used, but it was never subjected to the constructive criticism that publication would have brought. We should have remembered that all research is, in a sense, preliminary, and that to withhold work for long serves scholarship badly, however good the motives for withholding may be.

The delay has not been all a waste. In the years since we wrote the original manuscript I have managed to do most of the things we had planned: I have carried out additional tests, thoroughly revised the old estimates (here and there substituting new series), added estimates of important elements of the capital stock that were not treated in the old manuscript, and extended the series to earlier years.[1] This does not mean, of course, that the work is now complete—sound and durable in every respect. It is certainly not. Gaps remain (for example, there are no figures for the value of roadways), and there are any number of ways in which the existing estimates could be improved. But additions and improvements must be left, for the time being, perhaps to be carried out eventually by other hands. The existing estimates seem to me ready for formal presentation to the scholarly community, at long last.

Part, but not all, of the formal presentation will take place in this paper. There is not space enough here to include estimating details: the notes describing our procedures now run in excess of 200 manuscript pages, more than the Conference would happily publish. In the present paper I will be able to deal only with the types of estimating procedures and tests adopted and their general results, the identity and character of the principal sources used, and the theoretical concepts that guided the work. These subjects are treated in section 4.2. Section 4.3 is concerned with the theoretical and quantitative relationships between the new estimates and those already in the field: the Goldsmith and Kuznets series, as well as the original Gallman and Howle figures (Kuznets 1946; Goldsmith 1952; Gallman and Howle, n.d.; Gallman 1965). Section 4.4 considers the ways in which the new series illuminate the nature of the nineteenth-century United States economy and the course of United States economic development.

The new series contain estimates of the value of land (except agricultural land in 1840). I will use the term "national wealth" to refer to the value of reproducible capital, land, stocks of monetary metals, and net claims on foreigners. "Domestic wealth" will mean the value of reproducible capital and land. Notice that paper claims are excluded from both of these aggregates, as are consumers' durables and human capital. The terms "national capital" and "domestic capital" refer to national wealth and domestic wealth, respectively, minus the value of land. The concepts I refer to as "wealth" and "capital" are sometimes called (by others) "capital" and "reproducible capital," respectively.

## 4.2   Concepts, Sources, and Methods

### 4.2.1   Uses of Capital Stock Estimates

There are at least four scholarly uses for aggregate capital stock series.

1. They can be used in place of national product series—or in addition to national product series—to describe the scale, structure, and growth of the economy. There is no reason why, over short or even intermediate periods, the capital stock should grow at exactly the pace of the national product, but over the long run there should be a considerable degree of similarity. For this reason capital stock series have sometimes been used as proxies for national product series in the measurement of long-term growth (Jones 1980). But one could easily make a case for the use of such series as independent indexes of growth, not simply as proxies for national product. Looked at (and measured) in one way, the capital stock of a given year describes the accumulated savings of the past; looked at (and measured) in a different way, it is a vision of future production (see below). Either way, we have a picture of the economy that is different from the one provided by the national product, and one that is analytically useful.

2. Capital stock series have appeared as arguments in consumption functions and, thereby, in the analysis of the level of economic activity, cyclical variations, and economic growth. Land and consumers' durables are helpful additions to capital in these uses, as are paper claims.

3. The capital stock is a consequence of savings and investment decisions, with which are tied up choices of technique. The level and structure of the capital stock emerge out of these decisions, and capital stock series are used in studying them.

4. Finally, capital stock series are used in the analysis of production relationships and the sources of economic growth, a practice that has been at the heart of one of the major theoretical disputes of the postwar period.

In this paper the capital stock series are put chiefly to the first use and, to a limited extent, to the third and fourth.

### 4.2.2   Methods of Estimating the Capital Stock

Capital stock estimates may be made in two ways: they may be cumulated from annual investment flow data (Raymond Goldsmith's perpetual inventory method [Goldsmith 1956]) or they may be assembled from censuses of the capital stock. If census and annual flow data were perfectly accurate, if the identical concepts were embodied in each, and if appropriate estimating procedures were used, then perpetual inventory and census procedures would yield the same results. In fact, they rarely do, although given the rich opportunities for discrepancies to arise, it is surprising how narrow the margins of difference often are.

The choice between the two techniques turns on the types and quality of data available. From 1850 through 1900 there were six reasonably comprehensive federal censuses of wealth, while for 1805 and 1840 we have census-style estimates constructed by able and informed contemporaries—Samuel Blodget (1806) and Ezra Seaman (1852)—chiefly from federal data. Investment flow data, from which perpetual inventory estimates might be made, are less generally available. But there are some that offer opportunities for estimates superior to those derivable from nineteenth-century census-style data. The best were assembled in the extraordinarily well conceived and careful work of Albert Fishlow (1965, 1966) on the railroads. We used Fishlow's estimates as the bases for our railroad series and similarly exploited the work of Cranmer (1960), Segal (1961), North (1960), Simon (1960), and Ulmer (1960) on canals, the international sector, telephones, and electric light and power. We also built up our own perpetual inventory figures for the telegraph industry and for consumers' durables. No doubt other sectoral estimates could be constructed, with profit, from flow data, although I doubt that the remaining opportunities are quantitatively important. The estimates described in this paper are chiefly (and by necessity) drawn from census-style data (see table 4.1).

There are also some aggregate flow data which, while not very helpful in the derivation of sectoral estimates, proved useful in the construction of aggregate perpetual inventory estimates of manufactured producers' durables and structures—estimates that we have used for checking the census-style figures and for constructing annual capital stock series. That story is told elsewhere; I will also make brief reference to it subsequently in this paper (see Davis and Gallman 1973; Gallman 1983; Gallman 1985).

## 4.2.3 Valuation of Capital

In principle, capital stocks might be valued in any number of ways.[3] In practice, there are only three ways of any importance, two of which exist in two variants. (I refer here to current price estimates; constant price estimates are discussed below.) Capital may be valued at acquisition cost (which I will also refer to as "book value"), at reproduction cost, and at market value.[4]

Acquisition cost corresponds to the notion (expressed above) of the capital stock as piled-up savings. The great difficulty posed by such

**Table 4.1**  Estimation Methods, Valuation Bases, and Principal Sources, National Capital Stock Estimates, Current Prices, 1840–1900

| | Estimation Methods[a] | | Valuation Bases[b] | | | Principal Sources[c] [d] | |
|---|---|---|---|---|---|---|---|
| | Perpetual Inventory | Census | Book Value | Reproduction Cost | Market Price | U.S. Census | Other |
| **A. By Sectors** | | | | | | | |
| Agriculture | | X | | X | X | X | X |
| Mining | | X | | | X | X | |
| Manufacturing | | X | | | X | X | |
| Nonfarm residences | | X | | | X | X | X |
| Trade | | X | | | X | X | X |
| Shipping | | X | | | X | X | X |
| Canals and river improvements | X | | X | | | | X |
| Railroads | X | | X | X | | | |
| Street railroads | | X | | X | | X | |
| Pullman and express cars | | X | | | | X | |
| Telephone | X | | | X | | | X |
| Telegraph | X | | | X | | | X |
| Electric light and power | X | | | X | | | X |
| Pipelines | | X | X | | | | X |
| Churches | | X | | | X | X | X |
| Government buildings | X | X | X | | | | X |
| Schools | | X | | | X | | X |
| Inventories (excluding animals) | X | | | | X | X | X |
| International sector | X | X | X[e] | | | | X |

(continued)

**Table 4.1** (continued)

|  | Estimation Methods[a] | | Valuation Bases[b] | | | Principal Sources[c] [d] | |
|---|---|---|---|---|---|---|---|
|  | Perpetual Inventory | Census | Book Value | Reproduction Cost | Market Price | U.S. Census | Other |

B. *Percentage of the Total Value of the National Capital Stock (Current Dollars) Corresponding to Each Description, by Years*

|  | Perpetual Inventory | Census | Book Value | Reproduction Cost | Market Price | U.S. Census | Other |
|---|---|---|---|---|---|---|---|
| 1840 | 19 | 81 | 3 | 38 | 59 | 20 | 80 |
| 1850 | 23 | 77 | 2 | 34 | 64 | 50 | 50 |
| 1860 | 23 | 77 | 2 | 33 | 65 | 50 | 50 |
| 1870 | 27 | 73 | 1 | 27 | 72 | 50 | 50 |
| 1880 | 29 | 71 | 1 | 30 | 69 | 55 | 45 |
| 1890 | 26 | 74 | 1 | 26 | 73 | 60 | 40 |
| 1900 | 27 | 73 | 3 | 25 | 72 | 60 | 40 |

[a]"Perpetual inventory" is used here to refer to any and all cases in which estimates were derived from flow data; "census" means any and all cases in which estimates were derived from stock data.

[b]There remain some doubts concerning valuation bases (see text). In particular, a number of the estimates identified as expressed in market prices may, in fact, refer to net reproduction cost.

[c]Both columns are checked (panel A) in cases in which the census was the principal source in certain years, but not in others, and in those cases in which the census and some other source were about equally important in all years.

[d]The percentages in panel B are rough estimates of the relative importance of census and noncensus sources.

[e]Less bad debts.

estimates is that the capital stock of each year is valued in the prices of many years, so that no meaningful comparisons (at least none that comes to my mind) can be made. This difficulty can be overcome by adjusting the data by means of a general price index—a consumer price index would be best—so that all elements of the capital stock of a given year are expressed in the prices of that year. A capital stock so valued retains the sense of acquisition cost: the valuation expresses the capital stock in terms of forgone consumption. The forgone consumption consists of the consumption goods given up in the year of investment, expressed in the prices of the year to which the capital stock estimate refers. Unambiguous comparisons can thus be drawn—with the national product of the same year, for example.

The capital stock may also be valued at reproduction cost. Each item is valued at the cost of the resources that would be required to replicate it in the year to which the capital stock estimate refers, given the factor prices and techniques of production of that year. The capital stock thus has the sense of congealed productive resources, valued consistently, so that a summation has a precise meaning. Such estimates are well adapted to the study of production relationships. They avoid, in some measure, the circularity problem implicit in market value estimates. Compared to acquisition cost estimates, they express the capital stock in terms of current productive resources rather than historical forgone consumption.[5]

The third system values the capital stock in market prices; that is, each item of capital is appraised at the price it would bring in the current market. The market value of a piece of capital is presumably a function of its productivity, its expected life, and the going rate of interest. The capital stock, so valued, expresses the income that capital is expected to earn, discounted back to the year to which the estimate refers. Such a measure would be useful in consumption function applications, as well as in describing the scale and structure of the economy.

Book and reproduction cost measures differ, theoretically, in that the former measures the capital stock in terms of what was given up to obtain it, while the latter measures the capital stock in terms of what would have to be given up in the current year to reproduce it. In an unchanging economy in equilibrium, these measures would be identical. In an economy in which there were no changes except in the price level, they could be made identical by means of the deflation adjustment described above. In the absence of this adjustment, book value would exceed reproduction cost whenever the price level was falling, and vice versa. Changes in relative prices could lead to the divergence of the two measures, even after adjustment. Thus if the prices of capital goods fell relative to the prices of consumption goods, adjusted book value measures would exceed reproduction cost, and vice versa. (All of the above analysis rests on the assumption that the market price of new capital goods equals the reproduction cost of these goods. If that is not the case, matters become more complicated, as will appear.) In fact, we know that the price indexes of neither consumption nor capital goods exhibited a very pronounced trend over the last four decades of the antebellum period, although the latter fell slightly as compared with the former (see Brady 1964; *Historical Statistics* 1960, ser. E1, 7, 8). Between 1859 and 1869–78, the former rose dramatically, while the latter did not (Gallman 1966). The two then fell pronouncedly until nearly the end of the century, the latter declining the more markedly. Thus, for the dates of concern to this paper, book value (adjusted and unadjusted) probably exceeded reproduction cost modestly, 1840–60, and more markedly, 1880–1900; adjusted book value also probably exceeded reproduction cost in 1870.

Book value measures look to the past—what was given up to obtain capital—while market values look to the future—earnings potential. In an unchanging economy in equilibrium, and with perfect knowledge, book value and market value would differ only in that the former treats each piece of capital as though it were new, while the latter does not. Even in an unchanging economy, fixed capital would gradually wear out. Therefore old fixed capital would sell for less than new fixed capital, and a capital stock expressed in market values would be smaller than one expressed in book values. The disparity could easily be removed by deducting capital consumption from the book value measures, producing estimates of net book value.

The effects of changing prices (levels and relative prices) on the relative magnitudes of net book and market values are presumably much the same as the effects of changing prices on the relative magnitudes of book and reproduction cost values (see above). Once we drop the assumption of perfect knowledge, other opportunities for divergences between capital stock estimates based on these two concepts emerge. Specifically, deviations between the expected life of individual pieces of fixed capital (on which capital consumption allowances rest) and their actual life may arise. These deviations may prove, in practice, not to be serious, in view of the opportunity for errors of opposite direction to offset in the aggregate, although a general change in the rate of innovation could produce an uncompensated deviation.[6] Changes in the interest rate produce systematic shifts in the relative values of assets of differing life expectation, in the market, but do not influence aggregate net book values. Actual changes in the interest rate over the last 60 years of the nineteenth century seem likely to have raised market values above net book values from 1870 onward, but not by much, except perhaps for the year 1900 (Gallman 1983, 1985).

Once allowance is made for capital consumption, reproduction cost (that is, net reproduction cost) ought to be similar to market value.

Indeed, if the economy were in equilibrium—such that the market price of new capital equaled its reproduction cost[7]—and if capital consumption allowances followed the pattern implicit in the structure of the sales prices of capital goods of differing vintage, then market value and net reproduction cost would be identical. In fact, however, these conditions are not met. Market prices deviate from the value of resources used up in production (there are profits or losses), and capital consumption allowances fail to reflect precisely the structure of prices of capital of differing age. Thus divergences arise between market value and net reproduction cost, divergences of a type discussed previously in connection with book and market values.

Finally, it should be said that the deviations among net book value, net reproduction cost, and market value are least marked for items recently produced; in equilibrium, there is no deviation at all for new goods. The faster a capital stock grows, ceteris paribus, the lower the average age of capital and the narrower the differences among book value, reproduction cost, and market value. As will appear, the United States capital stock grew at an extraordinarily rapid pace in the nineteenth century. Thus the application of the three concepts might produce net valuations that differed little from one concept to the next. The market value and reproduction cost of inventories also will normally differ little. Thus the more important inventories are in the total capital stock, the smaller the disparity between aggregate reproduction cost and aggregate market value, ceteris paribus. Inventories were, in fact, an important element of the nineteenth-century capital stock, partly because agriculture bulked large in the economy and agriculture held large inventories (e.g., of animals).

If data were readily available and estimates costlessly made, it would be desirable to have sets of capital stock estimates based on acquisition costs, reproduction costs, and market values. Comparisons among the estimates would have interesting analytical uses (e.g., Tobin's q). Unfortunately, these conditions do not obtain. Data are less than abundant and less than perfect; the assembly of estimates is not costless.

In recent times the data that have been most abundant have been acquisition cost data, since firms maintain records of sales and purchases and keep books on their capital stock. Given good price data, evidence on purchases and sales can also be converted into perpetual inventory reproduction cost estimates, although the procedure is not problem-free. Market values and census-type figures on reproduction cost are very much harder to obtain. Few elements of the capital stock (apart from goods held in inventory) are sold in any given year. If the capital stock is to be valued at market prices, imputations must be drawn from recorded prices in markets that may be very thin.[8] Estimating reproduction cost is even more difficult, since it sometimes requires that one work out the cost, in a given year, of producing a good which, in fact, was not produced in that year. These are familiar points. But we should not lose sight of the fact that market and reproduction costs are constantly being estimated, and that there are experts who spend their lives at these tasks—experts hired by insurance companies, the loan departments of banks, and various tax offices. Indeed, most of us here today who own homes have a fair idea of what they would bring on the market, or how much it would take to rebuild them, despite the recent gyrations of the real estate market.

In the nineteenth century, book value data were much less common than they are today. Until late in the century, most firms charged off capital purchases on current account. Thus there were few books to refer to when the census taker came around. Perhaps equally important, businessmen did not think in terms of book value. It was much more natural for them to appraise plant and equipment in terms of what it would take to replace it should it all burn down, or what it might sell for. This was even more clearly the case for farmers and householders viewing their property. These notions of value seem to have influenced the designers of census questions. While the questions are by no means always crystal clear, they seem to refer most often to market value or net reproduction cost. (The two concepts are not always clearly distinguished.) There is little doubt—especially for the first three or four census dates—that book value was only rarely sought by census takers. How rarely is a matter on which there is not full agreement. Howle and I decided that most of the census returns we used were expressed in market values or net reproduction costs (see table 4.1). But I grant that we sometimes stand in opposition to very good authority. For example, Kuznets (1946) and Creamer et al. (1960) believe that the manufacturing censuses, 1880–1900, returned book value. Howle and I disagree.

I do not have the space here to argue Howle's and my case with respect to this matter, although I will do so on another occasion. As my previous remarks have suggested, the distinctions among book value, market value, and reproduction cost may not have great practical significance, in any case, so far as the nineteenth-century capital stock is concerned,[9] especially in view of the wide margins for error that must be assigned to the estimates. What is more important is the question of whether the census measurements of fixed capital are net or gross. Here we have access to a test that does not rely on the interpretation of nineteenth-century language. We can check the census data (land improvements and manufactured producers' durables, separately) against perpetual inventory estimates based on reproduction cost. The story of these tests has been told elsewhere (Davis and Gallman 1973; Gallman 1983, 1985), so I offer only a brief summary here: The net reproduction cost estimates check quite closely with the census aggregates before the Civil War, suggesting that the latter are, indeed, net valuations. There is also some support for the notion that the census valuations refer to reproduction cost and that they are accurate. The postwar fit is poorer, but the evidence for the belief that the census figures are net is strong: the perpetual inventory figures typically exceed the census figures.

Our estimates of agricultural land improvements (clearing, breaking, fencing, draining, irrigating) depend chiefly on census physical stock data (e.g., acres of improved land) and various coefficients developed from the work of Martin Primack (1962). Given the form of the data, we were restricted to the construction of reproduction cost figures. Fishlow's (1965, 1966) estimates of railroad investment also rest on physical data, as do our estimates for the telegraph industry. In these cases, however, the form of the data left open the possibility of constructing book value series. In order to maintain consistency with most of the rest of the work—and because we believed they would prove more useful—we chose to produce reproduction cost estimates instead.

The capital stock figures, thus, consist chiefly of net reproduction cost or market value estimates, as table 4.1 indicates. The assignment of items to the reproduction cost category in that table is sure, but the same cannot be said of the estimates referred to as "market value." For a number of these, the valuation may, in fact, refer to net reproduction cost. The practical distinctions between these two types of measures on the dates to which the capital stock estimates refer, however, are unlikely to be very important, for reasons previously given.

All of the data—including the federal census data—underwent considerable processing and testing during the construction of the estimates. The estimating and testing notes are much too extensive to be included here. Some general statements of appraisal can be ventured, however.

The evidence is considerably weaker for 1840 and 1870 than for the other census dates. The 1840 census provided much less information on wealth than did the censuses in subsequent years (although with respect to the trade sector it was unusually helpful). Also, prices fell dramatically across that census year, which means that it is very important to date the available evidence correctly. We cannot be absolutely sure that we have done so. The census dragged on for an inordinate length of time, so that the dating of census magnitudes is problematical. We also were obliged to depend heavily on the work of Ezra Seaman (1852), who was not always entirely clear about his valuation base. The 1870 census came at a difficult time, and it is widely believed that Southern wealth was badly returned (Ransom and Sutch 1975). Nonetheless, it must be said that the results of the perpetual inventory tests for these two dates do not impugn the stock estimates.

Of course the test is particularly difficult to run for 1840 and 1870, and the results must be regarded as particularly chancy. Still, it is moderately reassuring that the stock and flow estimates are about as consistent at these dates as at any others in our series.[10]

The test for 1880 is less successful. It suggests that our stock estimates at that date—for both equipment and improvements—may be too low. These are matters to which I will return below. It is perhaps sufficient to say here that the capital stock figures are much more likely to tell an accurate story of the long-term rate of growth and structural changes of the capital stock than of the decade-to-decade changes, and this is particularly true after 1860.

### 4.2.4    Constant Price Series

The best capital stock deflators available are to be found among the price index numbers assembled by Dorothy Brady (1966) to deflate components of the GNP. The Brady indexes are the best for several reasons: they are true price index numbers of capital goods (including structures); they are available in considerable detail; they were constructed with careful regard to their theoretical meaning; and their theoretical meaning makes them reasonably apt deflators for capital stock series valued in terms of reproduction cost or market value (see also Brady 1964). They are not perfect, but, in the absence of price data for old capital, they are as close to perfection as can be had. They are linked price indexes describing, in principle, the movement of the prices of capital goods of unchanging quality. If the economy were in equilibrium in all the relevant years, such that market prices and reproduction costs of new goods were identical, and if the prices of new and old goods moved closely together over time (i.e., the interest rate was the same at each relevant date and the rate of obsolescence was unchanging), then deflation of capital stock estimates valued in market prices or net reproduction costs would yield a constant price series expressed in net reproduction costs. That is, it would produce a series in which each element measured the net reproduction cost of the capital stock, given the factor prices and techniques of producing capital goods of the base year. Of course these conditions were surely not met: I have already pointed out that the interest rate changed, affecting the relative magnitudes of market value and reproduction cost. Nonetheless, the constant price capital stock series approximates more nearly to a reproduction cost series than it does to any other coherent concept. I will treat it as such, therefore, throughout the rest of this paper.

While the Brady indexes were the chief deflators we used, other price data figure in important ways in the construction of the constant price capital stock series. Some important components of the capital stock were built up by placing values on counts of capital goods, described in physical terms. In these cases—improvements to agricultural land (structures apart), railroads, the telegraph, farm animal inventories, crop inventories—constant price estimates could be made directly from the evidence on physical counts and base year prices, and we could be sure that the series so constructed were true reproduction cost series, or very close thereto. Inventories of manufactured goods and imports were deflated with price indexes germane to the types of products incorporated in these inventories, drawn from sources other than the Brady papers (Gallman 1960; *Historical Statistics* 1960, ser. U-34, E-1, E-70).

The Brady indexes refer to the census years (beginning on June 1 of the years ending in 9 and ending on May 31 of the years ending in zero) before the Civil War, and to calendar years ending in 9 after the Civil War. The current year capital stock valuations to which the Brady indexes apply refer to June 1 of the years ending in zero. I was therefore obliged to adjust the Brady indexes, on the basis of other available price data, to make them conform to the appropriate dates. Gaps in the coverage of the Brady indexes were filled similarly.

### 4.3 Old and New Capital Stock Series Compared

There are both conceptual and substantive differences between the old Gallman-Howle capital stock estimates and the new ones reported on in this paper. The conceptual differences are the more important.

When Howle and I estimated the value of property employed in agriculture we decided to extract from the value of agricultural land (and to list separately) the value of agricultural structures, but to treat all other agricultural improvements as part of the value of land. We wanted to be able to link our series with series extending into the twentieth century, and we believed that this treatment of agricultural land and improvements would bring our work into conceptual alignment with the twentieth-century estimates.[11] When I came back to this work I decided that a second set of estimates should be made, in which all land improvements are treated as capital, as of course they are. These estimates would go to make up a capital stock series roughly corresponding, conceptually, with the GNPII series of my paper in Volume 30 of Studies in Income and Wealth (Gallman 1966). For purposes of analyzing nineteenth-century developments, the GNPII series is certainly more appropriate than the GNPI series; similarly, the broader capital stock series would be superior for these purposes to the narrower one.

I made estimates of the reproduction cost of clearing and breaking farmland, fencing it, and draining and irrigating it, all of these estimates based on the work of Martin Primack (1962), as I have previously indicated. The value of fences was taken net of capital consumption. Retirements were deducted from the other items, but no allowance was made for capital consumption, on the ground that normal maintenance would prevent physical deterioration of these improvements. Clearly some deduction in value should have been made to account for the deterioration of improvements on land withdrawn from production but not yet returned, for census purposes, as unimproved (i.e., retired), but I could devise no system for making this type of adjustment. The improvements estimates are therefore almost certainly overstated, as compared with the values recorded for other elements of the capital stock. How important this matter may be, I do not know, although I doubt that it is of great importance.

Farm improvements (exclusive of structures) constituted a very large part of the capital stock, but a part that declined in relative importance as time passed. Thus roughly six-tenths of the agricultural capital stock consisted of these improvements in the years 1840 and 1850, a fraction that fell to less than half, in current prices, in 1900, and something over one-half, in constant prices. The fraction of total domestic capital accounted for by these improvements fell from between three-and-a-half and four-tenths, in 1840, to just over one-tenth in 1900 (see table 4.2). It should be clear, then, that the new Gallman-Howle capital stock series, inclusive of improvements, is substantially larger than the old one, and exhibits a substantially lower rate of growth. These are matters to which I will return below.

As I have already indicated, I also made a number of substantive changes to the old Gallman and Howle series. So far as the current price series are concerned, the chief changes are as follows: I substi-

Table 4.2    **Ratios of the Value of Farm Improvements (Exclusive of Structures) to the Value of United States Farm Capital and the Value of United States Domestic Capital, Current and Constant Prices, 1840–1900**

| | Ratio of Value of Improvements to Value of | | | |
|---|---|---|---|---|
| Year | Farm Capital | Domestic Capital | Farm Capital | Domestic Capital |
| | (Current Prices) | | (1860 Prices) | |
| 1840 | .58 | .34 | .61 | .38 |
| 1850 | .59 | .30 | .61 | .34 |
| 1860 | .56 | .27 | .56 | .27 |
| 1870 | .51 | .22 | .55 | .24 |
| 1880 | .51 | .18 | .58 | .22 |
| 1890 | .48 | .14 | .55 | .14 |
| 1900 | .49 | .13 | .54 | .12 |

*Sources:* See text.

*Note:* The denominators include farm improvements.

tuted Weiss's estimates of government buildings for the very preliminary estimates Howle and I originally used (Weiss 1967); I changed the
original animal inventory estimates, making them more comprehensive
(Howle and I had originally included only mature animals); I altered
the estimates of nonagricultural residences and trade capital for 1870,
the adjustments resting on evidence unavailable to Howle and me when
we built up our original series; I improved the price indexes for shipping
and railroad capital, which affected only the current price series, since
the constant price series were estimated directly from data on physical
capital. On balance, these changes are small so far as the years 1840,
1850, 1860, and 1880 are concerned: in these years the new and old[12]
national wealth series are within 1½% of each other, once allowances
are made for differences in coverage between the two series.[13] In the
remaining 3 years, the margins are much wider: about 8½% in 1870
and about 4% in 1890 and 1900, the new estimates being below the old
in each year. For 1890 and 1900, the principal explanation lies in the
changes I have made in the price indexes used to convert the constant
price railroad improvements series into current price. Originally, Howle
and I had used Ulmer's (1960) index, despite Fishlow's (1965, 1966)
warning that the price series incorporated therein and the weights attached to them made the index inadequate for our purposes. I have
now replaced this index with a new one, in which I have considerably
greater confidence.[14]

The new railroad improvements price index and the new price index
for vessels in the merchant marine and fishing fleets also affected the
1870 estimates, making the new ones lower than the old ones. Much
more important, however, is the fact that I have now reworked the
1870 estimates of nonfarm residences and of the capital of the "trade"
sector (the "other industrial" sector, in Kuznets's [1946] terminology).
The new estimates were adopted as the result of tests based on evidence
supplied by Lee Soltow (1975), evidence that was not available to
Howle and me when we constructed our original series. The new estimating procedures are very much stronger than the old ones were,
and a test for internal consistency provides strong support for the
results. Nonetheless one cannot be sure that the new estimates are
actually closer to the truth than were the old ones. Both sets depend
upon data from a census that underenumerated the population and
probably undercounted property as well (Ransom and Sutch 1975).
Since the new estimates are lower than the old ones, it may very well
be that they reflect the true value of the relevant property less accurately than do the old estimates, despite the fact that they rest on
technically superior procedures.

Some, but not all, of the changes in the current price series, described
above, affect the constant price series as well. I also made a few small
alterations in those constant price series that were built up from counts

of physical capital (e.g., the railroads). More important is the fact that I made some adjustments to the price index numbers. Howle and I received many of the price indexes we used in correspondence with Dorothy Brady. In a few cases, Brady subsequently revised her figures. Howle and I also used the Brady indexes without adjustment, although, in fact, they did not refer to precisely the dates we required (see the discussion of this point above). When I returned to the estimates, I corrected the price indexes, so that they reflected Brady's last word on the subject and so that the indexes were more nearly relevant to the dates to which the censuses refer. The principal changes, substantively, were to raise the 1840 estimates of agricultural buildings and nonfarm residences, and to lower the estimates of machinery and equipment in manufacturing, 1890 and 1900, and the "trade" sector, 1870–1900. Of these alterations, the ones referring to 1840 are most doubtful. In these cases I was obliged to build up new price indexes for structures to replace an index number abandoned by Brady. It may very well be that my new indexes—based, as they are, on materials prices and wage rates—actually understate the price levels of structures in 1840.[15] If that is the case, using these indexes to deflate the 1840 values may have produced an overstatement of constant price values in that year. However, all the tests I have run so far suggest that this has not happened. On balance, the changes I have made in the constant price series have not been of overwhelming quantitative significance (in no year do they amount to more than 10% of the value of the domestic capital stock), but they are far from negligible, and since the adjustment for 1840 is in an upward direction, and the ones for 1870–1900 in a downward direction, the rates of long-term growth are lower when computed with the new series than when computed with the old one, even when the two series are put on the same conceptual basis.

The old series, expressed in constant prices, was never published, but a set of index numbers based on it appeared in *American Economic Growth: An Economist's History of the United States* (Davis et al. 1972). These index numbers provide the best bases for comparing the old with the new series.

The comparisons can be made with data in table 4.3, which show that the new series describe lower long-term rates of growth than do the old (panels A and C). The disparities are the wider when the new series, inclusive of all farmland improvements (variant A in the table), is compared with the old series. That is reasonable enough, in view of the conceptual difference between the two series and the well-known fact that the agricultural sector grew at a slower pace, over the last six decades of the century, than did the rest of the economy. But even when the conceptual difference is removed—the variant B series is substituted for the variant A series—the new estimates exhibit some-

**Table 4.3**  Comparisons of the New and Old Gallman-Howle National Capital Stock Series, 1860 Prices, 1840–1900

### A. Index Numbers on the Base 1860 = 100

|  | 1840 | 1850 | 1860 | 1870 | 1880 | 1890 | 1900 |
|---|---|---|---|---|---|---|---|
| (1) New series, variant A[a] | 38 | 57 | 100 | 118 | 178 | 328 | 475 |
| (2) New series, variant B[b] | 31 | 51 | 100 | 121 | 189 | 385 | 570 |
| (3) Old series | 28 | 51 | 100 | 143 | 220 | 437 | 656 |

### B. Annual Rates of Growth, Short Intervals (%)

|  | 1840–50 | 1850–60 | 1860–70 | 1870–80 | 1880–90 | 1890–1900 |
|---|---|---|---|---|---|---|
| (1) New series, variant A[a] | 4.2 | 5.8 | 1.6 | 4.2 | 6.3 | 3.8 |
| (2) New series, variant B[b] | 5.1 | 6.9 | 2.0 | 4.5 | 7.4 | 4.0 |
| (3) Old series | 6.1 | 7.0 | 3.7 | 4.4 | 7.1 | 4.2 |

### C. Annual Rates of Growth, Long Intervals (%)

|  | 1840–1900 | 1850–1900 | 1860–1900 | 1870–1900 | 1880–1900 |
|---|---|---|---|---|---|
| (1) New series, variant A[a] | 4.3 | 4.3 | 4.0 | 4.8 | 5.0 |
| (2) New series, variant B[b] | 5.0 | 4.9 | 4.4 | 5.3 | 5.7 |
| (3) Old series | 5.4 | 5.3 | 4.8 | 5.2 | 5.6 |

*Sources*: New series: Derived from data in or underlying Appendix.
Old series: Derived from data in Davis et al. 1972.

[a]Includes all improvements to farmland.
[b]Excludes all improvements to farmland except structures.

what lower long-term rates of growth than do the old. The margins are not great, however—less than half a percentage point in every case, an adjustment of less than one-tenth in each of the long-term rates of growth. The data on the decadal rates of growth show, moreover, that in only two decades—1840–50 and 1860–70—are the disparities in growth rates at all wide (panel B). These are the decadal growth rates that are affected by the major estimating changes described above, of course. It should also be pointed out that the new and old series exhibit the same patterns of change over time, the rate of growth rising from 1840–50 to 1850–60, falling to 1860–70, rising again to 1870–80 and 1880–90, and finally falling to 1890–1900.

On the whole, then, the new series differ from the old in important respects, but once allowance is made for differences in concept and coverage, they appear to tell roughly the same story with respect to the rate of growth of the capital stock. (The subject is treated further, below.)

When Howle and I first came to this topic there were in the field two sets of comprehensive capital stock estimates covering a substantial part of the nineteenth century, Simon Kuznets's series, reported in *National Product since 1869* (1946), which cover the years 1880, 1890, and 1900, and Raymond Goldsmith's revisions to the Kuznets figures and extension of them to 1850, reported in *Income and Wealth*, series 2 (1952). There were also a good many sectoral estimates for the late nineteenth century, deriving from a major program at the NBER in which Creamer, Dobrovolsky, and Borenstein (1960), Ulmer (1960), Grebler, et al. (1956), and Tostlebe (1957) participated. (See also Kuznets 1961; Kendrick 1961.) Finally, there were a number of helpful independent pieces of work, some of them developed in connection with the Volume 24 and 30 meetings of this Conference: work by Fishlow (1965, 1966), Cranmer (1960), Segal (1961), Primack (1962), Lebergott (1964), North (1960), and Simon (1960) (see also Gallman 1960). Since then the research of Soltow (1975) and Weiss (1967) has provided additional materials that I have found helpful.

Howle and I began with Kuznets's *National Product since 1869* (1946), which provided us with the framework within which we have subsequently worked. The volume contains very detailed estimates, together with full descriptions of estimating procedures. Our idea was to modify Kuznets's estimates in light of the work that had come forward since *National Product since 1869* was published, and to extend the estimates to the years 1840, 1850, 1860, and 1870. The Goldsmith (1952) estimates for 1850, while available in less detail, were to serve as an antebellum benchmark.

The extent to which the new Gallman-Howle series now deviate from the Kuznets and Goldsmith estimates is exhibited in table 4.4. It will

**Table 4.4**    **Ratios of the Goldsmith (1850, and Elsewhere Where Indicated)**
**and Kuznets (1880–1900) Capital Stock Estimates (Current Prices),**
**to the New Gallman-Howle Estimates**

|  | 1850 | 1880 | 1890 | 1900 |
|---|---|---|---|---|
| *A. Fixed Reproducible Capital* | | | | |
| (1) Agriculture (variant B)[a] | 1.07 | 0.97 | 0.97 | 1.00 |
| (2) Mining | | 1.21 | 1.15 | 1.32 |
| (3) Manufacturing | | 0.72 | 0.80 | 0.85 |
| (4) Other industrial (trade) | | 1.56 | 1.27 | 1.28 |
| (5) Nonfarm residences | | | | |
|      Goldsmith | 1.10 | 1.20 | 1.15 | 1.28 |
|      Kuznets | | 0.83 | 0.72 | 0.81 |
| (6) Steam railroads | | 1.54 | 1.56 | 1.71 |
| (7) Street railroads | | 1.37 | 1.38 | 1.32 |
| (8) Pullman cars | | 1.32 | 1.37 | 1.57 |
| (9) Telephones | | 2.81 | 1.98 | 1.95 |
| (10) Shipping, canals, and river improvements | | 0.85 | 0.92 | 0.95 |
| (11) Electric light and power | | | 1.63 | 1.42 |
| (12) Waterworks | (not estimated by Gallman and Howle) | | | |
| (13) Irrigation | | 1.00 | 1.00 | 0.78 |
| (14) Pipelines | | 1.00 | 1.00 | 1.00 |
| *B. Inventories (Goldsmith)* | | | | |
| (1) Farm livestock | 0.92 | 1.05 | 0.96 | 1.06 |
| (2) Monetary metals | 1.00 | 1.20 | 1.00 | 1.00 |
| (3) Net international debits | 1.36 | 0.69 | 0.97 | 1.12 |
| (4) Other inventories | 0.52 | 0.96 | 1.06 | 0.94 |
| *C. Totals* | | | | |
| (1) Fixed reproducible capital (Kuznets)[a] | | 1.10 | 1.04 | 1.11 |
| (2) National capital (Goldsmith)[a] | 0.89 | 1.17 | 1.16 | 1.20 |

*Sources:* Goldsmith (1952); Kuznets (1946); data underlying Appendix.
[a]Excluding farmland improvements, other than structures.

be seen that in the cases of fixed reproducible capital in farming, street railroads, shipping, canals, river improvements, and pipelines and in the cases of inventories of farm livestock and monetary metals, the differences are slight. (In the cases of street railroads and pipelines there are none at all.) For the rest, there are substantial differences. As they relate to the Kuznets and Gallman-Howle estimates, they tend to cancel out, so that the values of aggregate fixed reproducible capital fall within 11% of each other in each year, the Kuznets figures being the higher. The net gaps between the Goldsmith and the new Gallman-Howle estimates are wider, and they also run in opposite directions in 1850 and the later years. Thus the Goldsmith series describes a substantially higher rate of growth across the nineteenth century than does the Gallman-Howle series, even when differences of concept and coverage are eliminated.[16]

The differences between our work and that of Goldsmith and Kuznets have emerged in part because we had available evidence unavailable to them, in part because we have interpreted some of the evidence available to all of us in a new way, and in part because we have adopted, here and there, different concepts. In the cases of the estimates relating to agriculture, the "other industrial" (or "trade") sector, nonfarm residences, steam railroads, telephones, canals and river improvements, electric power and light, irrigation, tax-exempt property, and international claims, we were the beneficiaries of substantial amounts of research that came forward only after Goldsmith and Kuznets had published. We did a certain amount of new research particularly with respect to inventories and the telegraph, and we worked out new interpretations of existing evidence in a number of places, notably in the cases of mining and manufacturing (we believe that rented real estate was inadvertently left out of Kuznets's manufacturing estimates). Finally, in a number of cases (e.g., steam railroads, the telegraph) we chose to substitute estimates of net reproduction cost for book value.

In summary, then, the new Gallman-Howle capital stock estimates are net of retirements and net of capital consumption. While a few of the components (current prices) are expressed in book values, most are in market prices or in net reproduction costs. Conceptually, the new series differ importantly from the old; substantively, somewhat less. The substantive differences between the new series and the Goldsmith and Kuznets nineteenth-century series are wide enough that one might anticipate that accounts of economic structure and change based on the new series would offer an element of novelty. It is to this matter that I now turn.

## 4.4  Capital and Economic Growth

### 4.4.1  Rates of Growth

To say that the nineteenth-century United States capital stock increased rapidly or slowly is to make a comparative statement. It is to say that the stock increased rapidly or slowly compared to other times—earlier or later—or to other places. So far as earlier times are concerned, Alice Jones's (1980) wealth data for 1774 and my own figures for the early part of the nineteenth century would provide bases for a relevant comparison. But my own estimates for the early part of the century are not quite ready to be put to this use, and I am thus obliged to defer this matter.

There is no reason to defer consideration of subsequent times, however. Raymond Goldsmith's recent extension of his estimates to 1980 provides us with data covering virtually the entire twentieth century

(Goldsmith 1982). These data differ from the Goldsmith series discussed in the previous section. The latter consisted chiefly of census-style estimates, whereas the twentieth-century series were built up by perpetual inventory procedures. In concept, the new Gallman-Howle variant B estimates are virtually identical to Goldsmith's twentieth-century series.[17] Where the two overlap—at 1900—they are also substantively quite similar. Where differences of detail appear, aggregating up to the next relevant level virtually removes them. For example, the estimates of agricultural structures and equipment differ, in the two series, in 1900, but the sums of the two—agricultural fixed capital—are virtually identical. The same is true with respect to nonfarm residential land and nonfarm residential structures.[18] Thus the two series link together reasonably well, providing coverage for a period of 140 years, the link being particularly good at the level of what I have called "domestic wealth" (see sec. 4.1, above). Here, however, I will be comparing Goldsmith's domestic capital series with the Gallman-Howle national capital series. For present purposes, the consequences of the conceptual and substantive differences between the series are trivial.

According to Goldsmith, domestic capital (reproducible tangible assets, narrow definition), in current prices, increased at an average annual rate of 5.79% between 1901 and 1929, 5.00% between 1930 and 1953, and 8.20% between 1954 and 1980. These are, on the whole, higher rates of change than are exhibited by the Gallman-Howle series over similarly extended periods (see table 4.5), and this is true whether one looks at the variant A or the variant B series. The explanation lies in the price history of the two centuries. While prices rose and fell dramatically in both the nineteenth and twentieth centuries, the long-term drift in the former period was neither powerfully upward nor powerfully downward. That is not true of the twentieth century, however. Prices moved strongly upward, on average, between 1901 and 1929, 1930 and 1953, and 1953 and 1980. Thus, deflating on the base 1929, one finds that the real capital stock increased at rates of only 3.60%, 1.68%, and 3.60% in the three periods, lower than most of the rates exhibited in table 4.5.[19] Over the full sweep of the years 1900 through 1980, the current price series rose 6.36% per year, on average, while the constant price series increased only 2.80%, the former substantially higher and the latter substantially lower than the long-term nineteenth-century rates (see table 4.5). Comparing the experiences of the two centuries, then, we find marked retardation of the rate of growth of the real magnitudes, just as had been previously discovered with respect to the real national product (Gallman 1966).

By the standard of twentieth-century experience, the capital stock grew rapidly between 1840 and 1900. My guess is that further work will show that it also grew rapidly by the standard of what had gone

Table 4.5              Rates of Growth of the National Capital Stock and the National
                       Product, 1840–1900

| | Variant A[a] | | Variant B[a] | |
|---|---|---|---|---|
| | Capital Stock | GNP[b] | Capital Stock | GNP |
| A. Current Price Data | | | | |
| **Long-term** | | | | |
| 1840–1900 | 4.4% | 3.9% | 5.0% | 4.0% |
| **Intermediate** | | | | |
| 1840–60 | 5.9 | 4.9 | 6.5 | 5.1 |
| 1860–1900 | 3.7 | 3.4 | 4.2 | 3.5 |
| 1870–1900 | 3.7 | (2.9)[c] | 4.1 | (2.9)[c] |
| 1860–80 | 3.3 | 4.1 | 3.9 | 4.2 |
| 1880–1900 | 4.1 | 2.7 | 4.5 | 2.7 |
| **Short-term** | | | | |
| 1840–50 | 4.9 | 3.8 | 5.6 | 4.2 |
| 1850–60 | 6.9 | 6.1 | 7.5 | 6.0 |
| 1860–70 | 3.8 | (4.3)[d] | 4.4 | (4.3)[d] |
| 1870–80 | 2.9 | (3.7)[e] | 3.4 | (3.9)[e] |
| 1880–90 | 5.1 | 2.5 | 5.7 | 2.6 |
| 1890–1900 | 3.1 | 2.8 | 3.3 | 2.8 |
| B. Constant Price Data | | | | |
| **Long-term** | | | | |
| 1840–1900 | 4.3% | 4.0% | 5.0% | 4.1% |
| **Intermediate** | | | | |
| 1840–60 | 5.0 | 4.7 | 6.0 | 5.0 |
| 1860–1900 | 4.0 | 3.6 | 4.4 | 3.7 |
| 1870–1900 | 4.8 | (4.0)[c] | 5.3 | (4.1)[c] |
| 1860–80 | 2.9 | 3.6 | 3.2 | 3.7 |
| 1880–1900 | 5.0 | 3.6 | 5.7 | 3.7 |
| **Short-term** | | | | |
| 1840–50 | 4.2 | 4.4 | 5.1 | 5.0 |
| 1850–60 | 5.8 | 4.9 | 6.9 | 4.9 |
| 1860–70 | 1.6 | (3.0)[d] | 2.0 | (3.0)[d] |
| 1870–80 | 4.2 | (5.4)[e] | 4.5 | (5.6)[e] |
| 1880–90 | 6.3 | 4.1 | 7.4 | 4.2 |
| 1890–1900 | 3.8 | 3.1 | 4.0 | 3.1 |
| C. Implicit Price Index Numbers | | | | |
| 1840 | 84 | 97(94)[g] | 90 | 99(94)[g] |
| 1850 | 89 | 91(95)[g] | 94 | 91(96)[g] |
| 1860 | 100 | 100 | 100 | 100 |
| 1870 | 123 | (123)[h] | 126 | (123)[h] |
| 1880 | 108 | 113 | 113 | 115 |
| 1890 | 97 | 97 | 97 | 97 |
| 1900 | 91 | 94 | 90 | 94 |

*Sources:* (1) Data underlying Appendix.
(2) GNP estimates: Variant B—Gallman (1966), p. 26, table A-1. (See note b above.)
Variant A—computed from Gallman (1966), pp. 26 and 35, tables A-1 and A-4, variant
I, and the implicit price index of improvements to farmland (exclusive of structures)

**Table 4.5**    (continued)

computed from data underlying the Appendix. GNP A is defined as conventional GNP plus the value of improvements to farmland (table A-4 in Gallman 1966). I assume that average annual improvements, 1849–58, were equal to improvements in 1859. Constant price improvements (table A-4 in Gallman 1966) were converted to current prices by means of the price index of agricultural land improvements (exclusive of structures) implicit in the data underlying the Appendix. I assumed that the value of improvements (current and constant prices) in 1839 and 1849 were equal to the mean value, 1834–43 and 1844–54, respectively.

[a]The variant A measures include improvements to agricultural land; the variant B measures exclude all such improvements other than structures.

[b]The dates to which the GNP estimates refer differ slightly from the dates in the stub:

| Stub | GNP estimates |
|------|---------------|
| 1840 | 1839 |
| 1850 | 1849 |
| 1860 | 1859 |
| 1870 | Mean of 1869–78 |
| 1880 | Mean of 1874–83 |
| 1890 | Mean of 1884–93 |
| 1900 | Mean of 1894–1903 |

[c]These rates of growth were computed from data for 1869–78 and 1894–1903 (means of annual data) and thus refer to the period 1873.5–1898.5.

[d]These rates of growth were computed from data for 1859 and 1869–79 (mean of annual data) and thus refer to the period 1859–73.5.

[e]These rates of growth were computed from data for 1869–78 and 1874–83 (means of annual data) and thus refer to the period 1873.5–78.5.

[f]The dates to which the GNP estimates refer differ slightly from the dates in the stub:

| Stub | GNP Estimates |
|------|---------------|
| 1840 | Mean of 1834–43 |
| 1850 | Mean of 1844–53 |
| 1860 | 1859 |

For the rest, see note b above.

[g]The implicit price indexes were computed from annual current price data (1839, 1849) and decade average constant price data (1834–43, 1844–53)—see notes b and f above. The index numbers in parentheses were computed from annual data above (1839, 1849).

[h]Refers to the period 1869–78.

before. But what of the third standard mentioned above, that of experience in other places? I am not yet in a position to make meaningful direct comparisons of this type, but a fairly obvious indirect one can be made. We know that the United States real national product increased between the 1830s and 1900 at an exceptionally high rate, the judgment resting on observations for many countries (Gallman 1966; Davis et al. 1972, ch. 2). Unless the rates of change of capital stocks and national products diverged widely—which is highly improbable—the United States capital stock must also have grown rapidly, compared with experience elsewhere. That means that the United States capital stock was probably a relatively young one, with a high proportion of the stock embodying best-practice techniques (Gallman 1978).

In fact, the data of table 4.5 show that the capital stock actually grew faster than the national product, in both current and constant prices, in both variants, over long periods and over most of the short periods identified in the table. That fact has a rather important set of implications. But before considering them, it will pay us to look at other aspects of the evidence in the table.

Rates of change of both variants A and B of the capital stock are contained in table 4.5. It will be observed that the rates of change of the variant B series are always at least as large as the rates of change of the variant A series, and usually larger. One should recall that the variant A series includes investment in agricultural land clearing, fencing, and the construction of drainage and irrigation ditches, while the variant B series does not. The variant A series grew the more slowly because this component of the capital stock increased at a below-average pace. This, in turn, was a consequence both of the fact that the value of improvements of this type (measured in reproduction costs) constituted a declining fraction of the value of the agricultural capital stock (in both current and constant prices) and of the fact that the agricultural sector—including the capital stock thereof—grew more slowly than the rest of the economy. The former development reflected both a slowing in the rate (percentage) at which agricultural land was being added to the stock and the continued high rates of increase of the stocks of agricultural structures and equipment, particularly the latter. Agriculture was becoming more highly mechanized.

A second feature of the table worth remarking is that the rates of growth recorded therein exhibit, on the whole, a downward long-term movement. This is true of both of the GNP series, in current and constant prices; both of the capital series, in current prices; and the variant B series, in constant prices. The variant A series, in constant prices, is only a moderate exception. It exhibits lower rates of growth for the periods 1860–1900 and 1870–1900 than for 1840–60, which makes it consistent with the variant B and GNP series, but if the period is broken into three equal lengths, the variant A series shows equal rates of growth for 1840–60 and 1880–1900, the rate for the period 1860–80 being considerably lower. This is the one bit of evidence running against a conclusion of general retardation in rates of growth across the latter part of the nineteenth century. The exception is not a very important one, however, in view of the reservations expressed above concerning the 1880 capital stock figure. If the estimate for that date is, indeed, biased downward, then an appropriate adjustment would remove this one exception to the general finding of retardation in the rates of growth of the GNP and the capital stock, a development begun in the nineteenth century and continued in the twentieth.

A third piece of information emerging from the table is that the decade-to-decade variations in the rates of growth of the GNP and the capital stock are reasonably consistent. Thus the long-swing boom of the 1850s clearly emerges from the record provided by table 4.5, rates of growth rising above the levels attained in the 1840s (exception: the current price GNP variant B series), while the rates of change of all series drop sharply in the Civil War decade, 1860–70.[20] Between 1870 and 1880 the rates of change of the current price series continue to fall, reflecting the price deflation of the period, while the rates of change of the real series all rise. All of these variations are reassuring. They correspond to what one might have expected, from a knowledge of the qualitative history of the period and of quantitative studies of a micro variety. It is also reasonable to expect the rates of change of the GNP and capital stock series to move together as they do. These features of the table thus enhance one's confidence in the capital stock series, but (necessarily) offer no new insights into the period.

The consistency in the movements of the rates of change of the two sets of series ends with 1880. Thereafter, the rate of growth of the GNP series, expressed in constant prices, falls persistently, while the rate of growth of the current price series falls and then rises. The rates of change of the current and constant price stock series follow neither of these patterns, rising between 1880 and 1890 and falling between 1890 and 1900. Thus the variations in the rates of growth of the GNP and capital stock series diverge across the last two decades of the century. Once again, if the capital stock estimate for 1880 is, indeed, too low, adjusting it might bring the patterns of change of the two series more nearly into line.

### 4.4.2   Sources of Growth

Finally, the data in table 4.5 offer the opportunity to rework the "sources of growth" calculations that I derived on the basis of the old Gallman and Howle series and presented on two earlier occasions (Davis et al. 1972; Gallman 1980). The results of this reworking, together with the old figures, appear in table 4.6. In making my revisions I have left everything unchanged from the earlier set of calculations, with the following exceptions: in the case of the new calculations based on the variant B series, I recomputed the contributions of the capital stock and productivity; in the case of the new calculations based on the variant A series, I recomputed the contributions of capital, productivity, and land. The variant B series is conceptually identical to the old Gallman-Howle series, it will be recalled. It was therefore possible to substitute it into the calculations without changing anything else, except, of course, for the contribution of productivity change to economic growth. Since productivity change is taken as a residual, the introduction of a new capital stock series necessarily produced changes in the productivity figures. The variant A series differs conceptually from the old Gallman and Howle series, incorporating elements of value

Table 4.6          **Contributions of Factor Inputs and Productivity to the Growth of Net National Product and Net National Product per Capita, 1840-1960**

| | | 1840–1900 | | 1900–1960 |
|---|---|---|---|---|
| | Old Estimate | New Estimate | | Old Estimate |
| | | Variant A | Variant B | |
| *A. Average Annual Rates of Growth* | | | | |
| I. Net national product | | | | |
| 1. Labor force | 1.88% | 1.88% | 1.88% | 1.09% |
| 2. Land supply | 0.38 | 0.13 | 0.38 | 0.08 |
| 3. Capital stock | 1.03 | 1.12 | 0.94 | 0.58 |
| 4. Productivity | 0.69 | 0.85 | 0.78 | 1.38 |
| 5. Totals | 3.98 | 3.98 | 3.98 | 3.12 |
| II. Net national product per capita | | | | |
| 1. Labor force | 0.17% | 0.17% | 0.17% | 0.11% |
| 2. Land supply | 0.05 | 0.02 | 0.05 | −0.01 |
| 3. Capital stock | 0.55 | 0.42 | 0.46 | 0.28 |
| 4. Productivity | 0.69 | 0.85 | 0.78 | 1.31 |
| 5. Totals | 1.46 | 1.46 | 1.46 | 1.69 |
| *B. Percentage Distributions* | | | | |
| I. Net national product | | | | |
| 1. Labor force | 47.2% | 47.2% | 47.2% | 34.8% |
| 2. Land supply | 9.6 | 3.3 | 9.6 | 2.5 |
| 3. Capital stock | 25.9 | 28.1 | 23.6 | 18.6 |
| 4. Productivity | 17.3 | 21.4 | 19.6 | 44.1 |
| 5. Totals | 100.0 | 100.0 | 100.0 | 100.0 |
| II. Net national product per capita | | | | |
| 1. Labor supply | 11.6% | 11.6% | 11.6% | 6.7% |
| 2. Land supply | 3.6 | 1.6 | 3.6 | −0.6 |
| 3. Capital stock | 37.5 | 28.6 | 31.5 | 16.4 |
| 4. Productivity | 47.3 | 58.2 | 53.3 | 77.5 |
| 5. Totals | 100.0 | 100.0 | 100.0 | 100.0 |

*Sources:* All of these figures, except the ones labeled "Land supply, variant A," "Capital stock, variants A and B," and "Productivity, variants A and B" were taken from Davis et al. (1972), table 2.12, and Gallman (1980), tables 1 and 2 or were computed from these tables or their underlying data.

The productivity figures in panel A were taken as residuals. The data in panel A labeled "Capital stock, variants A and B" were derived by weighting rates of change with appropriate income share weights. The rates of change were taken from table 3.5, above (in the case of panel A, part I) or were computed by subtracting the rate of change of population from the rate of change in table 3.5 (in the case of panel A, part II). The income share weight for the variant B series (0.19) was taken from the notes to table 2.12 of Davis et al. (1972). The income share weight for the variant A capital series (0.26) was computed by raising the variant B weight in the same proportion as the variant A capital stock figure (current prices) exceeds the variant B figure, in 1860. The average annual rate of change of the variant A land supply figure was computed from *Historical Statistics* (1960), ser. K-2, 1850–1900. The income share weight (0.06) was computed by subtracting the capital stock weight (0.26) from the sum of the land and capital stock weights (0.32) employed for the variant B calculations.

attributed to land in the old Gallman-Howle framework. Substituting variant A into the calculations therefore required reestimating the land supply and the system of weights to be attached to the rates of change of capital and land.[21] The details of these calculations are given in the notes to the table.

Table 4.6 is organized as a set of "sources of growth" calculations of the type made popular by Edward Denison. Panel A shows the contribution of each factor of production and productivity change to the rate of growth of real net national product and real net national product per capita. Panel B displays these figures in the form of percentile distributions.

The calculations based on the old series invited the conclusion that nineteenth-century growth could be attributed chiefly to increases in the supply of factors of production, in contradistinction to that of the twentieth century, in which productivity change was the leading source of growth. The new capital stock series do not oblige us to change this view dramatically. But they do argue for the assignment of a somewhat larger importance to nineteenth-century productivity change than recent custom has accorded it. In particular, use of the variant A series leads to the conclusion that productivity change accounted for almost six-tenths of the growth of per capita NNP in the nineteenth century. This is lower than the figure recorded for the twentieth century (almost eight-tenths), but is by no means low. The term "productivity" covers, of course, the influences of a multitude of forces operating on output. Perhaps a more meaningful way to put the conclusion is to say that the calculations in table 4.6 (variant A) assign to the factor inputs, narrowly defined, responsibility for only a little more than two-fifths of the increase in per capita real national product across the last six decades of the nineteenth century. The role of other forces, therefore, cannot be regarded as small.

### 4.4.3 Capital/Output Ratios

The capital stock increased faster than the national product, according to the data of table 4.5. This means that the capital/output ratio was rising; the economy was engaged in capital deepening. Table 4.7 is organized to describe this process. The data leave something to be desired because, for the period before the Civil War, some of the ratios depend upon data referring to individual years. The ratios, therefore, are influenced by events peculiar to these years and may not be fully representative of the period, 1840–60. The postwar estimates are less susceptible to this criticism, since the national product data are decade averages, centered roughly on the years to which the capital stock figures refer (see the notes to the table). One should remember, also, that the estimates are not equally reliable; those for 1840, 1870, and

**Table 4.7    Capital/Output Ratios, Current and Constant Prices, 1840–1900**

| | | | | Numerators[a] | | |
| | | | | | Farm[b] | Other | |
| Year | Variant A | Variant B | Inventories | Improvements | Improvements | Equipment |
|---|---|---|---|---|---|---|
| | | | *A. Current Prices* | | | |
| 1840 | 2.37 | 1.63 | .67 | .84 | .74 | .23 |
| 1850 | 2.64 | 1.87 | .73 | .81 | .88 | .24 |
| 1860 | 2.86 | 2.14 | .72 | .78 | 1.14 | .25 |
| 1875 | 2.58 | 2.08 | .74 | .54 | 1.19 | .24 |
| 1880 | 2.45 | 2.00 | .69 | .48 | 1.16 | .24 |
| 1890 | 3.14 | 2.71 | .75 | .45 | 1.72 | .36 |
| 1900 | 3.25 | 2.84 | .74 | .43 | 1.73 | .40 |
| | | | *B. Constant Prices* | | | |
| 1840 | 2.75 | 1.79 | .85 | 1.10 | .76 | .15 |
| 1850 | 2.69 | 1.82 | .79 | .92 | .84 | .17 |
| 1860 | 2.92 | 2.19 | .73 | .79 | 1.17 | .26 |
| 1875 | 2.78 | 2.17 | .75 | .65 | 1.18 | .34 |
| 1880 | 2.57 | 2.02 | .71 | .58 | 1.06 | .33 |
| 1890 | 3.16 | 2.72 | .75 | .46 | 1.40 | .70 |
| 1900 | 3.36 | 2.95 | .70 | .42 | 1.38 | .91 |

*Sources:* See the source notes to table 4.5.

[a]All the denominators, except for those for col. 2, are GNP, variant A (see table 4.5); the denominators for col. 2 are GNP, variant B.

[b]Exclusive of structures.

1880 rest on capital stock data that are probably less strong than the data for the other years. Differences in ratios between one year and the next should not be given undue importance. It is the general drift of the ratios that should be the focus of our interest.

The aggregate capital/output ratios (first two columns) do, in fact, rise over time, and this is true of both the variant A and variant B series, in current and constant prices. The variant A ratios are much larger than the variant B ratios, indicating the great quantitative significance of the component of capital consisting of farmland clearing, fencing, and so on (see, also, the fourth column), components included in variant A but not variant B. The variant A ratios also rise less rapidly than the variant B ratios, reflecting the declining relative importance of these forms of agricultural land improvement. But both series, in current and constant prices, exhibit a fairly marked increase, or perhaps it would be best to speak of two increases. All of the series show some rise before the Civil War, a decline to the first two postwar dates for which we have ratios, and then a more pronounced increase to the end of the century.

The last four columns show that the increase of the aggregate capital/output ratio reflects exclusively developments with respect to equipment and improvements (other than agricultural land improvements). In current prices, inventories increased about as fast as the national product, the inventory/output ratio changing little. In constant prices it actually declined moderately. The ratio of farm improvements to national product fell quite dramatically, especially in constant prices, for reasons discussed above. On the other hand, the ratios of "other improvements" and of machinery and equipment to output rose vigorously, the latter particularly in the constant price variant; the relative prices of machinery and equipment were falling dramatically. By the end of the century the structure of the capital stock had changed strikingly. Whereas in 1840 farm improvements were the most important components of capital, accounting for over two-thirds of the value of the stock in constant prices, by 1900 their share had fallen to about a third. Machinery and equipment, composing barely one-twentieth of the stock (constant prices) in 1840, were over one-quarter of the stock in 1900. Accompanying the capital deepening there was, then, a substantial reshaping of the stock, with new forms of capital rising to prominence.

The last four columns of the table also throw some light on the nature of the decline in the capital/output ratio between 1860 and 1875. Changes in the ratios of inventories, equipment, and "other improvements" to output clearly are not responsible. The first rose moderately, in both current and constant prices, whereas the other two either changed very little (equipment, in current prices), or rose vigorously (equipment, in constant prices; "other improvements," in current prices). But the ratio of "farm improvements" to GNP declined very sharply (especially in current prices) and played a major role in the observed capital shallowing for the economy as a whole. This development may reflect the effects of the Civil War. In the South, some improved land was allowed to return to nature during the War, while in the North the pace at which land was improved slackened for lack of labor. One would think that the effects of the War on improved land would have been largely removed by 1875, but it may be that the value of improvements had not yet attained the level it would have reached had there been no war.

A second factor also bears on the change in the aggregate capital/output ratio between 1860 and 1875. Bear in mind that the numerator of the ratio is the national capital stock, an aggregate (variant A) composed of the four components discussed above—inventories, equipment, farm improvements, and other improvements—plus net claims on foreigners. The latter is represented only indirectly in the table; that is, there is no column containing estimates of "net claims"/output ratios, paralleling the last four columns. The reason is that net claims represented a negative value in all the years of the table, a relatively small one in most of them. Between 1860 and 1875, however, the size of this variable increased, going from a small negative value in 1860 to a very large one in 1875. This was also probably a consequence of the Civil War, which increased the volume of negotiable American debt, altered the disposition of American savings, and changed the American balance of trade. In any case, this phenomenon also played a role in the decline of the capital/output ratio between 1860 and 1875 (Williamson 1974).

An indication of the importance of this matter is easily obtained. The sum of the ratios in the last four columns of the table in each year approximates the variant A ratio of domestic capital to GNP. The difference between this sum and the value in the first column measures the effect of net claims on foreigners on the national capital/output ratio. The sums and the entries from column 1 for 1860 and 1875 are as shown in the unnumbered table below. The sums are almost identical with the first column values in 1860, but larger than the first column values in 1875. More to the point, the sums drop slightly between the two years, in constant prices, while they fall more dramatically, in current prices. The decline in the aggregate national capital/output ratio, then, reflects both changes in the international circumstances of the United States and changes in the agricultural sector, both sets of changes probably being legacies of the Civil War.

In table 4.8 I have gathered together data at the industrial sectoral level, with the object of seeing how pervasive the trend toward higher capital/output ratios was. The table should be approached with great

| | Current Prices | | Constant Prices | |
|---|---|---|---|---|
| Year | Sum | Column 1 | Sum | Column 1 |
| 1860 | 2.86 | 2.86 | 2.95 | 2.92 |
| 1875 | 2.71 | 2.59 | 2.92 | 2.78 |

caution. All of the sectoral output data (value added) are discrete, being distributed at 10-year intervals from 1840 to 1900. Ratios measured from such data are likely to be unstable, particularly when computed for narrow industrial sectors. Furthermore, since I am unable to distribute all inventories accurately among industrial sectors, I was obliged to leave them out of account here and measure only fixed capital. The variations among these sectoral ratios in the table may not accurately represent sectoral variations in more comprehensively defined capital/output ratios. In particular, the ratios in the table probably understate the relative degree to which the "commerce" sector held capital. Additionally, the agricultural value-added data underlying lines 1(a) and (b) and 8(a) and (b) should have been adjusted to conform precisely to the variant A and B concepts. I did not make these adjustments, taking the data exactly as they came from the source. Other adjustments could easily be imagined, and I preferred not to be drawn into work along these lines at this time, work which is quite unlikely to alter the general results emerging from table 4.8 in any case.

Finally, it should be said that the sectoral value-added data have never been fully reconciled with the GNP data forming the bases of tables 4.5 and 4.7. When obvious conceptual or measurement differences between the two are eliminated (differences pertaining to the handling of the international sector and farm improvements), the sum of the value-added series exceeds the value of the GNP series in all years but one, the margin between the two widening over time. That is a reasonable result, in a general way. The aggregated value-added series are less net than the GNP series, the value of intermediate services being double-counted in the former but not in the latter. One would suppose that such duplication probably increased in relative importance as time passed. The value-added and GNP series, then, may be fully reconcilable. But since the former exhibits a higher rate of growth than the latter (due to the double-counting of intermediate services in the former), it follows that capital/output ratios computed from the former will show less tendency to rise over time than will capital/output ratios computed from the latter. That must be borne in mind when tables 4.7 and 4.8 are compared.[22]

I begin with three sectors: agriculture; mining, manufacturing, and hand trades; all other private business. The estimates for these sectors

**Table 4.8    Sectoral Depreciable Capital/Value-Added Ratios, Current and Constant Prices, 1840–1900**

| | 1840 | 1850 | 1860 | 1870 | 1880 | 1890 | 1900 |
|---|---|---|---|---|---|---|---|
| *Current prices* | | | | | | | |
| 1. Agriculture | | | | | | | |
| (a) Variant A | 2.67 | 3.23 | 3.25 | 2.51 | 2.73 | 3.21 | 3.31 |
| (b) Variant B | 0.75 | 0.91 | 1.02 | 0.90 | 0.97 | 1.18 | 1.27 |
| 2. Mining, manufacturing, and hand trades | 0.53 | 0.52 | 0.53 | 0.61 | 0.72 | 0.80 | 0.88 |
| 3. All other private business (excl. residences) | 0.90 | 1.08 | 1.31 | 1.21 | 1.29 | 1.45 | 1.46 |
| (a) Transportation and public utilities | 2.85 | 4.95 | 4.57 | 4.27 | 4.27 | 3.99 | 4.15 |
| (b) Commerce and all other private business | 0.35 | 0.42 | 0.57 | 0.45 | 0.53 | 0.73 | 0.68 |
| 4. Government and education | 1.36 | 1.76 | 1.32 | 1.27 | 1.70 | 1.45 | 1.82 |
| 5. Farm and nonfarm residences | 4.75 | 5.33 | 7.87 | 6.28 | 8.86 | 11.30 | 10.99 |
| 6. Weighted averages, Lines 1–4 | | | | | | | |
| (a) Fixed (1860) V.A. weights; variant A | 1.47 | 1.86 | 1.87 | 1.56 | 1.70 | 1.93 | 1.99 |
| (b) Fixed (1860) V.A. weights; variant B | 0.74 | 0.97 | 1.03 | 0.94 | 1.03 | 1.16 | 1.22 |
| (c) Fixed K/O weights; variant A | 2.10 | 1.82 | 1.87 | 1.82 | 1.77 | 1.54 | 1.52 |
| (d) Fixed K/O weights; variant B | 1.10 | 0.95 | 1.03 | 1.02 | 1.07 | 1.07 | 1.07 |
| 7. Weighted averages, Lines 1–5 | | | | | | | |
| (a) Fixed (1860) V.A. weights; variant A | 1.77 | 2.17 | 2.41 | 1.98 | 2.34 | 2.77 | 2.80 |
| (b) Fixed (1860) V.A. weights; variant B | 1.10 | 1.35 | 1.63 | 1.42 | 1.72 | 2.06 | 2.09 |
| (c) Fixed K/O weights; variant A | 2.69 | 2.48 | 2.41 | 2.36 | 2.23 | 1.96 | 1.93 |
| (d) Fixed K/O weights; variant B | 1.77 | 1.70 | 1.63 | 1.62 | 1.61 | 1.54 | 1.53 |
| *Constant (1860) prices* | | | | | | | |
| 8. Agriculture | | | | | | | |
| (a) Variant A | 3.01 | 3.19 | 3.27 | 3.18 | 2.76 | 2.72 | 2.90 |
| (b) Variant B | 0.65 | 0.75 | 1.02 | 1.05 | 0.81 | 0.87 | 1.04 |
| 9. Mining and manufacturing | 0.63 | 0.43 | 0.55 | 0.99 | 0.83 | 1.54 | 1.79 |

*Sources:* The value-added data are from Gallman (1960) and Gallman and Weiss (1969). The same agricultural value-added series were used to compute the ratios in lines 1(a) and 1(b). (That is, no adjustments were made to bring them into closer conformity with the variant A and B concepts.) The same is true of lines 8(a) and 8(b). Value added by construction (variant A) was included in the data from which lines 3 and 3b were computed. The numerators of the ratios of line 5 include the value of all farm buildings. The mining and manufacturing ratios, in current prices, are as follows:

| 1840 | .60 | 1860 | .58 | 1880 | .77 | 1900 | .95 |
|---|---|---|---|---|---|---|---|
| 1850 | .56 | 1870 | .66 | 1890 | .85 | | |

Lines 6(a), 6(b), 7(a), and 7(b) were computed by weighting the capital/output ratios in the body of the table by the

| | Lines 6(a) and (b) | Lines 7(a) and (b) |
|---|---|---|
| | 1860 | 1900 |
| Agriculture | .38 | .35 |
| Mining, etc. | .24 | .22 |
| Transportation, etc. | .07 | .06 |
| Commerce, etc. | .29 | .26 |
| Government, etc. | .02 | .02 |
| Residences | | .09 |

Lines 6(c), (d), 7(c), and (d) were computed by multiplying the 1860 capital/output ratios in the body of the table by annual sectoral shares in total value added.

The shares are

| | 1840 | 1850 | 1860 | 1870 | 1880 | 1890 | 1900 |
|---|---|---|---|---|---|---|---|
| **Lines 6(c) and (d):** | | | | | | | |
| Agriculture | .45 | .39 | .38 | .36 | .31 | .21 | .20 |
| Manufacturing, etc. | .19 | .25 | .24 | .24 | .27 | .32 | .33 |
| Transportation, etc. | .08 | .05 | .07 | .07 | .09 | .10 | .10 |
| Commerce, etc. | .26 | .29 | .29 | .31 | .31 | .34 | .34 |
| Government, etc. | .02 | .02 | .02 | .02 | .02 | .03 | .03 |
| **Lines 7(c) and (d):** | | | | | | | |
| Agriculture | .41 | .35 | .35 | .33 | .28 | .19 | .18 |
| Manufacturing, etc. | .17 | .22 | .22 | .24 | .25 | .30 | .31 |
| Transportation, etc. | .07 | .04 | .06 | .06 | .08 | .09 | .09 |
| Commerce, etc. | .23 | .26 | .26 | .26 | .29 | .32 | .32 |
| Government, etc. | .02 | .02 | .02 | .02 | .02 | .03 | .03 |
| Residences | .10 | .11 | .09 | .09 | .08 | .07 | .07 |

are relatively strong (that is, compared with the estimates on which the other ratios in the table depend), the capital and value-added estimates are independent in each case, and the sectors are sufficiently broad so that one can hope for a modicum of stability in the ratios.

All of the series, except for agriculture, variant A, show quite pronounced upward movements over time. The variant A series shows no very clear trend, in either current or constant prices. The variant B series and the ratios for the "all other private business" sector rise strongly before the Civil War, flatten out between 1860 and 1880, and then rise again strongly, while the "mining, manufacturing, and hand trades" sector exhibits a ratio that neither rises nor falls before the War, but increases strongly from 1860 to 1900, in both current and constant prices. It would be fair to say, then, that the upward movement of the national capital/output ratio (table 4.7) represents a fairly pervasive movement, affecting the chief industrial sectors.

These conclusions are moderated only slightly if we look within the "all other private business" sector and observe the ratios for its two dissimilar components, "Transportation and Public Utilities" and "Commerce and All Other Private Business." The ratios for the former are fairly volatile but show no long-term trend. That is not the case for the latter, the ratios for which move strongly upward to 1860, show no trend for the next twenty years, but rise pronouncedly again across the last twenty years.

The ratios for the remaining two sectors, government and education, and farm and nonfarm residences, also rise strongly and quite persistently, but there are reasons to place less emphasis on these data. The first sector is a very small one, and the capital stock data, with respect to government, refer only to buildings, while the education capital data include land as well as capital. Thus the evidence is not entirely apposite.

There are even more serious problems with respect to the residential sector. The denominator of the ratio includes the shelter value of all residences, farm and nonfarm. Since the capital stock series do not distinguish farm residences, I was obliged to include all farm buildings in the numerator, which means that all of the ratios for this sector are biased upward. Furthermore, the denominator was initially estimated on the basis of capital stock data (see Gallman and Weiss 1969), although not the capital stock data appearing in the numerators of these ratios. Thus the ratios cannot be taken very seriously. I include them for the sake of completeness and because the data do figure, in another form, in table 4.7, and the reader is therefore entitled to know something about them.

Whether or not the estimating procedures were proper (for the purpose of measuring the capital/output ratio), the relationships obtained between value added and the capital stock of the "residences" sector are plausible. Reversing the ratios and adding land to residential capital, we have estimates of the rate of return (gross) to residential property. The computed rate follows fairly closely the pattern of the interest rate (at least from 1860 onward), a result which might have been anticipated on theoretical grounds. Thus at least the value-added and capital stock data for this sector seem consistent.

The point draws attention to a factor that figured in the upward drift of all the capital/output ratios. The interest rate was falling through most of the postwar period. This was certainty true of the nominal rate, and probably true of the real rate as well (see Davis and Gallman 1978). This development affected the capital/output ratio—as I have measured it—in two ways. First, a declining interest rate, ceteris paribus, leads to a rise in the market value of the existing capital stock. (Bear in mind that many of the capital values underlying table 4.8 are market values.) The increase in market value, ceteris paribus, induces investment, since market price exceeds reproduction cost. A falling interest rate, then, produces a temporary rise in the capital/output ratio, reflecting nominal changes only, but in the long run it produces an increase based on real phenomena: capital deepening. The actual interest rate reductions of the postwar period were sufficiently gradual that I think we are entitled to suppose that the increases in the ratios described in tables 4.7 and 4.8 rest chiefly on real, not nominal, developments.

The capital/output ratios in table 4.8 differ widely from one sector to the next. In some measure this reflects no more than the fact that the data exclude certain types of capital. But that is certainly not all there is to it. The residential and transportation and public utilities sectors were, in fact, more capital intensive than were the secondary sectors, for example. Since the structure of the economy was changing in important ways, the level of the aggregate capital/output ratio may have been influenced by the shifting relative importance of the various sectors. Lines 6(a)–(d) and 7(a)–(d) were computed to help settle that issue. The lines contain various weighted average capital/output ratios, sets of calculations appearing for both variant A and B estimates, and for both all sectors and all except the questionable "residences" sector. In one set of calculations, 6(a) and (b) and 7(a) and (b), sectoral value-added weights were held constant and sectoral capital/output ratios were allowed to vary over time; in the other, 6(c) and (d) and 7(c) and (d), capital/output ratios were held constant while value-added weights were allowed to change over time. The first set of calculations shows the effects of rising sectoral ratios on the aggregate ratio, no allowance being made for the effects of structural changes. In the second set, only structural changes influence the weighted averages.

The calculations show that the structural changes of the economy either produced no direct net long-term effect on the aggregate ratio, as in line 6(d), or else reduced the ratio. The entire increase in the aggregate ratio was occasioned by developments within sectors. The explanation lies, of course, in the nature of the structural change that took place. The two sectors that exhibited the most pronounced alterations in their relative importance were agriculture and industry (mining, manufacturing, and hand trades), the former experiencing a pronounced loss in its share in aggregate value added, the latter a pronounced gain. The former had a high depreciable capital/output ratio (especially in the variant A form), the latter a very low one. The clear tendency of the exchange in degrees of relative importance of the two sectors was to force down the overall capital/output ratio. Two less pronounced compositional shifts in aggregate value added had the same effect. The "residences" sector, with a very high capital/output ratio, experienced a moderate loss in relative importance, while the "commerce, etc." sector, with a low ratio, gained in relative importance.[23] The one structural change that worked against the downward movement of the overall ratio was the growing relative size of the transportation and public utilities sector, with its exceptionally large capital/output ratio.

All of these structural developments were interrelated: all were part of the general process of modernization, which consisted of the transfer of economic activities into the orbit of the market, increasing specialization and trade, and the movement of information and goods over longer distances and at faster rates.

While these structural changes had no pronounced direct effect on the depreciable capital/output ratio,[24] they did influence the means by which the capital stock was assembled. In the antebellum years, almost half of the depreciable capital stock (constant prices) consisted of agricultural land improvements, many of them created by family labor, or the labor attached to the plantation on which they were constructed, or by other local sources of labor. These works were typically carried out in the off season—in the spaces in the agricultural year when there were no pressing tasks, such as planting or harvesting, associated with the growing crops. Little external finance was required to carry them out. But the structural changes of modernization brought to the fore industries, forms of capital, and organizational scales of operation that enhanced the roles of markets and of external finance in the provision of capital.[25] Thus the relative stability in the weighted averages of lines 6(c), 6(d), 7(c), and 7(d) mask important developments with respect to American capital formation and finance.

The capital/output ratio can rise if the rate of growth of output falls (without a compensating fall in the net investment proportion) or if the net investment proportion (net investment to output) rises (without a compensating increase in the rate of growth of output), or if some combination of these developments occurs.[26] The data of table 4.5 show that the rate of growth of output—GNP—did, in fact, decline during the nineteenth century. But what happened to the net investment proportion? Table 4.9 is organized to answer this question.

There are two ways of measuring the United States investment proportion during the last six decades of the nineteenth century. Net investment can be measured across each decade after 1840 as the increment in the capital stock between the terminal dates of the decade. It can then be combined with estimates of the value of flows of commodities and services to consumers (1839–48, 1849–58, etc. [Gallman 1960, p. 27]) to form estimates of net product (table 4.9, cols. 1, 2, and 4). This procedure does not result in useful estimates if current price stock data are employed; thus the estimates in table 4.9 all rest on constant price data. It should be said, however, that even the constant

**Table 4.9**  **Capital Formation Proportions, Constant Prices, 1839–48 through 1889–98**

| | National Capital | | | Depreciable Capital | | | |
|---|---|---|---|---|---|---|---|
| | Variant A | Variant B | | | Variant B | | |
| Year | Net | Net | Gross | Net I | Net II | Gross I | Gross II |
| 1839–48 | 12.1% | 9.6% | 14.3% | 6.0% | 5.6% | 11.1% | 10.6% |
| 1849–58 | 15.7 | 13.3 | 18.8 | 10.7 | 8.8 | 16.5 | 14.8 |
| 1869–78 | 12.8 | 10.7 | 18.4 | 7.3 | 15.4 | 15.5 | 22.3 |
| 1879–88 | 18.3 | 17.5 | 25.9 | 15.4 | 13.4 | 24.1 | 22.6 |
| 1889–98 | 14.8 | 13.8 | 26.4 | 11.1 | 15.7 | 24.5 | 27.9 |
| 1839–58 | 14.4 | 12.0 | 17.4 | 9.0 | 7.3 | 14.8 | 13.1 |
| 1869–98 | 15.6 | 14.5 | 25.1 | 11.9 | 14.3 | 23.0 | 25.0 |

*Sources:*
The denominator of each ratio is the sum of the numerator plus the value of flows to consumers, prices of 1860 (Gallman 1960, p. 27, col. 5). The numerators are as follows:

*Col. 1:* Increment to the national capital stock, Variant A, 1860 prices, 1840–50, 1850–60, etc.

*Col. 2:* Increment to the national capital stock, Variant B, 1860 prices, 1840–50, 1850–60, etc.

*Col. 3:* The numerators from col. 2 plus capital consumption, the latter estimated at 10% of the value of machinery and equipment and 4% of the value of improvements (exclusive of farmland clearing, etc.). These estimates approximate straight-line capital consumption on the assumptions that machinery and equipment had a useful life of 15 years and that the stock was, on average, 5 years old, and that improvements had a useful life of 40 years and that the stock was, on average, 15 years old.

*Col. 4:* Increment to the depreciable capital stock (machinery, equipment, and improvements), exclusive of farmland clearing, etc.

*Col. 5:* The numerators of col. 7 minus the capital consumption allowances underlying col. 3.

*Col. 6:* The numerators of col. 4 plus the capital consumption allowances underlying col. 3.

*Col. 7:* Gallman (1960), p. 34, col. 1 plus col. 2.

price estimates leave something to be desired, in view of the moderately ambiguous conceptual character of the stock estimates (see sec. 4.2 above).

In the second procedure, net investment flows are estimated by subtracting from gross investment flows (Gallman 1960, p. 34) the value of capital consumption (table 4.9, col. 5). The latter can be estimated from the capital stock data, given estimates of the average age and useful life of the various components of the depreciable capital stock. The flow data are of such a character that investment proportions can be estimated for depreciable capital. Given estimates of capital consumption, it is also possible to generate gross investment shares, in which the measurement of gross investment depends exclusively on stock data (table 4.9, col. 3, 6). Of course, gross share estimates can also be made directly from the flow data (table 4.9, col. 7). Since, as I have previously indicated, the stock and flow data are not fully consistent, I have chosen to make estimates of investment proportions based on both sets of data, so that the full range of results obtainable from the data is exhibited. The table does not exhaust all of the possible investment proportion estimates, however. To keep it from becoming unduly complex I have restricted myself to four estimates of the net proportion and three of the gross proportion.

All of the columns of table 4.9 devoted to the net proportion show it drifting upward over time. The movement is not uniformly persistent: the ratio actually falls between 1849–58 and 1869–78, as well as between 1879–88 and 1889–98, in the series depending exclusively on the stock estimates. This is not, however, altogether unexpected. As I have previously indicated, the 1880 stock estimate may be too low. Adjusting it upward appropriately might eliminate the first decline, although not the second. In any case, it would be expecting too much to hope to establish the timing of the upward movement of the proportion exactly with data of this type. More important is the fact of the long-term upward movement, a fact that emerges clearly in the data in the last two lines of the table—more clearly from the flow data (col. 5) than from the stock data (cols. 1, 2, 4), however, and from the measures incorporating a narrow definition of capital (cols. 2 and, particularly, 4) than from the ones based on a broad definition (col. 1).[27]

The increase in the net investment proportion required an even more pronounced increase in the gross investment proportion (cols. 3, 6, and 7). The explanation is not far to seek: the rising depreciable capital/output ratio meant that, ceteris paribus, the share of capital consumption in national product was rising. But other things were not, in fact, equal: the structure of the depreciable capital stock was changing, the shorter-lived machinery and equipment increasing in importance relative to the longer-lived improvements. This structural change increased the share of national product accounted for by capital consumption.

These two developments meant that the share of the GNP (concept adopted by Gallman 1960) accounted for by gross investment more than doubled between the 1840s and 1890s. One must further remember that the forms of investment and their relationships with the market were changing. The requirements for a rich and well articulated system of intermediation were expanding.

The forces operating to raise the investment proportion, while they have already received considerable attention in the literature, would surely reward additional work. This paper—intended to introduce the new capital series—is not the place to pursue them. But it does seem to me that the definitive work on this subject will have to come to terms with the changing structure of the economy and the developing system of intermediation. The pursuit of this topic will surely be made easier and more successful with the publication of Raymond Goldsmith's forthcoming book on national balance sheets through history.

### 4.5  Concluding Remarks

Section 4.4 is a brief precis of some of the main results derivable from the new capital stock series. Limitations of space prevent me from adding to these results and showing more clearly the place of capital in nineteenth-century history. I have been concerned here chiefly to introduce the new series, to explain their pedigrees and character, and to show the principal conclusions to which I have been drawn as a result of mulling them over and comparing them with related variables.

# Appendix

**4.A.1**    **Capital Stock Estimates, Variants A and B, Current and Constant (1860) Prices, 1840–1900 (Billions of Dollars)**

|  | 1840 | 1850 | 1860 | 1870 | 1880 | 1890 | 1900 |
|---|---|---|---|---|---|---|---|
| | | | *Current Prices* | | | | |
| **Variant A** | | | | | | | |
| 1. National wealth | | 7.89 | 16.39 | 24.21 | 32.22 | 54.92 | 73.12 |
| 2. Domestic wealth | | 7.95 | 16.51 | 25.24 | 33.30 | 56.66 | 73.93 |
| 3. National capital | 3.89 | 6.27 | 12.27 | 17.80 | 23.79 | 38.98 | 52.97 |
| 4. Domestic capital | 4.07 | 6.33 | 12.39 | 18.83 | 24.77 | 40.71 | 53.79 |
| 5. Improvements | 2.59 | 4.02 | 8.23 | 12.00 | 15.78 | 26.94 | 35.15 |
| 6. Equipment[c] | 0.38 | 0.58 | 1.09 | 1.60 | 2.31 | 4.47 | 6.59 |
| 7. Inventories[a][c] | 1.10 | 1.74 | 3.07 | 5.23 | 6.68 | 9.30 | 12.05 |
| 8. International sector[b][c] | −0.18 | −0.06 | −0.12 | −1.04 | −1.08 | −1.74 | −0.82 |
| **Variant B** | | | | | | | |
| 1. National wealth | | 5.96 | 13.06 | 20.12 | 27.61 | 49.31 | 66.17 |
| 2. Domestic wealth | | 6.03 | 13.18 | 21.15 | 28.70 | 51.04 | 66.99 |
| 3. National capital | 2.52 | 4.35 | 8.94 | 13.71 | 19.08 | 33.37 | 46.02 |
| 4. Domestic capital | 2.69 | 4.41 | 9.06 | 14.74 | 20.17 | 35.10 | 46.83 |
| 5. Improvements | 1.22 | 2.09 | 4.90 | 7.91 | 11.18 | 21.33 | 28.20 |
| | | | *Constant Prices* | | | | |
| **Variant A** | | | | | | | |
| 1. National capital | 4.65 | 7.02 | 12.30 | 14.52 | 21.90 | 40.38 | 58.38 |
| 2. Domestic capital | 4.83 | 7.09 | 12.43 | 15.23 | 22.91 | 42.35 | 59.31 |
| 3. Improvements | 3.14 | 4.58 | 8.26 | 9.99 | 13.98 | 23.71 | 31.32 |
| 4. Equipment[c] | 0.25 | 0.44 | 1.09 | 1.55 | 2.85 | 9.02 | 15.75 |
| 5. Inventories[a][c] | 1.44 | 2.06 | 3.07 | 3.69 | 6.08 | 9.63 | 12.25 |
| 6. International sector[b][c] | −0.18 | −0.07 | −0.12 | −0.71 | −1.00 | −1.97 | −0.93 |
| **Variant B** | | | | | | | |
| 1. National capital | 2.80 | 4.62 | 8.97 | 10.91 | 16.94 | 34.53 | 51.12 |
| 2. Domestic capital | 2.97 | 4.69 | 9.10 | 11.63 | 17.94 | 36.50 | 52.05 |
| 3. Improvements | 1.29 | 2.18 | 4.93 | 6.39 | 9.02 | 17.85 | 24.06 |

*Sources:* See text.

[a]Excluding inventories of monetary metals.

[b]Including inventories of monetary metals.

[c]Same in Variants A and B.

# Notes

1. This paper, however, is concerned exclusively with the period 1840–1900.

2. The topics treated in sec. 4.2 are of a type that has been discussed at earlier meetings of the Conference. See, in particular, volumes 2, 12, 14, 19, 25, 29, and 45, and especially the papers by Edward Denison, Raymond Goldsmith, Simon Kuznets, Nancy and Richard Ruggles, and Dan Usher, and the comments on them.

3. The following discussion was developed with fixed capital chiefly in mind, although it can also be made to apply to inventories and international claims, with two exceptions: there is no clear correspondence between "acquisition cost" and any single system of inventory accounting. For present purposes, that is not an important matter. All inventories treated herein are valued at market prices. So far as international claims are concerned, there is no good counterpart of reproduction cost (other than market price).

4. A fourth method—not relevant to the series of this paper, and therefore left undiscussed here—measures capital in terms of its current capacity to produce output. The problems of defining capacity and of measuring it, in a meaningful way, are ably discussed in the papers by Denison and by Nancy and Richard Ruggles and the comments on these papers in vols. 19 (1957) and 26 (1961) of Studies in Income and Wealth.

5. But see n. 3.

6. Whether loss of value due to obsolescence should figure in capital consumption has been hotly debated. See, e.g., the Denison and Ruggles papers, cited above, and the comments on them in vols. 19 (1957) and 26 (1961). As a practical matter, it almost always does. In this paper, I bow to practice and take no final stand on the theoretical issue, although the case of those who accept obsolescence as a factor in capital consumption seems to me the stronger of the two. (Similar arguments apply to casualty losses.)

7. I ignore here the problems posed by taxes and subsidies, problems of modest dimensions throughout most of the nineteenth century.

8. See also Kuznets's objection, voiced in his paper in Vol. 2 of Studies in Income and Wealth (1938).

9. This is particularly true with respect to the manufacturing sector, which was experiencing extraordinarily high rates of growth.

10. That is, the fit for 1840 is almost as good as the fit for 1850 or 1860; the fit for 1870 is at least as good as the fit for 1880, 1890, or 1900. See Gallman (1985), table 4.

11. Following Kuznets (1946), we produced a separate set of estimates—distinct from the agricultural estimates—of irrigation improvements, which we treated as part of the capital stock.

12. For present purposes, the "old" series is the one published in Gallman (1965), which includes some components of wealth (e.g., inventories) missing from the original Gallman and Howle series.

13. Since in these years most of the adjustments have the same sign, the *gross* differences are about the same as the net ones.

14. The index depends on Lebergott's (1964) wage series, the Warren and Pearson building materials index (1932), and data on rail prices from the American Iron and Steel Association (1912).

15. The Brady building price indexes exhibit more pronounced long-term downward movements than are observable in construction wages and materials prices series.

16. Goldsmith and Kuznets apparently include farmland improvements—other than structures—with land, rather than with capital.

17. See Goldsmith (1982), p. 32, for a statement of the valuation system followed in assembling the series. The Goldsmith series excludes net claims on foreigners.

18. These results were worked out from Goldsmith et al. (1963), 2:71, which is the source of the 1900 data in Goldsmith (1982).

19. It is well known that the deflation base selected can affect the rate of change of a real capital stock series, earlier bases typically producing higher rates of growth than late ones. It is therefore fortunate, for present purposes, that the deflation bases of the two series being considered here occupy similar relative temporal positions. Thus the

Goldsmith series is deflated on the base 1929, 28 years from the first year in the series and 51 from the last; the Gallman and Howle series, on 1860, 20 years from the first year in that series and 40 years from the last.

20. Throughout I use the dating scheme relevant to the capital stock series (1840, 1850, etc.). Notice that the GNP series is dated to different years from these, the disparity being particularly wide in the case of the first post–Civil War date. See the notes to table 4.5.

21. Land, in these calculations, is restricted to agricultural land.

22. The ratios of the sum of the value-added measures to GNP, variant A, are:

| 1839 | 1849 | 1859 | 1869 | 1879 | 1889 | 1899 |
|------|------|------|------|------|------|------|
| 1.03 | .98  | 1.01 | 1.03 | 1.04 | 1.17 | 1.16 |

Correcting the value-added and GNP estimates to put them both on the same basis, with respect to the treatment of farm improvements (variant A concept) and the international sector (i.e., leaving changes in claims against foreigners out of both sets of measures), and deducting from the value-added series those elements that are most likely to involve double-counting (value added by steam railroads, public utilities, banks, fire and marine insurance, lawyers and engineers, "all other" professionals, and the independent hand trades), the ratios become:

| 1839 | 1849 | 1859 | 1869 | 1879 | 1889 | 1899 |
|------|------|------|------|------|------|------|
| 1.05 | .94  | .96  | .92  | .93  | 1.00 | 1.00 |

The reconciliation between the two series is by no means perfect; the upward movement of the ratio from 1879 to 1889 is more than negligible. Nonetheless, the long-term trend is much reduced in the second tabulation, as compared with the first, and the variations from one year to the next are not large, in the context of the observed annual changes in GNP.

23. If the measure of capital employed here had included inventories, this result might have been different.

24. The indirect effects, through changing supply and demand conditions for capital goods, constitute another matter. The rapid expansion in the stock of machinery and equipment, for example—a development that, we have seen, played a role in the rise of the overall capital/output ratio—was related to the revolutionary growth of the industrial sector (mining, manufacturing, hand trades).

25. See Davis and Gallman (1973) for a treatment of these ideas in the context of the changing financial structure of the United States.

26. See Davis and Gallman (1973) for an effort to work through an analysis of this type in quantitative terms, making use of the old Gallman-Howle capital stock estimates.

27. Notice that the postwar pattern of change differs between the estimates based on the stock and flow data. In the former series, the net proportion peaks in the 1880s; in the latter, the net proportion is higher in both the 1870s and 1890s than in the 1880s.

# Comment    Raymond W. Goldsmith

This is an important subject and an important, interesting, and well-done paper. It could be discussed in at least four ways. One could, first, discuss the reliability of and possible improvements in the numerous series used in building up the estimates. Or one might mull over some of the conceptual problems. Or one could indicate one's agreement or disagreement with the interpretation of the estimates. Finally, one could discuss the needs for and the possibility of further

Raymond W. Goldsmith is professor emeritus in the Department of Economics at Yale University.

work on estimates of capital formation in the nineteenth century or even during the whole life of the Republic before World War I.

A detailed technical discussion of Gallman's estimates is well worth doing, but it does not fit into the format of this meeting. It would require a full session with not one but half-a-dozen discussants, including specialists on agriculture, housing, railroads, and inventories, at least, to mention only the four sectors which account for about four-fifths of the nineteenth-century capital stock in 1900. If I had been so foolhardy as to assay it by myself it would have cost me several weeks hard work (possible since Gallman was kind enough to provide me with a copy of the detailed updated Gallman-Howle paper) without ensuring corresponding results. My appetite for discussion of concepts is limited, and I feel they have for quite a while produced nothing that is new in this field. I shall, therefore, make only a few remarks on techniques of estimation or concepts and shall limit myself to a few aspects of the interpretation of the figures given the numerous problems which the paper discusses, and to some suggestion for further work in the field, a subject which Gallman has omitted, undoubtedly reserving it for another occasion.

I refrain from summarizing Gallman's paper. To do so would absorb all the time allotted to me and would be of little help to those who have not read the paper. Suffice it to say that it is the most thorough treatment of the subject; that it presents estimates for the capital stock of the United States for seven decadal benchmark dates between 1840 and 1900 for a good dozen of sectors in current and constant (1860) prices separating land and reproducible tangible assets; that most of the estimates are of the census type but that perpetual-inventory-type estimates are used for some components, rising from one-fifth to over one-fourth of the total value; that the main innovation is the estimation of the value of agricultural land improvements (such as clearing, fencing, and drainage) which are in effect shifted from land to reproducible assets; and that otherwise it contains no surprises—thus the value of the total capital stock for 1900 in current prices is $76 billion, which does not include roads or consumer durables, the latter of which I very roughly estimated 30 years ago to have risen from 8% to 11% of other reproducibles during the second half of the nineteenth century—compared to $78 billion, in the estimate of Goldsmith et al. published 20 years ago.

In the broad field of individual estimates I shall limit myself to one item: residential real estate, in part because it accounts for more than one-fourth of the total capital stock—and one should always remember the often forgotten advice given by Richard Stone over 30 years ago, that research efforts should be allocated in proportion to the importance of each item in the final result—and because I have difficulties in accepting the use of a land/structure ratio as high as 0.57 and in particular its application to all benchmark dates. I also feel that it is advisable to separate farm residences from other farm buildings.

The main innovation in the estimates is as just mentioned, the estimation of farmland improvements and their addition to the components in previous estimates of the stock of reproducible assets, an item accounting for over one-half of farm reproducible assets though its share in the national total declines from over one-third to one-eighth. The effect of this innovation on what may be regarded as the single most important ratio derivable from the new estimates, the rate of growth of the real stock of reproducible capital, is striking. For the period from 1840 to 1900 the rate of growth of that stock is 5.0% compared with one of 5.4% in the old Gallman-Howle estimate and 5.2% in an antique like my estimate made over 30 years for 1850–1900 (Gallman, 5.3%). However, if farmland improvements are included the rate of growth falls to 4.3%—virtually identical with Berry's estimate of 1978—14% less than the new narrow series and 20% below the old series. We are now in a different ballpark. So much for the national aggregates. The effect of the innovation is, however, still more pronounced on the per head rates of growth (per head of population of labor force of per man-hour) which are more significant for many analytical purposes, but which are not shown or discussed in the paper except incidentally in table 4.6, a defect which I hope will be remedied in the published version. Now, with an average annual rate of growth of population of 2.5% of labor force of 2.2%, and of man-hours of 1.8%, the difference between the new and the old estimates becomes spectacular. For capital stock per head of the population the average rate of growth falls from 2.9% to 1.8%. That is a substantial difference which sharply changes the comparison with earlier and later periods in the United States and with other countries during the same and other periods. It also changes the movement of the ratio between 1840 and 1900. While the decadal growth rates formerly fell from 6.1% in the 1840s to 4.2% in the 1890s, or by one-third, the decline is now only from 4.2% to 3.7% or by one-tenth. Per head of the population the decline from 3.1 to 2.3 in the old series is changed to an increase from 1.1% to 1.8%, quite a different story.

The new series will also require a sharp revision of estimates of saving and their interpretation. First, of course, the new estimates increase total national net saving, and hence the saving ratio substantially, for the period 1841–1900 by slightly more than one-tenth or by nearly 1.5% of national product. (The change would be somewhat lower if expenditures on land improvements were, as I would prefer, depreciated rather than, as I understand their present treatment, carried at the same value until retirement, i.e., using a straight line, concave, or convex rather than a rectangular downward schedule.) As the new estimates increase saving relatively more in the early than in the later part of the eight decades, they also change the movements of the saving rate over the period. Second, and more important, they greatly change the distribution of total saving among sectors, sharply increasing the share of agriculture; among regions; among income and wealth groups, increasing the share of the lower strata; and among forms of saving, raising the share of direct saving where saving and capital formation take place within the same economic unit and reducing that of indirect saving through financial instruments. Since no estimates of saving exist before 1896 which break down national saving (except those that can be derived from my 1952 estimate), the extent to which the inclusion of saving in the form of farmland improvements will affect these breakdowns is uncertain, but it is very likely to be substantial, particularly for the earlier part of the period.

Now for suggestions for further work. My main suggestion here, influenced no doubt by my own work, is to develop perpetual inventory estimates for additional components of the stock of reproducible capital to bring up their share from the present level of one-fifth to one-fourth to as near 100% as possible. I am making this suggestion not to produce annual estimates of the stock, but in order to ascertain the effects on different estimates of capital formation, of different assumptions regarding length of life, form of depreciation, retirement distribution and scrap value, and of different deflators on the estimates. It is therefore not essential to start from annual figures of capital expenditures, but 3-year or even 5-year averages will do. The most important candidates for this treatment are nonagricultural residential structures. I do not have the time or the knowledge of the sources to back up my conviction that a perpetual inventory estimate of this component is possible, though it may require that development of new sources, but shall just mention Gottlieb's annual series starting in 1840 of new units built. Two other candidates are the railroads and, more doubtfully, agriculture. These three components alone account for over 70% of the total stock in current prices in 1900. A perpetual inventory estimate for total capital formation is, of course, within reach even back to the early nineteenth century, using Berry's and Gallman's series for capital expenditures.

I would also suggest extending the estimates to include consumer durables and possibly semidurables, roads, and standing timber, an item whose treatment in the estimates is not clear to me, three items (excluding roads) which I have estimated, again very roughly, in my recent attempt to construct a national balance sheet of the United States to have amounted in 1900 to nearly one-fifth of the reproducible tangibles included in Gallman's estimates. Except for semidurables I can see no conceptual reason for exclusion. Even if perpetual inventory estimates cannot be made for the entire period, it would be worthwhile to construct them for the period after the Civil War for which I feel confident they are not beyond reach. In particular, use of the series which the Bureau of Economic Analysis has developed as a basis for its perpetual inventory of the reproducible capital stock from 1929 on should be considered.

Finally, I would like Gallman to discuss, at least verbally, the probable margins of error in the main component series if he is not willing to follow Simon Kuznets's bold example of half a century ago—as always ahead of the crowd—of indicating quantitatively the range of the margins.

There has not been a chance, unfortunately, to comment, among other things, on Gallman's interesting interpretation of movements of the capital formation and capital output ratios with which I generally agree. All I can say is, go and read the entire paper carefully if you have not already done so.

# References

Abramovitz, Moses, and David, Paul. 1973. Economic growth in America: Historical realities and neoclassical parables. *Economist* 121:251–72.

American Iron and Steel Association. 1912. *Statistics of the American and foreign iron trades*. Part 1. Philadelphia: American Iron and Steel Association.

Blodget, Samuel. 1806/1964. *Economica, a statistical manual for the United States of America*. Washington. (Reprint edition, Augustus M. Kelly, New York, 1964.)

Brady, Dorothy S. 1964. Relative prices in the nineteenth century. *Journal of Economic History* 24:145–203.

———. 1966. Price deflators for final product estimates. In *Output, employment, and productivity in the United States after 1800*, ed. Dorothy S. Brady. Studies in Income and Wealth 30. New York: National Bureau of Economic Research.

Conference on Research in Income and Wealth. 1938. Studies in Income and Wealth 2.

———. 1950. Studies in Income and Wealth 12.

———. 1951. Studies in Income and Wealth 14.

———. 1957. Studies in Income and Wealth 19.

———. 1961a. Studies in Income and Wealth 25.

———. 1961b. Studies in Income and Wealth 29.

————. 1980. Studies in Income and Wealth 45.

Cranmer, H. Jerome. 1960. Canal investment, 1815–1860. In *Trends in the American economy in the nineteenth century*, ed. William N. Parker. Studies in Income and Wealth 24. New York: National Bureau of Economic Research.

Creamer, Daniel; Dobrovolsky, Sergei; and Borenstein, Israel. 1960. *Capital in manufacturing and mining: Its formation and financing.* New York: National Bureau of Economic Research.

Davis, Lance E.; Easterlin, Richard A.; Parker, William N. et al. 1972. *American economic growth.* New York: Harper & Row.

Davis, Lance E., and Gallman, Robert E. 1973. The share of savings and investment in gross national product during the 19th century, United States of America. In *Fourth international conference of economic history*, ed. F. C. Lane. Paris: Mouton.

————. 1978. Capital formation in the United States during the nineteenth century. In *The Cambridge economic history of Europe*, ed. Peter Mathias and M. M. Postan. Vol. 7, Part 2. Cambridge, London, New York, Melbourne: Cambridge University Press.

Fishlow, Albert. 1965. *American railroads and the transformation of the ante-bellum economy.* Cambridge: Harvard University Press.

————. 1966. Productivity and technological change in the railroad sector, 1840–1910. In *Output, employment, and productivity*, ed. Dorothy S. Brady. Studies in Income and Wealth 30. New York: National Bureau of Economic Research.

Gallman, Robert E. 1960. Commodity output, 1839–1899. In *Trends in the American economy in the nineteenth century*, ed. William N. Parker. Studies in Income and Wealth 24. New York: National Bureau of Economic Research.

————. 1965. The social distribution of wealth in the United States of America. In *Third international conference on economic history.* Paris: Mouton.

————. 1966. Gross national product in the United States, 1834–1909. In *Output, employment, and productivity*, ed. Dorothy S. Brady. Studies in Income and Wealth 30. New York: National Bureau of Economic Research.

————. 1972. Changes in total U.S. agricultural factor productivity in the nineteenth century. *Agricultural History* 46:191–209.

————. 1978. Comments on "Investment strategy in private enterprise and the role of the state sector, 19th–20th centuries." In *Proceedings of the Sixth International Congress on Economic History.* Copenhagen: Daniels Society for Economic and Social History.

————. 1980. Economic growth. In *Encyclopedia of American economic history*, ed. Glenn Porter. Vol. 1. New York: Charles Scribner's Sons.

———. 1983. How do I measure thee? Let me count the ways: Investment and the capital stock in the nineteenth century. Paper presented to the Cal Tech/Weingart/Social Science History Association Conference; *The Variety of Quantitative History*, Pasadena, California.

———. 1985. Investment flows and capital stocks: U.S. experience in the nineteenth century. Symposium on American Economic History, Wesleyan University, Middletown, Connecticut.

Gallman, Robert E., and Howle, Edward S. n.d. Fixed reproducible capital in the United States, 1840–1900. Mimeographed.

———. 1971. Trends in the structure of the American economy since 1840. In *The reinterpretation of American economic history*, ed. Robert W. Fogel and Stanley L. Engerman. New York, Evanston, San Francisco, London: Harper & Row.

Gallman, Robert E., and Weiss, Thomas J. 1969. The service industries in the nineteenth century. In *Production and productivity in the service industries*. Studies in Income and Wealth 34. New York: National Bureau of Economic Research.

Goldsmith, Raymond. 1952. The growth of reproducible wealth of the United States of America from 1805 to 1905. In *Income and wealth of the United States, trends and structure*, ed. Simon Kuznets. Income and Wealth Series 2. Baltimore: Johns Hopkins Press.

———. 1956. *A study of saving in the United States*. Vol. 3. New York: National Bureau of Economic Research.

———. 1982. *The national balance sheet of the United States*. Chicago: University of Chicago Press.

Goldsmith, Raymond; Lipsey, Robert E.; and Mendelson, Morris. 1963. *Studies in the national balance sheet of the United States*. Vol. 2. New York: National Bureau of Economic Research.

Grebler, Leo; Blank, David M.; and Winnick, Louis. 1956. *Capital formation in residential real estate: Trends and prospects*. New York: National Bureau of Economic Research.

Historical Statistics of the United States. 1960.

Jones, Alice. 1980. *Wealth of a nation to be*. New York: Columbia University Press.

Kendrick, John W. 1961. *Productivity trends in the United States*. New York: National Bureau of Economic Research.

Kuznets, Simon. 1946. *National product since 1869*. New York: National Bureau of Economic Research.

———. 1961. *Capital in the American economy*. New York: National Bureau of Economic Research.

Lebergott, Stanley. 1964. *Manpower in economic growth*. New York: McGraw-Hill.

North, Douglass. The United States balance of payments, 1790–1860. In *Trends in the American economy in the nineteenth century*, ed.

William N. Parker. Studies in Income and Wealth 24. New York: National Bureau of Economic Research.

Primack, Martin. 1962. Farm formed capital in American agriculture, 1850 to 1910. Ph.D. dissertation, University of North Carolina.

Ransom, Roger, and Sutch, Richard. 1975. The impact of the Civil War and emancipation on southern agriculture. *Explorations in Economic History* 12:1–28.

Seaman, Ezra C. 1852. *Essays on the progress of nations*. New York: Charles Scribner.

Segal, Harvey. 1961. Cycles in canal construction. In *Canals and American economic development*, ed. Carter Goodrich. New York: Columbia University Press.

Simon, Matthew. The United States balance of payments, 1861–1900. In *Trends in the American economy in the nineteenth century*, ed. William N. Parker. Studies in Income and Wealth 24. New York: National Bureau of Economic Research.

Soltow, Lee. 1975. *Men and wealth*. New Haven: Yale University Press.

Tostlebe, Alvin. 1957. *Capital in agriculture: Its formation and financing since 1870*. New York: National Bureau of Economic Research.

Ulmer, Melville J. 1960. *Capital in transportation, communications, and public utilities: Its formation and financing*. New York: National Bureau of Economic Research.

Weiss, Thomas. 1967. *The service sector in the United States, 1839–1899*. Ph.D. dissertation. University of North Carolina.

Williamson, Jeffrey G. 1974. Watersheds and turning points: Conjectures on the long-term impact of Civil War financing. *Journal of Economic History* 34:636–61.

# 5    Choices, Rents, and Luck: Economic Mobility of Nineteenth-Century Utah Households

J. R. Kearl and Clayne Pope

## 5.1  Introduction

Is individual poverty permanent or temporary? This question lies at the heart of our interest in economic mobility and its relationship to economic justice. When we speak of the "rich" or the "poor," we imply that there are groups of households that display stability in economic position through time. Moreover, discussion of economic inequality or social mobility often presupposes the existence of classes or barriers to upward movement by individuals or households with certain characteristics. Yet research over the past few decades seems to contradict this assumed view of household immobility. The United States economy seems to be characterized more accurately by cross-sectional distributions of economic rewards that change slowly while many individual households experience substantial social and economic mobility as measured by occupational change or by movement over time of households within these distributions of income and wealth.[1]

The problem of measuring mobility has attracted a good deal of attention from sociologists, primarily, who have generally measured movement within an occupational hierarchy.[2] However, occupational change is not a particularly good measure of mobility if a large share of the labor force works in agriculture since "farming" covers a heterogeneous mixture of economic positions so that movement into or out of farming does not carry any clear signal as to the actual economic mobility of a household. In addition, measurement of economic mo-

J. R. Kearl and Clayne Pope are professors of economics at Brigham Young University and research associates of the National Bureau of Economic Research.

This research has been supported by the College of Social Sciences of Brigham Young University and the National Science Foundation through grant SES8218799NSF.

bility by occupational movement in any economy requires scaling or ordering occupations by economic or social status, that is, imposing a hierarchy on the economy's occupational structure. These imposed normative orderings encounter additional problems when mobility is measured over extended periods of time with changing economic and social status within the mix of occupations. The principal alternative measure is the movement of individuals within distributions of income and wealth.[3] This alternative is used less frequently, however, because of the paucity of panel data with sufficiently long histories.

Post–World War II developments in economic theory and measurement suggest the likelihood of economic mobility measured by movement in either the distribution income or wealth. For example, the permanent income hypothesis, with its focus on permanent and transitory income, suggests that a portion of cross-sectional inequality does not reflect long-term differences in income among individuals.[4] That is, permanent income is more equally distributed than income in a particular year. Consequently, one would expect mobility as measured by transition matrices that trace movement of households from one segment of the income distribution in the initial year to another segment of the distribution in the terminal year or interyear correlations of income. The larger the transitory component of income, the greater the observed mobility. Alternatively, life-cycle theories suggest that concave life cycles of household income and wealth would provide a basis for observed economic mobility in more permanent measures of economic position.[5] The more concave the life cycle of income or wealth, the greater the observed economic mobility for a particular group against a population with a reasonably stable age distribution.

Economic mobility generated by either the transitory component of income or movement along a concave age profile of income excites no great admiration or rush to the conclusion that reality and some egalitarian ideal are synonymous. But such theory does suggest that both cross-sectional inequality and economic mobility must be carefully measured and carefully interpreted.

Human capital models suggest that the paths of income and non-human wealth are partially under the control of the individual or household through investments in education, on-the-job training, and other skills.[6] Different household choices about the accumulation of human capital would also contribute to the economic mobility of households. Investment in human capital leads to changes in income or wealth measured by shifts of intercepts and changes in slopes of age-earnings profiles, causing the profiles of households who have made different investment choices to intersect and reverse relative positions, thus generating added measured mobility. If human capital is an important part of general capital accumulation, one should also observe mobility within the distribution of nonhuman wealth since households will be making portfolio adjustments between human and nonhuman wealth through time.

Many of the theories of the distribution of income are based on stochastic processes that generate inequality.[7] These theories have been stimulated, in part, by a large number of empirical studies attempting to explain earnings or income utilizing household data which have generally been able to account for less than half of the total variance of earnings in most cases.[8] The large unexplained variance in earnings or income may or may not be related to mobility. If this large unexplained residual is due to the omission of unobserved household characteristics, one would not necessarily expect economic mobility because the error terms of the cross-sectional equations would be correlated. On the other hand, if these stochastic elements are uncorrelated through time or distributional position is determined by some type of stochastic process, the observer should find substantial economic mobility.

There are clearly a variety of issues that direct attention to economic mobility. Since the normative importance of mobility is also clear, the measurement of the patterns and trends in economic mobility is of considerable interest. Unfortunately, the data sets that allow extended observation of individual households useful for measuring economic mobility are limited. This paper utilizes one such data set to lay out the patterns of economic mobility in a western frontier state being settled rapidly in the latter half of the nineteenth century. The rich data sources for nineteenth-century Utah have allowed us to create such a panel to measure mobility as movement within cross-sectional distributions over several decades (e.g., movement from a poor decile in one year to a richer decile in another year).[9] Using a variety of measures, we find substantial inequality in cross-sectional distributions and substantial economic mobility in nineteenth-century Utah, although the norm used to determine the level and significance of mobility is unclear. We argue that random economic shocks, decline in rents to permanent household characteristics, and household choice all contribute to this high degree of mobility within a generation. Intergenerational economic mobility is not considered in the analysis reported here.[10] Section 5.2 describes the data. Section 5.3 reviews patterns of household movement within distributions of income and wealth. Section 5.4 divides the elements affecting economic mobility into three categories—stochastic, rents to fixed characteristics of households, and household choices—and assesses the influence of each category on the economic position of households. Section 5.5 attempts to measure the importance of the various influences on economic mobility. The final section brings together the various aspects of mobility, linking occupational and locational choices, individual household characteristics, and changes in relative positions within cross-sectional distributions of income and wealth.

## 5.2   The Data Set

The data set was created by linking households in some or all of the following sources: census manuscripts of 1850, 1860, 1870, 1880, and 1900; probate inventories; tax assessment records of 1870, 1880, 1890, and 1900; financial records of the Church of Jesus Christ of Latter-day Saints (Mormons) for 12 years between 1855 and 1900; and "family group sheets" of the Genealogical Library of the Church.

Estimates of wealth were obtained from the census manuscripts of 1850, 1860, and 1870, tax assessment records, and probate inventories, although we have not used probate inventories in this paper. Census wealth estimates and wealth estimates drawn from the tax records overlap for 1870, allowing us to estimate the consistency of the two sources. The mean of tax assessment wealth is 40% lower than the census wealth estimate for the same year. The correlation of the two wealth estimates for 1870 is quite high with ln (census wealth) = 1.99 + .759ln (tax wealth). Both sources give estimates of gross rather than net wealth.

Estimates of income are obtained from the financial records of the LDS Church. Consequently, any statements involving income mobility or the determinants of income are confined to those households who contributed financially to the LDS Church. The records indicate the contribution an individual made to the Church with an understood moral obligation to contribute 10% of one's income. In nine of our 12 sample years, we also have a record of the percentage that an individual's contribution was relative to a full tithe. These assessments of tithing were done at a local level by local Church leaders who personally knew the individual. The individual was also consulted as to the percentage that he or she had paid. Families usually made their contribution under the name of the male spouse if there was one, although some young men also contributed to the Church. The combination of the amount contributed with the percentage that this amount was of a full tithe yields an estimate of income. If percentage of a full tithe is not given, we have used the average percentage paid by that individual and excluded those for whom we have had less than two observations of the percentage contributed.

Occupational data has been collected from the manuscripts of the five censuses listed above. The occupations were transcribed into a three-digit code that combined occupations that were essentially the same, such as lawyer and attorney. These codes were then aggregated for analysis into five categories. White-collar workers, managers, and proprietors were combined into one classification (W). Farmers, ranchers, dairy owners, and so on, were combined as another (F), as were the crafts (C). Laborers, farm laborers, and any other occupation that appeared unskilled were combined together (L). This left a heterogeneous mixture of occupations that were largely services, such as hotel clerks, policemen, lower-level clerks, and so on, that were classified as service workers (S).[11]

The census and the genealogical records both provide place of birth so that variables on nativity could be formed. If the two sources disagreed, the genealogical record was used. The family group sheets list most vital events for the household. We have used birth and death information as well as some place information from the genealogical records. Each time the household is observed the place information has been retained to provide a record of residence of the household. Internal migration has been measured by movement across county boundaries since the boundaries of towns shifted through time as new communities were formed so that one cannot accurately identify a true move within a county.

The core of the linked sample was formed by linking households from the census manuscripts of 1850, 1860, and 1870. We then added a random sample of the households that could not be found in more than one of these censuses. LDS financial records and tax assessment data were then added to this sample. Obviously, there were households for whom we could add no records as they either were not LDS or were LDS but were not contributing to the Church. While there are over 17,000 households in the sample, fewer households will be represented in any given source such as a particular census year or an income observation. Still fewer households will be represented when two years are linked together for observation of mobility or the formation of particular regressions that require observation at two points in time. To illustrate: of the 17,000 households in the sample, 3,741 and 4,787 households have census records in 1860 and 1870, respectively, while 2,951 households have census records in both years.

A longitudinal sample of this kind has obvious selection biases. Households disappear from the sample or enter the sample after some point of measurement. Further, households may be omitted from observation in one or more of the records. The most serious omissions are probably the lack of income observations from non-Mormons and the omission of households, Mormon and non-Mormon, from a particular census. A large number of individuals making sizable contributions to the Church are not listed as heads of household in the census. Such individuals are largely of two types—young men who have not yet established their own household and parents who live with one of their children in their elderly years. We have omitted both of these types of individuals from most of our measures of mobility and the regressions used to explain mobility. The effect of this omission is to reduce the overall level of mobility since the omitted individuals tend to change their economic position dramatically as they move to or from head of household. A young man who is not a household member usually has little or no wealth, but he accumulates wealth as he establishes a household. Similarly, the act of retiring or moving to live with married children usually accompanies a decline in wealth and income. Consequently, the focus on household heads will understate the mobility of all individuals within certain age ranges. Specific issues of selection and generality will be addressed throughout the paper.

Perhaps the most important weakness of the data set is the absence of educational data. However, longitudinal data sets of this kind are rare, so this Utah data set represents one of the best opportunities to study economic mobility over an extended time period.

### 5.3   Patterns of Economic Mobility

The most direct measure of income or wealth mobility uses a transition matrix of the sort illustrated in table 5.1. The values in each cell represent maximum likelihood estimates of the probabilities of moving from one cell to another. For example, the estimated probability of moving from the poorest quintile to the richest over the 1860–70 decade is .09. The probability of dropping out of the richest quintile over the same decade is .47. Such matrices may be constructed for any two years. They are, however, cumbersome and it is useful to have a single summary measure of mobility. A number have been suggested including an index by Shorrocks based on the diagonal of the matrix, $S = (N - \sum_{i=1}^{N} r_{ii})/(N - 1)$, where $r_{ii}$ is the stayers of row $i$ and $N$ is the number of categories or divisions in each year.[12] Since the diagonal measures the proportion of stayers in each division, the Shorrocks index measures the movement out of the original division but does not distinguish the distance of the movement. For example, the index would be the same in the case where 80% of each division moved up or down one level as the case where 80% of each division was evenly distributed across the other divisions. The Shorrocks index is but one of several measures of mobility. Tables 5.2 and 5.3 summarize some alternative measures of mobility drawn from transition matrices for income and wealth.

#### 5.2.1   Income Mobility

Table 5.2 provides a picture of income mobility by comparing cross-sectional distributions and the movement of households within these

**Table 5.1**   Transition Matrix as Measure of Mobility

| 1860 Wealth | 1870 Wealth | | | | |
|---|---|---|---|---|---|
| | Poorest Quintile ($0–$400) | Quintile 2 ($401–$750) | Quintile 3 ($751–$1,200) | Quintile 4 ($1,201–$2,300) | Quintile 5 ($2,301–$275,000) |
| Poorest quintile ($0–$260) | .35 | .27 | .17 | .12 | .09 |
| Quintile 2 ($261–$500) | .25 | .27 | .25 | .16 | .07 |
| Quintile 3 ($501–$795) | .19 | .21 | .26 | .24 | .10 |
| Quintile 4 ($796–$1,390) | .16 | .18 | .23 | .25 | .18 |
| Quintile 5 ($1,391–$49,500) | .00 | .06 | .11 | .23 | .53 |

Table 5.2    Patterns of Mobility within the Distribution of Income

| | 1855–61 | 1861–70 | 1870–80 | 1880–90 | 1890–1900 | 1861–80 | 1870–90 | 1880–1900 |
|---|---|---|---|---|---|---|---|---|
| Percentage who do not change quintiles | | | | | | | | |
| Poorest quintile | 28% | 29% | 36% | 41% | 44% | 29% | 30% | 35% |
| Fourth quintile | 21 | 25 | 26 | 29 | 29 | 23 | 24 | 21 |
| Middle quintile | 22 | 24 | 23 | 27 | 23 | 24 | 22 | 23 |
| Second quintile | 17 | 26 | 27 | 25 | 30 | 23 | 24 | 20 |
| Richest quintile | 35 | 40 | 47 | 48 | 53 | 38 | 38 | 40 |
| All | | 24 | 29 | 32 | 34 | 36 | 27 | 28 |
| Shorrocks measure | .94 | .89 | .85 | .83 | .80 | .91 | .91 | .90 |
| Percentage moving at least two quintiles | 43% | 35% | 32% | 29% | 26% | 39% | 38% | 37% |
| Pearson correlation | .26 | .37 | .35 | .49 | .56 | .32 | .31 | .45 |
| Number of households | 1,519 | 2,705 | 2,986 | 2,924 | 2,709 | 2,117 | 2,052 | 2,325 |

Source: Income and Wealth data.

distributions from 1855 to 1900. The quintiles used in table 5.2 are based on boundaries defined by the distributions of income for those households that we find in the two years being compared rather than boundaries defined by the population. Hence, we are observing mobility *within* a sample of households. Thus, for 1870–90, we have selected those households for whom we have an estimate of income in both 1870 and 1890. We then draw quintile boundaries based on that group rather than other households that we may observe in one of the two years but not the other. These boundaries ensure that we should expect 20% of each row or column to be in each cell if the income position of the household in the initial year were independent of its position in the second year.[13] The number of households observed in any two years ranges from 1,519 in the 1855–61 comparison to over 2,000 for all other years. Quintile boundaries differ by reasonable amounts so that a household cannot move through two or more quintiles with an income change of a few dollars. The lower boundary for the richest quintile is usually about five times the upper boundary for the poorest quintile.

The first six rows of table 5.2 report the percentage who stay within the same quintile for the two years being observed. For example, 28% of those in the poorest quintile in 1855 were also in that quintile in 1861. Similarly, 35% of those in the richest quintile in 1855 remained there in 1861, while 24% of those observed in these two years remained in the same quintile in the two years. Each of the transition matrices displays a U-shape in terms of the percent "stayers." That is, the percentage is higher in the tails of the distribution (the first and fifth quintiles) while those in the middle approach 20%—implying that the expected value of a household's later position is independent of its prior position if the household is in the middle of the distribution.

The Shorrocks measure, essentially a normalization of the percentage of stayers, will range from zero with no mobility to one when initial position has no expected effect on final position. This measure, reported in tables 5.2 and 5.3, ranges from .80 to .94. This pattern suggests a slight decline in mobility from 1855 to 1900 when decade intervals are used but essentially a constant level of mobility when two-decade intervals are used. Since income contains a transitory component, it is not surprising that there is considerable movement in terms of a quintile change. Therefore, we have also reported the percentage of the households that move at least two quintiles. About one-third of the households move at least two quintiles over a decade while just under 40% move that much over two decades. Finally, the Pearson correlation coefficient shows the simple correlation of incomes for the two years. While it is clear that there is a correlation in the incomes as measured by the Pearson correlation coefficients, all of which are statistically significant, these matrices evidence substantial income mobility.[14] However, a household's initial position in the income distribution is importance since the middle quintiles tend to be characterized by greater mobility while the tails display more rigidity. For the entire sample, from 24% to 34% do not change quintiles over a decade.

An interesting aspect of table 5.2 is the rising immobility with time. Most of the measures suggest increasing rigidity within the distribution of income, with the percentage of stayers rising in the tails of the distribution by 50% and the percentage of stayers for the whole matrix exhibiting comparable change. However, the 20-year intervals show no particular increase in rigidity, by any of the measures except the Pearson correlation coefficient. The 20-year intervals also show higher observed mobility as one would expect.

Even though the increases in mobility, comparing one-decade to two-decade measures, are not large, the differences are important because they suggest that the observed mobility is not due merely to transitory changes in income. Rather, a part of the observed mobility reflects more permanent changes in economic position. If all mobility were due to transitory influences, the one-decade and two-decade transition matrices would be virtually the same since it cannot matter when one draws truly random shocks unless there is a very strong autocorrelation in the random component. For example, the decades of the 1880s and 1890s produce Shorrocks measures of .83 and .80 which rise to .90 for the two decades combined. While 29% and 26% of the households move more than two quintiles in the 1880s and 1890s, respectively, 37% make such moves for the two decades combined. Thus, the two-decade measures show an increase in mobility suggesting that the observed mobility is influenced by factors in addition to stochastic shocks. This conclusion, that the observed mobility involves nonstochastic changes, is strengthened by the observed wealth mobility. For if all of the income mobility were due to transitory components, there should be little wealth mobility. Conversely, income mobility due to choice or other factors would also lead to wealth mobility.

Table 5.3 reports the same kind of summary statistics as table 5.2 for wealth rather than income. Wealth estimates come from two different sources. Wealth estimates for 1850 (real estate only), 1860, and 1870 come from the census manuscripts, while estimates for 1870 through 1900 come from the tax assessment rolls. Obviously, these two sources are substantially different. The census is self-declared and has no relation to taxes. Tax assessment was the responsibility of county officials, and estimates may have been less likely to change.

Wealth mobility appears to us, like income mobility, to be substantial.[15] While the Shorrocks measure is generally above .8, there is less mobility in the wealth distribution than in the income distributions.

**Table 5.3    Patterns of Mobility within the Distribution of Wealth**

| | 1850–60 | 1860–70 | 1870–80[a] | | 1880–90 | 1890–1900 | 1850–70 | 1860–80 | 1870–90 | | 1880–1900 |
| --- | --- | --- | --- | --- | --- | --- | --- | --- | --- | --- | --- |
| | | | C | Tx | | | | | C | Tx | |
| Percentage who do not change quintiles | | | | | | | | | | | |
| Poorest quintile | 31% | 35% | 33% | 50% | 43% | 41% | 26% | 29% | 30% | 29% | 32% |
| Fourth quintile | 23 | 27 | 27 | 35 | 31 | 31 | 24 | 21 | 23 | 21 | 21 |
| Middle quintile | 23 | 26 | 29 | 31 | 30 | 29 | 17 | 26 | 26 | 20 | 24 |
| Second quintile | 21 | 25 | 32 | 32 | 33 | 32 | 17 | 27 | 27 | 23 | 27 |
| Richest quintile | 45 | 53 | 54 | 61 | 56 | 48 | 43 | 43 | 40 | 45 | 46 |
| All | 28 | 33 | 35 | 42 | 39 | 36 | 25 | 29 | 29 | 28 | 30 |
| Shorrocks measure | .89 | .84 | .81 | .72 | .77 | .80 | .93 | .89 | .89 | .90 | .88 |
| Percentage moving at least two quintiles | 36% | 29% | 29% | 19% | 27% | 26% | 37% | 34% | 36% | 39% | 32% |
| Pearson correlation | .44 | .45 | .35 | .70 | .43 | .39 | .31 | .41 | .26 | .15 | .39 |
| Number of households | 937 | 2,933 | 2,168 | 1,334 | 1,586 | 1,432 | 793 | 1,504 | 976 | 1,080 | 1.007 |

[a]In 1870 there are two wealth estimates: census and tax assessment. The first column (C) compares 1870 census wealth with 1880 tax assessment wealth. The second column (Tx) compares tax assessment wealth for 1870 and 1880.

This result is to be expected. As with income, there is more rigidity in the tails of the distribution and more mobility in the middle quintiles. The trend in mobility is difficult to ascertain because of the change in the source of measurement in 1870. Clearly the tax assessment distributions which are used in the last half of the period show much less mobility with Shorrocks measures from .72 to .80. As few as 19% of the households move at least two quintiles. Wealth transition matrices measured over two decades display significantly more mobility than the matrices based on a single decade comparable, once again, to the pattern for income. Adjustment for age or other factors does not substantially reduce this observed wealth mobility.[16] Certainly these comparisons of mobility for income and wealth suggest that the income mobility is not simply due to transitory elements of income alone.

Tables 5.2 and 5.3 present a picture of what appears to us to be substantial movement and change. The transitional matrices of income and wealth display a high degree of economic mobility but with some noticeable rigidity in the tails of the distributions. These patterns are not attributable to age since adjustment for age changes the pattern little. The next section of the paper examines those elements that may generate the observed economic mobility.

## 5.4    Influences on Economic Mobility

Tables 5.4 and 5.5 report cross-sectional regressions that explore the relationship of the logarithm of wealth and income (LNTW and LNY) and the portion of variance explained by individual characteristics such as occupation, nativity, duration in Utah, residence, and age. A notable feature of the equations is their lack of success in explaining a large part of the variance in economic success. The explained variance of income is never as great as 15% while the explained variance of wealth is never as great as 40%. Why might the explained variance be so low?

### 5.4.1    Market Adjustment and Measurement of Influences on Income and Wealth

Different economic rewards for different individuals have at least three components: those differences that result from different choices made by individuals (e.g., labor-leisure choices, savings decisions, occupational choices); those differences that result from market rewards for different individual characteristics that cannot be chosen but which an individual "inherits" (examples might, but need not necessarily, include race, gender, genetic traits); and those differences that result from purely stochastic sources (e.g., "luck"). It should be clear that many things that one cannot choose for oneself may have been choices for someone else. Prominent among these individual attributes would

**Table 5.4    Cross-Sectional Regressions on LNTW**

| Variables | 1860 B | 1860 $\|t\|$ | 1870 B | 1870 $\|t\|$ | 1880 B | 1880 $\|t\|$ | 1890 B | 1890 $\|t\|$ | 1900 B | 1900 $\|t\|$ |
|---|---|---|---|---|---|---|---|---|---|---|
| Age | .022 | 5.04 | .026 | 5.19 | .050 | 6.62 | .064 | 7.02 | .078 | 6.58 |
| Age$^2$ | -.0002 | 3.40 | -.0002 | 4.35 | -.0005 | 7.06 | -.0006 | 7.71 | -.0007 | 7.10 |
| W | .617 | 8.00 | .563 | 10.15 | .305 | 5.56 | .292 | 4.90 | .076 | .99 |
| C | -.326 | 8.52 | -.160 | 4.52 | -.228 | 5.59 | -.126 | 2.35 | -.43 | 5.67 |
| S | -.209 | 2.17 | -.097 | 1.56 | -.069 | .94 | .020 | .23 | -.26 | 2.36 |
| L | -.734 | 18.70 | -.591 | 14.00 | -.515 | 10.20 | -.325 | 5.19 | -.455 | 5.03 |
| FBE | -.284 | 9.84 | -.192 | 7.39 | -.052 | 1.67 | .002 | .05 | -.010 | .19 |
| T | .067 | 16.31 | .033 | 12.98 | .031 | 13.20 | .016 | 6.26 | .008 | 2.94 |
| R | -.083 | 2.62 | -.526 | 15.71 | -.557 | 14.99 | -.599 | 12.24 | -.126 | 1.91 |
| Constant | 6.04 | 65.66 | 6.48 | 58.39 | 5.425 | 30.45 | 5.87 | 26.03 | 4.77 | 14.54 |
| $R^2$ | .28 | | .21 | | .25 | | .14 | | .06 | |
| N | 4005 | | 4014 | | 2609 | | 2609 | | 2209 | |

*Source*: Utah Income and Wealth Project.
*Control group*: United States–born farmers in Salt Lake County.

Table 5.5            Cross-Sectional Regressions on Income

| Variables | LNY55 B | $|t|$ | LNY61 B | $|t|$ | LNY66 B | $|t|$ | LNY70 B | $|t|$ | LN75 B | $|t|$ |
|---|---|---|---|---|---|---|---|---|---|---|
| Age | .047 | 5.07 | .058 | 7.93 | .078 | 8.00 | .070 | 7.34 | .052 | 5.77 |
| Age$^2$ | −.00053 | 4.69 | −.00067 | 8.06 | −.00086 | 8.23 | −.00076 | 7.82 | −.0006 | 6.88 |
| FBE | .084 | 2.56 | −.027 | 1.01 | −.0071 | .21 | .085 | 2.51 | .065 | 1.96 |
| T | .024 | 3.67 | .034 | 8.32 | .018 | 4.19 | .026 | 7.00 | .030 | 10.03 |
| W | .032 | .33 | .064 | .97 | .236 | 3.22 | .238 | 3.31 | .319 | 4.77 |
| C | .05 | 1.11 | −.121 | 3.38 | −.070 | 1.51 | −.037 | .80 | .023 | .51 |
| S | −.159 | 1.20 | −.136 | 1.42 | .103 | 1.02 | −.046 | .44 | −.012 | .13 |
| L | −.144 | 2.57 | −.222 | 5.59 | −.212 | 3.79 | −.173 | 3.15 | −.255 | 4.91 |
| R | −.032 | .95 | −.057 | 1.87 | −.236 | 5.44 | −.150 | 2.97 | −.189 | 4.33 |
| Constant | 5.27 | 29.10 | 4.94 | 33.27 | 4.708 | 22.839 | 4.30 | 20.60 | 4.72 | 23.70 |
| $R^2$ | .05 | | .08 | | .06 | | .07 | | .10 | |
| N | 1448 | | 3160 | | 2891 | | 2854 | | 2959 | |

Source: Income and Wealth Project.
Control group: United States–born farmers of Salt Lake County.

be those associated with one's family (e.g., parental choices about early home environment, child spacing, location, family size).

Individuals have some characteristics such as occupation and residence that can be acquired and affect one's economic rewards and, hence, relative position in the distribution of those rewards across a population. Since acquisition is generally costly, such choices have many of the characteristics of an investment decision—an individual incurs a cost at the time of change with the expectation that the future path will be superior to the path without the change. Costs of change may vary because of the nature of one's human and nonhuman capital.[17] If rewards are perceived to be correlated with acquirable characteristics, and if individuals pursue maximizing strategies, individuals will tend to acquire those characteristics necessary for participation in the relatively high return activities. Maximizing choices, the acquisition of a higher expected relative return characteristic, will arbitrage return differences causing a decline in the relative return to the higher return activities as more and more households acquire such characteristics. Acquisition of attractive market characteristics should continue until the cost of acquiring the associated characteristic equals the difference between the return in the current activity and the return to the activity requiring that characteristic. This arbitrage process will narrow the distribution of returns to the distribution of the costs of acquiring beneficial characteristics (assuming no stochastic shocks).

Obviously, if individuals do acquire characteristics consistent with differential returns across activities, attempting to maximize returns, those doing less well in any current activity are more likely to choose

| LN80 | | LN85 | | LNY90 | | LNY95 | | LNY00 | |
|---|---|---|---|---|---|---|---|---|---|
| B | \|t\| | B | \|t\| | B | \|t\| | B | \|t\| | B | \|t\| |
| .063 | 8.29 | .049 | 7.20 | .047 | 6.03 | .044 | 4.29 | .030 | 3.39 |
| −.00070 | 9.57 | −.00055 | 8.96 | −.00054 | 7.65 | −.00046 | 5.30 | −.00033 | 4.60 |
| .047 | 1.55 | .055 | 1.93 | .032 | .978 | .086 | 2.13 | −.012 | .325 |
| .016 | 6.87 | .013 | 6.36 | .012 | 5.63 | .0065 | 2.56 | .00083 | .405 |
| .378 | 7.02 | .29 | 5.93 | .593 | 11.09 | .56 | 9.12 | .600 | 10.63 |
| .005 | .14 | −.07 | 1.70 | .017 | .39 | −.086 | 1.51 | −.026 | .52 |
| −.131 | 1.80 | −.14 | 2.07 | .107 | 1.35 | .111 | 1.16 | −.238 | 2.73 |
| −.274 | 5.34 | −.300 | 6.00 | .209 | 3.95 | −.147 | 2.07 | −.294 | 4.96 |
| −.336 | 8.89 | −.354 | 8.52 | −.52 | 11.82 | −.369 | 7.09 | −.400 | 8.64 |
| 4.68 | 27.29 | 5.14 | 32.05 | 5.20 | 26.86 | 4.83 | 17.93 | 5.61 | 22.75 |
| .11 | | .10 | | .14 | | .09 | | .13 | |
| 4004 | | 3325 | | 2826 | | 2327 | | 2382 | |

alternative characteristics consistent with higher return activities. Thus, the percentages of individuals in low-income or low-wealth groups changing activities or acquiring characteristics are likely to be greater than for those finding themselves in more attractive positions.

Since characteristic acquisition is comparable to an investment decision, there should also be a systematic correlation between changes in acquirable characteristics and the age of the individual. That is, if choices are costly, with costs uncorrelated or positively correlated with age, older individuals, who have shorter time horizons over which to exploit the investment, will be less likely to acquire different characteristics. Thus, one would expect the following patterns relative to our current data:

1. More occupational change and residential change for younger age groups.
2. Higher probabilities of movement for those with lower wealth and/ or income.
3. Less movement among those households holding "specific" human capital.

While these effects follow from an arbitrage model of market choices, the market also acts as a filter, making the observation of these very effects difficult. Assume, for present purposes, that the costs of acquiring a relatively attractive characteristic are low and essentially the same for all individuals. Suppose further that market adjustments create, at some moment, a spread of different returns across activities. If all high return characteristics may be acquired, then rapid market adjustment would arbitrage these differences in returns. This implies, however, that the observed distributional outcome, after choices about characteristics have been made, would be an egalitarian one, net of the random disturbances that affected economic rewards. This means that a cross-sectional regression would have little explanatory power since the market adjustments narrowed or eliminated the original systematic differences that stimulated the choices made by households. If acquisition costs differ for individuals, market responses would level to these differences but such differences would be, in general, indistinguishable from stochastic influences. More generally, this argument suggests that the choice-market response mechanism per se is a leveling or egalitarian mechanism so long as the individual characteristics associated with differential returns are matters of choice. Clearly this leveling process would be more pronounced the lower the costs of characteristic acquisition for all individuals. Hence, if adjustment is rapid, there will be little ex post facto correlation between characteristics and rewards even though it is precisely the ex ante correlation to which individuals respond when making choices. One would have to observe the adjustment process, not the final result, in order to measure the effects of choice.

This argument suggests that there will be difficulties in testing for a choice-market response mechanism using ex post outcomes unless the choice-market response mechanism has some residual effect that can be identified in the observable outcome. If acquisition costs are low and adjustment rapid, it would be difficult to find evidence of the influence of choice. Moreover, finding little or no correlation between individual characteristics *does not* allow one to infer that "nothing matters" or "nothing matters very much."[18] Finally, it should be noted that market and individual characteristics may be of considerable importance and stochastic elements of less importance, but the stochastic element dominates in observed outcomes by virtue of the market filtering process.

### 5.4.2 Ricardian Elements

Markets may also reward individual characteristics that are not volitional and that therefore cannot evoke the choice-market-response leveling process just outlined. Individuals possess characteristics such as race, gender, birthplace, age, or physical characteristics that might be rewarded, for whatever reason, with a higher income or wealth. These characteristics may not be a matter of choice for the individual and hence cannot be changed or acquired regardless of the associated relative return or penalty. We think of these characteristics as "Ricardian" since they have in common the essential element that land possessed in Ricardo's classic model of distribution, namely, inelastic supply. Since the essential element of the choice-market-response leveling process is characteristic acquisition in response to differential returns, if acquisition is precluded because the characteristics are nonvolitional, there is no reason to expect that rewarded or penalized Ricardian characteristics will be subject to either the leveling or filtering processes suggested earlier. Hence, Ricardian characteristics that have importance in the market will always be correlated with ex post observable outcomes.[19]

Indeed, if acquisition costs are low for any characteristics that can be acquired so that the choice-market-response filtering process works well, Ricardian characteristics will be the only identifiable characteristics from observed distributions of economic rewards—the only mechanism for generating systematic individual differences is Ricardian. This does not suggest, obviously, that the Ricardian mechanism is the only or even dominant mechanism responsible for the distribution of economic rewards; rather, Ricardian characteristics will dominate the explainable variance in the distribution.

Individuals may overcome the effect of Ricardian characteristics by labor/leisure or savings/consumption choices even though they cannot change the characteristic or its market reward. Moreover, there is an important sense in which choice itself has Ricardian aspects—the history of some group or some individual with an attractive characteristic cannot be chosen. For example, if the return to some characteristic, say a particular occupation, is relatively high, others will acquire that characteristic, driving down the return. However, there will be individuals who will have had that particular characteristic for differing lengths of time. The one thing that cannot be acquired is the characteristic yesterday or, more generally, a history for oneself that includes the high-valued choices (ex post) at each moment of time. Hence some choice paths will be more attractive, ex post, than others in the specific sense that such choice paths will be correlated with observed outcomes. Not all people currently farming, for example, are the same. Some were farming earlier; others just chose to become farmers. Moreover, among those who chose to become farmers, some came from one occupation, some from a different occupation.

The Ricardian nature of choice paths suggests that these paths should have an observable correlation within the distribution. Thus it is possible to test, in a different way, the importance of certain choices that individuals can make (or could have made) on the distribution of rewards. Moreover, if choice paths are important, there will be a heterogeneity for any observable individual characteristic that will account for part of the variance of outcomes within that characteristic class. This affect is more likely to be more pronounced for wealth than for income for the following reason. Assume that some characteristic is particularly attractive. Those not having that characteristic will acquire it, driving down the return to that characteristic. Hence, assuming no taste differences (particularly over leisure-labor choices), the incomes of those holding the characteristic, both newly acquired and historical, will tend to be equalized. However, unless adjustment is instantaneous, those already having the attractive characteristic will gain the benefit of the higher-than-average return until entry has moved it toward the average, and this will be reflected in wealth positions. The market-response mechanism cannot level wealth, a stock, in the same way that it can income, a flow. Hence, we should observe a smaller effect of choice paths on income than on wealth. Indeed, with wealth, choice paths could matter a good deal since that market signals desired adjustments in an economy by changing returns, but those already in the desired or attractive area benefit from that market mechanism. This suggests that the distributions of wealth and income are likely to be quite different even if one could appropriately adjust for the life-cycle effects. More precisely, the distribution of income should be less dispersed than that for wealth. The determinants of income and wealth distributions may also differ as a consequence of the effect described above. For example, a characteristic could be positively associated with wealth and negatively associated with income.

The stochastic element of the regression reflects the combined influence of true stochastic elements and unobserved individual characteristics, including differences in the costs of acquiring different characteristics. For reasons discussed above, the true stochastic elements are likely to dominate the cross-sectional regressions even though they may not dominate the process by which income or wealth is generated. The influence of the unobserved characteristics may also be important if they are characteristics such as IQ or education that are costly or difficult to acquire.

A cross-sectional regression could be specified in the following way for the $i$th individual.

$$\text{LNTW}_i \text{ or } \text{LNY}_i = \alpha_0 + \sum_{j=1}^{n} \beta_j X_j + \sum_{k=1} \gamma_k Z_k + \epsilon_i + \mu_i,$$

where the $X_j$ are the characteristics that may be acquired, such as occupation or place of residence; the $Z_k$ are the characteristics that may not be acquired; $\epsilon_i$ represents the variance due to the unobserved characteristics of the household, while $\mu_i$ represents the true stochastic variance.[20] The market mechanism should reduce the returns to the $X_j$ so the $\beta_j$ reflects the costs of acquisition in equilibrium. The $\gamma_k$ will rise or fall as the returns to particular fixed characteristics are changed by movement in the economy.

Mobility within the distributions of income and wealth would depend upon any of the following:

1. Stochastic variance ($\mu_i$). Given the market filtering argument this should be a primary source of mobility within the two distributions.
2. Choices (acquiring $X_j$ with high returns). The extent of their contributions to mobility will be difficult to measure because the market process changes the return to choices and masks the influence of such returns ($\beta_j$).
3. Changing returns to Ricardian characteristics ($\gamma_k$).

The distribution of Ricardian characteristics ($Z_k$) and the variance due to unobserved household characteristics ($\epsilon_i$) stand as the primary barriers to economic mobility. The following section considers their relative contribution to the mobility observed in the nineteenth-century Utah economy.

## 5.5 Household Characteristics, Stochastic Elements, and Mobility

While it is easy to categorize characteristics conceptually, the separation of the variables in the regressions of tables 5.4 and 5.5 into choice variables and fixed or Ricardian characteristics is arbitrary to some degree. Age and nativity (FBE) are obviously fixed characteristics. The unique settlement pattern of Utah suggests that duration in Utah (T) is also a Ricardian characteristic since most households in Utah were converts to the LDS faith who migrated to Utah shortly after conversion. Hence, while there is a clear choice component to duration in most economies, the reason individuals came to this economy when they did suggests that duration is more properly considered a fixed characteristic in this context. Occupation and residence are considered as choice variables.

Several patterns in these cross-sectional regressions on income and wealth are worth noting.[21] The ordering of the effects of occupation on wealth is quite uniform through time. We should note that we did not use either wealth or income to determine occupational categories as is often done when creating indices of occupational status. (It is possible that individuals self-classify depending on their wealth or income.) Households with a white-collar classification consistently have a higher level of wealth and income. In most years this advantage is substantial. While there is some tendency for the wealth advantage of the white-collar group relative to the control group (farmers) to decline over time (a 60% advantage in 1860, dropping to a 30% advantage in 1890 with no statistically significant advantage in 1900), the income advantage of the white-collar households shows no such tendency. Indeed, the income advantage of the white-collar households increases through time. One would suspect that farmers were making capital gains that increased their wealth, but which they did not consider as income. Craftsmen consistently had lower wealth than farmers ceteris paribus, but their income was not significantly different from that of farmers. The service classification is a collection of very heterogeneous occupations (as well as a small subset of the total), and the difference between this group and the control group is rarely statistically significant although the sign is usually negative. Unskilled laborers held lower wealth than the other occupational classifications, with perhaps a slight tendency for their wealth disadvantage to decline with time. Laborers also had lower incomes than farmers, the control group, but their income disadvantage was relatively less than their wealth disadvantage.

Those households residing outside Salt Lake County (R) had both lower wealth and lower income. The income disadvantage grew through time from 6% in 1861 to a high of 52% in 1890, dropping to 40% in 1900. The wealth disadvantage shows no strong trend but does have an anomalous decline in 1900 to 13%.

These cross-sectional regressions suggest that a household could improve its position through choice by acquiring higher return characteristics such as residence in Salt Lake County or the occupations of white-collar worker or farmer. (We return to the measurement of this choice process later.) Certainly these characteristics that we have labeled as choice variables did matter. However, an examination of the low explained variance of these regressions suggests that such choices are not the dominant observed determinants of income or wealth. In general, the variables explain more of the variance of wealth than of income. This would be expected if transitory elements were important and relatively larger for income than wealth.

For those variables that are considered as fixed characteristics, there are persistent effects for both foreign birth (FBE) and duration in Utah (T) on wealth. However, the effect of both characteristics declines through time. Foreign birth reduced wealth by 36% in 1860, but only 5% in 1880, and it was not significant as a determinant of wealth in 1890 or 1900. Foreign birth had a much different effect on income. By 1870, this characteristic was positively associated with income, and this correlation persisted until the latter part of the century. Migration from Northern Europe to Utah reduced the nonhuman wealth for many households to zero. Lower wealth may have induced a higher labor/leisure ratio that produced higher income in spite of the low wealth.[22] There may also have been a selection process at work among the foreign born selecting out individuals with higher levels of ambition, etcetera, who were willing to migrate to the American West as well as to adopt an unusual religion. Clearly by the end of the century, any economic disadvantage that the foreign born may have had was eliminated, in part because individuals could make decisions that changed the effect of the fixed characteristic of birthplace.

There were rents to early entry into the Utah economy in terms of both income and wealth. This rent was substantial from initial settlement and persisted throughout the period. For example, entry into Utah in 1850 increased wealth in 1860 by 68%, 72% in 1870, and 93% in 1880. By 1900, the effect of early entry declined to 42%. The effects of duration on income were lower but impressive. Entry in 1850 increased income in 1861 by 34% ceteris paribus, 52% in 1870, 75% by 1875. The effect declines after 1875 and is not significant after 1890. The rent per year of duration declines steadily through time. This fact does not mean that the total effect of duration will decline for particular households since T may be increasing faster than the decline in rent per year duration. While the rent to United States birth becomes relatively unimportant through time, the rent to duration continues to play a role until the very late years in the sample.

The concave age patterns are quite robust for both income and wealth. The peaks in the age profiles for income are at earlier ages than those for wealth, a relationship explored elsewhere.[23] While the life-cycle pattern could explain mobility against a population with a relatively stable age distribution, the samples used in tables 5.2 and 5.3 are composed of fixed groups of people whose age relationships are constant. Therefore, only concavity contributes to mobility.

In summary, the decline in the effect of nativity on wealth would generate some wealth mobility, while nativity must have been relatively unimportant as a source of income mobility. Duration remains an important barrier to mobility since the rents to duration persist and cannot be acquired. The concave age pattern generates a modest amount of mobility.

The cross-sectional regressions of tables 5.4 and 5.5 provide reference points for a closer examination of each of the three elements that generate mobility—stochastic variance, returns to choice, and changes in the rents to fixed characteristics. But the cross-sectional regressions mask many of the important issues. Such equations tell us the average return to a characteristic, not the return for acquiring the characteristic. Fortunately, longitudinal data allow us to gain richer insights into the very issues that are elusive with cross-sectional data.

At first glance, the explained variance of the regressions of tables 5.4 and 5.5 implies that much of the mobility in income and wealth observed in nineteenth-century Utah was due to stochastic processes, since $R^2$ on the income regressions never exceeds .14 while the explained variance of the wealth regressions is never above .28. However, these low explained variances are underestimates of the actual amount of the variance in income and wealth that is patterned or potentially explainable for two reasons. As noted earlier, the market adjustment processes amplify the relative importance of stochastic variance and dampens the relative importance of choice in observable outcomes. Also the regressions estimated in tables 5.4 and 5.5 confound the stochastic elements and the variance due to unobserved variables in the error term. We can estimate the variance explained by unobserved individual characteristics which are time invariant by correlating the household-specific residuals of cross-sectional regressions between different years. If the residual calculated by subtracting the predicted value of a household's wealth (given age, nativity, occupation, residence, and duration) from actual wealth was low for both 1860 and 1870, it would suggest that there were unobserved individual or household characteristics that were correlated with wealth. The measure being used, called the intraclass correlation, is defined as

$$ r = \frac{2\sigma_{12}}{\sigma_1^2 + \sigma_2^2} , $$

where $\sigma_{12}$ is the covariance of the residuals for years 1 and 2 and $\sigma_1^2$ is the variance of the residuals in year $i$.[24] The intraclass correlation is also a measure of the percentage of the unexplained variance of the cross-section attributable to unobserved characteristics.

The unobserved household-specific effect on both income and wealth have been measured for a number of pairs of years and summarized in table 5.6. There are large and significant correlations in these residuals

| Table 5.6 | Intraclass Correlations for Selected Pairs of Years | |
|---|---|---|
| | Years | Correlation |
| Wealth | | |
| | 1860–70 | .37 |
| | 1870–80 | .35 |
| | 1880–90 | .42 |
| | 1890–1900 | .36 |
| Income | | |
| | 1855–61 | .14 |
| | 1861–70 | .32 |
| | 1870–80 | .43 |
| | 1880–90 | .37 |
| | 1890–1900 | .45 |

*Source:* Utah Income and Wealth Project.

*Note:* This correlation coefficient is estimated by estimating lnTW or Y as a function of Age, Age$^2$, FBE, T, R, W, C, S, and L for the two years indicated. Then the residuals of the regressions are "stacked." If $U_{60}$ is the residual for 1860 and $U_{70}$ for 1870, two variables are formed:

$$ N_1 = \begin{pmatrix} U_{60} \\ U_{70} \end{pmatrix} \quad \text{and} \quad N_2 = \begin{pmatrix} U_{70} \\ U_{60} \end{pmatrix} . $$

Then $N_1$ is correlated with $N_2$. The correlation is the covariance of the residuals divided by the sum of the variances.

suggesting that there are unobserved individual effects of importance. It appears that about a third of the unexplained variance in the wealth distribution is due to unobserved fixed characteristics that the household possessed. The unobserved characteristics might include ability, work ethic, or education (as long as there was no change in education between observations). Thus, the variance of income or wealth can be broken down into components:

|  | LNTW1860 | LNY1880 |
|---|---|---|
| A. Variable explained by the variables of the regression | 28% | 11% |
| B. Variance accounted for by unobserved variables | 37% | 37%–43% |
| C. Stochastic variance | 35% | 46%–52% |

This procedure estimates stochastic variance as about 50% total variance for income with higher estimates for early years. The estimate of stochastic variance for wealth is somewhat lower. Thus, stochastic variance continues to play a dominant role in generating mobility within the distribution of income and wealth. On the other hand, the influence of both observed and unobserved individual or household characteristics accounts for 40–60% of total variance which reduces stochastic variance well below the unexplained variance of the cross-sectional regressions. One should, of course, expect higher income mobility since income is likely to have a relatively larger transitory component.

### 5.5.1  Patterns of Occupational and Residential Choice

Table 5.7 summarizes some interesting aspects of occupational and residential change as observed in each of the censuses from which we have drawn data. It should be reemphasized that the data set under analysis here is not a random sample of the census population for each of the noted years. Rather, the sample consists of those households that have been traced through several records so that longitudinal analysis of the household was possible. The percentages reported in Table 5.7 are based on those who were "at risk" for the indicated change. For example, 7% of the rural population of 1850 had moved to Salt Lake County (our classification as an urban area) by 1860.

About two-fifths of the households shifted from one occupational class to another within any of our census decades. Obviously, finer classification of occupations would produce a considerable increase in occupational change. Forty-seven percent of those observed in 1860 and 1870 made an occupational change where a change represents substantial change in occupation (white-collar to farmer, laborer to farmer, etc.) rather than small changes in arbitrary naming such as

**Table 5.7    Patterns of Occupational and Residential Change**

|  | 1850–60 | 1860–70 | 1870–80 | 1850–70 | 1860–80 | 1880–1900 |
|---|---|---|---|---|---|---|
| Number of households[a] | 937 | 2,933 | 2,168 | 793 | 1,504 | 1,007 |
| **Occupation** | | | | | | |
| Percentage who change occupation[b] | 42% | 40% | 37% | 45% | 43% | 39% |
| Percentage of farmers shifting out of farming | 18 | 25 | 25 | 25 | 27 | 32 |
| Percentage of nonfarmers entering farming | 54 | 35 | 33 | 47 | 41 | 41 |
| Percentage of unskilled laborers who remain unskilled laborers | 16 | 23 | 15 | 18 | 13 | 12 |
| Percentage of unskilled laborers who become farmers | 65 | 49 | 49 | 58 | 55 | 64 |
| Percentage of unskilled laborers who become craftsmen | 15 | 13 | 17 | 10 | 17 | 9 |
| Percentage of nonlaborers who become laborers | 6 | 9 | 7 | 9 | 6 | 8 |
| **Residence** | | | | | | |
| Percentage who change county of residence | 39 | 34 | 17 | 57 | 27 | 20 |
| Percentage moving to an urban area (SL County) | 7 | 4 | 5 | 8 | 3 | 3 |
| Percentage moving to a rural area | 37 | 34 | 9 | 56 | 45 | 13 |
| **Combined** | | | | | | |
| Percentage who change county of residence and occupation | 16 | 15 | 8 | 25 | 18 | 8 |
| Percentage who change county of residence but not occupation | 23 | 18 | 7 | 32 | 21 | 9 |
| Percentage who change occupation but not county of residence | 25 | 24 | 29 | 20 | 24 | 30 |
| Percentage who change neither | 36 | 42 | 56 | 24 | 37 | 53 |

*Source*: Utah Income and Wealth Project.

[a]This is the number of households with occupations in the indicated years. County residence is observed on some households not in census.

[b]There are five occupational classes: (1) white collar, consisting of professionals, owners, and managers; (2) craftsmen; (3) service workers; (4) unskilled laborers including farm laborers; (5) farmers (those who owned farms).

carpenter to woodworker or physician to doctor. The most difficult change to interpret is that from farm laborer to farmer since it is not clear that this is a substantial change in occupation. Such a change has been classified as a shift from unskilled laborer to farmer. While such changes in occupation (farm laborer to farmer) are important in the Utah economy, they are by no means the bulk of the occupational changes. Eliminating all such movements would reduce occupational change by less than 15% in the seven years considered here. There are substantial movements of individuals from farmers to crafts, or white-collar employment, or vice versa. There are also substantial movements among the nonfarm occupations. For example, only one-third of the households classified as having a white-collar occupation in 1870 were so classified in 1860. In fact, more of the households that were classified as white-collar in 1870 were classified as farm than as white-collar in 1860. Over 40% of craftsmen in the 1870 sample were classified in some other category in 1860. It seems reasonable to conclude that there is substantial movement among occupations when one considers the rather broad categories that are used here to define occupational change.[25]

It is of interest to know how much of this occupational movement is simply a response to the life cycle. Perhaps one starts as a laborer, shifts to farming or crafts during middle age, and then shifts back to some sort of semiretired position with advancing years. (Persons who designated themselves as retired from an occupation were classified in that occupation in our fivefold classification scheme.) Occupational mobility does vary somewhat by age, but the general pattern of movement remains. Those under the age of 30 change occupations about 15% more than the total sample, while those over 50 change occupation classification very slightly more than does the total sample. In general, the age effect is present but not a dominating factor.

There are two other aspects worth noting about the percentage who change occupations. The proportion changing occupation seems to decline through time as the economy matures. In 1850, Utah is definitely a frontier area being settled rapidly by immigration largely from Europe. At the end of the period, the large migration has ended and the arable land was largely under cultivation. Perhaps the decline in opportunities to shift into farming combined with the maturing of the economy outweigh the factors we would expect to increase the opportunities for occupational change—more education, increased specialization in the economy, and structural shifts in the labor force toward crafts and white-collar employment. The second interesting characteristic concerns the very small increase in the percentage changing occupation when the occupations are observed over two decades rather than one. The increase is never more than 3%. This result suggests that occupational change is confined to a subset of the population. Longer intervals between observation increases the percentage slightly, but there appears to be a substantial percentage of the population that never changes occupation. For the households traced through three censuses (1860, 1870, 1880), just over half did not change occupational class. Of the remaining households, a substantial number (36%) changed occupation twice.

The proportion of farmers who shift into other occupations rises as the economy matures from 18% in the 1850–60 decade to 25% between 1870 to 1880. This is consistent with general trends in the economy as more nonfarm opportunities become available. Similarly, the fraction of the nonfarmers moving into farming declines from 54% to 33% as the economy matures. (The 20-year intervals show the same general patterns.) These movements into and out of farming highlight the difficulty of assigning status change to occupational movements. Farming represents a heterogeneous occupation associated with a wide variance of income and wealth such that unskilled labor is the only definitive case of lower economic status than farmer, and yet only white-collar occupation has unambiguously higher status than farming (assuming that wealth and income are closely associated with status).

The movement of unskilled workers is of special interest since normative judgments are often premised upon some barrier to upward mobility for this group. In nineteenth-century Utah, most unskilled workers were able to move into other occupational classifications. At most, less than one-fourth of the unskilled stayed in that classification between any two censuses. The majority moved into farming with another sizable group moving into the crafts. For the two-decade comparisons (1850–70, 1860–80, 1880–1900), those trapped as unskilled laborers declined slightly as the economy matured. Those moving from the higher status occupations into the unskilled labor classification showed no trend, being less than 10% throughout.

Residential mobility shows a pronounced tendency to decline with time. The percentage choosing to change counties declines quite dramatically from 57% in the initial two decades to levels around 20% at the end of the century. (A small part of the initial county change, especially in the 1850–60 period, is spurious due to the realignment and formation of new counties.) It should be emphasized that all migration observed here is being conducted by household heads so that the initial move of leaving home is not being measured. Moreover, virtually all the males who "headed" households were married, so that the migration would undoubtedly be larger for the general population in contrast to the particular households in our sample. In spite of this selection bias, there was substantial movement across county lines in the Utah economy.

In spite of the fact that the individuals in the urban area of Salt Lake County (6,157 persons in 1850, 19,337 in 1870, and 77,725 in 1900) enjoyed higher wealths and incomes, migratory flows were largely from rural counties to other rural counties and from Salt Lake County to rural counties. However, the movement from Salt Lake County to the rural areas sharply declines over time. It is likely that this type of migration was associated with desires for land ownership that might gradually lead to more wealth accumulation. The movement from a rural county to Salt Lake County was quite small throughout the period.

The interaction of residential and occupational change reported at the bottom of table 5.7 shows that a significant share of the population (24% in the 1850–70 period rising to 53% in the 1880–1900 period) made neither residential nor occupational change. The next largest category tends to be those who change occupation but not county of residence. Like those who change neither, this category tends to rise through time as one might expect with the increased population allowing more extensive specialization. The percentage of those who change both county of residence and occupation falls through time as does the percentage of those shifting counties but not occupation. As will be seen later, there is a relationship between occupational and residential changes, but the changes do occur separately more often than together.

Table 5.7 exhibits a pattern of substantial occupational and residential change as measured by one-decade intervals. The rates of change in both areas show tendencies to decline as this frontier economy matures. Selection biases in the sample probably lead to an understatement in both the rate of occupational and residential change. However, the gradual increase in the average age of this sample contributes somewhat to the observed decline in occupational and residential change. If one considers only those age 50 in the initial census, the trends are very similar. For those below the age of 30, the patterns of decline are less noticeable.

### 5.5.2 Determinants and Consequences of Occupational and Residential Change

Table 5.8 reports probit regressions estimating the effects of various influences on the probability of changing occupational class as defined by the fivefold classification. Wealth (interacting with occupation), age, and initial occupations influence the probability of changing occupation. While the coefficients of a probit regression are not marginal effects, the significance and relative importance of each variable may be assessed from the equations reported here (the results were very similar with a logit specification). In table 5.8, age has a flattened U effect upon the probability of changing occupation, with a higher probability of change in younger years, a decline in probability to about age 50, and a slight increase in later years as individuals retire or shift to lighter work. Lower wealth increases the probability of occupational change. The effect is statistically significant and fairly large in mag-

**Table 5.8**      **Probit Regressions on Change in Occupation**

| Variables | 1860–70 | | | | 1870–80 | | | |
|---|---|---|---|---|---|---|---|---|
| | B | \|t\| | B | \|t\| | B | \|t\| | B | \|t\| |
| Age | −.023 | 2.25 | −.019 | 1.78 | −.051 | 3.47 | −.053 | 3.41 |
| Age² | .00026 | 2.14 | .00024 | 1.89 | .0004 | 3.10 | .0004 | 3.03 |
| LNTW | −.069 | 5.19 | −.008 | .52 | −.071 | 3.96 | −.005 | .25 |
| T | −.013 | 1.91 | .005 | .67 | −.0001 | .02 | .008 | 1.19 |
| FBE | .044 | .87 | .007 | .14 | .049 | .80 | .08 | 1.17 |
| R | −.086 | 1.67 | .16 | 2.85 | −.094 | 1.13 | .19 | 2.05 |
| W | — | — | .66 | 5.12 | — | — | .46 | 3.43 |
| C | — | — | .57 | 8.42 | — | — | .42 | 4.77 |
| S | — | — | .28 | 1.75 | — | — | 1.17 | 6.66 |
| L | — | — | 1.41 | 18.99 | — | — | 1.79 | 14.94 |
| Constant | .717 | 3.39 | −.427 | 1.88 | 1.54 | 3.94 | .408 | .97 |
| N | 2903 | | 2903 | | 1894 | | 1894 | |

*Source:* Income and Wealth Project.

*Control group:* United States–born farmers in Salt Lake County.

nitude relative to the other variables in the regression. The effects of both age and wealth on occupation are consistent with the investment view of occupational change outlined earlier. Duration in the Utah economy (T) reduces the probability of changing occupation but is not significant in the 1870–80 regression. Foreign birth has no effect on occupational change while rural residence has a statistically marginal effect in the 1860–70 regression.

When occupations are added to the regression, wealth loses its statistical significance. The nonfarm occupational classes have higher probabilities of changing occupation than farmers when other characteristics are controlled. The addition of the occupational classes to the regression also produces a positive effect of rural residence on the probability of changing occupational class.

Table 5.9 with estimates of the probability of moving as measured by changing the county of residence is quite similar to table 5.8. However, the probability of changing county of residence tends to decline with age. The wealth of the household again has an inverse relationship to the probability of change. Duration is marginally important at best. The major difference in the determinants of the probability of changing occupations or residence is the effect of foreign birth on residence change. Clearly, the foreign born are reluctant to shift their residence. The effect is relatively large and robust under a variety of specifications. The foreign born were apparently more likely to live near others of similar nationality for perhaps cultural and informational reasons—a settlement pattern comparable to the immigrant experience elsewhere.[26] Perhaps this reluctance to move to new economic opportunities explains some of the early disadvantages in wealth holdings that the foreign born apparently had in the Utah economy. This effect of foreign birth on choice illustrates another aspect of interaction of Ricardian and choice variables.

The introduction of initial occupations into the probit regression does not eliminate the effect of wealth on the probability of moving in contrast to the interaction of occupation and wealth in determining occupational change. In an alternative specification not detailed in table 5.9, change of occupation was added to the regression predicting change of residence. Occupational change increases the probability of moving, but wealth still reduces the probability of moving independent of the occupational change. Thus, being poor influences occupational change, but it also influences residential change independent of the occupational effect.

The equations in tables 5.8 and 5.9 confirm the importance of wealth, ex ante occupation, and age as influences on the occupational choice and the influence of age, wealth, and foreign birth on residential choice. The patterns of coefficients are consistent with maximizing strategies.

Table 5.9     **Probability of Changing County of Residence (Probit Regression)**

| Variables | 1860–70 | | | | 1870–80 | | | |
|---|---|---|---|---|---|---|---|---|
| | B | \|t\| | B | \|t\| | B | \|t\| | B | \|t\| |
| Age | −.0068 | .63 | −.0066 | .61 | −.036 | 2.6 | −.035 | 2.07 |
| Age² | −.00007 | .55 | −.00008 | .58 | .0002 | 1.72 | −.0002 | 1.33 |
| Ln TW | −.028 | 2.10 | −.029 | 2.04 | −.056 | 2.98 | −.066 | 3.03 |
| (Initial year) | | | | | | | | |
| T | −.01 | 1.45 | −.011 | 1.51 | .010 | 1.56 | .005 | .65 |
| FBE | −.21 | 3.99 | −.218 | 4.18 | −.129 | 1.94 | −.154 | 1.90 |
| R | −.08 | 1.56 | −.076 | 1.34 | −.116 | 1.40 | −.119 | 1.09 |
| W | — | — | −.21 | 1.54 | — | — | .056 | .31 |
| C | — | — | .10 | 1.42 | — | — | .253 | 2.31 |
| S | — | — | −.185 | 1.12 | — | — | .320 | 1.56 |
| L | — | — | −.009 | .13 | — | — | .335 | 2.79 |
| Constant | .316 | 1.45 | .314 | 1.39 | .574 | 1.55 | .358 | .77 |
| N | 2903 | | 2903 | | 1894 | | 1894 | |

*Source*: Income and Wealth Project.

*Control group*: United States–born farmers in Salt Lake County.

### 5.5.3 Occupational Change and Economic Mobility

Occupational mobility is usually studied independently of income or wealth mobility. The model of choice discussed earlier implies that the two types of mobility are intertwined. The importance of the path of choices taken may be explored by forming variables representing the alternative paths taken and regressing wealth on such variables. There are three ways of examining the data. Choice paths (occupational paths such as farmer to white-collar or residential paths such as urban to rural) may be correlated with ex ante wealth in order to see the relationship of wealth or income to subsequent occupational or residential movement. For example, one could use the correlation of occupational choice paths taken from 1860 to 1870 as observed in the census with 1860 wealth to analyze who took such paths. One may then reverse the process to examine the consequence of a particular path on subsequent wealth by regressing ex post wealth on the paths taken. Finally, one may examine the effect of choice paths on the rate of wealth accumulation between two years observed, testing whether changes in occupation and residence enhanced economic mobility.

If individual characteristics determine the rate of growth of wealth, $R$, then

(2) $$W_{70} = e^{Rt}W_{60}$$

where $t$ represents time and the subscripts indicate the census year. Taking logarithms and transforming, we have

(3) $$\ln(W_{70}) - \ln(W_{60}) = Rt.$$

The left-hand expression is the dependent variable for some of the behavioral regressions that we consider. We assume, given our earlier arguments, that $R$ is a function of choice, Ricardian, and random elements.[27]

The number of potential paths with two observations is equal to $N^2$ where $N$ is the number of available choices. Thus, with five occupational alternatives and two residential alternatives, there are 49 possible choice paths. Even a large data set does not make this kind of specification particularly useful or productive. Consequently, the variable set will be shortened in different ways to try to illustrate some of the important results of choices on wealth.

Table 5.10 starts with the simplest possible specification, looking at the effect of change versus no change. The control group is composed of households who change neither occupational category nor county of residence. The regression on ex ante wealth (1860) confirms the results of the previous analysis. It is the poorer households that choose to change occupations and residence holding the effects of age, duration, and birthplace.

Table 5.10          General Effects of Occupational and Residential Change on
                    Wealth (1860–70)

| Variables | LNTW1860 | LNTW1870 | ΔLNTW from 1860 to 1870 |
|-----------|----------|----------|-------------------------|
| Age | .046 | .032 | −.014 |
| Age$^2$ | −.00043 | −.00039 | .00004 |
| FBE | −.408 | −.194 | .214 |
| T | .080 | .053 | −.027 |
| ChgRes | −.106 | −.330 | −.224 |
| ChgOcp | −.194 | −.076 | .118 |
| Constant | 5.43 | 6.46 | 1.03 |
| $R^2$ | .23 | .10 | — |
| N | 2,534 | 2,534 | |

Note: All coefficients significant at the .05 level.

Column 2 of table 5.10 gives the effects of the choices on subsequent wealth. Once again, note that the effect of foreign birth and duration decline in influence on the cross-section of the 1870 regression relative to the regression of 1860 shown in table 5.4. The reason for decline is clear in table 5.10. Households with a foreign-born head have less wealth, but they enjoy higher rates of wealth accumulation, while those with longer duration in the economy have more wealth but lower rates of wealth accumulation. Changing residence is costly and reduces the rate of wealth accumulation relative to those who do not change. (No counterfactual statement about the paths of the two groups—those who change and those who do not—is intended here.) Those who change occupation enjoy higher rates of growth of wealth relative to the control group. These results highlight a finding that is consistent through different years and different specifications. That is, recovery and gain from occupational change occur more quickly than recovery and gain from residence change.

In table 5.11 the possible choices are expanded by considering the following paths: (1) Those who change neither occupation nor county of residence—the control group; (2) those who change their residence classification from urban to rural or vice versa—ChgResCl; (3) those who change occupation in a narrow sense within a classification but do not shift out of the occupational class—ChgOcpS; (4) those who change their occupational class—ChgCl; and (5) those who change their county of residence within the rural sector—ChgRRes.

Those who move from urban to rural, or vice versa, are poorer than the control group in 1860, with wealth holdings 16% below the wealth of the control group ceteris paribus. The relative position changes little by 1870 with their wealth now 17% below the average so that their rate of wealth accumulation over the decade is essentially the same as that

Table 5.11    **General Effects of Occupational and Residential Change on
Wealth (1860–70)**

| Variables | LNTW60 | LNTW70 | ΔLNTW from 1860 to 1870 |
|---|---|---|---|
| Age | .046 | .032 | −.014 |
| Age² | −.00043 | −.00039 | .00004 |
| FBE | −.401 | −.202 | .199 |
| T | .080 | .052 | −.208 |
| ChgResCl | −.159 | −.169 | −.010 |
| ChgRRes | −.069* | −.433 | −.364 |
| ChgOcpS | .023* | .164 | .141 |
| ChgCl | −.232 | −.136 | .096 |
| Constant | 5.43 | 6.46 | 1.03 |
| R² | .23 | .10 | — |
| N | 2,534 | 2,534 | |

*Not significant at .05 level.

of the control group. Those changing county of residence within the rural sector are different from those making an urban-rural shift. Moreover, their wealth is not statistically different from the wealth of the control group in 1860 but is 43% below that group in 1870. Their rate of wealth accumulation is the lowest of any of these possible general paths.

Those changing occupation *within a general class* are not statistically different in 1860 wealth holdings from those who make no change. However, they do enjoy a higher rate of wealth accumulation ending the period with wealth holdings 14% larger than those of the control group, ceteris paribus. The causation of this pattern is not clear. Occupational change could be a name change to ratify the increased wealth position, or it could reflect choice that led to a higher return. However, those changing occupational *classifications* obviously are poorer than others with wealth holdings 23% below the control group. It seems clear that the change across classes is fundamentally different from the changes within classes; for those changing classes enjoyed a high rate of growth or wealth making up nearly half of the disadvantage by 1870 that they suffered in 1860.

The regressions of table 5.12 are designed to look backward from 1870 occupational classifications and demonstrate the heterogeneity that exists in any cross-sectional classification because of the different paths by which individuals have reached a particular position. These regressions also show the Ricardian nature of different paths even though individuals have arrived at the same occupation or place of residence by a certain date. In each occupational class except laborers, those households in other occupations choosing to shift into an oc-

**Table 5.12**            **Consequence of Choice on Wealth (Same Terminal Occupations)**

| Variables | LNTW60 | LNTW70 | ΔLNTW from 60 to 70 |
|---|---|---|---|
| Age | .042 | .012 | −.03 |
| Age$^2$ | −.00038 | −.00007 | .00031 |
| WW | .649 | 1.188 | .539 |
| OW | −.025* | .386 | .411 |
| CC | −.318 | −.158 | .160 |
| OC | −.264 | −.327 | .063 |
| SS | .149* | .098* | −.051 |
| OS | −.337 | −.356 | −.019 |
| LL | −.886 | −.890 | −.004 |
| OL | −.314 | −.688 | −.374 |
| OF | −.448 | −.116 | .332 |
| FBE | −.379 | −.201 | .178 |
| T | .074 | .045 | −.029 |
| RR | −.113 | −.571 | −.458 |
| UR | −.228 | −.576 | −.348 |
| RU | −.030* | −.302 | −.272 |
| Constant | 5.68 | 7.05 | 1.37 |
| $R^2$ | .28 | .21 | — |
| N | 2,534 | 2,534 | |

*Control group:* Native farmers in Salt Lake County (in both 1860 and 1870).
*Not significant at .05 level.

cupation tended to have lower wealth, ceteris paribus, than those already in that occupation in 1860. For example, the farmers, craftsmen, service workers, and laborers shifting to white-collar occupations (collected together as OW) had about the same wealth as the control group of households who remained farmers in both census years. The white-collar workers from whom they were taking cues (W60) were doing significantly better than the control group in 1860. This result holds for white-collar and service occupations and farmers. The pattern described above is also true of those in the urban area choosing to move to the rural area. Not only were they doing more poorly than other households of Salt Lake County when they chose to move, they also were worse off than rural households. On the other hand, rural households choosing to move to the urban area of Salt Lake County were richer than those choosing to remain in the outlying counties. The choices seem consistent with a set of cues drawn from the economy. Households choosing a characteristic, generally, were poorer than those who possessed the characteristic. Thus, households tried to acquire characteristics with high return.

We now come to the question of whether or not they could expect to attain the position of those they emulated. The answer is clearly no in the short run. The middle column of table 5.12 once again illustrates the importance of duration. In every case except laborers, those who moved to an occupation were less well off than those who had been in the occupation at least 10 years. Some of those choosing to change were able to narrow the gap through increased growth rates, such as those moving into farming, but not even this narrowing occurred for the other occupations. All residence choices except staying in the urban county produced disappointing growth in wealth. Notably, those households moving to the urban area had lower growth rates of wealth than households in the urban area in both censuses but higher than households staying in a rural county or moving to the rural counties. Table 5.12 also illustrates the difficulties of interpretation of cross-sectional regressions such as those in tables 5.4 and 5.5 that appear to show strategies for increasing income or wealth. Choosing a characteristic is not the same as having it. Households could not acquire an advantageous earlier position such as urban in 1860 or white-collar occupation in 1860. The only choices in 1860 were ones given occupation and county of residence in 1860. We turn to table 5.13 for an examination of this type of choice process.

Table 5.13 is designed to help answer two basic questions about occupational and residential choices. Given each occupation or place of residence, who chooses to change? If a change is made, how does

**Table 5.13**      **Impacts of Occupational and Residential Change on Wealth and Income (Same Initial Occupations)**

| Variables | LNTW60 | LNY60 | LNTW70 | LNY70 | Growth of TW | Growth of Y |
|---|---|---|---|---|---|---|
| WW | .68 | −.03* | 1.04 | .38* | .36 | .41 |
| WO | .47 | −.83 | .39* | .26* | −.08 | 1.09 |
| CC | −.28 | −.19 | −.19 | −.05* | .09 | .14 |
| CO | −.36 | −.38 | −.11* | −.40 | .25 | −.02 |
| SS | 2.79 | .40* | 3.31 | 1.47* | .52 | 1.07 |
| SO | −.30* | −.10* | .25* | −.30* | .55 | −.20 |
| FO | .05* | −.24 | −.13* | −.19* | −.18 | .05 |
| LL | −.98 | −.66 | −.85 | −.12 | .13 | .54 |
| LO | −.59 | −.41 | −.24 | −.18 | .35 | .23 |
| RR | −.20 | −.16* | −.51 | −.25 | .31 | −.09 |
| RU | −.17* | −.25* | .17* | .21* | .34 | .46 |
| UR | −.23 | −.33 | −.58 | .04* | −.35 | .37 |
| $R^2$ | .39 | .11 | .21 | .06 | | |
| N | | 1,213 | | 1,213 | | |

*Control group:* United States–born farmers living in Salt Lake County who make no changes.

*Not significant at .05 level.

the growth rate of those who change compare with those starting from the same position who did not change?

In the analysis summarized in table 5.12, those who converged to the same occupation or residence can be analyzed by the paths they had chosen to reach that position. Table 5.13 reverses the perspective of table 5.12 by examining individuals who start with ostensibly the same characteristics and subsequently choose different paths. Table 5.13 also reports regressions on the log of income in addition to those for wealth. The table is limited to the choice variables since the parameter specifications for the other variables are largely independent of the choice specification. The patterns of table 5.13 are generally consistent with the market adjustment model suggested earlier. Those with lower income and wealth in each class (such as WW compared to WO) tend to be those who move to other occupations or residence, with the exception of the unskilled laborers where those doing best are also those likely to move. Shifting occupation or residence has some cost associated with it, so that wealth in 1870 or the rate of growth of wealth may at first be adversely affected by movement. Income, however, adjusts more quickly so that choices, in general, improve the income position of those who change relative to others.

White-collar households provide a good illustration of the basic pattern postulated. White-collar households who shift to other occupations have lower wealth in 1860 than those who remain white collar. Their income is also significantly lower. This pattern holds for craftsmen, farmers, and service workers (perhaps), but not laborers. Those shifting out of white-collar employment did not improve their wealth position in 1870 relative to the control group or those remaining in that occupation. This was also true of those households shifting out of farming. But the shift in occupation did help the income position of both groups (WO, FO), moving them from well below the control group to a position of at least equality or perhaps above. This difference between the effect of choice on income and wealth seems to be strong evidence supporting the investment explanation of choice. It also suggests an important explanation for the differences between wealth and income mobility that does not rest on the relative importance of transitory elements.

Do the paths taken tend to produce convergence in the income and wealth distributions in and of themselves? Obviously many other factors such as the stochastic elements of the distribution will keep inequality and economic mobility high. But do choices tend to at least ameliorate the inequality and generate added economic mobility? The results of table 5.13 suggest that choice ameliorates inequality with some exceptions. The white-collar workers who remain in their occupation have higher wealth in 1860 and the same income level ceteris paribus. Since the growth profile of their wealth between 1860 and 1870 is steeper than those of the control group, inequality is increased in terms of both income and wealth. This result suggests that there may be barriers to successful penetration of the highest return occupations and that these barriers create inequality and prevent some mobility. Both those craftsmen who change and those remaining in the occupation have low wealth in 1860 but steep growth profiles producing some wealth convergence. Most important, both laboring groups enjoy wealth and income profiles that are steeper than the control group. Since their wealth and incomes were well below those of the control group in 1860, this effect produces convergence. The group shifting out of farming suffers a wealth loss, producing some divergence in the wealth distribution although their income gain moves the income distribution in the other direction. (The service sector is too heterogeneous and small to give consistent results.) Those changing residential classification enjoy high gains in income and start from a position below the control group so that some convergence occurs. Those moving from Salt Lake County to the rural area lose in terms of wealth growth but gain a high rate of income growth. The most important changes involve laborers who move to other occupations. This group clearly benefits from their choices. Since this group is rather large, their gains in income and wealth are important sources of economic mobility. In sum, the choices produce convergence in the distribution of income with less effect on wealth. The total effect of all such change would be marginal.

## 5.6  Conclusion

We have considered economic mobility from a variety of vantage points including movements within the income and wealth distributions as well as residential and occupational change. Measurement from these different viewpoints leads to several conclusions about mobility in this nineteenth-century enconomy:

1. The Utah economy was characterized by substantial mobility within the income distribution with only slightly less mobility within the wealth distribution. (See tables 5.2 and 5.3.) Both wealth and income distributions evidence substantial cross-sectional inequality. There is no well-defined reference point against which to measure this economic mobility. Nevertheless, movement of at least two quintiles within the income distribution by over one-third of all households seems convincing evidence of mobility. This conclusion is not meant to imply that there was no rigidity or inertia within the income or wealth distribution. Clearly, initial position in either tail of the distributions greatly influenced the future income or wealth of the household. Mobility appears to decline somewhat over the 50-year period.

2. The stochastic elements in the determination of income and wealth contribute significantly to economic mobility, but the unexplained variance of the cross-sectional regressions of tables 5.4 and 5.5 overestimates the actual stochastic influence. The unobserved, but patterned, component of the variance of income and wealth may be estimated using the intraclass correlations of table 5.6. The combination of these intraclass correlations with the cross-sectional regressions leaves a stochastic residual of 35–40% for wealth and about 50% for income. No doubt these large stochastic elements contribute a large share of the observed mobility. This remaining stochastic element is also an overestimate of the relative importance of pure chance in determining outcomes because market adjustments filter other elements. A substantial stochastic element probably remains, even accounting for this measurement problem.

3. Occupational and residential changes were common in the economy. In most cases, more than half of the households observed over a decade or two decades changed occupation, county of residence, or both. (See table 5.7.) The probability of both occupational and residential change decreased with wealth, while the foreign born were more reluctant to change residence. (See tables 5.8 and 5.9.)

4. Those households acquiring a particularly attractive characteristic such as an occupation or county of residence did not quickly acquire income or wealth equivalent to those who acquired the characteristic earlier. (See table 5.12.) That is, the path of choice-making matters. This is not a surprising result, but it does emphasize the point that cross-sectional regressions overstate the gain from acquiring characteristics that appear to yield a high marginal return. In addition, there will be considerable heterogeneity within any occupation because of the paths individuals chose in acquiring the occupation.

5. Occupational change, especially from laborer to other categories, was positively correlated with the rate of growth of income and wealth. On balance, occupational change contributed to mobility within income and wealth distributions.

6. Residential change was negatively correlated with both wealth and the rate of wealth accumulation. (See tables 5.10, 5.11, and 5.12.) This suggests that residential change was costly, requiring some loss of capital. However, residential change improved income quite rapidly. (See table 5.13.) Presumably, these income gains eventually lead to wealth accumulation.

7. Rents on fixed characteristics such as nativity and duration in Utah declined through the nineteenth century. This produced some economic mobility. In particular, the foreign born overcame their disadvantage in income very early and were able to eliminate their wealth disadvantage by the end of the century through higher incomes

and faster rates of wealth accumulation. (See tables 5.4, 5.5, and 5.12.)

These conclusions as well as others detailed in the paper suggest an economy with high mobility within the distributions of income and wealth. This mobility, generated by luck, choices, and changes in rents, must have made inequality more palatable. To go from homespun clothing, if not rags, to modest riches was within the reach of many households, even though the extremes of success eulogized by Horatio Alger were less likely. Social stratification was not an apt description of this large sample drawn from a frontier state.

How general are these results? What of those households who enter and disappear within the sample? Are they fundamentally different from those studied, so that the sample presents a distorted view of mobility within the Utah population? We have no reason to believe that the selection processes operating were such as to invalidate the basic findings of this paper. Because of the religious nature of the settlement, relatively few households migrated out of Utah. Those who did migrate in and out of the state often had not intended permanent settlement (e.g., soldiers). A few households migrated from Utah to Mormon settlements in surrounding states, although the settlements in California, Nevada, Arizona, and Idaho tended to be settled by Mormons with only a temporary or no stay in Utah. Households omitted from the census are also omitted from much of the analysis. Of the 1891 individuals of whom we have record in Utah in 1859 and again in 1861 in our sample, approximately 224 were not found by us in the census of 1860. It is possible that name resemblance is slight so that the individual has been missed. Some individuals may have left the state temporarily. A sample of these households ommitted from the census had an average income of $740 compared with $710 for the households found in the 1860 and 1870 census. The only other important group likely to be underrepresented in our sample would be disaffected Mormons who had stopped paying contributions to the Church and left Utah. We have no information about this group. Thus, we have no evidence that the sample is biased in a way that distorts the results.

Will these results generalize for the United States in general in the nineteenth century? It would seem likely that frontier states like Utah offered increased economic mobility. This is what made the frontier attractive. There is no particular reason to believe that Utah was unusual for a frontier state other than the cultural or religious milieu. Most of the forces we have examined such as occupational or residential choice, decline in rents to fixed characteristics and stochastic influences are not greatly influenced by the cultural and religious context. It remains to be seen if more settled states to the east had different patterns of economic mobility.

# Appendix
## Definition of Variables

Occupations and Occupation Paths

There are five occupational categories:

W—White-collar and self-employed professionals
F—Farmers and ranchers
C—Craftsmen
S—Service workers
L—Unskilled laborers

When occupational paths are observed, they are formed as two letters. The first letter is the occupational class in the initial year and the second letter the class of the second year. For example, WF would be a dummy variable equal to one if the occupation is white-collar initially with a change to farmer in the second period. Most times we have aggregated changes such as WO (white-collar and a change to any other occupation).

Residence

We have just two classifications:

U—Urban - Salt Lake County
R—Rural - All other counties

Paths are formed in the same way as occupations (i.e., UU, UR, RU, RR).

Other Variables

FBE—Foreign birth

T—Duration in Utah calculated as year of the dependent variable (e.g., 1870TW) less year of first observation in Utah

ChgRes—Dummy variable equal to one if initial county not equal to terminal county

ChgOcp—Dummy variable equal to one if initial occupation (not necessarily occupational class) not equal to terminal occupation

ChgResCl—Dummy variable equal to one if residential class changes (i.e., UR or RU = 1)

ChgOcpS—Dummy variable equal to one if occupation changes but not occupational class

ChgCl—Dummy variable equal to one if occupational class changes

ChgRRes—Dummy variable equal to one if household moves from one rural county to another

$Y_{60}$ or $_{70}$ etc.—Income calculated on tithing paid, adjusted for percentage tithing paid was of a full tithe (10% of income)

$TW_{60,70,80}$ etc.—Total gross wealth from either the census or tax assessments.

# Notes

1. See McCall (1973), Hart (1976), Lillard and Willis (1978), and Klevmarken and Lybeck (1980), for studies on contemporary mobility, and Blinder (1980) for a summary of contemporary United States income inequality.
2. For examples, see Lipset and Bendix (1963) or Blau and Duncan (1967).
3. Most historical studies of income or wealth mobility concentrate on wealth; see Curti (1959), Pessen (1973), and Doherty (1977). Contemporary studies usually focus on income; see McCall (1973), Lillard and Willis (1978), Shorrocks (1976), and Schiller (1977).
4. See Kearl and Pope (1983a, 1984a).
5. We have analyzed intergenerational effects in Kearl and Pope (1984b).
6. See Friedman (1957).
7. See Modigliani and Ando (1957), Miller (1965), and Lilliard and Weiss (1979).
8. See Mincer (1974).
9. For a survey see Sahota (1978).
10. For surveys see Mincer (1970) and Blaug (1976).
11. All symbols are defined in table 5.1.
12. See Shorrocks (1978).
13. In fact, quintile boundaries are drawn in a way that does not divide the sample into five groups of equal size. There is heaping on values such as $500 or $1,000 so that boundaries would normally fall on such values. The boundaries are adjusted up or down so that all persons with the same wealth or income are in the same quintile. That procedure yields groupings that deviate from 20% of the sample.
14. This mobility can be compared to the income mobility found in McCall (1973), p. 78. When the Utah data are rendered "comparable" to McCall's data, there appears to be more mobility in Utah. Schiller (1977, p. 932, table 1) suggests that there is much less contemporary mobility. We have found no nineteenth-century data with which to compare.
15. Again, there are few sources with which to compare. Fragmentary evidence may be drawn from Pessen (1973), Curti (1959), and Doherty (1977). The mobility in Utah seems to exceed the norm, although there is little evidence about income or wealth mobility.
16. The effect of such adjustments is reported in Kearl and Pope (1984b).
17. These issues are explored extensively in the literature. For examples, see Sjaastad (1962) and Becker (1967).
18. Jencks et al. make such an inference in chap. 1 and 9 of *Inequality* (1972).
19. This correlation was emphasized in Kearl et al. (1980).
20. This is a variant of an error-component model. See Judge et al. (1980, pp. 328–59).
21. The regressions may be compared to those in Soltow (1975, p. 80) Atack and Bateman (1981).
22. Chiswick (1978) finds higher income after 13 years for immigrants in contemporary data.
23. The life-cycle patterns have been analyzed in Kearl and Pope (1983b).
24. See Haggard (1958).
25. Unfortunately, most historical studies (e.g., Thernstrom, 1973; Griffen and Griffen, 1978) have focused on more urban economies. Utah certainly displays more occupational

mobility than most of the other historical studies with so much shifting between farming and other occupations. See Thernstrom (1973, p. 234, table 9.4). Contemporary studies such as Lipset and Bendix (1963, pp. 165–81) suggest less occupational change.

26. For examples, see Handlin (1941) Schnore and Knights (1969), and Chudacoff (1972).

27. The three specifications on initial wealth, terminal wealth, and the rate of growth are not independent. Any two equations will yield the coefficient estimates of the third. That is, $b_{70} = (X'X)^{-1} X' \ln(W_{70})$ and $b_{60} = (X'X)^{-1} X' \ln(W_{60})$ while $B = (X'X)^{-1} X' [(\ln W_{70}) - (\ln W_{60})] = b_{70} - b_{60}$.

## Comment    Lee Soltow

Certainly Kearl and Pope are to be admired for this fascinating study of the Mormon population from 1850 to 1900. Their ability to trace given individuals for 10 or 20 years, or longer, considering their wealth, income, age, occupations, residence, urbanity, and length of residence in Utah in any decade generates a dynamic dimension not otherwise available to those of us who try to unravel the mysteries of economic growth and the constancy or change in income and wealth inequality. The tracing of individuals from one census to the next is an exacting and frustrating task because the paths of so many persons become lost from view. Kearl and Pope tell, with admirable candor, that only 2,951 households, or about 17% of the 17,000 in the Mormon sample can be found in the two federal censuses of 1860 and 1870 and that some of their tables dealing with income changes involve samples of less than 2,000. In this work, I am afraid that there is also a tendency to eliminate extremes from distributions—the young men and parents who are not heads of households and often those with zero wealth— perhaps in an attempt to be conservative in reporting results. Those who find themselves uncomfortable with tables of data limited to Mormons in Utah must understand that the Mormon sets and subsets may be our best general information source concerning the poor and rich, and they may be our only source for individual incomes in a broad spectrum of a population in the United States in the nineteenth century.

First Kearl and Pope present transition matrices for wealth and income for quintile groups that demonstrate considerable mobility from 1860 to 1870 (see table 5.1); household heads in the narrow middle range for wealth in 1860 were not often found in the same range in 1870. This middle range unfortunately has a small class interval, I suspect. The poor in the lowest quintile range were more likely to linger, and the rich in the highest range were even more likely to

Lee Soltow is professor of economics at Ohio University.

maintain their position. The overall immobility index produced a U-shaped pattern, a form generally found in data for both income and wealth from 1850 to 1900. This pattern certainly would be predicted if distributions are unimodal, with two tails, and it is unfortunate that none of the characteristics of the 10 precious income distributions are given so that we might better understand changes in relative dispersion for various ranges of the distribution in a given year as well as changes from year to year.

The paper's second major analysis deals with cross-sectional regressions, that is, with wealth or income in a specified year, related to census variables: age, occupation (considering five broad classes), nativity, years of residence, and urbanity in that year. The amazing aspect of this analysis is that the explained variation of the logarithms is, at most, 28% in the case of wealth in five separate years, and 14% in the case of income, for the ten precious income years in the half-century (table 5.5). Income variation, explained by occupation, might have doubled, with 10 or 20 occupations (as is the case with present-day distributions), but there is one undeniable conclusion: a theory of income distribution based on occupations or on noncompeting occupational groups is indeed weak as it pertains to Utah development. It would be exceedingly interesting to have access to tables like those of Kearl and Pope for some European country to see if those counterparts to our census variables had more explanatory power. Right now, I would settle for a glimpse at Kearl and Pope's income distributions for laborers, white-collar workers, and so on. Measures of dispersion for each occupation and the extent of overlap would be most revealing.

What is not properly understood is the dispersion within occupational or age groups. Consider some reasons offered by Mormon officials in 1857 for low incomes: "Been sickly nearly all the time." "Been sick since he came into the valley." "Aged and sick 2 months." "Sickly consumptive." "A very small man in a small business." "Lost 5 acres of grain by grasshoppers." "Affected seriously with rheumatism for two years." "5 acres destroyed by frost." "Crop destroyed by frost." "Old and feeble" (Soltow and May 1979).

Most of these hardships could have occurred within any occupation or age group. Some are in the nature of irregularities that might not occur in future years, but others could be permanent.

One of the great findings reported in the paper is the tendency for an individual to maintain his relative position, above or below the average, from decade to decade, in a fashion that must be due to factors outside of the census variables in a given year. By correlating residuals in one year with those in another, it was determined that explained variation can be increased to as much as 50% for income, and to even a little more for wealth. These increases might be explained in part by education, inheritance, wealth of parents, and so on. It is strange that these authors do not state the effect of wealth on income or of income on wealth in some multiple regression form. Kearl and Pope offer only tantalizing statements—that income does not properly reflect capital gains, or that the relationship between the two choice variables may be weak.

Census variables for the constrained Utah set explain 25% of total variation. Previous wealth or income explains another 25%. The authors attempt to resolve the balance of unexplained variation by investigating the dynamic variable changes in occupation and changes in residence of household heads from decade to decade. It is difficult to determine to what degree these changes enhance explained variaton in wealth, in comparing tables 5.4 and 5.12. Nevertheless, there are several noteworthy findings: laborers who changed occupations benefited in terms of both income and wealth; changes in occupations and residence tended to "ameliorate" inequality.

What is more clearly shown from the matching of names is the degree of mobility enjoyed by the population. About 40% of households heads in the matched subset had different occupations, broadly defined, in 1860 than in 1850, and this ratio dropped slightly later in the century. The percentage changing county of residence started at 39% but dropped after 1870. Unmeasured interstate movement would only enhance this strong degree of mobility.

Finally, we must face the possibility that the Utah group is exceptionally homogeneous, particularly the matched household subset. I do wish there were some brief cross-classifications of characteristics for matched and unmatched Mormon groups. Even more, I wish that Kearl and Pope in some way might ferret out a subset of the Mormons, perhaps a random sample of 100, who moved from Utah to Washington or California or elsewhere so that we could better understand interstate movement, the characteristics of these restless people.

Nevertheless, we must recognize the beauty of the Mormon records. I can't help but admire these meticulous, glorious, columns of ascertained facts from the past. The best is still to come from our indefatigable searchers as they study the numbers of children in families as well as father-son and father-daughter relationships. These will help shed light on the more permanent aspects of transition matrices. Kearl and Pope find, from their residual analysis and their transition matrices, that there is a fair degree of permanence in the position of an individual from one decade to the next. Will they find that this permanence persists from one generation to the next, or will they find the great mobility found in studies of present-day generations?

# References

Atack, Jeremy, and Bateman, Fred. 1981. Egalitarianism, inequality, and age: The rural North in 1860. *Journal of Economic History* 41:85–93.

Becker, Gary S. 1967. *Human capital and the personal distribution.* Ann Arbor.

Blau, Peter M., and Duncan, Otis D. 1967. *The American occupational structure.* New York.

Blaug, Mark. 1976. The empirical status of human capital theory: A slightly jaundiced survey. *Journal of Economic Literature* 14:827–55.

Blinder, Alan. 1980. The level and distribution of economic well-being. In *The American economy in transition,* ed. Martin Feldstein. Chicago: University of Chicago Press (for NBER).

Chiswick, Barry R. 1978. The effect of Americanization on earnings of foreign-born men. *Journal of Political Economy* 86:897–922.

Chudacoff, Howard P. 1972. *Mobile Americans: Residential and social mobility in Omaha, 1880–1920.* New York.

Curti, Merle. 1959. *The making of an American community.* Stanford, Calif.

Doherty, Robert. 1977. *Society and power.* Amherst, Mass.

Friedman, Milton. 1957. *A theory of the consumption function.* Princeton: Princeton University Press.

Griffen, Clyde, and Griffen, Sally. 1978. *Natives and newcomers.* Cambridge: Harvard University Press.

Haggard, Ernest A. 1958. *Intraclass correlation and the analysis of variance.* New York.

Handlin, Oscar. 1941. *Boston's immigrants: A study in acculturation.* Cambridge.

Hart, P. E. 1976. The dynamics of earnings, 1963–1973. *Economic Journal* 86:551–65.

Jencks, Christopher, et al. *Inequality.* New York.

Judge, George C., et al. 1980. *The theory and practice of econometrics.* New York.

Kearl, J. R., and Pope, Clayne L. 1983a. Wealth mobility: The missing element. *Journal of Interdisciplinary History* 13:461–88.

———. 1983b. Life cycle patterns in income and wealth. NBER Working Paper.

———. 1984a. Mobility and distribution. *Review of Economics and Statistics* 66:192–99.

———. 1984b. Unobservable family and individual contributions to the distribution of income and wealth. NBER Working Paper no. 1425.

Kearl, J. R., et al. 1980. Household wealth in a settlement economy. *Journal of Economic History* 40:477–96.

Klevmarken, N. Anders, and Lybeck, John A., eds. 1980.*The statistics and dynamics of income.* Clevedon, G. B.

Lillard, L. A., and Weiss, Y. 1979. Components of variation in panel earnings data: American scientists, 1960–70. *Econometrics* 47:437–54.

Lillard, Lee A., and Willis, Robert J. 1978. Dynamic aspects of earning mobility. *Econometrica* 46:985–1012.

Lipset, Seymour M., and Bendix, Reinhard. 1963. *Social mobility in industrial society.* Berkeley: University of California Press.

McCall, John J. 1973. *Income mobility, racial discrimination and economic growth.* Lexington, Mass.: D. C. Heath.

Miller, H. P. 1965. Lifetime income and economic growth. *American Economic Review* 55:834–43.

Mincer, Jacob. 1970. The distribution of labor incomes: A survey with special reference to the human capital approach. *Journal of Economic Literature* 8:1–26.

———. 1974. *Schooling, experience and earnings.* New York.

Modigliani, F., and Ando, A. 1957. Tests of the life cycle hypothesis of savings. *Bulletin of the Oxford Institute of Economics and Statistics* 19:99–124.

Pessen, Edward. 1973. *Riches, class and power before the Civil War.* Lexington, Mass.: D. C. Heath.

Sahota, Gian S. 1978. Theories of personal income distribution: A survey. *Journal of Economic Literature* 16:1–55.

Schiller, B. R. 1977. Relative earnings mobility in the United States. *American Economic Review* 67:926–41.

Schnore, Leo F., and Knights, Peter R. 1969. Residence and social structure: Boston in the antebellum period. In *Nineteenth-century cities,* ed. Stephan Thernstrom and Richard Sennett. New York.

Shorrocks, A. F. 1976. Income mobility and the Markov assumption. *Economic Journal* 86:566–78.

———. 1978. The measurement of mobility. *Econometrica* 46:1013–24.

Sjaastad, L. A. 1962. The costs and returns of human migration. *Journal of Political Economy.* 70:80–93.

Soltow, Lee. 1975. *Men and wealth in the United States, 1850–1870.* New Haven: Yale University Press.

Soltow, Lee and May, Dean L. 1979. The distribution of Mormon wealth and income in 1857. *Explorations in Economic History* 16:151–62.

Thernstrom, Stephan. 1973. *The other Bostonians.* Cambridge: Harvard University Press.

# 6 Inheritance on the Maturing Frontier: Butler County, Ohio, 1803–1865

William H. Newell

## 6.1 Introduction

In his review of Gagan's paper on inheritance patterns in nineteenth-century Ontario, McInnis observes that

> while there is a long and well-established tradition in European history of making inheritance central to analyses of social, economic, and demographic change, inheritance has played a much smaller role in American historiography. There are some descriptions of inheritance patterns in Colonial New England but only the most scattered references to nineteenth century midwestern practices. There seems to be a fairly wide presumption that an egalitarian, partible inheritance system was typical of the U.S., but the presumption is based only on very scattered evidence. (P. 142)

This study seeks to add to that evidence through an extensive micro study for Butler County, Ohio, of the evolution of prevailing patterns of testation and their underlying causes, for the 62 years from the county's formation in 1803 through the end of the Civil War.

The seminal work on inheritance in America is Philip Greven's *Four Generations,* a study of colonial Andover. Greven writes of his use of probate records, "My focus has been principally upon the problem of inheritance and the methods of transmission of estates, especially of

William H. Newell is professor in the School of Interdisciplinary Studies at Miami University, Oxford, Ohio.

I wish to acknowledge the financial support of a Summer Research Appointment from the Miami University Faculty Research Committee, and of NSF grant SOS-07995 that supported initial data collection by Alex Echols, Keith Johnson, Rebecca Kennard, Debra Kocar, Anastasia Peterson, and Christine Pryately. Also valuable have been comments by Kathleen Conzen, David Gagan, and Carole Shammas on earlier versions of this paper presented at meetings of the Social Science History Association.

land, from one generation to the next. By examining patterns of inheritance from generation to generation, it is possible to see how men used their land for the purpose of perpetuating their families and providing for the settlements of their offspring" (p. 11). Greven concludes that a system of partible inheritance held during the seventeenth and eighteenth centuries through which fathers retained control over their sons by restrictions on their bequests of land in order to provide for themselves in their old age. He does not, however, identify distinct patterns of inheritance (other than to demonstrate that primogeniture was not found in colonial Andover), trace their evolution over time, nor identify their underlying causes.

A number of other scholars have mined the probate records of colonial America for evidence on patterns of testation. Lockridge also argues that a system of "partible descent" held in Massachusetts and Connecticut during the eighteenth century (p. 156). His emphasis is on the consequent division and redivision of landholdings which put economic pressure on subsequent generations that out-migration was unable to alleviate. The result, according to Lockridge, was increased age at marriage and increased social and economic inequality. Auwer's study of colonial Windsor, Connecticut, suggests an essentially partible system as well, though from her study of the wills of male testators only, she finds that "Daughters normally received their portions in 'movables' rather than land" (p. 142). Daniel Scott Smith, citing findings from Hingham, Massachusetts, wills, claims that one common pattern was for male testators to favor sons over daughters, a pattern he notes was not followed by female testators (p. 8). He specifically recommends that nineteenth-century Midwest wills be examined for comparison to colonial wills, since "I suspect women will have a more favorable status and make more real choices" (p. 15).

When one turns to the nineteenth century and further west to observe the evolving patterns of testation as the new frontier developed into settled agricultural regions, the empirical evidence becomes even more sparse. Easterlin bemoans the fact that "we have no studies comparable to Greven's for the nineteenth century—a research gap that badly needs to be filled" (p. 68). He puts together some impressionistic evidence in support of his hypothesis that parents reduced their fertility as the declining returns on their investment in the farm made it harder to leave their children with a start in life equal to their own (and his impression that sons received two to three times the legacy that daughters did), but Bogue questions his evidence: "The plain fact is, and I am sure Easterlin agrees, we know very little about the history of inheritance and intergenerational assistance within the farm population of this country. Did practices remain more or less as established by the early British settlers? Was the system in practice indeed one of more or less equal multigeniture? Were there significant cultural differences in the assistance and inheritance patterns?'' (p. 78). This study was designed to answer these questions as well as to test out the impression and hypothesis advanced by Easterlin.

There are, in fact, a handful of studies carried out earlier in the century of Midwest farm succession that draw on data as far back as 1860. Typical are publications of the Wisconsin Agricultural Experiment Station from the 1920s and 1940s that focus on the inheritance practices of Wisconsin farmers that allowed their farms to remain intact and within the family through several generations. Because of their exclusive focus on the farms themselves, these studies provide little insight into the question posed above. Similar research strategies were followed in the few studies published in the academic literature, such as economist George Wehrwein's "The Problem of Inheritance in American Land Tenure" and sociologist James Tarver's "Intra-Family Farm Success Practices." In his paper on Wisconsin farm families from 1848 to 1948, Tarver at least compares the homestead legacies of sons and daughters, finding that sons received the family farm in 902 out of 1307 cases. Unfortunately, he lumps the entire period together, ignoring any changes in farm inheritance practices, and has no information on the relative values of legacies within each will, nor on the socioeconomic characteristics of the testators from which to formulate hypotheses about the sources of the patterns. This study is able to provide such information.

More recently, inheritance research has focused on the role of ethnicity as a determinant of testation practices. Sonya Salamon's comparison of a German with an Irish community in East Central Illinois, for example, reaches back to their formation in the latter half of the nineteenth century. She finds sharply divergent inheritance patterns that she attributes to "historical ethnic values": partible inheritance for the Germans, de facto impartible for the Irish. The partible system was linked with reduced fertility after the first generation and declining farm size; the impartible with continued high fertility, stable farm size, higher out-migration, and celibacy. Kathleen Conzen finds a different but equally dominant pattern of land transfers—intervivos bequests of farms to sons as they reached marriageable age—in her micro study of St. Martin (Stearns County, MN) from the late 1850s through the 1920s. She attributes this partible (for sons) system to the interaction of abundant land and low settlement rates with traditional German values (even though those include impartible inheritance from some members of her community). Since these studies all focus on culturally homogeneous communities, one wonders how ethnic values related to inheritance fared in more culturally diverse settings such as Butler County, Ohio.

By far the most ambitious published study of nineteenth-century inheritance patterns is Gagan's analysis of 1500 estates probated in Peel County, Ontario, between 1840 and 1900. In his 1976 paper Gagan identifies three basic systems of inheritance:

> the perfectly partible system which involved the more or less equitable distribution of the estate among the surviving heirs, and the perfectly impartible systems which favored one principal heir to the exclusion of all other claims to the estate. The third system was a curious variation of the other two. In effect the estate was devised impartibly on one, but sometimes two principal heirs who in turn were legally obligated to satisfy out of their own inheritances, or other resources, the more or less equitable provisions made by the deceased for his remaining dependents. The farmers of Ontario employed all three systems, but it was the latter one which prevailed and in turn dictated the expectancies of the survivors. (p. 129)

The systematic linkage of virtually all archival records by the Peel County Project gives Gagan the opportunity to measure the association of inheritance patterns with a wide array of socioeconomic variables, though he chooses to focus his attention on occupation, family size and composition, wealth, and farm size. In his recent book, *Hopeful Travelers,* Gagan moves beyond the cross-sectional analysis of his paper to examine the changes over time in inheritance patterns and their correlates. He finds that after the first decade, when impartible inheritance was more and the "Canadian" (favored heir plus obligations) less prevalent, the relative importance of the three patterns remained stable throughout the rest of the period. The Canadian pattern, with farmers, extensive acreage, and large families as its primary correlates, Gagan calls Canada West's solution to "dividing the indivisible," the family farm (pp. 50–58). Gagan's study provides the most appropriate comparison available for this study of Butler County.

Evidence on nineteenth-century inheritance patterns for the East Coast is now beginning to appear. Mary Ryan's *Cradle of the Middle Class* includes some quantitative data on inheritance practices in Oneida County, New York, from its frontier days in 1790 to 1865. She finds that "simple equality" increased in both rural and urban areas from an average of 20% in 1798–1824 to 50% in 1845–65, while "unequal by age and sex" declined after the first period and "unequal by sex" declined after the second, but she does not search for the source of this dramatic change. She also observes that most farmers left land to each son and household goods to each daughter. While making no attempt to determine the extent of inequality in the legacies of daughters, she notes that "about one-third of the bequests to women were clearly of lesser value than their brothers' legacies." Beyond the startling trend in equal treatment, her study leaves one with more questions than answers about the nature and determinants of inheritance practices in early Oneida County (presumably because the focus of her study is on the relation between family and community).

An unpublished dissertation by Toby Ditz on Weathersfield, Connecticut, and the surrounding agricultural communities from 1750 to 1820 provides a final point of comparison for Butler County. She finds that few daughters were excluded from land in the wills, varying from a high of 45% excluded in urban Weathersfield in 1772–74 to a low of 10% in the surrounding rural areas in 1820–21. Daughters consistently received legacies of smaller value than sons, though the proportions fluctuated widely between time periods and between rural and urban areas; in general, however, urban testators gave daughters higher proportions of the estate than did rural ones. She also finds that the "favored heir plus obligations" strategy labeled "Canadian" by Gagan was the rule in rural areas of Connecticut as well, with proportions varying from 50% to 62% of landed testators leaving their children with heavy obligations. The small sample size (less than 25 from any one time period and region) and the limited statistical analysis make her project more suggestive than definitive, but she does provide important quantitative evidence available nowhere else in the literature.

In sum, a review of the literature indicates a substantial need for a study from the Midwest on nineteenth-century inheritance patterns. Ideally, the study should provide time series data on inheritance and intervivos bequest patterns, including the value of each legacy, the sex and age of each legatee, and the extent of any obligations between legatees. It should correlate those patterns and their evolution with the socioeconomic characteristics of the testators. It should also provide time series data on such social and economic variables as age at marriage, fertility, land prices and availability, credit availability, tenancy, and out-migration so their evolving relation with inheritance can be evaluated. This study meets most, but not all, these criteria.

## 6.2  Inheritance Patterns in Butler County, Ohio

### 6.2  The County

The choice of the county was dictated primarily by ease of access to Miami University, but it proved fortuitous. The county boasts a complete set of will, deed, testamentary, tax, and inventory records. Probably because of its proximity to Cincinnati, it was settled earlier and more rapidly and its land was of higher value at midcentury than almost any other rural county in Ohio, so that the full effects of the transition from frontier to mature settlement can be observed before the Civil War. In addition, its agricultural lands were all settled at about the same rate, planted with the same crops, and grazed by the same livestock. Its ethnic groups were scattered over the county: Germans, for example, the largest identifiable ethnic group, were distributed fairly uniformly across the county. And while the county was largely rural, it did include two small manufacturing cities with a combined population of over 9,000 in 1860, allowing some glimpses into rural/urban differences. In short, Butler County appears to be an appropriate unit of analysis for a study of inheritance.

## 6.2.2   The Data

The 1,151 wills filed in the county between 1803 and 1865 provide information on place of residence, sex, marital status, number and sex of children, signature literacy, the nature and extent of obligations between heirs, and the use of intervivos bequests, as well as the nature of each legacy. These wills were linked to deed, in-lot, out-lot, inventory, tax, and testamentary records to determine wealth and the value of each legacy, as well as to verify or complete the other information. In addition, the deed records provide data on land prices. Age, place of birth (hence ethnicity), and occupation were found by linking wills to manuscript censuses of population. Again, the census serves as a check on the information from the wills such as number of children. Finally, marriage records linked to the population censuses yield age at marriage, agricultural censuses provide land use data, and death records (available only for 1856–57) allow a comparison of characteristics of testators and intestators. (For example, testators, representing about 20% of all decedents in 1856–57 aged 40 or over, were older than intestators, and a higher percentage were male.) Most of these variables, and the data collection techniques underlying them, are discussed at length in my earlier article, "The Wealth of Testators and Its Distribution: Butler County, Ohio, 1803–65" so the discussion below is limited to data collected since that paper was written.

The largest ethnic group in the county was the Germans. Two categories of Germans were used in this paper, testators born in Germany and testators of clear German ancestry. Birth in Germany was determined largely from the population censuses, though several more were identified through the wills. German ancestry was imputed in addition through evidence from wills such as religion and spelling, and through independent identification of clearly German surnames by two German scholars. Since both categories yielded similar results, the later category is reported here since the observations are more numerous if more open to question.

Obligations of a favored heir to other heirs mentioned in the wills were divided into light and heavy. In practice the distinction rested largely on whether or not land was involved, since land was much more valuable than personal property for most testators.

Average family size was calculated for all married, widowed, or divorced testators in each time period. This measure has so many limitations as an estimate of completed family size that it must be viewed as a crude indicator of fertility at best. Since it includes young testators still in the family formation portion of the life cycle, it has a downward bias; since the proportion of young testators declined steadily (from 15% under 40 in the 1830s, to 10% in the 1840s, to 4% in the 1850s, with similar figures for testators in their forties), the bias is greater in the earlier decades. Consequently, fertility was probably higher than indicated, especially in the earlier decades.

Age at marriage was estimated for the county as a whole by linking a sample of marriages for each time period before 1850 with the 1850 manuscript census of population. For the midyear of each time period, couples were selected randomly from the marriage records by the first letter of the husband's last name and linked when possible to the 1850 census, using the wife's first name for confirmation. Sampling continued until 20 matches were achieved for each time period. In order to better approximate age at first marriage, couples were dropped from the sample when the husband was over 50 at the time of marriage. Then age at marriage was calculated separately for husbands and wives.

The data on testator's age have been extended from the previous study by linking testators to the manuscript census of population for 1840 as well as for 1850 and 1860. Since that census gives 10-year age categories instead of specific ages, testators were attributed the midpoint age of their category.

## 6.2.3   The Trends

Equality in the treatment of children by Butler County testators increased substantially during the first two-thirds of the nineteenth century. Figure 6.1 sets the trends in three measures of equal treatment. The most stringent measure, labeled *absolute equality,* refers to wills calling explicitly for identical treatment of all children. After an initial decline from less than 30% to more than 20%, absolute equality increased monotonically to almost 50% by the Civil War. The second measure—*rough equality*—refers to wills that left the children legacies that varied in monetary value by no more than 10%. Rough equality increased steadily from 10% in 1803–19 to 20% in the 1830s, while absolute equality declined and leveled off; then it slowly returned to its original level while absolute equality increased dramatically. The third measure, called here *presumptive equality,* refers to the occasional will that treated all children equally except for one or more children "already taken care of." This measure never accounted for even 4% of the wills. *Comprehensive equality,* or the sum of these three measures, increased consistently from 40% in 1803–19 to just over 60% in 1860–65. While absolute equality is of some interest for its embodiment

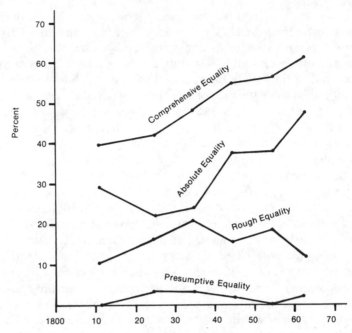

**Fig. 6.1**    Equality of treatment of children by Butler County, Ohio, testators.

of an ideal, comprehensive equality seems most relevant to a study of inheritance practices and will be the measure of equality employed in this study.

Figure 6.2 shows that the increase in equality was accompanied by an even more dramatic decline in the proportion of wills that favored sons over daughters. This study refers to such wills as *sexist,* not because the term necessarily best describes the attitudes underlying such wills, but because it draws attention to the historical roots of such behaviors in contemporary society. *Overall, sexist* wills declined in importance from nearly 40% in 1803–19 to 15% during the Civil War. The decline was most rapid at the beginning and end of the period, with the percentage leveling off just over 30% from the 1820s to 1840s.

Like the measure of equality used in this study, sexist treatment is the sum of three distinct inheritance patterns which were of roughly equal importance in antebellum Butler County. *Unigeniture,* where one or two sons were favored over daughters and other sons, declined from over 15% in 1803–19 to 5% in 1860–65, though it increased by a couple of percentage points between the 1820s and the 1840s. *Sexist equality* treated sons equally and daughters equally but favored sons over daughters. This pattern fluctuated between 12% and 15% until the 1860s,

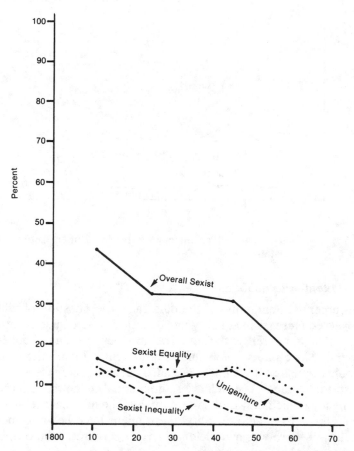

**Fig. 6.2**       Sexist treatment of children by Butler County, Ohio, testators.

when it dropped to under 8%. The last pattern, labeled *sexist inequality* here, refers to wills that favored sons over daughters while treating at least one sex unequally. This pattern exhibited the most pronounced decline. It started just under 15% in 1803–19, fell sharply to 7%–8% in the 1820s and 1830s, and fell sharply again to over 3% in the 1840s, leveling off between 2% and 3% by the end of the period.

Equal and sexist wills combined account for 80% of the testators from 1803 to 1865 who had two or more surviving children. Figure 6.3 shows that 14% of the remaining 20% wrote apparently idiosyncratic wills, with no discernible pattern to their legacies. Two other minor patterns are identified, one favoring younger children over older ones, the other favoring daughters over sons. These represent 2% and 4% of all wills, respectively, and they will be discussed commensurately in this study.

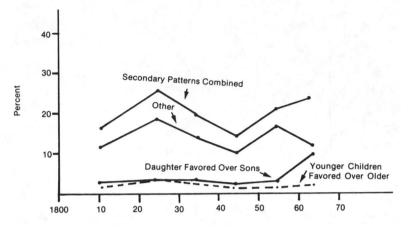

**Fig. 6.3**    Secondary inheritance patterns for Butler County, Ohio, testators.

### 6.2.4 Potential Limitations

Two potential limitations of the data raise the question of whether the observed increase in equality and decrease in sexism are statistical artifacts that do not reflect the actual behavior of testators or decedents in general. Since intervivos bequests are excluded from the analysis, one could argue that there might not have been any increase in equality because such bequests (which are seldom equal) might have increased in frequency (which they did). Alternatively, one might argue that since intestacy meant de facto equality, there might have been no increase in equality if there was a sufficiently large decrease in the proportion of decedents who died intestate.

The second question is most easily met. A sampling of decedents from the inventory records revealed in increase in intestacy. The proportion of decedents in the inventory records who wrote wills decreased from 36% (1804–9) and 38% (1815–16) to 26% (1825–26) and then to 20% (1835) and 22% (1845). (Sample sizes were between 50 and 80 for each time period.) If anything, the observed increase in testator equality actually understates the increase in equality for all Butler County decedents.

The first question is of potentially more concern, because intervivos bequests played an important role in the intergenerational transmission of wealth in some communities. However, their use appears to have increased only slightly during the period under study. The proportion of wills mentioning any intervivos bequest increases from 10% (1803–19), to 17% (1820s) and 14% (1830s) and 16% (1840s), and then to 21% (1850s), before the disruption of the Civil War (when it dropped to 8%). Even so, testators were under pressure to make mention of all legal heirs in the will to forestall disgruntled heirs left out of the will altogether from contesting it (especially if the will stipulated equal treatment), and there is strong evidence from the other documents linked to the wills that all living children were indeed mentioned in the wills. With the exception of the presumptive equality category, where all other children are treated equal except the one or two "already taken care of," all other instances where intervivos bequests were mentioned caused the will to be categorized under some form of unequal treatment—in other words, the trend toward equality occurred *in spite of* the slight increase in intervivos bequests.

## 6.3   Sources of the Trends toward Equality and away from Sexism

### 6.3.1   Characteristics of Testators Related to Equality

There are a number of interrelated testator characteristics associated with equality and its increase set out in table 6.1. Also included is one characteristic, ethnicity, that is of interest precisely because it is not related to equality or its increase.

*Wealth*

Log-wealth (in 1967–69 dollars) was strongly and inversely associated with equality. Of the poorest testators, 66% chose equality compared with only 36% of the wealthiest ones, and the percentage declined systematically with increasing wealth. The contribution of wealth to the increase in equality over time, however, came not from the least but from the most wealthy. The wealthiest testators were much less likely (24%) than testators in general (40%) to write equal wills in 1803–19, but their tendency increased much faster than the average. By the end of the period, the wealthiest were as likely as testators in general to choose equality. Testators of intermediate wealth increased much more slowly, their proportion treating all children equally. And the least wealth had no tendency to increase their already high proportions who treated all children equally.

*Occupation*

Farmers dominated the occupations in largely rural Butler County, so it comes as no surprise that their proportions over time practicing equality followed closely the trend for all testators. Other occupations, however, started with much lower proportions practicing equality but increased them much more rapidly, so by the end of the period their percentage of equal wills was identical to that of farmers. Testators identified in the 1850 or 1860 population census as not in the labor force had levels half that of farmers: 33% versus 67% in 1860–65. Their

Table 6.1 Contributions of Socioeconomic Characteristics of Testators to Increasing Equal Treatment of Children (% of Testators)

| Characteristics | N | 1803–19 | 1820–29 | 1830–39 | 1840–49 | 1850–59 | 1860–65 | 1803–65 |
|---|---|---|---|---|---|---|---|---|
| All testators | 792 | 40 | 42 | 48 | 55 | 56 | 61 | 51 |
| Log-wealth | 792 | +++ | ++ | | | | | ++66 |
| 0 | 64 | 100* | 75 | 52 | 60* | 54 | 77 | 59 |
| 0.1–0.9 | 37 | | | | | | | 47 |
| 1.0–1.9 | 357 | 40 | 38 | 43 | 57 | 51 | 57 | 53 |
| 2.0–2.9 | 323 | 24 | 31 | 53 | 52 | 61 | 60 | 36 |
| 3.0–3.9 | 11 | | | | | | | |
| Occupation | 602 | | | | | ++ | | ++51 |
| Farmer | 485 | 35 | 44 | 44 | 54 | 59 | 67 | 50 |
| Other | 80 | 80* | 25 | 38 | 44 | 60 | 67 | 27 |
| Not in LF | 37 | – – | – – | – – | 0** | 27 | 33 | |
| Residence | 792 | | | +++ | +++ | | ++ | 51 |
| Rural | 690 | 39 | 42 | 49 | 55 | 58 | 62 | 43 |
| Small town | 49 | [ | 27 | 65 | 57 | 44 | 56 | 62 |
| City | 53 | [ | 69 | 43 | 50 | 56 | 62 | |
| Children | 784 | +++ | +++ | +++ | +++ | | ++ | ++80 |
| 2 | 105 | 63 | 100* | 92 | 91 | 65 | 85 | 65 |
| 3 | 119 | 67 | 86* | 65 | 57 | 59 | 72 | 49 |
| 4 | 107 | 67* | 12* | 43 | 50 | 57 | 47 | 44 |
| 5–6 | 194 | 30 | 34 | 41 | 50 | 51 | 47 | 38 |
| 7+ | 250 | 21 | 28 | 38 | 41 | 50 | 50 | |

| | N | | | | | | | |
|---|---|---|---|---|---|---|---|---|
| Age | | | | | ++ | ++ | + | +++ |
| Less than 30 ⌐ | 379 | -- | -- | 61 | 74 | 80 | 83 | 72 |
| 30–39 | 74 | -- | -- | 50 | 43* | 75 | 70 | 60 |
| 40–49 | 43 | -- | -- | 43 | 41 | 50 | 50 | 46 |
| 50–59 | 84 | -- | -- | 44 | 33 | 50 | 46 | 44 |
| 60–69 | 178 | -- | -- | | | | | |
| 70+ | | | | | | | | |
| Marital status | 779 | | | | +++ | +++ | +++ | +++ |
| Married | 534 | 41 | 46 | 51 | 58 | 64 | 73 | 56 |
| Widowed | 245 | 38 | 31 | 42 | 46 | 43 | 45 | 42 |
| Sex | 792 | | | | | | | |
| Male | 708 | 40 | 42 | 48 | 54 | 58 | 65 | 61 |
| Female | 84 | 43* | 33* | 47 | 62 | 48 | 44 | 48 |
| German | 792 | ++ | ++ | | + | | | |
| Yes | 49 | 20* | 100** | 40 | 100** | 56 | 55 | 55 |
| No | 743 | 41 | 40 | 49 | 54 | 56 | 62 | 51 |
| Literate | 780 | | | | | | | ++ |
| Yes | 600 | 40 | 42 | 50 | 56 | 59 | 64 | 53 |
| No | 180 | 35 | 42 | 42 | 48 | 46 | 58 | 45 |

+ = .10 significance level.

+ + = .05 significance level.

+ + + = .01 significance level.

*$N \le 5$.

**$5 < N < 10$.

proportion of equal wills may have increased over time as well, but the data are too scattered to tell.

## Place of Residence

Much as farmers dominated the trend for occupations, rural testators dominated it for residency: the proportions over time of rural testators treating children equally was almost identical to the proportions of all testators. As best we can judge from the few nonrural testators prior to midcentury, the trends for small-town and city testators are quite distinct, from each other as well as from rural testators. Small-town testators started with a much lower proportion treating children equally, but the proportion increased more rapidly than for rural testators, ending at only a slightly lower level. City testators, on the other hand, simply maintained already high proportions. By midcentury, rural testators had caught up with them, and the proportions were nearly identical.

## Children

There was a strong inverse relationship between the number of children and the proportion of testators treating them equally. Eighty percent of testators with only two children treated them equally, whereas only 38% of testators with seven or more children did, and the proportion declined steadily with the number of children. Over time, however, it was the testators with the largest families that contributed most to increasing equality, primarily those with five or more children. Testators with only two or three children showed no trend because they had attained at the beginning of the period proportions attained by testators with larger families only at the end of the period.

## Age

There was also a strong inverse association between the age of testators and their tendency to treat children equally. Seventy-two percent of testators under 50 did so, while only 44% of those 70 or over did. The biggest differences were between testators over and under age 60. It was also the youngest that contributed most to the trend toward increasing equality: those under age 50 increased their proportion most rapidly, while those 70 and older showed no increase.

## Sex and Marital Status

Married men dominated the trend toward equality. Widowed testators showed a much weaker trend, and female testators showed no clear-cut trend, even though the proportion of female testators increased from 7%–8% at the beginning of the period to 18%–19% at the end.

## Literacy

Literate testators were consistently and significantly more likely to treat children equally, but illiterate testators contributed as much to the trend toward quality as literate ones.

## Ethnicity

Whether German-born or of German heritage, foreign born or a native of any particular region of the United States, or a native of Ohio, ethnicity and place of birth in general show no systematic relation to equal treatment of children, either cross-sectionally or over time.

## Summary

Equal treatment of children in the antebellum wills of Butler County, Ohio, was systematically associated with wealth, age, number of children, and literacy (and perhaps with residency and labor force participation as well). Younger, literate testators with less wealth and fewer children (perhaps city dwellers in the labor force as well) treated children equally most often. Contributions to the growth in equality came disproportionately from the most wealthy and those with the most children (who caught up with the least wealthy and those with only a few children) and from the youngest (who widened the gap with the oldest). Nonfarmers and small-town testators may also have caught up with farmers and rural testators (even though they both contributed as well), though the paucity of data precludes any confidence in the trend. The least wealthy, those with small families, and perhaps city dwellers made no contribution—their proportions treating children equally were already high at the beginning of the period; the oldest made no contribution in spite of their low initial proportions treating children equally.

## 6.3.2   Characteristics of Testators Related to Sexism

Table 6.2 presents the same set of testator characteristics as in table 6.1 in order to compare the sources of the decline in sexism with the increase in equality. Not surprisingly, very similar correlates are found, both for the extent of sexism and for its decline over time. The few differences appear minor: occupations other than farmer contributed less clearly to the decline in sexism than to the increase in equality; and all ages contributed to the decline in sexism while younger testators were most responsible for the increase in equality. In general, it appears appropriate to treat both trends as part of the same process—the sub-

Table 6.2　Contributions of Socioeconomic Characteristics of Testators to Decreasing Sexist Treatment of Children (% of Testators)

| Characteristics | N | 1803–19 | 1820–29 | 1830–39 | 1840–49 | 1850–59 | 1860–65 | 1803–65 |
|---|---|---|---|---|---|---|---|---|
| All testators | 792 | 44 | 33 | 32 | 31 | 23 | 15 | 29 |
| Log-wealth | 792 | +++ | | | | | | ++ |
| 0 ⎤ | | | | | | | | |
| 0.1–0.9 ⎦ | 101 | 0* | 8 | 29 | 20 | 19 | 8 | 15 |
| 1.0–1.9 | 357 | 44 | 34 | 35 | 30 | 25 | 17 | 32 |
| 2.0–2.9 ⎤ | | | | | | | | |
| 3.0–3.9 ⎦ | 334 | 54 | 44 | 31 | 33 | 22 | 15 | 29 |
| Occupation | 602 | | | | ++ | | | + |
| Farmer | 485 | 52 | 40 | 40 | 32 | 24 | 21 | 34 |
| Other | 80 | 20* | 42 | 31 | 11* | 20 | 6 | 21 |
| Not in LF | 37 | – – | – – | – – | 100** | 23 | 17 | 27 |
| Residence | 792 | +++ | | | +++ | | ++ | +++ |
| Rural | 690 | 45 | 33 | 31 | 32 | 24 | 16 | 30 |
| Small town | 49 | [—— 40 ——] | | | | 22 | 19 | 27 |
| City | 53 | [—— 19 ——] | | | | 6 | 10 | 11 |
| Children | 784 | +++ | +++ | + | +++ | | ++ | +++ |
| 2 | 105 | 21 | 0* | 8 | 9 | 13 | 0** | 10 |
| 3 | 119 | 25 | 0* | 15 | 14 | 24 | 12 | 18 |
| 4 | 107 | 11* | 75* | 30 | 33 | 20 | 26 | 29 |
| 5–6 | 194 | 64 | 34 | 41 | 32 | 26 | 5 | 32 |
| 7+ | 250 | 60 | 38 | 38 | 47 | 27 | 33 | 41 |

| | N | | | | | | | |
|---|---|---|---|---|---|---|---|---|
| Age | | | | | | | | |
| ⎡ Less than 30 | 379 | — | — | — | — | — | — | + |
| ⎣ 30–39 | | | | | | | | |
| 40–49 | 74 | — | — | 25 | 21 | 13 | 0 | 18 |
| 50–59 | 43 | — | — | 29 | 43* | 17 | 20 | 26 |
| 60–69 | 84 | — | — | 38 | 41 | 22 | 7 | 27 |
| 70+ | 178 | — | — | 44 | 45 | 24 | 29 | 33 |
| Marital status | 779 | | | | | | | |
| Married | 534 | 46 | 36 | 34 | 31 | 20 | 15 | 30 |
| Widowed | 245 | 38 | 28 | 29 | 32 | 26 | 14 | 27 |
| Sex | 792 | + | + | + | | | | ++ |
| Male | 708 | 46 | 35 | 35 | 31 | 22 | 16 | 30 |
| Female | 84 | 14* | 0* | 16 | 31 | 26 | 6 | 18 |
| German | 792 | | | | | | | |
| Yes | 49 | 80* | 0** | 50 | 0** | 25 | 18 | 31 |
| No | 743 | 42 | 34 | 31 | 32 | 22 | 14 | 29 |
| Literate | 780 | | | | | | + | |
| Yes | 600 | 40 | 36 | 33 | 29 | 21 | 19 | 28 |
| No | 180 | 58 | 25 | 29 | 39 | 27 | 4 | 31 |

+ = .10 significance level.

++ = .05 significance level.

+++ = .01 significance level.

*$N \leq 5$.

**$5 < N < 10$.

stitution of equal for sexist provisions in wills—with a single set of underlying causes.

### 6.3.3    Characteristics of Testators Favoring Daughters over Sons

Female testators chose this pattern three times as often as men ($p$ = .005). Professionals and small-town testators may have chosen it disproportionately as well, but the sample sizes are too small to tell with certainty. It is clear than when daughters were favored, it was because they got more than their share of land, as one might expect since land was the major form of wealth in largely rural Butler County. One final discovery is that "favored heir plus obligations" really meant "favored son plus obligations": daughters were almost never saddled with obligations to their siblings.

### 6.3.4    Interpretation

The first step in drawing hypotheses from the socioeconomic correlates of the substitution of equality for sexism is to disentangle the effects of wealth, age, number of children, and literacy, since these variables might well be expected to be correlated. (There are too few observations on testators not in the labor force or living in urban areas to determine their independent effects, even though they were undoubtedly interrelated with some of the other variables.) The statistical technique employed here is logistical regression analysis, which is preferable in this case to ordinary regression analysis since the dependent variable is dichotomous—either testators treated their children equally, or they did not.

The following equation presents the significant results of the logistic regression of wealth, age, number of children, and literacy on equal treatment of children.

$$EQUAL = -0.13\,NCLD - 0.02\,AGE + 0.57\,WRITE + 1.88, N = 366$$
$$\phantom{EQUAL = }(0.04) \phantom{NCLD} (0.0007) \phantom{+ } (0.27)$$
$$Model\,chi\,square = 39.6$$

The major result of the logistic regression analysis is that number of children ($p$ = .003), age ($p$ = .004), and to a lesser extent literacy ($p$ = .04) all retain statistically significant effects on equal treatment while the effects of wealth are removed if either number of children or age are held constant.

Since data on age are restricted to after 1840 and to those testators who could be linked to the manuscript censuses of population, the logistic regression was rerun excluding age:

$$EQUAL = -0.21\,NCLD + 0.31\,WRITE + 1.13, \phantom{xxxxx} N = 762$$
$$\phantom{EQUAL = }(0.03) \phantom{NCLD + } (0.18) \phantom{xxx} Model\,chi\,square = 68.4$$

While the significance of the overall model is increased, as in the literacy variable, by doubling the number of observations, the major finding remains the same: the apparent effect of wealth on equality of treatment merely reflects the effects of number of children or age; while age, number of children, and literacy all appear to have independent effects on equal treatment.

The modified portrait of a testator who was especially likely to treat his children equally is of a young literate testator with few children (possibly living in a city). Contributions to the increase in equality came disproportionately from the youngest testators (possibly non-farmers in small towns) and from the wealthiest testators with the largest families.

The first portrait suggests the hypothesis that equal instead of sexist treatment of children may have been a progressive, more modern approach to dividing one's estate. The fact that wealthier testators with more children caught up with their less wealthy counterparts with few children suggests that this modern approach spread to more traditional sectors of the population during the antebellum period. Because the youngest testators (perhaps nonfarmers in small towns) increased their tendency toward equality substantially even though they started the period already more likely to treat children equally, the substitution of equality for sexism does not appear to be related to any one cohort; rather it seems likely that some factor had increasing effect on young adults over time. And the tendency, if it was real, of small towns to act like rural areas only more so—increasing equality even more rapidly than rural areas did—supports the hypothesis that the factor affecting young adults was connected with the transformation of the county from frontier to mature settlement. Small towns were intimately connected to the surrounding farms and are a hallmark of settlement, unlike cities with their base in manufacturing (whose inhabitants could be expected to adopt more modern values). In sum, the hypothesis extracted from these data is that some feature of the process of transforming the frontier into mature agricultural settlement, affecting everyone but young adults most strongly, caused traditional members of the population as well as increasing proportions of young adults to adopt a modern practice that was already well accepted by more progressive members of the population.

## 6.4  Patterns of Land Inheritance

In order to develop this hypothesis further, and to compare the findings of this study to any other study in the published literature, it is necessary to focus on the primary component of the wealth being transmitted through wills, namely, land. Figure 6.4, drawn from my

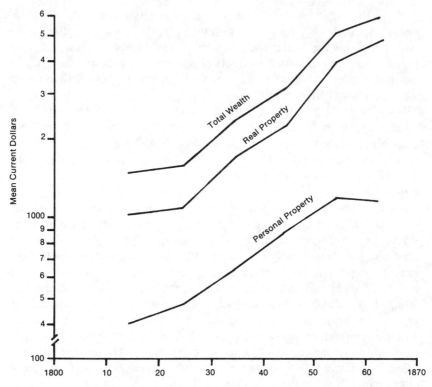

**Fig. 6.4**        Testator wealth and its components, Butler County, Ohio.

earlier study of wealth in Butler County, documents the importance of land in the total wealth of these testators. Three land inheritance patterns are examined, namely, equality, daughters preferred, and sons preferred. Two subpatterns—sons preferred but daughters included, and sons preferred and daughters excluded—are examined as well since the third pattern was the main alternative to equality and because there might be different attitudes underlying those subpatterns.

## 6.4.1  Equality

Table 6.3 presents data on the frequency of this pattern for the same time periods and testator characteristics used in the analysis of comprehensive equality. Equality in the distribution of land followed a trend so similar to that for comprehensive equality, as might be expected, that the analysis here is limited to differences in the testator characteristics associated with it.

Wealth, occupation, number of children, place of residence, sex, and marital status all had the same relations to land equality as comprehensive equality, both cross-sectionally and over time. The younger

**Table 6.3**     **Land Equality in the Wills of Butler County, Ohio, 1803–65 (%)**

| Characteristics | N | 1803–19 | 1820–29 | 1830–39 | 1840–49 | 1850–59 | 1860–65 | 1803–65 |
|---|---|---|---|---|---|---|---|---|
| All testators | 233 | 34 | 29 | 46 | 42 | 44 | 57 | 42 |
| Log-wealth | 233 | +++ | | | | | | + |
|   0–0.9 | 25 | 73* | | | | 47* | 40* | 57 |
|   1.0–1.9 | 101 | 36 | 31 | 43 | 45 | 40 | | 39 |
|   2.0–3.9 | 107 | 19* | | 43 | 40 | 47 | 62 | 42 |
| Occupation | 188 | + | | | | + | ++ | ++ |
|   Blue collar | 12 | 40* | | 42* | | 58 | 90 | 50 |
|   White collar | 18 | 34 | 32 | 40 | 44 | 42 | 58 | 56 |
|   Farmer | 155 | | | | | | | 40 |
|   Not in LF | 3 | – – | – – | – – | 0** | 25** | 0** | 17** |
| Residence | 233 | | | +++ | | + | ++ | +++ |
|   Rural | 202 | 34 | 29 | 46 | 42 | 43 | 55 | 41 |
|   Small town | 7 | 40** | | 41* | | 26* | | 23* |
|   City | 24 | | | | | 81 | | 75 |
| Children | 232 | + | +++ | +++ | | | | +++ |
|   2 | 29 | 68 | | 82* | | 58* | | 69 |
|   3 | 32 | 38** | | 58 | | 84 | | 51 |
|   4 | 32 | 21** | | 46 | | 48 | | 43 |
|   5–6 | 57 | 28 | | 30* | | 39 | 50* | 36 |
|   7+ | 79 | 21 | 33* | 41 | 36 | 49 | 46* | 37 |

(continued)

**Table 6.3** (continued)

| Characteristics | N | 1803–19 | 1820–29 | 1830–39 | 1840–49 | 1850–59 | 1860–65 | 1803–65 |
|---|---|---|---|---|---|---|---|---|
| Age | 116 | | | ++ | + | | | +++ |
| < 50 | 30 | – – | – – | 67 | 57* | 57* | 57* | 61 |
| 50–59 | 15 | – – | – – | 44* | 45 | 57* | 57 | 50 |
| 60–69 | 32 | – – | – – | 45 | 45 | 58 | 58 | 52 |
| 70+ | 39 | – – | – – | 22 | 22 | 37 | | 30 |
| Marital status | 231 | | | | + | +++ | | ++ |
| Married | 184 | 36 | | 42 | 47 | 52 | 59 | 44 |
| Other | 49 | 21* | 35 | 54 | 26* | 29 | 53 | 34 |
| Sex | 233 | | | | | | | |
| Male | 225 | 34 | | 46 | 43 | 45 | 57 | 43 |
| Female | 8 | 12** | 31 | 17** | | 40* | | 28* |
| Ethnicity | 233 | | | | | | | |
| Non-German | 223 | 34 | | 46 | 42 | 44 | 58 | 42 |
| German | 10 | 29** | 29 | 29** | | 38* | | 33 |
| Literacy | 228 | | | | | + | + | +++ |
| Illiterate | 30 | 29 | | 31 | 31 | 25* | | 29 |
| Literate | 198 | 36 | 27 | 47 | 45 | 47 | 60 | 44 |
| Comprehensive equality | | +++ | +++ | +++ | +++ | +++ | | +++ |
| Unequal | 35 | 6** | 19* | 18 | 7** | 6** | 17** | 11 |
| Equal | 196 | 83 | 55 | 80 | 86 | 80 | 93 | 81 |

+ = .10 significance level.

+ + = .05 significance level.

+ + + = .01 significance level.

*$N \leq 5$.

**$5 < N < 10$.

testators most favored land equality as they did comprehensive equality, but the contributions to the increase over time in land equality came from the oldest, not the youngest testators. The literate were more prone than the illiterate to land equality as well as comprehensive equality, but only the literate (instead of both) contributed to its increase. And Germans were less likely than non-Germans to favor land equality, and they contributed less to its increase.

### 6.4.2   Daughters Preferred to Sons

Table 6.4 shows that, while this pattern was quite uncommon, its use was more prevalent for land than for wealth in general, and it increased modestly in popularity over the period. Observations on this pattern are so scattered that any of its socioeconomic correlates must be treated as tentative, but several interesting relationships emerge from the data.

The principal finding is that females favored this pattern three to five times more often than males, an even clearer difference than for total wealth. The less wealthy contributed more to the increase in this pattern, even though wealth was not correlated with its level. Testators not in the labor force, and to a lesser extent farmers, started to adopt it late in the period, but other occupations never did. Small-town testators favored it more than rural ones, increasingly so after 1830. Married testators consistently chose it less than the widowed, single, and divorced. And the illiterate contributed much more to its increase than the literate.

### 6.4.3   Sons Preferred to Daughters

Table 6.5 shows that this pattern was more popular than overall sexism by some 15 percentage points, but their trends were again very similar. Wealth, occupation, number of children, place of residence, sex, and marital status all have the same associations with this pattern as with overall sexism. Ethnicity, literacy, and age all have the associations with it expected from land equality, thought they are different than for overall sexism.

### 6.4.4   Sons Preferred and Daughters Excluded

Table 6.6 shows that this subpattern accounted for two-thirds of the preference of sons over daughters and all of its decrease. Occupation, residency, marital status, sex, and literacy were the same as for sons preferred. The associations for age and ethnicity were like those with sexism, though different from those with sons preferred. The catching-up process for larger families was completed earlier (by the 1850s); in fact, there was an insignificant reversal after 1850—smaller rather than larger families were more likely to choose this subpattern. The biggest

**Table 6.4**  Daughters Preferred over Sons in Legacies of Land (%)

| Characteristics | N | 1803–19 | 1820–29 | 1830–39 | 1840–49 | 1850–59 | 1860–65 | 1803–65 |
|---|---|---|---|---|---|---|---|---|
| All testators | 48 | 8* | 4** | 5* | 8* | 13 | 12* | 9 |
| Log-wealth | 48 | | | | | ++ | | |
| 0–0.9 | 5 | 0** | | 6** | | 27** | | 11** |
| 1.0–1.9 | 23 | 5** | | 7* | | 18 | | 9 |
| 2.0–3.9 | 20 | 10** | | 7* | | 8* | +++ | 8 +++ |
| Occupation | 33 | | | ++ | | | +++ | |
| Blue collar | 0 | 0** | 0** | 0** | 0** | 0** | | 0** |
| White collar | 4 | 0** | 0** | 21** | | 0** | 0** | 13** |
| Farmer | 24 | 0** | 0** | 6 | | 9 | | 6 |
| Not in LF | 5 | – – | – – | – – | 0** | 33** | | 29** |
| Residence | 48 | | | | | + | | +++ |
| Rural | 40 | 0** | 7 | 6 | | 12 | | 8 |
| Small town | 7 | 0** | 0** | 11** | | 32* | | 23* |
| City | 1 | 0** | 0** | 12** | | 0** | 0** | 3** |
| Children | 48 | | | | | | | |
| 2 | 2 | 5** | | 0** | | 8** | | 5** |
| 3 | 9 | 15** | | 16** | | 13** | | 14* |
| 4 | 7 | 7** | | 7** | | 12** | | 9* |
| 5–6 | 16 | 10** | | 5** | | 17** | | 10 |
| 7+ | 13 | 3** | | 6* | | 10** | | 6 |

| Group | N | | | | | | |
|---|---|---|---|---|---|---|---|
| **Age** | 25 | | | | | + + | + + + |
| < 50 | 4 | - - | - - | | 3** | 21** | 8** |
| 50–59 | 3 | - - | - - | | 19** | 0** | 10** |
| 60–69 | 4 | - - | - - | | 3** | 10** | 6** |
| 70+ | 14 | - - | - - | | 6** | 15 | 11 |
| **Marital status** | 47 | | + + + | + | | + | + + + |
| Married | 25 | | 3** | 6 | | 8 | 6 |
| Other | 22 | | 13** | 11** | | 20 | 15 |
| **Sex** | 48 | | + + | + + + | | + + + | + + + |
| Male | 39 | | 5* | 6 | 6 | 11 | 7 |
| Female | 9 | | 25** | 33** | 33** | 33** | 31* |
| **Ethnicity** | 48 | | | | | | |
| Non-German | 45 | | 7* | 7 | | 12 | 9 |
| German | 3 | | 0** | 0** | | 19** | 10** |
| **Literacy** | 48 | | + | + + | + + + | + + + | + + + |
| Illiterate | 13 | | 3** | 10** | | 33* | 13 |
| Literate | 35 | | 8* | 6 | | 10 | 8 |
| **Comprehensive equality** | | | + | + + + | + + + | + + + | + + + |
| Unequal | 41 | 11* | 8* | 14* | 21 | 25* | 13 |
| Equal | 4 | 3** | 2* | 0** | 3** | 0** | 2** |

+ = .10 significance level.

+ + = .05 significance level.

+ + + = .01 significance level.

*N ≤ 5.

**5 < N < 10.

**Table 6.5**     Sons Preferred over Daughters in Legacies of Land (%)

| Characteristics | N | 1803–19 | 1820–29 | 1830–39 | 1840–49 | 1850–59 | 1860–65 | 1803–65 |
|---|---|---|---|---|---|---|---|---|
| All testators | 278 | 58 | 66 | 50 | 50 | 43 | 31 | 50 |
| Log-wealth | 278 | +++ | | | | | | ++ |
| 0–0.9 | 14 | 27** | | 39* | | 31* | 0** | 32 |
| 1.0–1.9 | 134 | 57 | 65 | 52 | 47 | 42 | 40* | 52 |
| 2.0–3.9 | 130 | 70 | 73 | 52 | 51 | 46 | 29 | 51 |
| Occupation | 236 | | | | | | | |
| Blue collar | 12 | 60* | | 42* | | 33 | 10 | 50 |
| White collar | 10 | | | | | | | 31 |
| Farmer | 204 | 70 | 68 | 57 | 57 | 48 | 38 | 53 |
| Not in LF | 10 | – – | – – | – – | 60* | | 33** | 56 |
| Residence | 278 | +++ | +++ | +++ | | | | +++ |
| Rural | 255 | 58 | 67 | 48 | 51 | 45 | 33 | 51 |
| Small town | 16 | 60* | | 25** | 67* | 42* | | 53 |
| City | 7 | | | 40* | 25** | 19** | | 22* |
| Children | 277 | +++ | +++ | +++ | | | | +++ |
| 2 | 11 | 26** | | 18** | | 33** | | 26 |
| 3 | 22 | 46* | | 25** | 29 | 35 | | 35 |
| 4 | 36 | 71 | | 40* | 54 | 39 | | 48 |
| 5–6 | 84 | 56 | 68 | 67 | 50 | 42 | | 54 |
| 7+ | 122 | 77 | 63 | 55 | 55 | 42 | | 57 |

| | N | | | | | | | |
|---|---|---|---|---|---|---|---|---|
| Age | 132 | – – | – – | + + + | + + + | | | + + + |
| < 50 | 15 | – – | – – | 29 | 43 | | | 31 |
| 50–69 | 12 | – – | – – | 33* | 43* | 21** | | 40 |
| 60–69 | 26 | – – | – – | 53** | 50** | 43* | 32 | 42 |
| 70+ | 79 | – – | – – | 77* | 68* | 49 | 46* | 42 |
| Marital status | 276 | | | | | | | |
| Married | 202 | 57 | 65 | 54 | 47 | 38 | 34 | 49 |
| Other | 74 | 62 | 68 | 38* | 61 | 51 | 26** | 51 |
| Sex | 278 | | | + | + | | | |
| Male | 266 | 59 | 66 | 51 | 48 | 44 | 34 | 50 |
| Female | 12 | 62** | 66 | 50** | 48 | 27** | | 41 |
| Ethnicity | 278 | | | + + + | | | | |
| Non-German | 261 | 57 | 66 | 48 | 50 | 44 | 29 | 49 |
| German | 17 | 71** | 69 | 71** | | 44* | | 57 |
| Literacy | 276 | + | + + | + + + | + | | | + + |
| Illiterate | 61 | 75 | 57* | 52 | 67 | 42 | 42 | 59 |
| Literate | 215 | 52 | 69 | 49 | 46 | | 33 | 48 |
| Comprehensive equality | | + + + | + + | + + + | + + + | + + + | | + + + |
| Unequal | 231 | 83 | 74 | 74 | 80 | 73 | 59 | 75 |
| Equal | 43 | 13 | 45 | 18* | 14 | 17 | 7 | 18 |

+ = .10 significance level.

+ + = .05 significance level.

+ + + = .01 significance level.

*$N \leq 5$.

**$5 < N < 10$.

**Table 6.6**    Sons Preferred and Daughters Excluded in Legacies of Land (%)

| Characteristics | N | 1803–19 | 1820–29 | 1830–39 | 1840–49 | 1850–59 | 1860–65 | 1803–65 |
|---|---|---|---|---|---|---|---|---|
| All testators | 194 | 45 | 53 | 29 | 39 | 29 | 6 | 34 |
| Log-wealth | 194 | + | | ++ | | | | +++ |
|   0–0.9 | 12 | [—— 18** ——] | | [—— 33* ——] | | [—— 27** ——] | | 27 |
|   1.0–1.9 | 107 | 49 | 50 | 41 | 43 | 36 | 7** | 42 |
|   2.0–3.9 | 75 | 48 | 67 | [—— 28 ——] | | 25 | 6** | 29 |
| Occupation | 162 | | | | | | | |
|   Blue collar | 10 | [—— 55* ——] | | [—— 26** ——] | | [—— 18** ——] | | 42 |
|   White collar | 139 | [—— 25** ——] | | | | | | 19* |
|   Farmer | 7 | 44 | 56 | 35 | 38 | 30 | 8** | 36 |
|   Not in LF | 6 | – – | – – | ;– | 67** | 42** | 0** | 39* |
| Residence | 194 | | | | | | | +++ |
|   Rural | 180 | 45 | 53 | 30 | 41 | 30 | 9** | 36 |
|   Small town | 12 | [—— 60** ——] | | [—— 29** ——] | | 27* | 0** | 40 |
|   City | 2 | | | | | | | 6** |
| Children | 193 | | | | | | | ++ |
|   2 | 8 | [—— 21** ——] | | [—— 9** ——] | | [—— 25** ——] | | 19* |
|   3 | 15 | [—— 31** ——] | | [—— 21** ——] | | [—— 23* ——] | | 24 |
|   4 | 24 | [—— 43* ——] | | [—— 32* ——] | | [—— 21* ——] | | 32 |
|   5–6 | 57 | [—— 51 ——] | | 40 | 44 | [—— 17* ——] | | 36 |
|   7+ | 88 | 56 | 56 | 33 | 43 | 33 | 8** | 41 |

| | N | | | | | | | |
|---|---|---|---|---|---|---|---|---|
| **Age** | 85 | | | | | | | |
| < 50 | 10 | – | – | 23* | | 14** | | 20 |
| 50–59 | 6 | – | – | 25** | | 14** | | 20 |
| 60–69 | 20 | – | – | 42 | | 23* | | 32 |
| 70+ | 49 | – | – | 44 | | 31 | | 37 |
| **Marital status** | 193 | | | | | | | |
| Married | 138 | 46 | 50 | 30 | 36 | 27 | 6** | 34 |
| Other | 55 | 53 | 53 | 43 | ++ | 34 | 5* | 37 |
| **Sex** | 194 | | | | | | | |
| Male | 183 | 45 | 53 | 31 | 38 | 23 | | 35 |
| Female | 11 | 50* | | 50** | | 27** | | 38 |
| **Ethnicity** | 194 | | | | | | | |
| Non-German | 183 | 45 | 54 | 29 | 39 | 29 | 6** | 35 |
| German | 11 | 43** | | 57** | | 25** | | 37 |
| **Literacy** | 193 | ++ | | | | | | |
| Illiterate | 43 | 62 | 43* | 38 | 38 | 32* | 0** | 41 |
| Literate | 150 | 39 | 57 | 31 | 38 | 29 | 7** | 33 |
| **Comprehensive equality** | | +++ | ++ | +++ | +++ | + | | +++ |
| Unequal | 165 | 63 | 53 | 48 | 68 | 48 | 12** | 54 |
| Equal | 26 | 13** | 32* | 8** | 6** | 12* | 0** | 11 |

+ = .10 significance level.

+ + = .05 significance level.

+ + + = .01 significance level.

*N ≤ 5.

**5 < N < 10.

difference is that the inverse association with wealth was no longer apparent.

### 6.4.5   Sons Preferred but Daughters Included

Since only 84 testators chose this particular subpattern, characteristics associated with its adoption must be viewed with caution. According to table 6.7 there was no consistent trend in this subpattern, unlike the sharp downward trend in the other one. On the other hand, the association between wealth and preference to sons clearly came from this subpattern: there was a strong and consistent tendency for wealthier testators to adopt it. Beyond that, there may have been a weak tendency for literate testators, and those with larger families, to adopt it. The other associations of occupation, residency, and ethnicity with preference to sons were contributed by the other subpattern.

This subpattern is of considerable interest, however, because it permits a test of Easterlin's impression that sons received twice as much land as daughters. We have already seen, of course, that the major development in antebellum Butler County was the substitution of equal inheritance of land for preference of sons over daughters as the dominant pattern; and even within the preferential treatment of sons, the most common practice was to give all land to sons. Still, for the 15% of all testators who chose to give land to both but more to sons, it would be useful to know what proportions they chose. In fact, the results provide a limited but startling confirmation of Easterlin's hypothesis: for every time period, the mean, median, and modal proportion of land to sons fell between 66% and 68% (with an average standard deviation of 11 percentage points). Those few testators who chose this pattern may well have been motivated by a sense of compensatory justice, as Easterlin suggests.

### 6.4.6   Favored Heir Plus Obligations

It is also possible to test the prevalence in antebellum Butler County of this land inheritance practice, also called the "Canadian" pattern by Gagan, which played such a prominent role in studies by Ditz and Gagan. The strategy employed here is to count every instance where a will mentioned an obligation of one heir to another, whether or not the obligated heir was "favored." Overall, 80% of the testators made no use of any obligations and another 5% stipulated only light obligations. These percentages were quite stable until the 1860s when the proportion employing no obligations jumped to 92% and those using heavy obligations dropped correspondingly. The pattern of favored heir (favored son, as we saw earlier) played a minor role in Butler County. It is unclear why Gagan in particular should find heavy use of obligations to accomplish equal overall treatment of heirs while this study

**Table 6.7    Sons Preferred but Daughters Included in Legacies of Land (%)**

| Characteristics | N | 1803–19 | 1820–29 | 1830–39 | 1840–49 | 1850–59 | 1860–65 | 1803–65 |
|---|---|---|---|---|---|---|---|---|
| All testators | 84 | 13 | 13 | 20 | 10 | 14 | 25 | 15 |
| Log-wealth | 84 | | | +++ | | ++ | | +++ |
| 0–.09 | 2 | 9** | | | 6** | 0** | | 4 |
| 1.0–1.9 | 27 | 12 | | | 8* | 13 | | 10 |
| 2.0–3.9 | 58 | 17* | + | | 23 | 22 | | 22 |
| Occupation | | | | | | | | |
| Blue collar | 2 | 13** | | 16** | | 5** | | 8** |
| White collar | 4 | 15 | | 16 | | | | 12*** |
| Farmer | 65 | | | 16 | | 17 | 31* | 17 |
| Not in LF | 3 | – – | | – – | 33** | 8** | 33** | 17** |
| Residence | | | | | | | | |
| Rural | 75 | 13 | | 14 | | 16 | 24* | 15 |
| Small town | 4 | 0** | | 18 | | 15* | | 13** |
| City | 5 | | | | | + | | 16** |
| Children | 84 | | | | | | | |
| 2 | 3 | 5** | | 9** | | 8** | | 7** |
| 3 | 7 | 15** | | 5** | | 13** | | 11* |
| 4 | 12 | 14** | | 14** | | 18** | | 16 |
| 5–6 | 27 | 10** | | 16 | | 25 | | 17 |
| 7+ | 34 | 15 | | 18 | | 13* | | 16 |

*(continued)*

**Table 6.7** (continued)

| Characteristics | N | 1803–19 | 1820–29 | 1830–39 | 1840–49 | 1850–59 | 1860–65 | 1803–65 |
|---|---|---|---|---|---|---|---|---|
| Age | 85 | | | | | | | + |
| < 50 | 10 | - - | - - | 11** | | | 7** | 10 |
| 50–59 | 6 | - - | - - | 12** | | | 29** | 20 |
| 60–69 | 20 | - - | - - | 10** | | | 10** | 10 |
| 70+ | 49 | - - | - - | 37 | 47 | | 18 | 23 |
| Marital status | 83 | | | ++ | | | | + |
| Married | 64 | 10 | | 17 | | | 16 | 16 |
| Other | 19 | 13** | | 6** | | | 18 | 13 |
| Sex | 84 | | | | | | | + |
| Male | 83 | 13 | | 15 | | 15 | 28 | 16 |
| Female | 1 | 12** | | 0** | | 0** | + | 3** |
| Ethnicity | 84 | | | | | | | |
| Non-German | 78 | 12 | 12* | 19 | 10 | 15 | | 15 |
| German | 6 | 29** | | 14** | | 19** | 23 | 20* |
| Literacy | 83 | | | | | | | |
| Illiterate | 18 | 13** | | 21 | | 18* | | 17 |
| Literate | 65 | 12 | | 13 | | 11 | | 15 |
| Comprehensive equality | | +++ | | ++ | | +++ | | +++ |
| Unequal | 66 | 20 | 12** | 26 | 12* | 24 | 46 | 22 |
| Equal | 17 | 0** | 14** | 10** | 8** | 5** | 7** | 7 |

+ = .10 significance level.

+ + = .05 significance level.

+ + + = .01 significance level.

*N ≤ 5.

**5 < N < 10.

should find so little. Differences in the availability of credit come to mind, but it seems more likely that it stems from the cultural tradition of primogeniture that was the law in Canada West until 1856 but never accepted in the United States.

### 6.4.7  Summary and Interpretation

For the most part, the levels and trends of land equality and sons preferred to daughters, with their socioeconomic correlates, confirm the findings for comprehensive equality and overall sexism, the comparable inheritance patterns for overall wealth. Two exceptions seem noteworthy: ethnicity becomes a factor (Germans favored equality less but contributed more), and older (rather than younger) testators become the primary contributors to the substitution of equality for sexism in the distribution of land.

The findings that Germans distributed their land more to sons than to daughters, and that they contributed more than non-Germans to the increase in land equality, are consistent with the hypothesis developed earlier. German landowners, especially German farmers, were likely to be among the more traditional members of the population, who were found earlier to favor less the "modern" pattern of equality while contributing more to its substitution for sexism. Indeed, when the data are restricted to farmers, the percentage of Germans favoring sons with land increases some 13 percentage points, while their contribution to the trend over time remains the same.

Still, these findings are at variance with a growing literature stressing the role of ethnicity in inheritance, since German heritage was only one of several factors influencing inheritance patterns; in fact, the underlying cause of the shift in patterns appears bound up in the settlement process, which was probably unrelated to ethnic origin. My suspicion is that these studies have been carefully focusing on anomalies: their choice of distinctive ethnic communities has led to unrepresentative results. It may well take a culturally exclusive community to maintain old-world inheritance practices. Certainly that has been the experience for the maintenance of other distinctive cultural traditions by various ethnic groups in American cities, for example. Areas like Butler County, with its mixture of ethnic groups, were presumably the rule rather than the exception for rural America in the nineteenth century, and the inheritance patterns and their underlying causes found in this county may well be representative rather than those of the more colorful, ethnically distinctive communities.

The finding that older rather than younger testators contributed most to increasing land equality does not have so obvious an explanation in terms of the hypothesis developed earlier. It is possible, however, that the settlement factor underlying the shift in inheritance patterns operated on total wealth for young testators but on land for older testators. If that factor were an attribute of the land itself, the price or its availability, then it might affect younger testators primarily through their ability to establish themselves and their families, while affecting older testators directly through the value of their land holdings. The next section will examine the trends in land availability and prices to explore this hypothesis further.

## 6.5    The Underlying Cause of the Substitution of Equality for Sexism

Figure 6.5 sets out the trends in land prices, land use, and potential labor force originally presented in my study of testator wealth for Butler County. The proportion of land use in farms shows that settlement came rapidly after the county was formed in 1803. Eighty percent of the agricultural land was in farms by 1820, though much of that acreage was unimproved. Settlement continued thereafter at a slower pace, but land under cultivation still reached 90% by the 1830s when it leveled off. The male population ages 15–69, a proxy for the labor force and the demand for farmland, grew very rapidly till 1830; its growth continued at a slower but steady rate up to the Civil War. Slowly growing and then constant supply combined with rapidly increasing demand to bring about very rapid increases in the price of land throughout the period.

The consequences of the tremendous growth in land prices are quite apparent for young men trying to put together a farm and raise a family: the cost became prohibitive. What may not be so apparent are the consequences for the parents of these young men and their prospective brides. It is generally agreed in the literature that parents were concerned with establishing their children, perhaps with the "start in life for each of his offspring at least as good as that which his father gave to him" that Easterlin suspects. The norm for testators at the beginning of the period, when the county was frontier and land prices were low, seems to have been to provide each son with enough land to set him up with a farm (perhaps comparable value to the one the testator started with) and to provide each daughter with an outfitting of bed, bedding, horse, and so on, sufficient for her to attract a husband. As the county became settled and land prices soared, it became impossible to set up sons with enough land to support themselves and a family (much less a farm as large as that on which the testator started raising a family). By the same token, it was no longer sufficient to outfit a daughter with the traditional dowery, since a prospective husband required a more substantial economic contribution from his bride. Daughters needed land as well as personal property for their dowery because land was the one commodity of substantial economic value most testators owned,

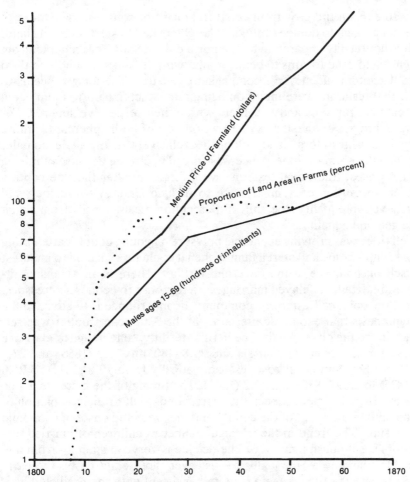

**Fig. 6.5**              Male labor force, land use, and land prices. *Sources:* Males—
United States census of population for 1810, 1830, 1840, 1850,
1860; land area—United States Census of Agriculture for
1840, 1850, Butler County tax duplicates for 1807, 1812, 1813,
1820.

but also because a small tract of land that might be inadequate as a
farm might be sufficient for the daughter and prospective son-in-law to
use as a homestead while he plied one of the trades that were becoming
feasible as the county matured and small towns sprang up. Sons could
no longer receive enough land, and daughters had to start receiving
land. The norm for inheritance had to change, for sons *and* for daughters.

To explain the growth in equal treatment of sons and daughters, it is not enough to demonstrate that daughters had to start receiving land. It is not readily apparent why the norm did not shift, for example, from leaving all land to sons to bequeathing two-thirds to sons and one-third to daughters—Easterlin's compensatory justice. The answer seems to be that testators were intent on being fair, which meant to them equal treatment for sons and daughters within their respective spheres. For more progressive testators, land was a part of both spheres; for more traditional testators, land belonged exclusively in the male domain. When the norm for inheritance was forced to change because of raising land prices, traditional testators were forced to alter their perception of a woman's proper inheritance to include land. Because they still believed in equality, the shift in perception meant a shift from sexist to genuine equality.

If there was growing economic pressure on young couples attempting to set up a home and start a family, then it could be expected to manifest itself on both age at marriage and fertility. There is an extensive literature detailing delayed marriage as a response to economic pressure, and the point of Easterlin's comments on inheritance is to advance the hypothesis that economic pressures at the American frontier was settled led to the observed decline in rural fertility. In fact, age at marriage rose for men from 24.3 (1811) and 25.8 (1825) to 28.3 (1835) and 27.1 (1845). For women, it rose less dramatically from 19.8 (1811) to 21.0 (1825) to 22.9 (1835) and 22.2 (1845). The timing of the increase in age at marriage for men, especially, corresponds well to the completion of the initial settlement of the county and the predicted onset of economic pressure. The trend in the average number of children of married testators is set out in figure 6.6. The decline is very substantial, from five children as late as the 1830s to just over three children by the early 1860s, and the timing again is quite consistent with the predicted economic pressure. (The unusually low level for the 1860s compared with other Ohio counties no doubt reflects the earlier settlement of Butler County as well as the downward biases in the measurement because some testators died while still in family formation years while others outlived some of their children.)

There is at least some evidence in the literature that these trends in inheritance and the process argued to underlie them are not peculiar to Butler County or this time period. Ryan finds at least as rapid increases in equality for the same time period for Oneida, New York, which was settled at about the same time as Butler County. Ditz discovers much higher proportions of land bequeathed to daughters and much higher proportions of daughters receiving at least some land in 1820 for Weathersfield, Connecticut, and vicinity. She also finds that these proportions increased from 1750. Since that area was settled much

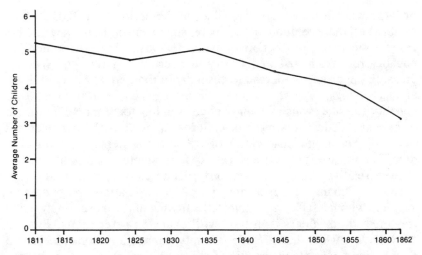

**Fig. 6.6**  Average number of children of ever-married testators.

earlier than Ohio, these results are consistent with the hypothesis that the same process operated both places, but was simply further along in the earlier settled region.

The recognition that economic pressures can affect inheritance patterns is not new. The literature on European inheritance practices is replete with arguments that particular inheritance patterns are the product of the type of agriculture practiced. Conzen presents a case for the modification of European inheritance in the context of the greater availability of land on the American frontier. Gagan argues that changing land availability in Ontario led to the development of the "Canadian" pattern of inheritance.

What this study makes clear for the first time is that pressure toward equality is inherent in land settlement process. Indeed, the change in attitude toward women in antebellum America may have been as much a product of the settlement of the frontier as of its opening; and both may have been more important (since they were grounded in hard economic realities) than the cult of true womanhood described by Barbara Welter that was being promoted by a few publishing houses.

## Comment    Lee Soltow

William Newell addresses himself to a most intriguing concept—the equal treatment of children-heirs in the division of estates. His study

Lee Soltow is professor of economics at Ohio University.

of 1,151 wills in Butler County, Ohio, in the period from 1803 to 1865 establishes the evolution of an increasingly egalitarian view in this respect since the proportion of wills demonstrating comprehensive equality rose from 40% in 1803–19 to over 60% in 1860–65. The increasing importance of intestate cases, with their equal estate division among siblings, only strengthen this finding. His general measure of equality classifies wills by their explicitly calling for identical treatment or almost identical treatment of children, as well as the achievement of equality through consideration of previous transfers to selected children. I suppose this measure is a proxy for enlightenment or liberalism, at least relative to the inegalitarian procedures of primogeniture, opposed by Thomas Jefferson and others in this nation so abundantly supplied with land. Certainly, Newell's finding of the increasingly equal treatment of daughters is in tune with changing perceptions. Even in New Jersey, which had a Butler County connection, sons received a double share in estate distribution for a few years after the Revolution.

Newell studies equal treatment of children by considering nine variables: wealth, occupation, residence, number of children, age, marital status, sex, German origin, and literacy. These influences are handled within a framework of classification tables (rather than by means of multiple regression analysis), a process leaving many cells with rather few cases in some of his two- and three-way cross-classification tables. The author finds that wealth was inversely related to equality in any decade, but the greatest movement toward equality, over time, was within the wealthiest group. Adjustment for either age or number of children seems to temper these results, but Newell finds that wealth is an important dimension. The young, the literate, and those in small towns enhanced the probability of equality. A special study of *land* inheritance shows similar results, with two important exceptions. Testators of German extraction demonstrated less inequality in any given period, but contributed more toward the move to equality over the long run. In the case of land, the old contributed more to the trend in equality.

Newell's cogent argument is that increased land scarcity and the rapid rise in land values forced the trend toward equal shares of real and personal estates inherited by children. He shows this scarcity in two ways: the average age at marriage increased 3 or 4 years for males, and the number of children decreased from more than 5 to about 3. It is asserted that after 1850 daughters needed land as much as did sons as they married and formed farm families. But couldn't one also argue that the early deprivation in Ohio, be it in land, buildings, dwellings, or farm animals was even more crucial? Wouldn't the rapid rise in per capita wealth in Ohio allow at least some differentiation in sibling portions? The considerations of testators are indeed complex, as shown by Marvin Sussman in his study of family inheritance in Cleveland, and by Carl Shoup in his study of estate planning by the rich. Very real is the attention, the care given to the old by one child compared to another, or the number of years of farm labor given by one child compared to another. Fairness in payment for past service to the testator may demand *inequality* in sibling portions. These productivity considerations can be related in a complex fashion to demographic and economic change, to a society which is aging, to one having fewer children, to one which is increasingly urban.

If equality in the distribution of estates increased because of general enlightenment, then it should appear in the strategic variable, literacy, or literacy adjusted for wealth. The diffusion of knowledge and culture in early nineteenth-century Ohio would have come from books and newspapers in the home as well as from the great surge in common school attendance (but only among the young by 1860). Again, this is an exceedingly difficult movement to quantify. Edward Stevens (1981) has studied numbers of books in both testate and intestate inventories in Washington (Marietta) and Athens Counties, in eastern Ohio, before the Civil War. He found that the majority of decedents had owned books, of which 63% were religious in nature, so we face the issue of whether this type of literature would lead to the concept of equality in treatment. At that time there were few scientific or philosophical books, the reading of which would have forced one to examine alternative ways of thinking—to break from past traditions. Some almanacs of the day, in rather wide use, included will forms for the use of the owner as well as consideration of sibling shares in estates.

Alternative treatment of some of the variables might have uncovered other causal relationships in Newell's data. Wealth and literacy could have been cross-classified because they are highly related. Perhaps a multiple regression equation of cases, with and without age data, would better reveal the characteristics of the set of persons not found by Newell in the censuses, presumably those who were more mobile. The fascinating downward trend in the number of children per testator, ending with an average of a little over three, seems quite shy of the 1860 census average for the United States, particularly if we are dealing with families with two or more children. Testators represent what proportion of those dying and of those with inventories? Were testator characteristics significantly different from those of the intestate group? Was there an increasing proportion of female testators? Finally, was Butler County typical, either of the state or the county? The cash value of its acreage of improved and unimproved land ranked second among Ohio's 88 counties in 1850, three times the national average; its land was sought after in the first surge of settlers into Ohio in 1795. Newell may have captured the more dynamic features of the trend toward family equality in America in this impressive study of Butler County.


# Reply

Professor Soltow's comments seem to fall into three categories: interpretation, statistical methods, and data. I have answered his substantive questions about the data by placing additional information in the text. His quite appropriate methodological criticisms have been met by replacing cross-classification tables with logistical regression analysis. Consequently, this reply focuses on his questions of interpretation.

If I understand his argument, Soltow advances two alternative explanations for the trend toward substituting equal for sexist treatment of children. The first is that the rapid rise in per capita income following an initial period of economic deprivation made possible some "differentiation in sibling portions." The second is that what I have called compensatory justice "may demand inequality in sibling portions" since children were more likely to have provided unequal "past service to the testator" as farms operated for more years since the opening of the county to settlement around the turn of the century. These arguments, however, appear to me to provide two of several possible explanations for *increasing* inequality in the treatment of children as the county was settled, when in fact the observed trend is toward *decreasing* inequality.

Soltow questions my interpretation of the trend toward equality on the grounds that literacy should then appear as a "strategic variable." In fact, literacy is significantly related cross-sectionally to equal treatment: on average, more literate testators were more likely to opt for equal treatment—they were more likely to accept the "modern" practice. What literacy does not explain is the trend toward equality—the adoption of that modern practice by more traditional members of the population. I do not believe, however, that literacy had its effect through knowledge of inheritance practices as much as through values. It seems plausible to me that more traditional testators abandoned the inheritance practice that their education (and other factors) had predisposed them toward, when that practice was no longer functional; and they replaced it with another practice long familiar to them that was now more functional given the altered assumptions forced on them by the changing circumstances associated with the settlement of the frontier.

If I am correct that the settlement of the frontier set economic processes in motion that necessitated changes in social norms such as inheritance practices, then it would be reasonable to expect that patterns of testation established by the end of the settlement period might persist. In fact, a sample of wills filed in Butler County in the 1890s (roughly 30 years after the end of this study) showed exactly the same proportion specifying equal treatment as did the wills of the 1860s.

This study, along with my earlier one of Butler County, suggests that we need to pay much closer attention to the ramifications of the settlement of the frontier. If the resulting increases in land prices in Butler County brought about substantial increases in the equality of inheritance within families and in the inequality of the distribution of wealth among families, then we need to ask what other major economic, social, or political changes might have the same source. Did other counties in other states experience the same extent of price increase? Did they undergo similar changes in wealth distribution or inheritance practices as a result? Finally, these two studies of Butler County point up the need for caution in interpreting the consequences of settling the frontier. For example, this study might seem to suggest that the settlement process improved the economic status of women (by replacing sexist with egalitarian inheritance practices), yet my previous study seems to suggest just the opposite (because women owned a small proportion of the land, which was the source of most of the increase over time in wealth). In fact, the two studies taken together show that settlement and the increasing land prices that resulted from it had more than one consequence for any one group or collectivity. Any analysis of the significance for that group of settling the frontier must examine the full range of its effects. I suspect that we have just started to discover the profound consequences of the settlement process.

# References

Auwers, Linda, 1978. Fathers, sons, and wealth in colonial Windsor, Connecticut. *Journal of Family History* 3:136–49.

Bogue, Allan. 1976. Comment on paper by Easterlin. *Journal of Economic History* 36:76–81.

Conzen, Kathleen. 1985. Peasant pioneers: Generational succession among German farmers in frontier Minnesota. In *The countryside in the age of capitalist transformations: Essays in the social history of rural America,* ed. Steven Hahn and Jonathan Prude. Chapel Hill: University of North Carolina Press.

Deen, James. 1972. Patterns of testation: Four tidewater counties in Colonial Virginia. *American Journal of Legal History* 16:154–77.

Demos, John. 1965. Notes on life in the Plymouth Colony. *William and Mary Quarterly* 22.

Ditz, Toby. 1981. Family, law and economy: Inheritance practices in five Connecticut towns, 1750–1820. Ph.D. dissertation, Columbia University.

Easterlin, Richard. 1976. Population change and farm settlement in the northern United States. *Journal of Economic History* 36:45–75.

Friedman, Lawrence. 1964. Patterns of testation in the nineteenth century: A study of Essex County, New Jersey wills. *American Journal of Legal History* 8:34–53.

Gagan, David. 1976. The indivisibility of land: A micro-analysis of the system of inheritance in nineteenth century Ontario. *Journal of Economic History* 36:126–41.

———. 1981. *Hopeful Travelers*. Toronto: University of Toronto Press.

Greven, Philip. 1970. *Four generations: Population, land and family in Colonial Andover, Massachusetts*. Ithaca, N.Y.: Cornell University Press.

Hibbard, Benjamin, and Guy Peterson. 1928. How Wisconsin farmers become farm owners. Bulletin 402. Madison: Agricultural Experiment Station, University of Wisconsin, Madison.

Lockridge, Kenneth. 1970. Land, population, and the evolution of New England society, 1630–1790. In *Class and society in early America*, ed. Gary Nash. Englewood Cliffs, N.J.: Prentice-Hall.

McInnis, Marvin. 1976. Comment on paper by Gagan. *Journal of Economic History* 36:145–46.

Newell, William. 1980. The wealth of testators and its distribution: Butler County, Ohio 1803–65. In *Modeling the distribution and intergenerational transmission of wealth,* ed. James Smith. Chicago: National Bureau of Economic Research.

Parsons, Kenneth, and Waples, Eliot. 1945. Keeping the farm in the family: A study of ownership processes in a low tenancy area of eastern Wisconsin. *Research Bulletin 157*. Agricultural Experiment Station at the University of Wisconsin.

Ryan, Mary. 1981. *Cradle of the middle class: The family in Oneida County, New York, 1790–1865*. London: Cambridge University Press.

Salamon, Sonya. 1980. Ethnic differences in farm family land transfers. *Rural Sociology* 45:290–308.

Salter, Leonard, Jr. 1943. Land tenure in process: A study of farm ownership and tenancy in a Lafayette county township. *Research Bulletin 146*. Agricultural Experiment Station of the University of Wisconsin.

Smith, Daniel Scott. 1974. Inheritance and the position and orientation of colonial women. Paper delivered at the second Berkshire Conference on the History of Women, Radcliffe College.

Stevens, Edward, Jr. 1981. Books and wealth in the frontier, *Social Science History* 5:417–43.

Tarver, James. 1952. Intra-family farm succession practices. *Rural Sociology* 17:266–71.

Wehrwein, George. 1927. The problem of inheritance in American land tenure. *Journal of Farm Economics* 9:163–75.

Welter, Barbara. 1973. The cult of true womanhood: 1820–1860. In *The American family in socio-historical perspective,* ed. Michael Gordon. New York: St. Martin's Press.

# III    Population and Labor Force

# 7     Rudimentary Contraceptive Methods and the American Transition to Marital Fertility Control, 1855–1915

Paul A. David and Warren C. Sanderson

## 7.1   Overview: Historical Issues, Evidence, and Argument

The economic and social history of the American nation in the nineteenth century was distinguished by the fact that the fertility of its people underwent one of the most dramatic declines recorded in the

Paul A. David is William Robertson Coe Professor of American Economic History at Stanford University. Warren C. Sanderson is associate professor of economics at the State University of New York at Stony Brook.

In the course of this monograph's long history, we have accumulated intellectual and other debts too numerous to acknowledge fully. Some of these have been noted at appropriate places in the text and footnotes, and in notes to tables, but others deserve mention here.

Carl Degler was encouraging and generous with comments and suggestions from the very first point at which we expressed interest in his archival find. Dr. Paul Gebhard, former director of the Institute for Sex Research at Bloomington, Indiana, kindly undertook to provide us with a special research tape based on the Kinsey data. William Nye and Edward Steinmueller carried out the initial coding of the Mosher Survey. Michel Matel recorded, devised additional questions, and painstakingly applied her insight and ingenuity to the task of deducing missing dates of vital events from the internal evidence of the survey responses. With Nilifur Cagatay, Matel also performed much of the actual computational work underlying successive editions of the present tables. Thomas Mroz programmed calculations made from the Kinsey tape (only some of which are presented here).

Presentation of some of this material in preliminary form to the Newberry Center Conference on Women and Quantitative History, July 5–8, 1979, in Chicago, brought insightful criticisms from Sheila R. Johansson on that occasion and subsequently, as well as suggestions from Maris Vinovskis and Daniel Scott Smith. For many other comments and references that have found their way into the present version, we thank Tony Wrigley, Peter Laslett, and members of the Cambridge Group for Population and Social Structure Seminar (1978); John Hajnal, Charles Rosenberg, Karen Paige, Dudley Kirk, John Whiting; Matilda W. Riley, and members of the Seminar on the Life Cycle and Aging at the Center for Advanced Studies in Behavioral Sciences (1979); and Michael Haines and participants at the NBER Williamsburg Conference on Long-Term Factors in American Economic Growth (1984). The research was sustained by grants to the Stanford Project on the History of Fertility Control from the National Science Foundation (Economics) and the National Institute of Child Health and Human Development.

whole of the Western world. Only the French preceded the white population of the United States in initiating a sustained decline in birthrates and total fertility which owed more to the reduction of total marital fertility rates than to a secular rise in marriage age and increases in the proportion of women who remained celibate. Moreover, the reduction of total fertility in America had commenced from levels that were among the highest achieved anywhere in the West when the nineteenth century opened. White women who entered marriage about 1800 and remained fecund to the normal age of menopause, in their later forties, would have given birth to 8 children on the average, whereas the comparable total fertility rate had fallen to the neighborhood of 3.3 by the second decade of the present century (Coale and Zelnik 1963, pp. 34–35; Sanderson 1979).

The magnitude and importance of the fertility decline in the United States, once virtually ignored by economic and social historians, increasingly has come to be recognized as a central factor in the nineteenth-century transformation of American society, one whose ramifications are to be discerned in almost every aspect of the evolving economy and culture of the world's first modern republic. As the descendants of the European settlers became less prolific, the entailed alterations in demographic structure touched many aspects of individual lives and social organization, ranging from savings behavior and labor force participation to popular education and the "status" of women (Easterlin 1972; David 1977; Guttentag and Secord 1984).

Given the perceived importance of this demographic revolution, is it not remarkable that only lately there has been something like a concerted effort to understand how it came about? Although the quantitative importance of enhanced control over marital fertility is now generally accepted, particularly by demographic historians who have analyzed the aggregate statistics pertaining to the native white population in the period 1860–1920, we are just beginning to be able quantitatively to describe the complex patterns in the adoption of family limitation goals and strategies that lie beneath the smooth downward progression of the aggregate fertility indexes. The purpose of this paper is to explore the morphology of the transition to low average levels of completed marital fertility, and the manner in which this was achieved among the native white segment of the population; not why it happened, but how it was managed by successive cohorts of couples who first entered marriage in the period stretching from the eve of the Civil War to the turn of the century.

Aggregate demographic measures tell us what needs explanation but are not inherently informative as to the best explanatory approaches. This is particularly so when the intent is ultimately to understand the motivations and constraints that shaped the behaviors of the individuals involved. In fashioning an account of the American fertility transition, no less than in the case of such transitions elsewhere, it will make a difference whether the decline of marital fertility can be portrayed as reflecting a gradual reduction of completed fertility by some representative couples, or as the consequence of a rise in the proportion of the population which had managed to achieve a reduced but essentially unchanging level of marital fertility. These are, of course, the polar alternatives. In the latter case, one would be justified in approaching the fertility decline purely as a form of "diffusion phenomenon," and seeking to account for it in congruent terms.

It should not be supposed, however, that identifying the fertility decline in postbellum America as "the diffusion of family limitation" would be sufficient to dispose of the problem of explanation. The term "diffusion" means different things to different people.[1] Contrary to the dichotomy suggested by Carlsson (1966), one may conceptualize diffusion as an equilibrium process in which at every point in time family limitation is the dominant, utility-maximizing strategy for just those couples in the population who have adopted it, or, as an "equilibrating" adjustment process (for the population as a whole) between uncontrolled marital fertility and some state of "controlled" fertility. The adjustment process often is portrayed in the latter vision as a disequilibrium phenomenon akin to the spread of an epidemic. Indeed, there is an abundant literature which would have us understand the adoption of family limitation in terms of the propagation of information about the benefits and methods of birth control, emphasizing the diffusion of (costless?) information through education and other media as the mechanism by which the new mode of behavior was extended throughout the society (see, e.g., Rogers 1973; Zei and Cavalli-Sforza 1977). We do not hope on this occasion to resolve the issues raised by the juxtaposition of these alternative interpretations. Indeed, until a better description of the proximate sources of the American marital fertility decline can be provided, in terms of the extent and effectiveness of the use of fertility control strategies, one cannot even make a sensible start toward understanding it.

### 7.1.1 Macrodemographic Outlines of the Postbellum Fertility Transition

To outline briefly the quantitative dimensions of the transition to lower marital fertility levels among the United States' native white population in the postbellum era, we may draw upon preliminary findings obtained by a new method of demographic analysis, applied to the age- and marital duration–specific parity distributions from the censuses of 1900, 1910, and 1940.[2] What these reveal is that the nineteenth century witnessed not one continuous process of transition to effective limitation of family size, but at least two chronologically and geographically distinct phases of movements among the native white population.

The earlier of these had its origins in the Northeastern region of the country during the antebellum era and was already well advanced there by the early 1870s. Over 26% of couples among the marriage cohort of 1855–59 in the United States had managed successfully to avert some births during their completed reproductive life span. The corresponding proportion for the resident population of the Northeast was over 41%. And typically they had averted many births. The later-marrying members of the birth cohort of 1840–44 (to which those women belonged), specifically, those who had been brides at ages 20–29, were particularly effective in restricting their completed family size. We estimate that their completed fertility rate was 4.07, compared with a rate of 7.41 for earlier-marrying women from the same (1840–44) birth cohort in the United States as a whole. Even among women who bore at least one child, the average number of children ever born to those who were active (effectual) controllers at some point in their completed reproductive span, was as low as 3.1 in the Northeast.

This was a standard not to be matched by the whole of the nation's native white urban-dwelling population for another two decades, that is to say, not until the later-marrying (ages 20–29) women among the marriage cohort of 1885–89. By then, as it appears from an analysis of the distribution of births among those effective controllers who did have children, the "two-child family" norm which had for some while been established in the Northeast was emerging ubiquitously among the native white urban population. Furthermore, the pattern was being carried thither to other parts of the country, most notably the states of the Far West.

The foregoing, essentially northern urban and rural nonfarm pattern in the extent and effectiveness of fertility control diverged starkly from the situation that prevailed among native-born whites in Southern states. The latter, largely rural population showed scant indication of any effective marital fertility control, right up to and including the marriage cohorts of the late 1850s.

In this respect, as in so many others, the antebellum South differentiated itself from the predominantly rural North Central region of the country. There, more than one-fourth of the native white residents who had married during the 1850s were active controllers, whereas among Southern native whites marrying during the 1870s fewer than one-fifth ever controlled effectively. Indeed, it was not until the late 1880s and the early 1890s that recently married couples in the South were swept up in a sudden and widespread transformation of fertility behavior. This movement was sufficiently rapid to be able to bring the later-marrying, and presumably the urban, segments of the white Southern population into substantial conformity with the standards of marital fertility control that prevailed in the rest of the nation by the 1920s.

Between the two phases we have discerned in the postbellum American fertility transition, there was a clear morphological change that reflected itself in the proximate sources of the decline recorded in the total marital fertility rate of the native white population. Among the segment of the married population that were actively controlling, average completed fertility (number of children ever born to a woman aged 45–49) decreased by one-fifth from the marriage cohort of 1860–64 to the marriage cohort of 1885–89. This change accounted for about 55% of the aggregate reduction in average completed fertility, leaving the smaller part attributable to the growth in the proportion of active controllers within the native white population.

The remainder, rather less than half of the decline, can be attributed to the expansion of the proportion of the population that was engaged in some form or other of effective control. This share had risen at a rate approaching 2% per annum, from 0.346 of the 1860–64 marriage cohort to 0.566 of the 1885–86 marriage cohort. Over the following quarter-century the pace of diffusion slowed appreciably, as was perhaps to be expected since the main arena for new recruitment to the ranks of the family limitation movement was largely confined to the South and the rural sections of the North Central region. Among the marriage cohort of 1910–14 nationwide, the proportion of active controllers stood at 0.756, with the South itself no longer far behind at the 0.70 level.

Nevertheless, the diffusion of active control constituted the proximate source of the 1.2 births per woman reduction in the total marital fertility rate for the United States native white population which took place during the second 25-year phase of the postbellum transition. All but 6% of that change is attributable to the more widely extended implementation of essentially the same standards of effective control as had been established among the actively controlling portion of the population during the 1880s. Looking at the comparison between the marriage cohorts of 1885–89 and 1910–14 in greater detail, one finds that while the number of children ever born to all active controllers was, on average, virtually stable, this stabilization was the result of two opposing tendencies. Higher mean levels of completed fertility typical of active controllers within the segments of the population (especially in the farm South) among whom family limitation was diffusing most rapidly, served largely to offset a slowed but continuing downward adjustment of mean family size among the social strata in which marital fertility control had been widely accepted for at least a generation, if not longer.

The impressive degree of family limitation achieved by the end of the first phase of the postbellum transition, and its uniformity throughout the ranks of active controllers, are worth remarking upon. Once-married women who reached the altar during their twenties in the years 1885–89, and who subsequently managed to avert at least one birth before reaching the end of their reproductive span (at ages 45–49), are estimated to have borne 3.18 children on the average. This figure pertains to the native white population of the United States at large, and stands a good bit above the average of 2.80 that prevailed among the residents of the Northeast. Leaving aside the active controllers who remained childless, the corresponding mean level of completed fertility was 3.35 nationwide, and 3.09 in the Northeast. Just as the geographical differentials were less pronounced within the ranks of the childbearing active controllers, urban-rural differences in completed fertility also were comparatively small. For comparable couples belonging to the same (1885–89) marriage cohort, the deviations of the urban, nonfarm rural, and farm-dwelling subpopulations from the 3.35 national average rate just cited were only −0.20, +0.03, and +0.38 births per woman, respectively.

It should be noticed, too, that the urban-Northeastern levels of completed fertility were so low even among childbearing active controllers that these couples could barely have been expected to replace themselves in the population. Based on the mortality experience of the period 1870–85, only 0.734 of the children born to women in the 1885–89 marriage cohort could have been expected to survive to ages 20–24, implying that no more than 2.3 mature offspring would have been on hand to take their parents' place. Still more remarkable is the fact that the same situation obtained in the Northeast as early as the marriage cohort of 1860–64, in which childbearing active controllers could have expected to see no more than 2.2 of their children survive to ages 20–24.[3]

To summarize these preliminary findings: from the beginning of the postbellum era, if not before, among those strata of the native white population of the Northeast in which women characteristically deferred marriage until their mid-twenties, even fertile couples were managing to hold their expected completed fertility remarkably close to the replacement level. The closing decade of the century saw this impressive standard approached by active controllers in other regions, and throughout the urban segment of American society, and the maintenance of the same degree of effective control as the ranks of birth controllers were swelled by new converts. Thus, it may be said that the approximate halving of the native white population's completed marital fertility rate, which occurred between the birth cohorts of 1840–44 and 1890–94, reflected the popular extension—or, to use Himes's

(1936, 1970 ed.) phrase, the "democratization"—of a pattern of successful reproductive control that was already being achieved at the outset among a substantial minority.

### 7.1.2 Toward Understanding the Microdemography of the Transition

The preceding quantitative overview directs our immediate attention to the task of understanding how such low levels of marital fertility were achieved and maintained in the latter part of the Victorian era. Thus motivated to probe further beneath the surface of the macrodemographic trends, we shall turn in section 7.2 to examine an important set of microdemographic clues provided by the remarkable body of information that has become known as the Mosher Survey. On the basis of this evidence we are led to suggest that during the last quarter of the nineteenth century, and quite possibly earlier still, the key to the success of the native-born urban fertility controllers lay in combining the application of rudimentary contraceptive methods with a very considerable measure of sexual restraint within marriage. If these Victorian pioneers of successful family limitation resembled us to a surprising degree in their fertility goals and their acceptance of the latest in available contraceptive technologies, their sexual life-style will be seen to have been, by choice and necessity, very "unmodern."

To lend a measure of credence to the relevance of the testimony concerning sexual, contraceptive, and reproductive experiences provided by the small group of married women who responded to the remarkably thorough and candid questions posed by Clelia Mosher starting in the early 1890s, we first go to some lengths to show that in their fertility experience these women were representative of the larger social and economic stratum from which they had been drawn. This is to say our historical "informants" testified to a pattern of reproductive experience that matched the urban wives of men in professional occupations. The latter group, in turn, closely resembled the entire contemporaneous segment formed by the effective fertility-controlling couples among the urban native white population.

A second line of support for the hypothesis advanced in section 7.2 is provided by the results obtained in section 7.3 with a simple microdemographic simulation model, using historically relevant parameters. This serves to establish the consistency between the range of contraceptive methods reported by the Mosher Survey interviewees, the low level of marital coitus to which they testified, and their actual fertility. It further demonstrates the possibility of effective use of rudimentary contraceptive methods, if one were prepared to bear the costs in terms of the sacrifice of what today would be judged a normal regime of marital sexual intercourse. The findings of this section (7.3) also lend some additional support to the proposition that "spacing behaviors" played an integral role in the nineteenth-century United States fertility transition. Recognition of the inherent unreliability of the available means of contraception, and the hazards entailed in effectual efforts to induce abortions, led couples in this era not only greatly to reduce the frequency of coitus but also to initiate positive measures of control at a very early stage of marriage (see David and Sanderson 1984).

The concluding discussion in section 7.4 addresses broader themes briefly, considering the significance of Victorian culture and sexual ideology among the formative elements of the strategies of fertility regulation which appear to have become most typical of American urban middle-class couples during the postbellum era. Rather than treat the Respectable Victorian ideology of sexual restraint as a wholly ex-ogenous cultural phenomenon affecting the "supply side" of fertility control, its emergence and persistence into the early twentieth century may be explained in part by reference to the contraceptive objectives and the technological constraints relevant to the situation of many middle-class couples. We suggest that the role models, or prescriptive behavioral stereotypes, which this ideology projected had acquired a positive functional value for individual couples who were seeking ef-fectively to utilize the rudimentary, inherently unreliable contraceptive technologies which became available during the nineteenth century. The acceptance within the society's educated middle classes of the life-style of marital sexual continence, in varying degrees, at both the individual attitudinal and behavioral levels, was, on this reading, pro-moted by the emergence of a transitional technological context that made the indicated course of sexual behavior consonant with their family-limiting goals.

## 7.2  How Did They Do It? Family Limitation Strategies among the Urban Middle Class

Exactly how near-replacement levels of marital fertility were achieved during the postbellum era by the vanguard of birth controllers among the urban, native-born population in the Northeast has remained some-thing of a mystery. It is widely supposed that the spread of contracep-tive practices during the latter part of the nineteenth century somehow played a key role in enabling individual couples to regulate their fertility, but the direct evidence for this presumption is meager, to say the least. Little is known quantitatively about the extent to which the various methods and devices available for the "the prevention of pregnancy" actually were employed by different socioeconomic groups in the American population before the 1920s. Still less may be ventured with any confidence as to the temporal and geographical patterns of adoption of specific methods. Indeed, the lack of close attention to the technological, physiological, and pharmacological aspects of historical methods of fertility control has given rise to something of a puzzle: How could an assortment of rudimentary contraceptive methods, which by today's standards appears both cumbersome and disastrously unreliable, have come to be so extensively and effectively employed?

No longer is it possible to attribute the persisting vagueness of discussions of the means of family limitation in nineteenth-century America to the delicacy or inhibitions of historians in addressing matters inextricably related to the subject of human sexuality. Modern scholars, such as Linda Gordon (1976), James C. Mohr (1978), James Reed (1978), Carl N. Degler (1980), and, most recently, Peter Gay (1983), are frank enough. But they have found it hard to cast off legacies of the tradition through which social historians became reconciled to discussing these questions despite the difficulties of furnishing documentary evidence about the fertility-regulating behaviors of populations in the past.

Insofar as a traditional speculative consensus can be said to have emerged on these matters, it maintained that low marital fertility could be achieved by premodern populations (and where such are observed, were most probably achieved) through a combination of abstinence, abortion, and coitus interruptus. Since these three methods of family limitation are often presumed to have been generally known and understood in America from colonial times onward—if not necessarily put into practice—most of the attention among social, economic, and demographic historians concerned to understand the nineteenth-century fertility decline has become focused upon the forces creating a demand for smaller families (see, e.g., Easterlin 1976; Lindert 1978; Haines 1979; Vinovskis 1981; Tolnay and Guest 1982, 1983; continuing an older tradition from Yasuba 1962; and Forster and Tucker 1972).

We hold no brief against this important line of inquiry, and seek here only to point out that there may be a value to attempting to redress the balance between the "demand side" and the "supply side" of the determination of effective family-limiting behavior. After all, the "why" of the story cannot properly be explained in abstraction from the question: How did they do it? One is not likely to be successful either in accounting for the diffusion of family limitation, or in understanding the emerging patterns of fertility among the effective controllers, without considering the full range of circumstances and attitudes that motivated the people involved. In addition to learning what prompted married couples to wish to inhibit their reproductive power, we must try to understand more about the means that were available to them for that purpose, and the behaviors entailed in implementing those methods successfully. Desired family size is not determined without reference to the pecuniary and psychic costs of control, as economists are ready to point out. (See Easterlin 1978 and David and Sanderson 1978a for theoretical formulations.) If this insight is to be fruitful, it should lead to fuller considerations of the factors determining the costs of marital fertility regulation. These costs must be gauged in terms of the behavioral demands of maintaining an effectual contraceptive regime, as well as pecuniary outlays for contraceptive appliances. The differing abilities of various groups within the society to sustain them may well have played an important role in generating the patterns of differential fertility that emerged among the native white population of the United States during the postbellum era (Rainwater 1960).

The key to the differential success of the contraceptive efforts of educated, native-born couples in the Northeastern states, and particularly the members of the professional classes who belonged to the marriage cohorts of the 1870s and 1880s, most probably was sexual restraint within marriage. The rudimentary state of development of the broadening array of contraceptive methods and devices which they sought to employ required that, for success, sexual "continence" had to be practiced to a degree which, by the standard of more recent times, can only be described as extreme.

Our reasons for advancing this hypothesis, and for believing that coital frequencies within marriage were exceptionally low among this particular segment of the population, derive from an analysis of material contained in the Mosher Survey, which is now widely accepted by American social historians as the earliest extant set of detailed and quantifiable responses to explicit questions concerning sexual and contraceptive behavior (MaHood and Wenburg 1980). The historical significance of the Mosher Survey and its broader relevance for the social history of sex and reproduction has been considered elsewhere (Degler 1974, 1980; Rosenberg 1982, esp. pp. 98–99, 180–87; Gay 1983, pp. 135–44, 258). Here, in section 7.2, we shall discuss the characteristics and import of this small but illuminating body of information as it applies to the study of the historical interrelationship between sexual and contraceptive behavior.

The group of women whose interview responses are recorded in the questionnaire forms of the Mosher Survey were mothers; all had borne at least one child. Despite the smallness of the sample and the serendipitous way in which it was collected, we show that the fertility experience of the respondents closely matched that of all childbearing wives of urban professional men in the United States who belonged, as they did, to the marriage cohorts of 1870–94. Considering just the urban "professionals" marrying in 1885–89 and taking brides in the 20–29 age group, the average completed fertility of those who bore children is found to have been 3.20. This is essentially the same as the figure (3.15) for the entire group of fertile (i.e., childbearing) but actively controlling couples among the contemporary native white urban population. What has previously been referred to as the "urban standard of effective control" for the marriage cohort of 1885–89 was thus reflected in the marital fertility of the Mosher Survey women. We therefore may hope to derive from the confidences of these candid few some pertinent hints to understanding the reproductive behavior of the reticent many, that multitude of successful birth controllers who at the time composed upward of 60% of the country's native white urban-dwelling couples.[4]

### 7.2.1  The Mosher Survey and Its Representativeness

Previous efforts to fashion an account of nineteenth-century sexual and reproductive behavior have proceeded largely on the basis of inferences drawn from diaries, letters, novels, marriage manuals, and other literary evidence. What follows takes the alternative tack of formulating a historical account of these matters largely on the basis of quantifiable information about the lives and behavior of a small sample of couples married during the late nineteenth and early twentieth centuries. At this stage tentative hypotheses rather than firm conclusions are in order. But our hypotheses, hedged and qualified as it is appropriate for them to be, do derive directly and indirectly from the microdemographic clues that we have extracted systematically from data which, until a decade ago, lay unnoticed in the Stanford University Archives.

Carl Degler first brought to our attention the presence in the Archives of the papers of Clelia Duel Mosher, and the existence among them of the responses to a questionnaire she had developed and administered in the period from 1892 to 1920.[5] The Mosher Survey, as Degler (1974) first called it, dealt with the sexual and reproductive experience of 44 married women, virtually all of whom were wedded to members of the professional classes and many of whom were the wives of university professors.

Clelia Mosher herself was neither wife nor mother. The early interest she displayed in these subjects derived from what would become for her a lifelong professional concern with issues relating to women's health. An exceptional woman in her time, she made a place for herself first as a physician and later among the Stanford professoriate. A dutiful daughter, she had remained in the family home following her secondary schooling, occupying herself in a little greenhouse business as her father wished. But in that capacity she unexpectedly accumulated enough money to strike out on an independent course, commencing her undergraduate education at the age of 25 by enrolling in Wellesley College (Jacob 1979). In her junior year, Mosher transferred to the University of Wisconsin at Madison to major in biology. It was there during 1892, when prompted by a request from the Mothers' Club of the University to speak on the "marriage relation," that Mosher designed and administered the first six of the existing questionnaires to which we have referred.

The following academic year, Mosher moved again, this time to Stanford University where she received her B.Sc. (in biology) in 1893. After completing her baccalaureate studies Mosher stayed on at Stanford as a graduate student in biology, and working also as an assistant in hygiene. She received her M.Sc. in 1894, and in the autumn of 1896 left Stanford to join the first cohort of women students admitted to study medicine at The Johns Hopkins University in Baltimore. During her initial sojourn at Stanford, Mosher collected sixteen questionnaires, and in the course of her medical student career at Johns Hopkins she administered four interviews. After she received her M.D. degree in 1900 and served an additional year at the Hopkins Hospital, Mosher returned to Palo Alto, California, where she engaged in private practice. No questionnaires were completed during this period. It was only after Mosher gave up her practice to become an assistant professor of personal hygiene at Stanford in 1910 that she resumed collecting the data analyzed below. In 1913, fifteen more questionnaires were added, and in 1920 the final five forms were completed.[6]

The respondents to her questionnaire were, in a literal sense, daughters of the early Victorian era: virtually all were drawn from the birth cohorts between 1835–39 and 1870–74. Fourteen of these women were born before the beginning of the Civil War, two as early as the decade of the 1830s. The largest birth cohort among the sample, numbering 19 to be precise, belonged to the decade 1860–69 in which Clelia Mosher herself was born. Nine of the women she interviewed were her juniors, seven having been born in the 1870s. But only one among the interviewees was born during each of the two closing decades of the century.[7]

Although the survey respondents as a group did not match Clelia Mosher's educational and professional attainments, they were nonetheless a highly educated group of women for the time. All those about whom educational information is available had completed high school, and roughly three-quarters of them continued their education beyond that point. About half the Mosher Survey women received at least one college degree. Their husbands were highly educated too: at the time of the survey, most were teachers and college professors, but a few businessmen and engineers appear among them.

The remarkable character of this data set, however, resides not in the fact that it pertains mostly to educated middle-class women born before 1870, but in the range and nature of the information elicited by the interviews.[8] Although we have but 44 usable sets of responses, there is an extraordinary wealth of detail about each individual's life and that of the household in which she resided. These afford glimpses of patterns of covariation among physiological, situational, attitudinal, and behavioral characteristics, some of which are only infrequently revealed in modern surveys dealing with reproductive behavior. Family backgrounds, educational careers (of both the respondent and her spouse), work experience, health history and status, attitudes, experience and habits in sexual matters—all these are inventoried. In addition, and most crucial for our purposes here, the responses provide records of marriage, conceptions, miscarriages, births, infant deaths, lactation period, as well as collateral information concerning knowledge and use of contraceptive methods.

The first point which must be established here about such a small and serendipitously collected sample concerns its usefulness for the purpose of suggesting hypotheses about the sexual and reproductive behavior of a broader segment of the American population. Deriving from the origins of Clelia Mosher's inquiries, the Survey respondents all were mothers, but conditional upon that fact that their fertility experience was quite representative of the social and occupational class of native white American's from which they were drawn.

Table 7.1 presents a comparison of the fertility of mothers in the Mosher Survey sample classified by age and marital duration with the fertility in 1910 of similarly classified native white, once-married mothers living in urban areas, whose husbands had a professional or semi-professional occupation. The cell means derived from 1910 census data are based on large numbers of observations, whereas the Mosher Survey cell means are based on very small numbers of cases. To take into account the greater biological and behavioral heterogeneity of the national sample, the figures obtained from the 1910 census source have been suitably adjusted to render them comparable with the Mosher Survey observations.[9]

Visual comparison of the fertility of the paired entries in table 7.1 conveys the correct impression that in their fertility, if in nothing else, the Mosher Survey respondents were quite representative of the larger group. This can be confirmed by more formal statistical tests. Consider the following regression model:

$$B_M(i,j) = \alpha + \beta [B_C(i,j)] + e(i,j),$$

where $B_M(i,j)$ is the mean number of births to mothers in the Mosher Survey who were of age $i$ and of marital duration $j$; $B_C(i,j)$ is the comparable figure in table 7.1 derived from the census data; $\alpha$ and $\beta$ are parameters; and $e(i,j)$ is a random variable with mean zero. Were the Mosher Survey responses truly an unbiased reflection of the un-

**Table 7.1**  Representativeness of Fertility Experience of Mothers in the Mosher Survey Sample: Average Numbers of Children Born to Mosher Sample Mothers in Specified Age and Marital Duration Groups, Compared with Corrected Averages for White Mothers Married to Urban Men in Professional Occupations in the United States in 1910

| Age | Duration of Marriage (years) | | | | | | | | | Total Number of Mosher Observations | Unweighted Average[a] |
| --- | --- | --- | --- | --- | --- | --- | --- | --- | --- | --- | --- |
| | Under 3 | 3–4 | 5–9 | 10–14 | 15–19 | 20–24 | 25–29 | 30–34 | 35–39 | | |
| | (4) | (3) | (6) | (4) | (2) | (4) | (4) | (3) | (2) | | |
| 25–29 | 1.0 | 1.0 | 2.0 | | | | | | | (4) | 1.3 |
| | *1.26* | *1.60* | *2.17* | | | | | | | | *1.68* |
| 30–34 | 1.0 | 1.0 | 2.4 | 2.0 | | | | | | (11) | 1.6 |
| | *1.26* | *1.60* | *2.29* | *2.86* | | | | | | | *2.00* |
| 35–39 | | | | 4.0 | 4.0 | | | | | (2) | 4.0 |
| | | | | *2.86* | *3.43* | | | | | | *3.14* |
| 40–44 | | | 1.0 | 2.0 | 2.5 | | | | | (4) | 1.8 |
| | | | *1.94* | *2.86* | *3.43* | | | | | | *2.74* |
| 45–49 | | | | 3.0 | | 3.0 | 5.0 | | | (3) | 3.7 |
| | | | | *2.29* | | *2.66* | *4.11* | | | | *3.35* |
| 50–54 | | | | | | 4.5 | 5.0 | 4.0 | | (5) | 4.5 |
| | | | | | | *3.31* | *3.89* | *4.69* | | | *3.96* |
| 55–59 | | | | | | | 4.0 | 2.5 | | (3) | 3.3 |
| | | | | | | | *3.43* | *4.23* | | | *3.83* |
| 60–64 | | | | | | | | | 5.5 | (2) | 5.5 |
| | | | | | | | | | *4.23* | | *4.23* |
| Unweighted Average[a] | 1.0 | 1.0 | 1.8 | 2.7 | 3.2 | 3.7 | 4.7 | 3.3 | 5.5 | (34) | Mosher |
| | *1.26* | *1.60* | *2.13* | *2.91* | *3.43* | *3.48* | *3.81* | *4.46* | *4.23* | | *Census* |

*Note:* Roman figures show means computed from Mosher Survey women reporting one or more live births. Italic figures show means computed from United States census of 1910 data, after correction for heterogeneity.

[a]Unweighted averages of cell means appearing in this table; these are not arithmetic averages of underlying individual observations.

*Technical notes and sources:*

**Mosher Survey Mothers, 1892–1920:** The average numbers of children ever born (live) to women in the indicated age and marital duration groups who had one or more live births have been computed from the unpublished source: "The Mosher Survey, an Edited, Machine-readable Version," prepared by Paul A. David and Warren C. Sanderson, with Michelle Matel, May 1979. (This source is referred to hereafter as the "Mosher Survey Tape.")

**United States White Mothers Married to Urban Men in Professional Occupations, 1910:** See United States Bureau of the Census (1947), table 19, pp. 116–41, for underlying 1910 census data (Sample W) from which were computed age- and marital duration–specific means of the number of children ever born to wives (of men classified by the 1910 United States Census as having a professional occupation) who reported at least one birth.

For comparisons with the age- and marital duration–specific means for the Mosher Survey (mothers), it is necessary to adjust the census sample means to allow for the much greater degree of heterogeneity in the effective fecundity in the population(s) to which these refer. As may be seen from the next to the rightmost column in table 7.1, there are very few Mosher sample observations in each cell; in addition, the geographical location, nativity, religious, and occupational composition of the Mosher Survey respondents render it a virtually homogeneous sample for purposes of comparison with the census sample of white women married to urban professionals. Cf. Bongaarts (1976), pp. 234–35, for derivation of the correction factor (1.143) which has been used to multiply the published census cell means.

derlying census data, we would expect that the parameter $\alpha$ would be insignificantly different from zero and that the parameter $\beta$ would be insignificantly different from unity.

The regression results are as follows, where the numbers in parentheses are standard errors of the coefficients:

$$B_M(i,j) = -0.507 + 1.157 \, [B_C(i,j)] \, , \, \bar{R}^2 = .660.$$
$$(0.589) \quad (0.190)$$

(standard error of the regression = .887)

The expected results clearly obtain at the conventional 95% confidence level: the intercept is insignificantly different from zero and the slope coefficient is insignificantly different from unity. To confirm that the slope coefficient remains insignificantly different from unity when the intercept term of the regression equation is constrained to be zero, examine the following regression equation:

$$B_M(i,j) = 1.002 \, [B_C(i,j)] \quad \text{(standard error of the regression} = .881)$$
$$(0.062)$$

An $F$-test ($F = .73$) indicates that constraining $\alpha = 0$ does not significantly reduce the explanatory power of the model—at any reasonable level of statistical significance that one might care to name. These results support the view that the Mosher Survey observations on fertility by age and marital duration are an unbiased sample of the relevant national subpopulation from which Clelia Mosher's informants were drawn, as reflected in the United States census data for 1910.

This fortuitous coincidence, taken altogether with the scope of the personal information inventoried, makes the Mosher Survey a veritable Rosetta Stone for the study of the demographic and social history of a significant segment of the American population—namely, the social, occupational, and residential stratum that appears to have formed the vanguard of the American family limitation movement during the postbellum era. It is not, of course, a suitable statistical testing-block for old and new theories concerning fertility behavior. The dangers of overanalysis, or of "overfitting" in the process of seeking internal regularities within this data set can scarcely be ignored. In view of the small number of respondents involved, it seems most appropriate to utilize their testimony in the way that social anthropologists make use of informants who belong to a culture other than their own. As such, this trove of information legitimately may serve as the inspiration for hypotheses that can eventually be subjected to rigorous statistical tests by indirect means, employing other bodies of historical data that are less comprehensive in scope yet offer wide coverage of a few important dimensions of fertility behavior.[10]

### 7.2.2  Extent and Methods of Contraception—From Mosher to Kinsey

In table 7.2 are assembled clues which have been gleaned from three historical sources concerning the quantitative extent of contraception and the distribution of methods used. To the Mosher sample we have added information from two better-known, twentieth-century surveys: the Terman sample and the Kinsey sample. All of these data sets refer to educated middle-class women.[11] The reproductive experiences spanned in this table extend from 1856, when the earliest marriage among the Mosher Survey women was celebrated, to the mid-1930s when the Terman survey was conducted. By the latter date most of the women in the Kinsey sample of those marrying before 1915 would have completed their reproductive spans.

The questions concerning contraceptive practice in the Mosher and Kinsey surveys were essentially inquiries into the array of contraceptive methods ever used by respondents, whereas the question in the Terman Survey (see table 7.2, n. 3) was apparently designed to elicit information on current use. The responses, however, led Terman to believe that many people were answering this question as if it referred to methods ever used (see Terman 1938, pp. 347–48). With this in mind, it is interesting to glance at the figures on the proportion of noncontraceptors among respondents shown on the second line from the bottom. One may see that only 12.5% of the Mosher respondents interviewed in the nineteenth century reported that they never used contraceptive methods, whereas only 5.9% of those interviewed in the twentieth century reported no contraceptive use.

The former of these figures fits in nicely with the preliminary estimates we have obtained, using the cohort parity analysis methods referred to in section 7.1. Those findings, based on ample census samples, confirm the relatively small dimensions of the "noncontrolling remnant" left among the native white women of the Northeast, whence many of the Mosher survey respondents originally had come. For women who married in their twenties during 1885–89, the CPA estimate of the proportion of dedicated noncontrollers, based upon completed reproductive lives, is found to be 14.6%. We also can report a close match with the subsequent, still lower estimate of the fraction of noncontraceptors among the women interviewed by Mosher after 1900. Most of the latter were married in the late 1890s, and for that marriage cohort the "noncontrolling remnant" in the population of native white women who wed in their twenties has been estimated at 7.0% in the case of couples remaining in the Northeast, and at 4.5% in the case of those residing in the West at the end of their reproductive lives. The Mosher survey respondents interviewed in Palo Alto after 1900 obviously be-

**Table 7.2**  Contraceptive Use Experience among Married Upper Middle-Class American Women: From the 1850s to the 1930s (Frequency Distributions of Methods Reported as Ever Used)

| | Mosher Survey Sample,[1] 1892–1920 | | | | Kinsey Survey:[2] Wives of College Men, Married before 1915 | | Terman Sample[3] 1935 | |
| | Full Sample | | 1892–97 | 1913–30 | 1938–50 | | | |
| Methods Ever Used | Number | Percent | Percent | Percent | Number | Percent | Number | Percent |
|---|---|---|---|---|---|---|---|---|
| **Positive methods** | | | | | | | | |
| Douche | 18 | 32.2 | 41.4 | 25.0 | 23 | 27.4 | 242 | 19.7 |
| Safe period/rhythm | 12 | 21.4 | 25.0 | 18.8 | 0 | 0.0 | 74 | 6.0 |
| Withdrawal | 8 | 14.3 | 16.7 | 12.5 | 21 | 25.0 | 233 | 18.9 |
| Condom | 11 | 19.6 | 12.5 | 25.0 | 22 | 26.2 | 259 | 21.1 |
| Pessary, diaphragm | 4 | 7.1 | 0.0 | 12.5 | 9 | 10.7 | 137 | 11.1 |
| Suppository, jelly (and foam powder) | 2 | 3.6 | 0.0 | 6.2 | 9 | 10.7 | 233 | 18.9 |
| Other | 1 | 1.8 | 4.1 | 0.0 | 0 | 0.0 | 53 | 4.3 |
| Total positive usage (above) | 56 | 100.0 | 100.0 | 100.0 | 84 | 100.0 | 1231 | 100.0 |
| Abstinence | 4 | 6.2 | 10.0 | 3.0 | 0 | 0.0 | n.a. | n.a. |
| No method used | 4 | 6.2 | 10.0 | 3.0 | 7 | 7.7 | 19 | 1.5 |
| Total instances reported | 64 | 100.0 | 100.0 | 100.0 | 91 | 100.0 | 1250 | 100.0 |
| Number of respondents | 41 | 100.0 | (24) 100.0 | (17) 100.0 | 41 | 100.0 | 792 | 100.0 |
| Noncontraceptors among respondents | 4 | 9.8 | (3) 12.5 | (1) 5.9 | 7 | 17.1 | 10 | 2.4 |
| Positive usage per user | 1.51 | | 1.14 | 2.00 | 2.47 | | 1.59 | |

*Note:* The observations presented in the upper and middle sections of this table are "instances of use" (or nonuse) of the indicated methods of contraception. More than one method may be reported by a given user. Observations pertaining to the survey respondents (contraceptors and noncontraceptors) are presented in the lower panel.

*Technical notes and sources:*

1. **Mosher Survey Sample:** Observations from coded responses to Mosher's question, "Have you ever used any means to prevent conception? If so, what?" as tabulated from David and Sanderson, with Matel, "Mosher Survey Tape" (May 1979). The data here pertain to the subsample of women currently married (at time of interview) who responded positively or negatively to this question.

Notes: (a) The "other" method mentioned, one instance, among the 1892–97 interviews, was coitus reservatus. (b) The exact questionnaire date cannot be determined in one case: Form 27 has been assigned to the 1892–97 period.

2. **Kinsey Survey Sample:** From the unpublished Kinsey Data Tape: Married Women (ISR Compilation, December 1978), kindly made available to the authors by Dr. Paul H. Gebhard. A subsample was created consisting of those once-married women who were married before 1915 to men who had attended at least one year of college. Within that subsample, tabulations were made of the responses of those 41 women who reported having ever used or never used the contraceptive methods listed in the table. See Gebhard and Johnson (1979), tables 309–14, for the form of the original Kinsey interview questions and marginal tabulations of the responses for the whole sample.

3. **Terman Sample:** Computations based on data in Terman (1938), table 130, p. 347, derived from responses to the question (asked of both husband and wife in each couple: "What method of contraception (birth control) do you use? (check) condom _____, pessary _____, jelly _____, powder _____, douche _____, withdrawal _____, 'safe period' _____, other methods."

longed to the second of the two groups: 5.9% of them reported themselves innocent of experience with contraception.

Only 2.4% of the California married couples interviewed by Louis Terman in the early 1930s labeled themselves as noncontracepting. This figure in table 7.2 also fits into the pattern of CPA-based estimates showing a steady shrinkage in the noncontrolling remnant in the West, until that proportion reached 2.5% among women belonging to the 1915–19 marriage cohort who were married at ages 20–29. These points of agreement with measures obtained by entirely independent methods from extensive census samples, offer a modicum of reassurance that small sample bias and self-selection biases in these early surveys are not leading us seriously astray regarding the pattern of contraceptive use among this stratum of middle-class American society.[12]

The indications from table 7.2, however, are strikingly at variance with Oscar Handlin's (1957) impression that the dire warnings issued by some Victorian authors of medical and marriage manuals must have persuaded educated middle-class couples to put aside all positive contraceptive methods as undesirable or ineffectual. As far as actual behavior is concerned, it seems quite incorrect to suppose that the combination of such individual exhortations with late-nineteenth-century legislation (inhibiting the distribution of contraceptive information and materials) had succeeded in making abstinence "the law" for those concerned to limit family size. Instead, the Mosher Survey evidence, in conjunction with the more broadly based indirect measures reviewed in section 7.1, suggest that, among native-born urban dwellers toward the upper end of the American socioeconomic hierarchy, the process of "quiet percolation" of contraceptive knowledge described by Norman Himes (1970 ed.) was already far advanced toward completion when the nineteenth century drew to its close. In the same vein it may also be remarked that, despite the influential role of nineteenth-century religious perfectionism, which Linda Gordon (1976) recently has discerned in tracing the development of feminist birth control thought in America, the perfectionists' "rejection of mechanical or chemical contraception in favor of changes in the nature of sexual intercourse itself" would appear to have exerted no decisive influence upon the modes of contraception adopted by women such as those interviewed by Clelia Mosher.[13]

Still more revealing is the distribution of contraceptive methods shown in table 7.2. In the full Mosher sample, the traditional "male-implemented" forms of contraception (withdrawal and condom) accounted for only one-third of all mentions of contraceptive use. Among the Mosher respondents who completed their questionnaires in the nineteenth century, douche was clearly the most prevalent form of contraceptive, followed by safe-period methods, withdrawal, and condom, in that order. The extent of use of safe-period methods may come as something of a surprise, especially since the timing of ovulation in the human menstrual cycle was not generally understood by the medical profession during the nineteenth century, indeed before the work of Knaus and Ogino in the 1930s. Nonetheless, widespread use of various primitive safe-period methods is quite consistent with much of the medical advice literature of the day (David and Sanderson 1979; Degler 1980, ch. 9). The possibility that safe-period methods may have played a role in the nineteenth-century United States fertility decline is one of those tantalizing suggestions which abound in the Mosher Survey data, to which we shall return briefly in section 7.3.

Starting with the nineteenth-century Mosher Survey responses in table 7.2, and reading across to the right, gives us several clues as to the changing patterns of contraceptive use. These trends may be followed up to the middle of the present century by consulting table 7.A.1. Douche and safe-period methods decline in popularity over time and are replaced with the more effective, female-implemented techniques of diaphragm, suppositories, and foams. The prevalence of male-implemented methods, particularly the condom, increases from the early to the late period in the Mosher responses but then remains roughly constant.

These observations lend further weight to the emerging consensus that middle-class couples were actively experimenting during the postbellum decade with a variety of contraceptive techniques, among which female-implemented methods of comparatively recent origins figured prominently. The latter included not only the new-fangled vulcanized rubber cervical caps and diaphragms of the 1870s and 1880s, but postcoital vaginal douching using syringes, as first advocated during the 1830s and 1840s by the western Massachusetts physician, Charles Knowlton; and systems of periodic continence, based upon the idea of a "safe period," that had been introduced into America from France during the 1850s (Himes 1970 ed.; La Sorte 1976; David and Sanderson 1979).

As far as educated, middle-class Americans were concerned, then, there is simply no foundation for continuing to suppose that couples desiring to avert pregnancies had been relying mainly upon the traditional "tried and true" methods of coitus interruptus and abstinence until 1915, when supposedly they were liberated to employ a better contraceptive technology by the political movement which coalesced around Margaret Sanger's catchy slogan—"birth control."[14] Few couples in the reproductive age range appear to have resorted to total abstinence from sexual intercourse for any prolonged duration, and the Mosher respondents mentioned using either douche or safe-period methods far more frequently than they mentioned the use of withdrawal.

Although it is clearly unwarranted to imagine that the contemporary medical and marriage manuals generally dissuaded readers from experimenting with the various methods of contraception described critically therein, perhaps their unanimously dire warnings against the use of coitus interruptus actually were heeded by substantial number of educated, middle-class couples who were inclined to suspect the worst of anything "old-fashioned." Surely, it appears unfounded for historians to venture the sophisticated interpretation, namely, that the great frequency of admonitory references concerning the damage done to mind and body by "pullbacks" (withdrawal) confirms an almost universal reliance upon this method by contracepting couples. Whether or not the virtually universal denunciations of coitus interruptus by writers of marriage manuals and tracts during the postbellum era in America is properly to be held responsible for a shift to other means of contraception among educated middle-class couples, must remain a matter for conjecture.

The Mosher Survey data do serve, however, to underscore the dubious nature of the argument that because coitus interruptus was the method of contraception most widely denounced, it must therefore have been "the most common method in actual practice."[15] On the same point, the evidence drawn from clinical surveys and retrospective investigations conducted in the 1920s (and later) appear to be no less treacherous as a basis for quantitative conclusions about nineteenth-century contraceptive practice, at least that among the professional classes. Wrigley (1969) and other students of British population history have been inclined to view the findings of Lewis-Fanning (1949) as providing corroboration for the view that withdrawal, having become a widespread practice among the French population as early as the eighteenth century, remained the dominant method of marital fertility control among the English—abortion aside—right up until the modern era.[16] This may yet be found to be true as a statement about the nineteenth-century American population as a whole, but the Mosher Survey evidence raises serious doubts that the generalization holds when applied specifically to the Victorian middle classes.

Further, since withdrawal is the male-implemented method of contraception par excellence, there have been those who have taken its putatively dominant position among the techniques actually in use as grounds for arguing that male motivation to control fertility held the key to successful contraception during the nineteenth century and before.[17] It is necessary now to reconsider this position, not only in light of the evidence we will present as to the effectiveness with which methods such as postcoital douching and the safe period could be used, but in view of the foregoing indications of the importance of these female-implemented methods among middle-class strategies of fertility regulation.

## 7.2.3    The Question of Abortion

What of abortion? The problem we face here is that the women interviewed by Clelia Mosher were asked no direct questions concerning induced abortion, nor did any of them volunteer explicit information on the subject. Quite apart from legal considerations and attitudes prevailing in respectable middle-class society at the end of the nineteenth century, the question of abortion doubtlessly would have been a matter of particular delicacy even in confidential communications between a regular medical practitioner and her patients (see Mohr 1978, chaps. 4, 6, 7). Fortunately, however, in the Mosher questionnaires the number of conceptions was reported separately from the number of children ever born, and so it is possible to examine the frequency and distribution of miscarriages within a subsample of the population.

The relevant data on conceptions and intrauterine mortality are summarized by table 7.3. Considering only the 40 women who had at least one recognized conception (missed menstruation) and for whom complete information is available as to the outcome of every pregnancy, the average rate of miscarriage was 0.185 in a total of 128 conceptions. From this, and from the fact that slightly under one-third of the subsample of these fertile women had ever aborted a recognized pregnancy (spontaneously or otherwise), it is evident that *successful* recourse to induced abortion among this group of middle-class wives was not at all the ubiquitous phenomenon decried by antiabortion campaigners within the American medical profession.[18] The Mosher Survey women belonged to another world than the real or imaginary one described by the Chicago physician Edwin M. Hale, who, in his work *On the Homeopathic Treatment of Abortion* (1860), held that it could be "safely asserted that there is not one married female in ten who has not had an [induced] abortion or at least attempted one!" (quoted in Mohr 1978, p. 90).

Unsuccessful efforts to induce abortions were probably widespread, fostering suspicions (or misplaced confidence) regarding the cause of miscarriages which in fact were of spontaneous origin. Such indications of a widespread willingness among women to attempt to terminate pregnancies, even by means so emotionally and physiologically "costly" as the techniques of abortion then available, are not without significance for our understanding of the strength of the desire to control fertility. Modern authorities have noted that interest in abortion and the actual incidence of induced abortion may sometimes increase with the initial diffusion of contraception, because couples become committed to the goals of family limitation before contraceptive control techniques are adequate to the task (Omran 1972, p. 100). But this is quite different

Table 7.3         Total (Spontaneous or Induced) Abortion Rates among Fertile Women in the Mosher Survey Sample, 1892–1920

|  | Mosher Survey Women Reporting One or More Pregnancies, the Outcome of Each of Which Is Known | |
|---|---|---|
|  | 1. Aggregate Average Rates of Occurrence | |
|  | Total Sample | Women Ever Aborting |
| Conceptions per woman | 2.98 | 5.33 |
| Abortions per woman | 0.55 | 1.83 |
| Abortions per conception | 0.185 | 0.343 |
| Number of women | 40 | 12 |

|  | 2. Probability of Pregnancy Terminating in Abortion (for Specified Individuals) | | | | | |
|---|---|---|---|---|---|---|
| Woman's contraceptive use experience (groups of methods ever used) | N. Obs. (Women) | Mean | S.D. | N. Obs. (Women) | Mean | S.D. |
| I.   Diaphragm, condom included: | 12 | 0.091 | 0.142 | 4 | 0.271 | 0.095 |
| II.  Withdrawal included, but not in (I) | 7 | 0.119 | 0.209 | 2 | 0.417 | 0.118 |
| III. Douche, safe period, other, but not in (I) or (II): | 17 | 0.127 | 0.191 | 6 | 0.361 | 0.125 |
| IV.  No contraception: | 4 | 0.000 | 0.000 | 0 | n.a. | n.a. |
| Totals | 40 | 0.102 | 0.170 | 12 | 0.340 | 0.118 |

*Technical notes and sources:*
1. **Aggregate Average Rates of Occurrence:** Each pregnancy (among those having a known outcome) that did not terminate in a live birth or a stillbirth was classified as having been "aborted." Tabulations were made for all qualified pregnancies (119 conceptions) recorded on the Mosher Survey Tape (May 1979). In four cases respondent was pregnant at time of interview; for the purposes of this table these conceptions are treated as if they had not occurred. The average rates presented for abortions per woman implicitly weights each woman's experience by her number of conceptions. The average abortion rate presented under (1) is thus a per conception rate, treating each *conception* as an independent observation.

2. **Probability of Pregnancy Terminating in Abortion:** From the Mosher Survey Tape (May 1979), an average frequency of abortions (as defined above) per conception was computed for each of the women who reported one or more pregnancies, the outcome of each of which is known. The mean and standard deviation of abortion probabilities presented in this portion of the table are calculated by treating each woman's average abortion rate as a single observation—rather than weighting by the number of conceptions she reported.

The women in the subsample for whom the foregoing abortion frequencies could be computed were then classified into one or another of the four, mutually exclusive contraceptive experience categories defined in detail in the stub of table 7.6.

from saying that successful abortion was quantitatively important among the factors responsible for the high degree of fertility control actually achieved by urban professional couples in postbellum America.

When one takes into account the prevailing standards of prenatal care and the age structure of the Mosher sample population (most of these women not having begun to bear children before they were 25), it would not be implausible to suppose that the observed average rate of miscarriage was wholly a reflection of spontaneous abortions. The findings of Leridon (1973), for example, indicate 0.19 as an overall average rate of *spontaneous* abortion.[19]

Another indirect approach to detecting significant reliance upon abortions is to compute individual average rates of induced or spontaneous abortion for groups of women who differed in regard to their reported experience in the use of contraceptive method. On the hypothesis that all abortions were spontaneous, we should expect to find abortion rates which did not differ significantly across contraceptive-experience groups. That is indeed the result that appears in the lower panel of table 7.3. Taken by itself, this last unfortunately falls short of being a conclusive test, because data for a sample in which there was a uniform rate of induced abortion also could have satisfied the "no relation" criterion. Although it may be concluded that the pattern in these quantitative data do not suggest the presence of a substantial number of induced abortions, the latter possibility cannot be completely dismissed. This residual element of ambiguity notwithstanding, it should be observed that the idea that induced abortion provided an important *alternative* to the strategy of contraception for successful controllers receives no support whatsoever. None of the handful of noncontraceptors among the women in table 7.3 had experienced abortions—induced or spontaneous.

Consideration of the available qualitative information in the Mosher Survey similarly tends to weigh against the impression that "criminal abortion" was especially rampant among the married middle classes in the postbellum era (Gordon 1976, pp. 51–60; Mohr 1978; Degler 1980; Gay 1983, pp. 253–54). Whatever the propaganda of the "regulars" in the American medical profession may have claimed, a reading of the individual medical histories contained in the Mosher Survey materials fails to disclose any indication immediately contradicting a bold surmise that the miscarriages experienced among this group of women were virtually all spontaneous in origin. None of the interviewees reported uterine infections, punctures, rupture, or other gynecological complications that would support suspicions that an abortion had been instrumentally induced or obtained by reflex methods. On the other hand, it is possible that these women were less than completely candid in divulging such aspects of their gynecological histories to Dr. Mosher. Had they been aborted by competent physicians—to which their income and social position would have helped give them access—there need not have been the sort of telltale injuries that often marked the work of the "quack" abortionists who ministered to the needs of less well-situated members of society. Further, the use of chemical abortifacients would not be expected to have left obvious physiological indications of this sort.

The matter simply resists closure on the basis of the available evidence. While one cannot justifiably assert that none among the 17.2% of pregnancies terminated represented induced abortions, the Mosher data remain consistent with the surmise that successful inducement of abortion was far from a commonplace experience in the lives of educated, urban, middle-class, married women during the closing decades of the nineteenth century.

If we are even approximately correct holding to the latter position, how is one to account for the "expert" testimony of contemporary physicians regarding the prevalence of induced abortions among the "well-to-do" and "so-called respectable classes," and their assignment of responsibility for the declining fertility of married middle-class American women to this supposed "slaughter of innocents"? (See e.g., Gay 1983, p. 254.) Perhaps mid-nineteenth-century American physicians, like Horatio Robinson Storer, for want of any hard evidence as to the actual extent of the midcentury "wave" of abortion against which they inveighed, were merely giving rein to their suspicions that essentially all miscarriages that came to their notice had somehow been produced by "criminal" interventions. It appears that it was indeed Storer's view that most miscarriages were intentionally produced. (See, e.g., Storer and Heard 1868, 1974 ed., p. 27, pp. 82–83.) Were such the case, and were the Mosher Survey women's miscarriage rates more generally typical of the frequency of spontaneous and induced abortion combined, then one could understand how these "expert contemporary observers" could have arrived at the erroneous consensus accepted by modern social historians, namely, that one pregnancy in five was being intentionally terminated by abortion (Mohr 1978, pp. 74–82; Degler 1980, pp. 231–32).

Some historians of the American fertility transition who have ventured beyond the evidence proffered by such "interested parties" as Storer and Heard have perpetuated the tradition of confounding observations on spontaneous and induced abortions. Reed (1978), for example, makes the following statement: "A 1917 study by a physician of 464 indigent women who received care in the dispensaries of New York's Department of Health revealed the stark reality of the frequency of *resort to abortion* among the poor. Of the 192 of these women who never used contraceptives 104 had a history of abortions. There were 202 abortions, or an average of almost two apiece" (p. 82, emphasis added).

A reexamination of the source of Reed's information (Kahn 1917, pp. 790–91), which we present as table 7.A.2, reveals three points. First, the 202 abortions mentioned by Reed were "miscarriages or abortions"—that is, both spontaneous and induced abortions in our terminology. Second, the ratio of spontaneous and/or induced abortions to conceptions among the 192 women who never used contraceptives is found to have been 0.135—a figure quite consistent with the hypothesis that the group members had not induced any abortions. Third, the women who did contracept had a ratio of (spontaneous and/or induced) abortions to conceptions of 0.132—almost identical to the rate of noncontraceptors. Thus, Reed's inference about the quantitative "resort to abortion" is contradicted by the very source he cited.

Reed is not the only social historian who has been misled by data which are often treacherous and at best difficult to interpret. In at least one passage of an otherwise generally informative study, James Mohr (1978, p. 79) was similarly carried astray: "Storer and Heard reach their most important single conclusion: 'The reported early abortions of which the greater number of course escape registry, bear the ratio to living births of 1 to 4.04 [in New York (Mohr's interpolation)], while elsewhere [in the world (Mohr's interpolation)] they are only 1 in 78.5.' In other words, on the basis of officially recorded figures alone, it appeared that fully 20 percent of all pregnancies in New York were being aborted."

Although Mohr's quotation from Storer and Heard's 1868 volume ([1974 ed.], p. 34) is technically accurate, there are two very serious flaws. One lies in the quotation itself, and the other in the interpretation placed upon it.

First, the sentence as it appears in Storer and Heard contains a serious typographical error. To show what it is we quote from Storer and Heard's detailed discussion of the underlying statistics elsewhere in the same volume: "In 41,699 cases registered by Collins, Beatty, La Chapelle, Churchill, and others, there were 530 abortions and miscarriages. Here all abortions were known: their proportion was 1 to 78.5. In New York from 1854 to 1857, there were 58,323 births at full time reported, and 1,196 premature. Here all the abortions were not known, probably but a very small fraction of them: the proportion was 1 to 40.4" (Storer and Heard 1974 ed., p. 27).

Thus the 4.04 figure quoted by Mohr, and cited by so many others who refer to his book, is the product of a nineteenth-century typographical error which misplaced the decimal point one digit too far to the left! Moreover, when the underlying statistics assembled for New York by Storer and Heard are correctly divided, the correct proportion turns out to be 1 to 48.77. This tells us that one pregnancy in 49.8 had ended either in a miscarriage or in an induced abortion, whereas we now know that about one pregnancy in five or six ends in a *spontaneous* miscarriage (Leridon 1976, p. 322). It is obvious that Storer and Heard examined data which suffered from a substantial undercount of miscarriages, as anyone familiar with the deficiencies of even twentieth-century public health statistics on the subject would suspect. Indeed, the undercount is so great that they can shed no light whatsoever on the frequency of induced abortion in nineteenth-century America.

Some of the most widely noted quantitative pronouncements made by modern social historians with regard to the frequency of induced abortion among married women in nineteenth-century America have thus been found to be essentially baseless. We suspect that a more throughgoing reexamination of the original sources than we have been able to undertake on this occasion would further deflate the legacy of exaggeration bequeathed to us by the anti-abortion campaigns of the 1860s and 1870s; in so doing it would corroborate the indirect testimony of the Mosher Survey, concerning the limited role of induced abortions as a means of family limitation among educated, urban middle-class couples.

In comparison with contraception, abortion as a regular method of fertility control imposes much heavier costs both in emotional and pecuniary terms and still entails far greater physical risks. It is perhaps not so surprising after all to find that educated upper-class women during the latter part of the nineteenth century resorted only infrequently to such effectual abortion techniques as were then available. We shall see, in section 7.3 below, that the existing array of contraceptive methods rendered fertility control aspirations largely attainable for this segment of the population, thereby greatly reducing their need to employ abortion except occasionally as an ancillary, "back-up" method.

Thus, to recapitulate the argument on this point, we have found several good reasons to doubt that abortion was utilized comparatively more intensively by the married women of the upper occupational and educational strata of American society during the final quarter of the nineteenth century. In the absence of empirical foundations such a view seems to rest largely upon the idea that, from the 1860s on, anti-abortion legislation and self-policing by the new masters of organized medicine "drove up the price of abortions and thus increasingly reserved them for the prosperous and enterprising" (Gay 1983, p. 254). Yet there were at least two distinct markets for abortions, and surely it was the artificial restriction of supply in the market for therapeutic abortions performed by socially respectable, "qualified" physicians which constituted the shift most relevant for potential upper-middle-class customers. The supply of self-performed, informal, and illicit abortions of undetermined but appreciable risk was far more elastic. Furthermore, the greater availability of contraception as an alternative form of effective fertility control meant that the middle classes' demand for "qualified medical" abortions was the more elastic, and so the quantity sought by them would fall more sharply in response to an increase in the relevant price. On both counts, then, we should expect that the negative quantitative impact of criminalization upon the frequency of abortions was most pronounced in respectable, higher-income circles.

Of course, married women belonging to the lower occupational and educational strata of American society were not the more fortunate for being left to the ministrations of "unqualified" abortionists. Lack of access to safe and dependable procedures—of the sort that have only recently come into widespread use in the United States—undoubtedly was responsible for much anguish and hardship in the lives of individual women. Estimates made by Sanderson (1979, table 5) indicate that for the entire United States population of ever-married white women born around the middle of the nineteenth century, induced abortion could have been quite significant as a means of control in comparison with contraception; even so Sanderson (1979) concludes that induced abortions in all likelihood accounted for less than half of all births averted by ever-married white women. Higher rates of induced abortion may indeed have prevailed among lower-income groups, the foreign born, and particularly among unmarried women, as a reflection there of less widespread diffusion of contraceptive knowledge and less effective contraceptive practice. This is but another respect in which the nineteenth-century American fertility decline was marked by divergent experiences rather than social and geographical uniformity.

### 7.2.3   The Frequency of Marital Coitus in the Era of "Careful Love"

The Mosher Survey data summarized in table 7.4 provide the first quantitative evidence, or at least the first of which we are aware, that the Respectable Victorian ideology of sexual continence had a definite counterpart in the marital sexual behavior of middle-class couples.[20] Age-specific frequencies of marital coitus computed from this source have been compared with those calculated for the Terman sample and the Kinsey sample. The frequencies of the respondents to the Mosher Survey were almost uniformly lower than those reported by either the 1935 Terman study sample or the Kinsey survey. As may be seen from table 7.A.3, the Mosher Survey observations also fall considerably below the coital frequency rates found by the 1965 and 1970 National Fertility Surveys. The one exception to this general rule is itself suggestive: among the Mosher Survey respondents who were interviewed at ages 45–59, the reported level of coital frequency was the same as, if not higher than, the rates found by the studies in the 1930s and 1940s.

How seriously ought one to take the contrast that appears in table 7.4? The observations available from the Mosher Survey are, after all, pitifully few in number. Might the apparent differences have arisen merely from random sampling variations? Such severe doubts as to the

**Table 7.4  Trends in Monthly Frequency of Marital Coitus Reported by Upper-Middle-Class Married Women in the United States, 1892–1950**

| Interview Dates | Mosher Survey Sample:[1] Currently Married Women | | | Terman Sample:[2] "Active" Married Women | Kinsey Survey Sample:[3] "Active" Women Married to College Men | |
|---|---|---|---|---|---|---|
| | 1892–97 | 1913–20 | Total 1892–1920 | 1935 | 1938–43 | 1944–50 |
| Ages 25–34 | | | | | | |
| Mean | 4.12 | 3.50 | 4.05 | 6.52 | 7.67 | 7.90 |
| SD | 2.48 | 0.00 | 2.33 | 3.99 | 4.77 | 4.56 |
| N | 15 | 2 | 17 | 332 | 28 | 424 |
| Ages 35–44 | | | | | | |
| Mean | 2.66 | 4.07 | 3.60 | 4.99 | 6.11 | 5.43 |
| SD | 1.26 | 2.48 | 2.17 | 3.36 | 4.61 | 3.99 |
| N | 3 | 6 | 9 | 277 | 15 | 298 |
| Ages 45–59 | | | | | | |
| Mean | 3.44 | 5.86 | 4.98 | 3.92 | 6.18 | 4.89 |
| SD | 2.61 | 4.77 | 4.15 | 2.80 | 4.45 | 4.93 |
| N | 4 | 7 | 11 | 108 | 3 | 114 |

*Technical notes and sources:*

1. **Mosher Survey Sample:** Computed from coded responses to Mosher's question, "Habit of intercourse," average number of times per week? per month? per year?" as tabulated from the Mosher Survey Tape (1979). The data here pertain to the subsample of women currently married (at time of interview) who reported their sexual relations with their present spouse. All such respondents reported some positive frequency of intercourse on this question.

For women reporting a range of coital frequencies as most did, e.g., "2–3 times per month," the midpoint of the range has been taken as the rate. Where an upper- or lower-bound rate was reported alone, e.g., "3 times or less," an estimate was interpolated for the other, missing end of the range, and the midpoint then calculated. Interpolations were made using the mean of ratios of individual maxima to minima among those women in the same age group who reported both explicitly. Of the 3 cases where such interpolations have been made, 2 occur among the 45–59 age group, and 1 among the 25–34 age group.

Coital frequencies originally reported as weekly rates have been converted to a monthly equivalent at the rate of 3.5 weeks per month. The latter figure was used to obtain comparability with the practice followed in the case of the Kinsey interview data. See n. 3, below.

2. **Terman Sample:** Computed from underlying data in Terman (1938), table 83, p. 270. Terman's questionnaires explicitly asked about the monthly frequency of marital intercourse. The published distributions of monthly frequency for (married) women of specified ages actually refer to a measure of the couple's sexual activity: the mean of the frequencies of marital intercourse reported separately by each of the spouses. To achieve comparability with the Mosher Survey Sample data, means and variances were computed for women (couples) who were sexually active—i.e., reporting some positive frequency of marital intercourse. A further adjustment was indicated, to achieve greater comparability with the *female*-reported frequencies secured from the Mosher and Kinsey Survey's for this table. Terman (1938, p. 269) noted that as a group, the women in his sample reported marital intercourse rates that exceeded those reported by their husbands. From tables 82 and 83 of Terman (1938, p. 270) we calculate that the mean monthly frequency as reported among the sexually active wives of all ages was 5.735, whereas the corresponding mean of their (self-reportedly "active") husbands was 5.435. (The differential is virtually the same cited by Terman as pertaining to the active and inactive couples as a group.) To adjust Terman's published age-specific measures to a female-report basis, we have multiplied them by the uniform factor of 1.027, that being the ratio of 5.735 to the midpoint (5.585) between the female- and male-report means. The unadjusted age-specific means corresponding to those presented in the table are: 6.35 for women 25–34, 4.86 for women 35–44, and 3.82 for women 45 or over (87% of women were in the 45–54 age group).

The uniform adjustment just described has the effect of raising the coital frequencies for women 25–44 somewhat less than is appropriate, while raising the rates for women 45 and over rather more than is appropriate. It has been found by Wallin and Clark (1958) that reporting discrepancies between spouses are correlated with the relationship between "preferred" and actual (mean of reports) frequencies of the partners. When one partner's preferred rate exceeds the "actual," that partner's reported rate is lower than the actual; the opposite holds when the preferred rate is below the "actual." In the Terman sample the mean age-specific rates "preferred" among husbands exceed the mean of the spouses' pooled reports at all ages, but especially below 45. The age-specific rates preferred among wives exceed the mean of the spouses' pooled reports among women in the under-45 age group, but the reverse is the case among older women (cf. Terman 1938, table 85, p. 272). Thus the presumption of a downward bias in the husbands' reports may be thought to be offset by the opposing upward bias in wives' reports, leaving the pooled estimate for the couple below the wife's reported frequency among women in the age group under 45. On the other hand, among older women there would be some (slight) underreporting bias by both partners, and the female-reported rate cannot be presumed to exceed the pooled rate to the same extent that is the case among the under-45s. Hence a uniform adjustment factor calculated from the Terman sample means across all ages—such as the 1.027 figure we have applied—tends to yield estimates of female reported frequencies of marital coitus which exhibit an insufficiently strong negative age gradient over the range above age 35.

3. **Kinsey Survey Sample:** Computed from current weekly frequencies of marital coitus reported by sexually active, currently married women, whose husbands had attended one or more years of college, as tabulated from the Kinsey Data Tape: Married Women, ISR Compilation, December 1978.

Our analysis of the coded current (and retrospective) observations on the frequency of marital coitus prepared by the staff of the Institute from the original interview records indicates that frequencies reported on a monthly basis were converted to a weekly basis by applying a factor of 0.29, which, allowing for rounding, corresponds to taking one month as the equivalent of 3.5 weeks. The latter figure has been used here to convert all the observations back into monthly frequencies.

Although interviewing by the staff of the Institute for Sex Research continued into the period 1951–63, the number of cases thus added to the basic sample of married women used here was negligible. We thus date the observations as referring to the period 1938–50, although those reported under the 1944–50 heading refer to all interviews conducted after 1943. Cf. Gebhard and Johnson (1979), pp. 31–35, for a description of the timing and location of the interviews conducted by Kinsey and his co-workers.

meaningfulness of the contrasts can be laid to rest. Consider for a moment the comparison between the coital frequencies of sexually active women married to college-educated males who were interviewed by the Kinsey team between 1944 and 1950, and the coital frequencies of the Mosher respondents. For 24–34-year-olds the difference appears quite large. The probability that 17 observations whose mean was 4.05 or lower would be chosen at random from the Kinsey subpopulation is less than one-half of one percent. Clearly in the case of women aged 25–34, by the usual standards of statistical significance, a test of the Mosher Survey respondents' average coital frequency against the sample mean for the corresponding Kinsey Survey women (interviewed in 1938–43 when married to men who had attended college) would require us to reject the null hypothesis that the coital frequencies of the two groups were identical.[21] For 35–44-year-olds, the probability that 9 observations having a mean of 3.26 or lower would be chosen at random from the 35–44-year-olds in the Kinsey subpopulation interviewed in 1944–50 is about 8%. It is possible also to reject the null hypothesis that the Mosher mean coital frequency among survey respondents age 35–44 *exceeded* that among the small sample of wives of college men interviewed by Kinsey and his colleagues during 1938–43, although the null hypothesis here can be rejected only at the 90% level. For 45–59-year-old women, as already noted, the coital frequencies reported in the Mosher Survey and the Kinsey 1944–50 interview data hardly differ, and the excess of the Mosher mean above that reported for the same age group in the Terman sample is not statistically significant.

We are thus led to conclude that during the years of exposure to reproductive risks the average frequency of marital coitus among the portion of the postbellum population represented by the Mosher Survey women was significantly lower than the norms that became established among more or less the same social strata of the American population in the second quarter of the twentieth century.

### 7.2.4  Covariation of Coital Frequencies with Contraceptive Methods

Some aspects of the relationship between contraceptive practice and coital frequencies among the Mosher Survey sample are presented in table 7.5, along with comparative data from the 1965 and 1970 National Fertility Surveys of the United States. One may note that the coital frequency levels are uniformly much lower in the Mosher Survey sample, within each of the comparable categories of contraceptive experience. As for the within-sample patterns of association, both the NFS and the Mosher Survey indicate that those who used "safe period" methods of contraception had relatively low coital frequencies. In the National Fertility Survey data, however, women using douche have the next lowest coital frequencies, while in the Mosher survey data they had the highest coital frequencies among the women who ever contracepted. Table 7.5 thus gives no clear hint that the Mosher Survey respondents resembled the respondents to the National Fertility Surveys in displaying positive covariation of the frequency of marital coitus with the inherent reliability of the contraceptive methods employed.

Nevertheless, variations in the frequency of marital coitus observed among couples in the Mosher Survey population were not unrelated to differences in their reported use of contraceptive methods. Beneath the surface of the summary figures in table 7.5 there existed a pronounced pattern of positive covariation between the current "habit of intercourse" and the (past and present) employment of methods of contraception whose characteristics belonged to the following set: (a) comparatively high inherent reliability, as indicated by modern demographic findings, and/or (b) involvement of an appliance-device during copulation, and/or (c) male implementation of the practice.

The vertical stub of table 7.6 lists the reported methods in the lexicographical ordering we have formed by reference to the three characteristics just cited. By this means we have been better able to accommodate the varied patterns of individual contraceptive experience that are described in the Mosher Survey responses. The contraceptive experience subset containing "diaphragm, condom, withdrawal, and douche" is placed at the top, as it involves—in order of listing—the two methods which entail use of an appliance-device, and two practices that are male implemented.

Although the five principal groupings of methods are set out in general conformity with modern notions of the inherent reliability of the methods denoted with capital letters, the arrangement as a whole does not guarantee a strict descending ordering of submethods with respect to this single dimension. "Condom only," prior to the introduction of liquid latex, and Federal Drug Administration testing in the late 1930s, is usually rated roughly on a par with "withdrawal only," but as the former member of this pair of male-implemented methods involves an appliance-device, it occupies a higher position in our ordering. "Withdrawal only" is generally held to be inherently more reliable than the nonappliance female-implemented techniques, and within the latter group "douche only" is likewise thought to dominate "rhythm only"— here taken to refer to all methods based upon the safe period.[22] A briefer explication suffices for the horizontal stub of the table: here the observations are arrayed according to four classes of coital frequency, and within each of those classes by the duration of the woman's exposure. The period of "exposure" for this purpose has been measured as the interval between marriage and the first of either the questionnaire date or the woman's fortieth birthday.[23]

**Table 7.5**  Patterns of Variation in the Mean Monthly Frequency of Marital Coitus with Contraceptive Methods Used: Mosher Survey and National Fertility Survey Findings Compared

| Category Code Numbers | Methods Ever Used | Number of Women | Mosher Survey, 1892–1920: Mean "Habitual" Frequency | | Current Method Used | National Fertility Survey: Age-Standardized Frequency[a] | | | |
|---|---|---|---|---|---|---|---|---|---|
| | | | Unstandardized | Age-Standardized | | 1965 | (Obs.) | 1970 | (Obs.) |
| a, b, b', c, d, e, f | Diaphragm and/or condom, included | 11 | 3.88 | 3.89 | Pill | 8.4 | (690) | 9.2 | (1211) |
| | | | | | IUD | 9.6 | (41) | 8.9 | (267) |
| | | | | | Diaphragm or condom | 7.2 | (900) | 8.6 | (679) |
| g, h, i | Withdrawal included but not a–f | 5 | 3.34 | 3.14 | Withdrawal | 7.5 | (112) | 8.6 | (74) |
| j, k, l | Douche included but not a–i | 12 | 4.86 | 4.87 | Douche | 7.1 | (196) | 7.6 | (126) |
| m, n | Safe period, but not a–l | 4 | 1.84 | 1.80 | Rhythm | 5.9 | (285) | 7.6 | (206) |
| o | None | 3 | | | None[b] | 6.7 | (1244) | 7.9 | (1462) |

[a]Marital coitus during 4-week period prior to interview; "contraceptive method used" refers to same time interval.

[b]Noncontraceptors other than women currently pregnant or lactating.

Note: Category numbers (letters) correspond to those in table 7.6 for Mosher Survey data.

*Technical notes and sources:*

1. **Mosher Survey:** Monthly Frequency of Marital Coitus, for Women, Classified by Contraceptive Use-Experience: The unstandardized and "age-standardized" means were computed from a tabulation of the Mosher Survey Tape (May 1979) coital frequency observations, described in note 1 of table 7.4. The underlying observations are the midpoints of the ranges reported by currently married women.

The contraceptive experience categories are formed by simple aggregation of the detailed categories which appear on the stub of table 7.6. See discussion in note 1 of table 7.2 for the definition of contraceptive use experience adopted in analyzing the Mosher Survey data.

To adjust the mean method-specific coital frequency estimates to remove the influence of intermethod differences in the age distribution of the respondents, the $(\bar{x}^s)$ "age-standardized" measure has been computed as follows: $\bar{x}^s = (\bar{x}) [\bar{x}_{\cdot j}/\bar{x}^s_{\cdot j}]$, where $\bar{x}$ is the grand mean $(\bar{x} = \Sigma_j \Sigma_i \bar{x}_{ij} (N_{ij}/N))$, $i$ being an index of the age groups 25–29, 30–34, 35–44, 45–59, and $j$ being an index of the five "experience" categories identified in the table. $\bar{x}_{\cdot j} = \Sigma_i (\bar{x}_{ij}) [N_{ij}/N_j]$ is the unstandardized mean, reported in the second column of the table, $N_j$ being the number of women in the $j$th category. $\bar{x}^s_{\cdot j} = \Sigma_i \bar{x}_i [N_{ij}/N_j]$ is an "experience" category-weighted average of the age-specific mean coital frequencies, where the latter are computed for the sample as a whole as follows: $\bar{x}_i = \Sigma_j \bar{x}_{ij} [N_{ij}/N_i]$. When the age distribution of women in each experience category is identical $\bar{x}^s_{\cdot j} = 1$ and the age standardization employed here has no effect.

The foregoing standardization is designed to improve the internal comparability of the method-specific mean frequencies, not to render the levels of the Mosher Survey rates strictly comparable with the NFS rates presented in the table. See further discussion, below.

2. **National Fertility Survey:** Age-standardized mean frequency of marital coitus among women using specified contraceptive methods during the 4 weeks prior to interview, in 1965 and 1970.

See Westoff (1974), table 3, p. 138, for underlying data, rearranged here. In describing the mean age–standardized rates, Westoff reports that the 1970 NFS age distribution was used "to eliminate effects of different age distributions associated with different exposure (contraceptive use) categories and changes in age distribution from 1965 to 1970."

The age standardization renders the NFS figures for these two dates comparable, but of course they are not fully comparable with the Mosher Survey mean method-specific rates, since the effects of differences between the 1970 NFS age distribution and the Mosher Survey sample age distribution have not been eliminated.

**Table 7.6  Distribution of Mosher Survey Respondents by Contraceptive Experience, Typical Frequency of Marital Coitus, and Duration of Marriage at Date of Interview**

| Contraceptive Experience Category Code Numbers | Methods Ever Used | Married over 10.5 Years 13+ | 5–12 | <5 | Married 10.5–7 Years 13+ | 5–12 | <5 | Married 6.99–3.5 Years 13+ | 5–12 | <5 | Married under 3.5 Years 13+ | 5–12 | <5 |
|---|---|---|---|---|---|---|---|---|---|---|---|---|---|
| I | Diaphragm (pessary) | | | | | | | | | | | | |
| a | & condom & c.i.[a] & douche | | | | | | | 4 | | | | | |
| b | & condom & c.i. & safe period | | | 7 | | | | | | | | | |
| b' | & condom & douche | | | | | 4 | | | | | | | |
| c | Only | | | | 8 | | | | | | | | |
| | Condom | | | | | | | | | | | | |
| d | & safe period & "jelly or douche" | | | | | | | 5 | | | 5 | | |
| e | & safe period | | | | | | | | | | | | 1 |
| f | Only | | | | | | | 5,2 | | | 4 | | 0 |
| II | Withdrawal (c.i.) | | | | | | | | | | | | |
| g | & abstinence | | | | | | | | 3 | | | | |
| h | & only | | | | 3 | | | 3,12 | 3 | | | | |
| i | coitus reservatus only | | | | | | | | | | | | 1 |
| III | Douche | | | | | | | | | | | | |
| j | & suppository & safe period | | | | | | | | | | 6 | | |
| k | & safe period | | | | | | | | | 2 | | | |
| l | Only | 6 | | | 6 | | 2 | 2,0 | 2 | 3 | 4 | 2 | |
| m | Safe period & abstinence | | | | | | | | | | 3 | 2 | |
| n | Only | | | | | | | | | | | 1,3 | |
| IV 0 | None | | | | | | 1,1 | | | | | | 0 |

*Source:* Tabulated from the Mosher Survey Tape (May 1979), prepared by David and Sanderson, with Matel. Exact marital durations are unknown in two cases: form 8 and form 44 have been assigned to the "13+" category.

*Note:* Each entry in the cells of the array records the number of conceptions reported by an individual woman.

[a] c.i. = coitus interruptus.

Each number entered in the body of table 7.6 represents an observation on the experience of one couple, and indicates the number of recognized *conceptions* reported by the wife. In all, there were 37 women for whom these four pieces of information—contraceptive experience, coital frequency, marriage duration, and number of conceptions—were available jointly. Other than the tendency for the number of conceptions to vary positively with coital frequency, no significant pattern of variation is immediately discernible in the *magnitudes* of these entries. Yet there is a statistically significant relationship between coital frequency and contraceptive experience within the cross-section. The latter stands out graphically from the location of the entries themselves, which will be seen to be concentrated in the cells forming the principal diagonal of the array. The comparative emptiness of the off-diagonal cells is strikingly illustrated by the next-to-lowest row of the table: every one of the (4) women who reported having relied exclusively upon the safe-period methods also reported that her modal frequency of marital coitus was less than 3.5 times in the month—and this was the case among older and younger women alike. The usual chi-square test for statistical independence—in this case, of coital frequency and contraceptive method-type—is immediately obtained from table 7.6 by converting the latter into a $4 \times 5$ contingency table. We simply count the frequency with which the sample of 34 observations *of women* are distributed among the main cells of the array, deleting the entries in the (bottom) row relating to noncontraceptions. At the 0.01 significance level, with $df = (5 - 1)(4 - 1) = 12$, the critical value $\chi_0^2 = 32.91$. The actual value of $\chi^2$ calculated from the array is 34.0, allowing us to reject the null hypothesis of statistical independence with a very high measure of confidence.

Focusing on the observed positive covariation of the Mosher Survey respondents' coital frequencies with the inherent reliability of the contraceptive methods they had employed, at least two explanatory hypotheses present themselves immediately for consideration. The first lays emphasis upon behavior in a stochastic environment, and would have us interpret the cross-section association between these intermediate fertility variables as reflecting the operation of a selection process. Those couples who fortuitously experienced low fertility when employing douche or safe-period methods, on this argument, would have been more likely to persist in those practices—rather than switching to other methods and so being led toward methods farther up the scale of reliability. At low coital frequency levels there would be a reduction in the probability of couples unluckily exceeding some pre-specified fertility norms, and a reduction, therefore, in the likelihood of their receiving a stimulus strong enough to induce a change in their mode of contraception. Thus it is quite possible that the observed covariation may have been generated by differentially higher continuation rates on the part of those couples who had begun to practice contraception by using douche and safe period, but who happened also to have established a regimen of infrequent sexual intercourse.

The second hypothesis is more straightforward: contraceptive methods such as postcoital douching and the premodern safe-period method may actually have proved much more effective in use than modern discussions of contraceptive reliability would intimate, especially when these supposedly ineffectual techniques were applied by couples who did not have intercourse with anything like the frequency observed among modern populations. In this vein, the conjunction of the evidence just examined with the observations reviewed above might be taken to suggest the existence of hitherto unrecognized interactions between low coital frequency and the "technologically inherent" reliability of contraceptive methods. If such interactions materially enhanced the use-effectiveness of what today appear to be extremely rudimentary techniques of fertility control, this could account for the remarkable large proportion among the Mosher Survey respondents who, though they reported having used only douche or the safe-period method, nevertheless as a group experienced low average conception rates for women of their ages and marital durations.[24] Among this subgroup the range of coital frequencies appears to have been low not only by modern standards but in relation to the other practitioners of contraception in the Mosher Survey population.

Was the fertility-regulating behavior of Victorian couples affected by an awareness of the existence of such interaction effects? Although suggestive, the evidence provided by the Mosher Survey itself is not at all conclusive on this point. Nor does it furnish a suitable statistical basis for evaluating the effects of coital frequency upon contraceptive effectiveness in order to establish that there is indeed a valid "technological" premise for this hypothesis. Fortunately, the latter task is one that may be approached by other means—and carried through to an affirmative conclusion, as shall be shown in section 7.3. For the moment, however, it is sufficient to notice that the hypothesis just proposed would complement the previously formulated "selection process" explanation. It would suggest a reason why couples at the lower end of the coital frequency distribution might tend (more than others) to begin to practice contraception using the less inherently reliable methods among those that were available.

At the core of the foregoing interpretation lie two notions: that a readiness to employ contraceptive means of family limitation already was widely established among the segment of the population represented in the Mosher Survey, and that persisting efforts to hold individual fertility below some generally accepted norm, or target level, caused these couples' choices among methods to become systematically adapted to their habitual frequencies of sexual intercourse.

But rather than implicitly regarding each couple's characteristic range of coital frequency as having been essentially predetermined, and therefore envisaging processes whereby the usage of contraceptive methods of different inherent reliabilities could come to be adjusted to accord with the goal of fertility control, the story could be turned around. Notice that our lexicographic ordering of contraceptive methods also arrays the latter in the "appliance/nonappliance-device" dimension, and according to the sex of the partner implementing the technique. Thus it is equally possible to suppose that for a given couple the selection of particular subsets of methods would be more or less determined by limitations in their knowledge of available techniques, their access to the necessary appliances, and/or the dominant preference of one or the other partners with regard to convenience, "naturalness," and still other considerations. Among the latter, concerns about the psychological and physiological side effects of regularly employing one or another particular method—whether or not these were scientifically justified—may have played a role. This has been suggested in the case of attitudes regarding the practice of coitus interruptus. In circumstances where selections of methods were thus constrained, there could well be a tendency for frequency of sexual intercourse to be adjusted in consonance with the couples' desire to achieve a target level of fertility.

The two microdemographic processes for the selection of contraceptive strategies that we have just set out are merely polar cases, and not competing or mutually exclusive alternatives. Thus it is not really necessary to take up the problem of deciding which of them is the more nearly correct, a determination that in any case could hardly be made simply on the basis of cross-section observations such as those culled from the Mosher Survey. Instead, it will be far more sensible to entertain the still broader view that in the experience of a representative population of late Victorian middle-class couples, family limitation efforts resulted in some degree of mutual adaptation between the methods of contraception employed and the "habitual" frequency of marital coitus. The resulting pattern of behavior would necessarily have reflected the profound influence of underlying technological (and biological) constraints that defined the set of possible fertility-regulating strategies.

### 7.2.5  Toward Interpretation

Two styles of possible explanation may be suggested for the temporal trends, and the pattern of cross-sectional variation suggested by table 7.6. The first is behavioral, whereas the second involves the nature of the questions in the two surveys. A behavioral story would go something like this: the Mosher women and their husbands had available to them contraceptive techniques which were perceptibly less reliable and more cumbersome than those at the disposal of the Terman and Kinsey survey couples. To lower their fertility without recourse to abortion with all its hazards, the Mosher women had learned to combine low coital frequencies with the relatively rudimentary methods which they employed. As they grew older, however, two changes occurred. Some of these women may have become infecund, "suffering" secondary sterility as a normal physiological development. For others, their experience with contraception may have been sufficiently successful so that it was no longer necessary to reduce coital frequency to the extent that they had done earlier in marriage. Finally, when they reached menopause and no longer faced any reproductive risks warranting the continued imposition of sexual self-restraints, their coital frequency rose and essentially matched that which the Kinsey study found among sexually active women married to college-educated men.

A different style of explanation threatens the foregoing plausible story. It focuses upon possible biases arising from the nature of the several survey questions regarding coital frequency. The Kinsey data presented in table 7.4 are coital frequencies at the date of interview.[25] The Mosher data, on the other hand, are not exactly comparable: they are responses to a question concerning the woman's "habit of intercourse," and it is possible that this elicited answers in terms of some marital lifetime average, rather than an average cast over the previous year. Were that the case, the true current coital frequencies of 35–44-year-old and 45–59-year-old Mosher respondents would actually have been lower than those appearing in table 7.4, augmenting the contrast with the chronologically later surveys but conforming to a more normal, "modern" pattern of gradual decrease with (male) age and marital duration.

This latter possibility raises further suspicions that the low reported frequencies of marital intercourse could somehow be artifactual or, alternatively, caused by circumstances other than purposive sexual restraint linked to the desire to avert pregnancies. Such circumstances would have obtained were the husbands of the Mosher Survey women much older, for it is observed in modern populations that coital frequency decreases with male age, and especially beyond age 45 (Kinsey et al. 1948; p. 252; Kinsey et al. 1953, pp. 353–55, 394; James 1973).

Examination of the actual distribution of the age differences between the spouses represented in the Mosher Survey, however, allows us to put aside this particular worry. The women in the age range from 25 to 45, virtually all of whom had been interviewed in the period 1892–97, belonged by and large to the marriage cohorts of the later 1870s and the 1880s. As one might have expected, postponement of marriage on the part of professional men was still very much the norm. The husbands of women who were 25–34 at the time of the interview had married at an average age of 28.5 (± 6.8) years, much like the husbands of the older interview group, who were 29.5 (± 8.0) years old, on the average, at the time of their espousal. But neither had their brides hastened to the altar, and so the interspousal age differences were quite small.[26] The mean age difference between husband and wife was 2.8 (± 6.6) years for Mosher's 25–34-year-old interviewees, −1.6 (± 6.9) for those who were 35–44, and 6.6 (± 13.9) for those aged 45–59. While that latter differential would suggest, if anything, that the women of postreproductive age should have reported relatively lower coital frequencies, just the reverse was the case.

A different source of doubt remains to be considered: a potential reporting bias other than the one initially examined. Quite conceivably, even married women of the *fin du siècle,* having grown up in the shadow of the higher Victorian era, were more prone to understate their true frequencies of marital intercourse than were the daughters of the early twentieth century's "sexual revolution" (Burnham 1973; Smith 1973). There is no direct way to evaluate this suspicion, but several considerations weigh against supposing this kind of reporting bias was responsible for the very low rates recorded among interviewees in the reproductive age range. The Mosher Survey questionnaires gave respondents the opportunity to distinguish between their desired ("ideal") frequency of marital coitus and their actual frequencies, and these women, as a group, indicated the latter to be significantly higher than the former. In a study of reporting biases in coital frequency information, however, Wallin and Clark (1958), found that spouses whose actual frequency exceeds their desired frequency tend to *overstate* the actual levels, as the theory of cognitive dissonance suggests they might (see n. 2 to table 7.4 for further discussion).

Hence we cannot find compelling reasons in the psychology of the situation to suppose that the low coital frequencies of reproductive-age women in the Mosher Survey population are an artifact of reporting biases. Moreover, as the analysis of section 7.3 will serve to establish, the coital frequency rates and the reported methods of contraception are entirely consistent with the degree of control over fertility which the Mosher Survey respondents had in fact achieved.

## 7.3 Possibilities of Effective Birth Control with Rudimentary Contraceptive Methods

As fascinating and suggestive as the microdemographic clues contained in the Mosher Survey materials are, the number of observations remains worrisomely small. Small-sample biases, not to mention the biases inherent in personal interview information on sexual and contraceptive behavior collected in the Victoran era, may be substantial. How much credence can be placed in generalizations based on such a source? How plausible is it that the large population of professional men and their wives, from which the Mosher Survey sample was constituted, managed effectively to control fertility by following similar strategies—combining the use of postcoital douching, or coitus interruptus, or the so-called safe-period methods, with a regime of comparatively infrequent sexual intercourse?

One style of answer to these questions would be that of the conventional empirical researcher and the traditional historian: gather additional historical information from similar sources and see whether it is consistent with the Mosher Survey indications. And indeed, this is sound advice. Without further direct corroborative material one must be extremely cautious in extrapolating from the behavioral patterns revealed by the Mosher Survey. Of course, the best sort of supporting evidence to be obtained would be a larger set of observations similarly detailing coital frequencies, contraceptive practices, and the reproductive histories of other such couples. But such advice, while sound, is not terribly encouraging. To date the Mosher Survey remains unique as a repository of information about these questions, as far as concerns couples who lived during the latter half of the nineteenth century. Researchers in American archives may turn up more fragmentary data pertaining to these and related aspects of fertility history, but it is doubtful that such finds will substantially enlarge the direct evidentiary base available at comparable levels of completeness and integration. Were we to come into possession of several additional sets of data just like the Mosher Survey, the same fundamental issues would be raised by seeking directly to extrapolate from the behavioral patterns in these small samples to conclusions about the population at large.

Fortunately, another approach is available: combining the analytic methods of mathematical demography with fragmentary historical evidence. Use of such techniques, and the still more complex business of microdemographic simulation in a stochastic framework, will allow researchers to proceed in a more immediate fashion to assess the plausibility of hypotheses suggested by the Mosher Survey and other small but potentially illuminating sources.[27]

Here we confine ourselves to reporting the outcome of a first and fairly obvious step in the direction of full-scale simulation experiments: to check the consistency between the average fertility experience of the larger population of couples belonging to the urban professional classes, on the one hand, and the pattern of contraceptive and marital sexual practices indicated by the sample of respondents to the Mosher Survey, on the other hand. Given the inherent unreliability of the methods being employed, was their use at reduced levels of coital frequency an effectual strategy of fertility regulation for a normally fecund, well-nourished population that did not rely significantly upon induced abortion as a "back-up method"? Some of the basic modeling techniques of analytical demography can be applied to answer such a question; to ascertain, in effect, the consequences of alternative patterns (including the Mosher Survey respondents' pattern) of fertility-regulating behavior within the framework of a general mathematical model of the reproductive process.

The outcome of such an exercise is of considerable intrinsic interest in exploring the way key intermediate fertility variables entered into the determination of completed marital fertility during the American fertility transition. Further, although it can amount to nothing more than a consistency check of the proposition that middle-class couples at large achieved comparably low fertility by adhering to patterns of sexual and contraceptive behavior resembling those of the Mosher Survey respondents, even obtaining this limited measure of confirmation is of value.

To see this one need only consider the implications of various conceivable results of the analysis. For example, it is imaginable that given the coital frequencies they reported, the Mosher Survey women's fertility could be accounted for only on the assumption that no *effective* contraceptive means were being employed. Were this the case, then we should have to conclude either that the reported methods of contraception were not really used, or were virtually ineffective, or that the Mosher Survey respondents as a group were of above average fecundity. Any of these inferences certainly would cast doubt on our general thesis. A different conceivable outcome of the exercise might be a finding that the range of contraceptive methods used by the couples in the Mosher sample were, after all, sufficiently reliable to make low fertility levels attainable even when marital coitus was as frequent as is observed in the modern American population. This result would be surprising and would undermine the argument that the ideology of sexual continence and its behavioral concomitants played an important role in the nineteenth-century diffusion of family limitation through contraception. There are in principle many other outcomes possible when comparisons are made between fertility predicted by a micro-demographic model with broadly representative biological parameters and the level of marital fertility observed among a historical population such as the professional classes in postbellum America. Any gross inconsistency between the two would suggest that the specification of a pattern of contraceptive and sexual behavior based upon the Mosher Survey finding is not likely to be generally valid as an indication of behavior in the corresponding social stratum at large.[28]

### 7.3.1  The Model

To carry out this test we shall start with a quite general microdemographic model of human reproduction viewed as a Markov renewal process, and proceed to adapt it so as to make explicit the relationship between expected fertility, on the one hand, and average coital frequency and contraceptive practice, on the other.[29] For a homogeneous group of fecund women the average level of completed fertility over an extended reproductive span may be closely approximated by

$$(1) \qquad B = \frac{M}{\left(\dfrac{1}{1-a}\right)\dfrac{1}{\Pi} + \left(\dfrac{a}{1-a}\right)I_a + I_g + I_p} .$$

In this expression $B$ is the expected number of live births during a reproductive life span of $M$ months. The probability that a recognized conception will terminate in a spontaneous or induced abortion is represented by $a$. $\Pi$ is the monthly probability of a recognized conception (a missed menstruation). $I_a$ is the mean length of the entire period of nonsusceptibility associated with miscarriages, that is, the sum of the lengths of the mean interval of terminated gestation and the mean duration of post-abortum nonsusceptibility. $I_g$ is the mean gestation interval in the case of a live birth, and $I_p$ is the mean length of the period of nonsusceptibility following a live birth.

The monthly probability of a recognized conception, $\Pi$, depends upon the biological effects of the pattern and frequency of marital intercourse over the menstrual cycle, and their interactions with the technical and behavioral determinants of contraceptive effectiveness. Treating time as a discrete variable, measured by the "days" of a standard "month," a suitable quantitative specification for this biological-technological relationship is given by

$$(2) \qquad \Pi = \theta \sum_{c=1}^{v} [\tbinom{v}{c}n^c(1-n)^{v-c}] \cdot [1 - (1-f)^c] ,$$

where

$$(3) \qquad f = \mu + (1 - \mu)\, \alpha_m.$$

Here $\theta$ is a parameter of inherent biological fecundity, denoting the probability of a fertile menstruating woman conceiving as a result of unprotected coitus during the fertile interval. The latter interval is $v$, representing the number of days within each menstrual cycle when unprotected intercourse may result in pregnancy. The summation index $c$ indicates the number of such susceptible days in the cycle on which intercourse does occur.[30] Finally, completing the ingredients of equation (2), $n$ is the probability that intercourse will occur on any given day and $f$ is the probability that (as a result of contraceptive failure) any given act of coitus will be rendered "unprotected" and therefore capable of leading to pregnancy.

As equation (3) indicates, the per-trial probability of contraceptive failure ($f$) depends on behavioral as well as essentially technological factors. $\mu$ is the per-trial probability that contraception will be omitted when intercourse occurs, whereas $\alpha_m$ is the $m$th method's inherent accident rate—the probability that the contraceptive method on any given trial will fail to eliminate possibility of a conception.

A number of assumptions are embedded in equations (2) and (3). These need not be labored over here, but it is necessary to state them explicitly and note some of their implications before proceeding to the stage of empirical implementation. In equation (2) the actual frequency and temporal pattern of marital coitus within the menstrual cycle are treated as stochastic variables whose distribution is governed by a single parameter $n$, the daily probability of intercourse. In effect, we assume a Bernoulli process—in which the probability of intercourse on a given day is constant and independent of the occurrence or non-occurrence of coitus between spouses on any preceding day.[31]

The specification based on the assumption of randomly timed coitus—a conventional assumption in mathematical studies of fertility determination—may be taken as a reasonable representation of the behavior of randomly chosen couples who do not practice contraception or who do contracept using such methods as douche, coitus interruptus, vaginal suppositories, condom, or diaphragm. On the other hand, it is obviously inappropriate as a representation of the behavior of couples who employ modern rhythm methods, or who follow an adaptive regime of contraception based on primitive safe-period methods. Theoretical investigations of fertility determination within such contraceptive regimes require other, rather more complex modeling approaches which need not be described here.[32] Salient findings of some of our exploratory work along these lines, however, will be mentioned below.

Insofar as the average frequency of marital coitus has been found to decline systematically with increases in the age of the male, the specification of a constant value of $n$ for any appreciable portion of the reproductive life span is unlikely to provide a close approximation to reality. But if the average daily probability of coitus over the reproductive span is used in equation (2) in place of the true age-dependent average frequencies, the average monthly probability of a conception indicated by this expression will be biased upward.[33] Since biases in this direction are unfavorable to the argument that we are advancing here, our case will be strengthened by accepting equation (2) and interpreting $n$ as the average daily probability of marital coitus over the reproductive life of a representative couple.

An analogous point can be made concerning the formal representation of methods and modes of contraception. The per-trial rate of contraceptive failure, denoted by the parameter $f$ is expressed in equation (3) as a sum of two constant probabilities: the probability $(\mu)$ of omission of all contraceptive protection, and the probability $(1 - \mu) \cdot (\alpha_m)$, of the $m$th method being employed but failing on any given trial.[34] It is quite appropriate to thus characterize contraceptive methods by a constant, technologically determined rate of per-trial failure $(\alpha_m)$ which we shall refer to as the "inherent accident" rate. On the other hand, there is modern evidence indicating that among contracepting couples the average omission rate is parity dependent and tends to decline as the couples approach some "target" level of fertility.[35] The combined probability of failure due to accidents and omission, $f$, is thus likely to decline during the course of a continuously contracepting couple's reproductive span. But if the parameter $f$ is interpreted as the average per-trial failure rate applicable over that period, we may be assured that the corresponding average monthly probability of a conception indicated by equation (2) will be biased upward on this account.[36]

A third set of remarks is in order, concerning our assumptions about the way biological and physiological factors enter into the determination of the monthly probability of a conception. In form, equation (2) is the sum of products of two terms. The first term in brackets represents the probability that coitus occurs exactly $c$ times within the fertile interval $v$. The second term in brackets represents the probability that at least one contraceptive accident or omission occurs on those occasions.

Two assumptions are implicit in this specification. The first is that intercourse occurs at most once per day during the fertile period. This is not a wholly unrealistic assumption with regard to couples whose coital frequencies are as low as those reported in the Mosher Survey. Moreover, relaxation of this restriction poses no particular formal difficulties and would yield results which are insignificantly different from those reported here.[37] The second, and the more significant assumption is that the monthly probability of a conception depends upon the probabililty of one or more contraceptive failures occurring during the fertile interval but is independent of the precise number of such instances.

We have two reasons for assuming that the likelihood of conception is not raised by the occurrence of multiple contraceptive failures within the brief period of susceptibility of impregnation. The first is essentially one of mathematical and computational convenience: although the specification undoubtedly is not precisely accurate, it leads to tractable expressions whose properties do mimic the quasi-concave functional relationship (between coital frequency and the probability of conception) that has been observed in detailed physiological and statistical studies of human fertility.[38] Second, when compared with other possible specifications that would more closely represent the complex dependence of the monthly conception probability upon the frequency of unprotected coitus during and immediately preceding the fertile interval, equation (2) yields results that least favor the empirical propositions we seek to establish.[39]

### 7.3.2  Historically Relevant Parameter Values

To implement our model it is necessary first to specify historically appropriate values of the parameters $a$, $I_a$, $I_g$, $I_p$ in equation (1) and to fix corresponding values for the biological parameters $v$, and $\theta$ in equation (2). Table 7.7 presents the numerical estimates we shall employ, and the notes appended thereto briefly describe the sources and procedures used in their derivation. The important point to notice is that, in keeping with our purpose of evaluating the general applicability of the particular array of fertility control strategies revealed by the Mosher Survey, we have employed values for the primarily biological parameters ($\theta$, $v$, $I_a$, and $I_g$) that are appropriate for the larger population of married fecund women belonging to the American professional classes during the nineteenth century. Equivalent care has been taken to employ values for the probability of spontaneous and induced abortion ($a$), and the mean duration of the interval of postpartum nonsusceptibility ($I_p$), that accord with observations derived from the Mosher Survey data. In principle the latter parameters could reflect significant fertility-regulating behavior. From the discussion in section 7.2 it should be recalled, however, that internal evidence from the Mosher Survey, and comparisons with data for larger historical populations, suggest that this (.184) rate of recognized miscarriage largely reflected spontaneous abortions. Further, we may note that our estimate of 7 months for $I_p$, based on the Mosher Survey's information about the mean length of the interval from birth to resumption of menstruation and the average duration of lactation, is somewhat shorter than estimates usually employed in simulation studies of historical noncontracepting populations.[40]

We now possess a suitably parameterized mathematical structure which predicts average completed fertility in a reproductive lifetime of $M$ months, given the corresponding average frequency of marital coitus ($n$) and the per-trial rate of contraceptive failure ($f$).[41] But, to be able to translate the results into statements about the efficacy of various historical strategies of fertility control one additional step is necessary.

Table 7.7          Parameter Values for Equations (1) and (2)

| Parameter | Symbol | Numerical Value |
|---|---|---|
| Probability of abortion | $a$ | 0.184 |
| Postabortum interval of nonsusceptibility | $I_a$ | 4 months |
| Gestation interval | $I_g$ | 9 months |
| Postpartum interval of nonsusceptibility | $I_p$ | 7 months |
| Fertile period | $v$ | 3 days |
| Mean inherent fecundity | $\theta$ | 0.2461 |

*Notes and sources:*

$a$: The value of $a$ is taken from the Mosher Survey data but accords quite well with modern estimates of the spontaneous miscarriage rate. See our discussion of this point in Sec. 7.4 above.

$I_a$: Two studies referring to populations during the first half of the present twentieth century, one for the United Kingdom and one for Indianapolis, show mean durations of pregnancies terminated before the seventh month as 3.25 and 2.78 months, respectively. The underlying data for these computations appears in United Nations (1954), table 3, p. 16. A recent, but also more careful study by French and Bierman (1962), p. 835, puts the mean duration of a spontaneously aborted pregnancy at approximately 2 months. Adding one month for postabortum nonsusceptibility we have a choice of setting $I_a$ either at 3 or 4 months. Since the studies referring to periods when maternal medical care was less preventive of miscarriage suggest that the 4-month estimate is more appropriate, and since a choice of the larger value would bias the computation reported in table 7.7 against our argument, we have chosen to set $I_a$ equal to 4 months rather than 3.

$I_p$: The Mosher Survey provides two sorts of information concerning the length of the period of postpartum nonsusceptibility. There are 48 direct observations on the interval between a birth and the first subsequent menstruation. The average duration of that interval is 5.17 months. The second source of data relates to lactation. The mean lactation period for 44 observations is 7.48 months. Both sorts of data are available in 25 cases and in this subset the mean interval from a birth to the first menstruation is 6.36 months and the mean lactation period is 6.76 months. Given these data and the fact that susceptibility may resume only after one or two menstrual periods (see Tietze 1961, p. 132, and Perez et al. 1971, p. 499–503), we have taken the mean period of postpartum nonsusceptibility to be 7 months. We may have as easily chosen 6 months as the mean period of postpartum nonsusceptibility. Given our procedure for determining $\theta$ described below, an $I_p$ value of 7 is less favorable to the thrust of our argument than is an $I_p$ value of 6.

$v$: An excellent survey on the length of the susceptible period can be found in Nag (1972). The literature reviewed there suggests that the susceptible period is about 2 days long. An identical conclusion is reached by Bongaarts (1976), pp. 236–37, although by a somewhat different route. Physiological evidence, on the other hand, suggests that the susceptible period may be as long as 3 days (cf., e.g., Hartman 1962, chap. 9, esp. 74). The latter value has been employed by Tietze and Potter (1962) in theoretical investigations of the modern rhythm method's effectiveness. We have chosen to set $v$ equal to 3 instead of 2, because given the procedure followed here in determining $\theta$, this choice is less favorable to our argument.

$\theta$: The value we have used for $\theta$ takes into account all the other parameters in table 7.6. It was set so that a population of noncontracepting women whose average daily probability of marital coitus was $n = .333$ (over their reproductive lives) would bear, on the average, the same number of children over a 20-year reproductive life span as would a group of married women between the ages of 20 and 39 who had the age-specific marital fertility rates which Coale and Trussell (1974) have associated with natural fertility. Age-specific marital fertility rates which occur in the absence of volitional contraception tend

**Table 7.7**     (continued)

to vary in level across times and places but not in any systematic pattern. Sanderson (1979) shows that the level of the age-specific marital fertility rates associated with natural fertility in Coale and Trussell (1974) is appropriate for nineteenth-century America. The value selected for $n(=.333)$ is consistent with modern coital frequencies reported in sec. 7.3 (table 7.3) above, and with the data analyzed in James (1971, p. 159). Bongaarts (1976, pp. 236–237) accepts the same average frequency as appropriate for historical populations displaying natural fertility.

In the process of computing $\theta$ (but not in table 7.7) a sterility rate of 8.2% was assumed. Our treatment of sterility here is a simple one. Sterility varies with age, but for ease of computation we have used the sterility rate of 25–29-year-old women in Tourouvre au Perche (1665–1765), as estimated by Charbonneaux (1970).

A correspondence must be established between $f$ and specified contraceptive methods employed with specified degrees of "regularity"— that is, omission probabilities. Since methods may be characterized by their inherent probability of failure when used with perfect regularity, it is natural to seek to determine the values of $\alpha_m$ associated with the relevant historical methods, using for this purpose observations of the "use-effectiveness" of contraceptives in situations where the omission rate is exactly known. The principal difficulty that stands in the way is the unavailability of such observations, even for periods more recent than the late nineteenth century.

As an alternative approach, we have utilized historical information pertaining to the use-effectiveness of various contraceptives under conditions in which it is reasonable for us to assume that the average per-trial frequency of contraceptive omission was negligibly low. The use-effectiveness measures in question derive from data gathered in the early 1930s and related to the experiences of a large sample of women during the period shortly following their having contacted a family planning clinic in the Bronx.[42] The technical appendix summarizes the procedures we have derived for retrieving estimates of the parameter $\alpha_m$ from conventional measures of postclinic use-effectiveness, and discussion of these complexities need not further detain us here.[43] For the three methods most relevant to the present discussion, douche, coitus interruptus, and condom, our computations produced the following values of $\alpha_m$: 0.118, 0.047, and 0.016, respectively. As satisfactory as these values may be in characterizing the state of contraceptive technology circa 1935, we shall find it necessary to consider the possibility that around the turn of the century the average inherent unreliability of the douche solutions and condoms in use may have been substantially greater than this.

### 7.3.3   Simulation Results

Our findings on the quantitative relationship between average completed fertility over a 240-month reproductive span, on the one hand,

and coital frequency, contraceptive method, and the regularity of contraceptive practice, on the other, are summarized in table 7.8. Since the latter two variables exert their influence by jointly determining the per-trial rate of contraceptive failure ($f$), it is best to begin by considering the general properties of the function $B(n,f)$ exhibited in this table. As one would expect, $B(n,f)$ is a positive and concave function of each of its arguments—holding the other constant.[44] For the values of $f$ greater than 0.125, the concavity of $B(n|f)$ appears here as being most pronounced when the coital frequency rate varies within the range below 0.250, that is, when intercourse occurs on fewer than 6 days of a 28-day "month" ($\tau < 6$). But as $f$ is parametrically reduced below .125, the $B(n|f)$ function becomes progressively more linear over the entire domain of $n$ and slopes upward less steeply.

Greater marital sexual continence, therefore, turns out to be quite ineffective as a means of averting births when the per-trial probability of contraceptive success $(1 - f)$ is as high as or higher than 0.97, which is essentially the range attainable by regular use of *modern* contraceptive methods. One may see that when $f = .03125$, drastically reducing the average monthly frequency of coitus from 12 to 4 only averts an additional 1.21 expected births over the reproductive span, thereby lowering completed fertility from 1.92 to 0.71. Nor is greater continence any more effective as a means of averting births in the absence of positive contraception, unless the average frequency of marital coitus is reduced to extremely low levels. When $f = 1$ it is possible to avert 1.21 births, on the average, by decreasing the monthly frequency of (unprotected) coitus from 12 to 6; but the proportional change in $B$, from 10.62 to 9.41, is a small one. Even when the average frequency of unprotected intercourse is held to as low a rate as twice in 3 months ($n = .0625$), 5.31 births would be expected over the course of the 20-year reproductive span. Near abstinence by itself could not account for the low average levels of completed marital fertility attained by couples belonging to the professional classes in Victorian America, even if it were plausible to suppose such a practice was ubiquitous among this segment of the population.

The foregoing observations pertain to the extreme situations of populations that either are using highly effective, modern contraceptives, or are not contracepting at all. They turn out to be quite misleading as guides to the quantitative significance of coital frequency variations in situations where rudimentary contraceptives are being employed—or where inherently quite reliable methods are applied only irregularly. Indeed, the interaction between reduced coital frequency and the application of rudimentary contraceptives is the most notable, and perhaps most surprising general feature of the relationships summarized in table 7.8. Whereas a reduction in $\tau$ from 12 to 4 averts 1.21 expected

**Table 7.8**  Expected Number of Births (B) to Completed Unions: Homogeneous Populations Following Specified Contraceptive Strategies throughout a Reproductive Life Span of 240 Months

| Per-Trial Probability of Contraceptive Failure (f) | Equivalent Contraceptive Practice Method (m) | Per-Trial Probability of Omission (μ) | Average Daily Frequency of Random Coition (τ); Frequency in 24-Day Period (τ) | | | | | |
|---|---|---|---|---|---|---|---|---|
| | | | $\tau = 12$ $n = .5000$ | $\tau = 8$ $n = .3333$ | $\tau = 6$ $n = .2500$ | $\tau = 5$ $n = .2083$ | $\tau = 4$ $n = .1667$ | $\tau = 3$ $n = .1250$ |
| 1 | No contraception | | 10.62 | 10.01 | 9.41 | 8.96 | 8.36 | 7.50 |
| 0.5 | Douche | 0.43 | | | | | | |
| | Withdrawal | 0.48 | 9.41 | 8.36 | 7.50 | 6.93 | 6.22 | 5.31 |
| | Condom | 0.49 | | | | | | |
| 0.25 | Douche | 0.15 | | | | | | |
| | Withdrawal | 0.20 | 7.50 | 6.22 | 5.31 | 4.75 | 4.11 | 3.35 |
| | Condom | 0.24 | | | | | | |
| 0.125 | *Douche* | 0.01 | | | | | | |
| | Withdrawal | 0.08 | 5.31 | 4.11 | 3.35 | 2.91 | 2.44 | 1.92 |
| | Condom | 0.11 | | | | | | |
| 0.0625 | *Withdrawal* | 0.02 | 3.35 | 2.44 | 1.92 | 1.64 | 1.35 | 1.04 |
| | *Condom* | 0.05 | | | | | | |
| 0.03125 | *Condom* | 0.02 | 1.92 | 1.35 | 1.04 | 0.88 | 0.71 | 0.54 |

*Source:* Equations (1) and (2), and parameter values summarized in table 7.7, with $M = 240$, generate the estimates shown for B.

[a] The standards of reference for inherent reliability and "perfect regularity" of use correspond to postclinic experience with the indicated methods during the early 1930s, as observed by Stix and Notestein (1940). See text for discussion of the procedures followed in establishing correspondences between (f) and indicated contraceptive practices. In eq. (3) the $\alpha_m$ estimates used are: douche (0.1186); withdrawal (0.0471); condom (0.0158).

births when $f = .03125$, the same drop in average coital frequency may be seen to avert 3.19 expected births when $f = .50$, 3.39 expected births when $f = .25$, and 2.87 when $f = .125$. Thus, in place of the 10% decrease in $B$ which the drop in $\tau$ from 12 to 4 yields in the absence of any contraception, with $f$ at these intermediate reliability levels we find the completed fertility rate is decreased by roughly 33%, 45%, and 54%, respectively.

What does the information in table 7.8 tell us about the effectiveness of the contraceptive methods which the Mosher Survey respondents reported having employed? It has long been maintained that the method of withdrawal can be quite effectual, if it is practiced with complete regularity and care to avoid postejaculatory reintromission. This is confirmed by the figures in the second row from the bottom of the table, which indicate an equivalence between the postclinic practice of withdrawal with 90% regularity, and the use of 1930s-standard condoms with 95% regularity. Either technique would yield a per-trial failure rate of $f = .0625$, easily sufficient to hold completed fertility below 2.5 children with the average frequency of marital coitus as high as 8 times per month.[45] Very regular postcoital douching, using solutions whose spermicidal effectiveness matched those employed by the New York birth control clinics' clients in the 1930s, is found to yield a per-trial failure rate twice as great ($f = .125$), and therefore would provide the same expected measure of lifetime fertility control for couples whose average coital frequency was only half as high.

Of course, one cannot assume that the condoms or douche solutions in use during the latter part of the nineteenth century typically were as reliable as those available to the clients of birth control clinics 40 or 50 years later. The historically relevant per-trial probability of failure with these methods, at any specified omission rate, may well have been substantially larger than is indicated by the equivalences established in table 7.8. Suppose, for example, that in 48% of the cases the inherent reliability of the douche solution and its method of application was on a par with the 1930s postclinic standard, and that for the remainder of the users the action of douching was subject to an inherent probability of failure three times greater than that standard. The representative user of "douche" would thus have been subject to a per-trial probability of contraceptive accident as high as $\alpha = .2424$, and the corresponding per-trial failure rate for very regular postcoital douching (i.e., with .01 probability of omission) would be $f = .25$ rather than .125. Similarly, whereas 1930s-standard condoms applied with probability of $(1 - \mu) = .89$ are shown as giving rise to a per-trial failure rate of $f = .125$, one may readily calculate that if 14% of the condoms were certain to be defective and the rest subject to the 1930s standard of inherent reliability, the historically relevant rate of per-trial contraceptive failure among common users (assuming the same .11 omission rate), again, would be as high as $f = .25$.[46]

Although the foregoing seem to us to be rather generous allowances for the inferiority of nineteenth-century contraceptive technology, to make them serves further to reinforce the general point that at low coital frequencies these rudimentary methods could afford couples a surprising measure of control over their expected fertility. The significance of the popularization of douche among middle-class women from the mid–nineteenth century onward, and the indications of the method's prominence which the Mosher Survey data provide, deserves particular notice in this regard. As may be seen from the following illustrative calculations, the introduction of even so unreliable a method as this provided women—or at least women who could purchase a syringe and conveniently prepare a douche solution—a means to reduce their fertility rather substantially.

To begin, let us suppose that the husband were to practice coitus interruptus only irregularly, say, with a probability of .52 on any given occasion of intercourse. The corresponding per-trial failure rate is found, from table 7.8 (withdrawal: $\mu = .48$), to be $f_h = .5$. Now assume that, independent of his actions, the wife were to adopt extremely regular postcoital douching using *inferior* solutions which alone as in the previous example would give rise to a typical per-trial rate of contraceptive failure of $f_w = .25$. The per-trial probability of failure for the couple's *combined* conti æceptive practice would therefore be $f_h f_w = .125$, which is equivalent to regular postcoital douching practice matching 1930s postclinic standards of effectiveness. Such a contraceptive regime, when maintained with an average monthly coital frequency of 4, would give the couple an expectation of substantially fewer than 2 births over a 15-year period: $(180/240)(2.44) = 1.83$ births, to be precise. Let us suppose, then, that the woman in question was 25 years old when she married, and, without having undertaken any positive contraceptive action on her own part, had borne two children and resumed menstruation by the time she reached age 30. Under the foregoing assumptions, having her take up the secondary, female-implemented regime of regular postcoital douching from that point onward would make the difference between the couple's completed fertility being 3.83, on average, rather than the 5.91 births that could be expected were they to rely solely upon continuation of the husband's irregular practice of coitus interruptus.[47]

### 7.3.4  No Safety in Numbers—Simulation Findings on Primitive "Rhythm" Methods

Among the means of preventing conception that had been used by the women whom Clelia Mosher interviewed during the 1890s, only the douche was cited more frequently than was the safe-period method. Prompted by this finding, and by the observation (from tables 7.5 and 7.6) that the women who had relied solely upon the safe-period method also reported extremely low frequencies of marital coitus, we have elsewhere undertaken to investigate the potential effectiveness of an adaptive strategy of contraception based on the primitive principle of the rhythm method.[48] By this we refer simply to the notion that susceptibility to impregnation is a periodic occurrence in the menstrual cycle, and that there must consequently exist some interval of absolute or comparative "safety." Premodern "safe-period" recommendations came in many forms, frequently conflicting, often treacherous, and generally lacking in any scientifically accurate physiological foundations.

Nevertheless, there scarcely can be any doubt as to the contraceptive success experienced by those women who adopted one specific formulation of safe-period advice current from the 1850s onward, and rigorously avoided intercourse during the fortnight following the cessation of their menses.[49] Such an antinatal regime would certainly be easier to maintain if intercourse occurred more often than three times a month. But infrequent coitus may equally accommodate a perversely pronatal regime of periodic continence. There is scant doubt that contraceptive failure must have awaited those women who accepted the advice, no less current in supposedly informed medical circles, to avoid intercourse through the week immediately before menstruation, during the menses, and in the week immediately following.[50]

Thus, in considering the subject, it is essential to distinguish between the principle of seeking the woman's period of minimal (or maximal) susceptibility to impregnation, and the various specific recommendations that have been made, down through the ages, as to where within the menstrual cycle one should first look. Historians of fertility control have generally failed to draw this distinction, and in so doing they have overlooked the possibility that the informal practice of *searching* for the elusive safe period could in itself constitute an effective means of limiting individual fertility. Not for every individual involved, alas, but at least for the representative couple of such a population.

Authorities on the modern rhythm methods (e.g., Tietze and Potter 1962) would be predisposed to dismiss such an adaptive strategy of fertility control as utterly hopeless. According to Christopher Tietze: "Self-taught rhythm, haphazardly practiced is a very ineffectual method of contraception and deserves its facetious designation, 'Vatican roulette' " (Tietze 1965, reprinted in Nam 1968, pp. 449–500). But just how ineffectual is "very ineffectual"? In the preceding statement the standard of comparison implied clearly is the array of far more dependable methods at the disposal of modern couples who seek to space pregnancies or terminate childbearing completely, methods whose appearance derives precisely from the fact that their proper application does not entail a process of trial and error. That is hardly the level of expectation appropriate in a discussion of nineteenth-century contraceptive efforts. Moreover, modern coital frequency norms apparently are higher than those relevant to the historical context of the present discussion, and it is only to be expected that antinatal "learning" would prove considerably more difficult when a regime of frequent intercourse was being maintained. Quite apart from the lower probability of chance avoidance of the susceptible interval, in the event of a recognized pregnancy there would be a larger number of days (on which coitus had occurred) during the preceding month to which the "responsibility" for the conception could be assigned.

We have made computer simulation experiments with simple, behaviorally plausible algorithms of heuristic information processing, and these confirm the importance of the coital frequency level as a determinant of the efficacy of adaptive safe-period strategies. When the frequency is maintained at a constant level in the modern range of 8 times per month, and above, average completed fertility is found not to differ significantly from that expected with a regime of purely randomly timed coitus at the same average monthly frequency. But the simulations also reveal that the contraceptive effectiveness of the same adaptive strategy is dramatically enhanced when coital frequency is (parametrically) reduced. With the latter rate ($\tau$) continuously maintained at 4 times per month it seems quite feasible to adaptively modify the timing of intercourse so as to hold the average level of completed fertility over a 240-month span in the range below 2 births.

In other words, referring back to table 7.8, it appears that at these low coital frequencies the effectiveness of a consistently maintained adaptive safe-period method rivaled that of coitus interruptus practiced with a fairly high ($1 - \mu = .92$ to $.98$) degree of regularity throughout the same reproductive life span. It is therefore understandable why one finds, in table 7.6, that the Mosher Survey respondents who reported having employed no method of contraception other than "the safe period" all belonged to the lowest coital frequency class in the sample—those having marital intercourse at an average rate below 3.5 times per month.

### 7.3.5   Further Implications

The final implications of the information summarized in table 7.8 can be brought out by drawing some comparisons with the average age- and marital-duration-specific fertility figures for the wives of men in the professional occupations at the time of the 1910 census. In table 7.1 the completed fertility rates for women aged 45–49 and married 20–24 years, or aged 50–54 married 25–29 years, are those most immediately comparable with our predictions of expected completed fertility over a 240-month (fertile) time span. Note that it is appropriate to restrict attention to the fertility of women who were mothers, as is done in the table, because our simulation model assumes a homogeneous *nonsterile* population. It is also proper to make allowance, as has been done in the entries in table 7.1, for the fact that the completed fertility of the homogeneous analogue would be greater than that for the heterogeneous population of couples in the professional classes that was actually censused. From table 7.1, one may see that the figures for the 1910 census population range from 3.66 to 3.89 births per fertile woman centering on 3.77 births. As one would be led to expect from the discussion in section 7.2, there is a remarkably close coincidence between this and the 240-month completed fertility average (3.86) that can be obtained from the handful of comparable observations provided by the Mosher Survey sample.[51]

Returning now to table 7.8, it is seen that the same level of completed fertility could be expected by couples practicing withdrawal continuously, and with fairly high regularity ($1 - \mu = .92$), at coital frequencies that averaged between 6 and 8 times per month over the course of a 20-year reproductive span. The midpoint between the predicted completed fertilities of 4.11 and 3.35 is 3.73 births. But what of those educated, middle-class couples who had taken to heart the warnings of dire physiological and psychological consequences that attended the practice of coitus interruptus? We have also seen that those like the Mosher Survey respondents—who were having marital intercourse only 3–4 times per month on average—would have found it equally feasible to keep their completed fertility close to 3.77 births by adopting other contraceptive practices involving the more recently popularized methods of douche and condom (even in forms substantially inferior to the standards of the 1930s) that were characterized by per-trial failure rates as high as $f = .25$; alternatively, they could have been following an adaptive practice of period continence based on the safe-period principle.

To suggest that the observed levels of marital fertility among the professional classes could be accounted for in this fashion might appear to require the implicit assumption that the adoption of positive contraceptive measures had become universal in this segment of the American population by the close of the nineteenth century. Such an assumption does strike us as too extreme: even though virtually all of the women interviewed by Clelia Mosher during the 1900–1914 period reported having used some contraceptive method(s), table 7.2 revealed that a somewhat larger group (12.5%) of those interviewed prior to 1900 claimed to have had no contraceptive experience. But the assumption of universal adoption of contraception is not really called for by our argument. We have previously noted that several sources of bias in the specification of our model that almost guarantee that the figures for completed fertility predicted in table 7.8 (for values of $n$ below .333, equivalent to $\tau \leq 8$ times per month) overstate the true levels of fertility that are to be expected when coital frequency and the per-trial probability of contraceptive failure have the indicated values as an average over the entire reproductive period. The presence of this margin of error means that we can make allowance for the adoption of contraception having been considerably less than universal, and still account for the observed population averages of completed marital fertility on the hypothesis that those who were contracepting adhered to a pattern of practice resembling that revealed by the Mosher Survey.[52]

A second point which had been left implicit in the foregoing discussion must now be brought out. We have supposed here that all of the various contraceptive regimes examined would have been maintained continuously from the initiation of the marriage, or at very least from the first birth. By implication this would seem to tell us that the use of unreliable contraceptive methods obliged would-be controllers to become "spacers," inhibiting fertility early in their marriage rather than permitting themselves a period of unregulated fertility followed by attempts to terminate childbearing completely.

Although some recent students of the American fertility transition have subscribed to the opposing view, which holds that spacing behavior was not important (Tolnay and Guest 1984), others have found indications that "spacing" of births played a role in the transition to controlled fertility, at least among the Mormons of Utah (Anderton and Bean 1985). There is a good bit to be said for the latter conclusion on a priori economic grounds: considerations of risk aversion would tend to militate against a strategy of unregulated fertility followed by efforts to stop when "target fertility" had been attained—unless the costs of falling short of the target level were smaller than those associated with bearing additional, unplanned children (David et al. 1985). Moreover, the available evidence for the nineteenth century suggests that the age-specific marital fertility rates for women in their early twenties did not remain undiminished in the course of the American white populations' transition to lower total marital fertility rates.[53]

Finally, we may mention in this connection that our preliminary estimates, derived from comparisons of the parity distributions for 1900 and 1910 relating to those couples who belonged to the same marriage cohort (1875–79) and can be classified as having controlled fertility effectively prior to those census data, indicate that deferral of the first birth and "spacing behavior" in the interval preceding the second birth remained a widespread practice among those native white women who were effectively controlling marital fertility at the very end of the nineteenth century (see David and Sanderson 1984). There is reason to conjecture that this sort of "spacing" was still more extensive among earlier cohorts of controllers. Of course, whether the motives for this truly derived from concerns to achieve some optimal separation between live births, or whether these couples were attempting—with nonnegligible probabilities of failure—to terminate childbearing very early in their marriage, cannot be clarified from the indirect information at our disposal.

## 7.4  Technology and Ideology in the Middle-Class Transition to Family Limitation

The Mosher Survey findings have been seen to characterize a set of fertility-regulating strategies that could have been in use much more widely throughout the urban middle-class married population in the late Victorian era. One cannot suppose that in such matters there was complete uniformity; the very absence of open, public discussion must itself have tended to foster the persistence of a wide variety of quite different sexual and contraceptive strategies. Some couples may have rejected positive contraception in favor of prolonged abstinence, in accord with the precepts of the radical feminist ideology of "voluntary motherhood." Indeed, there may even have been some groups in the population who made extensive use of esoteric techniques such as coitus obstructus and coitus reservatus or "karezza" (prolonged intromission without ejaculation), and others who, by employing the more popular contraceptive methods in multiple combinations, managed to curtail their family size while maintaining the frequency of marital intercourse at essentially modern levels. Almost surely there were some married middle-class women who relied upon induced abortions to a degree far beyond the apparent experience of the Mosher Survey respondents. On balance, however, it remains most probable to conclude that the pattern of contraceptive usage at reduced coital frequencies—which has been preserved for our study like a fossil in the matrix of the Mosher Survey questionnaire forms—was widespread among low-fertility married couples in late nineteenth- and early twentieth-century urban America.

There is ample reason to conclude that the comparatively low frequency of marital coitus revealed by the Mosher Survey was a cultural phenomenon, and not simply a biologically determined consequence of the age distribution of the marital partners represented in this sample. Such Victorian sexual restraint, if we permit ourselves to call it that, can be held to have been entirely consonant with the evident concerns of these middle-class couples to limit their fertility. Whether it should be seen, further, to have been an outcome of individual choices rationally directed toward the goal of family limitation—rather than as a pattern of behavior that was in some more general context "socially learned," or consciously directed toward goals having little connection with fertility control—remains a more problematic issue.

The systematic positive covariation found within the Mosher Survey cross-section observations on coital frequency and contraceptive usage (table 7.6) certainly is consistent with the interpretation that a commonly held set of low fertility goals was playing a powerful role in shaping these dimensions of individuals' reproductive behavior. But the pattern of coital frequency variations in question constituted a distribution whose mean lay distinctly below that found in comparable modern populations, and quite probably below the norms prevailing earlier in the nineteenth century and among other contemporaneous socioeconomic strata. And at the same time, the suppositions of Oscar Handlin (1957) and Linda Gordon (1976) to the contrary notwithstanding, it appears that these "sexually restrained" representatives of the late Victorian middle classes were quite advanced in their acceptance and extensive employment of positive contraceptive methods.

These observations pose an intriguing historical paradox. While reduced coital frequency and resort to positive contraceptive methods would appear from the microdemographic cross-section observations in the relationship of substitutes, when viewed from the dynamic and societal perspective these two aspects of middle-class reproductive behavior appear to have gone hand in hand during the Gilded Age. As it seems likely that the style of marital relations characterized by sexual continence had become more widely established among upper-middle-class households than elsewhere in postbellum American society, one is left with the rather pardoxical implication that the life-style of sexual restraint was embraced most firmly by the very same groups that were taking the lead in the initial phases of the movement toward the control of fertility by more effective contraception. Indeed, this feature of nineteenth-century middle-class culture now appears quite instrumental in the successful practice of contraception using the rudimentary methods available, and therefore integral to the emerging socioeconomic differentials in the diffusion of family limitation and the level of marital fertility.

Putting the matter this way invites the immediate comment that these two historical developments, although confluent, need not have been causally interrelated. Perhaps conjugal relations among middle-class Victorians were governed more by the dominantly repressive tone of late nineteenth-century public attitudes and social policies pertaining to sexual conduct and less by individual considerations of the possible fertility consequences that would flow from marital indulgence of the sexual appetites. But as plausible as it may seem to invoke the influence of respectable Victorian sexual mores, this simple explanatory gambit remains less than entirely satisfying.

How certain and immediate was the nexus between individuals' views (and behavior patterns) in sexual matters and the respectable Victorian belief system? The ideology which enjoined "considerate" husbands and wives to accept a regime of sexual intercourse once per month as the "ideal" had been introduced in America, beginning in the 1830s, by exhortations both spiritual and physiological on behalf of the continent life; it was propagated subsequently, from the 1870s onward, through more organized efforts "to enforce chastity upon the unwilling," such as were personified in the career of Anthony Comstock.[54] Were such prescriptions and proscriptions effective?

Carl Degler (1974, 1980) has questioned the presupposition that personal beliefs mirrored contemporary sexual ideologies, pointing out that during the late Victorian era the attitudes of middle-class men and women were not thoroughly permeated with the repressive doctrines regarding female sexuality that pervaded so much of the medical and marriage advice literature of the times. His argument, documented in considerable part by references to the attitudinal evidence contained in the Mosher Survey, offers a caution that is well taken. On the other hand, the behavioral evidence reviewed here must occasion, at very least, some skepticism of a portrayal of educated middle-class Victorians as having remained quite untouched by the prescriptions and proscriptions of their cultural milieu, and really rather modern in their notions about the proper objectives and conduct of sexual relations within marriage.

It is true that only a few of the women interviewed by Clelia Mosher were products of mid-nineteenth-century Victorian culture. Most of them had been raised and entered marriage in an era of growing interest and candor regarding sexual matters. Still, the authorities of their day continued to urge a rather Spartan sexual regime as the basis for an ideal life both prior to and after entering the marital state, and even those who encouraged married couples to enjoy the sexual aspects of their relationship were agreed that in a choice between extremes, too little was certainly better, healthier, and even emotionally more satisfactory than too much. Even if the public moral climate of the era of Anthony Comstock had not militated against developing a relaxed and positive attitude toward sexual expression within the privacy of marriage, the risk of pregnancy and childbirth remained substantial, and there was little objective basis for confidence in the protection afforded by contraceptive methods or the safety of remedial abortion. A couple immune to such influences, and able to sustain confidence in their ability to have sex freely and utilize existing methods of contraception without repeated failures, would have to have been far more atypical then the men and women whose intimate lives the Mosher Survey has allowed us to characterize.

Even a clear resolution of this point in social psychology would not fully dispose of the larger problem. In the end it seems just too facile to invoke an ideological explanation while leaving the emergence of the ideology itself unexplained. The real issue that has been broached is thus seen to run deeper, and to involve greater subtleties, requiring recognition of the interrelationships between two complex and contemporaneous society developments: the crystallization of respectable Victorian standards for sexual conduct, and the growing acceptance of family limitation as a proper middle-class objective to be pursued by contraceptive means. While the intellectual origins and psychological sources of the formalized system of beliefs were largely independent of fertility control considerations, insofar as individuals' behavior was influenced by the sex-role models thus defined,[55] the emergence of Victorian sexual ideology has to be reckoned among the forces that shaped the historical diffusion of effective contraceptive practice. At the same time, it may be argued, an awareness on the part of contracepting couples of the antinatal effects of reducing coital frequency could have promoted tacit acceptance of the accompanying ideological rationale.

The ideological framework into which individuals fitted their sexual attitudes, combined with the difficulties and uncertainties connected with using the available modes of control, both reinforced the effects of middle-class worries about producing too many offspring. It may ultimately have led some husbands to have recourse to mistresses and prostitutes. But it also encouraged many to opt for a sexually rather restricted home life as part of the cost of protecting their wives from the hazards of pregnancy and childbirth, of allowing their offspring more time and care before the arrival of the next sibling, and of ultimately keeping the number of their surviving children not far in excess of the emerging two-child norm.

# Technical Appendix

1. Estimation of Per-Trial Failure Rates ($f$) from Stix-Notestein Measures of Contraceptive Use-Effectiveness

Stix and Notestein (1940) measured use-effectiveness ($\bar{e}$) as the ratio of pregnancies per month of exposure, defining the latter as the months of observation ($M$) less "months in puerperium plus one" for each pregnancy. No reduction of exposure was made for the interval of postpartum amenorrhea ($I_p$). Thus, for the $j$th method,

$$(A1) \qquad \bar{e}_j = 1 - \frac{\dfrac{C_j}{M_j - [(1 - a) (I_g + 1) + aI_a] C_j}}{\dfrac{C_o}{M_o - [(1 - a) (I_g + 1) + aI_a] C_o}} ,$$

where $C_j$ is number of pregnancies with the $j$th contraceptive method; $j = o$ denotes no contraceptive; $M_j$ is number of months of observation of subjects using $j$th method.

The modern conventional definition of (monthly) use-effectiveness is

$$(A2) \qquad \hat{e}_j = \frac{\pi_o - \pi_j}{\pi_o} = \frac{M_j - M_o}{M_j} ,$$

where $\pi$ and $M$ are defined as in section 7.3 above and are interpreted as population means.

Assuming $M_j = M_o$, it may be shown that the two measures are related as follows:

$$(A3) \qquad \hat{e}_j = \bar{e}_j[1 + (1 - a) (I_p - 1)\pi_j] .$$

## 2.   The Relationship between $\bar{e}$ and $f$

For a heterogeneous population, if the homogeneous $\pi-$ function is given the continuous time analogue of equation (2) in the text at section 7.3, namely,

$$(A4) \qquad \pi = \theta(1 - e^{-vnf}) ,$$

the mean monthly probability of conception may be approximated from

$$(A5) \qquad \bar{\pi} = \theta \left[ 1 - \left( 1 + \frac{(cnv)^2}{2} f_j^2 \right) e^{-nvf_j} \right],$$

where $c = \sigma_n/n$, the coefficient of variation of coital frequency, $n$ being interpreted as the mean (population) frequency of intercourse.

From equations (A2) and (A3) we can derive a relationship between $\bar{e}$ and the mean monthly probabilities of conception, $\bar{\pi}_o$ and $\pi_j$ ; solving for $\bar{\pi}_j$ we have

$$(A6) \qquad \bar{\pi}_j = \frac{1 - \bar{e}_j}{\dfrac{1}{\bar{\pi}_o} + \bar{e}_j(1 - a) (I_p - 1)} .$$

Substituting (6) into (5), the following implicit function is obtained

$$
\text{(A7)} \quad e^{nvf_j} \left( 1 - \frac{(1 - \bar{e}_j)}{\{1 - [1 + \frac{(cnv)^2}{2}]e^{-nv}\} + \bar{e}_j\,(1 - a)(I_p - 1)\theta} \right)
$$

$$
- f_j^2 \frac{(cnv)^2}{2} - 1 = 0.
$$

Given estimates of the parameters based on table 7.6, and using $c = .62$ from Barrett (1964) as suggested by Bongaarts (1976), we have

$$
B_o = nv
$$

$$
B_1 = \theta(1 - a)(I_p - 1) = 1.2049
$$

$$
B_2 = \frac{(cnv)^2}{2} = 0.4258.
$$

With $B_3 = [1 - (1 - \bar{e}_j)/(B_o + \bar{e}_j B_1)]$ ,

we can solve the following formulation of equation (A7),

$$
\text{(A8)} \qquad e^{B_o f_j} B_3 - f_j^2 B_2 - 1 = 0 ,
$$

for $f_j$ corresponding to $\bar{e}_j$ at a constant $n$. Solutions are readily obtained by iteration using Newton's method.

**Table 7.A.1**  Contraceptive Use-Experience among Predominantly Urban Population Samples of American Married Women: From the 1920s to the 1950s (Frequency Distributions of Methods Reported as Ever Used)

| Methods Ever Used | Pearl[1] (Urban U.S., 1932–33) | | Kopp[2] (New York City, 1933) | | Kinsey Women Married after 1914[3] (1938–50) | | | | Growth of American Families[4] (1955) | | Kinsey Weights[b] |
| | | | | | All Husbands, | | College Husbands, | | GAF Weights | | |
| | Number | Percent | Number | Percent | Number | Percent | Number | Percent | Number | Percent | Percent |
|---|---|---|---|---|---|---|---|---|---|---|---|
| Positive methods reported | | | | | | | | | | | |
| Douche | 1350 | 42.2 | 1225 | 8.0 | 475 | 11.8 | 276 | 10.3 | 533 | 16.7 | 14.5 |
| Safe period/rhythm | 102 | 3.2 | 303 | 2.0 | 142 | 3.5 | 102 | 3.6 | 645 | 20.2 | 14.8 |
| Withdrawal | 612 | 19.1 | 5894 | 38.5 | 753 | 18.6 | 498 | 17.4 | 284 | 8.9 | 8.0 |
| Condom | 813 | 25.4 | 4759 | 31.1 | 1256 | 31.1 | 883 | 30.8 | 818 | 25.6 | 30.8 |
| Diaphragm, pessary | 83 | 2.6 | 748 | 4.9 | 1136 | 28.1 | 900 | 31.4 | 684 | 21.4 | 25.0 |
| Suppository, jelly | 199 | 6.2 | 1751 | 11.4 | 278 | 6.9 | 188 | 6.6 | 192 | 6.0 | 5.7 |
| Other | 41 | 1.3 | 697 | 4.1 | | | | | 38 | 1.2 | 1.2 |
| Total positive usage (above) | 3202 | 100.0 | 15,317 | 100.0 | 4040 | 100.0 | 2867 | 100.0 | 3194 | 100.0 | 100.0 |
| | | | | | | | | | | | |
| Abstinence[a] | 2849 | 47.1 | 1121 | 6.5 | | | | | 38 | 0.9 | 1.2 |
| No method used | | | 666 | 3.9 | 143 | 3.4 | 60 | 2.0 | 815 | 20.1 | 26.9 |
| Total instances reported | 6051 | 100.0 | 17,164 | 100.0 | 4183 | 100.0 | 2927 | 100.0 | 4047 | 100.0 | 100.0 |
| | | | | | | | | | | | |
| Number of respondents | 4932 | 100.0 | 9916 | 100.0 | 1903 | 100.0 | 1301 | 100.0 | 2716 | 100.0 | 100.0 |
| Noncontraceptors among respondents | 2849 | 57.8 | 1787 | 18.0 | 143 | 7.5 | 60 | 4.6 | 815 | 30.0 | 25.7 |
| Positive usage per user | 1.54 | | 1.65 | | 2.29 | | 2.31 | | 1.68 | | 1.70 |

*Note:* The observations presented in the upper and middle panels of this table are "instances of use" (or non-use) of the indicated methods of contraception. More than one method may be reported by a given user. Observations pertaining to the survey respondents (contraceptors and noncontraceptors) are presented in the bottom section.

[a]Lactation is included with abstinence in the Pearl (1934) and Kopp (1934) data.

[b]GAF contraceptive use-experience rates within religious groups reweighted using religious distribution of Kinsey sample of married women. Figures in this column may be compared with those for Kinsey Survey married women.

*Technical notes and sources:*

1. **Pearl, 1932–33:** See Pearl (1934, table 13, p. 383) for original data (rearranged here) on women interviewed in urban hospitals.

2. **Kopp, 1933:** See Kopp (1934, p. 134) for original data (rearranged here) on women interviewed in New York City hospitals and clinics.

3. **Kinsey Survey Sample, 1938–50:** Once-married women, married after 1914, who responded to interview questions regarding contraceptive use or non-use, as tabulated from the unpublished Kinsey Data Tape: I.S.R. compilation, December 1978. See n. 2 to table 7.2. The heading "All Husbands" refers to the total sample described above. "College Husbands" refers to the subsample of women married to men who reportedly attended at least one year of college.

4. **Growth of American Families, 1955:** See Whelpton et al. (1966, table 156, p. 278) for original data on frequency of use of positive methods and abstinence and (table 128, p. 218) for the proportion ever using contraceptives in the national sample of married couples conducted by the Michigan Survey Research Center in 1955. The same source also provides data separately for the three principal religious affiliation groups: Protestant, Catholic, and Jewish. The latter were presented in the 1955 GAF sample in the proportions 0.73, 0.24, and .03, respectively. In the column headed "Kinsey Weights," we present the result of reweighting the three religious-specific distributions of contraceptive use experience according to the relative representation of Protestant, Catholic, and Jewish women in the Kinsey Survey sample. The latter proportions are found from Gebhard and Johnson (1979, table 8) to be 0.64, 0.10, and 0.26, respectively.

**Table 7.A.2**  Estimates of "Miscarriage or Abortion" Rates Recorded among New York City Department of Health Dispensary Patients (Married Women) Interviewed about 1917

| | All Married Women Interviewed | | Married Women Ever Aborting or Miscarrying | |
|---|---|---|---|---|
| | Knowledgeable about Contraceptives (N = 272) | Ignorant of Contraceptives (N = 192) | Knowledgeable about Contraceptives (N = 72) | Ignorant of Contraceptives (N = 104) |
| *Aggregate Average Rates of Occurrence* | | | | |
| "Miscarriages or abortions" per woman | 0.45 | 1.05 | 1.69 | 1.94 |
| Reported conceptions per woman | 3.28 | 7.84 | n.a. | n.a. |
| "Miscarriages or abortions" per conception | 0.137 | 0.134 | n.a. | n.a. |

*Technical notes and sources:*

**Aggregate Average Rates of Abortion and Conception:** Data published by Kahn (1917, pp. 790–91) permit reconstruction of the aggregate number of births to the total sample of patients and to each of the two groupings of women based on previous contraceptive knowledge, when supplemented by the following two assumptions.

1. Among married women having 9 or more births, 69% had 10 or more births. This figure is based on the experience of the (natural fertility) population of rural Ireland in 1911, whose relevance here is justified by Kahn's (1971, p. 791) report that among the (44) women reaching parity 9 all were "ignorant of contraceptives."

2. The married women having 10 or more births averaged 11.56 births apiece. The latter estimate is derived from data on United States white women married for 30–34 years in 1940, having married at ages 22–24. The fertility of such women, belonging to the marriage cohort of ca. 1906–10, probably approximates closely the fertility of the high-parity women in the Kahn (1971) sample, who had first married, on average, in 1901. Cf. David and Sanderson (March 1979, table 3) for further discussion of the sources of the two estimates used.

From the estimated births to women knowledgeable about (771) and ignorant of (1,303) contraceptives, and the respective numbers (122 and 202) of "abortions or miscarriages" reported for these two groups by Kahn (1917, p. 790), the number of conceptions and the total abortion rates (per conception) can be computed for each.

The numbers of "miscarriages or abortions" per woman can be computed directly from Kahn's published figures for each contraceptive-experience group, whence the average conception rate for the two groups can be derived.

**Table 7.A.3**    **Monthly Frequency of Marital Coitus Reported by Married Women in the United States, 1938–70**

| | Kinsey Survey, 1938–50[1] | | | | National Fertility Survey[2] | |
|---|---|---|---|---|---|---|
| | Married Women: Current Observaions | | | | Married Women: Current Observations | |
| | College Husbands | | All Husbands | | | |
| | Active Sample | Total Sample | Active Sample | Total Sample | 1965 | 1970 |
| Ages 25–34 | | | | | | |
| Mean | 7.9 | 7.3 | 8.1 | 7.5 | 7.1 | 8.5 |
| SD | 4.6 | 4.8 | 5.1 | 5.4 | n.a. | n.a. |
| N | 452 | 488 | 637 | 685 | 1741 | 2240 |
| Ages 35–44 | | | | | | |
| Mean | 5.5 | 5.3 | 5.5 | 5.3 | 5.5 | 6.4 |
| SD | 4.0 | 4.0 | 4.1 | 4.2 | n.a. | n.a. |
| N | 313 | 321 | 409 | 424 | 1824 | 1842 |
| Ages 45 and over | | | | | | |
| Mean | 4.9 | 4.4 | 4.6 | 4.0 | | |
| SD | 4.9 | 4.9 | 4.8 | 4.8 | | |
| N | 117 | 131 | 171 | 194 | | |

*Technical notes and sources:*
1. **Kinsey Survey Samples, 1938–50:** Computed from current (monthly equivalent) frequencies of marital coitus for individuals in the indicated age groups, as tabulated from the unpublished Kinsey Data Tape: Married Women, I.S.R. Compilation, December 1978, described in n. 3 to table 7.4. The same procedure for converting weekly to monthly rates, at the rate of 3.5 weeks per month, was followed. "College Husbands" refers to the subgroup of women whose spouses reportedly attended one or more years of college. "Active Sample" refers to the subset of women who reported some positive frequency of marital coitus, whereas "Total Sample" refers to all women (in the age and spouse's education category) from whom an interview response to the question was obtained.
2. **National Fertility Survey Samples, 1965 and 1970:** Westoff (1974, table 2, p. 137) provides comparable mean coital frequencies, pertaining to the 4-week period prior to interview, for 5-year age groups. We have presented unweighted averages for age groups 25–29 and 30–34, and for the age groups 35–39 and 40–44. Aggregation of the respective 5-year age group means for each survey date, using uniform weights derived from the 1970 survey sample, yield 10-year age group means identical to the unweighted rates shown here—within the margin of rounding errors. Similarly, a reweighting of the 1965 NFS 5-year group means using weights corresponding to the age distribution of the Kinsey Survey Sample of Married Women (Total Sample), yields the following means: 7.13 for women 25–35, 5.55 for women 35–44.
   Westoff (1974) does not contain standard deviations corresponding to the mean age-specific coital frequencies.

# Notes

1. On the contrast between sociopsychological and economic models of diffusion, and the "equilibrium" vs. "disequilibrium" process distinction, see David (1969), Stoneman (1983), and references therein. Cavalli-Sforza and Feldman (1981, esp. pp. 180–89), suggest the applicability of various cultural transmission models—resembling those developed for population genetics—to the historical spread of behaviors consistent with the "small family ideal."

2. The methodology referred to as Cohort Parity Analysis (CPA) has been developed with this purpose in mind by the Stanford Project on the History of Fertility Control, an undertaking in which the present authors have had numerous collaborators, most notably Thomas Mroz, Kenneth Wachter, and David Weir. See David and Sanderson (1980) and David et al. (1983) for descriptions of the measures on which we report here.

3. These estimates are based on the survival rates to ages 20–24 for white males and white females (weighted at 0.514 and 0.486, respectively) computed as averages from the quinquennial life tables covering the periods 1845–60 and 1870–85 in Kunze (1979), table 14. The survival rates are .702 and .734, respectively.

4. Whether the small size, and more to the point, the self-selected nature of the sample casts more serious doubts upon the representativeness of the sexual *attitudes* expressed by the respondents, seems to us to be a valid issue which some critics of Degler's (1974) interpretation have raised (see, e.g., Faderman 1981, p. 440). But this is an issue quite separable from the questions of *behavioral* representativeness addressed here.

5. See Mosher (n.d.), Stanford University Archives. The descriptive title affixed to the set of questionnaires by Mosher was: "Statistical Study of the Marriage of Forty-seven Women." This is inaccurate as to the true number of individuals involved (44) and the number of separate questionnaires completed (48). See MaHood and Wenburg (1980) for a typed transcription of the handwritten responses; it is more accessible than the original, and is reasonably free of errors, although its subtitle errs in supposing that 45 individual women's sexual attitudes are represented.

6. There is one questionnaire whose date of completion (although most probably prior to 1900) cannot be ascertained precisely. There are a total of 48 questionnaires which refer to 44 women, since one woman reported two marriages, and several were interviewed more than once in the same marriage.

7. There are two questionnaires for which the respondent's precise date of birth and exact marital duration remain undetermined: form 8 has been assigned to the 20–24-year marital duration interval, and form 44 to the 10–14-year interval, for purposes of analysis in table 7.1.

8. The edited, "machine-readable" version of the Mosher Survey (David and Sanderson, with Matel 1979) codes 415 items to each questionnaire form; on many items there are no responses, however, and about half are repeated questions dealing separately with each conception, pregnancy, miscarriage, parturition, and so forth, for the respondent.

9. A correction factor of 1.143, derived from Bongaarts (1976) was used to multiply the census means, as noted in table 7.1. The need for a differential heterogeneity adjustment arises because of our concern with demonstrating that the behavior observed in the Mosher Survey could have produced the pattern of fertility outcomes observed in the 1910 census data. Average fertility rates depend not only on the average fertility-related behavior of group members but on the variability of that behavior as well. Therefore, in order to show that the behavior of the Mosher Survey respondents is consistent with the observed census figures, the average fertility rates for both groups must be measured in such a manner that group differences in the degree of behavioral heterogeneity are removed.

10. See David and Sanderson (1976) for various proposals along these lines.

11. See Terman (1938), table 6, for socioeconomic status and educational attainment of the couples surveyed; Gebhard and Johnson (1979) on the background of the Kinsey Data Tape from which subsamples used here have been constructed.

12. The 17.1% noncontracepting reported among the wives of college graduates—in the pre-1915 marriage cohorts—interviewed by Kinsey and his colleagues starting in 1938 is rather more problematic. It should be noted that the bulk of these early interviews involved Indiana couples and drew upon the marriage cohorts of 1895–1914. (See Geb-

hard and Johnson 1979.) From our CPA estimates we find the mean proportion of non-controllers among the later-marrying native white women belonging to those marriage cohorts, and resident in the North Central states in 1940, was about 11%. The latter population was undoubtedly much more urbanized than the one Kinsey encountered in the environs of Bloomington, Indiana. Nevertheless, since the corresponding CPA estimate of the dedicated noncontrolling remnant was 20% among all native white Southern residents, the 17.1% figure obtained from this Kinsey survey subsample must still be regarded as being anomalously high.

13. These conclusions are in agreement with the surmise which Degler (1980, pp. 196–99) offers, apparently on grounds of sheer implausibility, that the increasing practice of abstinence alone could not have brought about the decline in the total fertility rate observed during the nineteenth century.

14. This view was suggested by Himes's (1970, ed.) classic work, and continued to be echoed in the contributions of economic demographers, e.g., Easterlin (1972) and Lindert (1978). The latter, being primarily concerned to identify demand-side factors underlying the nineteenth-century American fertility decline, therefore tended to gloss over the possible role of changes in the state of the available contraceptive technologies. For the more recent consensus, especially as it is reflected in the writings of social historians of the middle class in America and Europe, see Degler (1980, chap. 9) and Gay (1983, chap. 3). Degler makes use of our preliminary findings from the Mosher Survey on these points.

15. See Smith (1973b), p. 50. Smith himself went on to recognize the possibility that the genre of literary evidence he cites might prove misleading as a guide to actual behavior, however sophisticated the interpretations placed upon it. He remarked, anticipating Degler (1974): "[e]ven among the urban middle classes (presumably the consumers of these manuals and tracts) reality and ideology probably diverged considerably."

16. See Grebenik and Glass 1965, pp. 113–18; Wrigley 1966, pp. 104–5, 1969, pp. 124–88. There is some circularity here, since the English nationwide survey findings reported by Lewis-Fanning (1949), esp. pp. 8–9 and table 91, have not been without influence in sustaining historical demographers suppositions as to the importance of coitus interruptus as a method of contraception among the population of France during the eighteenth century (see also Bergues et al. 1960). In turn, the writers of England cite those on France to bolster their argument that withdrawal as a regular technique was imported from France where it was the dominant method.

17. See Wrigley (1969), pp. 124–200, and citations therein. See Degler (1980), chap. 9, for the opposing view.

18. As one would expect, the average frequency of miscarriage among the 12 fertile women in the Mosher sample who reported one or more such events was much higher than the mean rate for the group as a whole: it was 0.343, more than twice the average. Assuming the subsample was homogeneous with respect to the probability of abortion, and assuming that probability was a constant, $a$, independent of previous occurrences of abortion for any cause, then the probability of having at least one abortion in $c$ conceptions could be reckoned as $P(A) = 1 - (1 - a)^c$. These assumptions, however, are not fulfilled even when all abortions are spontaneous, and it is to be expected that the actual proportion recording one or more abortions would be lower than the proportion $P(A)$ indicated by the formula. This is in fact the case, since with $a = 0.185$ and $c = 2.98$ (the mean number of conceptions) per fertile woman in the subsample of 40, we can calculate that $P(A) = 0.46$, whereas the actual proportion is 0.343 in table 7.3.

19. This estimate has been accepted recently by Bongaarts (1976, p. 234) as appropriate for use in simulating the fertility behavior of historical populations not engaged in fertility control. In a still more recent study of data obtained from a clinic near Paris, Leridon (1976, p. 322) reports the following age-specific rates of spontaneous abortion: age 20–24 = 0.127, age 25–29 = 0.155, age 30–34 = 0.182, age 35–39 = 0.216.

20. On the ideology of sexual continence and the realities of marital sexuality in England and America, see Cominos (1963); Nissenbaum (1968), to whom we are indebted for "Careful Love"; Burnham (1973); Rosenberg (1976); Degler (1980), chap. 11; Rothman (1978); Gay (1983), chap. 1.

21. Where the comparison samples are much larger, a fortiori there will be an increase in the confidence with which the Mosher Survey mean coital frequency can be said to fall below the other populations represented in table 7.4. For procedures in carrying out

these tests based upon the *t*-distribution of student's ratio, see e.g, Burington and May (1953, pp. 157–58).

22. See, e.g, Tietze (1965) for modern evidence on the reliability of the intermediate contraceptive methods. Measured use-effectiveness, however, depends on the regularity of use and coital frequency, as is pointed out in greater detail in sec. 7.3.

23. Some such measure of "exposure" would be required were one to read the table for information about contraceptive effectiveness. A warning is in order, however, against placing much weight on the data in the latter connection: the information about contraceptive use is retrospective and does not in general disclose the durations of use of the various methods. Since we do not attempt to ascertain contraceptive use-effectiveness directly from the Mosher Survey data, the "duration of exposure" information conveyed by the table serves mainly as a rough indication of the ages of the women and the duration of experience on which they were reporting.

24. The fact that the users of douche, safe period, and vaginal suppositories constituted half the subsample of contraceptors, as may be seen from the bottom two major-row entries in table 7.6, makes it rather unlikely that couples in this group represented a subfecund fringe *within* the Mosher Survey population. This view is further supported by the finding that among this group the average number of conceptions per woman was not significantly different (even at a 0.20 error level) from that among the remainder of the sample of contraceptors—holding constant the "exposure duration" classes indicated in table 7.6.

25. These differ, incidentally, from the published frequencies of marital coitus, e.g., Kinsey et al. (1953, table 93, p. 394), which mix retrospective and current report data.

26. The prevalence of such comparatively minor differences between the ages of once-married spouses appears to have been a relatively recent development. It represented a sharp departure from urban middle-class marriage customs of the pre-1870 era, and a transition to the nuptiality patterns established among the more educated strata during the interwar period of the present century. In a study of middle-class households in Union Park (Chicago) based upon the 1880 Manuscript Census, Sennett (1970, pp. 105–7) found that in a majority of all married couples the husband was at least 5–10 years senior to the wife. These data, however, were not analyzed by marriage cohort and so fail to shed light on the precise timing of the suspected shift in middle-class nuptiality patterns—a subject that clearly deserves further study.

27. See, e.g., Wachter et al. (1978) for recent applications of microdemographic simulation to historical questions.

28. The preceding illustrative statements are premised on the biological parameters of the model having been chosen to be representative of the larger population, with the behaviorally determined parameters set to correspond to the (Mosher) sample population levels. We pursue this approach, with suitable modifications designed to strengthen the power of the test.

29. The basic (Markov) renewal model of the stochastic birth process has been extensively analyzed by mathematical demographers. See Sheps and Mencken (1973), and references therein. For a nontechnical exposition of the approach, see Keyfitz (1971). Bongaarts (1976) neatly exemplifies the empirical implementation of a formal model resembling the one we present.

30. The combinatorial expression $\binom{v}{c} = v!/(v - c)!c!$ denotes the number of different ways in which $c$ (daily) occurrences can take place within $v$ days.

31. Strictly, we need only to assume that the frequency and pattern of marital coitus within the period of susceptibility ($v$) can be closely approximated by a Bernoulli process—in which, in effect, a coin with a constant loading is tossed to determine whether intercourse will occur on the given day. If other factors governing sexual activity, such as a taboo against intercourse during menstruation (see Paige and Paige 1981, chap. 6), merely affect the time pattern of coition outside the brief fertile period, our specification remains valid. See James (1971) for findings that individual distributions of coitus within the intermenstruum do not follow such random processes. But one must consider the effect of averaging over many individuals with different nonrandom patterns. In the subsequent implementation we do suppose that couples abstain from coitus during 4

menstrual days of an average 28-day menstrual "month." The average frequency of intercourse in the month ($\tau$) is therefore given by $\tau = 24n$.

32. See Tietze and Potter (1962) on the modern rhythm method; David and Sanderson (1976, sec. 2.2.4; 1979) treat adaptive safe-period methods.

33. This follows immediately from the fact that (when $v$ exceeds one day, as in the case under normal biological conditions) the monthly probability $\Pi$ is represented (properly) by eq. (2) as a concave function of $n$.

34. Since contraceptive failure is also represented as a Bernoulli process, the remarks in n. 31 apply correspondingly in this connection: we need, strictly speaking, only to assume the validity of the Bernoulli process as an approximation for contraceptive failures during the brief fertile period of each month.

35. For discussion of the relevant empirical evidence and its interpretation in the demographic literature dealing with "motivation effects," see David and Sanderson (1980).

36. This may be seen by expanding eq. (2), taking $v$ as any value equal to or exceeding one, and noticing that in the resulting expression $n$ and $f$ appear everywhere as multiplicative factors. From the preceding statement regarding the concavity of the $\Pi$-function in $n$ (when $v$ exceeds one), it follows that under the relevant biological conditions $\Pi$ must also be a concave function of $f$.

37. See Bongaarts (1976) for a continuous-time version of eq. (2), in which the distribution of marital coitus is assumed to be generated by a Poisson process. The technical appendix makes use of the latter specification in a distinct but related connection.

38. See the discussion and references in Hartman (1962), and MacLeod and Gold (1952, 1953a, 1953b), as the work of Lachenbruch (1967) and Tietze and Potter (1962). Two sorts of effects are at work. First, the probability of conception depends not only on intercourse occurring during the susceptible period, but also on the interval of male continence preceding coitus. Frequent intercourse decreases the concentration of sperm within the ejaculate and reduces the probability of a conception. Multiple acts of coitus within a 3-day period, then, may not cause the monthly probability of a conception to rise much above what it would be if coitus occurred only once during the susceptible period. The second effect relates to the level of the conception probability in a propitious menstrual cycle. Suppose for a moment that if intercourse occurred once in the susceptible period of a menstrual cycle the probability of a fertilized ovum would be as high as 0.8 (the probability of a *recognized* conception may be much lower due to early implantation failure and fetal loss), then there is little scope for multiple acts of intercourse to increase the probability of conception.

39. In eq. (2), as already noted, $\Pi$ is a positive concave function of $n$. The degree of concavity depends on the assumption that the probability of a conception is identical for one, two, or three acts of coition within the susceptible period. Relaxing this assumption, and allowing multiple occurrences to have some positive effect on the likelihood of conception, will render the relationship less concave. (See, e.g., David and Sanderson (1976, table 2.3.4:1, and accompanying discussion.) Given the manner in which we proceeded in setting the level of the parameter $\theta$, as briefly described in the notes and sources to table 7.7, the more concave the relationship between $\Pi$ and $n$, the higher are the monthly probabilities of a conception when $n < .333$. This raises fertility levels at low relative coital frequencies, biasing the results of our computations against the assertion that low fertility could be attained through the use of rudimentary contraceptive methods at relatively low coital frequencies.

40. See Henry and Gautier (1958) and Charbonneaux (1970) for estimates placing the mean interval of postpartum amenorrhoea at 7.1 and 9.1 months, respectively. Bongaarts (1976, p. 223), employs 8.1 as an estimate for $I_p$.

41. The period $M$ must be a fairly extended one if the birthrates predicted from the renewal model are to be taken as closely approximating their equilibrium values. With no contraception and low rates of pregnancy wastage, the oscillatory deviations of the birthrate from its equilibrium are found to become negligibly small (less than 1%) after roughly 120 months, given an interval of postpartum nonsusceptibility in the neighborhood of 15 months. Convergence occurs much more quickly when the monthly probability of conception is reduced or the pregnancy wastage rate is as high as 0.3. See Sheps and Menken (1973, pp. 213–18) for theoretical discussion and numerical examples. The

estimates of expected total fertility are less sensitive to such deviations, and may be regarded as highly accurate if $M$ exceeds 60 months. In table 7.8, $M$ is taken as 240 months and the estimates of $B$ cited in the text, below, all refer to reproductive spans exceeding 120 months.

42. See Dickinson (1938, p. 10) for postclinic use-effectiveness measures based on work of Stix and Notestein (1935). It has been possible to support the general assumption of negligible postclinic omission rates by analysis of other data presented by Stix and Notestein (1940, pp. 109, 122) on the causes of postclinic contraceptive failure among users of the diaphragm method prescribed by the same clinic.

43. See technical appendix. The conventional measures of use-effectiveness from which we started are as follows: douche, 69%; withdrawal, 86%; condom, 95%.

44. In fact, because $n$ and $f$ appear symmetrically in eq. (2) when $v = 3$, and enter eq. (1) only via the variable $\Pi$, all statements about the relationships $B(n|f)$ must hold equally for the relationships $B(f|n)$. We may therefore confine the text discussion to describing the former family of functions.

45. On the other hand, it may seem that with coital frequencies around $n = .333$ and omission rates in the range between .08 and .20, coitus interruptus would avert only something like five births within the course of a 20-year reproductive span. These figures seem quite consistent with the report of Lella Secor Florence (1930, p. 19) on the experience of the first 300, predominantly working-class clients of the first birth control clinic established in Cambridge, England, by the Cambridge Women's Welfare Association in 1925: "In our own clinic, for instance, we have many cases of parents employing *coitus interruptus* throughout all or part of their married life, despite the fact that it had failed on four or five occasions. The assumption that there might have been ten children instead of five if these efforts at limitation had not been made seems perfectly justified."

46. The illustrative calculations are made by applying eq. (3). For the case of douche, we set $f = .25$, $\mu = .01$, $\alpha^* = .1185$ (the estimate based on postclinic 1930s data), and solve for $x = .477$ (or approximately 48%) from the following equation:
$$0.25 = .01 + (1 - .01)[.1185)x + 3(.1185)(1 - x)] .$$
The term in the square brackets $= \bar{\alpha} = .2424$, the "average" inherent accident rate, is more than twice the level of $\alpha^*$ for douche.

For the case of condom, we set $f = .25$, $\mu = .11$, $\alpha^* = .0158$ (the estimate based on postclinic 1930s data), and solve for $x = .856$ (or approximately 86%) in the following equation:
$$0.25 = .11 + (1 - .11)[(.0158)x + 1(1 - x)] .$$
The term in the square brackets $= \bar{\alpha} = .1573$, the "average" inherent accident rate, is almost 10 times the magnitude of $\alpha^*$ for condom. It should be noted that the 1930s standard for condoms still represented the state of affairs prior to government regulation and inspection under the 1930 Pure Food and Drug Act.

47. The assumption that the wife has had 2 births and returned to the state of susceptibility 5 years after her marriage is entirely plausible for our hypothetical late Victorian middle-class couple. Consider the following scenario: since their average coital frequency up to the time of first conception was $n = .250$ (i.e., 6 times per month), and no contraception was practiced during this period, the mean date of resumption of menstruation following the first live birth would be 18.5 months ([240/9.41)] $-$ 7) after the woman's marriage. At that point, out of concern to space the next birth, the couple's average frequency of coitus was reduced to 4 times per month and the husband commenced the practice of coitus interruptus—but only slightly more often than not, i.e., with omission probability $\mu = .48$. From tables 7.8 and 7.7 it may be found that the next conception leading to a live birth would be expected in 22.58 months ([240/6.22] $-$ 16), and the woman could be expected to resume menstruating after her second live birth in the 58th month (18.5 + 22.58 + 16) of her marriage. From table 7.1 it may be seen, further, that among women age 25–29 who did not suffer primary sterility, and who were married to professional men for 4 years or longer, the average level of fertility was close to 2. This figure is quite consistent with both our assumptions and the foregoing scenario.

48. A more detailed, technical account of this line of research will be available in our forthcoming paper, "Contraception through Stochastic Learning: An Analysis of Adaptive Rhythm Methods."

49. Among American writers on birth prevention, see, e.g., American Physician (1855, pp. 59–61), Lewis (1874, pp. 94–98), and Trall (1881, pp. 205–9). See also the earlier influential work of the Frenchman Pouchet (1847). Drysdale (1854, p. 348), who was quite unorthodox in describing the *sterile* period as commencing two or three days before the menses and ending on the eighth day following, continued to claim some adherents among influential purveyors of birth prevention advice in England. See Himes (1970 ed., pp. 234–35) on Drysdale (1887) and Albutt (1887). If one pressed to the latter end of Drysdale's "sterile" interval, however, there was a nonnegligible probability of having coitus close enough to the time of ovulation for the sperm to survive to fertilize the ovum.

50. In addition to the prescriptions of Hollick (1850) and Gardner (1856), see Ashton (1865, pp. 14–15) and the more influential writings of Stockham (1887, pp. 29, 324–26) for examples of nineteenth-century American contraceptive advice in this perverse vein.

51. One may roughly approximate the average fertility of the Mosher Survey women (mothers) who had experienced 20 years of marriage within the reproductive span, by averaging the entries along the subdiagonal cells in table 7.1, starting with women aged 45–59 and married 20–24, and proceeding downward to the women in the age group 60–64 who were married 35–39 years. From the data underlying the table it is found that the women involved had an average completed fertility of 3.86. Note that allowing for the effect of greater heterogeneity in the United States population—compared with the Mosher sample—tends to eliminate the large (positive) discrepancies between the boldface and italicized entries, which appear among the older, higher-fertility women in table 7.1.

52. For example, start with a calculated figure for contraceptors (following practices yielding $f = .25$, with $\tau = 3$–4) of 3.8 births over 240 months, as suggested in table 7.8. Then, assume that 20% of the population did not control fertility by any contraceptive means and had an average completed fertility as high as 7.5. (the latter figure would be lower if the noncontraceptors were less fecund or resorted to abortion). If the true level of expected fertility for low coital frequency, contracepting couples were 0.79 of the level represented in table 7.8, one could account for the average fertility of the entire population being approximately 3.9.

53. Sanderson's (1979) findings for the white population are the most comprehensive, but the conclusion emerges also in other studies of extensive samples based on reconstitution and genealogical data, most notably Kunze (1979, chap. 5).

54. The phrase has been borrowed from Rosenberg (1976, p. 73). On the influence of Sylvester Graham and his followers in the antebellum period, see Nissenbaum (1968). For an account of Comstock's career and the "social purity" crusade as a moral reform movement, see Pivar (1973). Howe (1976) contains a number of illuminating essays on late Victorian attitudes regarding public and private sexual morality.

55. See Rosenberg (1976, chap. 3) for a view of Victorian sexual ideology as affecting individual behavior by delineating particular sexual stereotypes and influencing choices among alternative sex-role models.

# Comment    Michael R. Haines

This paper summarizes rather lengthily some of the recent and ongoing research of the co-authors on the nature of the fertility transition in

Michael R. Haines is professor of economics at Wayne State University.

Comments were originally written for the National Bureau of Economic Research Conference on Income and Wealth on Long-Term Factors in American Economic Growth, Fort Magruder Inn, Williamsburg, March 22–24, 1984. The present comments have been revised to reflect a number of changes in the original paper.

the United States in the nineteenth and early twentieth centuries. Earlier work by Warren Sanderson (1979) established that the dramatic decline in the American total fertility rate (from over 8 in about 1800 to about 3.3 by 1910) was more due to declines in marital fertility than to adjustments in nuptiality (rising female age at first marriage and increasing proportions of women never marrying). Both, however played an important role. Given the paucity of adequate vital statistics in the nineteenth century and the heavy reliance on census child/woman ratios to measure fertility, Paul David and Warren Sanderson turned to other techniques and sources to illuminate the problem.

The major sources that underlie this paper are (1) the published results of the censuses of 1910 and 1940 on children ever born by age, marital duration, race, and nativity of women; (2) similar data from a sample of the 1900 United States census; and (3) the remarkable information collected by Clelia Mosher between 1892 and 1920 on the reproductive behavior of 44 middle-class white women with professional husbands. The latter is so unusual because it constitutes the earliest instance of detailed survey data (albeit a small and unsystematic sample) on the sexual behavior of American women. Since that time there has been a rapid increase in survey research in this area, but the Mosher survey is unique in its period of coverage.

The initial issue was to establish some of the dimensions of the nineteenth-century fertility decline. This was done by Sanderson, who estimated total marital fertility rates and proportions of women married in the nineteenth century and assigned a precise role to declines in marital fertility (a neo-Malthusian transition) and to adjustments in nuptiality (a Malthusian transition) (Coale 1974). Then, using some new methodological developments, which David and Sanderson refer to as Cohort Parity Analysis (CPA), parity data from the censuses of 1900 (a sample of the manuscripts) and 1910 and 1940 (published data) were exploited to gain a more detailed picture. These results are summarized in section 7.1, but the reader is given no explanation of the methodology used in deriving them. While this is perhaps understandable, and forgivable, in a paper already over long, the result is to deprive readers of a basis for evaluating the statements made about the timing and pattern of diffusion of fertility control in the American native white population.

In consequence, the authors' methodological advances in connection with CPA deserve some mention, because they are very useful and important in their own right. I will therefore devote the bulk of my comments to this aspect of their work. First, it was necessary to correct the calculated mean parity data for older women for selectivity due to mortality and marital dissolution ("differential postreproductive attrition"). This has been done using a group of models for correcting censored distributions, where the censoring is not independent of the attributes which are to be estimated—in this case the status of having been a "controller" or a "noncontroller." Second, it was then necessary to exploit parity data using a model population of noncontrollers as a basis for estimating the proportion of controllers (both "active" and "passive," i.e., those who would control if it were necessary). One of the unique features of this method was the incorporation of the observation by Page (1977) that model marital fertility schedules which incorporate only age (such as those of Coale and Trussell [1974] and Brass [1975]) can produce seriously misleading results if marital duration is not considered. Pursuant to this, the authors develop, using parity data by age and marital duration from the 1911 census of Ireland, a model distribution of natural fertility (fertility not subject to deliberate control) to be applied to the American data.

Without going too much into detail, the authors then are able to estimate the full distribution of completed marital parity, the proportion of American marriage cohorts 1855–59 to 1915–19 ever controlling actively during completed reproductive lifetimes, aggregate effectiveness of control (the ratio of active controllers to couples desiring control), and the mean completed parity of controlling women. Their methods yield standard errors for these estimated population parameters, although these are not reported by the discussion in section 7.1 of the present paper. While the robustness of these methods has yet to be demonstrated (to me, at least), I believe that this methodology is very imaginative. (One possibility for verification would be some application to the English data on parity and marital duration from censuses of 1911 onward in conjunction with published and other vital and census data generating standard reproductive measures.)

Among the principal findings are that, from at least the middle of the nineteenth century onward, native white women in urban areas of the northern states (and especially the Northeast), as well as, increasingly, in northern rural areas, were able to exercise increasingly effective control of marital fertility. This was combined with a rising age at marriage. This pattern did not begin to characterize the South until rather late in the nineteenth century (approximately 1880). In the Northeast, for example, the marriage cohort of 1855–59 (with women married at ages 15–24) had over 40% "effective" controllers (defined as those who had managed over the course of their reproductive lives to avert one or more births). They achieved a mean parity of 3.78 children. The cohort of women in the Northeast married during 1865–69 at ages 20–29 achieved a parity of only 3.07 children. This pattern spread to other parts of the country, first the North Central region and the West, and finally the South. I would suggest the authors develop a single parameter from their age-duration model (analogous to Coale and Trussell's "m") that could be used to describe the degree of departure from natural fertility over time and by region. I wondered, however, how the earlier (pre-1850s) decline in total fertility rate (from over 8) was achieved with such a low proportion of women controlling (26% for the marriage cohort of 1855–59). Perhaps the simulation model in section 7.3 could be used to investigate this issue. An additional important finding is that both the spread of desire for fertility control and the reduction in average births to those who were successful in the application of contraception were about equally important. This is quite significant because it sheds light on supply-side constraints in family limitation. Much previous work on nineteenth-century American fertility, including my own, has focused on demand factors, assuming that traditional contraceptive measures were sufficient. Much of section 7.3 consists of the development of the supply side.

The basis for the hypothesis presented in the paper is the Mosher survey, which is characterized as "a veritable Rosetta Stone for the study of demographic and social history of a significant segment of the Amerian population." (I will not comment on the extensive comparisons of the Mosher data with other results (e.g., Kinsey and Terman). Suffice it to say that the authors have convinced me that the survey gives a reasonable picture of the reproductive lives of this particular socioeconomic stratum in this era. A description of Mosher and her survey, for the curious, may be found at the beginning of sec. 7.2.) The main conclusion is that in the regime of *inefficient* contraceptive technology (both in application and effectiveness) which characterized the late nineteenth and early twentieth centuries (douche, rhythm, condoms, and withdrawal were apparently the major methods), couples who desired to limit family size had to make love *very* carefully. Evidently abortion or "farming out" of unwanted children, which was widely practiced in France and which greatly increased child mortality, were not desirable options. However, abortion, though not common in the Mosher survey, may well have been important in the nineteenth century. The paper takes note of this and in the end concludes that induced abortion may well have accounted for somewhat less than half of births averted in the mid–nineteenth century, especially among lower-income groups and the foreign born. More investigation of this possibility is definitely an item for future research. In addition, the role of changes in infant and child mortality is not dealt with. With high mortality, neither contraception nor abortion assumes as much importance. In any event, the consequences of this inefficient technology were low coital frequency, delayed marriage, and apparent practice of contraception from the outset of marriage.

All these points are quite fascinating. The hypothesis (and that is what it is) of the "era of careful love" is consistent with the data and has a great deal of intuitive appeal. It is, moreover, a challenge to the use of Coale-Trussell types of model fertility schedules, which assume a lack of controlling behavior early in the marriage. I would note, however, that the new data presented in this paper did not confirm the notion that fertility control behavior in the nineteenth-century United States was largely spacing rather than stopping. The authors cite other work, some of it their own, in defense of this view, and point out that the simulation model presented in section 7.3 is certainly consistent with the argument that contraception would have had to have been consistently practiced with a low frequency of intercourse in order to have achieved the actual outcome. A recent paper by Anderton and Bean (1985) is cited. It uses the extensive database of genealogies in the Mormon Historical Demography Project to reconstruct fertility patterns in the nineteenth century and finds that spacing as well as stopping was characteristic of the fertility decline in this sample. But more work, such as the comparison of parities of the same young cohorts from the 1900 and 1910 censuses with the natural fertility model, seems to be a promising direction of inquiry. The authors have made a start in this direction already (David and Sanderson 1984). Overall, the present paper is imaginative and challenging, and opens a number of prospects for future work.

# References

Albutt, H. A. 1887. *The wife's handbook*. 3d ed. London: W. J. Ramsay.

American Physician. 1855. *Reproductive control, or a rational guide to matrimonial happiness . . . .* Cincinnati.

Anderton, Douglas L., and Bean, Lee L. 1985. Birth spacing and fertility limitation: A behavioral analysis of a nineteenth century population. *Demography* 22:169–83.

Ashton, J. 1865. *The book of nature*. New York.

Barker-Benfield, Ben. 1972. The spermatic economy: A nineteenth century view of sexuality. *Feminist Studies* 1:45–74.

Barrett, J. 1970. An analysis of coital patterns, *Journal of Biosocial Science*, vol. 2.

Bergues, H., et al. 1960. *La prévention des naissances dans la famille*. Institute d'Etudes Démographiques, cahier no. 35. Paris.

Bongaarts, John. 1976. Intermediate fertility variables and marital fertility rates. *Population Studies* 30 (July): 227–41.

Brass, William. 1975. *Methods for estimating fertility and mortality for limited and defective data*. Chapel Hill, N.C.: Laboratories for Population Statistics, Carolina Population Center.

Burington, Richard S., and May, Donald C., Jr. 1953. *Handbook of probability and statistics*. Sandusky, Ohio: Handbook Publishers.

Burnham, John C. 1973. The progressive era revolution in American attitudes toward sex. *Journal of American History* 59:885–908.

Carlsson, Gosta. 1966. The decline in fertility: Innovation or adjustment process? *Population Studies* 20:149–74.

Cavalli-Sforza, L. L., and Feldman, M. W. 1981. *Cultural transmission and evolution: A quantitative approach*. Princeton: Princeton University Press.

Charbonneaux, H. 1970. *Tourouvre au perche au XVII$^e$ et XVIII$^e$ siècles: Etude demographique historique*. Paris: Presses Universitaires de France.

Coale, Ansley J., and Trussell, James. 1974. Model fertility schedules: Variations in age structure of childbearing in human populations. *Population Index* 40:185–258.

Coale, Ansley J., and Zelnik, Melvin. 1963. *New estimates of fertility and population in the United States*. Princeton: Princeton University Press.

Cominos, Peter. T. 1963. Late-Victorian sexual respectability and the social system. *International Review of Social History* 8:8–48, 216–50.

David, Paul A. 1969. A contribution to the theory of diffusion. Research Memorandum no. 71. Stanford: University Center for Research in Economic Growth, June.

———. 1977. Invention and accumulation in America's economic growth: A nineteenth century parable. In *International organization, national policies and economic development*, ed. K. Brunner and A. H. Meltzer. Amsterdam: North-Holland.

David, P. A.; Mroz, T. A.; Sanderson, W. C.; Wachter, K. W.; and Weir, D. R. 1983. The quantitative history of modern fertility control: Summary report to NICHD. Stanford Project on the History of Fertility Control (SPHFC), Stanford University Department of Economics, October.

David, P. A.; Mroz, T. A.; and Wachter, K. W. 1985. Rational strategies of birth-spacing and fertility regulation in rural France during the ancien régime. SPHFC Working Paper no. 14, March.

David, Paul A., and Sanderson, Warren C. 1976. Contraceptive technology and family limiting behavior: Toward a quantitative history of the diffusion of contraceptive practices in America, 1850–1920. SPHFC Report, May.

————. 1978a. Intermediate contraceptive technology and the microeconomics of fertility regulating behavior. Working Paper for History of Contraceptive Technology and Family Limitation Project, Economics Department, Stanford University, January.

————. 1978b. The role of experience and adaptive behavior in contraceptive efficiency. SPHFC Working Paper no. 1, December.

————. 1980. Contraceptive technology and family limiting behavior: Second summary report to NICHD. SPHFC Report, April.

————. 1984. Spacing versus stopping in the past: Marital duration specific patterns of fertility control among U.S. native white women, 1880–1910. SPHFC Working Paper no. 13, April. Abstracted in *Population Index* 50:390.

Degler, Carl N. 1974. What ought to be and what was: Women's sexuality in the nineteenth century. *American Historical Review* 79 (December): 1467–90.

————. 1980. *At odds: Women and the family in America from the Revolution to the present.* New York: Oxford University Press.

Dickinson, Robert L. 1938. *Control of conception.* 2d ed. Baltimore: Williams & Wilkins.

Drysdale, G. R. 1854. *Physical, sexual and natural religion: By a student of medicine.* London.

————. 1887. *The elements of social science, or Physical sexual and natural religion. An exposition of the true course and only cure of the three primary social evils: Poverty, prostitution and celibacy, by a doctor of medicine.* 26th ed. London.

Easterlin, Richard A. 1972. The American population. In *American economic growth: An economist's history of the United States,* ed. Lance Davis et al. New York: Harper & Row.

————. 1976. Population change and farm settlement in the northern United States. *Journal of Economic History* 36 (March): 45–75.

————. 1978. The economics and sociology of fertility: A synthesis. In *Historical studies of changing fertility,* ed. Charles Tilly. Princeton: Princeton University Press.

Faderman, Lillian. 1981. *Surpassing the love of men: Romantic friendship and love between women from the Renaissance to the present.* New York: Morrow.

Florence, Lella Secor. 1930. *Birth control on trial.* London: Allen & Unwin.

Forster, Colin, and Tucker, G. S. L. 1972. *Economic opportunity and white American fertility ratios, 1800–1860.* Yale Series in Economic History. New Haven and London: Yale University Press.

French, F. E., and Bierman, J. 1962. Probabilities of fetal mortality. *Public Health Reports* 77:835–47.

Gardner, Augustus K. 1856. *Causes and curative treatment of sterility with a preliminary statement on the physiology of generation.* New York: DeWiltt & Davenport.

Gay, Peter, 1983. *The bourgeois experience: Victoria to Freud.* Vol. 1. *Education of the Senses.* New York: Oxford University Press.

Gebhard, Paul H., and Johnson, Alan B. 1979. *The Kinsey data: Marginal tabulations of the 1938–1963 interviews conducted by the Institute for Sex Research.* Philadelphia: W. B. Saunders.

Glass, D. V., and Grebenik, E. 1954. The trend and pattern of fertility in Great Britain. *Papers of the Royal Commission on Population,* vol. 6, part I. London: H.M.S.O.

Gordon, Linda, 1976. *Woman's body, woman's right: A social history of birth control in America.* New York: Grossman.

Guest, A. M., and Tolnay, S. E. 1983. Children's roles and fertility: Late nineteenth-century United States. *Social Science History* 7 (Fall): 355–80.

Guttentag, Marcia, and Secord, Paul F. 1984. *Too many women? The sex ratio question.* Beverly Hills and London: Sage Publications.

Haines, Michael. 1979. *Fertility and occupation: Population patterns in industrialization.* New York: Academic Press.

Handlin, Oscar. 1957. *Race and nationality in American life.* Boston: Little, Brown.

Hartman, C. G. 1962. *Science and the safe period.* Baltimore: Williams & Wilkins.

Henry, L., and Gautier, E. 1958. *La population de Crulai: Paroisse normande.* Travaux et Documents de l'Institut National d'Etudes Demographiques, Cahier no. 33. Paris: Presses Universitaires de France.

Himes. N. E. 1936. *Medical history of contraception.* Baltimore: Williams & Wilkins. (Reprinted, New York: Schocken Books, 1970.)

Hollick, Frederick. 1850. *The marriage guide, or natural history of generation: A private instructor for married persons and those about to marry.* New York: T. W. Strong.

Howe, Daniel W., ed. 1976. *Victorian America.* Philadelphia: University of Pennsylvania Press.

Jacob, Kathryn Allamong. 1979. Clelia Duel Mosher. *Johns Hopkins Magazine* 3 (June): 3–12.

James, W. H. 1971. The distribution of coitus within the human intermenstruum. *Journal of Biosocial Science* 3:159–72.

James, William H. 1973. The fecundability of U.S. women. *Population Studies* (November): pp. 493–500.

Kahn, Morris H. 1917. A municipal birth control clinic. *New York Medical Journal* 54 (April 28): 790–91.

Kennedy, David. 1970. *Birth control in America: The career of Margaret Sanger.* New Haven: Yale University Press.

Keyfitz, N. 1971. How birth control affects births. *Social Biology* 18:109–21.

Kinsey, A. C., et al. 1948. *Sexual behavior in the human male.* Philadelphia: W. B. Saunders.

———. 1953. *Sexual behavior in the human female.* Philadelphia: W. B. Saunders.

Kopp, M. 1934. *Birth control in practice.* New York: Robert M. McBride.

Kunze, Kent. 1979. The effects of age composition and changes in vital rates on nineteenth century population estimates from new data. Ph.D. dissertation, University of Utah.

Lachenbruch, P. H. 1967. Frequency and timing of intercourse: Its relation to the probability of conception. *Population Studies* 21:23–31.

LaSorte, Michael. 1976. Nineteenth century family planning practices. *Journal of Psychohistory* 4:163–83.

Leridon, H. 1973. *Aspects biometriques de la fecondité humaine.* Paris: Presses Universitaires de France.

———. 1976. Facts and artifacts in the study of intra-uterine mortality: A reconsideration from pregnancy histories. *Population Studies* 30 (July): 319–35.

Lewis, D. 1874. *Chastity, or Our secret sins.* Philadelphia.

Lewis-Fanning, E. 1949. *Report on an enquiry into family limitation and its influence on human fertility during the past fifty years.* Papers of the Royal Commission on Population, vol. 1. London.

Lindert, Peter H. 1978. *Fertility and scarcity in America.* Princeton: Princeton University Press.

Macleod, John, and Gold, Ruth Z. 1952, 1953a, 1953b. The male factor in fertility and sterility. *Fertility and Sterility.* Part 5, vol. 3, no. 4, pp. 297–315; Part 6, vol. 4, no. 1, pp. 10–35; Part 7, vol. 4, no. 3, pp. 194–209.

MaHood, James, and Wenburg, Kristine. 1980. *The Mosher Survey: Sexual attitudes of 45 Victorian women.* New York: Arno.

Mohr, James C. 1976. *The nineteenth century origins of American abortion policy.* Typescript.

———. 1978. *Abortion in America: The origins and evolution of national policy, 1800–1900.* New York: Oxford University Press.

Mosher, Clelia Duel. n.d. Statistical study of the marriage of forty-seven women. Vol. 10, Mosher Papers, Leland Stanford Junior University Archives.

Nag, Moni. 1972. Sex, culture, and human fertility: India and the United States. *Current Anthropology* 13 (April): 231–38.

Nam, C. B., ed. 1968. *Population and society.* Boston: Houghton Mifflin.

Nissenbaum, Stephen, 1968. Careful love: Sylvester Graham and the emergence of Victorian sexual theory in America, 1830–1840. Ph.D. dissertation, University of Wisconsin.

Omran, Abel R. 1972. Abortion in the demographic transition. In *Rapid population growth: Consequences and policy implications.* Baltimore: National Academy of Sciences Press.

Page, Hilary J. 1977. Patterns underlying fertility schedules: A decomposition by both age and marital duration. *Population Studies* 31:85–106.

Paige, Karen Ericksen, and Paige, Jeffery M. 1981. *The politics of reproductive ritual.* Berkeley: University of California Press.

Pivar, David. J. 1973. *Purity crusade: Sexual morality and social control, 1868–1900.* Westport, Conn.: Greenwood Press.

Potter, R. G. 1972. Births averted by induced abortion: An application through renewal theory. *Theoretical Population Biology* 3:69 ff.

Pouchet, F. A. 1847. *Théorie positive de l'ovulation spontanée.* Paris.

Rainwater, Lee. 1960. *And the poor get children.* Chicago: Quadrangle.

Reed, James. 1978. *From private vice to public virtue: The birth control movement and American society since 1830.* New York: Basic Books.

Rogers, Everett M. 1973. *Communication strategies for family planning.* New York: Free Press.

Rosenberg, Charles E. 1976. *No other gods: On science and social thought in America.* Baltimore: Johns Hopkins University Press.

Rosenberg, Rosalind, 1982. *Beyond separate spheres: The intellectual roots of modern feminism.* New Haven: Yale University Press.

Rothman, Ellen K. 1982. Sex and self-control: Middle-class courtship in America, 1770–1870. *Journal of Social History* 15 (Spring): 409–25.

Sanderson, Warren C. 1979. Quantitative aspects of marriage fertility and family limitation in nineteenth century America: Another application of the Coale specifications. *Demography* 16:339–58.

Sennett, Richard. 1970. *Families against the city: Middle class homes of industrial Chicago, 1872–1900.* Cambridge: Harvard University Press.

Sheps, Mindel C., and Menken, Jane A. 1973. *Mathematical models of conception and birth.* Chicago: University of Chicago Press.

Smith, Daniel Scott. 1973a. The dating of the American sexual revolution: Evidence and interpretation. In *The American family in Social-historical perspective,* ed. Michael Gordon. New York: St. Martin's.

———. 1973b. Family limitation, sexual control and domestic feminism in Victorian America. *Feminist Studies* 1, (Winter/Spring): 40–57.

Stix, Regine K., and Notestein, Frank W. 1935. Effectiveness of birth control: A second study. *Milbank Memorial Fund Quarterly* 13 (April): 162–78.

———. 1940. *Controlled fertility: An evaluation of clinic service.* Baltimore: Williams & Wilkins.

Stockham, A. B. 1887. *Tokology.* Chicago: Sanitary Publishing.

Stoneman, Paul L. 1983. *The economic analysis of technological change.* Oxford: Oxford University Press.

Storer, Horatio R., and Heard, Franklin Fiske. 1868. *Criminal abortion: Its nature, its evidence and its law.* Boston: Little, Brown. (Reprinted New York: Arno Press, 1974).

Terman, L. M. 1938. *Psychological factors in marital happiness.* New York: McGraw-Hill.

Tietze, C. 1962. The use-effectiveness of contraceptive methods. In *Research in family planning,* ed. C. F. Kiser. Princeton: Princeton University Press.

Tietze, C., and Potter, R. G. 1962. Statistical evaluation of the rhythm method. *American Journal of Obstetrics and gynecology* 84:692–98.

Tolnay, S. E., and Guest, A. M. 1982. Childlessness in a transitional population: The United States at the turn of the century. *Journal of Family History* 7:200–219.

———. 1984. American family building strategies in 1900: Stopping or spacing. *Demography* 21:9–18.

Trall, R. T. 1881. *Sexual physiology.* New York: M. L. Holbrook. (Reprinted New York: Arno Press, 1974).

Uhlenberg, Peter. 1969. A study of cohort life cycles: Cohorts of native-born Massachusetts women, 1830–1920. *Population Studies* 23 (November): 407–20.

United States Bureau of the Census. 1947. *Sixteenth census of the United States: 1940, population, differential fertility 1940 and 1910, fertility by duration of marriage.* Washington: Government Printing Office.

Vinovskis, Maris A. 1981. *Fertility in Massachusetts from the Revolution to the Civil War.* New York: Academic Press.

Wachter, Kenneth W., et al. 1978. *Statistical studies of historical social structure.* New York: Academic Press.

Wallin, Paul, and Clark, Alexander. 1958. Cultural norms and husbands' and wives' reports of their marital partners' preferred frequency of coitus relative to their own. *Sociometry* 21 (September): 249–54.

Westoff, C. F. 1974. Coital frequency and contraception. *Family Planning Perspectives* 6 (Summer): 136–41.

Whelpton, P. K., et al. 1966. *Fertility and family planning in the United States.* Princeton: Princeton University Press.

Wrigley, E. A. 1966. Family limitation in pre-industrial England. *Economic History Review* 19:82–109.

———. 1969. *Population and history.* London: Weidenfeld & Nicolson.

Yasuba, Y. 1962. *Birth rates of the white population in the United States, 1800–1860: An economic study.* Baltimore: Johns Hopkins Press.

Zei, G., and Cavalli-Sforza, L. L. 1977. Education and birth control. *Genus* 33:15–42.

# 8    New Results on the Decline in Household Fertility in the United States from 1750 to 1900

Jenny Bourne Wahl

## 8.1  Introduction

It is clear that a decline in fertility occurred in the United States during the nineteenth century. But exactly when it began, how rapidly and steadily it proceeded, the best method of measuring it, its proximate determinants, the subgroups of the population chiefly responsible for it, and the socioeconomic forces that produced it are all open questions, despite the fact that each has been subject to considerable scholarly discussion.

Several authors have presented evidence suggesting regular and persistent fertility decline since 1800, while Yasuba (1962) points to the wide regional differences in fertility at that date as evidence of possible prior reduction in fertility, at least in some regions. However, the data on which these conclusions rest are imperfect. National birth and death registration systems were not completed until the 1930s, although there are some data (not necessarily representative of the entire population) from city and state registration systems for the early and middle nineteenth century. Therefore, a large part of the analysis of the fertility decline has had to rely on data from the decennial federal censuses, which did not classify the population by single year of age until 1880.[1]

Jenny Bourne Wahl is an international economist at the Office of Tax Analysis, United States Treasury Department. All opinions are solely the author's.

My thanks go to Gary Becker, Thomas Mroz, Larry Wimmer, and Clayne Pope, to fellow research assistants at the University of Chicago and Brigham Young University, especially Jon Moen, and to an anonymous referee. Special thanks go to Robert Fogel, Michael Haines, Robert Gallman, Stanley Engerman, and Robert Katzmann, and to Catherine Mardikes, Carol Miterko, Marilyn Coopersmith, and Edward Wahl. I appreciate the support of the Walgreen Foundation, the National Bureau of Economic Research, and the American Association of University Women.

Child/woman ratios have been the most common measure of fertility calculated from the census data.[2] Clearly, the ratio is an ambiguous index of fertility since it is influenced by mortality experience and population structure. Thus, two populations with very different underlying fertility schedules might record the same child/woman ratio, given appropriate counterbalancing differentials in mortality and population structure.

In view of these considerations, it is not surprising that the timing and pace of the decline in American fertility remain uncertain. To settle these questions, scholars require household information for the nineteenth and earlier centuries, including comprehensive natality and mortality data for each sample household. The centerpiece of this paper is just such a data set. It is described and appraised in a subsequent section and then used to establish the timing and pace of decline in American fertility before 1900.

The new micro data set is also required to work out the effects of the proximate determinants of fertility and changes thereto. The number of children born to a couple depends on the number of their fertile years that they spend together, the frequency of their intercourse, how often (if at all) and how effectively they use contraception, and their fecundity. The censuses contain no direct information on any of these questions. The new micro data set introduced in this paper has direct information on the first question and considerable information bearing directly on the last three. It also includes data on the incidence of marriage.

The socioeconomic factor that has figured most prominently in the discussion of United States fertility levels in the nineteenth and earlier centuries is the availability of farmland. Benjamin Franklin and T. R. Malthus, among others, proposed that fertility is affected by land availability, and in recent decades this been brought up again by Yasuba and Easterlin. Easterlin's "bequest" model was applied exclusively to farm families, and it focused on planning across two generations. However, his model is readily adapted to nonfarm circumstances and can take account of other possible factors influencing fertility, such as the economic costs and benefits of children. In this respect, the adapted model can move in the general direction of the work of T. W. Schultz, T. P. Schultz, and Gary Becker, among others, who have sought a general cost-benefit framework for the analysis of fertility. Their models have included such variables as parents' wealth, parents' opportunity costs, life expectation of children, the consumption value of children, production in the family, and so forth. To apply such models to historical questions requires household demographic and economic data. The micro data set that forms the foundation of this paper has been matched to the census so that eventually comprehensive analyses of the socioeconomic determinants of fertility change will be possible. These possibilities are discussed in a subsequent section.

This paper makes use of a new household data set to establish both the timing and speed of the American fertility decline before 1900 and the proximate determinants of this development. The paper also outlines a plan for investigating the effects of socioeconomic factors on fertility.

The data set (discussed in some detail in the following section and in the appendix) consists of demographic information on households, with links established from one generation to the next, and, in some cases, with links to economic data. The data run from the mid–seventeenth century through the nineteenth century and include only white individuals. Three samples are discussed in this paper: samples A and B, the first with a broader geographical coverage than the second, and sample C, a subsample of B that contains economic data. The samples are not representative of the entire population, but they do cover a variety of circumstances and experiences and thus can be used to obtain insights into the broad developments with which this paper is concerned.

The next section describes and appraises the data set. It is followed by sections devoted chiefly to evaluating fertility differences over time and among families which have been grouped by socioeconomic characteristics.

## 8.2  Description of Data

The empirical work was performed using a large intergenerationally linked genealogical sample of American families to which additional household and economic information has been linked from the decennial federal censuses for 1850–80.

The data are remarkably detailed: birth, marriage, and death dates and places were coded for each individual.[3] For individuals who were found in the census, observations on the value of personal property, the value of real estate, occupation, literacy, age, sex, birthplace, and relationship to the head of household were coded from the information obtained in each of the four census years.[4] An elaborate identification scheme was used first to group individuals into nuclear families and then to connect families through generations. Currently, there is linked information on fertility for three generations and on wealth for two generations.

The data set is also quite large. Sample A was constructed by drawing random samples of the nuclear families contained in each of approximately 1,400 published family histories.[5] The working file for sample A consists of 15,748 individuals from 4,467 nuclear families. Sample B was constructed by recording all data contained in nine published family histories. The working file for sample B contains 16,820 individuals in 5,632 nuclear families.[6] Nuclear families at risk to be found in one of the four censuses must have had at least one family member alive during the census year. The number of families at risk to be found in at least one census year was about 2,500; the number actually found in at least one census was 2,042. The total number of families found in each census was 782 in 1850, 649 in 1860, 661 in 1870, and 706 in 1880.

Recent economic analyses of fertility suggest that the costs and benefits of children varied over time, among regions, between farm and nonfarm families, and by household income (which depended upon the occupation of the head of the household) and wealth.[7] Fortunately, the data in samples A, B, and C were quite well represented over time, space, and occupational and wealth classes. Families in sample A were evenly distributed among the mother's birth cohorts of 1650–1799, 1800–1849, and 1850–99. Half of the families in sample B fell into the 1800–1849 birth cohort and a fourth each into the 1650–1799 and 1850–99 cohorts. In sample A, 40% of all families resided in the New England or Mid-Atlantic states (70% of these in the states of Massachusetts, Pennsylvania, and New Jersey), 17% each in the Midwest or Western states, and 9% in the South. Two-thirds of the families in sample B lived in New England or the Mid-Atlantic states, one-fifth in the Midwest or Plains states, and 7% each in the South and in the West. The percentage of families in sample C who lived on farms was 68% in 1850, 70% in 1860, 68% in 1870, and 52% in 1880. As shown in table 8.1, a large majority of adult males in sample C reported their occupation as "laborer," of which most were farm laborers.

Although sample C was wealthier than another census sample which was drawn by Soltow,[8] nevertheless a wide range of reported wealth

**Table 8.1**         **Distribution of Occupations for Adult Males**

|  | Census Years | | | |
| --- | --- | --- | --- | --- |
| Occupations | 1850 | 1860 | 1870 | 1880 |
| Professionals and proprietors | 12.0% | 15.0% | 18.0% | 24.0% |
| Craftsmen | 12.0 | 10.0 | 11.0 | 11.0 |
| Laborers | 73.0 | 73.0 | 70.94 | 61.0 |
| Not in labor force | 3.0 | 2.0 | 0.06 | 4.0 |
| Total | 100.0% | 100.0% | 100.0% | 100.0% |
| Number of observations | 592 | 486 | 488 | 507 |

*Source:* Sample C (see text).

*Note:* Males who were 20 years of age or older in the census year of observation.

values was present. Families that held no reported wealth were especially well represented.[9]

The subsample linked to the census consists of white, native-born, and literate individuals (98% of the adults in sample C reported themselves as literate).

## 8.3    Trends in Fertility

### 8.3.1    Trends in Unstandardized Measures of Fertility

The data in the genealogical samples permit the computation of such unstandardized measures of fertility as the period total fertility rate and child/woman ratios, which have been the principal fertility measures constructed from published censuses and other types of data previously available to historical demographers. The genealogical samples, however, also permit the construction of age-specific marital fertility schedules and cohort total marital fertility rates.[10] Unlike the total fertility rate or child/woman ratios, changes in marital fertility rates reflect only shifts in the marital fertility schedule and are thus independent of changes in average marriage ages, mortality rates, or the age structure of the population. Changes in the total fertility rate would occur even if the fertility schedule is constant if there are changes in such variables as the average age of a woman at her marriage, the mortality rates of husbands and wives, and the percentage of the population ever married.[11] The child/woman ratio is affected by all of the aforementioned variables plus the age distribution of the population and the mortality rates of children. Neither the period total fertility rate nor the child/woman ratio can pinpoint shifts in the underlying age-specific fertility rates.

Trends in the period total fertility rate and the child/woman ratio are shown in table 8.2. There is a general downward trend in these fertility measures, although the timing of the decline in the two series did not always coincide.[12] One may note that, although the trend in the period total fertility rate was similar in samples A and B, the level differed somewhat. However, by the nature of its construction, sample A has a greater proportion of families who lived in regions of higher fertility (see sec. 8.4.2) and of immigrant families, who had more children than native-born Americans (see sec. 8.4.3). Therefore, the difference in the level of the period total fertility rate is partly explained by the difference in distribution of the two samples. The period total fertility rates for sample A are comparable to those calculated by Thompson and Whelpton for 1800–1855 and by Coale and Zelnik for 1860 onward (see Coale and Zelnik, p. 36) for the white population.

The level of the child/woman ratio, at least in the years 1850–90 in sample B, is lower than the level calculated from the censuses of the

**Table 8.2**    **Two Unstandardized Measures of Fertility Computed from the Genealogical Samples, 1700–1889**

| Years of Observation for Women Aged 15–44 (1) | Child/Woman Ratio (a) (2) | Period Total Fertility Rate (b) (3) | Number of Families (4) |
|---|---|---|---|
| *Sample A* | | | |
| 1700–1709 | 531 | 7.0 | 28 |
| 1750–59 | 658 | 7.2 | 42 |
| 1800–1809 | 561 | 7.0 | 245 |
| 1810–19 | 570 | 7.1 | 328 |
| 1820–29 | 625 | 6.9 | 386 |
| 1830–39 | 631 | 6.6 | 400 |
| 1840–49 | 641 | 6.1 | 370 |
| 1850–59 | 664 | 5.3 | 284 |
| 1860–69 | 746 | 4.8 | 187 |
| 1870–79 | 850 | 4.8 | 98 |
| 1880–89 | 686 | 3.7 | 31 |
| *Sample B* | | | |
| 1700–1709 | 625 | 6.0 | 6 |
| 1750–59 | 1228 | 7.2 | 17 |
| 1800–1809 | 908 | 5.0 | 234 |
| 1810–19 | 717 | 4.8 | 202 |
| 1820–29 | 627 | 4.4 | 172 |
| 1830–39 | 527 | 4.2 | 128 |
| 1840–49 | 415 | 3.8 | 90 |
| 1850–59 | 296 | 3.5 | 69 |
| 1860–69 | 215 | 3.4 | 51 |
| 1870–79 | 289 | 3.3 | 29 |
| 1880–89 | 313 | 3.5 | 11 |

*Source:* Samples A and B (see text).

*Note:* Secular movement of two unstandardized measures of fertility, including: (a) The child/woman ratio (equal to the number of children aged 0–4 per every 1,000 once- or never-married women aged 15–44 in the period given in col. 1). The secular movements in the ratio show interesting patterns, although the underlying forces producing the patterns are not explored in detail in this paper. (b) The period total fertility rate for women aged 15–44 sums the age-specific fertility rates for women of the given ages during the period. For example, the number of children born to women aged 20–24 during the given period divided by the number of women of that age, multiplied by 5, is the age-specific period fertility rate for the 20–24-year age interval. Note that only those women either once- or never-married are included. Therefore, women who remarried after the death of their first spouse are not included.

Data are available to construct fertility measures for the years 1710–49 and 1760–99 for both samples, but they have not been processed yet.

total population (not shown). The most likely explanation for this difference is that the census population of women aged 15–44 includes women who remarried after the death of a spouse, while my samples include only once- and never-married women. Therefore, my samples have greater fractions than the census population of women who were not at risk to bear children but who were included in the child/woman ratio calculations. Other factors are also important. Families of sample B were native-born, highly literate, primarily of Northeastern residence, and more likely to be located in urban areas than the total population (at least in 1880). All of these characteristics were associated with lower than average fertility, as will be seen in subsequent sections.

The declines in the series shown in table 8.2 may be due to shifts in the underlying marital fertility schedule, to changes in mortality rates, or to various structural changes. The most likely explanation for a shift in the fertility schedule over time is the onset of attempts to control fertility within marriage. For example, parents could have begun deliberately ending their childbearing before one or both parents became sterile, spacing their children farther apart, or using both methods of control. Families which ended childbearing before secondary sterility set in would have had lower ages at the last birth for the mothers who remained at risk to bear children and lower age-specific fertility rates in the last age intervals than families who continued childbearing. Families which spaced their children farther apart than other families would have had lower age-specific fertility rates in all age intervals in which longer spacing had occurred. Individuals also could have controlled their fertility by marrying later, which would have reduced their time at risk to bear children, or by not marrying at all. However, whereas the individual controls would have been reflected in such measures as the child/woman ratio and the period total fertility rate, they would have had no effect on the marital fertility schedule.

### 8.3.2   Explaining the Decline before 1850 in the Average Number of Children Ever Born

How much of the variation in the unstandardized measures of fertility shown in table 8.2 was due to a shift in the marital fertility schedule and how much was due to other determinants? Table 8.3, which presents both marital fertility schedules and total marital fertility rates for 10 cohorts of women, indicates that the fertility schedules of cohorts born prior to 1850 were quite stable. The data in table 8.3 reveal that intramarital fertility regulation did not become important in determining the number of children ever born to a family until the latter half of the nineteenth century. Except for the puzzling fall in total marital fertility in the 1800–1812 birth cohort in sample B, age-specific and total marital fertility rates were similar for cohorts prior to 1863 in sample A and for cohorts prior to 1850 in sample B. In subsequent birth cohorts, age-specific marital fertility rates fell primarily in the later age intervals (ages 30–44).

The conclusion that intramarital fertility regulation was not important until the latter half of the nineteenth century, especially in sample A,

**Table 8.3.**  Marital Age-Specific and Total Fertility Rates for the Genealogical Samples, 1700–1899

*Sample A*

Birth Cohorts

| Age Intervals | 1650–99 (43) | 1700–1749 (33) | 1750–99 (55) | 1800–1812 (69) | 1813–24 (62) | 1825–36 (132) | 1837–49 (145) | 1850–62 (201) | 1863–74 (121) | 1875–99 (87) |
|---|---|---|---|---|---|---|---|---|---|---|
| 20–24 | .487 | .492 | .536 | .484 | .497 | .526 | .506 | .486 | .476 | .514 |
| 25–29 | .407 | .372 | .420 | .408 | .437 | .408 | .449 | .413 | .355 | .362 |
| 30–34 | .374 | .406 | .355 | .339 | .376 | .377 | .362 | .345 | .245 | .245 |
| 35–39 | .313 | .338 | .294 | .300 | .376 | .328 | .315 | .275 | .204 | .207 |
| 40–44 | .226 | .199 | .261 | .228 | .223 | .195 | .236 | .166 | .096 | .139 |
| Total fertility rate for women aged 20–44 | 9.0 | 9.0 | 9.3 | 8.8 | 9.5 | 9.2 | 9.3 | 8.4 | 6.9 | 7.3 |

## Sample B

| Age Intervals | Birth Cohorts | | | | | | | | |
|---|---|---|---|---|---|---|---|---|---|
| | 1700–1749 (25) | 1750–99 (204) | 1800–1812 (130) | 1813–24 (68) | 1825–36 (62) | 1837–49 (51) | 1850–62 (75) | 1863–74 (28) | 1875–99 (41) |
| 20–24 | .630 | .438 | .285 | .434 | .495 | .400 | .338 | .393 | .388 |
| 25–29 | .345 | .367 | .259 | .371 | .340 | .411 | .251 | .320 | .308 |
| 30–34 | .346 | .305 | .218 | .310 | .273 | .261 | .222 | .180 | .151 |
| 35–39 | .260 | .258 | .191 | .266 | .235 | .248 | .191 | .106 | .178 |
| 40–44 | .236 | .166 | .135 | .150 | .150 | .148 | .118 | .026 | .008 |
| Total fertility rate for women aged 20–44 | 9.1 | 7.7 | 5.4 | 7.7 | 7.5 | 7.3 | 5.6 | 5.1 | 5.2 |

*Source:* Samples A and B (see text).

*Note:* Age-specific marital fertility rates and total marital fertility rates are given for birth cohorts of women in each genealogical sample. The sample size for the 1650–99 birth cohort of women in sample B was too small to permit calculation of marital fertility rates. The age-specific rate for women aged 20–24 in sample B in the 1700–1749 cohort is probably higher than average because this age group was composed of a small number of women who were more fertile than average. The manner in which sample B was constructed explains both the small sample size and the higher than average fertility of early cohorts. See the text and the appendix.

The measures in this table differ from those in table 8.2 for two reasons: (1) Women included in the calculations of this table must have been married at the time of observation, while in table 8.2 women did not have to have been married to have been included. (2) Within a birth cohort, the age-specific rates in this table were calculated for the same group of women (although women who died at a certain age naturally were excluded from further calculations). Within a period, age-specific rates in table 8.2 were calculated for women who fell in a certain age interval during the given period. Therefore, the cohort rate (this table) was calculated for a birth cohort of women; the period rate (table 8.2) was calculated for women who were alive at a certain point in time.

The numbers enclosed in parentheses for each birth cohort equal the total number of woman-years lived in the 30–34-year age interval divided by 5. Therefore, these numbers represent the hypothetical number of women who would have been at risk to bear children from ages 30–34 if each woman had lived for the entire 5-year interval.

is supported by the trend in the age of the average mother who was at risk to bear children at least until she was 45 years old (see table 8.4). These mothers continued to bear children to an average age of about 38 years until 1850 in sample A and until 1820 in sample B.[13] In subsequent time periods, the average age fell to approximately 32 years for sample A and 33 years for sample B by 1890. This age pattern also supports the conclusion that stopping childbearing before the parents became sterile was probably a more important method of fertility control after 1850 than longer spacing of births.

Although fertility within marriage did not fall substantially until at least the 1850–62 birth cohort, the period total fertility rate declined throughout the nineteenth century. Therefore, other proximate determinants of fertility must have been changing prior to 1850. The average mother's age at marriage was steady throughout the nineteenth century, especially for sample A. However, there was an increase in the average marriage age of about 1½ years in sample A and about 2 years in sample B from 1700 to 1800. Although the sample sizes were too small in the early years to permit much speculation, it is possible that the underlying decline in family size during that time was partly due to a rising marriage age.

The two factors which explain the divergence between the total marital fertility rate and the unstandardized fertility indices in their movement between 1800 and 1850 are the increase in the percentage who never married (see table 8.4) and the rise in the mortality rate (see Fogel's fig. 9.1 in this volume).[14] The increase in the proportion of spinsters indicates that fewer women were exposed to the risk of childbearing than had been before; the decline in life expectation indicates that those who did marry were exposed to the risk of childbearing for a shorter period of time. Life expectancies at age 10 for both sexes during the period 1835–59 were about 20% below those in the quarter-century between 1765 and 1789. After 1860, life expectancies began to increase, so that mortality trends no longer contributed to the decline in family size.

Table 8.5 contains an index of the degree of fertility regulation within marriage, by cohort, which was developed by Coale and Trussell.[15] The results support the hypothesis that intramarital fertility regulation was not an important force in the genealogical samples until the latter half of the nineteenth century. The results also confirm that intramarital fertility regulation appeared slightly earlier in sample B than in sample A, probably owing to regional variations in fertility and differences in regional composition of the two samples.

Table 8.6 contains the conditional parity-specific probabilities,[16] by cohort, of having an additional child. Sample A shows constancy in the parity-specific probabilities, at least through cohorts born in 1825–

**Table 8.4**    **Some Proximate Determinants of Fertility**

| Years of Observation for Women Aged 15–44 during the Period (1) | Number of Families (2) | Average Mother's Age at Marriage (3) | Average Mother's Age at First Birth (4) | Average Mother's Age at Last Birth (5) | Average Mother's Age at Last Birth for Women at Risk to Age 45 (6) | Percentage Ever Married (7) |
|---|---|---|---|---|---|---|
| | | | *Sample A* | | | |
| 1700–1709 | 28 | 20.8 | 22.3 | 37.0 | 39.7 | —[a] |
| 1750–59 | 42 | 22.0 | 23.3 | 38.8 | 39.0 | — |
| 1800–1809 | 245 | 22.4 | 23.7 | 38.1 | 40.5 | — |
| 1810–19 | 328 | 22.1 | 23.4 | 38.1 | 40.3 | — |
| 1820–29 | 386 | 22.0 | 23.3 | 37.6 | 39.8 | — |
| 1830–39 | 400 | 22.0 | 23.3 | 37.1 | 39.2 | — |
| 1840–49 | 370 | 22.0 | 23.4 | 36.4 | 38.3 | — |
| 1850–59 | 284 | 22.0 | 23.5 | 35.1 | 36.8 | — |
| 1860–69 | 187 | 22.0 | 23.7 | 34.4 | 35.6 | — |
| 1870–79 | 98 | 21.7 | 23.3 | 34.0 | 34.6 | — |
| 1880–89 | 31 | 22.1 | 23.7 | 31.5 | 32.9 | — |

(*continued*)

**Table 8.4** (continued)

| Years of Observation for Women Aged 15–44 during the Period (1) | Number of Families (2) | Average Mother's Age at Marriage (3) | Average Mother's Age at First Birth (4) | Average Mother's Age at Last Birth (5) | Average Mother's Age at Last Birth for Women at Risk to Age 45 (6) | Percentage Ever Married (7) |
|---|---|---|---|---|---|---|
| | | | *Sample B* | | | |
| 1700–1709 | 6 | 22.0 | 23.6 | 35.5 | 42.0 | |
| 1750–59 | 17 | 22.5 | 24.2 | 39.5 | 40.3 | 97 |
| 1800–1809 | 234 | 24.0 | 25.8 | 35.9 | 38.2 | 90 |
| 1810–19 | 202 | 24.3 | 26.1 | 35.5 | 37.8 | 85 |
| 1820–29 | 172 | 24.0 | 26.0 | 35.0 | 36.4 | 83 |
| 1830–39 | 128 | 23.8 | 25.9 | 33.7 | 34.7 | 80 |
| 1840–49 | 90 | 23.1 | 25.3 | 33.1 | 34.0 | 78 |
| 1850–59 | 69 | 22.7 | 25.0 | 32.6 | 33.7 | 79 |
| 1860–69 | 51 | 23.2 | 25.3 | 32.5 | 33.5 | 80 |
| 1870–79 | 29 | 22.7 | 24.6 | 33.4 | 35.0 | 85 |
| 1880–89 | 11 | 21.5 | 23.6 | 32.8 | 32.9 | 86 |

*Source*: Samples A and B (see text).

*Note*: The fertility measures listed are useful for evaluating the relative strengths of the proximate determinants of the number of children. Columns 3, 4, and 5 were calculated over the same set of women.

Two important trends are in the average age at last birth for women who were at risk to bear children at least until they reached age 45 and in the percentage of women ever married during their fecund years. The former fell substantially only in the latter half of the nineteenth century, which supports the proposal that fertility regulation within marriage was not strong until after 1850. The latter was significantly lower between 1820 and 1860 than in previous and subsequent periods. Therefore the decline in the period total fertility rate during the first half of the century (shown in table 8.2) was partly due to lower incidence of marriage among fecund women.

[a]Data are available to construct averages for 1710–49 and 1760–99 and percentages married for all periods for sample A, but they have not yet been processed. Sample sizes for the period after 1890 were too small to permit calculations.

**Table 8.5**            **Coale-Trussell $M$ and $m$ Tests for Fertility Control**

|            | Birth Cohorts | | |
|------------|:---------:|:---------:|:---------:|
|            | 1825–49 | 1850–74 | 1875–99 |
|            |         | *Sample A* |         |
| $M$        | .957    | .970    | .944    |
| $m$        | −.105   | .182    | .346    |
|            |         | *Sample B* |         |
| $M$        | .674    | .732    | .741    |
| $m$        | −.057   | .308    | .333    |

*Source:* Samples A and B (see text).

*Note:* $M$ measures the overall level of fertility in the samples relative to the level of fertility in a natural fertility population (see n. 15); $m$ measures the degree of fertility control within marriage which was present in the samples. An increase in $m$ signifies an increase in intramarital fertility regulation.

49 and possibly through cohorts born in 1850–74. In sample B, however, the decline in parity-specific probabilities appears to have begun a half-century earlier. Clearly, not all families who had an additional child wanted one. However, suppose that child mortality was not changing through time and that successive generations of parents desired fewer children on average. Under these circumstances, parents would have attempted more stringent regulation of fertility than previous generations of parents. Therefore, the trend in the observed conditional probabilities of having an additional child would reflect the trend in desires to have an additional child. Of course, a downward trend in the observed probabilities could also reflect improving mortality conditions, for parents could have borne fewer children in order to have a given number of surviving children. Therefore, inferences from these probabilities about the timing of the onset of fertility regulation should be made only in conjunction with evidence previously presented in the paper.

It seems likely that differences in socioeconomic characteristics of the families in the two samples will account for the somewhat earlier entry of individuals from sample B into the regulation of fertility than was true of the individuals in sample A. So far, the linking of the genealogies to information on wealth and most of the other reported socioeconomic variables has been limited to sample B, so it is not yet possible to identify specifically the factors which explain the overall lag in the onset of regulation in sample A as compared with sample B. However, there is enough variation of both fertility behavior and socioeconomic characteristics in sample B to shed some light on the probable impact of socioeconomic variables on the decline in fertility.

**Table 8.6    Observed Parity-Specific Probabilities of Having an Additional Birth**

| Probabilities | Birth Cohorts | | | | | | Percentage Change from the 1800–1824 to the 1875–99 Cohort in the Probability of Having an Additional Birth |
|---|---|---|---|---|---|---|---|
| | 1650–1749 | 1750–99 | 1800–1824 | 1825–49 | 1850–74 | 1875–99 | |
| | | | | *Sample A* | | | |
| pr12[a] | 95.24 | 94.59 | 98.02 | 97.48 | 94.52 | 88.61 | 9.6% |
| $N$[b] | 63 | 37 | 101 | 278 | 292 | 79 | |
| pr23 | 94.29 | 97.67 | 94.44 | 95.29 | 90.14 | 87.84 | 7.0% |
| $N$ | 70 | 43 | 108 | 297 | 284 | 74 | |
| pr34 | 90.41 | 89.36 | 92.23 | 90.66 | 90.49 | 80.00 | 13.3% |
| $N$ | 73 | 47 | 103 | 289 | 263 | 65 | |
| | | | | *Sample B* | | | |
| pr12 | 73.33 | 79.65 | 64.12 | 54.47 | 47.06 | 44.44 | 30.7% |
| $N$ | 60 | 226 | 170 | 123 | 68 | 36 | |
| pr23 | 80.43 | 87.91 | 77.68 | 69.70 | 60.00 | 52.94 | 31.8% |
| $N$ | 46 | 182 | 112 | 66 | 35 | 17 | |
| pr34 | 87.18 | 86.83 | 82.02 | 63.04 | 59.09 | 66.67 | 18.7% |
| $N$ | 39 | 167 | 89 | 46 | 22 | 9 | |

*Source:* Samples A and B (see text).

[a] $pr(x)(x + 1)$ is the probability of observing an additional birth given that an $x$th birth occurred.

[b] $N$ is the number of families at risk to have an additional birth. Although women can (and do) become pregnant shortly after giving birth, there is generally a period of postpartum amenorrhea during which women are infecund. Therefore, families were included in the calculation of $pr(x)(x + 1)$ only if both spouses lived at least 2 years after the birth of the $x$th child.

## 8.4 Variations in Fertility and Nuptiality across Subgroups in the Sample

### 8.4.1 Introduction

Theoretical arguments, sometimes supported by evidence on child/woman ratios, have been put forward regarding the effect of changes in socioeconomic characteristics on the decline in fertility after 1800. Several scholars have argued that fertility declined first in the Northeast (Yasuba 1962; Forster and Tucker 1972; Easterlin 1976). Easterlin's formal model proposed that the parents' fertility was positively related to the expected growth of their capital, which was lower in the rural Northeast.[17] An alternative explanation stressed the rapid rise in urbanization as the principal factor explaining the fertility decline in the Northeast (Potter 1965). It is likely that both the direct (food, clothing, and shelter) and the indirect (especially the forgone labor of the mother) costs of children were higher in the cities than in the rural areas.

A third issue concerns the effect of ethnicity on fertility. Some scholars have suggested that immigrants were likely to have had larger numbers of children than native-born Americans because they were influenced by cultural patterns in their country of birth (Vinovskis and Hareven 1975). Others have argued that while this may have been partly true toward the end of the nineteenth century, before then immigrants came from countries that had smaller families than America.

Wealth is a fourth factor bearing on fertility patterns. One might expect the relationship of household wealth to household fertility to be positive if children are a normal good. However, the empirical results have not been clearcut, for negative relationships of fertility and wealth have been reported, at least in some ranges of wealth (see Simon [1974] for an excellent review). It is possible that the observed fertility/wealth relation is composed of a true wealth effect (which would cause wealth and fertility to be positively related) and a price effect.[18] If the effective price of children were rising with wealth in a certain range of wealth and the price effect dominated the true wealth effect in that range, the observed fertility/wealth relation would be negative.

### 8.4.2 Fertility Differences among Families Living in Different Regions

The total marital fertility rate was high and fairly steady for a long series of cohorts in each region of the country. It then began falling during the nineteenth century. However, although there was no significant decline in marital fertility prior to the nineteenth century in any region, there were differences across regions in the timing of the decline once it began (see table 8.7).

Table 8.7    Two Fertility Measures, by Region, Sample B

| | Birth Cohorts | | | | | | | | | |
|---|---|---|---|---|---|---|---|---|---|---|
| | 1650–99 | 1700–1749 | 1750–99 | 1800–1812 | 1813–24 | 1825–36 | 1837–49 | 1850–62 | 1863–74 | 1875–99 |
| *Mid-Atlantic region* | | | | | | | | | | |
| Number of children ever born | 7.3 | 6.7 | 6.8 | 5.1 | 4.9 | 4.3 | 3.7 | 4.3 | | 4.1 |
| Total marital fertility for women aged 20–44 | 7.9 | 8.3 | 9.0 | 7.2 | 6.8 | 6.7 | 7.1 | 6.9 | | 6.1 |
| Number of families | 8 | 10 | 100 | 132 | 40 | 53 | 58 | 159 | | 34 |
| *Midwest region* | | | | | | | | | | |
| Number of children ever born | | | | 5.5 | 4.8 | 4.4 | 4.4 | 4.6 | 3.6 | 4.1 |
| Total marital fertility for women aged 20–44 | | | | 8.3 | 8.1 | 7.2 | 7.0 | 6.3 | 5.3 | 6.1 |
| Number of families | | | | 43 | 10 | 19 | 21 | 50 | 13 | 34 |
| *Southern region* | | | | | | | | | | |
| Number of children ever born | | | 9.6 | 5.7 | | | | 3.6 | | |
| Total marital fertility for women aged 20–44 | | | 7.9 | 12.8 | | | | | | |
| Number of families | | | 15 | 11 | | | | 16 | | |
| *New England region* | | | | | | | | | | |
| Number of children ever born | 8.6 | 7.4 | 6.7 | 4.8 | 3.8 | 3.9 | 3.7 | | | |
| Total marital fertility for women aged 20–44 | 8.7 | 8.4 | 7.8 | 8.1 | 6.9 | 6.7 | | | | |
| Number of families | 17 | 26 | 123 | 49 | 28 | 20 | 7 | | | |
| *Western region* | | | | | | | | | | |
| Number of children ever born | | | | | | 7.3 | 8.6 | 7.7 | 5.6 | 4.4 |
| Total marital fertility for women aged 20–44 | | | | | | 8.1 | 10.9 | 7.8 | 5.8 | 5.7 |
| Number of families | | | | | | 33 | 49 | 78 | 49 | 59 |

*Source*: Sample B (see text).

*Note*: Average number of children ever born to a cohort of women contrasted with the total marital fertility rate of the same women, by region of the country.

Fertility regulation within marriage began earliest in the East and moved westward through time. Families in the New England and the Mid-Atlantic regions began controlling fertility as early as the 1800–1812 birth cohort of women, while families in the Midwest had higher marital fertility than Northeasterners until the 1837–49 birth cohort, and Western families had much higher marital fertility than families in other regions at least until the 1863–74 birth cohort. The data for Southern families indicate that their pre-nineteenth-century marital fertility was comparable to marital fertility in other regions. The total marital fertility rate for the South for the 1800–1812 birth cohort exceeded the rate found elsewhere; however, the sample size for this time period for the South was quite small.

Trends in the average number of children ever born (to once-married women) give quite a different picture of fertility than the total marital fertility rate. Although the level varied by region within cohorts, levels in all regions declined continuously across cohorts throughout the nineteenth century. Families living in the New England, Mid-Atlantic, and Midwest regions had similar average family sizes; families living in the West had persistently larger families than those in other areas until the 1875–99 cohort.

It is not surprising that the two indices of fertility have different secular patterns. Variations in the total marital fertility rate come about only by shifts in the marital fertility schedule. These shifts are manifested by changes in birth spacing or lengthening of the open interval after the last child is born and before death or sterility of the parents occurs. However, variations in the number of children ever born result not only from shifts in the marital fertility schedule but also from variations in the average times of entry into and exit from the schedule. The sample sizes are not large enough to permit me to make definitive statements. However, the following paragraphs do shed some light on the degree to which family size varied over time because of marital fertility schedule shifts vis-à-vis other proximate determinants of family size.

Table 8.8 includes the average woman's age at marriage, at first parity, and at last parity. Each average was calculated over all women for whom data were available. Therefore, the averages do not necessarily represent the same set of individuals; however, sample sizes become quite small in some cohorts if regional averages are calculated only on the set of women for whom all three variables had nonmissing values.

The average birth intervals between marriage and first birth and between first and second birth varied only slightly through time.[19] Therefore, shifts in the marital fertility schedule did not occur because of differential spacing over time of early births. However, a lengthening of the open interval after the woman's last birth was an important

**Table 8.8    Fertility Means, by Region, Sample B**

| | | | | | Birth Cohorts | | | | | |
|---|---|---|---|---|---|---|---|---|---|---|
| | 1650–99 | 1700–1749 | 1750–99 | 1800–1812 | 1813–24 | 1825–36 | 1837–49 | 1850–62 | 1863–74 | 1875–99 |
| *Mid-Atlantic region* | | | | | | | | | | |
| Mother's marriage age | 24.2 | 22.5 | 24.0 | 23.7 | 24.1 | 24.4 | 26.6 | 25.8 | | |
| Mother's age at her first birth | 25.3 | 24.9 | 23.9 | 24.4 | 25.4 | 25.5 | 27.8 | 25.8 | | |
| Mother's age at her last birth | 41.8 | 40.4 | 37.9 | 37.0 | 35.6 | 35.1 | 36.6 | 35.3 | | |
| Number of families | 8 | 10 | 100 | 132 | 40 | 53 | 58 | 159 | | |
| *Midwest region* | | | | | | | | | | |
| Mother's marriage age | | | | 22.0 | 23.7 | 21.4 | 24.6 | 22.9 | 23.3 | 22.1 |
| Mother's age at her first birth | | | | 24.2 | 25.6 | 23.6 | 25.9 | 23.3 | 23.2 | 24.3 |
| Mother's age at her last birth | | | | 38.5 | 34.3 | 34.9 | 35.2 | 35.2 | 29.6 | 32.6 |
| Number of families | | | | 43 | 10 | 19 | 21 | 50 | 13 | 34 |
| *Southern region* | | | | | | | | | | |
| Mother's marriage age | | | 24.0 | 23.0 | | | | 22.5 | | |
| Mother's age at her first birth | | | 25.2 | 19.0 | | | | 24.3 | | |
| Mother's age at her last birth | | | 38.3 | 33.0 | | | | 30.6 | | |
| Number of families | | | 15 | 11 | | | | 16 | | |
| *New England region* | | | | | | | | | | |
| Mother's marriage age | 22.2 | 23.9 | 22.9 | 23.2 | 23.8 | 24.0 | 24.8 | | | |
| Mother's age at her first birth | 25.8 | 24.0 | 23.4 | 25.1 | 25.2 | 25.3 | 25.7 | | | |
| Mother's age at her last birth | 36.0 | 38.5 | 37.6 | 37.0 | 33.6 | 34.8 | 32.7 | | | |
| Number of families | 17 | 26 | 123 | 49 | 28 | 20 | 7 | | | |
| *Western region* | | | | | | | | | | |
| Mother's marriage age | | | | | | 23.3 | 22.4 | 20.5 | 21.1 | 21.8 |
| Mother's age at her first birth | | | | | | 24.4 | 23.7 | 21.7 | 22.5 | 23.6 |
| Mother's age at her last birth | | | | | | 39.5 | 41.1 | 37.1 | 35.0 | 33.1 |
| Number of families | | | | | | 33 | 49 | 78 | 49 | 59 |

*Source:* Sample B (see text).

*Note:* Proximate determinants of the number of children ever born (shown in table 8.7). The number of families on which number of children ever born could be calculated; however, all averages in this table are calculated on nonmissing values of the variables. Therefore the average mother's age at her first birth can be less than the average woman's age at marriage. The calculations were not constrained to the subset of women on whom all variables were nonmissing because sample sizes for the subset were quite small in some cohorts.

movement through time in all regions. A woman stops bearing children if she or her partner dies, if she or her partner becomes sterile, or if she and her partner decide to have no more children. The average mother's age at her last birth reflects these three factors. Although not shown in table 8.8, the trend in the average mother's age at her last birth if she was at risk until she was 45 years old parallels the trend in the total marital fertility rate for each region. This measure controls for mortality, although it cannot control for women who experienced secondary sterility before age 45. Hence, shifts in the marital fertility schedule, as evinced by the trends in the total marital fertility rate and the average mother's age at her last birth if she was at risk to age 45, explain part of the fall in the average number of children ever born after the 1800–1812 cohort for Northeastern families, after the 1837–49 cohort for Midwestern families, and after the 1863–74 cohort for Western families.

Throughout the nineteenth century, trends in the average time of entry into and exit from the marital fertility schedule were also key in explaining both the decline in the average number of children ever born before the 1850 cohort and the difference in family sizes across regions. The average age at marriage for women rose by 2 years from the 1750–99 cohort to the 1837–49 cohort in the Mid-Atlantic and New England regions. The average age also rose by 2 years in the Midwest from the 1800–1812 cohort to the 1837–49 cohort. An age-specific fertility rate of .5 for women who married at the average age implies a loss of about one child per family in these regions due to an increase in marriage age. The larger family size among Western families was partially due to their low average age at marriage. The average woman's marriage age in the West was 4–5 years lower than the average in the Mid-Atlantic for the 1837–49 and 1850–62 birth cohorts. Therefore, Western family sizes exceeded family sizes in other regions largely because the average Western woman married earlier than the average woman living in regions other than the West.

Marriage ages may have varied over time and across regions because of variations in the desire to limit family size. It is also possible that persons married later because they had more difficulty in acquiring a given level of income that they felt was necessary to establish a home. Of course, the decision to reach a threshold income before marrying may have been tied to decisions on family sizes. However, there is simply not enough evidence at this point to settle the interesting questions of why marriage ages varied over time and space, and how strongly fertility and marriage age decisions were related. It is true, however, that persons who married at later ages had higher age-specific fertility rates in a given age interval than persons who married at earlier ages (not shown). Therefore, within a cohort, variations in marriage ages may not have necessarily reflected differences in the degree of deliberate fertility control by time of entry into the marital fertility schedule. However, it is possible that higher overall average marriage ages through time may have resulted from conscious decisions to increasingly limit family size.

The individual woman exited the marital fertility schedule either by death or by the death of her spouse. As mentioned previously, the average age of the mother at her last birth reflects both the deliberate decision to end childbearing and the mortality of the wife and husband. The evidence points toward increasing fertility regulation through time for all regions. However, the trend downward in the average age of the mother at her last birth prior to the time of the onset of fertility regulation reflects increasing mortality through that period. Therefore, part of the decline in average family size prior to the 1800–1812 cohort in the Northeast, the 1837–49 cohort in the Midwest, and the 1863–74 cohort in the West can be attributed to increasing mortality, which reduced exposure to the risk of childbearing. In particular, the combined effects of increasing fertility regulation and mortality which caused the average mother's age at last parity to fall by 5 years in New England from the 1750–99 cohort to the 1837–49 cohort, with an age-specific fertility rate of .2 for the interval, were responsible for reducing the average New England family by about one child.

How do the results from the genealogical samples compare with others' results? First of all, my comparison of alternative measures of fertility contributes to the knowledge of the importance of the timing of shifts in the marital fertility schedule relative to shifts in other proximate determinants in explaining declines in family sizes. In a similar fashion, one may contrast Yasuba's measure of fertility, the child/woman ratio, with my fertility measures. His finding of substantial regional variation in child/woman ratios caused him to speculate that fertility decline occurred prior to the nineteenth century in the earlier-settled regions of the United States (principally the Northeast). As we know, I found no significant decline in the total marital fertility rate in any region until at least the 1800–1812 birth cohort of women (whose childbearing years were from 1815 to 1857). The difference in the two fertility indices may be reconciled by examining the nature of their construction. For the first several decades of the nineteenth century, the average age of women of childbearing years in the earliest-settled states was higher than the average age in the later-settled states (not shown).[20] Although the total marital fertility rate is not affected by the proportion of women in each age interval, the child/woman ratio is highly sensitive to the age distribution of women. Hence, even if the marital fertility schedule were the same for all states, states with a large proportion of women in later age intervals (who have low age-specific fertility rates) would have a low child/woman ratio relative to states with a large proportion in early age intervals. This effect is exacerbated by the later marriages (and thus later childbearing) of women in the earlier-settled states. The child/woman ratio, but not the total marital fertility rate, is affected by the average age of entry into the marital fertility schedule.

The regional variations in fertility and nuptiality in my sample also allow us to evaluate Coale and Zelnik's (1963) results on United States fertility and nuptiality patterns. Applying stable population models to aggregate birthrates, they found that the period total fertility rate fell rapidly from the 1830s to the 1890s. They also reported that the average marriage age of women rose steadily throughout the latter half of the nineteenth century. Although data were not available to them for the first half of the century, they assumed that the average also had risen throughout the first half of the century. The results from the genealogical samples indicate that although the aggregate population experienced a secular fertility decline, shifts in the marital fertility schedules were timed differently across regions. Similarly, although the average age at marriage for women approximated the simple linear trend suggested by Coale and Zelnik, this aggregate trend masks substantial regional differences in nuptiality patterns through time.[21]

### 8.4.3   Fertility Differences between Native-born and Foreign-born Parents

The average number of children ever born was higher for the foreign-born parents than for the native-born.[22] There are at least two factors responsible for this difference. First, total marital fertility was higher for the foreign born. This was partly a result of closer birth spacing by immigrants (only the interval between marriage and first birth is reported in table 8.9). Higher infant mortality rates among the foreign born are associated with their closer spacing of births.[23] Shorter open intervals after the last birth for the foreign born (not shown) also contributed to their higher marital fertility. Thus, it seems that regulation was more prevalent among the native born, especially in the form of early cessation of childbirth. The second factor responsible for the larger numbers of children ever born to foreigners results from a selection bias. The average woman's age at marriage was similar for the two groups, as was average life expectancy for the native born and the immigrants whose marriages took place in the United States. However, the time at risk to bear children for foreign-born parents was longer on average. This was due chiefly to the fact that some emigration occurred after marriage. Since immigrants could not be observed in the genealogical samples until they arrived in America, those marrying before emigrating were not at risk of dying during the period of time between marriage and emigration. Therefore, foreign-born parents were

**Table 8.9    Average Fertility and Mortality Measures for Foreign- and Native-born Parents**

Birth Cohorts and Generation of Family

| | 1750–99 | | 1800–1812 | | 1813–24 | | 1825–36 | | 1837–49 | | 1850–62 | | 1863–74 | | 1875–99 | |
|---|---|---|---|---|---|---|---|---|---|---|---|---|---|---|---|---|
| | 1 | >1 | 1 | >1 | 1 | >1 | 1 | >1 | 1 | >1 | 1 | >1 | 1 | >1 | 1 | >1 |
| Mother's death age | 69.6 | 66.3 | 68.8 | 61.9 | 69.9 | 60.4 | 66.5 | 68.5 | 70.8 | 67.8 | 70.0 | 68.2 | 69.3 | 66.2 | 62.9 | 62.5 |
| Father's death age | 71.7 | 79.6 | 71.3 | 75.8 | 72.6 | 67.2 | 70.0 | 70.5 | 73.5 | 66.9 | 71.2 | 71.7 | 72.7 | 63.0 | 66.7 | 66.5 |
| Mother's marriage age | 23.1 | 21.5 | 22.6 | 22.2 | 22.4 | 21.6 | 22.4 | 22.1 | 22.4 | 22.6 | 21.2 | 22.6 | 22.2 | 22.6 | 22.3 | 22.6 |
| Number of children ever born | 6.3 | 6.5 | 7.2 | 5.4 | 7.2 | 4.1 | 6.7 | 5.3 | 7.3 | 5.4 | 7.0 | 4.4 | 5.3 | 3.3 | 4.8 | 3.8 |
| Interval between marriage and first birth in months | 11.3 | 17.2 | 17.1 | 16.8 | 15.6 | 18.8 | 13.7 | 17.0 | 14.5 | 14.6 | 13.2 | 19.0 | 15.0 | 22.2 | 17.3 | 21.0 |
| Total marital fertility for women aged 20–44 | 9.6 | 8.8 | 9.1 | 7.6 | 9.4 | 9.5 | 9.4 | 8.3 | 9.6 | 8.1 | 8.5 | 8.1 | 6.7 | 6.2 | 7.2 | 5.5 |
| Number of families | 44 | 147 | 91 | 107 | 56 | 51 | 103 | 57 | 124 | 59 | 153 | 125 | 74 | 73 | 71 | 83 |

*Source:* Sample A (see text).

*Note:* Fertility and mortality means listed separately for families with parents who were immigrants to the United States and for families with parents who were born in the United States.

at risk to die, on average, for a shorter period of time than were native-born parents. As a result, the selection process, rather than nuptiality or parental mortality differences, yielded longer average childbearing spans for foreign-born parents.

What might explain the differential marital fertility among the foreign born and the native born? First of all, immigrants tended to be poorer on average than the native-born population. Therefore, as suggested by Becker and Tomes's finding of regression to the mean in wealth (1984), the expectation that children would be better off than their parents was more reasonable for the average immigrant parent than for the average native-born parent. Assuming that parents cared about the welfare of their children, this encouraged higher fertility among immigrants. Second, at least in urban areas, children of immigrants probably began to earn income at an earlier age than children of native-born parents. Therefore, the net cost of children was lower to immigrants and so encouraged higher fertility among them.

The increase through time in the percentage of native-born parents, with their associated lower fertility, contributed to the overall fertility decline.

### 8.4.4  Fertility Differences among Occupational Groups

Occupational differences partly reflected earnings differentials across families. Therefore, if families were grouped only by the occupation of the head of household, it is likely that fertility differences were more related to wealth differences rather than to occupational differences. Table 8.10 shows that, across all occupations, the percentage of large families fell in later census years.

Families whose heads of household were professionals, proprietors, and craftsmen tended to have a higher percentage of zero- to two-child families than did families whose heads of household were unskilled workers. The fraction of all families who were part of the former group was also larger in later census years. Thus, fertility fell for two reasons: all occupational groups had fewer children, and the weights within the sample shifted so that occupations with low fertility had persistently higher weights.

### 8.4.5  Fertility Differences between Farm and Nonfarm Families

Both farm and nonfarm residents had smaller families in later census years, as shown in table 8.11. The decline in fertility of farm families resulted primarily from a decrease in the percentage of families who had six or more children and an increase in the percentage of families who had three to five children. In nonfarm families, the average level of fertility was lower in each census year and declined by a greater percentage than the average level of fertility of farm families. The

| Table 8.10 | Distribution of Family Size, by Occupation of Household Head | | | |
|---|---|---|---|---|
| | Professional | Proprietor | Craftsman | Laborer |
| *1850 Census* | | | | |
| Number of children | | | | |
| 0 | 13% | 13% | 10% | 5% |
| 1–2 | 16 | 13 | 28 | 18 |
| 3–5 | 37 | 31 | 23 | 28 |
| 6 or more | 34 | 43 | 39 | 49 |
| Total | 100% | 100% | 100% | 100% |
| Number of households | 24 | 16 | 40 | 248 |
| Mean number of children | 4.4 | 4.9 | 4.5 | 6.7 |
| *1860 Census* | | | | |
| Number of children | | | | |
| 0 | 16% | 5% | 0% | 7% |
| 1–2 | 26 | 45 | 27 | 18 |
| 3–5 | 27 | 18 | 40 | 37 |
| 6 or more | 31 | 32 | 33 | 38 |
| Total | 100% | 100% | 100% | 100% |
| Number of households | 19 | 22 | 30 | 180 |
| Mean number of children | 3.9 | 4.5 | 4.6 | 5.9 |
| *1870 Census* | | | | |
| Number of children | | | | |
| 0 | 17% | 0% | 4% | 6% |
| 1–2 | 31 | 21 | 43 | 17 |
| 3–5 | 17 | 42 | 29 | 42 |
| 6 or more | 35 | 37 | 24 | 35 |
| Total | 100% | 100% | 100% | 100% |
| Number of households | 23 | 28 | 28 | 174 |
| Mean number of children | 3.9 | 5.0 | 3.7 | 5.9 |
| *1880 Census* | | | | |
| Number of children | | | | |
| 0 | 8% | 5% | 7% | 6% |
| 1–2 | 31 | 32 | 34 | 15 |
| 3–5 | 37 | 25 | 34 | 52 |
| 6 or more | 24 | 38 | 25 | 27 |
| Total | 100% | 100% | 100% | 100% |
| Number of households | 38 | 43 | 29 | 151 |
| Mean number of children | 3.9 | 4.5 | 3.9 | 5.6 |

*Source:* Sample C (see text).

*Note:* Family sizes distributed separately for each occupational classification for the head of household.

**Table 8.11    Distribution of Family Size for Farm and Nonfarm Families**

| Number of children | 1850 Census Farm | 1850 Census Nonfarm | 1860 Census Farm | 1860 Census Nonfarm | 1870 Census Farm | 1870 Census Nonfarm | 1880 Census Farm | 1880 Census Nonfarm |
|---|---|---|---|---|---|---|---|---|
| 0 | 6% | 6% | 7% | 4% | 6% | 5% | 6% | 7% |
| 1 | 7 | 9 | 6 | 12 | 7 | 14 | 6 | 15 |
| 2 | 7 | 14 | 10 | 20 | 9 | 17 | 7 | 17 |
| 3–5 | 26 | 31 | 32 | 30 | 38 | 31 | 45 | 39 |
| 6 or more | 54 | 40 | 45 | 34 | 40 | 33 | 36 | 22 |
| Total | 100% | 100% | 100% | 100% | 100% | 100% | 100% | 100% |
| Number of households | 294 | 140 | 237 | 102 | 222 | 103 | 180 | 163 |
| Mean number of children | 5.6 | 5.2 | 5.2 | 3.9 | 4.9 | 3.6 | 4.6 | 3.1 |

*Source*: Sample C (see text).

*Note*: Family sizes distributed separately for farm and nonfarm families.

difference in levels can be plausibly ascribed to lower effective prices of children on the farm, the difference in percentage declines to differences in rates of change in effective prices of children. The shift in weights toward nonfarm families was a force contributing to the secular fertility decline.

### 8.4.6   Fertility Differences among Wealth Classes

Previous studies have found conflicting empirical evidence on the relationship of household wealth to household fertility. In general, fertility and wealth are reported to have been positively related in pre-nineteenth-century populations and in nineteenth-century rural populations.[24] However, there is evidence of a negative relation of household wealth to fertility in more urbanized populations, at least in some ranges of wealth.[25] An economic approach suggests that the effective price of children was rising with wealth in the ranges where a negative relation appeared.

The total number of children ever born to a couple is related both to lifetime wealth of the family (which equals total lifetime earnings of the family plus net bequests) and to the timing of receipts of income. Most of the previous work done in this area has had to rely on household income as a proxy for household wealth, because large household-level data sets with wealth information simply have not been available. For a number of reasons, reported wealth measures (such as the ones in this data set), especially for two generations of a family, are more valuable than reported income measures in assessing the wealth/fertility relationship. These reasons include: (1) measured income is highly sensitive to transitory components; (2) measured wealth smoothes out at least some of the transitory components and so more accurately reflects lifetime wealth; (3) reported wealth of grandparents can be used to construct measures of expected bequests; (4) reported wealth for persons not earning income is a more accurate measure of resources available to spend than income is; and (5) some timing of receipts of income can be observed for families which were found in more than one census.

The relationship of 1860 household wealth (standardized to age 45 of the household head) to household fertility for all families together, for nonfarm families, and for farm families is graphed in table 8.12. For all families together, the relationship of wealth to fertility was negative in the low ranges of wealth ($0-$3,000), positive in the middle to upper ranges of wealth ($3,000-$10,000), and negative in the highest ranges of wealth.[26] The relationship held for both nonfarm and farm families, although the ranges in which fertility and wealth were negatively associated were different for the two groups.

Intuitively, the observed wealth effect is a combination of a true wealth effect and a price effect. The number of children should have

**Table 8.12**    **Relationship of Family Wealth to Family Size**

Number of children

```
8

7    (3) farm families        $
                        $              $
                   $                 $
6    $                                    $
          $                        #   *   #
                                   *       #*
5
     (1) all families            *              #*
     *                    *       #
4         *
                    *          #
3                 *
               *
     #                    #
2         #            #
              #
                 #
1
     (2) nonfarm families
0

     0  1  2  3  4  5  6  7  8  9  10  11  12  13
        Family wealth (thousands), Adjusted for life cycle effects
```

*Source:* Sample C (see text).

*Note:* Relationship of family wealth (standardized to age 45 for the head of the household) to the average number of children. The separate lines are for:
(1) All families together *******.
(2) Nonfarm families #######.
(3) Farm families $$$$$$$.

been positively related to true wealth if children were a normal good; this effect dominated in the wealth range where fertility and wealth were positively related. The number of children should have been negatively related to their effective price. It seems likely that the effective price of children was rising in the ranges where fertility and wealth were negatively related, and that the price effect dominated the true wealth effect in those ranges. A detailed theoretical model which explains the observed relation between fertility and wealth is currently being developed (Bourne 1985).

From 1860 to 1870, mean household wealth in 1860 dollars (corrected for differences in age structure) increased from $5,700 to $6,400.[27] Most of the rise stemmed from shifts in the percentage of families holding $100–$1000 to families holding $1000–$3000 in wealth and in the percentage of families holding $10,000–$11,000 to families holding more than $11,000 in wealth. The cross-sectional relation of fertility to wealth was similar in 1860 and 1870; therefore, some of the secular decline in fertility may be ascribed to a shift in wealth classes toward classes which had lower fertility.

### 8.4.7   Fertility Differences among Lineal Families

There is some evidence that fertility across two generations of the same family is significantly correlated.[28] For the genealogical samples, family size was positively correlated for all families grouped together, as well as for families in which both the mother and the grandmother were at risk to bear children until the end of their fecund years (see table 8.13).

Variations in nuptiality and the degree of fertility regulation across lineal families are key in explaining the correlation. Averages of mother's age at marriage, at first birth, and at last birth (see table 8.14) differ significantly at the 95% level; spacing of low-parity births was not significantly different across families. As an example of differences across lineal families, families descended from John Edminster of Scotland (history 4) had fewer children than families descended from Robert Winchell of England (history 5) because marital fertility was relatively low, age at marriage relatively high, and age at last birth relatively low compared to the same measures for the Winchell descendants.

Although it is helpful to break down the differences in family sizes across lineal families by examining proximate determinants, it is likely that the differences both in proximate determinants and in fertility outcomes arose chiefly because of familial variations in underlying socioeconomic variables. A detailed analysis (Bourne 1985) suggests that wealth differences and residence (nonfarm or farm) explained nearly all of the variation in family sizes across lineal families.

**Table 8.13**   **Correlation of Family Size Across Two Generations**

|  | Correlation | Number of Families | Significance |
|---|---|---|---|
| | | *Sample A* | |
| Total children | .184 | 2658 | 99% |
| Total children, mother and grandmother at risk to age 45 | .139 | 460 | 95% |
| | | *Sample B* | |
| Total children | .192 | 2694 | 99% |
| Total children, mother and grandmother at risk to age 45 | .144 | 503 | 95% |

*Source:* Samples A and B (see text).

*Note:* Sizes of families correlated across two generations. These correlations are uncorrected for wealth and the birth cohort of the mother.

**Table 8.14    Average Fertility Measures, Grouped by Family History**

| | Number of Family History | | | | | | | | |
|---|---|---|---|---|---|---|---|---|---|
| | 1 | 2 | 3 | 4 | 5 | 6 | 7 | 8 | 9 |
| Number of children ever born | 5.1 | 5.2 | 3.3 | 3.9 | 5.9 | 5.8 | 4.8 | 5.0 | 4.3 |
| Mother's marriage age | 22.8 | 23.6 | 27.3 | 22.8 | 22.1 | 23.4 | 22.3 | 24.2 | 22.0 |
| Mother's age at her first birth | 24.6 | 24.2 | 37.3 | 24.9 | 23.3 | 25.0 | 24.0 | 25.6 | 24.0 |
| Mother's age at her last birth | 35.3 | 36.0 | 38.8 | 32.5 | 35.8 | 37.0 | 33.0 | 35.9 | 32.8 |
| Total marital fertility for women aged 20–44 | 7.9 | 5.7 | 10.8 | 5.9 | 7.3 | 9.7 | 3.8 | 8.2 | 5.9 |
| Number of families | 74 | 54 | 3 | 148 | 96 | 95 | 14 | 483 | 81 |

*Source*: Sample B (see text).

*Note*: Separate calculations of fertility variables for each of the nine family histories in sample B. The averages are calculated for the set of women on whom all variables are nonmissing. The differences in the averages (excluding histories 3 and 7) are significant at the 95% level.

## 8.5    Conclusion

The preliminary analysis of the new genealogical data answers questions regarding when the historical fertility decline began in the United States, what methods of fertility control were most prevalent through time, and what socioeconomic characteristics of the household were especially important in influencing fertility.

The number of children ever born to the average woman in the sample declined throughout the nineteenth century. Up until the 1850–62 birth cohort of women the principal factors responsible for the decline were decreases in the proportion of women ever marrying and in the life expectancy of women of childbearing years. Thereafter, the decline was chiefly due to the restriction of childbearing within marriage, primarily through early cessation of childbearing rather than by increases in the intervals between births.

The sample exhibits no important regional differences in the marital fertility schedule prior to the nineteenth century. During the nineteenth century, the number of children ever born to the average married woman fell more rapidly in New England and the Middle Atlantic than in other regions, principally because of earlier regulation of fertility within marriage and declining life expectation for women of childbearing years. Intramarital fertility regulation was perceptible as early as the 1800–1812 birth cohort of women in families who lived in the New England and Mid-Atlantic regions. However, regulation within marriage was not strongly apparent among families who lived in the Midwest until the 1850–62 cohort. Furthermore, families who lived in the West did not control fertility within marriage to a large degree until the 1875–99 cohort. The average age at marriage for women differed both in the level and in the rate of change over time for the various regions of the country.

Up to the 1800–1812 birth cohort, the number of children ever born per woman was about the same for foreign-born and native-born women. But after the 1800–1812 birth cohort, the average for the native born lay below that of the foreign born. There was somewhat earlier fertility regulation among the native born. However, a primary determinant of the larger family size among immigrants was their longer average time at risk to bear children. This result is related to the sample selection process rather than to mortality or nuptiality differences: immigrants were not observed in the genealogical sample until the time of their arrival in the United States. Hence, the period of time between marriage and emigration was not one in which immigrants could have died, although native-born husbands and wives, who differed only in that they did not emigrate, could and did die during a comparable time period.

Families whose heads of households were not laborers (i.e., professionals, proprietors, and craftsmen) had fewer children than other families, but families of all occupational groups experienced lower fertility as time passed. Farm families were larger than nonfarm families. The relationship of household wealth to fertility was quite interesting: fertility and wealth were negatively related in the lowest and highest ranges of wealth and positively related in the middle range. The weights of the sample also shifted over time, with the nonlaborer occupational groups, nonfarm families, and wealth classes which experienced lower fertility receiving ever larger weights as time passed. Some fertility differences were also exhibited among the genealogies, although elsewhere I deduce that these differences were explained principally by wealth and residential differences.

The size and detail of the new intergenerationally linked household data set have been exploited to substantiate the speculation that household fertility differed sharply both in level and in trend over time across socioeconomic subgroups in nineteenth-century America. The next step will be a thorough theoretical and empirical examination of the relative strengths of the socioeconomic variables which have been shown to underlie the historical decline in household fertility in the United States.

# Appendix

## Construction of Sample A

Within a family history, the first male immigrant to the United States with recorded country of departure and state of destination was located. All information on him, his spouse, and his children and grandchildren was recorded. This information includes the day, month, year, and place of birth, marriage, and death for each individual. In some cases, an additional set of three later generations of the family was selected randomly from the same history. Therefore, from any one history, the data (from the first three generations) are structured as follows:

first male immigrant and spouse

child 1 and spouse ........ child $n(1)$ and spouse

| child 1 and spouse | ..... child $n(2)$ and spouse | child 1 and spouse | .... child $n(3)$ and spouse |

The entire sample may be diagrammed over time and space as a set of these triangles, with each triangle representing data from a different history.

REGIONS

COHORTS

1650          △

                                    △

1750

                        △

1800                              △

        △

1850

As mentioned in the text, there are 15,748 individuals from 4,467 nuclear families in about 1400 published family histories in sample A. One-third of the families fell into the mother's birth cohort of 1650–1799, one-third in the 1800–1849 cohort, and one-third in the 1850–99 cohort. Regionally, 40% of the families lived in New England or the Mid-Atlantic, 17% each in the Midwest or West, and 9% in the South.

Analytical work was done only for once- and never-married individuals, although the working file contains individuals with multiple marriages. Fecund women who did not remarry after the death of a spouse (and thus had no more children after the spouse's death) are included in calculations of the child/woman ratios and period total fertility rates of table 8.2, but fecund women who remarried (and possibly had more children after the death of their first spouse) are not. On the other hand, both are included in others' calculations of these measures from overall census data. Therefore, my measures tend to be lower than reported measures compiled from the censuses.

### Construction of Sample B

Currently, all information from nine published family histories is contained in the working file. A total of 16,820 individuals from 5,632 nuclear families are represented. As in sample A, the first immigrant to the United States with recorded departure and destination places was located in the history. Date and place information on him, his spouse, and all his descendants was recorded. Therefore, for each of the nine histories, the data are structured as follows:

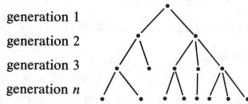

generation 1

generation 2

generation 3

generation n

The diagram makes it clear that nuclear families from a given history were concentrated heavily in the cohorts born near the end of the recorded history. All nine histories were published in the nineteenth or twentieth century; all of the first male immigrants were born in the seventeenth century. Therefore, most of the observations were clustered in the 1800–1849 birth cohort (50%), while the rest were divided evenly between the 1650–1799 and 1850–99 cohorts. Unlike sample A, which consists of over 40% immigrants, sample B has but nine immigrant families. For comparative purposes, the Statistical History of the United States reports 12% of the population as foreign born in 1850, 16% in 1860, 17% in 1870, 16% in 1880, 18% in 1890, and 16% in 1900. Sample B is also less representative regionally than sample A.

Construction of Sample C

Individuals from sample B were matched by hand to the same individuals in the 1850, 1860, 1870, and 1880 federal manuscript census schedules. Families were reconstructed from the matched data and then linked through generations. As a result, an observation in sample C contains both genealogical and census information on individuals and their spouses, children, and parents. Some information on siblings is also present. As in sample B, sample C consists chiefly of native-born bloodline individuals, although spouses may have been foreign born.

# Notes

1. In the 1800–1820 censuses, the relevant age groups (by sex) for fertility analyses were ages 0–9, 10–15, 16–25, and 26–44. In 1830 and 1840 the relevant groups were changed to ages 0–4, 5–9, 10–14, 15–19, 20–29, 30–39, and 40–49. In 1850 and 1860 an age-class of under one year was added, and in 1870, single year ages were tabulated for those under age 5 and quinquennial age groupings were tabulated for those aged 5–79.

2. A child/woman ratio is the ratio of the number of children in a certain age group to every thousand women in a certain age group. The age groups used for the children are usually either 0–9 years or 0–4 years; the age groups used for the women are 15–44, 20–44, 15–49, or 20–49. Clearly, the structure of the available data determines which age groups are used. See, e.g., Yasuba (1962), Forster and Tucker (1972), Potter (1965), Haines (1977), and Easterlin (1968).

3. Birth years were recorded for 91% of the individuals in the sample and death years for 72% of the individuals.

4. The data were quite consistent internally. Ages reported from the census differed from ages reported from the genealogies for only 3% of the observations. Birthplaces, if recorded in both sources, differed in only 5% of the observations.

5. Family histories are compiled by individuals or family organizations and attempt to list all the descendants of a patriarch, with dates and places of their births, deaths, and marriages.

6. Sample A was collected first, with an eye toward geographical representativeness of the sample. As collection proceeded, we realized that it would be less costly to collect all information from each family history as raw data, then to select and reweight the various family characteristics by computer rather than by hand. Therefore, sample B

consists of data on all individuals represented in a family history. The linkage to census data of genealogical data from a few family histories was also much less costly than the linkage of data from numerous histories. Since the former group was composed of many more people with the same surname than the latter group, the search for names in the manuscripts was cheaper for the former group.

7. For example, see Yasuba (1962), Coale and Zelnik (1963), T. W. Schultz (1974), Simon (1974), Becker (1981), T. P. Schultz (1981), and Haines (1984).

8. The average value of real estate holdings of adult males in 1850 was $3,034 in sample C; Soltow (1975) reported the average as $1,103 for his sample of the 1850 census.

9. Families who reported no wealth made up 62% of all families in 1860 and 60% in 1870. Soltow (1975) reported figures of 62% for both census years from his sample.

10. An age-specific fertility rate equals the number of children born to women in a specific age interval (usually a 5-year interval) divided by the number of woman-years lived during the interval. The total fertility rate is the sum of the age-specific rates multiplied by the interval length. An age-specific marital fertility rate is calculated similarly to an age-specific fertility rate, except the denominator equals the number of woman-years in the interval during which women are married and both spouses are living. The total marital fertility rate is the sum of the age-specific marital rates multiplied by the interval length.

A period rate sums the age-specific rates of women alive during the period, whereas a cohort rate sums the age-specific rates of a birth cohort of women.

11. The period total fertility rate reported in table 8.2 equals the sum, over all age intervals, of the total number of children born to women in a given age interval during the period divided by the total number of women within the interval, multiplied by the interval length. The denominator includes both once- and never-married women. Therefore, a change over time in the percentage of lifelong spinsters would affect this index of fertility without affecting the marital fertility schedule.

12. The increase in the child/woman ratio for sample A from 1800 to 1880 is puzzling, for child/woman ratios obtained from censuses of the total population show a continuous decline during the period. However, the recording of vital events, particularly deaths, was more complete in later years in my samples. Since it is necessary to have birth and death dates for both women and children in order to compile a child/woman ratio from my samples, it is possible that secular variations (by actual age at death) in the recording of death dates caused the apparent rise in the child/woman ratio. A greater proportion of young women, who have higher fertility than older women, contributes to increases in the child/woman ratio. If age structure and underlying fertility patterns were not changing through time, but a higher percentage of younger women could be included in the ratio because of increasing accuracy in recording of death dates of women who died young, the observed child/woman ratio would increase. Changes in the age structure and in fertility patterns could, of course, mitigate or exacerbate this effect.

13. In the Mineau et al. study (1979) of a Mormon natural fertility population (a population exhibits "natural fertility" if there is no apparent tendency of couples to prevent additional births after a certain number of births have occurred), the average age at last birth for women who were at risk to age 45 was 40.5. In Smith's study (1977) of an eighteenth-century French natural fertility population, the average age was 40.1.

14. Again, I have not found a completely satisfactory explanation for the secular increase in the child/woman ratio in sample A. See n. 12.

15. Coale and Trussell (1978) have derived a standard natural fertility schedule of age-specific marital fertility rates from a set of empirically observed populations and have devised two statistics: $M$, which measures the overall level of fertility in the observed marital fertility schedule as compared to the standard natural fertility schedule, and $m$, which measures deviations from the standard schedule. They hypothesized that the pattern of deviations departs from the natural fertility schedule in a typical way if fertility control was present in the population being studied. The value of $m$ is independent of the level of fertility and depends solely on the age structure. It is calculated such that if the observed fertility schedule deviates from the natural fertility schedule in a typical fashion, the value of $m$ at all ages greater than 24 is identical. The value of $m$ should be

zero if no fertility control was present. The value of $m$ was approximately one for populations observed in Western countries in the early 1960s.

16. The observed conditional probability of having a $(k + 1)$th birth is also called the $k$th parity progression ratio. See, e.g., Curtin et al. (1979).

17. Easterlin (1976) hypothesized that parents want to provide their children with as good a start in life as they themselves had. Therefore, the number of children parents can afford depends upon the prospective return to parents' capital within the parents' lifetime. Suppose the parents were part of an agricultural society based on family units, with a multigeniture system of inheritance and favorable mortality conditions. In such a society, the expected rise in land prices would give a fair indication of the expected growth in parents' capital. Within the context of nineteenth-century America, land prices were increasing by much higher percentages in the later-settled regions than in the earlier-settled regions. Therefore, parents living in the later-settled regions would have been able to provide more children with as good a start in life as they had than parents living in earlier-settled regions.

18. Michael Haines has pointed out to me that the manner in which wealth is received should have a bearing on the "price effect." That is, a windfall, perhaps in the form of a bequest, would probably have little or no "price effect" on fertility. However, increases in wealth which result from increases in wage earnings would be more likely to be associated with both a "wealth effect" and a "price effect." See sec. 8.4.6 for a more complete discussion.

19. The table does not report these averages. For instance, the average interval between marriage and first birth cannot be calculated directly from the table because the average age at marriage was calculated over all married women, including those with no children. The mother's age at her first birth, obviously, could be calculated only for those who reported at least one birth.

20. The period 1800–1860 was one of remarkable East-West migration, and the migrants were heavily concentrated among people aged 18–30 (see Villaflor and Sokoloff 1982).

21. Although the simple average of marriage ages of women from the genealogies fluctuated through the century, the weighted average, with appropriate regional weights assigned from census population estimates, had a general upward trend (not shown).

22. Tolney et al. (1982) also reported larger families among immigrants to the United States. Correspondence from Michael Haines indicates that a similar result is suggested by the 1900 census recall data.

23. Breastfeeding prolongs the period of reduced fecundity following a birth. If an infant were to die, the mother would return to a normal level of fecundity earlier than if the infant were still breastfeeding. Therefore, the mother would be at risk to have another child earlier than a mother whose child did not die. Although infant mortality was higher in sample A for children born to foreign-born parents (which led to closer birth spacing), the average number of surviving children, as well as total children ever born, was higher for foreign-born parents than for native-born parents.

24. Examples of populations in which a positive relation of fertility and wealth was found include fifteenth-century Tuscany (Klapisch 1972; Herlihy 1977), fifteenth- and eighteenth-century Italy (Livi-Bacci 1977), rural Canada in 1861 (McInnis 1977), rural United States in 1865 (Bash 1955), and rural nineteenth-century Germany (Knodel 1979).

25. Knodel (1974) found a negative relation of fertility to wealth for families living in German cities in the early 1900s. Becker and Lewis (1974) found a negative relation for twentieth-century United States families for the lowest ranges of wealth. There is also some evidence that members of the patrician class in ancient Rome had small families relative to lower-wealth families.

26. Michael Haines reports a similarly shaped curve for a nineteenth-century Philadelphia sample.

27. Reported wealth in 1870 was deflated by the Warren-Pearson wholesale price index for all commodities (see the Statistical History of the United States 1965).

28. For example, see Johnson and Stokes (1976), Ben-Porath (1975), and Becker (1981).

## Comment    Michael R. Haines

This paper makes use of a new data set to study the decline in fertility in colonial America and the United States between roughly 1750 and 1900. The data consist of longitudinal information on individuals and families collected from family histories kept at the Genealogical Society's libraries in Utah. The work is fundamentally descriptive and demographic, although an economic perspective on the costs and benefits of children (e.g., Becker 1981) is provided. The basic analysis presents calculation of fertility, nuptiality, and mortality measures, usually on a cohort basis but sometimes in period form, for women born between about 1650 and 1900. (This implies, of course, that the cohort rates in, for example, table 8.3 extend to periods beyond 1900. Period rates are given in table 8.2 up to 1889.)

Two principal data sets are used. Both contain the demographic information from a number of published family histories. They provide data on dates and places of births, deaths, and marriages and on family relationships for parents, children, spouses, and other relatives. These data permit the calculation of derivative demographic information (e.g., age and marital status by date) and also standard measures of fertility and mortality. Sample A contains 15,748 individuals from 4,467 nuclear families, and sample B consists of 16,820 individuals in 5,632 nuclear families. Sample C is a subset of sample B to which economic data (including occupation and wealth) have been linked from the manuscripts of the United States censuses of 1850–80. The reason for the existence of two separate samples seems related to sampling strategy, if my interpretation of note 6 is correct. Sample A was apparently an attempt to gain spatial and temporal representativeness by sampling the original male immigrants from selected family histories and then, in some cases, following the family for three generations. (Wahl does not explain why the three generations were sampled in some cases and not in others.) Sample B apparently abandoned this goal and followed all the descendants of a male immigrant in nine family histories. The reason was apparently easier logistics.

In any event, Wahl acknowledges that these samples are not representative of the United States population over this period, nor are they geographically representative. (For example, New England appears overrepresented relative to the South.) It is important thus to emphasize that the results in this paper, while extraordinarily valuable for the insights they provide, must be used and interpreted with care.

Michael R. Haines is professor of economics at Wayne State University.

These comments were originally written for the NBER Conference on Income and Wealth, "Long-Term Factors in American Economic Growth." The present version has been rewritten to reflect a substantial revision of the original paper.

The samples contain white, largely literate, and mostly native-born individuals. They are geographically concentrated in the Middle Atlantic and (earlier at least) New England regions. This was owing to settlement patterns to some extent, but the South is, by any standard, underrepresented. For 1850–80, it seems that laborers (a category which unfortunately lumps farm laborers and other laborers together) had a large representation relative to craftsmen and proprietors (especially farmers). Finally, even with such large initial samples, some fairly small cell sizes appear when subdivision is made over time and across regions, occupations, and so forth. Thus the samples do not replicate the whole population nor do they probably provide, in a few cases, very accurate estimates.

One way to pursue this further is to compare results from Wahl's samples with standard demographic measures from other sources. In table C8.1 I compare the child/woman ratios (children 0–4 per 1,000 women aged 15–44) from unadjusted published census data for the white population with those reported in table 8.2 of the paper. I also compare period total fertility rates for the white population given in Coale and Zelnik (1963, p. 36) with those given in Wahl's table 8.2.

The results for the child/woman ratios are, frankly, rather discouraging. While the national pattern from census data exhibited fairly steady declines over time from relatively high levels, sample A showed a monotonic *increase* from low to high levels. Early in the nineteenth century, sample B experienced a high level not out of line with the national child/woman ratios. On the other hand, the rate of decline in sample B was much more rapid than for the country as a whole. Wahl recognizes this problem and advances the explanation that it occurred because only once- and never-married women were included. Fecund women who remarried after the death of the first spouse were excluded, at least for sample A (app. 8.A.1). It is not explained whether the same exclusions characterized sample B; and, if so, why the child/woman ratios in sample B showed a decline whereas those in sample A did not. Also, why would the exclusion of remarried women have caused a rise in the ratios in sample A? It must be assumed that remarried women had systematically higher fertility and either that their incidence decreased over time (despite a suggestion that mortality was increasing prior to the Civil War) or that the fertility differential diminished. In note 12, Wahl suggests that possibly improved recording of death dates led to more younger women being included in the sample. This is possible, but the effect would have had to have been quite large. It could bias other analysis. And it could be examined directly by just looking at the age-sex distribution over time. The *very* low levels of child/woman ratios in sample B toward the end of the nineteenth century are troubling as pertains to representativeness.

Table C8.1    Fertility Measures: A Comparison of the Wahl Genealogical
              Samples with Measures for the White Population of the United
              States, 1800–1890

| | Child/Woman Ratios[a] | | | Total Fertility Rates[b] | | |
|---|---|---|---|---|---|---|
| | Wahl | | United | Wahl | | United |
| Period | Sample A | Sample B | States | Sample A | Sample B | States |
| 1800 | | | 943 | | | 7.04 |
| 1800–1809 | 561 | 908 | | 7.0 | 5.0 | |
| 1810 | | | 944 | | | 6.92 |
| 1810–19 | 570 | 717 | | 7.1 | 4.8 | |
| 1820 | | | 897 | | | 6.73 |
| 1820–29 | 625 | 627 | | 6.9 | 4.4 | |
| 1830 | | | 828 | | | 6.55 |
| 1830–39 | 631 | 527 | | 6.6 | 4.2 | |
| 1840 | | | 876 | | | 6.14 |
| 1840–49 | 641 | 415 | | 6.1 | 3.8 | |
| 1850 | | | 654 | | | 5.42 |
| 1850–59 | 664 | 296 | | 5.3 | 3.5 | |
| 1860 | | | 668 | | | 5.21 |
| 1860–69 | 746 | 215 | | 4.8 | 3.4 | 4.61 |
| 1870 | | | 610 | | | 4.55 |
| 1870–79 | 850 | 289 | | 4.8 | 3.3 | 4.47 |
| 1880 | | | 586 | | | 4.24 |
| 1880–89 | 886 | 313 | | 3.7 | 3.5 | 4.18 |
| 1890 | | | 579 | | | 3.87 |
| 1900 | | | 508 | | | 3.56 |

*Source:* Wahl, table 8.2; United States Bureau of the Census (1975), ser. A, pp. 119–34;
Coale and Zelnik (1963), table 2.
[a]Children 0–4 per 1,000 women aged 15–44.
[b]The sum of age-specific overall fertility rates for women 15–44.

The period total fertility rates are much more encouraging, since
both samples exhibited declines over the nineteenth century. Peculiarly,
however, sample A had higher total fertility rates in the early nineteenth
century than did sample B, exactly the reverse of the situation with
the child/woman ratios. It is noted that sample A had more families
from higher fertility regions and from among the foreign born (who also
had higher fertility). This makes the differentials in total fertility rates
in table 8.2 more plausible, but it tends to make results from samples
B and C less convincing. Perhaps it is best at this point to consider
sample A as more representative, to regard samples B and C as special
subgroups (i.e., white, literate, largely living in the Northeast), and to
disregard the child/woman ratios as possibly an aberration of tabulation
procedures. They are, however, disturbing and remain a nagging reminder that the results in this paper may not be as informative as could
be hoped.

At this point, it should also be pointed out that only husband-wife nuclear families are used for fertility analysis, which is appropriate for analysis of marital fertility. It is not clear, however, whether this had any effect on the tabulations related to the child/woman ratios. Also, were families with greater complexity excluded from analysis? Would this impart biases? Further, at the end of the paper there is a discussion of fertility differences among extended families. It appears that the extension considered is only upward or downward and that nuclear families alone were related. It is also not clear if extension is applied to coresident kin (the usual definition). If so, this is a place where household fertility (used in the title) and family fertility differ.

Among the major findings: "The number of children ever born to the average woman in the sample declined throughout the nineteenth century," which is quite consistent with the previous work (Thompson and Whelpton 1933; Yasuba 1962; Coale and Zelnik 1963; Forster and Tucker 1972). The more interesting result is the fact that early in the century, fertility declines were caused by changes in nuptiality (increases in proportions of females who never married) and increases in adult female mortality. The divergences between cohort children ever born and cohort total marital fertility rates (for women aged 20–44) that are observed in table 8.7 (with the total marital fertility rates always being higher) are traceable to nuptiality and mortality differences. Cohort total marital fertility rates did not decline for sample A until the birth cohort of 1850–62, although decline in total marital fertility rates may have set in for sample B as early as the birth cohort of 1813–24. The declines were not large until the birth cohort of 1850–62 for sample B. The declines in total marital fertility rates for both samples in the seventeenth and eighteenth centuries must, I believe, be taken with some caution. These were likely natural fertility populations, and, historically, natural fertility populations have exhibited fluctuations in marital fertility (Smith 1977).

One question remains, however: If those *were* natural fertility populations, why were the total marital fertility rates *consistently* lower in sample B than in sample A (table 8.3)? As table 8.4 indicates, although the average age of woman at first marriage was somewhat higher in sample B than in sample A in the nineteenth century, the mean age at first birth was greater by a larger amount (in B relative to A). This implies a longer delay, and perhaps spacing behavior, in sample B. This result is confirmed by the low values of $M$ (table 8.5) for sample B relative to sample A in the Coale-Trussell (1974, 1978) model fitted to these data. The conclusion must be that some spacing was taking place early or that there were biological and/or non-fertility-related behavioral differences between the samples. Age-specific marital fertility rates at ages 20–24 and 25–29 were also lower in sample B than in sample A for the birth cohorts of 1750–99 and later, also indicating some differences between the samples in behavior at this early age not usually characterized by controlling behavior.

In terms of fertility control within marriage, it becomes evident in the Coale-Trussell $m$ index in table 8.5 for sample B only for the birth cohort of 1850–74 and in sample A only for the birth cohort of 1875–99. On the other hand, stopping behavior at older ages is evident in table 8.4, controlling for mortality (i.e., "average mother's age at last birth for women at risk to age 45"), for both samples early in the nineteenth century (on a period basis). The decline in age at last birth was, however, more pronounced in sample B. This is also seen in the lower levels and more rapid declines in age-specific marital fertility rates at ages 30–44 in sample B over the nineteenth century, as well as in the higher $m$ values in table 8.5.

The peculiar nature of sample B in relation to sample A is evident throughout: lower age-specific marital fertility rates at almost all ages for all birth cohorts after 1750–99; consequently lower total marital fertility rates; lower period total fertility rates; higher average age at marriage; proportionately still higher mother's average age at first birth; lower average age at last birth, even taking into account mortality; earlier apparent fertility control within marriage. There is some evidence that spacing as well as stopping behavior was characteristic of this group from early in the nineteenth century. Both samples, however, did exhibit the more conventional pattern of stopping as the century progressed. Table 8.6, which gives the probabilities of progressing from one parity to the next, shows another anomaly. At very low parities (i.e., one, two, and three) sample B had lower parity progression probabilities at these early parities which declined more than those for sample A. It is unfortunate that the parity distributions and the parity progression probabilities for higher parities were not given. Overall, however, unless there was some higher incidence of subfecundity and sterility at early ages and parities in sample B (which is possible by chance considering the small genetic pool of only nine family histories), there is evidence that sample B was peculiar in that it gave evidence of early spacing, early stopping, *and* later marriage.

This peculiarity, or at least difference, concerning sample B is disturbing because sample B is the basis for analysis by region (tables 8.7 and 8.8), by occupation (table 8.10), by farm-nonfarm residence (table 8.11), and by wealth (table 8.12). (Remember that sample C is derivative from sample B.) The fertility differentials are, in some cases, not too surprising: laborers had higher fertility than other groups, farm families had more children than nonfarm families, the foreign born had larger families than the native born. (There is some confusion concerning rural/urban differences. Farm versus nonfarm residence is not equivalent to rural versus urban residence, and so the discussion should reflect this.)

Regional differences are a bit hard to summarize (tables 8.7 and 8.8). It does seem that declines began earliest in New England and the Middle Atlantic regions and gradually spread to the Midwest and West. (Results for the South are based on such small numbers and intermittent observations as to be of little value.) This, of course, fits with the findings and views of Yasuba (1962), Forster and Tucker (1972), and Easterlin (1971, 1976). Unfortunately, the New England region is lost to observation after the birth cohort of roughly 1825–36. The Midwest and Middle Atlantic regions appeared to converge over time. The West exhibited early marriage and high fertility until quite late. (Were any of the Western families in sample B Mormons, a high fertility group?) These regional differences are difficult to analyze easily because of small cell sizes and irregular coverage. The results seem to confirm prior work.

Results on wealth are of interest, in that a curvilinear pattern was found. This has interesting implications for the relationship of wealth (and permanent income) to fertility and holds possibilities for future research on the relative importance of wealth versus price effects over various ranges of wealth. Unfortunately, the sample is restricted to the linked families (for the censuses of 1850, 1860, and 1870 for sample C), and so the analysis must be limited in time and to the peculiarities of sample B.

The analysis of correlation across generations is unclear. Are these truly coresident extended households, or are they merely linked non-coresident households? The positive correlation between fertility across generations is of interest, although the effect of behavioral differences aimed at differential fertility regulation across lineages may be confused with biological differences and behavioral differences not related to fertility. Table 8.14 does reveal substantial differences across family histories, although some histories with few cases (e.g., nos. 3 and 7) should probably be excluded from analysis.

This paper reveals that much of the early decline was through nuptiality adjustment (a "Malthusian" transition, to use the terminology of Coale 1974). It is asserted in the paper that there was an important effect from interruption of marriage via mortality, which apparently was increasing prior to the Civil War. (See Robert Fogel's paper in this volume.) The effect of mortality is, however, possibly overrated. Its effect should have been expressed in a larger gap (relative or absolute) between average mother's age at last birth (which takes mortality into account) and average mother's age at last birth for women at risk to age 45 (which removes the mortality effect). I have taken these values from table 8.4 and calculated the absolute difference and the ratio of the mean age at last birth to the mean age at last birth at risk to age 45. The results are given in table C8.2. The idea is that mean age at last birth to risk at age 45 revealed the stopping age without mortality,

Table C8.2        Comparison of Mother's Average Age at Last Birth with Mother's
                  Average Age at Last Birth at Risk to Age 45: Genealogical
                  Sample, 1700–1899

| Years | Sample A | | | | Sample B | | | |
|---|---|---|---|---|---|---|---|---|
| | (1) | (2) | (2) − (1) | (1)/(2) | (1) | (2) | (2) − (1) | (1)/(2) |
| 1700–1709 | 37.0 | 39.7 | 2.7 | .9320 | 35.5 | 42.0 | 6.5 | .8452 |
| 1750–59 | 38.8 | 39.0 | .2 | .9949 | 39.5 | 40.3 | .9 | .9801 |
| 1800–1809 | 38.1 | 40.5 | 2.4 | .9407 | 35.9 | 38.2 | 2.3 | .9398 |
| 1810–19 | 38.1 | 40.3 | 2.2 | .9454 | 35.5 | 37.8 | 2.3 | .9392 |
| 1820–29 | 37.6 | 39.8 | 2.2 | .9447 | 35.0 | 36.4 | 1.4 | .9615 |
| 1830–39 | 37.1 | 39.2 | 2.1 | .9464 | 33.7 | 34.7 | 1.0 | .9712 |
| 1840–49 | 36.4 | 38.3 | 1.9 | .9504 | 33.1 | 34.0 | .9 | .9735 |
| 1850–59 | 35.1 | 36.8 | 1.7 | .9538 | 32.6 | 33.7 | 1.1 | .9674 |
| 1860–69 | 34.4 | 35.6 | 1.2 | .9663 | 32.5 | 33.5 | 1.0 | .9701 |
| 1870–79 | 34.0 | 34.6 | .6 | .9826 | 33.4 | 35.0 | 1.6 | .9543 |
| 1880–89 | 31.5 | 32.9 | 1.4 | .9574 | 32.8 | 32.9 | .1 | .9967 |

*Source:* Bourne (1985), table 4.
*Note:* (1) Mother's average age at last birth.
(2) Mother's average age at last birth at risk to age 45.

and the mean age for all women revealed the effect with mortality. The table reveals no trend in favor of *reducing* fertility between 1800–1809 and 1870–79 for sample A. In fact, the absolute and relative differences declined, pointing to an effect acting to *increase* actual fertility (and to close the gap between total marital fertility rates and children ever born). The results for sample B also showed a decline in the gap between 1800–1809 and 1840–49 and then an increase to 1870–79. For this sample, then, fertility decline was counteracted by mortality prior to 1850 and then modestly assisted by it. The real effect of mortality in reducing fertility by shortening the childbearing period was between the period 1750–59 and the beginning of the nineteenth century (1800–1809).

The evidence presented in the paper does suggest that a "neo-Malthusian" transition (i.e., control of marital fertility) was beginning in the early nineteenth century, more in sample B than in sample A and also more related to stopping than spacing behavior. This is not a case of "either/or" but of "more or less." The data point to stopping via declines in mother's average age at last birth to risk at age 45 as early as 1800–1809 in both samples (table 8.4). The analysis of spacing behavior must await a study of birth interval lengths, which is not provided here. Also, further study is needed of the role in the fertility decline of shifting weights among subgroups and regions having differential fertility.

The results in this paper form a complement to earlier work by Warren Sanderson (1979) and the paper in this volume by Paul David and Warren Sanderson. Sanderson (1979, table 2) found that nuptiality changes were important in fostering declines in total fertility rates in the nineteenth century, but the effect was not dominant except during the decade 1880–90. More than half of the declines in total fertility rates were due to declines in marital fertility. It is important to reconcile these findings.

Overall, this paper constitutes an important first step in analyzing what is potentially a most valuable window on the past. There are many other possible uses for the data (e.g., the mortality paper by Robert Fogel in this volume). More can be done with the fertility analysis, and I am confident that it will be. But doubt as to the representativeness of this sample remains: the low fertility of samples B and C; the differences between samples A and B; the peculiar child-woman ratio results; the fact that the samples are white, literate, and mostly native born. There are thus reasons to regard the findings as pertaining to a "leading" group in the demographic transition. As such, it is an important source of information on the fertility decline in the United States, peculiar because it occurred in a largely rural, agrarian context early in the nineteenth century.

# References

Adams, J., and Kasakoff, A. 1983. Migration and life-cycle in the American north: Age-specific migration rates, 1700 to 1850. Discussion paper.

Alter, G. 1984. Fertility analysis with linked and unlinked population register samples from nineteenth century Belgium. Working paper.

Amemiya, T. 1981. Qualitative response models: A survey. *Journal of Economic Literature,* vol. 19.

Barclay, G. 1958. *Techniques of population analysis.* New York: Wiley.

Bash, W. 1955. Differential fertility in Madison County, New York, 1865. *Milbank Memorial Fund Quarterly,* vol. 33.

Bean, L., et al. 1978. The Mormon historical demographic project. *Historical Methods.*

Becker, G. S. 1965. A theory of the allocation of time. *Economic Journal,* vol. 75.

———. 1976. *The economic approach to human behavior.* Chicago: University of Chicago Press.

———. 1981. *A treatise on the family.* Cambridge: Harvard University Press.

Becker, G. S., and Lewis, H. G. 1974. Interaction between quantity and quality of children. In *Economics of the family,* ed. T. W. Schultz. Chicago: University of Chicago Press.

Becker, G. S., and Tomes, N. 1984. The rise and fall of families. National Opinion Research Center discussion paper.

Ben-Porath, Y. 1975. First-generation effects on second-generation fertility. *Demography,* vol. 12.

————. 1980. Child mortality and fertility. In *Population and economic change in developing countries,* ed. R. Easterlin. Chicago: University of Chicago Press.

Bongaarts, J. 1978. A framework for analyzing the proximate determinants of fertility. *Population and Development Review.*

Bourne, J. 1985. An intergenerational model of household fertility with a new approach to wealth estimation. Working paper.

Coale, A. 1975. The demographic transition. In *The population debate: Dimensions and perspectives.* New York: United Nations.

Coale, A., and Demeny, P. 1966. *Regional model life tables and stable populations.* Princeton: Princeton University Press.

Coale, A., and Trussell, T. J. 1974. Model fertility schedules: Variations in the age structure of child bearing in human populations. *Population Index* 40:185–258.

————. 1978. Technical note: Finding the two parameters that specify a model schedule of marital fertility. *Population Index* 44:203–13.

Coale, A., and Zelnik, M. 1963. *New estimates of fertility and population in the United States.* Princeton: Princeton University Press.

Curtin, L., et al. 1979. A note on the analysis of parity progression ratios. *Demography,* vol. 16.

David, P., and Sanderson, W. 1984. Rudimentary contraceptive methods and the American transition to marital fertility control, 1855–1915. NBER Working Paper.

Easterlin, R. 1961. Influence in European overseas emigration before World War I. *Economic Development and Cultural Change,* vol. 9.

————. 1968. *Population, labor force, and long swings in economic growth.* New York: National Bureau of Economic Research.

————. 1971. Does human fertility adjust to the environment? *American Economic Review* 61:399–407.

Fogel, R. W. 1977. The economics of mortality in North America, 1650–1910. Research proposal submitted to the National Science Foundation.

Fogel, R. W., et al. 1982. Uses of intergenerational data sets: The problem of time scales. Preliminary draft.

Forster, E., and Tucker, C. 1972. *Economic opportunity and white American fertility ratios, 1800–1860.* New Haven: Yale University Press.

Gautier, E., and Henry, L. 1958. La population de Crulai, paroisse Normandie au XVII^e et au XVIII^e siècles. Paris: INED.

Grabill, C., et al. 1958. *Fertility of American women.* New York: Wiley.

Haines, M. 1977. Fertility decline in industrial America: An analysis of the Pennsylvania anthracite region, 1850–1900, using own-children methods. *Population Studies,* vol. 32.

———. 1979. *Fertility and occupation: Population patterns in industrialization.* New York: Academic Press.

———. 1984. Ethnic differences in marital fertility during the fertility decline: Philadelphia, 1850–1880. Conference paper for the Population Association of America.

Henry, L. 1956. Anciennes familles genevoises: Etude demographique: 16$^e$-20$^e$ siècles. INED cahier 26. Paris: Presses Universitaires de France.

———. 1961. Some data on natural fertility. *Eugenics Quarterly,* vol. 18.

Herlihy, D. 1977. Deaths, marriages, births, and the Tuscan economy (ca. 1300–1550). In *Population patterns in the past,* ed. R. Lee. New York: Academic Press.

Hershberg, T., and Dockhorn, R. 1976. Occupational classification. *Historical Methods.*

Johnson, N., and Stokes, C. 1976. Family sizes in successive generations: The effects of birth order, intergenerational change in lifestyle, and familial satisfaction. *Demography,* vol. 13.

Karlin, S., and Taylor, H. 1975. *A first course in stochastic processes.* New York: Academic Press.

Kearl, J., and Pope, C. 1983. Wealth mobility: The missing element. *Journal of Interdisciplinary History,* vol. 13.

Keyfitz, N., and Flieger, W. 1968. *World population.* Chicago: University of Chicago.

Klapisch, C. 1972. Household and family in Tuscany in 1427. In *Household and family in past time,* ed. P. Laslett. London: Cambridge University Press.

Knodel, J. 1974. *The decline of fertility in Germany, 1871–1939.* Princeton: Princeton University Press.

———. 1977. Family limitation and the fertility transition: Evidence from the age patterns of fertility in Europe and Asia. *Population Studies,* vol. 32.

———. 1979. From natural fertility to family limitation: The onset of fertility transition in a sample of German villages. *Demography,* vol. 16.

Kunze, K. 1984. The effects of age composition and changes in vital rates on nineteenth century population estimates from new data. Ph.D. dissertation. University of Utah.

Kuznets, S. 1958. Long swings in the growth of populations and in related economic variables. *Proceedings of the American Philosophical Society,* vol. 102.

Leasure, J. 1962. Factors involved in the decline of fertility in Spain, 1900–1950. Ph.D. dissertation, Princeton University.

Lee, R. 1978. *Econometric studies of topics in demographic history.* New York: Arno.

Livi-Bacci, M. 1977. *A history of Italian fertility.* Princeton: Princeton University Press.

McInnis, R. 1977. Childbearing and land availability: Some evidence from individual household data. In *Population patterns in the past,* ed. R. Lee. New York: Academic Press.

Malthus, T. 1798. An essay on the principle of population. London.

Mineau, G., et al. 1978a. Introduction of family limitation in a natural fertility population. National Institute of Health Research Working Paper.

———. 1978b. Natural fertility of once married couples. National Institute of Health Research Working Paper.

———. 1979. Mormon demographic history II. The family life cycle and natural fertility. *Population Studies,* vol. 33.

Okun, B. 1958. *Trends in birth rates in the United States since 1870.* Baltimore: Johns Hopkins Press.

Potter, J. 1965. The growth of population in America, 1700–1860. In *Population in history,* ed. D. Glass and D. Eversley. Chicago: Aldine.

Razin, A., and Ben-Zion, U. 1975. An intergenerational model of population growth. *American Economic Review.*

Rosenzweig, M., and Schultz, T. P. 1984. The demand and supply of births: Estimating a production function for U.S. Fertility. Conference paper for the Population Association of America.

Saad, A. 1981. Intergenerational occupational mobility in 19th century America. Thesis seminar paper, University of Chicago.

Sanderson, W. 1979. Quantitative aspects of marriage, fertility and family limitation in nineteenth century America: Another application of the Coale specification. *Demography* 16:339–58.

———. 1984. New interpretations of the decline in the fertility of white women in the United States, 1800–1920. Working paper.

Schultz, T. P. 1981. *Economics of population.* Reading, Mass.: Addison-Wesley.

Schultz, T. W. 1974. *Economics of the family.* Chicago: University of Chicago Press.

Simon, J. 1974. *The effects of income on fertility.* Chapel Hill, N.C.: Carolina Population Center.

Smith, D. S. 1977. A homeostatic demographic regime: Patterns in West European family reconstitution studies. In *Population patterns in the past,* ed. R. Lee. New York: Academic Press.

Soltow, L. 1975. *Men and wealth in the United States, 1850–1870.* New Haven: Yale University Press.

*The statistical history of the United States from colonial times to the present.* 1965. Stamford, Conn.: Fairfield.

Thompson, W., and Whelpton, P. 1933. *Population trends in the United States.* New York: Wiley.

Tolney, S., et al. 1982. Own-child estimates of U.S. white fertility, 1886–99. *Historical Methods,* vol. 15.

Tomes, N. 1981. The family, inheritance, and the intergenerational transmission of inequality. *Journal of Political Economy.*

United States Bureau of the Census. 1975. Historical statistics of the United States: Colonial times to 1970. Washington: Government Printing Office.

van de Walle, E. 1976. Household dynamics in a Belgian village, 1847–1866. *Journal of Family History,* vol. 1.

Vielrose, E. 1965. *Elements of the natural movement of population.* Oxford: Pergamon.

Villaflor, G., and Sokoloff, K. 1982. Migration in colonial America: Evidence from the militia muster rolls. *Social Science History.*

Vinovskis, M., and Hareven, T. 1975. Marital fertility, ethnicity, and occupation in urban families: An analysis of South Boston and the South End in 1880. *Journal of Social History.*

Weir, D. R. 1982. Life under pressure: Questions for a comparative history of economics and demography in France and England, 1670–1870. Center Discussion Paper 407, Economic Growth Center, Yale University.

Willigan, J., and Lynch, K. 1982. *Sources and methods of historical demography.* New York: Academic Press.

Willis, R. J. 1974. Economic theory of fertility behavior. In *Economics of the family,* ed. T. W. Schultz. Chicago: University of Chicago Press.

Wrigley, E. 1966. Family limitation in preindustrial England. *Economic History Review,* 2d ser., vol. 19.

———. 1968. Mortality in preindustrial England: The example of Colyton, Devon, over three centuries. *Daedalus,* vol. 97.

———. 1975. Baptism coverage in early 19th century England—the Colyton area. *Population Studies,* vol. 29.

Wrigley, E., and Schofield, R. 1981. *A population history of England, 1541–1871: A reconstruction.* London: Edward Arnold.

Yasuba, Y. 1962. *Birth rates of the white population in the United States, 1800–1860.* Baltimore: Johns Hopkins Press.

Young, C. 1978. French historical demography. *Working Papers in Demography,* vol. 9.

# 9    Nutrition and the Decline in Mortality since 1700: Some Preliminary Findings

Robert William Fogel

## 9.1 The Issues

Between 1700 and 1980 there was a decline of about 35 points in the standardized American death rate (see table 9.1). Between the same years, the British rate declined by about 21 points. About 70% of the American decline and about 50% of the British decline took place before 1911.

Robert W. Fogel is Charles R. Walgreen Professor of American Institutions at the University of Chicago, director of the Center for Population Economics at the University of Chicago, and program director for the Development of American Economy Program of the National Bureau of Economic Research.

This paper is a progress report on two projects jointly sponsored by the National Bureau of Economic Research and by the Center for Population Economics of the University of Chicago. Aspects of the research reported here were supported by grants from the National Science Foundation; the Social Science Research Council, London; the British Academy; the Exxon Educational Foundation; the Walgreen Foundation; Brigham Young University; the University of California at Berkeley; Harvard University; Ohio State University; the University of Pennsylvania; Princeton University; the University of Rochester; and Stanford University. I have drawn on the work of fellow collaborators in the two projects including S. L. Engerman, R. Floud, G. Friedman, C. D. Goldin, R. A. Margo, C. Pope, K. Sokoloff, R. H. Steckel, T. J. Trussell, G. Villaflor, K. W. Wachter, and L. Wimmer. J. Bourne Wahl, C. Ford, M. Fishman, J. Moen, and J. Walker have been effective research assistants. C. Miterko efficiently typed and corrected the various drafts. A. M. John has generously made material from her study of Trinidad available to me, and D. Levy permitted me to cite some of the results of his study of life expectancy in colonial Maryland. I am especially indebted to J. M. Tanner for his encouragement and advice since the beginning of both projects and to P. H. Lindert for insightful comments and criticisms and for the correction of several errors in the draft presented at the Williamsburg conference.

An earlier version of this paper was commissioned by Gunter Steinmann and other organizers of the "Conference on Economic Consequences of Population Change in Industrialized Countries," which was held in Paderborn, West Germany, during June 1983. Successive versions of the paper were presented to seminars at Caltech, the London School of Economics, the Graduate Institute of International Studies (Geneva), Harvard,

Table 9.1          The Probable Decline in Standardized Death Rates between 1700
                   and 1980 in the United States and Great Britain

| Approximate Date | United States | Great Britain |
|---|:---:|:---:|
| A. Standardized Death Rates (per thousand) | | |
| 1. 1700 | 40 | 28 |
| 2. 1850 | 23 | 24 |
| 3. 1910 | 15 | 17 |
| 4. 1980 | 5 | 7 |
| B. Percentage of the Total Decline Which Occurred between ca. 1700 and the Specified Date | | |
| 5. 1850 | 49 | 19 |
| 6. 1910 | 71 | 52 |
| 7. 1980 | 100 | 100 |

Sources:
United States: The age distribution is standardized on the weights computed from persons alive in 1700 in the pilot sample of genealogies that is described in the next section of this paper. Line 1, Fogel et al. 1978, p. 76, with the New England and Chesapeake rates weighted by the New England and Southern populations for 1700 as given in United States Bureau of the Census 1975, p. 1168. Line 2, unpublished mortality tables for whites in 1850, cited in Haines, 1979. Line 3, Preston et al. 1972, pp. 728, 730. Line 4, United States National Center for Health Statistics 1983, p. 12.
Great Britain: The age distribution is standardized on the weights given in Wrigley and Schofield 1981, p. 529, for 1701–5; male and female death rates were equally weighted. Line 1, ibid. Lines 2 and 3, Case 1963, pp. 41, 53, 65, 76. Line 4, Great Britain Central Statistical Office 1983, p. 43.

The causes of this remarkable decline remain a puzzle. Until the mid-1950s it was widely attributed to improvements in medical technology. During the past 3 decades Thomas McKeown vigorously disputed that view in a series of highly influential papers and books. McKeown agreed that there had been a considerable expansion of hospital services and important advances in medical knowledge during the eighteenth and nineteenth centuries, but he argued that such ad-

Chicago, Birkbeck College, Minnesota, Northwestern, Pennsylvania, Toronto, Rochester, and Indiana. Numerous revisions were made as a consequence of points raised during these sessions. I have also benefited from comments and criticisms by M. J. Bailey, R. K. Chandra, M. G. Coopersmith, E. Crimmins, J. Cropsey, P. A. David, L. E. Davis, N. Davis, G. R. Elton, A. Fishlow, R. A. Easterlin, F. Furet, D. Galenson, R. E. Gallman, H. Goldstein, M. R. Haines, R. Hellie, J. A. Henretta, S. Horton, T. A. Huertas, H. C. Johansen, D. G. Johnson, W. Kruskal, P. Laslett, E. P. Lazear, S. E. Lehmberg, M. Livi-Bacci, W. H. McNeill, L. Neal, D. C. North, G. H. Pelto, S. Peltzman, S. H. Preston, M. G. Reid, J. C. Riley, A. Sen, W. C. Sanderson, R. S. Schofield, T. W. Schultz, N. S. Scrimshaw, S. G. Scrikantia, J. L. Simon, S. Stigler, C. E. Taylor, B. Thomas, R. H. Tilly, E. van de Walle, S. C. Watkins, S. B. Webb, E. A. Wrigley, and W. Zelinsky.
    The findings presented in this paper are tentative and subject to change. They do not necessarily reflect the views of the NBER or any of the other cooperating institutions or funding agencies.

vances had little effect on the decline in death rates until the twentieth century. An epidemiologist, McKeown gained prominence for biomedical research, including his studies of the relationship between birthweight and perinatal mortality rates in Birmingham after World War II (Gibson and McKeown 1950, 1951; McKeown and Gibson 1951), before turning his attention to long-term changes in medical practices and demographic rates.

### 9.1.1  The Nutritional Contribution: The English Experience

McKeown's explanation for the decline in mortality rates after 1700 is most fully set forth in his book on *The Modern Rise of Population* (1976a), and he subsequently restated and cogently summarized his argument in 1978 and 1983. In the place of medical technology, McKeown substituted improvement in nutrition as the principal factor affecting the decline in mortality. He does not make his case for nutrition directly but largely through a residual argument in which he rejects the other principal explanations. The alternatives to nutrition are advances in medical technology; reductions in the virulence of pathogens; human acquisition of immunity through natural selection, genetic drift, or acquired immunities; personal hygiene; and public sanitation.

McKeown's analysis turns on a careful consideration of the British pattern of decline in death rates due to specific infectious diseases between 1850 and 1971. During this period the standardized death rate attributable to infectious diseases declined from 13.0 per thousand to 0.7 per thousand. About 54% of the decline was associated with airborne diseases, 28% with water- and food-borne diseases, and 18% with diseases spread by other means (McKeown 1976a, pp. 54–63). This simple classification permits McKeown to assess the probable impact of public health measures and personal sanitation. Cleaning up the public water supply and improving sewage systems, he argues, would have had little effect on the airborne diseases. Moreover, as long as water supplies were polluted, individuals could not protect themselves against such waterborne diseases as typhoid and cholera by washing regularly. Under such circumstances "the washing of hands is about as effective as the wringing of hands" (McKeown 1978, p. 540). In his view public health measures did not become effective until the very end of the nineteenth century. The sharp declines in food- and water-borne diseases (which he dates in England and Wales with the start of the eighth decade) were not only due to better water and sewage systems but to improvements in food hygiene, especially pasteurization. He attributes the rapid decline of infant mortality between 1900 and 1931 mainly to the development of a "safe milk supply" (McKeown 1976a, p. 122; 1978, p. 540). McKeown argues that improvements in personal or public hygiene would not have reduced deaths from airborne diseases unless they reduced crowding, and crowding generally increased during the nineteenth century.

McKeown's skepticism about the efficacy of early medical measures is based on his study of the temporal pattern of decline in the death rates of the most lethal diseases of the nineteenth century. Tuberculosis, the leading killer in England and America during much of the nineteenth century, is a case in point. During 1848–54 tuberculosis caused nearly one out of every six English deaths from all causes, and one out of every four due to infectious diseases. It was not until 1882 that the tubercle bacillus was identified, and an effective chemotherapy for this disease was not developed until 1947. Nevertheless, the death rate of respiratory tuberculosis declined to just 43% of its 1848–54 level by 1900 and to just 10% of that level before the introduction of streptomycin in 1947. Similarly, the major decline in the death rates from bronchitis and pneumonia, whooping cough, measles, scarlet fever, and typhoid all preceded the development of effective chemotherapies. McKeown also doubts the efficacy of the lying-in hospitals which were established during the eighteenth and nineteenth centuries, noting that well into the third quarter of the last century "hospital death rates were many times greater than those of related home deliveries" (McKeown 1976a, p. 105).

McKeown is skeptical of the contention that the decline in mortality rates was due to a decline in the virulence of pathogens. He notes that scarlet fever and influenza have fluctuated in their severity in short periods of time and acknowledges that these fluctuations were due to changes in the character of these diseases. He lists typhus as another disease that might have declined due to changes in the pathogens. However, the fraction of the total decline attributable to these three diseases is small. On a more general plane he notes that infectious diseases that are now relatively benign in developed nations are still quite virulent in less developed countries and argues that it is quite unlikely that pathogens would have lost their virulence only in developed countries. McKeown also minimizes the impact of natural selection, arguing that in the case of tuberculosis too much of the population had been exposed to the bacillus for too long a period before the decline, and the decline itself was too rapid, to be consistent with natural selection.

McKeown's arguments in favor of a nutritional explanation fall into two categories. First, he cites evidence that per capita food supplies in England increased sporadically during the late eighteenth and early nineteenth centuries and then regularly in the late nineteenth and in the twentieth centuries. Second, he emphasizes findings of medical researchers currently working in the developing countries who have concluded that there is a synergistic relationship between malnutrition and infection, and that malnutrition significantly increases the likelihood that a victim will succumb to an infection. In this connection he cites a report of the World Health Organization which concluded that malnutrition was an associated cause in 57%–67% of the deaths of children under age 5 in Latin America (1976a, p. 136).

### 9.1.2   The Nutritional Contribution: The American Experience

McKeown's argument has been extended to the American experience by Meeker (1972) and by Higgs (1973, 1979). According to Meeker, the period from 1880 to 1910 witnessed both a substantial rise in per capita income and a decline in mortality rates. In cross-sectional regressions for 1890–1900, city mortality rates are significantly related to housing density variables and state mortality rates are significantly related to income. In his 1973 paper Higgs estimated the decline in rural mortality rates for the period from 1870 to World War I. Despite the absence of direct observations on rural mortality, Higgs was able to infer a series by making use of three other series (the aggregate crude death rate, the urban crude death rate, and the share of the population that was urban) and an identity that related the rural crude death rate to these series. This procedure produced a rural crude mortality series which declined at approximately the same rate as the urban mortality series, the total decline over 50 years amounting to 30%–40%. Higgs argues that whatever role public sanitation and medical care might have played in the urban context, they were of minor consequence in rural areas which were undersupplied with physicians, and which continued to draw water mainly from wells, springs, and cisterns, continued to rely on privies, and continued to consume unpasteurized milk. Like McKeown, Higgs concluded that "the great bulk of the decline in rural mortality before 1920 is probably attributable to rising levels of living among the rural population" (1973, p. 189).

### 9.1.3   Objections to the Nutritional Argument

Virtually all those who are attempting to explain the secular decline in mortality rates in Europe and America agree that improvements in nutrition made a contribution. But some scholars believe that McKeown and others have greatly exaggerated the case (Livi-Bacci 1983). The doubts arise partly because of major gaps in the evidence. Razzell, for example, doubts McKeown's claim that the food supply in England grew more rapidly than the population before 1840. He argues that at least for the eighteenth century the evidence is "much more consistent with a reversed hypothesis—that the standard of the diet was a function of population change" (Razzell 1973, p. 8). Even more basic is the absence of adequate evidence on mortality rates. Before 1837 in Great Britain and before 1900 in the United States information on death rates is so sparse that historical demographers are at odds not only on the levels of mortality but even on the direction of change (Vinovskis 1972; Easterlin 1977; Lindert 1983).

In the American case, for example, fragments of evidence led Thompson and Whelpton (1933) to believe that mortality rates declined fairly steadily from the middle of the eighteenth century to 1900. On the other hand, Yasuba's (1962) examination of available urban death registrations and some scattered registrations from rural communities led him to conclude that mortality rates increased between 1800 and 1860. More recently, a study of Deerfield, which has vital records that extend back to the early eighteenth century, revealed that mortality was low and stable within this rural town of western Massachusetts until the turn of the nineteenth century. Between 1795–99 and 1840–44, however, mortality rates nearly doubled (Meindl and Swedlund 1977, p. 398).

It is not merely the evidential gaps in the argument of McKeown and others that aroused the concern of critics. Certain facts seemed to contradict the case for nutrition. The absence of a significant gap between the mortality rates of the peerage and those of the laboring classes in England before 1725 was particularly vexing. "If the food supply was the critical variable," Razzell argued (1973, pp. 6–7), mortality reductions should have been "concentrated almost exclusively amongst the poorer" classes and the mortality rates of the aristocracy should have been "unaffected." Yet as table 9.2 shows, between the fourth quarter of the sixteenth century and the beginning of the second quarter of the eighteenth century, the mortality rates of the aristocracy were about as high as those of the general population. Both the high mortality rates of the nobility before 1725 and the rapid fall in these rates thereafter, although there was no apparent change in the diet of the peerage, predisposed Razzell "to look at the food supply hypothesis very critically."[1]

Efforts to relate both short- and long-term variations in the mortality rates to variations in bread or wheat prices have also undermined the nutritional explanation. Appleby's (1975) regressions, which related London deaths from specific diseases to bread prices over the period from 1550 to 1750, led him to conclude that there was no correlation between the supply of food and deaths due to plague, smallpox, or tuberculosis and only slight correlations between bread prices and deaths due to typhus and "ague and fever." More sophisticated analysis by Lee (1981) revealed statistically significant but weak relationships between short-term variations in death rates and in wheat prices. According to Schofield (1983, p. 282), short-run variations in English mortality were "overwhelmingly determined" by factors other than the food supply and the long-run trend in mortality was unaffected by the trend in food prices.

**Table 9.2**        Cohort Life Expectancy ($e_0^0$) in the English Peerage and in the
             English Population as a Whole

| Birth Cohort (century and quarter) | Peerage (both sexes) | England and Wales (both sexes) |
|---|---|---|
| 16th: | | |
| III | 38.0 | 35.6 |
| IV | 37.2 | 38.0 |
| 17th: | | |
| I | 34.7 | 37.3 |
| II | 33.0 | 35.5 |
| III | 31.9 | 34.2 |
| IV | 34.2 | 33.5 |
| 18th: | | |
| I | 36.2 | 35.1 |
| II | 38.1 | 33.8 |
| III | 40.2 | 36.3 |
| IV | 48.1 | 37.0 |
| 19th: | | |
| I | 50.6 | 41.5 |
| II | 55.3 | 44.6 |
| III | 58.6 | |
| IV | 60.2 | |
| 20th: | | |
| I | 65.0 | |

*Sources: Column 1:* Hollingsworth 1977, table 3. *Column 2:* The observations for 16–III through 18–IV are from Wrigley and Schofield 1981, p. 530; the observations for 19–II and 19–III are computed from the cohort life tables in Case et al. 1962, pp. 1–28, which were derived from registration data.

Lindert's (1983) examination of the work of Lee, Wrigley, and Schofield confirmed their conclusions on the absence of a notable relationship between food prices and mortality rates. Nevertheless, he was discontented with results that implied that living standards "left little or no mark on mortality." The puzzle, he acknowledged, extended to his own work with Williamson, since they have not yet been able to "find a firm casual link behind the obvious correlation between income and life expectancy after 1820." He suggested that the resolution to "the mystery of independent mortality" trends might require more complex attacks on the issue. That would be the case if the "life-extending" effect of income "was hidden behind the shift toward earlier death in the growing unhealthy cities." He also suggested that diets may "have improved in ways unmeasured by income" (pp. 147–48).

Other investigators have found evidence which suggests that Mc-Keown underestimated the impact of public health measures on the decline in mortality during the nineteenth century. Estimates of the cause of mortality rates in the three largest urban areas of France during the nineteenth century by Preston and van de Walle (1978) led them to the conclusion that water and sewage improvements played a major role in the urban mortality decline. Not only were the declines concentrated in the waterborne diseases, but the rate of decline was much more rapid in the two cities that introduced vigorous sewage and pure water programs than in the one that did not. On the other hand, deaths due to tuberculosis did not decline in Paris over a 33-year period, although deaths due to other airborne diseases showed small declines. Even these declines could have been due to the cleanup of the water supply. Preston and van de Walle stress that diarrheal and other waterborne diseases have important nutritional consequences because they "reduce appetite, reduce the absorption of essential nutrients, increase metabolic demands and often lead to dietary restrictions" (p. 218). Thus, cleaning up the water systems not only reduced deaths caused by waterborne diseases but also contributed to the reduction in deaths due to airborne diseases because the reduction in waterborne diseases improved the nutritional status of the population, especially of infants and young children.

### 9.1.4  The Concepts of "Nutritional Status" and "Nutritional Adequacy"

The last point calls attention to a terminological issue that has confused the debate over the contribution of improvements in nutrition to the decline in mortality. Although some investigators have equated the term *nutritional status* with the amount of food that is consumed, epidemiologists and nutritionists use the term in a different way. To them *nutritional status* denotes the balance between the intake of nutrients and the claims against it. It follows that adequate levels of nutrition are not determined solely by the level of nutrient intake but vary with individual circumstances. Whether the diet of a particular individual is nutritionally adequate depends on such matters as his level of physical activity, the climate of the region in which he lives, and the extent of his exposure to various diseases. As Nevin S. Scrimshaw put it, the adequacy of a given level of iron consumption depends critically on whether an individual has hookworm.[2] Thus, it is possible that the nutritional status of a population may decline even though that population's consumption of nutrients is rising if the extent of exposure to infection or the degree of physical activity is rising more rapidly. It follows that the assessment of the contribution of nutrition to the decline in mortality requires measures not only of food consumption but also of the balance between food consumption and the claims on that consumption. To avoid confusion, in the remainder of this paper I will use the terms "diet" and "gross nutrition" to designate nutrient intake only. All other references to nutrition, such as "nutritional status," "net nutrition," "nutrition," "malnutrition," and "undernutrition" will designate the balance between nutrient intake and the claims on that intake.

## 9.2  New Sources of Evidence

The major obstacle to a resolution of the debate on the causes of the decline in mortality is the absence of data rather than the absence of analytical ingenuity or credible theories. Recognition of this point has led to numerous attempts to find sources of data that could fill the gap. The most impressive of these undertakings have been the work with parish records in England and France which have produced important new series on population and vital events that reach back to the first half of the sixteenth century. The publication of *The Population History of England* and of a summary of the second volume in the series (Wrigley and Schofield 1983) reveal that we are now coming into possession of a new long-term series that will greatly illuminate the evolution of demographic processes in England. Similar promise for French demography resides in the parish data assembled by INED, a part of which has been insightfully analyzed by Weir (1982), and in the new project based on the collection of a random sample of genealogies that has been launched by J. Dupâquier and his colleagues. Despite the demonstration by Henripin (1954) and his colleagues that genealogies could be used to reconstruct the population history of French Canada during the eighteenth century, historical demographers made little use of this type of evidence during the three decades following the publication of that study. The situation now appears to be changing. In Germany samples of genealogies are also being employed as the principal source of evidence in attempts to reconstruct long-term series on population and vital events in that nation (Imhof 1977).

It has been far more difficult to obtain data on standards of living and nutrition that could be used in conjunction with the demographic series that are now coming on line. Wrigley and Schofield (1981), for example, were forced to rely on a wage series of a small class of workers in a single region and to treat the price of wheat as a proxy for the consumption of food (cf. Thirsk 1983). This difficulty is also being addressed, and promising new sources of data on economic variables are now being exploited. It has recently been demonstrated that probate records, bailiffs' accounts, tax lists, and similar archival records can provide data on economic information suitable for both cross-sectional and time-series analysis. From these sources scholars have been able to measure such variables as grain yields, meat supplies, rental prices of housing, changes in occupational structure, income, and wealth (Overton 1979, 1980; Lindert 1980; Schuurman 1980; Lindert and Williamson 1983a; Campbell 1983).

Although European scholars have led the way in the exploitation of many of the new data sources, Americans have not been far behind. Much of the work on this side of the Atlantic has been pioneered by historians of the colonial period who have exploited the full array of these difficult but now highly valued documentary sources to produce evidence on demographic, economic, and social behavior (Lockridge 1966; Demos 1970; Greven 1970; McCusker 1970; Smith 1972; Walsh and Menard 1974; Menard 1975; Kulikoff 1976; Fischer and Dobson 1979; Rutman and Rutman 1979; Carr and Walsh 1980; J. Gallman 1980; Jones 1980; McMahon 1981; Galenson 1981; R. Gallman 1982; Main 1982; Rothenberg 1984; Levy 1984). Although for the most part these studies have focused on local communities and particular periods, collectively they adumbrate regional and national patterns and demonstrate the feasibility of extending this approach to the national level and to the entire span of United States history.

In 1977 the NBER launched a new Program in the Development of the American Economy (DAE) which is investigating long-term changes in the United States economy that have occurred at the microeconomic level. To facilitate this objective the DAE has organized several studies of the feasibility of creating representative data sets consisting of intergenerationally linked households. Such data sets could open up entirely new possibilities for examining the interaction of economic and cultural factors and their mutual influence on such variables as the saving rate, the rate of female entry into the labor force, fertility and mortality rates, the inequality of the wealth distribution, migration rates, and rates of economic and social mobility. These data sets cannot be created from a single set of records but require the linking of several different types of records. The pilot studies have been aimed at determining whether the creation of the projected data sets is economically feasible and whether it is likely that such data sets will yield the desired information. The results to date have been encouraging on both counts.

### 9.2.1  The DAE/CPE Genealogical Sample

One of the projects in the DAE program is called "The Economics of Mortality in North America, 1650–1910." Jointly sponsored by the Center for Population Economics of the University of Chicago, this project turns on the collection of a large sample of genealogical records. The demographic information in the genealogical sample is being linked, on an individual or household basis, to economic information contained in probate records, tax lists, manuscript schedules of federal and local censuses, military and pension records, and eventually with medical records. The projected size of the ultimate sample is approximately 1 million individuals in 200,000 families that will be linked intergenerationally for up to 10 generations (see table 9.3).

During the past 5 years we have retrieved a sample of approximately 80,000 persons who were born or entered the United States between 1640 and 1910. Our objective during this phase has been to investigate the various categories of genealogical records in order to determine which types of records would yield the most desirable properties and which are most cost effective. Of the various categories of genealogies that we have examined the two most promising are *published family histories* and *family group sheets*.

There are at least 40,000 published histories of families that contain information on over 20 million people who have lived in North America. The largest collection, with 24,000 volumes, is in the Library of Congress, but the New York Public Library, the Library of the American Antiquarian Society, the Genealogical Society Library in Salt Lake City, and the Newberry Library have extensive collections. We have surveyed the resources in these and other collections and have put information from a sample of the family histories into machine-readable form. At the present time the sample of published histories consists of about 65,000 individuals drawn from about 275 books.

Most of the family histories begin with an immigrant to North America or some other individual who may be viewed as a patriarchal or matriarchal figure. The book then records the descendants of this initial

Table 9.3    Tentative Estimates of the Temporal Distribution of Observations in the Completed Genealogical Sample

| Period | Families Established during the Period | | Persons Born or Entering United States during the Period | |
|---|---|---|---|---|
| | Number (1) | Percent (2) | Number (3) | Percent (4) |
| Before 1700 | 1,000 | 1 | 8,000 | 1 |
| 1700–1750 | 3,000 | 2 | 26,000 | 3 |
| 1751–1800 | 6,000 | 3 | 51,000 | 5 |
| 1801–50 | 34,000 | 18 | 246,000 | 26 |
| 1851 or after | 144,000 | 77 | 608,000 | 65 |
| Totals | 188,000 | 100 | 939,000 | 100 |

*Source:* Fogel et al. 1978. A family is defined by a marriage of a bloodline individual, whether or not that marriage produces progeny. See Fogel et al. 1978, app. B, for a description of the simulation model on which this table is based. It should be kept in mind that children in one family are parents in the next one. Since col. 3 does not count such individuals twice, the ratio of col. 3 to col. 1 for a generation is not equal to the average size of completed families during the period covered by that row.

individual so that a descending tree or a pyramid is described within the family history. Dates of birth, death, and marriages are recorded in the family history, along with the place of each vital event, although omission of some vital information is common. The typical family history in the pilot sample covers six to eight generations and contains about 2,000 individuals. Families of New England are overrepresented in the histories but a significant number of books exist for each region of the country. The paucity of black family histories is the most serious shortcoming of this source. But the source is sufficiently diverse with respect to religion, European origins, places of settlement in North America, and period of immigration to be useful for studies of the white population.

We have experimented with a variety of strategies in sampling from these books. An initial concern was the distribution of the sample over the largest feasible number of books in order to insure geographic and other forms of diversity. More recently we have been experimenting with the recording of all of the information in a book, which may be the most cost-effective procedure. This new approach was encouraged by the discovery that whatever the initial location of the patriarch, subsequent generations were so mobile that each book generally had wide geographic coverage.[3]

Of the 75,000 observations in machine-readable form, only two-thirds have been integrated into the two files currently employed for demographic analysis. For the analysis of fertility we created an intergenerationally linked file of about 10,000 families embracing about 41,000 unduplicated individuals. The subsample currently being used to investigate mortality consists of about 19,000 individuals at risk from birth. About 15% of the individuals in these two working subsamples have been linked so far to economic information obtained from probate records and from the manuscript schedules of the federal censuses.[4]

Family group sheets are also family histories, but each sheet consists of just three generations. It is possible to link successive group sheets together in order to form longer genealogies, but we have not yet attempted to do so. So far we have used them mainly for the period between 1830 and 1900 when foreign immigration was heavy. The group sheets are well suited for that purpose since patriarchs who arrived during the second half of the nineteenth century would only have had one or two generations of eligible descendants. The family group sheets were constructed by Mormons, and there are about 10 million of these records in the files of the Genealogical Library in Salt Lake City. Although the compilers were Mormons, the ancestors included in the group sheets usually were not.[5] Much of our work with the group sheet sample has been concerned with whether its members are similar enough to the members of the published family histories to consider both samples as constituting a single pool of information. So far the results of our tests indicate that they do, and for many of our runs we have been pooling the two samples, although we continue to test for differences. The current working sample of group sheets consists of about 9,500 individuals who belonged to 1,500 families.

A priori considerations suggest that genealogies are likely to be a biased source of information on demographic and other socioeconomic characteristics. For example, it seems reasonable to assume that the probability that a family history will be constructed is proportional to the fertility of the family and inversely proportional to its mortality. It follows that genealogies may yield upward-biased estimates of fertility rates and downward-biased estimates of mortality rates. Whether the magnitude of such biases is large or small and whether they are correctable cannot, however, be determined on a priori grounds and the investigation of the direction and magnitude of various biases has been at the center of our work.

One approach to this problem has been to run a series of regressions of the form:

$$(1) \qquad D_j = g_j(X_{ij}, B_{ij}),$$

where

$D_j$ = a dichotomous variable for persons in the $j$th age group that takes the value one in the event of a death,

$X_{ij}$ = the $i$th behavioral factor affecting the mortality rate of the $j$th group,

$B_{ij}$ = the $i$th distortion in the data set which spuriously affects the probability of dying in the $j$th group.

The regressions described by equation (1) can be used to produce values of $_nQ_x$ corrected for the biases measured by the $B_{ij}$. At the present time only a proportion of the $X_{ij}$ variables that we intend to consider have been brought into analysis. Still missing are the main economic variables, which we are now in the process of linking to the demographic variables. Nevertheless, the initial runs on age-specific risk of death (for each sex, on each of the seven age intervals, for each of four birth cohorts) are rather promising. Birth order is statistically significant and has a relatively large impact on the probability of dying in most of the age intervals, with first and last births having a higher probability of dying than intermediate births in families with at least four live births. Place of birth has a significant impact on the probability of dying, and the high-risk regions change over time.

The bias variables ($B_{ij}$) indicate that practices by the compilers of genealogies had a small but statistically significant effect on the measured level of risk. So far these biases do not appear to have had much effect on the coefficients of the $X_{ij}$, generally changing the values only of the second or third significant digit. Much remains to be done, however, on investigating alternative ways in which the bias variables may be introduced into the regressions. But so far the impact of the various biases identified on a priori grounds appears to be small in well chosen and carefully screened genealogies. Even in the case of wealth, the upward bias in the genealogies is smaller than had been conjectured. Adams and Kasakoff have collected a sample of genealogies for northern states which they linked with the manuscript schedules of the 1850 census. They then computed mean wealth of the men in their sample who were age 20 or over in 1850, by occupation. Table 9.4 compares their results with the means reported by Soltow (1975) for his random sample from the 1850 census schedules. Table 9.4 shows that although the means in the sample of Adams and Kasakoff (1983) are biased upward as one would expect, the differences in means are not very large. Moreover, the large standard deviations indicate that the genealogies cover virtually the whole range of wealth holders.[6] Consequently, by including wealth as an argument of equation (1), it is possible to adjust for errors in estimates of mean mortality rates due to the overrepresentation of rich individuals and underrepresentation of poor ones.

Potential biases in the mortality rates because of the nature of different categories of genealogies raise more troublesome issues. One of the first issues we investigated was whether the family histories were truly family histories or merely pedigrees. Family histories include all of the descendants of the patriarch but pedigrees include only the direct ancestors of the compiler (his father, his grandfather, his great grandfather, and so on). Quite clearly pedigrees would bias mortality rates downward severely since the individuals in a pedigree had to live at least long enough to have procreated. The creation of a pedigree is the first step in the compilation of a family history since the compiler must

Table 9.4    The Mean Value of Real Estate of Native-Born Males Age 20 and over in 1850 in Two Samples (in Dollars)

|  | Genealogical Sample | | | Random Sample of 1850 Census | | |
|---|---|---|---|---|---|---|
|  | N | Mean | S.D. | N | Mean | S.D. |
| Farmers | 325 | 1,547 | 1870 | n.a.[a] | 1,401 | n.a. |
| Nonfarmers | 276 | 1,037 | 2803 | n.a. | 805 | n.a. |

Source: Adams and Kasakoff 1983.
[a]Not available.

trace his lineage to the patriarch. Only then can he come forward in time to construct a complete family history. The simplest test of whether a book is a family history or a pedigree is to observe the fullness of the tree. Some books can be discarded because it is obvious that the compiler traced only a few lines. Such inspection will not, however, reveal more subtle omissions. To get at these we devised other tests, such as whether the number of lines that died out in a given genealogy was consistent with the predictions generated by reasonable guesses at appropriate life tables and fertility schedules. The results of the various tests have indicated that the majority of the family histories in our sample are indeed what they purport to be. It appears that once they determined who their patriarchs were, the compilers usually sought to fill in the entire family tree, although they were not always completely successful.

Other tests of potential bias have involved evaluation of the behavior of various fertility and mortality statistics in order to determine if they conform to patterns observed in comparable populations. We have, for example, compared age-specific fertility schedules and the mean birth intervals at various parities with those obtained from a variety of family reconstitutions and found them to be normal for noncontraceptive populations. We are currently comparing the age structure of the individuals in the sample who are alive at given dates with the age structure in censuses performed at the same date but have not yet completed these tests. We have also computed both period and cohort life tables from the data in our sample in order to determine whether the internal structures of these tables are consistent with known characteristics of life tables and these are (Bourne et al. 1984).

One such life table has been constructed for 920 native-born white males in the pilot sample who were at risk to die during the decade of the 1850s (see panel A of table 9.5). It should be emphasized that during the pilot phase of data collection the individuals included in the sample have been chosen in such a way as to be representative of the collections of genealogies that have been the focus of our concern. Consequently, the observations in the pilot sample are not necessarily representative of the national population to which the final sample will pertain. Although the individuals at risk during the 1850s come from all of the major regions, the Northeast is overrepresented and the South and Midwest are underrepresented. The rural areas are also overrepresented and urban areas are underrepresented. In principle the deficiencies in the sample could be remedied by reweighting each of the cells in an appropriate manner. I have not engaged in such an exercise for two reasons. First, the current sample is too small; on average there are only about 13 observations for each of the 70 cells that need to be

Table 9.5    A Comparison of a Period Life Table for United States Males Derived from the Genealogical Sample with Two Other Period Life Tables

| Age (years) | A Native-Born Whites, 1850–60, Derived from the Genealogical Sample | | | B All Whites, 1850–60, Average of Haines's Tables for 1850 and 1860 | | | C All Whites, 1900, Registration States | | |
|---|---|---|---|---|---|---|---|---|---|
| | $1000Q_X$ | $l_x$ | $e_x$ | $1000Q_X$ | $l_x$ | $e_x$ | $1000Q_X$ | $l_x$ | $e_x$ |
| 10 | 29.4 | 1000 | 46.7 | 48.6 | 1000 | 46.6 | 38.3 | 1000 | 49.5 |
| 20 | 253.7 | 971 | 37.9 | 192.8 | 951 | 38.7 | 155.2 | 962 | 41.3 |
| 40 | 280.2 | 724 | 27.4 | 328.2 | 763 | 25.8 | 289.9 | 812 | 27.1 |
| 60 | 344.3 | 521 | 14.2 | 360.0 | 512 | 13.5 | 346.3 | 577 | 14.0 |
| 70 | 539.7 | 342 | 9.0 | 656.9 | 328 | 8.3 | 603.6 | 377 | 8.8 |
| 80 | 1000.0 | 157 | 4.5 | 1000.0 | 113 | 4.4 | 1000.0 | 149 | 4.7 |

*Sources and notes: Panel A:* See the text and n. 7 for the sources. The number of observations on which each $_nQ_x$ value was computed ranged between 126 and 212. The value of $e_{80}$ was computed from the approximation in Coale and Demeny (1966, p. 20). *Panel B:* This table was built up from the average of the $_nQ_x$ values in the unpublished tables for 1850 and 1860 of Haines (1979). Since Haines did not estimate the $_{10}Q_{70}$, I used the value of $_{10}Q_{70}$ in Model West (Coale and Demeny 1966) consistent with $e_{10} = 46.6$. *Panel C:* Constructed from the $_nQ_x$ values in the 1900 life table in Preston et al. 1972. The use of longer age intervals in the estimation of $l_x$ resulted in a value of $e_{10}$ slightly below that reported in the source.

reweighted. Second, the life tables which are available for comparison suffer from sample selection biases which cannot, at present, be defined with the precision required for reweighting.

Panel B of table 9.5 presents the average of the 1850 and 1860 life tables recently estimated by Haines (1979) from the data in the censuses of mortality for these two years. Because these censuses suffer from substantial underreporting, Haines fitted model life schedules to data for persons aged 5–19, ages during which the reporting tends to be most complete. Nevertheless, it is still likely that the mortality rates in his tables are to some degree biased downward. The downward bias is likely to be present even at the ages he focused on because underreporting was greater in the South than in the North and because underreporting was severe in urban areas at all ages (cf. Kahn 1978; Condran and Crimmins 1980). Panel C presents the life table for 1900 constructed by the Bureau of the Census for the 10 original death registration states. Unlike the Haines tables it is difficult to know the direction of bias in this table because the biases run in both directions. The exclusion of the South from the original registration states tends to bias mortality rates downward. It was not until 1933 that all 48 states were included in the death registration system (United States Bureau of the Census, 1975 p. 44). On the other hand, the states included in the original registration area are overrepresented, in comparison with the nation as a whole, in two high-risk groups: the foreign born and residents of large cities.

Table 9.5 indicates that life expectation at age 10 during the decade of the 1850s in the genealogical sample is 46.7 years, which is almost identical with the corresponding figure in the average of the Haines tables for 1850 and 1860 (46.6 years) and about 3 years less than that indicated by the 1900 table (49.5 years). These results are generally consistent with what is known about the extent of improvement in mortality between the 1850s and 1900. There are some differences in the $_nQ_x$ values between the genealogical sample and the average of the Haines tables, but because of the relatively small sample sizes, these are within the range of sampling variability. Sampling variability can, however, be reduced by further aggregation, and for this reason the preliminary findings presented in section 9.3 turn on 25-year averages (averages of five quinquennial intervals). All in all, the life tables derived from the genealogies conform well to those derived from registration data and other sources even before adjusting the sample for the underrepresentation of various sections of the reference population. The prospect for further improving the genealogical sample by both fuller sampling of underrepresented groups and various statistical adjustments is quite good.

### 9.2.2 The Height-by-Age Samples

One of the variables that we wanted to include in the regressions run on equation (1) was a measure of nutritional status. Measures of the mean consumption of various foods are so scarce for modern populations that it is unlikely that even the most assiduous search of archival documents would produce reliable annual estimates of the consumption of the principal nutrients for any significant number of individuals, certainly not for the whole span of time that we wish to consider. Moreover, since nutritional status depends not only on the amount of nutrients that are consumed but also on the claims against that consumption, a measure of food intake alone would be insufficient.

Fortunately, there is a class of measures that are relatively abundant, that reach far back into time, and that are sensitive to variations in nutritional status. Both laboratory experiments on animal populations and observational studies of human populations have led physiologists and nutritionists to conclude that anthropometric measurements are reliable indexes of the extent of malnutrition among the socioeconomic classes of particular populations. Measures of height and weight at given ages, the age at which growth of stature terminates, attained final height, and the rate of change in height or weight during the growing ages "reflect accurately the state of a nation's public health and the average nutritional status of its citizens" (Eveleth and Tanner 1976, p. 1). Consequently, these measures are now widely used by the World Health Organization and other agencies to assess the nutritional status of the population of underdeveloped nations.

The use of anthropometric measures as measures of nutrition rests on a well-defined pattern of human growth between childhood and maturity. The average annual increase in height (velocity) is greatest during infancy, falls sharply up to age 3, and then falls more slowly throughout the remaining preadolescent years. During adolescence, velocity rises sharply to a peak that is approximately one-half of the velocity achieved during infancy, then falls sharply and reaches zero at maturity. In girls the adolescent growth spurt begins about 2 years earlier, and the magnitude of the spurt is slightly smaller than in boys.

This growth pattern reflects the interaction of genetic, environmental, and socioeconomic factors during the period of growth. According to Eveleth and Tanner (1976, p. 222),

Such interaction may be complex. Two genotypes which produce the same adult height under optimal environmental circumstances may produce different heights under circumstances of privation. Thus, two children who would be the same height in a well-off community may not only both be smaller under poor economic conditions, but one may be significantly smaller than the other. . . . If a particular environmental stimulus is lacking at a time when it is essential for the child (times known as 'sensitive periods'), then the child's development may be shunted, as it were, from one line to another.

The relative importance of environmental and genetic factors in explaining individual variations in height is still a matter of some debate. For most well-fed contemporary populations, however, systematic genetic influences appear to have very little impact on mean heights. Thus, the mean heights of well-fed West Europeans, North American whites, and North American blacks are nearly identical. There are some ethnic groups in which mean adult heights of well-fed persons today do differ significantly from the West European or North American averages, presumably due to genetic factors. However, since such ethnic groups have represented a minuscule proportion of American and European populations, they are irrelevant to an explanation of the secular trends in mean adult heights in the United States and in the various European nations since 1750. Nor do they contribute significantly to differences, at various points of time, between the height means of the United States population and of the principal populations from which the United States population was drawn. In this connection, it should be noted that today the mean final heights of well-fed males in the main African nations from which the United States black population is derived also fall within the narrow band characteristic of Western Europe (Eveleth and Tanner 1976; Fogel et al. 1983).

Biologists, epidemiologists, and nutritionists have charted the effect of nutritional deficiencies on the human growth profile. Nutritional insults in utero are reflected in birth length and birthweight. Short periods of severe undernutrition or prolonged periods of moderate undernutrition merely delay the adolescent growth spurt; severe, prolonged undernutrition may diminish the typical growth-spurt pattern and contribute to substantial permanent stunting. If undernutrition is both prolonged and moderate, growth will continue beyond the age at which the growth of well-fed adolescents ceases. Hence, average length at birth and in early childhood, the average age at which the growth spurt peaks, the average age at which growth terminates, the mean height during adolescent ages, and the mean final height are all important indicators of mean nutritional status (Frisancho 1978; Tanner 1978; Kielmann et al. 1983). Any one of these factors can be used to identify secular trends in nutrition. The more of these measures that are available, the more precise the determination of the severity and duration of periods of malnutrition.

In considering the relationship between nutrition and height, it is important to keep in mind that height is a net rather than a gross measure of nutrition. Moreover, although changes in height during the growing years are sensitive to current levels of nutrition, mean heights reflect the accumulated past nutritional experience of an individual over all of his growing years including the fetal period. Thus, it follows that when the final heights are used to explain differences in adult mortality rates, they reveal the effect, not of adult levels of nutrition on adult mortality rates, but of nutritional levels during infancy, childhood, and adolescence on adult mortality rates. Similarly, when heights at age 8 are related to mortality at age 8, the exercise reveals the effect of nutritional experience up to that age.

The measure of net nutrition represented by mean heights depends on the intake of nutrients, on the amount of nutrients available for physical growth after the necessary claims of work and other activities (including recovery from infections), and on the efficiency with which the body converts nutrients into outputs. The body's ability to generate a surplus for growth will vary with such factors as age, the climate, the nature of the available food, clothing, and shelter, the disease environment, the intensity of work, and the quality of public sanitation. In other words, the same nutritional input can have varying effects on physical growth, depending on environmental conditions. Consequently, mean height corresponds quite well to the type of measure of nutritional status called for in section 9.1.4: it is a measure of the balance between food consumption and the claims on that consumption.

Some social scientists have suggested that height (or weight) at given ages should not be called measures of "nutritional status," but "generalized indexes of health" or "non-specific indicators of health status" (cf. Moseley and Chen 1983).[7] The definition of "nutritional status" that I have set forth here is not my own, but rather the definition employed by medical nutritionists, epidemiologists, and physiologists. It is an unfamiliar concept to most economists (and other social scientists) because we are not steeped in the medical literature. Moreover, "nutritional status" sounds too much like "diet" to most of us, although medical nutritionists and epidemiologists draw a sharp distinction between the two terms. To some social scientists the use of the term "nutritional status" seems to be a subtle way of supporting the oversimplified view that low levels of nutritional intake are the only sources of malnutrition, and so use of the term appears to give covert support to oversimplified theories of the relationship between diet and mortality.

Will the use of such alternative terms as "health" or "non-specific indicators of health status" avoid the problems? These terms have been advanced as though their meaning were unambiguous; yet as F. K. Taylor (1979) has pointed out, "health" is difficult to define rigorously. We can try to give it rigor by using available information on morbidity and mortality rates. Then "healthy" populations may be defined as populations having rates in these dimensions that fall within a "normal" range. The difficulty with this procedure is not only that reliable measures of mortality and, especially, of morbidity are often lacking; there is the more fundamental issue that "normal" ranges of morbidity and mortality vary so widely with time, place, and circumstances that epidemiologists often turn to anthropometric measures in order to determine what is "normal" in a given environment (Meredith 1970; Hytten and Leitch 1971; Goldstein 1976; Thomson and Billewicz 1976; Waterlow et al. 1977; Habicht et al. 1979; Naeye 1981; Raman 1981). So the mere substitution of one term for another, of "generalized indexes of health status" for "nutritional status," will not remove conceptual ambiguities or prevent oversimplified characteristics of the empirical relationships we seek to uncover.[8]

Quite the contrary, striking out on our own, without adequate attention to and connection with the extensive medical investigations on which we must base our own work, is far more likely to be misleading than acceptance of medical terminology that now seems strange or even questionable.[9] Long experience with the problems of the interrelationship between nutritional status and infectious diseases has led medical specialists to the conclusion that anthropometric measures are the best single index of the average nutritional status of a population and of the relationship between undernutrition and the outcome of a significant range of infections (Habicht et al. 1979). Both clinical studies and laboratory experiments have shown that body wasting, retardation in the rate of physical development, and stunting are usually caused by undernutrition during the developmental years, which reduces both the rate of cell accumulation and the size of cells (Winick and Brasel 1980). These findings do not, however, imply that inadequate nutrient intake is the primary source of undernutrition or that undernutrition can be remedied merely, or even primarily, by increasing nutritional intake, since the source of the undernutrition may be a disease which makes it impossible for the body to assimilate those nutrients which are ingested.

Moreover, both laboratory experiments on animal populations and field studies of human populations have identified a set of infections whose outcome is sensitive to the nutritional status of the population at risk. The most carefully controlled of these field studies has been underway in the Narangwal district of India for more than a decade (Kielmann et al. 1982, 1983; C. E. Taylor 1982). The Narangwal project has revealed that perinatal mortality is particularly sensitive to the nutritional status of mothers. Perinatal mortality rates were reduced by more than 40% when the diets of pregnant women were supplemented by various nutrients, particularly iron and folic acid. Public health measures, such as the immunization of mothers for neonatal tetanus and improved delivery procedures, also were effective, contributing about half as much to the reduction in perinatal mortality rates as did nutritional supplementation. Infant mortality during the balance of the first year and mortality between ages 1 and 3 were also reduced by both measures. Interestingly, public health measures were more effective than nutritional supplementation in curbing late infant mortality, and the two types of intervention were about equally effective in curbing mortality at ages 1–3. Both nutritional supplementation and public health measures had marked effects on height and weight at given ages, and deviations from the 50th percentile of prevailing standards for height and weight were strongly correlated with death rates. Whatever the nature of the infections to which they were exposed, children whose diets were supplemented grew more rapidly up to age 3 (the final age of the test) than children in the control group.

In other words, improvements in nutritional status, whether the consequence of nutritional supplementation (which enables the body to resist infections) or medical intervention (which reduces the virulence of infections) were associated with reductions in morbidity and mortality rates. However, these associations are not identical or even symmetrical. Increases in nutritional intake and medical or public health measures often have different effects on particular diseases (and these effects vary with different stages in the life cycle) as well as on the pattern of human growth. For the range of issues that we are exploring it is particularly important to stress that every infection affects nutritional status; the survivors of an infection suffer a deprivation of nutrients required for growth which slows down the rate of cell accumulation and reduces cell mass (Winick and Brasel 1980). It does not follow, however, that improvements in nutritional status necessarily reduce morbidity and mortality rates. Not all infections are nutritionally sensitive, and the body's capacity to resist a nutritionally sensitive infection may be inconsequential if the pathogen is sufficiently virulent. In other words, nutritional status is likely to be "a determining factor" in the outcome of an infection when that infection is both nutritionally sensitive and of an intermediate degree of virulence (*Journal of Interdisciplinary History* 1983, p. 506). Physiologists have also identified the "mechanisms responsible for the increased number and severity of infections in the malnourished host" (Feigin 1981, p. 18).

Furthermore, although mean height is a good measure of nutritional status, it does not by itself indicate whether fluctuations in net nutrition are due to fluctuations in the consumption of food, in the claims on the food intake, or in the efficiency with which food is converted into outputs. Such decomposition is possible because of the asymmetries to which I have referred. Although both infection and inadequate nutritional intake retard the process of growth, they do not do so in precisely the same way. Because the body draws more heavily on nutritional stores when it is fighting an infection than when it is not, an infection may cause growth to cease during a period of infection. However, if a child is normally well fed, and if there is sufficient time between infectious episodes, there will usually be full catch-up in growth when an infection ceases. Normal, well-fed children do not grow at equal daily rates but alternate periods of growth well in excess of the daily average with periods of little or no growth, as disease and other claims on nutritional intake wax and wane. In well-fed children with sufficient time between infectious episodes these lacunae in growth have no effect on final heights, because of full and rapid catch-up, but in malnourished children they contribute to permanent stunting (Fogel et al. 1983).

The more data which are available on heights at each age, the more numerous and disaggregated the links between age- and disease-specific death rates, not only with anthropometric data, but with a variety of other socioeconomic variables, the more complete the decomposition of the determinants of the decline in mortality will be, including the determinants of nutritional status. It is not easy to construct a database as varied and abundant as I have indicated, but the objective is not out of reach. Some initial stabs at decomposition with the data currently in hand are undertaken for a few specific cases that are considered in sections 9.3.2, 9.4.2, 9.4.3, and 9.4.4.

The collection of a modest sample of height-by-age data was launched in early 1978 as an adjunct of the mortality project in order to produce a measure that could be employed in equation (1). However, it quickly became apparent that this body of evidence was filled with so much useful information on economic behavior that the scope of the sampling effort was enlarged and the work on this body of evidence became the foundation for a new NBER project called "Secular Trends in Nutrition, Labor Welfare and Labor Productivity," which is also cosponsored by the Center for Population Economics.

The nutrition project currently involves a set of 16 samples (see table 9.6) containing information on height by age, weight, and various socioeconomic variables. The samples, which cover the period from 1750 through 1937, reveal aspects of physical development in the United States, Trinidad, Great Britain, Austro-Hungary, and Sweden. Ten of the samples were drawn from military records and hence pertain to males of military age. One of the British samples is composed of poor teen-age boys taken in by the Marine Society, a charitable organization, from 1750 to 1910; another is composed of upper-class boys admitted to Sandhurst. Three of the samples contain information on both sexes from infancy to old age. One sample is of birthweights and lengths in Philadelphia from the 1840s to the end of the 1870s. The data in these samples are being linked with additional data obtained from probate records, tax lists, pension records, and manuscript schedules of censuses. Such linking increases both the range of variables that can be brought into the analysis and the complexity of the interrelationship between height, nutritional status, and economic and social behavior that we can investigate. As of mid-1984, information had been collected on about 400,000 individuals, which is about 70% of the anticipated final number.

Much of our work on the height data between 1977 and 1982 dealt with problems of estimating and correcting biases that arose from using military records to estimate the mean height of the population from which the recruits were drawn. These biases fall into three categories. First, there are the self-selection biases that are peculiar to volunteer armies. Then there are a variety of more general measurement biases, some relating to the accuracy of the age information and others to the accuracy of the height information. Finally, there is the bias that arises because military organizations may have height limits. Most frequently these organizational restrictions produced a jagged truncation of the left tail of the height distribution, but right-tail truncation is also encountered. Since we have published several papers dealing with the

**Table 9.6    The Principal Samples in the Nutrition Project**

| Title of Samples | Number of Observations Originally Planned | Number of Observations Currently on Tape | Main Categories of Information Included | References |
|---|---|---|---|---|
| **Civil War Samples:** | | | | |
| 1. Union army, whites | 40,000 | 53,000 | Height, age, mortality, cause of death, various socioeconomic characteristics; covers mainly ages 18–45 | Margo and Steckel (1983) |
| 2. Union army, blacks | 5,000 | 10,000 | Same as 1, plus complexion | Margo and Steckel (1982) |
| 3. Amnesty records, white southern males | 5,000 | 5,000 | Height, age, place of residence, occupation, ages 12–80 | Steckel (1982a) |
| 4. Union army, rejects | 5,000 | 5,000 | Same as 1 (except mortality information) plus reason for rejection | Steckel (1984b) |
| **Other U.S. Samples:** | | | | |
| 5. Regular U.S. army, 1790–1910 | 100,000 | 43,000 | Same as 1 | |
| 6. Ohio National Guard, 1870–1925 | 13,000 | 13,000 | Height, age, birthplace, residence, occupation, marital status, mainly ages 18–49 | Steckel (1982b) |
| 7. Coastwise manifests, 1807–62 | 75,000 | 51,000 | Height, age, color, sex, dates, and points of embarkation and arrival; covers all ages of both males and females | Margo and Steckel (1982) |
| 8. Colonial muster rolls, 1750–83 | 20,000 | 14,000 | Same as 1, except no mortality information | Sokoloff and Villaflor (1982) |

| No. | Sample | | | Description | Source |
|---|---|---|---|---|---|
| 9. | Philadelphia Alms House, 1847–77 | 4,500 | 3,000 | Birthweight and birthlength, gestational age, birth order, characteristics of labor, mortality of child and mother during hospital stay, sex of child, race, characteristics of mother (age, ethnicity, residence, marital status, health status [e.g., venereal disease, drunkenness]) | Goldin and Margo (1984) |
| 10. | Cost of living surveys, 1934–77 | 3,000 | 3,000 | Height for all family members by age, sex, and various socioeconomic characteristics including occupation, wages, days ill, education, and family wealth | Goldin (1979) |
| 11. | Trinidad, 1813–34 | 30,000 | 25,000 | Height, age, color, births, deaths, and various other socioeconomic variables for all ages and both sexes | Friedman (1982) |
| **British Samples:** | | | | | |
| 12. | Marine Society, 1750–1910 | | 50,000 | Height, age, and various socioeconomic characteristics including occupations of fathers and sons, literacy and vaccination (or inoculation); ages mainly 13–17 | Floud and Wachter (1982) |
| 13. | Sandhurst boys, 1750–1910 | 11,000 | 11,000 | Height by age, date of recruitment, fees paid | Floud (1983a) |
| 14. | Military recruitment records, 1750–1910 | 130,000 | 130,000 | Same as 11, except for father's occupation | |
| **Other European Samples:** | | | | | |
| 15. | Swedish conscript rolls, 1750–1910 | 30,000 | 30,000 | Height by age, years of service, and various other socioeconomic characteristics for males | Sandberg and Steckel (1979) |
| 16. | Hapsburg monarchy, 1720–1920 | 75,000 | 19,000 | Height by age, occupation, residence, mainly ages 19–50 | Komlos (1984) |

techniques developed for coping with these problems (Trussell and Bloom 1979; Wachter 1981; Wachter and Trussell 1982; Fogel et al. 1982, 1983; Floud 1983a; Floud and Wachter 1983; Trussell and Wachter 1984), I will not attempt to describe them here but merely state that both simulation techniques and practical experience have demonstrated the effectiveness of the procedures.

## 9.3    Some Preliminary Findings on the Relation between Improvements in Nutritional Status and the Decline in Mortality

At present we have three pieces of evidence linking mortality rates with nutritional status (as measured by height). Before presenting these findings, I wish to reemphasize that they are provisional. Although the work on the height data is fairly advanced, we are still in the pilot phase of the drawing of the genealogical sample. The pilot sample is still relatively small, lacking in the geographical diversity we desire, especially before 1750, and only partly linked to the economic, medical, and social information that we will eventually have. Nevertheless, there are several suggestive findings that have arisen out of these data sets, and which appear to be sufficiently robust to warrant their presentation.

### 9.3.1    The Secular Trends in the Height and in the Life Expectancy of United States White Males, 1700–1930

Figure 9.1 compares the time series that we have developed so far in both the height and the life expectancy of United States white males. Before considering this diagram some characteristics of the series and their limitations should be kept in mind. First, the secular trend in height is controlled for shifts in the distribution of the region of birth, of occupation, and several other relevant characteristics while the life-expectancy series is not, but merely gives the mean life expectancy at age 10 of all of the individuals at risk during each period.[10] Second, Southerners are underrepresented in both the height and the life-expectancy series. The correction of these deficiencies, which we hope to make in the near future, will probably have a greater effect on the $e_{10}$ series than on the height series, especially before approximately 1750.[11]

It is possible to estimate tentatively the effect of the mortality correction by making use of Levy's (1984) estimates of the life expectancy of Maryland legislators. The value of $e_{10}$ estimated from his data for 1700–1749 and 1750–99 are shown in the lower portion of the diagram.[12] Also shown is the effect of averaging his observations and those in the genealogical sample, using weights that correct for the undercount of Southerners in the genealogical sample.[13] As can be seen, the impact of the correction will be greatest before 1750, partly because the dif-

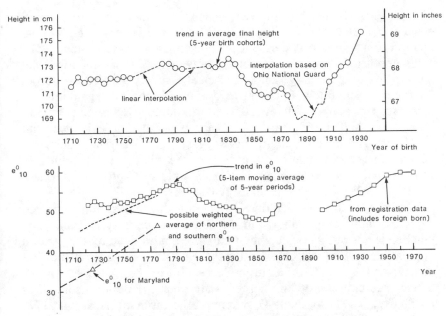

**Fig. 9.1**    A comparison between the trend in the mean final height of native-born white males and the trend in their life expectancy at age 10 ($e^o_{10}$) (height by birth cohort; $e^o_{10}$ by period).

ferential in mortality between the regions closed rapidly during the first half of the eighteenth century and partly because the current representation of the South in the sample improves considerably after 1750. Thus, I expect a more representative sample to show a more rapid rise in $e_{10}$ between 1700 and 1750. The beginning of the peak may be shifted by one or two decades and the level of the peak may be lowered slightly.

These corrections will not change the suggestive and unexpected similarities in the two series. Both series appear to be rising during most of the eighteenth century, attaining both substantially greater heights and life expectations than prevailed in England during the same period (Floud 1985a). Life expectancy began to decline during the 1790s and continued to do so for about half a century. There may have been a slight decline in the heights of cohorts born between 1785 and 1820, but the sharp decline, which probably lasted about half a century, began with cohorts born around 1830. A new rise in heights, the one with which we have long been familiar, probably began with cohorts born during the last decade of the nineteenth century and continued for about 60 years.[14]

We do not, at present, have data on final heights in America for cohorts born before 1710, but the relatively flat profile between around 1710 and around 1750 and the tall stature compared with the English in 1750 suggests that heights were probably rising rapidly for several decades before our series begins. This inference is supported by data on food consumption in Massachusetts discovered by McMahon (1981). Wills deposited in Middlesex county between 1654 and 1830 indicate a sharp rise in the average amount of meat annually allotted to widows for their consumption. Between 1675 and 1750 the average allotment increased from approximately 80 to approximately 168 pounds per annum: about half the increase took place by 1710. The evidence both on stature and on food allotments suggests that Americans achieved an average level of meat consumption by the middle of the eighteenth century that was not achieved in Europe until well into the twentieth century (McMahon 1981; Holmes 1907; Fogel 1986).[15]

Figure 9.1 and table 9.7 reveal not only that Americans achieved modern heights by the middle of the eighteenth century, but that they reached levels of life expectancy that were not attained by the general population of England or even by the British peerage until the first quarter of the twentieth century. Correction of the $e_{10}$ series for the underrepresentation of Southerners may push the period estimate of $e_{10}$ in around 1725 to about 47 years and the estimate for around 1775 to about 54 years, but these would still be remarkably high values for $e_{10}$. Although a more refined downward adjustment will eventually need to be made to obtain a reliable national average, there is at present no obvious reason for believing that the figures shown were not representative of the Northeast.

The early attainment of modern stature and relatively long life expectancy is surprising, and for that reason alone calls for further verification. Yet in light of the evidence that has accumulated in recent years it is by no means unreasonable. By the second quarter of the eighteenth century, Americans had achieved diets that were remarkably nutritious by European standards, and particularly rich in protein. The American population was low in density, probably below the threshold needed to sustain major epidemics of such diseases as smallpox. The low density probably also reduced exposure to the crowd diseases of the nineteenth century that took a heavy toll of life in both England and America. This is not to say that there were no epidemics in America between 1725 and 1800, but with the exception of a few port cities, outbreaks of epidemic diseases appear to have been much milder than in England.

The discovery of the cycling in both height and $e_{10}$, especially of the amplitude of the movements, is so new and so surprising that many issues will have to be pursued before doubts about the discovery can be set aside. Not least of the tasks is the need to enlarge the genealogical sample and to investigate characteristics that might be inducing spurious cycles or exaggerating the amplitude of the cycles in the uncon-

Table 9.7      **A Comparison among the Cohort Life Expectations for Native-Born United States White Males, British Peers, and the English Population, 1700–1925**

| Birth Cohort (century and quarter) | (1) England and Wales (both sexes) $e_0$ | (2) British Peerage (males) $e_0$ | (3) British Peerage (males) $e_{10}$ | (4) United States Native-Born Whites (males) $e_{10}$ |
|---|---|---|---|---|
| 18th: | | | | |
| I | 35.1 | 34.9 | 39.4 | 50.3 |
| II | 33.8 | 38.8 | 44.4 | 55.5 |
| III | 36.3 | 44.6 | 46.3 | 55.8 |
| IV | 37.0 | 46.9 | 46.1 | 51.9 |
| | | $e_{10}$ (Males) | | |
| 19th: | | | | |
| I | | 49.3 | 48.3 | 52.3 |
| II | 41.5   47.1 | 52.2 | 49.5 | 48.9 |
| III | 44.6   50.6 | 54.7 | 51.4 | 55.3 |
| IV | | 53.7 | 47.4 | |
| 20th: | | | | |
| I | | 60.1 | 54.0 | 56.9 |

*Sources:* Column 1: table 9.2, above. The two observations of $e_{10}$ (males) for 19–II and 19–III were computed from Case et al. 1962 in the manner described in table 9.2. *Columns 2 and 3:* Hollingsworth 1977, p. 328. *Column 4:* The genealogical sample (N = 4,210) for all observations except 20–I, which is derived from United States registration data in the sources listed in appendix A and from United States National Center for Health Statistics 1983. The $_nQ_x$ values for late ages reached after 1980 were projections of the entries in the 1980 life table using the rate of decline in age-specific death rates obtained from medical records during 1968–78 and reported in Wilkin (1981). The entry for 20–I is the average of $e_{10}$ for cohorts born in 1900, 1910, and 1920. This entry includes the foreign born, while all the other entries in col. 4 do not. Consequently, a comparison between 19–III and 20–I may understate the extent of the improvement in $e_{10}$ for cohorts born in the United States during the first quarter of the twentieth century.

trolled trend. In this paper, however, it is the hitherto unsuspected pattern in the height series and its strong correlation with the mortality series that I want to emphasize.

### 9.3.2   Slaves, Poor London Boys, and Adult English Workers

The second piece of evidence linking mortality and nutritional status comes from data on slaves, on poor London boys, and on a more typical cross-section of English workers. Under abolitionist pressures the British colonial office conducted two registrations of slaves in Trinidad within a 20-month period, the first in 1813 and the second in 1815. Because the aim of the registrations was to prevent smuggling of slaves, physical characteristics, including height, were recorded. The second registration also included information on the disposition of all the slaves who were registered in 1813. Friedman (1982) was the first to investigate the differences between the height of the slaves who died and those who survived. The difference is evident in table 9.8, which presents the heights of surviving and nonsurviving males under age 26. The extent of the difference is more apparent in a regression format. Table 9.9 shows that Trinidad-born males under age 26 who died between 1813 and 1815 were 1.2 inches shorter than those who survived. The corresponding figure for females is 0.9 inches.

Table 9.8 shows not only that nonsurvivors were shorter than survivors, but that even the survivors were exceedingly short by modern standards. Figure 9.2 indicates how bad their nutritional status was. In this diagram the heights of Trinidad-born male slaves, at ages from

**Table 9.8**    Mean Heights by Age and Mortality, 1813–15, Trinidad-Born Males

|      | Survivors | | | Nonsurvivors | | |
|------|--------|------|-----|--------|------|-----|
| Age  | Height | S.D. | N   | Height | S.D. | N   |
| 0    | 23.9   | 3.29 | 118 | 22.2   | 3.44 | 26  |
| 1    | 26.6   | 3.38 | 159 | 26.4   | 2.91 | 30  |
| 2    | 29.9   | 3.22 | 131 | 28.1   | 2.96 | 16  |
| 3    | 33.8   | 3.09 | 177 | 33.1   | 3.75 | 11  |
| 4    | 36.2   | 4.09 | 158 | 36.7   | 2.90 | 11  |
| 5    | 38.6   | 3.39 | 128 | 37.0   | 4.38 | 8   |
| 6    | 41.2   | 3.72 | 134 | 39.9   | 2.27 | 7   |
| 7    | 43.0   | 3.22 | 119 | 43.2   | 4.09 | 5   |
| 8    | 44.5   | 3.95 | 104 | 45.0   | 3.16 | 5   |
| 9    | 46.8   | 2.70 | 67  | 44.5   | 3.54 | 2   |
| 10   | 49.7   | 3.75 | 110 | 42.0   | —    | 1   |
| 11   | 49.9   | 3.25 | 70  | —      | —    | 0   |
| 12   | 52.3   | 2.75 | 84  | 54.0   | —    | 1   |
| 13   | 52.7   | 3.34 | 60  | 52.0   | —    | 1   |
| 14   | 56.1   | 3.96 | 68  | 59.5   | 0.71 | 2   |
| 15   | 58.3   | 3.86 | 59  | 60.0   | —    | 1   |
| 16   | 59.4   | 2.99 | 43  | 59.0   | 1.41 | 2   |
| 17   | 61.6   | 4.05 | 30  | —      | —    | 0   |
| 18   | 62.5   | 3.05 | 50  | 61.5   | 2.12 | 2   |
| 19   | 63.7   | 2.87 | 18  | —      | —    | 0   |
| 20   | 64.6   | 3.29 | 48  | 64.0   | 5.66 | 2   |
| 21   | 64.8   | 2.17 | 16  | —      | —    | 0   |
| 22   | 65.0   | 3.07 | 40  | —      | —    | 0   |
| 23   | 66.3   | 2.69 | 9   | —      | —    | 0   |
| 24   | 65.3   | 2.99 | 20  | —      | —    | 0   |
| 25   | 65.2   | 3.00 | 33  | 65.0   | —    | 1   |

*Source:* Friedman 1982. Age and height are those recorded in 1813. Owing to a transcription error the standard deviations of nonsurvivors were misreported in the original source. Those shown here, supplied by Friedman, are the correct ones.

**Table 9.9    Height Regression for Slaves under Age 26, Trinidad-Born (Dependent Variable = Slave's Height)**

| Variable | Males | | | Females | | |
|---|---|---|---|---|---|---|
| | Mean | Coefficient | t Ratio | Mean | Coefficient | t Ratio |
| Intercept | — | 9.2 | 4.64 | — | 15.8 | 7.77 |
| Age | 6.7374 | 5.0927 | 27.05 | 6.8528 | 4.9525 | 26.05 |
| Age$^2$ | 77.4127 | −0.4148 | −11.71 | 81.0743 | −0.3533 | −9.93 |
| Age$^3$ | 1,155.665 | 0.0227 | 9.50 | 1,243.841 | 0.0177 | 7.47 |
| Age$^4$ | 20,048.90 | −0.0005 | −8.90 | 22,013.99 | −0.0004 | −7.13 |
| Number of slaves on the unit | 75.6142 | 0.0054 | 0.95 | 76.8831 | 0.0006 | 0.10 |
| Number of slaves$^2$ | 9,109.826 | 0.000016 | 0.63 | 9,349.246 | 0.000034 | 1.34 |
| Sugar unit | 0.6975 | −0.1437 | −0.42 | 0.6722 | 0.1958 | 0.56 |
| Sugar × number of slaves | 63.9059 | −0.0032 | −0.78 | 62.8478 | −0.0031 | −0.80 |
| Cotton unit | 0.04796 | −0.0918 | −0.22 | 0.0577 | 0.4115 | 1.02 |
| Light child of dark mother | 0.0496 | 0.9285 | 2.41 | 0.0432 | −0.5840 | −1.38 |
| Creole mother | 0.2436 | 2.9238 | 0.74 | 0.2803 | −8.5058 | −2.33 |
| Creole mother × her height | 15.0205 | −0.0561 | −0.87 | 17.1799 | 0.1420 | 2.38 |
| Crude death rate on unit | 0.0399 | −4.5974 | −1.85 | 0.0373 | −3.1587 | −1.12 |
| Mother's height | 60.8135 | 0.1983 | 6.13 | 60.7987 | 0.0830 | 2.49 |
| Died 1813–15 | 0.0652 | −1.1687 | −3.33 | 0.0812 | −0.8538 | −2.61 |
| Mean of dependent variable | 40.3 | | | 40.4 | | |
| $R^2$ | | 0.92 | | | 0.91 | |
| F-ratio | | 1,358.35 | | | 1,296.09 | |
| Degrees of freedom | | 1749 | | | 1857 | |

Source: Friedman 1982.

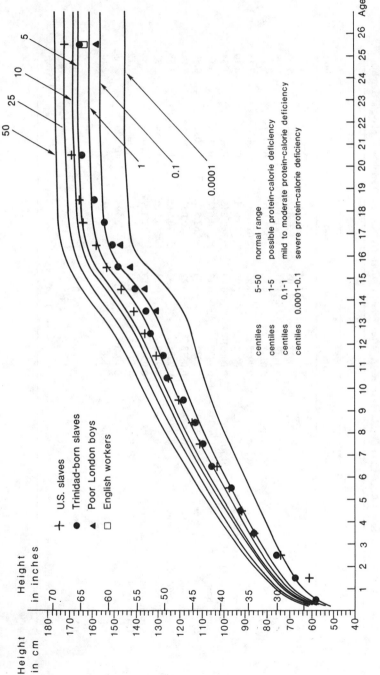

**Fig. 9.2**  The extent to which mean heights of male slaves, poor London boys, and English workers deviated from the modern height standard.

infancy to maturity, are superimposed on a set of curves which describe the current British standard for assessing the adequacy of physical development. The curve marked "50th centile" gives the average height at each age among generally well-nourished persons in Great Britain today. Also shown on the diagram are the heights of United States male slaves (which come from documents designed to prevent smuggling of slaves into the United States), the height of poor adolescent boys in London during the last half of the eighteenth century, and the height of more typical English workers at maturity about 1800.

Figure 9.2 shows that during early childhood slaves in both Trinidad and the United States were exceedingly malnourished. The figures for ages 0.5 and 1.5 are probably biased downward because the legs of the children were not fully stretched out when they were measured. But at ages 2.5 and 3.5 the children were walking and would have been measured in a standing position. Yet they were still exceedingly short by modern standards, falling at or below the 0.1 percentile. Such poor development is indicative of kwashiorkor and other diseases caused by severe protein-calorie malnutrition (PCM). Although the gap with modern height standards was reduced after age 3, it remained in a range suggesting at least mild to moderate PCM through age 8. Between ages 10 and 17 the growth patterns of United States and Trinidad slaves diverged, with the heights of United States slaves climbing into the normal range, while the heights of Trinidad slaves fluctuated in the range of moderate to severe PCM. By the mid-twenties, United States slaves were well into the normal range and Trinidad-born slaves were borderline normal. Thus, it appears that the diet that United States slaves received when they began working at adult tasks was good enough not only to sustain their work effort but to permit a substantial degree of catch-up growth as well. In the case of Trinidad slaves, however, the diet appears to have been inadequate to permit the same degree of catch-up, given the character of the physical environment.

Figure 9.2 suggests that nutritional deficiencies in utero and in early childhood, rather than the overwork or underfeeding of adults, were the main cause of the relatively high death rate of United States slaves. This possibility is supported by available data on the death rates. Figure 9.3 indicates that it was excess death rates of slave children under 5 that accounted for the difference between the overall death rates of United States slaves and United States whites during the late antebellum era. Moreover, the fact that United States slaves and whites had similar life expectancies after age 20 suggests that it was not the general virulence of the disease environment but conditions specific to young children. Campbell's (1984) examination of a large cotton plantation in Georgia revealed a correlation between the infant death rate and the intensity with which planters worked pregnant women. Steckel (1984a)

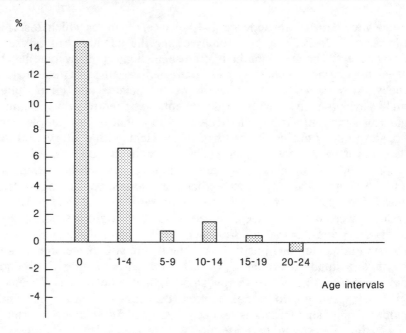

**Fig. 9.3**        The difference between age-specific death rates of U.S. slaves and whites, estimated for the late antebellum Era (slave death rate minus white death rate). *Sources:* Haines and Avery, 1980; Steckel, 1984a; Fogel, 1986.

has also found evidence that overwork of pregnant women increased the stillbirth and neonatal death rates. His examination of the monthly pattern of a sample of such deaths indicated that these rates were highest among the babies of women whose first trimester coincided with the planting season and who were in their third trimester when the peak period of harvesting occurred.

The small heights at ages 2.5 and 3.5 suggest not only that fetal malnutrition was prevalent but that chronic undernourishment was widespread during infancy and early childhood. Breastfeeding of slave babies was common throughout the South, but its average duration is uncertain. On some of the larger plantations most of the infants may have been at least partially weaned within 3 or 4 months. Plantation records which describe the diets of weaned infants and young children suggest that it was ample in calories but low in protein. Gruels and porridges, usually made with cornmeal and sometimes containing milk, were common fare. After age 3 these were supplemented to some extent by vegetable soups more likely to contain lard than meat, potatoes, molasses, grits, hominy, and cornbread. These more balanced diets contributed to catch-up growth between ages 3 and 8, although even the 8-year-olds were still quite short by modern standards (Fogel 1986).

Both the available descriptions of the diets of young children and the small stature of children, especially those under age 3, are consistent with the evidence on protein deficiency culled from the antebellum medical reports by Kiple and King (1981). They argue that frequent descriptions of the "glistening fat and corpulent paunches" of young children, the frequent listing of "dropsy" and "swelling" as a cause of death, and the concern of Southern physicians with "the distention of slave children's stomachs," suggest that kwashiorkor or prekwashiorkor was prevalent.

In Trinidad as in the United States the exceedingly small stature of slaves under 3 years suggests intrauterine malnutrition of fetuses. But in the case of Trinidad consumption of alcohol during pregnancy, which retards fetal development and induces a number of other abnormalities that are referred to as the Fetal Alcohol Syndrome, may have been a complicating factor. On sugar plantations liberal rations of rum were usually provided to slaves, especially during harvest time. Thus, although the absence of catch-up growth before age 3 may indicate that the early childhood diet was very low in protein, it could also reflect the residual effect of Fetal Alcohol Syndrome. However, since Trinidad slaves had a weaker adolescent growth spurt and a lower final height than United States slaves, the nutrients available for adolescent growth were obviously less in Trinidad than in the slave South. Not only was the nutrient intake of Trinidad slaves relatively low, but the more virulent disease environment of Trinidad undoubtedly exercised relatively greater claims against that intake. It is doubtful that adult slaves in Trinidad could have worked harder than United States slaves; the nutrient value of their diet would not permit it (Sheridan 1985). But in combination, the claims of work and disease and the dysfunctions caused by alcohol appear to have left Trinidad slaves with a lower net nutrition to sustain an adolescent growth spurt than United States slaves.

There are no measurements of the stature of the poor London boys during infancy or early childhood, but their heights between ages 13 and 16 are 1 to 2 inches less than those of Trinidad-born slaves of the same ages (Floud and Wachter 1982). Nor is it likely that much of this gap was made up during the late years of adolescence. These boys appear to have been drawn from the poorest section of the English working class—that one-fifth of English families that were unemployed or at best partially employed. They lived in the most crowded and virulent slums of London, and many were orphans or for other reasons lived with guardians (Floud and Wachter 1982). Evidence that the nutritional status of most English workers was superior to that of the poor London boys is also presented in figure 9.2, which shows the mean final height of the pool of men from which the recruits into the Royal Marines were drawn about 1800. Although this pool included

Londoners, most were residents of the southern and northern counties and of the Midlands. Artisans and craftsmen from both rural and urban areas were well represented in the ranks of the Royal Marines, and so were common laborers from both rural and urban areas. Analysis of this broad cross section indicates that the mean height of the English working class as a whole near the beginning of the nineteenth century was about 64.5 inches (Floud 1985a).

Tanner (1982) has estimated that the height of poor London boys at maturity was just 62 inches, about 3 inches below the adult height of Trinidad slaves. It thus appears likely that some combination of intra-uterine malnutrition, poor weaning diet, and an adolescent diet inadequate to sustain catch-up growth (under the conditions of their environment) stunted the physical development of these poor London boys between 1750 and 1800. When Tanner assessed this evidence (1981, p. 158) he said that such short stature, which persisted into adulthood without an acute retardation of the teenage growth spurt, probably stemmed from conditions in utero and in early childhood: "Severe malnutrition of the pregnant mother followed by chronic and severe undernutrition of the infant could cause this result. More likely still is a low birthweight and/or a low weight gain in infancy caused by injurious substances breathed or eaten by the pregnant mother and the newborn child." The substances to which he referred included opium, laudanum, and morphia, which were the ingredients of popular patent medicines for children that are thought to have been widely used by mothers, unaware of their contents, to keep their children quiet while they worked at home or in factories (Pinchbeck and Hewitt 1969; Berridge and Edwards 1981).

Although malnutrition in utero and in early childhood may contribute to severe permanent stunting, it should not be assumed that these early experiences rigidly determine the entire pattern of physical growth. Such an inference is contradicted by the information in figure 9.2. Although both the Trinidad and the United States slaves were severely stunted in early life, their development patterns diverged markedly after age 10. Since the distribution of tribal origins of the United States and Trinidad slaves was similar, differences in their adolescent growth patterns were due principally to environmental rather than genetic factors (Steckel 1984a; Fogel 1986). Correlations between indicators of early childhood experience and later-life morbidity and mortality rates (Forsdahl 1977; Marmot et al. 1984) may thus reflect not so much the long reach of these childhood experiences as the normally strong correlations between childhood and later-life experiences, correlations that appear to have broken down in the case of American slaves. Thus it appears that even severe malnourishment in utero and in early childhood may be largely offset by improved conditions during adolescence.

### 9.3.3 Evidence from Regressions between Height and Mortality

Table 9.9 revealed a strong correlation between height and mortality in Trinidad. This relationship has been investigated further by John (1984), who ran a series of logit regressions relating the probability of dying between 1813 and 1815 to a number of variables including height. Among adults and children under age 15, the elasticity of the death for believing that the effect of height (or length) on mortality rates would be greatest for infants, especially neonates, although this proposition cannot be tested against the Trinidad sample because both infants and infant deaths were undercounted by margins that render them of little use.

Floud (1983b, 1985b) has assembled data for eight European nations over the years from 1880 to 1970 which permit an examination of the relationship between adult male height and mortality.[17] Equations (2) and (3) present the results of regressions which related both the crude death rates and infant mortality rates to height (numbers in parentheses are $t$-values):

(2)
$$\hat{C} = 30.7877 - 5.3851\hat{H} - 0.0363\hat{Y} - 0.006647T$$
$$(5.292)\ (-4.534)\ (-0.382)\ (-4.040)$$
$$\bar{R}^2 = .85;\ N = 64$$

(3)
$$\hat{I} = 88.9781 - 15.9106\hat{H} - 0.3889\hat{Y} - 0.00837T$$
$$(12.327)\ (-10.797)\ (-3.294)\ (-4.213)$$
$$\bar{R}^2 = .96;\ N = 64$$

where

$C$ = the crude death rate per thousand
$I$ = the infant mortality rate per thousand
$H$ = adult male height measured in centimeters
$Y$ = per capita income measured in United States dollars of 1970
$T$ = time (year 1 = 1880)
$\hat{}$ = a hat over a variable indicates the natural logarithm of that variable

From these equations it can be seen that a 1% increase in height was associated with a change in infant mortality rates that was three times as large as the corresponding change in crude mortality rates. In both equations height has an independent effect on mortality rates, even after controlling for per capita income and time. Indeed, the addition of time to these regressions had virtually no effect on the coefficients of height, although it reduced the coefficient on per capita income in equation (2) by more than half, and in equation (1) it made the coefficient of per capita income statistically insignificant. Equation (2) implies that the rise in heights accounted for 39% of the decline in the infant mortality rate and per capita income accounted for another 27%, leaving only about 33% attributable to the unknown factors which are measured by time.[18]

There is a question regarding the interpretation that should be placed on the coefficients of height and per capita income when both are included in the regression. Steckel's (1983) analysis suggests that when per capita income is held constant, height becomes a proxy for the degree of inequality in the income distribution. His regression on adult height implies that a 1% change in the Gini ratio (holding the level of income constant) had about four times as large an effect on mean heights as a 1% change in the level of per capita income (holding the Gini ratio constant).

Equations (2) and (3) suggest that height and income together were only about half as important in explaining the decline in the crude death rate between 1880 and 1970 as in explaining the decline in infant death rates in the eight countries covered by these equations. Even this last statement tends to exaggerate the effect of improvements in income and nutrition on the decline in adult mortality rates since infant death rates represent as much as a quarter of the crude death rate in high-mortality regimens such as those which existed in Europe during the nineteenth century. Of course, the crude death rate is a poor proxy for life expectancy since it is so sensitive to variations in age structure. Nevertheless, when considered in conjunction with the Trinidad regressions, equations (2) and (3) add to the evidence that the mortality rates of infants and and very young children are more sensitive to nutritional status than the mortality rates of adolescents and adults.[19]

## 9.4  Discussion

In combination, the several pieces of evidence make a fairly strong case for the view that nutritional status had a significant impact on mortality rates. Yet even those scholars who are skeptical of nutritional arguments acknowledge that nutrition is a relevant consideration. The real issues are the size of the nutritional contribution to the long-term decline in mortality and the locus of its impact. Much work remains before it will be possible to provide an adequate resolution of these issues. But I believe that a provisional estimate of the nutritional contribution is possible and might be useful.

### 9.4.1  A Provisional Estimate of Improvements in Nutritional Status on the Long-Term Decline in Mortality

I will first estimate the impact of improvements in nutritional status on noninfants. Because of the absence of data a more indirect approach is required for infants. This illustrative calculation will be applied to the British case.

Let us begin by supposing that the nutrition of working-class English males about 1800 had been improved to the point that they were able to achieve modern stature. Then their mean final height would have increased from 64.5 to 69.5 inches, which is an increase of 7.75%.[20] How much impact would such an improvement in nutritional status have had on mortality? As previously noted, the Trinidad sample revealed that the elasticity of the death rate of non-infants with respect to height is about −1.4. Hence, a 7.75% increase in the final height of males would have reduced the non-infant death rate by about 11% (−1.4 × 7.75 = −10.85).

The Trinidad registrations undercounted mortality so badly that they cannot be used to estimate reliably the elasticity of infant mortality with respect to height. We can circumvent this problem by using the schedule that relates the neonatal death rates to birthweight.[21] The probability of dying at given birthweights is very high at weights below 2501 grams (5.5 pounds). The schedule which relates the probability of dying to birthweight is stable below 2501 grams. It varies little from one socioeconomic group to another within a nation or even across nations. This stability is evident in figure 9.4.[22]

Mean birthweights vary greatly with the nutritional status of populations (Eveleth and Tanner 1976; WHO 1980). This point is illustrated in figure 9.5. The lines on this graph are normal approximations of the frequency distributions of birthweights.[23] Birthweight is represented on the vertical axis, and the horizontal axis represents $z$-scores (deviations of birthweight from the mean measured in units of the standard

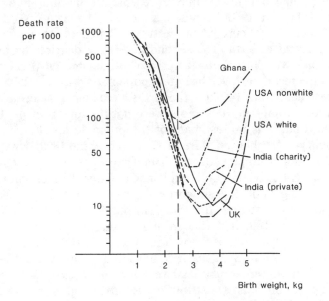

**Fig. 9.4**    Perinatal mortality by birth weight in Ghana, India, U.K., and United States. *Source:* Hytten and Leitch, *Physiology of Human Pregnancy* 2d ed.) p. 324.

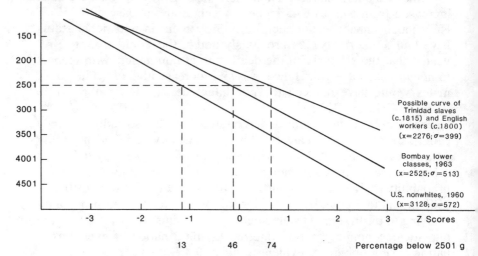

Grams

Possible curve of
Trinidad slaves
(c.1815) and English
workers (c.1800)
(x=2276; σ=399)

Bombay lower
classes, 1963
(x=2525; σ=513)

U.S. nonwhites, 1960
(x=3128; σ=572)

Z Scores

13    46    74    Percentage below 2501 g

**Fig. 9.5**    The percentage of male births with weights below 2,501 grams
in two modern populations and the possible percentage among
Trinidad slaves and English workers during the early nineteenth century.

deviation). Hence, the cumulative frequency distribution is represented
by a straight line. The lowest line represents the distribution of United
States nonwhites in 1960. They had a mean birthweight of 3128 grams
and, as indicated by figure 9.5, about 13% of the neonates weighed less
than 2501 grams at birth. The second line is the distribution of birthweights for lower-class women in Bombay (Jayant 1964). Figure 9.5
indicates the mean birthweight in this population was just 2525 grams.
In this case nearly half (46%) of the births were below the critical level,
although the women in the sample were not the lowest of the low.

The third curve is my estimate of the probable distribution of the
birthweights of the children of English workers about 1800.[24] In deriving
this distribution I employed established correlations between height
and birthweight as well as both published and unpublished information
on the final heights of English workers developed by Floud and Wachter. These sources suggest that the distribution of the birthweights in
this class around 1800 had a mean of 2276 grams, which is about 249
grams (about half a pound) below the average in the deliveries of the
lower-class women in Bombay. It follows that about 79% of the births
among English workers around 1800 were at weights below 2501 grams.[25]

The implication of this distribution of birthweights is revealed by
table 9.10. Column 2 represents the actual schedule of neonatal death
rates by weight for nonwhite United States males in 1950, and column
3 gives the actual distribution of their birthweights. The product of

**Table 9.10**    **Effects of a Shift in the Distribution of Birthweights on the Neonatal Death Rate, Holding the Schedule of Death Rates (by Weight) Constant**

| Weight (grams) (1) | Neonatal Death Rate of Single Nonwhite U.S. Males in 1950 (per 1,000) (2) | Distribution of Birthweights of Single Nonwhite U.S. Males in 1950 ($\bar{x}$ = 3,128 g; $\sigma$ = 572 g) (3) | Distribution of Birthweights in a Population with $\bar{x}$ = 2,276 g $\sigma$ = 399 g (4) |
|---|---|---|---|
| 1,500 or less | 686.7 | 0.0117 | 0.1339 |
| 1,501–2,000 | 221.3 | 0.0136 | 0.2421 |
| 2,001–2,500 | 62.1 | 0.0505 | 0.3653 |
| 2,501–3,000 | 19.7 | 0.1811 | 0.2198 |
| 3,001–3,500 | 10.7 | 0.3510 | 0.0372 |
| 3,501–4,000 | 12.1 | 0.2599 | 0.0017 |
| 4,001–4,500 | 13.0 | 0.0865 | — |
| 4,501 or more | 23.2 | 0.0456 | — |
| Implied neonatal death rate (per 1,000) | | 26.8 | 173.0 |
| Possible infant death rate (per 1,000) | | 48.9 | 288.3 |

*Sources: Cols. 2 and 3:* United States National Office of Vital Statistics 1954; *Column 4:* See nn. 21, 23, 24, and 26.

*Note:* The infant death rate in the last line of col. 4 is estimated at 1.67 times the neonatal rate.

these two columns yields an implied neonatal death rate of 26.8 per 1,000 which, of course, was also the actual death rate. If, however, this United States population had had the distribution of the birthweights of the English workers about 1800 which I have estimated, their neonatal death rate would have been 173.0 per thousand (see col. 3). The implication of table 9.10 is that improvements in nutrition sufficient to have shifted the mean birthweight from 2276 grams to 3128 grams would have reduced the infant death rate by 83% [$1 - (48.9 \div 288.3) = 0.83$].[26]

Equation (5) can be used to estimate the overall contribution of improvements in nutritional status to the decline in English mortality between 1800 and 1980.[27]

(5)        $\dot{S} = \phi\dot{I} + (1 - \phi)\dot{S}_n,$

where    $\dot{S}$ = the counterfactual percentage decline in the standardized death rate due to improvements in nutritional status

$\dot{I}$ = the percentage change in the infant death rate due to improvements in nutritional status

$\dot{S}_n$ = the percentage change in the standardized non-infant death rate due to improvements in nutritional status

$\phi$ = the share of infant deaths in total deaths around 1800 as indicated by the data in Wrigley and Schofield.[28]

Substituting into equation (5), we obtain

(6)                    $28 = 0.24 (83) + 0.76 (11)$.

Since the age-standardized death rate actually declined by about 69%, equation (6) implies that improvements in nutritional status accounted for about 41% of the total decline in the age-standardized English mortality rate since 1800. This figure is neither inconsequential nor everything. It shows that although improvements in nutrition made a substantial contribution to the decline in English mortality, other factors accounted for the majority of the decline. The main impact of the nutritional contribution was on the infant death rate. The reduction in noninfant deaths that may be attributed to nutrition account for just 12% of the total decline in English mortality since 1800.[29] Plausible upper and lower bounds on the variables in equation (5) indicate that 41 ± 10 probably bounds the nutritional contribution at all ages. It should be emphasized that these figures refer not merely to the diet but also to the other factors that affected the nutrients available for growth.[30]

### 9.4.2. A Possible Explanation for the Peerage Paradox

Although the calculation suggests a more modest role for nutrition than some have argued, other scholars may find even four-tenths is much too high a number, since the question about the peerage is still unanswered. If nutrition was so important, why did the English peerage have virtually the same mortality as the general population until the beginning of the eighteenth century? And why did life expectation of peers improve so rapidly after 1750 when no great change in their diet is apparent?

First, there is a general point which may not be of great quantitative significance in the resolution of the peerage paradox, but which bears on the context in which that issue ought to be considered. Some of the work on the changing epidemiology of Europe suggests that the potential leverage of nutritional status on mortality rates may have increased during the eighteenth and nineteenth centuries. Since nutritional status does not have an equal influence on the outcome of every disease, the prevalence of different diseases among different classes, and within different geographical areas, will obviously affect the impact of nutritional factors on fluctuations in mortality rates. Table 9.11 classifies diseases according to whether nutritional status is likely to influence their outcome. Taken in conjunction with studies of the epidemiology of medieval and early modern Europe by Creighton (1891),

Table 9.11    **Nutritional Influence on Outcomes of Infections**

| Definite | Equivocal or Variable | Minimal |
|---|---|---|
| Measles | Typhus | Smallpox |
| Diarrheas | Diphtheria | Malaria |
| Tuberculosis | Staphylococcus | Plague |
| Most respiratory infections | Streptococcus | Typhoid |
| Pertussis | Influenza | Tetanus |
| Most intestinal parasites | Syphilis | Yellow fever |
| Cholera | Systemic worm infections | Encephalitis |
| Leprosy | | Poliomyelitis |
| Herpes | | |

*Source:* JIH 1983.
*Note:* Outcome includes morbidity and mortality.

Helleiner (1967), McNeill (1976), Hatcher (1977), Appleby (1980), Kunitz (1983), and others, this classification suggests that diseases in which nutritional influence is minimal or equivocal (such as plague, malaria, smallpox, typhus, and influenza) may have had a greater impact on mortality before 1750 than after. For reasons that are still unclear, the prevalence of these diseases declined in Europe between 1700 and the mid-nineteenth century, and there was an increase in the prevalence of those infectious diseases in which the influence of nutrition is large. The possibility that there was a shift in the distribution of diseases suggests that the impact of nutritional status on mortality rates may have increased after 1750. However, whether such a shift actually took place, and its quantitative significance if it did, is still in dispute.[31]

A point more directly relevant to the resolution of the peerage paradox is that investigators searching for the possible influence of nutrition on the longevity of peers appear to have dwelt on the wrong issue: the diet of adults. As we have seen, nutritional status has its greatest impact on the mortality of infants, not on adults. That dukes and earls had an abundance of food as adults does not mean they were well nourished in infancy or in early childhood. Weaning peers of the eighteenth century did not eat joints of beef, but like weaning peasants, dined on a pap or watery gruel. During this era privilege and wealth did not ensure a diet or a nutritional status for the upper-class infants and young children that was better than that experienced by the common people. Although the housing, the clothing, and some aspects of the personal care of upper-class infants probably was better than that received by their lower-class counterparts, these advantages do not appear to have affected the infant and early childhood mortality rates of the peerage during the first half of the eighteenth century. Examination of the Hollingsworth (1977) mortality schedules indicates that 60% of the increase in the life expectancy between the cohorts of 1700–

1724 and of 1900–1924 was due to the decline in deaths under age 10. Indeed, if the peerage had continued to suffer the $_{10}Q_0$ value of 1700–1724 in 1900–1924, but experienced the improved mortality rates of the twentieth century at all other ages, then the life expectancy of the peers (both sexes combined) born during 1900–1924 would not have been 65.0 but only 46.4.

Furthermore, the fact the English nobility was rich enough to afford a good diet does not imply that they actually enjoyed a good diet. Considerable evidence suggests that, as G. R. Elton recently put it, the English nobility of the late medieval and early modern eras was often afflicted by "bad nutrition" (an abundant but unhealthy diet) while the lower classes often suffered from an "inadequate diet (hunger)."[32] Studies of per capita rations and annual food expenditures in the estate account books of noble households indicate that although aristocratic diets were abundant in calories and proteins, they were deficient in vitamins A, C, and D, owing partly to a dietary theory that viewed "greenstuff as a danger to health" and partly to a class prejudice against milk, cheese, and eggs (Dyer 1983, pp. 196, 207). Consequently, lower-class diets, though often inadequate in quantity, were often "more varied" than those of the upper classes. Peasants "ate all types of corn, not just wheat" and "the peasant table was more likely to carry the dairy produce and vegetables that the nobility despised" (Dyer 1983, p. 209). The hallmark of aristocratic diets before 1700, aside from their abundance (or superabundance) in calories and meats, was the regular availability of wines and spices.

The huge quantities of wine and ale consumed in aristocratic households, not only in England but throughout Europe, raises still another issue, one that bears on both neonatal and late-age mortality rates. The standard ration of drink for the inferior members of noble households was a gallon of ale per day, while the superior members drank both ale and wine, with wine constituting as much as half of the daily intake of fluids (Drummond and Wilbraham 1939; Pullar 1970; Wilson 1973; Dyer 1983; Thurgood 1984). So prominent were these alcoholic beverages in aristocratic diets that they accounted for one-quarter or more of the daily consumption of calories (Drummond and Wilbraham 1939; Heckscher 1954; Dyer 1983). The lavish consumption of ale and wine was stimulated by the fact that even in aristocratic households much of the fish and meat were heavily salted.[33] A diet heavy in salt and alcohol probably increased the incidence of liver, renal, gastrointestinal, and cardiovascular diseases among peers who survived to middle and late ages and may have contributed to the high mortality rates of peers at ages 40 and over. But it was in utero that dietary habits of the peerage were most deadly, since ladies of the realm were apparently consuming an average of between three and nine ounces of absolute alcohol per day—more than enough to produce a high incidence of Fetal Alcohol Syndrome and Fetal Alcohol Effects.[34]

Thus, despite their enormous wealth and command over resources, the diet of the English aristocracy during the sixteenth and seventeenth centuries was deleterious to health. Their diet was bad partly because of nutrients that were excluded but mainly because of toxic substances that were included. Alcohol may have been the most lethal of these substances. In the quantities in which it was apparently consumed by pregnant women, it not only increased late fetal deaths and the neonatal mortality rate of the peerage, but also increased the risk to surviving infants into the second and third years of life (Abel 1982). By impairing the ability of the body to assimilate nutrients for 3 years or more after birth, Fetal Alcohol Syndrome severely exacerbated the deficiencies in the weaning and early childhood diets and may have undermined the health of many peers for the balance of the life cycle.

The peerage paradox thus appears to have arisen from the mistaken proposition that because the adult diet of English aristocrats was abundant in grains and meat, it was a "good" diet. That proposition overlooked the role of toxic substances in upper-class diets, substances which were harmful to adult health and disastrous for fetal development as well as for development during infancy and early childhood. The proposition also overlooked the critical nature of the weaning diet, which was as inadequate for peers as for peasants. These neglected factors are certainly relevant to an explanation of the exceedingly high infant and childhood mortality rates of the peerage before 1725. They also help to account for the decline in these mortality rates after 1725. The relevant point here is not merely what was added to the aristocratic diet between 1700 and 1900 but also the gradual elimination from that diet of the toxic substances that were so lethal to the young and the unborn (Mingay 1963; Pullar 1970; Wilson 1973). The children of the upper classes were the beneficiaries of the reform in manners that were in part a lagged response to Puritanism and other austere religious movements of the seventeenth century, in part a reflection of the Enlightenment, and in part a reaction to the devastating consequences of the gin mania of 1720–50 (Trevelyan 1942; Warner and Rosett 1975). One of the by-products of this reform that affected both the nutritional status and mortality rates of infants was the gradual disappearance of the upper-class practice of putting out infants with wet nurses (Mingay 1963; Pullar 1970; Sussman 1975, 1977; Stone 1977; Trumbach 1978; Flinn 1981).

The suggested resolution to the peerage paradox points to the need for further research on past practices that affected nutritional status during infancy, the weaning ages, and in utero. What was the temporal pattern by which the new manners diffused through the upper classes of England, and how did this pattern affect the consumption of alcohol, opiates, and other toxic substances by pregnant mothers, infants, and young children? Was it fashionable in court during some periods for pregnant women to keep their weight gain low? To what extent did the weaning diet of peers expose them to virulent infections from contaminated water or raw milk, and when did this risk diminish? Research into these issues should, of course, be extended to cover the experience of the lower as well as of the upper classes. Study of the leads and lags between changes in the cultural standards of the upper and lower classes may go a long way toward explaining the leads and lags between the changes in their respective mortality rates.

### 9.4.3    The Wrigley-Schofield-Lee Paradox

In interpreting the regressions between mortality rates and wheat prices, it has often been assumed that the price of wheat was so highly correlated with all other grain prices that it could serve as a proxy for the price of food. It has also been assumed that food shortages would be reflected in their price. Although the second assumption is quite reasonable, it does not follow that a large rise in prices necessarily implies an equally large decline in the supply of food. That would be the case only if the demand elasticity ($\epsilon$) for food was one. However, if the demand elasticity for grains was only between 0.25 and 0.1, then even the so-called exceptionally high fluctuations in grain prices (20% or more above trend) would imply shortfalls in grain yields that were only between 2% and 5% below the trend (see table 9.12). With a highly inelastic demand for grains, even the weak relationship between mortality and wheat prices found by various investigators would be consistent with the nutritional case. Their regressions would then imply that mortality rose even when declines in the supply of food were quite small. Thus, the critical question raised by the studies of correlations between wheat prices and mortality is the size of demand elasticities for wheat, for grains, and for food as a whole in England during the early modern era.

**Table 9.12    The Changes in the Price of Grains Associated with Changes in the Quantity, for Elasticities of 1.0, 0.5, 0.25, and 0.1**

| Percentage Increase in Price | Percentage Decline in Quantity of Grain if | | | |
|---|---|---|---|---|
| | $\epsilon = 1$ | $\epsilon = 0.5$ | $\epsilon = 0.25$ | $\epsilon = 0.1$ |
| 10 | 9.1 | 4.7 | 2.3 | 0.9 |
| 20 | 16.7 | 8.7 | 4.5 | 1.8 |
| 30 | 23.1 | 12.3 | 6.3 | 2.6 |
| 40 | 28.6 | 15.4 | 8.0 | 3.3 |
| 50 | 33.3 | 18.3 | 9.6 | 4.0 |

The analytical framework recently developed by Amaryta Sen (1981) facilitates the marshalling of the evidence needed to answer this question. Sen called attention to the fact that certain recent famines in underdeveloped nations occurred despite abundant harvests. These famines were caused not by natural disasters but by dramatic redistributions of "entitlements" to grain. The mechanism which promoted the redistribution of entitlements was a sharp rise in the price of grain relative to wages or other types of income received by the lower classes. In the "great Bengal famine" of 1943, for example, the exchange rate between wages and foodgrains declined by 86%, despite an "exceptionally high" supply of grain. In this case the rise in grain prices had nothing to do with the bountifulness of the harvest, but was driven by forces outside of the agricultural sector. The Bengal famine, Sen points out, was a "boom famine" caused by "powerful inflationary pressures" unleashed by a rapid expansion of public expenditures (pp. 66, 75).

The relevance of the entitlement approach to the interpretation of the economic demography of the early modern era does not depend on the source of the rise in grain prices that triggers the redistribution of entitlements. It is the similarity in the structural characteristics of traditional societies of the past and of low-income countries today that makes the entitlement approach pertinent (Flinn 1974; Post 1976; Appleby 1979a; Hufton 1983: Tilly 1983). At the root of these structural similarities is the highly unequal distribution of wealth and the overarching importance of land as a source of wealth. These twin characteristics lead directly to two other structural features. First, they cause the price elasticity of the total demand for grains to be quite low. Second, they drive a large wedge between the grain demand elasticities of the upper and the lower classes, with the elasticity of the lowest classes having a value that may be 10 or 20 times as large as the elasticity of the class of great land magnates.

It is these large class differences in demand elasticities (caused by social organization) rather than wide year-to-year swings in harvest yields (caused by variations in weather or other natural phenomena) that were the source of the periodic subsistence crises that afflicted late medieval and early modern England. Once the yield-to-seed ratio reached four and carryover inventories exceeded a month or two of the annual supply (which probably occurred in England before 1400), large weather-induced reductions in the normal national supply of foodgrains probably became exceedingly rare. The evidence at hand suggests that during the 331 years covered by the analysis of Wrigley et al. there were probably not more than 7 or 8 years (and there may have been as few as 3) during which the average food supply fell below its normal level by as much as 7%. One implication of the proposition that the national subsistence crises of the pre-industrial era were the products of entitlement shifts (rather than natural disasters that cut deeply into the food supply) is that the impact of these crises on average national mortality rates was fairly limited.[35]

Equation (7) is a convenient starting point for the estimation of the relevant elasticities:

$$(7) \qquad \bar{\epsilon}_i = (\theta_i - \beta_i)\psi_i - \epsilon_i$$

where

$\bar{\epsilon}_i$ = the income-compensated price elasticity of the demand for grain
$\psi$ = the income elasticity of the demand for grain
$\epsilon_i$ = the income–fixed price elasticity of the demand for grain
$\beta$ = the share of grain in total consumption expenditures
$\theta$ = the share of income arising from the ownership of grain
$i$  = a subscript designating the $i$th class.

Equation (7) states that the income-compensated elasticity of demand for grains of a given class depends not only on $\epsilon_i$ (the income–fixed price elasticity, which is often referred to as the "substitution" elasticity) but the relative magnitude of $\theta_i$ and $\beta_i$. It follows from equation (7) that wealthy landlords would have a much more inelastic demand for grain (because the share of their income arising from ownership of grain-producing lands equaled or exceeded the share of their income that was spent on the consumption of grains—that is, because $\theta_i \geq \beta_i$) than landless laborers (for whom $\theta_i = 0$ and $\beta_i$ is large).

Table 9.13 divides the English population at the middle of the Wrigley-Schofield-Lee period (ca. 1700) into four classes that correspond to the aristocracy and gentry, the yeomanry, artisans and shopkeepers, and common laborers (including the unemployed). Servants working in the households of the upper classes are included with these classes, since their masters provided the grains which they consumed. In other words, the population embraced by the landlords (class 1 in table 9.13) includes not only the landlords and their immediate families but all of their retainers, high and low. Table 9.13 also presents my estimates of share of the English population represented by each of the classes, the normal share of each class in the annual consumption of grain ($\phi_i$), and of $\theta_i$, $\beta_i$, $\psi_i$, and $\epsilon_i$. The population shares are based on King's table (Laslett 1984).[36] The values of $\phi_i$ follow from the population shares and estimates of the per capita consumption of grains and calories in each class indicated by recent studies (including Drummond and Wilbraham 1939; Everitt 1967; Kerridge 1968; Appleby 1979b; Dyer 1983; Shammas 1983, 1984; Lindert 1985; Williams 1985). The values of $\phi_i$ shown in column 2 imply that landlords and yeomen consumed about 50% more grain per capita than the national average (much of it as ale and spirits), that shopkeepers and craftsmen consumed the national average, and

**Table 9.13** Estimates of the "Normal" Shares in Foodgrain Consumption and of the "Normal" Price Elasticities of the Demand for Foodgrains by Socioeconomic Class in England about 1700

| Class of Household Head | Share in Population (1) | Normal Share in Consumption of the Foodgrains (2) $\phi_i$ | Share of Grain in Total Consumption of a Class (3) $\beta_i$ | Share of Grain in Income (4) $\theta_i$ | Income Elasticity (5) $\psi_i$ | Income-Fixed Price Elasticity (6) $\epsilon_i$ | Income-Compensated Price Elasticity (7) $\bar{\epsilon}_i$ |
|---|---|---|---|---|---|---|---|
| 1. Landlords (including servants and retainers) | 0.11 | 0.16 | 0.20 | 0.50 | 0.24 | 0.05 | −0.02 |
| 2. Farmers and lesser landlords (including servants) | 0.34 | 0.51 | 0.30 | 0.50 | 0.38 | 0.12 | 0.04 |
| 3. Shopkeepers, minor professionals, and craftsmen (including servants) | 0.11 | 0.11 | 0.40 | 0.00 | 0.52 | 0.20 | 0.41 |
| 4. Laborers and the unemployed (not including servants covered in lines 1, 2, and 3) | 0.44 | 0.22 | 0.70 | 0.00 | 0.96 | 0.50 | 1.17 |

*Source:* Fogel 1985.

that common laborers and paupers consumed about 50% of the national average. Allowing for waste and storage losses, these values of $\phi_i$ imply that the average caloric intake of the poor was at about the mean level of Afghanistan or Bangladesh today (World Bank 1984), while the landlords and yeomen were at the level of United States farmers about 1850 (Fogel and Engerman 1974). The values of $\theta$, $\beta_i$, $\psi_i$, and $\epsilon_i$ are based on available evidence regarding the share of gross farm income originating in grains during the early modern era and cross-sectional studies of less developed countries today with income levels and agricultural sectors similar to those of early modern England (Fogel 1987).[37]

One important implication of table 9.13 is that although laborers were about 44% of the population, they accounted for only 22% of the normal consumption of foodgrains, and that landlords (who with their retainers and servants represented only 11% of the population) accounted for nearly as large a share of consumption. Another implication of table 9.13 is that both the magnitude and the direction of the effect of a rise in grain prices on elasticities was quite different for different classes (see col. 6 and 7). In the case of landlords the income–compensated price elasticity is positive, even though the income–fixed price elasticity is negative. This change in sign reflects the fact that landlords were not only consumers of grain but owners of large surpluses. In their case the rise in prices had two effects: the rise in grain prices increased their income as owners of surpluses, while it reduced their income as consumers. For landlords the producer's effect was so much stronger than the consumer's effect that rising grain prices would have led them to increase their consumption of grain. In the case of yeomen both effects were also present, but the income effect was not strong enough to have increased their grain consumption with rising prices; however, it did cut the income–compensated price elasticity to one-third of the income–fixed price elasticity. In the case of laborers only the consumption effect was present. Although the income–fixed price elasticity is already high, the income–compensated price elasticity is more than twice as high.

The values set forth in table 9.13 make it possible to estimate aggregate elasticity of the consumption demand for grains ($\bar{\epsilon}_c$), by making use of the relationship set forth in equation (8):

$$(8) \qquad \bar{\epsilon}_c = \phi_1 \bar{\epsilon}_1 + \phi_2 \bar{\epsilon}_2 + \phi_3 \bar{\epsilon}_3 + \phi_4 \bar{\epsilon}_4.$$

Substituting the appropriate values of $\phi_i$ and $\bar{\epsilon}_i$ into equation (8) yields

$$(9) \quad \bar{\epsilon}_c = (0.16)(-0.02) + (0.51)(0.04) + (0.11)(0.41)$$
$$+ (0.22)(1.17) = 0.320.$$

Thus, the estimates of class elasticities in table 9.13 imply that the elasticity of the aggregate consumption demand was well below 0.5, even though common laborers and paupers, who accounted for nearly half the population, had an elasticity in excess of one. However, as equation (8) indicates, it is shares in consumption rather than in population that determine the value of $\bar{\epsilon}_c$. If it were the population share that mattered, $\bar{\epsilon}_c$ would be nearly twice the indicated size and would fall between demand elasticities of artisans and laborers, who constituted the majority of the population. As it is, $\bar{\epsilon}_c$ falls below the demand elasticity of artisans because of the heavy weight given to the elasticities of landlords and yeomen who, although a minority of the population, accounted for two-thirds of consumption.

Although $\bar{\epsilon}_c$ is the price elasticity of the aggregate foodgrain demand, it is not the price elasticity of aggregate demand, which is given by equation (10):

$$(10) \qquad \epsilon_t = \delta\epsilon_s + (1-\delta)\bar{\epsilon}_c,$$

where

$\epsilon_s$ = the price elasticity of demand for grains used as seed and feed
$\delta$ = the share of the total crop normally used as seed and feed.

Available evidence suggests that about 25% of grains were reserved for seed and feed and that the demand for this intermediate product was moderately inelastic (about 0.6) but not as inelastic as is often implicitly assumed.[38] Substituting these values into equation (9) results in

$$(11) \qquad \epsilon_t = 0.25 \times 0.6 + 0.75 \times 0.32 = 0.39.$$

Equation (11) gives the "normal" value of $\epsilon_t$—the value of $\epsilon_t$ when yields are close to the mean (within plus or minus one standard deviation). We have not yet considered the case in which the deviation from normality is large enough to trigger significant declines in exchange entitlements. Table 9.14 shows that such declines could be triggered with surprisingly small shortfalls in output. Even a shortfall in output as small as 8% triggers significant shifts in the shares of grain consumed by different classes. In the case of landlords, the rise in their share more than offsets the decline in output so that their per capita consumption rises slightly. In the case of laborers, however, the decline in their share reinforces the decline in output so that their per capita consumption is down by 23%. It is worth noting that although output declines by 8%, aggregate foodgrain consumption only declines by 6% because grain reserved for feed and seed declines by twice as much (13%) as foodgrain consumption. As a result the feed and seed share of the reduced crop declines from 25% to 22%. With a supply that is 15% of the normal level, the interclass distribution of per capita consumption is so greatly exacerbated that the per capita grain con-

**Table 9.14  Consequence of Shifting "Entitlement" Exchange Ratios on the Share of Each Class in the Reduced Crop and on the per Capita Consumption of Each Class**

| Class of Household Head | Normal Share of Each Class in Foodgrain Crop $Q_d = Q_s = 1$ $p = 1$ $\epsilon_t = 0.39$ (1) | Case Where $Q_s = 0.92$ | | Case Where $Q_s = 0.85$ | |
|---|---|---|---|---|---|
| | | Share of Each Class in Reduced Output of Foodgrain at Market-Clearing Price (2) | Percentage Decline of Each Class from Normal per Capita Consumption of Foodgrains (minus signifies rise in consumption) (3) | Share of Each Class in Reduced Output of Foodgrain at Market-Clearing Price (4) | Percentage Decline of Each Class from Normal per Capita Consumption of Foodgrains (minus signifies rise in consumption) (5) |
| 1. Landlords (including servants and retainers) | 0.16 | 0.172 | −0.5 | 0.186 | −1.0 |
| 2. Farmers and lesser landlords (including servants) | 0.51 | 0.540 | 0.9 | 0.570 | 2.0 |
| 3. Shopkeepers, minor professionals, and craftsmen (including servants) | 0.11 | 0.107 | 8.8 | 0.100 | 18.6 |
| 4. Laborers and the unemployed (not including servants listed under 1, 2, and 3) | 0.22 | 0.181 | 23.2 | 0.145 | 44.4 |

*Source:* Fogel 1985.

sumption of laborers and paupers falls to less than 60% of its normal level.

The sharp decline in consumption of the laboring class (when $Q_s = 0.85$) is due to the combination of its high elasticity of demand ($\bar{\epsilon}_4 = 1.17$) and the sharp rise in price ($P$ goes to 1.65). It should be noted that more than a fifth of the indicated price rise is due not directly to a decline in $Q_s$ from 1 to 0.85, but to the rise in the value of $\epsilon_t$ as the price increases. If $\epsilon_t$ had remained constant, the decline in $Q_s$ would have led to a 52% increase in prices instead of a 65% increase. In other words, one of the effects of the shifting distribution of entitlement is to reduce both $\bar{\epsilon}_c$ and $\epsilon_t$ (to 0.23 and 0.30, respectively). It follows that an initial rise in prices tends to feed on itself, even in the absence of a speculative demand or irrational hoarding, by increasing the share of grain entitlements held by classes with a highly inelastic demand.

The estimates in table 9.14, together with the distribution of deviations in grain prices from their trend, make it possible to assess the extent of harvest failures in years of "exceptionally" high prices.[39] Perhaps the most important feature of the price distribution is that there are only 23 out of 198 observations (0.1162) between 1540 and 1737 in which the price index deviates positively from the trend by as much as 25%. Using 0.37 as an estimate of $\epsilon_t$ (the value implied by table 9.14 for a 25% rise in prices), this fact implies that the aggregate quantity of grains fell below the trend (or mean level) of quantity by as much as 0.0792 in only 11.62% of the years. With the deviations in quantity ("yields") normally distributed,[40] the preceding points imply equation (12):

$$(12) \qquad 1.20\sigma_g = 0.0792\bar{X}_g,$$

where

$\sigma_g$ = the standard deviation (S.D.) of deviations from the "normal" level (or trend) of quantity

$\bar{X}_g$ = the "normal" level (trend level) of quantity, which is set equal to one.

Solving equation (12) for $\sigma_g$ results in a value of 0.066.[41]

Thus, the standard deviation of the distribution of grain "yields" (deviations in the quantity of all grains) is far smaller than the standard deviation of the distribution of deviations in wheat prices, which over the same 198 years was 0.251.[42] This is an important finding for the assessment of investigations that have used the price of wheat as a proxy for the physical quantity of all grains. The large difference between the two standard deviations (of grain "yields" and of deviations in wheat prices) implies that the elasticity of grain "yields" with respect to wheat prices was substantially below that of $\epsilon_r$. This result is immediately apparent from equation (13):

(13)
$$\frac{\dot{Q}_g}{\dot{P}_w} = \epsilon_{gw} = \frac{\sigma_g}{\sigma_w} r_{gw},$$

where

$\dot{Q}_g$ = percentage deviations in the quantity of grain
$\dot{P}_w$ = percentage deviations in the price of wheat
$\epsilon_{gw}$ = the elasticity of the quantity of grain with respect to the price of wheat
$r_{gw}$ = the coefficient of correlation between deviations in grain quantities and deviations in wheat prices
$\sigma_g$ = the S.D. of deviations in grain quantities
$\sigma_w$ = the S.D. deviations in wheat prices.

Hence

(14)
$$\epsilon_{gw} = 0.263 r_{gw}.$$

Although it is often assumed that, except for the very rich, grains were virtually the equivalent of the food supply in early modern England, recent studies have revealed that meat, fish, game, dairy products, vegetables, fruits, and nuts formed a significant part of the diet of other classes, even of common laborers and paupers (Fussell 1949; Everitt 1967; Kerridge 1968; Richardson 1976; Dyer 1983; Oddy 1983; Shammas 1983, 1984; Skipp 1978; Drummond and Wilbraham 1958; cf. Webster 1845). The difficulty with the stylized approach to food supply is that it implicitly assumes that $\sigma_g$ (the S.D. of deviations around the trend in the quantity of grain) is identical with $\sigma_f$ (the S.D. of deviations around the trend in the total food supply). As it turns out this assumption is unwarranted. In the case of the all-agricultural-products price series, only five out of 198 observations (0.0253) between 1540 and 1737 deviate positively from the trend by as much as 25%. Hence, instead of equation (12) we have equation (15):

(15)
$$1.95\sigma_f = 0.0792\bar{X}_f,$$

which yields a value for $\sigma_f$ of 0.041.[43] Now $\epsilon_{fw}$ (the elasticity of the quantity of food with respect to the price of wheat) follows from equation (16):

(16)
$$\epsilon_{fw} = \frac{0.041}{0.251} r_{fw} = 0.163 r_{fw},$$

where $r_{fw}$ is the coefficient of correlation between deviations in the quantity of food and deviations in wheat prices.

Equations (14) and (16) reveal the pitfall in the interpretation of studies that used wheat prices as a proxy for shortfalls in the supply of grain and of food. It was assumed that because wheat prices were highly correlated with other food prices, that large positive deviations of wheat prices implied not only large declines in the supply of wheat but in the supply of grains as a whole and in the total supply of food. Equation (14) shows that even if the correlation between grain "yields" and wheat prices were perfect, what has been termed an "exceptional" deviation in wheat prices (20% above trend) would only imply about a 5% decline in the total supply of grains and (taking account of the shift away from feed and seed) only about a 4% decline in the supply of foodgrains. Consequently, far from representing serious nutritional deprivation, most "exceptional" deviations in wheat prices fell within the range of "normal" consumption of grains (although not necessarily of wheat). Even among common laborers, who would have suffered from the adverse effect of a shift in entitlements, a positive deviation in wheat prices of 20% would imply a decline in per capita food consumption of about 9%—not a catastrophe, but not trivial either for a class suffering from the chronic malnutrition that accompanied a diet that probably averaged below 2,000 calories per capita. For the other three classes, the implied decline in per capita consumption is negligible.

The estimate of $\sigma_g$ and $\sigma_f$ developed from equations (12) and (15) makes it possible to assess the extent to which the English population suffered from generalized harvest failures during 1541–1871. A decline in grain "yields" of as much as 10% ($1.52\sigma_g$) was a relatively rare event, occurring less than 1 year in 15. It is unlikely that England suffered more than one 10% shortfall in the overall food supply ($2.44\sigma_f$) after 1540. The estimated value of $\epsilon_{fw}$ (assuming $r_{fw} = 1$) implies that even in 1556 when the positive deviation in wheat prices was at its highest post-1540 level (98%), the decline in the overall food supply was about 10.5%. All but seven of the other poor harvests imply grain shortfalls of less than 10%, foodgrain shortfalls of less than 8%, and overall food shortfalls of less than 7%.[44]

The information in column 3 of table 9.14 provides a basis for estimating the effect of post-1540 harvest failures on the mortality rate. That column shows that with total grain shortfalls of 8%, only the two lowest classes would have had nonnegligible reductions in their normal supply of grain. In the case of the artisan class, much of the 8.8% reduction in the apparent consumption of grains could have been offset by shifting from inefficient to efficient forms of the extraction of calories (from beer and ale, e.g., to gruels and porridges) and by reducing storage losses and waste (Fussell 1949; Drummond and Wilbraham 1958; Mathias 1959; Stern 1964; Walford 1970; Walter 1976; Appleby

1978). Consequently, the demographic effect of harvest failures would have been confined largely, if not exclusively, to the class of common laborers and paupers, many of whom were unrelieved by public or private charity (Lindert 1980; Lindert and Williamson 1983b). In this case, the gap between apparent and effective consumption was probably quite small because the lower classes could not indulge in inefficient forms of grain processing and consumption to the same extent as the other classes. Moreover, lacking the wherewithal to hold inventories of food, they were also spared the large inventory losses of the period.

On the other hand, part of the decline in the grain consumption of laborers would have been offset by an increased consumption of other foods, some normally considered inferior to grains, including nuts, rootcrops, garden vegetables, milk, and milk products (Fussell 1949; Drummond and Wilbraham 1958; Stern 1964). Equations (14) and (16) together imply that about 40% of the decline in grain consumption would have been offset by the increased consumption of other foods. Consequently, in order for the food consumption of laborers to have declined by 23%, the shortfall in the grain supply would have had to have been about 13% ($0.08 \div 0.615 = 0.130$), an event that would have occurred just one year in every 41. If we continue to assume an elasticity of the death rate with respect to nutritional status of $-1.4$ (although that figure may be too high for a single year's deprivation), then a shortfall in grains yields sufficient to reduce the food consumption of common laborers by 23% would have raised their mortality rate by 32%—more than enough to constitute a grave social crisis. Nevertheless, the effect of such a rise on the crude death rate (cdr) of the entire population (which is the statistic that has entered into studies which attempt to relate wheat prices to mortality rates) would be much smaller. During an age in which the trend value of cdr was about 28 per thousand, and assuming that the normal cdr for laborers was 10% above the average, the national cdr in a famine year would have risen by about 4.4 per thousand ($0.44 \times 1.4 \times 0.232 \times 0.028 \times 1.1 = 0.0044$), to a level which is about 16% more than the average cdr.

Thus, even if the elasticity of mortality rates with respect to nutritional status was as large in early modern England as the Trinidad data suggest, one would hardly expect to discover that the elasticity of wheat prices with respect to famine-induced deaths (as opposed to deaths due to regular and persistent malnutrition) was large since only one-fifth of the years identified as famine years using wheat prices would represent years in which there was actually a substantial increase in the national cdr due to a shortfall in food. The basic point, however, is not that regressions have been misspecified and the results misinterpreted. It is rather that after approximately 1400 or 1500, famines in England were rare events, affecting a minority of the population, and accounting for a minuscule proportion of accumulated deaths. Over the entire 331 years covered by the Wrigley-Schofield-Lee analysis it is unlikely that *famine* deaths accounted for as much as 0.4% of the accumulated total deaths (0.16 × 0.024 = 0.0038).[45] Given the exceedingly small proportion of deaths due to famines, the many factors (including nonfamine malnutrition) that affected annual death rates and the lack of controls for most of the relevant factors, the highly aggregated level of the time-series analysis, and the use of wheat prices as a proxy for food shortfalls, it is impressive that Lee was able to pick up any mortality effect at all, let alone one which appears to be quite close to the mark.[46]

The Wrigley-Schofield-Lee results seemed paradoxical only because it was widely assumed that the large swings in wheat prices represented correspondingly large swings in the aggregate supply of food.[47] When it is recognized that food shortfalls of 7% or more were quite rare, it becomes evident that their results neither contradict nor confirm the nutritional hypothesis. They do demonstrate that *famine* mortality was a minor factor in explaining both cumulated deaths and secular trends in the death rate during 1541–1871, but this finding does not eliminate *chronic* malnutrition as a significant component of pre-industrial mortality rates.[48] The "normal" distribution of shares in grain entitlements shown in table 9.13 and what is known about the course of agricultural production suggests that until the end of the Napoleonic Wars, English laborers were about as badly fed as the lower classes in such countries as India, Pakistan, and Bangladesh shortly after World War II. This conclusion is consistent with the currently available data on the heights of English laborers between 1760 and 1810. The impact of chronic malnutrition on English mortality rates during the preindustrial era remains an open issue.

### 9.4.4 Some Implications for the Standard of Living Controversies in Europe and America

The long and sustained upward movements in physical growth schedules in Europe and the United States that began late in the nineteenth century and continued through most of the twentieth century were a sharp break with the past. Before the last quarter of the nineteenth century, only the United States had experienced a long period of relatively rapid upward movement in growth schedules, with most of it occurring before 1710. Between cohorts born in 1710 and in 1780 final heights of native-born white American males increased at a rate of only 0.25 centimeters per decade.[49] During the next century the final heights of Americans oscillated in a narrow band or declined fairly sharply, losing about 3 centimeters in just two decades beginning with cohorts born about 1830. Rapid upward shifts in growth schedules probably did not resume until the last decade of the nineteenth century. The new period of increase in final heights which lasted for about 60 years was more rapid than the increase experienced during the late seventeenth and early eighteenth centuries (Sokoloff and Villaflor 1982; Fogel et al. 1983; Margo and Steckel 1983).

The principal upward shift in English growth schedules before 1900 came later and was shorter than that experienced in the United States. The mean final height of English working-class males born about 1760 was about 64.5 inches (which was about 9 centimeters below that of United States whites) and remained more or less at that level for the next half century. The succession of cohorts born between approximately 1810 and 1840 appears to have experienced a fairly rapid upward shift in growth schedules, so that the 1840 cohort was about 3 centimeters taller at maturity than the 1810 cohort. Thereafter, the upward shift in growth schedules slowed down so that cohorts born half a century later were only about a centimeter taller at maturity than their 1840 counterparts (Floud and Wachter 1982, 1983; Sokoloff and Villaflor 1982; Floud 1983a, 1983b).

There were also relatively constant growth curves for France between approximately 1820 and 1900, and for Belgium between about 1830 and 1900. In both countries heights at age 20 remained below 65.5 inches down through the end of the nineteenth century (Floud 1983b). In the Netherlands and the Scandinavian countries the laboring classes appear to have experienced improved living conditions sometime during the third quarter of the nineteenth century. In the case of the Netherlands, for example, mean adult heights between 1865 and 1905 increased at about 1 centimeter per decade, which is about five times as large as the British rate of increase during the same period. Even so, the Dutch rate of increase during the late nineteenth century was only half as great as the rate of increase during the half-century following World War I (Van Wieringen 1978).[50]

Although the standard of living of the laboring classes in the United States was quite high early in the nineteenth century by European standards, it appears that the difference narrowed considerably over the course of the nineteenth century, partly because United States height declined for about half a century and partly because the heights of Europeans increased somewhat. At the end of the nineteenth century when the United States entered a new phase of rapid upward shift in growth curves, living standards for United States workers, as measured by final heights, were quite similar to those prevailing in northwestern Europe, but they were still significantly better than those of southern Europe. As late as 1900 the mean height of adult Italian males was below 65 inches (Terrenato and Ulizzi 1983).

In recent decades economists and economic historians have tended to assume that if the "real wage" (an index of nominal wages divided by an index of prices) was rising, then the standard of living of workers was rising. Beginning with the late nineteenth century, but especially after 1930 when large investments were made in the gathering of wage and price data, older measures of the standard of living, such as weight, housing conditions, and mortality rates began to be abandoned in favor of the newer and presumably more comprehensive index. Criticisms have been made of the quality of the data from which long-term series of real wages were constructed (Von Tunzelmann 1979; Thirsk 1983), and far-reaching questions have been raised about what real wages actually measured, even when the indexes were ideally constructed (Taylor 1975). Nevertheless, the tendency has been to employ real wages not just as *a* measure (or even as the principal measure) of the standard of living but sometimes to convert it into a synonym for the standard of living.

The point is not that real wage measures should be discarded but that the interpretation that has been placed on them needs to be reconsidered. We may be able to obtain a deeper understanding of the changing standard of living of workers, develop a subtler appreciation of the manifold dimensions of the phenomenon, if the information embodied in both real wage indexes and measures of per capita income is reviewed in the light of the information contained in anthropometric measures, mortality and morbidity rates, and other measures of living conditions that are now becoming available.

What, for example, are we to make of a situation in which real wages were rising rapidly, as apparently occurred in England during the last half of the nineteenth century (Mitchell and Deane 1962; Matthews et al. 1982) while working-class heights remained at relatively low levels, showing little increase over half a century? How should we characterize conditions of workers in the United States between 1820 and 1860 if real wages were generally constant or rising, sometimes quite rapidly (Williamson 1976; David and Solar 1977), but heights and life expectation were decreasing? During an era in which from 50% to 75% of the income of workers was spent on food, is it plausible that the overall standard of living of workers was improving if their nutritional status and life expectations were declining? These are not questions that can easily be resolved, and I will not attempt to do so here. Rather, I want briefly to sketch some of the new issues about the course of the standard of living that are suggested by the anthropometric and demographic data. When real wages, per capita income, and other measures all move in the same direction there is little need to probe into their exact meaning. The interesting issues arise when the measures diverge, and it is on some of these issues that I wish to focus.

The evidence so far developed on height and mortality rates suggests that improvements in the living conditions of workers during the nineteenth century may have been more sporadic and uneven (both in time and among subgroups of workers) than is suggested by indexes of real wages or the movements in per capita income. In England the period of rapid improvement in the nutritional status of workers seems to have been confined largely to the 3 decades following the end of the Napoleonic wars. In France there was little change from the end of the Napoleonic wars until the beginning of the twentieth century. In the United States, the nutritional status of the laboring classes, which was initially quite high by European standards, appears to have deteriorated during the middle decades of the nineteenth century.

Although the substantial declines in both heights and life expectation shown by figue 9.1 are too new and provisional to be accepted without substantial additional evidence, let us suppose for the moment that further investigation supports the provisional findings. Will these series then contradict prevailing estimates of fairly rapid increases in conventional measures of per capita income? Since Williamson and Lindert (1980) have provided evidence that the inequality in the income distribution increased during this period, the question does not have an obvious answer. It is now necessary to probe more deeply into the magnitude, nature, sources, and locus of both gains in income and the increase in inequality. Rising inequality provides one way, although not the only way, of resolving the apparent anomaly between current estimates of rapidly rising per capita income and of declining heights during the middle quarters of the nineteenth century. Steckel's (1983) analysis of the relationship between mean final height, per capita income, and the Gini coefficient (a measure of the inequality of income or wealth distributions) reveals that with respect to final heights an increase of 100% in per capita income would just offset an increase in the Gini ratio of 0.066. It follows that current estimates of the increase in per capita income and the estimated decline in mean heights of 1.5 inches together suggest that the Gini ratio increased by about 0.17, going from perhaps 0.30 in c.1830 (the current figure for Australia) to about 0.47, which is a plausible estimate of the Gini ratio for the United States near the turn of the twentieth century (Lebergott 1976; Sawyer 1976; Williamson and Lindert 1980).[51] Thus, the decline in final heights of native-born United States white males may add to the evidence recently developed by others which indicates that the middle quarters of the nineteenth century witnessed significant increases in the inequality of the American income distribution (Pessen 1973; Williamson and Lindert 1980).

It may seem odd to those unfamiliar with this body of evidence that changes in height should be used as a measure of changes in the inequality of the distributions of income and wealth. However, as Floud and Wachter (1982) have recently pointed out, there was a time when height was the most compelling and the most widely used index of inequality. Moreover, because of the abundance of height data and their wide coverage of geographic regions and socioeconomic groups, it is possible to probe more deeply into vexing issues regarding variations in the conditions of the population of particular regions and occupations than has so far been possible with wage data which are skimpy in their coverage of particular categories. Two examples suggest the possibilities that now appear to be emerging.

The first is drawn from the work on British sources. Data recently collected by Floud on the British upper classes (1984) when combined with his data on the lower classes make it possible to estimate how much of the improvement in the average nutritional status in Great Britain over the past century and a half has been due to a closing of the gap between the upper and lower classes and how much was due to an upward shift in attainable average height. By "attainable" I mean not genetically attainable but, within genetic constraints, attainable under the most favorable prevailing socioeconomic circumstances. Floud's research indicates that about three-quarters of the increase in the mean final height of British males since about 1820 was due to the decrease in class differentials in height and the balance to an upward shift in the mean final heights of the upper class (which may be taken as a measure of the attainable mean height at any point in time).[52] In this connection it is worth noting that Sweden and Norway, which have two of the lowest after-tax Gini ratios, are the only countries in which height differentials by socioeconomic class have disappeared (Lindgren 1976; Sawyer 1976; Brundtland et al. 1980). The means of adult height in these nations now exceed those of high-Gini-ratio nations, such as the United States and Great Britain, by several centimeters (United States Bureau of the Census 1983).

The second example pertains to the effect of urbanization on both the level and distribution of real income. Previous research has revealed an association between the increase in the inequality of the American distributions of income and wealth during the nineteenth century and urbanization (Gallman 1969; Soltow 1971). Analysis of the height data in the samples drawn from the Union and the regular army rolls supports this finding but calls attention to the complexity and often roundabout nature of the influence of urbanization. Figure 9.6 shows the beginning of the long downward trend in the aggregate series on native-born whites (cf. fig. 9.1). It also shows that when this series is disaggregated into occupational and residential groups, the series for farmers exhibits a rising trend until around 1830 and then declines for the next two cohorts. The trend for urban laborers is basically flat at the beginning, rises slightly between 1825 and 1830, and then declines. These curves indicate that about 85% of the initial decline in the aggregate series was due to a decline in the mean heights of farmers and other rural

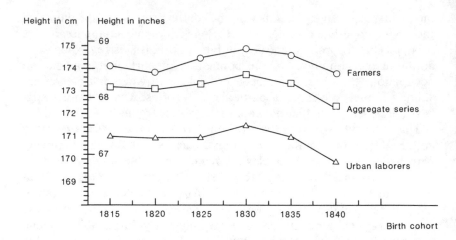

**Fig. 9.6**            A comparison of the aggregate time profile of final height for native-born white males with those for native-born white farmers and urban laborers. *Source:* unpublished data.

residents. The balance of the decline in the aggregate series was due to the increased proportions of the population experiencing the poor nutritional health conditions of the cities as well as to declining heights among urban residents (cf. Margo and Steckel 1983).

The deterioration in the mean final height of farmers apparent in the last two cohorts of figure 9.6 continued in subsequent decades. Native-born farmers who were born about 1860 were about 1.5 inches shorter than those who were born 3 decades earlier. Over the same period the final heights of urban laborers declined by about 0.8 inches. Thus, although deteriorating conditions in the cities and the shift of population from the countryside to the cities played a role, they explain only about one-fifth of the decline in the aggregate series shown in figure 9.1 for cohorts born between 1830 and 1860. About four-fifths of the decline was due to a deterioration of conditions affecting growth in the rural areas.

Current research is aimed at explaining this surprising decline in rural heights. One possibility is that an increasing proportion of the native-born rural males were children of foreign-born parents. It is likely that foreign-born mothers were relatively malnourished during their own developmental years and that foreign-born parents generally had lower incomes than native-born parents. Both factors would have made the children of foreign-born parents shorter than the children of native-born parents. Support for this hypothesis is found in a subsample of the Union Army recruits which has been linked to the manuscript schedules of the 1860 census. This subsample reveals that in the rural areas native-born males of foreign parents were 0.4 inches shorter in final height than native-born males of native-born parents. The effect of parental ethnicity was even greater in the cities, with children of foreign-born parents averaging 1.2 inches less in final heights than children of native-born parents. It thus appears that the low incomes of foreign-born parents and the poor nutritional status and health of foreign-born mothers had an effect on children both in the cities and in the countryside, but that effect was greater in the cities than in the countryside. It is plausible that as much as half of the urban-rural differential in native-born heights was associated with parental ethnicity.[53]

The decline of heights in the rural areas is particularly puzzling. The ethnic effect could only have accounted for a small share of the rural decline, and the available evidence strongly suggests that the per capita production of food, especially in the Midwest, increased between 1840 and 1860. There is, of course, the possibility that rural food consumption declined, despite the increase in output. Steven B. Webb has recently suggested that improved transportation links between farms and the cities might have had two negative health effects in the rural areas:[54] "First, while railroads were lowering food prices in the cities and improving nutrition there, they may have raised farm gate prices and lowered nutrition there. Giving farmers the opportunity to trade corn for calico may raise their utility, or at least the parents' utility, but may also reduce caloric intake. Second, increased contact with the urban disease environment may have increased the spread of communicable diseases in the rural sector."

Both of these possibilities certainly ought to be pursued, and they may turn out to be right. Yet the evidence on the growth of per capita income in the Midwest between 1830 and 1860 is so compelling, and midwestern farmers as a class seem to have prospered so much during this era, that it is not easy to accept the hypothesis that their food consumption declined, let alone that it declined by enough to explain a decrease in height of more than 1.5 inches (Bidwell and Falconer 1925; Berry 1943; G. R. Taylor 1951; Easterlin 1975).[55]

Of course, not all rural residents were farmers, and not all farmers shared equally in the agrarian prosperity. As much as 40% of the rural labor force of the North was employed in manufacturing, construction, and trade (Yang 1984; Moen 1985). This was an age in which many sectors of manufacturing, including iron production, milling, textiles, and many handicrafts were located largely in rural areas, partly because access to water power and raw materials were significant considerations (Temin 1966). There is a good deal of evidence that the nonagricultural sector of rural labor force, particularly native-born craftsmen, may have suffered from the rise in the cost of living to which Webb refers (Fogel 1986). Moreover, the competition from foreign-born labor and a rise in unemployment may have led a fair number of native-born craftsmen to shift into agriculture, either as laborers or at the low end of the distribution of farm owners and operators. Yet, even if half of these workers suffered income declines large enough to induce a 1.5-inch decline in the final heights of their children, the deprivation of this class would explain only about a fifth of the rural height decline.[56]

Perhaps Webb's second point holds the key. Recent studies have demonstrated a strong link between immigration rates and urban mortality rates both before and after the Civil War (Higgs 1979; Meckel 1985). Public health studies of the antebellum era demonstrated not only that mortality rates were much higher in the immigrant wards than in the wards in which the native-born were preponderant, but that epidemics often began first in the foreign-born wards and then spread outward, not only to other wards in the cities but to the rural areas as well.

The cholera epidemic of 1848–50 is the most dramatic case in point. This epidemic was brought to American shores in December of 1848 by two ships carrying German immigrants, one bound for New York, the other for New Orleans. Although New York-bound passengers who were sick with cholera when the ship arrived were kept in quarantine, others were allowed to enter the city. Within a few days cholera broke out in the immigrant districts of New York; then it spread to the predominantly native-born, lower-class districts nearby; and eventually to upper-class districts. In the case of the ship bound for New Orleans, public health officials were able not only to tie the spread of disease to New Orleans with the disembarkation of the immigrants there, but to follow the movement of cholera up the Mississippi and its tributaries. As immigrants from the infected ship boarded river steamers, cholera broke out aboard these ships and then in the cities at which the steamers called, including Memphis, Nashville, Louisville, Cincinnati, Wheeling (West Virginia), Pittsburgh, and Saint Louis (United States Surgeon-General's Office 1875). Soon after it reached these cities, cholera broke out in the surrounding countryside.

Cholera was the most dramatic disease of the antebellum era because it struck the nation suddenly, spread quickly, had a high case fatality rate, and its victims often succumbed within 24 hours after they became sick (Rosenberg 1962; *Encyclopaedia Britannica* 1961, 5: 615–18). But such diseases as malaria, typhoid, typhus, tuberculosis, smallpox, yellow fever, and dysentery took far more lives than cholera between 1800 and 1860. So severe was the increase in epidemic diseases during these decades that one historian of public health characterized it as a "period of great epidemics" (Smillie 1955). It seems likely, therefore, that increased exposure to disease was a major factor contributing to the decline in both the height and life expectation series shown in figure

9.1. The wide variations in the prevalence of particular diseases, by localities and over time, opens up the possibility of being able to measure the effect of variations in exposure to diseases on the variation in mortality rates with controls for height and a variety of socioeconomic variables.[57]

If cholera and other diseases that afflicted the United States during the nineteenth century were acts of God, unrelated to the functioning of the economic system, they would pose no special problem for the resolution of the standard-of-living controversy. However, economic growth, the spread of disease, and the concomitant increase in morbidity and mortality rates were intricately intertwined. Not only was internal migration responsible for as much as 50% of the increase in measured per capita income during the antebellum era (Fogel and Engerman 1971; Gallman 1972; Easterlin 1975; Fogel 1986), it was also a principal factor in the spread of cholera, typhoid, typhus, malaria, dysentery, and other major killer diseases of the era (Boyd 1941; Ackerknecht 1945, 1952; Smillie 1955). Increasing population density, another concomitant of economic growth, also increased the prevalence of various diseases, raising the level of malaria, enteric diseases, and diseases of the respiratory system (Ackerknecht 1945; Smillie 1955; May 1958; Kunitz 1983; New York State Board of Health 1867).

The increase in mortality between 1790 and 1860, therefore, calls for a downward adjustment in the measured growth of per capita income. Such an adjustment is necessary even if wage rates in high disease localities fully reflected the bribe which workers demanded for the increased risks of living in these areas, since national income accounting procedures treat the bribe as an increase in national income when it is merely a cost of production. Jeffrey Williamson's recent application of the bribery principle, using differences in wage rates between regions of high and low mortality to measure the disutility of English industrialization (Williamson 1981a, 1981b, 1982), represents an important advance in the assessment of both the short- and long-run costs and benefits of economic growth during the nineteenth century. The debate set off by his estimates (Pollard 1981; Floud 1984) involves such issues as whether workers had enough information to properly assess differences in risks, whether the measures of mortality used by Williamson were precise enough to gauge the differential risks that workers actually suffered in particular occupations and localities, and whether the various labor markets were all in equilibrium (or all out of equilibrium by the same degree). The resolution of these issues will no doubt add greatly to our knowledge about the costs and benefits of industrialization to the workers who experienced it.

There is an alternative approach to the computation of the mortality correction which, while not as comprehensive as the correction implied by the bribery principle (Williamson 1984), is easier to measure. Equation (18) is derived from the theory of human capital:

(18)                       $$w_n = (i + \delta_n)V_n$$

where

$w_n$ = the wage rate (rental rate) at age $n$ of a worker
$i$   = the market rate of return on capital
$\delta_n$ = the annual rate of depreciation in the stock of human capital
     at age $n$ (the probability of dying at age $n$)
$V_n$ = the cost of producing a new worker aged $n$ (the long-run equilibrium price of such a worker if he could be sold as a slave).

Differentiating equation (18) totally yields

(19)                       $$\overset{*}{w}_n = \phi \overset{*}{i} + (1 - \phi)\,\overset{*}{\delta}_n + \overset{*}{V}_n,$$

where
$\phi = [i/(i + \delta_n)]$
$\overset{*}{}$  = an asterisk over a variable indicates the rate of change in that variable.

Equations (18) and (19) indicate that increases in mortality rates will lead to spurious increases both in "real" wages (wages adjusted only for the price level) and in "real" per capita income. That is because conventional measures of "real" wages and per capita income fail to distinguish between rises in wages that are due to, say, technological change and those that are due to a more rapid consumption of human capital, treating both as if they represented net additions to human welfare.[58] Equations (18) and (19) indicate that increased mortality rates raise wages not only because they increase $\delta$ (the probability that someone in the labor force will die), but also because they increase $V$ (the cost of producing a new entrant into the labor force). The higher the mortality rate, the greater the number of live births (and associated costs) needed to produce a new entrant into the labor force.[59] There is, of course, a corresponding increase in cost due to extra expenditures on nonsurvivors at all the other ages between birth and entry into the labor force.

The estimates of $\overset{*}{\delta}$ and $\overset{*}{V}$, which can be derived from the decline in life expectation shown in figure 9.1 and appendix A, indicate that rising mortality may have accounted for about two-fifths of the average annual increase in the conventional measure of "real" per capita income over the 70 years between 1790 and 1860.[60] In principle, this correction is a lower bound on the correction that one would obtain from the implementation of the bribery principle, since no account was taken of the psychic cost involved in the loss of loved ones, and since it was implicitly assumed that workers were risk neutral with respect to their own fate.

The preceding estimate is merely meant to illustrate the new possibilities that are arising for refining our measures and conceptions of the changes in standards of living during the various stages of the industrialization process. The data on stature should provide additional information, beyond that conveyed by the mortality series, because they pertain to survivors, to individuals who lived to maturity (Floud 1984). Although the calculation based on equation (18) suggested the magnitude of the correction needed to net out the effect of rises in mortality rates on conventional measures of per capita income, it did not provide adjustments for the consequences of increased morbidity rates experienced by those who survived exposure to virulent diseases. Such corrections are needed to take account of medical expenditures and a variety of investments which merely offset the deterioration in the environment, and of diseases which degraded the quality of life and reduced the productivity of the labor of survivors. The data on stature promise to provide such adjustments, although we will need to learn more than we now know about how to separate out the effect of morbidity from other influences on stature before we can implement such an adjustment.

One issue which I have not yet probed in this discussion but which now leaps to the fore is the transfer of income and wealth between immigrants and native-born workers. Until now discussions of real economic growth by economic historians have tended to slight this issue, although it has been of great concern to many social, political, and labor historians (Hoagland 1913; Commons et al. 1918, I; Ernst 1949; Benson 1969; Handlin 1979; Pessen 1978; Hannon 1984). Whatever the long-run benefits of unrestricted immigration to native workers, it appears that in the short run it created severe hardships for them, not only by increasing the competition for jobs but also by increasing their exposure to disease and by reducing their life expectancy. The extent of the losses to native workers has been shrouded by the tendency to average over the experience of native and foreign-born workers. The available evidence suggests that the conditions of immigrants improved fairly rapidly after they arrived in the United States, not only because the disease environment was less virulent in America than in their native lands, but also because their wages rose fairly rapidly with time in the United States (Chiswick 1978, 1979; Lebergott 1984; Kearl and Pope 1986). Native workers, on the other hand, experienced declines in real income during the periods of most rapid antebellum immigration, even though the average level of their conventional income and their levels of health and longevity were higher than those of immigrants. This, then, is a case in which averaging over subgroups gives quite misleading impressions of the fate of the different groups. Even if the average real wages of all United States workers rose between 1840 and 1860, as seems likely, such a highly aggregated index tends to underestimate the substantial gains of foreign-born workers and obscures the declines in the real income of native-born workers in the nonagricultural sectors during the intervening years (Fogel 1986).

## 9.5  Conclusion

The decline in mortality rates since 1700 is one of the greatest events of human history.[61] I was inclined to say "one of the greatest achievements of humankind," but the fact remains that we still do not know how much of that achievement was due to causes beyond human control. The paper published by McKeown and Brown in 1955 marked a turning point in the effort to provide a warranted explanation of the decline in mortality. Bridging the worlds of social scientists and of medical specialists, they brought into the discussion most of the range of issues that have been under debate for the past 3 decades. That debate not only defined the issues more clearly than previously, but also revealed that the critical differences were quantitative rather than qualitative. Nearly all the specialists agree on the range of factors that were responsible for the decline in mortality, but they have had quite different views about the relative importance of each of the factors.

The unresolved issue, therefore, is not really whether a particular factor was involved in the decline, but how much each of the various factors contributed to the decline. Resolution of the issue is essentially an accounting exercise of a particularly complicated nature, which involves measuring not only the direct effect of particular factors but also their indirect effects and their interactions with other factors. Our preliminary investigations indicate that the construction of data sets rich enough to permit such a complex accounting is critical to the successful outcome of the exercise. What is needed is a data set that can cope with the changes in the cause-of-death structure which, as Preston (1976) indicated, has varied significantly over time and place. To identify the locus of influences of each of the principal factors that contributed to the decline we need not only disease-specific but age-specific and generation-specific information, because the influence of both risk-increasing and risk-averting factors appears to vary markedly both over lifetimes and over generations.

The findings on the extent and the locus of the nutritional contribution presented in this paper are preliminary in two respects. First, we anticipate that more complete data will lead to revisions in the estimates we have presented. Second, nutritional status is only the first of numerous factors which contributed to the mortality decline in America since 1700 that we hope to measure. Our preliminary results indicate that the contribution of improvements in nutritional status was neither inconsequential nor overwhelming; although it made a substantial contribution, the factors which contributed to the majority of the decline are still unmeasured. Moreover, although our preliminary estimates indicate that improvements in nutritional status may have accounted for about four-tenths of the mortality decline, this contribution was confined largely to the reduction in infant deaths, particularly to late fetal and neonatal deaths and to deaths during weaning. The concentration of the impact of improved nutrition in these age categories raises the possibility that increases in diarrhea and other diseases which diverted ingested nutrients from growth both before and after birth, rather than a decline in food intake, was the main cause of the decline in nutritional status and the rise in mortality during the middle decades of the nineteenth century.

Several important issues have been obfuscated by the confusion between diet (the gross intake of nutrients) and nutritional status (the balance between nutrient intake and the claims on that intake). The blurring of these concepts has diverted attention from the ingestion of harmful substances, which not only are devoid of nutritional value but prevent the body from assimilating nutrients at critical ages, especially in utero and in early childhood. Alcohol may have been the most devastating of these substances because it was long and widely consumed by pregnant women. But the administration of opiates to infants also appears to have been widespread for some stretches of time and may have been as widespread among the upper classes as it was among the lower ones. Even salt, in the quantities in which it was consumed prior to the development of refrigeration, was a toxic substance that may have taken a heavy toll at later ages. We are just beginning to become aware of the full range of ingested toxic substances and their role in the high mortality rates of the early modern and early industrial eras. More attention needs to be paid to the role of a variety of contaminants, including lead, arsenic, snakeroot, and mold poisoning (Ackerknecht 1952; Scrimshaw 1983; Matossian 1984).

Preoccupation with diet, especially the excessive focus on adult diets, has diverted attention from an array of intrauterine occurrences that undermined nutritional status and raised mortality rates during infancy and early childhood. Overwork of pregnant mothers and bacterial infections of minor consequence to mothers could have caused serious retardation of fetal development, especially when the insult occurred during the first trimester (Hurley 1980; Kielmann et al. 1983; Moore 1983; Steckel 1985). Intrauterine infections not only contributed to the large proportion of low-weight births, but increased the incidence of birth anomalies that severely affected the respiratory, circulatory, renal, skeletal, immune, and neurological systems and thus undermined physical development throughout the first year, and often well into the second year and beyond (Fitzhardinge and Steven 1972a, 1972b; Bjerre 1975a, 1975b; McFarlane 1976; Shapiro et al. 1980; Christianson et al. 1981; McCormick 1985). Whether caused by a poor diet, by toxic substances, by overwork, or by intrauterine infections, low birthweight increased not only perinatal death rates but also late infant and early childhood death rates. Recent studies suggest that the incidence of arteriosclerotic diseases at middle and late ages may be promoted by adverse intrauterine and infant environments (Forsdahl 1977; Marmot et al. 1984).

The preliminary results indicate that the factors contributing to the unanticipated cycles in heights and mortality were concentrated at particular ages, and that the routes of influences might have been quite round about. These findings point to new issues in the standard-of-living controversy. It may turn out that the difficulties created by improved transportation and rapidly growing cities carried over into the rural regions surrounding the cities, so that urban disamenities imposed costs on the rural populations that have not yet been measured (Pollard 1981; Williamson 1981a, 1981b, 1982). In the American case it is difficult to believe that per capita food consumption was declining during the last two-thirds of the nineteenth century since there is so much evidence pointing in the opposite direction (Gallman 1960; Towne and Rasmussen 1960; Bennett and Pierce 1961). Yet there could have been more unequal distribution of food products, especially of meat, which adversely affected the nutritional status of the poor. This appears to have been the case with blacks, whose nutritional intake apparently declined and whose mortality increased, between 1860 and 1880 (Frissell and Bevier 1899; United States Department of Labor 1897; Atwater and Woods 1897; Fogel and Engerman 1974; Meeker 1976). A more subtle and possibly more pervasive effect on the living standards of laborers and their families, both in the cities and in the countryside, may have come from increased exposure to risks (not captured or only partially captured by current measures of real wages) that more than offset the rises in consumption. This possibility does not invalidate indexes of real wages which were designed to cope with a specific set of issues. Rather it raises new issues which require new measures, measures that will supplement the information obtained from the older ones.

The new findings suggest that much more attention needs to be given to the way that population pressures, urbanization, and other economic factors affected not just those of working age but the very young. It may well be that the main damage to the standard of living of workers occurred at exceedingly young ages, in ways that no one at the time fully appreciated, and in a manner that does not conform well to current scenarios regarding the factors and individuals responsible for the hardships of working-class life during the nineteenth century. Nutritional and other health insults delivered in utero or early life appear not only to have affected adult health and longevity but to have reduced significantly the later productivity of those who recovered from early insults (cf. Fogel et al. 1983).

The search for data sources capable of dealing with both the new and the old issues on the interrelationship between demographic and socioeconomic variables has gained considerable force in recent years. Scholars have pushed in many different directions, and nearly all of the work has borne fruit. Careful examination of published data on disease-specific causes of death in United States cities have revealed that expenditures on sewers and waterworks had a relatively small effect on the decline in urban mortality before the beginning of the twentieth century (Condran and Crimmins-Gardner 1978), that the main diseases in which rural death rates were consistently lower than urban death rates in 1890 and 1900 were those which are nutritionally sensitive, and that the urban-rural differential was greater for infants and young children than for older persons (Condran and Crimmins 1980). These findings, although consistent with the nutritional hypothesis, raise questions about the role of exposure to disease, a variable that could not be measured in these studies. The weak relationship between public health expenditures and mortality rates could reflect the propensity of cities with the most virulent environments to make the heaviest expenditures. Similarly, urban-rural differences in disease-specific mortality rates might be more a matter of differences in exposure rates than in nutritional status. Such issues have led to a search for data sources that make it possible to measure exposure rates.

In this connection, there is much to be gleaned from a reexamination of published data in both state and local sources which can now be more effectively exploited than previously because of computers. Close examination of such published sources have revealed subtle aspects of the mortality structures (Preston 1976) and of influences upon them that were not adequately appreciated in the past. Condran and Cheney (1982), for example, have found that in Philadelphia during 1870–1930, medical intervention was effective, despite the absence of "high-tech" chemotherapy, because of the role of medical personnel in spreading knowledge about the environmental sources of diseases and in isolating carriers of diseases. Among the more suggestive findings of these recent studies of published data was the discovery by Higgs (1979) of marked cycles, around a declining trend, in the mortality rates of 18 large American cities between 1871 and 1900 that are strongly associated with variations in the rate of immigration.[62]

Work on the manuscript sources is still at an early stage, but as the studies of Wrigley and Schofield (1983), Preston and van de Walle (1978), Haines (1983), and Preston and Haines (1983) have already indicated, these sources will permit us not only to push the empirical analysis of the causes of the decline in mortality further back in time but also to shed light on factors that are not apparent in published data. Linked micro data sets will make it possible to disentangle factors that are intricately convoluted in aggregate data. The ability to measure the separate and joint effects of nutritional status, disease exposure rates, medical practices, public sanitation, and intergenerational transmission of behavioral patterns will illuminate the past and directly contribute to a better understanding of important issues in current economic and social policies.

# Appendix A
## On the Construction of Figure 9.1

Table 9.A.1 gives the time series on height and on $e_{10}$ used in the construction of figure 9.1.

### The Height Series

The entries from 1710 to 1875 give the mean adult heights of native-born whites who were ages 25–49 at the time of measurement. Each observation is the mean height of a 5-year birth cohort centered on the indicated date. The various cohort averages in the time series were obtained from regressions on height with dummy variables for each 5-year birth interval. To prevent changes in the socioeconomic composition of recruits into the army from introducing spurious variations in the trend, a variety of control variables were introduced, including civilian occupation, state or region of birth, state or region of residence at time of enlistment, date of enlistment, number of previous enlistments, rural and city-size variables, and migration variables. The effects of alternative functional forms for the time trend and various transformations of the other variables were also investigated. The time trend proved to be robust to these alternative specifications. We chose to present the time trend generated by the dummy variables since this specification put the least constraint on that trend. The results of the regression analysis will be more fully reported at a later date. Some of the findings have been reported in Sokoloff and Villaflor (1982) and Margo and Steckel (1983).

There are three gaps in the time series on height (1760–75, 1800–1810, and 1880–1900). The data needed to close these gaps have been retrieved from the muster rolls but work on the processing of these data has not yet been completed. Consequently, the first two gaps were

**Table 9.A.1        Data for Figure 9.1**

| $e^0_0$ | | Height | |
|---|---|---|---|
| Years on Which Observation Is Centered | Entry | Year on Which Observation Is Centered | Entry (cm) |
| 1720–24 | 51.8 | 1710 | 171.5 |
| 1725–29 | 52.7 | 1715 | 172.2 |
| 1730–34 | 52.0 | 1720 | 171.8 |
| 1735–39 | 51.2 | 1725 | 172.1 |
| 1740–44 | 52.9 | 1730 | 172.1 |
| 1745–49 | 52.3 | 1735 | 171.7 |
| 1750–54 | 52.5 | 1740 | 172.1 |
| 1755–59 | 52.9 | 1745 | 172.0 |
| 1760–64 | 53.9 | 1750 | 172.2 |
| 1765–69 | 53.7 | 1755 | 172.1 |
| 1770–74 | 54.8 | 1760 | |
| 1775–79 | 55.2 | 1765 | |
| 1780–84 | 56.4 | 1770 | |
| 1785–89 | 56.5 | 1775 | |
| 1790–94 | 56.7 | 1780 | 173.2 |
| 1795–99 | 55.4 | 1785 | 173.2 |
| 1800–1804 | 55.2 | 1790 | 172.9 |
| 1805–09 | 53.0 | 1795 | 172.8 |
| 1810–14 | 52.3 | 1800 | |
| 1815–19 | 51.9 | 1805 | |
| 1820–24 | 51.4 | 1810 | |
| 1825–29 | 51.1 | 1815 | 173.0 |
| 1830–34 | 51.0 | 1820 | 172.9 |
| 1835–39 | 50.2 | 1825 | 173.1 |
| 1840–44 | 48.7 | 1830 | 173.5 |
| 1845–49 | 48.2 | 1835 | 173.1 |
| 1850–54 | 47.9 | 1840 | 172.2 |
| 1855–59 | 47.8 | 1845 | 171.6 |
| 1860–64 | 49.2 | 1850 | 171.1 |
| 1865–69 | 51.4 | 1855 | 170.8 |
| 1870–74 | | 1860 | 170.6 |
| 1875–79 | | 1865 | 171.1 |
| 1880–84 | | 1870 | 171.2 |
| 1885–89 | | 1875 | 170.7 |
| 1890–94 | | 1882.5 | 168.9 |
| 1901 | 50.6 | 1887.5 | 169.2 |
| 1910 | 51.3 | 1892.5 | 169.0 |
| 1920 | 54.1 | 1897.5 | 170.0 |
| 1930 | 55.0 | 1902.5 | 170.0 |
| 1940 | 57.0 | 1906.5 | 171.6 |
| 1950 | 59.0 | 1911 | 172.2 |
| 1960 | 59.6 | 1916 | 172.9 |
| 1970 | 59.8 | 1921 | 173.2 |
| | | 1931 | 175.5 |

closed by linear interpolation. The third gap was closed by interpolation on the trend in the height of native-born recruits into the Ohio militia (Steckel 1982b).

The observations on the birth cohorts for 1905.5–1931 were obtained from Fogel et al. (1983). They pertain to all whites, foreign as well as native.

### The Series of $e_{10}$

The first step in the construction of time series on $e_{10}$ was the construction of period life tables for 5-year intervals extending from 1710–14 through 1875–79. The value of $e_{10}$ for each of these life tables was then computed. The series was smoothed by taking a five-item moving average of the $e_{10}$'s. In other words, each observation of $e_{10}$ listed in table 9.A.1 reflects mortality experience over a 25-year period centered on the midyear of a given interval.

Time series of $e_0$ and $e_5$ were also constructed. The secular trend in these series are quite similar to that generated by $e_{10}$. However, there appears to be a significant undercount of infant deaths among cohorts born before 1850 and a smaller undercount in ages 1–4. There are data in the genealogies that may permit us to correct the deficiency but the work on this problem is still in progress. Although the listing of deaths at ages 5–9 appears to be virtually complete, we chose to work with $e_{10}$ until we completed our analysis of the problem of undercounting at younger ages.

The observations from 1901–70 give $e_{10}$ for all whites, foreign as well as native. The life tables from which these statistics were computed are based on the states in the death registration system which expanded from 10 states in 1900 (with 26% of the national population) to the entire nation in 1933 (United States Bureau of the Census 1975, p. 44). The observations for 1901, 1910, 1920, 1930, 1940, and 1950 are each for 3 years centered on the designated year (United States National Office of Vital Statistics 1963). The observations for 1960 and 1970 are each based on data for a single year (United States National Center for Health Statistics 1963, 1974).

# Appendix B
## *The Derivation of Equation* (5)

Equation (5) may be derived from the identity:

(5.1)
$$S = \frac{D_i}{B} \cdot \frac{B}{P} + \frac{D_n}{P_n} \cdot \frac{P_n}{P}$$

which may be rewritten as

(5.2) $$S = I\alpha + S_n\beta.$$

Total differention of (5.2) yields

(5.3) $$\frac{dS}{S} = \frac{I\alpha}{S}\left(\frac{dI}{I} + \frac{d\alpha}{\alpha}\right) + \frac{S_n\beta}{S}\left(\frac{dS_n}{S_n} + \frac{d\beta}{\beta}\right).$$

Since

$$\frac{I\alpha}{S} = \frac{\dfrac{D_i}{B}\cdot\dfrac{B}{P}}{\dfrac{D_i + D_n}{P}} = \frac{D_i}{D_i + D_n} = \phi,$$

equation (5.3) may be rewritten as

(5.4) $$\dot{S} = \phi\,(\dot{I} + \dot{\alpha}) + (1 - \phi)\,(\dot{S}_n + \dot{\beta}),$$

where

$D_i$ = the number of infant deaths
$D_n$ = the number of non-infant deaths
$B$ = the number of births
$P_n$ = the number of non-infants alive at midyear
$P$ = the total number of individuals at all ages alive at midyear
$S$ = the age-standardized death rate
$I$ = the infant death rate
$S_n$ = the age-standardized non-infant death rate
$\alpha$ = the crude birthrate ($B/P$)
$\beta$ = the proportion of non-infants in the population ($P_n/P$)
$\cdot$ = an asterisk over a variable indicates the rate of change in that variable
$\phi$ = $[D_i/(D_i + D_n)]$ = the share of infant deaths in total deaths

It follows that if the birthrate and the age structure of the population are held constant, which is the assumption of the computation presented in the text, then equation (5.4) reduces to equation (5), since $\dot{\alpha} = \dot{\beta} = 0$.

The preceding derivation rests on two assumptions which require further consideration: First, the mortality schedule was treated as if it consisted of just two ages, without demonstrating that the reduction of the number of age intervals from $z$ to 2 does not invalidate the results. Second, since the percentages employed in equation (6) are large, there is the question of the appropriateness of applying an equation derived from differential approximations to discrete changes.

The first question can be addressed by beginning with the definition of an age-standardized rate, which is given by equation (5.5):

$$(5.5) \qquad S = \frac{P_0}{\Sigma_0 P_i} M_0 + \frac{P_1}{\Sigma_0 P_i} M_1 + \ldots + \frac{P_z}{\Sigma_0 P_i} M_z,$$

where

$P_i$ = the number of individuals at age $i$
$\Sigma_0 P_i$ = the total population
$M_i$ = the age-specific death rates.

Here, the $P_i/\Sigma_0 P_i$ are fixed from one time period to another; in other words, only the $M_i$ change so that $S_0 \neq S_i$ is due only to temporal differences in the $M_i$. If we let $\alpha_i = (P_i/\Sigma_0 P_i)$, equation (5.5) becomes

$$(5.6) \qquad S = \alpha_0 M_0 + \alpha_1 M_1 + \ldots + \alpha_z M_z.$$

Total differentation of equation (5.6) yields

$$(5.7) \quad \dot{S} = \frac{D_0}{\Sigma_0 D_i}(\dot{M}_0 + \dot{\alpha}_0) + \frac{D_1}{\Sigma_0 D_i}(\dot{M}_1$$

$$+ \dot{\alpha}_1) + \ldots + \frac{D_z}{\Sigma_0 D_i}(\dot{M}_z + \dot{\alpha}_z).$$

However, since by definition $\dot{\alpha}_i = 0$, equation (5.7) reduces to

$$(5.8) \quad \dot{S} = \frac{D_0}{\Sigma_0 D_i}\dot{M}_0 + \frac{D_1}{\Sigma_0 D_i}\dot{M}_1 + \ldots + \frac{D_z}{\Sigma_0 D_i}\dot{M}_z = \frac{\Sigma_0 D_i \dot{M}_i}{\Sigma_0 D_i}.$$

Now the sum of all the terms on the right-hand side of equation (5.8), except for the first term, is

$$(5.9) \qquad \frac{\Sigma_1^z D_i \dot{M}_i}{\Sigma_0^z D_i} = \dot{M}_x.$$

By induction, from equation (5.8), the average rate of change in the age-standardized rates above age 0 is

$$(5.10) \qquad \dot{S}_n = \frac{\Sigma_1 D_i \dot{M}_i}{\Sigma_1 D_i}.$$

If we let $\Sigma_1 D_i = D_n$ and $\Sigma_0 D_i = D_0 + D_n$, then it follows from equations (5.9) and (5.10) that

$$(5.11) \qquad (D_0 + D_n)\dot{M}_x = D_n \dot{S}_n, \text{ or } \frac{D_n}{D_0 + D_n}\dot{S}_n = \dot{M}_x.$$

Substituting equation (5.11) into equation (5.8) yields

(5.12)
$$\dot{S} = \frac{D_0}{D_0 + D_n} \dot{M}_0 + \frac{D_n}{D_0 + D_n} \dot{S}_n.$$

Then letting $\phi = \dfrac{D_0}{D_0 + D_n}$ and $\dot{I} = \dot{M}_0$, yields

(5.13)
$$\dot{S} = \phi\dot{I} + (1 - \phi)\dot{S}_n,$$

which is the same as equation (5).

The discrete analogue to equation (5.4) may be derived as follows:

(5.14)
$$S_1 = I_1 \alpha_1 + S_{n1} \beta_1,$$

(5.15)
$$S_0 = I_0 \alpha_0 + S_{n0} \beta_0,$$

(5.16)
$$\alpha_1 = \alpha_0 + \Delta\alpha$$

(5.17)
$$S_1 = S_0 + \Delta S$$

(5.18)
$$S_{n1} = S_{n0} + \Delta S_n$$

(5.19)
$$\beta_1 = \beta_0 + \Delta\beta.$$

(5.20)
$$I_1 = I_0 + \Delta I$$

Subtracting equation (5.15) from (5.14) and making the substitutions indicated in equations (5.16) – (5.20) yields

(5.21)   $\Delta S = \alpha_0\Delta I + I_0\Delta\alpha + \Delta I\Delta\alpha + \beta_0 \Delta S_n + S_{n0} \Delta\beta + \Delta S_n \Delta\beta.$

Then, dividing both sides of (5.21) by $S_0$ and multiplying the first right-hand term by $I_0/I_0$, the second by $\alpha_0/\alpha_0$, etc., yields

(5.22)   $\dot{S} = \phi(\dot{I} + \dot{\alpha} + \dot{I} \cdot \dot{\alpha}) + (1 - \phi)(\dot{S}_n + \dot{\beta} + \dot{S}_n \cdot \dot{\beta}),$

where

$$\phi = \frac{I_0\alpha_0}{S_0} = \frac{D_{i0}}{D_{i0} + D_{n0}}.$$

Equation (5.22) is the discrete analogue to equation (5.4), and these two equations differ only by the two interaction terms $\dot{I} \cdot \dot{\alpha}$ and $\dot{S}_n \cdot \dot{\beta}$. Since by nature of an age-standardized death rate $\dot{\alpha}$ and $\dot{\beta}$ are equal to zero, equation (5.22) also reduces to equation (5).

# Notes

1. Richard Hellie has called my attention to "the coincidence of the lowest life expectation [in table 9.2 above] with the Maunder Minimum (the Little Ice Age)," and notes that "the declining life expectations of the English peerage parallels the worsening

of the enserfment process in Russia, with the nadir of life expectations coinciding with the completion of the enserfment process." He suggests "that low yields and the generally unhealthier-than-usual climatic conditions" may have "played a role in driving both processes." From a letter to R. W. Fogel dated July 17, 1984.

2. From comments made at the Bellagio Conference on Hunger and History, June 1982.

3. The principal disadvantage of an emphasis on whole books is that a single aberrant book will have a large influence on the whole sample. Although such instances can be handled by reweighting, the aberrations reduce the efficiency of the sample and diminish its usefulness for some purposes. This problem will diminish as the sample size increases. The final sample will contain over a thousand books.

4. The mortality file is smaller than the family file partly because a requirement for entry into that file is that both the birth and the death dates of an individual are known. Nonbloodline spouses, who are at risk only after their marriages, have not yet been integrated into the mortality file. Their inclusion will increase the size of the mortality file by about 25%.

A family is defined by the existence of marriage, whether or not the family produces progeny. Families with multiple marriages have not yet been integrated into the family file, but they are a relatively small percentage of the families already in the file. Bloodline individuals who marry will appear in both their families of birth and the families formed by their marriages. The number of families suitable for the computations of various statistics varies because of the completeness of information. For example, it is possible to compute total births in completed families for about 77% of the families. In most of the other 23% of the families, date of publication of the genealogy preceded the end of the childbearing period of families at risk to have children. However, mother's age at last birth can be computed only for about 35% of the families since computation of this statistic not only requires that the date of publication of a genealogy follow the end of the childbearing period, but also requires information on the date of birth of both the mother and of the last child.

The small percentage of the individuals in the sample who have been linked to economic information reflects the recent start on this task. As of May 1984 we had searched for economic information on only 20% of the individuals in the sample. In other words, so far we have been able to obtain economic information on about 75% of the individuals for whom this information was sought.

5. The Mormon Church was not founded until 1830. The religious objective behind the compilation of family group sheets required the identification of ancestors who had not been Mormons. There are three parts to the collection of family group sheets. The *Main Section* consists of about 4.7 million sheets submitted mainly before 1962 and contains information on about 25 million individuals, only a small proportion of whom are Mormons. The *New Patrons Section* was started in 1962 when members of the Mormon Church were asked to submit sheets on the most recent four generations of their families. There are about 1 million sheets in this part of the collection, and a fairly large proportion of the individuals in these sheets are Mormons. The *Old Patrons Section* was launched in 1924 and consists of any genealogical records held by Church members that they desired to place on deposit in the Genealogical Library. There are about 4 million sheets in this part of the collection. The DAE/CPE pilot sample of group sheets is drawn from the *Main Section*. See Wimmer 1984.

6. About 43% of males age 20 and over had zero real wealth. The largest endowment in the linked genealogical sample thus far is about $200,000 which falls into the top 0.01% of the national distribution estimated by Soltow (1975) for 1850.

7. The first term was suggested by P. H. Lindert at the Williamsburg meeting.

8. In practice "health" is usually defined as "freedom from clinically ascertainable disease" (Great Britain Department of Health Social Service 1980). Measures of health include morbidity rates, mortality rates, number of GP consultations, days absent from school, disability days, days absent from work, parental assessments, weekly laboratory cultures, and weekly clinical diagnosis. Responses to key questions (e.g., "Do you have any physical difficulty with shopping?") are also used (Balinsky 1975; Blaxter 1976; McKeown 1976b; Sackett et al. 1977; Martorell 1980).

9. I do not mean to argue that average stature cannot be employed to assess factors affecting the general level of health in a population, but only to argue against the notion

that the health and stature are synonyms. The relationship between growth retardation and disease is complex, varying from one disease to another, and from one context to another. Consequently, while it may be possible to use data on stature to make valid statements about the probable level of exposure to certain diseases, a great deal more will have to be learned than is now known about complex interactions within a multivariate context. (The same caveat applies to attempts to infer diet from stature without controlling for exposure to disease and other relevant variables.) An oversimplified approach which assumes strict proportionality or some other simple relationship between stunting, or its absence, will miss or greatly underestimate nearly all respiratory diseases, most chronic diseases, many infectious fevers, and most nonspecific disorders—much of the range of diseases occurring among well-fed populations. Indeed, in one study anthropometric measures and the incidence of nonspecific health disorders were positively and significantly correlated (Butler 1974; Martorell et al. 1975; Condon-Paoloni et al. 1977; Briscoe 1979; Beisel 1977; Cole and Perkin 1977; Mata et al. 1977; Frisancho 1978; Martorell 1980; Baumgartner and Mueller 1984). On the other hand, I believe that there is enough evidence around to permit us to investigate and establish the robustness of these complex interrelationships. Given adequate patience, caution, and a good deal of ancillary information, we may be able to establish the likely combination of factors which affected growth profiles. In secs. 9.3 and 9.4 of this paper attempts are made to identify situations in which such inferences may be tenable.

10. Because the series of $e_{10}$ is not yet controlled for the variables that were controlled in producing the height series, considerable caution needs to be exercised in interpreting leads and lags which are evident in the two series of fig. 9.1.

11. See appendix A for a discussion of the procedures employed in constructing the two time series displayed in fig. 9.1. Table 9.A.1 gives the values of each of the entries.

12. Levy's life tables begin with age 25. The $e_{10}$ values shown for his data in figure 9.1 were extrapolated to age 10, using the model West tables of Coale and Demeny (1966).

13. Levy also has a life table for 1650–99 which was used to establish the location and slope of the line segment between 1715 and 1725 which shows the effect of a possible correction for the undercount of southern observations in the genealogical sample employed in fig. 9.1.

14. At the Williamsburg meetings Paul A. David and Warren C. Sanderson called our attention to a time series of $e_{10}$ contained in a dissertation by Kent Kunze (1979) which overlaps with our series. Kunze covers the period from 1800 to 1880 in 14 life tables for males (and an additional 14 for females). His first table is based on a 15-year period (1800–1815), the second on a 10-year period (1815–25), and the remaining 12 are for quinquennia centered on years ending with zero or five. Kunze's data were obtained from samples of the family group sheets in the files of the Genealogical Society of the Church of Jesus Christ of Latter-day Saints. Only information on individuals who resided outside of Utah were included in his computations. Foreign-born as well as native-born white individuals were included.

Over the years in which they overlap, Kunze's series and the DAE/CPE series depict quite similar patterns. Both show a fairly steady decline after 1805. His series bottoms out in 1865 and then rises. The DAE/CPE series bottoms out 1857 and then rises. The decline of $e_{10}$ in Kunze's series from 1807 to 1865 is 10%, which is the same decline as that shown in the DAE/CPE series between 1807 and 1857. However, between the peak of the DAE/CPE series (which occurred 1792, about 15 years before Kunze's first observation) and its trough, the decline in about 16%. (All dates are approximate.)

15. An improvement in the diet is not by itself a sufficient basis for inferring an increase in final heights, since a substantial secular deterioration in environmental conditions could have offset the potential improvement in nutritional status associated with a better diet. Based on current knowledge of the epidemiology of Massachusetts during 1675–1720, however, such a deterioration seems unlikely (Duffy 1953; Vinovskis 1972).

16. The elasticity of the mortality rate with respect to height in Trinidad was estimated from regressions (and the mean values of the variables in these regressions) reported in a memorandum from Meredith John to Robert W. Fogel dated November 30, 1983. I used four of John's logit regressions relating the probability of surviving to a series of variables including height. These regressions were for males ≥ age 15 (p. 36), females ≥ age 15 (p. 39), males ≤ age 15 (p. 42), females age ≤ 15 (p. 43). The elasticities for

these four groups (estimated over the arc between the average height of each group of Trinidadians and the current British height standard for the mean age of each group) were: $\epsilon_{m<15} = -2.00$, $\epsilon_{f<15} = -1.54$, $\epsilon_{m\geq15} = -2.50$, $\epsilon_{f\geq15} = 0$. The average of these four elasticities (weighted by the share of each group in the total population of Trinidad) was $-1.57$. If English population weights in 1801–5 are used (Wrigley and Schofield 1981, p. 529), the average elasticity is $-1.44$ (the sex ratio was assumed to be equal both above and below age 15, since Wrigley and Schofield do not give the sex ratio by age). United States population weights for 1980 (United States Bureau of Census 1983, p. 33) yield an elasticity of $-1.33$. Population weights for England and Wales for 1851 and 1961 (Mitchell 1975, p. 52) yield elasticities of $-1.41$ and $-1.32$.

17. The eight nations included in the Floud (1983b) study and the dates covered are Belgium (1880–1969), Denmark (1880–1975), France (1880–1960), Italy (1880–1952), Netherlands (1877–1970), Norway (1880–1960), Sweden (1880–1961), and Switzerland (1884–1957).

18. Total differentation of eq. (3) yields

$$（3.1) \qquad \dot{I} = -15.9106\dot{H} - 0.3889\dot{Y} - 0.00837,$$

where an asterisk over a variable indicates the rate of change in that variable. Regressions of the log of each of the variables in equations (2) and (3) on time yielded the following estimates of average annual rates of change:

| Variable | Average Annual Rate of Change (%) |
|---|---|
| $\dot{C}$ | $-1.05$ |
| $\dot{I}$ | $-2.51$ |
| $\dot{H}$ | $0.0610$ |
| $\dot{Y}$ | $1.75$ |

It follows that height accounts for 39% ($15.9106 \times 0.0610 \div 2.51 = 0.39$), income for 27% ($0.3889 \times 1.75 \div 2.51 = 0.27$) and time for 33% ($0.837 \div 2.51 = 0.33$) of the average annual decline in the infant death rate.

19. The similarity between the results of eq. (2) and (3) and John's (1984) set of logit regressions on the probability of dying in Trinidad should not obscure the significant differences in the nature of the two sets of regressions. The Trinidad regressions related the *own* height of an individual to *his or her* probability of dying between two points in time. Equation (3), on the other hand, relates the average height of males (mainly in their early twenties) to a nation's infant death rate. When used in this way adult heights have only indirect bearing on the nutritional status of infants. Since the adult heights measure the nutritional status of males during the preceding 2–3 decades, and since the mean nutritional status of a nation exhibits high serial correlation, such a lagged measure of average nutritional status may be a fairly good predictor of a nation's current nutritional status especially during a period when the nutritional status of particular nations has been changing in a fairly steady way. Adult heights also have a bearing on current infant mortality rates to the extent that they indicate the nutritional circumstances of mothers during their developmental years. When comparing several nations, lagged measures may be a good predictor of differences in current nutritional status if the different nations had different starting levels and different rates of change in nutritional status.

20. The figure 64.5 inches is the estimated mean height of the pool of adult males from which recruits into the Royal Marines were drawn. Floud and Wachter have not yet completed their examination of possible sample selection and other biases in their military samples. Consequently, the use of 64.5 inches as an estimate of the mean final height of English males reaching maturity around 1800 must be considered tentative and is subject to revision. However, no currently plausible revision (the possibilities of change are pretty well bounded by ± 1.0 inches) would substantially alter the estimates of the effect of improved nutritional status on the decline in non-infant mortality rates.

21. Neonatal deaths are those which occur within the first 28 days of life. Perinatal deaths are late fetal deaths (generally of 20 or 28 weeks of gestational age) plus early neonatal deaths (generally deaths during the first 7 days after birth). In the United States

and Great Britain during the early 1960s the distribution of infant deaths was approximately as follows (Shapiro et al. 1968):

| Days | % | Cumulative Percentage |
|---|---|---|
| 1 | 40 | 40 |
| 2–7 | 25 | 65 |
| 8–28 | 8 | 73 |
| 29–365 | 27 | 100 |

Late fetal deaths in Britain and the United States have recently been approximately equal to neonatal deaths (United States Bureau of the Census 1983, p. 77). For countries experiencing death rates in the range of 100 per thousand and over, neonatal deaths range between 35% and 70% (Bouvier and Tak 1976; Mata 1978, table 2.16; Ashworth 1982).

Wrigley and Schofield (1981, p. 97) estimate neonatal deaths in England during the seventeenth and eighteenth centuries at about half of infant deaths. However, the practice of treating infant deaths during the 7–9 days as stillbirths, common in England and America before 1900 and still common in some high-mortality societies today, suggests that neonatal death rates may have been substantially underestimated. Although Wrigley and Schofield wrestled with this problem, the procedure they developed for correcting the bias may only have captured a part of the undercount in infant deaths. Their procedure rests on the assumption that the count of deaths during the last 11 months of infancy is virtually complete, and that there is a linear relationship between cumulated deaths (per thousand births) during the course of the first year and the cube of the log of days (plus one) elapsed since birth. Their procedure is described briefly in Wrigley and Schofield (1981, pp. 98–100), and at greater length in Wrigley (1977); see Knodel and Kintner (1977) and Hogan (1976), for discussions of the linearity assumption. Other reasons for a possible substantial undercount of mortality by Wrigley and Schofield, especially after the turn of the nineteenth century, are suggested by Lindert (1983). The small stature of the English workers prior to 1820 and the high correlation between the infant death rate and stature at age 3 and at maturity (see Floud 1985a; Steckel 1985) also indicate that infant mortality rates were substantially higher than suggested by Wrigley and Schofield. However, because of the widespread consumption of alcohol and other toxic substances by pregnant women, and the probable undercount of deaths during the first 7–9 days, 0.6 seems to be a more appropriate figure. See n. 34 and sec. 9.4.2 below.

22. However, in recent years new high technology introduced into maternity hospitals in the more developed nations has led to some downward shift in this schedule, especially for births of less than 1,500 grams that are of early gestational age but not otherwise impaired (Jones et al. 1979; *Lancet* 1980, p. 481; Pharoah and Alberman 1981).

23. The distribution of birthweights is not normal, mainly because there are too many observations in the left tail. The fat left tail may be treated as the result of adding together a distribution of the weights of underdeveloped babies (which I will call "pre-term") to a much larger distribution of fully developed babies (which I will call "full term"). Nevertheless, for the purposes to which they are put in fig. 9.5, normal approximations to the distribution of the United States nonwhite and Bombay lower classes yield satisfactory results. The mean and standard deviation in the normal approximation to the United States distribution differs from those of the actual distribution by less than 1% (Chase 1969). In the Bombay case the difference in the means is less than 1% (the standard deviation of the sample was not reported) (Jayant 1964).

24. In this case it was necessary to estimate the heaping of preterm births on the left tail of the distribution of birthweights. My procedure was based on the proposition set forth in fn. 23 that the observed distribution of birthweights may be viewed as the result of a convolution of a small distribution of weights of preterm babies which is heaped on the left tail of a much larger distribution of weights of full-term babies that is normally distributed. Under this assumption the underlying normal distribution can be recovered by truncating the left tail of the distribution at (say) 2,001 grams and then using the QBE procedure described in Wachter (1981) and Wachter and Trussell (1982) to estimate the

complete normal distribution of full-term babies. It follows that the difference between the number of observations below 2,001 grams in the reconstituted normal distribution and in the original distribution yields an estimate of the distribution of preterm babies that have been heaped on the left tail.

In estimating col. 4 of table 9.10, which is graphed in fig. 9.5, I assumed that the underlying full-term distribution was $N(2,300; 420)$. To this distribution I then added the estimated number of preterm births at weights below 2,001 grams, using ratios obtained from Guha et al. (1973) which provides information on birthweight by gestational age for a Delhi sample quite similar to the Bombay sample. Basically, the number of births under 2,001 grams in the original normal distribution was inflated by the ratio of all births to full-term births in the Delhi sample, but the additional births were distributed over two intervals: under 1501 and 1,501–2,000. This adjustment for preterm births produced a convoluted distribution with a mean of 2,276 grams (down 24 grams from the underlying normal) and a standard deviation of 399 grams (down 21 grams from the underlying normal).

Although the mean birthweight of the hypothetical distribution is quite low, it is consistent with the final height of English workers 1800–1810 and the high infant death rates indicated by current estimates (before adequate allowance is made for the undercount of deaths during the first 9 days after birth). In this connection, I would emphasize the likelihood that the mean birthweight in rural areas of countries such as India and Bangladesh is below those prevailing in the hospitals of their large cities. This inference is consistent with evidence indicating that incomes and final heights are generally lower (and the infant death rates are higher) in the rural areas of these countries than in the cities. In the villages covered by the Narangwal experiment, e.g., the mean birthweight was below 2,500 grams (Kielmann et al. 1983). Moreover, babies born to women of a given socioeconomic class in hospitals are liable to be higher by several hundred grams than those born to women of the same class at home because of the phenomenas discussed in fn. 25.

See Steckel (1985) for an alternative procedure that produces similar results.

25. My estimate of the mean birthweight of lower-class children is about 590 grams (about 1.3 pounds) less than mean weights of about 27,000 births at the Maternité de Port Royal in Paris delivered during the first decade of the nineteenth century (Tanner 1981, pp. 255–56). I suspect that this differential was due partly to late third-trimester weight gains associated with much improved diets received by mothers while at the Maternité. Until the late nineteenth or early twentieth century lying-in hospitals, often called prematernity homes, functioned more as charities aimed at rescuing destitute women and their often illegitimate children than as scientific institutions. The aim of these hospitals was to provide food, clothing, and shelter to "poor and desperate" women who were awaiting delivery, rather than to offer a surgical type of facility (Vogel 1980, pp. 12–13). Destitute expectant mothers were often kept in these hospitals for several weeks or longer on a nutritious diet before their deliveries. A study of birthweights at English prematernity homes shortly after the turn of the twentieth century revealed that the birthweight of children whose mothers worked up to the day of confinement averaged 280 grams less than those of mothers who were confined to the homes for 10 days (Ashby 1915).

Since 45% of the increase in fetal weight normally takes place during the last 8 weeks of pregnancy (Thomson et al. 1968; Birkbeck 1976; Southgate 1978), birthweights at the Maternité may well have exceeded the average of babies born to working-class women in England and France during the first decade of the nineteenth century by the 590 grams suggested by the birthweight distribution of fig. 9.5. The combination of an enforced sedentary life together with a substantial increase in the intake of nutrients for several weeks could have led to a substantially larger gain in the weight of fetuses than would otherwise have been the case. The exceedingly high death rates among deliveries in the maternity hospitals of the nineteenth century, as much as seven times as high as home deliveries (McKeown 1976a), is consistent with this possibility. One would expect an unusually high rate of stillbirths and neonatal deaths among fetuses that suffered first trimester insults, even though they had high levels of nutrition during the third trimester (Hurley 1980; Moore 1983).

In the case of food-supplemented pregnancies (when supplementation begins late in, or after, the first trimester), mean birth size may not be as good a predictor or perinatal and neonatal mortality rates (Kielmann et al. 1983) as in unsupplemented feeding regimens. This discrepancy may be due to the diversity of responses to first trimester insults and later supplementation. Some pregnancies will abort early. Some fetuses that have suffered permanent impairment during the first trimester will continue to develop (at a retarded rate) and will be at high risk late in the third trimester and after birth. Still, others will fully recover from the first trimester trauma and, as a result of supplementation, will experience third trimester weight gains that are greater than they otherwise would have been. It seems likely, therefore, that a very poor first trimester diet (or other nutritional insult) combined with supplementation in the third trimester will increase the coefficient of variation in birthweights (with an uncertain effect on the mean weight, since supplementation may increase the proportion of small-for-dates fetuses that are born alive). This appears to have been the case in the Maternité. Its coefficient of variation is 26% higher than that of a sample of 43 populations with low mean birthweights (under 3,000 grams) reported in the WHO survey (1980).

Two recent studies, one on births between 1851 and 1905 at the University Lying-In Hospital in Montreal (Ward and Ward 1984), the other births between 1848 and 1865 at the Philadelphia Alms House (Goldin and Margo 1984), promise to increase our knowledge of nineteenth-century birth size and of its bearing on perinatal deaths during that century. The Wards have discovered a decline in mean birthweight of about 420 grams between the late 1860s and the beginning of the twentieth century. The Wards are also collecting birthweight data for the nineteenth and early twentieth centuries from a number of other lying-in hospitals in North America and Europe. Preliminary analysis of the Philadelphia data by Goldin and Margo not only indicates a decline in birthweights between the mid-1850s and the mid-1860s, but also reveals that the first-day death rate, even for live births in the range of 3,000–4,000 grams, was about twice as high as in the United States national sample in 1950. Goldin and Margo are also collecting data that will relate the duration of the stay in the Alms House prior to birth to birthweights and to perinatal mortality rates.

26. I have not distinguished birthweight and length by sex since it is a refinement not justified by the rough calculations which follow. At birth the mean weight of girls is less than that of boys, but the difference is only about 100 grams (about 3 ounces). The average difference in birth length between the sexes is about 0.6 centimeters (about a quarter of an inch) and shows less variation across nations than weight differences. Cf. Tanner et al. 1966; Hytten and Leitch 1971; Eveleth and Tanner 1976; Beal 1980; and the sources cited in WHO 1980.

I have used 0.6 rather than the 0.5 figure employed by Wrigley and Schofield as the share of infant deaths that occurred during the neonatal period, partly because of the widespread ingestion of toxic substances by pregnant women (cf. the discussion in nn.21, 33, 34, and in sec. 9.4.2 above).

The percentage reduction in the infant death rate due to a shift in the birthweight schedule is quite robust to the principal assumptions employed in table 9.10. If, for example, I had used assumptions which yielded an than indicated in table 9.10), the decline in the infant mortality rate due to the shift in the birthweight schedule would still be 76% $[1 - (48.9 \div 200.0) = 0.76]$.

27. See app. B for the derivation of eq. (5).

28. Wrigley and Schofield (1981, p. 529) give the following values for 1801–5:

$$e_0 = 35.89$$

$$cdr = 27.08$$

$$cbr = 37.71.$$

The appropriate value of $_1Q_0$ (179.0 per thousand) for the indicated value of $e_0$ was obtained from their table A14.5 (p. 714) by interpolating between their levels 8 and 9. Then $37.71 \times 0.179 = 6.42$ is the number of infant deaths per 1,000 persons in the total population. Consequently, infant deaths were 23.7% of all deaths ($6.42 \div 27.08 = 0.237$).

29. The age-standardized death rate in Britain circa 1980 was 8.32 per thousand, using the Wrigley and Schofield (1981, p. 529) age distribution for 1801–5 and the 1978–80 life table for the United Kingdom to estimate the $_nm_x$ values (Great Britain Central Statistical Office 1983, p.43). Since the crude death rate for 1801–5 in Wrigley and

Schofield (1981, p. 529) was 27.08, the decline in the standardized mortality rate is 18.76. Non-infant deaths were 20.66 per thousand in 1801–5 ($0.763 \times 27.08 = 20.66$). Then $20.66 \times 0.1085 = 2.24$ is the reduction in non-infant mortality due to improved nutrition. The last figure is 12% of the total decline in mortality ($2.24 \div 18.76 = 0.119$).

30. Some caveats about the foregoing estimates are in order. After maturity, height will not adequately measure nutritional status unless the relationship between nutritional status during the growing ages and after maturity is not only strong but of a simple form. Consequently, the computations presented in the text may miss part of the effects of improvements in nutritional status after maturity on the decline in adult mortality. The assumption that the elasticity between $_nQ_x$ and height is stable with respect to time, place, and circumstances (which is involved in the application of the Trinidad elasticity to the British case) requires confirmation and may have to be modified as additional evidence becomes available.

31. Roger Schofield has called my attention to evidence which suggests that diseases listed in the first column of table 9.11 might have accounted for the majority of deaths among the peerage well before 1750. I do not mean to suggest that the shift in the distribution of diseases is the main factor explaining the decline in the death rate of the peerage, but only that it might have played some role. The principal point of this paragraph is that improvements in nutritional status could not have played a significant role in reducing the death rates of either the peerage or of the lower classes as long as the main killer diseases were those whose outcome was unaffected by nutritional status. Just when this shift took place, or even whether it took place, is still an open issue. Some students of medieval demography believe that the outcome of epidemics of medieval plague, or at least some forms of it, may have been influenced by nutritional status. See, e.g., Hellie 1982.

32. From a letter to R. W. Fogel dated July 16, 1984.

33. A half-pound of hard-salted herring, bacon, or similarly cured meat per capita per day (and upper-class individuals may have consumed that much at breakfast alone—cf. n. 34) would have exceeded maximum "safe" levels of sodium consumption for an average individual by more than fivefold. Salt was also used much more heavily than today to cure and flavor butter (about 1.5 ounces of salt per pound of butter) and other dairy products, and in bread (five pounds of salt per sack of flour) and porridges. Sodium occurs naturally in significant quantities in various root vegetables, pulses, milk, beer, meats, and fish (Encyclopedia Britannica 1961, 2:888; Ashbrook 1955; Webster 1845, pp. 747, 773–833, 1135; Davidson et al. 1979; Meneely and Battarbee 1976; United States Senate 1977).

34. According to Dyer (1983, pp. 193–94) a gallon of ale was the standard ration for adult males in "lordly households" during the late medieval era, but superior members of the household consumed two or three pints of this amount as wine. At Northumberland the Lord and Lady split a quart of beer and a quart of wine at breakfast alone (along with two pieces of salt fish and six baked herrings), and even the children in the nursery consumed a quart of beer at breakfast. Children of all classes drank ale or beer, but usually of a weaker type than their parents (Pullar 1970; Wilson 1973). The per capita ration of ale for nuns at Syon was 7 gallons per week (Pullar 1970, p. 111). According to Thurgood (1984, p. 6) the accounts of the first Duke of Buckingham during the mid-fifteenth century indicate that daily consumption of wine among "upper members of the household" was about a half gallon per capita. If peeresses consumed two-thirds of a gallon of liquid, half as ale and half as wine, then their daily consumption of absolute alcohol would have been between 7.2 ounces (allowing 4% of absolute alcohol in ale and 11% in wine) and 9.1 ounces (if the percentage of absolute alcohol in ale is set at 8%). Even if peeresses drank only weak ale (4% absolute alcohol) their daily consumption of absolute alcohol would still have averaged about 3.4 ounces. Recent studies indicate that among women whose daily consumption of absolute alcohol during pregnancy equaled 2 or more ounces per day, about one out of five newborns suffered from symptoms of Fetal Alcohol Syndrome (Hanson et al. 1978; Abel 1982). Heavy salt intake further endangered fetuses by causing edema and by increasing the likelihood of kidney damage (United States Senate 1977).

35. The balance of this section presents a highly condensed version of the analysis set forth in Fogel (1987). See that paper for the derivation of the equations and the estimates of parameters that are merely reported in this section.

36. Estimates of the social distribution of the population based on revisions of King's table (Lindert 1980; Lindert and Williamson 1983b) would not significantly affect the analysis that follows.

37. The provisional nature of the estimates of these parameters and of those set forth in eq. (11) should be emphasized. Although consistent with the available evidence thus far developed for the early modern era, current research into estate and probate records and similar sources should permit improvements in these estimates. See Fogel (1987) for a discussion of the effects of plausible variations in these parameters on the estimates of entitlement shifts, foodgrain shortfalls, overall food shortfalls, and famine-induced mortality rates. Cf. the discussion in n. 40.

38. A yield/seed ratio of 8 implies that 12.5% of the crop was used for seed, and grains used as feed for work animals may have accounted for a like amount by the beginning of the eighteenth century. Hoskins (1964, 1968) and other economic historians have implicitly assumed that the seed elasticity of demand was close to zero. However, econometric estimates of agricultural production functions, as well as controlled experiments by plant breeders, suggest a fairly high elasticity of substitution between seeds and other inputs. That finding, together with the theory of demand for inputs, suggests that 0.6 is a reasonable estimate of $\epsilon_s$ (Fogel 1987).

39. The grain price series used here includes peas and beans, which were also used to make bread during the early modern era. The prices are from Bowden (1967, 1985). Missing entries in the peas and beans series were linearly interpolated. Peas and beans were then added to the Bowden grain series, using a weight of 0.165 each for peas and beans and 0.67 for Bowden's grain series.

40. The assumption that yields were lognormally distributed (there is a slightly better fit of grain prices to a lognormal than a normal distribution) would have little effect on the analysis that follows. Under the lognormal assumption the estimated value of $\sigma_g$ would rise by only 4% (from 0.066 to 0.069). In this paper I have, therefore, employed the normal assumption in order to simplify the exposition. See Fogel (1987) for the results obtained when the analysis is based on a lognormal distribution of yields.

41. I believe that this estimate of $\sigma_g$ is probably too high. Since I did not take account of a hoarding and speculative demand, my assumption that $\epsilon_t = 0.37$ probably biases the value of $\sigma_g$ upward. If, for example, hoarding demand reduced $\epsilon_t$ to 0.25, $\sigma_g$ would be just 0.045.

It is possible to estimate $\sigma_g$ directly for the first 30 years (1884–1913) that output and yield-per-acre data are available in Great Britain (Mitchell and Deane 1962). Yields on wheat, barley, and oats were combined into an index of grain yields (using equal weights), and then detrended by regressing the index on time. The S.D. of the errors divided by the mean of the index, $\sigma_g$, was 0.051. However, $\sigma_g$ is determined not purely by deviations in the per acre yields of these grains but by deviations from trend in the total supply of all grains. When total supply of all grains (broadly defined) was taken into account, the estimate of $\sigma_g$ for the period 1884–1913 dropped to 0.035 (Great Britain House of Commons 1899, 1917; Great Britain Ministry Agricultural Fishery 1927). These two figures (0.051 and 0.035) may be taken as reasonable estimates of the bounds within which $\sigma_g$ probably fell during 1540–1871 (cf. Fogel 1987).

If we now substitute 0.051 for $\sigma_g$ in eq. (12), that equation becomes $1.2 \times 0.051 = 0.061\bar{X}_g$. Hence, we can estimate $\epsilon_t$ from log $0.939 = \epsilon_t$log 1.25, which yields a value of 0.282 for $\epsilon_t$. Similarly, if we use 0.035 for $\sigma_g$, the estimate of $\epsilon_t$ becomes 0.192. These computations suggest that failure to take account of the speculative demand may have biased the estimate of $\epsilon_t$ used in the text upward by between 31% and 93%. The correction of $\sigma_g$ and $\epsilon_t$ would also reduce the estimates of $\epsilon_{gw}$, $\sigma_f$, and $\epsilon_{fw}$ by similar proportions. Cf. n. 46 below.

42. The S.D. of deviations of wheat prices from a 25-year moving average was computed from the price series of Bowden (1967, 1985). Lee (Wrigley and Schofield 1981, p. 374), using a somewhat different series of wheat prices, found that the SD of the deviations around an 11-year moving average was 0.25 during 1540–1640 and 0.24 during 1641–1745.

43. The S.D. in the total food supply ($\sigma_f$) was estimated from the "all-agricultural-products" price series developed by Bowden (1967, 1985). The deviations in food prices were computed from a 25-year moving average of this series. The weight of food in Bowden's series varies between 87% and 97%. When the Phelps Brown and Hopkins

series (1956) of the price consumables (in which food has a weight of 80%) is used, $\sigma_f$ is 0.043.

44. This estimate of the decline in the food supply is based on Bowden's (1967, 1985) all-agriculture price series. When the price series of consumables constructed by Phelps Brown and Hopkins (1956) is used, equation (16) becomes

(16.1)                          $\epsilon_{fw} = 0.172r_{fw}.$

This equation also implies that there were only 8 years with food shortfalls in excess of 7%. In setting up eq. (15), I assumed $\epsilon_f$ for all food was the same as for all grain, which probably biases the estimate of $\sigma_f$ upward.

45. The first figure in the parentheses is the proportionate increase in the national cdr due to a 23% decline in food consumption by the class of common laborers. The second figure is the proportion of years $(1 \div 41)$ in which such a decline occurred. For reasons explained in n. 41 and 46, the upper bound on famine deaths as a percentage of accumulated total deaths during 1541–1871 may be as low as 0.1

46. Lee (Wrigley and Schofield 1981, pp. 370–73) finds a sharp decline in fertility between 3 and 9 months after a rise in wheat prices, which he attributes to first and second trimester fetal mortality. Not all fetuses that suffered nutritional insults would have died. One would also expect an increase in neonatal death rates because impaired fetuses survived the entire gestation period but died shortly after birth. In other words, some part of the apparent fertility decline in year zero may be due to a rise in infant mortality that was unmeasured. If we add half of the zero-year elasticity of fertility decline to the zero-year elasticity of mortality rise, Lee's 5-year cumulated elasticity of mortality rates with respect to a rise in wheat prices becomes 0.163.

The last figure is not far from the elasticity implied by my computation, which is about 0.23. A 23% decrease in the food consumption of the class of common laborers requires (from eq. [14] and the accompanying text) a 70% increase in wheat prices and will lead to a 16% increase in the national cdr in such a year. Hence, the elasticity of the national cdr with respect to wheat prices is $0.16 \div 0.70 = 0.23$. For various reasons that I have suggested, this last figure is an upper bound. If, for example, I had made allowance for a speculative demand for wheat, the elasticity of the mortality rate with respect to wheat prices implied by my computations would have been between 0.163 and 0.094. Cf. n. 41.

47. This widely used assumption in the analysis of time series on grain prices was questioned by Landes in 1950, but his caveat has been largely unheeded.

48. A similar point was made by Flinn (1974, p. 315) in a different context. Citing the work of two French demographic historians (J. Meuvret and J. Lebrun), Flinn argued that after the beginning of the eighteenth century "improved social organization prevented the very poor from actually dying from starvation during a famine, but it did not rescue them from their more permanent state of undernourishment which left them vulnerable to both endemic and epidemic disease. This kind of social action, in other words, leveled the unevennesses of mortality without reducing it in aggregate."

49. Galenson (1981) has shown that the majority of English immigrants to North America were from the lower classes. If it is assumed that the mean height of adult male immigrants before 1650 was 64.5 inches (the approximate mean male adult height of the English laboring population for cohorts born ca. 1750), then the implied rate of increase in adult height between immigrants born ca. 1630 and native cohorts born ca. 1710 was about 1 centimeter per decade. There is no information currently available on the mean height of English cohorts born before 1750. However, the high mortality rates in England between 1625 and 1790 (Wrigley and Schofield 1981, pp. 528–29) suggest that there was little change in height schedules during this period. (Cf. Palliser [1982] on conditions during 1300–1640.)

50. Swedish and Norwegian adult heights appear to have increased fairly rapidly during the first third of the nineteenth century. However, the secular increase slowed during the middle third of the century and accelerated during the last third (Kiil 1939; Udjus 1964; Sandberg and Steckel 1980).

51. The estimate of the Gini ratio for the distribution of income ca. 1900 (0.47) was obtained from Steckel's regression, Gallman's income estimate for that year (converted in dollars of 1970), and the adult height estimate for ca. 1900 derived from the data in

fig. 9.1. Alternative specifications of Steckel's regression, with dummies for high-income countries raised the estimated Gini ratio for ca. 1900 to about 0.50. A Gini ratio can be computed from the income distribution for 1900 estimated by Lebergott (1976) from budget surveys. That computation yielded a Gini ratio of 0.56.

52. The equation used in this computation can be derived as follows:

(17.1) $$H = (1 - \pi) H_u + \pi(H_u - D).$$

Hence

(17.2) $$H = H_u - \pi D.$$

Differentiating (17.2) totally yields:

(17.3) $$\dot{H} = \psi \dot{H}_u - (\psi - 1)(\dot{\pi} + \dot{D})$$

where

$H$ = the mean height of the population
$H_u$ = the mean height of the upper class
$D$ = the difference between the mean height of the upper and the lower class
$\pi$ = the share of the lower class in the total population
$\psi$ = $H_u \div H$
$\overset{\cdot}{\phantom{a}}$ = an asterisk over a variable indicates the rate of change in that variable.

In eq. (17.3) both $\dot{D}$ and $\dot{\pi}$ only enter into the second right-hand term. Thus, we can measure the share of increase in the mean height of the English that is due to the growth of the upper class just by computing $\psi \dot{H}_u \div \dot{H}$. The values of the variables needed to compute this ratio and the sources of the estimates are as follows:

$H^0 = 64.7''$   (a weighted average of the mean height of the pool from which British soldiers aged 23–35 were recruited into the British armed forces in 1810 and of the implied final height of Sandhurst boys (1820), using a weight of 0.05 for the share of the gentry in the English population. The share is from Laslett (1984). The Sandhurst height data are from the unpublished files of Floud described in table 9.6).
$H^1 = 68.9''$   (Rona et al. 1978, table 3).
$H_u^0 = 68.9''$   (The Sandhurst sample, and the ratio of the final height to heights at age 15 computed from the United States Civil War sample).
$H_u^1 = 69.9''$   (Rona et al. 1978, table 3).

These data yield the following estimates (rates of change are in % per annum; the period of change was assumed to be 150 years):

$$\dot{H} = 0.042$$

$$\dot{H}_u = 0.010$$

$$\psi = 1.040 \; [0.5(68.9 \div 64.7) + 0.5(69.9 \div 68.9)]$$

and

$$\frac{\psi \dot{H}_u}{\dot{H}} = 0.25.$$

53. It is likely that immigrants too poor to provide their growing children with adequate nutrition (which may be viewed as an intergenerational transfer of human capital) also were unable to provide children with adequate transfers of ordinary capital.

54. The quote is from a letter to R. W. Fogel dated November 30, 1984. Similar points were called to my attention by S. Peltzman and P. A. David.

55. It is, of course, possible that the increase in Midwestern per capita income was accompanied by a rise in the inequality of the income distribution sufficient to impoverish a substantial percentage of the region's population. Even if it is unlikely that the per-

centage so impoverished would have been large enough by itself to explain the observed height decline, it could have been a nontrivial contributing factor.

56. There is also the possibility that part of the decline is a statistical artifact. It might be argued that children of the farm families who enlisted during the peacetime years of the 1880s came, on average, from poorer families than those who enlisted during wartime years. On the other hand, the mean height of the native-born population as estimated from the recruits who joined the regular army during the peacetime years of 1850–55 was 68.1 inches, which is just one-tenth of an inch below the corresponding figure for the Union army (Sokoloff 1984).

57. Our investigation of available data sources indicated that there is enough quantifiable information on the disease environment of localities in the recruiting and station records of the United States Army, in the surveys of medical societies and public health officials, and in mortality records to be able to construct time series on the extent of exposure to particular diseases by counties (by wards within large cities) or at least by congressional districts. We have, therefore, initiated a new project aimed at collecting and analyzing these data.

58. Meade (1955) and Kuznets (1959) called attention to the fallacies that may arise in growth accounting when the effect of mortality rates on the measured growth in per capita income is neglected.

59. This point was made in another context by Butlin (1971).

60. For the period 1790–1860 the best current estimate of the average annual rate of increases in United States "real" per capita income appears to be about 0.71% (David 1967; Engerman and Gallman 1983). The mortality increase between 1790 and 1860 involved a shift from the life table at level 16 to that at level 10 in West Model Female (Coale and Demeny 1966). The values of $\delta$ computed the $\int_x$ schedules of these tables during the prime working ages (taken to be ages 20–50) was 1.10% for level 10 and 0.58% for level 16. Hence, the average value of $\delta$ over the 70 years from 1790 to 1860 was 0.91%. The value of $(1 - \phi)$ was computed from

$$(1 - \phi) = \frac{0.5 \times 1.10 + 0.5 \times 0.58}{(0.5 \times 1.10 + 0.5 \times 0.58) + 6.0} = 0.123.$$

The values $V$ for 1790 and 1860 were computed as follows. First, the number of live births required to produce one survivor at age 20 was computed from $_{20}l_0$, which turned out to 1.18 births at mortality level 16 and 1.45 birth at level 10. Then, $V_{1860}/V_{1890}$ was computed from

$$\frac{V_{1860}}{V_{1790}} = \frac{1.45X_1 \, {_0\int^{20}} e^{(-\alpha_1 - \delta_1 + i_1)t} dt}{1.18X_0 \, {_0\int^{20}} e^{(-\alpha_0 - \delta_0 + i_0)t} dt},$$

where

$$X = \text{the net expenditures on child rearing at birth}$$

and

$$\alpha = \text{the average annual rate of decline in } X.$$

It was assumed that $X_1 = X_0$, that $\alpha_1 = \alpha_0 = 0.08$, and that $i_1 = i_0 = 0.06$. The values of $\delta_1$ and $\delta_0$ were computed from $_{20}l_0$ for mortality levels 10 and 16, respectively, and turned out to be 0.0170 for $\delta_1$ and 0.0075 for $\delta_0$. Consequently, $\dot{V} = \left(\frac{20.4915}{18.1527}\right)^{\frac{1}{70}} - 1 = 0.0017$. The result is fairly robust to alternative plausible assumptions regarding the values of $X$, $\alpha$, and $i$. It follows from eq. (19) that the average annual rate of increase in "real" wages due to the rise in mortality is 0.28% ($0.877 \times 0 + 0.123 \times 0.91 + 0.17 = 0.28$).

The relationship between the rate of change of "real" per capita income and the average "real" wage is given by

$$(19.1) \qquad \dot{w} = \dot{\beta} + \dot{Y} - \dot{L} = \dot{\beta} + \dot{Y} - \dot{\rho}$$

or

(19.2) $$\dot{\bar{Y}} = \dot{w} - \dot{\beta} + \dot{\rho}$$

where

$w$ = the "real" wage

$\bar{Y}$ = "real" per capita income

$\beta$ = the labor share in income

$Y$ = "real" national income

$L$ = the number of workers

$\rho$ = the labor force participation rate.

Hence, if $\dot{\beta}$ and $\dot{\rho}$ were unaffected by the rise in mortality (both appear to have been low during 1790–1860 [David 1967; Gallman 1972; Engerman and Gallman 1983]), then $\dot{\bar{Y}}$ will be equal to $\dot{w}$. It follows that the mortality adjustment reduces the rate of growth in "real" per capita income by about 39% ($0.28 \div 0.71 = 0.39$).

61. The decline in the mortality rates of low-income countries since 1950 is even more remarkable than the mortality decline in the industrialized nations between 1700 and 1980. The less developed nations have accomplished in 3 decades what took two centuries or more in the industrialized nations. A significant part of this acceleration is due to the transfer of medical and economic technology from the industrialized nations to the less developed nations (cf. Preston 1976, 1980, 1985).

62. That the debate launched in the mid-1950s still continues should not distract attention from the considerable advances in knowledge that have occurred because of the debate. Investigators have probed increasingly into aspects of issues that were obscure at the outset. The point is well illustrated by the evolution of research on the pathways of airborne diseases. McKeown (1976a) stressed direct exposure; Preston and van de Walle (1978) called attention to the risk-increasing effects of the lowering of resistance to airborne pathogens brought about by infections caused by waterborne pathogens. Thus, in the course of the debate the concept of nutritional status has been refined and the factors which affect it have been elaborated. Similarly, Condran and Cheney (1982) have provided evidence that medical intervention became increasingly effective before the dramatic chemical breakthroughs that became apparent during and after World War II. However, the extent of mortality reduction due to these less dramatic contributions has yet to be measured.

# Comment     Peter H. Lindert

Robert Fogel's excellent paper, and the larger research effort it draws upon, promises to be a durable landmark in the history of mortality trends. If subsequent documentation and independent estimates confirm key results that have only been sketched here, we will be citing his mortality time series and debating his interpretations for a long time. My task is to voice lasting praise and lingering questions on three fronts Fogel has opened: (1) his pioneering estimates of United States mortality trends from early colonial times through the Civil War, (2)

Peter H. Lindert is professor of economics at the University of California, Davis.

his emphasis on the role of changes in "nutritional status," and (3) his helpful suggestions on several puzzles about the effects of material living standards on life expectancy.

## United States White Male Mortality since about 1700

Thanks to the research team headed by Fogel, and to an independent study by Kent Kunze (1979), we are beginning to get a fresh look at changes in the length of life before the Civil War. The new estimates come from genealogical data, including the genealogies of ancestors of Mormons. The nature of this source imposes some limitations. The ancestral population was nearly all native white, precluding any measurement of nonwhite or immigrant life expectancy. In addition, serious underregistration of infant and early childhood deaths forces one to measure life expectancy only from later childhood, in this case from the tenth birthday, instead of from birth.

The tentative new contours of American mortality history are sketched in figure C9.1A. According to Fogel, life expectancy improved rapidly until the middle of the eighteenth century. This improvement first became noticeable in New England and then spread southward. By the 1750s white American colonists apparently lived longer than any other national population, even longer than British peers.[1] For the nineteenth century Fogel unveils a puzzling surprise: life expectancy for native white male 10-year-olds dropped by more than 4 years in the first half of the century, both in his sample and in that of Kunze. By the 1850s Americans faced shorter life spans than the English. This worsening of mortality was foreseen by only a slight plurality of previous studies, which lacked a clear consensus about antebellum mortality trends.[2] The new estimates present us with a

---

1. It should be noted that the pilot sample being used by Fogel and his associates contains very few observations per decade for the seventeenth and eighteenth centuries. Yet his tentative conclusions for the seventeenth and eighteenth centuries are at least consistent with the results of previous local studies. See the studies of colonial demography cited by Vinovskis (1972, pp. 184–213) and Fogel et al. (1978, pp. 75–108).

2. Some studies suggested improvement in life expectancy in some areas (e.g., Boston and perhaps the South) with no clear trend in others (e.g., in Massachusetts outside Boston). Again see Vinovskis (1972) and Fogel et al. (1978) and the sources they cite. Other studies, by contrast, saw an increase in antebellum mortality: (1) Duffy's study of New York City found that infant mortality and overall crude death rates both rose considerably across the first half of the nineteenth century (see Duffy, pp. 575–79). (I am indebted to my colleague Alan L. Olmstead for this reference.) (2) Meindl and Swedlund (1977, pp. 389–414) found that mortality worsened in two villages of central Massachusetts between 1790 and 1840. (I am indebted to Robert W. Fogel for this reference.) (3) Yasukichi Yasuba (1962, p. 89) found crude death rates rising in three cities, though not in two others, between 1804 and 1860. (4) See also the discussion in Kunze (1979, pp. 118–24).

Future acceptance of the Fogel-Kunze finding that mortality worsened will further discredit any comparison of Wigglesworth's 1789 life table with later tables for Massa-

major challenge: to explain a worsening in American health that lasted as long as three generations.

The surprising decline in life expectancy in the early nineteenth century cannot be explained by shifts in population toward less healthy areas. Urbanization was one such shift, but would have shortened life for 10-year-old males only by 1.3 years or less even if they shifted from being completely rural in 1800 to the true urban-rural mix of 1860.[3] This falls far short of accounting for the declines estimated by Fogel (a decline of 4.6 years from 1800–1815 to the trough of 1848–52) or Kunze (5.2 years from 1800–1815 to the peacetime trough of 1858–62). Nor is it likely that interregional shifts would explain the observed decline: the dominant westward shift was not a shift toward less healthy areas.

The early nineteenth-century fall from grace also clashes with what we would expect from the trend in real wages and income per capita. Even for the unskilled, real wages at least doubled between 1800–1809 and 1850–59.[4] Fogel rightly stresses the importance of such anomalous cases: What indeed do we make of historical periods in which real wages or incomes moved one way but life expectancy moved in the opposite direction? Such experiences warn against any simple belief that real income variables dominated life expectancy so strongly as to force the latter to rise and fall with the former.

---

chusetts. Even after Vinovskis's (1971) careful adjustments and warnings, Wigglesworth would imply a life expectancy of only 36.5 years (both sexes) back in 1789, whereas comparable figures from around 1830 and 1860 imply 47–48 years. This improvement cannot coexist with the Fogel-Kunze results unless one imagines radically different trends between Massachusetts and the national native white population.

3. The figure of a decline of 1.3 years or less due to urbanization is derived as follows: Let us overstate the rural-urban gaps in white male life expectancy ($e_{10}$) for 1860 by taking some extreme values from Vinovskis's study. Vinovskis estimates that $e_{10} = 52.7$ years for all rural areas. Extend this figure to towns smaller than 2500, even though the small towns had slightly lower $e_{10}$. Vinovskis further estimates that $e_{10} = 51.9$ for males in towns with population between 2500 and 4999 and $e_{10} = 52.6$ for towns 5000–9999. For towns over 10,000 let us use the pessimistic Boston rate, $e_{10} = 44.2$, instead of the true grand average rate ($e_{10} = 46.7$). Compute an average national rate by using the actual population shares for the United States in 1800 and 1860 (it is necessary to use shares for all races, all ages, and both sexes in place of the missing rural and urban shares for 10-year-old white males). The results are shown in the unnumbered table below.

| Mixture of places | $e_{10}$ |
|---|---|
| Entirely rural | 52.7 |
| Actual 1800 | 52.4 |
| Actual 1860 | 51.4 |

The extreme decline, from entirely rural to actual 1860, is only 1.3 years, even under the exaggerating assumptions just mentioned.

4. Specifically, the real wage rate rose 134% for Vermont farmhands and by 101% in the David-Solar estimates for nonfarm unskilled laborers (see Adams 1944; David and Solar 1977).

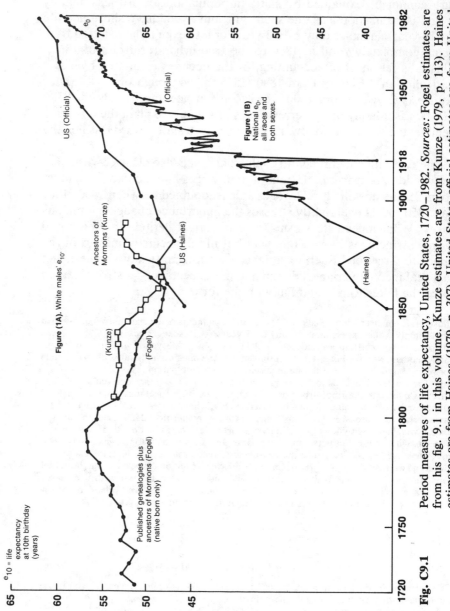

**Fig. C9.1** Period measures of life expectancy, United States, 1720–1982. *Sources:* Fogel estimates are from his fig. 9.1 in this volume. Kunze estimates are from Kunze (1979, p. 113). Haines estimates are from Haines (1979, p. 307). United States official estimates are from United States Bureau of the Census (1976, 1: 55; 1983, pp. 73, 74); United States Public Health Service (1970); and (for male $e_{10}$, 1900–1960) Preston et al. (1972, pp. 2–11).

The new estimates of early American mortality also serve to dramatize the extent to which improvements have been concentrated in the period since the 1850s. Indeed, if fuller investigations bear out Fogel's chronology, American life expectancy showed improving trends only before 1790 and since 1860, and not during the intervening 70 years. The improvement since 1860 has been especially dramatic for infants, women, foreign born, and nonwhites. Figure C9.1B presents a series on life expectancy from birth to remind us of the extent of the improvement of these groups, and to pose two questions:

1. Could the rise in life expectancy before 1790 and the decline from 1790 to 1860 have been as dramatic as the rise after 1860? If $e_0$ and native-white-male $e_{10}$ always followed the same life table relationship, sharing common tables from the same model, as they might have done after 1860, then yes, the earlier movements in $e_0$ were as dramatic as shown for years after 1860 in figure 9.C.2. We need more reliable estimates of $e_0$ before we can tell.

2. If the improvement in life expectancy since 1860 was indeed more dramatic than any swing that went before it, we need to renew past scholars' efforts to find out why.

The Role of "Nutritional Status"

Fogel goes beyond presenting new estimates and plunges into the difficult task of explaining his mortality results. His explanation features the concept of "nutritional status" so prominently that it dominates the title and substance of the paper. His careful conjectures about the possible role of nutritional status are a clear gain in knowledge. Yet he has chosen a concept that is sure to mislead at least some share of readers. To minimize that share, I must go beyond Fogel's own caveats and stress that "nutritional status" lacks most of the meaning that unwary readers are liable to assign it. Fogel defines nutritional status as "the balance between the intake of nutrients and the claims against it." What would enter into this balance? Almost every determinant of health and mortality would seem a candidate. To stress this vagueness, figure C9.2A's schematic portrayal simply refers to "other factors" as codeterminants, along with nutritional intake, of nutritional status. Furthermore, as shown in figure C9.2A, nutritional intake and the claims against it *jointly* determine this status, a jointness that complicates analysis. Fogel allows the search for determinants to be narrowed slightly by arguing at length that height is a good proxy for his concept of nutritional status (and a correlate of life expectancy). Some health and mortality factors are helpfully excluded thereby: childhood health factors that do not affect growth, plus influences impinging after the growth phase has ended. But this does not exclude much. We are left with a menu of possible influences on nutritional status that look

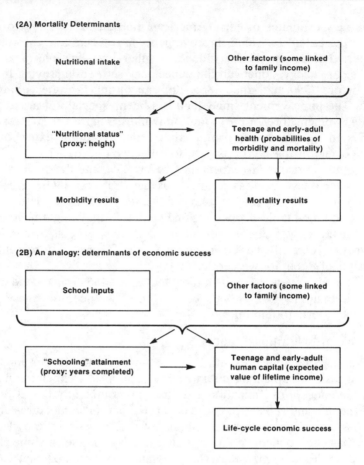

(2A) Mortality Determinants

Nutritional intake

Other factors (some linked to family income)

"Nutritional status" (proxy: height)

Teenage and early-adult health (probabilities of morbidity and mortality)

Morbidity results

Mortality results

(2B) An analogy: determinants of economic success

School inputs

Other factors (some linked to family income)

"Schooling" attainment (proxy: years completed)

Teenage and early-adult human capital (expected value of lifetime income)

Life-cycle economic success

**Fig. C9.2**    Illustrative schematic diagrams of determinants of mortality and of economic success.

very similar to the influences on health itself, at least for the teen and early adult years. Little progress has been made toward weighing exogenous influences on mortality.

Employing a concept that is a near neighbor to teen and early adult health is not too dangerous by itself. But if the concept is labeled "nutritional status" it will be hard to keep readers from thinking that something significant has been said about the role of nutritional *intake*. That is not the case.

The dangers here can be underlined with an analogy from the familiar literature on the determinants of the lifetime economic success of individuals, as is diagrammed schematically in figure C9.2B. Just as one could call on height as a measure of nutritional status, one could use years of schooling attainment as a measure of something called "schooling" and then proceed to argue that schooling is a good correlate of economic success. But little has been gained in our attempt to analyze the manipulable sources of economic success, since almost everything that might influence teen and early adult earning potential (human capital) and, through it, lifetime economic success, could influence the quality and years of one's schooling experience. Furthermore, emphasis on the importance of "schooling," like Fogel's emphasis on "nutritional status," invites misjudgment with its semantic link to school inputs. Precisely this confusion has led public debate to slip from the schooling-success correlation to overstate the case for extra investment in school inputs, overlooking the role of other schooling (and success) determinants such as family inputs into child development.

## Living Standards and Life Expectancy

Fogel's paper offers some helpful suggestions and some provocative questions on the broader issue of how general purchasing power affects mortality.

One clear contribution is his short section on the surprisingly small effect of early modern English *harvest failures* on death rates (the "Wrigley-Schofield-Lee paradox"). With a minimum of fuss, he inverts our view of the wide swings in grain prices and real wages in the wake of harvest fluctuations. The percentage fluctuations in the harvest or in available supplies must have been smaller than those in grain prices, since price elasticities of demand for such staples are notoriously low. Thus a 20% jump in grain prices could have resulted from only a 5% grain harvest deficiency, in a low-income early modern England with only imperfect international trade in grains. This may be a key reason death rates were not more sensitive to grain price movements. It serves Fogel's argument by keeping his emphasis on the importance of nutrition from suffering criticism based on the low response of English mortality to grain prices: if the harvest failures involved small percentage shifts in grain supply, a small mortality response is still consistent with great unit impact of nutritional intake.

To this point well put, one should add only the other key point about early modern English experience with food and death: a given percentage of national harvest failure had less and less mortality effect with the passage from the sixteenth century to the early nineteenth. Prices themselves varied less and less from year to year and from region to region as storage and transportation improved. In addition, government intervened to give special food entitlements to the poorest, especially with the spread of poor relief specifically tied to the price of food after 1795 (Schofield 1983).[5]

A second living-standards area explored by Fogel is "the peerage paradox": why didn't peers live longer than the rest of the population before about 1750 despite their much higher incomes, and why did their life expectancy improve so much faster thereafter? To some this looks like evidence against a nutrition-centered explanation of mortality (Livi-Bacci 1982). Fogel resourcefully counters with the possibility that perhaps the nutritional intake of infants in peerage families was as bad as that for common babes until 1750, and then somehow improved both absolutely and relatively. He presents good prima facie evidence for deleterious dietary habits in peerage families in early modern times. When and why these habits were reformed remains uncertain. The peerage paradox remains high on the research agenda of British demographic history.

The final section of this paper links mortality to overall living standards rather than to nutrition. Here he stresses a point that is familiar yet seriously underemphasized: *inequality* of income and wealth *causes extra deaths* for any given average income per capita. It can do so because the dependence of life expectancy (or average height) on income is very nonlinear: the same extra income extends life much more near the margin of malnutrition than it does at higher incomes.[6]

In one respect, Fogel may be pushing this point too far. Regarding the antebellum United States, he argues for strong causal links among rising economic inequality, declining heights, and declining life expectancy, drawing on Steckel's regression results showing a strong impact of Gini coefficients on height (and, by extension, mortality) for any given income per capita. The inequality-health link is so strong, he suggests, that we can use heights and other data to predict unobserved antebellum Gini coefficients, and we should ask whether living conditions really improved before 1860: During an era in which 50%–75% of the income of workers was spent on food, is it plausible that the workers' overall standard of living was improving if their nutritional status and life expectation were declining?

Readers should take care not to infer that the antebellum decline in life expectancy and health would outweigh gains in more conventional measures of economic resources, leaving us with a net decline in "living

5. Thus early modern England is not the best context for conjecturing that social food entitlements, à la Sen, may have tended to break down.
6. See, in addition to the studies by Floud and Steckel cited in Fogel's paper, Preston (1976) and World Bank (1980). The relationship is nonlinear whether the dependent variable is life expectancy, death rates, or heights. While the most accessible evidence relates to international cross-sections, the results for cross-sections of individuals look similar.)

conditions." Any such judgment must await quantification of the net change in the value of disamenities, including those associated with the threat of morbidity and mortality. I think it likely that such quantification will show that the antebellum gain in real annual incomes outweighed the shortening of life plus the psychological cost of ill health and death risks, even for low-income groups.

A starting point for weighing changes in the value of health against conventional real income gains is to combine lifetime consumption plus final savings with the disamenities associated with the average living situation to derive a measure of adult material well-being. Drawing on work by Usher (1973), Williamson (1984), and others, we can employ the following measures of average material well-being ($W$) in two cohorts ($_0$ and $_1$):

$$W_0 = C_0 L_0 (1 - d_0), \quad W_1 = C_1 L_1 (1 - d_1),$$

where  $C$ = average consumption and bequests, averaged over all persons in the relevant group and all years of the life cycle;

$L$ = expectation of life, but with each extra year's survival chance discounted back to the present (here, to age 10) at a rate of time preference, as is done in Usher and Williamson;

$d$ = the percentage disamenity discount associated with the living conditions of that cohort, as revealed in studies of adult's choices of jobs and places of residence.

To judge the impact of the antebellum changes in mortality Fogel has documented, let us compare a synthetic cohort based on conditions in 1800–1809 with one based on conditions in 1850–59. The ratio of the later to the earlier well-being is

$$(W_1/W_0) = (C_1/C_0)(L_1/L_0)(1 - d_1)/(1 - d_0).$$

If consumption plus bequests was in fixed proportion to the real wage rates for unskilled workers from 1800–1809 to 1850–59, then $(C_1/C_0)$ ≥ 2, as noted in n. 5. If life expectancy was proportional to the new $e_{10}$ estimates developed by Fogel, then over the same period $(L_1/L_0)$ slightly exceeded 0.866, a ratio based on comparing the low figure for 1855–59 with the high figure for 1800–1804. So far we have

$$(W_1/W_0) \geq 1.732 \, (1 - d_1)/(1 - d_0).$$

Material well-being clearly advanced across the antebellum period *unless* psychological disamenities became much more severe ($d_1 >> d_0$).

If the antebellum (nonslave) population found urban life more unpleasant than rural life in its nonconsumption dimensions, then we could make some headway toward judging disamenity values by breaking the departure of $(1 - d_1)/(1 - d_0)$ from unit into three changes: the change in the quality of urban life, the change in the quality of rural life, and the change in the quality of life implied by the migration of a fraction of the population from rural to urban life. We can put an upper bound on the third change. American cities in the 1850s cannot have been as much worse than the American countryside of 1800 as appalling Manchester was worse than bucolic rural Norfolk in the late 1830s. In this extreme English contrast, Manchester employers offered unskilled workers a 65% annual wage premium over the annual pay given to comparable workers in low-wage Norfolk (Lindert and Williamson 1983). In other words, the disamenity discount for the worst urban-industrial life was less than or equal to $1 - (1/1.65)$, or 39.4%. Suppose that conditions of urban American life in the 1850s were that much worse than conditions for America as a whole in the 1800s. Then, combining the 1860 urban share of 19.8% with the 65% extreme disamenity, and assuming that city life was no worse than country life in 1800–1809, we get

$$(1 - d_1)/(1 - d_0) = 1 - (0.198)(1 - 0.394) = 0.880,$$

$$(W_1/W_0) \geq (2)(0.866)(0.880) = 1.524 .$$

The changes in real wages, length of life, and the disamenity of ante-bellum urbanization together imply that average well-being improved by more than 52%.

The most important omissions from these calculations are the net changes in the quality of life *within* the cities and *within* the countryside between 1800–1809 and 1850–59. If these can be shown to have deteriorated enough to pull $(W_1/W_0)$ below unity, then Fogel will have led us to one of the most important findings in the history of modern economic well-being: a long era when things got demonstrably worse for the average American (or the average unskilled American worker) despite a large increase in annual purchasing power. Indeed, Fogel does help pave the way for such a conclusion by showing that heights (and, by presumption, life expectancy) dropped in both urban and rural settings before the Civil War. But the 52% improvement shown here is the mountain that must be removed if we are to believe that the best antebellum clues to overall material well-being were the mortality and health series he has unveiled.

Yet Fogel's key point about inequality and health remains. It carries an important policy suggestion: for countries whose poor are close to the malnutrition margin, poor relief (welfare payments) financed by the rich could lengthen life and increase the size of the labor force. In such settings, the life-extending effect of fiscal (or philanthropic) redistribution from rich to poor could even repay the taxed rich, partly or completely or even more, through its tendency to expand the labor supply and enhance the pretax returns to property and skills.[7] The result depends on several aspects of our economy, in particular the elasticities of demand and supply for common labor, the elasticity of labor supply with respect to disposable income, the elasticity of supply of property (land, capital, skills), the level of taxation, and the share of unskilled earnings in national income.

Preindustrial England might have been a case in which greater poor relief would have taken Fogel's point to this paradoxical extreme. A large share of the population was malnourished, the levels of taxation and philanthropy were low, and a large share of national income accrued to the owners of relatively inelastically supplied land. In such a setting poor relief could have brought a net gain to the taxed propertied and skilled classes, thanks to its tendency to raise the supply of common labor (even without any Malthusian effect of poor relief on fertility). If so, it would be paradoxical that England was so much more tight-fisted in its opposition to poor relief before the revolutionary fears of 1795 and before the modern welfare state. Perhaps English history, like today's global cross-section of nations, finds poor relief least generous when (or where) it was most clearly a matter of life and death. This is another of the issues illuminated by Fogel's important preliminary findings.

# References

Abel, E. L. 1982. Consumption of alcohol during pregnancy: A review of effects on growth and development of offspring. *Human Biology* 54:421–53.

Ackernecht, E. H. 1945. *Malaria in the upper Mississippi valley, 1760–1900*. Baltimore: Johns Hopkins Press.

———. 1952. Diseases in the Middle West. In *Essays in the history of medicine in honor of David J. Davis*. University of Illinois.

Adams, J. W., and Kasakoff, A. B. 1983. Migration and life-cycles in the American north: Age-specific migration rates, 1700 to 1850. Mimeographed. University of South Carolina.

Adams, T. M. 1944. *Prices paid by Vermont farmers . . . wages of Vermont farm labor, 1780–1940*. Burlington: Free Press.

---

7. This argument assumes, of course, that the poor relief expands the population of labor-force age enough to outweigh any work disincentive from the fact that income maintenance reduces the postbenefit wage rate. In a very poor country, it might.

Appleby, A. B. 1975. Nutrition and disease: The case of London, 1550–1750. *Journal of Interdisciplinary History* 6:1–22.

———. 1978. *Famine in Tudor and Stuart England*. Stanford: Stanford University Press.

———. 1979a. Grain prices and subsistence crises in England and France, 1590–1740. *Journal of Economic History* 39:865–87.

———. 1979b. Diet in sixteenth-century England: Sources, problems, possibilities. In *Health, medicine, and mortality in the sixteenth century*, ed. C. Webster. Cambridge: Cambridge University Press.

———. 1980. The disappearance of the plague: A continuing puzzle. *Economic History Review* 2d ser. 33:161–73.

Ashbrook, F. G. 1955. *Butchering, processing, and preservation of meat*. Toronto: Van Nostrand.

Ashby, H. T. 1915. *Infant mortality*. Cambridge: Cambridge University Press.

Ashworth, A. 1982. International differences in infant mortality and the impact of malnutrition: A review. *Human Nutrition: Clinical Nutrition*. 36c:7–23.

Atwater, W. O., and Woods, C. D. 1897. Dietary studies with reference to the food of the Negro in Alabama in 1895 and 1896. USDA Off. Exp. *Statistical Bulletin* 38:3–69.

Balinsky, W., and Berger, R. 1975. A review of the research on general health status indexes. *Medical Care* 13:283–93.

Baumgartner, R. N., and Mueller, W. H. 1984. Multivariate analyses of illness data for use in studies on the relationship of physical growth and morbidity. *Human Biology* 56:111–28.

Beal, V. A. 1980. *Nutrition in the life span*. New York: Wiley.

Beisel, W. R. 1977. Magnitude of the host nutritional responses to infection. *American Journal of Clinical Nutrition* 30:1236–47.

Bennett, M. K., and Pierce, R. H. 1961. Changes in the American national diet, 1879–1959. *Food Research Institute Studies* 2:95–119.

Benson, L. 1969. *The concept of Jacksonian democracy: New York as a test case*. New York: Atheneum.

Berridge, V., and Edwards, G. 1981. *Opium and the people: Opiate use in nineteenth-century England*. London: Allen Lane.

Berry, T. S. 1943. *Western prices before 1861: A study of the Cincinnati market*. Cambridge: Harvard University Press.

Bidwell, P. W., and Falconer, J. I. 1925. *History of agriculture in the northern United States, 1620–1860*. Washington: Carnegie Institution.

Birkbeck, J. A. 1976. Metrical growth and skeletal development of the human fetus. In *The biology of human fetal growth*, ed. D. F. Roberts and A. M. Thomson. London: Taylor & Francis.

Bjerre, I. 1975. Neurological investigation of 5-year-old children with low birth weight. *Acta Paediatrica Scandinairica* 64:33–43.

Blaxter, M. 1976. *The meaning of disability: A sociological study of impairment.* London: Heineman.

Bourne, J., et al. 1984. A description and analysis of the data in the DAE/CPE pilot sample of genealogies. Mimeographed. University of Chicago.

Bouvier, L. F., and van der Tak, J. 1976. Infant mortality: Progress and problems. *Population Bulletin* 31, no. 1.

Bowden, P. 1967. Agricultural prices, farm profits, and rents, and statistical appendix. In *The agrarian history of England and Wales.* Vol. 4. *1500–1640,* ed. J. Thirsk. Cambridge: Cambridge University Press.

———. 1985. Agricultural prices, wages, farm profits, and rents, and statistical appendix. In *The agrarian history of England and Wales.* Vol. 5. *1640–1750: II. Agrarian change,* ed. J. Thirsk. Cambridge: Cambridge University Press.

Boyd, M. F. 1941. An historical sketch of the prevalence of malaria in North America. *American Journal of Tropical Medicine* 21:223–44.

Briscoe, J. 1979. The quantitative effect of infection on the use of food by young children in poor countries. *American Journal of Clinical Nutrition* 32:648–76.

Bruntland, G. H., Liestøl, K., and Walløe, L. 1980. Height, weight, and menarcheal age of Oslo schoolchildren during the last 60 years. *Annals of Human Biology* 7:307–22.

Butler, N. 1974. Risk factors in human intrauterine growth retardation. In *Size at birth.* Ciba Foundation Symposium 27:379–97.

Butlin, N. G. 1971. *Ante-bellum slavery: A critique of a debate.* Canberra: Australian National University, Department of Economic History.

Campbell, B. M. S. 1983. Arable productivity in medieval England: Some evidence from Norfolk. *Journal of Economic History* 43:379–404.

Campbell, J. 1984. Work, pregnancy, and infant mortality among southern slaves. *Journal of Interdisciplinary History* 14:793–812.

Carr, L. G., and Walsh, L. S. 1980. Inventories and the analysis of wealth and consumption patterns in St. Mary's County, Maryland, 1658–1777. *Historical Methods* 13:81–104.

Case, R. A. M., et al. 1962. *Chester Beatty Research Institute abridged serial life tables, England and Wales 1841–1960.* Pt. I. London.

Chase, H. G. 1969. Infant mortality and weight at birth: 1960 United States birth cohort. *American Journal of Public Health* 59:1618–28.

Chiswick, B. R. 1978. Immigrants and immigration policy. In *Contemporary economic problems 1978,* ed. W. Fellner. Washington: American Enterprise Institute.

———. 1979. The economic progress of immigrants: Some apparently universal patterns. In *Contemporary economic problems 1979,* ed. W. Fellner. Washington: American Enterprise Institute.

Christianson, R. E., et al. 1981. Incidence of congenital anomalies among white and black live births with long-term follow-up. *American Journal of Public History* 71:1333–41.

Coale, A. J., and Demeny, P. 1966. *Regional model life tables and stable populations*. Princeton: Princeton University Press.

Cole, T. J. 1979. A method for assessing age-standardized weight-for-height in children seen cross-sectionally. *Annals of Human Biology* 6:249–68.

Cole, T. J., and Parkin, J. M. 1977. Infection and its effect on the growth of young children: A comparison of the Gambia and Uganda. *Transactions of the Royal Society of Tropical Medicine and Hygiene* 71:196–98.

Commons, J. R., et al. 1918. *History of labor in the United States*. 2 vols. New York: Macmillan.

Condon-Paolini, D., et al. 1977. Morbidity and growth of infants and young children in a rural Mexican village. *American Journal of Public Health* 67:651–56.

Condran, G. A., and Cheney, R. A. 1982. Mortality trends in Philadelphia: Age- and cause-specific death rates 1870–1930. *Demographics* 19:97–123.

Condran, G. A., and Crimmins, E. 1980. Mortality differentials between rural and urban areas of states in the northeastern United States, 1890–1900. *Journal of Historical Geography* 6:179–202.

Condran, G. A., and Crimmins-Gardner, E. 1978. Public health measures and mortality in U.S. cities in the late nineteenth century. *Human Ecology* 6:27–54.

Creighton, C. 1891. *A history of epidemics in Britain from A.D. 664 to the extinction of the plague*. Cambridge: Cambridge University Press.

David, P. A. 1967. The growth of real product in the United States before 1840: New evidence, controlled conjectures. *Journal of Economic History* 27:151–97.

David, P. A., and Solar, P. 1977. A bicentary contribution to the history of the cost of living in America. *Research in Economic History* 2:1–80.

Davidson, S., et al. 1979. *Human nutrition and dietetics*. Edinburgh: Churchill Livingstone.

Demos, J. 1970. *A little commonwealth: Family life in Plymouth Colony*. New York: Oxford University Press.

Drummond, J. C., and Wilbraham, A. 1939. *The Englishman's food: A history of five centuries of English diet*. London: Jonathan Cape.

Duffy, J. 1953. *Epidemics in colonial America*. Baton Rouge: Louisiana State University Press.

———. 1968. *A history of public health in New York City, 1625–1866*. New York: Russell Sage.

Dyer, C. 1983. English diet in the later Middle Ages. In *Social relations and ideas: Essays in honour of R. H. Hilton,* ed. T. H. Aston, et al. Cambridge: Cambridge University Press.

Easterlin, R. A. 1975. Farm production and income in old and new areas at mid-century. In *Essays in nineteenth century economic history: The old Northwest,* ed. D. C. Kingaman and R. K. Vedder. Athens: Ohio University Press.

————. 1977. Population issues in American economic history: A survey and critique. *Research in Economic History, 1 (suppl.):* 131–58.

*Encyclopaedia Britannica.* 1961. Chicago: Encyclopaedia Britannica Inc.

Engerman, S. L., and Gallman, R. E. 1983. U.S. economic growth. *Research in Economic History* 8:1–46.

Ernst, R. 1949. *Immigrant life in New York City, 1825–1863.* New York: King's Crown Press.

Eveleth, P. B., and Tanner, J. M. 1976. *Worldwide variation in human growth.* Cambridge: Cambridge University Press.

Everitt, A. 1967. Farm labourers. In *The agrarian history of England and Wales.* Vol. 4. *1500–1640,* ed. J. Thirsk. Cambridge: Cambridge University Press.

Feigin, R. S. 1981. Interaction of infection and nutrition. In *Textbook of pediatric infectious diseases,* ed. R. D. Feigin and J. D. Cherny. Philadelphia: Saunders.

Fischer, D. H., and Dobson, M. S. 1979. Dying times: Changing patterns of death and disease in England and America 1650–1850. Mimeographed. Brandeis University.

Fitzhardinge, P. M., and Steven, E. M. 1972a. The small-for-date-infant. I. Later growth patterns. *Pediatrics* 49:671–81.

————. 1972b. The small-for-date-infant. II. Neurological and intellectual sequelae. *Pediatrics* 50:50–57.

Flinn, M. W. 1974. The stabilization of mortality in pre-industrial Western Europe. *Journal of European Economic History* 3:285–318.

————. 1981. *The European demographic system, 1500–1820.* Baltimore: Johns Hopkins University Press.

Floud, R. 1983a. Inference from the heights of volunteer soldiers and sailors. Mimeographed. NBER.

————. 1983b. The heights of Europeans since 1750: A new source for European economic history. Mimeographed. Birkbeck College, London.

————. 1984. Measuring the transformation of European economies: Income, health and welfare. Mimeographed. Birkbeck College, London.

————. 1985a. Two cultures? British and American heights in the nineteenth century. Mimeographed. Birkbeck College, London.

————. 1985b. Human stature and inequality: A progress report. Mimeographed. Birkbeck College, London.

Floud, R., and Wachter, K. W. 1982. Poverty and physical stature: Evidence on the standard of living of London boys, 1770–1870. *Social Scientific History* 6:422–52.

————. 1983. The physical state of the British working class, 1860–1914: Evidence from army recruits. Mimeographed. Birkbeck College, London.

Fogel, R. W. 1986. *Without consent or contract: The rise and fall of American slavery.* New York: Norton.

————. 1987. Second thoughts on the European escape from hunger: Crop yields, price elasticities, entitlements, and mortality rates. Mimeographed. University of Chicago. Forthcoming

Fogel, R. W., and Engerman, S. L. 1971. The economics of slavery. In *The reinterpretation of American economic history,* ed. R. W. Fogel and S. L. Engerman. New York: Harper & Row.

————. 1974. *Time on the cross.* Boston: Little, Brown.

Fogel, R. W., et al. 1978. The economics of mortality in North America, 1650–1910: A description of a research project. *Historical Methods* 11:75–108.

————. 1982. Exploring the uses of data on height: the analysis of long-term trends in nutrition, labor welfare, and labor productivity. *Social Scientific History* 6:401–21.

————, et al. 1983. Secular changes in American and British stature and nutrition. *Journal of Interdisciplinary History* 14:445–81.

Forsdahl, A. 1977. The poor living conditions in childhood and adolescence: An important risk factor for arteriosclerotic heart disease? *British Journal of Social Medicine* 31:91–95.

Forster, E., and Forster, R., eds. 1975. *European diet from pre-industrial to modern times.* New York: Harper.

Friedman, G. C. 1982. The heights of slaves in Trinidad. *Social Scientific History* 6:482–515.

Frisancho, A. R. 1978. Nutritional influences on human growth and maturation. *Yearbook of Physical Anthropology* 21:174–91.

Frissell, H. B., and Bevier, I. 1899. Dietary studies of Negroes in eastern Virginia in 1897 and 1898. *U.S.D.A. Office of Experiment Statistical Bulletin* 71.

Fussell, G. E. 1949. *The English rural labourer: His home, furniture, clothing, and food from Tudor to Victorian times.* London: Batchworth.

Galenson, D. W. 1981. *White servitude in colonial America: An economic analysis.* Cambridge: Cambridge University Press.

Gallman, J. M. 1980. Mortality among white males: Colonial North Carolina. *Social Scientific History* 4:295–316.

Gallman, R. E. 1960. Commodity output, 1839–1899. In *Trends in the American economy in the nineteenth century.* Conference on Research in Income and Wealth, vol. 245. Princeton: Princeton University Press (for NBER).

———. 1966. Gross national product in the United States. In *Output, employment and productivity in the United States after 1800.* Conference on Research in Income and Wealth, vol. 30. New York: Columbia University Press (for NBER).

———. 1969. Trends in the size distribution of wealth in the nineteenth century: Some speculations. In *Six papers on the size distribution of wealth and income,* ed. L. Soltow. Conference on Research in Income and Wealth, vol. 33. New York: Columbia University Press (for NBER).

———. 1972. The pace and pattern of American economic growth. In *American economic growth: An economist's history of the United States.* New York: Harper & Row.

———. 1982. Influences on the distribution of landholdings in early colonial North Carolina. *Journal of Economic History* 42:549–75.

Gibson, J. R., and McKeown, T. 1950/1951. Observations on all births (23,970) in Birmingham, 1947. I. Duration of gestation. III. Survival. *British Journal of Social Medicine* 4:221–33; 5:177–83.

Goldin, C. D. 1979. Evolution of the female labor force in the United States. Mimeographed. NBER.

Goldin, C. D., and Margo, R. A. 1984. The poor at birth: Birth weights, infant deaths, and maternal mortality in the Philadelphia Alms House, 1840–1865. Mimeographed. University of Pennsylvania.

Goldstein, H. 1976. Birthweight, gestation, neonatal mortality and child development. In *The biology of human fetal growth,* ed. D. F. Roberts and A. M. Thomson. London: Taylor & Francis.

Great Britain, Central Statistical office. 1983. *Annual abstract of statistics,* no. 119. London: Her Majesty's Stationery Office.

Great Britain, Department Health Social Service. 1980. *Inequalities in health: Report of a research working group. London.*

Great Britain, House of Commons. 1899. *Parliamentary papers,* vol. 104.

Great Britain, House of Commons. 1917. *Parliamentary papers,* vol. 76.

Greven, P. J., Jr. 1970. *Four generations: Population, land and family in colonial Andover, Massachusetts.* Ithaca: Cornell University Press.

Guha, D. K., et al. 1973. Relationship between length of gestation, birth weight, and certain other factors. *Indian Journal of Pediatrics* 40:44–53.

Habicht, J. P., et al. 1979. Anthropometric field methods: Criteria for selection. In *Nutrition and growth,* ed. D. B. Jelliffe and E. F. P. Jelliffe. New York: Plenum.

Haines, M. R. 1979. The use of model life tables to estimate mortality for the United States in the late nineteenth century. *Demography* 16:289–312.

——. 1983. Inequality and child mortality: A comparison of England and Wales, 1911 and the United States, 1900. Mimeographed. Wayne State University.

Haines, M. R., and Avery, R. C. 1980. The American life table of 1830–1860: An evaluation. *Journal of Interdisciplinary History* 11:73–95.

Handlin, O. 1979. *Boston's immigrants: A study in acculturation.* Rev. ed. Cambridge: Harvard University Press.

Hannon, J. U. 1984. Poverty in the antebellum Northeast: The view from New York State's poor relief rolls. *Journal of Economic History* 44:1007–32.

Hanson, J. W., et al. 1978. The effects of moderate alcohol consumption during pregnancy on fetal growth and morphogenesis. *Journal of Pediatrics* 92:457–60.

Hatcher, J. 1977. *Plague, population, and the English economy, 1348–1530.* London: Macmillan.

Heckscher, E. F. 1954. *An economic history of Sweden,* trans. G. Ohlin. Cambridge: Harvard University Press.

Helleiner, K. F. The population of Europe from the Black Death to the eve of the vital revolution. In *The Cambridge economic history of Europe.* Vol. 4. *The economy of expanding Europe in the sixteenth and seventeenth centuries,* ed. E. E. Rich and C. H. Wilson. Cambridge: Cambridge University Press.

Hellie, R. 1981. Review of *Bubonic plague in early modern Russia: Public health and urban disaster,* by J. T. Alexander. *Journal of Interdisciplinary History* 12:710–13.

Henripin, J. 1954. *La population canadienne au debut du XVIIIe siècle: nuptialité-fecondité-mortalité infantile.* Paris: Presses University de France.

Higgs, R. 1973. Mortality in rural America, 1870–1920: Estimates and conjectures. *Explorations in Economic History* 10:177–95.

——. 1979. Cycles and trends of mortality in 18 large American cities, 1871–1900. *Explorations in Economic History* 16:381–408.

Hoagland, H. E. 1913. The rise of the iron moulders' international union. *American Economic Review* 3:296–313.

Hogan, H. R. 1976. Age patterns of infant mortality. Ph.D. dissertation, Princeton University.

Hollingsworth, T. H. 1977. Mortality in the British peerage families since 1600. *Population,* numéro spécial: 323–49.

Holmes, G. K. 1907. Meat supply and surplus, *United States Bureau of Statistics Bulletin* 55.

Hoskins, W. G. 1964. Harvest fluctuations and English economic history, 1480–1619. *Agricultural History Review* 12:28–46.

———. 1968. Harvest fluctuations and English economic history, 1620–1759. *Agricultural History Review* 16:15–31.

Hufton, O. 1983. Social conflict and the grain supply in eighteenth-century France. *Journal of Interdisciplinary History* 14:303–31.

Hurley, L. S. 1980. *Developmental nutrition.* Englewood Cliffs, N.J.: Prentice-Hall.

Hytten, F. E., and Leitch, I. 1971. *The physiology of human pregnancy.* 2d ed. Oxford: Blackwell Scientific.

Imhof, A. E. 1977. Historical demography in Germany: A research note, *History Methodology Newsletter* 10:122–126.

Jayant, K. 1964. Birth weight and some other factors in relation to infant survival: A study on an Indian sample. *Annals of Human Genetics* 27:261–67.

John, A. M. 1984. The demography of slavery in nineteenth-century Trinidad. Ph.D. dissertation, Princeton University.

Jones, A. H. 1980. *Wealth of a nation to be: The American colonies on the eve of the Revolution.* New York: Columbia University Press.

Jones, R. A. K., et al. 1979. Infants of very low birth weight: A 15-year analysis. *Lancet* 1:1332–35.

*Journal of Interdisciplinary History* 1983. The relationship of nutrition, disease, and social conditions: A graphical presentation. *Journal of Interdisciplinary History* 14:503–6.

Kahn, C. 1978. The death rate in Memphis in 1860: Application of an alternative estimating technique. Mimeographed. Harvard University.

Kearl, J. R., and Pope, C. 1986. Choices, rents, and luck: Economic mobility of nineteenth-century Utah households. In this volume.

Kerridge, E. 1968. *The agricultural revolution.* New York: Kelley.

Kielmann, A. A., et al. 1982. Nutrition intervention: An evaluation of six studies. *Studies in Family Planning* 13:246–57.

———. 1983. *Child and maternal health services in rural India: The Narangwal experiment.* Vol. 1. *Integrated nutrition and health.* Baltimore: Johns Hopkins Press.

Kiil, V. 1939. *Stature and growth of Norwegian men during the past two hundred years.* Oslo: I kommision hos J. Dybwad.

Kiple, K. F., and King, V. H. 1981. *Another dimension to the black diaspora: Diet, disease, and racism.* Cambridge: Cambridge University Press.

Knodel, J., and Kintner, H. 1977. The impact of breastfeeding patterns on the biometric analysis of infant mortality. *Demography* 14:391–407.

Komlos, J. 1984. Stature and nutrition in the Hapsburg monarchy: A study of secular changes in the standard of living and economic development, 1720–1920. Mimeographed. University of Chicago.

Kulikoff, A. 1976. Tobacco and slaves: Population, economy, and society in eighteenth-century Prince George's county, Maryland. Ph.D. dissertation, Brandeis University.

Kunitz, S. J. 1983. Speculations on the European mortality decline. *Economic History Review* 36:349–64.

Kunze, K. 1979. The effects of age composition and changes in vital rates on nineteenth-century population: estimates from new data. Ph.D. dissertation, University of Utah.

Kuznets, S. 1959. *Six lectures on economic growth.* Glencoe, Ill.: Free Press.

*Lancet.* 1980. The fate of the baby under 1501 g. at birth. *Lancet,* 461–64.

Landes, D. S. 1950. The statistical study of French crises. *Journal of Economic History* 10:195–211.

Laslett, P. 1984. *The world we have lost: England before the industrial age.* 3d ed. New York: Scribner's.

Lebergott, S. 1976. *The American economy: Income, wealth, and want.* Princeton: Princeton University Press.

———. 1984. *The Americans: An economic record.* New York: Norton.

Lee, R. 1981. Short-term variation: Vital rates, prices and weather. In *The population history of England, 1541–1871: A reconstruction,* ed. E. A. Wrigley and R. S. Schofield. Cambridge: Harvard University Press.

Levy, D. 1984. The life expectancy of colonial Maryland legislators. Mimeographed. University of Chicago.

Lindert, P. H. 1980. English occupations, 1670–1811. *Journal of Economic History* 40:685–712.

———. 1983. English living standards, population growth, and Wrigley-Schofield. *Explorations in Economic History* 20:131–55.

———. 1985. English population, wages, and prices: 1541–1913. *Journal of Interdisciplinary History* 15:609–34.

Lindert, P. H., and Williamson, J. G. 1983a. English workers' living standards during the industrial revolution: A new look. *Economic History Review* 36:1–25.

———. 1983b. Reinterpreting Britain's social tables, 1688–1913. *Explorations in Economic History* 20:94–109.

Lindgren, G. 1976. Height, weight, and menarche in Swedish urban school children in relationship to socio-economic and regional factors. *Annals of Human Biology* 3:501–22.

Livi-Bacci, M. 1982. The nutrition-mortality link in past times: A comment. *Journal of Interdisciplinary History* 14:293–98.

Lockridge, K. A. 1966. The population of Dedham, Massachusetts, 1636–1736. *Economic History Review* 19:318–44.

McCormick, M. C. 1985. The contribution of low birth weight to infant mortality and childhood morbidity. *New England Journal of Medicine* 312:82–89.

McCusker, J. J., Jr. 1970. The rum trade and the balance of payments of the thirteen continental colonies, 1650–1775. Ph.D. dissertation. University of Pittsburgh.

McFarlane, H. 1976. Nutrition and immunity. In *Nutrition reviews: Present knowledge in nutrition.* 4th ed. New York: Nutrition Foundation.

McKeown, T. 1976a. *The modern rise of population.* New York: Academic Press.

————. 1976b. *The role of medicine: Dream, mirage, or nemesis?* London: Nuffield Provincial Hospitals Trust.

————. 1978. Fertility, mortality and cause of death: An examination of issues related to the modern rise of population. *Population Studies* 32:535–42.

————. 1983. Food, infection, and population. *Journal of Interdisciplinary History* 14:227–47.

McKeown, T., and Brown, R. G. 1955. Medical evidence related to English population changes in the eighteenth century. *Population Studies* 9:119–41.

McKeown, T., and Gibson, J. R. 1951. Observations on all births (23,970) in Birmingham, 1947. II. Birth weight. *British Journal of Social Medicine* 5:98–112.

McMahon, S. F. 1981. Provisions laid up for the family, *Historical Methods* 14:4–21.

McNeill, W. H. 1976. *Plagues and peoples.* Garden City, N.Y.: Doubleday.

Main, G. L. 1982. *Tobacco colony: Life in early Maryland, 1650–1720.* Princeton: Princeton University Press.

Margo, R. A., and Steckel, R. H. 1982. The heights of American slaves: New evidence on slave nutrition and health. *Social Science History* 6:516–38.

————. 1983. Heights of native-born whites during the antebellum period. *Journal of Economic History* 43:167–174.

Marmot, M. G., et al. 1984. Inequalities in death-specific explanations of a general pattern. *Lancet* 1:1003–1006.

Martorell, R. 1980. Interrelationships between diet, infectious disease, and nutritional status. In *Social and biological predictors of nutritional status,* ed. L. S. Greene and F. E. Johnston. New York: Academic Press.

Martorell, R., et al. 1975. Diarrheal diseases and growth retardation in preschool Guatemalan children. *American Journal of Physical Anthropology* 43:341–46.

Mata, L. J., et al. 1977. Effect of infection on food intake and the nutritional state. *American Journal of Clinical Nutrition* 30:1215–27.

———. 1978. *The children of Santa Maria Cauque: A prospective field study of health and growth.* Cambridge: MIT Press.

Mathias, P. 1959. *The brewing industry in England, 1700–1830.* Cambridge: Cambridge University Press.

Matossian, M. K. 1984. Mold poisoning and population growth in England and France, 1750–1850. *Journal of Economic History* 44:669–86.

Matthews, R. C. O., et al. 1982. *British economic growth, 1856–1973.* Stanford: Stanford University Press.

May, J. M. 1958. *The ecology of human disease.* New York: MD Publishing.

Meade, J. E. 1955. *Trade and welfare.* Vol. 2. *The theory of international economic policy.* London: Oxford University Press.

Meckel, R. A. 1985. Immigration, mortality, and population growth in Boston, 1840–1880. *Journal of Interdisciplinary History* 15:393–417.

Meeker, E. 1972. The improving health of the United States, 1850–1915. *Explorations in Economic History* 9:353–73.

———. 1976. Mortality trends of southern blacks, 1850–1910: Some preliminary findings. *Explorations in Economic History* 13:13–42.

Meindl, R. S., and Swedlund, A. C. 1977. Secular trends in mortality in the Connecticut Valley. *Human Biology* 49:389–414.

Menard, R. R. 1975. Economy and society in early colonial Maryland. Ph.D. dissertation. University of Iowa.

Meneely, G. R., and Battarbee, H. D. 1976. Sodium and potassium. In *Nutrition reviews: Present knowledge in nutrition.* 4th ed. New York: Nutrition Foundation.

Meredith, H. V. 1970. Body weight at birth of viable human infants: A worldwide comparative treatise. *Human Biology* 42:217–64.

Mingay, G. E. 1963. *English landed society in the eighteenth century.* London: Routledge & Kegan Paul.

Mitchell, B. R. 1975. *European historical statistics, 1750–1975.* London: Macmillan.

Mitchell, B. R., and Deane, P. 1962. *Abstract of British historical statistics.* Cambridge: Cambridge University Press.

Moen, J. R. 1985. Labor force participation in the rural northern United States: 1860. Mimeographed. University of Chicago.

Moore, W. M. O. 1983. Prenatal factors influencing intrauterine growth: Clinical implications. In *Perinatal medicine,* ed. R. Boyd and F. C. Battaglia. London: Butterworths.

Moseley, W. H., and Chen, L. C. 1983. An analytical framework for the study of child survival in developing countries. Mimeographed. Bellagio Conference.

Naeye, R. L. 1981. Nutritional/nonnutritional interactions that affect the outcome of pregnancy. *American Journal of Clinical Nutrition* 34:727–31.

New York State Board of Health. 1867. *Annual report.* Albany: Van Benthuysen.

Oddy, D. J. 1983. Urban famine in nineteenth-century Britain: The effect of the Lancashire colton famine on working-class diet and health. *Economic History Review* 2d ser. 36:68–86.

Overton, M. 1979. Estimating crop yields from probate inventories: An example from East Anglia, 1585–1735. *Journal of Economic History* 39:363–78.

———. 1980. English probate inventories and the measurement of agricultural change. *A.A.G. Bijdragen* 23:205–15.

Palliser, D. M. 1982. Tawney's century: Brave new world or Malthusian trap? *Economic History Review* 35:339–53.

Pessen, E. 1973. *Riches, class, and power before the Civil War.* Lexington, Mass.: Heath.

———. 1978. *Jacksonian America: society, personality, and politics.* Rev. ed. Homewood, Ill.: Dorsey.

Pharoah, P. O. D., and Alberman, E. D. 1981. Mortality of low birth-weight infants in England and Wales 1953 to 1979. *Archives of Diseases of Childhood* 56:86–89.

Phelps Brown, E. H., and Hopkins, S. V., 1956. Seven centuries of the prices of consumables compared with builders' wage rates. *Economica* 23:296–314.

Pinchbeck, I., and Hewitt, M. 1969. *Children in English society.* Vol. I. *From Tudor times to the eighteenth century.* London: Routledge & Kegan Paul.

Pollard, S. 1981. Sheffield and sweet Auburn—amenities and living standards in the British industrial revolution: A comment. *Journal of Economic History* 41:902–4.

Post, J. D. 1976. Famine, mortality, and epidemic disease in the process of modernization. *Economic History Review* 2d ser. 29:14–37.

Preston, S. H. 1976. *Mortality patterns in national populations: With special references to recorded causes of death.* New York: Academic Press.

———. 1980. Causes and consequences of mortality declines in less developed countries during the twentieth century. In *Population and economic change in developing countries,* ed. R. A. Easterlin. National Bureau of Economic Research Conference Report, no. 30. Chicago: University of Chicago Press.

———. 1985. Resources, knowledge, and child mortality: A comparison of the U.S. in the late nineteenth century and developing countries today. Paper presented at International Population Conference, Florence, June.

Preston, S. H., and Haines, M. R. 1983. New estimates of child mortality in the United States at the turn of the century. Mimeographed. University of Pennsylvania.

Preston, S. H., et al. 1972. *Causes of death: Life tables for National Populations.* New York: Seminar Press.

Preston, S. H., and van de Walle, E. 1978. Urban French mortality in the nineteenth century. *Population Studies* 32:275–97.

Pullar, P. 1970. *Consuming passions: Being an historic inquiry into certain English appetites.* Boston: Little, Brown.

Raman, L. 1981. Influence of maternal nutritional factors affecting birthweight. *American Journal of Clinical Nutrition* 34:775–78.

Razzell, P. E. 1973. An interpretation of the modern rise of population in Europe—a critique. *Population Studies* 28:5–170.

Richardson, T. L. 1976. The agricultural labourer's standard of living in Kent, 1790–1840. In *The making of the modern British diet,* ed. S. D. Oddy and D. Miller. London: Croom Helm.

Rona, R. J., et al. 1978. Social factors and height of primary school children in England and Scotland. *Journal of Epidemiology and Community Health* 32:147–54.

Rosenberg, C. E. 1962. *The cholera years: The United States in 1832, 1849, and 1866.* Chicago: University of Chicago Press.

Rothenberg, W. B. 1984. Markets and Massachusetts farmers: A paradigm of economic growth in rural New England, 1750–1855. Ph.D. dissertation. Brandeis University.

Rutman, D. B., and Rutman, A. H. 1979. "Now-wives and sons-in-law": Parental death in a seventeenth-century Virginia county. In *Chesapeake in the seventeenth century: Essays in Angloamerican society and politics,* ed. T. W. Tate and D. L. Ammerman. New York: Norton.

Sackett, D. L., et al. 1977. The development and application of indices of health: General methods and a summary of results. *American Journal of Public Health* 67:423–28.

Sandberg, L. G., and Steckel, R. H. 1980. Soldier, soldier what made you grow so tall? *Economics and History* 23:91–105.

Sawyer, M. 1976. Income distribution in OECD countries. *OECD Economic Outlook: Occasional Studies,* July, 3–36.

Schofield, R. 1983. The impact of scarcity and plenty on population change in England, 1541–1871. *Journal of Interdisciplinary History* 14:265–91.

Schuurman, A. 1980. Probate inventories: Research issues, problems and results. *A.A.G. Bijdragen* 23:19–31.

Scrimshaw, N. S. 1983. Functional consequences of malnutrition for human populations: A comment. *Journal of Interdisciplinary History* 14:409–11.

Sen, A. 1981. *Poverty and famines: An essay on entitlement and deprivation.* Oxford: Clarendon.

Shammas, C. 1983. Food expenditures and economic well-being in early modern England. *Journal of Economic History* 43:89–100.

———. 1984. The eighteenth-century English diet and economic change. *Explorations in Economic History* 21:254–69.

Shapiro, S., et al. 1968. *Infant perinatal, maternal, and childhood mortality in the United States.* Cambridge: Harvard University Press.

———. 1980. Relevance of correlates of infant deaths for significant morbidity at 1 year of age. *American Journal of Obstetrics and Gynecology* 136:363–73.

Sheridan, R. B. 1985. *Doctors and slaves: A medical and demographic history of slavery in the British West Indies, 1680–1834.* Cambridge: Cambridge University Press.

Skipp, V. 1978. *Crisis and development: An ecological case study of the Forest of Arden, 1570–1674.* Cambridge: Cambridge University Press.

Smillie, W. G. 1955. *Public health: Its promise for the future.* New York: Macmillan.

Smith, D. S. 1972. The demographic history of colonial New England. *Journal of Economic History* 32:165–83.

Sokoloff, K. L. 1984. The heights of Americans in three centuries: Some economic and demographic implications. Mimeographed. NBER Working Paper 1384.

Sokoloff, K. L., and Villaflor, G. C. 1982. The early achievement of modern stature in America. *Social Scientific History* 6:453–81.

Soltow, L. 1971. *Patterns of wealthholding in Wisconsin since 1850.* Madison: University of Wisconsin Press.

———. 1975. *Men and wealth in the United States, 1850–1870.* New Haven: Yale University Press.

Southgate, D. A. T. 1978. Fetal measurements. In *Human growth: Principles and prenatal growth,* vol. 1, ed. F. Falkner and J. M. Tanner. New York: Plenum.

Steckel, R. H. 1982a. Height, health, nutrition, and labor productivity in the antebellum South. Mimeographed. National Bureau of Economic Research.

———. 1982b. Height, nutrition, and mortality in Ohio, 1870–1900. Mimeographed. National Bureau of Economic Research.

———. 1983. Height and per capita income. *Historical Method* 16:1–70.

———. 1984a. Adversity and diversity: The nutrition, health, and mortality of American slaves from conception to adult maturity. Mimeographed. Ohio State University.

———. 1984b. Characteristics of men rejected by the Union Army. Mimeographed. Ohio State University.

————. 1985. The health and mortality of slave children reconsidered: Were the abolitionists right? Mimeographed. Ohio State University.

Stern, W. M. 1964. The bread crisis in Britain, 1795–96. *Economica* 31:168–87.

Stone, L. 1977. *The family, sex, and marriage in England, 1500–1800*. New York: Harper & Row.

Sussman, G. D. 1975. The wet-nursing business in nineteenth-century France. *French Historical Studies* 9:304–653.

————. 1977. Parisian infants and Norman wet nurses in the early nineteenth century: A statistical study. *Journal of Interdisciplinary History* 7:637–53.

Tanner, J. M. 1978. *Fetus into man: Physical growth from conception to maturity*. Cambridge: Harvard University Press.

————. 1981. *A history of the study of human growth*. Cambridge: Cambridge University Press.

————. 1982. The potential of auxological data for monitoring economic and social well-being. *Social Scientific History* 6:571–81.

Tanner, J. M., et al. 1966. Standards from birth to maturity for height, weight, height velocity, weight velocity: British children, 1965. *Archives of Diseases of Childhood* 41:454–71., 613–35.

Taylor, A. J., ed. 1975. *The standard of living in Britain in the industrial revolution*. London: Methuen.

Taylor, C. E. 1982. Infections, famines, and poverty. Mimeographed. Johns Hopkins University.

Taylor, F. K. 1979. *The concepts of illness, disease, and morbus*. Cambridge: Cambridge University Press.

Taylor, G. R. 1951. *The transportation revolution, 1815–1860*. Vol. 4. *The economic history of the United States*. New York: Rinehart.

Temin, P. 1966. Steam and water power in the early nineteenth century. *Journal of Economic History* 26:187–205.

Terrenato, L., and Ulizzi, L. 1983. Genotype-environment relationships: An analysis of stature distribution curves during the last century in Italy. *Annals of Human Biology* 10:335–46.

Thirsk, J. 1983. The horticultural revolution: A cautionary note on prices. *Journal of Interdisciplinary History* 14:299–302.

Thomson, A. M., and Billewicz, W. Z. 1976. The concept of the "light-for-dates" infant. In *The biology of human fetal growth*, ed. D. F. Roberts and A. M. Thomson. London: Taylor & Francis.

Thomson, A. M., et al. 1968. The assessment of fetal growth. *Journal of Obstetrics and Gynecology of the British Commonwealth* 75:903–16.

Thompson, W. S., and Whelpton, P. K. 1933. *Population trends in the United States*. New York: McGraw-Hill.

Thurgood, J. M. 1984. Introduction to the account of the great household of Humphrey, First Duke of Buckingham, for the year 1452–

1453, ed. Mary Harris. In *Camden miscellany XXVIII*. London: Royal Historical Society.

Tilly, L. A. 1983. Food entitlement, famine, and conflict. *Journal of Interdisciplinary History* 14:333–49.

Towne, M. W., and Rasmussen, W. D. 1960. Farm gross product and gross investment in the nineteenth century. In *Trends in the American economy in the nineteenth century*. Conference on Research in Income and Wealth, vol. 255–315. Princeton: Princeton University Press.

Trevelyan, G. M. 1942. *English social history: A survey of six centuries, Chaucer to Queen Victoria*. London: Longmans.

Trumbach, R. 1978. *The rise of the egalitarian family: Aristocratic kinship and domestic relations in eighteenth-century England*. New York: Academic Press.

Trussell, J., and Bloom, D. E. 1979. A model distribution of height or weight at a given age. *Human Biology* 51:523–36.

Trussell, J., and Wachter, K. W., 1984. Estimating covariates of height in truncated samples. Mimeographed. National Bureau of Economic Research.

Udjus, L. G. 1964. *Anthropometrical changes in Norwegian men in the twentieth century*. Oslo: Universitetsforlaget.

United Nations Statistical Office. 1983. *Demographic yearbook*. New York.

United States Bureau of the Census. 1975. *Historical statistics of the United States, colonial times to 1970*. Washington.

United States Bureau of the Census. 1983. *Statistical abstract of the United States, 1984*. Washington.

United States Department of Labor. 1897. Conditions of Negroes in various cities. *Bulletin No. 10*.

United States National Center for Health Statistics. 1963. *Vital statistics of the United States 1960, Vol. II. Mortality, Part A*. Rockville, Md.

United States National Center for Health Statistics. 1974. *Vital statistics of the United States 1970, Vol. II. Mortality, Part A*. Rockville, Md.

United States National Center for Health Statistics. 1983. Advance report of final mortality statistics, 1980. *Monthly Vital Statistics Reports* 32, no. 4.

United States National Office of Vital Statistics. 1954. Weight at birth and its effect on survival of the newborn in the United States, early 1950. *Vital Statistics Special Report*, Vol. 39, no. 1.

United States Senate Select Committee on Nutrition and Human Needs. 1977. *Dietary goals for the United States*. Washington: Government Printing Office.

United States Surgeon General's Office. 1875. *The cholera epidemic of 1873.* Washington: Government Printing Office.

Van Wieringen, J. C. 1978. Secular growth changes. In *Human growth.* Vol. 2. *Postnatal growth,* ed. F. Falkner and J. M. Tanner. New York: Plenum.

Vinovskis, M. A. 1971. The 1789 Life table of Edward Wigglesworth. *Journal of Economic History* 31:570–90.

———. 1972. Mortality rates and trends in Massachusetts before 1860. *Journal of Economic History* 32:184–213.

Vogel, M. J. 1980. *The invention of the modern hospital: Boston 1870–1930.* Chicago: University of Chicago Press.

Von Tunzelmann, G. N. 1979. Trends in real wages, 1750–1850, revisited. *Economic History Review* 32:33–49.

Wachter, K. W. 1981. Graphical estimation of military heights. *Historical Methods* 14:31–42.

Wachter, K. W., and Trussell, J. 1982. Estimating historical heights. *Journal of the American Statistical Association* 77:279–303.

Walford, C. 1970. *The famines of the world past and present.* New York: Burt Franklin.

Walsh, L. S., and Menard, R. R. 1974. Death in the Chesapeake: Two life tables for men in early colonial Maryland. *Maryland History Magazine* 69:211–27.

Walter, J. 1976. Dearth and social order in early modern England. *P & P* 71:22–42.

Ward, W. P., and Ward, P. C. 1984. Infant birth weight and nutrition in industrializing Montreal. *American Historical Review* 89:324–45.

Warner, R. H., and Rosett, H. L. 1975. The effects of drinking on offspring: An historical survey of the American and British literature. *Journal of Studies in Alcohol* 36:1395–1420.

Waterlow, J. C., et al. 1977. The presentation and use of height and weight data for comparing the nutritional status of groups of children under the age of 10 years. *Bulletin of WHO.* 55:489–98.

Webster, T. 1845. *An encyclopedia of domestic economy.* New York: Harper.

Weir, D. R. 1982. Fertility transition in rural France, 1740–1829. Ph.D. dissertation, Stanford University.

Wilkin, J. C. 1981. Recent trends in the mortality of the aged. *Society of Actuaries, Transactions* 33:11–62.

Williams, M. W. 1985. Improvements in western European diets and economic growth. Mimeographed.

Williamson, J. G. 1976. American prices and urban inequality since 1820. *Journal of Economic History* 36:303–33.

———. 1981a. Urban disamenities, dark satanic mills, and the British standard of living debate. *Journal of Economic History* 41:75–83.

————. 1981b. Some myths die hard—urban disamenities one more time: A reply. *Journal of Economic History* 41:905–07.

————. 1982. Was the Industrial Revolution worth it? Disamenities and death in 19th century British towns. *Exploration in Economic History* 19:221–45.

————. 1984. British mortality and the value of life, 1781–1931. *Population Studies* 38:157–72.

Williamson, J. G., and Lindert, P. H. 1980. *American inequality: A microeconomic history.* New York: Academic Press.

Wilson, C. A. 1973. *Food and drink in Britain: From the Stone Age to recent times.* London: Constable.

Wimmer, L. T. 1984. Phases and strategies in the collection and linking of genealogical data: The status of the DAE/CPE pilot sample as of May, 1984. Mimeographed.

Winick, M., and Brasel, J. A. 1980. Nutrition and cell growth. In *Modern nutrition in health and disease,* ed. R. S. Goodhart and M. E. Shils. Philadelphia: Lea & Febiger.

World Bank. 1980. *World development report 1980.* Washington: World Bank.

————. 1984. *World development report 1984.* New York: Oxford University Press.

World Health Organization. 1980. The incidence of low birth weight: A critical review of available information. *World Health Statistics Quarterly* 33:197–224.

Wrigley, E. A. 1977. Births and baptisms: The use of Anglican baptism registers as a source of information about the numbers of births in England before the beginning of civil registration. *Population Studies* 31:281–312.

Wrigley, E. A., and Schofield, R. S. 1981. *The population history of England, 1541–1871: A reconstruction.* Cambridge: Harvard University Press.

————. 1983. English population history from family reconstitution: Summary results 1600–1799. *Population Studies* 37:157–84.

Yang, D. 1984. Aspects of United States agriculture circa 1860. Ph.D. dissertation, Harvard University.

Yasuba, Y. 1962. *Birth rates of the white population in the United States, 1800–1860.* Baltimore: Johns Hopkins Press.

# 10 The Female Labor Force and American Economic Growth, 1890–1980

Claudia Goldin

## 10.1 Introduction

When the labor force participation of a nation increases, measured national income per capita also rises. In the history of the American economy, as in other Western nations, the labor force participation rate has increased because the participation of prime-aged women has increased. Most other changes in the labor force have decreased this rate, most notably the decline in the age of retirement and the increase in age at which work begins.

By the definitions of the United States Population Census, the labor force participation rate of prime-aged females (15–64 years old) rose from 19.6% in 1890 to 59.9% in 1980, and the female component of the labor force increased from 17% to 43%.[1] Not only did the labor force participation rate of women expand, but the ratio of female to male full-time earnings increased as well, from 0.46 to 0.60 over the last century.

The expansion of the female labor force as conventionally measured and the rise in the female/male earnings ratio were associated with a growth of national income per capita that exceeded the growth in male earnings by 28%. Had the female labor force not expanded over this period, national income per capita would probably have been at least 14% lower than it actually was.

The labor force data underlying these calculations have been the subjects of substantial debate, and the degree to which the female labor

Claudia Goldin is professor of economics at the University of Pennsylvania and a research associate of the National Bureau of Economic Research.

This research has been supported by various grants from the National Science Foundation and is part of the author's ongoing study of women in the American labor force.

557

force actually increased over this century depends on the accuracy of the data for the period from 1890 to 1910.[2] Many have argued that the female labor force was severely undercounted in these censuses, although the goods and services it produced were incorporated into subsequent national income estimates. Alternatively, because of the change in the official labor force concept in 1940, others have argued that the female labor force may have been overstated in the earlier period.

The measurement of the female labor force raises fundamental problems in national income accounting procedures. As the market expands, goods and services once produced in the home are purchased in the marketplace. If women have traditionally produced such goods, then their later emergence in the paid labor force would increase economic well-being far less than measured national income.[3]

Different conclusions regarding the role of women in economic growth would emerge if the labor force data are inaccurate or if the theories underlying the calculations are mistaken. Revisions to the female labor force data for the period around 1890, in section 10.3, suggest that shifts in the locus of production across the twentieth century may produce a misleading picture of change in the economic role of women. These revised labor force estimates tend to support Durand's (1975) hypothesis that the labor force participation rate of married white women first shrinks and later expands as production moves from the home and the family farm to the more centralized marketplace. Thus the relationship between female labor force participation and economic development may be U-shaped.

Despite the substantial revisions to the female labor force data for the early period, the census statistics document an important trend. The emergence of a modern female labor force, with substantial life-cycle labor force participation, was a product of the movement of women out of the home and family farm and into the marketplace. Further, change in the economic marketplace flows into other spheres. As Carl Degler (1980, p. 362) observed, "Work for money as opposed to work for family generates different attitudes and relationships among family members."

The earnings data indicate that the ratio of female to male earnings rose from at least 1890 to 1950. This ratio, commonly called the "gender gap," has remained remarkably constant at about 0.60 from 1950 to 1980, that is, since the time the Current Population Reports with their detailed income data have been published. The relative constancy of this ratio over that period of time has prompted many to claim that it must have been constant over a much longer period. But for most of American history the ratio of female to male earnings has risen, and the relative constancy of the ratio over only these three decades is more easily understood in light of its movement across a longer period of time.[4]

## 10.2   The Dimensions of Change in Female Labor
##          Force Participation

The potential importance of the female labor force to understanding economic growth estimates is clear, but the accuracy and meaning of the labor force data must be explored. A brief review of labor force participation rates over the last century will stress the notion that while substantial change in the conventionally measured female labor force has only recently surfaced, it has been rooted in a longer history and has been determined by more distant factors. This point is more fully developed in Goldin (1983a).

Readily available labor force data dictate that the period under study begin with 1890. Data on the occupations of women were first collected in 1860, but the printed tabulations were aggregated at the state level and give little variation by age and other characteristics. Marital status was not requested until 1880.

The printed version of the 1890 Population Census (United States Census Office 1897) provides a fine start for a labor force series, with the data detailed by age, marital status, race, nativity, and region. The period from 1890 to the 1920s together with part of the earlier, less charted century witnessed the expansion in the market employment of the unmarried, particularly young single women. Similarly, the period beginning with the 1920s marks the expansion in the market role of married women.

### 10.2.1   Female Labor Force Participation Rates, 1890–1980

Labor force data for the aggregate female population, together with those by race, marital status, and nativity, are given in table 10.1. The overall trend for the aggregate from 1890 to 1980 is upward, but most of the movement comes from increases in the participation rate of married women, particularly after 1950. This increase is most apparent for white married women, but the aggregate nature of these data necessarily hides the most revealing trends. I turn therefore to a more detailed exploration of the data for white women, both single and married.

*Changes in the Labor Force Participation Rate of Unmarried Women*

The trend in the labor force participation rates of white single women across the entire United States, given in table 10.2 to 1970, suggests that the period should be divided at 1920. Participation rates for those 15–24 years old rise until 1920 when they reach a virtual plateau at about the 0.40 level. The data in table 10.2 have been disaggregated by nativity to point out substantial differences among these groups. Differences arise, in part, from the geographic location and age distribution of the groups. Accounting for the differences requires a decomposition by urbanization for the years before 1920, but this can only

**Table 10.1**  **Female Labor Force Participation Rates by Marital Status, Race, and Nativity, 1890–1980**

| | ≥ 16 Years Old | | | | ≥ 15 Years Old | | | ≥ 16 Years Old | |
|---|---|---|---|---|---|---|---|---|---|
| | 1890 | 1900[a] | 1920 | 1930 | 1940 | 1950 | 1960 | 1970 | 1980 |
| Total | 18.9 | 20.6 | 23.7 | 24.8 | 25.8 | 29.0 | 34.5 | 42.6 | 51.5 (49.9) |
| Total[b] | 19.0 | | | | | | | | 55.4 |
| Married | 4.6 | 5.6 | 9.0 | 11.7 | 13.8 | 21.6 | 30.7 | 40.8 | 50.1 (49.2) |
| Single | 40.5 | 43.5 | 46.4 | 50.5 | 45.5 | 46.3 | 42.9 | 53.0 | 61.5 |
| White | 16.3 | 17.9 | 21.6 | 23.7 | 24.5 | 28.1 | 33.7 | 41.9 | (49.4) |
| Married | 2.5 | 3.2 | 6.5 | 9.8 | 12.5 | 20.7 | 29.8 | 39.7 | 49.3 (48.1) |
| Single | 38.4 | 41.5 | 45.0 | 48.7 | 45.9 | 47.5 | 43.9 | 54.5 | 64.2 |
| Nonwhite | 39.7 | 43.2 | 43.1 | 43.3 | 37.6 | 37.1 | 41.7 | 48.5 | (53.3) |
| Married | 22.5 | 26.0 | 32.5 | 33.2 | 27.3 | 31.8 | 40.6 | 52.5 | 59.0 (60.5) |
| Single | 59.5 | 60.5 | 58.8 | 52.1 | 41.9 | 36.1 | 35.8 | 43.6 | 49.4 |
| Foreign-born | 19.8 | | | 19.1 | | | | | |
| Married | 3.0 | | | 8.5 | | | | | |
| Single | 70.8 | | | 73.8 | | | | | |

*Source:* Goldin (1977). The 1980 data are from United States Department of Labor (1982) and are the Current Population Survey figures. Those in parentheses are from United States Bureau of the Census (1983) and are the population census figures.

[a]The 1910 labor force figures have been omitted. See text for a discussion of the overcount of the agricultural labor force in that year.

[b]Adjusted for unemployment, by subtracting out the unemployed, and calculated for 15–64-year-olds for 1890 and 16–64-year-olds for 1980.

**Table 10.2**  Female Labor Force Participation 1890–1980 by Age, Marital Status, and Nativity for White Women in the Entire United States

### Never Married (Single)

| Year | Age = 15–24 NN | NF | F | Age = 25–34 NN | NF | F |
|---|---|---|---|---|---|---|
| 1890 | 24.0 | 41.9 | 71.1 | 42.3 | 55.7 | 78.9 |
| 1900 | 27.5 | 45.7 | 70.6 | 47.0 | 59.1 | 81.5 |
| 1910 | n.a. | n.a. | n.a. | n.a. | n.a. | n.a. |
| 1920 | 38.8 | 57.8 | 70.0 | (65.4) | (64.9) | (84.8) |
| 1930 | NN + NF 41.2 | | 71.4 | NN + NF 77.6 | | 94.1 |
| 1940 | NN + NF + F 40.8 | | | NN + NF + F 79.4 | | |
| 1950 | 42.9 | | | 80.6 | | |
| 1960 | 40.0 | | | 81.8 | | |
| 1970 | 51.8 | | | 83.4 | | |

### Currently Married

| Year | Age = 15–24 NN | NF | F | Age = 25–34 NN | NF | F |
|---|---|---|---|---|---|---|
| 1890 | 2.5 | 3.1 | 4.7 | 2.4 | 2.6 | 3.4 |
| 1900 | 2.7 | 3.1 | 4.4 | 3.0 | 3.2 | 3.4 |
| 1910 | n.a. | n.a. | n.a. | n.a. | n.a. | n.a. |
| 1920 | 7.7 | 9.2 | 9.8 | 6.6 | 6.7 | 8.3 |
| 1930 | 13.2 | | 14.9 | 11.5 | | 11.6 |
| 1940 | 14.7 | | | 16.7 | | |
| 1950 | 24.9 | | | 21.0 | | |
| 1960 | 30.0 | | | 26.7 | | |
| 1970 | 44.1 | | | 36.2 | | |
| 1980 | 60.1 | | | 56.0 | | |

*(continued)*

Table 10.2   (continued)

| | Age = 35–44 | | | Age = 45–54 | | | Age = 55–64 | | |
|---|---|---|---|---|---|---|---|---|---|
| 1890 | 2.3 | 2.6 | 3.1 | 2.1 | 2.5 | 2.5 | 1.7 | 2.2 | 1.9 |
| 1900 | 3.3 | 3.4 | 3.3 | 2.4 | 3.0 | 2.8 | 1.9 | 2.3 | 2.0 |
| 1910 | n.a. | n.a. | n.a. | n.a. | n.a. | n.a. | n.a. | n.a. | n.a. |
| 1920 | 6.6 | 6.3 | 8.1 | (5.0) | (4.7) | | (5.0)[b] | | |
| 1930 | 9.8 | | 10.0 | 8.2 | | 6.5 | 5.4 | | 4.1 |
| 1940 | | 13.8 | | | 10.1 | | | 6.4 | |
| 1950 | | 25.3 | | | 22.2 | | | 12.6 | |
| 1960 | | 35.4 | | | 38.6 | | | 24.6 | |
| 1970 | | 44.4 | | | 46.7 | | | 34.1 | |
| 1980 | | 59.1 | | | 53.4 | | | 36.8 | |

Widowed and Divorced

| | Age = 15–24 | | | Age = 25–34 | | |
|---|---|---|---|---|---|---|
| 1890 | 32.6 | 40.5 | 51.3 | 42.2 | 46.1 | 53.6 |
| 1900 | 29.3 | 37.8 | 47.5 | 51.8 | 58.2 | 53.6 |
| 1910 | n.a. | n.a. | n.a. | n.a. | n.a. | n.a. |
| 1920 | 41.1 | 81.2[a] | 31.1 | (56.0) | (93.3) | (54.9) |
| 1930 | 56.4 | | 65.7 | 71.9 | | (59.5) |
| 1940 | | 49.3 | | | 63.2 | |
| 1950 | | 52.0 | | | 60.9 | |
| 1960 | | 49.5 | | | 60.7 | |
| 1970 | | 58.5 | | | 66.8 | |
| 1980 | | 73.2 | | | 77.2 | |

| | Age = 35-44 | | | Age = 45-54 | | | Age = 55-64 | | |
|---|---|---|---|---|---|---|---|---|---|
| 1890 | 42.4 | 40.6 | 42.4 | 33.4 | 28.7 | 27.8 | 22.6 | 20.4 | 18.0 |
| 1900 | 54.0 | 53.2 | 53.8 | 42.0 | 36.5 | 31.8 | 26.8 | 23.1 | 18.9 |
| 1910 | n.a. | n.a. | n.a. | n.a. | n.a. | n.a. | n.a. | n.a. | n.a. |
| 1920 | (56.0) | (93.3) | (54.9) | | (17.8) | (28.9) | | | (15.4)[b] |
| 1930 | 60.2 | | (59.5) | 47.2 | | 38.4 | 26.9 | | 18.9 |
| 1940 | 59.3 | | | 44.1 | | | 25.2 | | |
| 1950 | 65.2 | | | 55.7 | | | 35.4 | | |
| 1960 | 68.4 | | | 57.1 | | | 47.8 | | |
| 1970 | 71.0 | | | 71.5 | | | 54.9 | | |
| 1980 | 77.7 | | | 73.8 | | | 54.0 | | |

*Sources:* Derived from United States Bureau of the Census and United States Census Office, Population Censuses, 1890–1970; United States Department of Labor, Bureau of Labor Statistics (1971) for widowed and divorced, 1970; and United States Department of Labor, Bureau of Labor Statistics, (1981) for 1980.

*Notes:*

NN = native-born white with native-born white parents.

NF = native-born white with at least one foreign-born parent.

F = foreign born.

Single includes unknown marital status for 1890, 1900, and 1920.

Widowed and divorced includes only widowed for 1890 and 1900; unknown and widowed and divorced for 1920 and 1930; and widowed and divorced and other for 1940, 1950, and 1960.

1920 figures in parentheses refer to 25-44-year-olds for single and married groups; 1920 figures in parentheses for widowed and divorced refer to 25-44-year-olds in 24-35 and 35-44 categories and 45+ in 45-54 and 55-64 categories.

1930 figures in parentheses for widowed and divorced refer to 25-44-year-olds in 24-35 and 35-44 categories.

1970 figure for single women 15-24 may reflect a change in definition.

Married spouse present for 1940-80.

[a] The NF figures derived from the 1920 census appear too high and may be the result of the statistical procedure employed.

[b] Refers to ages ≥ 45.

be computed for 1890. The participation rate in that year for young (15–24 years) single white women in cities with populations over 100,000 was 0.580. Those who were native born and of native parents (NN) had a rate of 0.429, those with foreign-born parents (NF) had a rate of 0.540, and the foreign born (F) had a rate of 0.822. Thus different geographic locations of young women account for some of the variation in their labor force participation rates, particularly between the two native-born groups, but do not account for the entire difference. Even within urban areas participation rates differed across ethnic lines, and evidence from disaggregated sources suggests that while higher family incomes reduced participation in the labor force, ethnicity had a separate influence on the daughters of the foreign born (Goldin 1979). The participation rate of 0.429 for the daughters of native-born parents in urban areas is, nonetheless, almost twice the U.S. aggregate rate in that age and marital status group (0.240).

What these data suggest is that the labor force participation rate for the entire population of young single women converged on that achieved by the urban native-born groups as early as 1890. The participation rate of urban single women, 15–24 years old, of native-born parents in 1890, as noted above, was 0.429; that of the entire population of single women between those ages was 0.408 in 1940, 0.429 in 1950, and 0.400 in 1960.

Despite the apparent stability in the percentage of single urban women in the labor force, there was, over this long time period, substantial variation in the activities of the approximately 60% who were not employed. In 1890 young women not in the labor force were overwhelmingly occupied "at home," ostensibly helping their mothers. Data for 1900 indicate that about two-thirds of the young women not in the labor force were not in school and were listed in the census as being "at home." With the proliferation of high schools in both urban and rural areas, the percentage "at home" dropped rapidly over the early twentieth century to less than one-tenth by 1930.[5] The increase in formal education exactly offset the decline in time devoted to home production by young single women. These changes in turn encouraged increased participation by married women (Goldin 1983a). More education enabled young women to obtain occupations which they would retain when married or reenter later. The decrease in their home production may have altered their preferences when married for work in the market. In this way the occupations of young single women early in this century may have affected those of married women more recently.

*Changes in the Labor Force Participation Rates of Married Women*

Participation rates of married women did not expand to any great extent until the 1920s, reinforcing the notion that the 1920s were a turning point for the female labor force. But if the change just after 1920 was an expansion, the change beginning with 1950 was an explosion in employment, first for women over age 35 and later for those under 35 years (Easterlin 1980; Goldin 1983a).

The participation rates for currently married women are disaggregated by nativity in table 10.2, but the variation in their employment is considerably smaller than that for single women. Indeed, the variation in the employment of married women across geographic regions, and particularly with urbanization and industrial development, was for the 1890–1930 period considerably less than it was for single women.

The strength of the demand for female labor determined the participation rate of single women, while the participation rate of married women was far less affected by it. Put another way, the long-run elasticity of supply of single women appears to have been considerably greater than that for married women for the period prior to 1930. Time-series changes in the employment of single women to about 1930 can be explained almost entirely by factors revealed in the cross-sectional analysis (Rotella 1980). The same cannot be said for married women, for whom time-series changes appear to arise from factors other than those varying in cross section.[6] Regional variation in female employment rates was mentioned in Lewis's (1954 [1958]) classic article on unlimited supplies of labor.[7] But while Lewis, referring to the English case, did not distinguish between the "wives and the daughters," such a division appears critical in American history.

The labor force participation rate of married white women may have varied far less by level of urban and industrial development than it did for single and widowed women from 1890 to 1930, but it was higher in cities than it was elsewhere. More significant with regard to the origins of the post–World War II rise in married women's labor force participation is that married women increased their participation rates earlier in urban areas. Participation rates for urban areas, in table 10.3, indicate the degree to which the 1920s shaped the structure of these data and the degree to which the 1930s were a decade of relative stagnation in female labor force participation. Seen in this light, the explosion of participation rates after 1950 becomes a contination of a pattern begun some thirty years before.[8]

Data identical to those in table 10.2 arrayed by birth cohort have been explored in detail elsewhere (Robinson 1980; Goldin 1983a). When arranged in this manner the large increase in the labor force participation of the older age group in the 1950s can be correlated with both economic and demographic circumstances at that time and cohort-specific factors. Cohorts born around 1900 achieved a much higher educational level than did those born before, enabling them to pursue occupations in the clerical and professional sectors (Rotella 1981; Gol-

**Table 10.3**     Labor Force Participation by Age and Nativity, for Married White Women in Urban Areas, 1890–1970

| Age | 1890 | | | 1920 | | | 1930 | 1940 | 1950 | 1960 | 1970 |
|---|---|---|---|---|---|---|---|---|---|---|---|
| | NN | NF | F | NN | NF | F | NN + NF | All | All | All | All |
| 15–19 | 4.8 | 5.5 | 4.2 | 15.4 | 15.5 | 15.3 | 17.8 | 20.1 | 26.1 | 33.2 | 46.8 |
| 20–24 | | | | 12.2 | 12.9 | 11.2 | 20.9 | | 31.2 | | 47.6 |
| 25–34 | 3.8 | 4.3 | 3.4 | 9.6 | 10.5 | 8.5 | 15.8 | 19.5 | 23.3 | 27.3 | 36.3 |
| 35–44 | 4.0 | 4.3 | 3.7 | 9.0 | 10.0 | 7.8 | 12.8 | 15.4 | 27.5 | 36.5 | 44.6 |
| 45+ | 3.8 | 3.8 | 4.0 | 6.4 | 7.3 | 5.4 | 8.4 | 9.2 | 17.5 | 29.8 | 40.4 |

*Notes:*

1890–1940: Urban includes cities of over 100,000 population.

1950–70: Urban includes cities of over 2,500 population.

1890–1930: Married is married spouse present or absent.

1940, 1960, 1970: Married is married spouse present.

1950: Married is wife of the head of household.

Procedure used to derive 1890 data: The number of women in the labor force by marital status, age, and nativity had to be constructed from the 1890 data. The original data were aggregated by nativity, age, and marital status separately for cities over 100,000 persons. The number of women in each cell was constructed from the number of women of each nativity under the assumption that the age–marital status distribution was the same as that of the nonagricultural female labor force, which was available from the census.

NN, NF, F defined in table 10.2.

din 1984a). These were the cohorts that later reentered the labor force in the 1950s. Cause and effect of the changes in female occupations, education, and labor force participation are not easily discerned. Evidence from other western nations suggests that changes in the structure of the economy and general educational levels have tended to precede the increase in participation of married women by several decades.[9] The increase in labor force participation rates among young married women in the last two decades can also be correlated with a change in schooling, in this case college education.

The marital composition of the female labor force given in table 10.4 provides further confirmation of the turning point suggested in table 10.2. By 1930 one female labor force participant in four was currently married, even though the participation rate of married white women was only 9.8%. Despite relatively low participation rates, the shift in the percentage of the labor force that was married from just over 10% to one-quarter altered the tone of public policy.[10] Sometime between 1950 and 1960 married white women became over one-half the white female labor force, although recent changes in the marital composition of the population have reversed this trend.

## 10.3    Some Further Considerations Regarding Female Labor Force Estimates

The labor force participation rates derived from the census for the 1890–1980 period were offered, in section 10.2, with few qualifications. The accuracy of these figures, their consistency over time, and their inclusiveness have been frequently questioned, but no changes of any substantial magnitude have yet been made.[11]

The definition of labor force participation changed in 1940 from the "gainful worker"concept to that of the "labor force," raising the issue of consistency over time. Closely related is the extent of part-time and intermittent work, and the degree to which each could have been differentially treated by the labor force constructs. Women might have been more reluctant to tell census marshals that they had an occupation when it was not the norm to work for pay.

The labor force data for the entire period, 1890–1940, need to be reexamined. Because the data for the earliest period ought to reveal the most severe biases, I have focused only on the interval from 1890 to 1910. Data from turn-of-the-century surveys at the national level provide independent evidence on the reliability and consistency of the census and on the possible omission of boardinghouse keepers and home workers in manufacturing. The censuses from 1890 to 1910 and various time-budget surveys of the 1920s will be used to revise the

**Table 10.4  Marital Composition of the Female Labor Force, 1890–1980, White Women, Entire United States**

| | 1890 | 1900 | 1910 | 1920 | 1930 | 1940 | 1950 | 1960 | 1970 | 1980 |
|---|---|---|---|---|---|---|---|---|---|---|
| *Percentage Single* | | | | | | | | | | |
| NN | 69.0 | 69.1 | | 66.4 | 61.0 | | | | | |
| NF | 89.9 | 86.4 | | 74.3 | | | | | | |
| F | 74.3 | 71.1 | | 54.1 | 49.6 | | | | | |
| All | 76.2 | 74.7 | | 63.6 | 59.5 | 52.3 | 33.6 | 24.3 (24.9)[a] | 22.5 | 24.3 |
| *Percentage Married* | | | | | | | | | | |
| NN | 10.0 | 11.3 | | 19.0 | 24.6 | | | | | |
| NF | 4.5 | 5.8 | | 11.6 | | | | | | |
| F | 9.4 | 11.6 | | 19.8 | 31.3 | | | | | |
| All | 8.3 | 9.7 | | 17.0 | 25.5 | 29.2 | 46.9 | 56.3 (55.3)[a] | 60.0 | 57.4 |
| *Percentage Other (widowed, divorced, unknown)* | | | | | | | | | | |
| NN | 21.0 | 19.6 | | 14.6 | 14.4 | | | | | |
| NF | 5.6 | 7.8 | | 14.1 | | | | | | |
| F | 16.3 | 17.3 | | 26.1 | 19.1 | | | | | |
| All | 15.5 | 15.6 | | 19.4 | 15.0 | 18.5 | 19.5 | 19.4 (19.8)[a] | 17.5 | 18.3 |

*Sources*: 1890–1960, United States Bureau of the Census and United States Census Office, Population Censuses; 1970, 1980; United States Department of Labor, Bureau of Labor Statistics (1982).

*Notes*:

NN = native-born with native parents.

NF = native-born with at least one foreign-born parent.

F = foreign-born.

Percentage married: includes only married spouse present 1940–80.

Percentage single: includes "unknown marital status" 1890–1900.

[a]Figures in parentheses are from the Current Population Reports for comparability with the 1970 and 1980 figures.

female agricultural labor force, and these surveys are also used to construct a value for home production.

The outcome of these corrections is that the "gainful worker" concept does not necessarily overcount, nor does it necessarily undercount, female workers. Evidence on days worked per year suggests that the two concepts may have been very close in empirical fact. The omission of particular female workers did occur in certain areas: The undercount of boardinghouse keepers was severe in cities, family farm laborers were more than often omitted in the cotton South, and casual family farm labor was not often counted in the rest of the country. The aggregate figures could be substantially altered by these corrections, but it is not clear that they all deserve to be incorporated into final time-series estimates of the female labor force.

### 10.3.1  Definitions of Labor Force Participation

Prior to 1940 the "gainful worker" concept of employment was used by the census, but in that year it was changed to the "labor force" concept we use today. Individuals were counted in the labor force under the gainful worker concept if they claimed to have had an occupation during the census year. The labor force concept includes individuals if they were employed for pay during the survey week, were employed for over 14 hours in unpaid family labor, or were unemployed and searching for work. Durand (1948, 1975) believed that gainful worker estimates, by asking an individual's primary occupation in the previous year, always overstated the labor force figures. For the female population this would imply that the earlier gainful worker estimates are biased upward and that the growth of the labor force is biased downward. There is, however, no simple theoretical relationship between the gainful worker and labor force concepts.

The precise relationship depends on a number of factors, among them the accepted norm for the number of days or weeks worked during the year that constituted having an occupation in the pre-1940 period and the distribution of actual days or weeks worked during the year. The gainful worker concept is an upwardly biased estimate of the labor force only if individuals work a large enough portion of the year to have some notion that they have an occupation. If instead they work only a small part of the year, say 15 weeks, they may not state they have an occupation even though a labor force estimate based on a large sample of such individuals would be at least (15/52), or 29%. The gainful worker criterion in this example would lead to a lower employment figure than the labor force construct.

Under certain circumstances the two definitions produce identical labor force percentages, and there is no particular reason why one definition should result in a higher value than the other. Suppose an individual in the pre-1940 period considered herself to have an occupation if she was employed for at least half the year, say 26 weeks or more. In the post-1940 period such an individual would stand a 50% chance of being counted in the labor force by census takers who define work as being employed in the survey week.[12] The gainful worker estimate of labor force participation would, in this case, be higher than the labor force concept. If the number of weeks worked were below 26, the labor force concept would result in a higher participation rate than the gainful worker criterion.

The distribution across the population of weeks (or days) worked will, in general, determine the overall labor force participation rate and the biases in using one construct or the other. A uniform or symmetric distribution around 26 weeks, in the example given, will produce similar results for both definitions, and, as a general rule, the concepts will always coincide with a symmetric distribution around the societal norm for time worked to constitute an occupation.

The distribution of days worked, however, was not symmetric, but had a long left tail and a substantial mass near the maximum days worked. A large-scale survey of women working in manufacturing in 1907, *U.S. Senate Report on the Condition of Child and Woman Wage-Earners* (United States Senate Documents 1910/11), hereafter the 1907 Senate Report, indicates that the mean number of days worked by single women over 15 years old was 249. Therefore approximately 83% (249/300) of those employed at all during the year would have been counted under the labor force definition. The "gainful worker" definition will depend on the societal norm for days worked during the year. If the norm were half the full year, or 150 days, 92% of these women would have been counted, and the two definitions would coincide if the societal norm were 200 days, or 67% of a full year.

The same report also surveyed married women, working primarily, but not exclusively, as manufacturing laborers in factories and in their homes. The mean for the entire group was 212 days, somewhat lower than that for single women. The labor force definition would have counted as employed 71% of this group. If the "gainful worker" definition held for those working over 150 days, 73% would have been counted, and the results of the two definitions would have coincided at 175 days, or 58% of a full year. Thus it does not appear that these two definitions would have produced very different labor force results for either single or married women.

### 10.3.2  Part-Time, Intermittent, and Home Work

Closely related to the issue of the changing definition of labor force participation is the possibility that a large fraction of married women felt reluctant to report their occupation early in this century. Those who question the census data hypothesize that such women may have been more hesitant to admit they worked when the work was done at home, regardless of the amount of time devoted to paid labors. Alternatively, and more probably, they may not have claimed they had an occupation when the work was done part-time or intermittently through the year, at home or away from home. Thus the issue is whether they were actually working a sufficient number of hours or days to have considered themselves to be gainful workers, and if not, what the implicit labor force estimate would have been.

Two surveys exist to address these issues. The *Sixth and Seventh Annual Reports of the Commissioner of Labor* (United States Commissioner of Labor 1890, 1891), hereafter the 1890/91 Report, were surveys of industrial families listing the income earned by all family members, including the wife plus payments from boarders.[13] The 1907 Senate Report contained a survey of married women working in manufacturing both within factories and in their own homes.

Data from the 1890/91 Report lend support to the census labor force data for married women in industrial areas. Even if census takers had counted in the labor force *all* women who earned *any* positive amount over the year, the percentage of married women (husband present) in the labor force would still have been quite small. In the glass industry, for example, only 2.2% of all wives reported positive earnings; in heavy industries only 1.3% did; and in textiles 12.1% did. These statistics are not surprising given the nature of the industrial settings and the available work for women. What is surprising is that among women who did earn income, earnings were on average one-half those of full-time, year-round single women working in industry in 1890. Although there were few married women who worked in industry at that time, these data suggest that those who did worked more than half the year.[14]

The data in the 1907 Senate Report, reported above, also bear on the issue of intermittent and part-time work.[15] The proportion of a year worked for the average married women was sufficiently high (212/300 = 71%) and the distribution tight enough that the gainful worker definition should have produced an unbiased estimate of the labor force.

Not only did the married women in this sample who worked in industry labor almost full time, but those working at home tended to work an even greater number of days per year than did those in the factories. Those working at home labored for 216 days on average, while those in factories worked 210 days. The work of the industrial home workers was apparently more regular than previously believed. The incomes of industrial home workers, however, were 49% less than those of women working in factories. The large difference could be due to a compensating differential, a lower intensity of work, a greater intermittency of work within the day, or to less on-the-job training, as was suggested by government investigators at the time.

The 1907 Senate Report also surveyed the extent to which home workers, typically finishers in men's ready-made clothing, were helped by family members and friends (United States Senate Documents 1910/11, vol. 2). Of the 674 home workers interviewed, 176, or 24%, had helpers "with more or less regularity." These helpers were typically young children and, less frequently, the woman's husband. In 36% of the cases this work involved another adult woman ($\geq$ 18 years), but in only 19% of these cases did it involve another married or widowed woman. Thus the regularity of industrial home work for these women indicates that the census probably did not undercount them, and the nature of their helpers suggests that other adult women were not omitted to any great extent. Further, because home workers were typically of foreign birth, the time series on native-born white women should not be affected.

### 10.3.2 Undercounts of Female Laborers in Particular Occupations and Sectors

It has been frequently claimed that women have been undercounted in certain occupations, particularly those that were performed in the home or on the family farm, and in certain sectors. Married women comprised the majority of boardinghouse keepers and unpaid family farm workers. Adjustments to cotton farm workers and to those in manufacturing are for the entire female labor force.

*Boardinghouse Keepers*

An undercount of boardinghouse keepers in the late nineteenth century is suggested by the fact that 14% of all white households in 1880 Philadelphia had boarders (Goldin 1979), but fewer than 1% of all dwellings in Philadelphia were enumerated in the 1880 United States Population Census as having a female boardinghouse keeper.

Data on income from boarders, as well as the number of boarders, are included in the 1890/91 Report on industrial families. Because the data are presumably gross, and not net, the following procedure was used to form the estimate of labor force participation:

a) About 23% of all husband-wife families in the industrial communities surveyed in the 1890/91 Report had at least one boarder or nonnuclear family member (the two were grouped together), and about 16% of all husband-wife families received income from boarders, a figure that is almost identical to that inferred from 1880 United States Population Census data for Philadelphia (Goldin 1979). Boarding varied by industry, with textile families having the highest percentage with income from boarders. Income from boarding was $201 per year on average across all husband-wife families having positive earnings from boarders.

b) The gross income figure must be adjusted for the additional costs of running a household with boarders. An equation regressing total rent paid on the number and composition of household members yielded a mere $2.70 for each additional boarder, only 3.4% of the total rent. Rent, it appears, was invariant to the presence of boarders. Food expenditures, however, were about 29% of average boarding income ($29 per boarder × 2, average number of boarders/$201, average income from boarders).[16] The net income from boarders was about $140 per year for each boarding household, a figure that translates into 47% of expected full-time income for women in comparable geographic areas.[17]

In summary, about 16% of all husband-wife couples and 20% of all female-headed households had income from boarders in industrial areas around 1890, figures that are similar to those from large cities at that time. Each boardinghouse keeper earned approximately half full-time earnings, a figure comparable to the earnings of industrial home workers.

The distribution of net earnings from boarding indicates that about 37% of all boardinghouse keepers should be counted under the gainful worker definition, if having an occupation was construed as earning over 50% full-time yearly income. The current labor force definition counts home workers if they work 15 hours or more during the survey week or 37.5% of a normal 40-hour work week. By applying this criterion, 46% of all boardinghouse keepers should be included in the labor force estimate. The correction for all married women in cities and industrial areas is somewhere between 5.9 and 7.4 percentage points, a substantial addition to the 4.0% labor force figure for married white women in cities in 1890.

It might be claimed, however, that all industrial home workers who logged as many days per year as factory workers but earned only one-half their pay should, on a days-worked-per-year basis, be included in labor force estimates. Using the same logic, all boardinghouse keepers should be included in the labor force as well. Under these conditions the correction for all married women in cities and industrial areas is the full 16%, a substantial addition to the census figure for married white women in cities in 1890.

c) These data must still be translated into aggregate statistics. In 1890, 17% of all dwellings were in cities with 25,000 or more inhabitants. If the data presented above apply only to urban areas, the adjustment is somewhere between 1.0 and 2.7 percentage points for married women and 1.3 to 3.4 percentage points for widows. Boarding must have been extensive on farms and in rural nonfarm areas, but we have no idea how widespread it was. It should be clear, however, that undercounting boardinghouse keepers overstates the later movement of married women into the labor force particularly in cities, and understates their participation in the economy of the nineteenth century.

*Agricultural Workers*

The understatement of female agricultural workers concerns the casual unpaid labor of farm family members. Those who designed the 1910 census were aware of this problem and instructed enumerators that "a woman working regularly at outdoor farm work, even though she works on the home farm for her husband, son, or other relative and does not receive money wages, should be returned . . . as a *farm laborer*."[18] These instructions produced an acknowledged overstatement of the female labor force and have led to the wholesale abandonment of the 1910 census as a source of occupational and labor force data.

The 1910 census may be a poor source for accurate labor force estimates, but it provides superb data to produce an upper-bound estimate of female employment in the agricultural sector. These data yield a measure of the excess number of female agricultural laborers in 1910 compared with previous censuses and an upper bound to that figure for 1890 and 1900. Two different, but complementary, procedures have been employed here, and they are in agreement that the number of female farm laborers would have been half the 1910 census estimate had previous survey procedures been used.

The overcount of agricultural workers was almost entirely concentrated in the category of unpaid family farm labor, and only the major cotton-producing states were affected.[19] White families tended to underreport their unpaid family labor far more than did black families, whose wives and daughters frequently were part of the paid labor force. In the first of the two procedures, the ratio of unpaid female family farm workers to all females in the population in 1910 is compared to that for 1900. The difference between these two figures is construed as the maximum shortfall in 1900. In 1910 the ratio was 0.063 for white women over 15 years old. Data from a special report of the 1900 census on working women indicate that only one-fourth of these women had been counted as unpaid family workers in that year.[20] Thus the undercount is 4.7 percentage points.

The second procedure computes the percentage of women who were working in agriculture in 1910 and compares it with the figure for 1890, adjusted for the relative decline that sector experienced over the twenty intervening years. In 1890, 8.4% of the white female labor force ($\geq 15$ years) was employed in agriculture; the 1910 census reported 10.5% of the white female labor force ($\geq 16$ years) employed in agriculture. The 1910 figure would have been 5.6% had the relative decline in the male agricultural labor force applied as well to females.[21] The difference between the figure for 1910 and the adjusted figure, 4.9 percentage points, is the shortfall.

The two procedures give almost identical results, a 4 to 5 percentage point shortfall in the labor force participation rate computed for white women over 15 years old in either 1890 or 1900. Using the entire shortfall as the adjustment assumes that all individuals who worked on family farms in 1910 should be included in the labor force estimate. For consistency with both the labor force and the gainful worker concepts the percentage of a full work year spent in family labor is needed to adjust the shortfall. One study of family cotton-farm labor (Allen 1931) gives a value of 3.7 months per year as the time women spent working on the farm for their families.[22] A labor force construct would include 31% (3.7/12) of the total number of women working on cotton farms for their families. The adjusted shortfall in the labor force would be 1.24 percentage points for all white female unpaid laborers in the cotton South.[23]

What of the unpaid farm labor of women on noncotton farms? Data from time-budget surveys of farm women can be used to address this issue. These surveys were conducted in the late 1920s, primarily among western farm families whose daily lives and chores were apparently unchanged in the thirty years that separate them from housewives in 1890. The seven surveys that have been consulted yield an average 9 to 10 hours per week spent by the housewife in unpaid family agricultural labor.[24] If all women performed 10 hours of unpaid work, then none of them would be counted by the "labor force" concept used today.[25] Rather than using either the current concept or that of "gainful worker," an expected value construct might be more appropriate. Given that the average laborer's work week was 50 hours in the 1920s, 20% (10/50) of these women should be included in the labor force. Multiplying by the appropriate percentages yields an undercount of 5.4 percentage points for all married women.[26] It should be noted that even the 1910 census with its vast overcount of unpaid family labor counted very few farm wives outside of the cotton areas in the labor force.

*Manufacturing Workers*

A divergence between the late nineteenth-century manufacturing labor force estimates derived from two census sources, that of population and that of manufacturing, was noted by Abbott (1910), Rubinow (1907), and Smuts (1960). The problem, quite simply, is that the two numbers differ and differ most severely for women and children. Abbott (1910) conjectured that part of the difference was due to the definitions of the labor force used in compiling the two censuses. The two definitions differ in exactly the same way that the gainful worker concept differs from that of the labor force. The labor force, as defined in the manufacturing census, was a full-time equivalent concept. Given the data above on the distribution of days worked in manufacturing, there can be no presumption as to which definition will produce the upper bound, and the two should have produced nearly similar labor force estimates.

The problem, then, must be traced back to two aspects of coverage. The manufacturing census did not survey many of the smaller shops and businesses that employed women in the production of clothing and hats. It is also likely that the population census undercounted women working in the larger manufacturing firms. The adjustment that will be made to the population census will assume that the population census data on women working as dressmakers and milliners are correct, but that the manufacturing census more accurately counted women working in the larger manufacturing firms.

There were 839,952 females ≥ 10 years old working in manufacturing in 1890 (excluding officers, firm members, and clerical workers), according to the manufacturing census (United States Census Office 1895a). The population census yields 1,027,242 (United States Office 1897). Note that the employment of women in manufacturing in 1890 accounted for almost one-third of all women in the labor force. There were, however, 602,677 females in the population census who had occupations in the making of clothing or hats, while the manufacturing census listed only 294,194. Given the assumption that the population census is more accurate for these occupations but that manufacturing is more accurate for the rest, the population census has a shortfall of 121,193 females working in larger manufacturing firms.[27] If correct, this number would translate into an increase of 3.1% in the female labor force (≥ 10 years old) in 1890, raising the population census estimate by 0.5 percentage points.

*Household Production*

Perhaps the most difficult of the necessary adjustments is the computation of the time spent by women in the household production of goods that were later supplied by the market. Of the various goods produced in the home around 1890 that later shifted at least in part to the market, clothing, meals, and baked items seem the most important.[28] Time budgets indicate that about 5 hours per week were spent in the production of clothing by farm wives around the 1920s and 2.5 hours, at a maximum, were devoted to baking. Total time spent in food preparation and cleanup dominated the time budgets, accounting for 35% on average. This figure is now 23% for full-time housewives, and 16% of the total eating time of all family members is spent consuming restaurant meals (Szalai 1972, p. 576). Had relative prices enticed families in 1890 to consume the same proportion of their meal time in restaurants as we do, they would have saved about 4 hours of meal preparation and clean-up time per week, given the 65-hour work week of the 1920 farm housewives.

It seems reasonable to assume that 5 hours is the combined net addition to household production of clothing and baked goods in 1890, compared to 1980, and that 4 hours is the saving from restaurant meals.[29] Thus (9/65), or 14% of the time of 1890 wives should be allotted to household production of goods that the market later supplied. This figure of 14% will be used to adjust the income figures in the growth calculation below.

## Summary of Adjustments to the 1890 Estimate

Table 10.5 summarizes the various corrections that have been noted in this section. For some we are on rather firm footing, such as the adjustment to the estimate of boardinghouse keepers. But for others, the adjustments are no more than educated guesses, as is the case for the estimate of unpaid family farm laborers outside the cotton South. The addition of these percentage points to the official census labor force estimates requires further thought in all cases, and only under certain assumptions would it be correct to use them to augment the original data.

**Table 10.5**   **Summary of Adjustments to the Female Labor Force Participation Rate, 1890**

| | Percentage Point Adjustments to the 1890 Census Female Labor Force Participation Rates for | | |
|---|---|---|---|
| Corrections owing to | Married[a] | Widowed | All[b] |
| A. Change in definition[c] | No correction needed | | |
| B. Omission of workers | | | |
| (1) Boardinghouse keepers | 1.0–2.7 | 1.3–3.4 | 0.69–1.84 |
| (2) Agricultural laborers, unpaid family farm | | | |
| Cotton | 1.33 | | 1.24 |
| All other | 5.40 | | 3.14 |
| (3) Manufacturing workers | 0 | | 0.50 |
| Total omission of workers | 7.73–9.43 | | 5.57–6.72 |
| C. Omission of household production from national income | 14% of 1890 household production value to be added to 1890 market production of females | | |

[a]The figure of cotton workers is adjusted for white women only; all others are implicitly for all races.

[b]"All" refers to 15–64-year-olds.

[c]The change in definition refers to that from "gainful worker" in the pre-1940 period to the "labor force" definition. See text.

## 10.4    Earnings of Females Relative to Those of Males: A Long-Term View

Full-time earnings for females and males are given in table 10.6 for six major occupational groupings for three benchmark years, 1890, 1930, and 1970. Average earnings are constructed by weighting them by the occupational distributions.

The ratio of female to male full-time earnings for the entire population increased from 0.463 to 0.603 from 1890 to 1970. The latter figure is unadjusted for differences in average hours per day for men and women working full-time and increases to 0.657 when the implied earnings per hour are used.[30] The rise in relative earnings from 1890 to 1970 would understate the true rise, corrected for hours, if the hours worked by males and females per week differed more in 1970 than in the two earlier years. One late nineteenth-century study that distinguished between male and female hours indicated that the ratio of male to female weekly hours was 1.076 in 1895/96 (United States Commissioner of Labor 1897). The ratio was 1.0893 in 1980. The adjustment for hours worked would increase the 1890 ratio to 0.498 (to be compared with the hours constant ratio of 0.657 in 1970), yielding an increase of 32%, rather than the uncorrected figure of 30%.

In part B the ratios of female to male earnings within each occupation are given and indicate a rise over time, particularly in the period from 1890 to 1930. Part C constructs the earnings data for each year using the earnings and occupational weights of that year. Average earnings data using the earnings of a particular year but the occupational weights of another year are also given. Part D uses these data to construct a matrix of female to male earnings ratios in which the occupational structure varies across the columns and the earnings data vary down the rows.

The matrix of part D suggests that the increase over time in relative earnings of females was due far more to changes in relative earnings within occupations than it was to changes in the distribution of occupations between men and women. The narrowing of skill premia from 1890 to 1930 with the increase in schooling levels raised relative earnings for women more than did any other single factor (Goldin 1984a,b). This finding is particularly noteworthy since it is generally presumed that the occupational distribution is the primary determinant of relative wages.

If women had the occupational distribution of the male labor force would their average earnings been substantially greater? The answer is no. Had females in 1890 the male occupational distribution given in the table for 1890, the ratio of female to male earnings would have been 0.473, but it was actually 0.463; had females in 1970 the male occupational distribution for 1970, the ratio would have been 0.629, but it was 0.603. While these findings hold for the limited number of occupations in table 10.6, there is reason to believe that they would hold as well for far more numerous occupational classifications.[31]

While the occupational distribution mattered far less than did earnings within occupations in determining the overall earnings ratio of females to males, the structure of occupations did experience considerable change. Over the first half of the 80-year period under consideration, the female labor force shifted relatively out of service and manufacturing jobs and into the clerical sector and, to a lesser degree, professional activities. The percentage of the total female labor force in the clerical sector rose from 4 to 21 and that in professional jobs increased from just under 10 to just over 16; in manufacturing it dropped from 28% to 20%, and the percentage working on farms was more than halved. The male labor force experienced somewhat similar shifts, although not nearly as extensive. In general, male laborers moved out of farm activities and into all other sectors.

The ratio of female to male earnings rose from 0.463 to 0.556 over the first 40-year period. Had the earnings figures by occupation remained at their 1890 levels but had the structure of occupations changed, the ratio would have increased from 0.463 to 0.489 (row 2, pt.D). Part of the remaining seven-tenths of the difference in relative earnings was due to changes in the structure of earnings, both between the sexes and across all occupations. Similar findings result from holding the structure of earnings at the 1930 and 1970 levels (rows 3 and 4, pt. D).

Over the last period, 1930–70, the male labor force moved relatively into the high-paying positions, out of the farm sector and into professional activities. The share of the male labor force in the professional category increased from 14% to 25%; that for females increased only from 17% to 19%, but the proportion of female employment in the clerical sector continued to expand. As in the previous 40 years, the ratio of female to male earnings rose during the 1930–70 period, from 0.556 to 0.603. But had the earnings figures remained at their 1930 levels, this ratio would have declined, from 0.556 to 0.507. Alternatively, had the 1970 earnings prevailed, the ratio would have been 0.610 in 1930 but would have declined to 0.603 by 1970. Thus the relative shift of both males and females across sectors from 1930 to 1970 reduced the relative earnings of women. That the aggregate ratio increased at all was due to the increase in the ratio of female to male earnings for professionals and to the reduction of skill differentials for men (Keat 1960; Lindert and Williamson 1980). Over the last 10 years (not in table 10.6) the average earnings of women relative to those of men have risen precisely because women have progressively shifted into the profes-

**Table 10.6**   Full-Time Earnings and Occupational Distributions of the Female and Male Labor Forces, 1890, 1930, and 1970

### A. Full-Time Earnings and Occupational Distributions

| | 1890 Male $ | 1890 Male % | 1890 Female $ | 1890 Female % | 1930 Male $ | 1930 Male % | 1930 Female $ | 1930 Female % | 1970 Male $ | 1970 Male % | 1970 Female $ | 1970 Female % |
|---|---|---|---|---|---|---|---|---|---|---|---|---|
| Professional | 1391 | 10.2 | 366 | 9.6 | 3713 | 13.6 | 1428 | 16.5 | 12250 | 24.9 | 8700 | 18.9 |
| Clerical | 943 | 2.8 | 459 | 4.0 | 1566 | 5.5 | 1105 | 20.9 | 8750 | 7.6 | 6000 | 34.5 |
| Sales | 766 | 4.6 | 456 | 4.3 | 1580 | 6.1 | 959 | 6.8 | 10150 | 6.8 | 4450 | 7.4 |
| Manual | 587 | 37.6 | 314 | 27.7 | 1532 | 45.2 | 881 | 19.8 | 8891 | 48.1 | 4950 | 17.9 |
| Craft, supervisory | | (12.6) | | ( 1.4) | | (16.2) | | ( 1.0) | | (21.3) | | ( 1.8) |
| Operative, laborer | | (25.0) | | (26.3) | | (29.0) | | (18.8) | | (26.8) | | (16.1) |
| Service | 445 | 3.1 | 236 | 35.5 | 1220 | 4.8 | 730 | 27.5 | 7100 | 8.2 | 3965 | 20.5 |
| Farm | 445 | 41.7 | 236 | 19.0 | 1220 | 24.8 | 730 | 8.4 | 7050 | 4.5 | 4151 | 0.8 |

### B. Ratio of Female to Male Earnings within Each Occupation

| | 1890 | 1930 | 1970 |
|---|---|---|---|
| Professional | 0.263 | 0.385 | 0.710 |
| Clerical | 0.487 | 0.706 | 0.686 |
| Sales | 0.595 | 0.607 | 0.438 |
| Manual | 0.535 | 0.575 | 0.557 |
| Service | 0.530 | 0.598 | 0.558 |
| Farm | 0.530 | 0.598 | 0.589 |

## C. Male and Female Earnings in Current Dollars ($e$ = Occupational Share)

| | 1890 | | 1930 | | 1970 | |
|---|---|---|---|---|---|---|
| | Male | Female | Male | Female | Male | Female |
| $\Sigma \theta_i w_i$ | 624 | 275 | 1741 | 968 | 9581 | 5776 |
| $\Sigma \theta_i w_{1890}$ | 624 | 289 | 683 | 325 | 809 | 368 |
| $\Sigma \theta_i w_{1930}$ | 1618 | 864 | 1741 | 968 | 2043 | 1035 |
| $\Sigma \theta_i w_{1970}$ | 8306 | 4834 | 8874 | 5411 | 9581 | 5776 |

## D. Ratios of Female to Male Earnings ($e$ Varies across the Columns)

| | 1890 | 1930 | 1970 |
|---|---|---|---|
| (1) $[w_{fi}/w_{mi}]$ | 0.463 | 0.556 | 0.603 |
| (2) $[w_f/w_m]_{1890}$ | 0.463 | 0.489 | 0.455 |
| (3) $[w_f/w_m]_{1930}$ | 0.534 | 0.556 | 0.507 |
| (4) $[w_f/w_m]_{1970}$ | 0.571 | 0.610 | 0.603 |

## E. Partitioning Change in the Ratio of the Log of Female to Male Earnings, (Average Earnings Are Geometrically Weighted Averages of the Six Occupations)[a]

| | 1890 Weights | 1970 Weights |
|---|---|---|
| 1. $\Sigma \theta_f (R^1 - R^0)$ | +0.1452 | +0.3018 |
| 2. $\Sigma R(\theta_f^1 - \theta_f^0)$ | -0.0880 | +0.0687 |
| 3. $\Sigma a(W_m^1 - W_m^0)$ | +0.0071 | -0.0981 |
| 4. $\Sigma W_m(a^1 - a^0)$ | +0.0679 | -0.0373 |
| 5. $\Sigma (R^1 - R^0)(\theta_f^1 - \theta_f^0)$ | +0.1567 | -0.1567 |
| 6. $\Sigma (W_m^1 - W_m^0)(a^1 - a^0)$ | -0.1052 | +0.1052 |
| Total change | +0.1836 | +0.1836 |

(continued)

**Table 10.6** (continued)

[a]Where $w = \Sigma w_i \theta_i$, for males and females. A geometrically weighted average enables a partitioning of the various factors accounting for change in the ratio of female to male earnings. $W = \log(w)$; $R = (W_f - W_m)$; $a = (\theta_f - \theta_m)$; $1 = 1970$; $0 = 1890$. Note that the total change in the ratio when earnings are a geometrically weighted average is considerably less than when average earnings are the arithmetic mean. The geometrically weighted results are: $(w_f/w_m) = 0.487$, but 0.463 for the arithmetic mean in 1890; the results for 1970 are 0.586 for the geometric weights, but 0.603 for the arithmetic means. Therefore the geometrically weighted averages understate the total increase. Columns may not add up owing to rounding error.

*Notes and Sources:*

OCCUPATIONAL DISTRIBUTION

*Historical Statistics*, ser. D 182–232, pp. 139–40. The 1900 occupational distribution was used for 1890. The professional category includes professional, technical, and kindred workers, and managers, officials and proprietors (lines 218 + 219).

EARNINGS. All earnings are annual, full time, and in current dollars.

*1890, Male, Professional:* Weighted average of professional (34%) and managerial (66%) workers. Professional earnings for six categories, representing over 75% of all professionals, were obtained from the following: Lebergott (1964, p. 500) gives $1,662 for first- to third-class postal workers (government officials); *Historical Statistics*, ser. D 793, p. 168, gives $731 for ministers (clergy); a value of $460 for male teachers was derived from *Historical Statistics* ser. D 763, p. 167, given the assumption that the ratio of female to male teacher salaries was 0.8 and given a value of $1,505 for the 5% who were college teachers; the figures for physicians ($2,540), lawyers ($2,691), engineers ($2,108), and college teachers ($1,505) were derived from *Historical Statistics*, ser. D 913–20, p. 176 for 1929, extrapolated back to 1900 on federal employee earnings, *Historical Statistics*, ser. D 764, p. 167. Managerial earnings were derived from United States Census Office (1895b), table 6, using the category "officers or firm members actively engaged in the industry or in supervision." A figure of $1,264 was converted into a 1900 figure of $1,285, based on nonfarm money (when employed) earnings, *Historical Statistics*, ser. D 735, p. 165. The final estimate of $1,391 ($1,414, for 1900) was constructed by weighting by the actual occupational distribution, and it is consistent with the notion that the ratio of full-time earnings in manufacturing jobs to those in professional occupations must have been smaller in 1890 than it was in 1930 (Lindert and Williamson 1980).

*Clerical:* United States Census Office (1895b, p. 10) yields data for urban clerical workers excluding salaried personnel.

*Sales:* Data for drygoods salesmen in United States Commissioner of Labor (1897) for 11 states yield a mean of $13.58/week or $706/year for 1895, and conversion to 1890 based on nonfarm money (when employed) earnings gives $766.

*Manual:* Brissenden's (1929, p. 94) full-time manufacturing earnings are used. Although these are given for 1899, the accompanying actual figures are identical to those for 1890. See also Rotella (1981, pp. 197–212), app. B, on the 1890 figures. The implied ratio of full-time to actual earnings is 1.18.

*Service and farm:* Lebergott's (1964) common laborer's wage × 310 days. The figure for service is almost identical to that in Salmon (1897, p. 96) of $6.93/week, given 52 weeks and $100/year board. Conversion was made to 1890 based on full-time annual earnings. The farm figure poses problems because no data exist for owner-operator farmers in 1890, and those for more recent periods indicate lower earnings than for farm laborers. Farm wage laborers received less than the wage for common laborers, but owner operators earned far more. The ratio of female to male farm wages for yearly contracts in 1909 was 0.578 and those for seasonal contracts (with board) was 0.538 (Holmes 1912), therefore the relationship between male and female earnings on farms does not differ significantly from that given by the rate for farm wage laborers.

*1890, Female, Professional: Historical Statistics*, ser. D 760, 763, p. 167, for 1900.

*Clerical:* Rotella (1981, pp. 197–212), app. B.

*Sales:* See source for male earnings. The 1895 figure is $421.

*Manufacturing:* United States Census Office (1895a).

*Service: Historical Statistics*, ser. D 758, p. 167, for 1900. Salmon (1897) gives an average of $3.23/week or $268/year, including $100 board. Lebergott's (1964, p. 542) estimate is $3.14/week in 1900.

*1930, Male, Professional:* A weighted average of the earnings of lawyers, physicians, engineers, and dentists (Friedman and Kuznets 1945), semiprofessionals, clergy, professors, and teachers (*Historical Statistics*, ser. D 793, D 792, D 913), $4,099. The earnings of proprietors, managers and officials are from United States Bureau of the Census (1943, p. 121) for males who worked 12 months in 1939, adjusted to 1929 dollars, $3,500.

*Clerical:* Rotella (1981, pp. 197–212), app. B.

*Sales:* United States Bureau of the Census (1943, p. 121), for males who worked 12 months in 1939, adjusted to 1929 dollars.

*Manual:* The weekly full-time wage from Beney (1936) for 50 weeks; also in *Historical Statistics*, ser. D 835, p. 172. The Beney data imply a ratio of female to male earnings for manufacturing workers of 0.575 in 1929 which might be too high in light of Brissenden's (1929) ratios for the 1920s which are lower than Beney's for the same period.

*Service and farm:* Unskilled manufacturing laborers, *Historical Statistics*, ser. D 841, p. 172, × 50 weeks.

*1930, Females, Professional:* A weighted average of professors, teachers, nurses, and attendants from *Historical Statistics*, ser. D 763, p. 167, and Department of Labor, Women's Bureau (1934a).

*Clerical and manual:* The weekly full-time wage from Beney (1936) for 50 weeks; Rotella (1981, pp. 197–212), app. B gives 868. Department of Labor, Women's Bureau (1934b), gives median clerical earnings for 1931 of between $1,044 and $1,308.

*Sales:* United States Bureau of the Census (1943, p. 125); see 1930, males, above.

*Service: Historical Statistics*, ser. D 758, p. 167, for 1929.

*1970, Male and Female, All Sectors:* United States Department of Labor, Bureau of Labor Statistics (1982, p. 732), table C-23. Median, full-time, weekly earnings for each sex-occupational group. The manufacturing group for males and the service group for females are weighted averages of subgroups. Earnings for the farm sector are those of nonfarm laborers. Annual wages are weekly × 50 weeks.

sional sector, a move previously accomplished by males from 1950 to 1970.

The matrix of table 10.6, part C provides a convenient way of tracking the impact of changes in earnings and occupational structure on the relative earnings of females to males, but it is not a complete partitioning of the two factors. A full partitioning must use a geometrically weighted average of earnings by occupation for each of the three benchmark years. The use of the geometric mean can be defended on the grounds that the underlying structure of earnings is a function of its log (Mincer 1974). But it is used here out of necessity, even though the geometric means are not entirely good substitutes for their arithmetic counterparts. The implied ratio of female to male earnings using the geometric means is 0.487 in 1890, rising to 0.586 in 1970, while the arithmetic means are 0.463 and 0.603.

There are six terms in the partitioning of table 10.6, part E. The first and the third are the change in relative earnings and in male earnings, given the structure and relative structure of occupations, using either 1890 or 1970 weights. The second and the fourth are the change in the structure of occupations and the change in the relative structure, given the relative earnings and male earnings for either of the two years. The last two terms are interactions.

This partitioning of the change in the relative earnings of females to males reinforces the results of the matrix of part D. Over the entire period 1890–1970, the change in relative earnings (terms 1 and 3) encompassed 83% to 111% of the entire change, while the change in structure (terms 2 and 4) encompassed only −11% to 17%, with the interaction terms adding the remainder.

The largest of the first four terms, the first, demonstrates that the rise in relative earnings of females to males within occupations greatly increased the overall ratio. The effect is greater given the structure of female occupations in 1970 than it is for the 1890 structure. The second, third, and fourth terms, while relatively small, change signs depending on the year chosen for the weights. The second term weights the change in the structure of female occupations by the ratio of female to male earnings. Females moved relatively into their more highly paying pursuits, thus the 1970 weights yield a positive effect and the 1890 weights a negative one. The same logic holds for the fourth term, which weights the relative occupational shift of females to males by male earnings. Females moved into those occupations which were high paying within the male earnings distribution. The third term, negative for the 1970 structure while small but positive for 1890, indicates for the 1970 weights male earnings increased relatively more in occupations that contained more males. In this manner it serves to diminish the effect of the first term.

Both the complete partitioning and the matrix demonstrate that the change in relative earnings within occupations was of greater importance in altering the overall earnings ratio than was the change in occupational structure between males and females.

## 10.5.   The Role of Women in Economic Growth

Increases in the female labor force participation rate and in the ratio of female to male earnings from 1890 to the present served to increase national income per capita, but by how much in comparison with the increase in male earnings alone? Put somewhat differently, in terms of a counterfactual conjecture: Had the female labor force participation rate remained at its 1890 level, how much lower would income per capita have been in 1980? It is far simpler to answer the first question than it will be to answer the second.

The answer to the first question can be treated in a straightforward manner using the accounting identity:

(1) $$(LY/P) \equiv w_m(\ell_m + \alpha\ell_f)\beta/2,$$

where $LY$ = labor income; $P$ = total population; $w_m$ = average annual earnings per male worker; $0 < \alpha \le 1$ is such that $w_f = \alpha w_m$; $\ell_f$, $\ell_m$ are the labor force participation rates of adult ($\ge$ 15 or 16–64 years old) females and males; $\beta$ = the proportion of the total population who are adults (15–64 years old); $P_a/P$, where $P_a = P_m + P_f$; and $P_m = P_f$ by assumption.

From 1890 to 1980 $\alpha$ rose from about 0.463 to about 0.603; $\beta$ fell slightly from 0.624 in 1890 to 0.616 in 1980;[32] $\ell_m$ has been roughly stable at about 0.80; and $P_f$ has been approximately equal to $P_m$. Therefore the growth of $(LY/P)$ from 1890 = 0 to 1980 = 1 may be simply stated as[33]

(2)   $(LY/P)_1/(LY/P)_0 = (w_{m1}/w_{m0}) [(0.8 + 0.603 \, \ell_{f1})/(0.8 + 0.463 \, \ell_{f0})]$

With $\ell_{f1} = 0.554$ and $\ell_{f0} = 0.188$,[34] the degree to which growth in per capita labor income exceeded growth in per capita male earnings is 1.28. Because labor income $(LY)$ has remained a relatively constant fraction of national income $(NY)$, $LY = (0.70)NY$,[35] these conclusions should hold for national income as well.

The above calculation has implicitly included in labor income the entire increase in female earnings. Two cases, with reference to figure 10.1, must be considered before accepting the procedure. The line $SS$ in figure 10.1 is the supply of female labor function, in per (female) capita terms, and at some maximum participation rate, given by $\ell_t$, the schedule becomes vertical. The participation rate in the base period is $\ell_0$ and that in the current period is $\ell_1$. The upward

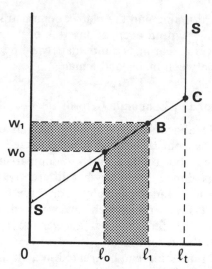

**Fig. 10.1**          Labor supply and household production.

slope of the supply function could reflect a number of factors, such as diminishing returns to home production or the more classic labor-leisure choice. If it is only the latter, or if home-produced goods are always excluded from measured national income, then one can include the entire shaded area, $[w_0ABw_1 + \ell_0AB\ell_1]$, in the increment to national income associated with changes in the female labor force. The procedure employed above would then be correct, at least in the context of the national income accounts. Two considerations could modify this procedure.

The first, to be called a *type A* error, concerns the inclusion in national income of goods produced by female workers although they are excluded from the aggregate participation rate (e.g., unpaid family farm labor, undercounted manufacturing workers). There are two kinds of type A errors. The simplest is the undercount by the census of women who worked in the marketplace at market wages. The adjustment, in terms of figure 10.1, would be to increase $\ell_0$ while keeping $w_0$ constant, thus by an imagined shift in the supply of labor function. The second is the omission of female laborers who produce goods in the home at wages unobserved in the marketplace. I will assume, in these cases, that the market wage is the correct proxy for the value of these women's marginal product.

The second consideration, to be termed a *type B* error, is the exclusion from national income of goods produced by women at home or on the farm who are, as well, excluded from the labor force estimates. The distinction between type A and type B errors is of less importance in the calculations that follow than in those that would adjust actual national income figures.

If the elasticity of supply of female labor were not zero, as $SS$ in figure 10.1 to $\ell_t$ is not, women and their families may have valued their labor within the family unit in terms of its productive capacity, that is, in the base period at a maximum of $[\ell_0 AC\ell_t]$. This productive value of female labor should be restricted to encompass only those goods and services also included in current period national income. The two areas $[0w_0 A\ell_0 + \ell_0 AC\ell_t]$ compose an upper bound measure of national income derived from female labor in the base period. The latter area is the value of home production, and the former is the value of market production.[36] The full value of home production $[\ell_0 AC\ell_t]$ need not be included if only a portion of the home-produced good is included in current period national income.

As the wage rate rises, say from $w_0$ to $w_1$, more women enter the market labor force, and their added contribution to national income is imputed at the prevailing market wage. But it would be incorrect to include the entire addition to national income if the value of home production were already included in base period national income. The error arises because the labor force had been understated in the base period. The correction involves more than an addition to the female labor force at market wages. It involves the estimation of the value of goods and services that are not traded at market wages and prices.

The assumption that the labor force data for 1890 and 1980 are correct and comparable and that the value of household production in 1890 was zero enabled the initial calculation of the role of changes in the female labor force on economic growth. The data presented in section 10.3 can now be used to adjust the initial estimate. These corrections will all involve assessing the female labor force and the goods and services produced by it around 1890.

The first errors were type A, those for which the labor force participation rate in the base period was biased downward although national income in the base period includes the productive services of this labor. The computed shortfall of unpaid agricultural workers, primarily on cotton farms, increases the aggregate participation rate for all women 15–64 years old from the initial estimate of 0.188 to 0.202. Adding the less reliable estimate of the labor force of all other married female family farm workers increases the figure to 0.234. Using the lower-bound figure has little impact on the initial calculation, reducing it from 1.28 to 1.27; the upper-bound figure reduces the measure to 1.25. The undercount of manufacturing workers is too small to affect the initial calculation.

Type B errors are of more quantitative importance and involve the understatement of the female labor force and of national income in the base period. Several adjustments must be made here, and on some we are on rather shaky ground.

One adjustment involves the value of previously home-produced goods now produced by the market and included in national income estimates in the current period. Section 10.3 discussed several of these goods which together comprise as much as 14% of the total time spent in household production. To produce an upper-bound measure of this time would require a value for the area $[\ell_0 AC\ell_t]$ in figure 10.1 and an estimate of the labor supply elasticity.[37] Under rather generous assumptions about the elasticity, the addition to total product of this labor reduces the growth calculation from 1.28 to 1.19.[38]

The shortfall in boardinghouse keepers might be considered in either type A or type B corrections because it is not clear that national income estimates excluded the value of their services. Because boardinghouse keepers earned income, I will impute to them the market wage rate. Using the maximum figure for all women given in table 10.5 of 1.84 percentage points lowers the initial calculation from 1.28 to just under 1.27; the minimum figure of 0.685 lowers the initial calculation to just over 1.27.

Combining the two type B errors with those of type A requires adjustments for consistency. Taking such care results in lowering the initial figure from 1.28 to 1.16 for the upper-bound case and to 1.18 for the lower-bound case.[39] Therefore the growth in the female labor force and the increase in the ratio of female to male earnings were associated with a growth in per capita income that exceeded by 16% to 28% the increase in male earnings.

It would be incorrect, however, to turn this statement around and claim that had the female labor force not expanded, income per capita would have declined by 16% to 28% or by some other percentage based only on these data. To answer the counterfactual conjecture posed above, one needs considerably more information, in particular knowledge of the aggregate production function.

One must also take care to pose the counterfactual as a particular experiment, say one in 1980 that reduces the female labor force to 1890 levels, or equivalently one in 1890 that increases the female labor force to 1980 levels. The fact that the ratio of female to male earnings increased along with the female labor force participation rate suggests that there may have been biased technical change or unbalanced growth at some time from 1890 to 1980 that served to increase female earnings more than it did male earnings. The earnings ratio increased rapidly to 1930, and, at that date, exceeded the 1970 ratio for several occupations (see table 10.6). These facts suggest that there may well have been biased technical change prior to 1930 and that the last 50 years witnessed an expansion of the female labor force in response to higher earnings levels in certain occupations.

In an aggregate production function with constant returns to scale the smaller is the elasticity of substitution between males and females, the larger will be the impact on total product of a reduction (or an increase) in the female labor force. With an elasticity of substitution equal to one, the case is that of the simple Cobb-Douglas. Using an average of the 1890 and 1980 weights and the census labor force data results in a 16.3% figure for the reduction (or increase) in national income had the female labor force in 1980 (1890) been reduced (increased) to that in 1890 (1980). The revised lower bound figure results in a 14.4% reduction and the revised upper-bound figure one of 11.5%.[41] All of these figures might be construed as lower-bound estimates because the elasticity of substitution between males and females was probably less than one.

## 10.6  Summary Remarks

The motivation for this paper was a desire to have a statistic giving the extent to which the expansion of the female labor force affected growth in real income per capita from 1890 to 1980. The initial calculation indicated a rather hefty effect associated with an increase in female labor force participation and an increase in the ratio of female to male earnings. The growth in per capita income exceeded that in male earnings alone by 1.28; had the female labor force not expanded, national income would have been lower by at least 14%.

But the consistency and completeness of census labor force figures have long been questioned, and the applicability of national income accounting procedures to earlier periods remains a problem. These defects are most apparent in the data for women, whose part-time, intermittent, home work, and unpaid family labors were far more frequent than were those of prime-aged males. Numerous revisions were offered, and several had large impacts on the labor force and underlying national income data. Taken together these corrections lowered the initial calculation of the extent to which the growth in national income per capita exceeded that in male earnings from 1.28 to 1.18.

Revisions to the female labor force figures, particularly those for married women, raise the possibility that participation rates declined sometime in the past. Participation rates on family farms could have been considerably higher than early censuses have recorded. The corrections for both family farm labor and boardinghouse keepers result in an estimate for married women in 1890 of 12.33% to 14.03%, figures that bracket the labor force participation rate for married women as late as 1940 (see tables 10.1 and 10.6). Additional evidence, for a period much earlier in our history, indicates that married women in eighteenth-century cities worked more frequently in small proprietorships with their husbands than was the case later in American history (Goldin

1986). John Durand's (1975) observation that married women's labor force participation rates are U-shaped over the course of economic development may well fit the American case.

The evidence on which many of the revisions rest is meager, but the results seem clear. The change in the locus of production from the family farm and home to the centralized marketplace must certainly have altered the nature of work for married women. Whether or not one chooses to add these figures to those of the census labor force estimates depends on the ultimate question. If one is interested in the role of women in increasing aggregate national income, then it would be correct to use these revised estimates. If, however, interest centers on the evolution of the labor market and on the accumulation of human capital, the original estimates might be more appropriate.

There is, however, another factor to consider in the calculation. If instead of using 1980 as the current year, we use 1950, the initial statistic is lowered to 1.12 and is lowered further with corrections for the various errors. The most substantial component of the century-wide calculation is the increase in labor force participation rate over the past three decades. But the discussion of the labor force data in section 10.2 stressed that the large increase in participation rates from 1950 had its origin in the changes of the previous decades. Indeed the long-run supply function of female labor may well have shifted over the last century, becoming more elastic sometime after 1930.

Shifts in the long-run supply function of labor raise additional problems with the comparability of the calculation over time. Of more importance, however, are the underlying reasons for such shifts. Long-run changes in the structure of the economy and in educational levels affected the participation rates of women decades later (Goldin 1983a, 1983b, 1984a.) The long-run nature of the determinants of female labor force participation supports the time dimension of the initial calculation and, thus, the conclusion—that the increase in the participation of women and in their relative earnings was associated with an increase in national income that was from 16% to 28% higher than was the increase in male earnings alone.

# Notes

1. The 1890 figure is from *Historical Statistics* (1975, p. 131), ser. D 29–41, for 15–64-year-olds. The 1980 figure is from United States Department of Labor (1982), tables A-3, A-4, for the civilian labor force 16–64-years-old. Including only employed laborers lowers the 1890 figure to 18.8% and the 1980 figure to 55.4%. The 1890 female unemployment estimate is ser. D 85, under the assumption that unemployment was distributed by sex in proportion to the labor force figures. The 1980 employed figure is from table A-10.

2. Edith Abbott (1910) questioned the occupational information in the late nineteenth-century population censuses; see Rubinow (1907) for a criticism of Abbott. Smuts (1960, p. 71) noted that "the basic criterion, the core of today's labor force concept, was not made explicit until 1910. This is the rule that defines a worker as a person who works for money." He also questioned the 1890 female farm laborer figures (1960, pp. 76–77). Durand, among many others, noted the anomalous 1910 female farm laborer estimates (1948, p. 195). Durand (1948, pp. 197–200) and Bancroft (1958, pp. 183–97) discussed the implications for the early census data of the change in the definition of the labor force in 1940. Jaffe (1956) argued that the growth in the female labor force was vastly overstated because of omissions in the 1890–1900 data. See Lebergott (1964, pp. 57–58), however, for a defense of the census labor force estimates.

3. Conventional accounting procedures have been criticized on other grounds. Boserup (1970), among others, has claimed that they necessarily bias policy in favor of market (male-produced) goods, particularly in less developed countries. Integrating the female labor force into economic growth calculations provides a response to these critics, but need not produce the results they anticipate. Accurate procedures for incorporating nonmarket production into national income accounts could increase the contribution of women to the base period income figure while reducing their contribution to the augmentation of national income.

4. Goldin and Sokoloff (1982) discuss the increase of this ratio from 1820 to 1850 with industrialization.

5. Approximately 35% of native-born single women of native-born parents between the ages of 16 and 24 were not in the labor force and not at school in 1900 across five cities, Boston, Chicago, New York, Philadelphia, and St. Louis. By 1930 this figure was between 2% and 9%. The 1900 figure was computed from labor force and schooling data in United States Bureau of the Census (1902) and the related volume United States Bureau of the Census (1907). Those for 1930 were computed from labor force and schooling data in United States Bureau of the Census (1933a, 1933b). The lower bound subtracts the entire number of women 16 years and older in school, and the upper bound subtracts only 80% of those 16–20 years old in school and none of those 21 years old and over in school.

6. That is, the labor force participation rate of single women in cross section varied by population density and the structure of demand. As the population became more urbanized and as more families lived closer to industrial areas, the participation rate for single women rose. The participation rate of married women varied far less in cross-section, and therefore the time series cannot be tracked by only these factors. There was, however, variation by wage and by husband's income. See Mincer (1962) for the use of cross-sectional information on income and substitution effects to track time-series changes from 1890 to 1960.

7. "[From] what sectors would additional labour be available if new industries were created offering employment at subsistence wages? . . . First of all there are the wives and daughters of the household. The employment of women outside the household depends upon a great number of factors . . . and is certainly not exclusively a matter of employment opportunities. There are, however, a number of countries where the current limit is for practical purposes only employment opportunities. This is true, for example, even inside the United Kingdom. The proportion of women gainfully employed in the U.K. varies enormously from one region to another according to employment opportunities for women" (Lewis [1954] 1958, pp. 403–4).

8. The role of fertility change in affecting female labor force participation cannot be adequately discussed here and is detailed in Easterlin (1980).

9. The relationship between educational and occupational change is apparent in data for almost all of the 12 countries represented in a conference on long-term trends in female labor force participation. See Layard and Mincer (1985). Goldin (1983b) presents cross-sectional evidence that a woman's occupation early in her life-cycle influences later life-cycle labor force participation.

10. Monographs about working women published in the 1920s differ from previous ones in their concern with married women. While none of them claimed that there was a large percentage of married women in the labor force, they looked to the percentage of the labor force consisting of married women as the basis for action. Note this perception in a 1925 study of mothers in industry: "We have known, vaguely enough, that in the

gray stream of women pouring into our industries at dawn there are many married women, and here and there is a mother of little children" (Hughes 1925, p. xiii).

11. Durand (1948, pp. 199, 207) adjusted the 1940 census data for comparability with both the 1930 "gainful worker" estimates and the Current Population Survey data, but the adjustment ratios for females are not substantial. The "gainful worker" adjustment was based on a special survey of the 1930 census and indicated that the "gainful worker" concept overstated the female workforce in 1930 by 2.72%. Bancroft (1958) also discusses changes in definition and the comparability of the decennial census with the Current Population Survey data. Lebergott (1964, pp. 71–73) summarizes the debate over the accuracy of the labor force estimates of the female population, particularly the doubts of Smuts (1959, 1960), and concludes by accepting the census figures as the proper standard.

12. This calculation assumes that work is done in weekly intervals.

13. See Haines (1979) and Goldin and Parsons (1984) for a discussion of these surveys which include about 6,000 families in industrial areas.

14. They probably worked more than half the year because older women earned somewhat less than did experienced younger women in industry (Goldin 1981), and average earnings for married women includes earnings for women who began work during the year and for whom days worked that year was artifically low.

15. It is not possible to distinguish between part-time and intermittent work in the sense of working part of a day. Part-time work usually refers to that which is done for less than the standard number of hours per week, while intermittent refers to work done for the full number of hours per week but not the full number of weeks per year.

16. Boarders and other family members were grouped together, and the estimate of two boarders per boarding household is based only on the families reporting income from boarding.

17. United States Commissioner of Labor (1889) gives a figure of $300 for full-time earnings in manufacturing.

18. United States Bureau of the Census (1914, p. 27). This volume contains few breakdowns of occupational data by age, marital status, race, and region, and therefore the data cannot be corrected for the overstatement of agricultural labor. Smuts, among others, has called for the inclusion of these women in the labor force. He noted that in 1890 although "there were perhaps 4 million married white women living on farms, the census reported only about 23,000 of them in agricultural occupations. In 1950, when the farm population was much smaller than in 1890, nearly 200,000 married white women were counted as unpaid family farm laborers" (1960, pp. 76–77).

19. The proportion of unpaid family workers among all agricultural workers for white females ≥ 15 years old is as follows, by state in 1910: Alabama (0.507), Arkansas (0.433), Florida (0.151), Georgia (0.367), Louisiana (0.165), Mississippi (0.507), North Carolina (0.399), Oklahoma (0.177), South Carolina (0.382), Tennessee (0.191), Texas (0.344), Virginia (0.074). All other states had proportions lower than 0.044 (Wisconsin), and averaged 0.007.

20. United States Bureau of the Census (1907, p. 32), gives 94,601 white female agricultural laborers, of whom 61% were members of the farmer's family. Therefore 57,707 white female family farm workers, or 1.6% of the total female population, were already counted in the 1900 census.

21. The assumption is that the male adult agricultural figures were not affected by the instructions to the enumerators in 1910. The proportion of the male labor force that was in agriculture declined from 0.403 in 1890 to 0.270 in 1920.

22. Ruth Allen (1931) surveyed non-Mexican female cotton farm workers in Texas. The number of women interviewed was 664 and included both the unmarried and married.

23. The 1.24-percentage-point figure is: 4.5 × 0.31 × 0.89 (percentage white in the adult female population).

24. A listing of these time-budget studies can be found in Vanek (1973). The published reports that were consulted, together with the mean number of hours worked in unpaid family farm labor and the number of observations, are: Idaho, 1927 (9.74; 49); Washington, 1929 (9.9; 137); South Dakota, 1930 (11.55; 100); Montana, 1929–31 (9.12; 48); ington, 1929 (9.9; 137); South Dakota, 1930 (11.55; 100) Montana, 1929–31 (9.12; 48);

Oregon, 1929 (11.3; 288); USDA, primarily California, 1924–28 (8.67; 559). These house-wives spent on average 65 hours a week on all work, of which 15% was unpaid dairy, poultry, orchard, and garden labor.

25. Only two of the studies gave the distribution of time worked. Using the 15-hour cutoff yields 12% who would have been counted in Montana and 30% who would have been counted in Oregon.

26. This calculation uses 40% of the population living on farms and 68% of all farms outside the South.

27. The 121,193 figure assumes that 30% of all children working in manufacturing in 1890 were female. It is derived as a residual. There were 545,758 (839,952 − 294,194) women enumerated in the manufacturing census after those in clothing production are netted out; equivalently 424,565 (1,027,242 − 602,677) remain in the population census after women in clothing production are subtracted. The difference between these figures, 545,758 − 424,565 = 121,193, is then the shortfall in the population census of women working in the larger manufacturing firms. It should be noted that it would be incorrect to adjust or compare the manufacturing employment figures from the two censuses on an industry by industry basis, as Smuts (1960) did. The population census listed workers in general classifications, such as "operatives," not necessarily associated with a par-ticular industry.

28. With the exception of meals, these were several of the items for which Gallman (1966) computed value added to augment the pre-1890 national income estimates.

29. The assumption made in this calculation is that married women currently spend about 2.5 hours per week in the household maintenance and production of clothing and the baking of foods.

30. O'Neill and Braun (1981, p. 60) give a value of 1.0893 for the ratio of weekly work hours of full-time male to female workers in 1980.

31. See Polachek (1984) who finds a similar result for recent data and who notes that the aggregation of occupations would have to be considerably smaller to overturn the conclusion that changes in occupational structure matter less than changes in relative wages within occupations.

32. *Historical Statistics* (1975, p. 15), all races, ser. A 19.

33. *Historical Statistics* (1975, p. 132), ser. D 30, for the 1890 figure and United States Department of Labor (1982) for the 1980 figure. The participation rate of adult males (16–64 years) was 0.853 in 1890 and 0.845 in 1980. Adjusting for unemployment lowers the 1890 figure to 0.817 and that for 1980 to 0.781.

34. The labor force participation rates adjusted for unemployment are used. See 1 above.

35. Estimates in Denison (1962) for the share of property income in national income range between 0.305 for 1909–13 to 0.270 for 1929–58. Budd's (1960) estimates for the earlier period indicate a rather constant share of about 0.36 from 1870 to 1910 broken only by a sharp decline in 1890.

36. The shaded area below line *AB* is the value of household production under a set of assumptions detailed in an appendix available upon request from the author.

37. The problem is actually more complicated since the computation is in terms of the ratio of female to male earnings. One needs the value of $\alpha$ when $\ell_t = 1$, that is, the value of time spent at home production for the last hour or last person together with the period of time it would take to achieve that result since the male wage must also be computed. In the absence of such data it is assumed that this value is 0.70.

38. The original calculation had 0.188 proportion of the female labor force earning 0.463 $w_m$. The addition from household production in the base period assumes that all married women not in the labor market give 14% of their time to the production of goods later valued in the market and that the value of $\alpha$ at maximum labor force participation is 0.70. The value of 0.70 is, in some sense, arbitrary, but was chosen because women have only recently achieved this ratio in the labor market on an hourly basis. It is entirely possible that the value of their time in home production was greater than that ever achieved in the market. In 1890 4.5% of all married women were in the conventionally measured labor force, and all married women were, in that year, 58.2% of the adult (15–64 years old) female population. Thus 95.5% of all married women were out of the labor

force, and each produced: $[0.955 \times 0.582 \times 0.463 \times 0.14] + [(0.955 \times 0.582 \times 0.70 \times 0.14)/2] = 0.0633 \times w_m$, where the division by 2 assumes a linear supply function within that range. The initial calculation is adjusted by adding $0.0633 \times w_m$ to the labor income produced by all female workers.

39. The upper and lower-bound corrections in table 10.5 are used. The female labor force participation rate rises to 0.2572 for the upper-bound case. The value of household production, however, must be lowered because the labor force participation rate of married women rises from 0.045 to 0.1393. For the case of the lower bound, the female labor force participation rate rises to 0.2143 and that for married women rises to 0.0683.

40. See Goldin and Sokoloff (1984) on unbalanced growth from 1820 to 1850 and its impact on the ratio of female to male wages.

41. The average weight is a share value of 0.14 for female labor, given labor's total share of 0.70. Perhaps a more reasonable production function would be one in which labor was produced by a constant elasticity of substitution production function embedded in a Cobb-Douglas. With an elasticity of substitution between male and female labor of 0.5 and an average of the 1890 and 1980 earnings, a reduction in the female labor force from 0.554 to 0.188 would have reduced national income by 42%, a figure much larger than that generated by a simple Cobb-Douglas. All of these calculations imply that the earnings ratio would have risen greatly with the reduction in the female labor force.

# Comment    Susan B. Carter

"Indispensable," "crucial," and "revolutionary" are commonly used today to describe the impact of women's work and its reallocation on the larger society. While this consensus is a healthy corrective to an earlier disregrad of women's contributions, it does not rest on any systematic, comparative evaluation of the role of women's work relative to factors such as technological change or increases in the capital/labor ratio. That the Industrial Revolution upon close empirical examination was found not to have made a distinctive contribution to the growth process should make us suspicious of claims for a quantifiable role for the "Subtle Revolution."

Claudia Goldin's paper is a first attempt to determine whether the history of women's work belongs in the chronology of *economic* events. Her conclusion, that "had the female labor force not expanded [between 1890 and 1980] . . . national income per capita would probably have been at least 14% lower than it actually was," implies a significant role for this aspect of labor reallocation, making it comparable to the deepening of capital in explaining twentieth-century economic growth. Quantification also permits her to identify the period 1950–80 as the one in which 90% of women's contribution to the growth process was made.

The conclusion proceeds from an accounting definition in which the growth of labor income per capita is equal to the growth of male earn-

Susan B. Carter is associate professor of economics at Smith College.

ings multiplied by a term which is a function of the male and female labor force participation rates and the ratio of female to male earnings in the base and end years. By assuming that changes in the female labor force participation rate do not induce changes in the male wage, and by using growth of labor income as a proxy for the growth of national income, she is able to equate the value of the labor force participation rate/relative earnings term with the contribution of the expansion of the female labor force to the growth in per capita income. The problem therefore breaks down into one of finding values for the female labor force participation rate and the relative earnings rate for the base and end years for which the calculation is made.

A desire for consistency between base- and end-year measures of material well-being dictates three types of adjustments to 1890 census estimates of female labor force participation rates. First, women whose services were included in the 1890 national income measure but who were absent from the 1890 labor force count must be filled in. Goldin's imaginative use of varied data sources to construct reasonable corrections for this undercount, largely of agricultural workers and boardinghouse keepers, is for me one of the most satisfying parts of the paper. Second, to avoid the overstatement of the growth of material well-being which comes about whenever goods formerly produced in the home come to be produced in the market, Goldin identifies the principal products which experienced this transition during the time period under study—baked goods, clothing, and some meal preparation—and includes a measure of the labor time devoted to them in the base year labor force estimate. Third, one service—housecleaning—which had been provided through the market in 1890 essentially reverted back to home production by 1980. For consistency's sake, Goldin removes domestic servants from the 1890 labor force figures.

I will focus my remarks on three steps in the approach: the criterion for selecting activities to be included in the base period measure of national income, the technique for valuing time spent in home production, and the assumption that male wages are unaffected by the growth of the female labor force.

First, the criterion for selecting activities to be included in base period labor force estimates which Goldin uses—include the activity if it was produced in the market in 1980—is not neutral with respect to the calculation of growth in per capita income. It is like the standard index number problem. In this case goods like bakery products and clothing whose production was moved from home to market are those which experienced higher productivity growth rates than the housecleaning or child care whose production processes were not so transformed. The result of the inclusion of only the most rapidly advancing productive uses of female labor is to insert an upward bias in the calculation of the contribution of the female labor force to material well-being.

I would have preferred to have seen the measure of material well-being defined more broadly still to include all the goods and services provided by women both in and outside of the market. Goldin rejects this as requiring "wholesale revamping of all accounting procedures," but in this case there seem to be both practical and theoretical reasons for using the most inclusive measure possible.

At a practical level, even child care and household maintenance are being rapidly transformed into market-produced services. Between 1960 and 1980 the proportion of mothers with children under six in the paid labor force rose from 18.6% to 45.0%. The increased need for substitute care implied by this trend was met by growing reliance on the market. Between 1958 and 1977 care by nonrelatives outside the child's home rose from 17.2% to 41.2% of all child care arrangements (Hacker 1983, pp. 133, 135). If these trends continue, child care will have to be treated as a market-produced service when the calculations are redone in 1990.

Theoretically the inclusion of child care and household maintenance into an index of material well-being is attractive because together they accounted for a significant share of total consumption, especially in the early years. Moreover, it has been argued that the level and quality of this output was strongly affected by the institutional arrangements under which it was carried out, the nuclear family. There are competing hypotheses about the efficiency of this institution. Feminist reformers such as Charlotte Perkins Gillman have argued that the nuclear family is inefficient, wasteful, and exerts a significant drag on the growth of economic welfare. Goldin's current estimates seem to support this position as women's biggest contribution to the growth process coincides with their wholesale entry into the labor force. Others, however, claim that small nuclear families with full-time homemakers made possible vast improvements in child quality (Lindert 1978). Given the demonstrated importance of human capital formation in economic growth, married, middle-class women's low labor force participation rates up to 1940 may have made a significant, heretofore unappreciated contribution to the growth process. Including the value of child care and household maintenance services in national income estimates could be a first step in assessing this possibility. Exactly how these activities should be valued, however, I do not know.

The second concern I want to raise is with the technique employed for valuing time spent in 1890 home production. Goldin invokes a model in which the allocation of time between home and market is determined by relative productivity in the two sectors. This allows her to equate the market value of the last hour spent in home production with the female wage rate. Finding an objective measure of this time is an extremely desirable thing to be able to do. Nonetheless the underlying assumption of the model, that the only significant difference between home and market work is the amount of the homogeneous good $G$ which can be produced in each setting, is not consistent with the weight of historical evidence. Cultural values stressing the importance of intimate involvement in one's child's development suggest it would have taken a very high wage to lure mothers away from this responsibility. On the other hand, labor market discrimination, limited availability of part-time work, and cultural values which labeled women's work outside the home incompatible with nineteenth-century ideals of womanhood suggest that women's home production may have been carried on at a point where productivity in the home was well below that in the market. Since a far higher percentage of women's time was devoted to household production in 1890 than in 1980, a female wage greater than the value of household production overstates the level of production in the base year relative to that in the end year and understates the growth in welfare due to the reallocation of women's labor.

My third point concerns the appropriateness of assuming that male earnings are unaffected by changes in the female labor force participation rate. For the short run this assumption may be plausible. Given the strength and prevalence of gender-based occupational segregation, a increase in the supply of women workers would simply increase competition within the female occupations, causing the female wage to fall, leaving the male wage unchanged. But for the 90-year period under study a different pattern for women's labor force entry would surely have meant a different pattern of wage growth for men.

The effect on men would probably have differed by skill type. Unskilled men and women seem to have been close substitutes in nineteenth-century manufacturing occupations. The New England cotton mills, for example, responded to a shortage of female labor and an influx of unskilled Irish men by hiring men into previously female operative categories (Nickless 1979). If, as Piore argues, the supply of unskilled males is perfectly elastic, then a different growth path for the female labor force might have left the wage of unskilled males unchanged (Piore 1979).

The wages of skilled males in blue-collar occupations would probably also have been unaffected by the growth path of the female labor force. Women could not compete directly with men for these jobs since women were denied access to the training necessary for proper performance.

However, in the white-collar occupations, especially those requiring high levels of formal education, a failure of the female labor force to expand might be expected to have dramatically raised the male wage. White-collar occupations were poorly paid relative to skilled blue-collar work in 1900 (Carter and Prus 1982). For example, median weekly earnings for male teachers were only $11.63 as compared with $27.50 for heaters and $35.00 for rollers in the iron and steel industry. Such low wages meant that boys who had access to training for skilled blue-collar trades opted for that rather than formal schooling. While in 1890 jobs with formal schooling requirements constituted less than 10% of total employment, by 1980 professional and clerical work alone accounted for over a third of all jobs (Collins 1979). White-collar work was over two-thirds of total employment. Such a rapidly growing demand for skills and affective characteristics learned in schools would have been difficult to meet without raising males' wages if it were not for the rapid growth of an educated female labor force.

While the relatively small bonus for schooled over unschooled labor was not sufficient to draw many boys to the schools in 1900, it was adequate for girls. Compared with the $6.50 per week they might average in cotton and woolen mills or $3.50 in candy, the $9.73 average weekly salary for teaching was attractive. Girls went to school to prepare for such occupations, outnumbering boys in the high schools by 50% in the 1890s and remaining in the majority until school attendance through age 16 became compulsory. These educated women then entered the labor force, forming a disproportionate share of the rapidly expanding white-collar work force. Their strong response to opportunities for skilled work actually compressed the wage differential between schooled and unschooled women's occupations between 1890 and 1930 (Rotella 1981).

An important implication of this line of thinking for an understanding of the impact of women's labor on the growth process is that all those developments which relied on a cheap and plentiful supply of educated labor would have had to have been reduced if not eliminated if women's labor force had not grown the way it did. The first to go might have been mass secondary and later higher education, for in the educational production process it is extremely difficult to substitute capital for labor and in the absence of women willing to teach for low wages it is plausible that mass education would have been too costly to have been politically feasible (Fishlow 1966, p. 435). Since the increase in the stock of education per laborer resulting from the expansion of mass education has been found to account for from 12% to 23% of the increase in real national income over this century, the failure of the female labor force to grow would have meant a substantially different character to twentieth-century economic growth. (Denison 1962, pp. 148, 266)

It is fascinating to consider the concrete ways in which a shortage of educated labor might have made itself felt. Since mass secondary education is connected to the rise of vocational education, it is plausible that many of the job-related skills which over the twentieth century have come to be taught in schools would have had to have been transmitted in the workplace. This would have meant substantially higher labor costs. In a study of two New York City department stores which Michael Carter and I just completed we found that the store which used idiosyncratic clerical and accounting procedures which employees had to learn in the store paid wages two-thirds higher than an otherwise similar store which used the standardized bookkeeping, billing, and correspondence techniques taught in commercial schools at the time. Employees in both stores were equally skilled in the sense of being able to get the job done. Wages were higher in the store with idiosyncratic accounting methods because high turnover costs (primarily the cost of in-house training) made the employer anxious to keep employees happy. The store which took advantage of standardized techniques taught in commerical schools had far lower turnover costs and could afford to pay lower wages. Its employees did not leave because they faced stiff competition from other commercial school graduates who were effective substitutes for them (Carter and Carter 1985). Higher costs resulting from the absence of generalized clerical skills might have hindered the development of the large-scale business enterprise which required cheap, effective coordination of its various divisions to maintain a cost advantage over smaller rivals (Chandler 1977). A reduction in the number of highly educated workers also might have slowed the introduction of capital embodying the most up-to-date technology since this capital was complementary with educated labor. In short, many of the characteristic features of twentieth-century economic growth appear to have required the cheap supply of educated labor which the rapid growth of the female labor force made possible.

In summary, I have suggested that some aspects of the estimation procedure may have overstated and others understated the effects of the female labor force on the growth process. On balance the conclusion that without the growth of the female labor force, United States economic growth would have been substantially less spectacular seems well founded. To become more precise about the role of women's labor in the growth process now requires an examination of the specific institutions through which its effects were worked out.

# References

Abbott, Edith. 1910. *Women in industry: A study in American economic history.* New York: Appleton.

Allen, Ruth. 1931. *The labor of women in the production of cotton.* University of Texas Bureau of Research in the Social Sciences Study, no. 3. Austin: University of Texas.

Bancroft, Gertrude. 1958. *The American labor force: Its growth and changing composition.* New York: Wiley.

Beney, M. Ada. 1936. *Wages, hours, and employment in the United States, 1914–1936.* National Industrial Conference Board Study no. 229. New York: National Industrial Conference Board.

Boserup, Ester. 1970. *Women's role in economic development.* New York: St. Martin's.

Brissenden, Paul F. 1929. *Earnings of factory workers, 1899 to 1927: An analysis of pay-roll statistics.* Washington: Government Printing Office.

Budd, Edward C. 1960. Factor shares, 1850–1910. In Studies in Income and Wealth, vol. 24, ed. William N. Parker, Princeton: Princeton University Press (for NBER).

Carter, Michael J. and Carter, Susan B. 1985. Up the down escalator: Internal labor markets in two New York department stores, 1913. *Industrial and Labor Relations Review.* In press.

Carter, Susan B. and Prus, Mark. 1982. The labor market and the American high school girl 1890–1928. *Journal of Economic History* 42 (March): 163–71.

Chandler, Alfred D., Jr. 1977. *The visible hand: The managerial revolution in American business.* Cambridge: Harvard University Press.

Collins, Randall. 1979. *The credential society.* New York: Academic Press.

Degler, Carl. 1980. *At odds: Women and the family in America from the Revolution to the present.* New York: Oxford University Press.

Denison, Edward. 1962. *The sources of economic growth in the United States and the alternatives before us.* New York: Committee for Economic Development.

Durand, John. 1948. *The labor force in the United States, 1890–1960.* New York: Social Science Research Council.

———. 1975. *The labor force in economic development: A comparison of international census data, 1946–66.* Princeton: Princeton University Press.

Easterlin, Richard. 1980. *Birth and fortune: The impact of numbers on personal welfare.* New York: Basic.

Fishlow, Albert. 1966. Levels of nineteenth-century American investment in education. *Journal of Economic History* 26 (December): 418–36.

Friedman, Milton, and Kuznets, Simon. 1945. *Income from independent professional practice.* New York: National Bureau of Economic Research.

Gallman, Robert E. 1966. Gross national product in the United States, 1834–1909. In *Output, employment, and productivity in the United States after 1800.* Studies in Income and Wealth, vol. 30, ed. Dorothy Brady. New York: National Bureau of Economic Research.

Goldin, Claudia. 1977. Female labor force participation: The origin of black and white differences, 1870 to 1880. *Journal of Economic History* 37 (March): 87–108.

———. 1979. Household and market production of families in a late nineteenth century city. *Explorations in Economic History* 16 (April): 111–31.

———. 1981. The work and wages of single women, 1870 to 1920. *Journal of Economic History* 41 (March): 81–89.

———. 1983a. The changing economic role of women: A quantitative approach. *Journal of Interdisciplinary History* 13 (Spring): 707–33.

———. 1983b. Life-cycle labor force participation of married women: Historical evidence and implications. National Bureau of Economic Research Working Paper no. 1251.

———. 1984a. The historical evolution of female earnings functions and occupations. *Explorations in Economic History* 21 (January): 1–27.

———. 1984b. The earnings gap in historical perspective. Paper presented to the United States Commission on Civil Rights, Consultation on Comparable Worth.

———. 1986. The economic status of women in the early republic: Quantitative evidence. *Journal of Interdisciplinary History* 16 (Winter): 375–404.

Goldin, Claudia, and Parsons, Donald. 1984. Parental altruism and child labor: An empirical analysis of late nineteenth century U.S. families. Revised version of National Bureau of Economic Research Working Paper no. 707.

Goldin, Claudia, and Sokoloff, Kenneth. 1982. Women, children, and industrialization in the early republic: Evidence from the manufacturing censuses. *Journal of Economic History* 42 (December): 741–74.

———. 1984. The relative productivity hypothesis of industrialization: The American case, 1820 to 1850. *Quarterly Journal of Economics* 99 (August): 461–88.

Gronau, Reuben. 1977. Leisure, home production and work—the theory of the allocation of time revisited. *Journal of Political Economy* 85 (December): 1099–124.

Hacker, Andrew. 1983. *U/S: A statistical portrait of the American people*. New York: Viking.

Haines, Michael. 1979. *Fertility and occupation: Population patterns in industrialization*. New York: Academic Press.

Holmes, George K. 1912. *Wages of farm labor*. Bulletin 99, Washington: Department of Agriculture, Bureau of Statistics.

Hughes, Gwendolyn. 1925. *Mothers in industry: Wage-earning by mothers in Philadelphia*. New York: New Republic.

Jaffe, A. J. 1956. Trends in the participation of women in the working force. *Monthly Labor Review* 79 (May): 559–65.

Keat, Paul G. 1960. Long run changes in occupational wage structure, 1900–1956. *Journal of Political Economy* 68 (December): 584–600.

Layard, Richard, and Mincer, Jacob. 1985. Conference on trends in women's work, education, and family building. *Journal of Labor Economics* 3 (January).

Lebergott, Stanley. 1964. *Manpower in economic growth: The American record since 1800.* New York: McGraw-Hill.

Lewis, W. Arthur. 1954/1958. Economic development with unlimited supplies of labour. *Manchester School* (May). Reprinted in *The economics of underdevelopment,* ed. A. N. Agarwala and S. P. Singh. Oxford: Oxford University Press.

Lindert, Peter H. 1978. *Fertility and scarcity in America.* Princeton: Princeton University Press.

Mincer, Jacob. 1962. The labor force participation of married women: A study of labor supply. In *Aspects of labor economics,* ed. H. Gregg Lewis, Princeton: Princeton University Press.

———. 1974. *Schooling, experience, and earnings.* New York: National Bureau of Economic Research.

Nickless, Pamela J. 1979. A new look at productivity in the New England cotton textile industry, 1830–1860. *Journal of Economic History* 39 (December): 889–910.

O'Neill, June, and Braun, Rachel. 1981. Women and the labor market: A survey of issues and policies in the United States. Washington: Urban Institute.

Piore, Michael J. 1979. *Birds of passage: Migrant labor in industrial societies.* New York: Cambridge University Press.

Polachek, Solomon. 1984. Women in the economy: Perspectives on gender inequality. Paper presented to the United States Commission on Civil Rights, Consultation on Comparable Worth.

Robinson, J. Gregory. 1980. Labor force participation rates of cohorts of women in the United States: 1890 to 1979. Paper presented at the annual meeting of the Population Association of America, Denver.

Rotella, Elyce. 1980. Labor force participation of married women and the decline of the family economy in the United States. *Explorations in Economic History* 17 (April): 95–117.

———. 1981. *From home to office: U.S. women at work, 1870–1930.* Ann Arbor: University of Michigan Press.

Rubinow, I. M. 1907. Women in manufactures: A criticism. *Journal of Political Economy* 15 (January/December): 41–47.

Salmon, Lucy Maynard. 1897/1972. *Domestic service.* Reprinted. New York: Arno.

Smuts, Robert W. 1959. *Women and work in America.* New York.

————. 1960. The female labor force: A case study in the interpretation of historical statistics. *Journal of the American Statistical Association* 55 (March): 71–79.

Szalai, Alexander, ed. 1972. *The use of time: Daily activities of urban and suburban populations in twelve countries.* The Hague: Mouton.

United States Census Office. 1895a. *Report on manufacturing industries in the United States at the eleventh census: 1890. Part I. Totals for states and industries.* Washington: Government Printing Office.

————. 1895b. *Report on manufacturing industries in the United States at the eleventh census: 1890. Part II. Statistics of cities.* Washington: Government Printing Office.

————. 1897. *Report on population of the United States at the eleventh census: 1890. Part II.* Washington: Government Printing Office.

United States Bureau of the Census. 1902. *Twelfth census of the United States, 1900. Part II: population.* Washington: Government Printing Office.

————. 1907. *Statistics of women at work: Based on unpublished information derived from the schedules of the twelfth census: 1900.* Washington: Government Printing Office.

————. 1914. *Thirteenth census of the United States, 1910. Volume IV: Population, occupation statistics.* Washington: Government Printing Office.

————. 1933a. *Fifteenth census of the United States: 1930. Population, volume V. General report on occupations.* Washington: Government Printing Office.

————. 1933b. *Fifteenth census of the United States: 1930. Population, volume II. General report statistics by subject.* Washington: Government Printing Office.

————. 1943. *Sixteenth census of the United States: 1940. Population. volume III: The labor force. Occupation, industry, employment, and income. Part 1: United States summary.* Washington: Government Printing Office.

————. 1975. *Historical statistics of the United States.* Washington: Government Printing Office.

————. 1983. *1980 census of population. Volume 1, chapter C: General social and economic characteristics. Part 1: United States summary.* Washington: Government Printing Office.

United States Commissioner of Labor. 1889. *Fourth annual report, 1888: Working women in large cities.* Washington: Government Printing Office.

————. 1890. *Sixth annual report of the commissioner of labor, 1890. Part III: Cost of living.* U. S. Congress, House of Representatives, House Executive Document 265, 51st Cong. 2d Sess. Washington.

————. 1891. *Seventh annual report of the commissioner of labor, 1891. Part III: Cost of living.* U. S. Congress, House of Representatives, House Executive Document 232, 52d Cong., 1st Sess. Vols. I and II. Washington.

————. 1897. *Eleventh annual report of the commissioner of labor. 1895–96. Work and wages of men, women and children.* Washington: Government Printing Office.

United States Department of Labor, Bureau of Labor Statistics. 1971. *Marital and family characteristics of the labor force, March 1970.* Special Labor Force Report 130. Washington: Government Printing Office.

————. 1981. *Marital and family characteristics of the labor force, March 1979.* Special Labor Force Report 237. Washington: Government Printing Office.

————. 1982. *Labor force statistics derived from the Current Population Survey: A databook. Volume I.* Bulletin 2096. Washington: Government Printing Office.

United States Department of Labor, Women's Bureau. 1934a. *The age factor as it relates to women in business and the professions.* Harriet A. Byrne. Bulletin of the Women's Bureau, no. 117. Washington: Government Printing Office.

————. 1934b. *The employment of women in offices.* Ethel Erickson. Bulletin of the Women's Bureau, no. 120. Washington: Government Printing Office.

United States Senate Documents. 1910–11. *Report on condition of woman and child wage-earners in the U.S. in 19 volumes.* Vol. 86–194. Washington: Government Printing Office.

Vanek, Joann. 1973. Keeping busy: Time spent in housework, United States, 1920–1970. Doctoral dissertation, University of Michigan, Ann Arbor.

Williamson, Jeffrey, and Lindert, Peter. 1980. *American inequality: A macroeconomic history.* New York: Academic Press.

# 11    Population and Labor in the British Caribbean in the Early Nineteenth Century

B. W. Higman

The early nineteenth century was a critical period of transition in the long-term development of the British Caribbean's labor force. The abolition of the British Atlantic slave trade in 1807 ended almost two centuries of dependence on the labor of imported African slaves. The effective abolition of slavery itself in 1838 was followed by a movement toward dependence on free wage labor, though a few colonies, notably Trinidad and British Guiana, continued to make extensive use of indentured, contract labor on plantations until World War I (Engerman 1983).

Before 1807, most British Caribbean colonies had shown long-term growth in the size of their slave populations, but this growth was sustained largely by the continued influx of slaves through the Atlantic trade since few of the populations had achieved a position of positive natural increase. Thus the ending of the trade was followed by decline in the slave populations of the major sugar-producing colonies, with the important exception of Barbados, and an internal slave trade developed briefly to redistribute slaves from the economically backward areas of the British Caribbean, such as the Bahamas and the Virgin Islands, to the frontier sugar regions. In the British Caribbean as a whole, the slave population declined from 775,000 in 1807 to 665,000 in 1834 (the date of formal emancipation). However, the abolition of the Atlantic slave trade was important not only for its impact on total population growth and decline but also for its effects on the structure of the slave labor force. Whereas the slave trade had permitted a degree

B. W. Higman is professor of history at the University of the West Indies, Mona, Kingston 7, Jamaica.

I am grateful to the Johns Hopkins University Press for permission to use here material originally published in Higman (1984).

of demographic selectivity, regulated by its price mechanism, the abrupt ending of importation in 1807 meant change in the structure of the potential labor force away from the planters' ideal model. During the long period of dependence on slave labor in the plantation sector, a set of principles had been worked out which determined the allocation of slaves to particular occupations, a blend of demographic and psycho-social perceptions balanced against the demand for labor in particular tasks. The abolition of the slave trade created stress within this system of allocation. Thus an examination of the period 1807–34 serves to illuminate the mature system of slave labor organization developed in the British Caribbean since the underlying assumptions were high-lighted under stress.

## 11.1  The Data

The most systematic data available for the study of British Caribbean slave populations are to be found in the slave registration returns made to the colonial governments by the masters between 1813 and 1834. The dates of these returns varied from colony to colony, as did the amount of information contained in them. Initial returns provided the name, sex, age, color, and birthplace of each slave belonging to an owner and, for some colonies, the slave's occupation, stature, bodily marks, and family relations. Subsequent, normally triennial, returns listed births, deaths, manumissions, transfers, and desertions within the slave holdings. Difficulties arise in the interpretation of these data, particularly as a result of the underrecording of births and deaths, but it is not possible to discuss all of these problems here (Higman 1984, pp. 6–39).[1]

Of the 20 British colonies in the Caribbean in the early nineteenth century, only the slave registration returns for Barbados, St. Kitts, Dominica, St. Lucia, St. Vincent, Tobago, Trinidad, Demerara-Essequibo, Berbice, British Honduras, the Cayman Islands, the Bahamas, and Anguilla included data on occupation. The most important omission from this list is Jamaica, which accounted for almost half of the total slave population. The original Trinidad Order in Council in-structed the masters to record in their returns "the particular trade, occupation, or ordinary employment of the slave, specifying, in the cases of mechanics, artisans, or handicraftmen, the particular art or business in which he or she is usually employed; and in cases of or-dinary plantation slaves, describing them as labourers only" (Higman 1984, p. 24). There is no doubting the capacity of the masters to know the occupations of the slaves, but problems of definition remain. Some slaves, especially those belonging to small units, performed a wide range of tasks from day to day. In making their registration returns, the masters either spelled out this multiplicity or adopted portmanteau labels. Field workers were the most likely to be described in general terms. Thus the St. Vincent registration act, following the Trinidad pattern, called for specific descriptions of the occupations of tradesmen and domestics, but "in case of ordinary plantation slaves, describing them as labourers only" (Higman 1984, p. 24). This results in a relative lack of information on the distribution of slaves between particular field gangs and other agricultural tasks, compared to the richer detail on skilled and house slaves.

Of equal importance is the problem of seasonality in occupational patterns. Since the returns were made at a specific time of year, the occupations listed may have been weighted to that particular point in the seasonal cycle. For example, would a slave be described as a "sugar boiler" or a "fiddler" only if the return was made during crop or close to Christmas revelry? The Trinidad, Barbados, St. Kitts, and Anguilla regulations all called for "ordinary" or "usual" employment, but it seems probable that specific skills were more likely to be mentioned than manual work, even though the use of these skills might be confined to one part of the year, since it was these skills that served best to identify the slave. The result, probably, is some overstatement of the amount of time spent in specialized occupations.

## 11.2 Economic Activities

The British invasion of the Caribbean fell into three major phases: the second and third quarters of the seventeenth century, the 1760s, and the nineteenth century. The first phase saw the establishment of the "old sugar colonies," Jamaica, and the "marginal" or nonsugar colonies. The second and third phases created the "new sugar colonies" (table 11.1).

By 1807, the territorial expansion of the British Empire in the Caribbean was complete. But the phasing of this expansion over almost 200 years meant that the colonies were inevitably at different states of economic and demographic development. They were also subject to differing political and cultural forces. But the plantocracy was generally strongest in the longest settled, most monocultural, most British of the colonies, and weakest in the recently settled colonies of diversified agriculture and cosmopolitan population. Thus the political power of the plantocracy was strongest where the ratio of slaves to free people was greatest. In general, the first-phase colonies tended to have the slighter slopes, the thinner soil, and the lighter rainfall, whereas the later settled tended to be rugged and wet. The nature of the economic

Table 11.1          British Colonies in the Caribbean, circa 1834

| Colony | Slave Population | Slaves per Km$^2$ | Year of British Colonization |
|---|---|---|---|
| *Old sugar colonies* | | | |
| Barbados | 83,150 | 193.4 | 1627 |
| St. Kitts | 17,525 | 104.3 | 1625 |
| Nevis | 8,840 | 95.1 | 1628 |
| Antigua | 28,130 | 100.5 | 1632 |
| Montserrat | 6,400 | 63.4 | 1632 |
| Virgin Islands | 5,135 | 33.6 | 1672 |
| Jamaica | 311,070 | 27.2 | 1655 |
| *New sugar colonies* | | | |
| Dominica | 14,165 | 17.9 | 1763 |
| St. Lucia | 13,275 | 22.0 | 1803 |
| St. Vincent | 22,250 | 57.2 | 1763 |
| Grenada | 23,645 | 68.5 | 1763 |
| Tobago | 11,545 | 39.1 | 1763 |
| Trinidad | 20,655 | 4.3 | 1797 |
| British Guiana | 83,545 | 0.4 | 1803 |
| *Marginal colonies* | | | |
| British Honduras | 1,895 | 0.1 | 1670 |
| Cayman Islands | 985 | 3.8 | 1734 |
| Bahamas | 9,995 | 0.7 | 1648 |
| Anguilla | 2,260 | 25.1 | 1650 |
| Barbuda | 505 | 3.2 | 1685 |

*Source:* Higman 1984, p. 41.

activities in which the slaves were employed was determined by the interaction of these contrasting physical environments with phases of settlement.

The principal factor underlying any classification of the British colonies' economic structure must be the relative dominance of sugar (table 11.2). In 1830 roughly 80% of the slaves in the old sugar colonies worked on sugar estates, compared to 71% in the new sugar colonies, 53% in Jamaica, and none in the marginal colonies. The proportion changed little between 1807 and 1834, except in the new sugar colonies where the crop significantly increased its share of the population. There was also a clear pattern of agricultural diversification outside of sugar, with cotton predominating in the old sugar colonies, coffee, pimento, and livestock in Jamaica, and coffee, cotton, and cocoa in the new sugar colonies. It is probable that this pattern, especially in the years immediately before emancipation, was the most monocultural in the history of the British Caribbean, since the peasantry which emerged after 1838 was quick to restore minor staples to a more important place. Thus the dominant role of the large sugar estate was at its most intense in this period. Even in 1830, however, more than one-third of the slaves

**Table 11.2    Estimated Distribution of Slaves by Crop Type: Classes of Colonies, 1810, 1820, and 1830**

| | Sugar | Coffee | Cotton | Other Agriculture | Live-stock | Salt, Timber | Fishing, Shipping | Urban | Number of Slaves |
|---|---|---|---|---|---|---|---|---|---|
| *1810* | | | | | | | | | |
| Old sugar colonies | 77.5 | – | 4.8 | 5.0 | 1.1 | 0.1 | 0.6 | 10.9 | 156,150 |
| Jamaica | 51.5 | 17.0 | – | 8.0 | 14.0 | – | 0.5 | 9.0 | 347,000 |
| New sugar colonies | 54.7 | 14.2 | 13.4 | 5.8 | 0.7 | 0.1 | 0.7 | 10.4 | 246,400 |
| Marginal colonies | – | – | 3.2 | 54.0 | 0.1 | 16.4 | 6.9 | 19.4 | 15,800 |
| Total | 56.8 | 12.3 | 5.4 | 7.6 | 6.8 | 0.4 | 0.7 | 10.0 | 765,350 |
| *1820* | | | | | | | | | |
| Old sugar colonies | 78.9 | – | 3.4 | 5.5 | 1.0 | 0.1 | 0.6 | 10.5 | 151,700 |
| Jamaica | 52.0 | 16.0 | – | 9.0 | 14.0 | – | 0.5 | 8.5 | 342,380 |
| New sugar colonies | 64.2 | 10.5 | 8.1 | 5.7 | 0.6 | 0.1 | 0.7 | 10.1 | 222,200 |
| Marginal colonies | – | – | – | 59.9 | 0.1 | 14.9 | 7.1 | 18.0 | 16,960 |
| Total | 60.1 | 10.6 | 3.2 | 8.5 | 6.9 | 0.4 | 0.7 | 9.6 | 733,240 |
| *1830* | | | | | | | | | |
| Old sugar colonies | 79.9 | – | 2.2 | 6.2 | 1.0 | 0.1 | 0.5 | 10.1 | 150,870 |
| Jamaica | 52.7 | 15.2 | – | 9.9 | 13.7 | – | 0.5 | 8.0 | 319,000 |
| New sugar colonies | 70.5 | 8.0 | 4.0 | 6.2 | 0.7 | 0.1 | 0.7 | 9.8 | 199,250 |
| Marginal colonies | – | – | – | 63.0 | 0.2 | 13.6 | 6.9 | 16.3 | 15,480 |
| Total | 62.7 | 9.4 | 1.7 | 9.2 | 6.8 | 0.3 | 0.7 | 9.2 | 684,600 |

Percentage of Slaves

*Source:* Higman, 1984, p. 71.

were not employed in sugar, but lived and worked in a variety of economic, social, and physical environments, each with a differing potential for their demographic experience.

## 11.3   Ownership Patterns

The strongest contrasts in the pattern of slaveowning were between rural and urban regimes. In the British Caribbean, most rural slaves belonged to absentee white males and lived in relatively stable communities of 100 and over. Town slaves, on the other hand, belonged to small fluid units, most of the owners being women and many of them colored and black freedpeople. The decline of the urban populations after 1807, together with negative natural increase on the larger plantations, resulted in a general concentration into holdings of about 50–200 slaves. But in some colonies, chiefly those described as marginal, the slaves lived typically in units of less than 10 and very few belonged to holdings of more than 50 slaves. In some of the relatively diversified new sugar colonies there was a concentration in units of less than 100 slaves, few of the sugar estates being really large but sometimes dominating isolated regions (table 11.3). In Jamaica, very large holdings, medium-sized plantations, and small units were intermixed in most regions of the island (Higman 1976, pp. 68–71).

The number of slaves possessed by a free person was determined chiefly by the individual's wealth. It depended on the rate of natural growth or decline in the slave population, but a slaveowner could always alter the extent of his or her holding through selective sale and purchase, within the constraints imposed by prevailing prices. Slaveowners also had definite preferences regarding the characteristics of their slaves, particularly in terms of sex, age, color, and birthplace. These preferences were determined partly by the type of work a slave-

Table 11.3     Slaves per Holding by Crop, in Five Colonies

| | Mean Slaves per Holding | | | | |
|---|---|---|---|---|---|
| Crop | Demerara-Essequibo, 1832 | Jamaica, 1832 | St. Lucia, 1815 | Dominica, 1827 | Trinidad, 1813 |
| Sugar | 233 | 223 | 121 | 112 | 56 |
| Coffee | 87 | 128 | 33 | 30 | 7 |
| Cotton | 149 | — | 23 | — | 12 |
| Cocoa | — | — | 24 | — | 12 |
| Provisions | — | — | 12 | — | 9 |
| Livestock | 28 | 99 | — | — | — |

*Source:* Higman 1984, p. 106.

owner wanted performed and partly by biological ideas and prejudices. In consequence, there were significant differences between the types of slave holdings in terms of their internal demographic structure as well as in their absolute numbers.

## 11.4  Demographic Structure

British Caribbean planters showed a preference for males as agricultural laborers, and this was reflected in the prices paid for slaves. About 1820 males of prime age fetched prices 110%–130% of those paid for females. In the last decades of the Atlantic trade slave cargoes had sex ratios varying between 150 and 180 males per 100 females (Klein 1978, p. 150; Sheridan 1981, p. 276). Thus the sex ratios of the slave populations differed according to the proportions of Africans they contained, and these differences in turn were determined chiefly by variations in stage of settlement. In general, abolition of the slave trade was followed by convergence toward a balanced sex ratio, most colonies having a female majority after 1815. By 1834, however, only the slave population of British Honduras (with 163 males per 100 females) approximated the sex ratio desired by the masters, and this was reflected in its peak slave prices.

The declining proportion of African-born slaves after 1807 was the most obvious result of the abolition of the Atlantic slave trade. In the first-phase sugar colonies the proportion varied from a minimum of 7.1% in Barbados in 1817 to a maximum 16.1% in St. Kitts. In the Windward Islands and Jamaica, however, the proportion exceeded 35%, and in Trinidad and British Guiana it exceeded 50%. Where Africans made up a substantial part of the total slave population, the sex ratio rose rapidly to reach a peak of almost 200 males per 100 females at age 45, around 1817, but the ratio fell even more rapidly after this age, because of the heavier mortality levels of males, to be evenly balanced among the oldest slaves.

In the period between the abolition of the slave trade and emancipation the slave populations of the new sugar colonies were aging. In Demerara-Essequibo, for example, the mean age of the slaves increased from 25 years in 1817 to 30 in 1832. At the same time the over 50 years group increased its share from 4.3% to 14.1%, while slaves under 10 years decreased from 22.3% to 18.7%. This trend was a product of the increasing maturity of the large African-born section of the slave population and its declining fertility. In some of the first-phase sugar colonies, however, the slave populations tended to become younger after 1807. This tendency was chiefly a result of increasing fertility levels. A similar trend occurred in most of the marginal colonies. In Barbuda the proportion of slaves under 15 years increased from 39% in 1817 to

46% in 1832. In Barbados, however, the amount of change was much slighter and the age structure was quite stable in this period. Beyond these contrasts between the types of colonies, there was a significant difference in the age structure of rural and urban slave populations. Because they contained relatively large proportions of Africans, the urban populations displayed a more prominent bulge, in the 20–34 year age group, about 1817. This reflected the specific labor demands of the towns. On the other hand, differences between the age structures of the various rural crop types were not marked.

The proportion of colored (mixed-race) slaves in the British Caribbean increased with length of settlement, varying from 4% to 12% around 1817. The differences between the colonies are reduced somewhat if the focus is shifted to the proportion of the creole population comprising colored slaves, but the ordering of the colonies remains much the same. In St. Lucia and Nevis 16.4% of the creole slaves were colored around 1817 and in Berbice 4.8%, at the extremes. The most striking contrast in the distribution of the colored slave population was that between town and country. In general, colored slaves were almost twice as numerous in the towns as in the rural populations, reaching a maximum of 25% in Bridgetown.

## 11.5  Occupational Allocation

For an overall view of the occupational structure of the British Caribbean slave population, the most comprehensive data available are those generated as a by-product of the compensation of the masters at emancipation. This compensation was calculated according to the money value of the slaves, on the basis of the average prices paid for slaves sold between 1823 and 1830 (a total of 74,000 transfers). The slaves were classified after actual inspection by the Assistant Commissioners for Compensation, except that in the Bahamas the occupations listed in the registration returns of 1834 were used.

In the British Caribbean as a whole, 81.7% of the slaves were classified as active in the labor force (table 11.4). Indeed the only slaves excluded were children under 6 years of age (13.6% of the population) and those classed as "aged, diseased, or otherwise noneffective" (4.7%). There were some significant differences between the colonies but only in Anguilla and Barbuda did the active labor force fall below 75% of the total slave population, and only in Trinidad, British Guiana, and the Virgin Islands did it exceed 84%. These variations were a product of differing age structures.

Predial slaves, who made up 85% of the total labor force, were those employed in agriculture or the extraction of other produce from the land (table 11.4). Many of the "nonpredial" slaves lived on agricultural

Table 11.4     **British Caribbean Slave Population as Classified for Compensation, 1834**

| Compensation Classification | Number of Slaves | Percentage of Slaves | Percentage of Employed Slaves |
|---|---|---|---|
| *Predial attached* | | | |
| Head people | 25,658 | 3.8 | 4.7 |
| Tradesmen | 18,735 | 2.8 | 3.4 |
| Inferior tradesmen | 5,999 | 0.9 | 1.1 |
| Field laborers | 241,177 | 36.2 | 44.3 |
| Inferior field laborers | 132,008 | 19.8 | 24.2 |
| *Predial unattached* | | | |
| Head people | 1,772 | 0.3 | 0.3 |
| Tradesmen | 1,639 | 0.3 | 0.3 |
| Inferior tradesmen | 643 | 0.1 | 0.1 |
| Field laborers | 22,218 | 3.3 | 4.1 |
| Inferior field laborers | 10,730 | 1.6 | 2.0 |
| *Nonpredial* | | | |
| Head tradesmen | 4,151 | 0.6 | 0.8 |
| Inferior tradesmen | 2,439 | 0.4 | 0.5 |
| Head people on wharves, shipping, etc. | 3,335 | 0.5 | 0.6 |
| Inferior people on wharves, shipping | 3,928 | 0.6 | 0.7 |
| Head domestic servants | 29,387 | 4.4 | 5.4 |
| Inferior domestic servants | 40,718 | 6.1 | 7.5 |
| Children under 6 years of age | 91,037 | 13.6 | — |
| Aged, diseased, or otherwise noneffective | 30,088 | 4.5 | — |
| Runaways | 1,075 | 0.2 | — |
| Total | 666,737 | 100.0 | 100.0 |

*Source:* Higman 1984, p. 47.

units, of course, but most of these served in the masters' households. The largest proportions of predials were found in the sugar colonies of Tobago and British Guiana (exceeding 90% of the active labor force) and the smallest in the marginal colonies of Anguilla and the Bahamas (less than 60%). Slaves working on lands owned by their masters were classified as "predial attached" and those employed elsewhere as "predial unattached." The latter were hired out by their masters under a variety of arrangements. Some led relatively settled lives, working for years on a single plantation, while others belonged to jobbers who moved them about frequently and some, especially tradesmen, were employed by the day.

Below these broad divisions, comparisons of the occupational composition of the colonies are affected more strongly by inconsistencies in classification. In particular, the principles used to separate "inferior" from other slaves in a class varied from colony to colony (Wastell 1932, p. 77). It is more useful to ignore this distinction and consider the five main occupational categories into which the slaves were grouped. Overall, "field labourers" accounted for almost 75% of the active labor force. Only in British Honduras and the Bahamas did this proportion fall below 60%. Low proportions were also found in Trinidad, Anguilla, and Nevis. After field laborers the most numerous category consisted of "domestics." In the marginal colonies of British Honduras, the Bahamas, and Anguilla, domestics made up more than 25% of the slave labor force. They were less numerous in the sugar colonies, where the proportion varied with the urban concentration of the slaves. More than half of the domestics lived in capital towns. Slave "tradesmen," employed in manufacturing processes or the production of intermediate goods on plantations, accounted for 6.2% of the labor force. The largest proportions occurred in the first-phase sugar colonies, whereas the marginal colonies with large numbers of domestics had the smallest. Although the compensation records rarely summarized the data by sex, it is clear that the trades were the occupations most strictly reserved for male slaves.

Slaves classified as "head people," the supervisors, overlapped the tradesman and field laborer categories. If they were distributed thus, there would be a significant inflation of the tradesman category (probably raising it to 10% of the labor force) and a slighter inflation of the field laborer class. Greater changes might result from this adjustment at the colony level, but there seem to have been inconsistencies in classification. It is obvious that head people would be more numerous in those colonies where the slave holdings were large. In the Bahamas, for example, no headman was assigned to a master unless he owned at least 10 slaves (Wastell 1932, p. 77). In the sugar colonies the proportion of head people was inevitably larger, a reflection of the structure of slaveownership and work organization, and of the internal hierarchy of the slave system.

## 11.6 Rural Patterns

At the end of the eighteenth century, a group of Barbadian planters instructed their fellow planters that a "judicious division of negroes into gangs" was essential to good plantation management, since "the application of their labor to works suited to their strength and ability requires the strictest attention." The first task of a new manager, they said, was "to examine individually the state and condition of every negro; and then to assort them in such manner, that they may never be employed upon any work to which their powers are not equal"

(Lascelles 1786, p. 22). The planters' evaluation of the slaves' "strength and ability" was based chiefly on the demographic characteristics discussed above: sex, age, birthplace, and color.

The general principles of occupational allocation on rural slave holdings can be stated fairly simply. Females were totally excluded from skilled trades other than sewing, and very rarely worked in transportation or fishing, or served as "watchmen." Males were excluded only from washing and sewing. Color was less exclusive than sex, but colored males generally were allocated to domestic work or skilled trades and colored females to domestic occupations. Ethnic origin or birthplace was of only minor significance and never accounted for actual exclusions. Within the framework of these fixed characteristics, occupational allocation depended above all on age. Children generally worked in the third gang between 5 and 12 years of age. The second gang comprised children of 12–18 years and weak adults, most of them over 40 years of age. The first gang comprised the strongest slaves on the holding, those aged between 18 and 45 years. On sugar estates, slaves in the first gang performed the heavy tasks of hoeing the soil, planting and cutting canes, and working in the mills during crop; those in the second gang molded, weeded, and trashed canes, and carried trash in crop; and those in the third gang weeded and gathered grass for the livestock. Domestics and stockkeepers also commenced work at an early age. Skilled tradespeople, transport workers, and fishers were generally drafted from the field gangs and domestics during their teens. Drivers emerged gradually from the first gang, most of them over 35 years of age. The duties of watchmen were confined to the old and weak. All of these general tendencies were affected by short- or long-term illness or physical disability, of course. The size and demographic structure of particular slave holdings also imposed constraints on the flexibility of the rules, as did changes in demographic structure consequent on the abolition of the slave trade.

Detailed occupational data are available in the slave registration returns for Trinidad, St. Lucia, Berbice, Anguilla, the Cayman Islands, and British Honduras, and these have been reduced to a simplified classification in table 11.5. Most of the analysis which follows is based on these examples, together with sample parish data from Barbados.

Field labor accounted for the majority of rural slaves between the ages of 10 and 60 years in the new sugar colonies of Trinidad and St. Lucia. But slaves entered the field much earlier in Barbados, and left earlier as well. More than 40% of Barbadian slaves were in the field by age 9 and more than 70% by age 14, compared with only 5% and 25% in Trinidad. Although the concentration of slaves in field labor in the marginal colony of Anguilla was not as great as in the sugar colonies, for any age group, the slaves tended to remain longer in field work

**Table 11.5    Occupations of Slaves: Trinidad, St. Lucia, Berbice, Cayman Islands, Anguilla, and British Honduras, 1813–34**

| | | | Percentage of Slaves | | | |
|---|---|---|---|---|---|---|
| Occupation | Trinidad, 1813 | St. Lucia, 1815 | Berbice, 1819 | Anguilla, 1827 | Cayman Islands, 1834 | British Honduras, 1834 |
| Field laborers | 57.3 | 57.0 | 62.4 | 61.0 | 50.1 | 2.9 |
| Drivers | 1.6 | 1.4 | 1.8 | 0.6 | 0.0 | 0.5 |
| Skilled tradespeople | 10.6 | 7.0 | 9.1 | 7.6 | 2.8 | 5.6 |
| Domestics | 22.7 | 21.4 | 10.2 | 21.9 | 43.7 | 39.0 |
| Stockkeepers | 1.6 | 2.7 | 1.9 | 3.4 | 0.0 | 0.8 |
| Transport workers | 1.6 | 1.8 | 0.8 | 0.9 | 1.5 | 0.9 |
| Watchmen | 0.4 | 2.3 | 1.1 | 0.9 | 0.0 | 0.0 |
| Fishermen | 0.4 | 0.5 | 0.2 | 1.5 | 1.6 | 0.0 |
| Sellers | 0.8 | 0.5 | 0.2 | 0.1 | 0.0 | 0.1 |
| Laborers | 0.7 | 1.3 | 5.6 | 0.0 | 0.0 | 49.9 |
| Hired | 0.0 | 0.4 | 0.0 | 0.0 | 0.0 | 0.0 |
| Nurses | 0.6 | 0.8 | 1.5 | 0.5 | 0.2 | 0.3 |
| Sick or disabled | 0.7 | 2.3 | 4.8 | 1.6 | 0.1 | 0.0 |
| Absent | 1.0 | 0.6 | 0.4 | 0.0 | 0.0 | 0.0 |
| Total | 100.0 | 100.0 | 100.0 | 100.0 | 100.0 | 100.0 |
| No occupation | 17.1 | 22.8 | 21.2 | 32.9 | 8.7 | 13.9 |
| Number of slaves | 25,571 | 16,078 | 23,760 | 2,503 | 985 | 1,923 |

*Sources*: Calculated from Higman (1984, pp. 559–79, 584) and Bolland (1977, pp. 108–9).

because there were fewer alternative occupations for the aging. In Anguilla there was little difference in the concentration of males and females in field work, but in the sugar colonies it is striking that a larger proportion of females than males worked in the field after about 20 years of age and until they reached 50. Indeed, the proportion of males in the field declined from an early peak of about 65% at 20 years in all of the sugar colonies, while females reached a higher peak of more than 80% only by about 30 years. The peak was reached earlier in Barbados than in the new sugar colonies, probably because Barbados had a larger proportion of young creoles in the population by 1817. It is important to note that this discussion is based on cross-sectional registration data and does not reflect the life experiences of individual slaves or secular trends in the structure of the slave populations. The concentration of females in field labor, then, does not mean that they necessarily outnumbered males in the gangs. Where the sex ratio was relatively high, as in the third-phase sugar colonies, males continued to dominate the field labor force. In Trinidad females made up only 43.6% of the field slaves in 1813, compared with 43.5% of the total rural population; and in Berbice in 1819 females accounted for 44.9% of field slaves, compared with 43.8% overall. Where the sex ratio was low, as in the old sugar colonies, Jamaica, and the marginal colonies excepting the Cayman Islands, females did indeed attain a numerical superiority in the field gangs soon after 1807 (table 11.6). The important point here is that females were always overrepresented in the field labor force, and that as the slave populations became increasingly creole and the sex ratio fell to low levels females came to dominate. The reason for this tendency is that males were put to a fairly wide range of occupations, whereas females were confined almost entirely to field or domestic tasks.

Females also dominated among the house slaves. In general, 70% of rural domestics were females, though the proportion was as high as 86.4% in Anguilla in 1827. In the new sugar colonies, a large proportion of the domestics were young. This pattern was most obvious in Trinidad, where 44% of rural females aged 10–14 years were employed as domestics in 1813 and 25% of males. The proportion dropped rapidly until it leveled out at about 30 years of age, when only 15% of females and 2% of males were domestics. A similar pattern occurred in St. Lucia and Berbice. In these new sugar colonies, then, many young slaves spent a few years in domestic work before being drafted to the field gangs or skilled trades. Anguilla showed a similar pattern, except that males never accounted for so many domestics and the concentration of females was clear at all ages. In the parish of St. John, Barbados, however, the proportion of the female slave population employed in domestic work increased fairly steadily with age, and the male pro-

**Table 11.6**    Percentage of Female and Colored Slaves by Occupation: Rural Barbados, St. Lucia, and Anguilla, 1815–27

| Occupation | Percentage Female | | | Percentage Colored | | |
|---|---|---|---|---|---|---|
| | St. John, Barbados, 1817 | Rural St. Lucia, 1815 | Anguilla, 1827 | St. John, Barbados, 1817 | Rural St. Lucia, 1815 | Anguilla, 1827 |
| Field laborers | 56.8 | 58.8 | 55.3 | 11.0 | 5.6 | 10.6 |
| Drivers | 51.6 | 3.0 | 0.0 | 6.6 | 14.8 | 0.0 |
| Skilled tradespeople | 6.7 | 7.9 | 21.1 | 33.3 | 26.2 | 37.0 |
| Domestics | 72.8 | 69.3 | 86.4 | 36.4 | 32.0 | 24.0 |
| Stockkeepers | 26.7 | 28.7 | 21.1 | 9.1 | 12.2 | 10.2 |
| Transport workers | 0.0 | 0.0 | 0.0 | 0.0 | 10.2 | 24.3 |
| Watchmen | 0.0 | 31.8 | 26.7 | 8.3 | 7.6 | 25.0 |
| Fishermen | — | 2.2 | 0.0 | — | 20.0 | 24.3 |
| Laborers | 68.6 | 36.6 | — | 0.0 | 18.3 | — |
| Nurses | 100.0 | 97.1 | 100.0 | 17.5 | 14.7 | 0.0 |
| Sick or disabled | 64.3 | 65.2 | 51.9 | 5.7 | 7.1 | 7.4 |
| None | 50.6 | 54.9 | 50.3 | 18.2 | 18.9 | 19.2 |
| Total | 53.2 | 54.2 | 54.6 | 15.8 | 13.5 | 17.3 |

*Source:* Higman 1984, p. 192.

portion showed a similar, though flatter, curve. Since the overall proportion of slaves employed was much the same in St. John and rural Trinidad, it is clear that the Trinidad domestics contained significantly fewer adult slaves. This contrast between the old and new sugar colonies can be explained by the greater demand for "able" field laborers in the expanding plantation frontier and the desire to minimize the loss in productivity resulting from the use of scarce labor in domestic service. It matched the significantly earlier entry of slaves to field work in Barbados.

The skilled trades were confined almost entirely to males, and the few females included in this category were usually seamstresses. The latter were often quite young, but skilled males were generally older than male field laborers or domestics and increased as a proportion of the population with age. Skilled males were drawn from the domestics or field gangs as they entered their later teens, while females employed as domestics or seamstresses in their youth were drafted to field labor. Apprentice carpenters, coopers, masons, and wheelwrights distinguished in the Barbados registration returns were aged between 8 and 18 years.

In most colonies all drivers were males. Not one female driver was identified in the registration returns of Trinidad or Anguilla, and only a handful were listed for St. Lucia and Berbice. But they were common in Barbados. Females accounted for 37.9% of the drivers in rural St. Michael, 44.8% in St. Andrew and 51.6% in St. John. They easily outnumbered males as supervisors of the second, third, or fourth gangs. Almost all of these female drivers were over 40 years of age, whereas males often began working as drivers in their thirties. The unusual importance of female drivers in Barbados must be traced to the early age at which Barbadian children were introduced to field labor and the resulting large squads of children under 15 years of age to be supervised. These two characteristics made the field labor system of Barbados unique, and they help to explain how Barbadian planters were able to maintain productivity while extracting relatively low levels of work time from their first gangs.

Females constituted about one-quarter of the slaves employed as stockkeepers, but they generally had responsibility for the smaller animals rather than cattle and horses. The age distribution of stockkeepers, both male and female, was bimodal, with peaks in the teens and over-50 age group. The tasks of watchmen overlapped with those of stockkeepers, to some extent, but females were generally not required to keep watch at night and males employed in this occupation were older than any other active group. Fishermen tended to be mature adults. So did nurses, but the females, who predominated, were generally older than the males.

Color was a significant factor in occupational allocation, especially for domestics and skilled tradespeople, but slaves of color never outnumbered blacks in any occupation. In St. Lucia, for example, 57.5% of employed colored slaves worked as domestics or skilled tradespeople in 1815, yet they composed only 32.0% of domestics and 26.2% of skilled tradespeople. Slaves of color were also overrepresented among the drivers, fishermen, and nurses of St. Lucia. In Anguilla slaves of color were overrepresented among domestics, skilled tradespeople, transport workers (most of them sailors), fishermen, and watchmen. A relatively large proportion of slaves of color remained unemployed, both because they tended to be younger than blacks and because they were sheltered from the rigors of plantation life. Slaves of color were everywhere underrepresented in the field gangs, though they followed the pattern for blacks in being introduced to field labor earlier in Barbados than elsewhere. The contrast between the sexes applied to colored as well as black slaves, so that colored males least often found themselves in the field, followed by colored females, black males, and black females. The proportion of colored males in the field began to decline at an earlier age than for any other group. Although females predominated overwhelmingly among domestics, a larger proportion of the male colored population was employed in the house than of the female black population. Female drivers were always black, but a small proportion of the males were colored. Seamstresses were much more likely to be colored than were skilled tradesmen. Within the female domestic group, however, washerwomen were rarely selected on the basis of color and most of them were relatively mature, suggesting that the strenuous nature of their work was recognized.

The preference given to colored slaves as domestics, skilled tradespeople, and nurses reflected the slaveowners' perception of them as relatively weak and unfitted for the hard work of field labor. In some cases it also reflected a conscious recognition of the obligations of paternity or an essentially unconscious appreciation of the hierarchy of status within the broader slave society. But the conviction that slaves of color made poor field laborers, and should be employed as domestics or put to skills, was placed under stress in the period after 1807 as the source of black field laborers was cut off and the proportion of colored slaves grew.

Birthplace was the least important of the demographic factors controlling occupational allocation. Creole slaves were generally regarded by planters as more "intelligent" than Africans, but this was believed to give them an advantage only in the skilled trades. In Berbice, for example, creole males were much more likely to be skilled tradesmen than Africans, even if slaves of color are excluded from the creole group. Africans and creoles of similar age were equally likely to be domestics, but Africans over 25 years of age were more often employed as field laborers and creoles as skilled tradesmen. In the other occupations birthplace mattered little. Similarly, among the Africans, regional or ethnic origins associated with particular skills seem not to have been considered in allocating slaves to occupations.

It can be concluded that rural slaveowners did allocate slaves to occupations on the basis of their "strength and ability," with some notable exceptions. The most important of these aberrations were the tendency to keep slaves of color from field work and other types of heavy manual labor and the failure to recognize the particular skills of Africans. In the field gangs females performed the same tasks as males, including the digging of cane holes and night-work in the factories, though some concessions were made to pregnant and nursing women. The early age at which children were put to work did not appear unusual to the slaveowners of this period, nor did the long hours children had to labor. There were few significant differences between the colonies in the principles used to allocate slaves to tasks, except that the Barbadian system of large gangs of children supervised by female drivers was unique.

## 11.7  Urban Patterns

Most urban slaves worked as domestics (table 11.7). In Bridgetown, for example, 50% of the slaves were domestics in 1817, compared with just 10% of the rural population of Barbados. Apart from domestics, the towns also contained many more sellers and transport workers than the rural slave populations, and roughly twice as many skilled tradespeople, fishermen, and general laborers.

Female slaves worked in a narrower range of occupations than males in both town and country, but whereas this meant large-scale allocation to field labor on plantations in the towns it meant concentration in domestic work. The occupations of urban females were somewhat more diverse than those of rural females, however, so that only slightly more than 60% of adult females were employed as domestics in most towns. Fewer than 20% of adult males were domestics in the towns. In Trinidad, for example, only 16.5% of urban males aged 30–39 years worked as domestics in 1813, compared with 2.0% of rural males, while 72.2% of urban females in this age group were domestics, compared with 13.4% of rural females. Thus a relatively larger proportion of males than females worked as domestics in the towns as against the plantations, even though they were always a minority. Females comprised all the seamstresses and washers, and most of the hucksters, while

Table 11.7          Occupations of Urban Slaves: Barbados, St. Lucia, St. Vincent, Trinidad, 1813–17

|  | Percentage of Slaves | | | |
| Occupation | Bridgetown, Barbados, 1817 | St. Lucia, 1815 | Kingstown, St. Vincent, 1817 | Trinidad, 1813 |
| --- | --- | --- | --- | --- |
| Field laborers | 0.1 | 10.4 | 0.0 | 21.7 |
| Drivers | 0.0 | 0.0 | 0.0 | 0.2 |
| Skilled tradespeople | 16.4 | 11.5 | 16.2 | 15.7 |
| Domestics | 69.9 | 60.9 | 53.8 | 52.6 |
| Stockkeepers | 0.4 | 0.5 | 0.0 | 0.4 |
| Transport workers | 6.4 | 6.6 | 10.8 | 2.8 |
| Watchmen | 0.0 | 0.4 | 0.0 | 0.0 |
| Fishermen | 1.0 | 1.5 | 0.8 | 1.2 |
| Sellers | 0.8 | 2.7 | 1.4 | 2.8 |
| Laborers | 2.9 | 3.7 | 14.8 | 1.3 |
| Hired | 0.6 | 0.6 | 0.0 | 0.0 |
| Nurses | 0.3 | 0.0 | 0.4 | 0.1 |
| Sick or disabled | 0.8 | 1.0 | 1.2 | 0.4 |
| Absent | 0.4 | 0.2 | 0.6 | 0.8 |
| Total | 100.0 | 100.0 | 100.0 | 100.0 |
| No occupation | 28.0 | 19.2 | 23.0 | 15.4 |
| Number of urban slaves | 9,254 | 1,957 | 2,255 | 6,170 |
| Percentage of colony slave population | 11.9 | 12.0 | 8.9 | 24.0 |

Source: Calculated from Higman 1984, pp. 413–15, 552–70, 580–83.

males had a monopoly of the skilled trades, fishing, and transport work. Thus males and females were equally likely to work out and live separate from their owners.

In urban Trinidad and St. Lucia large numbers of young children were employed as domestics, the proportion reaching a peak in the 10–14 age group for both females and males. There was also a minor peak in the sixties. In Bridgetown, however, the proportion of females employed as domestics increased steadily with age to a maximum at about 35 years and only males shared the early peak seen in the new colonies. Thus, while the planters of Barbados were particularly quick to put children to field work, the slaveowners of Bridgetown were relatively slow to put them to domestic tasks. It is difficult to explain this contrast, though the perceived abundance of labor was greater in town than country. Among the domestics, washerwomen followed a distinct pattern, being concentrated in the 25–50-years age groups. Seamstresses, on the other hand, reached an early peak, in the teens, and then fell to a small proportion of the female population. This suggests that sewing was seen strictly as a part of domestic work. Male skilled tradespeople emerged at later ages, as on the plantations, and always accounted for a larger proportion of the population than domestics after age 20. Transport workers emerged at even higher ages, and in Bridgetown outnumbered domestics and skilled males only after age 35. In part this reflected the concentration of African-born slaves in transportation, but it was determined also by the heavy nature of the work. Sellers also tended to be relatively old, approaching 10% of the female population only among those aged over 40 years.

Sex and age affected urban occupational allocation in much the same way as in the rural slave population. Color and birthplace, however, were less significant in the towns than on the plantations. More important, the general rule that colored females should be employed as domestics was not followed in the towns. In Bridgetown, for example, 69.6% of black females were employed as domestics but only 56.5% of the colored, and among the males 28.6% of black but only 26.2% of colored slaves. This pattern was little affected by differences in age structure, larger proportions of black than colored slaves working as domestics in almost every age group. In urban St. Lucia colored males and females did have a slight edge over black slaves, but it was nothing like that seen on plantations. This contrast between the rural and urban situations existed in spite of the much larger proportions of colored slaves found in the towns. It was a product of the fact that most urban slave holdings were small. Slaveowners had relatively few choices available to them and could not always afford to put colored slaves to domestic tasks or exclude blacks.

Skilled tradespeople and transport workers belonged to the larger urban slave holdings, and were purchased more selectively than domestics. Colored male slaves were employed more often in the skilled trades than blacks, and less often as porters, sailors, fishermen, or laborers. But the contrasts were less than seen on plantations. Colored females were more likely to work as seamstresses, but less likely to be sellers, most of whom belonged to small units. The sex and color of the owners had only a minor influence. Skilled tradesmen and transport workers belonged most often to males but domestics were evenly distributed. Although it was sometimes said that hucksters were generally the property of free colored women, the registration data for Bridgetown show that white and free colored women owned roughly equal proportions of sellers. Few belonged to males, certainly. In general, then, it may be concluded that the structure of urban slaveownership, particularly its dispersion, meant that occupational allocation in the towns was determined very largely by the slaves' age and sex but had relatively little to do with their color or birthplace.

## 11.8 Transition

The principles of occupational allocation developed in the British Caribbean under the system of slavery, and matured in the early nineteenth century, were essentially the creation of the slaveowners. Slaves were able to modify to some extent the manner in which they performed their tasks, but rarely were they able to influence the initial choice of occupational category. They were forced to recognize the hierarchy of statuses associated with occupations, particularly on large plantations, and elements of this hierarchy were internalized. Thus "demotion" to field labor was a common form of punishment for house slaves, and the parents of colored slaves sought for their children apprenticeship to skilled trades, for example. But the principles of allocation applied by the masters were never fully accepted by the slaves, as became clear after the abolition of slavery.

Emancipation did not in itself create freedom of occupational choice for the ex-slaves. Wherever the plantation system effectively occupied all the cultivable land, as it did in Barbados and the Leeward Islands, the ex-slaves had little choice but to continue laboring on the estates. Even where the plantation was not completely dominant and there were opportunities for the emergence of an economically viable peasant agriculture, as in Jamaica and the Windward Islands, those ex-slaves who worked either full time or part time on the estates remained subject to the planters' system of work organization and occupational allocation (Green 1976; Engerman 1982). The fundamental importance of emancipation, then, lay in the fact that ex-slaves were free to choose their employers and to refuse to work under specific regimes and in particular occupations. But they could do so only within the constraints imposed by the planters' variable control of resources and the necessity of survival. The first response of the ex-slaves to emancipation was not to flee the plantations but rather to seek a flexible system of work organization and residence rules within the context of the plantation (Hall 1978). Only when the planters attempted to connect rent, residence, and estate labor did the ex-slaves leave the plantations in large numbers, wherever alternative means of making a living existed. In turn, the planters sought to maintain their command over labor by introducing indentured, contract laborers who had little more control over the system of work organization than slaves (Engerman 1984).

Plantation labor continued to be organized on a gang system after 1838, though task-work and job-work became increasingly important during the nineteenth century. The composition of the gangs changed significantly, however. Wherever possible, females and young children were withdrawn from estate field labor and the gangs became increasingly male (Adamson 1972, p. 40; Craton 1978, pp. 282–83). This withdrawal was never complete, and its extent varied with the strength of the independent peasant economy. It made clear the high value placed on the household labor of women by the ex-slaves. Color continued to play a role in occupational allocation after emancipation, persons of color still being favored for the skilled trades and domestic service. But the great demand for construction workers in the immediate post-emancipation period meant that skilled carpenters and masons were able to find employment outside the plantations, and this permitted the entry of an increasing proportion of black males (Riviere 1972, p. 3). The demand for domestic servants, on the other hand, contracted after 1838, since their services were seen as relatively unproductive and estates were increasingly controlled by absentees. In this situation, persons of color continued to dominate, until a servant-employing black and colored middle class emerged at the end of the nineteenth century, and the occupation lost status (Higman 1983, p. 125). The importance of gender, differentiating skilled and domestic occupations, persisted throughout the century, however. In these ways, then, emancipation meant a sharp break in patterns of occupational allocation and work organization, altering the roles of male and female, while at the same time the significance attached to color under slavery had long-term implications for the distribution of status and wealth within British Caribbean society.

# Comment    Stanley L. Engerman

Barry Higman has presented some important economic and demographic information for the slave colonies of the British Caribbean for the years of the early nineteenth century, focusing on the period from 1808 (the ending of the legal slave trade from Africa) to 1834 (the ending of slavery—the transitional stage of apprenticeship was terminated in 1838). The topic of Caribbean slavery is of obvious importance, as are comparisons of slavery there with slavery in the United States, but in my comments I will be concerned chiefly with measures and interpretations of labor force participation and occupational structure.

From the perspective of American economic history, slavery, particularly Caribbean slavery, is an important topic. Down to the early nineteenth century, about four times as many black slaves as free white settlers came to the Americas, and reliance on crop production by

Stanley L. Engerman is the John H. Munro Professor of Economics and professor of history at the University of Rochester and a research associate of the National Bureau of Economic Research.

slaves was instrumental in the expansion of European powers (Eltis 1983). The pronounced difference between the migration rates of the races is obscured in the aggregate population data by regional differences in demographic performance, the Caribbean societies experiencing negative rates of increase in contrast with the very high rates of natural increase of the British mainland colonies. Unlike the mainland, where even in the South slaves were only about one-third of the population, the Caribbean areas were generally about 90% black slave, with relatively few whites and free blacks and coloreds—a point with obvious implications for the analysis of occupational distribution by race and status.

During the period with which Higman is dealing, the economies of the British Caribbean were generally expanding, particularly the newer sugar colonies (areas of low population density acquired in the late eighteenth and early nineteenth century, most importantly Trinidad and British Guiana). Thus whatever may be argued about broader issues of long-term prospects and the relationship between capitalism and abolition, the Caribbean slave economies were not economically stagnant and decaying. Nonetheless, the British Caribbean was undergoing demographic decline. While the rates of decline were lower than before the close of the slave trade, only Barbados (among the major sugar producers) and the marginal colonies (with only a few slaves and without sugar production) had positive rates of natural increase. For various reasons, political constraints on interisland migration of slaves had been introduced, so the large-scale movements of slave labor into new areas, which had been taking place in the United States, was precluded in the Caribbean. The closing of the slave trade meant fewer Africans in the West Indian populations and, since the slave trade had brought in almost two males for each female, a change in the sex composition to a greater number of females, a shift often accelerated by a marked difference in death rates by sex.

Sugar was the main crop grown in the British Caribbean, but there were other export crops (cocoa, coffee, cotton) as well as considerable production of foodstuffs, some on plots cultivated by individual slaves. While most slaves were on sugar plantations, Higman shows that in 1830 over one-third (the share varying by area) lived on agricultural units specializing in other crops, and about 10% resided in urban areas. Sugar plantations were large and heavily capitalized, generally averaging over 100 slaves, allowing for a considerable division of labor internally. They were among the largest business units in the Americas, eclipsed only by the New England cotton textile firms after 1820. And, it may be added, down to the 1890s there were no small-scale units producing sugar, a point relevant to the matter of potential technological flexibility and the possible variability of labor force distribution.

The major findings of Higman's analysis relate to labor force participation rates and occupational distribution. His findings pose important questions for the analysis of free labor populations. Most striking, no doubt, is the extremely high labor force participation rates observed; these are generally about 80% of the total population, with no marked differentials between males and females. With the exception of children under 6 (treated differently, for legal reasons, on the Compensation Returns Higman used, but shown by other evidence to be the age at which children usually began to labor), the aged, and the diseased, some labor force function was found for almost everybody. Within agriculture, most laborers were described as fieldhands, and this was true for both males and females. About 12% of slaves had artisan-like and skilled occupations, these jobs being restricted almost exclusively to males. Domestic service was primarily a woman's job. Within the limits set by the importance of field labor, jobs were allocated according to a life-course pattern; for example, among males the percentage of workers with skilled occupations rose with age.

Both physical and cultural factors play roles in the determination of labor force participation rates. The significance of the cultural factors can be seen in the disparities between labor force participation rates of women and children in slave and nonslave societies, disparities that have important implications for our understanding of measured national income and economic welfare. Not only were there differences in measured rates of female and child labor force participation between slave and free societies, the high percentages of females and children in the field labor force in sugar plantations suggests a significant difference in type of work performed by slave and by free females. Clearly freedom meant the ability to avoid certain types of labor, even if not the ability to avoid participation in the labor process. Higman's data highlight one of the benefits of slave emancipation—the relative withdrawal of women and children from the labor force, particularly from plantation work. By seeing what participation rates were for women and by observing at what ages children could do full-time work under different forms of labor institutions, we are better able to interpret the extent to which labor force participation in free societies is influenced by social and cultural, as well as economic, forces.

The life course of functions found in slave societies is based upon a different set of factors than in a free labor society. The pattern is set by planters; it does not reflect the free choices of individuals (as in a free labor society), and there is no prospect for wealth accumulation and intergenerational transfer by the slaves. The pattern of change of slave occupations over the life course apparently reflects a deliberate pattern of promotion of slaves, a pattern constrained by the influence of age and physical and intellectual maturity on the masters' capacity

to exploit opportunities. There were not only age-related shifts in occupations, but also, as reflected in price data, age-related changes in
the productivity of slaves within given occupations. The existence of
these age-related productive capacities in a slave society, even without
individual accumulation, indicates that there are physiological and/or
skill development factors in the age-income relationship. Measures
from slave societies could be used to indicate the importance of the
prospects for wealth accumulation in determining the life-cycle wealth
and income patterns within free labor societies.

Higman points out that it is often difficult to define the occupational
structure of the slave labor force. Individuals often performed more
than one type of job, but were generally assigned to only one job
classification in the records, either the one corresponding to the highest
skilled job they performed or the one at which they spent most of their
time. In an era of highly seasonal work, with different functions performed at different times of the year, these recording procedures can
produce serious problems for the student of labor force structure.[1]
These slave records may overstate the time spent in skilled work, and
thus the skill needs of the economy (see Higman 1984, p. 24). Such
problems are particularly serious in economies—such as those of the
Caribbean plantation sector—in which labor time is divided between
agricultural and industrial pursuits. It is not just that some agricultural
output (and labor time) might best be classified as industrial. In examining the early stages of industrialization, where such seasonal shifts
can be quite important, the measure of occupational change and of
industry productivity development can be quite sensitive to the principles by which occupational and industrial distributions of output and
labor are measured. Further, since the measured division of labor is
affected by the size of producing units, intertemporal comparison of
skill distributions, in a time of increasing unit size, may overstate the
extent of the changing skills embodied in the population.

More generally, there are questions concerning the reasons for preparing measures of skill distributions and also of the broader relationship between the level of technology and the distribution of skills. The
distribution of the labor force by occupation is used to measure changing fortunes of individuals, as well as to describe the overall sophistication of an economic system. In a free labor economy the attention
paid to occupations in studies of social mobility reflects the use of skill,
measured by occupation, as a proxy for individual returns from economic activity (see Thernstrom 1973). The higher the level of skills

---

1. For detailed information on the functional distribution of work done, prepared on
the basis of planter allocations of actual days spent performing different tasks on United
States slave plantations, see Anderson (1974) and Olson (1983).

observed, the more favorable, it is argued, are living standards, a basic consideration from the general relation of skills and incomes.[2] Skill levels are, of course, imperfect proxies for increased income, given learning by doing within specific occupations (particularly important in the agricultural sector, where little occupational reclassification over time might be noted). There is an obvious interplay between the occupational structure and the level of technology. The relative sophistication of a sugar-producing economy required certain skills and, as Higman shows, the plantation owners were aware of the need to have methods of job selection and planning to fill the necessary slots. The patterns—by sex, age, color, etc.—found by Higman reflect the constraints of demographic forces on the choices required to fill these slots. The skilled positions were filled by individuals with low levels of literacy and few of the correlates of skill among free laborers. In interpreting changing measured skill levels over time, we need to learn more about the precise meaning and nature of skills at different levels of economic development (e.g., What are the necessary skills acquired by those in what are commonly classified as unskilled jobs?) as well as the extent to which the technology at each time determines the measured level of skills and abilities within an economy (and vice versa).

# Comment    Gerald Friedman

Professor Higman's paper presents a superb summary of the demographic and occupational structure of slavery in the British West Indies (BWIs) in the period between the abolition of the African slave trade (1807) and emancipation (1834). Higman's paper covers a wide range of topics and draws on his detailed study of slavery in many of the islands of the BWIs to place each in a comparative context. Since the larger part of Higman's paper concerns slave occupations—that is, "labor" rather than "population"—my remarks will also focus on the occupational allocation of slave labor in the BWIs. I begin with a brief discussion of the demographic performance of the BWIs, focusing on the differences between the group of colonies that Higman designates the "new sugar colonies" (NSCs) and those he calls the "old sugar colonies" (OSCs). I follow with a few comments concerning the reli-

2. Skilled slaves, similarly, may receive pecuniary as well as nonpecuniary benefits relative to the unskilled. They nevertheless do not receive the full pecuniary benefits, since part was reflected in the higher prices of the skilled slaves.

Gerald Friedman is assistant professor of economics at the University of Massachusetts, Amherst.

ability of the data Higman uses on slave occupations, and some remarks on the high labor force participation rate of the slave labor force, the technological determinants of the share of slaves in nonfield occupations, and the effect of an individual slave's personal characteristics on that slave's occupation. I then conclude with a brief discussion of the BWIs after emancipation, returning here to a comparison of the NSCs and the OSCs.

Higman begins with data on the size and distribution of the BWIs slave population at the time of the abolition of the African slave trade in 1807. The point is not new (Curtin 1969, 1975; Fogel and Engerman 1974), but even a casual comparison of the population figures Higman presents in table 11.2 with data on the volume of the African slave trade shows the catastrophic demographic effects of West Indian slavery, especially compared with slavery in the United States. Higman reports that in 1810 there were fewer than 800,000 slaves in the BWIs, or fewer than half Curtin's estimate of 1.7 million Africans imported to these colonies. The comparison with the United States is striking: in 1807, the number of free blacks and slaves in the United States was over three times the number of Africans imported.

Because of this poor demographic performance, the slave population of the BWIs began to decline once the African slave trade was ended. Despite a lively interisland slave trade, the sharpest population declines were suffered by the NSCs which had been most involved in the African slave trade and had experienced the most rapid population growth before 1807. (This association between the African slave trade, a high proportion of Africans in the slave population, and rapid population growth with high rates of natural decrease was also found among the OSCs in their early years [Craton 1974].) Using the data in table 11.2 of Higman's paper, the population of the NSCs declined by 19% between 1810 and 1830, while the population of the OSCs and the marginal colonies fell by only 3%, notwithstanding the movement of slaves from the marginal colonies and the OSCs to the NSCs.

The abolition of the African slave trade, and later restrictions on the interisland slave trade, crippled slavery in Jamaica and the NSCs, including many of the most productive slave colonies with the lowest population densities and the highest priced slaves (Great Britain 1837–38, no. 700; Ragatz 1928; Ward 1978). Estate owners in the NSCs were denied access to foreign slaves when their own slave labor force was aging and dying. British abolitionists expected the slaveowners to institute a pronatalist policy, and, possibly reflecting a change in the slaveowners' policy, there is some evidence that the rate of natural increase rose among the slaves after 1807. Another response to relative labor scarcity appears in table 11.2 of Higman's paper. The proportion of slaves employed in sugar cultivation rises throughout the BWIs between 1810 and 1830, and the sharpest increase is in the NSCs. The proportion of the slave labor force involved in sugar cultivation rises by over 25% in the NSCs (from 55% to 71%), compared with much smaller increases in the OSCs (from 78% to 80%) and Jamaica (from 52% to 53%). This association of relative labor scarcity and an increasing concentration of slave labor in staple crop production has also been observed in the nineteenth-century American South, where it has been attributed to a relatively inelastic demand for slaves in gang labor cultivation as compared with more diversified urban labor or general farming (Goldin 1976).

Most of Higman's paper is devoted to the distribution of slaves across occupations in the BWIs, and is based on the masters' reports of the slave's occupation either at the time of a slave registration or at emancipation. Higman is properly concerned with possible biases in using these reports of the slave's "occupation" to infer the actual work activities of the slaves. He expresses two concerns in particular: first, that the proportion of the slave's time devoted to nonfield labor might be understated on smaller units if slaves classified as "laborer" actually performed a wide range of tasks, including some nonfield work. In addition, Higman is concerned that the proportion of nonfield labor might be exaggerated if masters classified their slaves by the highest occupation performed over the course of a year even if the slaves spent much of their time working as common laborers.

I suspect that Higman is correct that both of these biases exist, but his estimates of the occupational allocation of slave labor are probably quite accurate nonetheless. Both of the biases he discusses are probably relatively small, and the total error produced by the two biases together will be smaller than either individually since they work in opposing directions, one raising and the other lowering the estimate of the proportion of slave labor in nonfield activities. I have two specific points:

1. Among predial slaves in Trinidad in 1813, or slaves attached to rural estates, increases in the size of slave holdings are associated with very sharp increases in the proportion of workers listed as nonfield workers, especially tradesmen (or crafts workers). Some of this increase may be due, as Higman suggests, to the underreporting of nonfield labor performed by slaves listed as common laborers on smaller units. Slaves on larger units, however, may have performed a larger share of the nonfield work than did those on smaller farms since the proportion of units with resident owners is much lower on larger than on smaller units. Contemporary observers commented on the active involvement of small farmers in Trinidad (mostly French and Spanish) in the work routine of their holdings; absentee slaveowners may have employed slaves for nonfield craft and managerial work performed by resident owners on smaller estates.

2. There is considerable evidence, furthermore, that the occupation labels Higman uses do represent meaningful economic categories. The slaveowners' classification of slaves into occupations is clearly non-random and, as Higman notes, nonfield slaves are clearly distinguished from field laborers by their sex, age, physical condition, place of birth, and color. In addition, slaves listed in nonfield occupations are worth considerably more than field slaves and common laborers, possibly reflecting greater training, human capital investment, and productive potential. Michael Craton, in his study of one Jamaican plantation, Worthy Park, presents the range of values for slaves in different occupations in the period before emancipation. Comparing the midpoints of these ranges, drivers at £135 are worth 54% more than members of the great gang, while the head cooper is worth 60% more and tradesmen as a whole are worth 36% more. Domestic servants and members of the second gang were mostly females and either older or younger male slaves; the domestic servants are valued at 2% less on average than members of the great gang, while members of the second gang are worth 14% less. (It is revealing to note that the slaveowners anticipated a profit even from the labor of slaves without an occupation—including those listed as "superannuated" and "hopeless invalids"—since even these slaves have positive prices, albeit only a little over £5, or 6% of the value of a member of the great gang [Craton 1978; see also Higman 1976, pp. 190–205].)

Higman devotes much of his paper to discussing the factors determining a slave's occupation. Perhaps the most striking characteristic of the slave occupational structure is the very small proportion of slaves without an occupation, and the efficiency (or ruthlessness?) with which the slaveowners utilized their slaves' labor. Higman notes that in 1834 fewer than 20% of the slaves are listed without occupation, including 0.2% listed as runaways. Trinidad may be typical of the high labor force participation of the slaves. Even among predial slaves as young as 5 years of age in 1813, 14% are listed with occupations. The labor force participation rate for Trinidad children rises steeply with age; at age 10, 72% of the males and 76% of the females are listed with an occupation, and 98% of males and all females aged 15 years had occupations. The labor force participation rate remains over 98% for both sexes until age 40, and even among slaves over 60 years of age, 77% of the males and 59% of the females are listed with occupations. (It is interesting to note that while young females were more likely to have occupations than young males, the labor force participation rate declines faster for older females.) These labor force participation rates are significantly higher than those for most free societies, including the population of emancipated slaves in the BWIs after 1838 (Aufhauser 1974).

The high labor force participation rate among children reduced the cost to slaveowners of rearing children, and the relative advantage of buying Africans. There may have been hidden costs attached to this intense utilization of the slaves' labor, however, and I will suggest two in particular that may have contributed to the poor demographic performance of the BWIs:

1. The early exposure of young children to field labor may have contributed to the relatively high mortality rate among children over age 5 by increasing their exposure to stress and to diseases transmitted through human and animal wastes often used as fertilizer and gathered by the children's gang. (The deleterious effect of field labor on children's health may be concealed where only children who are otherwise relatively healthy are selected for employment in the fields. Barbados had the highest rate of natural increase of the sugar colonies and also, as Higman notes, a particularly high proportion of children employed in field labor.)

2. The high labor force participation rate among adult women was achieved, in part, by granting short "concessions" to the needs of pregnant and nursing mothers. Dr. Collins (1811), a St. Vincent physician, for example, proposes reducing the field labor demanded of pregnant women beginning 6–8 weeks before delivery and resuming some field labor about 4 weeks after delivery; he implies that at least some West Indian slaveowners expected even more field labor from mothers than these restrictions would allow. Heavy field labor performed by pregnant women may have reduced their capacity to support their fetus and led to relatively weak, underweight babies.

Higman demonstrates that the probability that a rural slave would be in a nonfield occupation depends on the technology of production, the crop and unit size, as well as personal characteristics of the slave, including sex, age, color, and place of birth.

The most striking feature of slave occupations in the BWIs to an American is the relatively low proportion of adult slaves employed as simple field laborers. In Trinidad, for example, only 71% of adult male predial slaves and 84% of the adult females are listed as simple laborers. Most studies of slave occupations in the United States have found a much higher proportion of adults employed as common laborers. Herbert Gutman and Richard Sutch, for example, have estimated that between 88% and 97% of adult male slaves were simple field laborers (Gutman and Sutch 1976, pp. 87–89). Gutman and Sutch's estimates of the share of field laborers among American slaves are almost certainly too high (Margo 1979), but even my estimate of the proportion of adult male slaves in the Fogel and Engerman probate sample employed as common laborers (79%) is significantly higher than the comparable figure for Trinidad, and this estimate is made for a sample of slaves including a disproportionate share from large sugar-growing units likely to have a high proportion of slaves in nonfield occupations. (John Olson, using a smaller subsample from the Fogel and Engerman probates including only 39 relatively large units with very good occupation data estimates that only 72% of the adult male slaves were in field occupations. Olson also finds the proportion of field workers is still lower on a sample he drew of 29 very large plantations with surviving records [Olson 1983].)

The technology of sugar production in the nineteenth century, and the large size of sugar estates, may account for some of the differences in the occupational allocation of slaves in the United States and the BWIs. In particular, the male share of slaves in nonfield occupations may have been higher in the BWIs than in the United States because unit size and crop have different effects on the proportion of slaves employed in predominantly male occupations (managers and tradesmen) than on the proportion in female occupations (such as domestic service).

Higman demonstrates in table 11.3 that sugar estates were significantly larger than units producing other crops and were, indeed, among the largest units of production in the world prior to the development of the modern textile industry (Chandler 1977). Because of their concentration on sugar production, farms employing slave labor in the BWIs were significantly larger than slave farms in the United States. Using data from Higman's earlier work on Jamaican slavery (Higman 1976) and from the United States *Census of Agriculture* for 1850, we can estimate that the average Jamaican slave lived on a unit with over 180 slaves, or more than four times as many as on the unit where the average American slave lived. These differences in scale served to reduce the proportion of both domestics and of male field hands on West Indian farms. Among slaves on predial units in Trinidad, 1813, for example, the proportion of adult females employed as domestics falls steadily with increases in the size of units, from 19% among women on units with under 16 slaves to 11% on units with over 99 slaves. By contrast, the proportion of adult males employed as tradesmen and managers rises steadily in Trinidad with increasing unit size and is nearly four times as high on units with over 99 slaves as on those with fewer than 16 slaves. Since females were virtually excluded from nonfield, nondomestic slave occupations, the proportion of females in nonfield occupations declines sharply with increases in the average size of slave holdings, even while the proportion of males in nonfield occupations rises because of the increased employment of tradesmen and managers.

The predominant crop grown in the BWIs may have also increased the employment of males in nonfield positions. Sugar cultivation using nineteenth-century technology requires the services of an especially large number of skilled tradesmen, including coopers to make barrels for transporting the sugar and boilers to refine the sugar syrup. In predial Trinidad, for example, even after controlling for unit size, the proportion of adult male tradesmen is nearly 40% higher on sugar estates than on nonsugar farms. In the United States, as well, there is evidence in the Fogel and Engerman probate sample that the proportion of tradesmen is significantly higher on units in sugar-growing counties.

Higman notes that women were virtually excluded from nonfield, nondomestic occupations in the BWIs, as they were from trades and managerial positions supervising the labor of adults (especially adult males) in all slave societies I am aware of (see, e.g., Goldin 1976; Van den Boogaart and Emmer 1977; Craton 1978). This male monopoly on nonfield, nondomestic labor may have been due to the masters' prejudice, or perhaps reflected the hostility of male slaves (including male craftsmen) to working with and training women. The restriction of women from trades and managerial positions may also be consistent with the relative exclusion from these positions of shorter, less healthy, and presumably weaker males and may reflect the slaveowners' desire to have only the strongest slaves in craft and managerial positions. Among predial slaves in 1813 Trinidad, adult male drivers and craftsmen are nearly an inch taller than are male field hands, and are over 4 inches taller than the average adult female. Only some 10% of the adult women in Trinidad are as tall as the average male craftsmen. Most domestic servants are children or female, but the few adult male domestics are among the shortest males (Friedman 1982). Adult male tradesmen and managers also had significantly lower rates of mortality and morbidity than did domestics or field hands—perhaps also reflecting the selection of stronger slaves for these positions.

Higman notes that many slaves did not remain in the same occupation throughout their lives. Because of occupational segregation by sex, the age pattern of occupations was different for males than for females. The proportion of predial Trinidad males and females employed as domestics, for example, falls sharply as slaves enter late adolescence and continues to decline until slaves are nearly 40 years old. Among males, the proportion of slaves employed as field hands also declines after late adolescence, and some of the slaves released from field and domestic labor became tradesmen or managers. The proportion of tradesmen and managers among males doubles between the 16–19 and the 20–29 age groups and then continues to increase more slowly until age 60. Since adult females were not employed in trade and managerial occupations to any significant extent, the proportion of adult females employed as field hands and common laborers varies inversely with the share of domestics. The share of adult female field hands rises steadily with age until around age 40 when the share of field hands falls as the proportion of domestics begins to rise.

Higman notes that creoles, or slaves born in the New World, were preferred to African-born slaves in the skilled trades, but otherwise argues that "ethnic origin or birthplace was of only minor significance" in selection of occupation. The data on slave occupations in Trinidad in 1813 may not be ideal to test this suggestion because of the island's recent development, but Trinidad creoles were much more likely to be in nonfield occupations than were slaves born in Africa. Among dark-skinned slaves, adult male creoles are over twice as likely to be drivers and nearly twice as likely to be craftsmen as are adult male slaves born in Africa, while the proportion of adult females employed in nonfield positions is nearly 2.4 times as high among creoles as among the African born. There is evidence as well that creoles were preferred to African-born slaves for nonfield work in both colonial Virginia and in at least one Jamaican estate (Mullin 1972; Craton 1978).

The slaveowners' preference for creoles may reflect the creole slaves' superior grasp of the master's language (a reason given in Virginia), as well as the masters' belief in their superior intelligence (as Higman notes). Creole slaves may have also been selected for nonfield positions because of their superior health; even 6 years after the abolition of the African slave trade, in 1813–15, male creole death rates in Trinidad were nearly 40% lower than were mortality rates for slaves born in Africa. In addition, it is also possible that some of the creoles inherited their trades from their fathers (Craton 1978).

Higman has only a few comments on the transition from slavery to freedom in the BWIs, although he notes that the principles of occupational allocation established by the masters under slavery, especially the high labor force participation rate, were not necessarily accepted by the freedmen. The freedmens' ability to act on their own principles of occupational allocation was constrained, however, where the former slaveowners maintained an effective monopoly over access to the means of production, especially land. The effect of emancipation on the economy of the former slave societies depended on the relative supplies of land and labor and the production technology available. Land abundance influenced the ability of the freed slaves to support themselves outside of the plantation economy, while the technology determined whether it was possible to renew staple crop production outside of large estates.

The plantation regime, with labor concentrated on large sugar estates employing gang labor, survived emancipation best in the OSCs where there was a high slave population density. The simple correlations between the slave/km$^2$ ratio and the ratio of sugar production in 1839–46 to production 1824–33 is 0.54 for the 13 colonies in table 11.1 of Higman's paper that did not experience the widespread use of imported indentured labor in the decade after emancipation. Sugar production declined sharply after emancipation in most colonies, with production increasing in only four. These four include three colonies where the ratio of slaves/km$^2$ was over 100 in 1834 (Barbados, St. Kitts, and

Antigua), and also Trinidad, where planters imported large numbers of indentured laborers from Asia soon after emancipation to replace the freedmen who ceased supplying regular field labor to the sugar estates. In the sugar colonies with relatively low population densities where semifree labor was not introduced, the preemancipation labor system broke down as the ex-slaves withdrew their labor from large-scale regimented sugar cultivation in gangs and established subsistence peasant properties. Sugar growers in the postemancipation British Caribbean were never able to pay sufficiently high compensating wage differentials to attract labor to gang cultivation of sugar where free peasant farming was an available alternative; consequently, the amount of labor employed on sugar estates declined after emancipation, and sugar production fell, wherever free land was available to freedmen. In Jamaica, for example, sugar production fell by over 50% between 1824–33 and 1839–46 (Deerr 1949, p. 377).

The effect of emancipation on the economies of the BWIs makes an interesting comparison with the postbellum American South. In the American South, as in Jamaica and other land-abundant sugar colonies, the newly freed slaves were able to avoid a return to gang labor; unlike Jamaica, however, the American South was able to restore staple crop production (of cotton) after emancipation, and it did so without the wholesale introduction of outside bound labor. The American success in reestablishing cotton production may be associated with the relatively small size of slave holdings before emancipation and the relatively small economies of scale in cotton production compared with sugar. Staple crop production in the United States was reestablished after emancipation because unlike sugar, which could be produced economically only on very large units with regimented labor, economically viable small cotton farms with semi-independent holdings could be operated without gang labor (Fogel and Engerman 1974; Engerman 1983).

# References

Adamson, Alan H. 1972. *Sugar without slaves*. New Haven: Yale University Press.

Anderson, Ralph V. 1974. Labor utilization and productivity, diversification and self-sufficiency: Southern plantations, 1800–1840. Ph.D. dissertation. University of North Carolina at Chapel Hill.

Aufhauser, Robert K. 1974. The distribution of income and leisure after emancipation in Louisiana and the Caribbean. Manuscript.

Bolland, O. Nigel. 1977. *The formation of a colonial society.* Baltimore: Johns Hopkins University Press.

Chandler, Alfred. 1977. *The visible hand.* Cambridge: Harvard University Press.

Collins, Dr. 1811. *Practical rules for the management and medical treatment of Negro slaves in the sugar colonies.* London: J. Barfield.

Craton, Michael. 1974. *Sinews of empire: A short history of British slavery.* Garden City, N.Y.: Doubleday Anchor.

———. 1978. *Searching for the invisible man: Slaves and plantation life in Jamaica.* Cambridge: Harvard University Press.

Curtin, Philip. 1969. *The Atlantic slave trade: A census.* Madison: University of Wisconsin Press.

———. 1975. Measuring the Atlantic slave trade. In *Race and slavery in the Western Hemisphere: Quantitative studies,* ed. Stanley Engerman and Eugene Genovese. Princeton: Princeton University Press.

Deerr, Noel. 1949. *History of sugar.* London: Chapman & Hall.

Engerman, Stanley L. 1982. Economic adjustments to emancipation in the United States and the British West Indies. *Journal of Interdisciplinary History* 13:191–220.

———. 1983. Contract labor, sugar, and technology. *Journal of Economic History* 43:635–59.

———. 1984. Economic change and contract labor in the British Caribbean: The end of slavery and the adjustment to emancipation. *Explorations in Economic History* 21:133–50.

Etis, David. 1983. Free and coerced transatlantic migrations: Some comparisons. *American Historical Review* 88 (April): 251–80.

Fogel, Robert W., and Engerman, Stanley L. 1974. *Time on the cross: The economics of American slavery.* Boston: Little, Brown.

Friedman, Gerald C. 1982. The heights of slaves in Trinidad. *Social Science History* 6:482–515.

Goldin, Claudia. 1976. *Urban slavery in the American South, 1820–1860.* Chicago: University of Chicago Press.

Great Britain. 1837–38. *Parliamentary Papers,* vol. 48. London.

Green, William A. 1976. *British slave emancipation.* Oxford: Clarendon.

Gutman, Herbert, and Sutch, Richard. 1976. Sambo makes good, or Were slaves imbued with the protestant work ethic? In *Reckoning with slavery,* ed. Paul David et al. New York: Oxford University Press.

Hall, Douglas. 1978. The flight from the estates reconsidered: The British West Indies, 1838–1842. *Journal of Caribbean History* 10/11:7–24.

Higman, B. W. 1976. *Slave population and economy in Jamaica, 1807–1834.* Cambridge: Cambridge University Press.

———. 1983. Domestic service in Jamaica since 1750. In *Trade, gov-*

*ernment and society in Caribbean history,* ed. B. W. Higman. Kingston: Heinemann Educational Books.

————. 1984. *Slave populations of the British Caribbean, 1807–1834.* Baltimore: Johns Hopkins University Press.

Klein, Herbert S. 1978. *The middle passage.* Princeton: Princeton University Press.

Lascelles, Edwin, et al. 1786. *Instructions for the management of a plantation in Barbados.* London.

Margo, Robert. 1979. Civilian occupations of free blacks and ex-slaves in the Union Army. Manuscript.

Mullin, Gerald W. 1972. *Flight and rebellion: Slave resistance in eighteenth-century Virginia.* New York: Oxford University Press.

Olson, John F. 1983. The occupational structure of plantation slave labor in the late antebellum era. Ph.D. dissertation. University of Rochester.

Ragatz, Lowell J. 1928. *The fall of the planter class in the British Caribbean, 1763–1833: A study in social and economic history.* New York: Century Co.

Riviere, W. Emanuel. 1972. Labour shortage in the British West Indies after emancipation. *Journal of Caribbean History* 4:1–30.

Sheridan, Richard B. 1981. Slave demography in the British West Indies and the abolition of the slave trade. In *The abolition of the Atlantic slave trade,* ed. David Eltis and James Walvin. Madison: University of Wisconsin Press.

Thernstrom, Stephan. 1973. *The other Bostonians: Poverty and progress in the American metropolis, 1880–1970.* Cambridge: Harvard University Press.

Van den Boogaart, E., and Emmer, P. C. 1977. Plantation slavery in Surinam in the last decade before emancipation: The case of Catherine Sophie. In *Comparative perspectives on slavery in New World plantation societies,* ed. Vera Rubin and Arthur Tuden. New York: New York Academy of Sciences.

Ward, J. R. 1978. The profitability of sugar planting in the British West Indies, 1650–1834. *Economic History Review* 31:197–213.

Wastell, R. E. P. 1932. The history of slave compensation, 1833 to 1845. M.A. thesis. University of London.

# 12 Revised Estimates of the United States Workforce, 1800–1860

Thomas Weiss

## 12.1 Introduction

Economic historians are wont to set the record straight. In part, this desire stems from the aesthetic value of seeing each jot and tittle in its proper place, and from the comfort found in believing that nothing is askew. We sleep a little better at night knowing that sound data are in the computer terminal. There is also a bit of the detective in each of us, and our risk aversion leads us to sleuth among wayward estimates rather than among hardened criminals. There is, of course, the more practical, and we suspect more valuable, purpose of assuring the users of historical time series that the data are accurate and consistent.

The accuracy and consistency of any time series rest on the replicability of the original estimates and procedures, and on a masochistic streak which occasionally compels some of us to examine in detail the original estimates, replicating the various parts and rendering an assessment of the data. In some cases revisions are forthcoming and the record is set straight again—at least for a while.

It has been almost 20 years since Stan Lebergott's estimates of the nineteenth-century workforce appeared in print and some initial revisions were suggested (Lebergott 1966; David 1967). These estimates

Thomas Weiss is professor of economics at the University of Kansas and a research associate of the National Bureau of Economic Research.

The paper has benefited from the comments of Paul David, Stan Engerman, Robert Gallman, and the research assistance of Terri von Ende. I also wish to thank Stan Lebergott for patiently answering my questions and for giving me access to his worksheets. The work was financed in part by the University of Kansas General Research Fund and the National Science Foundation (No. SES 8308569). This research is part of the NBER's program in Development of the American Economy. Any opinions expressed are mine and not those of the National Bureau of Economic Research.

are still the most recent comprehensive reconstruction of the labor force statistics, and are the only series to extend over the entire nineteenth century. Lebergott's work pushed our knowledge backward in time so we would have a picture of the changing industrial structure of a consistently defined workforce over a much longer period than could be found in previous work. His series was designed to link up with the Bureau of Labor Statistics data for the post-1940 period, giving a combined series which spans the nineteenth and twentieth centuries. Obviously, this evidence is a basic foundation of any analysis of long-term change in income and productivity, and it can serve as a starting point for more detailed investigations of labor force changes. It is my intention to extend Lebergott's series to the state and regional level. The assessments and small revisions in this paper are the first steps in that longer-term effort.

Previous work raised some doubts about the procedures, the execution, and the results of Lebergott's original work. Near the time of their publication, Paul David (1967) used the Lebergott figures to construct his conjectural estimates of economic growth before 1840. In the course of that work he discovered some "minor inconsistencies" in the implementation of the described procedures and revised the figures accordingly, and the revisions have been adopted by Lebergott (1984, p. 66). The chief alteration was a reduction in the 1800 workforce of 10.5% (200,000 workers), all of which occurred in the nonfarm sector. The main reason for this change was an adjustment in the number of workers aged 10–15 years. In constructing the 1800 estimate, Lebergott had used an 87.2% participation rate for males aged 10–15 years, while David substituted 25%, the rate Lebergott had used in other years. David also questioned Lebergott's ratios of farm laborers to farmers and the secondary worker ratio which prevailed among rural nonfarm workers. He also made minor revisions in 1820, 1840, and 1860, years in which Lebergott indicated he had used a slave participation rate of 87.2% instead of the 90% used in 1810, 1830, and 1850.[1]

A number of other ambiguities have been noted (Weiss 1983). Chief among these are the inconsistent treatment of adult female worker estimates, and the use of establishment based counts of workers in some industries rather than gainful worker estimates. Lebergott's detailed description of his estimation methods suggested other possible biases; among these are the double-counting of 15-year-olds in some years, the omission of free colored persons in 1810, an upwardly biased participation rate for males aged 10–15 years, the inclusion of females aged 10–15 years in 1860, an upwardly biased estimate of the 1800 urban population, and a downwardly biased estimate of the number of slaves in nonfarm activities.

This list is not meant to be exhaustive, but only illustrative of the possible biases and inconsistencies in the original estimates. An exhaustive list would serve no purpose, for we would have no idea whether that list was unusually long or short. More important, we would not know whether the items on it were of any consequence. In a work as complex, technical, and monumental as the estimation of the labor force for a century or more, there are bound to be some slips 'twixt the cup and the lip. Some zealot may wish to compile a complete listing and assess the significance of each flaw, but this seems unnecessary. As can be seen in the abbreviated menu, there are possibilities for offsetting biases. A more pertinent assessment would seem to be an estimate of the net effect of all the biases and inconsistencies, regardless of whether they are listed. This is the approach I have taken.

## 12.2  Reconstruction of Lebergott's Estimates

I have attempted to gauge the net effect of the known and possible errors or biases in the original estimates, and indirectly as well, the early revisions suggested by Paul David. I did this, not by replicating each of Lebergott's figures or assessing the magnitude of individual biases, but instead by following his procedures and revising the input data where appropriate. In some cases I had additional demographic detail that was unavailable to Lebergott.[2] In other instances, the revisions corrected some inconsistencies between the described procedure and the execution. I did have the immeasurable benefit of access to the original worksheets, which Lebergott generously made available. What I have produced with all this is a set of revised workforce figures for the antebellum years. While these revisions seem desirable, they are in fact fairly small and thus attest to the solidity of the original estimates.

The revisions have relied on the procedures set forth by Lebergott, which in principle are sound and efficient. Basically, his workforce figures are the sum of the estimates for four demographic groups: free males aged 16 years and over, free males aged 10–15 years, free females, and slaves. The estimates for the free male groups and slaves were derived as the product of the estimate of the population in each group times an appropriate participation rate.[3] The estimates of free female workers were the sums of estimates of workers in selected industries in which women predominated.

I made one substantial change of a conceptual nature in implementing the procedures, namely, I used a slightly different age breakdown for free males. Instead of using his groupings of ages 10–15 years and those 16 years and over, I used a 10–14-year age group and those 15 years and over. This seems more consistent with the data reported in the 1850 and 1860 censuses.

To be sure, there is some ambiguity surrounding the treatment of 15-year-old gainful workers in the 1850 and 1860 censuses. The census of

1850 called for reporting the occupation of all free males "over 15 years of age." The 1860 census apparently did likewise. At face value, these directives suggest that the census count of free male gainful workers is for those aged 16 and above. And, previous researchers seem to have interpreted the statistics this way. Whelpton made estimates of those aged 10–15 in certain industries, indicating clearly that he was dealing with the group "under 16 years of age" (1926, p. 338). Lebergott likewise made estimates of gainful workers aged 10–15 to supplement the figures for those 16 years and over. Paul David (1967) followed Lebergott's convention; and my own earlier interpretation accorded with these (Weiss 1975).

While Lebergott generally referred to the group of males 16 and over, he occasionally mentioned those "aged fifteen and over" (pp. 141, 144). More important, he estimated male workers in 1860 using the ratio of the 1850 census count of workers (presumably free males 16 years and over) to the free male population "fifteen and over" (p. 144). He did this for the obvious reason that the census reported the population figures that way.

Occasionally the census has engaged in some mischievous behavior, but it seemed strange that they would have categorized the population as being 15 and over but have recorded gainful workers 16 and over. This implies more work for the bureaucrats who were compiling these statistics by hand. Whatever the legislation had in mind, the key empirical issue is whether the census enumerators interpreted the category "over fifteen" to mean 16 and over, or as being one or more days over 15.

Two sets of evidence are available to shed light on this matter, a random sample of the manuscript census data for rural northern households in 1860 (Bateman and Foust 1976), and an unsystematic sample gleaned from the manuscript census records readily available to me for both 1850 and 1860. In the latter approach I looked at the records for only nine counties in five states in 1850, and three counties in three states in 1860. The 1860 sample of northern households is the more systematic evidence and has greater geographic coverage. My nonrandom search of selected counties, while less systematic, did produce evidence for 1850.

Although the evidence is incomplete and pertains to rural areas it does show clearly that 15-year-olds were reported as gainful workers in all states. In the broader sample, 36% of the males and 19% of the females reported occupations, while the selected county data show figures of 45% for males in 1860 and 30% in 1850.[4] These rates seem reasonable in light of evidence for later years. For 1900, the rate for 14- and 15-year-olds was 43% for males and 18% for females (Miller and Brainerd 1957, table L-3).

Given the incompleteness of the evidence, its rural bias, and the evident wide variation across states, it seems inappropriate to use this sample evidence to estimate a precise figure for 15-year-old workers in the United States. Instead I have chosen to assume that the census included 15-year-olds in the 1850 count with a tolerable degree of accuracy. This means that the participation rates derived from that census pertain to those aged 15 years and above, and should therefore be applied to a similar age grouping in earlier years. So instead of estimating the 15-year-old workers in 1850, my revisions required instead that I estimate the number of 15-year-olds in the population in the years 1800 through 1820. These estimates are described in appendix A. While this approach may contain inaccuracies, the series is consistent over time in its treatment of 15-year-old workers.

The interesting thing is that Lebergott's estimate for 1850 takes the 15-year-olds as being included in the census figure. His estimate of 280,000 boys was derived using the free male population aged 10–14, which the census reported. Thus if the census counted accurately 15-year-old workers and included them in the published total, Lebergott's 1850 figure would be an unduplicated count of gainful workers. To the extent the census undercounted 15-year-old workers or excluded them from the published figures, his total will be lower than the true value.

Unfortunately, the other years appear to have been treated differently by Lebergott. For the years 1800–1840, the 1850 participation rate for those 15 and over was applied to the population base 16 and over. Since the inclusion of 15-year-olds, even if counted accurately, would lower the participation rate, the estimated workforce for those 16 and over is too low in each of these years. The size of the bias depends on how accurately 15-year-old workers were counted in 1850.[5] The 1860 result is somewhat different. The population base used was 15 and over, so the accuracy and age coverage of male workers above age 15 would be comparable to the 1850 figure. But Lebergott then makes an estimate of the number of workers aged 10–15 years thereby double counting some 15-year-olds.

## 12.3   Total Labor Force

The original and revised figures are presented in table 12.1. I have also assembled there the revised estimates for each of the demographic components making up the labor force.

In the aggregate these comparisons enhance the credibility of Lebergott's estimates. The consequences of the inconsistencies and flaws in execution apparently did not cumulate to a substantial degree. The only difference of note is that for 1800. I have in fact used Paul David's estimate for that year, and while this minimizes the discrepancy there

Table 12.1     Estimates of the Labor Force, 1800–1860

|  | Total Labor Force (Thousands of Workers) | | | Composition of the Present Estimates (Thousands of Workers) | | | |
|---|---|---|---|---|---|---|---|
| Year | Lebergott | Present Estimates | Percentage Difference | Free Males 15+ | Free Males 10–14 | Females 10+ | Slaves 10+ |
| 1800 | 1,700[a] | 1,658 | −2.5 | 1,016 | 56 | 63 | 523 |
| 1810 | 2,330 | 2,358 | +1.2 | 1,393 | 75 | 150 | 740 |
| 1820 | 3,135 | 3,126 | −.3 | 1,904 | 99 | 160 | 963 |
| 1830 | 4,200 | 4,172 | −.7 | 2,634 | 126 | 235 | 1,177 |
| 1840 | 5,660 | 5,686 | +.5 | 3,652 | 164 | 390 | 1,479 |
| 1850 | 8,250 | 8,199 | −.7 | 5,330 | 228 | 675 | 1,966 |
| 1860 | 11,110 | 11,063 | −.5 | 7,395 | 195 | 920 | 2,452 |

Sources: Lebergott 1966, table 1; David 1967, table A-1; appendix table 12.A.2, below.
[a]This is David's revision of Lebergott's estimate. Legergott's estimate for this year was 1,900,000 workers. In his recent textbook, Lebergott has incorporated the David estimate into his series (1984, p. 66).

is still a difference of 2.5% between the two figures. Surprisingly, this does not reflect our use of different participation rates for those aged 10–14 and those 15 years old.[6] Instead the difference represents an overestimate of the number of free colored workers in the original figures. Both David and Lebergott used an estimate of the free colored male population 10 years and over of about 78,000. The census of 1800 reported a total free colored population of 108,000 (United States Census 1800, p. a). After deducting females (estimated as 52%) and males aged 0–9 (32% of the males), one is left with only 35,000 males aged 10 and over. The current estimate is a labor force of only 27,000 in comparison to the 57,000 estimated by David.[7] The present estimate of slaves is also lower than David's. For slaves, David believed Lebergott had underestimated by using a participation rate of 87.2%, so he increased the slave force to 547,000. The current figure is only 523,000, close to Lebergott's original figure which was in fact 91% of the slave population. These upward biases in David's figures are partially offset by his lower estimate of workers aged 10–15 years.

In other years, while the totals are extremely close, there are some observable differences among the component figures. In all years, the revised estimate of males aged 10–15 is higher than the original. A comparison of the estimates for this age group is beset by the problem that the revised estimates do not contain an explicit figure for 15-year-olds. The revised figures are biased upward in this comparison by my use of the average rate for all males 15 years and over, solely for the purpose of making these comparisons. My imputed rate for 15-year-olds is 87% versus Lebergott's figure of 25%. This bias shows up clearly in the years 1800–1830 where the revised figures are above Lebergott's. For the years 1840–60, however, this known bias serves to highlight an estimation problem. For those years I used the same participation rates as I did in the other years, whereas Lebergott used smaller rates in those years, and in 1850 also used the smaller population base of those aged 10–14 years. In that year his estimate of free male workers aged 10–15 is only 70% of the implicit revised value. Ironically, while he referred to his 280,000 estimate as pertaining to those aged 10–15 years, the figure in fact refers to those aged 10–14 years, and its addition to the census figure gives an unduplicated total. When confined to this smaller 10–14-year age group, the revised figure is below the original, reflecting my use of an 18.2% participation rate and his use of a higher rate 22.4% based on data for the broader 10–15 age group.

The other notable differences show up in the 1860 figures and affect every component. Since some of the differences are offsetting, the aggregate figures are quite close. A comparison of the two series for that year is presented in table 12.2. The revised slave figure was derived by applying the same formula as was used in other years, specifically, 90% of the slave population aged 10 years and over. For some reason, Lebergott chose to use a different method in this one year, using the participation rates for free males that prevailed in 1850 (p. 146). He did this on a state-by-state basis, carefully evaluating each state's ratio and adjusting those which seemed out of line. But given that the ratios were well below the 90% figure used in other years, ranging between 84% and 88%; and given that he did not think it appropriate to apply these same rates in 1850 when they originated (p. 143), it seemed desirable to drop this variation in making the revisions. The consequence is that the revised slave workforce is 113,000 greater than the original.[8]

The discrepancies in the 10–14 age groups reflect our use of different participation rates for males (22.6 vs. 18.2), while for females it reflects a difference in rates (6.2 vs. 5.1) and the use of the larger age group,

**Table 12.2     Comparison of the 1860 Estimates**

| 1860 Workforce | Lebergott | Present Estimates | Difference | Ratio |
|---|---|---|---|---|
| Total | 11,110 | 11,061 | 49 | 1.00 |
| Slaves | 2,340 | 2,453 | −113 | .95 |
| Males, 15 and over | 7,397 | 7,395 | 2 | 1.00 |
| Males, 10–14 | 365 | 293 | 72 | 1.25 |
| Females, 15 and over | 895 | 841 | 54 | 1.06 |
| Females, 10–14 | 113 | 79 | 34 | 1.43 |

*Source:* Appendixes below; Lebergott 1966, pp. 144–47. The figure for males 15 and over was not reported in Lebergott but was derived to make the total consistent with the sum of the components.

10–15 years, in the original estimates. In both estimations the figures for females aged 15 and over were derived by subtracting an estimate of free male workers from the reported census total for 1860. The estimate of male workers was obtained by weighting the free male population by the 1850 participation rates. The difference appears due to an arithmetical error, where some negative numbers were inadvertently treated as positive in Lebergott's calculations.[9]

## 12.4    Farm Workforce

I have also constructed a revised series on the farm workforce that is consistent with the revised total workforce figures, again following Lebergott's procedures but using new evidence where appropriate. The farm workforce was intended to be the sum of estimates for slaves and for free males. In principle, females were to be excluded in all years, but in fact some unknown, but small number were included in several years.[10]

Several dates are crucial in Lebergott's construction of the antebellum farm workforce figures. One of these is 1860, which provides some of the basic parameters used to derive the estimates in the earlier years. Fortunately, the census provided reasonably complete and detailed figures for that year. More critical is the estimation for 1800. Without this figure the series would likely have terminated in 1820, and would then not be such a substantial advance on the work of Whelpton. The estimate for 1820 is also important, for it influences heavily the estimation by interpolation of the figures for 1810 and 1830. The revised figures are presented in table 12.3.

In most years, but not all, there are only small differences in the number of workers and in the workforce shares. Again this exercise seems to confirm the solidity of the original figures. In spite of a number of potential biases in the original estimation, those figures approximated closely the corrected values. As with the totals, there were some offsetting revisions. For example, the revised 1860 slave workforce is 30,000 greater than the original, but this upward change is more than offset by an 86,000-worker decrease in the free farm workforce. The latter decline reflects entirely the elimination of the duplicate counting of 15-year-olds and the lower participation of those 10–14 years of age.[11]

In all years, except 1860, there is a slight reduction in the slave farm workforce. Lebergott specified that the slave farm workforce was to be derived by dividing the slave population 10 years of age and over into an urban share of 5% and a rural one of 95%; and then weighting the rural population by an assumed participation rate of 87% (pp. 150, 151). While this would appear to be inconsistent with the 90% rate

**Table 12.3    Estimates of the Agricultural Workforce, 1800–1860**

| Year | Farm Workforce (Thousands of Workers) | | | Workforce Shares | | Components of the Present Series (Thousands of Workers) | |
| | Lebergott | Present Estimates | Difference (%) | Lebergott | Present Estimates | Free Males | Slaves |
|---|---|---|---|---|---|---|---|
| 1800 | 1,400[a] | 1,263 | −10.2 | 82.4 | 76.8 | 783 | 480 |
| 1810 | 1,950 | 1,797 | −7.8 | 83.7 | 76.2 | 1,117 | 680 |
| 1820 | 2,470 | 2,462 | −.3 | 78.8 | 78.8 | 1,577 | 885 |
| 1830 | 2,965 | 2,944 | −.7 | 70.6 | 70.6 | 1,862 | 1,082 |
| 1840 | 3,570 | 3,520 | −1.4 | 63.1 | 61.9 | 2,160 | 1,360 |
| 1850 | 4,520 | 4,394 | −2.8 | 54.8 | 53.6 | 2,587 | 1,807 |
| 1860 | 5,880 | 5,822 | −1.9 | 52.9 | 52.6 | 3,570 | 2,252 |

*Sources:* Lebergott 1966, table 1; appendixes below.

[a]Paul David's revisions affected largely the total labor force, and the farm share, but not the farm workforce. His revised farm figure was 1,406,500 (David 1966, p. A-17).

used to estimate the total slave workforce, it is reconciled by Lebergott on the grounds that this lower 87% figure would "partially [compensate] for the inclusion of domestic servants, carpenters, etc., employed on the plantations and small slaveholdings" (p. 152). His execution, however, used the 90% figure, so that by following the described procedures one derives a lower slave farm workforce in each year, except 1860. In that year he estimated the number of slaves on a state-by-state basis using the participation rates for free males that prevailed in each state in 1850 (p. 152, n. 92). As noted earlier, this seems inappropriate, so I revised the slave estimate for the total and the farm workforce.

The estimates for 1800 and 1810, however, are substantially different, with important implications for our understanding of long-term changes in productivity and income. Since the 1810 figure is essentially an interpolation between 1800 and 1820, it is only necessary to examine the 1800 figure carefully.

The estimate of the 1800 farm workforce is quite simply the sum of agricultural slaves plus free colored farm workers plus the residual of free workers not allocated to other occupations. Lebergott made important distinctions among farmers, farm laborers, and family heads, but these were for use in assessing his results and were not necessary to derive the free farm workforce. The free white farm workforce is just the difference between the total number of white workers and those engaged in navigation, urban activities, and rural nonfarm occupations. A comparison of the components is contained in table 12.4.

There are several major differences in the estimation of the original and revised farm figures. The total number of white workers is sub-

**Table 12.4**    **Gainful Workers by Occupation, 1800 (Thousands of Workers)**

|  | Lebergott | Present Estimates | Difference |
|---|---|---|---|
| | *White Males* | | |
| Total | 1,240 | 1,047 | 193 |
| Navigation | 50 | 50 | — |
| Urban occupations | 116 | 75 | 41 |
| Rural nonfarm | 227 | 158 | 69 |
| Agriculture[a] | 847 | 764 | 83 |
| | *Agriculture* | | |
| White males | 847 | 764 | 83 |
| Free colored males | 63 | 21 | 42 |
| Slaves | 490 | 480 | 10 |
| Total in agriculture | 1,400 | 1,265 | 135 |

*Sources:* Lebergott 1966, table 1, pp. 134–37; appendixes below and text

[a]The agriculture figure equals the total number of white males less those in navigation, urban occupations, and rural nonfarm occupations.

stantially smaller, as explained in the previous section. Additionally, the revised figures for urban and rural nonfarm occupations are lower, as is the estimate of free colored farm workers. Of less importance is a minor revision in the estimate of the slave workforce.[12]

Lebergott derived his urban/rural breakdowns using the 1790 evidence for five cities (p. 135). I have used the 1800 census data to construct the urban/rural distribution for each demographic component, with the white population being disaggregated by age and sex. This latter detail provides more pertinent information on the geographic location of family heads. The 1790 figure Lebergott used to estimate the urban free male workforce is higher than the more pertinent 1800 figures. He estimated the urban workforce as 9.1% of free males 10 years of age and older. Additionally, he used a much higher participation rate for those aged 10–15 years. The 1800 census data show that only 7.3% of the free males aged 16 and over, and 5.5% of those aged 10–15 years, lived in cities. The differences in these urban shares accounts for approximately three-fourths of the 41,000-worker discrepancy, and the higher participation rate accounts for the remainder.

The difference between the estimates of rural nonfarm workers reflects a revision in the ratio used in the calculation. The number of rural nonfarm workers was derived as the product of the population base (free white males 10 years and over) times a ratio of rural nonfarm workers to population, the ratio being obtained from the 1840 census evidence for southern states. It appears that Lebergott's ratio of 17.6% referred to the male population 15 years of age and over, not to those aged 10 and over. As such, the ratio he used is very close to the 1840 United States figure for males 10 and over (19.7%). It is quite unlikely that the 1840 United States figure, or any ratio close to it, would be representative of the 1800 economy. The southern ratio is lower than the United States figure, and thus may be more representative of the 1800 economy. But even the southern ratio seems too high because it includes a very high ratio for Virginia, where 26.4% of the free males aged 10 and over were engaged in rural nonfarm occupations.[13] Since this figure is well above that for the United States, it seemed appropriate to calculate the ratio with Virginia excluded. I also converted the ratio to the appropriate population base of free white males aged 10 years and over. The resulting figure of 11.7% was rounded downward to compensate for the unknown upward bias arising from the inclusion of females and slaves in the 1840 worker count.

Two factors explain the 42,000-worker discrepancy in the free colored farm workforce. The major factor is that Lebergott's figure includes free colored females as well as males. The revised figure is restricted to males.[14] A second factor is that the 1800 urban share of the free colored population was 18%, a figure well above that derived from the 1790 census. The revision then places 82% in rural areas, and thus in farming, as opposed to the 92.6% implicit in Lebergott's estimates.

## 12.5   Caveats

Obviously, it is possible to obtain different estimates of the workforce by varying the estimates of the components used in the calculation. And, there are clearly some further refinements that would improve the estimates, perhaps especially the agricultural series. I have not incorporated these here, because I wanted to produce a series that was faithful to the original procedures, and because some adjustments would be quite arbitrary and would offset each other to some extent, perhaps fully. Nonetheless, let me suggest some possible revisions.

First, the farm workforce estimates for 1850 and 1860 may be low because no account was taken of a general category of workers called "laborers, not otherwise specified." It is well known that estimation of the industrial distribution of the workforce in the years 1870 through 1900 must contend with the problem of allocating this group of general laborers to the various industries in which they worked. This is no inconsequential problem for these unspecified laborers made up between 8% and 10% of the labor force in each of the postbellum years, and Lebergott allocated an average of 56% of them to agriculture on the basis of their rural residency. For 1850 and 1860 the census reported nearly a million of these laborers, comprising 8.7% of the workforce in 1860 and 11% in 1850 (United States Census 1900, p. liv); none of which have been included in the farm workforce estimates. Surely some of them worked there, but any estimate would be crude. We cannot simply extrapolate the postbellum distributions, for they include all whites and blacks, whereas the antebellum census data refer predominantly to free whites. In order to apply the urban/rural approach used in the postbellum period, we would need information on the location of at least a sample of these workers. Improved estimates, then, await additional evidence.[15]

The 1820 agricultural share of the workforce appears somewhat high, being 2 percentage points above the 1800 figure. It is of course possible that the latter figure is too low, but the procedure for estimating the 1820 figure suggests a likely upward bias. That figure was derived by combining the census count with an estimate of farm workers omitted from that count. In so doing, the share of the omitted free workers allocated to farming was based on the share implicit in the census data (83%). Since those data include slaves, the share is likely higher than it would be for only free whites.

Female workers are treated inconsistently across census dates. In all years an explicit estimate of women in selected occupations was included (see table 12.1). Additionally, there is an implicit count in several years, namely, 1820, 1840, and 1860. In 1860, the number implicit in the census count was made explicit by deducting free males from the census total. But some of these women must have been farmers and farm workers, and are thus included implicitly in the free farm workforce for that year. In 1820 and 1840, some women were probably included in the census count of farm workers, but their number is not specified in the present estimates, and moreover, they are not included in the total labor force figures for those years. By interpolation, then, some women are implicitly included in the farm workforce for 1810 and 1830, but again excluded from the total workforce. To be sure these numbers are small, but nonetheless they do cause the 1800 and 1850 figures to be somewhat different in scope.[16]

The possibility of offsetting adjustments can be seen in the 1800 estimation. One downward bias in the farm figure is that the nonfarm estimates of the free workforce double-count some workers, thus reducing the residual allocated to farming. Surely some of those engaged in navigation and rural nonfarm activities are also counted in the urban figure.[17] Then, too, the rural nonfarm figure may include some unspecified number of females and slaves, which again reduces the residual count of free males in farming. Working in the opposite direction is an upward bias in the number of slaves engaged in agriculture. The procedure used assumes that only 3% of the occupied slaves were engaged primarily in nonfarm activities. This seems low in light of other evidence (Weiss 1975; Crawford 1980; Higman 1984).

Whatever adjustments one might wish to make, a strength of Lebergott's procedure is its straightforwardness. The refinements are simply added to or subtracted from the prevailing level. From this perspective, the estimates are not unduly sensitive to changes in any of the components. In this regard the Lebergott procedure seems preferred over the balance equation approach devised by Paul David (1966). Estimation of the rural nonfarm and farm workforce by his method is quite sensitive to changes in some of the input data. For this reason, I have not used that approach to derive the farm workforce in the revised series.[18]

## 12.6 Conclusions and Implications

As already noted, this paper is but the first step in a longer-term effort to build up reliable estimates of the workforce at the state level. Given that those estimates will be derived using procedures set out by Lebergott, and that the sum of the state estimates should be consistent with the national figures, it seemed worthwhile to scrutinize and assess the original procedures and estimates. The exercise did indeed prove valuable, suggesting, on the one hand, possible pitfalls in the estimation procedures, but on the other hand, indicating that the existing figures are reliable. In spite of the many places to go awry, Lebergott produced a carefully constructed set of figures. Even if no revisions were made in those estimates, they would depict well the nation's workforce, its trend over time, and could serve as a standard for assessing the summation of the state estimates.

The exercise did, however, suggest a few revisions. In some years, there were offsetting differences in the estimates for various population components which netted out to small discrepancies in the aggregate (see table 12.2). Since all the differences are explained in the text and appendixes, here let me just highlight the key discrepancies between my revised figures and Lebergott's original estimates.

The most substantial revision lies in the 1800 figures, and Lebergott now accepts that the original estimate of 10–15-year-old workers was too high (Lebergott 1984, p. 66). His revised figure, based on Paul David's work, still exceeds my estimate by 1.3%, a difference arising from our estimates of free colored workers. Lebergott included free colored females, while I confined my estimate to free colored males and assumed that free colored female workers were included in the independently derived estimate of female workers. At the aggregate workforce level, there is only one other year, 1810, in which I would revise Lebergott's figure by as much as 1%. This difference reflects primarily our treatments of 15-year-old workers. I included them with the older segment of the labor force which had a participation rate of 87.2%, while Lebergott included them with youths, with a 25% participation rate. At the sectoral level there are notable differences in the farm workforce estimates for 1800 and 1810, and smaller differences in 1840 through 1860 (see table 12.3). The 10.2% difference in 1800 reflects a number of factors, as explained in the text (see table 12.4), while the 1810 discrepancy of 7.8% results in part from the difference for 1800, since we both obtained the 1810 figure by interpolation between 1800 and 1820. The remaining difference is due to our methods of interpolation (see app. A, especially table 12.A.4).

Of course, these revisions of the workforce figures have implications for our understanding of historical trends and issues. In particular, the revisions in the farm workforce in the earlier years bear on our view of the pace and timing of economic growth in the antebellum years, and on the behavior of productivity change in farming over the course of the nineteenth century. A careful reinterpretation of these issues would involve lengthy discussion of some other unsettled matters and underlying assumptions, and would take us far astray of the purpose of this paper. Let me suggest, however, the consequences for our view of antebellum economic growth.

The use of these revised figures would lower Paul David's conjectural estimate of per capita growth for the period 1800–1860 from 1.27% to 1.09% per year.[19] Moreover, the impact on the subperiods is to make it even more clear that our record probably followed the British pattern in that there was no discontinuity in trend, but rather the shift to "a higher secular rate was a much more gradual affair" (David 1967, p. 195). Instead of a one-time leap, the revised figures would show some acceleration during the antebellum period, with the rate rising from 0.98% in the subperiod 1800–1835 to 1.3% in the years 1835–55, and additional acceleration after the Civil War.

My cursory examination of implications such as this suggests that the new workforce figures present a quite plausible picture, thereby lending credence to the suggested revisions. Much more careful assessment is of course called for, and will be an ongoing activity. Presumably other researchers as well will continually test the plausibility of the estimates as they are used. In my view, the revisions in the total labor force are quite small, serving primarily to improve the consistency and precision of an already solid set of figures and enhancing our confidence in these national benchmark figures. At the sectoral level, the changes are more substantial, being large enough to alter our perception and understanding of economic development in the antebellum period. Even these larger sectoral changes are not a wholesale revision of the original estimates, but rather a refinement and strengthening of them. For the most part, the changes are due to the use of improved underlying data and the removal of some inconsistencies in the execution of the estimation procedures. In consequence of the solidity of the aggregate figures and these sectoral refinements, this revised labor force series should provide a firm foundation for extending the estimation to the state and regional level.

# Appendix A
## Nineteenth-Century Labor Force Estimation

The estimation of the labor force for the nineteenth century was derived as the sum of estimates for several demographic groups: free males, free females, and slaves. These groups in turn were broken down by age and race. The estimates for each component were calculated as the product of the population base for that group times an appropriate participation rate. The estimation, then, required evidence on these rates as well as figures for the population base for each of the groups.

Population Figures

The population data used in the estimation are presented in table 12.A.1. Unless otherwise noted, the data are from *Historical Statistics* (1975) series A, pp. 119–34. While population counts for some groups were readily available, others had to be estimated, especially in the earlier years. Where possible, I followed the procedures laid out by Lebergott (1966). Since I have used a different age breakdown, it was necessary to estimate the number of 15-year-old free white males in the years 1800–1820.

*Slaves*

For 1800, the number of slaves aged 10 years and over was estimated as 65% of the reported total slave population. The percentage was that which prevailed in 1830, and which was used by Lebergott (p. 137, n. 44). For 1810, the slave figure was calculated as 69% of the total slave population, a percentage derived from the 1820 calculation explained below. This was the percentage used by Lebergott (pp. 138–39) and was adopted here. For 1820, I first estimated the number of slaves under the age of 10 as 70% of the reported number of those under 14 years of age. This estimate was then deducted from the reported total slave population to obtain the number of those aged 10 and over (Lebergott, p. 140, n. 55). The resulting figure is equal to 69% of the total slave population.

*Free White Males*

Free white males aged 10–14 years were reported for the years 1830–60. For 1800–1820 those aged 10–14 were estimated as equal to the reported number aged 10–15 years minus an estimated number of 15-year-olds. The resulting figure for 10–14-year-olds is equal to 86.2% of those aged 10–15 years. The number of 15-year-old free white males in the years 1800–1820 was estimated as 13.8% of those aged 10–15 years, the group for which data were reported. The percentage figure used is that which prevailed for whites in 1880, the first year for which such evidence could be found in the published census (United States Census 1880, 1:548). Free white males aged 15 and over is the sum of the reported number aged 16 years and over plus the estimated number of 15-year-olds.

*Free Colored Males*

The total number of free colored persons was reported in the early census volumes, but no sex or age breakdowns were shown for 1800 or 1810 (United States Census 1830, p. 26). The sexes were distinguished in later years, with the shares being very steady between 1820

**Table 12.A.1  Population Data Underlying the Workforce Estimates (Thousands of People)**

| Year | Slaves 10 Years and Over | Free White Males by Age | | | Free Colored Males | | Free Females 10 Years and Over |
|---|---|---|---|---|---|---|---|
| | | 10–14 Years | 15 Years | 15 Years and Over | 10–14 Years | 15 Years and Over | |
| 1800 | 581 | 304 | 49 | 1,136 | 7 | 28 | 1,425 |
| 1810 | 822 | 403 | 65 | 1,549 | 13 | 48 | 1,962 |
| 1820 | 1,070 | 528 | 85 | 2,122 | 15 | 61 | 2,674 |
| 1830 | 1,308 | 670 | — | 2,936 | 19 | 85 | 3,617 |
| 1840 | 1,643 | 880 | — | 4,081 | 23 | 107 | 4,895 |
| 1850 | 2,185 | 1,226 | — | 5,956 | 26 | 124 | 6,937 |
| 1860 | 2,725 | 1,590 | — | 8,341 | 30 | 140 | 9,536 |

and 1860. The male share was 48% in each of those census years, and I have assumed that this figure applied in 1800 and 1810 as well. Those aged 10 years and over were then estimated to be 68% of the total number of free colored males, the share which prevailed in 1830, the first year in which the age breakdown was available. The share may actually be higher in the earlier years, as there does appear to be a trend in the data for the years 1830–60, but the numbers involved are so small that greater precision or more sophisticated estimation techniques do not seem necessary. The distribution between the age group 10–14 years and those 15 years and over was assumed to be the same as that derived for free white males in each year.

*Free Females*

The figures for free females were not used to estimate the female component of the workforce, but are included here for completeness. The figures are the sum of free white females and free colored females aged 10 and over. The number of free white females 10 and over was reported in each year, and that for free colored females was reported for 1830–60. For 1800 and 1810, free colored females were estimated as 52% of all free colored; and for these years, and for 1820, when females were reported separately, those aged 10 and over were estimated as 72% of all free colored females, the share which prevailed in 1830 and 1840 (*Historical Statistics* 1975, ser. A:119–34).

Labor Force Estimates

For all components of the workforce, except free females, the estimate is the product of each group's population base times a participation rate. The single exception is the figure for free males 15 years and over in 1850, which was obtained from the census of that year. The participation rates were taken from Lebergott, but adjusted to the revised age groupings. A few other changes were made in order to achieve consistency in the estimation procedures. The estimates are presented in table 12.A.2.

*Slave Labor Force*

The slave labor force includes males and females 10 years of age and above. For all years I used the 90% participation rate which Lebergott espoused. The description of his estimates suggests he used 90% in some years (1810, 1830, and 1850) but 87% in others. In fact, in his execution he used approximately 90% in all years except 1860. In that year he used the rates which prevailed for free whites in southern states in *1850*. Since he did not think these rates were appropriate for 1850, it seemed inconsistent to use them in 1860, so I opted for the 90% figure.

**Table 12.A.2  Revised Estimates of the Labor Force (Thousands of Workers)**

| Year | Slaves 10 Years and Over | Free White Males 10–14 Years | Free White Males 15 Years and Over | Free Colored Males 10–14 Years | Free Colored Males 15 Years and Over | Free Females 10 Years and Over | Total Labor Force 10 Years and Over |
|---|---|---|---|---|---|---|---|
| 1800 | 523 | 55 | 991 | 1 | 25 | 63 | 1,658 |
| 1810 | 740 | 73 | 1,351 | 2 | 42 | 150 | 2,358 |
| 1820 | 963 | 96 | 1,850 | 3 | 54 | 160 | 3,126 |
| 1830 | 1,177 | 122 | 2,560 | 4 | 74 | 235 | 4,172 |
| 1840 | 1,479 | 160 | 3,559 | 4 | 93 | 390 | 5,686 |
| 1850 | 1,966 | 223 | 5,222 | 5 | 108 | 675 | 8,199 |
| 1860 | 2,452 | 289 | 7,273 | 6 | 122 | 920 | 11,063 |

## Free Males

The participation rate for free males aged 10–14 years was derived from the 1900 census data. For that year a rate of 21.4% was found for all males 10–14 years old. Following Lebergott's lead, it was assumed that a rate for native whites would be more representative of the antebellum group of free males than would the rate for all males. In 1900 the native white race was reported for those aged 10–15 years. That rate of 22.1% was equal to 85% of the reported rate for all males aged 10–15 (26.1%), and so it was assumed here that the native white rate for those aged 10–14 was equal to 85% of the rate for all males aged 10–14 years (United States Census 1900, pp. lxvii, cxviii). This same rate was used for free colored males aged 10–14 years.

For free males aged 15 and over I used the 1850 participation rate of 87.2% as derived by Lebergott (p. 140 and elsewhere). I used this rate in all years, whereas Lebergott used it in all years except 1860. For that year, he divided the 1860 census figure into males and females by applying the 1850 participation rate for males on a state-by-state basis. The summation of the state estimates yields a slightly higher participation rate (88.6%) for all free males. The 1850 figure for free white males is the reported census figure, excluding students, less the estimated number of free colored workers.

## Free Females

The numbers for female workers were taken from Lebergott (1966). The ages were not always specified, so I have treated them as referring to those 10 years of age and over. For 1800, Lebergott (p. 136) indicated that in urban areas there were 40,000 female domestics "plus an arbitrary 10,000 addition for other females." There was no specific discussion of rural female workers, but an estimate of 13,000 free domestic servants was made, and Lebergott's worksheets indicate that these were female. Paul David (1966) treated these rural domestics as females. The addition of these 13,000 female domestics brings the total to 63,000 female workers. The 1810 figure (p. 139) had no age specification, but the 1820 estimates (p. 140, n. 55) were referred to as those 10 years of age and over. For 1830 (p. 141) he specified 75,000 in manufacturing, to which must be added his estimate of domestic servants. It appears that all servants were female (160,000), as was specified in 1810, 1820, and 1840. I assumed likewise for other years. I derived the 1840 figure as a residual of Lebergott's total free workforce less his estimates of free male workers (p. 142). Lebergott did specify that there were 240,000 domestics, which by subtraction from the 390,000 leaves 150,000 females in manufacturing. This figure is certainly consistent with the number he must have estimated in industrial pursuits. He did not cite a specific figure, but noted that one was derived by interpolation between the 1830 figure of 75,000 and the 1850 one of 220,000. He did specify clearly that the figures for 1840 pertained to females 16 and over. His discussion of the 1840 estimate implies that the 1830 and 1850 figures should pertain to those 16 years and over, but it is not specified in either of these years. For 1860, Lebergott explicitly included an estimate of females aged 10–15 years (p. 146, n. 73). I have therefore included an estimate for the 10–14-year age group. Lebergott used a rate of 6.4% for those aged 10–15 years (the 1900 rate for native whites), whereas I used a rate of 5.1% for those aged 10–14 years. This figure was based on the 1900 data (United States Census 1900, pp. lxvii, cxviii). The rate of 8.1% for all females aged 10–14 was converted to a rate for native whites on the basis of the participation rates for those aged 10–15. In 1900, the rates for 10–15-year-olds were 6.4% for native whites and 10.2% for all females, giving a ratio of .627. In 1860 there were 1,553,234 free females aged 10–14 years in the population (*Historical Statistics* 1975, ser. A:122), yielding 79,214 gainful workers in that age group. The bulk of the 1860 female workforce, those aged 15 and over, was calculated by subtracting the revised estimate of free male workers aged 15 and over (7,935,000) from the 1860 census count of gainful workers (8,235,557); the latter figure excluding 51,486 students, nuns, and sisters of charity (United States Census 1900, p. liii). The result is 840,557.

Agricultural Workforce Estimates

*Slaves*

I followed the procedures outlined by Lebergott for estimating the number of slaves in agriculture (see table 12.A.3). I obtained figures on the number of slaves 10 years of age and over, allocated 95% of

**Table 12.A.3**    Revised Estimates of the Agricultural Workforce United States, 1800–1860 (Thousands of Workers)

| | | Free Males in Agriculture | | | |
|---|---|---|---|---|---|
| Year | Slaves | 10–14 Years | 15 Years and Over | 10 Years and Over | Total |
| 1800 | 480 | — | —. | 785 | 1,265 |
| 1810 | 680 | — | — | 1,117 | 1,797 |
| 1820 | 885 | — | — | 1,577 | 2,462 |
| 1830 | 1,082 | — | — | 1,862 | 2,944 |
| 1840 | 1,360 | — | — | 2,160 | 3,520 |
| 1850 | 1,807 | 182 | 2,405 | 2,587 | 4,394 |
| 1860 | 2,252 | 234 | 3,336 | 3,570 | 5,822 |

these to the rural areas, and calculated the number in agriculture as 87% of this rural base. Lebergott, in fact, estimated the slave farm workforce as 90% of the rural figure (except in 1860), which implies that the entire rural slave workforce was in farming. The 87% approach allows for 3% to be engaged in nonfarm occupations, a figure which seems low in light of other evidence (see Weiss 1975; Crawford 1980).

The 1800 census data put the urban share of the slave population at 3%. In view of the fact that I have not adequately assessed this figure and have not revised the share in other years, I have adopted Lebergott's 5% figure for all years.

*Free Males*

For 1850 and 1860 Lebergott estimated the 10–15-year-old males in farming as equal to 17% of the population. Since I have used a much different participation rate for those aged 10–14 (namely, 18.2%), I could not assume the same agricultural participation rate of 17%. The share of 10–14-year-old gainful workers in agriculture might be higher than that for 10–15-year-olds, because the 15-year-olds would have had some greater freedom of job choice. Still it seems unlikely that the share would be as high as 93% (17 ÷ 18.2), when the 10–15-year-old share implicit in Lebergott's data was only 75% (17 ÷ 22.6). In 1900, the only year for which we have reliable data, the respective shares were 74% for 10–14-year-olds and 70% for 10–15-year-olds. By assuming that the same ratio of shares (74/70 = 1.06) prevailed in 1800, the 10–14-year-olds' share was placed at 80% (1.06 × 75%).

The 1850 and 1860 figures for males 15 and over are from the census (1900, *Occupations,* p. liii) and are the sum of farmers, planters, and overseers; agricultural laborers; dairymen; gardeners, etc.; and one-half the figure for stock raisers, etc. In 1850, laborers were *probably* included with farmers and planters, and some women were included in the 1860 census count.

The 1840 figure for males 10 and over was taken from Lebergott (p. 155) and is the 1840 census count of agricultural employment minus all rural slaves aged 10 and over. The 1820 figure for males 10 and over was derived by subtracting the slave farm workers from the total farm workforce. The latter was derived by following Lebergott's procedure (pp. 155, 156). The 1820 census figure of 2,491,000 workers was deducted from the revised labor force total of 3,126,000, obtaining 635,000. I then deducted the 160,000 females, allocated 83% of the balance to agriculture (393,000), and combined it with the 1820 census count for agriculture (2,069,000) (United States Census 1900, p. xxx).

For 1800, I produced two estimates of the free farm workforce, both of which are consistent with the revisions incorporated in the total workforce figures. The variant which is shown in table 12.A.3 was derived following Lebergott's procedures; the alternative, discussed subsequently, was based on David's procedures. In the reported version, the free farm workforce is the sum of estimates for free white males and for free colored males. The free colored farm workforce was derived by allocating the revised estimate of free colored male workers between urban and rural areas; the former being counted as nonfarm workers, the latter as farm workers. This is the procedure used by Lebergott, but his figures and mine differ for two reasons. First, he apparently included free colored females, and my revision is confined to males. Second, his urban/rural breakdown was based on the 1790 data for five cities, while my breakdown is based on the census counts for 1800, which show that 18.0% of the free colored population lived in cities (see text). The rural count of free colored gainful workers, then, is 82% of 26,000. The free white male farm workforce was derived as a residual, again following Lebergott's method. The residual is simply the difference between the total number of white workers and those engaged in navigation, urban, rural nonfarm occupations. Each of these was estimated independently by Lebergott. I have accepted his estimate of navigation employment (50,000), and followed his procedures to derive the other two but obtained different figures.

The revised urban estimate differs from his because I have used different urban population estimates, and a different participation rate for males aged 10–14 years. I used the 1800 census data to construct the urban/rural distribution for each age and sex category of the white population, while Lebergott used the 1790 census evidence for five cities (p. 135). The disaggregated evidence of the 1800 census shows that only 7.3% of the free males aged 16 and over, and 5.5% of those aged 10–15 years lived in cities, figures noticeably below the 9.1% figure used by Lebergott. My urban workforce statistic is lower as well, because I used a participation rate of .182 for males aged 10–14, while Lebergott used the much higher rate (.872) more pertinent to those aged 15 and over.

The rural nonfarm figures differ because I revised the ratios used to derive the number of workers. It appears that Lebergott multiplied the male population 10 years and over by a ratio of rural nonfarm workers to males over 15. I have adjusted the ratio (derived from the 1840 census data) to relate to males 10 years of age and over. Additionally, I excluded Virginia from the calculation on the grounds that in 1840 it showed a substantially higher ratio (22.2%) for the numerically important category of manufactures and trades than that in any other southern state, or for the United States (16%). Thus I used a ratio of 11% instead of the 17.6% used by Lebergott. The exact calculation of the ratio was

11.7%, but I rounded down to allow for the fact that the 1840 census worker counts included some females and slaves (United States Census 1900, p. xxx; United States Census 1940, pp. 373–74).

Lebergott does make important distinctions between farmers and farm laborers, but these are for use in assessing the results, and are not necessary to derive the workforce itself.

An alternative estimate of 533,000 free male farm workers was derived using Paul David's approach. I used his balance equation, his two assumed ratios of family heads to rural nonfarm workforce (.56) and farm labor to farmers (.4), and the same figure for navigation employment used by David and Lebergott. I substituted my revised figures for white male workers, urban white male workers, and free colored in farming, and also adjusted the number of white family heads used in the balance equation. This last revision has a decided impact on the results. Since this estimate was not used the details are presented in another section of the appendix.

Finally, the free farm workforce in 1810 and 1830 was estimated. Lebergott calculated his figures for these years as 150% of the number of free farmers (p. 155–56). The number of free farmers was apparently estimated on the basis of the ratio of farmers to rural white families in other years. This required that he derive a breakdown of the free farm workforce between farmers and laborers in these other years. I have chosen a more direct approach, bypassing the derivation of the farmer-laborer breakdown. I simply calculated the ratio of the free farm workforce to rural white families for the years 1800, 1820, 1840, 1850, and 1860; and estimated the 1810 and 1830 ratios by interpolation. In fact I used the mean of the ratios for the immediately adjacent years. The data are summarized in table 12.A.4.

### Alternative Estimates of the Farm Workforce, 1800

Paul David's revisions of Lebergott's figures included an alternative approach to estimating the industrial distribution of the workforce. His idea was to avoid making a direct estimate of the rural nonfarm workforce based on assumptions about the temporal stability of the relationship between nonfarm employment and population (1966, p. A-11). He preferred to use a balance equation, which enabled him to specify selected parameters about the workforce and its distribution, and then simultaneously solve for the number of rural nonfarm workers, white male farmers, and farm laborers.

In order to solve the equation, he had to have estimates of six items: the total white male workforce; the white male urban workforce; those engaged in navigation, fishing, and whaling; white male rural heads of families; free colored male farmers; and free colored male farm laborers; and he had to assume values for two ratios, the ratio of heads of

**Table 12.A.4**    **Estimating the Free Male Farm Workforce (Thousands) in 1810 and 1830**

| Year | Rural White Families[a] (1) | Free Males in Farming[b] (2) | Ratio Col. 2 ÷ Col. 1 (3) |
|---|---|---|---|
| 1800 | 700 | 783 | 1.119 |
| 1810 | 947 | 1,117 (est.) | (1.179)[c] |
| 1820 | 1,274 | 1,577 | 1.238 |
| 1830 | 1,685 | 1,862 (est.) | (1.105)[c] |
| 1840 | 2,223 | 2,160 | .972 |
| 1850 | 2,945 | 2,587 | .878 |
| 1860 | 3,978 | 3,570 | .897 |

[a]Lebergott's worksheets. My 1800 figure differs from his (708,000) because I divided the total number of families between urban and rural on the basis of the distribution of free males 16 and over. The rural share is 92.7%.

[b]The figures for all years except 1810 and 1830 are discussed in the preceding notes and are presented in table 12.A.3. The figures for 1810 and 1830 were derived using the interpolated ratios contained in col. 3.

[c]These figures are the means of the values in the two adjacent years.

families to white males among the rural nonfarm workforce, and the ratio of free farm laborers to free farmers.

The balance equation can be expressed in reduced form to solve for the number of rural nonfarm workers, $X$. Once that value is known, one can subsequently derive the number of white farmers and the number of farm laborers. The current workforce revisions include changes in a number of the input values, so the equation must be recalculated. The equation, the variables, the input values, and the solutions are presented in table 12.A.5 for the original and revised versions.

While five of the estimated inputs take on different values in the revised version, the one of significance is that for white, male rural family heads (658,000 vs. 610,000). Both of these figures rest on Lebergott's estimate of 755,000 white families in 1800 (p. 135). Assuming that the 87.2% participation rate for free white males applies to this group gives a total of 658,000 white heads of families in the workforce. This would appear to be how Paul David obtained his figure. However, this figure includes those family heads engaged in navigation or urban occupations, and an estimate of their number must be deducted to obtain the number of rural heads of families. I have assumed that family heads were distributed between urban and rural areas in the same proportion as males 16 years and over (United States Census 1800). This gives a rural share of 92.7%, or 610,000 white, rural heads of families in the workforce. This leaves 48,000 nonrural heads, and for this group, an implicit .38 ratio of heads to workforce. Lebergott's

Table 12.A.5    **Balance Equation Estimates of the Farm and Rural Nonfarm Workforce United States, 1800 (Thousands of Workers)**

|  | David's Values | Revised Values |
|---|---|---|
| **Estimated inputs** | | |
| $T$ = white male workforce | 1,033.8 | 1,047 |
| $U$ = white, urban male workers | 91.3 | 75 |
| $N$ = navigation, fishing, whaling employment | 50.0 | 50 |
| $H$ = white, male rural family heads | 658.0 | 610 |
| $CF$ = free colored farmers | 8.5 | 3 |
| $CL$ = free colored farm laborers | 45.0 | 18 |
| **Assumed ratios** | | |
| $hr$ = family heads/rural nonfarm workforce | .56 | .56 |
| $fr$ = farm laborers/farmers | .40 | .40 |
| **Solutions** | | |
| $X$ = rural nonfarm workforce | 60 | 387 |
| $F$ = white, male farmers | 624.3 | 393 |
| $L$ = white, male farm laborers | 208.2 | 140 |

*Sources:* David (1966), table A-2; tables 12.4, 12.A.2. The reduced form of the balance equation is

$$X = \frac{T - U - N - H - fr(H + CF) + CL}{1 - hr - fr \times hr}$$

White farmers $(F) = H - .56X$.
White farm laborers $(L) = .4 (F + CF) - CL$.

original figures implied a .34 ratio. Both of these ratios are below the .56 ratio David assumed for rural nonfarm families. An alternative approach would be to assume that the .56 ratio applied to this group, but this would reduce further the number of rural heads and the farm workforce.

The revised calculation showing 387,000 rural nonfarm workers, implies as well that the farm share of the workforce was only 62.4%, a figure which seems much too low. The result is of course influenced by the assumed ratios, and since the workforce figures have changed, these should probably change as well. Obviously one could alter these ratios to produce reasonable results, but I have not done so. Instead, I have explored the sensitivity of the estimates to changes in selected parameters. My judgment is that the results are very sensitive to changes in selected parameters, and therefore one must be very cautious about accepting figures obtained by this method. A summary of the sensitivity experiments is presented in table 12.A.6.

None of the input changes are extraordinary, all being based on some piece of evidence or imputing a tolerable error to the input variable. Consider just a few examples. An error of only 5% in the estimated number of rural family heads would lower David's figure from 658,000 to 625,000 and reduce the farm share of the workforce by 13 percentage

**Table 12.A.6**    **Sensitivity of the Balance Equation Method of Estimation**

|  | David's Figures | | Revised Figures | |
| --- | --- | --- | --- | --- |
|  | Rural Nonfarm (Thousands) | Farm Share (%) | Rural Nonfarm (Thousands) | Farm Share (%) |
| Base values (table 12.A.5) | 60 | 83 | 387 | 62 |
| New values of selected parameters | | | | |
| *Rural heads* | | | | |
| 658,000 (David's base) | 60 | 83 | 76 | 81 |
| 610,000 (revised base) | 371 | 64 | 387 | 62 |
| 634,000 (midpoint; 4% change) | 215 | 74 | 232 | 72 |
| *Head/worker ratio* | | | | |
| .3 (Lebergott: rural nonfarm) | 22 | 85 | 144 | 77 |
| .71 (David: farm sector) | 2,150 | −40 | 13,940 | −755 |
| .73 (David: white male workforce) | −586 | 121 | −3,803 | 315 |
| *Laborer/farmer ratio* | | | | |
| .3 (arbitrarily lower) | 293 | 69 | 533 | 54 |
| .52 (Lebergott) | −451 | 113 | 67 | 82 |

points. At certain levels, changes in the ratios produce bizarre results. If the head/worker ratio is set at .71, the ratio implicit in David's farm figures, the rural nonfarm workforce exceeds the total labor force. A further rise to the .73 ratio implicit in his total workforce data gives a negative number (David 1966, p. A-14, A-19, and tables 12.A.2, 12.A.3). Likewise a positive to negative swing occurs when the laborer to farmer ratio changes within a narrow range between David's ratio (.4) and the .52 ratio noted by Lebergott. Indeed, the rural nonfarm workforce becomes negative when the ratio equals .42.

# Appendix B
## *Census Evidence on Fifteen-Year-Old Workers*

There has long been ambiguity surrounding the census age coverage of gainful workers reported in 1850 and 1860. The odds are that the uncertainty regarding the inclusion of 15-year-old workers originated at the time of the census surveys and has persisted to the present. The exact treatment of these 15-year-olds was not crucial to the present workforce estimation, but since I did treat this group as being included in the census count in those years, it seemed pertinent to present some evidence in support of that decision. Moreover, since such data were not previously available, the evidence may be of interest in its own right to some other researchers.

There are two sets of data. The first (table 12.A.7) is a random sample of rural, northern households taken from the 1860 manuscript census (Bateman and Foust 1976). The sample is representative of the region, and not necessarily each state. I have reported the results on a state basis to suggest the possible variation that may have prevailed. The second body of evidence (table 12.A.8) is a less systematic collection of data from the censuses of 1850 and 1860. That evidence was taken from manuscript schedules that were readily at hand, and was not compiled as a representative sample of any state or region. Thus that evidence is presented by county, or counties in some cases, for which it represents a 100% sample. Its chief merit is that it contains data for 1850.

Both sets of data make clear that 15-year-olds were recorded as workers and that some of these youths were classified as farmers, not merely farm helpers. Moreover, it is also clear that females were included in the 1860 census count. Indeed, the search of the 1850 schedules also turned up four females, aged 15, who reported occupations.

**Table 12.A.7     Random Sample Evidence on 15-Year-Old Workers, 1860**

| State | Sample Sizes | | Percentage with Occupation | | Distribution of Those with Occupations | | |
|---|---|---|---|---|---|---|---|
| | Males | Females | Males | Females | Farmer | Laborer | Oth |
| Connecticut | 10 | 9 | 20% | 11% | 0 | 0 | 100 |
| Illinois | 96 | 91 | 16 | 21 | 3 | 44 | 53 |
| Indiana | 332 | 301 | 29 | 7 | 37 | 46 | 17 |
| Iowa | 47 | 53 | 45 | 25 | 12 | 29 | 59 |
| Kansas | 34 | 30 | 18 | 0 | 67 | 33 | 0 |
| Maryland | 41 | 30 | 15 | 3 | 0 | 57 | 43 |
| Michigan | 75 | 73 | 63 | 45 | 13 | 38 | 49 |
| Minnesota | 16 | 14 | 25 | 7 | 40 | 0 | 60 |
| Missouri | 68 | 68 | 40 | 9 | 27 | 52 | 21 |
| New Hampshire | 21 | 36 | 43 | 8 | 0 | 58 | 42 |
| New Jersey | 9 | 16 | 33 | 6 | 25 | 0 | 75 |
| New York | 192 | 194 | 60 | 46 | 0 | 55 | 45 |
| Ohio | 58 | 45 | 59 | 31 | 0 | 72 | 28 |
| Pennsylvania | 160 | 139 | 28 | 7 | 32 | 42 | 26 |
| Vermont | 9 | 8 | 22 | 25 | 0 | 75 | 25 |
| Wisconsin | 24 | 31 | 0 | 3 | 0 | 0 | 100 |
| Totals | 1,192 | 1,138 | 36 | 19 | 14 | 48 | 38 |

*Source:* Bateman and Foust (1976).

**Table 12.A.8    Unsystematic Evidence on 15-Year-Old Males, 1850 and 1860**

| County, State | Sample Size | Percentage with Occupation | Distribution of Those with Occupations (%) | | |
|---|---|---|---|---|---|
| | | | Farmer | Laborer | Other |
| 1850 | | | | | |
| Washington, White, and Yell, Arkansas | 253 | 18 | 20 | 72 | 9 |
| Frederick, Maryland | 405 | 27 | 21 | 58 | 21 |
| Rockingham and Rowan, North Carolinia | 214 | 29 | 8 | 82 | 10 |
| Venango and Warren Pennsylvania | 336 | 33 | 65 | 15 | 19 |
| Grant, Wisconsin | 131 | 56 | 44 | 29 | 27 |
| 1860 | | | | | |
| Frederick, Maryland | 413 | 31 | 1 | 79 | 20 |
| Warren, Pennsylvania | 156 | 42 | 59 | 8 | 33 |
| Grant, Wisconsin | 289 | 66 | — | 51 | 49 |

*Source:* Manuscript census schedules.
*Note:* The 1850 results include 4 females, aged 15 years, who reported occupations. For 1860, when females were to be counted we found 104 females aged 15 years who reported occupations; 27% of all 15-year-old gainful workers.

The evidence also shows great variation across states. For males the rates range from zero in Wisconsin to 63% in Michigan, while for females the range is zero (Kansas) to 46% (New York). Such wide variation suggests that the inconsistencies of census enumerators might have been at work, as well as real economic behavior; although the 1900 evidence also indicates a wide range of rates, 20%–72% for males and 4%–47% for females (Miller and Brainerd 1957, table L-3).

# Notes

1. For 1860 Lebergott estimated the slave workforce state by state, using the 1850 participation rates for free males. David assumed that the weighted average would approximate 87.2%, but in fact it equaled only 86%. The consequence is that David's revision for 1860, as well as Lebergott's original estimate, is still inconsistent with other years.

2. For example, Lebergott relied on the 1949 edition of *Historical Statistics,* a source that has been revised and expanded twice since then.

3. In several years, 1820, 1840, and esp. 1850 and 1860, the census provided data on the workforce, which enabled more direct estimation of free males aged 16 years and over.

4. The mean rate of 36% for males is above the 25% figure used by Lebergott. This surely reflects the fact that this sample evidence pertains to rural areas where the workforce participation of farm children would give an upward bias. On the other hand, the sample data exclude the South, where the participation rate for children was typically above that for the nation.

5. The 1900 data suggest that the inclusion of 15-year-olds lowers the participation rate by about 1.5 percentage points. The rate for those 16 and over was 90.7%. Using a participation rate of 43% for 15-year-olds (the rate which prevailed for 14- and 15-year-olds), the rate for those 15 years and over would have been 89.2% (Miller and Brainerd 1957, tables L-1 and L-2). If the 1850 census undercounted 15-year-old workers, the derived participation rate of 87.2% would further underestimate the number of workers 16 years of age and over.

6. I used a rate of 18.2% for those aged 10–14 years. In order to make the comparison for the 10–15-year group I used the 87.2% figure for 15-year-olds. The implied rate for the combined group aged 10–15 is 27.7, slightly above the figure of 25 used by David.

7. I have used an estimate of 63,000 females, the same figure used by David. There is some ambiguity surrounding this estimate as 13,000 domestic servants may be included with females or rural nonfarm male workers (Lebergott 1966, p. 136).

8. The revised slave figures, as well as the original ones, differ from Paul David's estimates of slave workers for 1820 and 1840. This is because he revised Lebergott's slave figures in light of text statements that the participation rate used was 87% in those years. However, the text was wrong, and the figures required no such upward revision.

9. The error raises serious doubts about this method and the estimate. The error arose because the method yields a negative number of female workers in several states (namely, Illinois).

10. In 1860, the estimate includes some unspecified number of females who were recorded in the census figures. The same is true for 1820 and 1840, and thus in 1810 and 1830 by interpolation.

11. Lebergott estimated the 10–15-year-olds in agriculture as 17% of the male population in that age group. Since 15-year-olds were counted in the census, this calculation resulted in an overcount of 44,000. For those 10–14 years of age, the revised calculation used a lower overall participation rate (18% vs. 25%) and thus a lower agricultural participation rate (14.4% vs. 17%). This resulted in 42,000 fewer farm workers aged 10–14 years.

12. The 1800 census also yields a lower urban share of the slave population (3.1 vs. 5.0). I have not used this revision as it would make the 1800 slave figures inconsistent with other years.

13. Paul David quite correctly asks whether the 1840 southern evidence is representative of conditions in 1800 (1966, A-11).

14. It is certainly true that some free colored females were employed in farming, but conceptually the estimates were to exclude females (Lebergott 1966, p. 139). It would be easy enough to add an appropriate number of free colored females once one had a reasonable estimate of their participation rate. I have estimated that the free colored female population included 9,000 aged 10–15 and 31,000 aged 16 and over. Using the male participation rates yields 28,600 workers, with 5,100 in urban areas and 23,500 in farming.

15. Extrapolation of the post-1870 ratios of urban laborers, not otherwise specified, to urban population would yield 664,000 rural laborers, n.o.s. in 1860 and 718,000 in 1850 (Weiss 1975, p. 108). The addition of these workers to the farm workforce would raise the farm shares to 62.3% in 1850 and 58.6% in 1860. Since this would raise the 1850 share above the 1840, the adjustment appears excessive. Nonetheless, it does suggest that the farm figures for these years may be substantially underestimated.

16. According to Lebergott, "examination of the unpublished Census schedules for 1820 and 1840 indicates [females] were not included in those years," so the only problem may be the inclusion of free nonwhite females in 1860 (1966, p. 139).

17. Assuming that the estimate of 158,000 (table 12.4) includes urban as well as rural, and in the same proportion as males 16 years and over, then the figure should be reduced by 11,500 workers and the farm sector increased by that amount.

18. The sensitivity of that approach can be seen in the results derived by revising the number of rural family heads used in the calculation. David used a figure of 658,000 which is that for all gainfully occupied family heads (87.2% × 755,000 heads). This figure includes heads of families engaged in navigation and urban occupations. By adjusting the figure to include only rural heads of families (610,000) the resulting solution for the rural nonfarm workforce is 387,000 instead of 60,000; and the farm share falls from 82.7% to 62.0%. This is discussed in greater detail in the appendix.

19. The revised growth rates were derived using David's formula, the present workforce estimates and David's other input data, some of which (e.g., farm productivity index) had to be revalued in light of the workforce changes (David 1967, table 1). David has revised his conjectural estimates of growth to 1.1% per year (1977, p. 194), a figure identical to the present calculation. The change, however, reflects the use of a broader measure of GDP, and if that broader measure were used in the present calculation, presumably the result would be a rate below 1.1%. The comparison of the present calculation of 1.09% and the original value of 1.27% more accurately suggests the impact of the workforce revisions.

# Comment    Stanley Lebergott

Weiss's paper divides into two parts, "revised estimates" and "implications."

## Revised Estimates

His revisions in my published estimates are readily summarized:

Percentage Revisions in
Lebergott Estimates[1]

| | By Thomas Weiss | | | By Paul David | | |
|---|---|---|---|---|---|---|
| | Labor Force | | | Gainful | | |
| Year | Total | Slaves | Agriculture | Workers | Slaves | Agriculture |
| 1800 | −1% | −1% | 10% | * | +3% | * |
| 1810 | 1 | * | −8 | * | * | * |
| 1820 | * | 1 | * | 1 | 3 | * |
| 1830 | * | * | * | * | * | 1 |
| 1840 | * | * | * | 1 | 3 | 1 |
| 1850 | * | * | −3 | * | * | * |
| 1860 | * | 5 | −2 | 1 | 3 | 1 |

*Under 1% (includes zero).

Stanley Lebergott is professor of economics at Wesleyan University.

1. Lebergott (1984, p. 66). An earlier version Lebergott (1964) and Volume 30 of the proceedings of this Conference had an arithmetic error for the 1800 labor force, noted in 1967 by Paul David. See Weiss, table 11.1, note a.

Surely this is very small beer indeed. (Weiss's few noticeable changes, for agriculture, far exceed the 1%—or smaller—revisions proposed by David.)

## Implications

His numbers may carry "important implications for our understanding of long-term economic changes in productivity." But Lady Cotton's question does come to mind. (Her husband—a sixteenth-century luminary and amateur scientist—once inspected a dusty object; wondering whether "it was Moses shoe, or Noah's, wond'ring at the strange Shape and Fashion of it: But 'Mr. Cotton,' says she, 'are you sure it is a shoe?' ")

Weiss is sure that his "revisions in the farm workforce do imply notable differences in farm productivity." Indeed, they do differ from the estimates by Robert Gallman.[2]

Factor Productivity in Agriculture
Annual Rate of Change

| Years | Gallman (1975) | Weiss (1984) |
|---|---|---|
| 1800–1850 | +.14 | +.43 |
| 1850–1900 | +.80 | +.49 |

That Gallman increased my 1850 farm worker figure by 600,000, while Weiss reduced it, partly accounts for their differing productivity estimates.

How did Weiss arrive at a surgically precise (3%) revision in the 1850 number of persons in agriculture—more than a century and a quarter ago? He outlines no procedure, but does cite two sources. One proves to be a collection of narratives to WPA interviewers by ex-slaves, some 70 years after slavery ended. The other source appears to be what he terms his "unsystematic sample."

---

2. Since reference to Gallman's (1975) work has been struck from Weiss's revised draft, I may usefully cite it. Weiss has retained the workforce estimates he presented at the conference, and description of his productivity estimation appears to be the same. The estimates he presented there presumably serve as basis for his assertion that they "alter our perception of development in the antebellum period." Weiss originally emphasized the strength of his work by noting that these productivity rates were much the same 1800–1850 and 1850–1900 as Gallman's 1971 work suggested, but unlike David's 1967 study. We cite Gallman's later work.

Without commenting on Gallman's 1975 farm productivity study, he goes on to the broader topic of total productivity, as treated by Paul David (1967).[3] Since his changes in the farm totals may yield compensating changes in the nonfarm totals of a fixed population, Weiss's "implications" may prove premature.

Some recognition is due to the many words and numbers Weiss presents for 15-year-olds. They lead to an unwarranted adjustment in my estimates (and those by others).[4] The adjustment rests on his unsupported guess that the occupation tables in the 1850 census, and the 1860, were incorrectly labeled (and incorrectly labeled by Walter Wilcox, Wesley Mitchell, and Alba Edwards in 1900 when summarizing the historic occupation record).

That improbable assumption rests on his discovery that some enumerators reported occupations for 15-year-olds. But since Jefferson American censuses have had editing and transcription instructions, plus review procedures—all to select, adapt, and correctly summarize the original enumerator schedules. We need a stronger basis than guess to conclude that the reported census figures for those "over 15 years of age" incorrectly include those aged 15.

One awaits with interest further work by the National Bureau of Economic Research project of which this study is part.

# Reply    Thomas Weiss

Lebergott makes three points about my paper, and I shall address each in turn.

His first point, that my effort produced few noticeable changes, simply underscores my main conclusion. My wording, that "Lebergott produced a carefully constructed set of figures," is not quite as eloquent as "this is very small beer indeed," but the point is the same. We can have some faith in our existing body of knowledge. It seems to me

---

3. David has since superseded his 1967 estimates.

4. No economic historian, old or new, has devoted so much attention to their role in the nineteenth-century labor force. His original table 12.A.8, labeled "unsystematic evidence on 16-year-old workers in 1860," is now accompanied by a table termed "Random Sample Evidence. . . ." Is the "random sample" evidence preferable? One would think so. But his estimates have not changed from the earlier paper, which presented only the "unsystematic evidence." Moreover, his "random sample totals" for 15-year-old males imply that 28% of them lived in Indiana. (The census locates fewer than 5% of United States 10–15-year-olds there.)

helpful that these assurances come from someone other than the researcher who produced the original figures.

His second point is that my revised agricultural figures are questionable. He is particularly skeptical about the 1850 revision, suggesting that I did not outline my estimating procedures and based my revisions on two unworthy sources, ex-slave interviews and an unsystematic sample. Obviously, my presentation must be unclear.

I cited the WPA interviews of ex-slaves only to suggest that more slaves worked at nonfarm tasks than was implied by his estimation. I did not use this evidence to reduce the estimate of agricultural slaves. Nor is the 3% difference in our estimates due to the use of an unsystematic sample of 15-year-olds working on farms. That evidence, along with a random sample containing similar information, was presented only for the purpose of showing that 15-year-old workers were already included in the census counts of 1850 and 1860.

Our 1850 farm figures differ because we used different participation rates for rural slaves. In the former case, Lebergott used the participation rate for those aged 10–15 years, while I used the more appropriate rate for those aged 10–14 years. My rate was not taken from the sample data, but from the same source that Lebergott obtained his figure, namely, the census of 1900. In estimating the slave farm workforce I used a farm participation rate for rural slaves of .87 instead of the .90 he used. This lower rate was not taken from the slave reminiscences, it was taken from Lebergott! He argued in his original article that the .87 figure would allow for those rural slaves engaged in nonfarm tasks. Unfortunately, and unbeknown to Lebergott, his research assistant did not agree and used the higher figure. In my opinion, it is these sorts of changes that make the revised figures more consistent and precise.

Finally, Lebergott sees little value in the evidence on 15-year-old workers (contrary to what he says, there is no evidence on 16-year-olds). I am sure he is correct in claiming that no economic historian has devoted so much attention to this group of workers. My reason for devoting any attention to them is simply to straighten out the record. As far as I can tell, all previous researchers, including Lebergott, David, and myself, behaved as if 15-year-old workers were not included in the census counts of 1850 and 1860. The fact of the matter is that they were included, and I am willing to admit I was wrong. I presented the evidence not only because it shows that 15-year-old workers were included in the census count, but also because it contains other information that might be of use to other researchers. Lebergott has, however, simply misinterpreted the evidence and my use of it.

# References

Bateman, Fred, and Foust, James. 1976. Agricultural and demographic records for rural households in the North, 1860. Manuscript Census Sample.

Carson, Daniel. 1949. Changes in the industrial composition of manpower since the Civil War. *Studies in Income and Wealth* 11. New York: National Bureau of Economic Research.

Crawford, Steven. 1980. Quantified memory: A study of the WPA and Fisk University slave narrative collections. Ph.D. dissertation. University of Chicago.

David, Paul. 1966. Technical appendices to U.S. real product growth before 1840. Mimeographed. Stanford University.

———. 1967. U.S. real product growth before 1840: New evidence, controlled conjectures. *Journal of Economic History* (June): 151–96.

———. 1977. Invention and accumulation in America's economic growth: A nineteenth century parable. In *Carnegie-Rochester Conference Series on Public Policy*, vol. 6, ed. Karl Brunner and Allen Meltzer. Amsterdam: North-Holland.

Durand, John D. 1948. *The labor force in the United States, 1890–1960*. New York: Social Science Research Council.

Edwards, Alba M. 1943. *Comparative occupation statistics for the United States, 1870 to 1940*. Washington, D.C.

Fabricant, Solomon. 1949. The changing industrial distribution of gainful workers: Comments on the decennial statistics, 1820–1940. *Studies in Income and Wealth* 11. New York: National Bureau of Economic Research.

Gallman, Robert. 1975. In *Essays in nineteenth-century economic history*, ed. David Klingaman and Richard Vedder.

Goldin, Claudia, and Sokoloff, Kenneth. 1981. Women, children, and industrialization in the early republic: Evidence from the manufacturing censuses. NBER Working Paper no. 75.

Goldsmith, Raymond. 1959. Long period growth in income and product, 1839–1960. *Hearings before the Joint Economic Committee*, 86th Cong., 2d Sess.

Higman, B. W. 1984. Population and labor in the British Caribbean in the early nineteenth century. In this volume.

*Historical statistics of the United States*. 1975. Washington, D.C.: Department of Commerce.

Kaplan, David, and Casey, Claire. 1958. Occupational trends in the United States, 1900 to 1950. United States Census Bureau, Working Paper no. 5.

Lebergott, Stanley. 1960. Population change and the supply of labor. In *Demographic and economic change in developed countries*. Princeton: Princeton University Press.

———. 1964. *Manpower in economic growth*. New York: McGraw-Hill.

———. 1966. Labor force and employment, 1800–1960. *Studies in Income and Wealth* 30. New York: National Bureau of Economic Research.

———. 1984. *The Americans: An economic record*. New York: Norton.

Long, Clarence D. 1958. *The labor force under changing income and employment*. Princeton: Princeton University Press.

Miller, Ann, and Brainerd, Carol. 1957. Labor force estimates. In *Population redistribution and economic growth, United States, 1870 to 1950*. Philadelphia: American Philosophical Society.

Thomas, Brinley. 1966. General comment. *Studies in Income and Wealth* 30. New York: National Bureau of Economic Research.

United States Census Office. 1800. *Second census, return of the whole number of persons*.

———. 1830. *Fifth census, population*.

———. 1840. *Sixth census, population*.

———. 1850. *Seventh census, population*.

———. 1860. *Eighth census, population*.

———. 1880. *Tenth census, statistics of the population of the United States*.

———. 1900. *Special reports: Occupations at the twelfth census*.

Weiss, Thomas. 1975. *The service sector in the United States, 1839 through 1899*. New York: Arno.

———. 1980. Productivity growth, factor substitutability and the rise of the service workforce, 1840 to 1900. Mimeographed. University of Kansas.

———. 1983. An assessment of the workforce statistics for the 19th century United States. Mimeographed. University of Kansas.

Whelpton, P. K. 1926. Occupational groups in the United States, 1820–1920. *Journal of the American Statistical Association* (September).

# IV    Sectoral Studies

# 13    Productivity Growth in Manufacturing during Early Industrialization: Evidence from the American Northeast, 1820–1860

Kenneth L. Sokoloff

## 13.1  Introduction

It has long been recognized that industrialization got under way in the United States early in the nineteenth century and was largely concentrated in the Northeast throughout the antebellum period. The dramatic sectoral reallocation of resources that accompanied this process is generally acknowledged to have yielded a significant gain in measured per capita income, if only because resources in that region were more productive in industries other than agriculture. The extent of productivity growth within sectors, however, remains unclear. This gap in our knowledge has been a serious obstacle to improving our understanding of this initial phase of industrialization, because the record of productivity is so closely related to issues of the sources, location, timing, and nature of this episode in American economic growth.

Evidence on the progress realized in manufacturing, in particular, would have a direct bearing on whether the surge of rapid industrial

Kenneth L. Sokoloff is associate professor of economics at the University of California, Los Angeles, and a faculty research fellow at the National Bureau of Economic Research.

This paper was substantially revised during the year following its presentation at the Williamsburg Conference. I thus had the opportunity to take full advantage of the penetrating comments received from Jeffrey Williamson, and the excellent advice offered by Robert Allen, Paul David, Lance Davis, Stanley Engerman, Robert Fogel, Gerald Friedman, Robert Gallman, Peter Lindert, Michael Waldman, and Thomas Weiss. I also benefited from seminar discussions of early versions of the paper at Northwestern University, UCLA, the University of British Columbia, the University of Chicago, Indiana University, the University of Iowa, and the All–University of California Conference in Economic History, held in Los Angeles in May 1985. I am grateful to James Lin for careful research assistance, and to the California Institute of Technology, where I was a visiting assistant professor during the reworking of the paper, for research support. Grants from the UCLA Academic Senate, the Institute for Industrial Relations, and the Foundation for Research in Economics and Education are also acknowledged.

expansion in the Northeast was driven by dynamic manufacturing industries that were generating sustained increases in productivity and income or by a declining agricultural sector that was finding it increasingly difficult to compete with producers outside the region. Moreover, industry- specific estimates would help determine to what degree early productivity growth in manufacturing was linked to capital- deepening or capital-augmenting innovations. Some scholars have suggested that these factors were virtual prerequisites for major gains in productivity, while others have emphasized that changes in the organization of labor, increases in the intensity of work, and other alterations in production processes that were not dependent on additional capital equipment per unit of labor may have been important sources of measured advances (Landes 1969, 1985; Marglin 1974; David 1975; Chandler 1977; Sokoloff 1984b; Lazonick and Brush 1985).

Despite the clear significance of the issues involved, there have been few studies of productivity growth during early United States industrialization due to the relative inaccessibility of evidence.[1] Recently collected samples of firm data from the schedules of the 1820 Census of Manufactures and the *McLane Report* of 1832 provide valuable new sources of information, however (Sokoloff 1982). Employing these bodies of evidence in conjunction with the Bateman-Weiss samples of firms from the schedules of both the 1850 and the 1860 Census of Manufactures, and the aggregate data from those censuses, this paper seeks to establish the record of productivity growth in northeastern manufacturing during this critical period of industrial development.

These sources are not without flaws, but the richness of the information they contain makes them together an unequaled collection of material for research on the subject. All of them provide reports of the value of outputs produced and the quantity or value of inputs utilized, and thus indexes of productivity can be estimated for many industries in each of the 4 years. Perhaps the primary concern involving the quality of the data is that the firms included in the four cross-sectional samples from the manufacturing survey and censuses may not be representative of the population of northeastern manufacturing firms during the respective years.[2] Problems of the representativeness of data are always a serious matter and require special care in conducting the analysis. Nevertheless, as will be discussed below, the sample selection biases that afflict these bodies of evidence seem unlikely to be responsible for the qualitative results uncovered.

This paper reports estimates of labor and total factor productivity for 13 manufacturing industries in the Northeast over the period from 1820 to 1860. It finds that although the highly mechanized and capital-intensive industries, such as cotton and wool textiles, realized somewhat more rapid progress than the others did, even the latter managed major advances. The evidence appears to support the conclusion that the manufacturing sector in the Northeast was quite dynamic during this stage of industrialization, and that much of its early productivity growth can be explained by changes in production processes that did not require mechanization or substantial increases in capital intensity. This suggests, as has been argued by a number of recent studies building on an old tradition, that developments such as increases in the division and intensity of labor within firms and other relatively subtle alterations in technique, perhaps stimulated by the expansion of markets, may have played important roles in accounting for the progress achieved.

Estimates of labor productivity over the period are presented in section 13.2 of the paper. The procedures employed in constructing them are discussed in some detail, and although they were consciously designed to yield conservative estimates of the increase in productivity, weighted averages indicate rates of labor productivity growth that are quite high by nineteenth- or twentieth-century standards. There is evidence of an acceleration in the pace of advance, particularly in the less mechanized and capital-intensive industries. Estimates of total factor productivity are presented in section 13.3. They reveal that if one treats firm valuations of their capital investments as relatively accurate assessments of the capital input, as I contend that one should, the data imply that most manufacturing industries realized large gains in total factor productivity over the period. As all classes of industries appear to have manifested similar rates of progress, doubts about the primacy of capital deepening or capital intensity in generating productivity growth are reinforced. Moreover, the estimated advances are of such a magnitude that they appear to account, together with increases in the ratio of raw materials to labor, for nearly all of the rise in labor productivity. Some general remarks on what these findings imply about the early stages of industrialization in the United States are offered in section 13.4.

## 13.2   Estimates of Labor Productivity

There are at least several reasons why the record of labor productivity deserves separate treatment from that of total factor productivity. Perhaps the major one is that movements in labor productivity convey information about the evolution of production methods that is not generally contained in the more comprehensive measure. Since several of the most important issues relating to the development of manufacturing technology during early industrialization concern the direction and extent of changes in factor proportions, it would seem desirable to examine both labor and total factor productivity. The availability of the two series is also useful in that investigation of apparent inconsistencies between them can help to identify problems with the data or of interpretation. Finally, it might be argued that, because movements in output per unit of labor are more closely related to those in per capita income, establishing the record of labor productivity, even in only this single sector of the economy, would by itself directly contribute to our understanding of economic growth during this critical period. The accounting exercise of decomposing the responsibility for increases in labor productivity between changes in factor proportions and total factor productivity, for example, may yield results suggestive of what similar calculations for per capita income would indicate.

Two measures of labor productivity are employed here, value added per equivalent worker and gross output per equivalent worker. Estimates expressed in current dollars are presented in tables 13.1 and 13.2, respectively, for 13 industries at the years 1820, 1832, 1850, and 1860. The industries examined were selected so as to cover both the major ones of the period and a broad cross-section of the manufacturing sector, subject to the limitations imposed by the need for each industry to be reasonably well represented in the samples of manufacturing firm data and a desire to maintain conventional industrial classifications.[3] Some industries do not have estimates of productivity reported for certain years, because of an inadequate number of observations, but the threshold for inclusion was set to keep the number of omissions low.

Three sets of estimates, A, B, and C, are reported for each industry. They are computed over different subsets of firms, with the variation in composition attributable to the progressive application of increasingly stringent standards for separating establishments likely to be operating part-time from those in full-time production. Part-time enterprises should be excluded from the subsamples over which the estimates are prepared, because the measured productivity levels of such firms are biased downward due to the general practice of reporting the average labor input over the period in operation, rather than over the entire year.[4] Since these firms generally failed to identify themselves explicitly, several methods of ordering the establishments by their probability of being part-time operators, so that selected proportions could be dropped from the subsamples over which productivity was estimated, were applied to the problem and yielded roughly similar results. The method and procedures underlying the construction of the three sets of subsamples employed in this paper are explained in the note to table 13.1. The logic behind reporting three sets of estimates is to provide evidence on the sensitivity of the results to the assumptions made about the prevalence of part-time operators in different years.[5] Although intended to yield somewhat conservative estimates of the rates of productivity growth over time, the B set represents the "best-guess" figures and will be the basis, unless otherwise indicated, for the results discussed below.

The major implication of the estimates reported in tables 13.1 and 13.2 is that nominal labor productivity, whether evaluated in terms of value added or gross output, increased substantially between 1820 and 1860. All of the 13 selected industries registered significant advances in product per equivalent worker, by each of the measures. Ten of the 13 managed a greater than 50% increase in gross output per unit of labor (GQLP) between 1820 and 1860, and eight did by the value-added gauge of labor productivity (VLP).[6] The unweighted averages of the growth over the period in the value-added and gross-output measures of labor productivity are 76% and 98%, respectively, whereas the weighted average increases are only slightly different, 68% and 99%.[7] This record of advance might not seem remarkable taken by itself, but, considered together with the evidence of sharp decreases in output prices (see table 13.3), the implied gains in real labor productivity are dramatic indeed.

It is fortunate that the principal qualitative finding seems to be insensitive to reasonable variation in the proportions of firms truncated from the samples to deal with the problem of the inclusion of part-time firms in the data. The A estimates imply much more substantial productivity growth than the "best-guess" B figures, and the C set suggests somewhat less progress, but all three provide evidence of an era of major increases in manufacturing productivity. This general robustness can be demonstrated by computing the implied growth in labor productivity that results from an especially extreme adjustment for the problem.[8] If, for example, one accepts the C estimates for 1820, thus assuming that an unrealistically high proportion of firms in the earlier year operated part-time and that an extraordinary decline in their prevalence occurred, weighted averages of the estimated growth in labor productivity over the 13 industries fall from 68 to 51 for value-added labor productivity and from 99% to 85% for gross-output labor productivity. These are not trivial alterations to the quantitative results, but the picture of labor productivity growth in manufacturing that emerges from the data remains essentially unchanged. Such sensitivity analysis suggests that although the initial truncation of establishments for likely part-time operations has major effects on estimated productivity levels and growth, the influence of successive truncations declines, to the point that no plausible revision of the proportion of firms assumed to be operating part time in 1820 could reverse the basic finding of major advances over the period.

There are several troubling features of the estimates that should be considered in interpreting them, but they do not seem to warrant a general rejection of the reliability of the figures. Perhaps foremost among

**Table 13.1**  Nominal Value Added per Equivalent Worker in Selected Manufacturing Industries, 1820–60

| Industry | 1820 | 1832 | 1850 Firms | 1850 Agg. | 1860 Firms | 1860 Agg. |
|---|---|---|---|---|---|---|
| **Boots/shoes** | | | | | | |
| A | $276.0 (22) | — | $283.5 (254) | $305.4 (8,110) | $430.7 (170) | $421.7 (7,326) |
| B | 323.3 (17) | — | 290.1 (247) | | 434.2 (161) | |
| C | 350.0 (15) | — | 306.7 (207) | | 454.7 (133) | |
| **Coaches/ harnesses** | | | | | | |
| A | 473.7 (33) | $330.6 (36) | 388.4 (96) | 435.4 (2,635) | 691.4 (122) | 600.1 (5,057) |
| B | 490.5 (31) | 359.6 (35) | 461.5 (88) | | 697.5 (118) | |
| C | 502.5 (28) | 368.9 (32) | 464.2 (77) | | 645.8 (98) | |
| **Cotton textiles** | | | | | | |
| A | 352.8 (64) | 504.3 (76) | 322.3 (24) | 460.0 (856) | 494.9 (23) | 772.7 (840) |
| B | 391.0 (45) | 505.5 (75) | 326.5 (23) | | 494.9 (23) | |
| C | 457.8 (25) | 513.6 (69) | 390.2 (18) | | 618.6 (20) | |
| **Furniture/ woodwork** | | | | | | |
| A | 395.0 (25) | 359.9 (26) | 380.6 (48) | 517.3 (2,299) | 664.7 (42) | 674.5 (1,804) |
| B | 434.2 (21) | 364.6 (25) | 421.7 (46) | | 695.8 (38) | |
| C | 496.5 (15) | 384.3 (22) | 426.7 (39) | | 722.2 (31) | |
| **Glass** | | | | | | |
| A | 488.3 (3) | 767.2 (6) | — | 593.5 (77) | — | 682.1 (79) |
| B | 488.3 (3) | 767.2 (6) | — | | — | |
| C | 519.6 (2) | 753.8 (5) | — | | — | |
| **Hats** | | | | | | |
| A | 417.6 (27) | 541.3 (13) | 591.1 (17) | 633.3 (814) | 788.9 (13) | 808.2 (281) |
| B | 485.5 (22) | 541.3 (13) | 595.7 (16) | | 788.9 (13) | |
| C | 413.8 (19) | 558.5 (10) | 631.9 (12) | | 776.6 (11) | |

| | | | | | | |
|---|---|---|---|---|---|---|
| **Iron** | | | | | | |
| A | 350.4 (32) | — | 328.9 (36) | | 564.1 (23) | 648.1 (1,288) |
| B | 585.4 (21) | — | 443.8 (33) | 470.5 (1,494) | 613.6 (21) | |
| C | 593.6 (15) | — | 479.3 (28) | | 702.5 (15) | |
| **Liquors** | | | | | | |
| A | 530.0 (177) | — | 635.8 (7) | | 1262.6 (13) | 1,469.4 (922) |
| B | 640.7 (132) | — | 699.7 (6) | 1052.5 (633) | 1339.7 (12) | |
| C | 667.1 (107) | — | 793.8 (4) | | 1514.3 (10) | |
| **Flour/ grist mills** | | | | | | |
| A | 563.0 (43) | — | 530.0 (109) | | 846.1 (105) | 906.4 (4,964) |
| B | 651.6 (32) | — | 549.3 (104) | 689.7 (5,128) | 900.4 (97) | |
| C | 735.9 (24) | — | 672.7 (64) | | 1051.3 (64) | |
| **Paper** | | | | | | |
| A | 426.0 (23) | 582.6 (27) | 982.0 (20) | | 706.4 (20) | 1,128.9 (472) |
| B | 432.1 (22) | 582.6 (27) | 982.0 (20) | 913.2 (361) | 720.3 (19) | |
| C | 445.7 (20) | 618.4 (23) | 909.8 (18) | | 817.0 (14) | |
| **Tanning** | | | | | | |
| A | 331.8 (120) | 582.2 (45) | 511.7 (98) | | 803.3 (77) | 1033.5 (2,670) |
| B | 419.0 (76) | 588.0 (43) | 531.0 (92) | 761.3 (3,256) | 825.7 (69) | |
| C | 499.9 (47) | 543.2 (33) | 562.1 (65) | | 896.0 (53) | |
| **Tobacco** | | | | | | |
| A | 305.6 (8) | — | 312.8 (15) | | 733.7 (12) | 667.1 (918) |
| B | 319.0 (7) | — | 312.8 (15) | 240.1 (628) | 733.7 (12) | |
| C | 337.1 (5) | — | 360.7 (12) | | 744.8 (11) | |
| **Wool textiles** | | | | | | |
| A | 373.4 (53) | 650.9 (59) | 730.7 (42) | | 871.5 (23) | 849.7 (1,041) |
| B | 466.4 (35) | 651.7 (58) | 739.2 (40) | 563.2 (1,375) | 871.5 (23) | |
| C | 571.9 (19) | 652.0 (48) | 738.8 (35) | | 840.7 (20) | |

(*continued*)

**Table 13.1** (continued)

*Notes and sources:* The firm-level estimates were computed from the samples of northeastern manufacturing firm data drawn from the schedules of the 1820, 1850, and 1860 Federal Censuses of Manufactures and the *McLane Report* (United States House of Representatives 1832). The aggregate estimates were computed from the industry-wide information reported by state in United States Census Office (1858, 1865). The figures reported for 1832, 1850, and 1860 are based on information that probably pertains primarily to the operations of firms in 1831, 1849, and 1859, respectively. The estimates were calculated as the ratio of the industry value added (or the value of output minus the cost of the raw materials) to the total number of equivalent adult male workers in the industry. The number of equivalent workers was computed according to the formulation: $TE = M + 0.5 (F + B) + E$, where $TE$ is the number of equivalent adult male workers, $M$ is the number of adult male employees, $F$ and $B$ are the numbers of female and boy employees, respectively, and $E$ is set equal to one per firm as the measure of the entrepreneurial input. In 1850 and 1860, firms generally did not enumerate adult males and boys separately. Accordingly, I decomposed the reported numbers of male employees in those years into adults and boys by assuming that boys accounted for the same proportions, by industry, of male employees as they had in 1820. In those industries in which boys had accounted for more than 33% of male employees in 1820, I assumed further that the shares had been reduced to 33% by 1850 and 1860.

The estimates based on firm data were computed over subsamples from the various years that have observations deleted from them in order to control for the effects of establishments that operated only part-time and other outliers. The method adopted to identify potential part-time firms utilized two distributions of firms for each year by total factor productivity, one computed with gross output as the measure of output (TFP) and the other treating value added as that measure (NFP). The guiding principle was that the lower the total factor productivity of a firm in a given year, the more likely the firm was a part-time operation and should be truncated from the subsample of establishments over which the productivity estimates were computed.

Three sets of productivity estimates have been prepared from three corresponding sets of firm subsamples. The sets of subsamples vary in composition by the successive truncations made primarily to exclude part-time firms from the calculations. The A set of estimates were computed over subsamples of firms with no adjustments for part-time operators. The establishments dropped from the samples of firms that reported all of the necessary information and did not explicitly identify themselves as part-time enterprises to obtain the A subsamples included those with negative value added, a few other large outliers, and those who placed in the top 3% of enterprises in the respective years by *both* measures of total factor productivity. These criteria led to 4% being truncated from the 1820 sample, 3% from that in 1832, *5%* in 1850, and 4% from the sample in 1860.

Set B is based on more severe truncations of the left tails of the distributions of firms by total factor productivity. For the 1820 subsample, establishments that ranked in the lowest 30% by both measures of total factor productivity were dropped from subsample A to get B. The corresponding percentages were 5% in 1832, 10% in 1850, and 10% in 1860. The smaller proportions truncated from the samples of later years reflect the presumed decline over time in the fraction of firms operating part time, as well as the desire to bias the estimated productivity growth rate downward. In order to achieve this latter goal, one would seek to overestimate the proportion of establishments in 1820 that operated parttime, and underestimate the proportion in 1860. A particularly small proportion was dropped from the 1832 sample because enumerators from the *McLane Report* indicated that nearly all of the establishments covered from the states considered here were operating throughout the year. The total proportions of firms excluded from the entire samples to obtain set B were 29% in 1820, 5% in 1832, 9% in 1850, and 10% in 1860.

For set C, even larger fractions of the firms in the samples were truncated. Firms that were in the bottom 40% of the 1820 sample, by either measure of total factor productivity, were left out of the subsample that was the basis for the C estimates of that year. The corresponding threshold points for truncations from the C subsamples for the other years are 10% for 1832, 20% for 1850, and 20% for 1860. In addition, those establishments that were in the top 3% of firms by *either* measure of total factor productivity in their respective years, and had not already been dropped from the A and B subsamples, were also truncated to produce the C subsamples. These criteria led to 48% being truncated from the 1820 sample, 17% from that of 1832, 28% from that of 1850, and 29% from that of 1860.

The numbers appearing within parentheses signify the number of observations on which the respective estimate is based. No estimates are reported for years in which there were less than three observations in the A subsample. The only industry whose estimates are based on such a limited number of firms is glass, but in this case the several firms appearing in the 1820 sample account for a substantial proportion of the regional output. No estimates are reported for the boots/shoes industry in 1832, because a large proportion of the firms in the sample from that year were putting-out establishments.

**Table 13.2**    Nominal Gross Output per Equivalent Worker in Selected Manufacturing Industries, 1820–60

| Industry | 1820 | 1832 | 1850 Firms | 1850 Agg. | 1860 Firms | 1860 Agg. |
|---|---|---|---|---|---|---|
| **Boots/shoes** | | | | | | |
| A | $517.6 (22) | — | $556.8 (254) | $563.0 (8,110) | $904.2 (170) | $803.6 (7,326) |
| B | 581.2 (17) | — | 564.1 (247) | | 910.1 (161) | |
| C | 594.6 (15) | — | 593.7 (207) | | 940.7 (133) | |
| **Coaches/harnesses** | | | | | | |
| A | 873.8 (33) | $574.4 (36) | 765.9 (96) | 763.4 (2,635) | 1,175.8 (122) | 987.5 (5,057) |
| B | 904.6 (31) | 614.0 (35) | 902.4 (88) | | 1,184.2 (118) | |
| C | 928.1 (28) | 622.1 (32) | 932.3 (77) | | 1,136.4 (98) | |
| **Cotton textiles** | | | | | | |
| A | 668.4 (64) | 927.7 (76) | 1,045.0 (24) | 1,073.7 (856) | 1,053.2 (23) | 1,497.0 (840) |
| B | 721.6 (45) | 928.6 (75) | 1,056.6 (23) | | 1,053.2 (23) | |
| C | 796.7 (25) | 933.7 (69) | 1,046.3 (18) | | 1,574.0 (20) | |
| **Furniture/woodwork** | | | | | | |
| A | 629.2 (25) | 677.3 (26) | 724.4 (48) | 830.9 (2,299) | 1,023.8 (42) | 1,027.4 (1,804) |
| B | 665.1 (21) | 685.8 (25) | 742.3 (46) | | 1,064.0 (38) | |
| C | 760.5 (15) | 721.0 (22) | 762.5 (39) | | 1,096.5 (31) | |
| **Glass** | | | | | | |
| A | 676.0 (3) | 1,300.4 (6) | — | 879.4 (77) | — | 1,030.5 (79) |
| B | 676.0 (3) | 1,300.4 (6) | — | | — | |
| C | 727.2 (2) | 1,299.6 (5) | — | | — | |
| **Hats** | | | | | | |
| A | 796.2 (27) | 1,027.5 (13) | 1,329.0 (17) | 1,278.2 (814) | 1,866.6 (13) | 1,605.3 (281) |
| B | 899.3 (22) | 1,027.5 (13) | 1,338.7 (16) | | 1,866.6 (13) | |
| C | 816.7 (19) | 1,061.2 (10) | 1,377.2 (12) | | 1,868.1 (11) | |

| | | | | | | |
|---|---|---|---|---|---|---|
| **Iron** | | | | | | |
| A | 762.2 (32) | — | 745.2 (36) | | 1,457.1 (13) | |
| B | 1,251.4 (21) | — | 872.2 (33) | 1,030.5 (1,494) | 1,588.2 (21) | 1,422.2 (1,288) |
| C | 1,347.1 (15) | — | 881.7 (28) | | 1,788.9 (15) | |
| **Liquors** | | | | | | |
| A | 1,554.5 (177) | — | 1,454.0 (7) | | 4,253.9 (13) | |
| B | 1,882.1 (132) | — | 1,606.0 (6) | 3,341.0 (633) | 4,508.9 (12) | 4,252.1 (922) |
| C | 1,954.0 (107) | — | 1,806.6 (4) | | 4,898.0 (10) | |
| **Flour/ grist mills** | | | | | | |
| A | 2,923.3 (43) | — | 3,895.9 (109) | | 5,756.9 (105) | |
| B | 3,419.8 (32) | — | 4,037.1 (104) | 4,900.8 (5,128) | 6,117.0 (97) | 6,154.7 (4,964) |
| C | 3,560.7 (24) | — | 4,794.6 (64) | | 6,599.5 (64) | |
| **Paper** | | | | | | |
| A | 667.9 (23) | 1,418.2 (27) | 2,153.1 (20) | | 1,619.1 (20) | |
| B | 673.3 (22) | 1,418.2 (27) | 2,153.1 (20) | 2,065.8 (361) | 1,648.4 (19) | 2,286.9 (472) |
| C | 690.2 (20) | 1,477.8 (23) | 1,953.5 (18) | | 1,874.9 (14) | |
| **Tanning** | | | | | | |
| A | 853.5 (120) | 1,535.7 (45) | 1,412.3 (98) | | 2,750.5 (77) | |
| B | 1,037.0 (76) | 1,550.2 (43) | 1,455.5 (92) | 1,909.3 (3,256) | 2,825.1 (69) | 3,573.5 (2,670) |
| C | 1,218.7 (47) | 1,450.2 (33) | 1,581.8 (65) | | 3,043.0 (53) | |
| **Tobacco** | | | | | | |
| A | 669.0 (8) | — | 727.2 (15) | | 1,781.4 (12) | |
| B | 682.6 (7) | — | 727.2 (15) | 715.0 (628) | 1,781.4 (12) | 1,120.3 (918) |
| C | 703.6 (5) | — | 838.2 (12) | | 1,809.8 (11) | |
| **Wool textiles** | | | | | | |
| A | 677.3 (53) | 1,662.8 (59) | 1,756.1 (42) | | 2,086.6 (23) | |
| B | 821.3 (35) | 1,664.8 (58) | 1,776.7 (40) | 1,530.8 (1,375) | 2,086.6 (23) | 2,143.4 (1,041) |
| C | 906.1 (19) | 1,681.3 (48) | 1,784.6 (35) | | 2,120.5 (20) | |

*Notes and sources*: See the note to table 13.1 The estimates were calculated as the ratio of the value of gross output to the total number of equivalent adult male workers.

these is the irregular pattern of advance that a number of the industries exhibit. Nominal labor productivity does not always increase continuously across the subperiods, and even in those industries where it does, the apparent rates of growth fluctuate widely over time. Some variability should be expected, however, since the nominal estimates are not adjusted for the substantial and erratic changes in the prices of many commodities, including outputs and raw materials, that occurred during the period. Moreover, a great deal of random variation in the estimates of productivity would also be generated by the limited numbers of observations.[9] This latter problem is quite serious for estimating the growth in productivity over individual subperiods, but would be expected to decline in significance for the study of long-term changes, because the proportion of the variation in estimated productivity due to substantive or actual movements in productivity should increase with the length of the period under examination.

Also puzzling are the sometimes large discrepancies between the estimates computed from the firm-level information and those from aggregate data in 1850 and 1860. The industry estimates drawn from these two sources are frequently similar but diverge substantially in some cases, particularly in 1850. One might have expected the figures based on aggregate data to be generally lower, because of the presumed inclusion of part- time establishments in those totals. However, where there are large disparities, it is typically these estimates which exceed those from the firm data. This might seem to imply that the prevalence, or the production, of part-time operators was rather modest in those years. In addition, the pattern is consistent with the view that the design of the 1850 and 1860 samples served to bias the productivity estimates for those years significantly downward.[10] Accordingly, one might suppose that the aggregate- based estimates would be more representative of the actual productivity levels in the respective industries than those computed from firm data. Whatever the reasons for the discrepancies, the close correspondence between the estimates in 1860 means that the qualitative results on productivity growth over the entire period are not sensitive to the choice between the firm- and aggregate-based figures for that year.

Although the series of current-dollar estimates are useful in roughly gauging the long- term trends in labor productivity, they are not nearly as informative as would be series expressed in constant dollars. Accordingly, a variety of price indexes have been assembled to construct estimates of real productivity from current-dollar values, and are reported in table 13.3. Measures of the changes in the prices of the outputs and of the raw materials for each of the 13 industries would of course be preferred for the calculation of the constant-dollar estimates. This goal could not be achieved, but a wide-ranging survey of available price

**Table 13.3          Price Indexes, 1820–60**

| Indexes | 1820 | 1832 | 1850 | 1860 |
|---|---|---|---|---|
| *General output price indexes* | | | | |
| Consumer price index | 156 | 119 | 93 | 100 |
| Wholesale price index | 114 | 99 | 88 | 102 |
| *Industry price indexes*: | | | | |
| Boots/shoes | | | | |
| Q | 166 | 155 | 111 | 100 |
| RM | 113 | 124 | 88 | 113 |
| K | 140 | 135 | 103 | 105 |
| Coaches/harnesses | | | | |
| Q | 178 | 141 | 95 | 100 |
| RM | 137 | 119 | 106 | 102 |
| K | 150 | 128 | 109 | 102 |
| Cotton textiles | | | | |
| Q | 179 | 115 | 78 | 98 |
| RM | 155 | 88 | 69 | 110 |
| K | 160 | 130 | 112 | 103 |
| Furniture/woodwork | | | | |
| Q | 200 | 149 | 111 | 100 |
| RM | 111 | 102 | 121 | 98 |
| K | 151 | 126 | 115 | 100 |
| Glass | | | | |
| Q | 190 | 109 | 81 | 100 |
| RM | 114 | 99 | 88 | 102 |
| K | 149 | 115 | 99 | 101 |
| Hats | | | | |
| Q | 166 | 155 | 111 | 105 |
| RM | 114 | 99 | 88 | 102 |
| K | 142 | 127 | 105 | 103 |
| Iron | | | | |
| Q | 171 | 145 | 113 | 100 |
| RM | 128 | 111 | 99 | 102 |
| K | 159 | 137 | 118 | 103 |
| Liquors | | | | |
| Q | 96 | — | 91 | 104 |
| RM | 57 | — | 83 | 96 |
| K | 124 | — | 106 | 102 |
| Flour/grist mills | | | | |
| Q | 91 | — | 87 | 98 |
| RM | 57 | — | 83 | 96 |
| K | 142 | — | 115 | 102 |
| Paper | | | | |
| Q | 319 | 244 | 125 | 104 |
| RM | 179 | 115 | 78 | 98 |
| K | 164 | 136 | 111 | 101 |
| Tanning | | | | |
| Q | 90 | 99 | 70 | 113 |
| RM | 65 | 72 | 51 | 113 |
| K | 104 | 101 | 81 | 108 |

(*continued*)

**Table 13.3**    (continued)

| Indexes | 1820 | 1832 | 1850 | 1860 |
|---|---|---|---|---|
| Tobacco | | | | |
| Q | 138 | 69 | 100 | 127 |
| RM | 138 | 69 | 100 | 127 |
| K | 140 | 81 | 103 | 122 |
| Wool textiles | | | | |
| Q | 161 | 138 | 133 | 102 |
| RM | 95 | 74 | 80 | 104 |
| K | 144 | 124 | 114 | 102 |
| *Capital component price indexes* | | | | |
| Machinery | 183 | 159 | 138 | 107 |
| Structures | 136 | 118 | 107 | 100 |

*Notes and sources:* Corresponding to the productivity estimates, the price indexes reported for 1832, 1850, and 1860 actually refer to the price levels in 1831, 1849, and 1859. The price indexes, however, are expressed relative to an 1860 standard of 100. The industry-specific capital price indexes were constructed as a weighted average of the price indexes for "structures" and "machinery," as well as of the industry-specific indexes for output and raw materials. The weights were obtained from firm-level data on the composition of the total capital investment contained in the *McLane Report* or, when there were insufficient observations from 1832, from aggregate information contained in the report of the 1890 Census of Manufactures. See Sokoloff (1984a) and United States Census Office (1895). The "structures" and "machinery" indexes were weighted by the shares of the total capital investment that they accounted for in the respective industries. The remaining proportion of the capital investment was assumed to consist entirely of inventories, which were divided equally between output and raw materials. Hence, the latter two indexes received half of the weight for inventories in constructing each industry's capital price series.

*General Output:* Consumer and wholesale price indexes (CPI and WPI henceforth) from United States Bureau of the Census (1975, E-135 and E-52).

Boots/shoes: Output price index for "shoes" from Brady (1966). Interpolation was based on the WPI (as were all interpolations of price indexes drawn from Brady). The index for raw materials was constructed from the 1850 and 1860 firm data, and from United States Bureau of the Census (1975, E-55).

Coaches/harnesses: Output index constructed from that for "carriages, buggies, and wagons" in Brady (1966) and from the 1850 and 1860 firm data. The index for raw materials also consists of a segment obtained from these data, spliced into the WPI.

Cotton textiles: Both the output and raw materials indexes are from United States Bureau of the Census (1975, E-128, E-126).

Furniture/woodwork: The output index is that for "furniture" from Brady (1966), and the raw materials index is from United States Bureau of the Census (1975, E-59) and the 1850 and 1860 firm data.

Glass: The output index is that for "window glass" from Brady (1964). The WPI serves as the index for raw materials.

Hats: The output index is that for "men's hats" from Brady (1964). The WPI serves as the index for raw materials.

Iron: The output index was constructed from several price series contained in Cole (1938). The raw materials index is the WPI, with a segment estimated from the 1850 and 1860 firm data spliced in.

Liquors: Both indexes are from United States Bureau of the Census (1975, E-62, E-123).

Mills: Both indexes are from United States Bureau of the Census (1975, E-124, E-123).

Paper: The output price index is that for "writing paper" from Brady (1966). The index for raw materials is from United States Bureau of the Census (1975, E-128).

**Table 13.3**    (continued)

Tanning: The same price index serves here as the basis for both the output and raw materials indexes, United States Bureau of the Census (1975, E-55). The two indexes differ slightly, however, in that the segments between 1850 and 1860 were obtained from the firm data for those years.

Tobacco: A price index for "tobacco" was constructed from several series appearing in Cole (1938). This index was utilized for both outputs and raw materials.

Wool textiles: The output index is for "woolen worsted goods" from Brady (1966). The index for raw materials was constructed from information in Cole (1938).

Capital component price indexes: The indexes for structures and machinery are for "factories, office buildings" and "machine-shop products," respectively. Both are drawn from Brady (1966).

series for the period yielded industry-specific indexes for the outputs of all 13 industries, and for the raw materials of nine.[11] The Warren and Pearson wholesale price index (henceforth referred to as the WPI) was employed as the index for the prices of raw materials in the remaining four industries. In cases where there was reason to doubt the representativeness of an index, and where the procedure was feasible, the change in price between 1850 and 1860 was estimated from the information in the samples from those years, and spliced into the original series.[12]

In addition to these price indexes for outputs and raw materials, table 13.3 also presents industry-specific estimates of the price of capital. These indexes of the price of capital will be utilized in the calculations of total factor productivity treated below, and were computed as weighted averages of the indexes for structures, machinery, outputs, and raw materials. The weights vary across industries, and were obtained from industry-specific proportions of capital invested in structures and land, machinery and tools, and inventories. Inventories were assumed to have been composed of equal amounts of outputs and of raw materials.

Perhaps the most striking general pattern that emerges from an examination of table 13.3 is that the prices of outputs declined significantly relative to those of raw materials and capital between 1820 and 1860. In all of the 13 industries but tobacco, where the same series was adopted for both outputs and raw materials, the index for output prices fell relative to that for raw materials; the index declined relative to that for capital in 10 of the 13. Since it is also clear that real wages rose substantially over the period, one can infer, by duality, that total factor productivity must have increased (Sokoloff 1983).

Indexes of real value added and real gross output per equivalent worker have been constructed for the 13 industries by applying the output price series to the conversion of the current-dollar labor productivity estimates to units of constant dollars. These indexes, which are presented in tables 13.4 and 13.5, respectively, indicate that all of

**Table 13.4    Index of Real Value Added per Equivalent Worker in Selected Manufacturing Industries, 1820-60**

| Industry | 1820 | 1832 | 1850 Firms | 1850 Agg. | 1860 Firms | 1860 Agg. |
|---|---|---|---|---|---|---|
| Boots/shoes | | | | | | |
| A | 100 | — | 154 | 165 | 259 | 254 |
| B | 100 | — | 135 | 142 | 224 | 217 |
| C | 100 | — | 131 | 130 | 216 | 200 |
| Coaches/harnesses | | | | | | |
| A | 100 | 88 | 154 | 172 | 260 | 225 |
| B | 100 | 93 | 176 | 166 | 253 | 218 |
| C | 100 | 93 | 173 | 162 | 229 | 213 |
| Cotton textiles | | | | | | |
| A | 100 | 222 | 210 | 299 | 256 | 400 |
| B | 100 | 201 | 192 | 270 | 231 | 361 |
| C | 100 | 175 | 196 | 231 | 247 | 308 |
| Furniture/woodwork | 100 | | | | | |
| A | 100 | 122 | 174 | 236 | 337 | 341 |
| B | 100 | 113 | 175 | 215 | 321 | 311 |
| C | | 104 | 155 | 188 | 291 | 272 |
| Glass | | | | | | |
| A | 100 | 274 | — | 285 | — | 265 |
| B | 100 | 274 | — | 285 | — | 265 |
| C | 100 | 253 | — | 268 | — | 249 |
| Hats | | | | | | |
| A | 100 | 139 | 212 | 227 | 299 | 306 |
| B | 100 | 119 | 184 | 195 | 257 | 263 |
| C | 100 | 145 | 228 | 229 | 297 | 309 |
| Iron | | | | | | |
| A | 100 | — | 142 | 203 | 277 | 318 |
| B | 100 | — | 115 | 122 | 180 | 190 |
| C | 100 | — | 122 | 120 | 203 | 188 |
| Liquors | | | | | | |
| A | 100 | — | 127 | 209 | 220 | 256 |
| B | 100 | — | 115 | 173 | 193 | 212 |
| C | 100 | — | 126 | 166 | 210 | 203 |
| Flour/grist mills | | | | | | |
| A | 100 | — | 98 | 128 | 140 | 149 |
| B | 100 | — | 88 | 111 | 128 | 129 |
| C | 100 | — | 96 | 98 | 133 | 114 |
| Paper | | | | | | |
| A | 100 | 179 | 588 | 547 | 509 | 813 |
| B | 100 | 176 | 580 | 539 | 511 | 801 |
| C | 100 | 181 | 521 | 523 | 562 | 777 |
| Tanning | | | | | | |
| A | 100 | 160 | 198 | 295 | 193 | 248 |
| B | 100 | 128 | 163 | 234 | 157 | 196 |
| C | 100 | 99 | 145 | 196 | 143 | 165 |

**Table 13.4**     (continued)

| Industry | 1820 | 1832 | 1850 Firms | 1850 Agg. | 1860 Firms | 1860 Agg. |
|---|---|---|---|---|---|---|
| Tobacco | | | | | | |
| A | 100 | — | 141 | 108 | 261 | 237 |
| B | 100 | — | 135 | 104 | 250 | 227 |
| C | 100 | — | 148 | 98 | 240 | 215 |
| Wool textiles | | | | | | |
| A | 100 | 203 | 237 | 183 | 368 | 359 |
| B | 100 | 163 | 192 | 146 | 295 | 288 |
| C | 100 | 147 | 173 | 132 | 256 | 259 |
| Average | | | | | | |
| Weighted (B) | 100 | [159] | [168] | 192 | [230] | 264 |
| Unweighted (B) | 100 | [158] | [187] | 208 | [250] | 283 |

*Notes and sources:* See the notes to tables 13.1 and 13.3. The estimates of value added per equivalent worker presented in table 13.1 were converted to constant dollars by employing the price indexes reported in table 13.3, and then normalized relative to a base of 100 representing the respective industry's level in 1820. The weights employed in computing the weighted averages are equivalent to the industry shares of the value added produced in the northeastern states in 1850, and were calculated from information contained in United States Census Office (1858). The weights were normalized so that their sum was equal to one whenever there were missing values. Averages based on fewer than 13 industries (affected by missing values) are reported within brackets.

the industries realized major advances in real labor productivity, by either measure, between 1820 and 1860. Weighted averages of the records of the industries yield, taking the estimates based on aggregate data as the standard for 1860, increases of 164% in value added per equivalent worker and 187% by the alternative gauge. Only very few failed to register gains of 100%. It is interesting to note that in most industries the progress in gross output per equivalent worker significantly exceeded that in value added per equivalent worker. This feature of the results presumably reflects a rapid growth in the amounts of raw materials processed per unit of labor during the period.

As for the reliability of these labor productivity estimates, it must be admitted that even after their conversion to constant dollars, there remain many anomalies where the productivity growth indicated for an industry over a subperiod is either implausibly high or low. These cases generally involve rather short spans of time, but not always. Many of them might be attributed to noise in the point estimates generated by a paucity of observations, inappropriate or inaccurate price indexes, rapid changes in the factor proportions utilized, varying degrees or types of sample selection bias over the years included, or cyclical effects, but their number is nevertheless unsettling. It is, however, reassuring to note that the frequency and magnitude of such

**Table 13.5    Index of Real Gross Output per Equivalent Worker in Selected Manufacturing Industries, 1820–60**

| Industry | 1820 | 1832 | 1850 Firms | 1850 Agg. | 1860 Firms | 1860 Agg. |
|---|---|---|---|---|---|---|
| **Boots/shoes** | | | | | | |
| A | 100 | — | 161 | 163 | 290 | 258 |
| B | 100 | — | 145 | 145 | 260 | 230 |
| C | 100 | — | 149 | 142 | 263 | 224 |
| **Coaches/harnesses** | | | | | | |
| A | 100 | 83 | 164 | 164 | 240 | 201 |
| B | 100 | 86 | 188 | 154 | 233 | 194 |
| C | 100 | 85 | 189 | 155 | 218 | 190 |
| **Cotton textiles** | | | | | | |
| A | 100 | 216 | 359 | 369 | 288 | 409 |
| B | 100 | 200 | 336 | 341 | 267 | 379 |
| C | 100 | 182 | 301 | 309 | 361 | 343 |
| **Furniture/Woodwork** | | | | | | |
| A | 100 | 144 | 207 | 238 | 325 | 327 |
| B | 100 | 138 | 201 | 225 | 320 | 309 |
| C | 100 | 127 | 181 | 197 | 288 | 270 |
| **Glass** | | | | | | |
| A | 100 | 335 | — | 305 | — | 290 |
| B | 100 | 335 | — | 305 | — | 290 |
| C | 100 | 312 | — | 284 | — | 269 |
| **Hats** | | | | | | |
| A | 100 | 138 | 250 | 240 | 371 | 319 |
| B | 100 | 122 | 223 | 213 | 328 | 282 |
| C | 100 | 139 | 252 | 234 | 362 | 311 |
| **Iron** | | | | | | |
| A | 100 | — | 148 | 205 | 329 | 321 |
| B | 100 | — | 105 | 125 | 218 | 195 |
| C | 100 | — | 99 | 116 | 228 | 181 |
| **Liquors** | | | | | | |
| A | 100 | — | 99 | 227 | 253 | 252 |
| B | 100 | — | 90 | 187 | 221 | 209 |
| C | 100 | — | 98 | 180 | 231 | 201 |
| **Flour/grist mills** | | | | | | |
| A | 100 | — | 139 | 175 | 183 | 196 |
| B | 100 | — | 123 | 150 | 166 | 167 |
| C | 100 | — | 141 | 144 | 172 | 160 |
| **Paper** | | | | | | |
| A | 100 | 278 | 823 | 789 | 744 | 1050 |
| B | 100 | 275 | 816 | 783 | 751 | 1042 |
| C | 100 | 280 | 722 | 764 | 833 | 1016 |
| **Tanning** | | | | | | |
| A | 100 | 164 | 213 | 288 | 257 | 333 |
| B | 100 | 136 | 180 | 237 | 217 | 274 |
| C | 100 | 108 | 167 | 201 | 198 | 234 |

**Table 13.5**   (continued)

| Industry | 1820 | 1832 | 1850 | | 1860 | |
|---|---|---|---|---|---|---|
| | | | Firms | Agg. | Firms | Agg. |
| Tobacco | | | | | | |
| A | 100 | — | 150 | 147 | 289 | 182 |
| B | 100 | — | 147 | 145 | 284 | 178 |
| C | 100 | — | 164 | 140 | 280 | 173 |
| Wool textiles | | | | | | |
| A | 100 | 286 | 314 | 274 | 486 | 500 |
| B | 100 | 236 | 262 | 226 | 401 | 412 |
| C | 100 | 216 | 238 | 205 | 369 | 373 |
| Average | | | | | | |
| Weighted (B) | 100 | [186] | [207] | 220 | [265] | 287 |
| Unweighted (B) | 100 | [191] | [235] | 249 | [305] | 320 |

*Notes and sources:* See the notes to tables 13.2 and 13.3. The estimates of gross output per equivalent worker in current dollars presented in table 13.2 were converted to constant dollars by employing the price indexes reported in table 13.3 and then normalized relative to a base of 100 representing the respective industry's level in 1820. The weights employed in computing the weighted averages are equivalent to the industry shares of gross output produced in the northeastern states in 1850, and were calculated from information contained in United States Census Office (1858). The weights were normalized so that their sum was equal to one whenever there were missing values. Averages based on fewer than thirteen industries (affected by missing values) are reported within brackets.

strange results are greatly reduced in the series of total factor productivity estimates discussed below.[13] The industry with the most puzzling record is paper, which appears, by both measures of labor productivity, to have realized astonishingly high rates of advance, particularly after 1832. Although substantial progress would be expected, because of the dramatic increases in the utilization of raw materials and capital per unit of labor over the period, the estimated gains are probably too large to be believed. Given that this qualitative result is not sensitive to the choice between the firm-level and aggregate estimates, the problem may stem from the output price index employed.[14] Anomalies in the productivity series for boots/shoes, tanning, and tobacco are also associated with suspicious movements in the relevant price indexes.[15].

The per annum growth rates of labor productivity presented in table 13.6 were computed from the B sets of indexes in table 13.4 and 13.5. Rates of advance are reported for the entire period from 1820 to 1860, as well as for several subperiods. The estimates indicate that labor productivity increased rapidly in virtually all industries, ranging from 0.6%–0.7% and 1.3% per annum for VLP and GQLP, respectively, in flour/grist mills to 4.3%–5.5% and 5.3%–6.2% in paper. Weighted averages of the performance of the 13 industries yield estimated ranges

**Table 13.6**    **Growth Rates of Labor Productivity in Selected Manufacturing Industries, 1820–60 (%)**

| Industry | 1820–32 | 1820–50 | 1850–60 | 1820–60 |
|---|---|---|---|---|
| **Boots/shoes** | | | | |
| VLP | — | 1.0–1.2 | 4.4–5.2 | 2.0–2.1 |
| GQLP | — | 1.3–1.3 | 4.7–6.0 | 2.2–2.5 |
| **Coaches/harnesses** | | | | |
| VLP | −0.7 | 1.8–2.0 | 2.7–3.7 | 2.0–2.4 |
| GQLP | −1.4 | 1.6–2.2 | 2.1–2.2 | 1.7–2.2 |
| **Cotton textiles** | | | | |
| VLP | 6.6 | 2.3–3.5 | 1.9–2.9 | 2.2–3.3 |
| GQLP | 6.5 | 4.3–4.3 | −2.3–1.0 | 2.5–3.5 |
| **Furniture/woodwork** | | | | |
| VLP | 1.1 | 1.9–2.7 | 3.8–6.2 | 2.9–3.0 |
| GQLP | 3.0 | 2.4–2.8 | 3.2–4.8 | 2.9–3.0 |
| **Glass** | | | | |
| VLP | 9.6 | 3.7 | −0.7 | 2.5 |
| GQLP | 11.6 | 3.9 | −0.5 | 2.8 |
| **Hats** | | | | |
| VLP | 1.6 | 2.1–2.3 | 3.0–3.4 | 2.4–2.5 |
| GQLP | 1.9 | 2.6–2.8 | 2.9–4.0 | 2.7–3.1 |
| **Iron** | | | | |
| VLP | — | 0.5–0.7 | 4.6–4.6 | 1.5–1.7 |
| GQLP | — | 0.2–0.8 | 4.6–7.5 | 1.7–2.0 |
| **Liquors** | | | | |
| VLP | — | 0.5–1.9 | 2.0–5.3 | 1.7–1.9 |
| GQLP | — | −0.4–2.2 | 1.1–9.4 | 1.9–2.1 |
| **Flour/grist mills** | | | | |
| VLP | — | −0.4–0.4 | 1.6–3.8 | 0.6–0.7 |
| GQLP | — | 0.7–1.4 | 1.1–3.0 | 1.3–1.3 |
| **Paper** | | | | |
| VLP | 5.3 | 6.0–6.2 | −1.2–4.0 | 4.3–5.5 |
| GQLP | 9.7 | 7.4–7.5 | −0.8–2.9 | 5.3–6.2 |
| **Tanning** | | | | |
| VLP | 2.2 | 1.7–3.0 | −1.7–0.4 | 1.2–1.7 |
| GQLP | 2.8 | 2.1–3.0 | 1.5–1.8 | 2.0–2.6 |
| **Tobacco** | | | | |
| VLP | — | 0.1–1.0 | 6.3–8.1 | 2.1–2.4 |
| GQLP | — | 1.3–1.3 | 2.1–6.8 | 1.5–2.7 |
| **Wool textiles** | | | | |
| VLP | 4.5 | 1.3–2.3 | 4.4–7.0 | 2.7–2.8 |
| GQLP | 8.1 | 2.8–3.4 | 4.4–6.2 | 3.6–3.7 |
| **Weighted average** | | | | |
| VLP | [4.3] | [1.8]–2.3 | 3.2–[3.2] | [2.2]–2.5 |
| GQLP | [5.8] | [2.5]–2.7 | 2.5–[2.7] | [2.5]–2.7 |

*Notes and sources:* These annual rates of growth were computed from the constant-dollar estimates of labor productivity presented in set B of tables 13.4 and 13.5. The VLP estimates refer to the growth of value added per equivalent worker, and the GQLP refer to the growth of gross output per equivalent worker. Ranges of estimates are often presented, reflecting the differences between the figures derived from firm data and those based on aggregate data. See the notes to tables 13.4 and 13.5.

of 2.2%–2.5% and 2.5%–2.7% for the rates of growth of the two measures of labor productivity. These figures are remarkable in that they are drawn from the experience of industries that together accounted for a large share of the entire manufacturing sector in the Northeast and yet are substantially higher than those that other scholars concerned with antebellum growth have calculated for the United States economy as a whole (David 1967, 1977; Gallman 1972a, 1972b).

These estimates of productivity growth in northeastern manufacturing during early industrialization may exceed what might have been expected from previous work on the era, but they seem quite reasonable by other historical standards. For example, McCloskey (1981) has computed rates of productivity growth for four manufacturing industries in Britain during that country's initial phase of industrial development, 1780 to 1860. His calculations suggest that the British record of advance was similar to that observed here in the American Northeast. Of perhaps even greater interest, our estimates of labor productivity growth during early industrialization are slightly larger than those computed by Kendrick (1961) for the United States manufacturing sector between 1869 and 1957.

Another finding that emerges from these estimates is that, on average, there is weak evidence for acceleration in the rate of labor productivity growth over the period. This claim is based primarily on a comparison of the experience between 1820 and 1850 with that between 1850 and 1860 and thus must be offered tentatively. An analysis focusing on the performance before and after 1832, of the eight industries for which we have estimates in that year, reinforces the grounds for skepticism about the occurrence of acceleration. When the thirteen industries are considered together, they exhibit a marked increase in the rate of labor productivity growth by the VLP measure, from 1.8%–2.3% per annum before 1850 to 3.2% following, but no change by the GQLP measure. According to the latter, labor productivity rose at a roughly constant 2.5%–2.7% per annum between 1820 and 1850, as well as between 1850 and 1860. On an individual industry basis, nine of the thirteen enjoyed faster growth during the latter subperiod, by either measure, than in the former. Whether or not the pace quickened over time, it is clear that rapid progress must have been realized as early as the 1820s. While evidence of acceleration would conform with the work of scholars who view the diffusion of mechanization across manufacturing industries during the 1840s and 1850s as the crucial development behind productivity growth in that sector, this perspective, even if it were more strongly supported by the data, contributes little to understanding how and why the impressive advances between 1820 and 1850 were achieved (Chandler 1977).

Given that the utilization of sophisticated machinery and highly capital-intensive production processes were essentially confined to but a few industries until late in the period, the finding that a broad range of manufacturing industries enjoyed substantial gains in productivity through-out the early nineteenth century might tend to enhance appreciation of the importance of the changes in labor organization and other relatively modest alterations in technique that seem generally to have been adopted sooner and more widely. Another reaction, however, would be to question the accuracy of the estimates of productivity growth. Comparisons between the rates reported here and those computed for other places or eras do provide some check on the plausibility of the results, but those drawn with alternative industry-specific figures for the same period would be even more informative. Unfortunately, such estimates are quite scarce, and the only prominent industry for which they are readily available is cotton textiles. As for that industry, the rates of labor productivity growth presented here are generally lower than what other scholars have found. Davis and Stettler (1966) calculated that gross output per worker in the entire United States industry increased at rates of 4.1% per annum between 1820 and 1860 and of 3.4% between 1832 and 1860, as compared to the 2.5%–3.5% and 1.9%–2.3% rates for the respective periods reported here. Their estimates for cotton textiles in Massachusetts indicate somewhat slower rates of advance in that state; but their figure of 2.2% per annum growth between 1832 and 1860, resembling the 2.0% and 2.5% rates of McGouldrick (1968) and Layer (1955) for mills in Lowell during roughly the same years, is near the upper end of our range. Nickless's (1979) analysis of Layer's data on three Lowell establishments yields an even higher estimate, 3.3% per annum, for the period from 1836 to 1860. Hence, the evidence from the only other industry for which independent estimates are easily obtained suggests that our figures on labor productivity growth are on the low side, as they were constructed to be.

A skeptic might not accept the number or relevance of the standards of comparison utilized, and continue to dispute the estimates of the rates of advances as too high, claiming that the results were an artifact due to some defect in the data or in the way they were derived. There are, indeed, several aspects of the estimation procedure that could be of sufficient importance to account for the findings of rapid productivity growth across a wide spectrum of manufacturing industries and, on average, in the sector at large. Perhaps the most obvious of these is the selection of price indexes. As is clear from the indexes listed in table 13.3, there were substantial fluctuations in both absolute and relative prices over the period from 1820 to 1860. In this context, it is conceivable that some of the price indexes utilized might diverge significantly from the actual movement of the relevant prices, particularly since the indexes frequently pertain only to one specific product or raw material of an industry and in several cases were drawn from the WPI. Nevertheless, in order for there to be a qualitatively important upward bias in the estimates of productivity growth, the respective price indexes would have to seriously overstate the decline in output prices relative to input prices. Given the absence of any evidence or argument that such a systematic pattern in the errors of the price indexes across industries exists, there would seem to be no basis for accepting the argument that inaccurate price indexes account for the general finding of rapid labor productivity growth.

There are several other reasons to doubt the severity of the problems with the price indexes. The first is that when multiple price indexes were available for an industry, the most conservative of them generally were selected for use, biasing the estimated rates of productivity growth downward. Another factor that mitigates the significance of possible errors in the indexes is that the value-added figures were deflated to constant dollars with only output price indexes, instead of converting the values of gross outputs and raw materials separately. In manufacturing industries in which the prices of the raw materials consumed fell relative to the output prices, this procedure would lead the advance over time in real labor productivity to be overestimated. The evidence, however, suggests that it was the relative price of the outputs that typically declined during the period. Of the eight industries included in table 13.3 that have separate and industry-specific indexes for outputs and inputs, all experienced a decrease in the former relative to the latter. To the extent that this pattern was characteristic of the manufacturing sector, the employment of output price series to deflate the nominal value-added figures should tend to bias estimates of productivity growth downward, not upward. Hence, the likelihood that the result of substantial advances was due to inaccurate price indexes seems even more remote. Given that there are undoubtedly some errors in the price indexes utilized, however, and that the magnitude and perhaps the direction of the biases referred to must vary across industries, one should be cautious about comparing the relative performances reported for individual industries. Although the rates of productivity growth should be biased downward in most industries, the variability in the extent of the biases at the industry level implies that the record of any particular industry relative to another might be quite fragile.[16]

The other feature of the construction of the estimates that the qualitative results might plausibly be sensitive to is the method of adjustment for the inclusion of establishments operating part-time in the samples. This is a potentially important problem, because such enterprises did not generally explicitly identify themselves as such, became less prevalent in manufacturing over time, and had their measures of productivity biased downward from the actual levels.[17] As discussed above, the logic of the procedure adopted to deal with the dilemma was based on the assumption that the lower the total factor productivity of an establishment, the greater the likelihood it operated only a fraction of the year. Generous assessments of the prevalence of part-time operations in the various years were made, and corresponding percentages of the least productive enterprises were dropped from the respective samples to obtain the subsamples over which the sets of estimates were computed. The B set of estimates was intended to represent conservative "best-guess" figures, and provides the basis for the rates of growth reported in table 13.6. If the adjustments to the samples underestimated the extent of part-time operations in 1820, or especially the decrease in their prevalence over time, then the rates of productivity growth would likely be biased upward. This is a possibility, but as an examination of the nominal figures in tables 13.1 and 13.2 indicates, the qualitative result of rapid productivity growth, on average, in manufacturing is not sensitive to reasonable variation in the proportions of firms presumed to have been operating part-time and truncated from the samples. Estimates of the advances in several of the industries, such as iron and tanning, might be substantially affected, however, as could the relative rates of progress in some industries versus others.

There are other aspects of the estimation procedures that might be expected to yield biased results, but they are more likely to lead to understatements of the advances in productivity than overstatements. The first concerns the manner in which value added was computed. Each of the bodies of data employed contains reports of the value of outputs produced and the value of raw materials consumed by the particular firm or industry. Value added was calculated in a straightforward fashion by deducting the value of the raw materials from the total value of output. The potential bias arises from the additional category of expenses specified by firms in the 1820 Census of Manufactures. This class of production costs was defined as "contingent expenses" and included the costs of items such as fuel, insurance, and repairs to equipment. Since none of the other surveys collected information on a similar category of expenses, "contingent expenses" were ignored in the calculation of the value-added figures for 1820. If, however, some of the expenditures on inputs counted among "contingent expenses" in that year were included as raw materials later, then the value added per firm would be overestimated in 1820 relative to that in other years, and the growth in the value-added measures of productivity underestimated.

Another possible source of systematic error in the preparation of the productivity estimates is the method of aggregating different classes of workers into units of adult male equivalents. Females and boys have been treated as equal, in terms of their labor input, to one-half of an adult male employee, with these weights having been drawn from evidence on the relative wages of the groups prevailing near the end of the period.[18] In both the 1820 Census of Manufactures and the *McLane Report* of 1832, each of the three types of workers was enumerated separately. There were only two classifications of employees utilized in the 1850 and 1860 censuses, however, males and females. For those years, the reported number of male workers in each industry was decomposed into adults and boys by assuming that the industry-specific proportions of males that were boys were the same in 1850 and 1860 as they had been in 1820.[19] Since the shares of male employees that were boys probably rose somewhat over the period, a small upward bias might be imparted by this procedure to the estimation of the labor inputs in the later, relative to the earlier, years (Goldin and Sokoloff 1982). As a consequence, estimates of productivity in those years, and thus of its growth over time, would tend to be biased downward.

One might also expect the estimates of productivity growth during the period to understate the actual record because of the problems in the sample selection that afflict the various bodies of data. First, the systematic undercounting of smaller establishments in the 1820 and 1832 samples should probably generate overestimates of the productivity levels in those years.[20] In addition, the unrepresentative character of the samples from 1850 and 1860 would be expected to yield underestimates. These two samples were designed to incorporate a certain minimum number of observations from each state that had surviving data, and hence they suffer from a disproportionate representation of manufacturing firms from states that had relatively limited industrial development or small populations (Atack et al. 1979). As the firms from such states tended to be less productive than those from other areas, at least partially because of their smaller scales of operation, the levels of productivity estimated from the samples should be lower than those actually prevailing in the Northeast at the respective years. Moreover, the inclusion of part-time establishments in the aggregate data from the 1850 and 1860 censuses means that the estimates obtained from these sources are downward biased as well. Hence, with productivity levels overestimated for 1820 and underestimated for 1850 and 1860, the rates of advance derived should be lower than those that were realized.

The above discussion has reviewed, in considerable detail, many of the features of the data sources and the estimation procedures that might have contributed to inaccurate or biased assessments of the productivity growth between 1820 and 1860. It has been argued that most of them would be expected to have led to estimates that were biased downward. The chief exception to this generalization about the impacts of the potential biases is the effect of a decline over time in the relative amount of manufacturing production carried out by firms operating seasonally. The disproportionate truncation of the least productive manufacturing establishments from the 1820 sample, however, should probably more than compensate for this problem, because the percentages dropped from the analysis for the 13 industries seem likely to have exceeded those of firms that were part-time enterprises. Even if the adjustments underlying the B set of estimates, on which the discussion focuses, are not quite sufficient, sensitivity analysis employing set C for 1820 indicates that the qualitative results would not be altered by any reasonable relaxation of the assumptions concerning the prevalence of seasonal operations in that year.[21] Particularly when one considers the net effect of all the biases, it appears likely that the estimates of productivity growth in manufacturing understates, on average, the actual record.

The evidence seems to support the conclusion that labor productivity growth in manufacturing during this initial phase of industrialization was remarkably rapid and significantly higher than scholars may have reckoned previously. What is one to make of this performance? One possibility is to attribute the progress to the combined effects of a variety of related developments marking the period that include the introduction and diffusion of machinery, increases in capital and raw materials intensity, changes in the organization of labor, the realization of scale economies, learning by doing, and the impact of expanding markets through the selecting out of inefficient producers and the stimulation of technical innovation. One might also explain the remarkably high rates of labor productivity growth as being at least partially accounted for by the severe contraction that occurred in the United States between 1816 and 1821, and might have dragged productivity in 1820 well below its trend level. From this perspective, the estimates could accurately reflect the actual amount of labor productivity growth between 1820 and 1860 but convey a misleading impression about the long-term record.

Although cyclical effects might, in principle, have been large, the qualitative findings with respect to productivity growth over the entire period from 1820 to 1860 are not fundamentally altered when one makes adjustments for them. In order to gauge the potential magnitudes of the cyclical effects on manufacturing productivity, estimates of the trend over time in gross output per worker were computed through regression analysis from the annual series on cotton textiles assembled by Davis and Stettler (1966) and by Layer (1955), and then the residuals were compared with the NBER classifications of cyclical behavior by year (Thorp 1926). Both sets of residuals indicate some procyclical variation, with the greatest deviations below trend in labor productivity being achieved, on average, one year before the trough of the business cycle. The Davis and Stettler series implies much greater cyclical variation than the Layer series, but even here the effect seems somewhat modest. In the average business cycle, labor productivity, as measured by gross output per worker, fell to only 4.2% below trend during the year before the trough.[22] Moreover,, over the limited period of time spanned by their data, the magnitude of the deviation from trend does not appear to have been systematically related to the duration of the cycle. It is not clear whether cyclical variation in labor productivity should be more or less in cotton textiles than in other industries. Nevertheless, even if the 4.2% figure is doubled and applied to all manufacturing industries, the adjustment for the business cycle in 1820 would not change the qualitative results concerning the pace of labor productivity growth over the period under study. Such refinements would be even less significant for the other years covered by the data, because none of them seem to have been associated with extreme cyclical activity.[23]

It is apparent that taking cyclical factors into consideration does not appreciably alter the interpretation of the finding that there were major increases in labor productivity across a wide range of manufacturing industries during the antebellum period. The relative importance of the various contributors, such as capital deepening or mechanization, to these developments, however, is less clear. That virtually all of the industries investigated realized impressive gains in labor productivity despite the rather modest degrees of mechanization and capital intensity in most of them suggests that other factors must have played a significant role. An indirect method of roughly gauging whether capital deepening or mechanization were the principal determinants of the rate of progress is to examine whether the records of productivity growth of the capital- and machinery-intensive industries compared favorably with those of their counterparts.

Instead of treating the relationship between the factor proportions employed and productivity growth through a discussion of the cases of individual industries, the 13 industries were ranked by both capital intensity and machine intensity, on the basis of information pertaining to 1850 and 1832, respectively, and divided into two groups for each dimension.[24] Weighted averages of the alternative measures of labor productivity were computed for the various classes of industries, and indexes and per annum rates of growth derived from them are presented in table 13.7.

Several findings of interest emerge from these estimates. Perhaps most important is that, over the entire period from 1820 to 1860, all categories of industries registered major increases in labor productivity. It does appear, however, that the more capital-intensive and machinery-intensive industries generally realized somewhat larger advances, particularly in terms of GQLP. For example, in the more capital-intensive industries this measure of labor productivity rose by 161%–202% (de-

**Table 13.7**    **Indexes of Labor Productivity for Classes of Manufacturing Industries, 1820–60**

| Year | Mechanized Industries | | Other Industries | | Capital-Intensive Industries | | Other Industries | |
|---|---|---|---|---|---|---|---|---|
| | VLP | GQLP | VLP | GQLP | VLP | GQLP | VLP | GQLP |
| 1820 | 100 | 100 | 100 | 100 | 100 | 100 | 100 | 100 |
| 1850 (firm) | [181] | [232] | [153] | [165] | [175] | [219] | [154] | [171] |
| 1850 (aggregate) | 204 | 239 | 179 | 187 | 205 | 235 | 170 | 174 |
| 1860 (firm) | [234] | [271] | [226] | [255] | [220] | [261] | [248] | [275] |
| 1860 (aggregate) | 296 | 311 | 228 | 247 | 278 | 302 | 240 | 244 |
| Per annum growth rates: | | | | | | | | |
| 1820–50 | [2.1]–2.5 | [3.0]–3.0 | [1.5]–2.0 | [1.7]–2.2 | [1.9]–2.5 | [2.7]–3.0 | [1.5]–1.9 | 1.9–[1.9] |
| 1850–60 | [2.6]–3.8 | [1.5]–2.7 | 2.5–[3.9] | 2.8–[4.5] | [2.3]–3.1 | 1.8–[2.5] | 3.5–[4.9] | 3.4–[4.9] |
| 1820–60 | [2.2]–2.8 | [2.6]–3.0 | [2.1]–2.1 | 2.3–[2.4] | [2.0]–2.7 | [2.5]–2.9 | [2.3]–2.4 | 2.3–[2.6] |

*Notes and sources:* These estimates were computed as weighted averages of the industry-specific figures underlying the indexes presented in table 13.4, 13.5, and 13.6. They were calculated with the same weights employed in those tables to construct the weighted averages. However, the weights of the industries in each class were normalized so that their sum was always equal to one. The mechanized industries include cotton textiles, wool textiles, paper, glass, mills, and iron. The capital-intensive industries include cotton textiles, wool textiles, paper, mills, iron, liquors, and tanning.

pending on whether the firm or aggregate data are employed) between 1820 and 1860, whereas those less dependent on capital managed an increase of 144%–175%. This differential is consistent with the view that the utilization of machinery or capital equipment may have facilitated changes in production processes that increased the rate at which raw materials could be processed into final products with a given amount of labor.

What is rather puzzling about these comparisons between the various classes of industries is that the qualitative results appear sensitive to whether the productivity estimates are derived from the samples of firm information or from the aggregate data. Especially in 1860, the aggregate figures suggest much greater productivity growth in the capital-intensive and machinery-intensive industries, relative to their counterparts, than do the estimates obtained from the firm reports. Since both sets of estimates would be expected to be biased downward, as discussed above, the substantial disparity might be thought to shed light on which sources of biases are most serious and accordingly to convey information about the structure of the manufacturing sector. In particular, it might seem to suggest that the disproportionate sampling of firms in 1860 from less developed states biases the firm-level productivity estimates downward by more than the aggregate productivity figures are affected by the inclusion of part-time operations in the census totals. Such an explanation does not hold up well, however, to the observation that no industries other than tanning and perhaps cotton textiles have large discrepancies of the same sign between the firm- and aggregate-level productivity estimates in both 1850 and 1860. Instead, the sensitivity of the finding of higher productivity growth in the capital-intensive and machinery-intensive industries to the choice between the two sets of estimates is primarily attributable to the enormous differences in 1860 for cotton textiles and paper that have not yet been satisfactorily accounted for.[25]

Regardless of the appropriate interpretation of the significantly more rapid progress of labor productivity implied by the aggregate data, one must be impressed with the extent of the advances realized by those industries with low levels of capital or machinery intensity. By either measure of labor productivity, these industries managed growth rates of over 2.0% per annum. Despite the evidence that industries with a greater reliance on capital and machinery did slightly better, this strong record would seem to bear against the view that the increasing utilization of these factors of production per unit of labor were the dominant forces in accounting for, or encouraging, growth in manufacturing productivity during this early phase of industrialization.

One might legitimately challenge the persuasiveness of this argument, on the grounds that a comparison of the rates of productivity growth between classes of industries defined by their factor intensities at one moment in time does not bear directly on the issue of how changes in the ratio of capital to labor over time contributed to advances in labor productivity. Such a procedure does, however, establish whether there was an association between the capital intensity of an industry at a point in time and the future capacity for, or history of, its productivity growth (depending on whether capital intensity is measured at the beginning or end of the period in question), but that is a somewhat different, if related, question. In this regard, the finding that the rates of advance achieved were nearly equal across classes of industries tends to suggest that any relationship between capital intensity and productivity growth was weak during this phase of industrial development. An alternative approach to the problem of how important capital accumulation was in promoting productivity increase would be to evaluate formally how much of the growth in labor productivity over some specified span of time can be directly attributed, in an accounting sense, to the accumulation of capital per unit of labor that occurred. Such an analysis entails the measurement of total factor productivity and will be carried out in the next section of the paper.

Another caveat to the interpretation of the comparisons between the rates of labor productivity growth in machinery- or capital-intensive industries and their counterparts is that the disparities are significantly smaller for the entire period from 1820 to 1860 than they are when attention is restricted to developments before 1850. For example, the gap in the rate of increase of GQLP between the mechanized industries and the less mechanized widens from between 2.6%–2.9% and 2.3%–2.4% per annum for 1820–60 to between 3.0%–3.0% and 1.7%–2.2% for 1820–50. This pattern reflects both impressive rates of advance throughout the period for all industries and an acceleration from 1850 to 1860 that is especially pronounced among, and perhaps exclusive to, the less mechanized and capital-intensive industries. The record of change in the capital-labor ratio is similar, in that the less mechanized and the less capital- intensive industries experienced an extraordinary rise between 1850 and 1860, while their counterparts failed to manifest any robust acceleration.

This perspective on the evidence tends to place somewhat greater emphasis on the roles played by mechanization and capital accumulation in promoting labor productivity growth. The estimates can be viewed as consistent with the notion that the advances were initially most rapid among industries such as cotton textiles that mechanized and were highly capital intensive early, and that the pace of progress in the rest of the manufacturing sector was boosted as sophisticated capital equipment began to be diffused more broadly during the 1840s and 1850s. Nevertheless, it is also clear that many industries, such as hats and furniture/woodwork, realized substantial increases in productivity while they were still utilizing small amounts of capital per unit of labor and little or no machinery.

The findings thus support the judgment that there may have been two general sources, or perhaps "stages," of productivity growth in manufacturing during early industrialization. The first wave of advances seems to have been associated, in many industries, with changes in the organization of labor and other alterations in production processes that did not involve large adjustments in the capital-to-labor ratio (Goldin and Sokoloff 1982; Sokoloff 1984b). The gains from these sorts of improvements eventually were to be exhausted, but a second class of innovations related to the introduction of sophisticated capital equipment followed, leading perhaps to an acceleration of labor productivity growth (Chandler 1977; Atack 1985). These stylized "stages" undoubtedly fail to describe the experience of all manufacturing industries; indeed, it is apparent that industries passed through them at different rates and periods, and that the timing of the diffusion of the new production methods may have varied across firms within industries with location and other characteristics. Moreover, changes in production techniques that encompassed aspects of both "stages" at once were implemented in some industries. It is difficult to determine precisely how important each development was in explaining labor productivity growth, particularly with only the bodies of evidence examined here. An exploration of more comprehensive measures of productivity should, however, help to improve our assessment of at least the relative significance of the various contributors.

### 13.3 Estimates of Total Factor Productivity

Although the estimates of labor productivity growth presented above are quite informative about the record of industrial development in the Northeast, broadening the investigation of productivity to include other factors as inputs can extend our knowledge further. It makes possible, in particular, the decomposition of the growth in labor productivity between the amounts attributable to increases in capital and raw materials utilized per unit of labor and that due to advances in total factor productivity. Such information in turn will contribute to our understanding of the evolution of production methods and help to determine how important physical capital accumulation was during the early stages of industrialization.

It is useful to begin the treatment of total factor productivity by examining the indexes of real partial factor productivity reported in table 13.8. These figures indicate the industry-specific movements over the period in the ratios of gross output to raw materials, capital, and labor. Several features of these estimates deserve comment. The first

**Table 13.8**    **Indexes of Real Partial Factor Productivity, 1820–60**

| Industry | 1820 | 1832 | 1850 Firms | 1850 Agg. | 1860 Firms | 1860 Agg. |
|---|---|---|---|---|---|---|
| **Boots/shoes** | | | | | | |
| GQ/RM | 100 | — | 107 | 113 | 141 | 156 |
| GQ/K | 100 | — | 181 | 217 | 115 | 220 |
| GQ/L | 100 | — | 145 | 145 | 260 | 230 |
| **Coaches/harnesses** | | | | | | |
| GQ/RM | 100 | 121 | 136 | 154 | 148 | 155 |
| GQ/K | 100 | 85 | 206 | 181 | 126 | 137 |
| GQ/L | 100 | 86 | 187 | 158 | 233 | 194 |
| **Cotton textiles** | | | | | | |
| GQ/RM | 100 | 89 | 68 | 82 | 112 | 123 |
| GQ/K | 100 | 124 | 222 | 215 | 301 | 219 |
| GQ/L | 100 | 200 | 336 | 341 | 267 | 379 |
| **Furniture/woodwork** | | | | | | |
| GQ/RM | 100 | 91 | 158 | 181 | 177 | 178 |
| GQ/K | 100 | 204 | 304 | 283 | 225 | 222 |
| GQ/L | 100 | 138 | 201 | 225 | 320 | 309 |
| **Glass** | | | | | | |
| GQ/RM | 100 | 103 | — | 155 | — | 140 |
| GQ/K | 100 | 179 | — | 218 | — | 188 |
| GQ/L | 100 | 335 | — | 305 | — | 290 |
| **Hats** | | | | | | |
| GQ/RM | 100 | 90 | 96 | 105 | 113 | 131 |
| GQ/K | 100 | 163 | 205 | 242 | 209 | 284 |
| GQ/L | 100 | 122 | 223 | 213 | 328 | 282 |
| **Iron** | | | | | | |
| GQ/RM | 100 | — | 127 | 115 | 119 | 134 |
| GQ/K | 100 | — | 150 | 125 | 180 | 142 |
| GQ/L | 100 | — | 105 | 125 | 218 | 195 |
| **Liquors** | | | | | | |
| GQ/RM | 100 | — | 180 | 148 | 146 | 157 |
| GQ/K | 100 | — | 83 | 143 | 114 | 97 |
| GQ/L | 100 | — | 90 | 187 | 221 | 209 |
| **Flour/grist mills** | | | | | | |
| GQ/RM | 100 | — | 143 | 144 | 148 | 148 |
| GQ/K | 100 | — | 103 | 124 | 100 | 102 |
| GQ/L | 100 | — | 123 | 150 | 166 | 167 |
| **Paper** | | | | | | |
| GQ/RM | 100 | 51 | 72 | 71 | 107 | 119 |
| GQ/K | 100 | 150 | 372 | 310 | 455 | 321 |
| GQ/L | 100 | 275 | 816 | 783 | 751 | 1042 |
| **Tanning** | | | | | | |
| GQ/RM | 100 | 97 | 95 | 100 | 117 | 116 |
| GQ/K | 100 | 93 | 112 | 143 | 114 | 117 |
| GQ/L | 100 | 136 | 180 | 237 | 217 | 274 |

**Table 13.8**     (continued)

| Industry | 1820 | 1832 | 1850 Firms | 1850 Agg. | 1860 Firms | 1860 Agg. |
|---|---|---|---|---|---|---|
| Tobacco | | | | | | |
| GQ/RM | 100 | — | 93 | 80 | 91 | 132 |
| GQ/K | 100 | — | 114 | 98 | 80 | 150 |
| GQ/L | 100 | — | 147 | 145 | 284 | 178 |
| Wool textiles | | | | | | |
| GQ/RM | 100 | 65 | 75 | 70 | 128 | 124 |
| GQ/K | 100 | 145 | 208 | 169 | 263 | 252 |
| GQ/L | 100 | 236 | 262 | 226 | 401 | 412 |

*Notes and sources:* See the note to table 13.1. The nominal values of the respective measures of partial factor productivity were converted to constant dollars with the industry-specific price indexes presented in table 13.3. These estimates were then normalized relative to a base of 100 representing the respective industry's levels in 1820.

is that in nearly all industries, each of these ratios of partial factor productivity increases between 1820 and 1860. Although the liquors and tobacco industries do diverge slightly from this pattern, neither case appears to contradict significantly the general result as the decreases they manifest are small and sensitive to the choice between firm- and aggregate-level estimates. Since the index of total factor productivity is equivalent to a weighted average of these individual ratios, it is accordingly obvious that any reasonable measure of the former would rise over the period in all industries.

Another pattern in the data that merits emphasis is that, in all industries, labor productivity increased much more over the period than either raw materials or capital productivity. While the gains in labor productivity between 1820 and 1860 typically were very large, the advances in raw materials productivity observed are quite modest. Capital productivity appears generally to have increased less than labor and more than raw materials productivity, although there are a few prominent deviations from this pattern where it also failed to keep up with the rise in the latter (i.e., liquors and flour/grist mills). This evidence suggests that, in general, manufacturing production methods evolved over time in such ways as to reduce the amounts of labor and, to a lesser extent, capital required to process a unit of raw materials into final product. It conforms well with the work of scholars who have argued that many of the innovations introduced by manufacturers during this period were intended to substitute relatively cheap raw materials for other inputs (Habakkuk 1962).

By dividing *GQ/L* by *GQ*/K or *GQ/RM,* one can calculate the change over time in the ratios of capital or raw materials to labor from the information provided in table 13.8. These latter ratios indicate that northeastern manufacturing did shift somewhat toward more capital-intensive production processes, as judged by the capital-labor ratio, between 1820 and 1860. However, the extent of this adjustment in factor proportions pales by comparison with the dramatic surge in raw materials intensity that occurred contemporaneously. Whereas the weighted-average growth in the ratio of raw materials to labor was in the 110%–118% range, the rise in capital per unit of labor amounted to only 59%–63%. It is striking that both of these increases in the utilization of other inputs per unit of labor are proportionally much lower than the estimated growth in GQLP during the period. This finding casts additional doubt on whether either raw materials accumulation or capital accumulation, but especially the latter, could play the dominant role in explaining the advance in labor productivity.

There is, of course, substantial variation across the industries in the extent of the movement toward greater capital intensity, and some of them experienced significantly larger shifts than the average did. Nevertheless, as will be shown below, the increase in the ratio of capital to labor was not sufficiently massive in any industry to account directly for a major share of the progress realized in labor productivity. Moreover, it is interesting that the industries that underwent the most extensive capital deepening during the period may have been those that were most capital intensive to begin with. Industries such as liquors, flour/grist mills, paper, tanning, and wool textiles, which were among the seven most capital intensive of the 13 in 1820, appear to have experienced the largest increases in the capital-labor ratio. Conversely, several of the less capital-intensive industries, boot/shoes, furniture/woodwork, and hats, were among those with the smallest percentage gains. Weighted averages of the two classes of industries reveal that the capital-to-labor ratio rose by 45%–79% over the period in the more capital-intensive industries (as identified at either 1820 or 1850), and by 16%–95% in their counterparts. Since the estimated range of increase for the former class of industries does not unambiguously dominate that for the latter, one cannot make an unqualified claim that those industries that were initially most capital intensive carried out more capital deepening. Nevertheless, it seems that the classes of industries were not converging in their degrees of capital intensity and that many industries remained highly labor intensive throughout the period.[26]

A final point to make about the indexes of partial factor productivity is that they imply that the doubts some scholars have raised concerning the accuracy of the census valuations of the capital invested in manufacturing firms are unwarranted. The chief question about the usefulness of the reported capital input has been whether establishments included working capital in their statements to census enumerators.[27]

If, as some have argued, they did not, then estimates of both the growth of capital intensity and total factor productivity over time would likely be confounded. The possible seriousness of the problem can be evaluated with the more detailed information on the composition of capital investments contained in the 1832 sample drawn from the *McLane Report*. These data include separate assessments of the value of capital invested in land and structures, tools and machinery, and inventories (Sokoloff 1984a).

Since the bulk of the capital investment was in working capital, and the 1832 estimates of total factor productivity and the capital-labor ratio were based on valuations of the capital input that included inventories, one would expect to observe some stark contrasts between the estimates from that year and those from 1820 or 1850 if working capital had not been incorporated as part of the reported capital investments into the censuses of the other years. More specifically, there would be large decreases in total factor productivity and substantial increases in capital intensity between 1820 and 1832, especially in those industries in which investment in working capital was relatively important. No such patterns emerge, nor do the differentials in total factor productivity across industries, varying with the relative investments in fixed and working capital, that would be evident in the 1820, 1850, and 1860 data if their information on capital investments did not include at least a major component of the working capital. It thus seems unlikely that undervaluation of working capital in manufacturing censuses was a serious defect, and correspondingly that the estimates of the growth in total factor productivity and capital intensity are significantly distorted as a consequence.

Indexes of real total factor productivity, based on the two alternative definitions of output, are presented for the 13 industries in tables 13.9 and 13.10. As with the labor productivity figures reported above, the estimates were computed for each of three sets of subsamples of firms so as to demonstrate the insensitivity of the results to the extent of adjustment for part-time firms, and the price indexes appearing in table 13.3 were employed to convert the nominal measures of gross output, value added, raw materials, and capital to constant dollars before productivity was calculated.

The results indicate that by either of the two measures, nearly all industries realized substantial growth in total factor productivity between 1820 and 1860. Weighted averages of the records of the individual industries yield estimated increases ranging from 104% to 130%, with output defined as value added (NFP), and from 68% to 76% by the alternative gauge (TFP). Each industry performed well by at least one measure. Flour/grist mills registered the smallest advance in NFP, only 10%–11%, but the estimated gain in TFP approached 50%; and although

**Table 13.9**    **Indexes of Total Factor Productivity: Computed with Value Added as the Measure of Output**

| Industry | 1820 | 1832 | 1850 Firms | 1850 Agg. | 1860 Firms | 1860 Agg. |
|---|---|---|---|---|---|---|
| Boots/shoes | | | | | | |
| A | 100 | — | 158 | 179 | 195 | 240 |
| B | 100 | — | 144 | 160 | 175 | 215 |
| C | 100 | — | 145 | 154 | 175 | 206 |
| Coaches/harnesses | | | | | | |
| A | 100 | 94 | 175 | 191 | 231 | 216 |
| B | 100 | 93 | 181 | 173 | 210 | 196 |
| C | 100 | 93 | 179 | 171 | 189 | 193 |
| Cotton textiles | | | | | | |
| A | 100 | 195 | 188 | 264 | 269 | 344 |
| B | 100 | 174 | 169 | 235 | 240 | 306 |
| C | 100 | 149 | 186 | 200 | 224 | 261 |
| Furniture/woodwork | | | | | | |
| A | 100 | 134 | 191 | 248 | 298 | 303 |
| B | 100 | 127 | 198 | 230 | 288 | 281 |
| C | 100 | 121 | 183 | 210 | 274 | 257 |
| Glass | | | | | | |
| A | 100 | 227 | — | 258 | — | 233 |
| B | 100 | 227 | — | 258 | — | 233 |
| C | 100 | 216 | — | 249 | — | 225 |
| Hats | | | | | | |
| A | 100 | 147 | 201 | 229 | 253 | 298 |
| B | 100 | 130 | 179 | 203 | 224 | 264 |
| C | 100 | 156 | 213 | 234 | 254 | 304 |
| Iron | | | | | | |
| A | 100 | — | 165 | 203 | 262 | 289 |
| B | 100 | — | 128 | 122 | 170 | 173 |
| C | 100 | — | 128 | 112 | 180 | 159 |
| Liquors | | | | | | |
| A | 100 | — | 121 | 184 | 173 | 193 |
| B | 100 | — | 113 | 160 | 158 | 168 |
| C | 100 | — | 122 | 156 | 174 | 164 |
| Flour/grist mills | | | | | | |
| A | 100 | — | 95 | 123 | 122 | 130 |
| B | 100 | — | 84 | 105 | 110 | 111 |
| C | 100 | — | 88 | 91 | 113 | 97 |
| Paper | | | | | | |
| A | 100 | 149 | 466 | 415 | 440 | 572 |
| B | 100 | 147 | 458 | 408 | 440 | 563 |
| C | 100 | 150 | 422 | 399 | 487 | 550 |
| Tanning | | | | | | |
| A | 100 | 139 | 168 | 247 | 157 | 187 |
| B | 100 | 114 | 141 | 201 | 129 | 152 |
| C | 100 | 93 | 127 | 175 | 120 | 132 |

**Table 13.9** (continued)

| Industry | 1820 | 1832 | 1850 Firms | 1850 Agg. | 1860 Firms | 1860 Agg. |
|---|---|---|---|---|---|---|
| Tobacco | | | | | | |
| A | 100 | — | 130 | 96 | 178 | 224 |
| B | 100 | — | 126 | 92 | 171 | 216 |
| C | 100 | — | 131 | 88 | 165 | 206 |
| Wool textiles | | | | | | |
| A | 100 | 180 | 227 | 171 | 332 | 318 |
| B | 100 | 141 | 179 | 134 | 260 | 248 |
| C | 100 | 123 | 157 | 118 | 212 | 218 |
| Average | | | | | | |
| Weighted B | 100 | [143] | [160] | 181 | [204] | 230 |
| Unweighted B | 100 | [144] | [175] | 191 | [207] | 240 |

*Notes and sources:* These estimates of total factor productivity were computed over the same sets of observations as the corresponding labor productivity estimates presented in tables 13.1 and 13.4 were. See the notes to tables 13.1 and 13.4. The index of total factor productivity for the weighted average of the industries was computed with the same weights, and in the same manner, as the index of labor productivity reported in the latter table. The output elasticities employed in the computation were selected from a range derived by estimating Cobb-Douglas production functions over each cross-sectional sample. These regressions yielded estimates of the capital coefficient between 0.25 and 0.30. The latter value was employed here so as to increase the estimates of the inputs in the later years relative to the earlier. The formulation of total factor productivity employed here is NFP = $(VA/K^{0.30}L^{0.70})$, where NFP is a measure of total factor productivity utilizing value added as the measure of output, $VA$ is value added, $K$ is the value of the capital invested, and $L$ is the labor input. The calculations of NFP were performed after the values of gross output, raw materials, and capital had been deflated to constant dollars, utilizing the price indexes reported in table 13.3. These "real" estimates of total factor productivity were then normalized relative to an 1820 standard of 100.

tobacco ranked at the bottom in terms of progress in TFP, its increases of 30%–48% in that measure, and of 71%–116% in NFP, are not unimpressive. The cotton textiles, wool textiles, and paper industries are among those attaining the largest estimated increases in total factor productivity, but major gains were also achieved by industries such as furniture/woodwork and hats, which were among the least capital intensive and mechanized throughout the period. These figures provide dramatic testimony to how dynamic the manufacturing sector was during the early stages of industrialization. Moreover, they serve to undercut the hypothesis that capital accumulation was the driving force behind productivity growth during this era. The substantial increases in total factor productivity demonstrate clearly that the bulk of the gains in labor productivity cannot be accounted for directly by capital or raw materials deepening within manufacturing firms. In addition, the wide range of industries that shared in this general advance of productivity suggests that the phenomenon cannot be attributed to

**Table 13.10    Indexes of Total Factor Productivity: Computed with Gross Output as the Measure of Output**

| Industry | 1820 | 1832 | 1850 Firms | 1850 Agg. | 1860 Firms | 1860 Agg. |
|---|---|---|---|---|---|---|
| Boots/shoes | | | | | | |
| A | 100 | — | 133 | 142 | 178 | 197 |
| B | 100 | — | 127 | 134 | 168 | 185 |
| C | 100 | — | 125 | 129 | 165 | 179 |
| Coaches/harnesses | | | | | | |
| A | 100 | 104 | 156 | 166 | 175 | 171 |
| B | 100 | 104 | 159 | 159 | 168 | 164 |
| C | 100 | 104 | 158 | 158 | 159 | 163 |
| Cotton textiles | | | | | | |
| A | 100 | 128 | 141 | 157 | 180 | 203 |
| B | 100 | 121 | 134 | 149 | 170 | 192 |
| C | 100 | 112 | 133 | 136 | 164 | 176 |
| Furniture/woodwork | | | | | | |
| A | 100 | 122 | 184 | 217 | 229 | 232 |
| B | 100 | 116 | 186 | 206 | 222 | 220 |
| C | 100 | 114 | 179 | 197 | 218 | 211 |
| Glass | | | | | | |
| A | 100 | 163 | — | 202 | — | 185 |
| B | 100 | 163 | — | 202 | — | 185 |
| C | 100 | 160 | — | 201 | — | 183 |
| Hats | | | | | | |
| A | 100 | 115 | 148 | 157 | 185 | 199 |
| B | 100 | 108 | 140 | 148 | 174 | 187 |
| C | 100 | 118 | 153 | 159 | 186 | 201 |
| Iron | | | | | | |
| A | 100 | — | 137 | 151 | 187 | 193 |
| B | 100 | — | 122 | 119 | 153 | 153 |
| C | 100 | — | 124 | 115 | 157 | 147 |
| Liquors | | | | | | |
| A | 100 | — | 134 | 170 | 169 | 173 |
| B | 100 | — | 129 | 159 | 162 | 162 |
| C | 100 | — | 134 | 157 | 168 | 160 |
| Flour/grist mills | | | | | | |
| A | 100 | — | 139 | 154 | 154 | 159 |
| B | 100 | — | 130 | 143 | 146 | 147 |
| C | 100 | — | 136 | 138 | 148 | 142 |
| Paper | | | | | | |
| A | 100 | 103 | 203 | 192 | 246 | 280 |
| B | 100 | 102 | 200 | 190 | 245 | 277 |
| C | 100 | 103 | 192 | 188 | 256 | 273 |
| Tanning | | | | | | |
| A | 100 | 118 | 129 | 153 | 155 | 169 |
| B | 100 | 108 | 120 | 139 | 143 | 154 |
| C | 100 | 98 | 115 | 131 | 138 | 145 |

**Table 13.10**     (continued)

| Industry | 1820 | 1832 | 1850 Firms | 1850 Agg. | 1860 Firms | 1860 Agg. |
|---|---|---|---|---|---|---|
| Tobacco |  |  |  |  |  |  |
| A | 100 | — | 113 | 102 | 132 | 151 |
| B | 100 | — | 111 | 100 | 130 | 148 |
| C | 100 | — | 114 | 98 | 128 | 145 |
| Wool textiles |  |  |  |  |  |  |
| A | 100 | 124 | 146 | 130 | 231 | 227 |
| B | 100 | 110 | 130 | 115 | 205 | 202 |
| C | 100 | 103 | 122 | 108 | 187 | 190 |
| Average |  |  |  |  |  |  |
| Weighted (B) | 100 | [114] | [133] | 142 | [168] | 176 |
| Unweighted (B) | 100 | [117] | [141] | 152 | [174] | 183 |

*Notes and sources:* These estimates of total factor productivity were computed over the same sets of observations as the corresponding labor productivity estimates preserved in tables 13.2 and 13.5 were. See the notes to those tables. The index of total factor productivity for the weighted average of the industries was computed with the same weights, and in the same manner, as the index of labor productivity reported in table 13.5. The output elasticities were selected from a range provided by Cobb-Douglas production functions estimated cross-sectionally. The choice was influenced by the desire to have the coefficients for capital and raw materials to be on the high side so as to depress the estimated rates of productivity growth. The formulation of total factor productivity employed here is TFP $= (GQ/RM^{0.54}L^{0.33}K^{0.13})$, where TFP is a measure of total factor productivity utilizing the gross value of output as the measure of output, $RM$ is the value of raw materials, $L$ is the labor input, and $K$ is the value of capital invested. All of the relevant variables were deflated to constant dollars, by the indexes in table 13.3, before the calculations were performed. These "real" estimates of total factor productivity were then normalized relative to a 1820 standard of 100.

developments such as the diffusion of new and more sophisticated capital equipment, which touched only a relatively limited number of industries until late in the period.

The consistency of the finding of large gains in total factor productivity, across industries and measures, bolsters confidence in the robustness of the qualitative result. Moreover, as the minor differences between the C and B sets of estimates suggest, the basic picture that emerges is not sensitive to any reasonable adjustments of the subsamples to account for the existence of part-time establishments.[28] It is also encouraging to note that there are fewer implausible fluctuations in these estimates than in the indexes of labor productivity, particularly with the TFP measure. Several industries do continue to manifest strange records of progress, but at least in the most troubling cases, paper, tanning, and tobacco, the price indexes relied on are suspect and likely the primary source of the problems. The other questionable features may also be attributable to the inappropriate or defective nature of the price series utilized, or an inadequate number of observations in some years. Whatever the explanation for these anomalies, however, the fundamental results do not depend upon their inclusion in the manufacturing averages.

Estimates of the per annum growth rates of total factor productivity have been computed from the indexes reported in tables 13.9 and 13.10 for the entire period between 1820 and 1860, as well as for several subperiods. They are presented in table 13.11, and confirm that a wide spectrum of manufacturing industries in the Northeast enjoyed rapid progress in total factor productivity during this initial phase of industrialization. Indeed, the weighted average per annum growth rates for these 13 industries match, if not exceed, the performance of the United States economy during other periods. Between 1820 and 1860, northeastern manufacturing appears to have achieved per annum rates of increase of 1.8%–2.2% in NFP and 1.3%–1.5% in TFP. These figures might be compared to the 1.8% rate for NFP estimated by Kendrick (1961) for the national manufacturing sector between 1869 and 1953, or to the 0.8%–0.9% and 1.4% rates computed by Gallman (1986) for the annual increase in TFP for the economy at large during the respective periods 1840–1900 and 1900–1960. Although some might react to the application of these standards by rejecting the early manufacturing rates of advance as implausibly high, it should be remembered that one would expect the pace of productivity growth in the most dynamic sector of the most burgeoning region during the period to have surpassed that for the national economy or for United States manufacturing in total. Hence, the finding that northeastern manufacturing might have realized faster rates of total factor productivity increase during its initial burst of expansion than economy-wide averages, pertaining to the same or other periods, should perhaps not be too surprising.

These estimates further suggest, more strongly than did those for labor productivity growth, that productivity rose, on average, more slowly between 1820 and 1850 than during the 1850s. The average rate of advance in TFP, for example, increased from 1.0%–1.2% per annum over the first 30 years to 2.2%–2.3% during the later 10. The pattern of acceleration is, admittedly, somewhat weaker if one focuses on the contrast between 1820–32 and 1832–60, and only on those industries for which 1832 figures are available. Nevertheless, even here, the weight of the evidence seems to favor a mild increase in the pace of total factor productivity growth. Many researchers have contended that such an acceleration may have resulted from a spurt in the accumulation of more and better capital equipment, during the 1840s and 1850s (Chandler 1977; David 1977; Williamson and Lindert 1980). They might tend to argue that the process of capital deepening only seems unimportant, because the conventional measures of input fail to fully detect the technical change that is embodied in newer vintages of capital. The acceleration of total factor productivity growth during a decade of more

**Table 13.11**    **Growth Rates of Total Factor Productivity in Selected Manufacturing Industries, 1820–60 (%)**

| Industry | 1820–32 | 1820–50 | 1850–60 | 1820–60 |
|---|---|---|---|---|
| Boots/shoes | | | | |
| NFP | — | 1.3–1.6 | 2.0–3.0 | 1.4–2.0 |
| TFP | — | 0.8–1.0 | 2.9–3.3 | 1.3–1.6 |
| Coaches/harnesses | | | | |
| NFP | −0.7 | 1.9–2.1 | 1.3–1.5 | 1.7–1.9 |
| TFP | 0.3 | 1.6–1.6 | 0.3–0.5 | 1.3–1.3 |
| Cotton textiles | | | | |
| NFP | 5.2 | 1.8–3.0 | 2.7–3.6 | 2.3–2.9 |
| TFP | 1.8 | 1.0–1.4 | 2.4–2.6 | 1.4–1.7 |
| Furniture/woodwork | | | | |
| NFP | 2.2 | 2.4–2.9 | 2.0–3.8 | 2.7–2.8 |
| TFP | 1.4 | 2.2–2.5 | 0.7–1.8 | 2.0–2.1 |
| Glass | | | | |
| NFP | 7.7 | 3.3 | −1.0 | 2.2 |
| TFP | 4.5 | 2.5 | −0.9 | 1.6 |
| Hats | | | | |
| NFP | 2.4 | 2.0–2.5 | 2.3–2.7 | 2.1–2.5 |
| TFP | 0.7 | 1.2–1.4 | 2.2–2.4 | 1.4–1.6 |
| Iron | | | | |
| NFP | — | 0.7–0.8 | 2.9–3.6 | 1.4–1.4 |
| TFP | — | 0.6–0.7 | 2.3–2.5 | 1.1–1.1 |
| Liquors | | | | |
| NFP | — | 0.4–1.6 | 0.5–3.5 | 1.2–1.2 |
| TFP | — | 0.9–1.6 | 0.2–2.3 | 1.2 |
| Flour/grist mills | | | | |
| NFP | — | −0.6–0.2 | 0.6–2.8 | 0.2–0.3 |
| TFP | — | 0.9–1.2 | 0.3–1.2 | 1.0–1.0 |
| Paper | | | | |
| NFP | 3.6 | 5.0–5.4 | −0.4–3.3 | 3.9–4.5 |
| TFP | 0.2 | 2.2–2.4 | 2.0–3.8 | 2.3–2.6 |
| Tanning | | | | |
| NFP | 1.2 | 1.2–2.4 | −2.7--0.8 | 0.7–1.1 |
| TFP | 0.7 | 0.6–1.1 | 1.1–1.8 | 0.9–1.1 |
| Tobacco | | | | |
| NFP | — | −0.3–0.8 | 3.1–8.9 | 1.4–2.0 |
| TFP | — | 0.0–0.4 | 1.5–4.0 | 0.7–1.0 |
| Wool textiles | | | | |
| NFP | 3.2 | 1.0–2.0 | 3.8–6.4 | 2.4–2.5 |
| TFP | 0.9 | 0.5–0.9 | 4.7–5.8 | 1.8–1.9 |
| Weighted average | | | | |
| NFP | [3.3] | [1.6]–2.1 | [2.4]–2.4 | [1.8]–2.2 |
| TFP | [1.2] | [1.0]–1.2 | [2.2]–2.3 | [1.3]–1.5 |

*Notes and sources:* These per annum rates of total factor productivity growth were computed from the set B estimates reported in tables 13.9 and 13.10. See the notes to those tables. The NFP estimates are of the growth of total factor productivity measured with value added as output. The TFP estimates are based on the measure of total factor productivity that employs gross output as the measure of output and explicitly treats the value of raw materials as an input.

rapid diffusion of machinery is certainly consistent with this interpretation, but alternative explanations of this feature of the economic record are also available.[29]

Although some of the technical change realized between 1820 and 1860 was undoubtedly embodied in capital goods, there are several reasons to doubt whether a proper accounting for this phenomenon would be capable of reversing the qualitative conclusion concerning the significance of capital accumulation for productivity growth in early manufacturing. First, even if one were to ascribe as much as half of the acceleration in total factor productivity increase to improvements of manufacturing capital not reflected in its price, the amount of productivity growth so generated would be quite small relative to the total realized over the entire period. One might claim that more of the estimated advance in total factor productivity should be credited to embodied technical change unincorporated in price, but the rationale for this appears weak. Not only did the less capital-intensive and less mechanized industries do quite well before the purported consequential developments of the 1840s and 1850s, but their investments in machinery and tools per unit of labor remained quite small in absolute terms, as well as in relation to their total investment in capital, at the end of the period. Even most of the counterpart industries, classified as more mechanized and capital intensive, had rather modest absolute and relative amounts invested in capital equipment that was directly involved in production (Sokoloff 1984a). Given that manufacturing industries had the bulk of their investments in structures and inventories, there would seem to be severe limits on the amount of embodied technical change that the capital input could plausibly be endowed with.[30]

One approach to evaluating the importance of embodied technical change is to compare the records of total factor productivity growth between the more capital-intensive and the less capital-intensive industries, or between the more mechanized and less mechanized ones. The logic underlying this procedure is that where new vintages of capital are endowed with embodied technical change, the measured increase over time in the inputs utilized by firms will be lower, relative to the outputs produced, and hence measured total factor productivity will be higher. Given that one would expect the realization of technical change embodied in capital and not incorporated in its price to be associated with either the size of the capital input relative to other inputs or the change in that relative size of the capital input over the period in question, the more capital-intensive and mechanized industries might seem likely to have enjoyed greater total factor productivity growth than the others if this component of embodied technical change was of much quantitative significance.[31] Although, as discussed above, the evidence of significantly more capital deepening over the period by these classes of industries is not entirely robust, it is clear that they did employ larger amounts of capital and machinery per unit of labor throughout the period, and carried out approximately as much capital deepening as their less capital-intensive and mechanized counterparts did. One might, accordingly, expect them to exhibit more total factor productivity growth.

When one examines the indexes of total factor productivity presented in table 13.12 for classes of manufacturing industries, however, only minor differences in performances emerge.[32] The discrepancies in the amount of productivity growth realized between the more and less capital-intensive industries are rather trivial in magnitude. As for the other system of classification, the more mechanized industries do seem to have experienced higher rates of advance than the less mechanized did. However, these disparities are small relative to the rates of increase, and are dependent on NFP serving as the gauge for total factor productivity. Another feature of these estimates that bears against the hypothesis that much of the technical change realized was embodied in physical capital and not reflected in its price is the relative decline in the rate of total factor productivity growth of the less mechanized and capital-intensive industries, as compared to their counterpart classes, between the subperiods 1820–50 and 1850–60. As already alluded to, the rates of increase of both capital intensity and labor productivity accelerated sharply between the two subperiods among the former classes of industries relative to the latter.[33] If the capital investments involved considerable embodied technical change, then one might have expected a relative increase in the pace of total factor productivity in the less mechanized and capital-intensive industries to have accompanied the relative surge in capital deepening and labor productivity.

Regardless of how persuasive these arguments for questioning the extent of embodied technical change are, it is informative to decompose the growth over the period in gross output per equivalent worker between the amounts directly attributable, in an accounting sense, to increases in capital intensity ($K/L$), in raw materials intensity ($RM/L$), and in total factor productivity (TFP). The results of such a procedure are reported in table 13.13, with separate estimates presented for the estimates obtained from the firm data and those from the aggregate data. They indicate that in most industries the increase between 1820 and 1860 in capital intensity explains less than 10% of the growth in labor productivity as measured by GQLP. Indeed, in no case does the share exceed 16%. Advances in total factor productivity, on the other hand, appear to be the principal force behind labor productivity growth, generally accounting for over half of the increase in GQLP and never

**Table 13.12**     Indexes of Total Factor Productivity for Classes of Manufacturing Industries, 1820–60

| Year | Mechanized Industries | | Other Industries | | Capital-Intensive Industries | | Other Industries | |
|---|---|---|---|---|---|---|---|---|
| | NFP | TFP | NFP | TFP | NFP | TFP | NFP | TFP |
| 1820 | 100 | 100 | 100 | 100 | 100 | 100 | 100 | 100 |
| 1850 (firm) | [166] | [133] | [155] | [134] | [159] | [131] | [162] | [141] |
| 1850 (aggregate) | 181 | 138 | 181 | 147 | 181 | 138 | 182 | 151 |
| 1860 (firm) | [221] | [169] | [186] | [166] | [204] | [165] | [205] | [175] |
| 1860 (aggregate) | 249 | 176 | 209 | 176 | 231 | 172 | 229 | 186 |
| Per annum growth rates: | | | | | | | | |
| 1820–50 | [1.8]–2.1 | [1.0]–1.1 | [1.5]–2.1 | [1.0]–1.3 | [1.6]–2.1 | [0.9]–1.1 | [1.7]–2.1 | [1.2]–1.4 |
| 1850–60 | [2.9]–3.2 | [2.4]–2.4 | 1.4–[1.9] | 1.8–[2.1] | 2.5–[2.5] | 2.2–[2.4] | 2.3–[2.4] | 2.1–[2.2] |
| 1820–60 | [2.0]–2.4 | [1.4]–1.5 | [1.6]–1.9 | [1.3]–1.5 | [1.8]–2.2 | [1.3]–1.4 | [1.9]–2.2 | [1.4]–1.6 |

*Notes and sources:* These estimates were computed as weighted averages of the industry-specific figures underlying the indexes presented in tables 13.9, 13.10, and 13.11. The weighted averages were constructed with the system of weighting employed in table 13.7. See the notes to those tables.

**Table 13.13**    **Decomposition of the Growth in Gross Output per Equivalent Worker between Proportions Accounted for by Increases in Capital Intensity, Raw Materials Intensity, and Total Factor Productivity, 1820–60 (%)**

| Industry | % Due to Δ (K/L) | % Due to Δ (RM/L) | % Due to Δ TFP |
|---|---|---|---|
| Boots/shoes | | | |
| F | 11 | 34 | 54 |
| A | 1 | 25 | 74 |
| Coaches/harnesses | | | |
| F | 9 | 29 | 61 |
| A | 7 | 19 | 74 |
| Cotton textiles | | | |
| F | −2 | 48 | 54 |
| A | 5 | 46 | 49 |
| Furniture/woodwork | | | |
| F | 4 | 27 | 68 |
| A | 4 | 26 | 70 |
| Glass | | | |
| F | — | — | — |
| A | 5 | 37 | 57 |
| Hats | | | |
| F | 5 | 48 | 46 |
| A | 0 | 40 | 60 |
| Iron | | | |
| F | 3 | 42 | 55 |
| A | 6 | 30 | 63 |
| Liquors | | | |
| F | 11 | 28 | 61 |
| A | 14 | 21 | 65 |
| Flour/grist mills | | | |
| F | 13 | 12 | 75 |
| A | 13 | 12 | 75 |
| Paper | | | |
| F | 3 | 52 | 44 |
| A | 6 | 50 | 43 |
| Tanning | | | |
| F | 11 | 43 | 46 |
| A | 11 | 46 | 43 |
| Tobacco | | | |
| F | 16 | 59 | 25 |
| A | 4 | 28 | 68 |
| Wool textiles | | | |
| F | 4 | 44 | 51 |
| A | 5 | 46 | 49 |

*Notes and sources:* The decomposition of the growth in gross output per equivalent worker was based on the accounting equation:

$$G\dot{Q}LP = T\dot{F}P + 0.13\,(\dot{K/L}) + 0.54\,(\dot{RM/L}),$$

where ˙ signifies a derivative of the log. Separate decompositions were computed for the firm-level (F) and aggregate (A) data from 1860. See the notes to tables 13.5 and 13.8.

less than 25%.[34] These findings dramatize how remarkably limited the importance of capital deepening was in generating labor productivity growth in manufacturing during early industrialization. They imply that if capital accumulation played a substantial role at all, it was due to improvements in capital that were not reflected in price. Given the basis for skepticism about the extent to which technical progress was embodied in capital outlined above, other sources of total factor productivity, and thus of labor productivity, growth appear to deserve more attention.

## 13.4 Conclusions

This paper has relied on four cross-sections of manufacturing firm data to study the growth of labor and total factor productivity during early industrialization in the United States. Although the bodies of evidence analyzed suffer from some defects, the procedures employed in constructing the estimates were designed to deal with the problems and yield growth rates that would be biased downward. Despite this concern for producing conservative estimates, the results indicate that a wide range of manufacturing industries realized major increases in both labor and total factor productivity as early as the 1820s, and continued to do so at an accelerated pace through 1860. The breadth, magnitude, and timing of the advances observed suggest that the northeastern manufacturing sector was a dynamic one, whose productivity growth, perhaps coupled with similar gains in agriculture, fueled the process of industrialization in that region. The evidence would seem to make it increasingly difficult to sustain the view that the onset of industrial expansion in the Northeast was primarily due to the release of labor and other resources from a stagnant and declining agricultural sector.

Of perhaps even greater interest, the estimates imply that increases in total factor productivity, sometimes referred to as the residual, accounted for most of the advance in labor productivity between 1820 and 1860. The deepening of capital, in contrast, appears to have made only a modest contribution. Although it is possible that a major share of the growth in the residual over the period consisted of technical change embodied in capital equipment, which would enhance the significance of capital in explaining the gains in productivity, the shreds of evidence that can be gleaned from these data do not support this notion. Capital accumulation may indeed have had important influences on the course of early industrial development, such as through allowing for the extension of the transportation network and other social overhead capital, but the introduction of sophisticated capital equipment and capital deepening in general were evidently not as central to the initial phase of industrialization as they have sometimes been depicted.

On the contrary, the material examined here seems to suggest that other sources of measured productivity growth in manufacturing, including the changes in labor organization and the intensification of work that have been emphasized in recent studies, played the leading roles (Goldin and Sokoloff 1982; Sokoloff 1984b; Lazonick and Brush 1985). Although many questions remain, the results also appear to be consistent with, if not actually to support, the view that the expansion of markets that accompanied the onset of industrialization unleashed powerful forces that acted to raise productivity. At least in the United States, pre-industrial manufacturing seems to have had the potential, which it was ultimately to realize, for substantial gains in efficiency without major additions to the stock of capital equipment utilized per unit of labor.

# Notes

1. Nearly all studies of productivity growth during this period have been based on information that was either highly aggregated or drawn only from a small number of cotton textile firms (Layer 1955; Davis and Stettler 1966; David 1967, 1975, 1977; McGouldrick 1968; Williamson 1972; 1972a, 2b, 1986; Nickless 1979).

2. Each of the data sets suffers from problems of sample selection bias. The coverage of the 1820 Census of Manufactures and the *McLane Report* differed substantially by geographic region and size of establishment, with an apparent net result of an under-sampling of smaller, and accordingly less productive, firms. The design of the samples from 1850 and 1860 led to a disproportionate representation of firms from states with limited industrial development. See Sokoloff (1982) and Atack et al. (1979) for details on the characteristics of these samples. Since the sample selection biases are likely to raise the estimated productivity levels for 1820 and 1832, and reduce them in 1850 and 1860, the rates of productivity growth computed from these sources should understate the actual record.

3. The industrial classification system employed in the 1850 census was in general adopted, but several of the industry definitions used here include two or more of the 1850 categories. The reluctance to combine data from different industries stemmed from a concern about the possibility of confusing increases in labor productivity within industries over time with variation in the estimates due to changes in industrial composition.

4. This generalization about the reporting practices of part-time establishments is based primarily on an examination of the schedules for roughly 200 firms in the 1820 and 1832 samples that specified the fractions of the year they were in operation. Rather than expunging observations of seasonal enterprises from the calculations, one would of course prefer to have accurate assessments of their inputs and outputs to work with so that their levels of performance would be reflected in the estimates. It is likely that part-time firms, whose relative importance declined over time, were indeed less efficient producers than their full-time counterparts. Accordingly, to the extent that the adjustments in the composition of the subsamples do succeed in excluding all part-time establishments from consideration, the estimates of productivity growth might tend to understate the advances realized over the period by failing to pick up the perhaps important gains to the economy of displacing seasonal operators with full-time producers.

5. It is admittedly unclear what fractions of manufacturing firms in the various years were operating significantly fewer than 50 weeks per year (fulltime). A general sense of the orders of magnitude has been obtained, however, from the reports by many firms in 1832 of the fraction of the year they were in operation, from an examination

of the cross-sectional distributions of establishments by industry, size, wage rates, and location, as well as from inspections of the distributions of firms by measures of total factor productivity. The approach adopted in preparing the three sets of estimates was not to attempt a precise delineation of the proportion of firms operating part time in the individual years, but rather to demonstrate that no plausible assumptions about the changes in their relative numbers would reverse the qualitative findings. Although ad hoc in nature, this manner of displaying the patterns in the data appears effective. One can check the sensitivity of the industry-specific results by comparing the figures from the three sets of estimates, or by evaluating the C figures for 1820 with respect to the B figures for the later years. The extent of the allowance for the decreasing prevalence of part-time firms implied by this latter comparison appears to be extremely generous.

6. In this paper, such summaries of the quantitative results are based on the choice of the 1860 estimates computed from the aggregate data as the standard for that year.

7. The weights employed to construct the averages consist of the industry shares of total northeastern value added and gross output, respectively, in 1850, and were calculated from United States Census Bureau (1858). The two point estimates available for 12 of the industries in 1850 and 1860, as well as the growth rates they enter into, will henceforth be expressed as a range of estimates (i.e., 72%–112%).

8. The general robustness of the results is apparent from the observation that the estimates of labor productivity in 1820 are greatly affected by the shift from the B subsample to the C in only a few industries. The value-added figures are considerably more sensitive to the subset of establishments employed in the calculations, but even by this measure, only three of the industries have their levels of labor productivity raised by as much as 15%.

9. Of greatest concern in this regard are the glass, liquor, and tobacco industries. All of these industries are characterized by having estimates based on very few observations in at least one of the years. Random variation in the estimates due to this source may magnify the impact of sample selection bias in some cases. For example, the extremely high levels of productivity estimated for the glass industry in 1832 is probably related to their being computed from information on a rather small number of glass-making enterprises in Massachusetts. The most advanced plants in that industry were located in Massachusetts (Davis 1949), and that state accounted for a disproportionate share of the firms included in the *McLane Report*.

10. The 1850 and 1860 samples were designed to ensure that each state accounted for a certain minimum number of observations. This feature of their collection led to an oversampling of manufacturing firms from smaller and less-developed states such as Maine, Vermont, and New Hampshire. The establishments located in such states operated, on average, at lower levels of productivity. Accordingly, one would expect that this source of sample selection bias would lead to underestimates of productivity. In principle, one should be able to correct for this sample selection problem by reweighting the observations. In practice, however, inconsistent evidence from the aggregate census reports and the firm samples on the industrial composition of state manufacturing sectors suggests that there are other defects in the samples that confound the identification of the appropriate set of weights.

11. It is, of course, important to recognize that the great majority of the price series pertain only to a single output or raw material of the respective industries. Hence, they undoubtedly introduce errors and must be applied with caution. The four industries for which raw materials indexes could not be retrieved are coaches/harnesses, glass, hats, and iron. The Wholesale Price Index constructed by Warren and Pearson was employed as a reasonable substitute in these cases, because it behaves more like the average of the other raw materials series than the alternative general indexes. Another deficiency is that in two industries, tobacco and tanning, the author was compelled to rely on basically the same price index for both outputs and raw materials. It is especially unfortunate that separate indexes could not be obtained for these industries, because the indexes, which pertain primarily to the price of raw materials, move quite erratically. Additional information on whether the prices of outputs and raw materials in each of these industries actually followed such peculiar paths would be quite helpful. It seems

likely that the extraordinary variability in these price indexes accounts for at least some of the irregular movements in the productivity growth estimates for these industries.

12. In cases where there were several alternative price indexes available, the most conservative, with respect to the estimation of the increase in productivity over time, were generally selected.

13. This suggests that a significant portion of the variability in the labor productivity estimates is due to sharp changes in the factor proportions utilized by the firms sampled.

14. The extreme decline in the price index for paper output invites skepticism. However, it should be noted that the general stability between 1820 and 1860 in the ratio of gross output to raw materials in that industry would seem to suggest that the output price index might not be far off in terms of the extent of the decrease over the entire period.

15. As was mentioned above, the price indexes for tanning and tobacco fluctuate wildly, particularly between 1859 and 1860. The erratic behavior of the index for "hides and leather" may also affect estimates for boots/shoes, because this series serves as the index for raw materials in that industry, as well as for both outputs and raw materials in tanning.

16. The argument presented in this paragraph applies to estimates of productivity growth that employ value added as the measure of output. Hence, it supplies a rationale for why the value-added figures might indicate less advance over the period than those relying on gross output as the appropriate measure of product. Given the uncertainty about the accuracy of the individual price indexes, however, any conclusions about the relative performance of two industries, regardless of the measure of productivity referred to, should be offered tentatively.

17. There are, admittedly, some scholars who judge part-time operations to be the rule during the early stages of industrialization, rather than the exception. Moreover, few would expect there to be many firms in industries such as flour/grist mills that were in production all year. Nevertheless, the enumerators for the *McLane Report* indicated that the overwhelming majority of the establishments included in that survey claimed to be in operation for at least 50 weeks a year. Although the level of production in any individual firm may have been characterized by enormous seasonal variation, there might have been tasks that required at least some workers to be employed throughout the year. As long as enterprises in such circumstances reported their average labor and capital inputs, they should, for our purposes, have been classified as full-time operators and included in the subsets of firms over which the estimates were prepared.

18. As is apparent from the evidence presented in Goldin and Sokoloff (1982), the ratio of female to adult male wages increased from roughly the 0.30–0.37 range in 1820 to roughly the 0.44–0.52 range in 1850 and beyond. Hence, to the extent that the wage ratio reflects the average relative productivity of the two groups, it might be argued that employing the same weights in all years leads to overestimates of the amount of productivity growth. The issue turns, however, on whether the change in the relative productivity of females is due to variation over time in the age or skill composition of workers, or to some other factors. In any case, a wide range of weights for females and boys was tested, and the general qualitative results were found to be insensitive to reasonable variation in them.

19. It was further assumed that in no industry at 1850 or 1860 did boys account for more than 33% of the male labor force. Such a constraint, probably serves to bias upward the estimates of the labor input for several industries. The ceiling on the proportion of males who were boys was introduced as another way of ensuring that the estimates of the labor input in the later years would err on the high side, if at all.

20. This would be expected, because of the scale economies present in most manufacturing industries (Sokoloff 1984b). The bias is likely to have been greater in the 1832 sample, because Massachusetts firms accounted for a highly disproportionate share of the enterprises covered by that survey, and generally were larger and had higher-than-average levels of measured productivity.

21. For example, the weighted average of the industry rate of growth in gross output per equivalent worker, as computed from the C estimates for 1820 and the B estimates for 1860, ranges between 2.4% and 2.6% per annum. These figures are only slightly

lower than the 2.5%–2.7% range derived from the employment of the B estimates for both years.

22. The Davis and Stettler series might be expected to yield estimates of the variation in output per worker over the business cycle that were downward biased, because their figures pertain to output per man-hour. See Davis and Stettler (1966).

23. One caveat to this generalization is that the iron and steel industry appears to have been quite depressed during the late 1840s and early 1850s. See Temin (1964).

24. The industries were ordered in terms of capital intensity by the information on their aggregate capital-labor ratios in the Northeast obtained from United States Census Bureau (1858), and then divided into groups. The same classification of industries is derived from the 1820 firm data. The ranking by machinery intensity was computed from information contained in the 1820 and 1832 samples of firm data, particularly the latter, as well as in United States Census Office (1895). Industries were placed in categories on the basis of estimates of the investment in machinery per unit of labor computed for 1832.

25. The cotton textile establishments in the firm samples were, on average, also smaller and substantially less capital intensive than their counterparts in the aggregate data. Their levels of total factor productivity were, however, not much lower. The massive disparity in measured labor productivity may be due to the less developed states', which were overrepresented in the samples, being characterized by a much different system or type of cotton textile manufacture.

26. It must also be admitted that these indexes of partial factor productivity not infrequently exhibit irregular, if not implausible, movements from one point in time to another, as well as discrepancies between the firm- and aggregate-level estimates for 1850 and 1860. As I contended above in discussing the labor productivity figures, many of the former type of problems may be due to inaccurate price indexes, excessive variability in point estimates because of a small number of observations, or sample selection biases. The disparities between the independent estimates for 1850 and 1860 are disturbing, but they might again be partially explained by many of the firm-level estimates being based on the characteristics of relatively few firms located in unrepresentative areas. These anomalies in the data indicate that much caution should be exercised in drawing conclusions, particularly with respect to changes over short periods, but they do not justify a blanket dismissal of the results.

27. The other principal issue has concerned whether firms reported the gross value of their capital investment or the net value. Recent work has tended to agree that some net measure of the capital stock was being reflected in the figures. See Gallman (1986) and Sokoloff (1984a).

28. If one computes the weighted-average growth in total factor productivity from the C figures for 1820 and the B figures for 1860, the estimates decline only slightly. NFP rises by 88%–112% over the period, while TFP increases by 61%–69%.

29. One could, for example, explain the acceleration in total factor productivity as arising from the expansion of product markets, which stimulated changes in the organization of production within the firm, technical change, and intraregional specialization between the more urbanized counties and the outlying areas within the Northeast (Lindstrom 1978; Sokoloff 1984b).

30. Although it is difficult to imagine that variation in the relatively small amount of tools and machinery per worker could account for much of the large changes observed in productivity, it would be helpful to know, by industry, how the former ratio moved over time. Unfortunately, of all the data sets being examined here, only the 1832 sample contains the detailed information on the composition of capital necessary to estimate the ratio. It seems likely, however, that the percentage changes in machinery and tools per equivalent worker would resemble the course of the capital-to-labor ratio, because the shares of capital invested in tools and machinery had not been altered much by 1890 (Sokoloff 1984a; United States Census Office 1895).

31. This conjecture does not necessarily hold, but if all else was constant, one would expect it to. The chief obstacles or objections to its applicability probably concern the variation across industries in the rates at which capital goods depreciated, old vintages were replaced by new, and output increased over the period. The complication arising from this latter situation is that the industries that grew most rapidly would tend to benefit relatively more from technical change embodied in capital even if their capital-

labor ratios were low and had not changed much, because a greater proportion of their capital stock would consist of new-vintage items.

32.  A series of pooled cross-section production functions were estimated with various measures of output serving as the dependent variable and measures of the inputs, year dummies, industry dummies, class dummies, and interactions appearing as independent variables. When variables for the interaction between dummies for the more mechanized or capital- intensive industries and the year 1860 were included in the specifications, the coefficients on them generally failed to indicate that these classes of industries realized significantly more productivity growth between 1820 and 1860.

33.  For example, the per annum rates of growth of capital per equivalent worker between 1820 and 1850 ranged from 0.8%–1.1% and −0.1% to +0.1% for the more and less mechanized industries, respectively. During the next decade, the less mechanized industries experienced a sharp acceleration in their absolute and relative rates of increase of this variable to 4.0%–6.8% per annum, as compared with the 0.8%–2.1% pace registered by their counterparts.

34.  If one decomposes the growth in value added per equivalent worker, the qualitative result is the same. Increases in the capital-labor ratio directly account for only a small fraction of the progress realized, leaving most of the rise in labor productivity to be explained by advances in total factor productivity.


# Comment     Jeffrey G. Williamson

### Motivation and Findings

Although most economic historians and development economists seem to share the view that technological change is the driving force behind all Industrial Revolutions, it is surprising what little we know about its quantitative dimensions. True, since Abramovitz and Solow pointed the way 25 years ago, we have learned something about aggregate rates of total factor productivity growth economy-wide. But we still know very little about sectoral rates of total factor productivity growth, and it is at the sectoral level that the issue is of most importance.

Why do we care about sectoral measures of total factor productivity growth? Because we think that many of the stylized facts of the Industrial Revolution that matter reflect unbalanced total factor productivity advance. For open economies with relatively price-elastic output demands, unbalanced rates of total factor productivity growth are likely to do most of the work fostering the shift in output mix toward the dynamic modern sectors. The shift in output mix has, in turn, important implications for other endogenous variables of critical interest to us. Since the dynamic sectors tend to be urban based, city job creation and urbanization are assured. To the extent that the dynamic sectors tend to be skill intensive, wage inequality is fostered. And to the extent that the dynamic sectors tend to be capital intensive (especially when the indirect requirements for urban dwellings and social overhead are considered), investment requirements are augmented, saving rates tend

Jeffrey G. Williamson is Laird Bell Professor of Economics at Harvard University.

to rise, and the rate of accumulation tends to accelerate. Apart from these important macro issues, information on productivity growth by industry clearly increases the opportunity to isolate the correlates of growth and thus to better understand the carriers of growth.

So it is that unbalanced total factor productivity advance during early industrialization must be better understood. Strangely enough, only a handful of Third World economies offer such evidence, and for Britain's First Industrial Revolution we still can only guess by reference to average labor productivities (Floud and McCloskey 1981).

There is an obvious reason for our quantitative ignorance: the data base is poor. This fact of life insures that the intrepid researcher is bound to stir critical debate. And so it is that Professor Sokoloff's "Productivity Growth in Manufacturing during Early Industrialization" is likely to stir critical debate here today.[1]

First, the database. Sokoloff has collected establishment production data for 1820, 1832, 1850, and 1860 in the American Northeast. The 1850 and 1860 data are taken from the Bateman-Weiss samples drawn from the *Census of Manufactures,* while Sokoloff (1982) himself has sampled the 1820 *Census of Manufactures* and the 1832 *McLane Report.*

Second, the findings. Using estimation procedures pioneered by Abramovitz, Kendrick, Denison, and others, Sokoloff emerges with the following impressive findings:

1. Antebellum labor productivity growth in manufacturing was much more rapid than has been appreciated (table 13.6);
2. Labor productivity growth was impressive enough in the 1820s and early 1830s so that there appears to be only weak evidence of trend acceleration over the antebellum period as a whole, especially in the gross output figures and especially over the first three decades of the antebellum period (table 13.6);
3. The estimated rates of total factor productivity growth are very rapid (table 13.11). They are highest in textiles, glass, paper, hats, furniture, and woodwork, but other sectors reveal impressive rates too;
4. Total factor productivity advance underwent modest acceleration up to 1850 before rising sharply in the decade following (table 13.11);
5. Total factor productivity growth typically "accounts for" more than 50% of labor productivity growth over the four decades as a whole, and capital deepening rarely "accounts for" more than 10% (table 13.13).

These are impressive findings. Can we believe them?

---

1. Professor Sokoloff has revised his paper extensively since the Williamsburg Conference. As a result, some of the remarks I made as a discussant no longer have relevance. This comment has been rewritten accordingly, although I have tried to retain the flavor of the debate.

## Three Problems
### Aggregation

What was manufacturing's overall performance? While Sokoloff supplies both weighted and unweighted averages, most of us would prefer the former. Otherwise it is difficult to assess exactly how important any given sector's performance was to manufacturing as a whole. Unfortunately, the weights employed are fixed at 1850 levels so that relatively dynamic sectors are not allowed to have their full impact on aggregate productivity performance as they increased their industrial output shares over time. But even if the aggregation was flawless, there is nothing to guarantee that those aggregates would coincide with the true rates of total factor productivity growth in manufacturing. After all, total factor productivity growth in manufacturing is composed of two parts, intra-industry total factor productivity growth, which Sokoloff reports in table 13.11, and *inter*industry total factor productivity growth, which he ignores. Much has been made of interindustry total factor productivity growth in the development and historical literature, the result stemming from improved resource allocation. For example, McCloskey (Floud and McCloskey 1981, p. 118–19) estimates a "Harberger Triangle" due to capital market imperfections in Britain—the area *ABC* in figure C13.1—and infers that its elimination between 1780 and 1850 would have added 0.1% per annum to economy-wide total factor productivity growth rates. If the same was true of labor markets, then the interindustry source might have been 0.2% per annum. The figures are likely to have been even larger for a faster growing economy with a larger boundary like America.

In short, the very modest acceleration in total factor productivity growth up to 1850 may or may not have been an attribute of American antebellum manufacturing—it depends on the importance of each of the sectors for which Sokoloff supplies productivity estimates, *and* it depends on the interindustry component which he ignores.

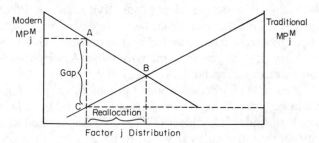

**Fig. C13.1**     Factor market imperfections and the Harberger Triangle.

## The Effective Labor Stock

How shall we aggregate heterogeneous labor inputs? American manufacturing employed adult males, females, and children during the antebellum period, and the labor input mix varied over time and across industries. Sokoloff uses a constant weight rule of thumb ("notes and sources" to table 13.1), namely,

$$TE = M + 0.5(F + B) + E$$

where

$TE$ = "equivalent" adult male workers = "effective" labor stock
$M$ = adult males
$F$ = females
$B$ = boys
$E$ = the entrepreneur.

This labor aggregation scheme is used throughout.

The first problem Sokoloff must confront is that the 1850 and 1860 censuses do not report adult males and boys separately. His solution is to assume that the 1820 distribution applies to 1850 and 1860 as well. Sokoloff thinks that this assumption is likely to impart a "small upward bias" to the measured growth of the effective stock of labor. I suspect that the bias may be larger than he admits, and that labor productivity and total factor productivity growth rates may be significantly understated, and further that the relative stability in productivity growth up to 1850 may be in part a spurious fabrication. I encourage Sokoloff to prove me wrong by sensitivity analysis.

The second problem which Sokoloff's procedure introduces is the constant weight applied to females and boys. The weight is guided by an average of the age/sex wage ratios prevailing in the 1850s (ranging between 0.34 and 0.55), when in fact it rose *sharply* over the antebellum period (from a range between 0.25 and 0.35 in the 1820s). While Sokoloff believes the constant-weight procedure tends to understate labor force growth, thus overstating labor productivity and total factor productivity growth, I would like to know more about which industries and which periods were most affected by the constant-weight assumption. In any case, it is not clear to me why *variable* weights cannot be used to construct the effective labor stock.

Certainly Paul David worried about both of these problems when looking at antebellum cotton textiles (David 1970), and Pamela Nickless (1979) did as well. Indeed, Nickless (1979, p. 902) estimated total factor productivity for cotton textiles 1836–60 to have grown far slower than Sokoloff's estimates for 1832–60 imply. Why? Sokoloff does not supply his effective labor stock estimates in the paper, but I suggest the answer may lie with his labor aggregation scheme.

*The Flow of Labor Services*

The 1820 census recorded "part-time" establishments which were of small size and seasonal. The share of establishments which were part-time varied over time and across industries: they appear to have been a far smaller share of all firms in the 1832 *McLane Report* as well as in the 1850 and 1860 censuses. To the extent that scale economies mattered during this era of the rise of large scale factories, and given that the smaller, part-time firms were less efficient, then the demise of the part-time firms was an important ingredient of industry total factor productivity growth. Indeed, Sokoloff himself supports this view in this paper and elsewhere (Sokoloff 1984). If I understand Sokoloff correctly, this important source of productivity growth has been purged from his samples B and C. Since it appears he has used B from table 13.6 onward, he understates total factor productivity growth, particularly for those industries in which the decline of part-time establishments was especially dramatic, and especially early in the antebellum epoch.

Sokoloff is faced with the following problem. The part-time firms record total employment stocks, rather than seasonally adjusted labor service flows. Rather than attempt to convert the part-time labor force to full-time estimates, Sokoloff chooses instead to truncate his samples. That is, those firms with "low" total factor productivity are purged from the sample on the grounds that they are the part-time firms in which labor inputs are overstated. Those purged from sample B amount to 29% in 1820, 5% in 1832, 9% in 1850, and 10% in 1860. Sokoloff also truncates his samples from the top, but the magnitudes are far smaller.

I have trouble with this treatment of part-time firms. Their demise was an important part of the technological process that Sokoloff is out to measure, and I believe the underlying total factor productivity growth rates are seriously biased as a result. Would the stability in productivity growth up to 1850 still be apparent if part-time firms were properly treated? I wonder.

How else might Sokoloff proceed? Here's one suggestion. Compute the average annual wage payment (by age and sex if possible) per worker by sector in the 1820 full-time firms (already identified by their "high" total factor productivity). Convert those annual wage rates to monthly wage rates. Assume that the monthly wage rates apply to the part-time firms, infer the number of months that the part-time firms were in operation, and scale down the labor input to the part-time firms accordingly.

# References

Atack, Jeremy. 1985. Industrial structure and the emergence of the modern industrial corporation. *Explorations in Economic History* 22:29–53.

Atack, Jeremy; Bateman, Fred; and Weiss, Thomas, 1979. An evaluation of nineteenth century censuses as sources of economic statistics. Paper delivered to the Cliometrics Conference, Chicago.

Brady, Dorothy S. 1964. Relative prices in the nineteenth century. *Journal of Economic History* 24:145–203.

————. 1966. Price deflators for final product estimates. In *Output, employment, and productivity in the United States after 1800,* Dorothy S. Brady. ed. Studies in Income and Wealth 30. New York: National Bureau of Economic Research.

Chandler, Alfred D. 1977. *The visible hand: The managerial revolution in American business.* Cambridge: Harvard University Press.

Cole, Arthur E. 1938. *Wholesale commodity prices in the United States, 1700–1861.* Vol. 2. Cambridge: Harvard University Press.

Cole, Arthur H., and Smith, Walter B. 1935. *Fluctuations in American business, 1790–1860.* Cambridge: Harvard University Press.

David, Paul A. 1967. The growth of real product in the United States before 1840: new evidence, controlled conjectures. *Journal of Economic History* 27:151–97.

————. 1970. Learning by doing and tariff protection: A reconsideration of the case of ante-bellum United States cotton industry. *Journal of Economic History* 30, no. 3 (September): 521–601.

————. 1975. *Technical choice, innovation and economic growth.* New York: Cambridge University Press.

————. 1977. Invention and accumulation in America's economic growth: A nineteenth century parable. *International organization, national policies and economic development,* ed. Karl Brunner and Allan Meltzer. Amsterdam: North-Holland.

Davis, Lance E., and Gallman, Robert E. 1978. Capital formation in the United States during the nineteenth century. In *The Cambridge economic history of Europe,* ed. Peter Mathias and M. M. Postan. Vol. 7, pt. 2. Cambridge: Cambridge University Press.

Davis, Lance E., and Stettler, H. Louis. 1966. The New England textile industry, 1825–60: trends and fluctuations. In *Output, employment, and productivity in the United States after 1800,* ed. Dorothy S. Brady. Studies in Income and Wealth 30. New York: National Bureau of Economic Research.

Davis, Pearce. 1949. *The development of the American glass industry.* Cambridge: Harvard University Press.

Floud, Roderick, and McCloskey, Donald, eds. 1981. *The economic history of Britain since 1700, Volume 1: 1700–1860*. Cambridge: Cambridge University Press.

Gallman, Robert E. 1972a. Changes in total U.S. agricultural factor productivity in the nineteenth century. *Agricultural History* 46:191–209.

————. 1972b. The pace and pattern of American economic growth. In *American economic growth*, ed. Lance Davis et al. New York: Harper & Row.

————. 1983. How do I measure thee? Let me count the ways: Investment and the capital stock in the nineteenth century. Paper delivered to the Caltech/Weingart/Social Science History Association Conference: The Variety of Quantitative History, Pasadena, Calif.

————. 1986. The U.S. capital stock in the nineteenth century. In this volume.

Goldin, Claudia, and Sokoloff, Kenneth. 1982. Women, children, and industrialization in the early Republic: Evidence from the manufacturing censuses. *Journal of Economic History* 42, no. 4:741–74.

Habakkuk, H. J. 1962. *American and British technology in the nineteenth century: The search for labour-saving inventions*. Cambridge: Cambridge University Press.

Kendrick, John W. 1961. *Productivity trends in the United States*. Princeton: Princeton University Press.

Landes, David S. 1969. *The unbound Prometheus: Technological change and industrial development in Western Europe from 1750 to the present*. Cambridge: Cambridge University Press.

————. 1985. What do bosses really do? Mimeographed. Harvard University.

Layer, Robert G. 1955. *Earnings of cotton mill operatives, 1825–1914*. Cambridge: Harvard University Press.

Lazonick, William, and Brush, Thomas. 1985. The "Horndahl effect" in early U.S. manufacturing. *Explorations in Economic History* 22:53–96.

Lebergott, Stanley. 1964. *Manpower in economic growth: The American record since 1800*. New York: McGraw-Hill.

Lindstrom, Diane. 1978. *Economic development in the Philadelphia region, 1810–1850*. New York: Columbia University Press.

McCloskey, Donald. 1981. The Industrial Revolution 1780–1860: A survey. In *The economic history of Britain since 1700*, ed. Donald McCloskey and Roderick Floud. (eds.), Vol. 1. Cambridge: Cambridge University Press.

McGouldrick, Paul. 1968. *New England textiles in the 19th century: Profits and investments*. Cambridge: Harvard University Press.

Marglin, Stephen A. 1974. What do bosses do? The origins and functions of hierarchy in capitalist production. *Review of Radical Political Economics* 6, no. 2:33–60.

Nickless, Pamela J. 1979. A new look at productivity in the New England cotton textile industry, 1830–1860. *Journal of Economic History* 39 (December): 889–910.

Smith, Adam. 1776/1976. *An Inquiry into the nature and causes of the wealth of nations*. Chicago: University of Chicago Press. Originally published in 1776.

Sokoloff, Kenneth L. 1982. Industrialization and the growth of the manufacturing sector in the Northeast, 1820–1850. Ph.D. dissertation, Harvard University.

———. 1983. The growth of real wages in northeastern manufacturing, 1820–1850. Paper delivered to Social Science History Association, Washington, D.C.

———. 1984a. Investment in fixed and working capital during early industrialization: Evidence from U.S. manufacturing firms. *Journal of Economic History* 44, no. 1:545–56.

———. 1984b. Was the transition from the artisanal shop to the non-mechanized factory associated with gains in efficiency? Evidence from the U.S. manufacturing censuses of 1820 and 1850. *Explorations in Economic History* 21 (October): 351–82.

Temin, Peter. 1964. *Iron and steel in nineteenth century America: An economic inquiry.* Cambridge: MIT Press.

Thorp, Willard L. 1926. *Business annals.* New York: National Bureau of Economic Research.

United States Bureau of the Census. 1975. *Historical statistics of the United States, colonial times to 1970.* Washington, D.C.: Government Printing Office.

United States Census Office. 1858. *Abstract of the statistics of manufactures, according to the returns of the seventh census.* Washington, D.C.: Government Printing Office.

———. 1865. *Eighth census of the U.S., 1860: Manufactures.* Washington, D.C.: Government Printing Office.

———. 1895. *Eleventh census of the United States: 1890. Report on the manufacturing industries in the United States.* Washington, D.C.: Government Printing Office.

United States House of Representatives. 1833. *Documents relative to the statistics of manufactures in the U.S.* 2 vols. Washington, D.C.: Duff Green.

Williamson, Jeffrey G. 1972. Embodiment, disembodiment, learning by doing and constant returns to scale in the nineteenth-century cotton textiles. *Journal of Economic History* 32:691–705.

Williamson, Jeffrey G., and Lindert, Peter H. 1980. *American inequality: A macroeconomic history.* New York: Academic Press.

# 14     Output and Productivity in Canadian Agriculture, 1870–71 to 1926–27

R. M. McInnis

## 14.1   The Study of Canadian Agricultural Development

Agriculture is widely acknowledged to have played a large and important role in Canadian economic development. Our knowledge of the quantitative dimensions of historical change in Canadian agriculture is, however, remarkably limited. We have census data at decennial intervals on numbers of farms and acres of land, on stocks of animals and production of crops. There are annual data on exports and imports of farm products, and there is a considerable abundance of other raw information of a less comprehensive or less continuously available form. Yet little has been done to assemble that information into an overview of Canadian agriculture over an extended period of history. To date there has been no systematic, quantitative history of Canadian agriculture. This paper is intended as a first step toward that.

Assuredly, there has been historical writing on agriculture in Canada. Much of it has focused on particular regions of the country or on particular sectors of the industry. R. L. Jones (1946) contributed an especially valuable monograph on the history of agriculture in Ontario up to 1880, and several important articles on farming in Quebec in the early years of the nineteenth century. Maurice Seguin's (1970) monograph on Quebec agriculture played an important role in the historiography of that province, and the condition of farming in early nineteenth-century Quebec has played a prominent role in the writings of Fernand

R. M. McInnis is professor of economics at Queen's University.

The research underlying this paper was carried out with financial support from the Social Sciences and Humanities Research Council of Canada, grant number 410-81-0673. At various times through the progress of the work I have benefited from the able assistance of Merritt Cluff, Robin Cowan, Jim Nugent, Steve Poloz, Shane Roherty, and Joanne Stewart.

Ouellet (1966, 1980). Andrew Clark's (1959) historical geography of Prince Edward Island quite naturally concentrates heavily on agriculture. The settlement of the wheat-growing region of Western Canada, which occurred mainly since the beginning of the twentieth century, at a time when statistical recording was quite well developed, has been extensively discussed. A series of monographs edited by Mackintosh and Joerg treated a number of aspects of settlement and economic change in the Prairie provinces (Mackintosh 1935; Morton and Martin 1938). Britnell's (1939) volume *The Wheat Economy* was an early attempt at a reasonably systematic treatment in statistical terms of one segment of Canadian agriculture. More recently, attempts to quantify the contribution of prairie settlement to Canadian economic growth have involved the estimation of the growth of production in the "wheat economy" and the increase in rent on prairie farmland (Chambers and Gordon 1966; Bertram 1973; Lewis 1975).

Only Fowke (1946) has attempted a comprehensive survey of agriculture in Canadian economic history. His valuable work offers an interesting interpretation but makes infrequent use of quantitative evidence to support his argument. There has been, then, no synthetic statistical study of Canadian agriculture in the period before the 1920s. There are no studies of aggregate output, carefully measured inputs, and productivity. Canada must be one of the few modern, developed countries that lacks studies of that sort.

The closest thing to an aggregate assessment of Canadian agricultural production is to be found in the work of O. J. Firestone (1958). It should be made clear that Firestone devoted a mere eight pages to a very cursory look at agriculture—clearly intended as only the most superficial sort of glance—and, on the whole, subsequent writers have not paid much attention to Firestone's agricultural data. Firestone estimated gross national product originating in agriculture for decennial census years from 1870, essentially as one step in obtaining overall estimates of gross national product. He was clearly more interested in the broader aggregate and its performance over the decades than in the agricultural sector alone. Nevertheless, his work represents the sum total of synthesized evidence on the quantitative dimensions of Canadian agricultural development.

There are several reasons why we might be less than satisfied with what Firestone has provided. For one thing, estimates for only 6 decennial census years over a span of half a century leave considerable uncertainty about the representativeness of those years. For another, while he does provide a constant dollar as well as a current dollar series, he is not very explicit about how he assembled the price deflator from a few specific wholesale price indexes. Consequently, Firestone's work on agriculture can be described as rather sketchy.

The most problematic thing about Firestone's estimates is that his method probably introduced a serious source of bias. His procedure was to aggregate estimates of production of each commodity made from data in the decennial censuses, and hinging critically on values of each category of production reported in the census of 1901, and then to reduce the aggregate by a fixed coefficient to account for duplication and deductions. That adjustment is to account for farm inputs purchased from other sectors and for crops included in the production aggregate that were used as inputs in the production of livestock and animal products. For this adjustment Firestone used a constant factor of 29.3% of the gross value of agricultural production. That was the average difference between total agricultural output and gross value added in agriculture as reported by the Dominion Bureau of Statistics in its annual *Survey of Production* over the years 1920–39.

The catch to Firestone's adjustment procedure is that it fails to take account of the major structural change that had occurred in Canadian agriculture. The 29.3% factor was derived from evidence covering a period when grain farming in western Canada comprised a large fraction of Canadian agricultural production. Firestone applies that coefficient to a historical period in which western grain farms made up a much smaller part of the total and livestock farming, which used considerably more of its crop production as input on the farm, was the predominant component of Canadian farming. Certainly for 1900 and earlier years, and possibly for 1910 as well, this must have led to an overstatement of gross value added in agriculture. By 1920 or so the adjustment coefficient used by Firestone would be reasonably accurate, so his procedure not only overstates the input of the farm sector in the nineteenth century, it understates the growth that occurred in the early decades of the twentieth century.

It is long since time that a fresh attempt was made to estimate a historical series of aggregate farm output in Canada for the years before 1926 when the official Bureau of Statistics series begins. That I have done in collaboration with M. C. Urquhart. This is part of a larger project organized and directed by Professor Urquhart to produce a new series of historical national income statistics for Canada, with work being carried out by several investigators on the various sectors. The estimates of gross value added in agriculture which are used in this paper are the McInnis-Urquhart estimates with only a few minor modifications. Only an abbreviated description is given here of the sources and methods used in the construction of these estimates, as the full details are intended to be reported elsewhere.[1]

The principal objective of this paper is to explore the pattern of development of Canadian agriculture implied by the new series and, especially, to examine its implications for changes in productivity. The difficulties of getting suitable measures of factor inputs are highlighted.

## 14.2  New Estimates of Agricultural Product

It is intended here only to give a brief outline of the procedure used in the estimation of the new Canadian historical agricultural output series. Some further specifics are provided in an appendix where the full annual series is also presented. In constructing the new series our concern was to develop a methodology that would avoid the main shortcomings of Firestone's estimates. That was possible, but at a cost that is perhaps unfortunate, given the considerable regional variation in Canadian agriculture. The series is a national aggregate only. No directly comparable provincial or other regional subaggregates could be provided. Work is underway on another project that uses a different methodology to estimate regional agricultural production estimates.[2] That work will have to be reported elsewhere.

In historical output estimation of the sort reported on here the nature of the available data is the critical matter of concern and, to a considerable degree, concepts and methods have to be tailored to the data. The evidence we have to go on comes primarily from two sources: decennial censuses of agriculture and annual statistics of the foreign trade of Canada. These are supplemented by a variety of other materials, often less than comprehensive and not continuously available. The most important of these are the reports of the *Ontario Bureau of Industries* on its annual surveys of agriculture. For the early twentieth century there are also some annual data reported by the provinces of Alberta, Manitoba, and Saskatchewan. That Ontario contributed about one-half of Canadian agricultural output in the later years of the nineteenth century and that when substantial settlement in the prairie region of the Canadian west occurred in the early twentieth century there were annual data reported by the provincial governments in that region, coupled with the fact that for many products international trade was relatively important in the Canadian case, has meant that it has been feasible to produce a reasonable set of annual estimates of agricultural gross output.

Some matters of definition and specification need first be attended to. The aggregate focused on in this chapter is gross value added in agriculture. That is a measure that is gross of the depreciation of farm capital but net of duplications and of inputs into agriculture from other sectors of the economy. There is potential for confusion of terminology here. Since the procedure that was followed was first to estimate a flow of final products from the agricultural sector and then separately to estimate inputs acquired from other sectors, a name must be given to the aggregate net production of agricultural goods before the deduction of inputs. I call this the final agricultural product to distinguish it from the even more gross aggregate of agricultural output including farm products used as further inputs on farms, or at least within the farm sector, that was measured by Firestone and in early work of the Dominion Bureau of Statistics.

Agriculture is here defined quite narrowly, in a way that falls short of the total output of farms. There are several reasons for this. Canadian farmers, especially in the nineteenth century, engaged in a range of production that typically went beyond what we would now think of as agriculture. Probably the most important element of this would have been forest products. That went far beyond firewood either for sale or for use on the farm, although that item alone is of considerable importance. By 1870 a few farms might still have been burning wood for potash but, more importantly, logs were often cut for the local sawmill, shingles and staves were made in otherwise slack time during the winter, fenceposts and rails were cut not just for farm use but also for sale, and, especially after about 1890, pulpwood became a really important product in some parts of the country. Farmers also provided both labor and draft animals for transport services and for construction. They processed agricultural products by curing meat and spinning and weaving wool. These and other adjunct products of the farm have not been included in the gross value added in agriculture as estimated here, nor has the rental value of farm dwellings. Moreover, no attempt has been made here to estimate farm capital accumulation in the form of land improvement through clearing, drainage, or fencing. That was not entirely by design. Additions to farm capital in the form of stocks of animals are included, and the original intention was to carry through to a more comprehensive estimate of farm production of new capital. This turned out not yet to be feasible.

Overall, then, what is being considered is a lean estimate of farm net output. In principle there are two ways of dealing with the situation. One is to aim at a comprehensive and widely inclusive estimate of output, reflecting all of the production to which the factors encompassed by the sector under consideration have contributed. Alternatively, one might measure output quite narrowly and restrictively and attempt to make the appropriate adjustment on the input side. It is the latter course that is attempted in the present paper—not always, admittedly, with complete success. Partly it is a matter of fitting the estimates for the agricultural sector into a wider project; more importantly, though, it is a matter of the data that were most readily available and adapting concept to data.[3]

Farm products have been valued at local markets rather than at the farm gate, thus implicitly attributing to agriculture the transport of output to primary markets. It is production that is being measured, though, rather than sales from farms. Hence, farm output includes production for consumption by the residents of the farm. That only makes sense in an age when one-third to one-half of the population still lived on farms and produced a lot of output for themselves. To overlook that would be a serious distortion, but it has important implications for the interpretation of the composition of agricultural output. Farm family demand must necessarily play a prominent role in the pattern of farm production.

The approach to the estimation of agricultural output that has been adopted here is, broadly speaking, to build up estimates of final agricultural product by estimating separate annual series of output and prices for each of the individual products of the agricultural sector. Such an approach makes the most effective use of such annual data on trade and production as are available. It also facilitates the construction of a constant price series. The main attraction of this approach is that it obviates the need to find some way to reduce aggregate output to a flow of final product to take account of intermediate products.

The direct estimation of final product considerably simplifies the treatment of many field crops—they can be ignored. Some, like turnips and corn for fodder, can just be left aside as wholly utilized within the farm sector for animal feed. In the case of other feed crops such as hay and oats, by far the greater part of the crop was used directly on farms, and it is necessary to estimate only that small fraction of production that contributed to net agricultural output. Often a significant part of that was exported. In this way of handling things the main farm products were dairy and animal products, wheat, potatoes, fruit, and vegetables.

A second prominent aspect of the procedure followed here is that where data on annual production are not directly available, the procedure is to estimate domestic consumption, in some cases just by interpolating between decennial census benchmarks, adjusting for year-to-year changes on the basis of international trade. This involves the not fully substantiated assumption that relatively stable domestic consumption demands took precedence and that exports were catered to out of left-over supply. The validity of this supposition still needs to be firmly established. In the late nineteenth century, Canada was still a predominantly agricultural country, producing a few commodities such as wheat, cheese, and to a lesser extent beef for export as well as domestic markets. An implication of this might well be that household demand took precedence and that exports came essentially out of surplus or "leftover" supply. This has to be recognized as a still insufficiently evaluated characterization of the Canadian agricultural sector. Tentatively, it may be worth proceeding so long as there is no imposing evidence to the contrary.[4]

The general case, then, is one in which the output of farm product has been estimated as the domestic consumption of that product, adjusted for international trade. In the case of livestock, outputs also include additions to or subtractions from the stock of animals. In cases where production could not be calculated directly, estimates of domestic consumption are made by starting with a benchmark level of per capita consumption. There is some considerable variation from commodity to commodity in the assurance with which these estimates are made. A few examples may provide both a clearer indication of methodology and some sense of the varying success it meets. Consider three of the most important items of farm input: wheat, cheese, and beef.

There are reasonably extensive data relating to wheat production in Canada, although, as is so often the case, coverage shrinks as one goes further back in time and a different procedure has to be followed in each of three time periods. From 1908–9 onward there is a national series based on a reasonably well-organized annual survey of agriculture. From 1881–82 through 1908–9 there were annual data only for two provinces, Ontario and Manitoba, but those were the two that predominated in wheat production. Decennial census benchmark data on national wheat production was for this period interpolated annually on the basis of the Ontario and Manitoba series. Between 1871 and 1881 there are no annual statistics of production. For those years a fixed per capita consumption of 5.5 bushels and a fixed provision for seed were modified by the amount of exports (net of imports) of wheat and flour. The seed provision is treated as an intermediate product and not as part of agricultural net production.

Cheese provides a good example of a commodity for which a heavy orientation toward export simplifies the estimation of annual output. Canadians were evidently never big cheese eaters. The industry developed very largely in response to opportunities in the export market in Great Britain. At a relatively early date exports comprised the greater part of output. That being the case, annual exports adjusted for a modest per capita addition of three pounds to take account of domestic consumption must give a reasonably accurate reflection of production.

The production of cattle for beef was in many years the largest single component of agricultural output. While from time to time exports reached significant levels, the production of cattle in Canada has been predominantly for domestic consumption, and a large part of that was within the localities where the animals were raised. Hence there are only limited market data pertaining to the cattle trade. Different procedures had to be followed for the years before and after 1890–91.

After that date there were annual data on sales and slaughter in Ontario, augmented by some of the western provinces after the beginning of the twentieth century. Annual estimates of the national stock of cattle were made by interpolating between decennial census counts on the basis of annual changes in the stock of animals in Ontario. Then the Ontario ratio of production to stock was applied to the entire national stock. For years before 1891, census benchmark estimates of domestic per capita consumption were made by adjusting the numbers of animals produced to take account of international trade in live animals and the live animal equivalent of processed meats. Annual figures for per capita consumption then were obtained by a straight line interpolation between census years. Annual estimates of net output were then made by converting per capita domestic consumption into a national aggregate by multiplying by population numbers and then adding exports, net of imports. This procedure was followed through the years after 1870–71 when, proportionally speaking, exports made up the greatest part of output.

In all cases the estimates were for the quantity of output of each commodity. Separate price series were prepared for each commodity. These were based for the most part on existing series of wholesale prices, supplemented in the case of some minor products by indexes of annual change in export or import unit values. The major shortcoming with this is that the price series are even more Ontario-centered than are the production series. Overall, the estimating procedure is too much tied to agriculture in Ontario, the province that carried the greatest weight in the national total. There is a real lack of infusion of any sense of the variety of regional experience that is such a prominent part of the Canadian scene. We are especially lacking in information on farming in the Maritime provinces and Quebec. Much additional research needs to be done before anything can be done to improve upon the situation. The assembly of price series for markets in those provinces would be a good starting point.

The estimates of final agricultural product are largely net of intermediate production and goods used as input in the farm sector. Exchanges of animals between farms, as for example exchanges between breeders and feeders, have been netted out. Only the export of feed crops or the sale to feed nonfarm draft animals, or the minor use of oats, corn, and barley for human consumption, has been counted as output. To go from final agricultural product to gross value added in agriculture only some relatively minor deductions have to be made. At least these are minor deductions until years in the twentieth century when tractors and fuel begin to become important. Over most of the period under examination the two principal items of purchased input were bran and other mill feeds and blacksmith services. By the 1890s binder twine had become a significant item. At no time in the period under review was purchased fertilizer an important input in Canadian agriculture. The other purchased items that have to be allowed for are mainly containers—cooperage, sacks, bags, and baskets. The total of these deductions never rose above 10% of final agricultural products before 1914. Some details of estimation are given in connection with table 14.A.2.

The full annual series of final agricultural product is presented in tables 14.A.1 and 14.A.2. The former shows the main commodity groups that make up agricultural product. The latter table provides a deflation of the current dollar estimates to constant 1913 prices. Since final agricultural product was estimated directly as a series of sums of price-quantity products, the constant dollar series was constructed simply by recalculating the entire $pq$ matrix. Any base price set could have been used. Many of the series for the United States are in terms of 1910–14 average prices. The use of 1913 prices alone here results in a series almost identical to that which would have been produced with 1910–14 average prices. The implicit price index that results from this calculation comprises a new price index for Canada, one that will bear some comparison with the long-existing wholesale price indexes of Coates (1910) and Taylor and Mitchell (1931).

There is little that can be done to evaluate the reliability of the agricultural production estimates, such as by comparison with other evidence. Usually all the available evidence is exhausted in making the estimates in the first place. The use of the estimates in analysis and interpretation—what we turn to next—is the main vehicle for assessing the plausibility of the estimates.

One partial check that can be reported in a tentative way entails a comparison of the new estimates of gross value added in agriculture in several census years with the sum of similar estimates by county across the whole country. The regional estimates are not entirely independent—they make use of a lot of the same basic data—but the method of estimation, particularly the method of netting out intermediate production, is quite different.[5]

The comparison between the new McInnis-Urquhart estimates of gross value added in Canadian agriculture and the national sums of county-level estimates of the same aggregate can be made for five decennial census years from 1881 through 1921. For the first and last of those years the two estimates come out, for what must be purely fortuitous reasons, virtually the same. For the three intervening census dates the sums of county estimates come out 7% or 8% above the McInnis-Urquhart national estimates. This is more in line with what might be expected since the county series probably was light on the estimation of some of the deductions required for purchases of inputs from other sectors. Overall the comparison is an encouraging one, although it has to be emphasized that it is more a check on method than on general accuracy. If there were major flaws in some important census aggregates they would put both sets of estimates in error. In light of the discussion of the ensuing section, where exceptionally slow growth of agricultural output in the 1881–91 intercensal decade is highlighted as one of the substantive results of the new estimates that calls for explanation, a note of caution should be entered. If the sum of the county estimates could confidently be expected to come out above the national estimate (something that probably cannot be said with sufficient confidence) then there may be an indication that the McInnis-Urquhart figure for 1881 might have some upward bias.

## 14.3   Canadian Agricultural Output, 1870–71 to 1920–21

The constant (1913) dollar series of gross value added in Canadian agriculture is shown in figure 14.1. Two features are notable. One is

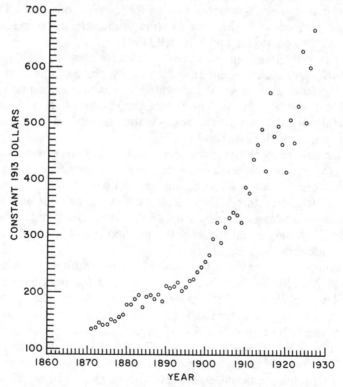

**Fig. 14.1**        Gross value added, Canadian agriculture, 1870–71 to 1926–27 (constant 1913 dollars).

that there is an evident break in the mid-1890s with output growing more rapidly in the years following. That is quite in accord with the usual account of Canadian agricultural development. The more rapid growth after about 1896 reflects the rapid settlement of the agricultural region the provinces of Alberta and Saskatchewan. An alternative characterization of the growth of agricultural output might be that between 1870–71 and 1882–83 it grew almost as rapidly as in the post-1896 period but that there was an intervening period from 1883 through 1895 when output grew very little. Throughout, however, the growth of agricultural output was associated with an expansion of the area farmed. That is obviously true of the period of western settlement, after 1896. In the years immediately following 1871, though, Canada was extended to include Prince Edward Island, British Columbia, and Manitoba.[6]

The second prominent feature discernible in figure 14.1 is the marked increase of instability associated with the greater weight in the total of the wheat growing region of the Prairie Provinces. Growth of output was fairly steady and year-to-year fluctuations relatively modest until 1909–10. In that year there was an especially large jump in output, associated with a 56% increase in wheat production. Thereafter, the output series fluctuates widely from year to year. That is not something introduced by the way in which the estimates are constructed but a consequence of the increased role of western Canadian wheat, grown under conditions of considerable uncertainty.

The principal interest of this paper is in the long-term development of Canadian agriculture. With that in mind, the following discussion is directed entirely to changes between decennial census dates. Estimates of factor inputs can be made only for census years, and those are the only years for which comparisons can be made with the Firestone estimates. With regard to the latter, it had earlier been pointed out that a shortcoming of the Firestone estimates was that, since they covered only decennial census years, they might offer a distorted picture depending upon the representativeness of those years. We can now examine this a bit more fully with the aid of data in table 14.1. In that table the new McInnis-Urquhart estimates of gross value added in Canadian agriculture are examined for decennial census years in terms of the estimates for census years alone and for 3- and 5-year averages centered on census years. It is still not possible to do much for the initial census year which, for want of estimates for years before 1870–71, is not averaged.

The census year 1881 was reputed to have been a poor crop year, and that shows up in an unusually low figure for wheat output. In 1881 and again in 1901, a rather poor census year was followed by a year of considerably higher yields. Overall, though, it makes little difference whether one focuses on the census years alone or on either 3- or 5-

Table 14.1          **Gross Value Added, Canadian Agriculture, Census Years, 1871–1921 (Millions of Constant 1913 Dollars)**

| Years | Census Year Only | 3-Year Average | 5-Year Average |
|---|---|---|---|
| 1870–71 | 136 | 136[a] | 136[a] |
| 1880–81 | 178 | 181 | 180 |
| 1890–91 | 208 | 210 | 206 |
| 1900–1901 | 266 | 272 | 277 |
| 1910–11 | 376 | 400 | 397 |
| 1920–21 | 508 | 463 | 477 |

*Source:* Calculated from table 14.A.2.
[a]Census year only.

year averages centered on those census years. The 5-year averages which are used in subsequent tables correspond closely to the figures for individual census years. The choice makes little difference in the nineteenth century. In the twentieth century the situation is somewhat different. The census year 1911 is itself on the low side, and 1921 is a relatively high year. In both of these cases the 5-year average probably offers a more representative number.

Any way one looks at it, the most rapid growth of agricultural production occurred in the first decade of the twentieth century when, in real terms, the growth was a little over 40%. The rapid growth continued through the following decade when output expanded by 35%. The other outstanding feature is that the decade between 1881 and 1891 was one of slow growth—only 17%. It would be of some considerable interest to track down the source of that slow growth in the 1880s. By contrast, by any way in which the data are organized, the first decade of the twentieth century was a period of remarkably rapid growth.

The composition of agricultural output is shown in table 14.2. There we see, on the whole, the simplicity of Canadian agricultural production. It was overwhelmingly oriented to the production of foodstuffs. Fibers and other agricultural inputs to other sectors never amounted to more than about 12% of agricultural output (1881). Wheat emerges as an outstanding element in final agricultural product only in the early years of the twentieth century. Even in 1910–11 the value of wheat production (net of provision for seed) still made up only 24% of the flow of final agricultural product. In most years the leading component of agricultural output was animals for meat—primarily beef and pork. That component contracted sharply in the 1870s but expanded again in the last decade of the nineteenth century. In the 1870s there was a notable contraction of a well-established Canadian export trade in cattle. Exports to Great Britain grew to substitute to some extent for the

**Table 14.2**    **Final Agricultural Product and Its Composition, Canada, 1870–71 to 1926–27**

| Years | Total Product | Dairy Products | Other Animal Products | Wheat | Other Field Crops | Other Outputs |
|---|---|---|---|---|---|---|
| | *Millions of Current Dollars* | | | | | |
| 1870–71[a] | 139 | 24 | 60 | 22 | 17 | 16 |
| 1878–79 to 1882–83 | 172 | 35 | 57 | 33 | 26 | 21 |
| 1888–89 to 1892–93 | 186 | 49 | 65 | 27 | 23 | 22 |
| 1898–99 to 1902–03 | 235 | 66 | 88 | 33 | 22 | 26 |
| 1908–09 to 1912–13 | 444 | 95 | 154 | 106 | 51 | 37 |
| 1918–19 to 1922–23 | 963 | 185 | 290 | 297 | 103 | 85 |
| | *Percentage of Total* | | | | | |
| 1870–71 | 100.3 | 17.3 | 43.2 | 15.8 | 12.2 | 11.5 |
| 1878–79 to 1882–83 | 100.0 | 20.3 | 33.1 | 19.2 | 15.1 | 12.2 |
| 1888–89 to 1892–93 | 100.0 | 26.3 | 34.9 | 14.5 | 12.4 | 11.8 |
| 1898–99 to 1902–03 | 100.0 | 28.1 | 37.4 | 14.0 | 9.4 | 11.1 |
| 1908–09 to 1912–13 | 100.0 | 21.4 | 34.7 | 23.9 | 11.5 | 8.3 |
| 1918–19 to 1922–23 | 100.0 | 19.2 | 30.1 | 30.8 | 10.7 | 8.8 |

*Source:* Table 14.A.1.
[a]Census years only.

loss of the American market, mainly in the last decade of the nineteenth century. Dairy production grew continuously in relative terms throughout the later nineteenth century. Rather interestingly, the most pronounced increase in the share of dairy products came in the otherwise slow-growth decade of the 1880s. It was not solely a matter of retreat in other sectors. In real terms the production of dairy products grew by 40% between 1881 and 1891. All other components of agricultural output were rather stagnant during that decade.

The new series of gross value added in agriculture is compared in table 14.3 with the earlier estimates by Firestone. The comparison is made in both current and constant dollars since the two series differ both in the pattern of real output they portray and in the price trends. In current dollars the relation of the new series to Firestone's estimates is pretty much as was expected. The two estimates compare closely in 1921. The McInnis-Urquhart estimate is 97% of the Firestone estimate. In earlier years, though, the Firestone estimates are considerably higher than the new series. The difference is greatest in 1901 when the McInnis-Urquhart estimate is only 70% of Firestone's figure. Part of the difference is in the implication of price changes. The main differences in the pattern of price change shown by the two series is in the first and the last decades. The new series indicates a more substantial fall in prices between 1871 and 1881 than did Firestone. The implicit

Table 14.3    Comparison of Firestone with McInnis-Urquhart Estimates of Gross Value Added in Canadian Agriculture, Census Years 1871–1921

| Years[a] | Current $GVA | Firestone Constant $GVA | Implicit Price Index | McInnis-Urquhart Current $GVA | McInnis-Urquhart Constant $GVA | Implicit Price Index |
|---|---|---|---|---|---|---|
| 1870–71 | 145 | 161 | 90 | 132 | 136 | 97 |
| 1880–81 | 186 | 214 | 87 | 151 | 178 | 85 |
| 1890–91 | 217 | 268 | 81 | 173 | 208 | 83 |
| 1900–1901 | 282 | 321 | 76 | 197 | 266 | 74 |
| 1910–11 | 509 | 509 | 100 | 380 | 376 | 101 |
| 1920–21 | 1,073 | 580 | 185 | 1,041 | 508 | 205 |

*Sources: Firestone,* Firestone 1958, tables 63, 69; *McInnis-Urquart,* table 14.A.2.
[a]Individual census years only.

price indexes for the two series are fairly similar from 1881 through 1911. The new series would indicate, though, that the rise in prices from 1911 to 1921 was greater than Firestone's estimates implied.

The main difference between the two series, however, is in real production rather than its valuation. For 1871 the McInnis-Urquhart estimate of real value added is only 84% of the level estimated by Firestone. The relationship was at about the same level a decade later. Thereafter, Firestone's series indicated greater growth, so that by the turn of the century the new estimate is only 72% of Firestone's. Earlier in the paper I explained why there was a strong presumption that Firestone may have considerably overestimated agricultural output. What may be a bit surprising is that the large differential persists right up to 1911. For that year the new estimate is only 74% of Firestone's figure. The convergence of the two series occurs almost entirely in the 1911–21 decade, although it should be noted that in the real output series the McInnis-Urquhart estimate is still only 88% of the Firestone estimate in 1921.[7] One implication of this is that the new series shows considerably less growth of real output in the first decade of the twentieth century and rather more growth in the second decade.

## 14.4    A Tentative Look at Inputs and Productivity Growth

It is not possible at this time to give a reasonably conclusive and well-grounded account of input growth and productivity change in Canadian agriculture. Too much remains to be done in explaining what might be squeezed out of the available data for anything like a definitive analysis to be provided. What follows is more in the nature of a preliminary exploration of what the rather meager data that can readily be assembled do imply. Mainly what they show is that there was a lot of growth in agricultural inputs, primarily because a vast area of new land was brought under cultivation.

Information on inputs into agricultural production comes essentially from the decennial censuses. It is only sensible, then, to concentrate on the change between census dates. Land is the most directly measurable input; moreover, it is the one in which the most dramatic growth is to be seen. Land, then, makes an obvious starting point.

### 14.4.1  Land

The amount of agricultural land is directly obtainable from the decennial censuses. Table 14.4 summarizes some basic census data on farms and farmland. The number of farms is measured rather restrictively as the number of farm units occupying more than 10 acres. This undoubtedly leaves out of account a few small but genuine farms. The size distribution in the published nineteenth-century censuses provide no break between 10 acres and very small plots of less than an acre. In some years the censuses included large numbers of small plots of an acre or less that were merely rural and suburban residences rather than farms. If these small units are not left out, the count of farms can be quite misleading. The numbers of farms shown in table 14.4 are undercounts by only slight amounts; the numbers of acres are affected hardly at all by this definitional proscription.

For the most part it is improved land that should really interest us. It is not the case that unimproved land did not enter into production at all, but mostly it entered into the production of goods such as firewood, pulpwood, and timber that are not included in the measure of agricultural output adopted here. Animals, especially cattle, were grazed on unimproved land. That should introduce only a minor distortion. There was a range cattle industry of some prominence in the years

**Table 14.4**    **Agricultural Land in Canada, Census Dates, 1871–1921**

| Years | Number of Farms (Thousands) | Acres Occupied (Millions) | Acres Improved (Millions) | Improved Acres per Farm | Gross Value Added per Improved Acre |
|---|---|---|---|---|---|
| 1871 | 328 | 36 | 17 | 52 | 7.49 |
| 1881 | 389 | 45 | 22 | 57 | 7.95 |
| 1891 | 429 | 59[a] | 28[a] | 65 | 7.19 |
| 1901 | 453 | 63 | 30 | 66 | 8.82 |
| 1911 | 616 | 110 | 49 | 80 | 7.76 |
| 1921 | 667 | 141 | 71 | 106 | 6.42 |

*Source:* Decennial *Censuses of Canada.*

[a]Adjusted to take account of the original tabulation of much of Quebec farm land in *arpents* rather than acres.

after 1891, but it was a small element in the overall picture. Even there, much of the land on which cattle grazed would not have been counted as "occupied."[8]

Agricultural settlement in the Canadian west was under way by the 1890s, but the most dramatic changes came after 1901. This shows up in table 14.4 with the much greater increases in land area after 1901. As a general expository device in this exploration of the evidence, the entire half-century will frequently be looked at as two subperiods: 1871–1901 and 1901–21. The first represents the period before western settlement had much effect. Improved acreage increased by 76% in the first 30-year subperiod. More than half of that occurred in the older-settled eastern provinces where the area of improved land used in agricultural production had increased by almost 40%. Acres occupied in the eastern provinces expanded by almost as much, so the last 3 decades of the nineteenth century have to be seen as a period in which considerable expansion was occurring in the older-settled areas. Canadian agricultural development in this period was not just a story of western settlement.

The picture would look even more striking if the time period were broken in 1891. From 1871 to 1891 improved acreage in eastern Canada increased by 59%. Western (mainly Manitoba) acreage made up only 5% of the stock of improved land in 1891, and 85% of the increase in improved acreage to that date had come in the eastern provinces. Growth accelerated in the west while, between 1891 and 1901, there was actually a 10% reduction in improved acreage in the east.[9] Figures spanning the last three decades of the century mask this more pronounced expansion and then retreat.

The considerable increase in acreage of improved land, mainly in eastern Canada, up to 1901 underscores the importance of the lack of a measure of capital formation in the form of land improvement in the estimates of gross value added. Unimproved land, labor, and capital in the form of implements, draft animals, and stocks of feed crops were being used to produce improved land, and this was going on at a fairly rapid pace. In principle one could account for this on the output side or, if it is too difficult to measure the value of farm improvement, by segregating agricultural inputs that go into the product "farm improvement."[10] So far I have not been able to estimate a satisfactory series of capital accumulation in the form of land improvement; hence we shall have to endeavor to make an adjustment in one way or another on the input side.

The great increase in acreage in western Canada after 1901 is problematic in another way. Western land was farmed much less intensively. Hence we find that improved land was growing quite a bit more rapidly than was output. Gross value added per acre of improved land declined considerably between 1901 and 1921. These were less productive acres, though. The physical yield of western land was lower and, in the extensive dry farming areas, more acres of improved land were required for every acre actually under crop. The situation, however, is quite complex. The inherent difference between eastern and western land is probably not enough to account for the change that occurred. A very large increase in available land—cheaply available in the form of free homesteads—brought about a shift to a more land-intensive form of agriculture.

Over the entire 50-year period between 1871 and 1921 the average annual rate of change in acreage of improved land (2.84%) was greater than the rate of growth of output (2.56%). What that may mean for productivity depends upon the weight assigned in the aggregate production function to the input of land. In the last three decades of the nineteenth century, output was growing considerably faster than land; in the first two decades of the twentieth century, though, improved acreage was increasing at an average annual rate of 4.35% while output was growing at only 2.77%.

## 14.4.2 Labor

The measurement of labor input into Canadian agriculture is a more complex matter. Here too there are decennial census data, but they have been much less critically examined by previous investigators, and the potential margin of variation is greater than in the case of land. Earlier work has taken entirely at face value the tabulations by Statistics Canada of agricultural workers at decennial census dates from 1881 through 1921. Those data are used by Firestone along with a very crude estimate of the number of agricultural workers in 1871. Closer examination reveals too many problems with these data for them to be accepted so unquestioningly.

First off there is the problem of female workers. Except for a small number of female farm operators, mostly widows, separately identified first in the census of 1881, there are no female workers attributed to the agricultural sector. This may not be an entirely unreasonable characterization of nineteenth-century Canadian agriculture. Women in Canada typically did not do field work. If they contributed it was only in peak periods of labor demand. On the whole, then, it seems appropriate not to attempt any measure of female agricultural workers.[11]

Much more problematical are male unpaid family workers, or "farmers' sons," as they were called in the Canadian censuses. Practice varied in the way that "farmers' sons" were classified in addition to some considerable uncertainty as to just who was counted. The census of 1891 does about the most explicit job of identifying agricultural workers. That was the first year in which it seems that farm operators themselves were clearly identified. In that year there was a reasonable alignment of persons identified as farmers with the number of genuine farms—units of 10 acres or more. Understandably the former were a bit less numerous than the latter, since there were always a few farms operated by persons whose primary occupation was something other than farmer. In 1891, though, the number of persons counted as "farmers" was 98% of the number of farm units of more than 10 acres. "Farmers sons" were generously enumerated. They amounted to 58% of the number of farmers. This is probably an overestimate of unpaid family workers in agriculture. Although it includes no female workers, the 1891 account adds up to a virtually complete tally of farmers sons aged 13 and above, whether or not they were attending school. In that same census agricultural laborers are separately identified. To get a complete count of agricultural labor one needs only to add in a small number of "servants" attributable to the farm sector. The total number of male "servants" is small and, unlike female servants, not predominantly urban. Almost one-third of male servants were under 15 years of age. The category appears to have been used largely to refer to unpaid workers other than family members in households. A plausible guess would put two-thirds of male servants in farm households. In any case the number is small.

The agricultural workforce may have been generously enumerated in 1891, but at least it is relatively well defined. That year has been taken as a pivotal one around which the estimates for the other census years were worked out. Table 14.5 presents estimates of the agricultural workforce, roughly divided by status. As previously indicated, the total for 1891 is essentially the same as given in various census publications and utilized by other writers such as Firestone. To be consistent with that number, the counts for other years have to be adjusted. There are two main problems. One is that the treatment of "farmer's sons" varies; the other is that the category "laborer" often includes more than just agricultural laborers.

**Table 14.5**    **Canadian Agricultural Workforce by Status, Census Dates, 1871–1921 (Thousands of Workers)**

| Year | Farmers | Family Workers | Paid Labor | Total |
|------|---------|----------------|-----------|-------|
| 1871 | 324 | 122 | 133 | 579 |
| 1881 | 386 | 151 | 130 | 667 |
| 1891 | 414 | 241 | 89 | 744 |
| 1901 | 445 | 236 | 86 | 768 |
| 1911 | 678 | 132 | 148 | 958 |
| 1921 | 658 | 212 | 171 | 1,041 |

*Source:* As explained in text.

For the two censuses prior to 1891 it is possible to examine the manuscript enumerations in order to establish just how occupational categories got assigned. For both 1871 and 1881 the number of "farmers" returned was much above the number of farms, whereas in 1891, when the occupational classification of the census was much clearer, the count of "farmers" was slightly less than that of farm units of 10 acres or more. That is a plausible result since some farms would have been operated by persons with different primary occupations such as millers, merchants, loggers, or carters, or in some cases a farmer operated farms in two different enumeration areas. In 1881 the number of "farmers" was 30% greater than the count of farms, and in 1871 it was 45%. The resolution for 1871 is straightforward. All male workers in farm households who did not indicate some other specific occupation were counted as farmers. Thus "farmers" includes farmers' sons 13 years of age or over, whether or not attending school. To get a full tally of agricultural workers one needs only to add some share of those enumerated as "laborers." No distinction was made in the census between agricultural and nonagricultural laborers. Indeed there was at the time no real distinction, since these persons would have been day laborers who divided their work between agricultural and nonagricultural pursuits. The best we could do would be to divided them roughly between rural and urban, where the latter includes all cities, towns, and villages. That appears essentially to have been the distinction made in the census of 1891. There the count of agricultural laborers appears to have encompassed all laborers with rural residences. If the estimates are made consistently, it may at least be possible to make adjustments to agricultural labor when undertaking analyses of production relationships.

The situation in 1881 differed again. Then, the category "farmers' sons" was made explicit in the census for the first time, but it referred only to farmers' sons from 13 through 20 years of age. Sons who were 21 or over were classified as farmers. In table 14.5 the number of farmers is estimated for 1881, as for 1871, by applying the ratio of farmers to farms that held in 1891. The remaining "farmers" were added to the category "farmers' sons." The number of farm "laborers" was estimated for 1871 and 1881 as 72% and 68% of all laborers for those two years, respectively. The fractions were derived from local tabulations of adult male population in rural and urban areas. The procedure is undoubtedly generous in that it is more a count of the labor pool available to agriculture than of actual farm labor input. Both farmers' sons and rural laborers are fully assigned to the farm sector when they would undoubtedly have been considerably less than full-time workers. Even with the adjustments that were made, however, the category "farmers' sons" grew too much between 1881 and 1891. Partly it is a matter of reassigning people for the category "laborer" to that of "farmers' sons" but there remains a considerable suspicion that the latter category may be upwardly biased. If that is not the case, then it must be downwardly biased in earlier years, especially in 1871. Considerably more research needs to be done before the measurement and categorization of labor can be satisfactorily resolved.

The census years after 1891 are not entirely without problems either. The treatment of laborers seems to have been more consistent, but there were continuing problems with family workers as the census definition became increasingly restrictive. In 1901 scarcely any farmers' sons under 16 years of age were enumerated as gainfully employed. The number in table 14.5 is based on an upward adjustment derived from the age structure of young males. A similar adjustment was made for 1911, although by then the number of farmers' sons in the workforce had dropped considerably. Partly this decrease was real. The shift of farming to the western provinces provided opportunities that accelerated the upgrading on the occupational scale of farmers' sons to independent farmers. At the same time, in eastern Canada rapidly growing opportunities for nonagricultural employment drew young men off the farm at earlier ages. Nevertheless, there remains a nagging suspicion that census enumeration had become more restrictive and that the number of family workers in agriculture in 1911 had a downward bias. The 1921 figures are those given in the census, without adjustment. The large increase in farmers' sons between 1911 and 1921 may be an indication that the category was even more seriously understated in 1911 than has been presumed here. One should not be too hasty in reaching that conclusion, though. The aging of farm families in the Western provinces meant that more farmers had sons of working age.

The labor estimates of table 14.5 can be used in conjunction with the estimates of real gross valued added to examine changes in labor productivity in Canadian agriculture. Keep in mind that the labor estimates are upwardly biased, although less so for years in the twentieth century. The estimates of gross value added per worker shown in table 14.6 point to an average annual rate of increase over the entire half-century of 1.36%. That is well above the 0.9% indicated for the United States from an amalgamation of estimates by Towne and Rasmussen (1960) and Kendrick (1961). Because these two slightly different series have to be put together for the United States, the calculation of productivity growth may be just an approximation. There is little question, though, that the Canadian rate is well above that of the United States. This result is due mainly to the pattern for the first two decades of the twentieth century, when productivity growth in United States agriculture flattened out almost completely. Between 1900 and 1920, Kendrick's figures for output per worker in agriculture rise by an average

Table 14.6          Gross Value Added per Agricultural Worker, 1871 to 1919–23

| Years | GVA[a] per Worker (Constant 1913 Dollars) | % Change over Preceding Decade | U.S. Gross Product per Worker (Constant 1910–14 Dollars) | Canada as % of U.S. |
|-------|------|------|------|------|
| 1871 | 235 | — | 334[b] | 70 |
| 1879–83 | 270 | 14.9 | 407[b] | 66 |
| 1889–93 | 277 | 2.6 | 424[b] | 65 |
| 1899–1903 | 361 | 30.3 | 490[b] | 74 |
| 1909–13 | 414 | 14.7 | 505[c] | 82 |
| 1919–23 | 458 | 10.6 | 524[c] | 87 |

[a]From tables 14.1 and 14.5.
[b]From Towne and Rasmussen (1960) adjusted to match concepts as closely as possible.
[c]From Kendrick (1961).

of only 0.33% per year. That is in considerable contrast to the 1.28% growth rate indicated by the Towne and Rasmussen (1960) series for the last three decades of the nineteenth century. In Canada the growth of output per worker in agriculture was not so much different between the two periods. In the first 20 years of the twentieth century the growth rate of labor productivity averaged 1.20%, almost as high as the 1.46% of the last 30 years of the nineteenth century. Productive growth in the latter period was highly variable across the three decades, being especially low in the decade 1881–91 and quite rapid in the succeeding one. A concern that this pattern may result from variations in the measurement of labor input has already been raised. It is interesting to note, however, that the evidence for the United States points to a very similar pattern.[12]

Agricultural gross value added per worker in Canada was about 70% of the level of the United States in 1870. By 1880 it had slipped to only 66%. These relationships are not at all implausible even though the Canadian figures are derived from especially generous measures of labor input. The agricultural comparison looks roughly the same as the longstanding relationship between per capita incomes of the two countries. United States agricultural output per worker was still relatively low in 1870 as that country worked its way through post–Civil War reconstruction. Canada began to catch up again on the United States in the last decade of the nineteenth century and pulled up sharply in the early twentieth century. Further investigation of the substance of Canadian agricultural development will probably reinforce the plausibility of this pattern as the waning years of the century are shown to be a period of decided agricultural improvement. The full evidence on that has yet to be assembled. In the meantime, a striking finding of this paper is that, despite one decade of slow productivity growth, the overall rise in agricultural output per worker was more rapid in the late nineteenth than in the early twentieth century. The first two decades of the twentieth century undoubtedly were a time of rapid expansion of agriculture, but they were primarily a time of growth of inputs. Intensive growth was less impressive. The rate of growth of output per worker slackened, and the expanding farm sector could not have been such a dramatic contributor to national per capital income growth.

With the rapid settlement of the Canadian west, a large addition was made to the agricultural workforce (35% in 20 years) and the amount of improved land was more than doubled. The increase in output was less spectacular, and gross output per worker increased by only 28% over the 1901–21 period—an annual rate of only 1.20%. To some extent the figures used here may understate the gain because they fail to take into account all of the capital accumulation in agriculture. The main point, though, may be a reminder that western settlement entailed substantial resource costs. It also meant that land and capital were being abandoned in eastern Canadian agriculture. Transferring labor from eastern Canada, leaving behind still usable physical assets, to work with low-yielding land in the west, may have had fairly limited benefits in the form of direct increases in per worker or per capita income. The net benefits of western settlement would have been even smaller if the attraction of the west tended to constrain supplies of capital to agriculture in eastern Canada.

### 14.4.3    Capital

The least satisfactory estimates provided in this paper are the following figures on capital. They are very tentative and should be treated with caution and viewed as little more than broad indications of likely magnitudes. Data for estimating the capital stock are very scanty. There are decennial census data on buildings and machinery from 1901 forward and on stocks of livestock for all census years. Some Ontario data on buildings and machinery go back to 1881. For nineteenth-century census years it is necessary to assume that the changes from decade to decade in buildings and machinery per farm followed the same time pattern as in Ontario.

Stocks of livestock made up between 55% and 65% of farm capital, as estimated here. That is about commensurate with Tostlebe's figures for the United States.[13] It is fortunate that the stock of livestock is such a large component of farm capital since that is the one element of the total that can be estimated with a reasonable degree of confidence. Numbers of each type of animal at each census date were valued at a fixed set of 1913 prices.

Buildings and machinery are measured much more dubiously. The starting point is 1901 and subsequent census measures of the values of buildings and machinery, projected backward to earlier years on the basis of a variety of indicators. Machinery and equipment is a relatively small element of the total. Only the value of nonresidential farm buildings should be included in the farm capital estimates made here, since no inputed rent on farm dwellings is included in the measure of agricultural output. The problem is that we have only the sketchiest idea of the relative importance of residential and nonresidential farm buildings. Mainly from evidence on farm investment requirements, or "farm-making costs," we get an indication that residences comprised at least 60% of the value of farm buildings. That proportion has been used here throughout, although there are indications that it may be on the low side of Prairie farming where grain was the principal product.

The broad composition of farm capital and the constant 1913 dollar values of it at each census date are shown in table 14.7. These must be taken as only the roughest sort of indicators. The pattern of growth over time is rather smoother than for other inputs but that may be partly contrived as a consequence of the way the figures were estimated. One of the most difficult issues concerns the estimation of constant dollar values of the stock of capital at a time when prices are changing drastically. That situation is met acutely in 1921 when prices had risen greatly. The value of buildings and machinery reported in the census of 1921 must have entailed a considerable lag in the valuation of assets. Deflating by any conventional price index of currently produced goods would lead to a considerable understatement of the value of capital. The figures shown in table 14.7 are as much guesswork as anything. They can do little more than provide a starting point for analysis.

Capital input in Canadian agriculture seems to have been increasing quite rapidly, just as were other inputs. The average annual rate of increase, 1871–1921, was 2.95%. There was a lower rate in the 1871–1901 period, but in the first two decades of the twentieth century the annual rate of capital increase rose to 3.89%. That again is greater than the rate of growth of output.

Table 14.7    **Estimated Stocks of Farm Capital, Canada, Census Years 1871–1921 (Millions of Constant 1913 Dollars)**

| Year | Machinery and Equipment | Nonresidential Buildings | Livestock | Total |
|------|------------------------|--------------------------|-----------|-------|
| 1871 | 46  | 90  | 284 | 420  |
| 1881 | 54  | 120 | 354 | 528  |
| 1891 | 67  | 166 | 453 | 686  |
| 1901 | 93  | 214 | 535 | 842  |
| 1911 | 273 | 326 | 770 | 1369 |
| 1921 | 443 | 368 | 993 | 1804 |

### 14.4.4    Total Factor Productivity

In the foregoing sections of the paper the rates of growth of both outut and inputs have been examined. It would be attractive to bring these together to compare the weighted sum of factor input growth with output growth in order to infer how much advance in total factor productivity there may have been.

We might take advantage of the fact that, from the many aggregate production function models of economic growth we can derive a straightforward expression of the growth of output as a weighted sum of the growth of factor inputs, where the weights are factor shares in national income. This approach has become fairly standard in applied work on economic growth and productivity advance. The catch is that for Canada in this period we have no studies of the factoral disposition of national income. Hence we have no reliable way of weighting the component series of inputs.

One way of proceeding that may be instructive is to compare the rate of growth of output with weighted combinations of input growth in Canada assuming that the factor shares used as weights are the same as in the United States. The other assumptions made are standard—an agricultural production function that is linear homogeneous of the conventional Cobb-Douglas sort; land, labor, and capital recognized as the primary inputs into production with no direct account taken of purchased inputs. The latter were indeed minor through most of the period. Artificial fertilizers were little used in Canadian agriculture, and only after World War I did fuel purchases emerge as a significant item of farming costs. In Gallman's (1972) study of productivity change in United States agriculture in the nineteenth study a relatively high value is given to the share of labor in agricultural production.[14] Kendrick (1961, table B–1), focusing on the period at the very end of the nineteenth and beginning of the twentieth century, puts the share of labor quite a bit lower. Kendrick, however, combines land and capital inputs into a single series, whereas I have retained separate indexes of the growth of capital and land inputs. If the same rate of return were earned on farm capital as on improved land, we might then crudely divide Kendrick's "capital" share into shares of reproducible capital and improved land on the basis of the ratios of values of the stocks of those two components in 1901 and 1911 (averaging 0.39).

Whether or not the choice of factor weights makes much difference to the results depends upon the questions of interest. The two sets of estimates of output, input, and total factor productivity growth rates, are summarized in table 14.8. They might be thought of as representing two bounds to the most likely representation of the actual situation. Over the entire half-century under examination, the findings are the

**Table 14.8**        **Output, Input, and Productivity Growth, Canadian Agriculture, 1871–1921 (Average Annual % Growth)**

| Years | Output Growth Rate | Accounted for by Input Growth | Total Factor Productivity Increase |
|---|---|---|---|
| | *High (Gallman) Labor Share* | | |
| 1871–1921 | 2.56 | 1.69 | 0.87 |
| 1871–1901 | 2.40 | 1.06 | 1.34 |
| 1901–21 | 2.77 | 2.33 | 0.44 |
| | *Low (Kendrick) Labor Share* | | |
| 1871–1921 | 2.56 | 1.79 | 0.77 |
| 1871–1901 | 2.40 | 1.32 | 1.08 |
| 1901–21 | 2.77 | 2.68 | 0.09 |

same. The growth of agricultural output was primarily the result of conventional factor inputs, and the increase in total factor productivity was relatively modest: 0.87% per annum on average with the higher factor share of labor, 0.77% with the lower. Those rates of productivity advance in agriculture are very similar to the results obtained by Gallman for the United States over the second half of the nineteenth century. For the 1868–1919 period, an average rate of total factor productivity increase of 0.42% can be computed from Kendrick's estimates. That would seem to indicate that Canada continued to enjoy appreciable, if not really rapid, productivity advance in agriculture after the rate of productivity growth in United States agriculture had begun to taper off. It is less than clear whether one should expect much similarity between the experiences of Canadian and United States agriculture. It is too easy to think of the two countries as similar, forgetting that there are important differences. Corn, for example, played a much less prominent role in Canadian agriculture, and Canada has nothing comparable to the cotton sector of the United States agricultural economy.

The choice of factor weights makes a greater difference to the account one would give of early twentieth-century experience. If one looks at the 1901–21 subperiod, the growth of agricultural output is even more a matter of factor input growth. The rate of productivity advance dropped markedly. Using the higher (0.70) share for labor, the average annual rate of advance of total factor productivity is only 0.44% compared with a vigorous 1.34% over the last three decades of the nineteenth century. With the lower (0.57) share of labor, there is virtually no productivity growth at all (0.09%). Labor's share need only be as low as 0.55 to eliminate productivity growth altogether. Without more firmly based evidence on factor shares, there is no resolution of the issue. That the first two decades of the twentieth century might have been a period when there was virtually no productivity growth in Canadian agriculture is far from implausible. In the United States over the same period, there appears to have been an actual decline in total factor productivity. Whether or not productivity growth in Canada had actually fallen to zero, it was almost certainly at quite a low rate. This was at a time when Canadian agriculture was undergoing a very rapid expansion and per capita income in Canada was increasing rapidly. The agricultural expansion is often supposed to have been at the heart of that per capita income growth. What the very low rates of productivity growth in agriculture suggest is that the farm sector as a whole cannot have made much of a direct contribution to Canadian per capita income growth in the first two decades of the twentieth century. Of course, per capita or per worker income growth need not in any relatively short period depend upon growth in total factor productivity. Output per worker can increase because the workforce gets more land and capital to cooperate with. That is in fact what was going on at the time. We have already seen in table 14.6, however, that gross value added per agricultural worker did not increase very rapidly between 1901 and 1921. We are left, then, with some serious questions about the direct contribution the agricultural sector could have made to Canadian per capita income growth in the period of the "Wheat Boom," the most glorified period of Canadian economic development. By contrast, the last three decades of the nineteenth century was a period of considerably greater productivity growth in agriculture. Even the lower of the two estimates puts total factor productivity advance at an average annual rate of more than 1%. In that period the agricultural sector would have made a proportionately much greater direct contribution to national per capita income growth. One implication of the productivity estimates made in this paper would be to redirect thinking about the nature and sources of economic growth in Canada.

Clearly, the quantitative record falls short of permitting a firm accounting of input, output, and productivity growth in Canadian agriculture. The weakest series—that for capital input—enters into the productivity calculation with only a small weight. There remain uncertainties about both the land and labor input series. Both might turn out to be quite sensitive to variations in the flow of factor services from generously measured stocks. A quality adjustment to the land input might reduce its rate of increase, although that point could be argued both ways. Land values cannot be used readily to indicate land quality so long as substantial amounts of land were available as free homesteads. The picture that seems to be visible behind the haze of data uncertainties is one of Canada opting for agricultural development in the form of large increases in factor inputs but with a relatively low rate of productivity growth.[15] The national picture may be concealing important contrasts in regional patterns. To clarify the situation it will be important to expedite the development of regional output and input series. The calculations made in this paper, however, suggest a degree of caution in regarding the extension of agriculture into the Canadian west as a major contribution to per capita income growth in Canada.[16]

# Appendix

**Table 14.A.1**    **Composition of Final Agricultural Product Canada, 1870–71 to 1926–27 (Millions of Current Dollars)**

| Years | Total Product | Dairy Products | Other Animal Products | Wheat | Other Field Crops | Other Outputs |
|---|---|---|---|---|---|---|
| 1870–71 | 139 | 24 | 60 | 22 | 17 | 16 |
| 1871–72 | 145 | 26 | 57 | 24 | 18 | 20 |
| 1872–73 | 144 | 24 | 59 | 26 | 16 | 19 |
| 74 | 145 | 29 | 58 | 25 | 17 | 16 |
| 75 | 154 | 39 | 53 | 20 | 22 | 20 |
| 76 | 147 | 33 | 53 | 24 | 21 | 16 |
| 77 | 141 | 33 | 50 | 26 | 15 | 17 |
| 78 | 147 | 36 | 48 | 24 | 18 | 21 |
| 79 | 136 | 30 | 41 | 26 | 21 | 18 |
| 80 | 162 | 30 | 50 | 37 | 24 | 21 |
| 1880–81 | 161 | 38 | 54 | 32 | 22 | 15 |
| 82 | 195 | 35 | 61 | 38 | 37 | 24 |
| 83 | 206 | 42 | 78 | 33 | 28 | 25 |
| 84 | 185 | 40 | 68 | 26 | 26 | 25 |
| 85 | 173 | 40 | 71 | 21 | 21 | 20 |
| 86 | 176 | 34 | 72 | 24 | 25 | 21 |
| 87 | 158 | 38 | 52 | 26 | 23 | 19 |
| 88 | 172 | 42 | 53 | 23 | 30 | 24 |
| 89 | 173 | 42 | 64 | 26 | 25 | 16 |
| 1889–90 | 181 | 42 | 66 | 25 | 24 | 24 |
| 91 | 189 | 48 | 65 | 27 | 22 | 27 |
| 92 | 193 | 54 | 63 | 34 | 22 | 20 |
| 93 | 193 | 57 | 66 | 25 | 21 | 24 |
| 94 | 170 | 60 | 44 | 21 | 21 | 24 |
| 95 | 177 | 55 | 62 | 19 | 19 | 22 |
| 96 | 170 | 50 | 58 | 30 | 15 | 17 |
| 97 | 162 | 51 | 54 | 23 | 16 | 18 |
| 98 | 193 | 54 | 60 | 36 | 18 | 25 |
| 99 | 197 | 58 | 70 | 26 | 18 | 25 |
| 1899–1900 | 214 | 64 | 75 | 31 | 19 | 25 |
| 1900–1901 | 217 | 68 | 82 | 28 | 18 | 21 |
| 02 | 255 | 67 | 96 | 37 | 27 | 28 |
| 03 | 295 | 74 | 116 | 45 | 29 | 31 |
| 04 | 279 | 74 | 96 | 39 | 32 | 38 |

**Table 14.A.1**    (continued)

| Years | Total Product | Dairy Products | Other Animal Products | Wheat | Other Field Crops | Other Inputs |
|---|---|---|---|---|---|---|
| 1900–05 | 291 | 71 | 115 | 49 | 26 | 30 |
| 06 | 319 | 86 | 112 | 56 | 28 | 37 |
| 07 | 329 | 87 | 125 | 54 | 29 | 34 |
| 08 | 368 | 92 | 122 | 70 | 42 | 42 |
| 09 | 353 | 98 | 110 | 77 | 35 | 33 |
| 1909–10 | 426 | 96 | 142 | 120 | 33 | 35 |
| 11 | 427 | 97 | 163 | 85 | 43 | 39 |
| 12 | 497 | 85 | 169 | 125 | 76 | 42 |
| 1912–13 | 515 | 101 | 187 | 121 | 70 | 36 |
| 14 | 565 | 95 | 217 | 137 | 73 | 43 |
| 15 | 539 | 98 | 220 | 128 | 56 | 37 |
| 16 | 753 | 115 | 213 | 299 | 80 | 46 |
| 17 | 850 | 134 | 256 | 281 | 128 | 51 |
| 18 | 1,014 | 148 | 308 | 377 | 122 | 59 |
| 19 | 995 | 176 | 361 | 275 | 108 | 75 |
| 20 | 1,034 | 200 | 328 | 291 | 131 | 84 |
| 1920–21 | 1,155 | 216 | 336 | 383 | 121 | 99 |
| 22 | 789 | 174 | 211 | 228 | 82 | 94 |
| 23 | 844 | 160 | 212 | 309 | 75 | 73 |
| 24 | 880 | 171 | 237 | 309 | 86 | 77 |
| 25 | 889 | 175 | 229 | 292 | 124 | 69 |
| 26 | 1,111 | 188 | 281 | 413 | 138 | 91 |
| 1926–27 | 1,035 | 187 | 273 | 387 | 117 | 71 |

*Sources and procedures:*
Dairy products
Cheese: Estimated as net exports plus a fixed allowance for domestic consumption of 3 pounds per capita. Prior to 1907 the exports are for the same fiscal year as the agricultural year identified in the aggregate output estimates. With the shift in the fiscal year in 1907 the estimates are changed to include the exports of the contemporaneous and the following fiscal years.
Butter: Census benchmark estimates of butter production are reconciled with export and import data for those years to obtain per capita estimates of "domestic disappearance" for those years. Annual levels of per capita consumption are then calculated by linear interpolation between census years and multiplied by population numbers to obtain an aggregate. Net exports are added to the national consumption estimates to get the quantity of national production. The total is valued at the wholesale price of butter less one cent per pound.
Fluid milk: Estimated by linear interpolation between census benchmark estimates of per capita consumption. The latter are fairly crude estimates derived from a reconciliation of estimates of butter and cheese production with plausbile levels of milk production per cow. Milk is valued at the farm price of butter converted into whole milk at a conventional rate of 23 pounds of milk to a pound of butter.
*Other animal products*
Cattle: Animal production is the sale or slaughter of cattle for consumption or export, adjusted for the change in farm inventories. Slaughter cattle are valued at higher prices than those being added to inventories. The stock of cattle is estimated for years from 1882 to 1921 by interpolating between decennial census benchmarks on the basis of annual provincial government reports for Alberta, Manitoba, and Ontario. Between 1871 and 1881 there are no annual reports for any province, and a smooth interpretation is

**Table 14.A.1**     (continued)

used. Production of cattle for export or slaughter is then estimated from the annual stock by the use of a ratio of production to stock derived from the annual reports for Ontario. Prior to 1891 there are no Ontario production reports, and annual production is based on interpolations between 1871, 1881, and 1891 census-based estimates of per capita consumption adjusted for net exports. One fortunate aspect of this procedure is that the 1871–81 decade is the period of the greatest relative importance of cattle exports; in some years they exceeded 25% of output.

Hogs: The estimating procedure is essentially the same as used for cattle.

Sheep and lambs: For 1871–91 the annual production is estimated as domestic consumption from figures for per capita consumption linearly interpolated between census benchmarks, adjusted annually for net exports.

For 1891–1921 the procedure is an elaboration of the foregoing. Annual estimates of "domestic disappearance" are first made in the same way as for the earlier period for both Canada as a whole and for Ontario. The ratio of sales and slaughter reported annually by the Ontario Bureau of Industries to the estimate for that province by smooth interpolation is then used to adjust the national, smoothly interpolated estimate.

For 1920–21 to 1926–27 the estimate is taken directly from the *Handbook of Agricultural Statistics* (Dominion Bureau of Statistics, various years).

Wool: For census years the quantities of wool produced on farms as reported in the censuses were valued at a farm price of wool projected backward from the 1920s on the time pattern of import unit values of raw wool.

Horses: Net agricultural production includes (1) exports of horses, (2) sales to the nonfarm sector, and (3) additions to the farm stock of horses. Separate series were constructed for farm and nonfarm stocks of horses. These were both based on census enumerations. Annual estimates for the nonfarm stock and the farm stock in the 1871–81 decade were made by smooth, linear interpolation. For the farm stock after 1881, the census number of Ontario and povinces to the east were interpolated on the pattern of annual stocks in Ontario. For the western region provincial government reports on the stock of horses in Manitoba were the basis for annual interpolations. All horses were assumed to be produced in the farm sector. Sales to the nonfarm sector were calculated as 10% of the previous year's stock plus the change in the stock between years. Exports were taken directly from the annual *Trade and Navigation* reports of the Canadian government. Exports were far from trivial and in several years were the largest component of production. The change in the farm stock of horses was then added (algebraically) to the sum of the other two components of production.

From 1891 onward the annual "production" of horses was valued at the 1911 census unit value adjusted annually on the pattern of unit values reported by the *Ontario Bureau of Industries*. For years before 1891 the price series is extended backward by multiplying the export unit value by a 12-year average of the ratio of *Ontario Bureau of Industries* (OBI) prices to export unit values.

Poultry: Based largely on the stocks of chickens reported in the censuses. Ratios of sales and slaughter to stocks are based on Ontario provincial government reports from 1891 onward. Prior to 1891 a fixed ratio is applied. Estimated sales and slaughter of chickens are adjusted for annual changes in inventories. Chicken production is then valued at the 1911 census unit values of sales projected backward on the basis of an average of OBI and Montreal wholesale prices. Prior to 1889–90 there are no available data on chicken prices and the pattern of variation in egg prices is used. The value of chicken production is adjusted upwardly by the ratio of total poultry to chickens in 1901 and 1911 to take account of poultry other than chickens. The maximum amount of that adjustment is 18%.

Eggs: From 1901 onward census data on egg production are used, interpolated annually on the basis of OBI reports for the province of Ontario. From 1881 to 1901 production per hen at the 1901 ratio is used to estimate egg production. For the decade 1871–81 production is estimated at a constant 1881 per capita consumption figure, adjusted annually for net exports. Prices are 1901 and 1911 unit values extrapolated on the time pattern of an average of export unit values and wholesale prices.

**Table 14.A.1**    (continued)

*Wheat*

This was by far the single most important field crop. A reasonably reliable national estimate is available for the years from 1908–09 onward. That is from the Dominion Bureau of Statistics *Handbook of Agricultural Statistics*. For earlier years the estimate of production is based on a fixed figure of 5.5 bushels per capita for domestic consumption, aggregated into a national consumption figure through multiplying by an annual population estimate and then adjusting for net exports either as wheat or flour. No provision is made for changes in farm-held stocks of grain. These appear to have been minor amounts in the years before the wheat economy of the Prairie provinces rose to prominence. A weighted average of eastern and western wheat crops is based on Toronto and Winnipeg wholesale prices.

*Other field crops*

These include oats, barley, potatoes, hay, corn, rye, and flaxseed. The first four are by far the most important until after 1903 when western flaxseed became significant. Production of flax, net of a seed allowance, is taken directly from annual surveys of crop production made by the federal Census and Statistics Office. Off-farm sales of hay were estimated from calculated feeding requirements of stocks of off-farm animals. The procedure followed for other crops was to adjust net exports for estimates of domestic human consumption based on fixed per capita consumption allowances. For barley there are good records of quantities of barley used for malt. The single most important of this list of crops, and the most precariously estimated, is potatoes. For census dates the estimates amount to reported production adjusted by what were essentially guesses about the proportion of the crop that went to animal feed or was lost as spoilage.

*Other outputs*

In approximate order of importance these are: vegetables, apples, other fruit, maple syrup and sugar, grass and clover seed, tobacco, hops, honey, and flax fiber. These are all assumed to be final products of the farm sector. Census production data are used, valued at 1911 unit values extrapolated on wholesale price series and unit values of international trade. Vegetables constitued by far the largest single item and, like potatoes, is probably quite precariously estimated.

**Table 14.A.2**    **Gross Value Added, Canadian Agriculture 1870–71 to 1926–27**

| Years | Final Agricultural Product | | Implicit Price Deflator | Constant $ Purchases from Other Sectors | Gross Value Added in Agriculture (Constant 1913 $) |
|---|---|---|---|---|---|
| | Current | Constant | | | |
| 1870–71 | 139 | 146 | 97 | 10 | 136 |
| 72 | 144 | 148 | 99 | 11 | 137 |
| 73 | 144 | 154 | 94 | 8 | 146 |
| 74 | 145 | 153 | 95 | 11 | 142 |
| 75 | 154 | 154 | 100 | 11 | 143 |
| 76 | 147 | 162 | 91 | 10 | 152 |
| 77 | 142 | 161 | 88 | 12 | 149 |
| 78 | 147 | 167 | 88 | 11 | 156 |
| 79 | 137 | 173 | 79 | 13 | 160 |
| 80 | 162 | 191 | 85 | 13 | 178 |
| 1880–81 | 160 | 190 | 84 | 12 | 178 |
| 82 | 194 | 202 | 96 | 14 | 188 |
| 83 | 206 | 210 | 98 | 15 | 195 |

**Table 14.A.2**    (continued)

| Years | Final Agricultural Product | | Implicit Price Deflator | Constant $ Purchases from Other Sectors | Gross Value Added in Agriculture (Constant 1913 $) |
|---|---|---|---|---|---|
| | Current | Constant | | | |
| 84 | 185 | 189 | 98 | 15 | 174 |
| 85 | 174 | 207 | 84 | 15 | 192 |
| 86 | 166 | 210 | 79 | 15 | 195 |
| 87 | 158 | 205 | 77 | 17 | 188 |
| 88 | 180 | 214 | 84 | 18 | 196 |
| 89 | 171 | 201 | 85 | 16 | 185 |
| 90 | 181 | 229 | 79 | 18 | 211 |
| 1890–91 | 189 | 228 | 83 | 20 | 208 |
| 92 | 193 | 230 | 84 | 20 | 210 |
| 93 | 194 | 240 | 81 | 23 | 217 |
| 94 | 185 | 226 | 82 | 23 | 203 |
| 95 | 177 | 233 | 76 | 24 | 209 |
| 96 | 171 | 244 | 70 | 23 | 221 |
| 97 | 162 | 249 | 65 | 26 | 223 |
| 98 | 193 | 264 | 73 | 28 | 236 |
| 99 | 197 | 274 | 72 | 29 | 245 |
| 00 | 214 | 285 | 75 | 30 | 255 |
| 1900–01 | 217 | 293 | 74 | 27 | 266 |
| 02 | 255 | 327 | 78 | 32 | 295 |
| 03 | 294 | 359 | 82 | 35 | 324 |
| 04 | 279 | 321 | 87 | 33 | 288 |
| 05 | 293 | 349 | 84 | 33 | 316 |
| 06 | 319 | 367 | 87 | 34 | 333 |
| 07 | 330 | 379 | 87 | 37 | 342 |
| 08 | 369 | 373 | 99 | 36 | 337 |
| 09 | 353 | 360 | 98 | 36 | 324 |
| 1909–10 | 426 | 430 | 99 | 43 | 387 |
| 11 | 426 | 422 | 101 | 46 | 376 |
| 12 | 497 | 487 | 102 | 51 | 436 |
| 1912–13 | 514 | 514 | 100 | 52 | 462 |
| 14 | 564 | 553 | 102 | 63 | 490 |
| 15 | 538 | 476 | 113 | 60 | 416 |
| 16 | 752 | 621 | 121 | 65 | 556 |
| 17 | 852 | 539 | 158 | 61 | 478 |
| 18 | 1,014 | 539 | 188 | 43 | 496 |
| 19 | 995 | 513 | 194 | 49 | 464 |
| 20 | 1,033 | 474 | 218 | 59 | 415 |
| 1920–21 | 1,155 | 563 | 205 | 55 | 508 |
| 22 | 788 | 540 | 146 | 73 | 467 |
| 23 | 829 | 619 | 134 | 86 | 533 |
| 24 | 879 | 715 | 123 | 85 | 630 |
| 25 | 888 | 569 | 156 | 66 | 503 |
| 26 | 1,111 | 677 | 164 | 76 | 601 |
| 1926–27 | 1,035 | 651 | 159 | 83 | 568 |

(*continued*)

**Table 14.A.2**    (continued)

*Sources and methods:*

1. Current dollar estimates of final agricultural product are from table 14.A.1.

2. Constant dollar final product is based on the quantity series underlying table 14.A.1 with each commodity valued at fixed 1913 prices. Because the price series used in table 14.A.1 are often weaker in quality than the quantity series, the constant dollar figures are probably more reliable than the current dollar figures.

3. The implicit price deflator is directly calculated from the relationship between current and constant dollar estimates.

4. Purchases from other sectors include the following:

Mill feed. Over most of the period this was the largest single item. Available quantities of bran, shorts, and middlings were calculated from the series on flour production on the basis of 15.8 pounds of by-product per bushel of wheat milled. Exports were deducted and the remainder valued at export unit values for bran.

Blacksmith expenses. For 1870–71, 1880–81, and 1890–91 this was calculated as an estimated rural share of census-reported production or sales of blacksmiths. For 1900–1901 through 1920–21 it was the number of own-account blacksmiths by occupation multiplied by an average wage rate for blacksmiths and marked up by a factor of 1.66.

Fertilizer. This was never an item of any real consequence in Canada. From 1891 and later it is census-reported production less exports plus imports. For earlier years only imports are included.

Binder twine. Introduced only in 1883, it was initially mostly imported. Domestic production of 1901 was projected backward on the time pattern of imports of undressed hemp and added to imports of twine.

Automobile and truck expenses. These are included only from 1904–5 forward. They were estimated by projecting backward the official estimate for 1926 on the trend in registered numbers of farm automobiles and trucks adjusted for changes in petroleum prices.

Tractor fuel. This is included only from 1907–8 onward. The procedure is the same as for automobiles and trucks.

Other expenses. This covers a variety of things including mainly bags, sacks, cooperage, and other containers. It is estimated as 4% of final agricultural product.

Current dollar estimates of farm expenses are deflated on an equally weighted index of prices of grain mill products and iron and steel products. This deflation procedure is very crude, but errors in it could make little difference to the final estimate of gross value added.

# Notes

1. This fuller report is at present in preparation. An early, abbreviated version was presented as R. M. McInnis and M. C. Urquhart (1981).

2. This study being done by the author of the present paper is part of a project to produce an economic and social *Historical Atlas of Canada*. That project is also supported by the Social Science and Humanities Council of Canada.

3. An example of how a lean estimate of output may be compared with inputs where an appropriate adjustment is made on the input side is Lewis and McInnis (1980).

4. Gavin Wright, in his comment on this paper, rightly seizes upon the procedure here as rather chancey, as I also point out in the text. The issue boils down to a question of how serious is the problem. The whole issue is even more complicated than Wright suggests. The problem he points to concerns the appropriateness of the estimating procedure if the expansion were demand led, by rising world prices. Several points should be made in connection with this problem. One is that the whole picture is complicated by the multiplicity of commodities and variations in the historical experience with regard to each commodity. Market conditions varied a great deal for each commodity. One might note that, generally, over much of the period under study, world prices were falling, not rising. It is relative prices that matter, however, and we do not have adequate data to be able to show that relative prices were in fact declining in the appropriate sense. Partly, the issue hinges on what is the appropriate way to model the expansion of an economy with strong export markets. Was it a matter of rising export demand, or mainly just a highly elastic foreign demand for Canadian agricultural products? A case could be made for the latter formulation. That in turn directs attention to whether demand should be conceived of as f.o.b. Canada or at the export market in Britain. Where much of the change involved concerns the wedge of transport and other transactions costs between the two markets, how much does the outcome depend on just how one chooses to set the problem up? Wright has certainly raised a valid point, but the answers are considerably more complex than he indicates.

5. These estimates of county net agricultural output have been prepared for the *Historical Atlas of Canada* project. Details have yet to be published. The methodology used, however, is similar to and builds upon that used for Quebec parishes in Lewis and McInnis (1980). Census data are used and the principles underlying the estimates are essentially the same, but the estimation is made at a low level of regional aggregation. When the county estimates for 1891, e.g., are aggregated across the country, they add up to a total that is only 4% short of the national total of the series being presented here.

6. In 1881 the improved land area of the regions added to Canada since the previous census amounted to a little less than 5% of the national total.

7. It should be pointed out that the new series merges quite smoothly with the officia Bureau of Statistics series in 1926.

8. Gavin Wright, in his comment on this paper, seems to think of unimproved farmland as essentially grazing land on which animal products were produced. In fact, wood lot and forest land was the predominant type of unimproved land. The products of that land have been excluded from the measure of output. The more serious concern is that the cooperating inputs, capital and labor, may have been used in production on unimproved land. For a fuller treatment of this problem, see Lewis and McInnis (1980).

9. The contraction of improved farmland between 1891 and 1901 was especially pronounced in Nova Scotia. The largest area was withdrawn in Ontario—almost 1 million acres—but that amounted only to 6.6% of the province's total area of improved land.

10. That is the procedure adopted in Lewis and McInnis (1980).

11. Female contributions to farm output consisted very largely of those products which have not been counted in the measure of output used here. The main exception would be the value added in butter making.

12. The substantial rise of the productivity in the 1870s probably reflects a recovery from the aftermath of the Civil War. The sudden and sharp rise in the 1890s shows up dramatically in Kendrick (1961, chart 18, p. 176).

13. See Tostlebe (1957). To make the comparison suggested it is necessary to make a rough and rather arbitrary separation in Tostlebe's figures of farm residences from other farm buildings.

14. See also Gallman (1975) on this point.

15. What I am arguing here, as Wright emphasizes in his comment, is that under some circumstances the growth of aggregate output and increasing productivity can be substitutes. The economy may benefit from the growth of a sector regardless of which source of growth predominates. The Canadian experience exemplifies the point that in some circumstances, at some points in time, output may grow rapidly for reasons that detract from productivity growth. On the other hand, productivity may be rising substantially in periods when resources are being shifted out of an industry, and hence net output grows relatively slowly.

16. The comment on this paper by Gavin Wright seems to me to give an impression of rather more disagreement between myself and him than is probably the case. Wright reminds readers that there is a broader context of Canadian economic development within which the agricultural change I have examined is set. In my presentation I have perhaps taken too much of that for granted. The prevailing interpretation of that development emphasizes a leading role for agricultural exports in fostering Canadian economic growth during what is popularly referred to as the "wheat boom era." My paper is considerably less than a full-blown commentary on the export boom based on western Canadian wheat. It is not the case, however, that the main conclusions reported here are at variance with the popular "staples" interpretation of the role of wheat in Canadian economic development. I show that one part of the direct contribution of agricultural expansion to overall economic development was quite modest. Agricultural expansion in Canada in the wheat boom era was not associated with big gains in total factor productivity. I am sure that comes as no great surprise to historians of Canadian economic development, but it is probably worth trying to determine the actual magnitudes. It has long been recognized that if there were big gains attributable to the wheat staple, they must have been in the indirect effects. It is well enough to reiterate that, but we can also recognize that there remains much to be done in putting numbers to those indirect effects. I have to agree, then, with at least part of what Wright has raised. It mostly concerns issues that I did not think I had space to pursue.

There remains an element of disagreement. Wright worries that I may have neglected a possibly important direct contribution to growth originating on the demand side. To the extent that there was an important shift in the terms of trade in favor of agricultural products, it would have to be acknowledged that a gain accrued to Canadian agriculture. Two issues remain unresolved. One concerns the construction of the terms-of-trade index given by Wright, the other is an empirical question of just how much gain in the terms of trade really did occur. On the first matter, Wright relates the implicit price deflator for agricultural output from my table 14.A.2 to a readily available index of import prices. Both, however, are current weighted indexes, and the resulting ratio reflects changes in the composition of the commodity weights as well as price changes. Indeed, we know that there were major changes in the commodity mixes in both indexes. Second, there is the matter of whether world demand for agricultural products increased in such a way as to produce the extent of improvement in the terms of trade that Wright suggests. I remain doubtful. The largest amount of the upward movement in the terms of trade depicted by Wright came in the second decade of the twentieth century, largely in connection with World War I. Moreover, the shift was mostly a result of a relative decline in import prices. The index used by Wright gives more a portrayal of what was happening to the prices of iron and steel and their products than of Canadian agricultural exports.

Admittedly, we do not yet have an adequate account of what really happened to Canada in the early years of the twentieth century. I am probably less content even than Gavin Wright with the state of what we think we know about this episode of economic development. The full story, though, is a lot more complicated than either my paper or Wright's comment might suggest.

# Comment    Gavin Wright

Marvin McInnis presents to us a new set of aggregate output and input measures for Canadian agriculture, for the 55 years prior to 1926 when the official Bureau of Statistics series begins. The research is part of the larger project directed by M. C. Urquhart on Canadian national income statistics. In this specialized study, however, McInnis goes on to develop indices of partial and total factor productivity, offering new evidence on the contribution of agriculture to Canadian growth and inviting comparison with the United States experience as portrayed by earlier work using similar methods. In this comment I review briefly the highlights of McInnis's techniques and conclusions, raise some questions about the measurement, and then discuss the interpretation of the figures.

## Summary

The information underlying the new annual production series is primarily foreign trade data. The strategy is to convert exports into production by adding estimates of domestic consumption for each major commodity, on-farm consumption included. The output concept is gross value added, gross of depreciation but net of farm products used within the agricultural sector and inputs from other sectors. The output measure is a substantial improvement over that of Firestone, which applied a fixed adjustment coefficient to the aggregate total of all agricultural outputs (including intermediates), thus missing a significant type of structural change. Since McInnis constructs both a current price aggregate (based on separate price series for each commodity) and a constant price aggregate (1913 price relatives), his efforts also generate an implicit price index for agricultural products.

The coverage of this output measure is much more limited than those used in the United States studies. It omits forest products, household manufactures, and the increase in land value attributable to improvement (e.g., clearing). The input measures are correspondingly narrowed, using improved acreage rather than total occupied farmland, and omitting female workers on the grounds that most of their production has also been excluded. Census year estimates of the agricultural workforce involve a substantial effort to correct inconsistencies in census categories, though McInnis fears there may still be an upward bias in the earlier years. Estimates of farm capital are scrappy and tentative, but it still may be that the broad output and productivity history does not depend crucially on precision in measuring the capital input.

Gavin Wright is professor economics at Stanford University.

The output picture which emerges (fig. 14.1) shows a plateau from 1883 to 1895, with the most rapid spurt coming in the first decade of the twentieth century. The McInnis series revises the Firestone estimates of growth between 1910 and 1920 *upward* by a factor of more than two. What McInnis presents as a "striking finding" of his paper, however, is not this output growth but the fact that labor productivity growth was more rapid in the late nineteenth century than in the early twentieth century. Turning to total factor productivity estimates (table 14.8), he finds that the falloff in growth was even more dramatic, from rates greater than 1% per year (1870–1900) to a ratio between 0.09% and 0.44% per year, 1900–1920. Total factor productivity accounts for almost half of output growth during the first period, a trivial share (between 3% and 15%) of output growth in the second period. These figures serve, according to McInnis, as "a reminder that western settlement entailed substantial resource costs." He concludes: "We are left, then, with some serious questions about the direct contribution the agricultural sector could have made to Canadian per capita income growth in the period of the 'Wheat Boom,' the most glorified period of Canadian economic development."

Aspects of the Estimates

The McInnis estimates are a significant new resource for students of Canadian and American agricultural history. The output measure clearly is preferable to Firestone's. McInnis expresses surprise that the gap between the new series and Firestone's remains wide even in 1911, but in fact this gap tracks closely the changing share of field crops in final agricultural product—precisely the structural change missed by Firestone. The share of field crops *declined* between 1880 and 1900, and was barely higher in 1911 than in 1871 (table 14.2). As Ankli (1980) has recently stressed, the big rise in wheat comes after 1910. The share of purchased inputs in gross value added has a different impact. It drifts up very gradually from 7%–8% in the 1870s to 11% in 1920–21, jumping sharply to 13%–15% in the 1920s (table 14.A.2). Both adjustments show the inappropriateness of applying structural coefficients from the interwar years to earlier periods.

The productivity estimates are also valuable, but here (as with all such figures) they should be used only with full awareness of their origins and characteristics. The adoption of a "lean" measure of agricultural output may be matched by "lean" measures of farm inputs, but a change in definitions like this is often not neutral with respect to total factor productivity. In this case, the measures becloud one of the true sources of rising efficiency, improved allocation of factors among types of production (Gallman 1975, p. 40). The change from "unimproved" to "improved" acreage status is really a transition from low-intensity to higher-intensity land use. The range cattle industry may not have had a giant share in total output, but this sort of shift may be a large part of overall efficiency growth in an era where the growth of factors generally predominated. If both inputs and outputs are restricted, this effect is missed. But if labor is measured grossly as men on farms, and no account is taken of the changing allocation of labor time between unimproved and improved acres, the effect is a mismeasurement of the main input, a much more serious bias in the other direction. This consideration may go a long way toward explaining the high rate of total factor productivity growth before 1900, to me the most remarkable finding in the paper.

It is also possible that the use of an export basis for estimating farm production neglects some inputs into food processing. Cheese, for example, was produced for export by hundreds of cheese factories which bought milk from farmers (Bogue 1947, pp. 164–66). Butter was in transition from a home industry for women to a factory basis during the 1870s (Lawr 1972, p. 249). The number of these factories grew rapidly in the late nineteenth century, and the share of dairy products in final agricultural product grew correspondingly, reaching a peak in precisely the census year 1900–1901 (table 14.A.1). The share of dairying declined after 1900, and the number of cheese factories and butter creameries in particular declined sharply, as they were outbid for the milk supply by the fresh milk trade, the condensed milk industry, and the rising ice cream market. This consideration may also contribute to the rise and subsequent decline in total factor productivity growth between the two periods.

The use of export data plus domestic consumption estimates raises a broader methodological issue. The passage of the text which describes the estimation procedure also describes a market process, but a peculiar one in which "relatively stable domestic consumption demands took precedence and . . . exports were catered to out of left-over supply." As a devotee of the safety-first model, I can hardly object to this characterization of a farm household's behavior with respect to its own consumption, but can this specification be extended to the level of a whole country, producing for domestic *buyers* as well as on-farm consumption? Especially a country which textbooks describe as one for which "the prices of many traded goods were established internationally" (Marr and Paterson 1980, p. 4)? I think it is unreasonable to do so as a specification of market dynamics, but estimation procedures do not have to map market dynamics. The question is, how does this procedure allocate measurement error? If we take the simplest model, in which domestic demand and supply have normal slopes but price is determined exogenously, we can reach the following conclusions: (1) So long as output increases because of *shifts of the supply curve* (either factor growth or productivity change), McInnis's procedure is exactly right. The rise in output will go entirely into exports, and domestic consumption will be unaffected; estimation of production should focus on the variable item in demand (exports), which fortunately happens also to be the best-measured component. (2) But if output rises because of a rise in the world price, domestic consumption will decline and exports will overstate the growth. The effect will depend on the elasticity of domestic demand, which may be greater for a commodity like meat, for which there are cheaper substitutes in the diet. It does not necessarily mean that the McInnis figures will be fundamentally misdirected over long periods, because he adjusts the consumption estimates at each census year. But the census year benchmarks thus acquire strategic importance for the output series as well as the input series, for reasons that may well be transitory.

### Aspects of Interpretation

I very much doubt whether any of the foregoing considerations would alter the overall contours of the evidence, given the basic conceptual framework. But do these figures justify the conclusion questioning the contribution of agriculture to per capita income growth during the wheat boom? The basic framework focuses on the supply side, and as the preceding paragraph points out, supply-side assumptions are built into the estimation procedure itself. But the wheat boom period has a demand side as well. McInnis gives it little emphasis, but as a by-product of his research he has produced a new price index, which may be used to follow the course of agricultural terms of trade. Using Taylor's import price index (Urquhart and Buckley 1965, pp. 300, 302) as the denominator (the quickest way to get a price series not heavily influenced by Canadian farm prices), I obtain the following:

| 1871–75 | 70 | 1891–95 | 85 | 1911–15 | 96 |
| 1876–80 | 75 | 1896–1900 | 82 | 1916–20 | 97 |
| 1881–85 | 81 | 1901–1905 | 80 | 1921–25 | 95 |
| 1886–90 | 81 | 1906–10 | 85 | | |

These figures seem to indicate that secular terms-of-trade improvement is part of the basic experience of Canadian agriculture before World War I, as it is for United States agriculture. But the years 1911–20 were characterized by extraordinary terms of trade, 20% higher than 1896–1905. Translated into growth rates, the effect adds 0.84 percentage points per year to productivity growth.

I do not see why this fact should be neglected. Demand-generated earnings are no less a part of income to those that receive them than supply-generated earnings. They may be consumed or invested in the same way. There seems to be an implicit view that our concerns are

with long-run factors, and economic growth is a supply-side phenomenon in the long run, demand effects being transitory. But if we take
that view, then we should not apply these tools to evaluating performances of relatively short periods, "glorified" in large part because of
beneficient demand conditions. And for a small open economy producing specialized resource-intensive goods, demand elements will always be a fact of life, and the effects may not be transitory over long
epochs.

But the supply-side interpretation should be questioned as well. In
recent years there has been a lively debate among Canadian economic
historians dealing with this very question, how to measure the effects
of the wheat boom on per capita income (Chambers and Gordon 1966;
Caves 1971; Bertram 1973; Lewis 1975). Many of the effects discussed
would not be reflected in *agricultural* total factor productivity, even if
the expansion originated in agriculture: induced domestic savings, induced capital inflow, scale economies in manufacturing, and the increase in the percentage of the population which is of working age, for
examples. Marvin McInnis, of course, never set out to measure all of
the indirect effects of the wheat boom, and it would hardly be fair to
criticize him for not doing so. But the discussion raises the question
whether the rise in agricultural factors is a measure of "resource costs"
involved in the expansion.

For a country with a vast reserve of land unutilized because it is
"outside the feasible region," the expansion of acreage under cultivation is not a good measure of resource costs. Depending as it did on
breakthroughs in farming techniques and transportation, the expansion
is in a sense a measure of the economy's achievement, not its costs
(Caves 1965; Marr and Percy 1980, p. 352; Lewis 1981). The fact that
land was being abandoned in the east is neither here nor there; it is
evident that western lands and eastern lands were not homogeneous.
The rise in western land values, which is omitted from the output index,
was quite large, large enough presumably to motivate the adventure
for many farmers (Bertram 1973). The expansion of farm capital is
harder to be certain about, but much of this may also have been induced
(internally or externally) by the very process of expansion under discussion. The main point is that we cannot get quick answers to these
questions from total factor productivity, and we should not try.

By far the larger share of nineteenth-century productivity growth in
United States agriculture (and indeed for the entire economy) was
factor growth rather than total factor productivity (Gallman 1971, 1975;
Abramovitz and David 1973), and in many ways the Canadian wheat
boom expansion may be viewed as a continuation of the same process.
By the straightforward standard of labor productivity, Canada gains
steadily on the United States from 1890 onward (table 14.6). The slow-

down in productivity growth after 1900 is extremely modest (from 1.46% to 1.20%) and would be an increase rather than a decrease if terms-of-trade effects were added. The *levels* of total factor productivity in the two countries may not be at all meaningful, but the 30-year trend in relative output per worker is not easily dismissed. For both countries, there is broad plausibility in the idea that factor expansion and productivity growth have a relationship of substitution; what is most interesting about the Canadian pattern is that an earlier period of high total-factor-productivity growth gives way to a new wave of resource growth, suggesting that there really was a breakthrough and a rejuvenation of Canadian agriculture after 1900. To me, these figures show that the wheat boom era amply deserves its glorification.

# References

Abramovitz, Moses, and David, Paul. 1973. Reinterpreting economic growth. *American Economic Review* 63:428–39.

Ankli, Robert E. 1980. The growth of the Canadian economy, 1896–1920. *Explorations in Economic History* 17:251–74.

Bertram, G. W. 1973. The relevance of the wheat boom in Canadian economic growth. *Canadian Journal of Economics* 6:545–66.

Bogue, Allan. 1947. The progress of the cattle industry in Ontario during the eighteen-eighties. *Agricultural History* 21:163–69.

Britnell, G. E. 1939. *The wheat economy.* Toronto: University of Toronto Press.

Canada. Dominion Bureau of Statistics. Various years. *Handbook of agricultural statistics.* Ottawa: Queen's Printer.

Caves, Richard. 1965. Models of trade and growth. In *Trade growth and the balance of payments,* ed. R. E. Baldwin et al. Chicago: Rand-McNally.

———. 1971. Export-led growth and the new economic history. In *Trade, balance of payments and growth,* ed. J. Bhagwati et al. Amsterdam: North-Holland.

Chambers, E. J., and Gordon, Donald F. 1966. Primary products and economic growth. *Journal of Political Economy* 27:315–32.

Clark, Andrew H. 1959. *Three centuries and the Island: A historical geography of settlement and agriculture in Prince Edward Island.* Toronto: University of Toronto Press.

Coates, R. W. 1910. *Wholesale prices in Canada, 1890–1910.* Ottawa: King's Printer.

Firestone, O. J. 1958. *Canada's economic development, 1867–1952.* London: Bowes & Bowes.

Fowke, Vernon C. 1946. *Canadian agricultural policy: The historical pattern.* Toronto: University of Toronto Press.

Gallman, R. E. 1972. Changes in total U.S. agricultural factor productivity in the 19th century. *Agricultural History* 46:191–210.

———. 1975. The agricultural sector and the pace of economic growth: U.S. experience in the nineteenth century. In *Essays in nineteenth century economic history,* ed. David C. Klingaman and Richard K. Vedder. Athens: Ohio University Press.

Jones, Robert Leslie. 1942. French-Canadian agriculture in the St. Lawrence Valley. *Agricultural History* 16:137–48.

———. 1945. The agricultural development of Lower Canada, 1850–1867. *Agricultural History* 19:212–24.

———. 1946. *The history of agriculture in Ontario, 1613–1880.* Toronto: University of Toronto Press.

Kendrick, John W. 1961. *Productivity trends in the United States.* Princeton: Princeton University Press.

Lawr, D. A. 1972. The development of Ontario farming, 1870–1914. *Ontario History* 64:239–51.

Lewis, Frank. 1975. The Canadian wheat boom and per capita income: New estimates. *Journal of Political Economy* 83:1249–57.

———. 1981. Farm settlement on the Canadian prairies, 1898 to 1911. *Journal of Economic History* 41:517–86.

Lewis, Frank, and McInnis, Marvin. 1980. The efficiency of the French-Canadian farmer, in the nineteenth century. *Journal of Economic History* 40:497–514.

McInnis, R. M., and Urquhart, M. C. 1981. The net output of Canadian agriculture, 1870–1926. Paper presented to the Eleventh Conference on Quantitative Methods in Canadian Economic History, Queen's University, 27–28 February 1981, Kingston, Canada. Mimeographed.

Mackintosh, W. A. 1935. *Economic problems of the Prairie Provinces.* Toronto.

Marr, William L., and Paterson, Donald G. 1980. Canada: An economic history. Toronto: Macmillan of Canada.

Morton, Arthur S., and Martin, Chester M. 1938. *History of prairie settlement and "dominion lands policy."* Toronto.

Ouellet, Fernand. 1966. *Histoire économique et sociale du Quebec, 1760–1850.* Montreal: Fides.

———. 1980. *Lower Canada, 1791–1840.* Toronto: McClelland & Stewart.

Sequin, Maurice. 1970. *La "Nation canadienne" et l'agriculture.* Trois-Rivières: Editions Boreal Express.

Taylor, K. W., and Michell, H. 1931. *Statistical contributions to Canadian economic history.* Vol. 2. Toronto: Macmillan.

Tostlebe, Alvin W. 1957. *Capital in agriculture: Its formation and financing since 1870.* Princeton: Princeton University Press (for the National Bureau of Economic Research).

Towne, Marvin W., and Rasmussen, Wayne D. 1960. Farm gross product and gross investment in the nineteenth century. In *Trends in the American economy in the nineteenth century.* Studies in Income and Wealth, vol. 24. Princeton: Princeton University Press (for the National Bureau of Economic Research).

Urquhart, M. C., and Buckley, K. A. H. 1965. *Historical statistics of Canada.* Toronto: Macmillan of Canada.

# 15     Growth and Productivity Change in the Canadian Railway Sector, 1871–1926

Alan G. Green

The written history of the Canadian railway sector focuses almost exclusively on the financial problems associated with the construction of specific railways.[1] Virtually no work on the growth of the Canadian railway system has been undertaken either in terms of its dimensions, and how they changed over time, or on the efficiency of this sector. This paper redresses part of this deficiency. It does so by setting out the growth of the railway system in Canada from 1871 to 1926 in terms of the net income generated by this industry. In addition, a preliminary attempt is made at estimating productivity change for the railway system.

The time period studied is from 1871 to 1926. These years span the decades from just after Confederation (1867) to approximately the peak of economic activity in Canada during the interwar period. By 1926 the railway system, as we know it today was largely in place. This is a far cry from the system which existed in the early 1870s. At that time there were only 2,700 miles of track in operation and they were located entirely in the Central (Ontario and Quebec) and Maritime (Prince Edward Island, Nova Scotia, and New Brunswick) Provinces and only in limited areas within these regions. The 55 years included here then cover the growth of the system from its infancy to full maturity.

Alan G. Green is professor of economics at Queen's University.

Although a number of people participated in the preparation of these estimates, two deserve special mention. Leighton Reid estimated interest and dividend payments, and Peter Wylie worked on the real output and capital stock estimates. I pulled the scattered pieces together while on leave at Harvard University. Robert Fogel kindly provided the space needed to do this research. The Social Sciences and Humanities Research Council of Canada provided a fellowship to take the leave. Much of the base funding was provided by a Killiam Grant. M. C. Urquhart was the principal investigator on this grant, and his support and assistance are gratefully acknowledged. Albert Fishlow's helpful comments on the paper at Williamsburg influenced my revision.

Railways provide the economic historian with a unique opportunity to study long-term economic development. Given their size and ultimate importance, governments sought information on them virtually from the day they were introduced. It was obvious to contemporaries that here was an innovation destined to touch, in some way, the lives of all citizens and hence the government needed to be informed about this new "gadget." This interest was often translated into a special effort to collect detailed data on the number of miles of track, revenue, expenses, engines owned, etc. The sector, then, may well provide the best window we have both on the development of a particular industry (how often do we get reasonably consistent annual data series that extend back 113 years?) and on the economy as a whole.

The paper is divided into three parts. Section 15.1 sets out the procedures used to estimate net income originating in the railway industry. These estimates were derived as part of a larger project on reestimating the Canadian National Accounts from 1871 to 1926 (reported on elsewhere in this volume). As such the railway figures discussed in this paper are only one segment of the income data devised for the Transportation and Communications sector.[2] Section 15.2 of the paper presents some analysis of the growth of railways in Canada over the study period, and in Section 15.3 a preliminary investigation is made of productivity change in this sector plus a look at factor share changes.

## 15.1 Estimating Procedures

The estimation procedure for railway net income is quite different from that used in the commodity sectors—at least that adopted in the reestimation of the Canadian national accounts. For the goods-producing sectors much of the evidence on sectoral growth comes from the decennial census. However, census reports do not contain information on output for railways as they do for agriculture, manufacturing, and so on. The only measure of railway size available from the census reports is on labor input and, as we shall see, even this evidence is suspect.

For Canada, at least, this omission did not present an insurmountable handicap to estimating railway output. From the beginning of railway development in Canada all levels of government have been interested in the progress of this industry and have, consequently, set out to record its development. Before 1867 (Confederation) such recording was carried out by the various colonial governments. Unfortunately this was not always done systematically. The newly formed Government of Canada decided to centralize the procedure and, commencing in the year ending June 30, 1875, required every railway operating in Canada to report annually on its operations to the Department of Railways and

Canals under the recently passed Railway Statistics Act of 1875. Annual collection of railway data has continued from then to the present. These annual estimates were published by the Department of Railways and Canals from 1875 to 1918 under the title "Railway Statistics" and appear in the Sessional Papers of Canada. Beginning in 1919 they were published by the Dominion Bureau of Statistics as "Railway Statistics of Canada" annually from 1919 to 1921 and thereafter as "Statistics of Steam Railways of Canada."[3] More will be said on the coverage of these annual reports in the discussion covering the actual estimation of income for this sector. In addition to the official source, evidence was drawn from Standard and Poor's and Moody's manuals on railways.

These annual publications provided the basic data for the calculation of net income originating in the railway sector. A factor-incomes approach was used. Thus net railway income is the sum of wages and salaries, interest and dividend payments, and net savings. The latter is estimated as a residual after dividend payments have been deducted from net operating revenue. Each factor income component has its own particular set of problems. Hence each will be discussed separately.

### 15.1.1 Wages and Salaries

Estimates of the total wage bill for railway employees were first published in 1907 and have appeared annually ever since that date. Unfortunately this series was not homogeneous over the period of inquiry. In the early years the series included workers in railway express. It is possible to divide these two series from 1919 on, but not for earlier years. Since such partitioning was not possible before this date, the wage bill estimates are the sum of the two groups.

Besides these annual reports, information on wages paid to railway workers was collected in the decennial census beginning in 1871. Unfortunately, the census estimates did not prove to be an entirely satisfactory alternative source for this type of information. The main reason is that those who assigned the results from the census to various components in the published reports saw the railway industry divided into two distinct parts. One part was composed of those activities which dealt exclusively with the provision of railway services, that is, the movement of people and goods. The other part was associated with manufacturing activity, the repair and rebuilding of railway equipment. Another component, and one even harder to separate, consists of unskilled workers who were partly engaged in track maintenance and partly on new construction. For our purposes inclusion of the latter would be inappropriate since they were not associated with the delivery of railway services in a given year.

The discrepancy is not small. If we take the censuses of 1911 and 1921, when annual estimates of total employment compensation are also available, the differences are as shown in table 15.1. There are two points to note. First, the absolute difference between the two series can be large. Second, the size of the difference is not stable. By 1921 it had grown to $81 million. The greater spread between the two series implies that as the system entered its slower expansion period more employees were engaged in repairing and rebuilding rolling stock, relative to operating workers, than was the case in 1911. The census estimates, for this reason (and for others to be discussed later), had to be abandoned.

The failure of the "augmented" census reports to provide reasonable estimates of the *level* of total wage payments forced us to find an alternative method. What was required, then, was to discover a reasonably constant relationship between an annual series that stretched over these earlier years and the railway wage bill. After some experimentation it was found that a fairly stable relationship existed between wages (the wage bill) and total operating expenses. For example, between 1907 and 1920 the ratio of wages and salaries to operating expenses averaged 59.1%, with only a small dispersion around this mean.

To check the stability of this ratio total annual compensation paid to United States railway employees was divided by total expenses for the system. The period chosen was from 1895 to 1910. Over these years the ratio averaged 61.0%, with only a small deviation about the mean. Interestingly, the United States ratio was within 2 percentage points of the Canadian ratio, and like the latter was trendless over the period reviewed.

It was decided then, on the basis of the stability of the wage/expense ratio, to extrapolate the wage bill for Canadian railways back from 1906 to 1875 on the basis of the total annual expenses record for the system, with one modification. Total expenses were broken down into "Maintenance of Way and Structures" and "Other Operating Expenses." The ratios of wages paid differs sharply between these two broad categories of expenses. "Maintenance of Way and Structures" exhibit a

Table 15.1    Railway Employees' Total Compensation, Census Estimates and the Annual Reports of Railway Operation in Canada: 1911 and 1921 (Millions of Dollars)

| Year | Census (1) | Annual Reports (2) |
|------|------------|---------------------|
| 1911 | 69.2 | 74.6 |
| 1921 | 167.0 | 247.8 |

*Sources:*
Col. 1: 1911, *Census of Canada;* 1921, *Census of Canada.*
Col. 2: *Canada Year Book of 1921* (Ottawa), p. 537.

higher ratio due, one suspects, to the amount of track maintenance, that is, replacing rails and ties, reballasting, snow removal, and so on, all of which is labor-intensive work. This breakdown then permitted us to incorporate, in the final estimates, any alterations between these two broad categories which occurred in the course of building and operating the railway system. Finally, estimates of total wages were carried back to 1871 on the basis of expenses recorded for the Grand Trunk Railway—the largest single railway operating in Canada at that time. The results of these calculations appear in table. 15.2.

## 15.1.2 Interest and Dividend Payments

Estimating annual costs associated with the use of capital proved to be a more difficult chore than was the procedure for obtaining a long-term series on the wage bill for Canadian railways. In setting out the procedures for estimating this component of total net income, the dis-

**Table 15.2**     Annual Estimates of Total Wages and Salaries Paid to Railway Employees, 1871–1926 (Thousands of Dollars)

| Year | Amount | Year | Amount | Year | Amount |
|------|--------|------|--------|------|--------|
| 1871 | 7,190 | 1891 | 19,834 | 1911 | 77,520 |
| 1872 | 7,819 | 1892 | 20,639 | 1912 | 97,654 |
| 1873 | 8,538 | 1893 | 20,668 | 1913 | 119,771 |
| 1874 | 10,964 | 1894 | 19,851 | 1914 | 116,136 |
| 1875 | 8,987 | 1895 | 18,479 | 1915 | 94,159 |
| 1876 | 9,054 | 1896 | 19,718 | 1916 | 108,358 |
| 1877 | 8,669 | 1897 | 19,779 | 1917 | 135,009 |
| 1878 | 9,164 | 1898 | 22,058 | 1918 | 158,824 |
| 1879 | 9,259 | 1899 | 22,956 | 1919 | 240,377[a] |
| 1880 | 9,573 | 1900 | 26,849 | 1920 | 299,875 |
| 1881 | 11,382 | 1901 | 28,617 | 1921 | 256,631 |
| 1882 | 12,673 | 1902 | 32,626 | 1922 | 240,428 |
| 1883 | 13,951 | 1903 | 38,436 | 1923 | 256,368 |
| 1884 | 14,471 | 1904 | 42,169 | 1924 | 241,359 |
| 1885 | 13,615 | 1905 | 45,450 | 1925 | 238,641 |
| 1886 | 13,725 | 1906 | 49,394 | 1926 | 254,689 |
| 1887 | 15,776 | 1907 | 58,719 | | |
| 1888 | 17,443 | 1908 | 60,377 | | |
| 1889 | 17,684 | 1909 | 63,217 | | |
| 1890 | 18,700 | 1910 | 67,168 | | |

*Sources and methods:*
1907–26: *Canada Year Book,* 1926.
1875–1906: "Annual Reports of the Department of Railways and Canals," various reports *Sessional Papers of Canada.*
1874–71: Poor's Manual—annual reports of expenses for the Grand Trunk Railway. See text for methods.
[a]Beginning with June 30, 1871, the estimates are for fiscal years until 1918. Beginning in 1919 estimates are for calendar years ending December 31.

cussion will be divided into two parts, since the method of estimating interest payments (i.e., the bond or fixed-income portion) differs substantially from that used to calculate dividend payments.

*Interest Income Payments*

Interest payments by Canadian railways are available from 1919 to 1926 and are recorded annually in the Dominion Bureau of Statistics publication, *Railway Statistics of Canada* from 1919 to 1921 and in *Statistics of Steam Railways of Canada: 1922 to 1926:* indeed, up to the present. Funded and floating debt payments from 1911 to 1915 can be found in the "Annual Reports of the Department of Railways and Canals," which appear in the *Sessional Papers of Canada*. The only problem with this series is that interest payments of the Canadian Pacific Railway's 4% debenture stock were excluded until 1919. However, with the introduction of the new publication they were properly recorded as part of interest payments. An adjustment for this omission was made for these years.

Before 1911 the "Annual Reports" did not calculate total interest payments (unlike the United States publications, which show total interest and dividend payments back to at least 1890). However, on very large spread sheets inserted in each "Annual Report" is shown the amount outstanding of the "Bonded" and "Floating" debt for each railroad in Canada, plus the coupon interest rate payable for the majority of these issues. This type of individual security information is available annually from 1875 to 1911.

The solution to our problem of obtaining total interest payments, then, seemed quite simple. We would multiply the outstanding security value by its own coupon rate and total across all railways. To check the validity of this approach, we calculated total interest payments using this method for 1911—a year for which we had the official total. Unfortunately the two estimates were very different. Our "calculated" total was much larger than the official estimate. In fact the difference was close to $2.5 million. On checking each of the 72 railways included in the estimation, we found that for many the difference between the calculated method and the official figures was small, and quite often the two estimates were identical. At least this was the case for the small railways. The problem centered on the large railways, such as the CPR and the Grand Trunk Railway. For example, for the CPR calculated interest exceeded the official estimate by $5.3 million. The excess of calculated over official for the Grand Trunk was about $2.0 million.

To eliminate this discrepancy, the estimation procedure was divided into two parts. For the small railways we calculated individual annual interest payments using the method described above. To this total we added interest payments for the Canadian Pacific Railway, the Grand

Trunk, the Canadian Northern, and the Canadian Northern Quebec Railway. Estimates of interest payments for these larger railways are recorded annually in Poor's *Manual of Railroads* back to the beginning of operation of each. Poor's proved to be an invaluable source of information on these larger Canadian railways. The manual recorded operating data for any Canadian railway which sought to issue securities in the United States, and did so annually from the middle of the nineteenth century. The information provided was quite extensive. It included such statistics as operating revenue and expenses, interest and dividend payments, capitalization by type of security, a history of the organization of each railway, and so on.

A number of the smaller railways did not report the coupon rate for their fixed interest securities. To solve this problem we calculated for each year an average interest rate from the lines which did report coupon rates. Table 15.3 sets out these average rates for each year from 1875 to 1916 for bonded and floating debt. They are unweighted

**Table 15.3**     **Average Interest Rates on Bonded and Floating Debt Paid by Canadian Railways, Annually, 1875–1916 (%)**

| Year (1) | Bonded Debt (2) | Floating Debt (3) | Year (4) | Bonded Debt (5) | Floating Debt (6) |
|---|---|---|---|---|---|
| 1875 | 6.42 | 7.06 | 1896 | 5.27 | 5.93 |
| 1876 | 6.42 | 6.25 | 1897 | 5.20 | 5.37 |
| 1877 | 6.28 | 7.20 | 1898 | 5.27 | 4.01 |
| 1878 | 6.28 | 7.06 | 1899 | 5.14 | 5.54 |
| 1879 | 6.13 | 7.06 | 1900 | 5.16 | 4.81 |
| 1880 | 6.20 | 7.27 | 1901 | 5.12 | 4.90 |
| 1881 | 5.92 | 6.50 | 1902 | 5.13 | 4.49 |
| 1882 | 6.06 | 6.29 | 1903 | 5.07 | 3.62 |
| 1883 | 5.63 | 6.70 | 1904 | 5.00 | 3.87 |
| 1884 | 5.72 | 6.30 | 1905 | 5.02 | 4.04 |
| 1885 | 5.82 | 6.63 | 1906 | n.a.[a] | n.a. |
| 1886 | 5.84 | 6.66 | 1907 | 4.95 | 4.04 |
| 1887 | 5.89 | 6.75 | 1908 | 4.98 | 4.04 |
| 1888 | 5.83 | 6.94 | 1909 | 4.95 | 4.04 |
| 1889 | 5.58 | 6.85 | 1910 | 4.94 | 4.04 |
| 1890 | 5.49 | 6.94 | 1911 | 4.86 | 4.04 |
| 1891 | 5.51 | 6.49 | 1912 | 4.91 | 4.04 |
| 1892 | 5.49 | 6.36 | 1913 | 4.92 | 4.04 |
| 1893 | 5.42 | 6.26 | 1914 | 4.85 | 4.04 |
| 1894 | 5.42 | 5.84 | 1915 | 4.89 | n.a. |
| 1895 | 5.40 | 5.74 | 1916 | 4.90 | n.a. |

*Source:* Department of Railways and Canals, "Annual Reports," *Sessional Papers of Canada,* 1875–1916.

*Note:* Unweighted average of reported coupon interest rates.

[a]n.a. = not available.

averages, and the number of observations varies from year to year, hence the results in terms of absolute levels for any one year must be treated cautiously.

These nominal interest rates trace out an interesting pattern over our study period. They dropped sharply from 1875 to 1915. For bonded debt the rates fell by 22% from 1875–80 to 1910–15, that is, from 6.29% to 4.90%. The full implication of this drop is seen if we compare average interest rates to price trends in general. Table 15.4 sets out these changes. For the last third of the nineteenth century, according to these results, real interest rates rose. The quality of these two data series precludes any closer judgment on the trend in real interest rates, even though the percentage changes suggest that prices fell slightly more slowly than longer-term nominal interest rates. Real interest rates dropped, however, in the opening years of the twentieth century, largely because of a reversal in the trend of prices. This changing pattern, as we will see, conforms closely to the level of railway investment over this period.

Columns 3 and 6 of table 15.3 show interest rates for floating debt, representing the rate on short-term securities. Behavior of this series parallels, over the whole period, the trend in bond debt; that is, the nominal rate falls. However, for the last decades of the nineteenth century the short-term rate is greater than the long-term rate, while after 1900 the short-term rate is below the longer-term rate. Whether these apparently divergent results are a product of the way interest rate averages were obtained or whether they signal different market prices for the two types of securities is a problem that will have to be studied elsewhere.

**Table 15.4    Index Numbers of Interest Rates Paid by Canadian Railways and GNP Implicit Price Series, Selected Years 1875–1916**

| | Annual Index for Years Shown of | |
| | --- | --- |
| Period<br>(1) | Annual Interest Rates<br>(1900 = 100)<br>(2) | Annual Prices<br>(1900 = 100)<br>(3) |
| | *Period A* | |
| 1875–77 | 123.5 | 109.6 |
| 1898–1900 | 100.7 | 98.0 |
| | *Period B* | |
| 1900–1902 | 99.5 | 101.7 |
| 1914–16 | 94.6 | 139.7 |

*Sources:*
Col. 2 See table 15.3.

Col. 3 M. C. Urquhart, "New Estimates of Gross National Product, Canada, 1870–1926: Some Implications for Canadian Development," in this volume, table 2.9.

Total interest income payments for the railway sector are shown in table 15.5. As in the case of wage payments, the interest income estimates were extrapolated to 1871 using the interest expense recorded by the Grand Trunk Railway during these years.

## Dividend Payments

Annual payments of dividends to shareholders in Canadian railways were not reported in the "Annual Reports" before 1911, as was the case for total interest payments. The sources of total dividend payments are the same over the period 1911–26 as those set out in the previous section.

Unfortunately, for the years before 1911 the "Annual Reports" did not carry any information on dividend payments. However, in 1911 the Department of Railways and Canals reported dividends paid by various Canadian railways (table 15.6). The CPR and the GTR, according to

**Table 15.5**    **Interest Payments Made by Canadian Railways, Annually, 1871–1926 (Thousands of Dollars)**

| Year | Amount | Year | Amount | Year | Amount |
|------|--------|------|--------|------|--------|
| 1871 | 3,123  | 1891 | 11,819 | 1911 | 21,581 |
| 1872 | 3,546  | 1892 | 12,724 | 1912 | 23,213 |
| 1873 | 3,684  | 1893 | 13,408 | 1913 | 25,073 |
| 1874 | 4,084  | 1894 | 14,620 | 1914 | 26,960 |
| 1875 | 4,004  | 1895 | 15,369 | 1915 | 27,765 |
| 1876 | 4,039  | 1896 | 15,603 | 1916 | 24,020 |
| 1877 | 4,129  | 1897 | 16,017 | 1917 | 43,795 |
| 1878 | 4,531  | 1898 | 15,968 | 1918 | 46,900 |
| 1879 | 4,254  | 1899 | 16,055 | 1919 | 54,697[a] |
| 1880 | 4,364  | 1900 | 16,326 | 1920 | 59,270 |
| 1881 | 4,490  | 1901 | 16,661 | 1921 | 74,750[b] |
| 1882 | 6,083  | 1902 | 16,910 | 1922 | 78,378[b] |
| 1883 | 4,644  | 1903 | 16,917 | 1923 | 54,666 |
| 1884 | 5,005  | 1904 | 17,933 | 1924 | 59,448 |
| 1885 | 8,766  | 1905 | 19,161 | 1925 | 60,498 |
| 1886 | 8,838  | 1906 | 19,672 | 1926 | 59,241 |
| 1887 | 9,405  | 1907 | 20,007 |      |        |
| 1888 | 9,715  | 1908 | 20,969 |      |        |
| 1889 | 10,296 | 1909 | 22,012 |      |        |
| 1890 | 11,139 | 1910 | 23,095 |      |        |

[a]See table 15.2, note a.

[b]The sudden increase in interest rate payments in 1921 and 1922 apparently is related to the amalgamation of several lines (i.e., Grand Trunk, Canadian Northern, etc.) into the government-owned railway, the Canadian National. In 1937, under the "Canadian National Railway Capital Revision Act" interest payments were adjusted downward beginning in 1923. Since these revised figures were the ones appearing in "Steam Railway Statistics," we used them here. The figures (in thousands of dollars) recorded annually were 1923, 84,444; 1925, 91,002; 1924, 89,761; and 1926, 90,415.

Table 15.6          Dividends Paid by Canadian Railways for the Year Ending June
                    30, 1911 (Dollars)

| Railway | Amount |
| --- | --- |
| British Yukon | 96,081 |
| Canada Southern | 450,000 |
| Canadian Pacific Railway | 26,413,556[a] |
| Grand Trunk Railway | 3,586,103 |
| Hereford Railway | 32,000 |

Source: Annual Report of the Department of Railways and Canals, *Sessional Papers of Canada* (1912), 13:104.

[a]This figure does not agree with the dividend figure shown in table 15.7, since the one in table 15.6 includes the 4% Consolidated Debenture stock payments which, for purposes of the National Accounts, have been moved to "Interest Payments."

those records, accounted for approximately 98% of the total dividends paid by all Canadian railways in this year.

To obtain dividend payments, then, only two railroads were used—the CPR and the GTR. The sum of dividends paid by these two companies was divided by .98 to inflate this total to include the whole system. Two problems were encountered with the GTR estimates. First, over the period from 1875 to 1911, the GTR reported all of its financial data in pounds sterling. The exchange rate used to convert these figures to Canadian dollars was £1 = $4.86 ⅔—the rate set under the terms of the Uniform Exchange Act, Statutes of Canada, 1871. The second problem is the way the GTR actually reported or failed to report dividends. For the years from 1899 to 1903 the published records show that no dividends were declared. However, a close check of the "surplus" account shows that in fact they were paid. Hence dividend payments are included in our estimates for these years. Poor's *Manual of Railroads* reocrds the dividend data. We also used the "Annual Reports" of the CPR.

The results of these calculations are shown in table 15.7. A word is necessary about this series since it moves around so much, especially in the early years. We should expect greater fluctuations in a dividends series than in an interest rate series since the ability, and willingness, of a company to pay dividends depends on the profitability of the company in a given year and that company's dividend policy. If the decision has been made to pay dividends at about the same level each year (i.e., adding to or drawing down from surplus), then the payout pattern would be much less volatile.

It is difficult to discern whether the CPR or the GTR had any such policy. Certainly the GTR's payout was very volatile, as one can see from the behavior of the series in 1883 and 1884. In 1883 the company, after several years of declaring low dividends, declared one of almost

**Table 15.7**    **Dividends Declared by Canadian Railways Annually, 1871–1926 (Thousands of Dollars)**

| Year | Amount | Year | Amount | Year | Amount |
|------|--------|------|--------|------|--------|
| 1871 | 100 | 1891 | 2,168 | 1911 | 24,989 |
| 1872 | 100 | 1892 | 2,200 | 1912 | 25,140 |
| 1873 | 100 | 1893 | 3,001 | 1913 | 27,333 |
| 1874 | 100 | 1894 | 1,920 | 1914 | 30,434 |
| 1875 | 100 | 1895 | 1,257 | 1915 | 32,341 |
| 1876 | 100 | 1896 | 2,231 | 1916 | 36,452 |
| 1877 | 100 | 1897 | 5,006 | 1917 | 30,145 |
| 1878 | 100 | 1898 | 4,944 | 1918 | 30,156 |
| 1879 | 100 | 1899 | 6,941 | 1919 | 30,157 |
| 1880 | 100 | 1900 | 6,954 | 1920 | 29,943 |
| 1881 | 100 | 1901 | 7,088 | 1921 | 30,157 |
| 1882 | 100 | 1902 | 7,516 | 1922 | 30,155 |
| 1883 | 2,985 | 1903 | 9,378 | 1923 | 30,356 |
| 1884 | 1,533 | 1904 | 9,318 | 1924 | 30,512 |
| 1885 | 100 | 1905 | 10,841 | 1925 | 30,410 |
| 1886 | 1,036 | 1906 | 12,198 | 1926 | 30,449 |
| 1887 | 1,872 | 1907 | 15,434 | | |
| 1888 | 906 | 1908 | 14,443 | | |
| 1889 | 2,101 | 1909 | 16,649 | | |
| 1890 | 2,612 | 1910 | 18,563 | | |

*Sources and methods:* See text.
[a]See table 15.2.

$3.0 million. This dropped by half the next year, and by 1885 there was only a token amount paid out. The large jump in 1883 and 1884 follows the acquisition of the Grand Trunk Western by the GTR on August 11, 1882. However, more work will have to be done both on the company's annual reports to shareholders and on the detailed reports submitted by the GTR to the Department of Railways and Canals before we will know why the Grand Trunk suddenly found that it could pay out such large amounts.

Another factor which needs to be examined is the way railways charged new capital items. Railways in Canada did not use depreciation accounting on their capital stock. Rather, they "expensed" such items as rail replacements, equipment renewals, and so on, against current revenue. Hence if the company chose to add an office building, or construct new bridges in one year, then this expenditure was charged against current revenue. The result was that net operating revenue (current receipts less current expenditures) dropped sharply and the amount available to pay for dividends declined or disappeared. For example, in 1898 the Grand Trunk built a new head office. The cost is listed at $900,000. This amount was charged against revenue earned in 1898. Such decisions will obviously distort dividend payment patterns.

## 15.2  Income and Investment, 1871–1926

The growth of the Canadian railway sector between 1871 and 1926 is set out in table 15.8. The estimates for income originating in this sector and for railway and telegraph capital investment are in current dollars.

Before we begin a discussion of this table, a word should be said about the link between estimates of labor and capital payments set out in the previous section and the total income figures shown in table 15.8. The latter is greater than the sum of wage and interest payments by two broad items: savings, and other fixed costs. Savings are defined as the difference between net corporate income and dividends paid out. Since information on net corporate income was not available before 1911, we used net operating revenue. This creates a slight upward bias in the recorded savings figure. In addition to savings, such items as taxes paid and income from renting equipment was included in the final figure. The final result for net income originating in the railway sector is shown in columns 1, 5, and 9 of table 15.8.

### 15.2.1  Income (Current Dollars)

During the first years of our study, Canadian railway income averaged about $10 million a year. By 1926 this annual income flow had increased to approximately $330 million. Even allowing for price changes, this is an impressive growth record. An additional perspective on this growth is provided in table 15.9, which sets out this expansion in terms of miles of track in operation. Between 1871 and 1926 Canada added 51,584 miles of railway track to its inventory, with 36,000 miles of this addition (or 70%) coming after 1900. The railway era for Canada is clearly a twentieth-century event, unlike the United States where the main building phase was over by the early 1890s.

The data show that within this 55-year span of time there were three periods of rapid expansion: 1871–76; 1880–84; and 1905–14. Each of these periods is associated with a particular aspect of Canadian development policy. At the time of Confederation there were two railway projects planned. One was to link the Maritime Provinces to Central Canada, and the other was to join British Columbia via a Canadian route to the rest of Canada.

A railway linking the Maritimes to Central Canada was begun in 1868 and completed in 1876. This line, known as the Intercolonial Railway (ICR), started in Truro, Nova Scotia, and ran westward terminating in Rivière du Loup. The Grand Trunk Railway ran eastward to this point. Given that the ICR was built over a fairly roundabout route (to keep it away from the United States border), private interests were unwilling to finance it; hence it was built as a government enterprise. The influ-

**Table 15.8** Income, Fixed Capital Formation and Investment/Income Ratio, in the Canadian Railway Sector, Annually, 1871–1926, in Current Dollars (Thousands of Dollars)

| Year | Income = O (Thousands of $) (1) | Gross Fixed Capital Formation = I (Millions of $) (2) | I/O (2) ÷ (1) (3) | Year | Income (4) | Gross Fixed Capital Formation (5) | I/O (6) | Year | Income (7) | Gross Fixed Capital Formation (8) | I/O (9) |
|---|---|---|---|---|---|---|---|---|---|---|---|
| 1871 | 9,413 | 12.4 | 1.32 | 1895 | 32,540 | 6.6 | 0.20 | 1919[a] | 279,644 | 95.1 | 0.34 |
| 1872 | 10,483 | 27.0 | 2.58 | 1896 | 34,986 | 7.4 | 0.21 | 1920 | 315,284 | 115.5 | 0.37 |
| 1873 | 11,322 | 29.3 | 2.59 | 1897 | 36,220 | 10.7 | 0.30 | 1921 | 287,821 | 100.0 | 0.35 |
| 1874 | 14,148 | 25.3 | 1.79 | 1898 | 42,207 | 18.6 | 0.44 | 1922 | 290,013 | 50.5 | 0.17 |
| 1875 | 11,606 | 24.1 | 2.08 | 1899 | 44,453 | 15.8 | 0.36 | 1923 | 295,723 | 102.9 | 0.35 |
| 1876 | 11,528 | 15.3 | 1.33 | 1900 | 49,986 | 18.7 | 0.37 | 1924 | 275,951 | 83.1 | 0.34 |
| 1877 | 11,030 | 8.7 | 0.79 | 1901 | 51,185 | 21.7 | 0.42 | 1925 | 296,740 | 52.2 | 0.18 |
| 1878 | 12,513 | 6.4 | 0.51 | 1902 | 58,898 | 24.3 | 0.41 | 1926 | 330,480 | 84.3 | 0.26 |
| 1879 | 12,008 | 8.7 | 0.72 | 1903 | 67,167 | 33.2 | 0.49 | | | | |
| 1880 | 15,191 | 14.1 | 0.93 | 1904 | 68,056 | 37.6 | 0.55 | | | | |
| 1881 | 17,992 | 18.3 | 1.02 | 1905 | 72,029 | 48.3 | 0.67 | | | | |
| 1882 | 18,482 | 44.0 | 2.39 | 1906 | 84,764 | 63.4 | 0.75 | | | | |
| 1883 | 21,848 | 57.5 | 2.63 | 1907 | 102,766 | 103.9 | 1.01 | | | | |
| 1884 | 21,642 | 72.5 | 3.35 | 1908 | 101,132 | 103.0 | 1.02 | | | | |
| 1885 | 20,997 | 33.8 | 1.61 | 1909 | 105,225 | 92.9 | 0.88 | | | | |
| 1886 | 24,739 | 23.7 | 0.96 | 1910 | 122,946 | 109.5 | 0.89 | | | | |
| 1887 | 26,222 | 23.4 | 0.89 | 1911 | 138,797 | 125.2 | 0.90 | | | | |
| 1888 | 28,280 | 20.7 | 0.73 | 1912 | 166,636 | 157.0 | 0.94 | | | | |
| 1889 | 28,318 | 22.1 | 0.78 | 1913 | 196,932 | 175.4 | 0.89 | | | | |
| 1890 | 32,099 | 15.3 | 0.48 | 1914 | 174,153 | 126.6 | 0.73 | | | | |
| 1891 | 32,119 | 14.2 | 0.44 | 1915 | 155,306 | 97.7 | 0.63 | | | | |
| 1892 | 34,951 | 12.0 | 0.34 | 1916 | 194,024 | 49.0 | 0.25 | | | | |
| 1893 | 35,006 | 12.9 | 0.36 | 1917 | 222,984 | 76.0 | 0.34 | | | | |
| 1894 | 32,457 | 8.8 | 0.27 | 1918 | 216,510 | 86.5 | 0.40 | | | | |

*Sources and methods:*

Col. 1: See text

Col. 2: Urquhart (in this vol.), table 2.2. Figures in millions of dollars.

Col. 3: Col. 2 divided by col. 1. Similarly for cols. 6 and 9.

[a]See table 15.2.

Table 15.9          Miles of Railway Track in Operation, Canada, 1871–1926

| Year | Miles | Year | Miles | Year | Miles |
|------|-------|------|-------|------|-------|
| 1871 | 2,695 | 1891 | 13,838 | 1911 | 32,559 |
| 1872 | 2,899 | 1892 | 14,564 | 1912 | 34,629 |
| 1873 | 3,613 | 1893 | 15,005 | 1913 | 38,223 |
| 1874 | 3,832 | 1894 | 15,627 | 1914 | 40,605 |
| 1875 | 4,331 | 1895 | 15,977 | 1915 | 45,833 |
| 1876 | 4,804 | 1896 | 16,270 | 1916 | 48,319 |
| 1877 | 5,218 | 1897 | 16,550 | 1917 | 50,253 |
| 1878 | 5,782 | 1898 | 16,870 | 1918 | 50,640 |
| 1879 | 6,226 | 1899 | 17,250 | 1919 | 50,691 |
| 1880 | 6,858 | 1900 | 17,657 | 1920 | 51,174 |
| 1881 | 7,194 | 1901 | 18,140 | 1921 | 51,747 |
| 1882 | 7,331 | 1902 | 18,714 | 1922 | 51,860 |
| 1883 | 8,697 | 1903 | 18,988 | 1923 | 51,936 |
| 1884 | 9,577 | 1904 | 19,431 | 1924 | 52,692 |
| 1885 | 10,273 | 1905 | 20,487 | 1925 | 54,100 |
| 1886 | 10,773 | 1906 | 21,353 | 1926 | 54,279 |
| 1887 | 11,793 | 1907 | 27,611 | | |
| 1888 | 12,184 | 1908 | 28,695 | | |
| 1889 | 12,585 | 1909 | 30,330 | | |
| 1890 | 13,151 | 1910 | 31,429 | | |

Source: Urquhart and Buckley (1968), ser. S28 and S77, pp. 528 and 532, respectively.

ence of this construction is seen in column 2 of table 15.8. Railway investment rises sharply from $12.4 million a year in 1871 to $29.3 million in 1873, remaining in the $24.0 million range until the ICR is completed in 1876. Note as well the sharp rise (col. 3) in the incremental capital/output ratio during these years of construction. It appears that excess capacity was being built into the Canadian railway system. Traffic to support this expenditure came after the railway was built.

The same sequence was followed by the other great political railroad of the period, the Canadian Pacific Railway (CPR). After years of negotiations, and not without scandal, a line running westward across the Prairies was started in 1880 and completed in 1885. Unlike the ICR, this was a privately built railroad but with substantial government subsidies. The initial subsidy was to grant the builders $25 million in cash and provide them with 25 million acres of land. The size of this undertaking can be seen in column 2 of table 15.8. Gross investment rose from an average of $7.9 million a year in 1877–79 to a peak in 1884 of $72.5 million. Within a decade the volume of investment had soared 10-fold. This massive undertaking, as in the period of the construction of the ICR, increased the investment/output ratio threefold—to levels never experienced at any other time in our period. Again the CPR was a railway built ahead of demand, although the sharp drop in this ratio toward the end of the 1880s and into the 1890s suggests that demand was not long in coming. By the 1890s, then, Canada was linked from the Pacific to the Atlantic by an all-Canadian railway route.

The third and final stage of rapid railway extension spanned roughly the first decade and a half of this century, peaking between 1905 and the beginning of World War I. These were the years of western settlement when the frontier pushed westward beyond Manitoba into Saskatchewan and Alberta (often called the "wheat boom" period). During these years, in addition to extensive branch lines being built, two additional transcontinental lines were constructed: the Canadian Northern, started in 1903 and completed in 1915, and the Grand Trunk Pacific, started in 1903, reaching completion at the outbreak of World War I.

The opening decades of the twentieth century were years of mass railroad building. As table 15.9 shows, the number of miles of railroad in operation increased by 26,800 between 1903 and 1915, an amount 10 times greater than the size of the whole system in 1871. The investment data reflect this rapid expansion. As column 5 of table 15.8 shows, the annual flow of gross fixed capital formation in railways, having reached a low of $6.6 million in 1895, increased to an annual level of $175.4 million in 1913 and averaged better than $120 million a year from 1907 to 1915. One must question whether, at the start of this railway investment boom, net investment was even positive. Between 1894 and 1895, for example, only 350 miles of track were brought into operation (see table 15.9). Prior to the boom, then, expansion of the railway system had virtually come to a halt. Expectations about economic returns to be made in the Canadian west after 1895 obviously proved to be a powerful magnet. CPR common stock, for example, rose from $47.50 a share in 1895 to $153.50 (Innis 1971, p. 284), in 1905—a threefold increase!

One interesting difference between this period of railway expansion and that which characterized the ICR and CPR periods is the lower absolute ratio of investment to income. Although the absolute change was quite spectacular—from .20 in 1895 to 1.02 in 1908 (table 15.8)— the "capping" at a level one-third of that observed in 1885 suggests that traffic generated by these new systems filled in very quickly behind completion of the lines. A steady state of about .30 was reached midway through the First World War and this held until the mid-1920s. This point will be studied more closely in the last section where real capital stock estimates are discussed.

The pattern of income growth, as one might suspect, is somewhat different from that of investment. The reason for this is related to the incentives for building these railways in the first place. In Canada, even more than in the United States, the majority of these new lines were really development railways, that is, railways sent into wilderness regions to open them for settlement. Transforming new land into productive farms takes time. Land must be broken, and "land-breaking" initial crops sown before crops for market can be planted. All of this takes time, but in the end it is moving the cash crop to market which generates traffic, and hence income growth in the railway sector.

One can see this lagged pattern quite clearly in table 15.8. Income growth from 1873 to 1880 was relatively flat, but from the latter date to 1886 it doubled. This increase was partly the reflection of better times, but it must also be due to business created by these new facilities. Even though the system was expanding slowly after 1885, nominal income grew substantially, that is, from about $28.0 million in the late 1890s to $50.0 million by 1900. As we saw earlier (table 15.4) prices actually fell during this period, so this gives a lower bound on nominal expansion. Finally, in the "wheat boom" period (1900–1914), much of the expansion in income occurred after the main phase of railway building was completed, that is, during and after World War I.

## 15.2.2  Physical Output

To complement the previous series (table 15.8) on nominal income growth in the railway sector, estimates of real output measured in physical terms—ton miles and passenger miles—have been derived for the period under review. These are shown in table 15.10. Official estimates of ton miles begin in 1907 and for passenger miles in 1910. Hence for the years before these dates, physical output figures had to be constructed from alternative data series.

The method used was that adopted by Fishlow (1966). This involves dividing freight and passenger receipts by the average charge for these services. Fortunately, receipts for the whole system are available back to 1875. For the years 1871–74 the ton and passenger miles derived for 1875 were extrapolated back on the trend of total expenses for the Grand Trunk Railway.

The main problem with this procedure lies in choosing the appropriate *average charges*. Freight rates proved to be more difficult than passenger tariffs. The former vary substantially on the basis of the type of good carried, that is, class of freight, and the distance goods are transported. Generally the average freight rate falls as one moves from higher-value but smaller items to lower-value, bulky goods. For example, boots and shoes are included in Class 1, while flour and lumber are included in the lowest class. Rates also varied by distance hauled, among regions, and among trunk carriers. To obtain an average freight rate we weighted the observed rates by regional mileage, the composition of freight carried, and freight shipped along the various trunks. We were fortunate in getting a basic source of freight rates from a publication submitted to the Royal Commission on Dominion-Provincial

**Table 15.10  Ton Miles, Passenger Miles, and the Weighted Total for Canadian Railways, Annually, 1871–1926 (All Figures in Millions)**

| Year | Ton Miles (1) | Passenger Miles (2) | Weighted Total (1) + (2) (3) | Year | Ton Miles (4) | Passenger Miles (5) | Weighted Total (4) + (5) (6) | Year | Ton Miles (7) | Passenger Miles (8) | Weighted Total (7) + (8) (9) |
|---|---|---|---|---|---|---|---|---|---|---|---|
| 1871[a] | 269 | 200 | 243 | 1891 | 2,184 | 583 | 1,615 | 1911 | 16,048 | 2,606 | 11,827 |
| 1872[a] | 307 | 228 | 278 | 1892 | 2,556 | 604 | 1,900 | 1912 | 19,558 | 2,910 | 14,547 |
| 1873[a] | 317 | 236 | 287 | 1893 | 2,745 | 629 | 2,015 | 1913 | 23,033 | 3,266 | 17,222 |
| 1874[a] | 352 | 261 | 318 | 1894 | 2,726 | 644 | 1,954 | 1914 | 22,063 | 3,089 | 16,333 |
| 1875 | 345 | 256 | 312 | 1895 | 2,955 | 566 | 2,133 | 1915 | 17,661 | 2,484 | 12,971 |
| 1876 | 360 | 254 | 321 | 1896 | 3,236 | 598 | 2,360 | 1916 | 28,195 | 2,727 | 21,701 |
| 1877 | 353 | 258 | 319 | 1897 | 3,529 | 619 | 2,569 | 1917 | 31,187 | 3,150 | 23,783 |
| 1878 | 438 | 255 | 370 | 1898 | 4,053 | 710 | 2,977 | 1918 | 31,029 | 3,190 | 23,791 |
| 1879 | 447 | 258 | 377 | 1899 | 4,221 | 741 | 3,114 | 1919[b] | 27,337 | 3,366 | 20,313 |
| 1880 | 596 | 283 | 490 | 1900 | 5,072 | 885 | 3,728 | 1920 | 31,894 | 3,522 | 24,432 |
| 1881 | 778 | 329 | 631 | 1901 | 5,185 | 946 | 3,807 | 1921 | 26,662 | 2,961 | 20,476 |
| 1882 | 771 | 401 | 629 | 1902 | 5,999 | 1,130 | 4,421 | 1922 | 30,368 | 2,814 | 23,700 |
| 1883 | 969 | 422 | 768 | 1903 | 7,009 | 1,275 | 5,231 | 1923 | 34,068 | 3,076 | 26,289 |
| 1884 | 988 | 448 | 786 | 1904 | 7,609 | 1,416 | 5,609 | 1924 | 30,514 | 2,872 | 23,438 |
| 1885 | 998 | 422 | 783 | 1905 | 8,024 | 1,524 | 5,905 | 1925 | 31,965 | 2,911 | 24,818 |
| 1886 | 1,115 | 410 | 864 | 1906 | 9,580 | 1,757 | 7,092 | 1926 | 34,153 | 2,999 | 26,801 |
| 1887 | 1,366 | 475 | 1,049 | 1907 | 11,688 | 2,050 | 8,633 | | | | |
| 1888 | 1,554 | 510 | 1,188 | 1908 | 12,962 | 2,082 | 9,426 | | | | |
| 1889 | 1,667 | 530 | 1,260 | 1909 | 13,161 | 2,033 | 9,622 | | | | |
| 1890 | 1,995 | 549 | 1,502 | 1910 | 15,712 | 2,467 | 11,619 | | | | |

*Sources and methods:* See text.

[a]Cols. 1 and 2 for the years 1871–74 were obtained by extrapolating backward on trend of total expenses for the Grand Trunk Railway.

[b]See table 15.2

Relations (Ottawa, 1939), entitled "Railway Freight Rates in Canada" (prepared by RAC Henry and Associates). In addition, the CPR "Annual Reports" carried details, annually, on average freight and passenger rates. Passenger rates did not show the same variation as did freight rates, although there were first-class and immigrant rates.

The final problem faced in calculating an average freight rate was to determine the average haulage distance. After plotting rates per mile against distance, it became clear that the average rate flattened out after 125 miles. Hence our estimates, by class and type of carrier (regional vs. national), were based on rates for 125 miles. Although by 1911 the average freight haul had increased from earlier years, it seemed that for the whole period the 125-mile figure could be used without seriously biasing the final results.

Finally, to combine these two series the weights used were the distribution of total earnings between freight and passenger service. These weights (i.e., shares of passenger and freight revenue) were calculated for each year from 1875 to 1926 and were used to obtain the total real output shown in columns 3, 6, and 9 of table 15.10.

The actual averages for freight and passenger rates are shown in the Appendix. Although any given rate should be treated with caution, the trends in passenger and freight charges per mile reflect, one suspects, the basic changes in the system over these decades. It is worth noting how rapidly average service charges for carrying freight dropped between 1875 and 1900 and again between the turn of the century and World War I. The rise in freight rates after the end of hostilities is an interesting reversal in trend. As far as one can tell, it reflected the awakening of the government to the fact that rates had not been allowed to rise in line with labor and other input costs caused by war inflation (more on this point later).

If we take the trends in the physical output series (table 15.10) for the total period, some interesting observations about the evolution of the system emerge. First, the volume of freight traffic being handled by the turn of the century was vastly greater than in 1871. This reinforces again the earlier contention that at the time of Confederation Canada had barely entered the railway era, but that with the completion of the ICR (1876) and the CPR (1885), plus the building of new branch lines, internal and external flows of goods (and people) were greatly enhanced. Second, note that although passenger traffic grew substantially (i.e., from 200 million to 741 million passenger miles from 1871 to 1900), freight volume growth was clearly the "leading" component, growing from 269 million to 5,072 million ton miles over these three decades. If we relate these volume differences to receipts, with freight rates falling relative to passenger rates, the distribution of earnings between the two services remained fairly stable. For example, in 1875 freight earnings accounted for 63% of total earnings, while in 1900 they accounted for 67%.

Twentieth-century expansion, although not as spectacular in rate-of-growth terms, nevertheless showed that we are dealing by the 1920s with a mature railway system. At the beginning of World War I ton miles of freight carried had increased fourfold from 1900, while between 1914 and 1926 the increase was about 50%. Hence over the whole period there are three distinct phases of growth. From the 1870s to the mid-1890s the annual compound rate of growth of freight traffic was about 10% per year. From 1900 to 1914, freight traffic grew at 11% per year, while from 1914 to 1926 the rate dropped to 3.6%. If we look back over the history of the period, it is obvious that much of this growth was associated with the geographic expansion of the system: the movement into the west and the linking of the Central Provinces with the Maritimes. For the years from 1914 to 1926 this rapid geographic expansion slowed, and so did total growth. In addition, road and canal transportation modes began to offer competition for freight business formerly held almost exclusively by the railways.[4]

## 15.3 Productivity Change

The written history of the role of railways in Canadian development is very different from that in the United States. Railways were central to much of the American growth experience in the nineteenth century. Schumpeter claimed that the economic history of the United States in the last half of the nineteenth century might well be written solely in terms of the railroad sector.[5] Indeed, Fishlow and Fogel introduced to economic history the concept of social savings in connection with their investigation into whether railroads were really as indispensable to United States economic growth as suggested by earlier economic historians.[6]

Railways in the context of this country's development did not fare so well in the hands of earlier Canadian economic historians. Most students read the history of Canadian railways as a series of scandals, for example, that surrounding the building of the CPR, especially in the final level of subsidy given to the contractors. Or the scandal which arose in connection with the building of the Canadian Northern Railway and the suspect role of the line's promoters, Mackenzie and Mann. Finally, the eventual takeover of all railways, except the CPR, in 1919 was clear testimony to two basic features of Canadian life. First, that the country from time to time was prone to excessive speculation, especially at the turn of the century; that is, the illusion that good times apparently always lead to better times. The main effect of this speculation during the wheat boom was the building of two new transcontinental railroads (in addition to the CPR) between 1903 and 1914. Again speculative investment got out of control, and the system was overbuilt, to the detriment of the economy.[7] The second contention is that some of these larger railways, like the Grand Trunk, experienced "irresponsible management" and hence made significant construction (and operations?) errors. This is hardly the stuff of which great myths are built.

In both countries recent research has modified such extreme positions.[8] Nevertheless, for Canada at least, the simple exercise of examining the growth and efficiency of the railway system has not yet been undertaken (Fishlow 1966). Before we can begin to study patterns of performance, information on the growth of the principal inputs—labor, capital, and fuel—must be acquired.

## 15.3.1 Growth of Labor Input

Data on the size of the railway labor force were first published in 1907, as in the case of total wages and salaries. Thus some method of estimating the growth of this input between 1871 and 1907 had to be found. Three possible approaches were available. One approach was that used by Fishlow (1965, app. C). With this method, total employment of railway workers is divided by total operating revenue to obtain an average relationship between these two magnitudes. If observation proves this to be a fairly stable relationship, then it can be used to calculate employment for earlier years, since we have gross revenue running back to 1871. Another method involves examining the relationship between employment and the number of miles of track in operation. This approach links the growth of the labor force used in the railroads to the growth of one of the principal pieces of fixed capital. Given the nature of technological innovation in this industry during the nineteenth century, estimates based on such a relationship probably are not out of line with what was indeed happening. Finally, the simplest method is to use decennial census estimates of the number of employees recorded for this industry.

There are two problems with using census estimates of employment for the railway sector. First, as in the case of wages and salaries referred to earlier, census authorities chose to assign some railway workers (such as those engaged in car repair and rebuilding) to the manufacturing sector rather than to the railway sector. Second, and more important, is the change in the method used to record workers in the census before 1901. Beginning in 1901 information was collected both on the number of gainfully occupied and on the number of wage earners attached to a particular industry. The latter total was collected from the individual industries surveyed, while the former was collected as part of the information obtained from individual households. For the censuses before 1901, only information on the gainfully occupied was obtained. The census takers were not interested in estimating the size of the Canadian labor force but were more concerned with the general socioeconomic characteristics of the population. As a result, where an individual worked for a number of employers in the census year, he or she was asked to name a main employer. This approach may have been adequate for workers with some skill, but for laborers who worked wherever they could find employment it meant listing them under the title "Miscellaneous Unskilled Labour." Many individuals who worked for the railroads fell into this category. For example, in a country like Canada where clearing the tracks of snow was a big job, a large number of workers who were actually on the payroll of the railway companies were not assigned to this sector. It is impossible to sort out how many of the unspecified laborers actually worked in this sector at any one census date. Indeed it is even impossible to estimate the trend. Since this was undoubtedly a large component, the census records could not be used even when the workers engaged in manufacturing activity were added to the base number of those listed as gainfully occupied workers in "Steam Railways."

With some doubt about whether the census approach would render the growth of labor input accurately, we were left with the Fishlow method and the ratio of workers to miles of track in operation. The Fishlow approach was tried,[9] but unfortunately for our case it gave misleading results. The problem which emerged was with the influence of price changes on the ratio during the turbulent years 1907–26. This period covered the last years of frontier settlement, the First World War, the inflation that accompanied it, and finally the postwar adjustment, not only to the economy, but also to the railroad sector which, with the exception of the CPR, was taken over by the government and amalgamated to form the Canadian National Railway system. These were not good years in which to establish a ratio of revenue to employment that could be used to project labor growth back from 1907 to 1871.

The method adopted, then, was to divide employment in the railroad sector by track mileage in operation. One possible benefit of this approach was that it put in the ratio two real factors, rather than mixing real (employment) with nominal elements (revenue). Further, the ratio of employment to track mileage proved to be a remarkably stable ratio over the years for which we had evidence on both figures, that is, after 1907. The ratio averaged about four employees per mile of track operated. The only deviation from this average occurred during periods of extensive railroad construction, when it rose to about 5.5 employees per mile of track. This is what one would expect, since the railroads would take on extra help during the startup of new lines. Accommodation for this variation was made by incorporating the higher ratio in our calculation of labor input during known periods of railroad expansion (e.g. during the building of the CPR). The results are shown in table 15.11.

### 15.3.2    Growth in Real Capital Stock

Estimates of real capital stock were never collected by the government. The only data available are on the book value of various railroad lines, investment figures, and the physical stock of certain assets. This is not a unique problem. Fishlow (1966) faced the same difficulty.

The method used to estimate real net capital stock for the Canadian railroad sector differs from that used by Fishlow. Here we adopted the "perpetual inventory" method. The "perpetual inventory" approach requires three basic pieces of information: current dollar gross fixed capital formation estimates, capital goods price indices, and data on the "average economic life" of capital goods. The sources of each of these series are set out below.

*Capital Formation Series*

We are fortunate to have two extant series on gross capital formation for the railroad industry. One series was completed in 1962 by Ken Buckley (1962); the other, by Statistics Canada (1978), as basic input

**Table 15.11        Employment in the Canadian Railway Sector, Annually, 1875–1926 (Thousands)**

| Year | Employment | Year | Employment | Year | Employment |
|------|-----------|------|-----------|------|-----------|
| 1875 | 21.62 | 1893 | 67.52 | 1911 | 141.22 |
| 1876 | 23.48 | 1894 | 62.51 | 1912 | 155.90 |
| 1877 | 26.02 | 1895 | 63.91 | 1913 | 178.65 |
| 1878 | 28.02 | 1896 | 65.08 | 1914 | 159.14 |
| 1879 | 30.86 | 1897 | 66.20 | 1915 | 124.14 |
| 1880 | 32.32 | 1898 | 67.48 | 1916 | 144.77 |
| 1881 | 36.66 | 1899 | 69.00 | 1917 | 146.18 |
| 1882 | 52.18 | 1900 | 75.04 | 1918 | 143.49 |
| 1883 | 58.06 | 1901 | 81.63 | 1919 | 158.78 |
| 1884 | 51.37 | 1902 | 93.57 | 1920 | 185.18 |
| 1885 | 48.48 | 1903 | 94.94 | 1921 | 167.63 |
| 1886 | 53.96 | 1904 | 102.01 | 1922 | 165.64 |
| 1887 | 60.92 | 1905 | 112.68 | 1923 | 178.05 |
| 1888 | 60.82 | 1906 | 117.44 | 1924 | 169.97 |
| 1889 | 63.14 | 1907 | 124.01 | 1925 | 166.03 |
| 1890 | 65.76 | 1908 | 106.44 | 1926 | 174.27 |
| 1891 | 69.19 | 1909 | 125.11 | | |
| 1892 | 72.84 | 1910 | 123.77 | | |

*Sources and methods:* See text; 1875–1918: "Railway Statistics," Annual Reports of the Department of Railway and Canals in the *Sessional Papers of Canada* until 1918; 1919–26: "Railway Statistics," Dominion Bureau of Statistics.

to its publication *Fixed Capital Flows and Stocks*. Both series are carefully constructed, and both are defined as covering railroad transport, including telegraph and cable systems. This study uses both series—Buckley for the earlier years, and the Statistics Canada figures for the more recent period. Buckley's estimates have the added advantage of beginning in 1850. Statistics Canada's figures start in 1871.

*Price Indices*

The availability of the Statistics Canada series entitled, "Price Indices for Capital Expenditure" allowed us to obtain real capital formation estimates back to 1871. These indices cover building and engineering construction as well as prices for machinery and equipment. To push the series back to 1850, a price index of "Iron and Its Products" and a "General Wholesale Price Index" were used."[10]

*Average Economic Life*

The ground rules on determining "average economic life" of railroad assets are very shaky. It was decided, therefore, that the service life estimates used by Hood and Scott (1957) were probably the most suitable. They estimated an average service life for all structures (not just railroad structures) at 50 years and for all equipment at 28 years. Ulmer (1960) found tht railroad structures accounted for 74% of total fixed reproducible assets in this industry, while machinery and equipment accounted for the other 26%. Hence average service life was calculated as follows:

$$50 (.74) + 28 (.26) = 45 \text{ years.}$$

Straight-line depreciation was assumed over the 45-year average service life of structures and equipment. The final estimates of net real capital stock are shown in table 15.12.

Unfortunately there are not extant alternative series against which to check our results. As a partial substitute, data were collected on the growth of physical stock in the Canadian railroad sector from 1870 to 1930. To test whether the real net capital stock provides a fair representation of the growth of this input, annual growth rates for several series (such as miles of rail in operation, number of engines in use, etc.) were collected to provide a rough comparison against which to judge our new estimates. These comparisons are shown in table 15.13. The unweighted growth rates of various physical assets shown in column 5 exhibit a very lose relationship to the growth of our estimates of real net capital stock. This is at least encouraging. During the critical period of railroad expansion, 1900–1915, 5-year average growth estimates were calculated (table 15.13, panel B). Again the correspondence is reasonably close and leads one to believe that the "perpetual in-

Table 15.12          Real Net Capital Stock in the Canadian Railroad Sector, Annually, 1875–1926 (Millions of Dollars)

| Year | Real Capital Stock | Year | Real Capital Stock | Year | Real Capital Stock |
|------|------|------|------|------|------|
| 1875 | 141.4 | 1892 | 448.3 | 1909 | 1,005.7 |
| 1876 | 154.9 | 1893 | 453.6 | 1910 | 1,133.2 |
| 1877 | 166.4 | 1894 | 454.4 | 1911 | 1,279.6 |
| 1878 | 176.3 | 1895 | 450.8 | 1912 | 1,466.7 |
| 1879 | 185.3 | 1896 | 450.1 | 1913 | 1,664.2 |
| 1880 | 191.6 | 1897 | 451.2 | 1914 | 1,792.0 |
| 1881 | 201.5 | 1898 | 465.7 | 1915 | 1,855.1 |
| 1882 | 230.6 | 1899 | 471.7 | 1916 | 1,837.3 |
| 1883 | 267.2 | 1900 | 478.7 | 1917 | 1,818.7 |
| 1884 | 309.1 | 1901 | 488.7 | 1918 | 1,801.8 |
| 1885 | 342.7 | 1902 | 500.6 | 1919 | 1,789.4 |
| 1886 | 363.2 | 1903 | 528.1 | 1920 | 1,779.8 |
| 1887 | 378.8 | 1904 | 560.6 | 1921 | 1,776.6 |
| 1888 | 393.8 | 1905 | 608.1 | 1922 | 1,740.3 |
| 1889 | 415.1 | 1906 | 670.1 | 1923 | 1,740.6 |
| 1890 | 431.0 | 1907 | 789.4 | 1924 | 1,729.8 |
| 1891 | 444.8 | 1908 | 901.3 | 1925 | 1,696.3 |

*Sources and methods:* See text.

Table 15.13          Annual Growth Rates of Rails, Engines, Passenger, and Freight Cars and in the Index of Real Net Capital Stock (%)

| Years | Rails (1) | Engines (2) | Passenger Cars (3) | Freight Cars (4) | Unweighted Average Cols. 1–4 (5) | Index of Net Capital Stock (1910 = 100) (6) |
|------|------|------|------|------|------|------|
| | | | *Panel A* | | | |
| 1875–1900 | 5.38 | 3.43 | 4.25 | 4.76 | 4.5 | 5.00 |
| 1900–1910 | 5.84 | 5.98 | 18.90 | 6.94 | 9.4 | 8.77 |
| 1910–20 | 5.00 | 3.99 | 4.26 | 6.53 | 4.9 | 4.62 |
| 1920–30 | 1.01 | −1.00 | −1.14 | −0.35 | — | 1.50 |
| | | | *Panel B* | | | |
| 1900–1905 | 2.94 | 4.95 | 0.40 | 5.79 | 3.5 | 4.90 |
| 1905–10 | 8.82 | 7.02 | 14.34 | 8.09 | 9.6 | 13.26 |
| 1910–15 | 7.84 | 6.10 | 7.93 | 11.24 | 8.3 | 10.14 |

*Source:* Cols. 1–4: Urquhart and Buckley (1968), pp. 528–32. col. 6: see table 15.12.

ventory" method (using the two series on capital formation) provides a good approximation to the long-term growth of railroad net real capital stock. Note that the rapid growth in passenger cars from 1905 to 1910 was followed in the next quinquennium by a a rapid growth in freight cars. The passenger car spurt was in response to accelerated immigration, while the freight car growth was in response to additions to output created by the influx of new settlers.

### 15.3.3   Growth of Fuel

Since the conversion of fuel into mechanical power is central to the operation of railroads, it was treated as a separate input. Table 15.14 sets out the number of BTUs consumed. Again from 1907 to 1926, the "Annual Reports" record tons of fuel consumed, in coal and coal equivalents. For the years prior to 1907 the only record of fuel consumed was that reported by the Intercolonial Railroad, a government railroad that reported separately on its annual operations. The Intercolonial listed fuel used annually over the full period plus the number of engine miles run by its locomotives during a given year. The number of engine miles run was also available for the entire railway system. Thus the tonnage used on the Intercolonial was scaled up to give a figure for the entire system, using the ratio of engine miles for the system to engine miles run on the Intercolonial. This ratio was remarkably stable, at about 10:1 over the period before 1907.

To compare Canada's consumption of fuel with the United States, I derived the figures shown in the unnumbered table below. These show pounds of coal and coal equivalents consumed per locomotive mile.

**Table 15.14**    Fuel Consumed in the Canadian Railroad Sector, Annually, 1875–1926 (Millions of BTUs)

| Year | Fuel | Year | Fuel | Year | Fuel |
|------|------|------|------|------|------|
| 1875 | 5.7  | 1892 | 20.7 | 1909 | 78.9 |
| 1876 | 6.1  | 1893 | 21.0 | 1910 | 72.2 |
| 1877 | 6.3  | 1894 | 21.0 | 1911 | 78.5 |
| 1878 | 6.8  | 1895 | 18.9 | 1912 | 89.9 |
| 1879 | 7.2  | 1896 | 20.4 | 1913 | 106.9 |
| 1880 | 7.3  | 1897 | 19.2 | 1914 | 98.7 |
| 1881 | 9.7  | 1898 | 20.8 | 1915 | 79.7 |
| 1882 | 9.6  | 1899 | 24.3 | 1916 | 103.8 |
| 1883 | 14.2 | 1900 | 26.3 | 1917 | 116.9 |
| 1884 | 11.1 | 1901 | 27.1 | 1918 | 117.4 |
| 1885 | 12.2 | 1902 | 29.9 | 1919 | 111.8 |
| 1886 | 12.3 | 1903 | 34.9 | 1920 | 124.0 |
| 1887 | 15.3 | 1904 | 39.1 | 1921 | 103.8 |
| 1888 | 15.3 | 1905 | 42.6 | 1922 | 106.9 |
| 1889 | 15.8 | 1906 | 47.7 | 1923 | 117.9 |
| 1890 | 17.2 | 1907 | 64.7 | 1924 | 107.5 |
| 1891 | 21.7 | 1908 | 68.9 | 1925 | 105.4 |
|      |      |      |      | 1926 | 111.3 |

*Sources and methods:* See text.

|      | Canada |      | United States (Fishlow) |
|------|--------|------|-------------------------|
| 1880 | 62     | 1880 | 65                      |
| 1890 | 80     | 1890 | 80                      |
| 1900 | 76     | 1900 | 100                     |
| 1907 | 125    | —    | —                       |
| 1910 | 132    | 1910 | 150                     |
| 1920 | 152    | —    | —                       |

These figures support our estimation technique, since they indicate that both countries were experiencing about the same trend in fuel consumed per locomotive mile. Increased consumption is mainly due to the shift to heavier engines over time.

### 15.3.4    Measures of Partial and Total Factor Productivity

Two measures of productivity change are used in assessing the performance of the railroad sector, partial and total factor productivity. These are shown in panel B of table 15.15. The ratios are derived from the indices on output and input recorded in panel A. A weighted sum of inputs is shown in line 5. The weights used for the labor, capital, and fuel are .55, .35, and .10, respectively. Fishlow used these shares

**Table 15.15**    **Index of Total Output, Inputs, Partial and Total Factor Productivity for the Canadian Railroad Sector, 1875–1920 (1910 = 100.00)**

|                        | 1875 (1) | 1880 (2) | 1890 (3) | 1900 (4) | 1910 (5) | 1920 (6) |
|------------------------|----------|----------|----------|----------|----------|----------|
| *A. Total Output and Inputs* | | | | | | |
| 1. Real output (O)     | 3.59     | 5.33     | 14.80    | 33.29    | 100.00   | 185.90   |
| 2. Labor (L)           | 17.48    | 26.15    | 53.14    | 60.62    | 100.00   | 125.37   |
| 3. Capital (K)         | 12.47    | 16.91    | 38.03    | 42.24    | 100.00   | 163.22   |
| 4. Fuel (F)            | 7.89     | 10.11    | 23.82    | 36.43    | 100.00   | 171.75   |
| 5. Total inputs        | 14.35    | 20.41    | 43.62    | 50.77    | 100.00   | 140.00   |
| *B. Partial and Total Factor Productivity* | | | | | | |
| 6. O/L                 | 20.56    | 20.40    | 27.85    | 54.91    | 100.00   | 148.28   |
| 7. O/K                 | 28.80    | 31.55    | 38.91    | 78.81    | 100.00   | 118.36   |
| 8. O/M                 | 45.52    | 52.76    | 62.12    | 91.38    | 100.00   | 108.24   |
| 9. TFP                 | 25.05    | 26.13    | 33.92    | 65.57    | 100.00   | 132.79   |

*Sources:* See tables 15.10, 15.11, 15.12, and 15.14.
*Note:*
Line 5: Weights for labor, capital, and fuel are .55, .35, and .10, respectively.
Line 6: Line 1 divided by line 2.
Line 7: Line 1 divided by line 3.
Line 8: Line 1 divided by line 4.
Line 9: Line 1 divided by line 5.
[a]TFP = total factor productivity.

in his study of United States railroads (1966, p. 626). A check on factor share costs for Canadian railroads in 1910, the same year used by Fishlow to obtain his shares, reveals an almost identical share distribution and since the cost share data appear more complete for the American case, the United States ratios were adopted.

## Partial Productivity

Per worker productivity (line 6) shows the most rapid advance of the three ratios. Its compound annual growth from 1875 to 1920 was 4.5%, while for capital the compound annual growth rate was 3.2%, and for fuel, the poorest performer, it was 1.9%. This rapid growth in labor productivity was not unrelated to the growth of capital, which exceeded the growth of labor; that is, 5.9 vs. 4.5, respectively. With a rise in the $K/L$ ratio, it is not surprising that labor productivity performed as it did over this period.

This advance in labor productivity, however, was not even. In the decades preceding the opening of the West (i.e., 1875–1900), labor productivity advanced at the annual rate of 4.0%, while for the frontier period it grew at 5.1%, or a full 25% faster. The reasons this occurred are complex, but differential rates of growth of labor and capital between the two periods tell part of the story. Between 1875 and 1900, labor grew at 5.1% and capital growth was virtually identical. After 1900 the rates diverged sharply. Labor growth slowed to 3.7% while capital growth grew at 7.0%, or almost double that of labor. It is little wonder that capital productivity fell behind that of labor after the turn of the century. The geographic expansion of the system after 1900 not only brought massive changes to the size of the system but clearly changed the relationship between capital and labor, raising the capital/labor ratio sharply.

Railroad building is a capital intensive and expensive activity. One would be surprised, then, if excess capacity were not built into the system initially. The Canadian system apparently is no exception to this rule, especially before 1800. The capital/output ratio (real capital stock divided by real output was about 14.1 in 1875 (compared to a United States ratio of 10.3). By 1900 the ratio had fallen to 5.2, and it continued to fall as we entered the twentieth century. Although we cannot say by how much, part of the observed growth in worker productivity must have come from these sharply increased capital utilization rates. These observations reenforce the points made early in the discussion on investment/output ratios.

## Total Factor Productivity

The measure of total factor productivity shown in line 9 of table 15.15 was derived by dividing the real output index by an index of weighted inputs (capital, labor, and fuel). It is simply the difference between the growth of output and weighted inputs. This residual measures the contribution of the growth in output not accounted for by measured inputs. It captures the influence of technological change, economies of scale, organization of business, and the effect of human capital improvements on productivity. The measure of total factor productivity shown here should be taken only as a first approximation. I hope that other writers will refine the estimate.

Between 1875 and 1920 total factor productivity, as measured in table 15.15, grew at an annual rate of 5.8%. The annual rate varied very little between our two periods, that is, 3.9% before 1900 and 3.6% between 1900 and 1920. In terms of the contribution of total factor productivity to total growth in real output, the story is quite different. Between 1875 and 1900 the residual accounted for 56% of output growth, while for the decades after 1900 it accounted for only 42%. This result is quite different from that for the economy as a whole. In calculating TFP for the Canadian economy, Lithwick (1967, p. 53) found that it grew at 0.75% a year between 1891 and 1910, rising to 1.2% between 1910 and 1926. The residual's contribution to the growth of national output was only 22% in the first period, rising to 47% in the second. Apparently technological change was playing a larger role in the total growth of the railroad sector than it was for the economy as a whole.

Fishlow (1966) also found that growth of TFP was high in the United States railroad sector over his period of study. In examining several factors which might have increased the quality of the capital input (such as the introduction of air brakes, the adoption of automatic couplers, the effects of building on a larger scale, and greater utilization), Fishlow (1966) came to the conclusion that the most important factor was apparently the substitution of steel for iron rails. Steel rails meant the railroads could run larger and heavier trains, hence saving on capital and labor inputs.

We have little information at this stage of our inquiry on the rate of adoption of such items as air brakes, automatic couplers, and so on, but information is available on the rate of adoption, in Canada, of steel rails. The ratios in table 15.16 indicate that Canada was ahead in the adoption of steel rails from 1875 to 1890. The rate of adoption is really quite amazing, given that the first large-scale adoption of steel rails was on the Pennsylvania Railroad system in the early 1860s. Within 2 decades, then, half of all rails used in Canada were steel. The use of steel rails, it is to be remembered, only provides an opportunity to use heavier equipment. It will be interesting to see whether Canadian companies actually exploited this potential advantage. The observation of an earlier adoption of steel rails is given only as a place to begin studying the factors which led to the high productivity gains in this sector between 1875 and the early 1920s.

| 15.16 | Percentage of Steel Rails to Total Rails, Canada and the United States 1875–1900 | |
|---|---|---|
| Year | Canada[a] | United States[b] |
| 1875 | 43 | — |
| 1880 | 57 | 30 |
| 1890 | 95 | 80 |
| 1900 | 100 | 100 |

[a]*Historical Statistics of Canada*, p. 528.
[b]Fishlow (1966), p. 635.

| Table 15.17 | Productivity Comparisons for Canadian and American Railroads 1880–1910 | | | |
|---|---|---|---|---|
| Year | O/L (1) | O/K (2) | O/F (3) | TFP (4) |
| 1880 | 80.5 | 107.8 | 135.7 | 95.2 |
| 1890 | 54.8 | 72.5 | 111.1 | 66.2 |
| 1910 | 54.6 | 63.7 | 103.7 | 62.1 |
| 1910 | 94.1 | 63.3 | 140.9 | 87.0 |

*Sources and methods:* The ratios were determined using the following relationships:

$$A_2/A_1 = \frac{Q_2/L_2}{Q_1/L_1}^{S_L} \quad \frac{Q_2/K_2}{Q_2/K_1}^{S_K} \quad \frac{Q_2/F_2}{Q_1/F_1}^{S_F}$$

where subscript 2 stands for Canada and 1 stands for the United States. The factor shares $S_L$, $S_K$, and $S_F$ are an average of these values for the year 1910. (see Allen, 1979, p. 916.) U.S., A. Fishlow (1966).

### 15.3.5 Productivity Change in Canada and the United States

Since the measurement techniques used by Fishlow (1966) and by me in estimating productivity change (partial and total) are very similar, it seemed reasonable to compare the relative performance of the two systems where we had estimates for both countries. These comparisons are shown table 15.17. It should be emphasized that we are only looking at productivity relatives at a particular date rather than as a trend, as in the case of productivity changes in the Canadian system discussed in connection with the results shown in table 15.16.

One does not want to make too much of these estimates, but as a preliminary glimpse of the relative performance of the two systems the effort seems worthwhile. The ratios suggest, but do not prove, that Canada's railroad system was relatively less efficient at the beginning of our study than was the United States system, and it fell slightly behind the latter during the balance of the nineteenth century. According to the estimates, this condition reversed itself in the first decade of this century. Was this due to the fact that the Canadian system was in the process of working off excess capacity, or was it due to other factors, such as added costs in running a northern railway system? These are obviously points that need to be investigated further.

Finally, the long-run evidence on productivity growth in the Canadian railroad sector gives us some perspective on the discussion earlier concerning the supposed overbuilding and ultimately the inefficiency which apparently plagued Canadian railroads after the completion of the third transcontinental railway. The reason given for the government takeover was that the supply of railroad services exceeded demand, forcing down returns and creating the potential for bankruptcy and major dislocations in the Canadian economy. The government was forced to step in and save the system from the overzealous railroad entrepreneurs. Was this really the case? The evidence seems to suggest that the answer is no.

First, there is no question that the some railroads' ability to pay fixed debt charges deteriorated sharply between 1913 and 1920. From 1912 to 1914 net operating revenue (out of which is paid all charges on fixed and floating debt, taxes, and equipment rentals) was averaging about $70 million a a year. By 1918 and 1919 net operating revenue was averaging $49 million. In current dollar cash flow terms, the fear of failure was not unfounded. However, this evidence on cash shortage was translated by earlier writers into overbuilding. The evidence we have seen implies that this is suspect. By the middle of World War I farm output from the Prairies—which had been the goal of railroad building from the beginning—had finally come on stream. For example, by 1918 the ratio of exports to GNP had climbed to 35.3%, more than double what they had been only 6 years earlier, in 1910.[11] The ratio remained at about 25% or greater until the end of our period. Most of these exports were bulky goods, grain, war materiel, and so on, virtually all of which moved by rail. As table 15.10, column 7 shows, ton miles carried, which had been running at roughly 15.7 billion in 1910, doubled by 1916 to 31.2 billion and remained around the latter level into the mid-1920s. Real output growth continued to expand at a rapid rate, at least until the end of the First World War.

Did real output grow more slowly than inputs? Regardless of the ratios used (panel B, table 15.15), none exhibit a downward trend, and we have used 1920 as the terminal year—the year that the takeover was under way. Apparently we must cast our net wider for an explanation of the failure of the system (with the exception of the CPR) to remain in private hands. The argument concerning inefficiency based on excess capacity has been substantially weakened with our new estimates. A starting place for a revision might be with the way railroads were regulated during this period. Briefly, the government regulated freight and passenger rates and held them constant during the course of the war. However, beginning around 1917 prices of all goods rose sharply, including wages. For railroads built just prior to the outbreak of hostilities the cost burden was high, since, among other reasons, they financed construction by borrowing rather than financing through equity. With high fixed costs and rising variable costs, but fixed tariffs, profits fell and the capacity of the railroads to meet debt obligations diminished. Ultimately, bankruptcy would have occurred, in the absence of either a change in rate regulations or, as did happen, the government's taking over railroad obligations and nationalizing the system (again with the exception of the CPR). The role of regulation in the operation of the railroads needs to be investigated more thoroughly before we know the full reasons for the nationalization of the system.

### 15.3.6  Long-Term Change in Labor's Factor Share

The way income in the railroad sector was estimated allows us to calculate the cost shares of capital and labor. Note that labor's factor share differs slightly from that used to estimate total factor productivity. Here the share is derived from an income approach, whereas in the earlier case an input cost-share method was adopted. The latter, for example, included a direct measure of fuel costs. Since our primary concern here is with trends, this difference should not affect the discussion. Labor's share has been estimated on a 5-year period basis from 1875 to 1924. The results are shown in table 15.18. Before discussing the results, a word needs to be said about the sudden rise in labor's share during the last period (1920–24). After the end of World War I, as discussed earlier, Canadian railroads ran into financial difficulty. The result was that the sector dissaved for much of the period from 1920 to 1924. The negative savings reduced the final estimate of income and hence pushed up the ratio of wages to income.

**Table 15.18**     **Labor's Factor Share, Average for Quinquennial Periods, 1875–1924 for the Canadian Railway Sector**

| Period (1) | Share (2) | Period (3) | Share (4) |
|---|---|---|---|
| 1875–79 | 0.68 | 1900–1904 | 0.57 |
| 1880–84 | 0.68 | 1905–09 | 0.60 |
| 1885–89 | 0.60 | 1910–14 | 0.60 |
| 1890–94 | 0.57 | 1915–19 | 0.69 |
| 1895–99 | 0.50 | 1920–24 | 0.87[a] |

*Sources:* Income originating, table 15.8; total wages and salaries, table 15.2

[a]If income originating in the railway sector is measured excluding saving (see text), this ratio becomes 0.73.

The ratios shown in table 15.18 suggest that the trend in labor's share was quite different between the nineteenth and the twentieth centuries. During the former, the share fell steadily, while during the first 3 decades of the century it rose. This type of break can be observed on an aggregate basis for the United States. Moses Abramovitz and Paul David (1973, table 2) show labor's share dropping steadily from 1800 to 1900 and then rising between 1900 and 1969.

The neoclassical explanation is that the bias of technical change tended to favor capital from 1875 to 1900 (taking into account the supply of investment funds and the elasticity of substitution). On the other hand, during the twentieth century the reverse is suggested. If, then, we assume, as is usually the case, that the elasticity of substitution between capital and labor is less than one and the capital/output ratio rises sharply (as was probably the case during part of the period), one might expect to find labor's share rising. Unfortunately, as we saw in table 15.8, the incremental capital/output ratio fell during the last decade of our period. It is obvious that we need to supplement the neoclassical explanation with an alternative hypothesis.

One suggested alternative would be a market-power approach.[12] The argument here is that as railroad unions became more powerful they increased labor's share of total income, that is, the railroad companies lost some of their monopsony power in the labor market. In this type of explanation it is necessary as well to understand conditions in the product market. If, as we suggested earlier, service rates on the railroad were regulated and could not be increased to offset the rise in wage rates, then labor's share would increase.

The neoclassical and market-power approaches are presented here more as interesting alternatives than as definitive explanations, although the fact that both may play a role either sequentially or simultaneously seems to be a line worth exploring. One benefit of a long-term approach in studying the phenomenon of sectoral or national growth is that it allows us to escape the strictures of believing that a single approach will suffice in what is inherently a complex process.

# Appendix

**Table 15.A.1**    **Average Freight and Passenger Rates per Mile, Canadian Railways, Annually, 1875–1926 (Cents per Mile)**

| Year | Passenger Rate | Freight Rate | Year | Passenger Rate | Freight Rate | Year | Passenger Rate | Freight Rate |
|------|------|------|------|------|------|------|------|------|
| 1875 | 2.50 | 3.50 | 1891 | 2.45 | 1.40 | 1907 | 1.91 | 0.81 |
| 1876 | 2.46 | 3.40 | 1892 | 2.45 | 1.30 | 1908 | 1.92 | 0.72 |
| 1877 | 2.50 | 3.20 | 1893 | 2.40 | 1.20 | 1909 | 1.92 | 0.73 |
| 1878 | 2.50 | 3.00 | 1894 | 2.40 | 1.10 | 1910 | 1.87 | 0.74 |
| 1879 | 2.50 | 2.80 | 1895 | 2.35 | 1.00 | 1911 | 1.94 | 0.78 |
| 1880 | 2.50 | 2.60 | 1896 | 2.30 | 1.00 | 1912 | 1.94 | 0.76 |
| 1881 | 2.50 | 2.40 | 1897 | 2.25 | 0.95 | 1913 | 1.97 | 0.76 |
| 1882 | 2.50 | 2.30 | 1898 | 2.20 | 0.95 | 1914 | 2.01 | 0.74 |
| 1883 | 2.50 | 2.20 | 1899 | 2.15 | 0.95 | 1915 | 2.02 | 0.75 |
| 1884 | 2.50 | 2.10 | 1900 | 2.10 | 0.90 | 1916 | 1.95 | 0.65 |
| 1885 | 2.50 | 2.00 | 1901 | 2.05 | 0.90 | 1917 | 1.95 | 0.65 |
| 1886 | 2.50 | 1.90 | 1902 | 2.00 | 0.90 | 1918 | 2.12 | 0.74 |
| 1887 | 2.50 | 1.80 | 1903 | 1.95 | 0.90 | 1919 | 2.59 | 0.98 |
| 1888 | 2.50 | 1.70 | 1904 | 1.90 | 0.85 | 1920 | 2.94 | 1.07 |
| 1889 | 2.50 | 1.60 | 1905 | 1.90 | 0.85 | 1921 | 3.04 | 1.20 |
| 1890 | 2.50 | 1.50 | 1906 | 1.90 | 0.85 | 1922 | 2.82 | 1.04 |
|      |      |      |      |      |      | 1923 | 2.76 | 0.99 |
|      |      |      |      |      |      | 1924 | 2.79 | 1.02 |
|      |      |      |      |      |      | 1925 | 2.69 | 1.01 |
|      |      |      |      |      |      | 1926 | 2.71 | 1.04 |

*Sources and methods:* 1875–1910, see text; 1911–26, "Railway Statistics," Department of Railways, and Canals; after 1919, Dominion Bureau of Statistics.

# Notes

1. The interested reader is referred to such standard texts as Easterbrook and Aitken (1956); Marr and Paterson (1980), chap. 10; and Pomfret (1981), pp. 99–107.
2. Similar estimates to those for the railway industry were made for the electric railways, water transport, road transport, telephone, and telegraph industries.
3. A complete description of the sources and assessment of railway statistics can be found in Urquhart and Buckley (1965), pp. 516 ff.
4. For a parallel growth pattern, although starting earlier, see Fishlow (1966), p. 628.
5. Quoted by Fishlow (1966), p. 583.
6. Fishlow (1965), esp. chap. 2, and Fogel (1964), chaps. 1–3.
7. For a discussion of this point, see Plumptre (1937).
8. For a review of whether the CPR did or did not receive excessive government subsidies, see George (1968).
9. For a full discussion on the application of the Fishlow method to the Canadian case, see A. Green (mimeographed).
10. Urquhart and Buckley (1965), ser. 40 and 165, p. 305.
11. See M. C. Urquhart's piece in this volume.

12. For a discussion of market power in explaining factor share trends, see Matthews et al. (1982), pp. 194–97.

## Comment    Albert Fishlow

There are three dimensions to the research reported here by Alan Green on the evolution of the Canadian railway sector from 1871 to 1926. The first is an estimate of annual income originating as a component of M. C. Urquhart's estimates of national income reported elsewhere in this volume. The second is determination of trend rates of increase in factor productivity over the same period. Last, but not least, is the use of these quantitative results to reassess generalizations about the performance of the Canadian railway sector in the early twentieth century. As is evident, this is an ambitious paper that a brief comment cannot do full justice. I shall be able to touch only lightly on these three subjects.

The principal tasks in estimating income originating are to calculate wages and salaries before 1907 and interest and dividends before 1911. Green is able to exploit the availability of relatively accurate annual data on railway operating expenses to ascertain the wage and salary totals. For interest and dividends he takes advantage of the concentration of the Canadian railway system to focus on large units like the Canadian Pacific and Grand Trunk, for which *Poor's Manual* provides detailed financial information.

His procedures are reasonable. The results for interest and dividends, in particular, are likely to be quite accurate. Residual profits are then obtained from the annual series on operating revenue. They are sensitive to variability in fixed charges and dividend policy; in particular, the decision of the Canadian government to change accounting practice in 1923 for the components of the Canadian National Railway system reallocates income between interest and residual profits.

The wages and salaries component is the largest. It is basically derived by extrapolation on the operating expense series. Despite Green's attempt to allow for differences in the relative importance of maintenance of way, the ratio of wages and salaries is a virtual constant: .566 between 1890 and 1906 with a standard deviation of only .003. Yet the actual ratio in the period 1907–13 is much more variable. The average is .598 with a standard deviation of .038. Green's lapse is to overstate the stability of the observed relationship and hence to exaggerate the reliability of the annual variations. For trend purposes the order of

Albert Fishlow is professor of economics at the University of California, Berkeley.

magnitudes will clearly serve, but it is of course the annual income originating that one wants.

An alternative procedure might be to start from operating expenses and seek to estimate material purchases. Train mileage is available on an annual basis and might serve as a measure of demand; some of the price indexes for materials later used to deflate capital formation might be of use. The advantage of approaching the problem from this other side would be an independent estimate that could provide some indication of the likely range of error.

The current income estimates are the easiest because of the annual aggregates already available. The physical output and input measures that occupy much of Green's efforts, and which are necessary for calculation of productivity change, are harder to come by.

For output Green utilizes freight and passenger receipts deflated by average fares estimated from rate schedules. He also might have applied a variant of the method he had earlier used for interest and dividends. By focusing on the largest lines, for which direct information was more readily available, he might have narrowed the degree of estimation considerably. At the least, such an alternative could have supplemented the series on ton miles and passenger miles actually constructed. The composite output series suffers from the defect of its weighting: the absolutes (rather than relatives) seem to be weighted by current ratios of freight and passenger revenues to total receipts. That yields an inconsistent index. Because the long-term physical trends dominate, the quantitative consequences over long intervals are not great. But readers fortunately can construct their own output indexes, either Paasche or Laspayres, because Green provides the necessary freight and passenger rates.

More serious questions arise with regard to the labor input series. Green derives his estimates by use of a constant ratio of employees to track mileage, but with an adjustment for a larger ratio during periods of construction. Once again, and even more so, he overstates the adequacy of the relationship: the correlation between employment and track in operation in the period 1907–19 when both are known is only .49 and with an elasticity of .38. This is hardly testimony in favor of "a remarkably stable ratio." Moreover, his variable adjustments seem arbitrary: in 1892 he applies a factor of 5; in 1893, 4.5; in 1894, 4. The increments in track in operation are respectively 726, 441, and 622, and estimated real investment is not very different either. It may have been that with falling revenues in 1894, employment was reduced. On the other hand, we are told that the Grand Trunk in *1891 and 1892* "had cut wages to the point where any further reductions would lead to strikes, and it had laid off men," (Currie 1957, p. 363). Green's employment cycle, and it is considerable, is apparently of his own creation.

For the estimation of labor input, other methods can be pursued. For purposes of long-term trend, for example, one might begin with the wage and salary series and deflate by an average annual wage to derive an employment total. Average remuneration in manufactures is available on a decennial basis from 1870 on. In 1910 the average railway wage was about 17% larger. Assuming the same differential earlier permits an estimate for employment in 1880, 1890, and 1900. The results differ from Green's series by about 10% in the first 2 years, and in the opposite direction. In 1890 employment was less than 60,000, and in 1880 more than 35,000. The implication is that productivity grew more rapidly between 1880 and 1890, and less rapidly in the subsequent decade, than Green's estimates suggest. For annual variation, the train mileage series seems a better indicator of the level of employment than sheer track mileage: maintenance as well as operating requirements are more dependent on intensity of use than extension. For the later period, the relationship with train mileage is quite more regular; the $R^2$ is .67 compared with .24 for track mileage.

To the information on labor input, Green adds estimates of fuel and capital inputs in order to calculate total factor productivity. For the former, Green uses the consumption per locomotive mile on the Intercolonial Railroad extended by the aggregate number of engine miles. Comparison with comparable United States estimates makes suspect the 1900 value, and hence the calculations of productivity increase between 1890–1900 and 1900–1910. One also would have liked some attention to later variance among different lines: fuel use depended on locomotive weight and size of trains.

Because railroads are so capital intensive, the capital input is important. There are two problems. One is an estimate of the capital stock; the other is an estimate of capital input in circumstances of deliberate construction ahead of demand. Green relies on a gross investment series published elsewhere to construct a net capital stock series. It is difficult to judge the validity of the procedures used to derive real investment in the absence of information in the proximate source. It is obviously encouraging to see a rough correspondence between rates of change of the capital stock series and of the mileage and equipment series assembled by Green. But caution is still indicated. Crude trends are undoubtedly right, but the purpose is finer calculation.

Nor do the stock series resolve the question of how to calculate capital inputs. Excess capacity built into a system will underestimate the efficiency with which current inputs are used, and overestimate productivity increases associated with technological change. For some purposes, one wants to single out the consequences of greater utilization; to do so, one might recalculate the productivity index by assuming an actual constant capital/output ratio and noting the difference. Despite Green's later interest in the question of construction ahead of demand and the increase in output after 1910, he does not do so. Had he, he would have found that utilization of the excess capacity (so measured) between 1900 and 1920 explains about one-fourth of the recorded total productivity increase.

Green also might have related his calculated productivity results to the trend decline in real freight rates. Then he would have noted that real freight rates fell less than productivity increased in the 1890s (even after allowance for changed labor and fuel inputs) but much more in the decade between 1910 and 1920. In the former case, it opened opportunity for greater return; in the latter, railways were being relatively taxed.

This last finding is very much in the spirit of Green's revisionism of the conventional story of Canadian railway nationalization during the First World War: "The reason given for the government takeover was that the supply of railroad services exceeded demand, forcing down returns and creating the potential for bankruptcy and major dislocations in the Canadian economy. . . . Was this really the case? The evidence seems to suggest that the answer is no."

But Green may be overstating his case and misapplying the productivity results. There are three reasons.

First, the entire system was not nationalized. The Canadian Pacific, paying handsome dividends, remained in private hands. Thus it is necessary to disaggregate the physical performance of Canadian railways. When one does, it is clear that the earlier completed line of the Canadian Pacific was a prime contributor to the great increase in railroad freight carriage rather than only the two new transcontinentals. Between 1910 and 1916 the number of bushels transported on the Canadian Pacific increased from 113 million to 277 million, proportionately more rapidly than the increase in total ton mileage (Innis 1971, p. 159).

Second, rates of change may be in the right direction without speaking to absolute levels of productivity. Here Green starts out correctly to compare the United States and Canadian levels but does not fully follow through. Because Canadian transcontinental rates were influenced by United States charges, the nexus is a critical one. Despite lower levels of productivity, partially explained by lesser revenues per mile of track and more frequent empty back hauls, Canadian freight revenues per ton mile fell from 60% more than the American in 1890 to equality in 1910. That is an important part of the story of eventual nationalization. The duplication of facilities by constructing parallel trackage as occurred after 1900 certainly did not help. Private gain seemed to call for monopolizing through haulage on a single system, but the systemic effect was overinvestment.

Third, productivity calculations are physical rather than financial. Nationalization occurred because, despite extensive governmental assistance, the Canadian Northern and the Grand Trunk Pacific coud not earn enough to meet even their fixed obligations. That is related to the cost of construction and capitalization, as well as to the expenses of operation. Green's point about regulation is obviously well taken. Keeping rates low, as was done, meant losses. But note that rates were also constrained by the competition of the profitable Canadian Pacific and could not be set arbitrarily.

Green's challenge to conventional wisdom on the nationalization issue thus is not decisive. His productivity calculations, particularly extended to absolute comparisons with the United States and disaggregated, are an important and new element in the discussion. And he is surely right to emphasize the developmental quality of Canadian railway investment.

In sum, Alan Green has left us all in his debt by his efforts. These new data, revised, extended, and used with care, permit new questions to be posed and examined. He has himself raised many, and in a fruitful and challenging way. In the last analysis, the purpose of quantitative research is not the numbers per se, but the substantive issues they illuminate.

# References

Abramovitz, Moses, and David, Paul. 1973. Reinterpreting economic growth: Parables and realities. *American Economic Review* 63 (May): 428–39.

Buckley, K. A. H. 1962. Capital formation in railway transport and telegraphs in Canada, 1850 to 1930. Paper presented to the Canadian Political Science Association Conference on Statistics, June.

Currie, A. W. 1957. *The Grand Trunk Railway of Canada.* Toronto: University of Toronto Press.

Easterbrook, W. T., and Aitken, Hugh. 1956. *Canadian economic history.* Toronto: Macmillan.

Fishlow, Albert. 1965. *American railroads and the transformation of the ante-bellum economy.* Cambridge: Harvard University Press.

———. 1966. Productivity and technological change in the railroad sector, 1840–1910. In *Output, employment and productivity in the United States after 1800,* ed. Dorothy S. Brady. Studies in Income and Wealth, vol. 30. New York: National Bureau of Economic Research.

Fogel, R. W. 1964. *Railroads and American economic growth.* Baltimore: Johns Hopkins Press.

George, Peter. 1968. Rates of return in railway investment and implications for government subsidization of the Canadian Pacific Railway. *Canadian Journal of Economics* 1 (November): 740–62.

Green, Alan. The measurement of net income originating in the transportation and public utilities sector. Mimeographed, Queen's University, Department of Economics.

Hood, W. C. and Scott, A. 1957. *Output, labour and capital in the Canadian economy.* Report prepared by the Royal Commission on Canada's Economic Prospects. Ottawa.

Innis, Harold A. 1923. *A history of the Canadian Pacific Railway.* Toronto: University of Toronto Press, reissued 1971.

Lithwick, N. H. 1967. *Economic growth in Canada.* Toronto: University of Toronto Press.

Marr, W. and Paterson, D. 1980. *Canada: An economic history.* Toronto: Macmillan.

Matthews; R. C. O.; Feinstein, C. A.; and Odling-Smee, J. C. 1982. *British economic growth, 1856–1973.* Stanford, Calif.: Stanford University Press.

Plumptre, A. F. W. 1937. The nature of economic development in the British dominions. *Canadian Journal of Economics and Political Science* 3 (November): 489–507.

Pomfret, R. 1981. *The economic development of Canada.* Toronto: Methuen.

Statistics Canada. *Fixed capital flows and stocks, 1926–1978.* Ottawa, 1978. Cat. 13–568.

Ulmer, M. J. 1960. *Capital in transportation, communications and public utilities: Its formation and financing.* Princeton: Princeton University Press (for NBER).

Urquhart, M. C., and Buckley, K. A. H. 1965. *Historical statistics of Canada.* Toronto: Macmillan.

# 16    Long-Term Trends in State and Local Finance: Sources and Uses of Funds in North Carolina, 1800–1977

Richard Sylla

Since "statistical" information in an etymological sense is information about "state" affairs, it is surprising that one of the yawning gaps in the quantitative record of United States history is detailed, year-by-year information on the finances of state and local governments. The gap is not a great one for the twentieth century. The bicentennial edition of *Historical Statistics of the United States* (United States Bureau of the Census 1975) contains 197 series under the heading "State and local government finances, 1902–1970." None of these is an annual time series covering the whole period, but the primary information to construct such series on a sound footing appears to be available, and indeed, scholars have used such information to explore quantitatively the changing roles of government activity and trends in government finance at all levels in the twentieth century. The NBER-sponsored studies of Simon Kuznets (1946, 1961), Solomon Fabricant (1952), M. Slade Kendrick (1955), John M. Firestone (1960), Morris A. Copeland (1961), and John W. Kendrick (1961), among others, come readily to mind. The emphasis of these studies was more on national totals and less on state and regional detail.

For the period of our history before the twentieth century, both existing comprehensive data and the sources from which better estimates might be derived are far less satisfactory. The 1890 and 1880

Richard Sylla is professor of economics and business at North Carolina State University and a research associate of the National Bureau of Economic Research. I thank Marilyn Miller Dutton, expert historian and master of archival searching, for her assistance in this research, Robert W. Fogel for support under the NBER program on the Development of the American Economy, Cindy Olsen for secretarial assistance, and Ellen Berry for help with data processing. At particular times and on particular questions Judy Gregory, Erin Newton, Ann Phillips, Marcus Phillips, James A. Seagraves, and Carol Smith were also of great assistance.

**819**

censuses contain extensive and detailed information on receipts, expenditures, and debts for states, counties, and cities and towns above specified levels of population. The 1870 census contains taxation and debt information but nothing on expenditures or nontax receipts. The 1850 and 1860 censuses each have a page on taxation, but the data appear to be understated as well as incomplete in coverage. Before 1850 there is essentially no comprehensive information on state and local finance in the United States.

During the first three decades of this century there was considerable interest among scholars in state and local finance, and a number of state studies were published. (See Davis and Legler [1966] for a list of the studies.) These and related but unpublished studies vary considerably in periods covered, levels of analysis, and quantitative detail, but they offer much guidance and encouragement to anyone going at the subject today. In the 1940s and 1950s, several provocative studies of the role of particular state governments in antebellum economic development attracted much attention (e.g., Handlin and Handlin 1947; Hartz 1948; Heath 1954). These studies were interested in government as regulator and promoter, and—if anything—they contain less quantitative information than the state studies done earlier in the century.

A concern for comprehensive quantitative information on nineteenth-century public finance surfaced in the 1960s in two studies, one by Lance Davis and John Legler (1966) and the other by Charles Holt (1970). Davis and Legler presented annual per capita state receipt and expenditure data, and—implicitly—annual per capita local government receipts for nine regions of the United States for the period 1815–1900. For the state estimates by region, approximately 70% of the underlying individual state data were observations taken from published reports and 30% were estimates based on regression estimates and regional averages assigned to individual states. Annual local receipts by region were estimates derived from regressions of local tax receipts on state receipts and other variables drawn from the six census-year studies 1850 through 1902. Total local receipts were obtained by multiplying local tax receipts by a factor of 1.44, the average ratio of local receipts to local tax receipts in the 1902 census. The estimates of local receipts were not presented by Davis and Legler; rather, they were embedded in annual per capita estimates by region of federal, state, and local receipts. Because of the level of aggregation, the estimates presented by Davis and Legler cannot be compared with existing data for individual states at either the state or local levels of government.

Charles Holt's study, a Ph.D. dissertation directed by Lance Davis, deals only with state receipts and expenditures for the period 1820–1902. National and regional totals and totals per capita, in both current and constant dollars, are presented in the form annual averages for overlapping decades. Holt also presents data on the composition of receipts and expenditures—sources and uses of funds—in a similar form. The underlying estimates are based on blowing up a sample containing 57% of the possible state-year observations by means of several formulas for deriving national and regional totals from partial information. The proportion of sample to total possible observations increased over time; the estimates for the earlier years of the period are based on a much smaller observational base than are those for the later years when the sample is much more complete.

The Davis-Legler and Holt studies make promising starts on the problem of developing comprehensive data on state and local finance for the nineteenth century. Their main weakness—as the writers freely acknowledge—is that they make only limited use of the information that is known to be, or likely will be found to be, available in both the published reports and the archives of state and local governments. They point to a large research agenda: the systematic construction, based on existing state and local records, of quantitative information on public finance from the earliest days of the nation. The historical and contemporary questions that such information would help us to answer are so numerous and obvious that an attempt to list them here would be tedious; indeed, they are the questions of the whole literature of public finance and of other literatures as well.

My purpose here is to make a start on the research agenda mentioned above by presenting a quantitative history of state and local finance in North Carolina. Most of the attention is focused on the period 1801–1930. Information of the kind I am seeking for years before 1801 is sparse indeed, and difficult to interpret because the handwritten accounts are given in several currencies. Information for the period after 1930 is abundant, readily available, and merits only summary treatment here. For the period of focus, I have virtually complete annual data on state receipts and disbursements, and fairly complete (though not annual) information on state debt. The state data are the basis for estimates in some detail of the sources and uses of funds.

In the local area, I have found data on the tax revenues of counties—by far the most important units of local government in North Carolina—from 1856 to 1930, and I have developed annual estimates of county tax revenues that I believe to be fairly accurate for determining levels and trends for the period 1801–55. Tables 16.A.1 and 16.A.2 present the state and county series and describe their construction as well as the underlying data sources. Cities, towns, and other minor civil divisions were not very important in North Carolina, a "rural" state, until late in the nineteenth century; I use the census data to establish this point and to provide details on municipal finance at census intervals from 1850 to 1930. Table 16.A.3 continues the state series to 1977 and presents a local (county, municipal, and district) tax revenue series for the years 1930–77.

## 16.1  North Carolina Public Finance, 1790–1930: Levels and Trends

Our searches uncovered only scattered data on state and local finance during the 1790s. A printed report from the Committee on Finance to the state House of Commons, dated December 15, 1790, gave the total of money in the treasury on November 1, 1790, as £49,355 and the Civil List (salaries of state officials and other "incidental expenses of government of every kind") for the year 1791 as £20,740, of which the largest single items were £12,000 for the legislature and £3,200 for judges of superior courts. (The North Carolina pound was reckoned as $2.50 before 1800, and $2.00 after that date.) In the report, the budgetary subcommittee recommended as follows, indicating, incidentally, the nature of taxation in the state for much of the antebellum era: "From the large sums of money due the public, and from the present wealth of the treasury, the subcommittee are led to propose a poll tax of two shillings only, and a land tax of eight pence on every hundred acres, and a tax of two shillings on every hundred pounds value of town property in this state, which in their opinion, with the other established taxes in aid of the revenue, will be fully adequate to the expenses of the year 1791."

A report of the 4th United States Congress, 2d Session, dated December 14, 1796, discussed the tax systems of the several states and estimated, from tax base, tax rate, and land sales data, that the state's revenue would be about £18,417 and that expenses were £15,000–£20,000 (*American State Papers* 1832, pp. 418 ff.). The state debt, consisting mostly of paper bills of credit, was given as approximately £150,000, and the report added, "the amount of the county taxes is supposed to be nearly the same, on an average, as the annual state tax."

Finally, we have a detailed and complete printed list of expenditures for the fiscal year 1798 (November 1, 1797–October 30, 1798). The total came to £27,146. Two years later, according to a contemporary, Archibald Debow Murphey (see Appendix), state expenses were $48,419, or about £24,000 with the North Carolina pound reckoned as $2.00.

The annual estimates of state receipts and disbursements and county tax receipts begin with the year 1801. Figures 16.1–16.4 plot the annual data on receipts (in logarithmic transformation) in current and constant dollars. (State disbursements are not plotted in fig. 16.1 and 16.3; the comprehensive nature of the state receipt and disbursement concepts yields a near identity of the two series in semilog plots.) The decade totals for 1801–10 to 1921–30, aggregate and per capita, in current

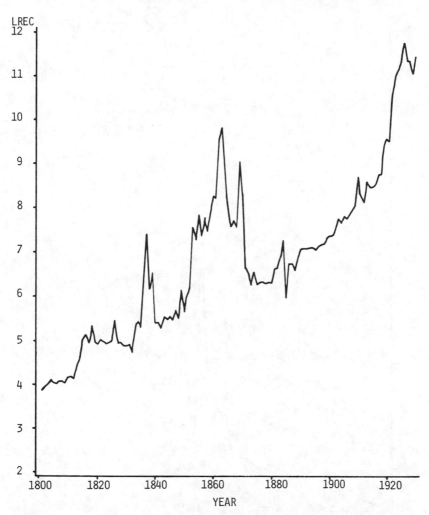

**Fig. 16.1**        State receipts in current dollars, 1801–1930. LREC is the
                     natural logarithm of state receipts, as given in table 16.A.1.

dollars are presented in table 16.1, along with the state and county
shares (cols. 9 and 10). Constant dollar estimates (1910–14 = 100) are
in table 16.2. I should emphasize that these data are decade totals; the
$1.30 of state spending per capita for 1801–10 in table 16.1, for example,
implies that on average the state spent $0.13 per person per year in
that decade.

The revenue share data in columns 9 and 10 of table 16.1 indicate
that in most decades the counties surpassed the state in collections;
since the county data are for tax revenues only whereas the state data

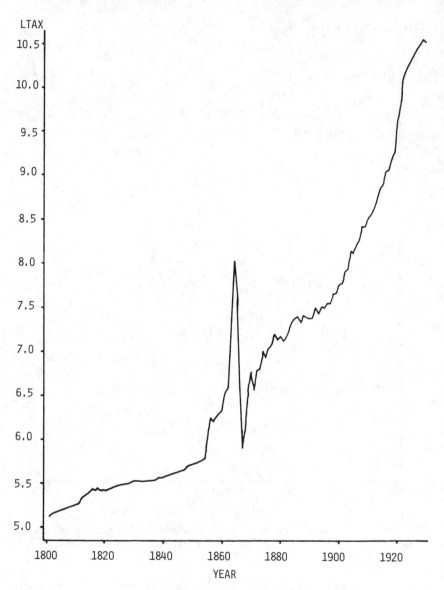

**Fig. 16.2**    County tax Revenue in current dollars, 1801–1930. LTAX is
the natural logarithm of county tax revenue, as given in table
16.A.2.

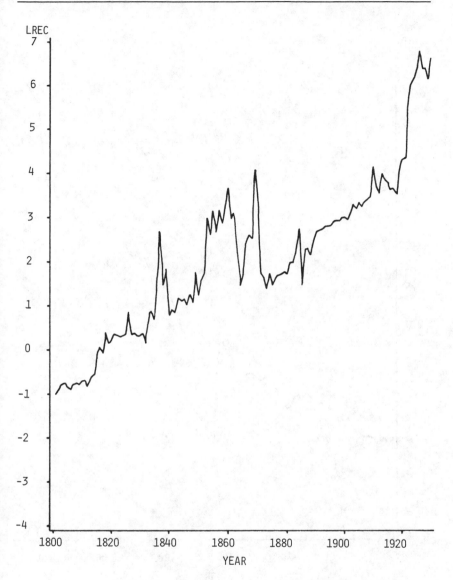

**Fig. 16.3**    State receipts in constant (1910–14 = 100) dollars, 1801–1930. LREC is the natural logarithm of state receipts deflated by the Warren-Pearson wholesale price index.

are for all revenues from whatever source, the greater relative importance of the counties in state and local finance in most decades seems firmly established. The exceptions are the 1830s when the federal government made a large transfer of surplus revenue to the state, the 1850s when the state was engaged in a large-scale program of railroad con-

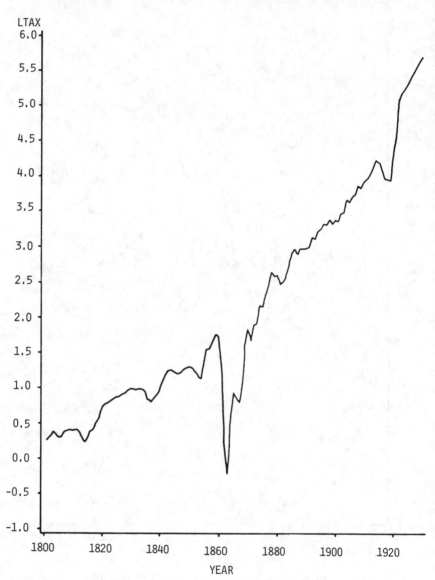

**Fig. 16.4**    County tax revenue in constant (1910–14 = 100) dollars, 1801–1930. LTAX is the natural logarithm of county tax receipts deflated by the Warren-Pearson wholesale price index.

struction, the 1860s when the state was at war, and the 1920s when North Carolina became "the good roads state" with a massive highway construction program under state auspices.

Real rates of growth of state and local government, total and per capita, may be seen in table 16.3. Given the comprehensive nature of

**Table 16.1** State Disbursements and Receipts and County Tax Receipts, Total and per Capita, by Decade, 1801–10 to 1921–30 (in Thousands of Current Dollars for Aggregates and in Dollars per Capita)

| Decade | State Disbursements (1) | State Receipts (2) | County Tax Receipts (3) | (2) + (3) (4) | (1) ÷ Pop. (5) | (2) ÷ Pop. (6) | (3) ÷ Pop. (7) | (4) ÷ Pop. (8) | (2) ÷ (4) (9) | (3) ÷ (4) (10) |
|---|---|---|---|---|---|---|---|---|---|---|
| 1801–10 | 670 | 564 | 1,804 | 2,368 | 1.30 | 1.07 | 2.73 | 3.80 | .24 | .76 |
| 1811–20 | 1,168 | 1,265 | 2,185 | 3,450 | 1.96 | 2.12 | 2.52 | 4.64 | .37 | .63 |
| 1821–30 | 1,398 | 1,507 | 2,393 | 3,900 | 2.03 | 2.19 | 3.51 | 5.70 | .39 | .61 |
| 1831–40 | 4,565 | 4,550 | 2,542 | 7,092 | 6.11 | 6.09 | 3.34 | 9.43 | .64 | .36 |
| 1841–50 | 2,749 | 2,728 | 2,837 | 5,565 | 3.39 | 3.36 | 4.21 | 7.57 | .49 | .51 |
| 1851–60 | 18,267 | 19,134 | 4,327 | 23,461 | 20.01 | 20.55 | 4.74 | 25.29 | .82 | .18 |
| 1861–70 | 59,087[a] | 61,978[a] | 7,627[b] | 69,605 | 57.26[a] | 60.06[a] | 2.09[b] | 62.15 | .91 | .09 |
| 1871–80 | 6,164 | 6,064 | 10,849 | 16,913 | 4.99 | 4.91 | 7.70 | 12.61 | .36 | .64 |
| 1881–90 | 8,986 | 8,985 | 15,105 | 24,090 | 5.95 | 5.95 | 11.00 | 16.95 | .37 | .63 |
| 1891–1900 | 13,246 | 13,178 | 19,170 | 32,348 | 7.54 | 7.50 | 14.75 | 22.25 | .31 | .59 |
| 1901–10 | 28,334 | 28,092 | 36,391 | 64,483 | 13.82 | 13.70 | 19.51 | 33.21 | .44 | .56 |
| 1911–20 | 64,495 | 67,401 | 88,235 | 155,636 | 27.07 | 28.28 | 26.26 | 54.54 | .43 | .57 |
| 1921–30 | 722,241 | 729,824 | 305,821 | 1,035,645 | 252.09 | 251.25 | 75.17 | 326.42 | .70 | .30 |

*Note:* For per capita estimates, I used the arithmetic mean of the state's population at the beginning and end of each decade.

[a] Nine years; no data for 1865.

[b] Seven years; no data for 1864, 1865, and 1869, and incomplete data for 1867, 1868, and 1870 when many counties did not report.

Table 16.2    State Disbursements and Receipts and County Tax Receipts, Total and per Capita, by Decade, 1801–10 to 1921–30
(in Thousands of Constant Dollars of 1910–14 for Aggregates, and in Dollars per Capita)

| Decade | State Disbursements (1) | State Receipts (2) | County Tax Receipts (3) | (2) + (3) (4) | (1) ÷ Pop. (5) | (2) ÷ Pop. (6) | (3) ÷ Pop. (7) | (4) ÷ Pop. (8) |
|---|---|---|---|---|---|---|---|---|
| 1801–10 | 523 | 441 | 1,409 | 1,850 | 1.01 | 0.86 | 2.73 | 3.59 |
| 1811–20 | 806 | 872 | 1,507 | 2,379 | 1.35 | 1.46 | 2.52 | 3.98 |
| 1821–30 | 1,412 | 1,522 | 2,417 | 3,939 | 2.05 | 2.21 | 3.51 | 5.72 |
| 1831–40 | 4,475 | 4,461 | 2,492 | 6,953 | 6.00 | 5.98 | 3.34 | 9.32 |
| 1841–50 | 3,312 | 3,287 | 3,418 | 6,705 | 4.08 | 4.05 | 4.21 | 8.26 |
| 1851–60 | 19,007 | 19,524 | 4,415 | 23,939 | 20.42 | 20.97 | 4.74 | 25.71 |
| 1861–70 | 20,592 | 21,560 | 2,156 | 23,716 | 19.95 | 20.89 | 2.07 | 22.96 |
| 1871–80 | 5,407 | 5,319 | 9,517 | 14,836 | 4.38 | 4.30 | 7.70 | 12.00 |
| 1881–90 | 9,875 | 9,874 | 16,599 | 26,477 | 6.54 | 6.54 | 11.00 | 17.54 |
| 1891–1900 | 17,900 | 17,808 | 25,905 | 43,713 | 10.19 | 10.14 | 14.75 | 24.89 |
| 1901–10 | 31,136 | 30,870 | 39,990 | 70,860 | 15.19 | 15.06 | 19.51 | 34.57 |
| 1911–20 | 45,741 | 47,802 | 62,578 | 110,380 | 19.19 | 20.06 | 26.26 | 46.32 |
| 1921–30 | 508,620 | 513,961 | 215,367 | 729,328 | 177.53 | 179.39 | 75.17 | 254.56 |

*Notes:* See the notes to table 16.1. The price deflator, with one exception, is based on the Warren-Pearson wholesale price index. See Warren and Pearson 1932, pp. 11–14. The exception is the Civil War period 1861–65 when I substituted an index based on Lerner's general price index of the eastern section of the Confederacy; see Lerner 1955, table 2.

Table 16.3    Real Growth Rates per Year of Receipts: Selected Periods, 1801–10 to 1921–30 (% per year)

| Decades | Real State Receipts | Real County Tax Receipts | Real State and County Receipts | Real State Receipts per Capita | Real County Tax Receipts per Capita | Real State and County Receipts per Capita |
|---|---|---|---|---|---|---|
| 1801–10/1811–20 | 6.82 | 0.67 | 2.52 | 5.29 | −0.80 | 1.03 |
| 1811–20/1821–30 | 5.57 | 4.72 | 5.04 | 4.15 | 3.31 | 3.63 |
| 1821–30/1831–40 | 10.75 | 0.31 | 5.68 | 9.95 | −0.50 | 4.88 |
| 1831–40/1841–50 | −3.05 | 3.16 | −3.63 | −3.90 | 2.32 | −1.21 |
| 1841–50/1851–60 | 17.82 | 2.56 | 12.73 | 16.44 | 1.19 | 11.36 |
| 1851–60/1861–70 | 0.99 | NMF[a] | −0.09 | −0.04 | NMF[a] | −1.13 |
| 1861–70/1871–80 | −14.00 | NMF[a] | −4.69 | −15.81 | NMF[a] | −6.49 |
| 1871–80/1881–90 | 6.19 | 5.56 | 5.79 | 4.19 | 3.57 | 3.80 |
| 1881–90/1891–1900 | 5.90 | 4.45 | 5.02 | 4.39 | 2.93 | 3.50 |
| 1891–1900/1901–10 | 5.50 | 4.34 | 4.83 | 3.96 | 2.80 | 3.29 |
| 1901–10/1911–20 | 4.37 | 4.48 | 4.43 | 2.87 | 2.97 | 2.93 |
| 1911–20/1921–30 | 23.75 | 12.36 | 18.88 | 21.91 | 10.52 | 17.04 |
| 1801–10/1841–50 | 5.02 | 2.22 | 3.22 | 3.87 | 1.08 | 2.08 |
| 1801–10/1851–60 | 7.58 | 2.28 | 5.12 | 6.39 | 1.10 | 3.94 |
| 1871–80/1910–20 | 5.49 | 4.71 | 5.02 | 3.85 | 3.07 | 3.38 |
| 1871–80/1921–30 | 9.14 | 6.24 | 7.79 | 7.46 | 4.56 | 6.11 |
| 1801–10/1871–80 | 3.56 | 2.73 | 2.97 | 2.30 | 1.48 | 1.72 |
| 1851–60/1921–30 | 4.67 | 5.55 | 4.88 | 3.06 | 3.95 | 3.28 |
| 1801–10/1891–1900 | 4.11 | 3.23 | 3.51 | 2.74 | 1.87 | 2.15 |
| 1801–10/1901–10 | 4.24 | 3.35 | 3.64 | 2.86 | 1.97 | 2.26 |
| 1801–10/1911–20 | 4.26 | 3.45 | 3.72 | 2.86 | 2.06 | 2.32 |
| 1801–10/1921–30 | 5.88 | 4.19 | 4.98 | 4.45 | 2.76 | 3.55 |
| 1851–60/1871–80[b] | | 3.84 | | | 2.43 | |

[a]The county data are so incomplete for the 1860s that no meaningful rates of growth can be calculated.
[b]The last row of the table gives the county rates of growth for 1851–60 to 1871–80.

the data on state disbursements and receipts, either series would yield approximately the same growth rates for any period, and so only the state receipts have been utilized in the table. If there is any bias in the growth rates, it would be in ones that involve the antebellum county data, which are my estimates rather than reported data. The bias, if there is one, is likely in the direction of overstating county tax revenues early in the nineteenth century. Such a bias would mean that growth rates based on these data are too low, and, indeed, the antebellum growth rates for the state exceed those for the counties by a good margin. There are historical reasons to account for such a pattern, however, and so I do not consider the bias to be self-evident. The counties did not get a massive gift from the federal government in the 1830s, and they did not engage in large internal improvement projects; moreover, the same relationship of state and county growth rates shows in the postbellum period when the data are reported, not estimated.

Because of the massive state-financed improvement projects of the 1850s (mainly railroads) and the 1920s (mainly highways), I consider the growth rates for 1801–10 to 1841–50 and 1871–80 to 1911–20 to be more representative of "average" antebellum and postbellum experience than the rates ending with the "improvement" decades. Similarly, the rates for 1801–10 to 1871–80, both decades in which governments were relatively inactive, probably reflect the long-term trend of state and local activity for the first three-fourths of the century more accurately than do the rates for any of the other periods.

What do the growth rates indicate? North Carolina is seldom described as a state known for its vigorous, dynamic government and economy in the nineteenth century. An opposite representation is indeed far more common. Yet North Carolina government, apart from some decadal fluctuations that have clear historical explanations, shows a steady if undramatic long-term expansion in real terms. The lowest per capita annual rate of growth of state and combined county revenues for any of the long-term (not decade-to-decade) periods shown in table 16.3 is 1.72% from the first to the eighth decades of the century. Since this rate is near or above most estimates of per capita real income growth for the United States in the period, and since North Carolina in most accounts apparently was not a high achiever in the economic growth sweepstakes, it seems evident that state and local government in North Carolina absorbed and disposed of an increasing share of their citizens' incomes as the century progressed. This trend continued and accelerated after the 1870s; per capita state and county revenues in real terms grew at 3.38% per year from 1871–80 to 1911–20, a rate that likely is well above the state's growth rate of per capita real income. Moreover, from all indications (see below), municipal government receipts and expenditures, which are not accounted for in the above analysis, were relatively insignificant before the 1870s and grew rapidly thereafter. Therefore, one may surmise that, on a real per capita basis, state and local government in North Carolina grew somewhat more rapidly than income before the 1870s and considerably more rapidly than income after the 1870s. (The more precise dimensions of the shift will not be known until the municipal data become more refined.)

What may be said, based on the North Carolina data, about the nineteenth-century place of state and local government in the United States federal system? In table 16.4, I relate the sum of state expenditures and county tax receipts (a proxy for county expenditures) to North Carolina's "share" of federal expenditures, calculated by multiplying North Carolina's share of United States population by total federal expenditures, for decade years 1800–1930. In only two of the years, 1860 (a "railroad" year) and 1930 (a "highway" year), did state and local spending exceed the state's federal "share." In each of the other years save one (1910), state and local spending was less than half of the state's "share" of federal spending. Based on these data, we may say that there was no early golden age of state and local government relative to federal government, no age when the state's responsibilities to its citizens exceeded the federal government's responsibilities to its citizens—at least not in North Carolina. Parenthetically, I note that Holt, in his study of state government expenditures, 1820–

**Table 16.4    State and Local Expenditures in North Carolina in Relation to State's Share of Federal Expenditures**

| Year | North Carolina "Share" of Federal Expenditures ($000) | North Carolina State and County Expenditures ($000) | (2) ÷ (1) (%) |
|---|---|---|---|
| 1800 | 971 | 226[a] | 23 |
| 1810 | 628 | 265 | 42 |
| 1820 | 1,205 | 348 | 29 |
| 1830 | 863 | 377 | 44 |
| 1840 | 1,069 | 415 | 39 |
| 1850 | 1,463 | 645 | 44 |
| 1860 | 1,957 | 4,429 | 226 |
| 1870 | 8,361 | 1,527[b] | 18 |
| 1880 | 7,494 | 1,807 | 24 |
| 1890 | 8,269 | 2,670 | 32 |
| 1900 | 13,021 | 3,999 | 31 |
| 1910 | 16,646 | 11,530 | 69 |
| 1920 | 152,584 | 28,331 | 19 |
| 1930 | 86,325 | 135,813 | 157 |

*Note:* Federal expenditures from *Historical Statistics* (1975), ser. Y-336, p. 1104.
[a]North Carolina data for 1801.
[b]North Carolina data for 1871.

1902, found that only in the period 1830–44 were aggregate state expenditures for the United States more than half of federal expenditures, the maximum being 65% in the period 1830–39 (Holt 1970, p. 22).

## 16.2 Sources and Uses of Funds

### 16.2.1 State Government, 1801–1860

Tables 16.5 and 16.6 provide a fairly complete portrayal in terms of percentage distributions of the state's sources and uses of funds by decades from 1801 to 1860. Most of the underlying data are annual breakdowns of state revenues and expenditures taken from state records by Hershal L. Macon in his Ph.D. dissertation, "A Fiscal History of North Carolina, 1776–1860" (Macon 1932). Macon's data were supplemented when additional and more complete data were discovered in the course of this research. His annual data for total receipts and disbursements are not exactly the same as the ones reported here, but they are so close (indeed, the same for most years) that it seemed pointless to make separate estimates of categories of receipts and disbursements by repeating his laborious efforts with our more complete set of records.

Taxation—land and poll taxes for the most part—and land sales provided virtually all of the state's revenue in the first decade, 1801–10. In 1808, the state invested in and began to receive dividend income from banks. Investment income from banks was a significant source of state revenue for the remainder of the antebellum period; in the 1850s dividend income from the state's investment in railroad stocks became another significant source, but it exceeded bank dividends in only one year, 1859. One aspect of the investment in banks deserves comment: in 1814, 1816, and 1823, the state issued treasury notes (akin to currency) totaling $262,000 to buy the bank stock. These note issues were the only long-term debts incurred by the state between 1786 and 1835, years when receipts typically exceeded expenditures exclusive of the burning of currency the state had issued before 1787 (an incendiary activity that was often a major item of state "disbursements" between 1810 and 1830). In issuing the treasury notes, the state used its credit to increase the resources of banks, a developmental effort made all the more attractive by the flow of dividends from the bank stocks to the state treasury.

Other significant sources of funds before 1860 that are evident in table 16.5 are (1) the federal surplus distribution of 1837, which brought $1.434 million to North Carolina, an amount representing nearly two-fifths of all state receipts for the entire decade 1831–40, and (2) borrowing in the 1850s, mainly to aid railroads, which supplied more than

**Table 16.5    State Government: Sources of Funds by Decades, 1801–60 (%)**

| | | | | Decade | | |
|---|---|---|---|---|---|---|
| Source | 1801–10 | 1811–20 | 1821–30 | 1831–40 | 1841–50 | 1851–60 |
| Taxation | 86.8 | 65.1 | 55.6 | 21.7 | 40.4 | 20.8 |
| Land sales | 12.4 | 4.7 | 8.6 | 4.8 | 5.9 | 0.5 |
| Dividends and other return on investments | 0.8 | 27.0 | 25.5 | 15.0 | 38.4 | 10.9 |
| Borrowing | | 3.2 | | 11.0 | 15.3 | 67.8 |
| Distribution of federal surplus | | | | 38.2 | | |
| Other | | | 10.3[a] | 9.2[b] | | |
| Total | 100.0 | 100.0 | 100.0 | 100.0 | 100.0 | 100.0 |

[a]Treasury note issue, restored defalcation, and federal payment for Cherokee Indian lands.
[b]Distribution of bank assets and restored defalcation.

**Table 16.6    State Government: Uses of Funds by Decades, 1801–60 (%)**

| Use | Decade | | | | | |
|---|---|---|---|---|---|---|
| | 1801–10 | 1811–20[a] | 1821–30 | 1831–40 | 1841–50 | 1851–60 |
| Current expenses | 90[b] | 46.6 | 63.8 | 22.4 | 76.8 | 30.3 |
| General government | | | | 16.7 | 24.0 | 4.5 |
| Education | | | | | 30.8 | 8.8 |
| Public welfare | | | | | 0.9 | 2.0 |
| Interest | | | | 1.2 | 13.8 | 13.3 |
| Miscellaneous | | | | 4.4 | 7.4 | 1.6 |
| Capital outlays | 10[b] | 30.7 | 22.3 | 68.5 | 18.8 | 46.6 |
| Public buildings | | | 5.0 | 11.5 | 1.9 | 1.0 |
| Bank stock | | | 12.9 | 17.7 | | |
| Navigation company stock | | | 4.4 | | 0.7 | 4.0 |
| Railroad securities | | | | 18.9 | 13.3 | 37.0 |
| Temporary loans | | | | 20.4 | 0.7 | 3.8 |
| Road and turnpike company securities | | | | | 2.2 | 0.8 |
| Debt retirement | | 22.7 | 13.9 | 9.1 | 4.4 | 23.1 |
| Total | 100.0 | 100.0 | 100.0 | 100.0 | 100.0 | 100.0 |

[a]Breakdown is possible only for the 3 years 1818–20.

[b]Rough estimate; the state probably spent some money on buildings and, in 1808, began to invest in bank stocks.

two-thirds of all receipts in that decade. (Brown [1928] provides a good account of the North Carolina railroad movement.) Not evident in table 16.5 is the significant broadening of the tax base in the 1850s; to the traditional sources—taxes on land and polls—were added new taxes on inheritances, interest, dividends and profits, salaries and fees, pleasure carriages, watches, jewelry, plate, musical instruments, pistols, knives, dirks, canes, capital in trade, and liquor traffic. None of the new taxes was individually significant compared to the traditional levies, but together they brought in about one-fourth of tax revenue in the 1850s.

The data on uses of funds in table 16.6 are not very helpful before the 1820s; only in 1818 did the state comptroller begin to list disbursements by category, and we were unable to find any earlier comprehensive breakdowns of expenditures. Before 1831—1818 to 1830—the interesting items are the investments in banks and navigation companies, and debt retirement, mainly (as noted) in the form of burning the old pre-Constitutional state-issued paper currency. In the 1830s, the federal windfall led to further investments in banks and in the securities of the state's first railroads, which needed the state investments to stay solvent. These federally financed investments swelled the resources of the state's Literary Fund and became the basis for financing the first common schools starting in 1840. Public common schools became an important category of state spending in the last antebellum decades. Only the purchase of railroad securities and paying interest on the money borrowed to do so were larger items of state expenditure.

### 16.2.2   Antebellum County Government

Other than estimating total tax revenues (as we have done), it is very difficult if not impossible to assemble comprehensive data on county spending for the whole antebellum era. The flavor of what county government did in these years can be gleaned from the sample of information in table 16.7. The table is titled "Sources and Uses of Funds" because antebellum North Carolina counties levied taxes (always on land—including town property—and polls) for specific purposes. In the records of the county court—the so-called court of pleas and quarter sessions, the appointed county government in antebellum North Carolina—of Edgecombe County, we uncovered a run of annual data on total revenues for the 1840s. Edgecombe, in the coastal plain, was a commercially oriented agricultural county with a population about evenly divided between whites and blacks at the time. In the 1840s it did not appropriate money for common schools under the 1839 schooling law, and it consequently did not receive the matching (2 for 1) state funds provided for under that law. Its experience may therefore reflect the spending pattern of a typical eastern county before the era of com-

Table 16.7          Antebellum County Government: Sources and Uses of Funds (%)

|  | Sample | | |
|---|---|---|---|
| Source and Use | Edgecomb County Revenue 1841–50 | Edgecomb County, Tax Revenue 1857 | 81 Counties' Tax Revenue 1857–58 |
| County purposes | 55.9 | 45.3 | 46.0 |
| Poor relief | 32.4 | 38.1 | 20.2 |
| Common schools |  | 16.7 | 17.9 |
| Jury |  |  | 2.4 |
| Railroad aid |  |  | 5.6 |
| Asylum for insane, deaf, and dumb |  |  | 1.8 |
| Public buildings |  |  | 5.6 |
| Patrol | 8.0 |  | 0.4 |
| Fines | 3.7 |  |  |
| Total | 100.0 | 100.1 | 99.9 |

mon schools. A little over half of the revenue was used for county
purposes, mostly general governmental functions. The more interesting
finding is the large proportion of county revenue gathered for poor
relief, a pattern that, judging by our more extensive information on
county tax levies (rates, not revenues), was fairly common throughout
the antebellum era. In olden days North Carolina county government
had few functions apart from providing *a* government, but it did look
after the poor at public expense. What today would be termed "welfare" was a major item of county spending in North Carolina. Among
the other items, the patrol function was a periodic one directed toward
the slaves when the county fathers deemed it necessary to provide
special surveillance, and it can be seen that fines were a small part of
total revenue compared to taxes. Not accounted for in these financial
data is the labor tax—days of road work required of able-bodied males—
which remained a part of county activity until the end of the nineteenth
century. The persistence of this tax, which possessed medieval, feudal
roots, lends an element of incongruity to modern public finance. Little
appears to be known about its relative importance in the aggregate of
resources commandeered by government.

By 1857 Edgecombe had adopted common schools and its distribution of spending and revenues at that date bears a resemblance to
that of the large sample (81 of 85) of counties for which complete tax
revenue data was published in the report of the state comptroller.
Edgecombe in 1857–58 spent relatively more of its revenue than other
counties on its poor. But even at that date, after the common schools
were well established in North Carolina, the counties spent more of
their revenues on poor relief than on education. This is not to deny

that in comparison with other southern states North Carolina was among the leaders in antebellum educational efforts—a point made by Albert Fishlow (1966)—but rather to put local spending priorities in perspective.

### 16.2.3   State Government, 1870s to 1920s

From the 1870s until the 1920s, the fiscal history of the state was relatively uneventful, apart from a large debt repudiation at the end of the 1870s (see below). Distributions of sources and uses of funds at 5-year intervals, 1872–1912, and for 1922 when the highway building program was underway, are reported in tables 16.8 and 16.9. Total receipts and disbursements for the indicated years are also given in the tables. After falling from 1872 to 1877, total receipts and disbursements grew steadily if unspectacularly to 1912, and then remarkably by 1922. The reader should keep in mind the totals when interpreting the percentage distributions; small decreases in the percentage for a particular category from one year to another may not have involved any decline in dollars received or spent. The same caveat applies to more substantial drops in the percentages for many categories between 1912 and 1922, when there was an approximate ten-fold increase in nominal receipts and disbursements of the state. Up to 1912 taxation provided most of the revenue, with a tendency for the general property and poll taxes (the latter were routinely turned over to the counties for education in this period) to decline and for taxes on business to increase as revenue sources. The main items of nontax revenue were the earnings of state institutions (mostly prisons) and investment earnings (mostly from the state's railroad holdings). The situation takes a dramatic turn in the 1920s; in 1922 fully two-thirds of state revenue was borrowed, mostly to construct highways. (Brown [1931] gives a good political account of the massive state highway program of the 1920s.)

Although tax structures are not a main concern of this research, it is worth noting at this point that in comparison with other southern states, political tensions over both tax structures and levels of taxation were relatively insignificant in postbellum North Carolina. One reason is that levels of state taxation and spending were low in the last three decades of the nineteenth century compared with previous years. The much higher levels of spending during the 1850s, the Civil War years, and the immediate postbellum years were financed to a great extent by debt, and the debt issues of those times were later repudiated entirely or in large part (see 16.4 below). In a sense, however, the same was true of other southern states, where tensions over taxation were nonetheless greater (see Wallenstein 1973; Thornton 1982). The lower tensions in North Carolina may be explained, I think, by antebellum differences between states in the relative importance of taxes on slaves and on land. In the antebellum years, North Carolina generally taxed

**Table 16.8    State Government: Sources of Funds by Years, 1872–1922 (%)**

Year (Total Receipts in Thousands of Dollars)

| Source | 1872 (700) | 1877 (567) | 1882 (769) | 1887 (855) | 1892 (1,225) |
|---|---|---|---|---|---|
| Taxation | 81.1 | 98.7 | 86.3 | 78.1 | 72.5 |
| General property and poll taxes | 43.2 | 49.5 | 69.9 | 59.8 | 50.1 |
| Specific business taxes | 2.9 | 8.6 | 16.2 | 13.8 | 11.7 |
| Excise taxes | | | | | |
| Income tax | | | 0.1 | | |
| Special taxes | 34.9 | 40.6 | | 4.4 | 10.6 |
| Nontax revenue | 32.0 | 25.6 | 32.5 | 24.3 | 6.9 |
| Licenses and fees | 0.2 | 0.7 | 2.9 | 7.4 | 2.4 |
| Land sales | | —a | | | |
| Penal and other institutional earnings | 10.4 | 9.1 | 16.5 | 6.1 | 2.5 |
| Investment earnings | 17.7 | 11.4 | 9.9 | 7.9 | 1.8 |
| Miscellaneous | 0.6 | 2.0 | 1.0 | 2.6 | 0.2 |
| Federal transfer | 2.9 | | 2.1 | | |
| Debt incurred | | 10.4 | | | 67.0 |

| Source | 1897 (1,316) | 1902 (1,924) | 1907 (2,653) | 1912 (3,414) | 1922 (40,096) |
|---|---|---|---|---|---|
| Taxation | 67.9 | 64.0 | 67.3 | 75.5 | 26.1 |
| General property and poll taxes | 41.8 | 36.2 | 34.1 | 39.8 | 5.0 |
| Specific business taxes | 18.2 | 18.9 | 22.9 | 28.2 | 4.6 |
| Excise taxes | | | | | 6.7 |
| Income tax | | | | | 5.5 |
| Special taxes | 7.8 | 8.7 | 10.2 | 7.3 | 4.3 |
| Nontax revenue | 32.0 | 25.6 | 32.5 | 24.3 | 6.9 |
| Licenses and fees | 0.2 | 0.7 | 2.9 | 7.4 | 2.4 |
| Land sales | | —a | | | |
| Penal and other institutional earnings | 10.4 | 9.1 | 16.5 | 6.1 | 2.5 |
| Investment earnings | 17.7 | 11.4 | 9.9 | 7.9 | 1.8 |
| Miscellaneous | 0.6 | 2.0 | 1.0 | 2.6 | 0.2 |
| Federal transfer | 2.9 | | 2.1 | | |
| Debt incurred | 10.4 | 10.4 | | | 67.0 |

aLess than 0.1%; because of rounding, the figures do not always sum to 100.0%.

**Table 16.9    State Government: Uses of Funds by Years, 1872–1922 (%)**

| Use | Year (Total Disbursements in Thousands of Dollars) | | | | |
| --- | --- | --- | --- | --- | --- |
| | 1872 (802) | 1877 (638) | 1882 (695) | 1887 (892) | 1892 (1,058) |
| General government | 51.5 | 57.2 | 34.1 | 36.6 | 34.0 |
| Administration | 32.1 | 33.4 | 14.0 | 20.6 | 11.8 |
| Regulation | 0.6 | 0.7 | 0.6 | 0.5 | 1.7 |
| Penal | 18.4 | 22.7 | 19.0 | 12.6 | 18.8 |
| Buildings | 0.3 | 0.2 | 0.2 | 1.8 | 0.1 |
| Defense | —[a] | 0.1 | 0.2 | 1.0 | 1.5 |
| Health and welfare | 21.5 | 23.6 | 31.6 | 25.0 | 34.2 |
| Health | 13.7 | 16.5 | 25.2 | 17.1 | 19.4 |
| Welfare | 7.7 | 7.0 | 6.3 | 7.8 | 14.7 |
| Natural resources | 0.9 | 0.8 | | | 1.3 |
| Social overhead | 0.8 | 8.4 | 10.8 | 8.6 | 9.1 |
| Transportation | 0.1 | 5.4 | —[a] | —[a] | —[a] |
| Education | 0.4 | 2.7 | 3.4 | 4.6 | 6.4 |
| Agriculture | 0.2 | 0.2 | 7.3 | 3.9 | 2.6 |
| Miscellaneous | —[a] | —[a] | | —[a] | —[a] |
| Financial investment | | | | | |
| Interest payments | | 9.7 | 23.3 | 29.5 | 21.0 |
| Debt paid | 24.8 | | | | |
| Short-term | 24.8 | | | | |
| Long-term | | | | | |

(continued)

Table 16.9 (continued)

| | 1897 (1,364) | 1902 (1,866) | 1907 (2,818) | 1912 (3,513) | 1922 (35,123) |
|---|---|---|---|---|---|
| General government | 29.8 | 21.1 | 22.0 | 21.3 | 9.6 |
| Administration | 17.0 | 8.2 | 10.6 | 10.8 | 2.3 |
| Regulation | 1.1 | 2.1 | 1.4 | 3.1 | 1.4 |
| Penal | 11.0 | 9.8 | 8.7 | 5.9 | 1.1 |
| Buildings | 0.1 | 0.3 | 0.5 | 0.3 | 4.6 |
| Defense | 0.5 | 0.6 | 0.7 | 1.2 | 0.2 |
| Health and welfare | 31.0 | 30.6 | 34.1 | 33.3 | 12.6 |
| Health | 15.7 | 17.4 | 22.1 | 13.8 | 7.8 |
| Welfare | 15.2 | 13.1 | 11.9 | 19.5 | 4.8 |
| Natural resources | 0.8 | 0.2 | 2.9 | 0.8 | 0.2 |
| Social overhead | 14.8 | 31.2 | 28.2 | 33.8 | 47.4 |
| Transportation | —a | —a | 0.3 | —a | 25.9 |
| Education | 10.6 | 26.9 | 23.7 | 27.2 | 20.2 |
| Agriculture | 4.3 | 3.7 | 4.1 | 6.5 | 1.0 |
| Miscellaneous | | 0.5 | —a | —a | 0.3 |
| Financial investment | —a | 0.2 | | 0.2 | 0.1 |
| Interest payments | 23.3 | 16.3 | 12.3 | 10.6 | 2.5 |
| Debt paid | 0.2 | | | | 27.5 |
| Short-term | | | | | 27.5 |
| Long-term | | | | | |

aLess than 0.1%; because of rounding, the figures do not always sum to 100.0%.

land at higher rates and slaves at lower rates than did the states of the lower South. As a result, North Carolina collected a considerably smaller portion of its revenue from taxes on slaves than did the others (Kruman 1983, p. 190; Thornton 1982). Hence, the end of slavery brought North Carolina fewer problems of tax structure adjustment in order to maintain a given revenue. Moreover, as tables 16.1 and 16.2 demonstrate, total state revenues, in both nominal and real terms, were lower in the 1870s, 1880s, and 1890s than in the 1850s and 1860s. For these reasons, there was less need in postbellum North Carolina to shift the burden of taxation from slaves to land than there was in other southern states.

State spending levels, although growing in both nominal and real terms, were not high before the 1920s; they ranged (see table 16.1) from an average of $0.50 per person per year in the 1870s to $1.38 in the 1900s and $2.71 in the 1910s. Within this rather constricted framework of state spending, health and welfare (a good portion of the latter being pensions for confederate veterans) and education (largely for colleges and universities) show rising shares.

### 16.2.4  County Sources and Uses, 1870s to 1920s

Property and poll taxes remained the overwhelming source of county tax revenues after the Civil War. In 1868 the state assigned its general poll tax to the counties for school purposes; although legally it was a state tax, de facto it was a county tax, and is so treated here. Table 16.10 indicates that financing schools became an increasingly important function of the counties from the inception of common schools in the 1840s until the early 1920s, when school taxes became more than half of all county tax revenues. The school tax share is modestly lower from 1901 to 1920 than it was in the 1890s because the counties were enacting special taxes for roads and bridges in these two decades. But, as table 16.1 indicates, real county tax revenues per capita were increasing at a rate of more than 3% per year from 1871–80 to 1911–20, so the small decline in the school tax share after the turn of the century

**Table 16.10**     **School Tax Share of Total County Tax Revenues, 1841–1923 (%)**

| Period | School Tax Share | Period | School Tax Share |
|---|---|---|---|
| 1841–50 | 14.6 | 1891–1900 | 43.5 |
| 1851–60 | 18.3 | 1901–10 | 37.6 |
| 1877–80 | 26.0 | 1911–20 | 40.0 |
| 1881–90 | 37.7 | 1921–23 | 52.3 |

*Sources:* School taxes, 1841–60, estimated as one-half of state expenditures for common schools since the state matched county school taxes $2 for $1. School tax revenues for 1877–1923 are given in the annual reports of the state auditor. Total county tax revenues are from appendix B.

is consistent with a steadily increasing educational effort throughout the postbellum decades. In the 1920s an educational spending boom at the county level, much of it for consolidated schools, went hand in glove with the highway spending boom at the state level. Improved roads facilitated transportation of students to the newer, larger schools that were opened in these years.

## 16.3 Municipal Finance

For most of the period on which this study is focused North Carolina was a predominantly rural state. As late as 1880 the United States Census classified only 3.9% of the state's population as urban. The census estimate rose to 9.9% in 1900 and 25.5% in 1930. The census urbanization estimates are far from perfect, but they point to two conclusions. The first is that public finance in North Carolina was virtually synonymous with state and county finance, the main subjects of this research, for most of the nineteenth century. The second is that the urban population began to grow quite rapidly toward the end of the century (in fact, using the census data, at 5.3% per year from 1880 to 1930), so that a thorough portrayal of state and local finance cannot ignore the municipalities from that time forward.

The revenue dimensions of municipal finance in North Carolina's state and local finance from 1860 to 1932 are indicated in table 16.11, which is based for the most part on census information. The data reported by the census are rough and not strictly comparable from one year to another. I believe, however, that in a broad sense they portray the trend of municipal revenues in North Carolina from the 1870s to the 1930s. The municipalities of the state accounted for about 10% of total state and local revenues in the 1870s and about 33% in the 1910s. If we add these factors to the estimates underlying the real growth rate calculations reported in table 16.3, the recomputed growth rate of total revenues (5.02% per year, 1871–80 to 1911–20, for the state plus the counties) becomes 5.49% per year for the state, counties, and municipalities combined. On a real per capita basis the growth rate rises from 3.38% to 3.85% of the same period. In North Carolina, a conservative southern state that prided itself—with the exception of occasional short bursts of active government activity—in limited government, the revenue measure of governmental growth yields a rate of almost 4% per capita per year from the 1870s to the 1910s. This rate very likely exceeded the state's growth rate of income per person, perhaps by a good margin. The economic, social, and political forces leading to the growth of governmental activity in these decades must have been strong indeed.

**Table 16.11 Municipal Finance, 1860–1932: Selected Data**

| Year | Municipal Tax Revenue ($000) (1) | (1) as % of State and Local Tax Revenue (2) | Total Municipal Revenue Excluding Loans ($000) (3) | (3) as % of State and Local Revenue (4) |
|------|------|------|------|------|
| 1860 | 2 | 0.2 | | |
| 1870 | 228 | 6.1–9.7[a] | | |
| 1880 | 222 | 10.6–11.6[b] | | |
| 1890 | 315 | 9.8 | 409 | 12.7 |
| 1902 | | | 1,974 | 27.8 |
| 1912 | | | 4,473 | 30.3 |
| 1922 | | | 16,815 | 35.4 |
| 1932 | | | 37,333 | 30.2 |

*Sources:*
1860: *Statistics of U.S. Census, 1860*, p. 511.
1870: *Compendium of the Ninth Census.*
1880: 1880 Census, *Valuation, Taxation and Public Indebtedness.*
1890: 1890 Census, *Wealth, Debt, and Taxation*, pp. 409, 440. The municipal data are for units of 4,000 to 50,000 in population.
1902: 1900 Census, *Wealth, Debt, and Taxation*, p. 990.
1912: 1910 Census, *Wealth, Debt, and Taxation*, pp. 34, 81, 417. The revenue concept is "revenue receipts", excluding "nonrevenue receipts" (mainly borrowing). Municipalities are places with a population of 2,500 or more.
1922: 1920 Census, *Wealth, Public Debt, and Taxation. Taxes Collected*, p. 15. Municipalities include incorporated places and specified civil divisions.
1932: 1930 Census, *Financial Statistics of State and Local Governments*, p. 1260. The municipal data are for cities, towns, and villages, school districts (excluding county schools), and other civil divisions.
[a]The smaller percentage relates to total state revenue, the larger one to state tax revenue.
[b]The smaller percentage relates to my estimates of total revenue; the larger to the census estimate.

## 16.4 State and Local Debt

North Carolina's state debt in 1790 was some $713,000, of which about $400,000 was the unredeemed portion of $500,000 of state currency (bills of credit issued in pounds in 1783 and 1785) and the remainder consisted of certificates issued during the Revolution. The certificate debt was redeemed by 1810, and in the next 15 years most of the bills of credit were also redeemed (Ratchford 1932). The redemption of the pre-Constitutional state bills (further issues were prohibited by the Constitution) took place between 1810 and 1825, and was aided by the state's new money-issuing creatures, three corporate banks (New Bern, Cape Fear, and State Bank), which paid a part of their dividends owed to the state in the form of the old bills. The state then proceeded to burn the old bills, terming the operation a "disbursement" of public funds. It was one of the largest items of state expenditure in these years.

Burning old, pre-Constitutional money did little to reduce North Carolina's debt, however, because the state issued $262,000 of non-interest-bearing and non-legal-tender treasury notes in 1814, 1816, and 1823—in denominations of 5 to 75 cents to relieve the banks and others from a shortage of change. The notes were used to purchase additional shares of stock from the banks. Most of these treasury notes were redeemed by 1835, when the state incurred its first funded debt, $400,000 in 5% certificates, in order to buy stock in the new Bank of the State of North Carolina. This issue was redeemed (but held in the treasury) with $400,000 of the 1837 federal surplus distribution. Between 1838 and 1841, the state endorsed $1.1 million of the bonds of two railroads (the Raleigh and Gaston, and the Wilmington and Raleigh), and when the railroad companies defaulted in 1842, the bonds became in effect state debt (Ratchford 1932). Some were redeemed before 1850, and in that year the state debt stood as $1.055 million (see table 16.12).

In the 1850s a railroad mania swept over North Carolina. The state borrowed some $8 million to finance an east-west trunk route constructed by three separate companies with state aid. The Civil War brought railroad building to a standstill, but borrowing for war purposes greatly swelled the debt of the state. The war-related debt was entirely repudiated in the fall of 1865, forcing all of the banks in the state into liquidation. In 1868, the "carpetbagger" legislature issued bonds for a net nominal value of $13 million, ostensibly to continue the railroads, but these bonds sold for only some $4 million and only $1.9 million of this amount was spent on the projects, the other $2 million apparently disappearing into the pockets of legislators and railroad officers. Because the state was not paying interest, the debt including arrears expanded to nearly $45 million in the late 1870s. In 1879, the carpetbag debt was entirely repudiated and the remainder was "adjusted," at 15–40 cents on the dollar, down to $6.4 million (Ratchford 1932). At that time the net debts of the counties and other local governments were about $2.5 million, little changed from a decade earlier (see table 16.12).

The state debt changed very little during the three decades after 1880, but the municipal (1880s) and county (1890s) debts began to grow toward the end of the century, and to grow rapidly indeed after 1902. The state joined the counties and municipalities in the borrowing binge after 1912, and it led the way in the massive debt financing of highways and schools in the 1920s. Public debt per person in North Carolina, according to the census studies on which table 16.12 is in part based, ranged from 21% to 38% of the national average of state and local debt per person between 1880 and 1912. By 1922, it had jumped to 86%, and in 1932 it was 117% of the national average. State and local debt per person was rising everywhere between 1890 and 1932; the national average rose from $18.13 to $141.17 in these years. In North Carolina,

**Table 16.12**              **Public Debt in North Carolina (Thousands of Dollars)**

| Year | State Total Gross Debt (Ratchford) (1) | Net Debt (Census) (2) | County (Net) (3) | Other Local (Net) (4) | Total State and Local Debt (Net) (5) |
|---|---|---|---|---|---|
| 1790 | 713 | | | | |
| 1810 | ca. 400 | | | | |
| 1825 | ca. 400 | | | | |
| 1835 | ca. 450 | | | | |
| 1850 | 1,055 | | | | |
| 1860 | 9,130 | | | | |
| 1864 | 31,442 | | | | |
| 1866 | 14,222 | | | | |
| 1870 | 33,085 | 29,900 | 1,733 | 841 | 32,474 |
| 1878 | 44,732 | | | | |
| 1880 | 6,385 | 5,707 | 1,525 | 963 | 8,195 |
| 1890 | 6,370 | 7,709ᵃ | 1,514 | 1,900 | 11,123 |
| 1900 | 6,528 | | | | |
| 1902 | | 6,755 | 2,398 | 6,195 | 15,348 |
| 1912 | | 8,059 | 7,049 | 19,236 | 34,344 |
| 1922 | | 34,713 | 67,012 | 80,986 | 182,711 |
| 1931–32 | | 164,534 | 158,859 | 209,354 | 532,747 |

*Sources:*
Col. 1: Ratchford 1932.
Col. 2: 1870, *Compendium of the Ninth Census*, p. 641.
   1880, *Compendium of the Tenth Census*, p. 1583.
   1890, 1902, 1912, 1922, *Wealth, Debt, and Public Taxation: 1922, Public Debt*, p. 15.
   1932, *Financial Statistics of State and Local Governments*, p. 1260.

ᵃThe 1890 census appears to have counted some prerepudiation bonds that had been converted to lower postrepudiation bonds at their prerepudiation value.

the rise was from $6.87 to $164.84. In a sense, North Carolina's new deal arrived well before Roosevelt's.

## 16.5   Since 1930

The financial history of state and local government in North Carolina in most respects does not seem exceptional after 1930. Revenues and expenditures, after falling off in the Great Depression, rebounded by the late 1930s. State debt and local tax revenue, however, did not return to 1930 levels—even in current dollars—until the late 1940s. Table 16.A.3 presents the current dollar series for the period 1930–1977.

Real average annual growth rates of state receipts and local tax receipts, both total and per capita, for various subperiods of the years 1930–77, are presented in table 16.13. Two points suggested by these

Table 16.13    Real Growth Rates per Year of Receipts in 1972 Dollars: Selected Periods 1921–30 to 1968–77 (%/Year)

| Decades | Real State Receipts | Real Local Tax Receipts | Real State Receipts per Capita | Real Local Tax Receipts per Capita |
|---|---|---|---|---|
| 1921–30/1931–40 | 5.17 | n.a. | 3.55 | n.a. |
| 1931–40/1941–50 | 7.29 | −1.15 | 6.04 | −2.39 |
| 1941–50/1951–60 | 4.10 | 2.82 | 2.92 | 1.61 |
| 1951–60/1961–70 | 3.50 | 4.55 | 2.38 | 3.44 |
| 1951–60/1968–77 | 4.85 | 4.49 | 3.67 | 3.32 |
| 1961–70/1968–77 | 6.78 | 4.42 | 5.51 | 3.14 |
| 1921–30/1968–77 | 5.28 | n.a. | 3.99 | n.a. |
| 1931–40/1968–77 | 5.31 | 2.52 | 4.11 | 1.31 |

Note: Current dollar data from table 16.A.3 were deflated by the implicit price deflation for state and local government purchases of goods and services, available for 1929–77 (see Economic Report of the President, February 1984, table B-3, p. 225). Missing years in the 1930s were taken from the implicit price deflator, 1958 dollars, in Historical Statistics of the United States (1975), ser. F-70, p. 212, converted to 1972 dollars. For the 1920s, it was assumed that movements in implicit price deflator for state and local government services exhibited the same relative movements as the Warren-Pearson wholesale price index, so that the latter could be used to estimate the former years before 1929.

data are of some interest. The first is that growth rate of state receipts (and also of state expenditures—not shown here) is virtually the same from the 1920s to the 1970s as from the 1930s to the 1970s. The Great Depression and the New Deal had no noticeable effect on the long-term growth of state government fiscal activity in North Carolina. The second point is that local tax receipts grew much more slowly than total state receipts in these recent decades, and even grew negatively from the 1930s to the 1940s. The impact of the Depression and the New Deal, as Wallis (1984) has argued and the North Carolina data confirm, was not so much in the direction of increasing government's overall share in the American economy as in that of altering the shares of federal, state, and local governments. The federal share increased greatly, the state share increased somewhat, and the local share was greatly reduced. North Carolina follows this pattern. Wallis contends that the impetus for the shift in the relative importance of state and local governments came from the federal government. The New Deal agricultural and relief programs, for example, created incentives for state governments to grow, whereas local governments, if anything, were induced to cut back on their own financing of local governmental functions. It is my impression, based on the North Carolina evidence, that not all of the impetus for these changes emanated from Washington. In North Carolina, the state increased its reliance on income and sales taxes—taxes that are sensitive to trends in income and spending—while local governments continued to rely for revenue primarily on the less sensitive property tax. The state also assumed—ahead of many other states—the obligation to finance elementary and secondary education, and it continued the emphasis begun in the 1920s on state-built and state-financed roads with state gasoline taxes. These changes resulted from initiatives within North Carolina; they were not merely responses to the incentives of New Deal programs.

Trends in sources and uses of funds—and in intergovernmental fiscal relationships—from 1942 to 1977 can be studied with the aid of table 16.14, based on materials from the census of governments. (The census data differ somewhat from the state and local data reported in table 16.A.3 because the census used a less comprehensive classification of revenue and expenditure than the receipts and disbursements data from state reports, and because of different treatments of debt and inter-governmental transactions.) A few observations based on the data contained in the table are warranted. The federal contribution to state and local revenues in North Carolina was negligible before 1930 (except for 1837); from 1942 to 1977, it rose from 7% to 27%. In 1930 and 1942, the state government raised and spent roughly twice as much as local (county and municipal government); by 1977, the state continued to raise substantially more revenue, but local governments ultimately received and spent much more than did the state. The federal largesse aided both state and local government, but primarily the latter: in 1977, local government financed 27% of total state and local government expenditures in North Carolina, but it spent 61% of the same total. The state financed 45% of the total, but spent only 39% of it. The remaining 28% of state and local financing of expenditures came from the federal government.

Looking at functional expenditures, the shares of education and health and welfare increased, those of highways and police, fire, and sanitation hardly changed, and that of interest payments fell. Part of the reason for the declining share of interest payments is that indebtedness grew much less rapidly than revenues and expenditures from 1942 to 1977, and also much less rapidly than it grew in the first three decades of this century when state and local governments in North Carolina borrowed a large part of their financial requirements.

## 16.5 Toward Interpretation

It may be a bit bold to generalize about the history of one's adopted state based on a study of its public finances. The purpose of this work is to reconstruct the long-term dimensions of the latter, as a prelude and perhaps a stimulus to further efforts along the same lines for other states, and—only then—serious comparison and interpretation. A sam-

Table 16.14    State and Local Revenue, Expenditure and Indebtedness: Selected Years, 1942–77 (Millions of Dollars)

| Category | Years | | | |
|---|---|---|---|---|
| | 1942 | 1957 | 1966–67 | 1976–77 |
| *General revenue* | 189 | 724 | 1,717 | 5,745 |
| By type of revenue | 14 | 118 | 312 | 1,558 |
| From federal government | 175 | 607 | 1,405 | 4,187 |
| From own sources | 159 | 503 | 1,129 | 3,275 |
| Taxes | 46 | 135 | 298 | 772 |
| Property taxes | 3 | 8 | 18 | 38 |
| State | 43 | 127 | 281 | 734 |
| Local | 114 | 368 | 831 | 2,503 |
| Nonproperty taxes | 110 | 361 | 823 | 2,347 |
| State | 16 | 208 | 439 | 1,129 |
| Sales | 23 | 98 | 287 | 986 |
| Income | 3 | 7 | 8 | 157 |
| Local | 15 | 103 | 276 | 912 |
| Charges and miscellaneous | | | | |
| By originating level | | | | |
| Federal | 14 | 118 | 312 | 1,558 |
| State | 117[a] | 411 | 957 | 2,795 |
| Local | 57[a] | 195 | 448 | 1,392 |
| By final recipient | | | | |
| State | 125 | 321 | 739 | 2,459 |
| Local | 65 | 404 | 978 | 3,286 |
| *General expenditure* | 179 | 723 | 1,728 | 5,492 |
| By function | | | | |
| Education | 45 | 295 | 805 | 2,405 |
| Highways | 14 | 151 | 278 | 499 |
| Health and welfare | 17 | 109 | 239 | 1,011 |
| Police, fire, and sanitation | 10 | 51 | 109 | 399 |
| Interest | 16 | 17 | 36 | 123 |
| By expanding level | | | | |
| State | 114 | 408 | 696 | 2,136 |
| Local | 65 | 315 | 1,032 | 3,356 |
| By financing level | | | | |
| Federal | 14 | 118 | 312 | 1,558 |
| State | 114[a] | 374 | 914 | 2,472 |
| Local | 51[a] | 231 | 502 | 1,462 |
| *Indebtedness* | 425 | 814 | 1,485 | 2,743 |
| State | 136 | 281 | 457 | 807 |
| Local | 296 | 533 | 1,028 | 1,935 |

*Sources:* 1942, "Revised Summary of State and Local Government Finances in 1942" Census State and Local Government Special Studies, no. 26 (June 1948); 1957, 1967, 1977, 1977 Census of Governments, *Historical Statistics on Governmental Finances and Employment,* p. 106.

[a]Estimate.

ple of one does not lend itself to compelling generalizations. Nonetheless, there are a few issues for which the findings here are pertinent.

In the 1940s and 1950s, a number of "state" studies, mostly by historians (e.g., Handlin and Handlin 1947; Hartz 1948; Heath 1954), argued that state governments played a decisive role in early nineteenth-century economic development, that laissez faire and the minimal state were ideas that had no real counterparts in United States history. One oft-cited review of this literature (Lively 1955, p. 81) said that the studies formed "a consistent report of economic endeavor in an almost unfamiliar land."

> There, the elected public official replaced the individual enterpriser as the key figure in the release of capitalist energy; the public treasury, rather than private saving, became the major source of venture capital; and community purpose outweighed personal ambition in the selection of large goals for local economies. "Mixed" enterprise was the customary organization for important innovations, and government everywhere undertook the role put on it by the people, that of planner, promoter, investor, and regulator.

In the 1960s and 1970s the pendulum of interpretation swung in the opposite direction as economists questioned the historians' conclusions and called for harder analysis:

> Was the social rate of return upon investments in certain areas higher than the private rate of return? . . . Did the government deliberately and purposefully invest in activities in which there was a significant difference between the private and social rate of return? . . . Was the magnitude of the social rate of return on government investment sufficiently large to make an appreciable contribution to the economy's rate of growth? (North 1966, pp. 100–101).

Doubts were raised about whether the affirmative answers given implicitly by the earlier studies of active state intervention would hold up under close scrutiny. Apart from a few successes (e.g., the Erie Canal), the states may actually have wasted a lot of the resources they directed into their improvement projects, and the debt problems of the 1840s—repudiation and so on—only transferred the burden of waste from taxpayers to bondholders (many of whom were foreigners).

North Carolina's experience lends some prespective to the issue debated by the historians and the economists. Before the 1850s, unlike the states of the "state" studies, its governmental activity, despite long-term growth, was quite modest, even when compared with a nearby state, Georgia, which also was an "original" state and had a similar land-based economy. Milton Heath's study of Georgia (Heath 1954, chap. 15), an "active" state, allows a comparison of per capita state spending levels with those of North Carolina. During the decades from

1801 to 1850, Georgia's spending levels per person were two to five times greater than North Carolina's. Did Georgia flourish under dynamic government while North Carolina languished? Or did North Carolina prosper with a minimal state government while Georgia wasted its citizens' resources?

Only suggestions toward answers can be made here, and the issues undoubtedly transcend public finance. Data do not exist to compare the pre-1840 income and product growth of Georgia and North Carolina, so other measures are needed. On the capitol grounds in Raleigh there is a statue of North Carolina's three native sons who became presidents of the Republic in its early history. They are Andrew Jackson, James K. Polk, and Andrew Johnson. Each left North Carolina in his youth to pursue his career and become president from another state, Tennessee. A more quantitative index of economic opportunity—perhaps—is population growth. In 1790, Georgia had 83 thousand people to North Carolina's 394 thousand. In 1850, Georgia had 906 thousand and North Carolina, 869 thousand. Richard Easterlin's estimates of per capita incomes by states in 1840 (Easterlin 1960) provide some additional evidence for that year; Georgia's was 88% of the United States average and North Carolina's, 78%.

Easterlin elsewhere (Easterlin 1975) shows agricultural income per worker by state and region for 1840. At United States prices, the North Carolina figure is 72% of the national average, the lowest of any state; the South Atlantic region as a whole came in at 81% and Georgia at 93% of the national average. One would be hard pressed, on the basis of such evidence, to make the case that limited government was associated with economic advancement in early United States history. Indeed, the verdict of North Carolina's historians (Lefler and Newsome 1973, p. 314) is quite the opposite: "During the first third of the nineteenth century North Carolina was so undeveloped, backward, and indifferent to its condition that it was often called the second Nazareth, the Ireland of America, and the Rip Van Winkle state." In looking only at "active" state governments, both historians and economists may have ignored a portion of the historical evidence pertinent to the issues they were debating from the 1940s to the 1970s—and continue to debate.

At the end of the 1840s, the common schools in North Carolina had been established for almost a decade and the state was ready to embark—belatedly—on its own internal improvement programs. The Civil War, reconstruction, and the return of quite limited government in the 1870s combined to undo much of the promise and progress of the 1850s. For example, when the state constitution's call for 4-month school terms conflicted with its limitation on combined state and county property and poll taxes, the state supreme court, in cases decided in 1870 and 1885, opted for low taxes and against education (Lefler and Newsome 1973, p. 537). Easterlin's estimates of personal income per capita by states (Easterlin 1957, table 4–1) show North Carolina at 37% of the national average in 1880 and 36% in 1900. The estimates imply economic growth because the nation itself was growing rapidly in these decades, but there was no decline in relative backwardness, which remained great as the new century dawned.

The twentieth century is a different story. Both the state and the local governments became more active promoters of economic development, and North Carolina's relative backwardness in the American economy declined considerably. The data of this paper document the former. The latter is apparent in trends of per capita income. Easterlin's per capita personal income estimates (Easterlin 1957, table 4–1) show a rise to 54% of the national average in 1919–21 and to 65% in 1949–51. The Commerce Department's estimates (United States Bureau of the Census 1963, p. 332; 1978, p. 449) show a rise from 48% in 1929 to 68% in 1950 to 85% in 1977. It is my impression, despite the finding that state and local governmental activity in real terms, both total and per capita, grew persistently throughout North Carolina's history, that for much of the nineteenth century it approached the political philosophers' concept of the "minimal state." In these decades—even in the antebellum prosperity that characterized many of the southern United States—North Carolina in relative economic development remained one of the most backward of all United States states. Early in the twentieth-century state and local governments assumed more active economic roles and enlarged fiscal responsibilities, and at the same time the state, from its relatively backward position, began to make impressive gains in economic growth and development relative to national averages.

Whether public finance and economic development are related to one another in any systematic way is, of course, still an open issue. And if they can be shown to be related, there is still the issue of the direction of causation. North Carolina's nineteenth- and twentieth-century experiences offer some food for thought on these matters. North Carolina's region, the South Atlantic (which contains the relatively "rich" states of Delaware and Maryland, as well as the District of Columbia) also gained on the national average per capita personal income in these years, with a rise from 66% in 1929 to 93% in 1977. These figures imply that North Carolina rose from 73% of its region's per capita income in 1929 to 91% in 1977. Evidence from North Carolina's history might thus allow one to advance the generalization that improved relative economic position and more active state and local governments went hand in hand. But comparable studies of other states will be needed, I think, before such discussions can advance beyond the initial stage of modest and tentative generalizations regarding government's role in economic development at the state and local levels in United States history.

# Appendix
## State Receipts and Disbursements, 1801–1930

The concepts of receipts and disbursements are comprehensive. Receipts include tax revenues, nontax revenues, and borrowing (including issues of near money). Disbursements include current and capital expenditures as well as repayments of debt (including the burning of money).

Basic sources of data were the annual reports of the state comptroller for the years 1815–67 (no report in 1865), and the state auditor for the years 1868–1930.

Before 1820, all receipts and disbursements of the state were from one fund. Beginning in 1820, one or more special funds with specially earmarked receipts or special expenditure purposes became part of the state's finances. The main fund was termed the Public Fund before 1906, when it was renamed the General Fund. In 1820 an Internal Improvement Fund was created; it lasted until 1847. The Literary Fund (for education) appeared in 1828. It became the Educational Fund in 1878, under which name it lasted well into the twentieth century even though by then it had become a small part of the state budget. An Agricultural Fund was in existence from 1828 to 1832. Today the General Fund and a Highway Fund are the two main components of state finance. The total receipt and disbursement data reported here combine the receipts and disbursements of these funds whenever more than one was in existence.

Receipts for the years 1801–14 are from Macon (1932, p. 70). Macon relied on reports of the Finance Committee in Senate Journals and reports of the Treasurer in House journals. Disbursements for 1801–14 are from Archibald Debow Murphey's (1819) "Memoir on the Internal Improvements Contemplated by the Legislature of North Carolina; and on the Resources and Finances of that State," as reprinted in Hoyt (1914, p. 173). Murphey was a state legislator and a leader of the early movement—largely frustrated—for a more active state government. His reported figures for 1815 and 1816 agree exactly with those of the auditor's reports for those years.

Fiscal years were November 1–October 31 prior to 1857. The 1857 fiscal year was November 1, 1856–September 30, 1857, 11 months. Fiscal years 1858 through 1882 were October 1–September 30. Fiscal year 1883 contained 14 months, October 1, 1882–November 30, 1883.

Fiscal years 1884–1920 were December 1–November 30. Fiscal year 1921 contained only 7 months, December 1, 1920–June 30, 1921. After 1921 fiscal years were July 1–June 30.

The state financial data located for this project convey an impression of great accuracy, being reported with a detail that included fractions of a cent, or, before 1816, fractions of a pence. But there are reasons to doubt that such accuracy in the small would carry over into the larger picture. The data for 1801–15 appear originally as pounds, shillings, and pence, the old North Carolina currency; these have been converted to dollars at the rate £1 = $2, the rate customarily reckoned at the time and fixed by law in 1812. But in the 1790s the rate was customarily £1 = $2.50, and some post-1800 transactions dealt with earlier moneys and debt instruments. Further, in the late 1820s when John Haywood, state treasurer from 1787 to 1827, died, a substantial shortage was discovered in his accounts; in the following years his estate paid back some but not all of this shortage. Finally, some of the North Carolina currency issues of the eighteenth century as well as some of the state's treasury note money issues of 1814, 1816, and 1823 were never presented for redemption or burning; these would show up in receipts in one period but would not be offset by disbursements in another. The remainder of these outstanding currency issues was declared to be null and void at the end of the 1840s.

To check on the accuracy of the pre-1860 data, I made use of an accounting identity involving reported receipts, disbursements, and cash balances. If the data are fully comprehensive and completely accurate, the receipts minus the change in cash balance (which could be plus or minus) would equal disbursements. The second column in the following table should be a column of zeros.

| Decade (1) | Receipts − (Cash Balance) − Disbursements (dollars) (2) | Absolute Value of Col. 2 ÷ Disbursements (%) (3) |
|---|---|---|
| 1801–10 | $ −28,140 | 4.0 |
| 1811–20 | −26,959 | 2.3 |
| 1821–30 | 160,693 | 11.5 |
| 1831–40 | −109,035 | 2.6 |
| 1841–50 | 50,723 | 1.8 |
| 1851–60 | 18,337 | 0.1 |
| | 65,619 | 0.2 |

In general, the discrepancies as a percentage of total disbursements are small and decline over time. The striking departure from this trend is the 1820s when receipts less change in cash balance substantially exceed reported disbursements. There was a large treasury note issue in 1823, and Treasurer Haywood's defalcation became known in 1827. The latter, at least, implied that some "disbursements" of earlier years were unrecorded, and that may account for the large discrepancy. Over the whole 6-decade period total receipts less change in cash balance exceeded total disbursements by some $65,000, a figure that is only 0.2% of total disbursements that were in excess of $29 million for the 6-decade period. One may conclude that, despite some unusual financial changes and events, the pre-1860 data on state finances are fairly consistent and accurate.

## County Tax Revenues

Before the twentieth century, the county was far and away the dominant local governmental unit in a rural state such as North Carolina. The 1870 census reported city and town tax revenues of $228,351 for North Carolina, a year in which county tax revenues reported to the state were $868,478, a figure that does not include 15 nonreporting counties (some of which were large ones). At that date, then, county tax revenues were at least 4–5 times city/town revenues. Similar data for 1902 imply that county tax revenues were still about twice those of municipalities and other minor civil divisions. For most of the nineteenth century, local finance in North Carolina was essentially county finance.

Counties reported their tax collections to state authorities starting in 1856. The state comptroller's (and later the state auditor's) annual reports contain a page for each reporting county showing its state and county tax collections. The latter aggregated over all reporting counties are the county data reported here for years after 1855. They are incomplete, especially in the Civil War decade, because counties sometimes did not report at all, and sometimes reported only partial returns. The data are thus minimum estimates of county revenues; they are incomplete in some years, and they exclude revenues such as fees, fines, and so on. (Scattered data for a few counties before 1856 indicate that nontax revenues such as fines were not more than 2%–3% of total county revenues.)

The main challenge in reconstructing North Carolina's financial history was to estimate aggregate county revenues before 1856. The starting point was the discovery that the county tax base was identical to the major part of the pre–Civil War tax base of the state. All county tax revenues and most state tax revenues were derived from taxes on polls and land (rural land and town property). The same official, the county sheriff, was responsible for collecting the county's and the state's land and poll taxes, and for forwarding the state's share to the state treasurer in Raleigh.

Initially, I thought that the near identity of the county and the state tax base, and the availability of state tax revenue data from that base, would allow estimating county tax revenue by taking ratios of county tax rates to state tax rates and multiplying these ratios (year by year) by state tax revenues derived from that base. In principle, this seemed a promising solution. In practice, it proved difficult. North Carolina had more than 80 counties in the 1850s, and the tax-rate data had to be gleaned very laboriously from records of the county courts of pleas and quarter sessions. Not all of these records are available. Moreover, the counties did not levy just land and poll taxes; they levied these taxes for a variety of purposes: for general county purposes, for schools, for juries, for building specific buildings (courthouses, jails), for roads and bridges, for railroads, and for patrols to look after slaves. Not all counties levied taxes for all of these purposes, and few levied them year after year. Often they were special taxes to collect enough money, say, until the courthouse or jail was built, or until the slaves behaved themselves so that patrols could be disbanded. After some experiments with sample tax-rate data for several counties, I gave up on this procedure.

The alternative procedure employed here to estimate county tax revenues before 1856 is based on regression analysis. The procedure is akin to that employed by Davis and Legler (1966) who posited a relationship for the entire United States between local revenues and, as independent variables, state revenues, urbanization, and regional differences captured by dummy variables. Davis and Legler were not very confident about their estimates, which used census data for the entire United States at the end of the nineteenth century to estimate local revenues back to 1815. The method is intriguing, however, and one may well have more confidence in it when it is applied to data for an individual state in which the local (county) and state tax bases are virtually identical.

One of the earliest North Carolina comptroller's reports to give detailed county and state tax collections is that for 1858. Only three of 85 counties gave no returns, and a fourth was discarded because the returns were incomplete. For the remaining 81 counties there are reports of land, town property, and poll tax collections for both the county and the state. To allow per capita analysis, population for each county was estimated for 1857 by linear interpolation of 1850 and 1860 census population values (the taxes were levied for 1857 although not collected until 1858). Finally, the state was divided into four regions (Tidewater, Coastal Plain, Piedmont, and Mountains) to capture regional differences between the older and more commercially oriented East, and the later settled, less commercially oriented Piedmont and Mountain areas. The model estimated is

$$\text{county tax revenues} = a_1$$

$$+ \ a_2 \left( \begin{array}{c} \text{state land and poll tax} \\ \text{revenues per capita} \end{array} \right)$$

$$+ \ a_3 \left( \begin{array}{c} \text{state town property tax} \\ \text{revenues per capita} \end{array} \right)$$

$$+ \ a_4 \ (\text{Tidewater dummy})$$

$$+ \ a_5 \ (\text{Coastal Plain dummy})$$

$$+ \ a_6 \ (\text{Mountain dummy})$$

$$+ \ \text{error term}$$

Specifying the town property tax as a separate variable was done, following the lead of Davis and Legler, to capture the effect of urbanization. It is a more refined variable than the census urbanization percentages by county or state, and it turned out to be highly significant. The constant term, $a_1$, is of course, essentially the Piedmont dummy, while $a_4$, $a_5$, and $a_6$ measure deviations of the other regions from the Piedmont.

The results of the 81-county cross-section estimation for 1857–58 are as shown in the unnumbered table below.

| Coefficient | $t$-ratio | Significance Level (%) |
|---|---|---|
| $a_1 = 0.214$ | 2.17 | 3.30 |
| $a_2 = 0.692$ | 1.85 | 6.77 |
| $a_3 = 3.655$ | 7.02 | 0.01 |
| $a_4 = 0.245$ | 4.20 | 0.01 |
| $a_5 = 0.126$ | 2.47 | 1.60 |
| $a_6 = 0.005$ | $-0.82$ | 93.47 |
| $R^2 = .62$ | $F$-ratio $= 24.45$ | Prob. $F = 0.001$ |

This cross-sectional relationship between county and state tax revenues for one of the earliest years when both types of data were reported was then used to estimate county tax revenues back to 1801. The transformed estimating equation for the whole state is:

$$\text{county tax revenues} = \ .46 \ (\text{Tidewater population})$$

$$+ \ .34 \ (\text{Coastal Plain population})$$

$$+ \ .21 \ (\text{Piedmont and Mountain population})$$

$$+ \ .69 \ (\text{state land and poll tax revenues})$$

$$+ \ 3.66 \ (\text{state town property tax revenues})$$

The independent tax revenue variables in this equation are available from the state reports. The regional population variables are available for census years; annual intercensal estimates were derived from linear interpolation. Since the Mountain coefficient was insignificantly different from the Piedmont coefficient, the two were combined.

The results of the estimation indicate that urbanization was a highly significant determinant of county tax revenue; for every dollar the state collected from its tax on town property, the county collected about $3.66, ceteris paribus. The significance is statistical rather than historical, however; since North Carolina was a rural state, neither the state nor the counties collected very much revenue from the tax on town property. The land and poll taxes generated much more revenue for both state and county governments. The regional effects are as expected. Both land values and commercial activity declined as one moved from east to west in antebellum North Carolina, and this shows up clearly in the regional coefficients.

How much confidence can one have in time series estimates of tax revenues derived from a cross-sectional relationship from a later year? It is difficult to say. We know that the state land and poll tax *rates* were unchanged from 1817 to 1853. If the county rates in general were increasing in these earlier years, then it is possible that our relationship overstates tax revenues in the earliest years. The tax-rate data I have for several counties do not seem on balance to show much trend from 1800 to 1855, but if there is any trend it is an upward one. So tax revenues for the earlier years may be overestimated. On the other hand, one of the reasons tax rates rose may have been that citizens preferred to pay taxes when their market opportunities increased rather than to pay the old and persistent labor service "tax" by working on the roads, and so on. That would seem to be normal expectation. So even if monetary tax revenues are overestimated in earlier years, the estimates may not exaggerate to the same degree the tax *effort* of the counties.

Some more direct tests of accuracy or reasonableness of the county estimates are possible. Hershal Macon, recognizing that the county and state tax bases were largely the same, used sample county tax rate data to estimate that county tax collections were $185,000–$275,000 annually in the mid-1830s (Macon 1932, pp. 197, 364–65). My estimates are about $250,000 for those years. Macon's similarly derived estimate for 1852 was $296,000; mine is $304,000. Macon also surmised that total county expenditures were about $100,000 annually between 1776 and 1814; my tax revenue estimates are 1½–2 times this figure, but they could be consistent with Macon's average and a rising trend. A more precise test is to compare actual tax collections with the estimates for a period when both are available—this being, to be sure, a period containing the year for which the estimating equation was developed. For 1856–60, my estimated total county tax revenues are $2,656,600; the reported figures total $2,633,800 for these 5 years. The estimates thus may not be far off, at least for much of the antebellum era. In the nature of the procedure, of course, they should be viewed as a smoothed series, not a portrayal of the tax revenue collected in each year.

The annual estimates for 1800–1860, and the actual reported data on county tax revenues for 1856–1930 are given in table 16.A.2.

## State and Local Finance, 1930–77

Table 16.A.3 continues the state receipts and disbursements series of table 16.A.1 to 1977, and presents a more comprehensive series of local tax revenue, 1930–77, than the county-only series, 1801–1930, of table 16.A.2.

**Table 16.A.1**    **Receipts and Disbursements of the State of North Carolina, Fiscal Years, 1801–1930 (Thousands of Dollars)**

| Year | Receipts | Disbursements | Year | Receipts | Disbursements |
|------|----------|---------------|------|----------|---------------|
| 1801 | 47.0 | 57.7 | 1824 | 140.3 | 87.3 |
| 1802 | 50.4 | 82.9 | 1825 | 144.7 | 135.4 |
| 1803 | 55.2 | 57.7 | 1826 | 237.7 | 223.7 |
| 1804 | 60.8 | 62.1 | 1827 | 139.8 | 125.2 |
| 1805 | 57.3 | 83.5 | 1828 | 144.0 | 127.5 |
| 1806 | 55.3 | 64.0 | 1829 | 131.6 | 134.1 |
| 1807 | 58.2 | 61.3 | 1830 | 131.0 | 125.3 |
| 1808 | 58.9 | 61.6 | 1831 | 137.3 | 103.4 |
| 1809 | 57.0 | 90.4 | 1832 | 110.7 | 128.9 |
| 1810 | 64.1 | 74.2 | 1833 | 218.7 | 140.2 |
| 1811 | 64.9 | 68.7 | 1834 | 230.3 | 311.8 |
| 1812 | 61.7 | 56.5 | 1835 | 201.0 | 219.6 |
| 1813 | 83.3 | 80.0 | 1836 | 588.4 | 619.1 |
| 1814 | 97.3 | 115.8 | 1837 | 1,691.8 | 1,701.5 |
| 1815 | 153.2 | 123.4 | 1838 | 485.8 | 481.0 |
| 1816 | 170.6 | 142.9 | 1839 | 667.0 | 705.7 |
| 1817 | 141.0 | 127.0 | 1840 | 219.5 | 154.0 |
| 1818 | 209.9 | 206.6 | 1841 | 223.5 | 214.3 |
| 1819 | 147.0 | 126.0 | 1842 | 195.7 | 198.2 |
| 1820 | 136.5 | 121.0 | 1843 | 253.7 | 285.4 |
| 1821 | 152.4 | 193.7 | 1844 | 240.9 | 263.7 |
| 1822 | 146.8 | 126.7 | 1845 | 260.0 | 230.5 |
| 1823 | 139.0 | 119.4 | 1846 | 238.9 | 233.9 |

**Table 16.A.1**    (continued)

| Year | Receipts | Disbursements | Year | Receipts | Disbursements |
|------|----------|---------------|------|----------|---------------|
| 1847 | 300.8 | 282.7 | 1889 | 989 | 1,047 |
| 1848 | 248.3 | 246.4 | 1890 | 1,204 | 1,063 |
| 1849 | 480.1 | 453.3 | 1891 | 1,204 | 1,180 |
| 1850 | 286.1 | 341.0 | 1892 | 1,225 | 1,058 |
| 1851 | 414.4 | 451.8 | 1893 | 1,243 | 1,320 |
| 1852 | 504.1 | 410.7 | 1894 | 1,233 | 1,196 |
| 1853 | 1,952.4 | 1,704.3 | 1895 | 1,167 | 1,379 |
| 1854 | 1,417.4 | 1,775.4 | 1896 | 1,261 | 1,247 |
| 1855 | 2,598.9 | 2,526.7 | 1897 | 1,316 | 1,364 |
| 1856 | 1,557.0 | 1,427.9 | 1898 | 1,343 | 1,288 |
| 1857 | 2,457.4 | 2,394.7 | 1899 | 1,556 | 1,597 |
| 1858 | 1,735.4 | 1,870.1 | 1900 | 1,630 | 1,648 |
| 1859 | 2,547.2 | 2,201.9 | 1901 | 1,620 | 1,686 |
| 1860 | 3,949.7 | 3,863.8 | 1902 | 1,924 | 1,866 |
| 1861 | 3,703 | 3,906 | 1903 | 2,372 | 2,322 |
| 1862 | 13,563 | 12,411 | 1904 | 2,150 | 1,953 |
| 1863 | 18,405 | 17,095 | 1905 | 2,510 | 2,563 |
| 1864 | 7,535 | 7,148 | 1906 | 2,354 | 2,254 |
| 1865 | | | 1907 | 2,653 | 2,818 |
| 1866 | 1,958 | 1,850 | 1908 | 2,922 | 2,637 |
| 1867 | 2,254 | 2,109 | 1909 | 3,212 | 3,663 |
| 1868 | 1,947 | 2,056 | 1910 | 6,375 | 6,571 |
| 1869 | 8,721 | 8,855 | 1911 | 4,013 | 3,771 |
| 1870 | 3,892 | 3,658 | 1912 | 3,414 | 3,513 |
| 1871 | 788 | 823 | 1913 | 5,506 | 5,277 |
| 1872 | 700 | 802 | 1914 | 4,812 | 4,981 |
| 1873 | 523 | 607 | 1915 | 4,803 | 4,883 |
| 1874 | 711 | 505 | 1916 | 5,094 | 5,012 |
| 1875 | 522 | 599 | 1917 | 6,424 | 5,584 |
| 1876 | 566 | 582 | 1918 | 6,391 | 6,427 |
| 1877 | 567 | 638 | 1919 | 12,546 | 11,299 |
| 1878 | 546 | 539 | 1920 | 14,398 | 13,748 |
| 1879 | 558 | 582 | 1921 | 13,278 | 16,119 |
| 1880 | 553 | 497 | 1922 | 40,096 | 35,123 |
| 1881 | 760 | 676 | 1923 | 61,039 | 51,263 |
| 1882 | 769 | 695 | 1924 | 70,286 | 77,872 |
| 1883 | 995 | 945 | 1925 | 86,838 | 90,297 |
| 1884 | 1,472 | 862 | 1926 | 130,783 | 118,748 |
| 1885 | 386 | 801 | 1927 | 85,546 | 83,294 |
| 1886 | 843 | 1,180 | 1928 | 84,038 | 84,827 |
| 1887 | 855 | 892 | 1929 | 62,364 | 66,210 |
| 1888 | 722 | 826 | 1930 | 95,556 | 98,487 |

Table 16.A.2    Tax Revenues of Counties in North Carolina, 1801–1930
(Thousands of Dollars)

| Year | Tax Revenue (Est.) | Year | Tax Revenue (Est.) | Year | Tax Revenue (Reported) |
|------|------|------|------|------|------|
| 1801 | 168.1 | 1846 | 283.6 | 1891 | 1,607 |
| 1802 | 172.0 | 1847 | 287.4 | 1892 | 1,814 |
| 1803 | 175.0 | 1848 | 298.3 | 1893 | 1,681 |
| 1804 | 177.1 | 1849 | 300.7 | 1894 | 1,831 |
| 1805 | 179.5 | 1850 | 304.4 | 1895 | 1,805 |
| 1806 | 181.9 | 1851 | 309.1 | 1896 | 1,915 |
| 1807 | 184.2 | 1852 | 313.6 | 1897 | 1,894 |
| 1808 | 186.5 | 1853 | 317.1 | 1898 | 2,128 |
| 1809 | 188.8 | 1854 | 325.0 | 1899 | 2,145 |
| 1810 | 191.2 | 1855 | 406.1 (reported) | 1900 | 2,351 |
| 1811 | 193.8 | 1856 | 450.9 (512.1) | 1901 | 2,395 |
| 1812 | 204.9 | 1857 | 498.4 (490.3) | 1902 | 2,733 |
| 1813 | 210.3 | 1858 | 502.4 (522.2) | 1903 | 2,829 |
| 1814 | 215.7 | 1859 | 598.3 (544.4) | 1904 | 3,424 |
| 1815 | 221.2 | 1860 | 606.6 (564.8) | 1905 | 3,357 |
| 1816 | 229.1 |  | (reported) | 1906 | 3,694 |
| 1817 | 226.6 | 1861 | 680 | 1907 | 3,908 |
| 1818 | 232.3 | 1862 | 736 | 1908 | 4,567 |
| 1819 | 224.2 | 1863 | 1,451 | 1909 | 4,528 |
| 1820 | 226.7 | 1864 | 3,061 | 1910 | 4,959 |
| 1821 | 226.2 | 1865 | n.a. | 1911 | 5,205 |
| 1822 | 229.4 | 1866 | n.a. | 1912 | 5,553 |
| 1823 | 232.9 | 1867 | 363 | 1913 | 6,176 |
| 1824 | 236.2 | 1868 | 467 | 1914 | 6,929 |
| 1825 | 238.9 | 1869 | n.a. | 1915 | 7,354 |
| 1826 | 241.3 | 1870 | 868 | 1916 | 8,424 |
| 1827 | 243.6 | 1871 | 704 | 1917 | 8,593 |
| 1828 | 245.2 | 1872 | 893 | 1918 | 9,810 |
| 1829 | 247.8 | 1873 | 891 | 1919 | 10,649 |
| 1830 | 251.6 | 1874 | 1,098 | 1920 | 14,583 |
| 1831 | 250.5 | 1875 | 1,020 | 1921 | 17,276 |
| 1832 | 250.6 | 1876 | 1,143 | 1922 | 24,002 |
| 1833 | 250.6 | 1877 | 1,189 | 1923 | 26,484 |
| 1834 | 251.9 | 1878 | 1,349 | 1924 | 28,476[a] |
| 1835 | 252.3 | 1879 | 1,252 | 1925 | 30,468[a] |
| 1836 | 252.7 | 1880 | 1,310 | 1926 | 32,460[a] |
| 1837 | 252.8 | 1881 | 1,235 | 1927 | 34,452[a] |
| 1838 | 259.9 | 1882 | 1,286 | 1928 | 36,444[a] |
| 1839 | 259.9 | 1883 | 1,372 | 1929 | 38,433 |
| 1840 | 260.9 | 1884 | 1,533 | 1930 | 37,326 |
| 1841 | 265.6 | 1885 | 1,614 |  |  |
| 1842 | 268.5 | 1886 | 1,644 |  |  |
| 1843 | 272.5 | 1887 | 1,525 |  |  |
| 1844 | 276.2 | 1888 | 1,662 |  |  |
| 1845 | 279.5 | 1889 | 1,626 |  |  |
|  |  | 1890 | 1,607 |  |  |

[a]Estimate.

**Table 16.A.3**     **State Receipts, Disbursements, Debt, and Local Tax Revenue, 1930–77 (Millions of Dollars)**

| Year | State Receipts | State Disbursements | State Debt | Local[a] Tax Revenue |
|------|------|------|------|------|
| 1930 | 96 | 98 | 178 | 65 |
| 1931 | 80 | 85 | 179 | 62 |
| 1932 | 79 | 79 | 183 | 50 |
| 1933 | 79 | 80 | 182 | 46 |
| 1934 | 89 | 86 | 177 | 36 |
| 1935 | 123 | 118 | 171 | 36 |
| 1936 | 105 | 103 | 167 | 37 |
| 1937 | 121 | 114 | 162 | 38 |
| 1938 | 133 | 132 | 155 | 43 |
| 1939 | 145 | 142 | 153 | 43 |
| 1940 | 145 | 146 | 148 | 44 |
| 1941 | 157 | 149 | 142 | 45 |
| 1942 | 174 | 154 | 134 | 47 |
| 1943 | 187 | 191 | 126 | 49 |
| 1944 | 261 | 257 | 118 | 49 |
| 1945 | 403 | 392 | 110 | 49 |
| 1946 | 278 | 256 | 100 | 50 |
| 1947 | 410 | 386 | 91 | 56 |
| 1948 | 366 | 348 | 83 | 68 |
| 1949 | 633 | 577 | 76 | 79 |
| 1950 | 529 | 554 | 201 | 87 |
| 1951 | 773 | 750 | 287 | 91 |
| 1952 | 647 | 726 | 274 | 102 |
| 1953 | 615 | 675 | 263 | 110 |
| 1954 | 703 | 678 | 298 | 116 |
| 1955 | 876 | 909 | 296 | 120 |
| 1956 | 783 | 782 | 277 | 130 |
| 1957 | 1,011 | 999 | 261 | 139 |
| 1958 | 1,101 | 1,110 | 255 | 153 |
| 1959 | 1,029 | 1,047 | 254 | 162 |
| 1960 | 1,018 | 964 | 251 | 178 |
| 1961 | 1,098 | 1,059 | 244 | 196 |
| 1962 | 1,489 | 1,220 | 239 | 211 |
| 1963 | 1,302 | 1,281 | 220 | 226 |
| 1964 | 1,480 | 1,440 | 212 | 243 |
| 1965 | 1,461 | 1,423 | 193 | 262 |
| 1966 | 1,866 | 1,799 | 211 | 285 |
| 1967 | 2,087 | 1,915 | 323 | 310 |
| 1968 | 2,451 | 2,465 | 339 | 343 |
| 1969 | 2,466 | 2,390 | 361 | 388 |
| 1970 | 3,108 | 3,104 | 325 | 441 |
| 1971 | 3,395 | 3,358 | 415 | 493 |
| 1972 | 3,745 | 3,720 | 425 | 558 |
| 1973 | 4,160 | 3,993 | 394 | 640 |
| 1974 | 4,984 | 4,860 | 362 | 714 |
| 1975 | 5,932 | 6,062 | 404 | 804 |

(*continued*)

**Table 16.A.3**   (continued)

| Year | State Receipts | State Disbursements | State Debt | Local[a] Tax Revenue |
|------|------|------|------|------|
| 1976 | 6,506 | 6,621 | 564 | 871 |
| 1977 | 7,071 | 6,975 | 658 | 960 |

*Source:* State receipts, disbursements, and debt from *Annual Report* of the State Auditor, 1930–77. Local tax revenue data from Annual Report of the Department of Revenue, Reports of the Tax Commission and the Local Government Commission, and Reports of the Department of Tax Research, various dates.

[a]Local tax revenue is the tax revenue of counties, municipalities, and special districts. Small amounts of miscellaneous nontax revenue may be included.

# Comment    Lance E. Davis

Twenty years ago, as Sylla notes, two graduate students and I became interested in the history of the "public finances." After some very preliminary studies, we recognized that the topic was important; but we concluded that further progress involved delving into 50 state (and perhaps several hundred county) archives. Given budget constraints, we suggested a cooperative effort that, when completed, could yield a single national data set. With that suggestion we sat back to await the profession's response to our "call to arms." And wait we did—for 20 years. Professor Sylla has almost convinced me that the wait was worthwhile. He has done for North Carolina most of the work we outlined, and more besides. I find it very difficult to criticize a paper that sets out to accomplish a task that I have long said was most important and that does it as least as well as I could have done. The subject is by agreement (Sylla's and mine) an important one, the research has been done in a straightforward and intelligent fashion; and Sylla has all the data in his possession, so it is impossible to check on his sources (I personally have always felt that possession is one of the most profitable products of archival research).

Sylla has, however, sent me a list of what he thinks are his most important conclusions; so, if we cannot debate the quality of the work, we can at least argue about Sylla's ability to recognize its merit. Sylla summarizes his work as follows: "The paper is light on interpretation; what to conclude about one state will not be altogether evident until we have more states to compare. Personally, I found the more interesting items to be (1) the real growth rates (table 3), which seem to imply a steadily rising 'share' for government even in a 'backward' state, (2) the county resources devoted to the poor, always a large part

Lance E. Davis is the Mary Stillman Harkness Professor of Social Science at the California Institute of Technology, Pasadena.

of the antebellum county budget, and (3) the contrast between the nineteenth and twentieth centuries, both in government activities and economic growth" (personal communication, March 5, 1984).

This list certainly provides a partial enumeration of the most interesting findings, but it proves that Sylla is either falsely modest or unable to judge the total merit of his own work. The growth rates do increase, but the rate of increase is far from steady. A comparison of the period 1801–50 with the period 1871–1920, for example, indicates a change in the real rate from 2.08% to 3.38%. A slight temporal change (consider the periods 1801–60 and 1871–1930) has a major impact on the levels in both periods: both rates increase by more than 80%.[1] A potential consumer of Sylla's results will quickly recognize that the 1850s and 1920s were periods of particular interest.

A glance at his estimate of the composition of expenditures confirms the substantial transfers to the poor at the county level in the antebellum decades, but equally interesting is the very low level of educational expenditure in that period. It is interesting to speculate about the political structure that produced this result—one that so neatly captures at least California experience in the present decade. Again, we (he and I) can agree that a single state is not the basis for reliable extrapolations, and we can both bemoan the fact that within a state a single county may serve only slightly better, and Sylla's conclusions do depend on both. The former is the product of the state-by-state approach, the latter may be more serious. A weakness of the study is the lack of data on county expenditures; however, that is probably an archival, not an investigatorial problem. It may be that some of those records are still aging and molding in the basements of some county courthouses, although the voracious appetite of the North Carolina State Archives makes this unlikely.

The county data seem particularly important in light of Sylla's very suggestive findings of the relative importance of federal, state, and county government. He indicates that, over the entire 130 years, state expenditures averaged less than three-fifths of North Carolina's "share" of federal expenditures; but that county expenditures, while lower than the federal index, exceeded the state's by about one-fifth. This ordering, if it proves generally correct, should directly affect the design of future research into the public finances. Moreover, his comparisons highlight periods in which the state did exceed the federal and county averages; and those periods must have been important from the viewpoint of the North Carolinian historiography (they were associated with surges in transport development and the Civil War).

---

1. The ratio of the second estimate to the first is 1.89 for the earlier period and 1.81 for the later.

Nor is interest in the functional distribution of receipts and expenditures limited to welfare and education. At least two other features of North Carolina's fiscal experience are of interest. Throughout the state's history earnings on investments in private economic activities have made a substantial contribution to the budget. Between 1811 and 1860, they averaged almost one-quarter of total revenues, and even in the period 1882–1912 the figure appears to have been more than one-tenth. In the earlier period, finance and transport appear to have been the major recipients of the transfers that led to these returns; it would be interesting to know who the recipients in the later years were.

Between the years 1887–1912, penal institutions absorbed about 10% of the state's resources; however, over the same period those institutions contributed about 12% of the state's revenue. Given the current problems raised by the costs of maintaining large prison populations, we might conclude that we have had institutional technological regression over the past half a century. It would be interesting to know if these trends (welfare, education, business support, and penal) are the result of a deliberate fiscal policy or the unintended results of a policy of very low taxes and expenditure coupled with some minimal sustainable levels for some categories of activities.

Three other points made lucidly in the paper but omitted in Sylla's summary seem worthy of note. First, the postbellum period was marked by a rapid increase in educational expenditures. For a state that had no public schools before 1840, the later growth seems particularly impressive. From 1872 to 1892, state school expenditures were only one-fifth of the expenditures on prisons; near equality was achieved in the 1890s, and from then until World War I, the state spent almost three times as much on education as on incarceration. At the county level (to the extent that receipts are a good proxies for expenditures), it appears that the proportion of effort devoted to education doubled between the 1840s and the 1870s, and doubled again between then and the early 1920s.

Second, the trend toward increased government appears to have been reinforced by the rapid growth in importance of the state's cities. Almost nonexistent in the 1860s, they still accounted for less than 10% of governmental activity in the late nineteenth century, but for almost a quarter in the twentieth. Moreover, while the turn-of-the-century surge is dramatic, there does not appear to have been further relative growth in that sector between then and the 1930s. Third, given the proclivity of the state to default on its debt obligations, one might wonder about the speculative nature of governmental securities, a question of considerable interest to British investors in the late nineteenth century. While all these observations pose interesting questions for the history of North Carolina, their overall significance will emerge only as we are able to compare Carolina with other states.

Thus far, I have performed more as illuminator than as critic; however, some questions remain. The study suffers from a shortage of both county and municipal data: Can those gaps be filled? Since local tax data are more plentiful than expenditure figures, the scarcity raises a second question: Just how good are taxes as proxy for expenditures? And a third: The county revenues reported by Sylla for the years before 1855 are "statistical" rather than "historical" artifacts. He has estimated them from an 1856 cross-section of county and state taxes; and he acknowledges that the procedure may present some problems, particularly in the early years. The estimation technique, although based on a much sounder foundation, is similar to one employed by Legler and me some 20 years ago. At that time I felt about our estimates much like the Duke of Wellington is said to have felt about a particularly scruffy draft of recruits: "I don't know what effect these men will have on the enemy, but by God they frighten me."[2] Two decades have not allayed all my fears. Finally, on a much more trivial note, would an adjustment for the county labor-road tax have significantly altered any of the findings for the earlier years?

Sylla has largely eschewed generalizations, certainly a wise course given the limited scope of his data, but he does provide some interpretation in a very tentative fashion. In so doing, he reveals the potential fruitfulness of his public finance project. He shows how research of this kind should be able to resolve once and for all the laissez-faire versus government-as-entrepreneur controversy and, of even more general interest, the relation between government activity and economic growth. Sylla compares Georgia and its activist government with North Carolina and its passive one; and he contrasts North Carolina in the nineteenth century (a passive government) and the same state in the present century (when government was much more active). He concludes, with appropriate caveats, that economic growth and an active government appear to have gone hand in hand. He quite rightly admits that even if the conclusion is correct (and data problems make even that result far from a certainty), there are serious questions about the direction of the causal connection. What he does not point out, but what his paper demonstrates conclusively, is that the kind of "data grubbing" that he has effected is not a substitute for analysis, but it is a *necessary* complement to it—a proposition all too often implicitly denied by "new" economic historians.

In summary: How can a study be faulted when the state selected for analysis includes as a major expenditure an item old "bills" paid by the state's banks as dividends, "which the state proceeded to burn,

---

2. Ascribed—probably apocryphally—to various statesmen and commanders: to the Duke of Wellington, on a draft of troops sent to him in Spain in 1809; to William Pitt, on being shown a list of English generals to be sent out to fight the colonists, etc. See Evans 1968.

terming the operation a disbursement of public funds." How is it possible to criticize a scholar who, when faced by a need to find a proxy for a state's relative income, cites the fact that the three native sons of Carolina who went on to become president of the United States (Andrew Jackson, James K. Polk, and Andrew Johnson) all "left North Carolina in their youth to pursue his career and become President from another state." How can you criticize a finished piece of work—the product of a major research effort—whose author refuses to speculate about the nature of a Turner seascape from the fact that one piece in the jigsaw puzzle is entirely blue. One might, however, criticize the rest of the profession for not filling in the other pieces—there is almost certainly a ship out there somewhere, and it may be a Spanish treasure galleon.

# References

*American state papers, finance.* 1832. Vol. 1. Washington, D.C.: Gales & Seaton.

Brown, Cecil Kenneth. 1928. *A state movement in railroad development.* Chapel Hill: University of North Carolina Press.

———. 1931. *The state highway system of North Carolina.* Chapel Hill: University of North Carolina Press.

Copeland, Morris A. 1961. *Trends in government financing.* Princeton: Princeton University Press (for NBER).

Davis, Lance E., and Legler, John B. 1966. The government and the American economy, 1815–1902: A quantitative study. *Journal of Economic History* 26:514–52.

Easterlin, Richard A. 1957. State income estimates. In *Population redistribution and economic growth, United States, 1870–1950,* Vol. 1. *Methodological considerations and reference tables,* prepared under the direction of Simon Kuznets and Dorothy S. Thomas. Philadelphia: American Philosophical Society.

———. 1960. Interregional differences in per capita income, population, and total income, 1840–1950. In *Trends in the American economy in the nineteenth century.* Studies in Income and Wealth, vol. 24. Princeton: Princeton University Press (for NBER).

———. 1975. Farm production and income in old and new areas at mid-century. In *Essays in nineteenth century economic history: The Old Northwest,* ed. David C. Klingaman and Richard K. Vedder. Athens: Ohio University Press.

Evans, Bergen, ed. 1968. *Dictionary of quotations.* New York: Delacorte.

Fabricant, Solomon. 1952. *The trend of government activity in the United States since 1900.* Publications of National Bureau of Economic Research, no. 56. New York: National Bureau of Economic Research.

Firestone, John M. 1960. *Federal receipts and expenditures during business cycles, 1879–1958.* Princeton: Princeton University Press (for NBER).

Fishlow, Albert. 1966. The common school revival: Fact or fancy. In *Industrialization in two systems: Essays in honor of Alexander Gerschenkron,* ed. Henry Rosovsky. New York, London, Sydney: Wiley.

Handlin, Oscar, and Handlin, Mary Flug. 1947. *Commonwealth: A study of the role of government in the American economy, Massachusetts, 1774–1862.* New York: New York University Press.

Hartz, Louis. 1948. *Economic policy and democratic thought: Pennsylvania, 1776–1860.* Cambridge: Harvard University Press.

Heath, Milton S. 1954. *Constructive liberalism: The role of the state in economic development in Georgia to 1860.* Cambridge: Harvard University Press.

Holt, Charles Frank. 1970. The role of state government in the nineteenth-century American economy, 1820–1902: A quantitative study. Ph.D. diss., Purdue University.

Kendrick, John W. 1961. *Productivity trends in the United States.* Princeton: Princeton University Press (for NBER).

Kendrick, M. Slade. 1955. *A century and a half of federal expenditures.* NBER Occasional Paper no. 48. New York: National Bureau of Economic Research.

Kruman, Mark W. 1983. *Parties and politics in North Carolina, 1836–1865.* Baton Rouge and London: Louisiana State University Press.

Kuznets, Simon. 1946. *National income: A summary of findings.* New York: National Bureau of Economic Research.

———. 1961. *Capital in the American economy: Its formation and financing.* Princeton: Princeton University Press.

Lefler, Hugh Talmadge, and Newsome, Albert Ray. 1973. *North Carolina: The history of a southern state.* 3d ed. Chapel Hill: University of North Carolina Press.

Lerner, Eugene. 1955. Money, prices, and wages in the Confederacy, 1861–65. *Journal of Political Economy* 62 (February): 20–40.

Lively, Robert A. 1955. The American system: A review article. *Business History Review* 29:81–95.

Macon, Hershal L. 1932. A fiscal history of North Carolina, 1776–1860. Ph.D. diss., University of North Carolina.

Murphey, Archibald Debow. (1819) 1914. Memoir on the internal improvements contemplated by the Legislature of North Carolina; and on the resources and finances of the state. In *The papers of*

*Archibald D. Murphey*, ed. William Henry Hoyt. Vol. 2. Raleigh: E. M. Uzzell.

North, Douglass C. 1966. *Growth and welfare in the American past.* Englewood Cliffs, N.J.: Prentice-Hall.

North Carolina, State Auditor. 1868–1977. *Annual report.* Raleigh: State Printer.

———. State Comptroller. 1815–67. *Annual report.* Raleigh: State Printer.

———. Department of Tax Research. 1942–48, biennial. *Report.* Raleigh: State Printer.

———. 1950–78, biennial. *Statistics of taxation.* Raleigh: State Printer.

———. Tax Commission. 1928–32, biennial. *Report.* Raleigh: State Printer.

Ratchford, Benjamin U. 1932. A history of the North Carolina debt, 1712–1900. Ph.D. diss., Duke University.

Thornton, J. Mills, III. 1982. Fiscal policy and the failure of radical reconstruction in the lower South. In *Region, race, and reconstruction: Essays in honor of C. Vann Woodward*, ed. J. Morgan Kousser and James M. McPherson. New York and Oxford: Oxford University Press.

United States Bureau of the Census. 1975. *Historical statistics of the United States, bicentennial edition.* Washington, D.C.: Government Printing Office.

———. 1963, 1978. *Statistical abstract of the United States.* Washington, D.C.: Government Printing Office.

Wallenstein, Peter Reeve. 1973. From slave South to New South: Taxes and spending in Georgia from 1850 through Reconstruction. Ph.D. diss., Johns Hopkins University.

Wallis, John J. 1984. The birth of the Old Federalism: Financing the New Deal, 1932–1940. *Journal of Economic History* 44:139–60.

Warren, George F., and Pearson, Frank A. 1932. *Gold and prices.* New York.

# Contributors

Susan B. Carter
Department of Economics
Smith College
Northampton, MA 01063

J. H. Dales
232 Rosepark Drive
Toronto, Ontario M4T 1R5
Canada

Paul A. David
Department of Economics
Stanford University
Stanford, CA 94305

Lance E. Davis
Division of Humanities and Social
    Sciences 228–77
California Institute of Technology
Pasadena, CA 91125

Stanley L. Engerman
Departments of Economics and
    History
University of Rochester
Rochester, NY 14627

Albert Fishlow
Department of Economics
University of California
Berkeley, CA 94720

Robert William Fogel
Center for Population Economics
University of Chicago
1101 East 58th Street
Chicago, IL 60637

Gerald Friedman
Department of Economics
University of Massachusetts
Amherst, MA 01060

Robert E. Gallman
Departments of Economics and
    History
University of North Carolina
Gardner Hall 017A
Chapel Hill, NC 27514

Claudia Goldin
Department of Economics
University of Pennsylvania
3718 Locust Walk/CR
Philadelphia, PA 19104

Raymond W. Goldsmith
Department of Economics
Yale University
37 Hillhouse Avenue
New Haven, CT 06520

Alan G. Green
Department of Economics
Queen's University
Kingston, Ontario K7L 3N6
Canada

Michael R. Haines
Department of Economics
Wayne State University
Detroit, MI 48202

B. W. Higman
Department of History
University of the West Indies
Mona
Kingston 7
Jamaica

J. R. Kearl
Department of Economics
Brigham Young University
Provo, UT 84602

Stanley Lebergott
Department of Economics
Wesleyan University
Middletown, CT 06457

Peter H. Lindert
Department of Economics
University of California
Davis, CA 95616

R. M. McInnis
Department of Economics
Queen's University
Kingston, Ontario K7L 3N6
Canada

William H. Newell
School of Interdisciplinary Studies
Miami University
Oxford, OH 45056

Douglass C. North
Department of Economics
Washington University
Saint Louis, MO 63130

Clayne Pope
Department of Economics
Brigham Young University
Provo, UT 84602

Warren C. Sanderson
Department of Economics
State University of New York at
Stony Brook
Stony Brook, NY 11790

Kenneth L. Sokoloff
Department of Economics
University of California
405 Hilgard Avenue
Los Angeles, CA 90024

Lee Soltow
Department of Economics
Copeland Hall
Ohio University
Athens, OH 45701

Richard Sylla
Department of Economics and
Business
North Carolina State University
P.O. Box 8110
Raleigh, NC 27695

M. C. Urquhart
Department of Economics
Queen's University
Kingston, Ontario K7L 3N6
Canada

Jenny Bourne Wahl
Office of Tax Analysis
Room 5121
Main Treasury Building
15th and Pennsylvania Avenue, NW
Washington, DC 20220

John Joseph Wallis
Department of Economics
University of Maryland
College Park, MD 20742

Thomas Weiss
Department of Economics
University of Kansas
Lawrence, KA 66044

Jeffrey G. Williamson
Department of Economics
Littauer Center 216
Harvard University
Cambridge, MA 02138

Gavin Wright
Department of Economics
Stanford University
Stanford, CA 94305

# Author Index

# Subject Index